BRANDO

BRANDO

THE BIOGRAPHY

PETER MANSO

HYPERION

NEW YORK

Library of Congress Cataloging-in-Publication Data

Manso, Peter.
    Brando: the biography / by Peter Manso.
        p. cm.
    Includes bibliographical references and index.
    ISBN 0-7868-6063-4
    1. Brando, Marlon. 2. Actors—United States—Biography.
    I. Title.
    PN2287.B683M36   1994
    791.43′028′092—dc20
    [B]   94-21250
                    CIP

Designed by Claudyne Bianco

First Edition
10   9   8   7   6   5   4   3   2   1

FOR MY FATHER, LEO MANSO
(1914–1993),

AND TO ELLEN HAWKES

"There are, it is true, those who lie consciously, coldly falsifying reality itself, but more numerous are those who weigh anchor, move off, momentarily or forever, from genuine memories, and fabricate for themselves a convenient reality. The past is a burden to them; they feel repugnance for the things done or suffered, and tend to replace them with others. The substitution may begin in full awareness, with an invented scenario, mendacious, restored, but less painful than the real one; in repeating its description to others but also to themselves, the distinction between true and false progressively loses its contours, and man ends by fully believing the story he has told so many times and still continues to tell, polishing and retouching here and there the details which are least credible or incongruous or incompatible with the acquired picture of historically accepted events: initial bad faith has become good faith. The silent transition from falsehood to self-deception is useful: anyone who lies in good faith is better off, he recites his part better, is more easily believed by the judge, the historian, the reader, his wife and his children."

—Primo Levi, *The Drowned and the Saved*

"Was you there, Charlie?"

—Marlon Brando

C O N T E N T S

CONTENTS

x

PHOTO SECTIONS FOLLOW PAGES 206, 590, AND 814

PROLOGUE

"I come from a long line of Irish drunks. My uncle, my mother's great-uncle . . . both my sisters were drunks. . . . I have been to Alcoholics Anonymous with my mother, with my father, and why it didn't get to me, I don't know. I have never been a drunk, although I have drunk in my life. It just jumped over me, and [I] never abused any kind of substance. It may be food, I guess, but that will appear in the papers."

Marlon Brando's attempt at humor brought only a smattering of nervous laughter from his audience—a packed courtroom in Santa Monica, California. It was the morning of February 28, 1991, the third day of the sentencing hearing that would determine the fate of the actor's oldest son, Christian, who had confessed to killing the boyfriend of his half-sister. Brando himself had been the last witness called to the stand, and he sat in the chair sideways to accommodate his massive girth. His long gray hair was swept back from his receding hairline into a ponytail fastened with a rubber band. His face was ashen, his eyes narrowed and seemingly lifeless as he went on with his testimony, describing his marriage to Christian's mother, Anna Kashfi.

"By that time I had achieved some measure of notoriety. I led a rather wasted life, chased a lot of women," he added, attempting to sway the judge to show his son clemency. "I tried to keep some measure of consistency in his life. [But] I think perhaps I failed as a father. The tendency is always to blame the other parent, but I am certain that there were things that I could have done differently had I known better at the time, but I didn't."

After two hours of testimony, Brando stepped down from the stand, his face streaked with tears. It was perhaps the most moving performance he had been asked to give in years: no brief cameo for huge amounts of money, no silly part that he could ham his way through and then sneer at afterward. To everyone in the courtroom that day Brando's appearance was startling, the source even of raw dismay. After all, this was once the actor who had affected generations of filmgoers with his extraordinary presence in *A Streetcar Named Desire, The Wild One, On the Waterfront,* and, more recently, *The Godfather.* Who, more than anyone, had rocked the culture with his T-shirts, tight jeans, leather jacket, and tough-guy sensibility. Now the myth that had long lingered in the American consciousness was shattered, replaced by this saddening persona: Marlon Brando, his weight in excess of three hundred pounds, a confused and weary man burdened by guilt and self-reproach, confessing his failure as a father.

How had this happened? How had this previously powerful, charismatic figure become the embodiment of regret and depression? What had brought America's quintessential rebel to this dark abyss of misery?

Reporters from around the world, some from as far away as the actor's legendary hideaway in Tahiti, could only look on, bewildered, from their seats in the courtroom's press gallery. Undoubtedly, Christian's ordeal had taken a toll. Yet in truth Brando had surrendered his lifeline fully twenty years before. Over the course of his troubled career he had given up the stage for films, films for social activism, and, finally, he had turned his back on his all absorbing causes for what he called "family." But family had not sustained him either, and he had retreated into self-imposed isolation. By forfeiting his genius as the world's most talented actor, by holding himself and his accomplishments beneath contempt, he had squandered his energy, even his identity and inner core. That was as much his failure as his self-acknowledged deficiencies as a father; indeed, the two were one and the same. In the context of Marlon Brando's own lifelong journey, his son's violent act seemed only an accident waiting to happen—the denouement of a tragedy that had been set in motion decades before.

BRANDO

1
O M A H A

1893–1930

M arlon Brando Jr. was born just before midnight on April 3, 1924, in Omaha, Nebraska. He was the third child of Dorothy Pennebaker Myers and Marlon Brando Sr. After the births of two daughters, the couple had longed for a son, and with his arrival, the infant was honored with his father's name.

The Brandos had been in the Midwest for several generations. As they had pursued success and respectability, their ancestors embodied a mixture of pioneering, adventurous, and questing spirits. The conflicting impulses of propriety and imagination, rigidity and freedom, practicality and mysticism, were as much a legacy for the Brando baby as they were emblematic of America's heartland.

Marlon Sr.'s mother was Marie Holloway, who had come from Illinois to marry Eugene Brando in 1893. She had one son, Marlon, but several years later she ran away with another man. Deeply embittered by his wife's defection, Eugene (of Alsatian stock—the name was originally spelled "Brandeau") went to live alone in a succession of rooming houses, leaving his only child with two maiden aunts in Wichita, Kansas. They dressed him in Little Lord Fauntleroy suits and combed his hair in long blond curls. He rarely saw his remote and taciturn father as he grew up.

"Eugene was a put-downer, and so was Papa," said Marlon Sr.'s elder daughter, Jocelyn. "Just before he died, I asked Papa, 'When you were a little boy, what did you want to be?' He said, 'The Mysterious Stranger.'

This was a character in a book of the time who had power, and that was Papa's goal. He felt inarticulate, shy, and alone, and he wanted to top those people who were mistreating him. He had a good friend in Omaha who hadn't invited him to a birthday party but Papa got dressed up and went over with a present anyhow, rang the doorbell, and the boy came to the door and said, 'What are you doing here?' Papa handed him the present, saying, 'To tell you that you're a silly fool,' and then he went away. He was a very sad boy—all alone, really—and early on he started dreaming of success as his revenge."

Entering the Shattuck Military Academy in the fall of 1909, Marlon Sr. quickly excelled academically as well as in sports. His grades were usually high Bs, and he earned five out of a possible seven silver stars for conduct. As a junior cadet he mixed with the scions of Midwest wealth at the prestigious military academy, studying the dress and habits of his betters, and on school records even listed his church affiliation as Episcopalian. Shattuck offered a structure, a regimen and conformity that he would forever equate with manners and "decency." Even then he was calculating the odds to achieve success and respectability, although for lack of money, he would have to transfer to and graduate from Omaha's Central High School. He then studied for a year at the University of Nebraska before enlisting in the army to fight in the Great War.

By that time he had already met his future wife, Dorothy Pennebaker Myers. Friends recalled "Dodie" as "vivacious," "talented," "beautiful," and "clairvoyantly sensitive." In the Omaha social columns, she was often hailed as one of the city's livelier forces, even as a teenager. She had a serene, sculpted face with high cheekbones. Her lips were curved and generous, her eyes blue, deep-set, and sparkling. She wore her dusty blond hair in a pageboy parted in the middle and falling smoothly to her shoulders. Her gaze was direct and open, suggesting a definite sense of poise and confidence.

She had been born on January 20, 1897, in Grand Island, Nebraska. Her father, William John Pennebaker, worked at a bank, but at heart he was a robust adventurer who prospected for gold in Mexico and dug silver in the Colorado Rockies. He died at an early age, succumbing to tuberculosis in 1899. "My mother's only memory of her father was of his lying in bed in a darkened room, stretching his arms out to her," Jocelyn said. "He was dying and somebody was holding her back, saying, 'No, no, you can't go.'

She was only two at the time, and afterward she had to wear flannel shirts because it was thought that this would ward off TB. So Mother thought of him as the father she never had."

At the time of his death, Pennebaker had been married only four years. Dodie's mother, Bessie J. Gahan, was the daughter of Dr. Myles J. Gahan, himself a legend in western Nebraska. A pioneer medical practitioner, Gahan had emigrated from Dublin in 1846, and in short order had become chairman of the Nebraska Medical Society, head surgeon for the Union Pacific Railroad, county coroner, director of the Grand Island Building and Loan Association, and one of the founders of Grand Island's St. Franciscan Hospital.

Prosperous, gregarious, and very much his own man, Dodie's grandfather had an eccentric side as well. His ruling passion, even as a man of science, was Spiritualism and Theosophy, the pursuit of ancient occult wisdom and the hidden truths of the East. A member of the Nirvana Lodge, he helped sponsor the first in a series of talks by William Q. Judge, the leading light of the Theosophical Society after his well-known associate Madame Blavatsky had quit America to make her famous pilgrimage into the Vale of Kashmir. Gahan's interest in the occult and Eastern ideas would be handed down through three generations, a gift that sustained the Brandos through thick and thin.

Bessie, born in 1876, was the oldest of the Gahan children; she was followed by Vine, June, and Myles Jr. The marriage then foundered, however, and the doctor's absences from home became more frequent, his practice slowly falling away as he continued to drink. After a decade he left altogether. In 1899 his simple country wife Julia petitioned for divorce on grounds of abandonment.

If Bessie thought that her own marriage to William Pennebaker offered an escape from her mother's hardships, she was soon disillusioned. Life with Will Pennebaker was never financially secure, and then she suddenly found herself a widow with a young daughter and no means of support; her options were to take shelter out on the prairie with her mother, sisters, and brother, or seek work as a single woman in Omaha, a move that was controversial at best by contemporary standards. Bessie, ever a Gahan, chose the latter course. By 1905 she had taken a secretarial job in the office of J. L. Webster, one of Nebraska's most distinguished attorneys, a former state legislator who had been nominated for the Supreme Court.

Two decades previously, Webster and his partner, A. J. Poppleton, had defended Standing Bear, chief of the Ponca tribe; this civil liberties case, which made judicial history, almost single-handedly paved the way for full U.S. citizenship for Native Americans.

Webster's mentoring influence on Bessie was immeasurable. The attorney regularly assigned her weekly readings from his personal library of more than 2,000 volumes. Building on the open-mindedness she had inherited from her iconoclast father, Webster guided her toward a more progressive, humanistic outlook in a time of enormous social flux and change. In the years to come, Bessie would prove herself a worthy student.

That same year, 1905, Bessie remarried. Her second husband, Frank A. Myers, was the son of a pioneer sheep rancher who had made it big. Omaha was the "last stop" before Denver, the nation's second busiest railhead after Chicago, and the family's Terminal Warehouse and Mercantile Storage Company was the largest in the state. A stalwart Republican and a Mason, Frank Myers was an odd match for the loud, energetic Bessie. Colorless and taciturn, "a man with a hole in the middle of his mouth where his cigar went," he rarely spoke at the dinner table and, according to family lore, was in the habit of pointing at whatever he wanted. Unintimidated, Bessie usually responded, "This, Frank? *This?*"

Still, Myers provided security. For the six years that Bessie had worked to support herself, the young Dodie had been boarded out, first with Gramma Julia on the family farm, then at the Sacred Heart School; she saw her mother only sporadically. But now Bessie removed her daughter from the Catholic boarding school and could settle her in a new home in one of Omaha's better neighborhoods. Myers was hardly a substitute father, but his silences could not dampen the joy of Dodie's reunion with her mother. Once the eight-year-old was enrolled in the local public school, she quickly emerged from her shell.

Meanwhile, the wedding hadn't changed Bessie's ways. Although she later gave birth to another child—Dodie's half-sister, Betty—Bessie continued to work for the high-profile Webster and became known for her outspokenness on such social issues as immigration, the woman's vote, and Negro rights. She smoked, she wore loose-fitting dresses and mesh stockings, and she cared not a whit for the talk at the Field Club, the center of Omaha's social life. These propensities greatly irritated her husband. The two fought, but Bessie still did as she pleased.

Bessie's independent-mindness seemed to stimulate her daughter, and with adolescence, Dorothy was transformed. She became a pretty girl—not tall, but possessed of a "nice" figure—and she dressed well, sometimes even with an eccentric panache, in reds, blues, and oranges; she was gregarious, her laughter infectious, and at Central High School, which she entered in the fall of 1911, her grades were adequate if uneven, with As and Bs in the humanities and barely passing marks in subjects that did not interest her. Bessie, though, did not push. Dodie, or sometimes "Dode," as she became known as a teenager, started dating, and boyfriends were in great supply. Dodie loved the attention, and she accepted a few marriage proposals, leading to some short-term engagements.

Then Marlon Sr. entered her life after he returned from Shattuck for his last year at Central High. He was seventeen, two years older than she, and always impeccably dressed. With his military bearing, he had a country-club handsomeness. His determination to prosper, even as a young man, had schooled him in the advantages of silence; and whether or not he spent long hours planning his moves in public, he impressed her as orderly and disciplined, tidy and responsible. Given her own chaotic childhood, Dodie found these qualities as irresistible as his good looks. Beneath his boosterism, she also saw his quiet sadness and mistakenly interpreted it as a sign of depth or sensitivity. For Marlon her prettiness coupled with rambunctious flapper energy were appealing, and the advantages of her stepfather's clout made her all the more attractive.

In 1916, Dodie graduated from Central High and enrolled at the University of Nebraska College of Nursing, or Clarkson, located in downtown Omaha. She shared a dormitory room with Margherite Schneider, a retiring, reticent girl. "My aunt was very proper while Dodie was most definitely not, and she was probably a little afraid of her," said Schneider's niece, Isabella Threlkeld. "She couldn't believe this gal was so wild."

A grainy photograph of the period shows Dorothy in full flapper outrage: a bolero jacket over a formal shirtfront, satin bow tie, broad-brimmed vaquero hat, ankle-length skirt, white spats, and high-heeled shoes. Her head and shoulders are thrown back challengingly, as if to say, What you see is what you get! In her right hand, reminiscent more of Montmartre than Omaha, is a lit cigar.

Schneider monitored her roommate's every move when Marlon was commuting from the University of Nebraska in Lincoln to court her. "In my aunt's nursing notes," added Threlkeld, "there's a handwritten note saying, 'Dorothy went out again last night, out through the window.' She used to laugh about this. She'd say, 'That's why she got expelled—she'd go out the window to meet Marlon.' Apparently Dodie took all kinds of risks and broke all the rules and she'd go out the fire escape to meet him in the middle of the night."

Once Marlon enlisted in the army, he was stationed at the Signal Corps' balloon training center at Fort Omaha, which only made their liaisons easier. He wrote Dodie long, passionate letters in which he expressed his hopes for the future. Although her decision to go into nursing had doubtless been influenced by her mother's stories of her grandfather Gahan's high purpose as a medical pioneer, it was also fueled by Dodie's intention of following her beau to France. Even so, she was still dating other men. "Marlon was just one of her boyfriends at the time," recalled a contemporary, "and she was flamboyant in the true sense of the word. She'd always speak loudly. She did what she wanted, even though her mother didn't always approve."

While Dodie's roommate thought she had been expelled, in fact she completed her first year of nursing school. She didn't return for her second year because in the spring of 1918 Marlon was posted to the West Coast. Faced with the thought of losing him, the twenty-one-year-old Dodie agreed to be married. On June 22, 1918, Marlon and Dodie were wed.

When the armistice was declared five months later, the newlyweds traveled south to San Francisco, where Dodie found them a small walk-up apartment near Golden Gate Park. Marlon then took a job with the new telephone company, since he had been trained as an engineer in the army and regarded the telephone business as offering future opportunities for advancement.

By then Dodie was pregnant with her first child, Jocelyn. When she was in her fifth month, a kerosene heater exploded near her, terrifying and almost killing her. As Jocelyn was later told, "Mother was wearing one of those long skirts of the day, and it caught fire. She ran down the hall, and there was a Chinese man who was cleaning rugs. She grabbed a blanket off the bed and told him to roll her into it. My Aunt Betty was also in the house. My mother had taken nurse's training, so she got her clothes off and told Betty, 'I'm going to lie down and you get two chairs from the dining room and put them over me, and then put some blankets on top of the chairs. Call the doctor, call Marlon.' "

Marlon rushed home from the office. The doctors told him that it was a critical burn, but in 1919 there was little to be done for it. They predicted a 50 percent chance of infection of the second- and third-degree suppurations that extended from her knees to her shoulders, across her back, and down to her hands.

"The doctors were advising Mother to abort," added Jocelyn. "But she kept refusing because she thought I was going to be Philip, the son she and Papa had talked about and had already named. Mother had lost her father when she was two, she had also lost a little brother, so she deeply wanted a boy."

Bessie came out from Omaha to nurse her daughter. For the remainder of her pregnancy Dodie could lie only on her side, swathed in wet sheets. The treatment worked, and on November 18, 1919, she gave birth to Jocelyn, whom they named after one of the two maiden aunts who had raised Marlon as a child.

"I was only three pounds at birth," said Jocelyn. "I was put in a cigar box and dressed in doll clothes. I was full term but I hadn't been fed very well in the womb."

The accident and the almost miraculous birth profoundly affected the family. Dodie would carry the scars throughout her life and often had to apply salves to her back to reduce the pain. But those difficult months of healing drew her and her mother closer; and within a month the Brandos were back in Omaha, living in a rented house on Thirty-first Street, only a few blocks from Bessie and Frank. Marlon had no job waiting for him, but he took office space at 702 South Tenth Street with MARLON BRANDO MANU-FACTURING painted on the door—though what his firm manufactured wasn't evident. His business address was that of the Terminal Warehouse Building, the property owned by Dodie's stepfather, Frank Myers.

"Nana," as Bessie was now called, meanwhile opened up a shop of her own at Sixteenth and Farnham, one of Omaha's busiest intersections. Having witnessed God's power to heal Dodie, and since her sister, June, was already a Christian Scientist, Bessie became a "practitioner," a lay healer, herself. "Nana had lots and lots of friends, all kinds," recalled her granddaughter, "from the woman who came to wash her hair, a little black lady, to Mrs. Sebesma, her Norwegian cook, and she never became doctrinaire. She would often tell patients, 'Well, if you have a headache, take an aspirin. I'm sure God won't mind.'"

Even so, Nana's faith in the teachings of Mary Baker Eddy was a little more complex than that. Philosophically, Christian Science was an offshoot of Spiritualism; as early as the 1870s, tens of thousands of Americans had sought to prove the immortality of the soul by establishing communication with the spirits of the dead. For iconoclasts and romantics alike, it provided an alternative to the established religious order and its repressive conventions. Spiritualists and their Christian Scientist cousins saw each individual (regardless of gender) as an embodiment of the laws of nature, with health itself as a natural condition restorable through a "reharmonizing" of the individual with the natural order. Women, in particular, were regarded as the most effective vehicles, both as occult mediums and healers. What Spiritualism did, as one commentator put it, was help an entire generation of American women "find their voice." In an era marked by sweeping progressive social reform, it produced the first group of female religious leaders as well as a model of women's capacity for action in a world dominated by men.

The appeal, for Bessie, of communicating with the dead should be obvious: She had lost her first husband, then her father, and finally, in the early years of her marriage to Frank Myers, an infant son. Her burden had been made heavier by Dodie's narrow escape in San Francisco. Christian Science's emphasis on "correct thoughts," on reason over ritual, was one answer, but she wasn't about to forsake the occult either. Her father, as Jocelyn recalled, "had all kinds of occult people—séancers—to dinner a lot, and that stuff was passed on to Nana, who was pretty psychic anyhow." Bessie would continue to try to "reach" her father with a Ouija board for the rest of her life: "We always used to get him when we rapped the table with her."

Bessie often showed up at the Brando house with the works of Madame Blavatsky or Krishnamurti, the famed student of Theosophy. Years later, when she suffered a stroke, Bessie had what mystics call a primal experience, "It was probably around '41 or '42," explained Jocelyn. "She was unable to communicate for three days, and when she came out of it, she said, 'I have never felt more alive.' I think she meant she had experienced life in its immensity. Life as an entity in itself. That 'alive' was more than 'living,' in our limited sense of it."

Bessie "lived her religion," as relatives and friends insisted. She put it to work on a one-to-one basis as a healer and also served as finance chairman for Omaha's Vocation Bureau, a local charity devoted to keeping poor children in school and educating the immigrants toiling in the city's stock-yards. In addition, she was a suffragist seeking reform through the Nebraska League of Women Voters and a supporter of the nascent birth-control movement under Margaret Sanger.

At times her husband grew weary of her enthusiasms. "She had a fight with Frank once in his office," said Jocelyn, recalling one of her favorite Nana anecdotes. "He got mad, walked out, and locked her in. It was a U-shaped building with a ledge running around the outside, and she knew a lawyer who had an office in the other wing. This was the era of hobbled skirts, which were tighter at the hem. But she climbed out of the window, three floors up, and walked completely around on the ledge. She knocked on the lawyer's window. He yelled 'Aghhh!' and let her in. 'Thank you very much,' she said, all self-composed, and went back to Frank's outer office, where he sat, thinking she was still locked in, and said, 'Don't you ever do that to me again!' "

With Dodie and Marlon's return to Omaha, mother and daughter saw each other often. They spent hours discussing history, art, philosophy, even their favorite pulp novels and magazines. The two took singing lessons together, often practicing on Dodie's upright when not listening to gramophone records of jazz and cowboy music. They would also sit around "hooting and hollering" at the world around them, and since they had no doubt that they had more brains, more pizzazz, than almost anyone they knew—including their husbands—neither begrudged the other her occasional snicker or snipe. Bessie helped Dodie through her second pregnancy with daughter Frances, born in September 1922, and when Marlon Jr. was born a year and a half later, she was devoted to her grandson.

Jocelyn recalled that her grandmother was the strongest influence on her own life, and on those of her sister and brother as well. She represented strength in a sea of troubles, unlimited supportiveness, and more: nothing less than the "norm" of heterodoxy that was to become synonymous with the name Brando in the years to come.

At the time of Marlon Jr.'s (or "Bud," as his grandmother nicknamed him) birth, the Brandos had moved to 3135 Mason Street, a comfortable wood-frame house fronted with wisteria and located in a neighborhood of merchants, insurance salesmen, and bank managers—the back of the city's prospering middle class. Marlon Sr., then twenty-nine, had given up his own company and gone to work for Western Limestone Products Company as a salesman whose territory included Missouri, Iowa, and Kansas. He put in seven-day work weeks and was often on the road, striving to expand his contacts during the region's boom years of mineral sales.

In the spring of 1926, two years after Bud's birth, the Brandos moved in with Nana at 1026 South Thirty-second Street. Dodie's half-sister, Betty, was off at college, and Frank was gone, too, having moved downtown to the Athletic Club. Bessie had grown tired of his contentious silences, but more than that she had discovered that his evening absences were as much devoted to women as business. The separation was amicable, though, and no divorce papers were filed. Frank still occasionally came to dinner but sat silently, puffing on his cigar. Four years later, terminally ill with cancer, he would move back home.

The house on South Thirty-second Street was constantly filled with visitors. Omaha was Omaha, no more sophisticated than Topeka or Moline, but somehow Dodie managed to find the bohemians and oddballs in its midst, people who were not necessarily rich but interesting, compelling, and *au courant.* These friends included Harry Berkeley, a lawyer who was the stepfather of actress Dorothy McGuire, and the Fonda and Abbott families. "There was even a Russian count," recalled Jocelyn, "as well as an artist who carved a chess set for us with cowboys and Indians that was stunning. Tepees and blockhouses for pawns, and the bishops were 'ranch cooks.' "

Informality was the hallmark. Dodie's favorite domain was her bed, which was always littered with crossword puzzles, pencils, pens, and books. The house itself looked just as lived in and was by conventional standards untidy, but even with guests, Dodie didn't worry about it. Marlon Sr., whose aspirations were much more conventional, mostly remained aloof from Dodie's entertaining. In the big living room he would characteristically stand with his elbow resting on the mantle, giving the impression that he was taller than his actual height of five feet nine. He drank as much as Dodie, but could hold his liquor better than either she or the guests. In his silences he made it clear that this was Dodie's scene—*her* friends, *her* interests, *her* pace and tempo.

For the kids, even then, he was slightly forbidding. "It was very strange," Jocelyn noted. "Everybody outside the family loved him and thought he was charming and marvelous and handsome and funny. But he saw us as extensions of himself. If we didn't toe the line, it reflected on him, and he wasn't rational about it. Anything we did that wasn't up to his standard wasn't good enough, and for him this discipline somehow translated to love. 'Eat in the kitchen until your table manners are good enough to come to the table.' If you spilled milk—every kid spills milk—the look was terrible. If you said, 'Papa, please could I have just a little bit of rutabaga, I don't like rutabaga,' he would serve you one spoon's worth and then he'd take another and give you double, and make us eat everything on our plate."

Still, on the surface, life on South Thirty-second Street during these pre-Depression years was almost idyllic. The house stood halfway down a dead-end street; Bud, Fran, and Jocelyn were free to roam. There weren't any other children on the block, so they ran as a pack. Hanscom Park was nearby and often they would take off to gawk at the monkeys in the greenhouse, or to sled in "the hollow," or in warm weather, throw crumbs to the fish in the still lily ponds. They stole their parents' cigarettes and tried to smoke. They played games like rummy and fish. And there were house pets, too, a bunch of bantam chickens, a dog, and several cats. One, the dwarf Sheba, black with silver tips, regularly brought back little field mice she'd caught, leaving her trophies lined up on the back porch to the children's shrieking delight.

As would be expected, their religious training was inconsistent. Like Nana, Dodie rarely went to church and the children were sent to doctors, even though they used their Christian Science "beliefs" to get out of their shots at school. Fran, who turned six in 1928, and perhaps the most proper of the three, would sometimes go to Sunday school alone, because (as she later explained) "all my little friends went, and we wished that our parents were more like the other parents."

For all her husband's "rigidity," Dodie's interest in people drew her into myriad social and political causes, and although she had never completed her nurse's training, when soon after she returned from the West Coast, the great influenza epidemic struck Omaha, she pitched in to help the sick. Later, more of her time was taken up with child labor issues, and with this effort, she was taking cues from Bessie as well as Grace Abbott, the legendary suffragist whose family had been close to the Gahans in Grand Island. Delinquent and neglected children, the education of unwed mothers, health and safety standards, as well as legislation to curb abuses in migrant labor camps—all were on the ballot in upcoming Nebraska elections. With Elizabeth Abbott, Grace's sister, Dodie threw herself behind the referendum heart and soul. With Fitzy Doyle, the wife of Marlon Sr.'s college classmate Lom Doyle, she drove a jalopy to the Colorado line, speechifying at every whistle stop along the way.

She next threw herself into Omaha's new Community Playhouse after friends, including Harriet Fonda, the sister of the then adolescent Henry, urged her to audition for a small part in February 1925. Less than two months later, with Arthur Wing Pinero's *The Enchanted Cottage,* she made her debut in a major role. Acting the female lead alongside L. C. ("Brick") Hawley and Henry Fonda's older sister, Jayne, she won rave reviews, despite never having taken a drama class or acted before. "The stage seldom sees a prettier scene than . . . Mrs. Brando made of the last few moments before the fall of the curtain," wrote the *World Herald.*

Over the next four years, the name Dorothy Brando would become synonymous with the Playhouse itself. Stepping into the role of the benumbed housemaid in Ferenc Molnár's *Liliom* opposite Harriet Fonda, her acting earned even more enthusiastic notices:

> Julie, the young wife of Liliom, is a characterization finely wrought by Mrs. Marlon Brando. The pathos of tragic grief in the death scene is profoundly moving. Many of the so-called emotional stars would have spoiled that phase of the play by overdoing it. Mrs. Brando, with her reserve, gives you the effect of benumbing sorrow.

Dodie was cast to play the leads in both productions announced for the following 1926–27 season, Eugene O'Neill's *Anna Christie* and George Bernard Shaw's *Pygmalion.* The schedule was a step up for the company since both demanded a level of psychological sophistication the players had never had to master before. Perhaps it was the controversy surrounding O'Neill's play—the story of a prostitute, a coal barge captain, and a steamship stoker—that prompted the Community Playhouse to preface its Playbill with testimonials from a college president, a noted drama critic, and the production's director. Nevertheless, justifications were hardly necessary after *Anna Christie* opened on October 24. Dodie was barely able to hide her pleasure at the rave reviews that compared the show to New York and Chicago productions and, once again, singled her out for praise:

Mrs. Marlon Brando's acting in *Liliom* was memorable, but as Anna Christie she far excels her earlier work. . . . The sincerity of the character and of Mrs. Brando's interpretation of it lies in the fact that Anna Christie speaks the truth and is the truth, ugly though it be. And there can be beauty even in that ugliness when the girl still keeps the desire to be clean again through the purification of the sea. The fine scene where Anna grows pensively near to tenderness during her first night in the fog, Mrs. Brando surpasses only when she scales the emotional heights in the tale of her early experiences.

She became the talk of dinner parties in the swanker parts of town, a "star" who was putting Omaha on the map. Otto Kahn, the president of New York's Metropolitan Opera Company and eminent patron of New York's Theatre Guild, who was in town with publisher Condé Nast and Frank Crowinshield, the editor of *Vogue,* had attended *Anna Christie.* He rose from his seat to pledge a not insignificant $500 to the Playhouse, praising the city's "growing love of music, the arts, and the finer things of life"; privately, it was said, he had urged Dodie to leave Nebraska for Broadway.

Pygmalion followed in May. Playing opposite Dodie's Eliza Doolittle was Rudyard Norton, the most renowned local actor in Playhouse history. "We worked together for at least six weeks," Norton recalled. "Dodie was no prima donna. We rehearsed under fairly primitive conditions, and she did Eliza's cockney accent beautifully through the whole show. She'd never been to England, and where she picked it up I never knew. It was remarkably dead-on, completely intuitive and unforced, so natural to the character that it didn't draw attention to itself."

"Amazingly true to life," her notices repeatedly said. Dorothy Brando could *identify,* suspend herself for the intricacies of a character. With the December 1927 Playhouse production of O'Neill's *Beyond the Horizon,* she prompted one ticket holder to recall: "The stage set was very shadowy, some old farmhouse in New England, and you sensed the heat of a summer night. It was with Dodie—her lines, and how she delivered them— that physically drenched you in the atmosphere. She made it that believable."

In this production Dodie was onstage with the twenty-one-year-old Henry Fonda for the first time. She had recruited Hank himself. Three

years before, he had flunked out of the University of Minnesota and returned to Omaha to face his father's wrath.

When Dodie called, Hank's mother had to rouse her son from his
lethargy. "Do me a favor," she said. "Dodie Brando's on the line. Just listen
to her."

Dodie asked him to see the Playhouse director, Gregory Foley, about
a bit part in *You and I*. For the rest of the season he built scenery, painted
sets, swept the stage, and ushered. He had caught the bug.

Months later, Foley offered him the lead in the next season's opener,
Merton of the Movies. Bill Fonda was apoplectic about Hank's new interest
in the theater and refused to speak to his son until Dodie, ever the manager, intervened: She went to Hank's father and wheedled, then argued on
behalf of the boy's talent. As usual, she wouldn't take no for an answer, and
in great part due to her effort, Fonda's star was born.

The show following *Beyond the Horizon* was Foley's last, and soon afterward, in September 1928, his replacement, Bernard Szold, arrived in
Omaha with impressive credentials. For a number of years, he had been in
the forefront of the Little Theater movement with the Goodman Memorial Theater in Chicago and New York's Theatre Guild, both among the
country's strongest showcases for modern drama. In short order Szold
"discovered" the thirteen-year-old Dorothy McGuire after seeing the
youngster in one of the Playhouse's Sunday afternoon children's plays.

To Dodie, the new director was elegant, intellectual, and certainly intense by Omaha standards. A tall, bronzed, thirty-year-old bachelor, Bernie Szold was not only committed to a life in the theater, but he also
painted and sketched. That he was the cousin of the famous American
Zionist Henrietta Szold only added to his exotic allure.

Szold's productions were like none Omaha had ever seen—always
challenging and controversial. In reviewing *Springtime for Henry*, a comedy, the *World Herald*, whose owner's wife was on the Playhouse board,
expressed dismay at the play's modernist setting, wondering aloud at the
propriety of "seeing a young man returning to a bedroom with another
man's wife." Szold, under attack, had no option but to reply in the paper's
pages. "If it will make anybody feel better," he wrote, "the people who
went off stage at the end of the show didn't go to a bedroom but straight to
the stage switchboard. They were all chaperoned by the electricians." Not
surprisingly, Szold would leave Omaha in disgust several years later.

• • •

Though becoming more and more popular with Omaha's smart set, Dodie never left her bohemian roots; unlike her husband, she had little taste for decorum. She was still close to her fellow campaigner Fitzy Doyle, and neither was beyond shocking their more proper acquaintances with words like *shit*. But perhaps her best-remembered outrage was the stunt she pulled one afternoon at Fitzy's posh country club in Lincoln.

"It was a big party that Mother threw for her," recalled David Doyle, the Doyles' youngest son and later a cast member of the television series "Charlie's Angels." "Dodie had been on her best behavior throughout the afternoon. All the society people were there—wives of bankers and other establishment types—and she had endured it for hours. Finally she and Mother were leaving, with the other women standing along the circular driveway waving good-bye. As the car started to pull away—Mother was driving—Dodie pulled out her bridgework, turned back, and gave them all this hideous, toothless grin. She was beside herself, absolutely in stitches. 'There!' she yelled out the window. 'That'll give you something to chew on!' All these society gals had come to see the bohemian with the reputation for raising hell," Doyle added, "and Dodie just wasn't going to disappoint them."

While Dodie had become absorbed by the Playhouse, her husband was increasingly absent from home. By 1927, his employer, Western Limestone, had absorbed three of its closest competitors, and as his workload expanded, so did his determination to prosper, leading to longer days on the road and frequent sales trips. "Marlon was just of another world from Dodie," Elizabeth Woolward, a Playhouse colleague, remembered. Nevertheless, as if to deny his distance from Dodie, he began to participate in the work of the Playhouse, banging nails, painting and constructing sets. For one production he even served as stage manager. But, try as he might to join in, he was not, and could never be, as open and spontaneous as his wife.

Liquor was already becoming a central part of their marital problems. Prohibition was then in effect, but from the time of the Volstead Act in October 1919, countless Americans found ways to supply themselves with illegal alcohol; in most cities wine and beer were made at home in tidal-wave quantities. In Omaha, the fixings were supplied by a local brewer, a chatty bohemian from across the river in Council Bluffs, Iowa, who regularly parked his truck at curbside along South Thirty-second Street to unload cans of malt syrup, sugar, hops, and barrels for home production. The Brando house was then filled with the smell of fermenting hops—"it smelled wonderful," recalled Fran. Sometimes one of the casks in the basement would explode loudly in the middle of the night, which amused the kids even more. There was also gin. Great bottles of spring water stood in the cluttered back pantry, where the contents were mixed with alcohol and juniper berries according to the standard recipe of the day. "They made it in bathtubs, then they put it in a big bottle," recalled Jocelyn, who watched from the sidelines.

Dodie's drinking, while not out of hand, was a way of denying her estrangement from her husband, as were her many outside activities. When not acting at the Playhouse, she was doing makeup for the Children's Theater as well as serving on the board of directors of the League of Women Voters, taking sketching classes, and frequently running off to her lunches at the trendy Aquilla Court, where she often talked with Szold and others for hours. She was on the move constantly, and began to rely more and more on Ermalene, the live-in housekeeper, to care for the children. Acquaintances began to wonder about her sense of maternal responsibility.

Marlon Sr. was also drinking and finding other outlets for his dissatisfactions. His drunken roistering at business conventions had become something of a standing joke among colleagues throughout the Midwest, if only because of his staid, gentlemanly veneer when sober. Now, though, Dodie knew that her husband was sleeping around, not only on the road but in town, and, worse, that people were talking.

"My mother spoke of how Marlon was the handsomest man she'd ever seen," recalled Geoffrey Horne, whose mother was a friend of the Brandos and often baby-sat for them. "She said that Dorothy in the beginning must have gone for his appearance. The implication was that he was a playboy."

Whether for retaliation or from a sense of adventure, Dodie was taking lovers of her own. She wasn't subtle about it, according to Belle West, who, like her friend Bidie Swift, wrote a column for the *Omaha Bee*. "In 1929 Bidie and I were down to Kansas City for the weekend in the spring," West said. "We stayed at the Athletic Club, and Sunday morning we were leaving the building when we ran into Dodie in the lobby. Dodie ran over to Bidie, and she made no bones about the fact that she was there to see some other man. Everything had been going great, she said, only she had just received word that her husband was on his way down. She had gotten rid of the boyfriend quickly and was then waiting for Marlon. But she wasn't saying to us, 'Look, you've seen me here, don't put any item in the paper.' She was just telling us as a friend, 'Isn't this a riot?' like, 'Hey, we're all in this together.' "

The Kansas City fling was not an isolated event, even though Jocelyn was going on ten, Fran was seven, and Bud five. Because of the differences in age, there was a natural bonding between the two younger kids, while Jocelyn, nearing adolescence, was cast in the role of surrogate mother.

"Fran and Bud were the babies," Jocelyn explained, "and in order to get approval I became the take-carer, helping Mother, telling her, 'I'll watch the other kids.' I was responsible for walking Fran and Bud to school every morning. But they would run away, and I came home and complained, 'They run off and I'm late.' So Mother bought this little harness—a leash, really—which embarrassed them.

"And who made cocoa and toast and got the kids off to school if Mother was sleeping and didn't want to get up because she couldn't face the day? Me. If Mother wasn't around, I was the mother."

But Dodie was rarely home, and there were long periods when Bud was left on his own, when even his incessant hectoring couldn't get the attention of his older sisters. Ermalene, the young housekeeper, was his most constant companion. When Ermy was too busy with housework, however, Bud went to see Isabel Kratville, a young housewife living directly opposite the Brandos.

"I didn't baby-sit him so much as he just came across the street on his own," she recalled. "But only during the week, not weekends. If it was lunchtime I'd say, 'Come on, let's have something to eat.'

"He was very serious and always minded me if I asked him to do something. He was curious but never asked questions, and never talked about his sisters, either. He just followed me around the house, and whatever I was doing he'd stand there, looking at me."

Sometimes Bud went there first thing in the morning, but if Isabel went out, he'd wait for her, watching from his window. As soon as she pulled into the garage, he raced across the street. "Once I tried to draw him out about his family," Kratville added. "The brewer's truck was out front and I said, 'I see you have company today.' He just replied, 'Oh, that's not company, that's somebody making beer!' "

The young Brando would continue to get himself "adopted" by substitute families in years to come. Alone and self-contained, he somehow intuited the power of silence and let his mute persona bespeak his sadness and solitude. At home, however, he was more demonstrative. Brighter, more commanding and adroit than Franny, he marshaled the younger of his two sisters to join him in antics designed to win attention or, with other adults present, gain their acceptance with laughter at his pranks and precociousness.

His looks helped—already visitors cooed over his "golden curls" and "delicate features," or "those eyes which were so vulnerable, so soft." But he had native cunning, too. He could surprise adults with his ready perceptions, his quickness and sensitivity to slights. Bud was once barred from using the playhouse built by a neighbor for his nephews and nieces, and for days afterward he watched the other children laughing from the shelter of their special place; aware that he had been brooding around the house, Nana asked what was bothering him. Bud shrugged, tossing his head in the direction of the off-limits playhouse. When his grandmother pressed him, he sneered, dismissing the neighbor and his live-in sister as "the little old man and little old woman across the street."

Closer to the bone but marked by the same bitterness was one of his rare outbursts at Dodie's departures. It was the spring of 1930. Marlon Sr. was away on business as usual, and Geoffrey Horne's mother had just arrived to baby-sit. Bud followed her into the house and loudly slammed the screen door behind them.

Dodie came down the stairs, dressed for a night on the town. Bud looked from one woman to the other. "You women stink!" he yelled and rushed back outside.

2
E V A N S T O N

1930–38

In June 1930, Marlon Sr. took a new job as general sales manager for the Calcium Carbonate Company. With a salary of $1,000 a month plus commissions, he believed that he'd found his niche at last. But the change meant that the family would have to leave Omaha and resettle in Evanston, Illinois, outside Chicago.

Although Dodie agreed to this move, she deeply resented it. Perhaps as a result, her alcoholism would worsen and tear at the family for the next fifteen years, causing wounds that would never heal. Perhaps the problem was genetic, as later medical research would suggest; on a simpler level, though, it would seem that drinking represented her way of denying the fissures in her marriage that were broadened by the move itself. The loss of her beloved theater, her sense of herself as having a place, a status, had all been subverted by the more pressing needs of "moving on," as her husband put it.

The Brandos' large shingled house on Evanston's Judson Avenue wasn't one of the grander edifices of the North Shore, but with four bedrooms, a marble fireplace, and a lawn fronting the serene, tree-lined street it was quiet and comfortable and fit Marlon's image of respectability. The Lincoln School, where Bud, now six, and Franny, now eight, were enrolled, was reputedly one of the best in the nation. With the ten-year-old Jocelyn baby-sitting them, they often traipsed to the Lake Michigan beach two blocks away, or to the public library, for even now, unprompted, all three were reading.

Dodie didn't attend Evanston's snobbish Glenview Club or join bridge parties in the afternoons. From the start she had little use for her conventional neighbors—"the tea-drinking Republicans," as she called them. Chicago, however, was less than a half hour away, and it wasn't long before she'd gathered another coterie of artistic types not all that removed from her clique in Omaha. Among them were Edgar ("Britt") Britton, a WPA muralist; Phil Baker and Erna Phillips, the creators of the well-known radio soap operas "Today's Children" and "The Guiding Light," and the puppeteer Bil Baird, who was the son of Nana's closest friend in Grand Island. It was a tightly knit, giddy group, playing on the fringes of Chicago's cultural scene. Mainly they drank together, barhopping along Rush Street or having a party at the apartment shared by Britt Britton and his live-in girlfriend. It was through Britton that Dodie met a banker named David Salinger, who quickly became her most steadfast and loyal friend.

"David felt that Dodie was an alcoholic, but didn't judge her," said Sylvia Salinger, who later became Salinger's wife. "I don't know that he ever really analyzed why she was drinking, except that she was so frustrated and felt trapped. She was creative and didn't have an outlet. She was also starting to neglect the kids, which made her feel guilty." Marlon Sr.'s remoteness—not to mention his frequent absences—had made the problem worse. Within a year after leaving Omaha, Dodie saw herself as a housewife rather than an actress, stymied in what she loved best.

"Dodie felt she got a little shortchanged, and she was also feeling that age was against her," recalled another close friend. "She blamed Evanston, the town itself, saying to me, 'You could never be happy in that place. *Never.* Evanston is old money and old names and social register.'

"She also used to quip, 'I'm the greatest actress *not* on the American stage.' She thought she was better than Katharine Cornell, and the only time I asked, 'Then why in hell are you letting it go?' all she said was, 'Three kids.' Was she evading my question? Now, I'd say yes. Then, I didn't know. The gal who jumped in a jalopy and took off to campaign for child labor laws, that was different. That was two weeks. With theater, she was talking a lifetime."

In 1931 Dodie began a love affair with an army officer in Omaha. The distance between them complicated their relationship, but it had been on-again, off-again for twenty months. Late in 1932, escaping Evanston to drive to Nebraska for a rendezvous, she crashed the family Ford and broke her left arm; Marlon had to be summoned to the hospital. By the time the dust settled, Dodie was forced to break off the affair, and the army man returned to his wife. Marlon and Dodie fought, but, as usual, nothing was settled. As usual, too, Marlon didn't confront the problems. Cold and distant, he'd never been able to engage openly, and the upshot was that Dodie's affairs proliferated in proportion to her drinking.

As a carryover from Omaha, the Brandos had continued brewing beer at home, but now it took on a far less jovial aspect. The parents' drinking led to arguments, which the kids often witnessed. Month by month, it got worse and the quarrels escalated with loud shouting matches into the night. Bud responded at one point by taking his parents' empty beer bottles and lining them up like duckpins on the sidewalk in front of the house; with Evanston as the home of the Women's Christian Temperance Union, it can be assumed his gesture did not go unnoticed.

Dodie's drinking was not confined to the house, however, even though Evanston had remained "dry" once Repeal was enacted in 1933. Often, she took off for the saloons outside the city limits on the west of town, and sometimes failed to return until thirteen-year-old Jocelyn had already cooked dinner. When Marlon Sr. chose to make an appearance, Dodie often faced his wrath all over again—the undertow of recrimination, guilt, and apologies was drowning the family in unhappiness.

"We had meetings every once in a while about what we were going to do," Jocelyn said. "Father, we three kids, and Mother. Mother would be crying, saying, 'Sorry, I don't know why it happens, I'll try not to do it again.' And Papa saying, 'We can't survive if this continues.'"

The worst of it was that no one knew what to expect next. Dodie's drinking was not daily, and as with many alcoholics her lapses varied in intensity and pitch. "It was like explosions, totally unpredictable," said a neighbor, who sometimes heard their quarrels. "They were drunks, both of them, so you never knew when they'd start yelling."

The kids lived with their uncertainties day to day; whether the altercations became physical, as Bud would later bitterly insist, may never be known. When any of the children's friends came over after school, there was no way of knowing if Dodie would be sober. When she wasn't, she demanded everyone's attention.

"She often wanted us to listen to classical music with her," Jocelyn recalled. "She insisted, 'Come on in, sit down, sit down!' and nobody could refuse. It was Mozart, Beethoven, but mainly Stravinsky's *The Rite of Spring,* which she liked because it was very emotional. She'd just keep us there, saying, 'Listen to this now. Isn't it beautiful? Really moving?' "

One of Jocelyn's boyfriends at the time, Jurgen Petersen, recalls the extra complication of Bud, who added to the chaos by making his own demands on everybody's attention. "He came home from school about the same time we did," Petersen recalled. "He was always alone, never with any friends. One day he wanted to sell me a revolver, maybe a .32 caliber. It was a little gun and it was sort of held together with a bent nail. The firing pin was missing—it wasn't a working gun at all—but he wanted a buck for it if I wanted to be alone with Jocelyn. It was a bribe, and I had to pay him just to get rid of him."

Another beau, William Valos, was held up for quarters. So hesitant were Bud's sisters to scold him—for fear of worse antics in response—that he seemed to have the run of the house.

"Basically, he was a pain in the ass, a firecracker just waiting to go off," said Petersen. "And Mrs. Brando? I met her only once. I sometimes asked Jocelyn, 'Where's your mother? How come I never meet your mom?' But she never gave me a clear-cut answer."

Word began to spread through the neighborhood: "The Brandos are crazy."

"Absolutely," said a classmate of Bud, who lived down the block, grimly recalling how the young Brando enlisted a mutual friend to join him in tripping the alarm on a corner firebox. "The father was never home, so Bud could do whatever he wanted. After a while my folks wouldn't let me go over there, because they were afraid he'd get me into trouble."

Another classmate, Betty Miller, remembered when Bud pushed his fist through a glass door at the Evanston Hotel, where she was living with her family. "I was with this group of girlfriends," she explained, "and we wouldn't let him in. He kept badgering us and when we still refused, he smashed the glass, then ran."

One of Bud's classmates, Byron Veris, realized that Bud could take over any situation with his no-holds-barred, frenetic behavior. On Saturdays the neighborhood kids usually went to the five-cent matinees on Chicago Avenue for a Flash Gordon, Tom Mix, or Tarzan serial. Afterward they regrouped at Howie Becker's house, which had a huge tree in the backyard. As the other kids watched, Bud would climb up to the roof over the Beckers' back porch, pause, then swing across to the garage at the end of a rope with a Johnny Weissmuller yell so piercing that it could be heard a block away. Like most of his contemporaries, he had a two-gun holster and even chaps to play cowboys. When he got "hit" by a bullet, he crashed down the steps or flung himself into the nearby bushes. "He'd get plugged, and he didn't just fall down," recalled Veris. "He really knew how to die. He made a specialty of it. I mean it was *real.*"

At home, his need for attention had escalated, too. "He wanted to win at everything," Jocelyn remembered. "If we played rummy he'd change the rules, then defend himself by saying, 'What do you mean, I always had this card.' 'We saw you. We say you cheated!' 'What do you mean,' he'd repeat. 'I was just sitting here.' "

Shadowboxing was another gambit. "He'd just touch your face, and goad you, 'Come on, come on.' You'd tell him to stop and he'd keep at it, and the goal was to get you discombobulated. He teased so much I broke windows throwing books at him," said Jocelyn. "Only then he'd duck, hooting, 'Why'd you get so mad? *Ha-ha-ha.*' "

At the Lincoln School, Bud's behavior was equally high profile, thanks to his rubber bands, spitballs, paper airplanes, and the frequent times he stuck his foot out in the aisle to trip his classmates. "He even chased us with a dead garter snake one day," recalled Nan Prendergast McChesney. "None of us were repulsed so much as it was, 'Gee, he sure has a lot of nerve, knowing what the consequences are going to be.' " Sure enough, the stunt meant another trip to the principal's office.

"Hyperactive" didn't begin to describe his mischief. "He was kicked out of class so many times," said one classmate, "that he had to know people were talking about him." One story that went around was how he used a can of lighter fluid to write *shit* on the blackboard; then, just before the teacher entered, he put a match to it. "He got kicked out for a few days, even a week," the classmate added. "Sometimes the parents had to come to get him. He was only ten at that point, but it was as if he had already made himself famous."

Although small-framed and wiry, Bud had started to broaden through the shoulders. His eyesight was poor and he wore glasses. Most of the time he spoke rapidly, without a hint of the languorous pauses that would later become his trademark. His most noticeable features were his large, liquid eyes, which were almost poetic in suggestion, yet week after week he often showed up for first-period class scratched and bleeding, his white shirt blotched with grass stains. Called upon to explain why he'd been fighting in the schoolyard, he ascribed it to "honor," the need to protect a classmate.

"He wasn't particularly affectionate or warm," said Mildred Milar, his fourth-grade teacher. "A little boy at that age will often have a fondness for his teacher, and they're still young enough that it's easy for them to express it. Sometimes they'll bring you a piece of fruit or flowers, or hang around to clean the blackboard. Not Bud, though. He always put on a tough exterior. His face would be all tied up in a scowl, and it was as though getting into fights answered a need for him. He was convinced that he was doing something that had to be done. It let him get something out, even though he couldn't or wouldn't talk about it."

It appears that the classmate Bud was defending was Wally Cox, later to become his friend and roommate in New York. Short and gangly, Wally was smaller than his protector, and he wore the same horn-rimmed glasses that would become his trademark as TV's Mr. Peepers. He was also brighter by far than most of the other kids at Lincoln—a whimsical extrovert and omnivorous reader who talked so much that his teachers constantly ordered him to silence.

Wally had come from Michigan, and, like Bud, was considered an outsider. His stepfather, Ben Pratt, a radio writer, was a friend of Merle Friedell, who had introduced him to Dodie. Nowhere in evidence was Wally's mother, an alcoholic who would shortly depart the household for parts unknown with a female lover.

The bonding between Bud and Wally was inevitable, given their personalities and their shared alienation from mainline Evanston. Both boys liked to argue. Their contests could be about anything, ranging from "I can stand on my left heel longer than you can" to guessing how many eggs were broken in the first soldiers' mess at Fort Bragg. It could go on endlessly. Wally, who always had the sharper memory, was often the victor.

Together the two went on hikes, with Wally extemporizing in his high, reedy voice as he'd point out particular larvae or rock formations, or posed mock philosophic questions like whether oysters could be called "a voluntary friend of man." It was goofy, even ludicrous, since everything was grist for Wally's offbeat sense of humor. But just as important, each boy found in the other an antidote to his own individual pain.

Jocelyn realized just how sensitive her brother was beneath his tough exterior. It was during this year that he came to the aid of a destitute bag lady, an alcoholic whom he encountered in the course of his wanderings.

"He was walking along by the beach with his bike," his sister recalled, "and he saw this woman in trouble. She was drunk—whether or not she was fainting, I don't know—but he went over to her and said, 'Can I help you?' He dipped his handkerchief in the lake and came back and put it to her face, and then brought her home with him.

"Mother and Papa were in Florida visiting some friends, but Dick Corrigan, this guy who'd been staying with us, was there. Eventually, he and our maid, Ermy, decided that the woman was nuts. They called a nearby hotel to get her a room. Bud had to be assured that she would be all right, so he insisted on going to the hotel with us."

While he was intent on protecting the underdogs and have-nots, as he had when coming to Wally's defense in the school yard, more often than not Bud simply raised hell. Once again his teacher, Mildred Milar, decided that his fractious behavior in the classroom dictated another parental alert. Again she called in Dodie, but as was often the case, the mother was hard to reach. "I'd have to make these complicated arrangements to see her," Milar said. "She was always busy with other interests, pursuits outside the home. When she finally came in, our conferences lasted about an hour. I'd emphasize the things that Bud was doing well, then get into the problems I wanted her help on. Had she encountered this sort of behavior at home? Was he upset when he'd leave for school in the morning? What did she think? She was cooperative enough, but preoccupied with herself. She couldn't get down to the commonsense kind of thing—she wasn't the solid, calm, motherly type, which would have been a lot more helpful."

Marlon Sr. never put in an appearance at the school—even on Parents' Day. Meanwhile, Bud continued to roam the neighborhood. Chicago Avenue, in addition to its many movie theaters, offered a run of ramshackle car lots usually left unattended after dark, and there he tagged along with older boys when they went joyriding late at night.

"There were always a lot of riders, four or five of us," recalled one of his cohorts. "We looked for a car with a full tank of gas, then pushed it down to the end of the alley before starting it up. The cars were Model Ts with foot pedals, or stick shifts you had to double-clutch. Mostly the excitement was a question of getting away with it, and we never got caught. Bud never got behind the wheel, but he'd ride with us, just sitting there waiting to see what was next."

If he was testing his nerve, at eleven the tests escalated. Despite the neighborhood's affluence there were a few abandoned homes that he had already explored with Fran in tow, but now he moved closer to the lake, to the corner of Lee and Judson, less than a dozen doors from the Brando home itself, and he enlisted a few classmates in the caper.

"The house was a sort of a Frank Lloyd Wright architecture," one of his neighborhood cronies explained. "It had wide overhangs, which made it easier to go up the drainpipe. The people were away on vacation, and we jimmied the lock on an upstairs door. Someone called the police, though, and there we were, not stealing anything but still inside, when all of a sudden a squad car squealed up and there was a cop yelling, 'Get down here!' "

There were five or six boys in the group, all caught red-handed. Outside on the street, they were lined up, and as one of the officers began interrogating them, Bud, smaller and less conspicuous than the others, began to slink away.

"It was as if he was just drifting off," added the friend. "I remember it that clearly, the exact way he was walking—head down, his limbs sort of folded into himself. It was a minute or two before the cops realized what was happening. 'Hey, you, come back here!' one of them yelled. But Bud kept walking. The cop yelled at him again, and it was only then that he turned around—very meekly now, as though he was some poor, innocent kid."

In June 1934, the family left the Judson Avenue house for an apartment several blocks south on Sheridan Square, a gesture toward simplified housekeeping since, as Jocelyn explained, "we did a lot of things on that basis when Mother was drinking." It was a lesser address, closer to Chicago and beset by noisy traffic, but it was supposed to be a new start. In the same spirit, almost immediately after they moved in, Dodie took Bud and Fran to a summer camp in southern Wisconsin, where she would work as a counselor, the children joining the other campers.

The vacation had been mutually agreed on because Marlon and Dodie realized that they both needed a rest from their arguments. Jocelyn, who had failed her sophomore year, stayed behind with her father to do remedial schoolwork.

The camp was coeducational—Camp Nagawicka for girls and St. John's for boys. Located outside Delafield, an hour and a half's drive north of Chicago, it provided a rustic setting for 600 campers, usually children of affluent society families from all over the country. Upon arriving there, Dodie immediately threw herself into coaching the camp's young thespians. She built sets, helped with costumes and makeup, and pitched in whenever her talents were needed. She was drinking, but apparently no more than the other staffers whom she joined at local roadhouses in the evening.

Bud also was involved in the theatrical productions, but within weeks of arriving, he drew attention to himself. "During the day, he was an outdoor kind of kid," said first-year counselor Bob Becker. "Basically he just went his own way. The gal who taught swimming, for example, claimed that he was the only kid who swam backward rather than forward in the water. Otherwise, he was all wrapped up in the plays his mother was putting on, even though she didn't push him. She staged *Good News,* a Broadway musical comedy at the time, then *A Midsummer Night's Dream.* Bud was in both, and though he wasn't that great, he went after it, since drama was the only thing that seemed to interest him."

He showed up regularly at the Thursday-night entertainments, which were the usual fare of musicals, pantomimes, and readings. Still, what caught everyone's attention was the way Bud spontaneously mimicked people around him. Soon he developed a pronounced southern accent that he picked up from a group of campers from Nashville. "It was startling," said one junior counselor. "He just loved the sound."

Returning to Evanston in September, Dodie found the Brando home lonely and saddening, especially with Jocelyn away at a Christian Science boarding school in St. Louis. In addition, Dodie had to acknowledge that the strategy of spending the summer at the camp hadn't achieved its desired effect. She had secretly been having another love affair during the previous year and had hoped that the self-imposed distance would put an end to it. Instead, faced with Marlon Sr.'s continued lack of attention, she soon found she couldn't stay away from the man who, she acknowledged to friends, was the "love of her life."

"She was profoundly involved," explained a woman in whom Dodie confided in later years. "The guy was a well-known ladies' man, a prominent brain surgeon in Chicago. The affair was very clandestine. He was a neighbor, they went to the same parties, and knew each other socially.

"I don't remember whether he eventually dumped her or she dumped him, although it might have been mutual," the friend added. "She knew she couldn't have any sort of life with him. He had a terrible reputation, and she realized that he was probably using her. Still, she couldn't let go."

She would not be free of the relationship for another eighteen months or so, and her medical records indicate that during this time Dodie underwent an abortion. The affair, along with the stress of coping with husband and children, triggered a return to the bottle.

As in the past, she turned to David Salinger, who was now living in New York, writing him long letters that simultaneously conceded and concealed her unhappiness:

> *I was struck drunk in the middle of my last letter and haven't the faintest idea what I may have written. . . . Liquor and I have had a feud, L. saying "I'll get you down" and me replying "Sez you," and liquor is ahead thus far. Not appetite, effect. Maybe I'll quit?*

Bud, Fran, and Tid (as Jocelyn was nicknamed) were her touchstones, too. Her youngest, she pointed out, had begun "to think Thoughts" that he enjoyed "discussing in detail," just as he carried himself as though "capable of licking Joe Louis." Fran's first formal gown, Jocelyn's dating, the whereabouts and doings of close mutual friends like Britt and Merle Friedell, and also her own reading filled her letters.

After a visit to Bernie Szold, just married and living in New Orleans, she returned to face another conference with Bud's teacher. Dodie was told that the boy's behavior at school was continuing to deteriorate and was again asked about Bud's home life. The inquiry was apt. The apartment on Sheridan Square, where the Brandos had remained for nearly a year, was a three-ring circus. Ermy, the housekeeper, had given birth to a child out of wedlock. Nana's brother, Myles Jr., the "Irish charmer," arrived for a visit, his presence provoking loud shouting matches. Nana, as usual, was high volume, and since she had not been back to California in months, Betty, Dodie's half-sister, visited, too, adding to the din.

There were periods when there wasn't enough money to pay bills, despite Calcium Carbonate's continued expansion. Marlon Sr. insinuated that Dodie was squandering house funds on the kids; from Dodie's side, it appeared he was frittering away money on his girlfriends. In fact, there was such chaos in the household that no one knew where his salary was going, and even one of Bud's contemporaries sensed that they "were living beyond their means."

In later years, in a burst of rare public candor, Bud himself summed up the situation, saying bitterly: "It used to bother me very much that my parents didn't act like other parents. They played undignified games, said what I considered startling, unparentish things." His response in those days was to stay away from home as much as possible and find himself a substitute family.

Byron Veris's parents were hardly mainline Evanston but, like many successful immigrants, they maintained their traditional European values of a warm and stable household. In her distinctly "unmodern" way, Mrs. Veris welcomed her children's friends and thought nothing of setting an extra place for Bud at the dinner table. "My dad came home at six o'clock sharp," Byron said. "We all sat down, and, bingo, Bud was there, bouncing a ball or just standing around, lingering. He should have been home, so in a way it was sad. My mother often asked him to come in and have something to eat. Later, when all five of us boys were in the service, he still was stopping by to see her. He almost seemed to revere her. Some of it was envying our family, longing for something like it. Even when he stuck around after dark, there were never phone calls from the Brando household looking for him."

By the summer of 1936, the tension in the Brando family reached overload, and Nana came up with a solution: Dodie needed time to cool out, and since Dodie's aunts Vine and June and half-sister Betty were on the West Coast, wouldn't it make sense for her to take the kids to California? It would not have to be acknowledged as a separation, she added. Marlon could visit, coming out over the holidays, and the family might yet get back on its feet.

"We all lived with Nana for a while on Parton Street in Santa Ana, then rented a house in back of her," recalled Jocelyn. "Vine and her husband, Art, lived two doors down; Betty and her husband, Ollie, moved in with Nana, too."

Almost as if to confirm that the move to Santa Ana might revive Dodie's Omaha happiness, Hank Fonda often visited her, driving the fifty miles down from Hollywood. Sometimes she brought the kids up to Paramount where, in the first years of his contract, Fonda was making films like *That Certain Woman, Slim, Blockade,* and *Spawn of the North.* In his essential decency, Fonda hadn't forgotten Dodie's role in launching his career; the relationship also took her back to her beloved Omaha Community Playhouse and all her earlier confidence. It may also have spurred her, not to return to the stage at the nearby Pasadena Playhouse, but to coach Jocelyn, a starstruck teenager who delighted in the Fonda friendship and had already thrown herself into dramatics at Santa Ana High.

"She was very good at elocution, by far the most knowledgeable, talented, trained actor in our class, and all of this she learned from her mother," said Jocelyn's boyfriend, Ben Blee, who recalled Dodie's efforts at instructing him, too. " 'Don't act! Don't act! Stop acting!' she would yell. 'Let the lines speak for themselves.' "

Even by southern California standards, the Brandos were perceived as being out of the ordinary. Nana was running her Christian Science practice out of the front-room parlor overlooking Parton Street. Fran, as usual, conformed and blended into the woodwork, while Jocelyn and Bud went their own ways. The older sister's success in school plays enchanted classmates, but it was rumored that she was no longer a virgin and was even permitted to smoke at home.

"They were all very colorful," said George Baird, brother of Bil, who was visiting the West Coast and saw that the flow of relatives in and out of the house was unceasing. Amid the hubbub Bud was louder than any of them—"a little brat, obnoxious and arrogant," said Ben Blee (from whom Bud extorted money in the same way he had coerced Jocelyn's boyfriends in Evanston).

At Lathrope Junior High School, Bud's grades were passing, but he pushed himself in sports. By the end of the eighth grade, when he was thirteen, he had earned letters in volleyball, basketball, football, and track. It was at home that he flew his true colors, stretched and let loose. Adolescence was part of it but he was also the center of attention because temporarily, at least, he was the man of the house. Nana doted, Dodie doted, and his sisters tried to stay out of the way. The role suited him, much as Dodie reported to David Salinger: "Bud has grown enormously but emotionally resembles a Fourth of July nigger chaser as much as anything. As for me, an irritated carrot will describe the situation. The whole plan has been beneficial I think however. . . . He is a grand kid but living with him is like climbing a greased pole in war torn Shanghai. And the worst won't come for another two or three years."

LIBERTYVILLE 3

1938–41

In the summer of 1938, Dodie made the decision to return to Marlon Sr., reuniting the family and giving their marriage another try in the rural tranquillity of Libertyville, Illinois, thirty-five miles northwest of Chicago. When the Brandos rented and moved into the "old Waller place" on Bradley Road, an unpaved, sparsely settled strip cutting between broad fields, they were immediately perceived as "different," outsiders with something of an air of mystery to them. "They might have moved out there intentionally because it was so isolated," said Jack Swan, later a high school classmate of Fran. "Living there they didn't have to mingle with local people."

Libertyville was the archetypal Midwest community on the eve of the Second World War. Settled in the 1830s by sodbusters gone west from New York and Pennsylvania, it had remained a rural hub for corn, beans, and grains; in the 1930s the population was still only 3,000 God-fearing and respectable citizens whose attendance at any one of the community's six churches was as mandatory as membership in the Masons, Women's Auxiliary, Lion's Club, American Legion, and Jay Cees.

High school football and basketball games and the wrestling matches at the American Legion Hall were the noteworthy entertainments, although the Libertyville Village Players, a community dramatics club, put on annual productions, as did the high school dramatics club. Otherwise, there were few social gatherings except for church suppers. Few of the high school students went on to college. They simply found local jobs, married, and fit in. Conservatism and conformity—values that neither Dodie nor her teenage son Bud were likely to appreciate—were the abiding norms.

As in any provincial community, gossip was rife, and a family's social standing, behavior, wealth, and attitudes were much discussed. "Everybody knew who had what or when someone got ill," said a town elder. "If any couple wasn't getting along, it would be all over town within a week. Nobody *really* knew, but it didn't matter, because there was nothing else to talk about." Not surprisingly, the Brandos would become the subject of what one neighbor called the "most vicious" rumors, especially since Dodie flouted the local rigid rules of propriety. "Basically, Dodie let it be known that she really didn't like Libertyville," said one of Jocelyn's boyfriends. "She had contempt for most of the people there, the small-town gossips, the Republicanism, and their anti-Semitism."

The Brandos now lived in an old rambling farmhouse, situated at the end of a high-bermed driveway, alongside of which Dodie planted a vegetable garden. Inside were four bedrooms, each with its own sleeping porch. The large living room was furnished with a worn sofa and easy chairs, an upright piano, and a threadbare rug—and, as if to insist on her liberal attitudes, Dodie hung a painting of abolitionist John Brown in full view. In the dining room was an oak table that the family had had forever. "Rich we were not," said Jocelyn. "Despite Papa's suits, money wasn't spent on appearances."

Nor was time spent on keeping up appearances, since Dodie hated housecleaning. The place was "usually a mess," recalled Jocelyn. "We wouldn't pay any attention until about five o'clock, when Papa was due to come home. Mother would say, 'Oh! Got to make a hole in the house!' Then we'd all scurry around—Fran, Bud, all of us—so it would be tidy when he got back from the office."

To the rear of the house, among several outbuildings, stood a stable where the local gentry boarded more than a dozen horses. Also on the grounds was a small house where the stablemaster and horse trainer, Bill Booth, lived. A six-foot, 200-pound hard-drinking womanizer, Bill was, like Dodie, another anomaly in Libertyville. He sometimes employed local kids as stable hands, including the Camellino brothers. "The stable was less than a hundred yards from the house," said Frank Camellino. "Bill lived on the south end of the property in a small house, probably forty feet from the big house, and he was on about his third or fourth wife. He was a big handsome guy, always dressed up, wore a Stetson and a sort of English riding outfit. He also had a $10,000 silver saddle at that time."

The Brandos also had a live-in maid, Margaret (she had come to work for them in Evanston, when Ermy had finally married and returned to Omaha). A short, chunky woman with white hair, an Irish brogue, and a philosophic temperament, she was devoted to the family and to Dodie especially. Sometimes a young black woman from Chicago came to help her out.

Completing the extended family were the kids' animals—chickens and a pet bantam rooster named Charlie Chaplin, house cats and barn cats. There was a Guernsey cow named Betsey that Bud was supposed to milk morning and evening; Bill always had to remind him to bring the cow in at milking time, and Bud often rode her backward as he returned her to the barn. There were also a beautiful but bad-natured black mare called Peavine's Frenzy; a black Great Dane, named Dutchie, who was Bud's constant companion; and several goats that Bill kept.

To the people of Libertyville, the family was a mystery from the beginning. "We thought of them as being kind of wild and wealthy," said Sheila Petry, one of Bud's classmates. "They seemed aristocratic from our point of view, because they dressed better and weren't local."

The Brandos had to be pegged and pigeonholed, fitted into the social hierarchy, and naturally money was the yardstick. Marlon Sr. was earning about $15,000 a year (the equivalent of approximately $75,000 in today's dollars). Still, their outlying house was a rental, with decor that fell considerably short of local standards, which made it all the harder to label them.

"Many of us thought they were in the upper class because of the way they handled themselves," said Ray Meyers, another local. "Dodie carried herself well. She had a bearing and a presence." It was well known that she had friends in Chicago, "arty types," and it wasn't long before townspeople were also aware of her friendship to Ellen Borden Stevenson (the wife of Adlai), who had a large estate on St. Mary's Road. Yet there was talk that the Brandos were chronically short of money.

"Dodie never complained about the lack of money," said one woman who knew her. "I just somehow got the impression that there was a certain struggle." At the grocery store, they were often late paying their bills, and the speculation was that Dodie was spending food money on drink. The gossip continued for months with the shared assumption that because the Brandos seemed reclusive, there was, as one resident put it, "something screwed up with the family."

Such opinions predominated and, with the start of the 1938–39 school year, were often reinforced by Bud's behavior. Photos of the period show the fourteen-year-old Brando going through an adolescent transition. His blond hair had started to darken. The familiar brow and aquiline nose were already pronounced, and he had started to broaden through the shoulders—even without the barbells he would soon begin to use unremittingly. He had the same full, sensuous lips of earlier snapshots as well as the long fluttery eyelashes and almost feline eyebrows. Still short, he had a "little boy" look, as one of Fran's friends put it; a late bloomer, his beard was little more than peach fuzz.

As a new arrival at Libertyville Township High School, he was at a huge disadvantage. His grades from Santa Ana were mediocre, but his classmates would not have been impressed if the new boy in their midst had been Einstein. Most of them had known one another all their lives, and like their parents, none was quick to accept a newcomer whose attitudes set him apart as an outsider from the beginning.

"My initiation into Libertyville was coincident with Bud's," said Joe Spery, whose family had just moved from Chicago. "As a freshman Bud was as mature as many seniors, and by this I mean he was able to understand human frailties, bullyism, values. Many of the kids in our class had an agricultural background, and they were unsophisticated. So they talked about him as crazy."

Most of the boys wore dress slacks and sweaters, but Bud often came to school in T-shirts, blue jeans, and sneakers. He was the only one to get away with such outfits, and he was also known for wearing brightly colored shirts, which prompted classmates to tease him that he was wearing pajama tops.

"A lot of times Bud came to school looking like he just crawled out from under a car," commented one former classmate, adding that he usually arrived late for class. If the teacher didn't say anything, he'd go right to his desk, no slinking, no making himself small; then he'd just drop his books and sit down, his entrance complete. Yet rarely would he *sit*. From his first days at Libertyville High, the newcomer was known for his trademark slouch.

"He'd sprawl in his seat, legs sticking out and splayed apart," said

William Roser, another classmate. "He'd just slouch out there, looking like he didn't give a shit." One day the slouch got out of control. The tile floor of chemistry lab was wet from the thick midwestern humidity, and Bud's chair slid out from under him; he landed flat on his back.

Most kids would have shrunk in embarrassment; not Brando. "Another day he had a pencil," continued Roser, who was in the same chemistry class, "which he was rotating very delicately between the thumb and forefinger of each hand. He was in his seat, looking at the pencil from all aspects, vertically, horizontally, you name it, and it was as if this damn pencil was the most fascinating object he'd ever encountered. Class hadn't started yet but the room was filling up, and as the kids came in one by one, they fastened on him playing with this pencil, which he continued to do even after the bell rang. When Pop Johnson, our teacher, came in and announced that class was about to begin, Bud kept on with the pencil. Finally Pop said, 'Bud, would you close the door, please?' Slowly, Bud rose from his seat, as if it was the greatest effort in the world, sauntered over to the door and closed it. Pop shook his head. 'No, Bud, I meant from the outside.' He looked back at Pop and blinked his eyes. Then he sauntered back to his seat with the same shuffle, picked up his books, and shuffled out."

It was as if he couldn't have cared less, and the incident was only one of many. Sometimes his testing stayed just within the letter of the law, sometimes not, and in the latter instances he would be sent out to the hallway or to the principal. "We joked about it," said another classmate. "After it happened again and again we'd be sitting out in the hall laughing, 'Bud got thrown out again today.' He made a name for himself *very* quickly."

Part of his reputation, because it was known that he'd lived in California, was that he was "worldly," which justifiably or not became the explanation for his "cocky airs." On more than one occasion, either because of lateness or his studied inattention, he "sat out a class on a chair in the hallway," said Carl Peterson, "either that or he got sent home." Which meant, everyone joked, that he went down and put pennies on the railroad tracks.

Peterson and his family lived near the Brandos out on Bradley Road, and he and Ed Sawusch, another neighbor, car-pooled to school, one or the other of the families driving the boys into town. "We didn't talk about the trouble he was getting into," said Sawusch, who was one of the few classmates who had ever been at the Brando house. "If he was having problems with his Mom and Dad, he never confided about that either. There were just periods of time when he was quiet when he might have been depressed. A fair amount of time he just stayed by himself alone, and he didn't seem interested in anything."

Bud soon fell behind his classmates in schoolwork, but hid his difficulties behind his usual mask of disinterest and noncooperation. He was a slow, uncertain reader, and his spelling was atrocious. To hide his embarrassment when asked to read aloud in class, he adopted an irritating slur that was bound to put a teacher's back up.

"There was definitely a mumble," said Joe Spery. "When he talked in class, he'd always be looking at his fingernails, his eyes at half-mast. He'd use a monotone, pause, then talk sotto voce and pause again, to be sure that everybody was listening. 'Well, I don' know whether I would wanna learn something like that, but . . . I mean, when ya . . .'" Another local agreed: "He had these gestures and phrasing that made him seem different."

"But he always was aware that he was onstage," added Spery. "The seeds of his style were all there; the things he did as a child to get what he wanted, his physical presence, the beauty of his face and body. He *knew* that by 'delivering' lines, one of the girls in the front row would turn and glance at him, and he knew they were thinking, 'What's he doing?' Bud-the-enigma—he reveled in that."

Mr. Russell, the stocky geometry instructor who resembled Herbert Hoover, had no tolerance for either his poses or his lateness. As luck would have it, Bud had drawn him for his homeroom teacher.

Homeroom began at 8:30 and ran for ten minutes. One morning, when handed a late warning, Bud had thrown the green slip in Russell's face. When Russell told him to come back and pick it up off the floor where it had fallen, Bud mimicked him, as much as telling him to shove it. In utter frustration Russell barreled down the aisle, grabbed him, and shook him violently.

Joe Spery recalled another classic incident, this one involving Mrs. Culbertson, the French teacher: "In class we all assumed French names, so 'Marlon' and 'Joseph' were not acceptable. Bud became Monsieur Alphonse. One day he said to Mrs. Culbertson, 'May I please go get my glasses?' He left the class which was the first class in the afternoon, and didn't come back. The next day she said, 'Monsieur Alphonse, I want your pass, a note from your mother.' He said, 'But you told me I could go get my glasses,' and then explained that he'd left them down by the river, which was a mile from school.

"He delivered the line perfectly straight, a bit indignantly even. 'But you told me I could go get my glasses. It's not my fault you didn't ask where I left them.' "

Some of his pranks were original, most clownishly silly:

• He took the pins out of the hinges on the door to one of his class-rooms.

• Once, when a class was in an uproar, the frazzled instructor hollered, "Order! Order!" Bud shot back, "A hamburger, french fries, and a Coke!"

• He hung a dead skunk on the football scoreboard, upwind of the classrooms.

• He rode his bike on the school's indoor, board running track.

• When no one was looking, he'd light up a string of "ladyfingers," little one-inch firecrackers, and casually toss them out the classroom windows in the middle of class.

• He poured hydrogen sulfide in the blower of the school's furnace, spreading a rotten egg smell throughout every classroom and hall-way. (In a separate incident, he used Limburger cheese.)

• One day he was reprimanded in French class for not having his homework; the next day he came in with his lesson done on toilet paper, and when called upon he stood up beside his seat and unrolled it yard after yard.

In class, Bud routinely stared into space, ignoring teachers' reprimands; the message seemed to be: I'm here, I'm not leaving. But don't expect me to open my book or pay attention because I could give a damn. The inevitable consequence was an escalation in his contact with Principal Henry E. Underbrink, who epitomized the rigidity of Libertyville. A tall, beefy Prussian, Underbrink had been around for years and had a heavy German accent. Bud could—and did—mimic the accent perfectly, which amused his classmates but only upped the ante, resulting in all-out war. "My father could never relate to Brando's persona or see any tenderness or complexity there at all," said Frank Underbrink, who himself now teaches at Libertyville High. "He tried to sympathize but couldn't. Dad was puzzled over what Marlon was doing to himself and his future. He just couldn't figure it out."

"Bud, you're a bum," the principal exploded on one occasion. "You're good for nothing, you'll never be good for anything. You'll never do anything but dig ditches!"

Mr. Russell took it further. One morning during homeroom Russell called him on the carpet, and when he'd finished with the usual dressing down, announced, "Bud, you're going to have to work harder. Your IQ test shows you're not too smart." It was hideous, "a hell of a thing to say in front of other students," observed one classmate, but Bud merely looked away, fastening his gaze out the window.

"To put it mildly, I don't think he particularly liked or trusted the teachers at Libertyville High School," said Robert Dunn, another classmate. "The one he really loved, I think, was Father Rogers, who offered him refuge."

The pastor of St. Lawrence's Episcopal Church, Reverend Tom Rogers, was another anomaly in Libertyville. Alleged to be homosexual, alcoholic, and liberal, he was always on call for his parishioners. "Up at the hospital, accidents came in at two, three o'clock in the morning," Ray Meyers remembered. "Who was there? Father Rogers." Later there would be a rumor he was using church funds to help ne'er-do-wells. When finally banished from town, Rogers would wind up in Chicago, running a ghetto parish until his death in 1983.

Rogers's drinking and homosexuality were gossiped about, but most of all he was known as openminded and a sympathetic listener. After school Bud often drifted over to his house next to the church, where Rogers lived with his mother and numerous cats. "Father Rogers recognized that Bud wasn't cut from the ordinary cloth," Spery said. "He was also aware of Dodie's drinking and the father's philandering and sympathized with Bud's problems."

Father Rogers was available to all of the Brando family. Fran confided in him every once in a while, and as much as her son, Dodie felt a real connection to the priest, largely because he fit right in with her ideas of spirituality and cared more about people than convention. For Bud, he was the only adult in town to whom he could talk without fear of condemnation and scolding.

After school, if Bud was not required to show up for detention—the so-called 3:15 Club—or didn't go to see Rogers, he'd usually just disappear, taking himself off on long walks; sometimes he was a solitary figure crossing the fields and cutting into the woods off Bradley Road, his only companion the dog Dutchie. Knowing that the school bus driver was running traplines for foxes and muskrats on the land surrounding the Brando farmhouse, he often went through them all, springing the traps.

"The only things Bud really seemed to care about were animals," Spery explained. "If somebody's dog died, I'd see him tear up. One of the Brando chickens died and Bud dug it up and brought it back in the house. His father got angry and reburied it. Bud dug it up again until his father, I assume in disgust, just threw it away. The thing was, he had liked the chicken and *he* wanted to be the one to bury it."

"He was nurturing," said another neighbor. "He was running away one day—either his father had thrown him out or he just was taking off on his own. He had a blanket and a frying pan, and was ready to leave home for good. But then he found some hurt animal." Bud buried his pride and took it back home. "It would have died if he left it in the open."

When Bud cut school, he often stayed home to read. "There was one room that their mother had given over totally to a library," said a friend of Fran. "They had red lacquered shelves, and Bud used to sit in there and read all day long. One day Fran made some comment—'You didn't go to school again?'—and he just said no, matter-of-factly." He would read T. S. Eliot, Shakespeare, F. Scott Fitzgerald, "all of the classics Dodie had," said Joe Spery. "And he was also looking at her books about Taoism and other religions. He raised questions pertaining to the cultures of the world, about peoples of different colors, lives, creeds."

In later years, Eastern religion would prove a mainstay in Brando's life, but one afternoon Ed Sawusch dropped by to find him poring over one of his father's few books, a Dale Carnegie motivational tract. Significantly, he was most interested in one statement that he read aloud to his friend: "It was something like, 'He's got guts,' " recalled Sawusch. "The sense of it was that a person had to have nerve to succeed. What Bud was doing was checking for a reaction from me. 'Yeah, that's reasonable,' I said.

I sensed that it seemed to help him justify the fact that he was always going out on the edge."

At the same time, he was perfecting his skills of observation. To others, he seemed always watchful but often inaccessible, in a world of his own. "If you could talk with him it was unusual," said Harvey Obenauf. "At school, he'd stand over by the building in the warm sun and watch people rather than carry on a conversation. He didn't want to be involved."

Sometimes after school he would go to Taylor's Drugstore, where the other kids hung out, but here, too, he would not join in. "He'd just be sitting there at the soda fountain staring at people, observing them," said Carl Peterson. "Maybe he was already studying people in order to become an actor, but he was also insulating himself, staying apart from everyone."

Dodie sometimes asked Frank Camellino, Bill Booth's stable hand, to pick Bud up from school when she was unable to (as was becoming more common). "He would just aggravate the shit out of me," said Camellino. "Either my brother, Dom, or myself, we'd go pick him up. He was supposed to be outside the school at a certain time and he wouldn't be there. Instead he would be uptown scooting around, like at Taylor's, or I might find him just walking the streets."

Bud's habit of observing from a withdrawn distance only added to his reputation. As an adult it would become his most characteristic mannerism, part of his arsenal of control, but even now he was "always looking, always hunting with his eyes." For Spery and others, it was clear that he sensed the power inherent to withholding, of keeping people at arm's length while basking in the aura of their attention.

"At pep rallies or dances he had a way of walking in and being casual," said Ed Sawusch. "He could smile and joke, but he had a peculiar laugh—'haw-haw-haw'—very mild, very gentle. He would also use his body. He would very gracefully hold his hand out, quiet and smooth and very easy, with almost a theatrical quality, an air of graciousness."

After he had everyone's attention, he severed the connection. "He'd just sort of mingle, walk around, get them laughing, and then he'd leave," added Spery. "The next time he could just step into the limelight because everyone was wondering what in hell they'd been deprived of. It didn't look stylized at the time, but his eyes would be doing the job."

He did this even more pointedly with girls. "I was a naive little farm kid," said Alice Calanca. "Marlon would stand by the lockers and stare at you, and you felt as if he was undressing you. But it was psychological more than sexual. . . . He hung back. He'd just watch you. It was like a challenge, a boast almost."

Anyone who tried to tell him to cut it out was met with his sullen resistance or worse. Bill Booth took him to task one afternoon. Bud's response was to smack him between the eyes with a wad of cow manure. Another time, at midnight he let the horses out of the stable, then phoned Dom Camellino; when Camellino arrived at the Brando place, twenty horses were running through the fields. "Bud helped my brother round them up," recalled Ann Camellino Scholl. "The next evening he came to our house to apologize, and my mother invited him to stay for pasta. Maybe that was the whole point—to get attention and to become like one of the family. My mother really took to him, and he really loved her—her warmth, her generosity, her broken English and Italian peasant enthusiasm, and after that he would drop by to eat the big *Italiano* meals that he loved." But in school, if anyone crossed him, his eyes "would become very cold, very icy," and "he'd just ignore you," recalled Sawusch. "The message was, You can't get to me."

Predictably, by midyear Bud had only a few close friends. In addition to Joe Spery, the other acquaintance who served as Bud's link to the clique of the most popular students was Bob "Bo" Hoskins. Bob was the youngest of the three sons of Glen Hoskins, the president of the First National Bank, a staunch Republican, and an owner of Libertyville's main employer, the Foulds Macaroni Company. Bob's mother was a Christian Scientist who attended the Presbyterian church and was a mainstay of Libertyville society. Bob himself was the rebel of the Hoskins family.

He and Bud soon became inseparable, if only because he too was considered a screwup. Although he was handsome, he wasn't all that bright. Joe Spery recalled, "Bob was a good athlete but a scatterbrained klutz, the kind of guy who scored the basketball at his own goal." He also played the trombone and hammed it up in a number of school plays, talents that appealed to Bud. In fact, Hoskins did a lot to get Brando on the basketball team, and the two even ran away together. "I think it was into Wisconsin," said Frank Underbrink. "They didn't ride the rails, but hitched a truck or something. They got quite a lot of miles away and then phoned back for money to come back home."

At school Bob ran with what might loosely be described as Libertyville's "proto-yuppies," who aspired to the values of families even richer than their own in nearby Lake Bluff and Lake Forest. At football and basketball games, track meets and school dances, the group clung together, and while Bud's participation was sporadic, he was appreciated for his outlandishness and daring. "One of the things we used to play a lot was charades," said one acquaintance. "I remember his antics trying to get across 'Nature's Way,' which was to act out someone taking a bowel movement."

As far as athletics went, Bud had natural talents, as he had discovered while in Santa Ana, and even though sports were taken more seriously at a midwestern high school, he might have excelled had his attitude in gym class not ensured low marks. He made a habit of not changing into his uniform or rebelling against the coach's instructions, and worse, he simply cut class: in the one team sport in which he was talented enough to make the varsity cut—football—he often missed practice on days he deemed "too cold to be outdoors." When he did show up, he usually clowned around.

Some called it laziness, but Ray Strand, a boyfriend of Fran, saw it differently. "Bud dropped football and then went out for track because he didn't like to get hit," he claimed. "After that, he went out for boxing because it was a show; we were a winning boxing team, and everybody looked good up there in the ring and got a lot of adulation. Then he found that he didn't like the sparring in practice, either, and he quit that, too."

Instead, he preferred to work out with weights, hour after hour, in the school gymnasium. Likewise, he had gotten more seriously into drums. His pal Joe Spery was also a drum fanatic and had earned the nickname "Drummer Boy," having worked with professional bands, and he had formed his own local group, too, the Sultans of Swing, to play high school dances and summer carnivals. Noting Spery's success, Bud tried to form a band of his own, calling it Bud Brando and His Keg Liners, after a beer advertised as being "keg lined." Unfortunately, the combo never got off the ground, since the band players rarely practiced.

Still, "his real passion was music, especially the big bands," recalled Spery. "He listened to Dorsey and Goodman, but even then he also was interested in Latin music and the bongos. Blues, too, and black jazz—Louis Armstrong, Jimmy Rushing, and Bessie Smith."

He had a set of Slingerland drums at home, a complete set of traps, as well as snare drums, and, characteristically, he drove his sisters to distraction with his playing. That Spery was performing professionally didn't sit all that well, and what rankled even more was that the Keg Liners played only one local roadhouse before disbanding. Nonetheless Bud, kept it up. "I remember him with his set of drums out in the middle of the living room," said Frank Ward, a classmate who lived nearby. "They were never put away, and he'd just sit there pounding, with the radio or phonograph turned up. He was totally inside himself, playing accompaniment." The drums were so loud that sometimes the stable hands complained about the racket, but Dodie never curtailed him.

He carried his drumsticks with him continually, practicing almost wherever he went. "He'd drum on our glass coffee table," said one of his girlfriends at the time. "He beat out little tattoos, which didn't go over too well with my folks."

He tried to form another band. "It was called Beau Brando and something," Jocelyn said. "Don't ask where the 'Beau' came from. He was looking for a catchy name for the roadhouse that he was dickering to play at, somewhere outside Libertyville. We went to see him once and he was very good. Other than acting, it was something he was absolutely super at."

As in so many other small towns, the Libertyville High School band stood at the center of everything—sports, school dances, local parades—and like his musical classmates, Bud gave it a try, but he never could get the hang of it. The director was always yelling, "Get in step, Brando!" At practice, while the band was rehearsing Sousa marches, he riffed, segueing into Gene Krupa. Fellow band members recall the director becoming so annoyed during one session that he threw his baton at him. Brando's response (as with so many other reprimands) was to shrug, as though to say *So what?*

But then there was acting.

A boy in the Dramatics Club was considered an oddball to begin with, but Brando joined in almost from his first day at the school. M. J. Bergfald, the dramatics coach, was a stoic Norwegian who dressed in three-piece suits, and like most of Bud's teachers, he had been in Libertyville for years.

"There was a very low level of inquisitiveness on the part of Bergfald," said Joe Spery. "He never asked, 'What can this kid do?' He was also apprehensive, I think, that Bud could come in and just walk away with any role that he was trying to direct him in."

For Bud, the teacher's personality was a recipe for trouble, exacerbated all the more by Dodie's input at home. Many years later, Bergfald still had distinct memories of their interactions. "There were small classes of fifteen or twenty kids who met two or three days a week," he explained. "The plays were modern ones, like [George S. Kaufman and] Moss Hart's *You Can't Take It with You*—no Ibsen, no Shaw, no Shakespeare. The material was upbeat, and that wasn't Brando's forte at all. What he did best was emotional and serious stuff, even though he had difficulty learning his lines.

"He was quite independent, and the problem was that he didn't enjoy being told what to do. Sometimes he was downright rude. One time I told him, 'Now look, if you're ever going to succeed, you're going to have to learn to fit in with the program, get things done on time and do them right.'

"We also did pantomimes," Bergfald added. "Students came up with their own stories, and Bud always brought in some really startling ones, like the time he played the gangster John Dillinger. His portrayal was so vivid that the group was squirming in their seats. That's where he excelled, in these pantomimes. He had a way of completely losing himself in a part."

One of the students in the class also recalled an improv in which Bud took the role of a woman. "He acted out a young girl taking a bath," said Janet Tiffany Keep. "First he put one toe in to test the water, then the other, then the soaping of the armpits and so forth—all of this done with great flourish."

Here Bud exhibited the same freedom and lack of self-consciousness he put into his "Nature's Way" charade, yet for all the young Brando's spontaneity, teacher and student continued to clash.

Ray Meyers, who worked the lights and curtains, said, "Bergfald would stand there and say, 'Reread the line and do it this way.' Bud would say, 'No, it doesn't sound right. That's wrong.' He would try to reason, explain his particular interpretation to the teacher, and you felt he actually knew what he was doing, that he wasn't just being a big shot. But when Bergfald wouldn't listen, he'd get so frustrated that he'd just leave. Storm out as if to say, There's no point in discussing it, you don't know what you're talking about."

The result, of course, was that while Bob Hoskins and Joe Spery were hamming it up in the holiday plays, Bud never appeared in any student productions. Spery himself believed that Dodie played a role in her son's rejection, since she had her own confrontations with Bergfald at meetings of the Village Players, where she argued for O'Neill and Shaw instead of the traditional light comedy fare endorsed by the drama coach.

"I think Mrs. Brando was very ambitious for her youngsters, all three of them," said Dorothy Bradford, the group's resident director, who usually opposed Dodie's attempts to stage more serious material—or at least to bring greater professionalism to the productions. However, Joe Spery, who as a director of television commercials would later encounter many stage mothers, saw the conflict in a different light. Dodie simply didn't fit into that category. Instead, she came across, he said, as a believer in "art and creativity."

"By Libertyville standards," he added, "she was an absolute progressive. She was not only active but didn't have any problem doing things in which there was profanity onstage, which engendered resentment. They were jealous of her ability as well as her imagination. Bergfald, who was regarded as the local expert, might want to do a musical play, but she kept pushing for Eugene O'Neill, and she also talked about the Omaha Community Playhouse. In a funny way, she was like Bud. She didn't give a shit, either."

Her position was bound to alienate Bergfald, in both the Village Players and, since Bud often brought a script home to ask for her opinion, in his drama class. "She would criticize, and Bud would say, 'But Mr. Bergfald . . .' Her final remark," said Spery, was usually, " 'Well, there's two ways to skin a cat.' What she was saying was, Hey, Bud, you've got to learn to get into these things, and make your own decisions. She was also telling him, Here's how you can improve the role. Do it. Go for the core."

Most of Bud's classmates couldn't understand Dodie any more than they could comprehend Bud's own investment in the Dramatics Club. "My personal feeling was that even then he had ambition," said Spery, "but he didn't want to show it. He was afraid he wouldn't make it. He also knew people would laugh at him." Ray Meyers remembered the same obliqueness: "He wouldn't specifically come right out and talk about it," he conceded, "but there would be remarks about this or that Hollywood film star. We'd be sitting in the hall on the railing, talking about a movie, and he'd forget himself and say, 'Boy, I'd like to act like that.' "

"When he did talk about it," Spery added, "it was done with complete detachment, almost in the same enigmatic manner as he said other

things. No cockiness, just an absolute positivity that could not be denied."
It was as if he were saying to himself, Yes, I'm going to be an actor, and it
was underscored by an implicit attitude of This is it, fellas, I'm going to
do it.

Rarely, though, did Bud say much to anyone, even to the one person
who might have understood—his mother. She had retreated into her
drinking again, so she was sometimes withdrawn and inaccessible. At
other times she was disorganized and chaotic, sleeping late and then in a
slapdash way trying to fulfill her motherly duties. She had already annoyed
Ruth Felgar, Principal Underbrink's secretary, with her routine of arriving
at the school every Friday.

"Without fail, Mrs. Brando showed up in the office those mornings,"
said Mrs. Felgar. "She had allowances for Bud and Fran in envelopes, for
the week, which I was supposed to give them. They were in different parts
of the building and had to have it in time for lunch. I would have to take
the envelopes to them, so we'd have another disruption to the classroom.
This went on for about six months. Finally I said, 'Mrs. Brando, I just cannot do this. I don't understand why you don't give your children the
money in the morning.' Well, she hadn't gone to the bank. I said, 'Then
you go to the bank on Thursday and give it to them before school on Friday.'

"Lots of times she would call," added the secretary, "and ask me to
give Bud messages, like 'Would you tell him to get a haircut tonight.' I
didn't think this was necessary for a school to do; she could have told him
herself in the morning."

Often, though, Dodie simply couldn't, and this only added to the general gossip that Brando's mother didn't get up in the morning because she
was hung over. Previously, Jocelyn had been Bud's solace, but at eighteen
she was embarking on a life of her own; she had completed one semester as
a theater arts major at Santa Ana Junior College as prelude for what everyone hoped would be a four-year college course. She looked a bit like
Frances Farmer, with a certain remote air, and she had learned that the
best response to Dodie's drinking was to keep her head down and stay out
of the chaos. By the end of the family's first year in Libertyville, she also
met her future husband, Don Hanmer, at the Lake Zurich Playhouse, the
most popular summer stock theater north of Chicago.

"I'd been there for two years after a scholarship at the Goodman The-ater," said Hanmer. "That summer of '39, Jocelyn came in as an appren-tice, and looked cuter than hell. At the time I'd been going with Carmelita Pope, the actress, who later became Marlon's friend. She was then four-teen. But then I saw Jocelyn, and it was just *boom.*"

A week or two into the summer program, one of Jocelyn's friends, Sheila Petry, went up to Lake Zurich with a group of girls to see her, but was turned away. "She sent a message out to the ticket booth," Petry re-called. "She said that she was too busy because she was in bed with her lover. Being very puritanical, it shocked me. It was also typical of Jocelyn, and Bud, too—this bohemian outlandishness, and that's why we plebeians were so enchanted with them."

That same summer of 1939, Bud was consigned to working as a mail-boy at the Blatchford Calf Meal Company in nearby Waukegan. Marlon Sr. had gotten him this job with a subsidiary of Calcium Carbonate, but Bud usually showed up late, rarely finished sorting the mail by the close of the day, and was "just generally a screwup." To lighten his routine, he made frequent visits to Lake Zurich, where he often showed up at parties with Bob Hoskins and Dutchie, the family's Great Dane, in tow. On the surface he seemed to be in search of a good time—sometimes he passed out by the end of the evening—but there was also a serious interest behind his visits to what in fact was a very real theatrical enterprise.

"He came alone once," recalled Hanmer. "There were all these actors around, sets being banged together, everyone doing their bit. Bud was walking across the lawn, and the first thing he did was faint. So right away he was the center of attention. Everyone rushed over. Then he 'revived.' But did he then acknowledge that it was a prank? He acknowledged noth-ing. He got up, smiled, and walked away."

"I'm not sure he ever saw a whole play that summer, although he came for many rehearsals," Carmelita Pope said. "He kept asking me, 'Why do you want to become an actress?' It wasn't clear to me if he was interested in me or the theater."

During the previous year, his sister Frances had thrown herself into school activities, writing for the school newspaper, becoming a cheerleader and a member of the choir, the Latin Club, and the Spanish Club. "She was a little picture-perfect doll," said her best friend and fellow cheer-leader, Dorothy Behm de Rivera. "Bright, gorgeous, wholesome—one hundred eighty degrees opposite of Bud. Later she graduated salutatorian of her class."

For Behm de Rivera and others, Fran was outperforming to gain approval from her father, while it was equally obvious that her mother favored Bud over her two daughters. But Dodie's care and enthusiasm were intermittent, with her drinking continuing in its established pattern: stretches of sobriety broken by a day or two of bingeing. If the children of alcoholics are cursed with the feeling that their family is "different," then within the aggressive, all-American normality of Libertyville the situation seemed worse. When Dodie was off on one of her toots, the children had to fend for themselves. Years before, in Omaha, a family friend had spoken of how "the peanut butter and jelly had to be kept down low so the kids could get to it themselves and wouldn't starve." But now, with the start of school again in the fall of 1939, this image was replaced with another—of Bud and Fran waiting for hours at Dorothy Behm de Rivera's house where, if the stable hands didn't pick them up, they were to wait for their father.

"We lived only a block from the high school," Behm de Rivera recalled, "and they would sit outside on our steps. Sometimes, when it was getting dark, my mother said, 'Why don't you all just come in and have something to eat?'

" 'No,' they'd say, 'Papa's gonna be here.' It would be after six o'clock and they'd still refuse to come inside."

Another aspect to Dodie's disappearances when drinking was that it fell to the kids to search for her in local saloons. Bill Booth, the stable master, sometimes helped; sometimes it would even be Marlon Sr., but most of the searching, according to Booth's assistant Frank Camellino, was done by Fran, who would come out to the stables to ask for help. "It was done in a way so that nobody would know what the hell was going on," he said. "It might be four or five o'clock in the afternoon, maybe even the next morning, but she couldn't come right out and say, 'My mother wasn't home last night.' Instead, she asked, 'Where do you think she could be?' She would ask me to take her where her mother might be, and she was embarrassed because she knew we realized what the problem was. As for Bud, he never showed it at all, and I don't recall him ever coming out and asking where she was."

For all his good intentions to put the family back together again, Marlon Sr. had begun slipping into his old patterns, too. More and more he was away on business trips; when he was at home, he maintained a curt but courteous distance, and not just from local townspeople. He had already joined AA in Chicago, trying to contain his own alcoholism, but that had never been the problem to begin with. It was more to try to get Dodie to join.

But he still dominated the family.

"Fundamentally, he was an impossible person to relate to," said Richard Loving, who was later Fran's husband. "He had this contained fury about the world. There was a sense of strong physicality, and he hid behind this bottled-up aggressiveness which he presented as manly composure."

"It was almost as if he erected a wall which you couldn't penetrate without running the risk of offending him," agreed a Libertyville neighbor, who described him as a curious mix of a passivity and bullying. Even while Marlon Sr. was on guard against Dodie's drinking and encouraged stableman Bill Booth to keep an eye out, too, he was aware that Booth could well be out drinking with Dodie. There were rumors that Dodie and the macho stableman were having an affair, which, doubtless, had reached him; nevertheless, given Brando Sr.'s own peccadilloes, he was in no position to object.

"The old man was no sweetheart," said Jack Swan. "He was a pompous bastard who always gave me the impression he was looking down his nose at people, as if he was doing you a favor."

"Papa couldn't do anything, he was inept," said Jocelyn, whose feelings echoed Bud's own hostility at the time. "All he could do was threaten. Franny always mispronounced words, and she once said, 'The trouble with Papa and Mama is that they dis*kip*line us when we don't need it, and they don't dis*kip*line us when we do.'

"Papa was very strict, very imposing, a put-downer," Jocelyn added. "There was always that heavy voice. I'd come down all dressed up, ready for a date, and he'd say, 'Oh, you look very nice, honey. But there's a little tear in your dress.'" The rest of the family simply dreaded his presence in the house.

Indeed, with his son he was even more demanding, ordering Bud to do his chores, get better grades, and even forcing him to milk the cow just before going out on dates—an episode so traumatic that years later Brando the actor would use it as his centerpiece in *Last Tango in Paris*. Among his friends in Libertyville, Bud might refer to his father's drinking, but he was less forthright in talking about his own pent-up hostility.

"He always covered it up," recalled Spery. "He'd examine his finger-nails, talking out of the side of his mouth, never looking at you. 'My old man wants me to get better grades,' he'd say. The father was habitually characterized as the taskmaster. Bud once made reference to the fact of his father's hitting him—'He gave me such a swat, I didn't know what I was doing.' "

The few times that there were guests at the Brandos—like Jocelyn's new acting coach, Tommy Tomlinson and his wife, from Lake Forest College—Marlon Sr. seemed to take particular relish in putting Bud in his place. During the visit the teenager became very talkative, obviously show-ing off to the drama coach. "At dinner he was constantly talking, in a cocky, bragging way," recalled Unity Tomlinson. "He kept butting into the conversation, very smart-alecky. Finally his father just raised his hand and looked at him and said, 'That's enough.' Two minutes later, Bud started all over again. Mr. Brando was a very disciplined kind of person, and he was sharp about it. He felt that Bud had overstepped his bounds. He just raised his hand and pointed at him again. 'That's enough.' The boy smiled, sort of shrugged his shoulders, and the minute dinner was over, he left the house."

Day to day, father and son jockeyed for power, circling each other like oedipal combatants searching for an opening. The house was paralyzed by the friction between them, even though everybody tried to ignore it.

"The arguments generally had to do with Bud's schoolwork," said Don Hanmer, who was coming by often to see Jocelyn. "There were shout-ing matches. Dodie would say to Marlon, 'All right, talk to him, but for God's sake, keep it down. Don't start yelling.' And he'd say, 'All right, I know what to do.' Then Marlon and Bud would go out on the porch or into another room and you'd hear mumbling in increasing levels of vol-ume, which ended in yelling. It would get louder and louder until there was a real fight."

The irony was that Marlon Sr. ultimately controlled nothing, since he was outnumbered and resented as an outsider in his own home, even ridi-culed when absent. Dodie not only sanctioned Bud's pranks and rebellions, she also laughed about them in public.

"You had the feeling," said Richard Loving, "that when Marlon Sr. was gone, everybody could do what they wanted to. They could drink, horse around, carry on just as they pleased. Eight hours of blissful freedom. When he was due to arrive at five-thirty, it was, Get ready for inspection."

But by and large, Dodie was the "powerhouse," the "glue," the "non-stop force" who set the pace despite her drinking.

Don Hanmer had also seen this from the start. "When Jocelyn brought me around to introduce me to the family," he recalled, "out came Franny, rushing around in her jodhpurs and riding clothes. Then we went into the living room, where Bud was playing the drums like a madman, with Krupa on the phonograph as loud as it could be. I was introduced to him, but he didn't stop."

Jocelyn then led Don out to the garden, where her father was working, bare-chested and sweating. She introduced them, and with a brief hello he went off with a rake in his hand.

Dodie announced that dinner would soon be ready, so the couple went back inside. Ten minutes passed, then twenty. Finally she invited them to the table. "Her voice was very controlled, very proper," said Hanmer. "But then she went to the foot of the stairs and let out this piercing whistle and hollered, 'Bud! Dinner!' Then she turned very politely to me and said, 'Won't you sit down?'

"I was just bug-eyed," he added. "It was the freedom that struck me, the atmosphere, the way they lived."

The way they talked was also freewheeling, shocking neighborhood guests. According to one story, the Brandos had people over and somebody remarked, "Oh! He has balls like a bull!" Dodie was in the next room, and suddenly she marched in to the guests and demanded, "*Who* has?"

Her laissez-faire attitude was best summed up by a conversation she once had with her mother about a neighbor. Dodie had joked about the local farmer, "Mama, Jamie's up on the hill and he's fucking his goat." Nana's reply was, "Well, it's Jamie's goat, isn't it?"

The retort became a long-cherished motto among the Brando offspring, one often applied to Marlon Jr. "It's Jamie's goat," meant "it's your life" and betokened the brother and sisters' acceptance of one another with no judgment passed.

It was "extraordinary, the kinds of things that went on in that house," said Hanmer, but it went beyond bawdy. "Judge not, lest ye be judged" was the underlying code, based on Dodie's sense that life was too fragile for the stalwart absolutes erected by her husband as a way of "holding back the tides of chaos." From the early days of their romance, she sanctioned Jocelyn's sexual intimacy with Don, simply because she believed that feelings were too important to waste on the conventions of middle-class behavior. The same supportiveness surfaced in any number of ways when she was sober, and the difference between Dodie and Marlon Sr. was no clearer than when Hanmer decided he wanted to marry the Brandos' eldest child.

"Just before Jocelyn and I got married," recalled Hanmer, "I went in to meet Marlon at his office. Dodie was there, too. It was the big sit-down, the I-want-to-marry-your-daughter deal. Jocelyn wasn't there, and what I got from her father was, 'Here's why you shouldn't.' What he said was, Fuck her if you want, but don't for Christ's sake marry her. You're an actor. You don't have a pot to piss in. Don't you realize she goes through a whole bottle of Listerine practically every two days? Do you know what it's going to cost you? How are you going to live? It was all about money, security, responsibility, sanctimonious stuff."

Dodie had been relegated to the outer office during this speech. Don had tried to object, telling the father that he and Jocelyn were in love, reassuring him that they would make it. "Marlon kept arguing," said Hanmer, "for over an hour. Finally Dodie opened the door and said, 'All right, this has gone on long enough. Don's stood up to you thus far, let's just cut it off right now. They're going to be married.' It was the same as her attitude toward Joce's becoming an actress," Hanmer added. "If that's what she wanted to do, fine. But it was up to her."

For all Dodie's enlightened common sense, and perhaps because she felt so stymied in her own choices, her drinking grew worse. There were any number of places around Libertyville where she indulged—not just bars but also a local gas station.

"My husband was a heavy drinker and they would meet down at this filling station on the corner of Milwaukee Avenue and Route 176," recalled Eleanor Purdy, who knew Dodie from the Village Players. "The owner was a drinker, too, and he kept booze in his office." Dodie continued to drink with Bill Booth, and even with her maid, Margaret, often at the Viaduct, a down-and-out workingman's place near the tracks to the east of town. From time to time she failed to come home, sometimes "forgetting" where she'd parked her car. Other times there were fender benders, and on at least one occasion she was thrown in jail for saloon brawling. Booth, not Marlon Sr., found her and bailed her out.

"When she'd take off, Papa would be very upset, and when he was hungry, he was more upset than usual," said Jocelyn. "I remember the only time I ever told him off—which I still feel wonderful about. He came home, and Mother wasn't there. I said, 'Dinner will be in ten minutes,' and I put the fish in the oven. He went upstairs but he didn't come down, and didn't answer me. The fish burned, so I turned off the oven, and he still didn't come down. Finally I went upstairs and found him packing his suitcase, taking shirts out of his drawers.

" 'Where are you going?' I said. He said, 'I'm going to the club.' I got furious and said, 'You're just going to leave us here? Your kids? You're going to leave us here to cope with all these things?'

"He didn't say a word. He took his shirts out of the suitcase, put them back in the drawer, and then came down and ate the burned fish. There was no discussion, no admission of anything—he was incapable of that—but without words, he acknowledged I was right."

Resolutely, the kids kept their pain to themselves. Bud was even more sensitive than his sisters, and the most he let on to friends Spery and Hoskins were in the form of vague remarks, like "Mother's under the weather today." He didn't speak at all about the violence when his father occasionally lost his temper and, as Bud would later claim, resorted to physical violence, except for the one time he alluded to it with Joe Spery.

"Bud was upset by it," recalled Spery, "but he was always oblique. More than anything he wondered why this was happening to his mother. Still he didn't ask 'Why me?' "

If he wasn't explicit, he was certainly acting out his resentment. At school, he was hiding behind the barriers of his pranks, poor grades, wisecracks, showboating, and manipulative "staring." But these ploys were as revealing as they were defensive, and his classmates, as well as their parents, kept on talking. Dodie's lapses made that inevitable—especially on those days when she was too drunk to function.

The gossip was vicious and oppressive. Dorothy Behm de Rivera remembered that Fran often wished her parents were more like the other parents in town. Carl Peterson, Bud's friend and commuting partner, once walked in on Dodie alone and was so shaken that he recalled the incident many years later: "Certainly I'd been aware of Mrs. Brando's problem," he said, "but that afternoon I knocked on the back door and heard her voice call, 'I'm down in the basement.' She added that Bud wasn't home, but that

I should come down. I went to the basement, and there she was, down there alone, in the semidark. I didn't see any booze around, but she was very strange, very talkative, and she wouldn't let me go. She was rambling, and it was scary as hell for me, a fifteen-year-old. She was slurring her words, repeating herself. She was obviously drunk—a sad drunk, not a happy one. She wanted company, and I stayed listening for twenty minutes, even though I just wanted to get out of there."

Dodie had tried going to Wauwatosa, a nearby clinic in Wisconsin, and she had also attended a few AA meetings at Marlon Sr.'s urgings, but nothing helped. By the autumn of 1940 she had hit bottom several times and also, reportedly, attempted suicide.

"She tried a couple of times," said Marian Johnsen, later her friend and a fellow alcoholic to whom Dodie described her worst episodes. "She took pills one time, and I think maybe she also used a razor. We had that in common because I too had attempted suicide, and she was quite ready to share this with me. Once we were in AA, there was no holding back."

As he worked behind the house in the stables, Frank Camellino saw her being brought home from the hospital twice that year. "Someone brought her in, holding her arm," he recalled. "It could have been six months or eight months between the two times. The explanation was that she'd had to be pumped out. Afterward I wouldn't see her for a week or two because she stayed inside and kept a low profile."

During the spring and summer of 1940, Bud was as bored as usual, and sometimes he went into Chicago and dropped in at his father's office. "He'd just make a nuisance of himself," said Doris Puffer, the firm's accountant. "He'd bang on the typewriters or play his drumsticks on the windowsills and desks, and also flirt with the temps. There was nothing Mr. Brando could do. Our office was open Saturday mornings, which was when he usually came in, but sometimes he came by when he was supposed to be in school."

Carmelita Pope lived on Monroe Street in Chicago with her parents, and with growing regularity, since they'd met at the Lake Zurich Playhouse the previous summer, Bud would arrive at the Popes for dinner. Often he stayed overnight, sometimes even for two or three days, much as he had at the Veris household in Evanston. It was another escape, silently planned, never explained.

"He just lingered," recalled Pope. "Then he'd announce, 'Oh, it's too late for me to go home, it's so far.' " The Popes had a sunporch attached to Carmelita's bedroom in which there was a studio couch. "He'd say, 'Oh, I can stay here. You've got room.' My mother would get upset and ask, 'But what about your parents, Bud?' He would reply, 'My mother hardly knows where *she* is, so how will she know I'm even gone?' "

"During the evening, after Mother and Dad went to bed, we would play records," Pope added. "Every time I hear 'Moonlight becomes you / It goes with your hair,' I think of Buddy Brando. His dancing was sort of klutzy, actually, but he could sure put on the charm."

The apartment was steam heated, and sometimes the heat would drive him out into the front hallway where he would curl up in his clothes and sleep. In the morning Carmelita's father would have to step over him to go to work. "Bud, what are you doing?" he would ask. "Oh, hi, Mr. Pope. I'm just sleeping," he would reply.

Most of the time he showed up without phoning, and as far as Carmelita remembered, no one from the Brando family ever called to track him down. "We didn't go out on dates so much as he just came over, hung around, and ate pasta with us," she added. "My mother fed him a lot. He'd hug her, and when she was in the hospital, he brought her violets, though he probably picked them out of somebody's garden."

Pope didn't see any of this as calculated or manipulative on Bud's part. "I just think there was a great need in him for family closeness," she said.

Bud especially liked talking to Carmelita's father, a lawyer who regaled him with stories of the Chicago mob, like the one about the time Ralph Capone, Al's brother, had taken Mr. Pope into an alley, put a gun in his back, and told him, "We don't want you to run for a judgeship. Get out or we'll take care of both your daughters."

"Bud asked him a million questions," recalled Carmelita. "He was fascinated by the Mafia, and intrigued with our Italian culture, the warmth, the genuineness of feeling. Once, we were talking about the hard or hurtful things you sometimes have to do. He said the most difficult thing for him was to make the rounds looking for his mother. That was the first time he revealed that she was an alcoholic. I realized then that he hated anybody prying into his life and would usually get angry if you asked too many questions."

The two of them dated, and Carmelita, who later understudied Kim Hunter's Stella in the Broadway production of *A Streetcar Named Desire,* recalled Bud's charm as well as his antics: "He once arrived to pick me up with a record album balanced on his head. We went downtown on the bus, and he kept the album on his head, trying to get my goat. We had an ice cream, got back on the bus, and came home again. He said good-night and went back to Libertyville, and the album was still on his head when he left."

In addition to his pranks, she soon became aware that he had great difficulty in telling the truth about anything, and she never knew when he was spoofing. In the beginning he had told her that he had been born in India, and while she learned that was untrue, she still remained gullible. "I was so naive I believed every word he said," she recalled. One time, he phoned and told her he was in the hospital.

"What are you in the hospital for?" she asked.

"I was collecting pigeons' eggs on the roof and I fell off," he said. "I broke my leg."

"Oh, what can I do?"

"Got a pencil? Write down these books."

He gave her four or five titles—"nonfiction, pretty heavy"—and then said, "Would you do me a favor? Since I'm going to be laid up, would you get me the books?"

The next day she ran out and did as requested. That night her doorbell rang, and there he was.

"Why did you tell me you were in the hospital?" she exclaimed.

"Well," he said, "I wanted those books and I knew you wouldn't get them for me unless I gave you a story."

"I just accepted whatever he said," Pope later explained. "I think he enjoyed that in me, because he could playact, and I was very controllable. I would just sit enthralled with all his stories, believing everything he said."

She was also enchanted because he could make her feel that she was "the only woman in his life," she said. "We necked, but that was about it. He put me in a different category of girls, and in fact, at the time I didn't think he had any sexual experience."

But Bud was much more experienced than his contemporaries, and he had let his classmates know it, not so much bragging but letting his body language do the talking. "He would make some oblique remarks," said Joe

Spery, "that a date had been hot and heavy, but he kept it an enigma. My father, who was street smart if nothing else, took one look at his appearance and his talk and gestures and said this guy was after the ladies. In my father's eyes, Bud was emblematic of sex."

By his own admission, Marlon had previously experimented sexually with Ermy, the family maid in Omaha and Evanston. Later, as he would brag to Wally Cox and other friends, he had also "fucked the family's black maid at the age of fourteen in Libertyville." In school he let it be known that "he was far ahead of us with girls," said one classmate. The simple truth was that this was part of his competition with Marlon Sr., not only in his dissembling but also in his attitude: He separated the "good girls" (like Carmelita), who couldn't fulfill his needs, from others whom he considered sexually available. Even then, his libido was boundless, and he seemed to have one thing in mind.

"There was an incredibly high level of sexuality," said his former brother-in-law, artist Richard Loving. "I connected this highly sexed individual with creativity, with a certain kind of primal energy. His pranks were fueled by the same sexual drive. There is a sensuality that results in fucking, and there is sensuality that gets channeled: with Bud there was naturally excess energy and it either went into fucking or into art."

To classmates, he gave the impression of knowing all the right moves, not through braggadocio but by conveying the sense of his own smug gratification. "It was the way he manipulated himself," said Richard Buehrer, who took several classes with him. "He had a certain body English, like cocking his hip or touching himself. It amounted to a direct kind of sexual overtness. He would touch people, just reach out while they were talking. He'd put his arm around the girl or take her hand, with great self-confidence."

The impression among his peers was that he could go out with any girl he chose, even older ones, and his high school dates all noted his aggressiveness.

"I went out with him once," recalled Mary Ann Meyers, "and sexually he was very forward. Forward then was a lot different from forward now, and forward then would be feeling the girl on the first date. With him, it was strictly what Bud thought he could get. There was nothing halfway. 'Let's get down to it' was his attitude. No foreplay, no style. He was basically a user."

"He tried to come on to my wife when we were going together in high school," added Buehrer, who later became a Chicago Bears center. "I had to tell him a couple of times to lay off. He had no choice because I could beat the shit out of him. He knew that Ruth and I were involved, but he was taking a shot at her anyway. To him she was just another notch on his belt."

Over the course of his three years at Libertyville High, Bud had no long-term steady. He took out a lot of girls, and about the only constant was that his dates were the prettiest catches in the class.

Sunshine Monroe, for example, was a sweet, angelic blonde with a good figure whom classmates recalled as a 1940 version of Ann-Margret. "A beautiful smile, lovely eyes," said Spery, "and, bang! Bud was right there. The guys were saying, 'Well, there he goes again.'" The chemistry was simple: He was trying to see if he could "tame her," as Dick Buehrer put it. If he didn't score immediately, it became a challenge and he'd sit and make conversation with them hour after hour, often stepping over the usual bounds of acceptable proprieties.

"He would get into talking about *Lady Chatterley's Lover*," said Spery. At the time the novel was considered risqué, but Dodie had permitted the kids to read a tattered copy. "He'd use descriptions from Lawrence, maybe even amplifying them a bit, and in Libertyville usually it worked."

At the same time he was frequenting the red-light district of Waukegan, not far from the waterfront. The gossip about his adventures added to his reputation at Libertyville High. "He went there some Saturdays," said Harvey Obenauf, repeating what was common knowledge at school. Bob Hoskins and his friends also showed up, but only to gawk at the hookers after taking in a matinee at the Genesee Theater. With Bud, though, "people talked about how he'd go over to Market Street for real," said Buehrer. "Bud was quite brazen about it."

During his three years at Libertyville High Bud had eked out only six credits from a possible fifteen, his grades an array of Ds, Es, and Incompletes. He had taken first-year French three times, repeated elementary algebra twice, and even in English had only squeaked by with two Ds and the unorthodox grade of "C-E" in his last semester. In gym, which required little more than regular attendance, he walked away with a string of Es.

Bud's lassitude and lack of application only compounded the problem made evident by his score on the Otis Intelligence Quotient test, which he had taken years before. The transcript of his grades noted an IQ test score of 96, indicating that his intelligence was slightly below average. For Libertyville, that might not have been so notable, except that his teachers seized on the mediocre rating as the ultimate reason for his failing grades. The faculty's perception of Bud as fractious, indifferent, and "strange" had become firmly rooted in the apparently incontrovertible fact that he was also stupid.

His impulsive random acts of aggression had also grown worse. One summer he had been hired as an usher at the town's brand-new movie theater. Bud had initially seemed proud of the usher's militarylike uniform, tan with gold buttons, and often wore it at dinner to impress Joce and Fran's friends. But, once again, his anger got the better of him: One night he tossed a string of firecrackers into the audience. However much he liked seeing the movies, mentioning them and actors' performances to his friends, he was out of control, and he was not only fired but also cited for disorderly conduct.

He was just as aggressive during the 1940–41 school year at Libertyville High, when his pranks took a more violent and mean-spirited edge, including a street-corner fight with a classmate and a set-to with Fran's friend Jack Swan. All students had science classes in the basement after lunch, and sometimes Bud lingered on the stairs, waiting until the last moment to make his entrance when the bell rang. "He kept kicking me, not hard, just annoying," said Swan, who'd be trying not to be late. "Every day I'd tell him to stop it, but he wouldn't. Finally I took my ruler and whacked him across the shin a good one. I didn't mean to hit him with the metal edge, but I did. He got a deep cut and probably still has the scar. But day after day he had kept at it, always with a grin. I guess he thought he was putting me on."

Bud's need for attention was obvious. With his mother's condition worsening, Jocelyn rarely home, and Fran now away at college, studying art at UCLA, he was even more isolated.

Dodie continued to look the other way. "It seemed to be left to Marlon Sr. to handle," said Don Hanmer, who was officially engaged to Jocelyn by then. "It would be something like the old cliché, 'Wait till your father gets home.' Dodie didn't seem worried about Bud's future. I never heard her crack the whip and say, 'You bring home at least Bs or you're in deep shit.' "

By the spring of 1941, however, both parents had been called in by Principal Underbrink several times. Even Dodie was forced to realize that Bud was in serious trouble, although she continued to say publicly that he would "outgrow it."

"I think she was concerned," Jocelyn said. "Any parent would be if their kid is getting in trouble all the time. And she probably blamed herself, because every alcoholic feels guilty. But she didn't talk about it to us."

In her more sober moments, she knew that Bud's problems had reached the boiling point. But it was Marlon Sr. who decided that the only solution was to send him to military school—specifically, to Shattuck, his alma mater—and he soon contacted the headmaster about transferring their son. The idea of Bud in dress grays was abhorrent and absurd to Dodie, yet she knew this was an argument she couldn't win.

"Maybe she'd been through this enough that she finally realized something had to be done," said Frank Underbrink, the principal's son. "I remember the Brandos came to my parents' house to discuss Bud's problems. She did most of the talking and was genuinely perplexed as to what to do. I got chased out of the room, but I listened anyway. They were saying, 'We're at a crisis. We've got to consider our son's future.' The decision to send him to Shattuck wasn't necessarily reached there and then, but the options were all explored. My father had talked to Bud himself any number of times and at school everyone had pretty much given up hope that he would ever graduate."

Whether Bud was actually expelled was a mystery to his classmates. Some recalled that he was finally booted out for roller skating in the school hallway; others said he'd been smoking in class. Most claimed there had been no crowning incident, only that he was quietly transferred at the end of the term.

Whatever the case, that spring Bud "just sort of disappeared" and never returned. Only Hoskins and Spery saw beneath Bud's show of indifference. "He was disappointed, disappointed in himself and the fact that he hadn't made it," Spery said. "Aside from his misgivings about military school, what he had to face was the plain fact that he'd lost."

Lost, indeed. Already seventeen, with three years of high school under his belt, he was slated to enter Shattuck in the fall of 1941 as a sophomore, an impossible handicap from the beginning. Even with Bud's well-stocked survival kit, he was destined to encounter what would be among the most excoriating and soul-wrenching experiences of his young life.

S H A 4 U C K

On a crisp September morning in 1941, Marlon Sr. delivered Bud to the Shattuck Military Academy with strict instructions to improve his attitude and his grades. Having reported for duty, the seventeen-year-old lined up with other incoming cadets to be issued his uniform. Much like entering prison or boot camp, the boys were being processed quickly, since the tailor took dimensions more with his eyes than a tape measure—"thirty-four," "thirty-six," "thirty-eight-short," he'd call out, then hand over a bundle of clothes.

When it was his turn, Marlon stepped forward and stopped the tailor, objecting that he wanted a more exact fit. The tailor looked him up and down, then shoved standard issue into his arms.

Marlon wheeled around. "How can you argue with an armadillo's asshole?" he muttered to John Fesler, the boy standing behind him.

Fesler was dumbfounded. Few people talked like that in his upper-middle-class family or in his midwestern hometown of South St. Paul; certainly such impertinence would not be tolerated at Shattuck, he thought. "I didn't even know what an armadillo was," said Fesler, "but from the beginning I realized that this guy was different. He was issued the usual crappy uniform, but he let everyone hear what he thought about it."

Marlon had fired his opening shot, as if he were already staking out his turf. The military academy was as rigid as the school's founder himself, the Right Reverend Henry Benjamin Whipple, the first Episcopal bishop of Minnesota. Set on a hilltop overlooking the small agricultural town of Faribault, Minnesota, Shattuck was a school established with the express purpose of developing "manly bearing, precision in movement, and the spirit of leadership." Most of the boys who enrolled each year were from wealthy Midwest and Plains families, and included the scions of the Burford oil dynasty of Oklahoma, the Mayos of the Mayo Clinic, and the Hormel meatpacking fortune.

For all Marlon Sr.'s hopes that the school would shape up his wayward son, he also recognized the advantages that might come Bud's way if he met the right people. As distinguished as their backgrounds were, however, many of the other boys at Shattuck were in fact there because of their own past "behavior problems." Like Marlon, their families had enrolled them in order to straighten them out. For example, although the great-grandfather of Marlon's classmate Stewart C. Dalrymple owned one of the largest wheat farms in the United States, Dalrymple had been shipped off to Shattuck because he'd been caught stealing war-rationed gasoline.

In 1941, with the war raging in Europe and the prospect of America's imminent involvement, the day-to-day routine had become even more rigorous; the school saw its mission as turning out ramrod straight, perfect soldiers: up early for chapel (on Sundays the boys were expected to attend two services), followed by physical training, then a half day of schooling, with most teachers demanding prompt recitals of facts-by-rote and memorized lines from classical authors. In the afternoon the students attended ROTC classes, perhaps the most important component of the Shattuck day. Taught by military officers assigned to active duty at the school, and paid for by the United States Army, the program had to meet rigorous standards. Every spring representatives of the War Department arrived for "government inspection," then issued "certificates of capacity" to the cadets who had measured up, which paved the way to advanced rank and Officer Candidate School. At Shattuck, ROTC was compulsory, and every day the students were drilling in formation, being taught how to take apart machine guns, and learning about military tactics or the horrors of venereal disease.

Following ROTC were two hours for organized athletics (students were expected to participate in one sport each season). After dinner they reported to compulsory study hall for two to three hours of homework, then it was back to the dorms for "lights out" at ten. On weekends cadets with a written pass were permitted to leave campus for downtown Faribault.

Into this constrained and uncompromising atmosphere stepped Bud. Already at his full height of five feet eight and three-quarters, and weighing a well-muscled 144 pounds, he was strikingly handsome with his Roman nose, sensuous underlip, and penetrating stare. His hair had turned a dirty blond, and he wore it unconventionally long. His most distinguishing feature, however, was the way he moved—at once seductive and threatening, catlike in its taut grace. Most of his classmates sensed a volatility in him, an energy that could erupt at any moment, and for the first few weeks they kept their distance.

Marlon himself must have been besieged by a welter of emotions. After his washout from Libertyville High, he knew he had to try to redeem himself. "Pop," as he called his father, was paying $1,500 a year in tuition, which he could ill afford. In fact, Pop was hoping that Bud would not only knuckle down but accelerate his studies, so that he could finish in two years instead of three. But his father's financial concerns were of less importance to Bud than the fact that he was two years behind, having been "demoted" to sophomore because of his poor academic record in Libertyville. Worse, his imaginative and spontaneous responses to life—ones that Dodie had always encouraged at home—were now labeled as signs of worthlessness and a failure of character by so many others around him.

At first Marlon seemed to make an attempt to take his classes seriously, but almost immediately he was discouraged to find how far behind he was in his studies. He had none of the verbal and mathematical skills of other students at his grade level. A more basic problem was his spelling: Often he reversed syllables in everyday speech, as well as in his writing, and while no one was likely to diagnose the condition in 1941—much less at a military academy—it would appear that he was slightly dyslexic. In early October the principal, Harry Drummond, wrote to Marlon Sr. with the disheartening news that his son was failing his classes.

Using his customary royal "we," Marlon Sr. wrote the principal that "we were neither surprised nor disappointed," but diagnosed the problem as Marlon's poor study habits, his inability "to apply himself," and his "needing to be taught concentration." Noting that Bud sounded "a little homesick and possibly still a little bewildered," Marlon Sr. explained to Drummond that he was urging his son not "to become discouraged" and "to build himself a new background by increased application."

Bud got back in touch with Carmelita Pope, now a college freshman in Davenport, Iowa. In his letters to her, Marlon vowed to make the trip to Iowa, even if it meant "going AWOL."

"I'm waiting to see you like a pregnant woman waits," he wrote. "I was kind of prudish at the time," Pope recalled, "and I was rather shocked by that language. Still, I could see how unhappy he was. He told me that his father had sent him off to Shattuck, a disciplinary thing, but even so, he never spoke of his difficulties in concrete terms."

For Pope, his communications had a "childish, self-absorbed quality, and were not always coherent." In her return letters, she questioned him more closely, trying to get a clearer picture of his situation. Marlon chose not to reply on those terms. "He was always very introverted, and it was nearly impossible to get any information out of him," Pope said. "He'd write about himself, but it was like, What's happening to my life, what are they doing to me here? If I asked for details, all I'd get was more philosophizing in general, or he'd just say, 'I can't wait to get out of here,' 'I can't wait till vacation,' 'I can't wait till summer.' "

Behind his poor class performance and his resistance to Shattuck's rituals and traditions lay his anger at having to be there in the first place. Rather than prompting the "increased application" advised by Marlon Sr., the added pressure sparked small brush fires in the son, repeated flare-ups in his insolent remarks and frequent pranks. From the first day, classmates had remarked upon his smart-ass language and cynical wisecracks. Soon his dormitory mates at Whipple Hall noticed that his capers went beyond the usual boarding-school tricks, like dumping buckets of ice water on cadets walking below his dorm window. Instead, he now offered up a variant of one of his Libertyville numbers by packing Limburger cheese into the study hall light fixtures, the pungent odor forcing the evacuation of the room. Similarly, he trailed a "fuse" of alcohol-based hair tonic down a hallway, into a classroom, and up a wall where he wrote *shit;* he then lit the fuse, and with a poof, indelibly the word was etched on the wall.

"He pulled all this stuff with great flair," said one Whipple Hall resident. "He was very creative, but it wasn't just on impulse. He knew exactly what he was doing, and his goal was to upset the routine as much as possible."

"He thought of pranks that no one else would have attempted," agreed Dalrymple, "and he didn't care how many demerits he got, as long as he pulled it off."

One morning after roll call at six A.M., the cadets turned out for calisthenics in the armory. In the midst of their exercises, Major Edward Thompson, the commandant of the military faculty, made an angry announcement: Someone had stolen all the silverware from the dining hall. There would be no breakfast until the guilty party confessed and returned the cutlery. After a few minutes of silence, the major ordered push-ups.

"And you'll keep at it until I know who did this," he thundered.

A half hour later, two cadets collapsed; ten minutes later, two more fainted. Marlon then rolled over on his back with a groan.

"Okay, let's go," he said with exaggerated indifference. "Follow me and we'll get it."

At one in the morning, he had sneaked into the dining hall and swept all the silverware into two laundry bags. He had then hauled them across the quad and hidden them in the basement of the chapel. Confessing to his prank, he was now forced to reset the tables, and another hour was lost before breakfast could be served. His schoolmates quickly saw that this was a prank with a point: He had virtually stopped the clock and forced the postponement of classes, hitting the school where it hurt most, smack in the center of its strict regimentation. "When we finally sat down to eat, the mood was electric," Dalrymple recalled with glee. "The students loved it, even the by-the-book guys, because they were learning something from Brando. He'd out-machoed all the macho guys, and he didn't even seem to care that he'd gotten a shitload of demerits for it."

In Shattuck's rigid environment, such small explosions were like cherry bombs in an echo chamber. From the beginning, his name was called every noon at formation as the commander read the day's disciplinary report, or "soak sheets," listing the cadets who had received demerits in the preceding twenty-four hours. Brando's repeated offenses ranged from the trivial, like buttons unbuttoned or shoes unshined, to the more serious, like cutting classes or "absent formation."

The faculty and their rules weren't the only objects of his rebellion. He also took on the "sadistic, macho" seniors who ruled the dormitory floors, and by resisting their bullying he became known for his toughness as well.

New students, or "yaps," were expected to submit when seniors inflicted kicks in the ass or thumps with closed fists between the shoulder blades—the time-honored practice of "bracing" to achieve a proper West Point stance. Every senior assigned himself one of the new cadets to act as his manservant, to shine his shoes, lay out his clothes, wake him in the morning, and help him dress. If the new underclassman failed to perform his duties, the seniors beat him with cut-off hockey sticks.

Not surprisingly, Marlon refused to kowtow. One night, Dick Denman, his neighbor from across the hall, was in Brando's room when a senior marched in to exact punishment.

"You lay a finger on me and I'm going to deck you," warned Marlon.

"Bend over and grab your knees!" the senior ordered.

"Screw you. You're not big enough to bend me over, and you're not going to hit me."

The upperclassman left, only to return with three football players. Together they managed to wrestle Brando into the ritual position. "They paddled his ass off," Denman recalled, "and Marlon took it without a word. There was no later revenge or retribution, but he made an impression. That was the only time in his years at Shattuck that anyone laid a hand on him."

In keeping with school requirements, he had signed up for the B-squad of Shattuck's football team at the start of term. Already strong and muscular from his two years of football at Libertyville High, Marlon also had speed and experience. It was the one area where he might have fit in, despite his denigration of Shattuck in general, since Coach Kenneth Relyea had assigned him to halfback and began to prepare him by teaching him plays—putting him through the drill of running the double reverse, for example. But Marlon usually had objections.

"I tried to explain to him that this was the way it had to be done," recalled Relyea. "I reminded him that the play would only work if he had the timing right and was in step with the rest of the guys. But he would argue back, and then I'd have to say, 'If you don't want to do it, that's all right with me. I got other guys who do.' Then he'd finally do it according to the plan."

There were other minor skirmishes at the beginning of the season. Shattuck players were required to travel to games at other schools in their military uniforms. As the team was boarding the bus for one of its first games, Marlon left the locker room already dressed in his football gear.

The coach told him, "Take off the gear or you don't go." Marlon stood for a moment, staring back at the coach, then returned to the locker room to change into his uniform.

Brando's need for attention, his love of the limelight, was also apparent during the most important game of the season, against a "civilian" prep school that was Shattuck's arch-rival. On a crucial play, the quarterback handed off to Brando. With a burst of speed, Marlon swept around the right end and took off downfield, his path clear to the goal line. But inside the ten-yard line, he began to showboat, holding the ball in one outstretched hand, waving it in the air, taking bows. "And wouldn't you know it?" said Denman. "He dropped the ball. Luckily no one was near enough to tackle him or recover the fumble, so he was able to pick it up and go into the end zone for a touchdown. But the coach was just a *little* upset with that stunt."

Marlon was in the doghouse for the next two weeks, the coach registering his disapproval by keeping him out of the lineup. His next game was against the Minnesota School for the Deaf, at home. It was a close game at halftime, so Relyea called the boys together in the locker room for a serious pep talk. "That's when Marlon got back at the coach," recalled Philip Ellwein. "Everyone was there listening to the coach's lecture, all very intense. Marlon was lying on the floor, and suddenly he let out a loud fart. Everybody cracked up laughing. Right then and there, Relyea lost control of the team."

By midterm Marlon was still having trouble in his classes, and his father registered his disapproval in a stern letter after his son's first report card at the end of October: English, 54; history, 50; modern language, 60; mathematics, 50—general average, 53.5. "I didn't expect you to fail in three subjects and barely pass in the fourth," he wrote. "Even more disappointing is the fact that you are not trying. . . . You are nearly eighteen years old and it is time you realized the only person you are kidding is yourself. You're not fooling me, or Dodie, or your instructors—only yourself. . . . Now get your butt in the saddle and get to doing what you should."

In response to his father's demand, Marlon explained that he had arranged to take special counseling from Don Henning, the school's headmaster. A tall, affable man, Henning was regarded by most students as more flexible and sympathetic than the stern military faculty. Most likely, he approached the problem directly—Marlon's poor concentration, short attention span, his impatience with rote work—but it is doubtful that he went any deeper during their closed-door sessions. Henning was a former Episcopal priest, not a trained psychologist, and even if he had probed, Marlon would doubtlessly have deflected his questions.

The one area in which Marlon took a more enthusiastic interest was the Dramatic Association, run by the head of the English department, Earle "Duke" Wagner, a teacher in his early forties. With chiseled features and a pencil-thin mustache, Wagner epitomized everything that Shattuck was not—urbane, witty, even sophisticated. Usually wearing a flowing cape tossed over his elegant British tweeds, bright neckties, and silk hand-kerchiefs, he quoted Byron, his favorite poet, and in good weather he liked nothing better than to arrive at the school's parade ground driving his shiny black Packard convertible with the top down, his English bulldog seated beside him. Students considered him "a gay blade" and "very suave," a man who "cultivated an image and never stopped living up to it."

Wagner was a bachelor and lived in Whipple Hall, too, in a small suite of rooms outfitted with Oriental rugs, overstuffed leather chairs, bookshelves filled with leather-bound classics, and, on the walls, eigh-teenth-century lithographs and steel-dye engravings. Shattuck's answer to Mr. Chips, he often invited students in after study hall. While they lolled on the floor at his feet, he entertained them with monologues on the state of the world or recited scenes from *Hamlet* or *Macbeth*, often injecting scatological jokes to keep them titillated.

As different as Wagner was from the other faculty, some students were uncomfortable with his behavior. "Sure, it was a boys' school and ev-erybody was thrown together," explained John Staver, a sophomore when he attended some of Wagner's soirees, "but this seemed almost too casual to me, with everybody lounging around on the floor of his apartment, like at a Roman dinner. It also seemed odd that the boys who spent a lot of time with him always seemed to do well in his class."

But Wagner didn't always indulge his students, and if they failed to live up to his expectations or faltered in their loyalty, he was as strict a dis-ciplinarian as any of the other faculty. He was particularly demanding of the boys he selected for his dramatic productions. Whether Marlon had been drawn by the teacher's flamboyance or by his own love for acting and pantomiming, he joined the drama group and was immediately cast in his first Shattuck production, *A Message from Khufu*, one of the three short plays to be presented over the Thanksgiving weekend. For once, Marlon Sr. received a positive report. "I have Marlon placed in a rather difficult role," wrote Wagner. "He seems to be taking hold fairly well and to be very much interested in trying to interpret the conception of the part which I have given him."

Marlon Sr. received the letter with mixed emotions, however. Wagner had obviously spotted Marlon's talent (Wagner's letter is, in fact, the first documented endorsement of Brando's skill) and was recommending that his dramatic abilities be cultivated. Having recognized the setbacks Marlon was having in his academic classes, Wagner also suggested that a new program be devised for him, one that would "strike at the root of the boy's weakness and give him the work he is best qualified for." Marlon Sr. would hardly be thrilled to hear that his son might be "best qualified" for the theater. Worse, he was indignant at Wagner's proposal that Marlon be dropped back a grade in both English and French, which would necessitate his staying at Shattuck an additional year.

By the time his parents arrived for Thanksgiving weekend, Bud's mood was up. Henning's tutorials had helped him raise his grades slightly, and his performance in the school play was considered a triumph, an accomplishment well beyond his years. No one was more pleased than Dodie when the review in the school paper heralded him as "a new boy who shows great talent." She had just returned from California, where she had been complaining to Bess of her husband's unilateral decision to enroll Bud at Shattuck. The militaristic atmosphere appalled her no less than the school's unimaginative academic program of Tennyson, Swinburne, and Greek mythology. Bud's performance in the school play at least held out the possibility that her son might have found a way to survive, even achieve some purpose in Faribault—and indeed, as she had suspected before, that he might actually have discovered his true calling.

While Marlon Sr. was visiting his old teacher, Nuba Pletcher, Dodie called on Wagner to ask his opinion of her son: Did he have real talent? Wagner reassured her, pointing out that he seemed more serious about it than just an idle pastime or fleeting respite from his studies. Dodie then took Bud for a walk, just the two of them strolling across the school green, to have a serious discussion of his future.

Years later, Jocelyn would claim that this weekend, and most particularly his conversation with his mother, had been a turning point for Bud—for the first time, he seriously started to consider becoming an actor. During their talk, Dodie praised him for his accomplishment, telling him that the performance he'd given was better than any of them could have expected. Despite that, despite Wagner's praise, she added, if he really wanted to become an actor, he would have to work at it. He would have to study the literature of the theater as well as the techniques of acting; he had to be prepared for the long haul, whether he chose to go to the American Academy of Dramatic Arts in New York or study with her old friend Bernie Szold. Was he committed to developing his talent? Did he have the patience to see it through, the discipline that went into becoming a professional actor? If the answer was yes, she would take his side against his father's demands and make sure he was allowed the extra year of study with Wagner, as well as try to finance his later enrollment in acting school.

Bud must have heard her promise to smooth the way with his father as so much wishful thinking. As Pop told him that weekend in their own heart-to-heart, his conversation with Pletcher had made one thing perfectly clear—despite Bud's slight improvement in his classes, his graduation at the end of two years was still in jeopardy. Whatever Wagner or Dodie said, Marlon Sr. still expected him to graduate according to *his* schedule and *his* terms. Back home, Dodie returned to her alcoholic withdrawal and would, or could, do nothing to persuade her husband to see things differently.

Whether or not his father's decision had undermined his resolve to work at becoming an actor, Marlon now began to distance himself from Wagner. Wagner had made the mistake of treating Marlon as his "showpiece." Since Wagner sometimes even tolerated his protégé's antics, Marlon lapsed into his usual testing of limits. Aside from his disappointment in his father's decision, there may have been other reasons for his rebellion. Perhaps Wagner's talk with Dodie had revealed too much about the family. There was even the possibility that the teacher's informality, which bothered other students because of its sexual undercurrents, was disconcerting. Whatever the basis for his resentment, Marlon began to show up late for rehearsals, then started to miss them altogether, forcing postponements. When he did show up, he either clowned around onstage or burst into angry tirades when classmates forgot their lines.

Adopting the role of a professional actor forced to work with amateurs, he also constantly argued with Wagner about interpretation, blocking, timing, costuming, even his inflection. Their discussions of technique were so far beyond the other students' experience that they would watch in dumbfounded silence. Marlon's performance as a self-confident, not to say arrogant, prima donna added yet another eccentric detail to his campus reputation.

In late November his academic performance was again suffering, so much so that the star of the drama society informed his father that he was dropping plane geometry on the grounds that he would be "able to put that one-fourth extra time over my three subjects." Brando Sr. was uneasy about the move and registered his disapproval in another letter to Principal Drummond in which he voiced his complaint that Marlon's decision had not been discussed with him, although it had apparently been sanctioned by Drummond and the director of mathematics and athletics. Reminding the principal that he had previously not allowed Marlon to drop English and French, he reiterated his expectation, "I feel that he must be in college in the fall of 1943 so that any changes should be made with this in mind."

Still, his report card of December 2 made it evident that he was passing in only one of his three remaining classes. Although he had squeaked by in history with a 60, he had failed French with a 35 and received an Incomplete in English. To make matters worse, Marlon's demerits had now climbed to nearly 200.

Bud returned home to a silent and joyless house for Christmas. Jocelyn was in New York City with fiancé Don Hanmer, searching for work in the theater, and Fran had chosen to remain at Aunt Vine's in Los Angeles. While neither sister was there to see the confrontations in the house during this holiday, a certain pall settled over the family's memories of the time, as if they later heard that the conflicts between Bud and his father had escalated. By and large, Marlon Jr. tried to steer clear of confrontations; Pop would take him out to the back porch, and while he tried to be on his best behavior, the two were soon shouting, firing accusations at each other. In later years Marlon would mention to his friends that there were times when he and his father had nearly come to blows.

For her part, Dodie tried to ignore the conflict. Once or twice she intervened, however, and her interruptions only brought down Marlon Sr.'s anger about her drinking and poor housekeeping. There were also the evenings when Marlon Sr. did not return until midnight. Officially, he was working late or meeting business associates at his club in Chicago. Although it was a relief not to hear his heavy tread clomping through the house, Bud was sure that the old hypocrite was actually carousing with one of his girlfriends. Dodie seemed to know, too, but drowned her loneliness in another bottle of gin.

That was too upsetting to watch, and Marlon Jr. would flee, usually with high school buddy Bob Hoskins, driving to Chicago, where they cruised the jazz joints along Rush Street, drinking and ogling the hookers.

During the holiday, people in Libertyville noticed that he went to see Father Rogers, too. The liberal and sympathetic priest was aware that Dodie's drinking had worsened, and as patiently as he had in the past, he pointed out to Bud that his mother had confided in him that she was going to try to make a go of AA. Rogers also sympathized with Marlon's hatred of Shattuck, and in this regard spoke of Dodie, too, explaining that she blamed herself for her son's exile to military school.

Saddened by this visit home, Marlon returned to the bitter cold of the Minnesota winter. During the second semester he made twelve visits to the infirmary, his stays varying from mere pit stops to four-day bed rests, his symptoms ranging from coughs, "tiredness," and headaches to diagnoses of fevers, colds, and flu. But several of his dorm mates knew that he was malingering, since he had told them how he was able to get a phony reading on a thermometer by rubbing it against the bedsheets. "He always laughed about it," said hall mate Dick Denman. "There was no way they could catch him, he'd boast, and it was always good for an 'overnighter.'"

It was during one of these stays in the infirmary that he met William Burford, one of the few cadets who became a good friend, although their relationship had its complications. Burford was laid up with the flu, and because of his high temperature had been placed in the room reserved for cadets with more serious illnesses. "I had just woken up," he recalled, "and there was Marlon in the next bed, not sick at all, but sticking the thermometer in his hot-water bottle."

They talked for a while, and after they were released from sick bay, the friendship grew. Burford sometimes dropped by his room and was struck by the books Marlon had. "He was reading philosophy," Burford explained, "books by Schopenhauer, Kant, more books than even an A student would have in his room—all because he was trying to find out the meaning of life. I realized even then that he was a complete anomaly at

Shattuck, sort of an advanced flower child. He thought of himself as having a half-mystical, half-mischievous sensibility, almost an existential outlook, and he acted as though he was seeking special knowledge. But he wasn't educated," added Burford, who later went on to become a professor of literature, "and knew nothing about the classics of literature or history. What he was reading was fringe, esoteric things, including people like Ouspensky."

Marlon adopted a superior air as he talked to Burford, insinuating that he had figured his new friend out. Burford was intelligent but was playing Shattuck by the book; he'd already made first sergeant, was the editor of the school paper, and worked hard in his classes. Marlon sneered at this, telling the cadet that while he might be conventional on the outside, he was sure he was quite different on the inside. "Marlon would begin by saying, 'Now Burford . . . ,' he recalled, "and soon he started making rather biting, caustic remarks. He said, 'You appear to be interested in becoming an officer and running for all these offices, but I know that's not really you.' "

Sometimes after Marlon had analyzed his friend, he would hand him a book, either one of the occult selections or, just as readily, Freud. " 'You should try this one,' he would say," added Burford. " 'I've observed you and I think it would be helpful.' For all his interest in psychology, though, his tendency was always to analyze the other person, not himself."

Cadet Fesler had also noticed Marlon's interest in psychology and thought that it was another sign of what he had come to recognize as a certain sensitivity behind the rebellious, angry shell. "They never taught anything like psychology at Shattuck," he explained, "but if they had, he could have challenged his teachers to the nth degree. He was constantly observing people, trying to figure them out, but always holding back, not letting anyone get close to him. Most students didn't know what to make of this, so there was a lot of joking about Brando as a washout, even a dope, because of his grades."

There was also something inside Marlon that never came out, that he would never reveal, and in the context of Shattuck's usual boarding-school banalities, it was this essential mysteriousness that set him apart. "He had a very strange laugh," said one cadet who was assigned to a table adjacent to Marlon's in the dining hall. "He would laugh sort of wildly and then become incredibly melancholy. And he had a rather curious smile that was disturbing and provocative. It was not an entirely nice smile, and people weren't quite sure what it meant. We never knew how far we could push him, how close we could try to get, because he had these incredible mood swings."

Sometimes he adopted a fatherly, gentle stance toward smaller, younger boys. Then, out of nowhere, he could erupt in violence, anger, or just plain cruelty. Stewart Dalrymple, who then stood five feet two and weighed only 112 pounds, felt the full force of Marlon's malicious streak in their morning military science and tactics class.

"Why don't we have a little warm-up session?" he would say to the smaller boy, then grab him and carry him across the room.

"Marlon, I'd rather you didn't do that," Dalrymple pleaded.

But Marlon ignored his objections and sat him down on the radiator, forcefully keeping him seated on the hot metal. "For Christ's sake, enough is enough!" Dalrymple argued. "You're ruining me for life." Marlon simply laughed and held him down.

"Maybe that was a way of showing he wanted to be friends," added Dalrymple. "I don't think he enjoyed hurting me. It was just that nobody had ever done it, so he had to try it. There was that kind of tension with him all the time, a kind of semicombustion. Whenever he walked into the room, you never knew what to expect."

"If someone said, 'I disagree with you,' Marlon would respond, 'You're crazy as hell and can go fuck yourself,'" classmate Jim Fite recalled. "There was a *simmering* explosiveness, something in him which, if it got loose, was going to be damaging. I was afraid to be near him. He made me ill at ease."

As usual, much of his anger seemed to originate in his feelings about his parents. One morning, during the fifteen-minute break when cadets were allowed to pick up their mail, Paul Rowsey came up behind him at his mailbox. Rowsey was a hail-fellow-well-met type, the epitome of the kind of cadet whom Marlon despised. He wanted to run for class president and, now when he called out a greeting to Brando and got no reply, he tapped him on the shoulder.

Marlon wheeled around, and with one smooth swing punched him in the jaw.

"Don't ever put your hands on me!" he shouted as Rowsey fell to the floor. Then, almost at once, he held out his hand to help Rowsey up.

"I'm sorry," he mumbled contritely.

Rowsey recalled that he accepted the apology. "He told me it was a letter from home, bad news, and so when he was interrupted he just took a swing at whoever was behind him."

However upset Marlon had been by the letter from home, he rarely talked about his family and instead made only vague references to "not getting along with the old man." This fooled no one, however. "We knew there were problems," recalled John Fesler, "and even though no one knew exactly what they were, the sense was that things were pretty rocky at home." Gradually word leaked out that alcohol was part of the problems.

Marlon's propensity to take a swing at someone was particularly threatening, since he had been building himself up and had already added four inches to his chest since first arriving on campus. Although he had already developed strange eating patterns—going on binges, slathering slices of bread with peanut butter, gulping down a quart of milk—he was converting the fat to muscle with strenuous exercise. Not only was he on the swim team (by the end of the year, he earned a letter in this sport), he also had his own private workout routine that consisted of climbing twenty to thirty feet of knotted rope in Shattuck's gym—hands only, without using his feet. (He would return to the same climbing exercise ten years later, playing a paraplegic in his first film, *The Men*.)

Hall mates at Whipple noticed that he often studied himself closely in the dresser mirror and also strolled about completely naked, not just making the trip to the shower bare-ass but roaming the corridors as if to make a point of his nakedness, often to the annoyance and embarrassment of cadets whose backgrounds had not prepared them for such abandon.

"He had this thing about the oils of his body," explained Burford. "I don't want to use the word *obsessed,* but he had this theory that he shouldn't wash very thoroughly because he wanted to protect the natural oils in his skin, which sounded pretty wacky to me. He was always saying, 'Burford, you mustn't bathe too much.' He didn't want to bathe at all, in fact, but he was forced to sometimes because the senior officers on the floor had already announced, 'Brando has a bathing problem.'"

Among his acquaintances, it was only Burford who noticed Marlon's softer inner self hidden behind the tough veneer. If he didn't always show it with human beings, he had great affection for animals, sometimes seeming to prefer their company to his peers. He often romped with Duke Wagner's slavering 100-pound bulldog, one of the few animals on campus—and it didn't matter if he was late to class or who might be watching. He'd wrestle with the dog and throw body blocks as the two of them slammed together, and when they played fetch with a ball, he would talk to the animal as he fearlessly pried open its great mouth.

He seemed to have a deep and responsive attachment to all animals, even insects. While most people would routinely step on bugs, Marlon watched and protected them. "We'd be sitting together, and an ant would crawl on his finger," recalled John Fesler. "Anyone else would have smashed it, but hell, he'd just study it for three or four minutes." One afternoon during drill formation, he incurred a few more demerits when he broke ranks to avoid crushing a caterpillar; stepping out of line, he stooped to pick it up and carry it out of harm's way.

In the same tender mode, during the spring he adopted a stray cat and against regulations took her home with him to his room where, a few weeks later, she gave birth to kittens. That semester Marlon had been temporarily stuck with an incompatible roommate, the son of a rich Minnesota farmer, a slow-witted, mean-spirited kid whom no one liked and Marlon despised. One evening after study hall, Brando returned to the dorm and found the roommate leaning out of the window, flinging the kittens, one by one, from the third floor onto the skating rink behind Whipple Hall. The student was laughing as he watched the animals splatter "like water balloons," according to the cadets below, who saw the kittens' bodies hit the paved surface.

Marlon stormed into the room, locking the door behind him.

"You son-of-a-bitch!" he shouted over and over again as he punched the sadist, then began bludgeoning him with a metal wastebasket. Dorm mates gathered outside the room, hearing his angry shouts, and pounded on the door to be let in. Marlon continued with his beating. Finally he unlocked the door, and the other cadets hurried in to see the roommate lying on his bed, cut and bleeding, the dented wastebasket thrown to one side. Brando was not finished, though; suddenly he pushed past them, picked up the roommate, and dragging him to the window, dangled him over the sill. Fearing that Marlon was about to kill the boy, the other cadets wrestled him back and separated the two.

For days afterward it wasn't safe to joke about the ugly prank, but

Tommy "the Meat Packer" Hormel, only twelve and the youngest cadet on campus, found that out the hard way. The incident was the talk of the campus, and the following afternoon Hormel was walking across the quad behind Marlon and Charles Mayo. "Hey, Charlie," Hormel shouted. "We just threw another cat off the third floor of Whipple and it was cut in half by the fence."

Marlon spun around and swatted the small, younger boy, knocking him across the walkway into a bush.

"God, I was just kidding!" Hormel called out as he struggled to his feet. "I had nothing to do with it."

But Marlon had barely broken stride, and refusing to acknowledge Hormel's apology, he continued down the path without so much as a backward glance.

Marlon's softer side also added to his extraordinary sex appeal. He was already more experienced than most other cadets, although like them he divided the opposite sex into "good girl" and "bad girl" stereotypes. The good girls that most Shads dated were at St. Mary's Hall, Shattuck's sister school, just 300 yards off the edge of the main campus. During the school term, St. Mary's held get-acquainted tea dances, or mixers. If a Shattuck boy then wanted to date a girl, he was allowed to visit her by appointment on Sunday afternoons—and then only in the presence of a faculty chaperon. During his first year, Marlon saw a few girls at St. Mary's, where he was regarded as something of a catch and indeed "very gentlemanly," if also mysterious.

Still, he devoted most of his energy to more adventurous sexual affairs, and fellow cadets heard rumors of dalliances with town girls, students at the public high school, or the daughters of local farmers. Here, too, Marlon adopted his usual secretive air, although he would drop vague hints, like "I was with this girl last night." Of course, a small number of other cadets played around, too, since local girls seemed "easy marks" for these wealthy boys in their spiffy uniforms. But very few dared to pursue what soon became Marlon's prey—the young women who worked as maids in Shattuck's vaulted, marble-tiled dining hall.

Some of the maids lived off campus, but the regular staff, about a dozen girls, were cloistered in the small dormitory behind the dining hall. A senior warden lived with them, and saw to it, at the threat of dismissal, that they kept apart from the cadets. Only Brando regularly trespassed.

"He made every effort he possibly could to fuck the maids," recalled Stewart Dalrymple. "It was his drive to excel, part of his strong need not to compromise. I don't think anybody else had the guts or the panache."

Several classmates reported a sighting of Marlon having sex with a maid underneath the bleachers inside the field house. Other times they were aware that he was ducking out of Whipple Hall under cover of darkness, sometimes using a tied sheet as though escaping from Sing Sing. He would skulk around the buildings, then climb up the ivy on the outside wall of the maids' dormitory. By the spring term he became notorious for these forays, and as Don Kirby, another resident of Whipple, exclaimed, "When it came to the maids, Mar had the balls of a burglar!"

With the end of the school year approaching, and Marlon's grades as bad as before, Marlon Sr. was reluctantly coming to grips with reality. He was aided in this by two candid letters (of May 16 and May 30, 1942) from Principal Drummond, who suggested that perhaps summer school was the answer. The principal cautioned that even if Marlon did well in summer school for two summers *and* passed all his courses the following year at Shattuck, he would still fall short of the requirements for graduating in June 1943, albeit by a single credit. Drummond wrote:

> *I wish I could be more optimistic in this letter, but I feel we should face the facts. Marlon leaves a good deal to be desired in the way of cooperation—for instance, last night, with examinations immediately before him, Marlon secured permission to be absent from study hall for the purpose of getting special help from another Master. He did not go to this Master, but was wandering around outside, and when he saw me, he very skillfully concealed himself in a clump of bushes.*

Drummond and other faculty were clearly at the end of their ropes, but Marlon had one last antic with which to distinguish himself before the close of the year. Despite his conflicts with Wagner, he had remained in the drama club. The most important production of the year was the commencement play, and Wagner had assigned Marlon only a small role in this year's production, *Is Zat So?* During rehearsals Marlon had continued to chafe against Wagner's direction. By the evening of the performance, the two had reached an unpleasant impasse, their egos openly in conflict.

The play was about boxing, with Marlon's role that of a cornerman, and after the first round the boxer was to stumble back to his corner.

Brando's character was then to step into the ring to sponge the fighter down. With parents and students in attendance, the play went smoothly enough for the first act. In the next act came the boxing match, and at the sound of the bell at the end of the round—Marlon's cue—he stepped into the ring with poise and exquisite timing. But suddenly he turned and looked out at the audience, and then, instead of sponging off the boxer's face and shoulders, he stretched back the waistband of his trunks and squeezed a stream of water down his crotch. "The boxer was supposedly trying to recover from fighting the first round," said Stewart Dalrymple, "and instead he jumped a foot from the cold water down his pants. The audience broke up laughing. They loved Marlon for it, but it stopped the play. Wagner, of course, went into orbit."

Marlon Sr. was equally furious with him when he returned to Libertyville. As predicted the month before by Drummond, Bud's grades were abysmal: English, 42.3; history, 57.8; French, 60; military science, 62.3. Worse, he had pulled down almost as many demerits as any cadet in Shattuck's history—244—although in a frenetic last ten days of nonstop marching, he had managed to walk off 240 of them. The remaining four demerits could be carried over to the following year—if there was a following year.

Ordinarily, any cadet with Bud's dismal record would have been expelled, and it is quite likely that his father had no compunction about telling him that he was being given a second chance in summer school only because Drummond and Pletcher had been reminded that Shattuck was "in the family." As much as young Marlon despised the school, he thus yielded to his father's plans and began commuting daily to New Trier High School in nearby Winnetka to make up his courses in English and plane geometry.

With Bud and Fran both home from school, the family resumed its usual patterns, although during these summer months there was a new addition to the household. Don Hanmer, recently married to Jocelyn, came to live with them while his wife was on tour understudying Omaha's Dorothy McGuire in *Claudia*. While awaiting induction into the air force, he was working as an understudy himself in a Chicago theater production. Feeding the cats, reading, driving into town for groceries and getting the mail, as well as the occasional trip to Lake Bluff for swimming all made up the typical day. "When Marlon Sr. wasn't around, it had a sort of aimless feel about it," said Hanmer. "Everyone just came and went, doing their thing, and that was because of Dodie's totally easygoing attitude."

When he was not at New Trier, Bud sometimes wandered downtown, meeting up with old friends like Bob Hoskins and Joe Spery. Usually he wore his uniform, for as much as he despised Shattuck, he found it necessary to announce to the community—now in the grips of war fervor and patriotism—that he too was a "soldier" and had a respectable standing. He occasionally mentioned to Spery how hard the year had been, telling him about his demerits or hazing incidents involving running the gauntlet of the seniors' paddles. "He was proud that he had been able to get through it and had been man enough not to cry," recalled Spery. "But all in all, I felt that while he didn't want to admit it, he had a sense that he was doomed at Shattuck."

Other times he dropped in at the Great Northern Theater in Chicago, where Carmelita Pope had started her first professional acting job. He was obviously fascinated, hanging around backstage and touching props so often that stagehands became annoyed. Nevertheless, he also expressed his ambivalence about acting, constantly questioning Pope, "Why do you want to be an actress? It's so phony. What kind of life is this, why do you find it intriguing?"

Periodically Don and Bud would play one-on-one football in the backyard, but Marlon seemed only to want to put his brother-in-law down; similarly he had earlier come to Hanmer "man to man" and informed him that just before their marriage, Jocelyn had caught the clap. Here was his strange, reckless, and hurtful streak, his desire, regardless of the circumstances, to gain power and control others.

Hanmer also found something else odd: While he had heard from Dodie that Bud had been a great success in school dramatics, the boy never questioned his brother-in-law about the theater. Despite the fact that Hanmer had already broken into professional ranks, had received several scholarships at repertory theaters, and was an understudy for *Papa Is All* in Chicago, Marlon resolutely showed no interest, as if any curiosity might leave him vulnerable. Instead he seemed intent on embarrassing and dominating Hanmer.

"He had a way of trying to make you feel uncomfortable, even *inferior*," Hanmer recalled. "We'd be sitting at the table having dinner, sometimes even including his father, and Bud would suddenly say something like, 'Don does such and such with his hands,' or 'Don does this with his fingers.' He was addressing everyone at the table, but talking about me and imitating me as if I weren't there. His observations were almost clinical: 'Don does this with his left eye,' or 'Have you noticed, whenever someone laughs, Don blushes?' He had made me an object of analysis, enlisting everyone at the table to call attention to a weakness. It made me feel very self-conscious. . . . What it all came down to was *him*," Hanmer added, "his need to manipulate."

Perhaps, too, it was Bud's effort to deflect the tension he felt at the table when his father was home. "Marlon [Sr.] was telling this kid how he should be this, be that," said Hanmer. "He expected him to be the paragon of all students and was always going on with that kind of pompous crap. Meanwhile, he had been out fucking and drinking. Did Bud know that his dad was a bullshit artist, a hypocrite? Of course, and if there was one thing Bud couldn't stand, it was bullshit. And it was doubly difficult for him, because by then Dodie had withdrawn from the situation. She had decided that grades and discipline were the old man's bailiwick, and whenever Bud and his father went at it, she just sighed and left the table."

Oblivious of his wife's unhappiness, Marlon Sr. was quite pleased when he learned that Bud had passed both his summer school courses. Even more welcome was the August 13 letter from Principal Drummond informing him that as a result of the summer class credits, Bud had qualified as a "full-fledged member of our junior class."

Returning to Shattuck that fall, Marlon seemed to continue his good-faith effort, going out for the Crack Squad, the school's prestigious fifteen-member exhibition drill team. He also returned to football and did well enough to be put in the starting lineup for the varsity team's first game. Likewise, he seemed to take more interest in joining in school activities, including an election bid for vice president of the Athletic Association, and joining the Tau Kappa Epsilon fraternity, whose membership for the most part consisted of the school's best athletes.

Most important, he had enough standing among his junior and senior classmates to be selected as an "adviser" at Whipple Hall. Here his softer side prevailed; perhaps remembering his antipathy to the senior cadets and their paddling rituals, instead of "soaking" younger students with demerits, he adopted a mentorlike stance toward his junior charges. He created a circle of young loyalists that even included George "Geordie" Hormel, the brother of the boy he'd flattened the previous year for his joke about the cats.

"Mar was sort of like a big brother to us," confirmed Charles B. Sweatt Jr., the heir to the Honeywell fortune. As a short, awkward underclassman, he was having his own fair share of difficulties adjusting to Shattuck's routine. "Anyone else, they'd spot something, slap you with a demerit, and just say, 'Tough shit.' Mar had more demerits than anyone else, but he didn't give a shit about the rules—not for himself, not for others. But he cared about us younger kids, and he shepherded us. He had a lot of sensitivity, and he could spot our confusions a mile away."

In late October, Drummond sent another progress report to Marlon Sr. and described a meeting with Bud that seemed to indicate a real attempt to turn over a new leaf:

> I have just had a very interesting talk with Marlon. He tells me very frankly that the trouble with his poor work in English and business arithmetic is with himself. He says that he would like to do things, but does not seem to be able to make himself keep to it. In other words, as Lady Macbeth says of her husband, "Art not without ambition, but without the illness should attend it." As an instance of this, he says he would love to play the piano but is unwilling to put forth the necessary effort. He tells me that he is now going to put on an efficiency drive, and I therefore feel that a letter from you encouraging him in this good resolution would be helpful.

By the end of October, his grades arrived: English, 55; history, 72; science, 66; business arithmetic, 56. General average: 62, hardly earth-shattering, but passing.

Meanwhile, Marlon returned to the dramatic society, where, despite his showstopping stunt at the commencement play, Wagner assigned him the leading role in the fall production of *Four on a Heath*. Perhaps the teacher realized that only someone with Marlon's talents could carry the part off. It called for a British accent (Marlon had already demonstrated his remarkable ability to imitate foreign tongues), and the play also featured a final, showy scene in which the character was to hang himself.

During rehearsals he entered into the scene with alarming realism, leaving his fellow cast members in awe over his death throes. At the close of the actual performance, he took it even a step further, achieving such an extraordinary intensity that when the final curtain came down, the audience sat in stunned silence for nearly thirty seconds, then erupted in wild applause that forced Marlon to take several curtain calls. "No one quite knew what to think," said Tommy Hormel. "They had never seen a performance like that from a student, or even from a professional actor."

Perhaps this gave Marlon his first real glimpse of what his prodigious talent could achieve. Nevertheless, while his performance was the talk of the campus, he said nothing about it, and if he had further thoughts about acting, he kept them to himself. Similarly, even with his few close friends like Burford, he still masked family problems. For all his attempts to fit in and control himself during his first term back at school, he could erupt in strange, inexplicable behavior, as he did several weeks after his theatrical triumph, when he took a weekend trip to the home of a fellow cadet.

Every year in the late autumn, Shattuck scheduled a "Hunter's Weekend," which allowed students to leave at noon Friday to join their male family members in the Midwest's annual bird-hunting rite. Faced with a bleak two days on a virtually empty campus, Marlon accepted the invitation of Phil Ellwein to join him and classmates Charlie Roberts and Lovell Adams for the weekend at the Ellwein home in Mitchell, South Dakota. Ellwein and Roberts were from wealthy families in the area—the Ellweins owned Pepsi-Cola distributorships, and the Robertses had major hotels, including the Woodman Hotel in Mitchell, where Marlon was to lodge with Roberts while Adams stayed with Ellwein's family.

When Shattuck closed at noon on Friday, the four boys hitched to Mitchell, arriving there at two in the morning. The next day Ellwein, Roberts, and Adams went off on the pheasant shoot, while Marlon remained behind at the hotel, claiming he was perfectly happy to spend the time reading and getting some extra shut-eye. But once his companions were gone, he made a beeline for the hotel bar. By evening he was smashed, too drunk for Ellwein to bring home to the family's ritual postshoot pheasant feast.

After dinner Roberts had a date, so it fell to Ellwein and Adams to look after their drunken compatriot. Ellwein had a date of his own scheduled for later in the evening, though. He decided that the best course of action was to pick Marlon up and drive, in his father's Cadillac, to the nearby dormitory of nursing students, some of whom Ellwein knew.

There was even one among them who was reputed to be a "bundle of sex," and he predicted that she would be ripe for Marlon's picking. But more to the point, given his classmate's reputation for sexual escapades, he was, as he remembered, "curious to see what Brando would do."

Marlon was still soused when they reached their destination and Ellwein introduced him to the nursing student he had in mind. The young woman lived up to her reputation. "Right away she started talking dirty," recalled Ellwein. "She was doing everything but screwing him right there and then. Marlon suddenly said, 'By God, I gotta go. I can't stand this.'"

Unable to get rid of Marlon, Ellwein and Adams took him along as they picked up Ellwein's date and drove to the Mitchell Gun Club. Soon they were all drinking, and at one point Ellwein excused himself and went to the bathroom. When he returned, his date and Marlon had disappeared, and Adams had no idea where they had gone. Twenty minutes later they went out to the car. "There was Marlo with my date, banging away in the backseat of my father's Cadillac," said Ellwein. He and Adams returned to the bar, and finally, close to one in the morning, Marlon and the girl came back in. Ellwein was ready to leave and announced that he would drop Marlon at the hotel.

"Just a minute," his date interrupted. "Marlo's coming with me." Ellwein was amazed, and even more to his surprise the girl actually took him into her family's apartment. "He must have slept with her right by her folks," added Ellwein, filled with admiration more than resentment.

The following morning Marlon returned to the hotel and headed for the bar once again. Ellwein's brother was to drive the four boys back to Faribault, but when they arrived to pick Marlon up, he was still drunk—in fact, they found him riding through the corridors on the back of Charlie Roberts's Chesapeake hunting dog as if it were a pony.

"I had never seen him so violently drunk before," said Ellwein. "We didn't know what to do, so we just put him in the car and started back to school."

Before they even reached Sioux Falls, Ellwein's brother had had enough. He pulled over to the curb and handed Marlon some cash.

"Okay, Brando, *out!*" he ordered. "You're not going to vomit in my car. Take the bus."

Too drunk to care or object, Marlon staggered away to the bus station, eventually arriving back at Shattuck late that evening.

In the meantime Charlie Roberts had already received a call from his father. "What kind of animal did you bring home with you?" he bellowed at his son. "He completely wrecked the room he was staying in—the lamps, the dresser, everything. You tell that boy he's going to pay for it!"

When Roberts confronted Brando, he just laughed and said he wouldn't be paying for anything. "He made some remark about 'cheap hotel furniture,'" Ellwein recalled. "Marlo was a charmer. He'd acted like an animal, but there was always something there that drew you back to him."

During the fall term, Marlon's charm again brought women's attention. As part of his early weeks of good behavior, he had attended another mixer at St. Mary's. One of his classmates had fixed him up with his sister, Barbara Wright, and Marlon had dutifully arrived at the girls' school to escort her to the tea dance. Over the course of the term, he took her to several more dances and sometimes called on her during Sunday-afternoon visiting hours. "He was very kind, very gentle," said Wright, "and never got fresh or made a pass."

Nevertheless, he soon returned to his forays with young women off campus. One evening in early December he slipped out of Whipple Hall to rendezvous with a salesgirl who had caught his eye the week before when he was downtown shopping. After Cokes and cigarettes in the backroom of Boosalis's Olympia Café, the two repaired to her parents' apartment, a second-floor unit located at one of the corner intersections along Main Street in Faribault. It was midnight or later, and it was not long before Marlon and his date were off the couch and onto the floor, committed to their sexual gymnastics. Suddenly the door to the living room opened to reveal the girl's father backlit in the hallway, and as the man stood there, peering into the darkness, he called out his daughter's name.

Brando bolted. Grabbing his jacket but with his trousers still bunched around his ankles, he hobbled to the window to the outdoor fire escape. Then, like a kangaroo, he jumped down the stairs, taking them three or four at a clip, until he reached the street and ran off.

"I thought I'd broken my goddamn legs," he later told Joe Spery during Christmas vacation when he recounted the escapade, convulsed with laughter. "The girl's old man was yelling from the landing up above, and I had to get out fast, so there I was, totally bare-ass, rolling in the snow."

By the end of the fall term, Marlon's good intentions and "efficiency drive" had all but ground to a halt. Brando Sr. received the report card at his office, and faced with Bud's grades of "Incomplete" in everything but history, he again pleaded with the administration for help. On January 5, 1943, Principal Drummond replied; he and senior faculty members had reviewed Marlon's record and arrived at the same unhappy conclusion: In addition to completing his present course load, he would have to complete an additional two credits' work by early June. Graduation at the end of the year was impossible. With this news, Marlon Jr. seemed ready to go for broke in every phase of his life at Shattuck, and by the end of March, he still had incompletes in all his subjects but one.

Any incentive to "turn in every day an honest day's work" was now blasted, and good guerrilla fighter that he was, Marlon escalated his war, targeting the ROTC program and Commandant Edward Thompson in particular. At morning formation he often showed up late, then stood at attention with his tie on backward or a shirttail sticking out of his unzipped fly. He resumed the ploy of frequently checking himself into the infirmary, and although a knee injury sustained during his Libertyville football days was listed only once as the reason for his visits, he began to use this as an excuse for ducking his ROTC drills.

Although Marlon frequently missed formation, he continued drilling with the Crack Squad, which was student-run and had nothing to do with the ROTC program. Even here, however, he seemed to be pulling out all the stops. The Crack Squad was undefeated in national precision drill, and that winter they were invited to perform before President Franklin Roosevelt. The cadets were bused to Washington, D.C., and lodged in a hotel for the evening. Marlon soon sneaked out of his room and found a nearby drugstore, where he purchased a bottle of henna dye, and the next morning everyone was aghast when he lined up with his fellow cadets. His hair had always been longer than regulation, falling over his collar, but now it was also a bright, reddish orange.

More sophisticated, more worldly than his classmates, Marlon skirted the edge like a high-wire artist, and while he was the school's undisputed clown-rebel, he was also using his precocious, even intuitive, sexuality as a weapon. By now he didn't seem to hesitate to proposition anybody, including a secretary in the bursar's office, who went to her boss when she couldn't get rid of him.

William Burford had remained Marlon's friend throughout the year, and the rebel had continued to try to "reform" Burford, analyzing his "true nature" and giving him advice during their "philosophical" discussions. "He thought of himself as a rather wise man, and he was pretty forward," explained Burford. "He still kept saying that the school activities I was involved in were all a sham, that none of it had any bearing on my 'real' self. He urged me to stop carrying on in this conventional way and liberate myself.

"His vision was of a philosophical, psychologically liberated life. It was a very strange anarchic world that undoubtedly included sex, but his overtures weren't the sexual advances of a promiscuous person. Rather, it was sort of an enveloping foam. He required you to enter entirely into his world. While I wasn't frightened, it was clear that what he was demanding of me was total intimacy, communication, and devotion. I felt as if he was pushing me to the brink of something I didn't want to get into."

These Svengali-like manipulations would later become the stuff of Brando legend, but even now Marlon seemed to have an innate sense of how to wheedle, exploit, and play off of personal doubts. It was similar to the one-upmanship that brother-in-law Don Hanmer had experienced over the previous summer, although with Burford it took the form of a boldness meant to encourage his friend to reach out, to exceed his day-to-day self. But Marlon persisted even in the face of Burford's admitted faint-heartedness, broaching a subject that he had never openly discussed before.

"In the course of trying to reeducate me, he started trying to suggest that relationships between men were all right," recalled Burford. "He assumed he knew what my real nature was, and he would say things like, 'If you would only loosen up, Burford, I'll introduce you to the person you'd really like.' Finally, he got around to telling me in more definite ways what was going on when he climbed out his window at night. He said, 'They think it's the maids, but it's not the maids. I have a friend'—he used the word *friend;* he didn't say, 'I have a lover,' because he didn't talk that way—'I have a friend downtown who I go to see.' He made it clear to me that the reason he was going out twice a week, sometimes more, was not to see the maids but to visit a boy."

Burford insisted that he never joined Marlon for any of these rendezvous, but said that another student did—another cadet who once claimed to have joined Marlon with two maids in a downtown apartment. The relationship with the young cadet had the makings of another Marlon-centered scandal, and the school, soon suspicious but without any proof, stepped in to prevent the two from rooming together.

The cadet in question was several years younger than Marlon, and finely featured to the point of almost being pretty. "At some point I accepted Marlon's statement that they were lovers," said Burford, "but I thought it was an unequal sort of relationship. Although I liked Marlon's friend, he was completely uninteresting mentally. He was rather soft and sweet, kind of moony and childlike, and not at all assertive. The two of them just sort of melted together, kind of entranced, but I never sensed that there was wild passion between them."

When together, the two seemed affectionate and made no attempt to hide it. Burford dropped by once to visit, finding Marlon lying on the bed with the boy. "They seemed comfortable and happy and made no move to get up," said Burford. "I was about to leave when Marlon started talking to me, as though to keep me there, as if to signal to me that it was okay."

Marlon had also discovered a hiding place, a small secret nook in the stone bell tower above the drama group's storage room for sets and props. Burford knew that Marlon used this as his private place to smoke, and now he realized that he and his friend often retreated there. If Burford had become aware of their behavior, it would not have escaped the notice of others on campus, and more than likely the rumor was added to the numerous others swirling around Brando that spring.

In another Marlon-inspired incident, one evening five or six freshmen marched into the dining room with their hair dyed green. Although their designated seats were at separate tables, they took over one table and sat down as a group, bravely flouting the rules as everyone stared.

"It was quite a shocker," said Cadet Captain Charles Betcher, who was second-in-command to Thompson. "It turned out that Brando had organized the prank; he was the ringleader." The following day came an even more shocking incident, Betcher explained: "Brando was apprehended in the act with four or five of them. One of the faculty discovered them in Whipple, so it was solid information, not just rumor."

If a faculty member did indeed report an incident that Brando had organized group sex with a circle of young cadets, this information, oddly enough, did not seem to have circulated among the students. Even though the "green hair" incident took place in the dining room with virtually the entire student body present, only Brando's classmates John Fesler and

Donald Ellsworth recalled the students' stunt, adding that the group had been dubbed the "Peroxide Kids." But neither they nor any other students had heard about a faculty member discovering a Brando-led orgy.

In later years Marlon would openly acknowledge the tie between his bisexuality and his search for meaning in life. But during this term at Shattuck, what his classmates noticed most of all was that some internal struggle had brought him to the point of leading a fugitive existence. Assiduously, he kept his friends apart. When he wasn't in class or at meals, no one could be sure where he was, or what he was up to, or with whom: the Crack Squad, the Dramatic Association, athletics, a Sunday reception at St. Mary's, as well as his off-campus exertions that raised more questions than anyone could answer. Each activity occupied a discrete spot on his private map. Despite the high-profile pranks and stage appearances, he wanted to be a mystery, and he was. Like some mythological creature, everyone was aware of Marlon but no one knew him at all.

Except, perhaps, for two people; Duke Wagner, the drama coach, and Mary Henning, the wife of his faculty counselor, Don Henning.

The parallels between Marlon's daring and Wagner's flamboyance escaped no one's attention, for each had been circling the other for the better part of a year and a half. But the exacerbated tensions between them could not be explained simply by Marlon's insistence on doing things his own way. Their competitiveness, verging on open hostility, pointed to something else, and given Marlon's sexual sophistication probably amounted to his delving into Wagner's personal secrets.

There had always been a darker side to the Duke, since he had the reputation of a rake and a womanizer. And he was a drinker, too. But the rumors that attached themselves to Wagner had less to do with "womanizing" than with sexual relations with cadets, thus leading to later speculation that Marlon's antagonism originated in his rejection of the teacher's overtures.

"They were very close and then they were estranged," recalled Geordie Hormel, another Wagner protégé. "Wagner would never tell me anything about it and Marlon wouldn't either, not even in later years, when we partied together in California." Had Marlon, in his own subtle way, been playing a cat-and-mouse game with the teacher who was so openly entranced with his acting abilities—and who, in turn, was put into a closet homosexual's fright by his student's X-ray vision? The scenario was more than arguable, given the events about to unfold.

With some ten weeks left before the end of the term, the commencement play had already been announced as Molière's *The Doctor in Spite of Himself*, chosen by Wagner to give his star student a prominent and complex role. Marlon, though, made a point of showing up late for rehearsals, which only heightened their conflict.

"They had violent arguments about how Marlon's role was to be played," said Dalrymple, who witnessed the unfolding struggle. "Wagner had very strong ideas, which Brando didn't like. The Duke was trying to rein him in. Remember, Wagner had suffered through a couple of Marlon's independent maneuvers in the past, and all the parents and alumni would be seeing the play during commencement week. It was supposed to be a feather in Wagner's cap, and he was using Marlon, no question."

Brando was not about to be co-opted, however, and as the two of them continued to jockey, it got increasingly acrimonious. Dick Denman stood by, asking Marlon, "What are you going to do next?" while the rest of the cast watched to see whether the student and the teacher would get into a fistfight.

"Marlon would throw his hands up in exasperation," Dalrymple recalled, "and look imploringly up at the ceiling and actually yell, 'This asshole!' Wagner's mustache was twitching and he'd shout back, 'Nobody calls me an asshole!' '*Asshole!*' Marlon would repeat, and then just walk off the stage. We'd all wait, wondering what Wagner would do about it. Eventually Marlon would return to the rehearsal. But, Christ, was he impressive. We all knew Brando had balls, but he was into this on a level that was staggering."

Was Marlon merely flexing muscle, aware that the production would not be possible without his presence? Dalrymple claims, in retrospect, that ultimately the play itself was the issue for Marlon, that the conflicts arose because he wanted to give the most creative, meaningful rendition he knew how. "Marlon wasn't just committed to the play, he was committed to his job as a player in the play," he explained. "So his blowups shouldn't have surprised any of us. This was the only area in Marlon's life where he could justify himself, the only legitimate outlet he had."

That might well have been the case, although he seemed to want to keep his fellow cast members on edge, too. Burford was in the play and Marlon often tried to shake him up, having switched from philosophy to fisticuffs. During one rehearsal, he substituted an ash broomstick for the harmless piece of balsa wood with which he was supposed to flail Burford's character. "He just laid into me," Burford said. "He beat me around the stage, laughing, 'How do you like that? Huh?' I didn't complain to Wagner, but it hurt, and I wasn't sure what was happening or why."

At the same time that Marlon and Wagner's conflicts were escalating, there were also persistent rumors involving Mary, or "Ma" Henning, as she was called by the students. Her husband, previously Brando's surrogate therapist, was away serving as a chaplain on the Italian front. There had been talk that in his absence she had carried on with other men, Duke Wagner among them. But there was also the story that Ma had formed a liaison with Marlon as well, and that perhaps it was this that had brought Brando and Wagner's competition to a head.

Like Dodie, Mary Henning was handsome in an upright Waspy way, as well as unconventional, lonely, and alcoholic. During the 1942–43 school year, with her husband away, she had remained behind in the headmaster's house. Regarded as a debunker, she often wore hats with veils, which she snipped full of holes to accommodate her omnipresent cigarettes. Often, she took young people under her wing.

"She was a lonesome woman, and Faribault wasn't the happiest place to spend the war," said Thomas Healy, a town local who came in contact with her through Red Cross bandage drives. "She'd have parties, invite townspeople as well as cadets over, and mix a few martinis."

Standish Henning was living with his mother at the time and recalled seeing Marlon often. "She liked him a lot," he said. "Whether there could have been a sexual relationship between them, that's the sort of thing I guess she would not do. But I don't rule it out. People came in and out of the place all the time. It was a turnstile."

Whatever the truth of the rumors about Wagner and Ma Henning, Henning and Marlon, or Marlon and his drama teacher, by late March Brando was announcing his intention of not returning to Shattuck the following fall. As if to prove his resolve, he continued to escalate his pranks, first by shinnying his way up into the Shumway Hall tower, where he cut the ropes to the campus chimes. Until repairs could be made, the school was forced to post buglers to signal reveille, as well as the beginning of every class period. The bugles proved worse than the bells, though, so he jumped to another plan, this one targeting the school's religious rituals.

First Brando, Dick Denman, and a younger cadet named Scott Kadderly scouted Whipple for a half-dozen alarm clocks. They set the alarms at five-minute intervals and sneaked into the chapel, where they taped them under the pews and even hid one deep inside the organ. During the next morning's service, the first alarm sounded shrilly. That one was located and shut off. Five minutes later, a second one sounded, and now the cadets were laughing. When the third one went off, the service was stopped and the cadets were instructed to find any more clocks under their pews.

"Finally, they thought they had found all the clocks, and started the service again," recalled Denman. "Reverend McKee, the vicar, was reading from the Bible when, *ting-a-ling-a-ling,* another went off. At that point the entire cadet corps was in stitches, and they had to vacate the chapel."

Marlon sat through the incident with only a wisp of a smile on his face. A few days later he let it be known that he wanted to know "what the body of Christ tastes like." At the next communion service, he received the wafer, but rather than taking it in the usual ritualized way, he turned back down the aisle and in front of the assembled student body and faculty ostentatiously chewed away as if he were working on a hunk of bubble gum. The following week he instructed cronies Denman, Dalrymple, and several others to position themselves at the end of the communion line, then gulp the last of the sacramental wine. "The last eight guys up can get a real snooker full," he told them, "and there's not a damn thing McKee can do about it."

He was right, of course. McKee, later the school's public relations head, was stymied. Marlon's antics had now been brought to the attention of Bishop Keeler of the Episcopal Diocese of Minnesota, which only added to the administration's woe. Behind closed doors, Drummond made it clear that regardless of Marlon's importance to the school's drama program, Shattuck was not about to jeopardize its standing with the diocese or with its own board of directors in Minneapolis.

Commandant Thompson had just about reached the end of his rope with Marlon as well. Thompson, a punctilious, by-the-numbers West Pointer, announced to the faculty that he wanted Brando dealt with severely. Since Marlon had repeatedly used the excuse of his knee injury to absent himself from drilling, Thompson argued that he should be removed from the ROTC program, thus removing him from the scrutiny of the army overseers who were due to make their annual on-campus inspection on May 20 and 21. In due course, by late April, when Brando was caught in downtown Faribault after excusing himself from a military drill to go to the infirmary, Thompson made good on his threat.

None of Marlon's classmates could recall hearing of any other cadet in Shattuck's history who had been kicked out of the mandatory ROTC program without also being expelled from school. The action, while quietly taken, dramatized the disarray into which the administration had fallen. The commandant's action wrested power from Pletcher, the acting headmaster, and was akin to announcing that if the school's civilian administrators didn't have the gumption to do what had to be done, then he, Thompson, would do what was necessary. It also had the impact of a dare. All that was needed now was one last provocation and Pletcher and the faculty would be forced to expel Brando.

He may or may not have seen the trap that had been set for him. He may not have cared. Suddenly, on May 21, an emergency faculty meeting was called. Marlon was sent to his room and instructed to wait there for the administrative decision on his fate.

What the precise incident was that had brought about this meeting remained unclear to Marlon's classmates. At least one incident was noted: Instead of performing with his classmates before the three-man army inspection team, he had been excused to the infirmary because of his knee injury. But instead of reporting there, he was caught smoking with some other cadets in the dormitory, discovered by Duke Wagner, who then became Marlon's chief accuser at the emergency faculty session.

Whatever his affirmations of loyalty to Shattuck and its traditions, the drama teacher would himself be unceremoniously bounced from the campus four years later—reportedly because of his association with Mary Henning. A more likely explanation, which may also indicate his resentment toward Brando, was the story that the Duke was discharged after another faculty member caught him having sex with a cadet—such, at any rate, was the clear, unhesitating recollection of Reginald Kramer, Wagner's friend, Shattuck's assistant headmaster, and one of the few surviving administrators from that era. According to Kramer, the Duke "was fired specifically for sexual activity with a cadet, relations with some boy. During the night he had to pack up and get out."

But what had actually happened to prompt the faculty meeting about

Marlon in May 1943 remained a mystery, even as it was obvious to most that Wagner was the main lobbyist against his former protégé.

Among the students, the sentiment that Marlon had finally gone too far was as ubiquitous as their puzzlement over the specifics. "There was never an explanation," classmate Jim Leigh recalled. "We speculated about it endlessly, like maybe he'd gotten some local gal in trouble and the sheriff's office called up to Pletcher, and they had to get him out of there fast."

For Charles Sweatt, it was more problematic still. His own father, president of the Honeywell Corporation, was one of the school's chief benefactors, and as a member of the board of directors was certainly privy to the truth of what had taken place. Yet, as Sweatt explained, "I could never get it out of him. And something *did* happen. Everyone knew it."

In later years Brando both excoriated the school and recounted his pranks to interviewers, friends, and even his own children. He called Shattuck "reactionary," "bigoted," and "not intelligently administered." He also notified the school to remove all traces of his attendance, including his signature, where he had daubed it on the backstage wall of Shumway auditorium as part of his initiation into the Dramatic Association. Repeatedly, he would claim he had been kicked out "unfairly" and attribute his dismissal to a fire in the school's bell tower. (This incident, however, occurred the next year, after he was long gone, and the guilty parties were two brothers. Their father simply arrived on campus, wrote a check for $100,000 to pay for a new bell tower, and managed to prevent the expulsion of his two boys.)

On May 22 Principal Drummond wrote a letter to Marlon Sr. to report the faculty's decision. The postmortem that Marlon "didn't keep to the rules and broke probation" seemed too mild to explain the secrecy surrounding the event, not to say the administration's angry and abrupt action only twelve days before the end of the term.

Marlon was waiting in his room while the faculty voted, and once expulsion was ordered, Commandant Thompson sent his second-in-command, Charles Betcher, to give him the news. Betcher was told to wait while Marlon packed and then escort him directly to the train for Chicago. Marlon said nothing, neither as he packed nor during the drive down to the depot in the school's station wagon. "He didn't show any emotion at all," Betcher recalled. "He just sat in the car, looking out the window."

Upset by the outcome of the faculty vote, Mary Henning had called

Marlon's friend Bill Burford and asked him to see Marlon off at the station. Betcher had been instructed not to leave before the train's departure, but Marlon was alone when Burford arrived. There was time before the train left for the two friends to go across the street for a beer at the Faribault Hotel.

"He didn't speak about his father," Burford recalled. "Nor did he say anything about how he was going to handle this at home. He was just rather silent and thoughtful."

As the two cadets sat over their beers, Marlon seemed resigned to the administrative decision. He didn't say anything for several minutes as he stared into his glass. Finally he looked up at his friend. "Burford, let's leave this terrible place together," he said quietly. "Get on this train, and come to New York with me."

5

N E W   Y O R K —
S A Y V I L L E

Once his train pulled into Chicago's Union Station, Marlon wandered the Loop for close to two hours until the start of the business day, then he presented himself at 43 East Ohio Street, the home of Calcium Carbonate. He had a cocky grin when he stuck his head through the door.

"Can I come in? This the right place?" he said.

"Bud was in civilian clothes," recalled Leo Knapp, Marlon Sr.'s assistant manager. "His gear was all stacked up outside in the hall. The door to his father's office was open and he came out and told his son to come inside. This was maybe ten o'clock, and I don't think Mr. Brando knew what had happened because the two of them went back into his office and didn't come out until lunchtime. There was a lot of talking but no yelling, so you really couldn't hear."

Marlon Sr. was always reserved, never showing his emotions, but that day he was so upset that he left with his son and didn't return to the office for the rest of the day. In his absence, rumors circulated among the staff that Bud had been expelled.

When father and son told Dodie the news, she wasn't surprised, but for several days afterward she openly blamed herself. Bud was without a high school diploma, he had no skills, and because of his bad knee neither the army nor the merchant marine was open to him.

"Papa was mad as hell," recalled Jocelyn, pointing out that the tension that filled the house stemmed from not only everyone's concern for Bud's future, but also the fact that no one was aware of the real reason for his sudden expulsion. The subject was off-limits; Bud wasn't talking, and if he had leveled with his father, Marlon Sr. wasn't sharing it, either. "We just didn't know," Jocelyn said. "But with Bud, nobody rejected any possibility. Hard as we tried, we couldn't get the straight story."

Back at Shattuck, Brando's fellow cadets heard that their classmate had been summarily expelled and sent packing, and his battalion did what was unthinkable in the spring of 1943: The senior cadet officers organized a meeting from which the faculty was barred by locked doors, and they threatened to go on strike. "People got up and gave speeches," recalled Charles Sweatt, "and everyone was saying what a shitty thing they'd done to him. One of the issues was that the cadet corps was supposed to police itself, and since we hadn't been consulted, the overwhelming sentiment was that Mar had got shafted because they didn't want him around when the military inspectors came in. With others they didn't want around, they would regularly give three-day passes, so we felt that Brando should be reinstated after the inspection."

They allowed Major Edward Thompson to address the group; he gave them no explanation but sternly announced that Brando was gone forever because he wasn't "good for the school." The cadets had vowed not to return to classes unless Marlon was reinstated and later that evening they staged a "silent meal." As a result, the administration agreed to hear from the official representatives of the protest, a group called the Committee of Five.

The following morning the consensus was that there might be a compromise. "The decision was made," said David Claypool, one of the committee, "that Marlon should be given the chance to complete his subjects by attending Shattuck's summer school. That way, he would at least be able to transfer to another school and graduate."

The cadet corps as a whole didn't think much of the compromise, according to Sweatt. They then wrote to Marlon to extend their sympathies, telling him about the strike and what they had done in an effort to get him reinstated. Several weeks later, Marlon would reply with a misspelled note, expressing his gratitude but declining any and all offers to return. (He would keep the cadets' letter of support for years—even framing it and hanging it on his bedroom wall in Beverly Hills as he, at age sixty-three, joined his son Christian and tried to complete a high school equivalency course.)

The school, however, had also telephoned Marlon Sr. to explain the expulsion. In his typical fashion, the patriarch had lambasted his son, but when the school then sent an official letter outlining reasons for the abrupt dismissal (that letter, strangely enough, would later be missing from Shattuck's Brando file), Marlon Sr. replied in a long and accusatory missive. The response made it clear that neither he nor Dodie had any idea why their son had been ousted, and in Marlon Sr.'s usual way, he chose to blame Shattuck for its dereliction in not keeping him fully informed of his son's problems during the previous two years.

But with all the secrecy and noncommunication about what had actually happened, the father imposed his own discipline, insisting that his ne'er-do-well son go to work that summer. Bud complied, and as the weeks passed into late June and July, the mood inevitably began to lighten. Dutifully, Bud had taken a job "laying tile," or digging agricultural drainage ditches, toiling in the hot sun side by side with a middle-aged laborer regarded as the town idiot. As things slowly returned to normal, first Dodie, then Jocelyn, began to hear Bud talk vaguely about acting.

Jocelyn, always the "propper-upper," jumped in. "I had already been in New York and done a play or so," she said. "Mother and Bud were talking about the American Academy of Dramatic Arts, where I'd been the year before. But I'd also heard a lot of good things about [Erwin] Piscator and his Dramatic Workshop down at the New School. You could perform a lot more there than at the academy, where you did one show at the end of the first year and maybe two shows the second year. Basically, the Dramatic Workshop was active—very, very busy. Papa eventually said, 'Okay, that's where Bud can go.' "

Apparently, money was not a problem. According to Darren Dublin, Marlon's best friend at the Workshop, "When he first arrived in New York, his parents were sponsoring him. Supposedly he worked at Best's for a day or two, but basically he never had a job. He always had plenty of money." The story circulated that when Marlon first arrived in Grand Central Terminal he tipped a shoe-shine boy five dollars. When he was later asked by a journalist why he had done that, he said, "Because I felt sorry for him." Richard Loving, later Frances Brando's husband, recalled that Marlon did the same with panhandlers on the street.

After two years at UCLA, Fran had come to New York as an aspiring artist. Marlon stayed with her on Patchin Place, a quaint Greenwich Village cul-de-sac not five minutes' walk from the New School. His sister worked part-time for Murray's Space Shoes and was now studying with the great abstract expressionist painter Hans Hofmann. She shared the apartment with an English girl, and, like her brother, was receiving money from home.

For Brando himself, New York was freedom. Compared with Libertyville or Shattuck, the big city offered anonymity, an outlet for exploration. His first girlfriend, whom he met within weeks of arriving, was Celia Webb, who was petite, exotic, and temperamental. She was about ten years Marlon's senior and had a child from a previous marriage. She worked as a window dresser and lived in a one-room apartment across the alley from Fran. Marlon soon moved in with her. Richard Loving remembered Celia as wise and competent: "There was a certain elegance about her, and a certain mystery which I suspect she cultivated. Even more enticing, she wore dresses with plunging necklines, open down to her waist."

Erwin Piscator's Dramatic Workshop had been established at the New School for Social Research in 1940; among its famous graduates are Harry Belafonte, Shelley Winters, Ben Gazzara, Beatrice Arthur, Anthony Franciosa, and Tony Curtis; Tennessee Williams took a playwriting workshop there. In the prebeatnik forties, it was a hotbed of student excitement. Walter Matthau, another Piscator graduate, referred to it as the "Neurotic Workshop of Sexual Research." "A lot of sexual research went on there," Matthau recalled. "That's why people become actors. They want to get fucked from here to China."

One of Germany's leading theater directors in the years between the wars, Piscator was also among the greatest innovators of the modern stage. His leftist, antiwar political productions had made theatrical history, and his concept of the Epic Theater was eventually developed into a major theory by Bertolt Brecht, who had worked for Piscator as a dramaturg in 1927.

Piscator had left Germany in 1931; his devotees claimed that he had done so because he was worried about the rise of fascism. In fact, it was legal problems and the threat of a paternity suit that prompted his flight, two years before the Nazis came to power in 1933. With his wife, Maria

Ley, a former Viennese dancer, he then left Paris in 1939 for New York, where he was asked by Dr. Alvin Johnson, director of the New School, to establish an acting program.

At the time, the New School was a haven for political refugees from Europe and a center of progressive thought. Its faculty included Karen Horney, Amédée Ozenfant, Hanns Eisler, and Wilhelm Reich. The Dramatic Workshop, as the new acting school was called, was a German-speaking reservation that had a distinct approach to theater arts and a strict and disciplinarian educational philosophy. In charge of the acting department was Herbert Berghof, a classical actor who performed under Max Reinhardt in Salzburg and also appeared in Theatre Guild productions. Mrs. Piscator taught the dance classes and started a successful children's theater. Leo Kerts and Lisa Jalowitz, both with extensive backgrounds in the German and Viennese theaters, were instructors in the design department then headed by Hans Sondheimer, a scenic and lighting designer from Munich.

Most prominent among the Americans on the faculty were the famous theater historian John Gassner; Theresa Helburn; James Light, who had worked with Eugene O'Neill; and the redoubtable Stella Adler, a veteran of the Group Theatre, which perhaps more than any modern theater company had revolutionized American arts during the turbulent 1930s.

In addition to actors' training, the Workshop offered courses in directing, design, dramaturgy, playwriting, community drama, and radio. Piscator taught a special course on the Epic Theater and in his classes often inveighed against the commercialism of Broadway, since his commitment was strictly to the avant-garde. Most of the readings and productions were from the classics—Shakespeare, Molière, Lessing—or from modern European drama—Shaw, Synge, Tolstoy, Kaiser, Chekhov. Producers would occasionally lecture on the practical side of the business, but the school— and especially the elitist Piscator—made little effort to invite agents, publicists, or even the mainstream critics to its productions.

The Workshop was as busy as it was stimulating. Full-time students like Marlon went from ten o'clock in the morning until midnight (and sometimes later), taking instruction in acting, movement, makeup, dance, acrobatics, voice and speech technique, as well as attending rehearsals and lectures on art history, literature, psychology, and other subjects. Not only did Piscator, Berghof, and Adler bring their rich professional experience but their renown drew in other luminaries. Sanford Meisner and Harold Clurman, Stella's colleagues from the Group Theatre, both gave guest lectures, and people like Bertolt Brecht and Paul Robeson attended the premieres.

In the opening months of the fall semester, most of Brando's classmates considered him charming and self-centered in an amusing way, yet with no outstanding talent or particular ambition. Some students had set themselves a goal, but, said Joy Thomson, a stage design student: "Marlon didn't seem dedicated to his work at all. If an assignment was easy, he'd do it, but if it was something he had to knock himself out for, forget it. He didn't sit up all night trying to do a good audition to play Hamlet. He wasn't really interested in anything but himself." In theoretical courses such as history of the theater, most of the time he didn't do the reading. Often he came to dance class wearing his pajamas instead of leotards.

The class that brought all the students together, the flagship of the Dramatic Workshop, was the March of Drama. Here, Professor John Gassner lectured on dramatic literature starting with the Greeks, and every Friday night, students presented a reading from assigned plays. The readings were usually staged by Piscator's assistant, Chouteau Dyer, and supervised by Piscator himself. Although only briefly rehearsed and often done with scripts in hand, they were performed with scenery, lighting, and costumes, so that students in the design department would also get experience. The most successful readings were later restaged as full productions at the Studio Theatre, located on the New School's main floor. Open to the public, these shows were reviewed by the press, and the leading parts were often given to professional actors and former graduates of the school who wanted a showcase. Occasionally an uptown agent would appear, trolling for new talent.

Marlon's first part in a March of Drama reading was as Brother Martin, the monk in Shaw's *Saint Joan,* on October 29, 1943. While one of his costars claims that Brando was "electrifying," Norman Rose, who came to the Dramatic Workshop as a guest actor, says that his performance was "less than adequate. My first impression of Marlon was that he was a very intense, kind of inner person who was trying terribly much to do something which I think proved to be foreign to him—namely, be a classical actor. Much to my present chagrin, I felt that of all the students in the class, he showed the least promise because he seemed to have less equipment than anybody else."

It wasn't until January, after four months at the Workshop, that Brando gave a widely acclaimed performance, in Gerhart Hauptmann's *Hannele's Way to Heaven,* about a waif who tries to drown herself and spends her last hours between waking and dreaming. Marlon was assigned a double role: He played Gottwald, the village schoolmaster who carries Hannele to the almshouse after her suicide attempt, and he was also the stranger who appears in Hannele's dream.

The reading received a full staging at the Studio Theatre, and Marlon's performance was a turning point. "People suddenly started looking at him," recalled Mae Cooper. "It gave you the chills, it was so good, so quiet, like the dawn of something great. I thought, I can't believe that this is Marlon. It was like suddenly you woke up and there's your idiot child playing Mozart. It made your hair stand on end."

George Freedley, the theater critic of the *New York Telegraph*, was also impressed. "Easily the best acting of the evening was contributed by Marlon Brando, a personable young man and a fine actor. . . . He has authority, smoothness, careful diction and an easy command of the stage to commend him."

Other successful March of Drama readings that turned into full productions were *Doctor Sganarelle* and *Twelfth Night. Doctor Sganarelle* by Milton Levene, a playwriting student, was an original adaptation that fused two Molière comedies, *The Imaginary Invalid* and *The Doctor in Spite of Himself.* Marlon played Cléante, Angélique's young lover, opposite Mae Cooper. Most of all, Cooper remembered Marlon's pranks, which seemed to escalate in step with his growing self-confidence as an actor. She added that during a rehearsal of one of their love scenes, Piscator didn't think Marlon had it right. "Piscator said, 'No, no, Marlon, you love her. Don't you know how a young lover looks at a girl?' Marlon started laughing. Piscator was sitting right there on the stage and Marlon pushed him on, grabbing him by the arm and exclaiming, 'Show me, show me!' So Piscator started to act out the scene and Marlon said, 'Oh, I see. You put your arms around . . . ?' He was just ribbing him. Piscator went along, he played the scene, and Marlon made believe that he had no idea what he was talking about."

In one performance of *Twelfth Night,* Sara Farwell, playing Olivia to

Marlon's Sebastian, recalls that he was constantly trying to make her laugh onstage during the dance scene in the final act: "Each time that we came full circle and his face was looking upstage, me looking down, he'd stick his tongue out to try to break me up. I was trying to remain in character, of course, and afterward I exploded at him, 'What were you doing?' and he just laughed. One really had to be careful with him. I don't think he had an evil bone in his body, but he wasn't serious about anything."

The contradiction between Marlon's wild, childlike behavior and the quality of his performances was obvious to others, too. While offstage it was as if he didn't have emotional complexity, once he was caught in character, he would let himself be transformed.

"I always regarded him as rather superficial, sweet-natured, and pleasant, with no depth," said Mae Cooper. "But suddenly he'd get onstage and these things came out of him that you wouldn't think possible. Maybe it embarrassed him that he was exposing something, because part of it was also that he didn't want to talk about it, as if it was some secret part of him."

He demonstrated his inventiveness in a walk-on part in *Bobino*, a Children's Theatre production written by Stanley Kauffmann, which transferred uptown to Broadway in the spring of 1944. Marlon did a brilliant little pantomime with classmate Elaine Stritch in this, his little-known first professional appearance.

Except for Dodie, Stella Adler would be the strongest influence on Marlon's life and career, first as a teacher, then as a mentor. She introduced him to agents and directors, but most of all she adopted Marlon, who dated her daughter, Ellen, and became part of the Adler tribe. "Marlon was in our house all the time," Ellen Adler said. "He was just a kid, nineteen or twenty, when he first came into our life like an angel. Through us he was introduced to this culturally rich, international world, because Stella and [my stepfather] Harold [Clurman] were part of a larger picture, not just Broadway. My grandmother, Sarah Adler, lived in the apartment, too, and it was in a sense a very Jewish atmosphere." For Marlon it was an instant education in sophistication and culture.

Elia Kazan recalled that whenever people later associated Brando with the Actors Studio or with Lee Strasberg, Brando would correct them: "No, I went to school with Stella." Likewise, Karl Malden claimed that during their time together acting in *A Streetcar Named Desire,* Marlon pointed at Stella Adler and said, "If it hadn't been for her, maybe I wouldn't have gotten where I am—she taught me to read, she taught me to look at art, she taught me to listen to music."

More than anything, she encouraged Brando to use his complex personality, to trust his intuition. "She gave him permission," as Jocelyn puts it, "to go into himself."

Adler was relatively new to teaching then. At age forty-one (give or take a few years, since Adler's age has always been subject to recount), she was a successful Broadway actress trying to build a Hollywood screen career. The youngest daughter of Jacob Adler, the titanic star of the Yiddish stage, she breathed theater from her first day. Her mother was the famous Sarah Adler, Jacob's third wife, and the rest of the Adler family—nine brothers and sisters, in-laws, nephews, and nieces—were all in show business, too. All had a large following of devoted fans, including John Barrymore, Isadora Duncan, and theater critics and intellectuals, many of whom did not understand Yiddish. Jacob's only performance on the American stage had been in 1903 when he played Shylock in Yiddish with the rest of the cast speaking Shakespeare's English.

Stella began acting professionally at the age of five and became a popular child prodigy, going on to play the best European repertoire in Yiddish translation. Her earliest memories involved being rushed from one Yiddish theater to the next; appearing as a sickly old-world infant in the first minutes of one Lower East Side melodrama, young Stella was then bundled up and limousined to her mother's Brooklyn theater, where she played the third-act, healthy product of the heroine's American marriage in yet another *yidishe* tearjerker. (No wonder that entrances were always so important to the adult, unaging Stella.) With her father's company, the teenage Stella toured Europe, North America, and South Africa, playing mostly character roles despite her obvious beauty. Her English-speaking debut was in Karel Čapek's *The World We Live In,* a Broadway hit in 1922. She then decided to take acting classes with Richard Boleslavsky at the American Laboratory Theatre, where she met Lee Strasberg and her future husband, Harold Clurman. Boleslavsky was a veteran of the famous Moscow Art Theatre, and taught the early version of the Stanislavsky Method: relaxation and concentration exercises, and an intensive exploration of the actor's personal memories and experiences. While taking classes, Adler continued to perform. For a time, she was the leading lady in Maurice Schwartz's Yiddish Art Theatre, and later headed her own company. In London she married the businessman Horace Oliashev and left him, pregnant, shortly afterward. Her daughter, Ellen, was born in New York in 1930.

In 1931 she was invited by Strasberg, Clurman and Cheryl Crawford to join their new company, the Group Theatre. Although she was the most experienced actor in the Group, she was not its star and continued to play mostly character roles. Her most memorable performance, alongside John Garfield, Morris Carnovsky, and her brother, Luther, was as the middle-aged Bessie Berger, the harassed matriarch in Clifford Odets's *Awake and Sing*—a look at the struggles of a financially strapped Jewish family.

Because Adler felt somewhat out of place among the "untheatrical" personalities in the Group and also disagreed with Strasberg's emphasis on the actor's personal emotion, which he claimed was the core of the Stanislavsky Method, she left for Paris in 1934. There she met the Russian director and persuaded him to coach her. When she returned to New York, she announced that Strasberg had, indeed, misunderstood Stanislavsky. What she had personally learned from the master, she said, was that dwelling excessively on the actor's psychology resulted in forced action; that "affective memory" exercises should be used as a last resort, and that a play's "given circumstances," its physical action, should be primary. The dispute with Strasberg was the beginning of a lifelong rivalry, and Adler's last performance with the Group was in 1937, three years before the collective disbanded.

According to Bobby Lewis, one of the original members of the Group Theatre, her ambition was to become an international movie star but her best work had actually been with the Group. Now she came into her own as a teacher, and would in fact become the most famous acting coach on the New School faculty. To the students she represented everything that was desirable in the theatre.

From the beginning, there was a rivalry between Stella Adler and Erwin Piscator. A fundamental philosophical difference arose as well: What Adler was looking for among the young actors were observers— sympathetic students of human behavior—while Piscator saw actors as the servant of their director, and the director himself at the beck and call of the playwright.

Adler was, in fact, running her own institution within the Dramatic Workshop—"an isolated acting class," as Piscator put it indignantly in the course of one of their fights. She did not work on plays, but rather on a variety of improvisations and exercises, focusing on the actors' own desires, fears, and inhibitions. Many of the students were torn. There was Stella, teaching downstairs in the basement, screaming, "Don't act! Stop acting!" at the slightest sign of overacting. Meanwhile, Piscator was upstairs, on the main stage, shouting "Be big!" when someone failed to project.

Adler's fundamentals of acting were concentration, attention to detail, and specific physical activities. At the very first session, the students were asked to examine the boards on the floor for spots, to count the folds in the curtains as well as the dust particles on them. Another exercise was "the lost watch": An imaginary watch had been "hidden" in the room, and the class was assigned to "hunt" for it. Then a real watch was hidden and the students were supposed to find it, this time "for real." The difference between the two exercises was the difference between playing an action and not playing an action; what Adler wanted was for the actor to always have a concrete physical task, never to perform without "a reason."

Sense-memory exercises, like sewing with an imaginary needle, came next. Again, the concentration was on the details of the specific action. For Marlon, these exercises were a lark. Norman Rose, who audited a few of Stella's classes, remembers how good he was. In one exercise without words, the task was to walk up a street, buy a newspaper, go home to one's apartment, enter, climb the stairs, put the key in the lock—all with imaginary objects. "He was very sharp. He could do it without the earnestness that plagued the rest of us."

Sara Farwell agreed. "He was a free spirit," she said, "and Stella had spotted that instantly. She saw this rambunctiousness, this easiness and talent all over the place."

Stella ordinarily flirted with every man within view, but only three of the roughly twenty students in the class were male. Blond, coiffed, with wonderfully long legs, a fancy suit, and matching hat, she would sometimes sweep in for her eleven o'clock class as late as 11:30. "Marlon, darling," she would say. "Darling, would you pay for my taxi?" She told wonderful stories about Clurman, how marvelous a husband he was but how she would punch him in his sleep, demanding, "Stop snoring like a great man! Snore like an ordinary man!" But she was reputed to have said at a left-wing May Day parade that she could live in any communist country if she were its queen.

Brando's fascination with and attachment to Adler seems all the more significant in the face of what many students saw as her phoniness. "Here she was coming in, all dolled up, the grande dame," Brando's sidekick Darren Dublin recalled, "but he thought it was amusing. He didn't have any respect for her heritage, but the 'Oh, yes, darling . . . ,' these big rings of hers, and how she'd make her entrance into class—all that phony stuff— he just loved the whole thing." Dublin added, "There was also a deep sense of respect, something bordering on awe."

Adler recognized Brando's raw talent as quickly as he had sensed her gift for reaching deep inside him. Their affinity was obvious from the first day he stepped into her class: She was a woman embattled, a crusader in search of a subject—while Marlon, as always, was in need of someone to trust.

Marlon was excellent in improvisations. Stella would proffer a fur piece and say it was a cat or a dog. Marlon would caress it, creating a real sense of how he loved it. Norman Rose remembers his impersonation of a chicken: "He was called and did not do it fully, and she was very sarcastic. I don't remember what she said exactly, but something jarred him out of his shyness and made him jump the barrier. He was silent for a moment and then—yes, he jumped into it and *was* a chicken."

Other students provided more details about this exercise, which point to just how interlocked Marlon's and Stella's impulses were. It was about becoming one of a coopful of chickens who have just learned that an atomic bomb is about to annihilate them. Naturally, most of the students in the class responded by leaping to their feet and running about the room, cackling wildly. Marlon alone sat still, miming the laying of an egg. His message was, What does a hen know about nuclear destruction? She does what she has to, what she has always done. For Stella, the imagination here, the *truth,* was precisely what was called for.

There was also Brando's "cash register routine," which proved equally imaginative: "The task was to impersonate an object in a drug-store, and we all did the usual things," said Sara Farwell. "But Marlon—I won't ever forget it—was sitting in a cross-legged yoga position with his 'cash' out in front of him and his arms out as the cash drawer. He would light up his face, his eyes popping in and out like the window of an old cash register, and his tongue was coming out like the sign of how much money it was. He made dreadful noises, funny noises, and you just visualized everything. His knees went in and out, his palms as the money tray, his whole body was moving, delighted with the idea of having all this money come in. After a while, we all stopped what we were doing, just stood there and watched."

Adler rejoiced in Brando's talent, telling friends that this "puppy thing," as she referred to him, "will be the best young actor on the American stage." The composer David Diamond was also an Adler protégé at the time. Along with Martha, "the black maid who drank all the liquor," he was in the Adler apartment on the corner of Fifty-fourth Street and Seventh Avenue daily. Stella, he said, recognized Marlon's potential at the very beginning of the semester. " 'David, wait till you meet this kid. . . . This is a genius,' she told me. I'd never heard her speak this way about anybody," Diamond added. "She used the word *genius,* absolutely. She made such a big to-do about it."

In later years Adler herself would confirm this, explaining, "I taught Marlon nothing. I opened up possibilities of thinking, feeling, experiencing, and as I opened those doors, he walked right through. . . . He's the most keenly aware, the most empathetical human being alive. . . . He's aware and he *knows,* he just knows. If you have a scar, physical or mental, he goes right to it. He doesn't want to, but he cannot be cheated or fooled. He's absolutely aware of everything that's going on in a person. If you left the room, he could *be* you."

For Brando, such bounty could not have come at a better time. He had no plans, no conception of himself as an actor. He was searching, and as his sister Jocelyn put it, "Encouragement meant a great deal" to him. But Stella was more than encouraging; she was the first person to give legitimacy to his inner contradictions, and also to sanction his lifelong habit of observation. In effect, their acting sessions amounted to therapy. "He trusted Stella because she was talking about his insides . . . and in a way, she put Bud in touch with himself as he had not been before," said his sister. "She gave him permission to try himself out, encouraged him to do what he *felt* like doing, even when he wasn't quite sure why he wanted to do it. Until then, he was usually going against the grain—it was resistance, rebellion, and it was only Stella who cared enough to say, 'That's interesting, your reaction to that. Go ahead, do more.' "

Brando himself, despite his usual reticence, would manage to verbalize his feelings years later. Stella Adler, he said, "was a very kind woman full of insights, and she guided and helped me. . . . Outside of her phenomenal talent to communicate ideas, to bring forth hidden sensitivity in people, she was very helpful in a troubled time in my life. She teaches people about themselves. . . . She imparts a most valuable kind of information—how to discover the nature of our own emotional mechanics and therefore those of others."

Nevertheless, a guided voyage into one's psyche is an extremely charged and intimate process—especially in a public classroom. For years Stella's friends as well as her foes had known her to be "carnivorous" when it came to men, and at the Workshop the common sentiment was that she "exuded female sex as much as Marlon exuded male sex." On another level, though, the relationship appeared to be no less entwined than that of a mother and child. Stella felt that it was "a bizarre and wonderful miracle," according to Diamond. "She never used those words, but it was there in the way she looked at him, the way he responded to her, the warmth he felt. It was love. Maternal love. I would say Stella might well have been the surrogate mother."

She was his port in a storm, and within weeks of enrolling at the New School, he had started coming around to Stella's apartment. There were her sisters, Celia, Lulla, and Pearly; brother Luther and his wife, Sylvia Sidney; their cousin, Francine Larrimore; but most of all Stella's mother, Sarah, who even though close to eighty thought nothing of sitting on the floor beside him doing three or four accents, leading him through scenes from Shakespeare and *Uriel Acosta*. The decor of the apartment was *yidisher* elegant—satin drapes, pink tasseled lampshades, French provincial furniture and on the walls, pastels by Numa Rabinowitz, the son of Shalom Aleichem. The atmosphere was anything but stiff, animated as it was by the Adler women with their skill and their warmth, "always hugging him—Marlon this, Marlon that." Adler's husband, Harold Clurman, brilliant and animated in public, usually sat and watched patiently while Stella and her mother ran things. When Stella said something, the place jumped.

Sometimes Stella and Harold would take Marlon to Stewart's Cafeteria, or to Childs on Columbus Circle, where he would nosh on coffee and bagels until closing time with Clifford Odets, John Garfield, or other Group Theatre alumni. Mostly, though, the love was back at the apartment. Marlon would show up in a sweater and loafers, invariably planting himself in a lotus position back on the floor, and often he mimicked Stella, affectionately teasing her with what came to be called the "parrot routine." Stella would have a glass of scotch before her and a cigarette in her hand. Marlon started by getting his own drink. He sat opposite her and aped her every movement—taking a sip or putting the glass back down in perfect syncopation. David Diamond was there one day when the routine kept going, because Stella wouldn't acknowledge it and Marlon wouldn't stop.

"She's talking, and when Stella talks nobody else talks. So Marlon is imitating every gesture. Now he gets up to grab his own cigarette, and here's the interesting manipulation: Stella does not have an ashtray near her, so she's flicking it on the carpet. So I get up and I run—they had a hand thing, a little carpet sweeper. 'David,' she says, 'please give the carpet a run-through.' She's still flicking, though, and only now does she acknowledge Marlon: 'What are you doing? You don't smoke.' He says, 'Oh, that's right.' He flicks the ashes onto the floor. She doesn't say a word and goes on. Now it starts again. She puts down the drink, she flicks, she picks up, he's following everything the same way.

"This goes on ten, fifteen minutes easily. Stella, as always, had one of those peignoir gowns where it's sort of to the floor. But it's always open, the tits half out with nothing on underneath. So I get up, I go get the thing to do the ashes, and suddenly, as I come back again, she crosses her legs, which are rather full down around the calves but gorgeous, gorgeous thighs. The peignoir just simply opened and this leg was there. So what does Marlon do? He takes off his pants, and there he is in his boxer shorts crossing his leg over, showing his thigh. What does Stella do? She looks over and says, 'Are you modeling?'

"Does he reply? Not a word. Finally I broke up. I said, 'Marlon, what a gorgeous hunk of leg that is.' Before he can respond, though, Stella says, 'There's nothing wrong with mine either.' "

The intimacy, not to say the humor, of these situations was a language all its own, and Marlon became no less engaged when Stella's mother would sit on the floor with him. "I can see his face when he'd hear stories about the great days of the Yiddish theater," Diamond recalled. "He felt enriched by the Jewish personalities, the family warmth, family sacrifice, families protecting each other. . . . He spoke to me of it: 'You know, I love being with Stella and the family, and when I see Lulla and Pearly . . .' "

Adler heard all about her protégé's beleaguered past. "He would pour it out to Stella," Diamond said. When Dodie was in New York in the spring, she even came to thank Stella for having saved Bud—his mother could see that he finally had direction. Stella, who regarded Dodie as a "very beautiful, lost, girlish creature," gave Marlon's real mother her own feelings about his talent. As she later explained, "Very quickly you could tell that he was brilliant. He tried to bluff a lot, and one day I said, 'Stop lying, Marlon,' and he stopped. He participated full-heartedly. . . . He found some of me that was adamant and strong and with a definite point of view . . . and he felt secure. Otherwise he would have forgotten the whole thing. . . . I told her this, and his mother understood completely."

As the relationship developed, Adler introduced Brando to the full circle of Jewish artists and intellectuals who regularly visited her apartment and whom she called *mishpocheh* (family): the composers Aaron Copland, Milton Babbitt, and Leonard Bernstein; the actor Joseph Schildkraut; critic Irving Howe; Oscar Levant; and others. Marlon's response, as always, was like a small terrier's—warm, because he felt safe.

One result was that he began buying books—not contemporary novels so much as Modern Library editions of Freud, Krafft-Ebbing, and Dostoyevsky—and contrary to his spotty reading habits of yore, the lengths to which he went were both moving and pathetic, if only because he was trying so hard to measure up.

"I would see him sometimes on Fifth Avenue and we'd stop and chat," said Norman Rose. "He looked like a nineteenth-century Russian character out of Chekhov or Turgenev, carrying loads of books. 'What do you have all these for?' I'd ask, and he'd say, 'I have to read. I have to study. I have to learn things. I must really educate myself.' "

So keen was Stella's sponsorship that she even showed up for the March of Drama performances (which she philosophically disapproved of). She brought Harold and also her daughter Ellen, who was about fourteen at the time, and for some observers, it appeared she was trying to arrange "some sort of a romantic thing between them." In fact, this may already have been going on.

Being Stella's protégé had put Marlon in a difficult position at the Workshop. On the one hand, Piscator recognized his talent, while on the other, what he demanded from his actors was different from—indeed contradictory to—what Adler was teaching. If you were faithful to Adler, you were bound to clash with Piscator.

Erwin Piscator is remembered by almost all of his students as difficult—strict and formal, and basically humorless. "You will show proper respect to the head of the Dramatic Workshop in future," he once wrote to Jack Bittner, who had addressed him casually. To this day, Mae Cooper hasn't forgotten how he refused to excuse her from a rehearsal to see her sister dance at Carnegie Hall: " 'An actress does not excuse herself from a performance or from a rehearsal to do something with her family,' he said. 'You must make a choice. If you do not want to be here, then don't come back.' "

Ever the self-centered disciplinarian, Piscator also looked the part. He was short, with a great mane of flowing silver hair, walked with a strut and wore only the most expensive clothes despite his talk of Marxism. Mel Brooks, later a Piscator student, was known for doing parodies of the director in the New School's hallways, and eventually used him as the model for the mad German playwright in *The Producers,* the author manqué of *Springtime for Hitler.*

In a word, Piscator was a martinet. Both he and his wife were foolish to have hoped for success with Marlon, who seemed outrageous even to his peers. It wasn't just the unpressed khakis and thrift-shop oddments that made up Brando's wardrobe. The young man was, in Stella's words, basically "against things," and for some observers, the Workshop's director became the father figure against whom he had to rebel. Marlon was never prepared and treated the work lightly, which Piscator would, of course, find frustrating—and doubly so, when the final result in performance was always stunning. Several students noticed a love-hate relationship between the two men.

During a rehearsal of *Twelfth Night,* Piscator asked him to do something in a much "larger" way than Adler would have. Marlon refused to follow the direction. There was no discussion. He just said, "I can't do it."

"He could go very low or sulk sometimes, be too slow in reacting to what was asked of him, and here Mr. Piscator was pacing up and down the aisles," recalled Sara Farwell. "Finally he said, 'Come here!' Marlon looked up without coming down off the stage, and after a moment he said, almost in a whisper, 'Don't you want me to go on with the rehearsal?' Perhaps it was more flippant, but Piscator blew up and yelled, 'Leave my theater! Out! *Now!*'

"We were all standing there in shock. None of us had ever seen this kind of confrontation before. Marlon danced down the aisle, making a point of showing that it didn't bother him at all."

It was not dissimilar to some of his tricks at Shattuck, and again he was making it clear that he wouldn't cross the line. "There was an honesty in him," said another student who witnessed his exit. "The rest of us would have done anything to earn the pleasure of our teachers, even though we were struggling to find the same truthfulness. Marlon was incapable of being anything he wasn't. He had his own criteria, and what he was doing he was doing for himself."

Judith Malina, one of Piscator's favorite students, and later a co-founder of the Living Theatre, adds another perspective: "Piscator had difficulty with his gifted pupils, and often made demands that they couldn't meet. He'd insist they understand his theory perfectly. If they didn't, they were betraying him and his whole ideology. Brando's attitude was basically, 'I don't give a shit.'

"Piscator was angry because while Marlon was clearly a bright light, he was also intractable, ungovernable, unteachable. It pained him that his best student was his most rebellious student, and the problem was compounded by everybody saying, 'You know what Marlon did in class?' "

Brando's rebelliousness was deeply merged with his gift, which bolstered the persona. His passion to resist authority was part of speaking "truthfully." That he didn't show any outward signs of wanting to capitalize on his talent, to carve out a career, only added to his prestige. Art for art's sake was part of the *Zeitgeist;* his air of someone taking a few courses because he could not think of anything better to do (courses that were being paid for by his parents) left many of Marlon's classmates convinced he was practically Byronic.

Jocelyn's explanation was that her brother's ambivalence was real— that at nineteen Bud still could not acknowledge or trust what it was he was doing, even with Stella's loving support.

But it was more complicated. Many male American actors have doubted the "virility" of their profession, and Brando was no different. Thanks, in part, to his father's Babbitt-like snipes, acting had never fit in with his idea of being "a natural guy." Using makeup and costumes in earnest only made it worse. Fran's artist boyfriend Richard Loving—Hungarian-Jewish, Viennese-born, and New York-raised, the son of two writers—had already left Bard College in order to pursue his painting more seriously, and in Marlon he detected "an underlying kind of embarrassment. He had an aversion to theater people, whom he saw as phonies, as narcissistic. . . . He viewed his own involvement in some way related to the idea of a joke, like he was putting something over on people, like it was an easy way to make a buck. He had many ways of bypassing the seriousness that a lot of people get involved in when they're talking about their art and career."

There was very little doubt, however, that professionally he was going to explode. If acting was somehow "sickly," as he later told Harold Clurman, in private there was another voice that came from some place deeper; he rarely acknowledged the conflict, but instead put on a cynical exterior—paradoxically enough, always acting. "You couldn't see what was happening, and in a sense he was very lucky because that helped save his life," said classmate Elaine Stritch. "He was laughing at all of us. I have a memory of him laughing at everything and everybody, like healthy and a little bit crazy and complicated with the no speaking and all that, but adorable."

For Farwell, he was "always ready, just as Mozart was always ready." Whereas everybody else labored, he showed no signs of effort. Eddie Grove, another Workshop member, remembered that Brando could find a script's subtext or spine almost immediately. The class might be asked: "Why does this character have this particular thought?" Students would sink deep in meditation, looking for the "correct" answer; Marlon would just quip, "He was hungry." It was always something very human and simple, and very often true.

It is impossible to analyze the ingredients that make for genius, yet a few qualities seem to be dominant: instinct, unswayable personal standards, and what Bobby Lewis calls "a profound ambivalence." Lewis, who later trained Brando at the Actors Studio, says he was "like an animal. He wasn't always able to put things into words, but at any given moment he could sniff out everything." Maureen Stapleton sees it as an extraordinary type of intelligence: "I think that he knows things that are so deeply rooted, maybe what you have to describe as the pain. . . . I don't think anybody could fool him." Dick Loving suggests yet another component, "a certain kind of consciousness about the importance of sexuality in life and art."

The most important quality, however, seems to be an unusual attention to detail, the habit of observation refined at Shattuck as a tool for survival. Marlon was extremely alert, always attentive even in the hurly-burly of Manhattan. "He would sort of look into your eyes and assess you," Sara Farwell explained. "Then he would trick you," she added, referring to how he might break the tension with some winning gesture like a compliment or softly planted kiss, abruptly inverting the mood to let himself off the hook.

Staring was Marlon's way of disarming people, just as it always had been, but he also internalized whatever he'd seen. Riding the subway, he studied the passengers, then imitated one of them, mimicking an old man's stoop, the rhythm of a black secretary's gait, or simply the tilt of a commuter's head. Another exercise: He would sit in the subway car reading the Yiddish newspaper *Forward* upside-down and observing the reaction of the startled Jews looking at him: Vas is dis, he's reading it the wrong way? "It was a minor prank of his, sure," said Dublin, "but at the same time he was aware that it was causing interest. The reactions interested him." He was in fact working, taking in everything, just as he did at the Central Park Zoo, where he'd often go to study the animals—the movement and gestures of the big cats, the chimpanzees, and the gorillas.

For Eddie Grove, he was "a snooper," a nineteen-year-old kid who was age forty in his insight." In Stella's class, Norman Rose recalls how Marlon would often sit apart from the others, as if pushing people away so his "camera" had room to focus. "He would sit quietly, eventually changing his position, and he'd be leaning back in his chair, never straining forward. It was always at a distance, and the eyes would go sleepy, go off. But he took in whatever was going on, what Stella was saying, what the actors were doing, so that *behind* this withdrawal was a very, very keen, if not calculating, mind."

His basic technique for getting into a part was to jump in, then refine it as he went along. Often he'd experiment, producing something different with each rehearsal, never relying on props. Like a professional race driver warming up slowly on an unfamiliar track, he underplayed, giving himself leeway to find what he was looking for; sometimes by the fifth or sixth run-through it still wasn't fully developed.

All of his characterizations were physical, which led Grove to realize that he was also "one of the greatest athletes of any actor I'd ever met." He would constantly play with matchbooks, twisting and turning them in order to limber up his fingers, to make them "more expressive." In Maria

Ley's dance class he "rolled" like a young horse, and when he'd move into character for Stella, what classmates saw was "the total security of the way his body moved."

One improvisation in particular, Farwell recalls, demonstrated Marlon's freedom about his physicality. Luther Adler had taken over Stella's class one morning and asked the students to ice-skate in an imaginary rink. "We were all working on our sense memory of how to put on the skates, and creepy crawling about pretending that we were having a hard time. . . . Marlon was twirling around, being much braver than the rest of us. He didn't care if he butted into somebody. He wasn't trying to be graceful, he just moved that much more freely than the rest of us."

Technically, Brando still had his share of difficulties. Reading classical plays was the major one, and undoubtedly it stemmed from his deep insecurity about his education and his dyslexia-like reading problem. Farwell recalls *Twelfth Night:* "Reading Shakespeare was impossible for him. He would just stumble over the words. He would look at a line a long time before he read it. I wanted to laugh, or help him, or something. There were long pauses, then muttering. One wondered how he could possibly do the role. I had a clarity here, the words were easy for me," Farwell added. "With Marlon, it took a while. He had to get into character—that seemed to be the only way he could do it."

But once Brando found that key, Farwell became the one who needed help. "I had to dig more to find the reality. Marlon encouraged me in that, not by touching, but by stopping and saying, 'Let's do it again,' or 'What do you mean, Sara?' He encouraged me to feel. I learned by watching him. . . . Something that would come from him would grab me, make me do a line or a scene differently."

Brando's difficulty with reading aloud was related to his most notorious problem as an actor, namely his diction.

"His mumbling speech was more a personality quirk than anything else, because he could speak beautifully when he wanted to," Farwell states. "He must have learned it on his own, or been born with a marvelous ear. With a script, he didn't want to read it, he had to *hear* it."

For the first time in his life, Marlon was successful. There was his growing status at school, the support of Stella and her *mishpocheh,* but no less, the "openness" of New York City, which permitted him to explore his own psyche. What he was finding may be glimpsed in a letter he wrote to Shattuck's headmaster, Don Henning, his confidant and counselor, in late January 1944:

> *To sum my activities up . . . I came to N.Y. Went to Drama School. Raised seventeen different kinds of hell, indulged in all emotional experiences wantonly . . . , found that I had an unusual drama talent—utilized it, made a successful promising actor out of myself, lost myself in Kantian metiphisics [sic], almost had a nervous breakdown from lack of security and direction, have decided that my soul is a part of a harmonious whole in which there is nothing ever to fear and if to fear—to fear consciously—To know that in the time of my life I shall know very little, that death (as an end) is non-existent—that change is inevitable and to give to it fully and willingly with all your [sic] is an arch virtue. . . .*

Discounting the braggadocio, what he was doing was an enormous undertaking, at least in his own eyes—pushing himself, using the city and everything that was happening to him as the source for growth. Things were happening so quickly, however, that the closer he got to what scared him, the more controlled, impenetrable, and even perverse his responses were becoming.

"Whatever is meant by 'raising seventeen different kinds of hell,' it brought him to a certain kind of brink," Dick Loving said. "His *life* had brought him to the brink. . . . Psychically he was pushing, testing some kind of emotional limit. I don't know how conscious an undertaking this was, but he was using his sexual exploits as a probe, and I'm sure it might have worried him [since at] some level he must have seen it as potentially if not actually destructive. . . . But he had to immerse himself in extremes. He felt the need as an actor to know everything. He saw every kind of indulgence as useful; at the same time, he could rationalize whatever he was doing, just because it was so 'useful.' "

Part of the search was social. After evening rehearsals at the New School, which could last past midnight, a group of acting and design students would tumble out onto the streets of the Village, needing to blow off steam. Marlon was the extrovert, sometimes actually dancing in the street.

"I remember one time when we all came out," Farwell recalled, "and it had been raining. We had jackets and it must have been a Sunday because the street was clear. There was no traffic and we just went booming out of the door on Twelfth Street, everybody arm in arm, and Marlon was somehow in the lead when he broke into a somersault—a complete somersault in the middle of the street, forward, over. We all laughed and a couple of other people may have tried it but didn't succeed."

Unlike many of his fellow students, he wasn't drinking much. He had already discovered a "health bar" on Fifty-seventh Street across from Carnegie Hall and talked constantly about the carrot and celery juice. Still, this did not preclude vendor hot dogs, nor the dollar spaghetti dinners at a place in the Village called the Grand Tacino.

Another popular hangout was the Rochambeau—a French café one block from the New School, where Piscator would occasionally drop in to hold court. Marlon took his pronunciamentos on an actor's "mission" less seriously than his companions, and not infrequently he launched into his parody of Piscator's German accent—sometimes while the teacher was still within earshot. Soon Piscator would be sending letters to the New School's dean chastising Brando's lack of "disciplined" behavior.

Staying up late and going to bars and restaurants was a problem for most students, since they had jobs, but for Marlon it was different. If the group went to a movie or to have spaghetti, it was almost commonplace for him to pay for everyone. When he ran out of cash, as he often did, he would borrow, sometimes forgetting to pay back. Money meant nothing to him, even when it came to the rent. "If his electricity was cut off, he'd just go live with somebody else," said Dublin. "If his socks got dirty, he'd go to someone's house and take a pair of theirs, because as he saw it, 'People love me.' He could say to a girl: 'All right, let's go to your place'—because that's where the clean underwear was. He never did laundry. Why should he do a wash? He could take his girlfriend's panties, or if his jeans were dirty he would just take her clean pants. When you've got money, you don't have to wash your clothes—you throw them away. And if somebody really complained, which no one ever did, he'd probably have said, 'I don't need them'—that or, 'Here's ten dollars, go buy yourself some others.' "

In retrospect, Farwell acknowledges that Marlon was also spending some sleepless nights in school, all by himself, playing his bongo drums in the basement dance studio. He would miss classes or show up groggy, and her guess is that he may have had an arrangement with Vincent, the doorman, who would let him stay overnight. "This would be his 'sleeplessness,' " she says, "and he may have been preventing himself from confronting certain serious things."

It was clear that he was suffering from more than the blues. When he wasn't upstaging everyone, he would withdraw, and Carmelita Pope, who had recently come to New York, recalls how difficult it was to help him out of these depressions. "He hated anybody prying into his private life, and would get angry if you asked too many questions about why he was unhappy." Her description of Marlon in one of these "down" states—falling silent, clamming up, detaching himself, or actually walking out of the room close to tears—is very similar to what many of his New York friends were to see even more clearly over the next few years.

Sara Farwell, who describes herself as "everybody's big sister," recalls that when the two of them were alone, walking or sitting in Washington Square Park, he'd find ways to gird himself without clamming up completely, as if he needed to maintain a front. His shyness was real, but he fought it: "He'd talk about what was around him . . . everything was just immediate with him," she says. "It would be how the light was falling on the snow, say, and he'd insist that we sit silently and watch it." It was easy to romanticize Marlon's moodiness, but Pope, undoubtedly because of their time together in Chicago, saw these withdrawals as part of a "manic-depressive cycle." Similarly, Dick Loving regarded them as hinging on "a kind of built-in trigger of anger and passion," as though Bud, internally, was at war with himself.

Marlon's brother-in-law believed the entire mechanism was essentially hereditary. "Bud conquers through withholding. It's what his father did, too. Marlon Sr. was much less imaginative about the whole process and used it maybe in a more brutal, one-track kind of way, but the tendency was there."

To those who were not as close to Brando, his behavior seemed eccentric and sometimes also fake. Paulette Rubenstein, a New School student, wondered: "He could be silent, [like a] kid who might be sullen and not answer when he was spoken to. The thing is, you couldn't tell if this non-cliché, nonaverage behavior . . . stemmed from his differentness as some kind of artist, or whether it was to some degree calculated, attention-getting as a mischievous, bad, naughty child can be."

Rubenstein recalls one particular incident that may explain her doubts: "I came into the dance studio downstairs, and Marlon was sitting on the corner of a table, holding a lit candle, and his other hand was totally covered with the wax drippings. He was all alone, and he kept right on doing this, not particularly noticing me. I said, 'What are you doing?' He didn't answer, and it struck me as strange, really. There was the air of preoccupation, like he may have been thinking through a problem."

For Eddie Grove, Marlon seemed "weird as hell," although it was nothing he could quite put his finger on. "I didn't get too close to him," he related, "largely because of the games he'd play, this business of his withholding. I had the feeling that he could turn on you, that something out of this imbalance might reveal itself, so I kept my distance. The sense was that Marlon was a user, even at those times when he could be terribly supportive and charitable. I was bigger than him and stronger and older, too, but I felt that something would happen, that there was a dangerous element to him."

One fellow actor, who wishes to remain anonymous, says he witnessed a sudden explosion during a rehearsal of *Saint Joan:* "I was on the stage doing a scene, and Marlon was in the wings with the other actors, when all of a sudden there was this tremendous scream from backstage—as if somebody were being murdered—and one of the actors came out, bleeding profusely from the face. Marlon came on as well, or somebody went backstage and got him. The story that was immediately told was that this actor had made a pass at Marlon, had grabbed him or whatever, and Marlon had struck him. It was horrendous. Piscator was appalled. We were all appalled.

"One can only theorize about why he behaved as he did," the witness added. "I mean, who goes around hitting somebody who makes a pass at you, rather than just removing yourself and saying, 'Hey, wait a minute, you're barking up the wrong tree, forget it.' [Later] I realized he was on the *qui vive* about this whole homosexual thing, this same guy who eventually adopted a macho persona, almost to the point of caricature."

Dick Loving recalls challenging Marlon to a boxing match that began as a game at a party: The two put on the gloves, went out in the hallway, and while Marlon kept a perfectly jovial expression on his face, things quickly started to get too serious. "He was playing with me, a cat-and-mouse kind of thing. He'd let me do everything, warding off the blows, then he decided to let fly a couple of good hard punches and that ended it. Abruptly."

Throughout this series of confrontations Marlon's strategy seems to have been to wait for the other person to make a move, then come in and dominate. Never trusting his own voice, the key was to counterpunch, literally and figuratively. Loving noted that there were a thousand such contests—some physical, some not. Invariably, Brando seemed to be asking himself, Is there something I can get from this person? Is there something I can learn? "You could write a whole chapter on the ways he could make people feel uncomfortable," Loving says. "There was this enormous urge, and if ever there was the possibility, he would get competitive and it could take virtually any form. Like how your shoelaces were tied, or guessing the number of hairs on the back of your hand, commenting on your watch, even. Like maybe he'd heard that somebody could throw their watch up in the air and tell the time while it was flying—anything, everything could get turned into a challenge or contest."

Even the devoted Sara Farwell recalls such challenges, like the night at a party where Marlon insisted that everyone in the group had to make the others laugh. "I hated it," Farwell relates. "He *liked* putting you on the spot. I didn't want to do it, but I wanted to be part of the group, so I did my best and felt foolish. But he was the one who set up the game . . . and the whole point was to see what the other person would do. He'd always do this, and he could make a fool of you."

Marlon's closest friend throughout this period was Darren Dublin. This strange, symbiotic relationship, in which the two saw each other literally every day, often spending twenty-four hours together, was to last nearly a dozen years—first in New York, then later in Hollywood. It would include shared girlfriends, create conflicts with Dublin's wife, and provide employment for Darren in several of Brando's films.

Physically, Dublin was the complete opposite of Marlon. He was small and bespectacled, somewhat like a young Woody Allen, but with a lot of big teeth. He came from a lower-middle-class Jewish family in the Bronx, and had a mean sense of humor. In 1942 he had started taking classes at the Dramatic Workshop, but soon afterward he was drafted. After only nine months in the army, Dublin was discharged on "psychoneurotic grounds." He returned to the New School and ran into Brando only weeks after Marlon arrived in New York.

The first time they met, the two spent the entire night talking in the basement of the New School, until they fell asleep on top of the piles of costumes in the costume room. The chemistry between them was instantaneous and was based, apparently, on three common grounds: their interest in the theater, their weird sense of humor, and girls.

While Brando's unusual talent had been recognized immediately, Darren did not show the same promise. Some classmates have described him as "talentless," and even Marlon would occasionally parody Darren's stage work. The two never discussed Darren's abilities, however. (Years later Marlon tried to arrange a job for him as an agent with MCA, a gesture that Darren interpreted as Marlon's way of saying, "You ain't gonna make it as a great actor, pal.")

When not in school, they often went to the movies on Forty-second Street, afterward grabbed a bite to eat, then went back into the dark for another movie, sometimes at one o'clock in the morning. The choice of films was always Marlon's—the latest foreign import, or Laurel and Hardy comedy, and always Chaplin—for what was important to Darren was spending time with Marlon. "He was so interesting to be with, that whatever he proposed was more exciting than what my life had been in the Bronx."

It did not appear to be a relationship of equals, and Eddie Grove is typical of the Workshop crowd in describing the two as "the king and his clown." Darren's role, principally, was to provide a stream of jokes that would buoy Marlon out of his depressions, and the irreverent Dublin knew how to do this better than anyone else. Once, on a crowded bus, he noticed an enormous woman and started talking to her protuberant behind, loudly making the introduction, "This is my friend, Marlon. Marlon, I'd like you to meet . . ." Another time, they were walking past construction workers using pneumatic jackhammers, and knowing Marlon's sensitivity to noise (on the subway, he would roll bread pieces and use them as earplugs), Darren stopped right where the men were working. "Come on, what the fuck are you doing?" Marlon yelled.

"Oh, that's what I like about the country," Dublin murmured, pretending to be lost in some pastoral silence.

It was always the gibe with Darren, since he was also a master of insult and could go to extended, diabolical lengths to puncture Marlon's self-absorption, to mock him and say, in effect, Hey, it's okay. Once, Brando was sulking and he had his shirt off, and Darren, standing behind him, started scrutinizing the pimples and eruptions covering his bare back, describing them in a German accent: "Ah, zo vee vent down here, but den vee invaded . . ." Marlon's body had become a mock battlefield, his pimples enemy shell holes, leaving Brando little choice but to laugh.

There were also practical jokes, macho contests where Darren would stand by watching, lending support of another kind. The roof of the New School was six stories above the street, and one evening the group snuck up there to walk the parapet that ran around the edge. Marlon had to tread farther, closer to the edge, than anyone, and while the others looked on silently, Darren was heard dryly commenting that arrangements could be made with UPS to ship the remains back to Libertyville.

The connection between Marlon and Darren—the bond—was also girls. Mae Cooper says, "They were always looking around to see who was going with whom, who's having an affair, and who's doing this or that. It was very funny in an unmasculine way, sort of like silly kids, like two girls would do." To others, their behavior was just adolescent. One young woman says she was later traumatized for years when, after being bedded by Marlon, she realized how much (and how indiscriminately) they were "fucking around": waitresses, waifs, strays, secretaries on the street, along with the pickings at the Workshop.

Marlon usually set the tempo, and often they would stay up all night. Darren remembers a time looking out the window of a friend's Brooklyn apartment after sunrise: "All these people were walking toward the subway, and we'd scream at them: 'There but for the grace of God go I!' We were about ready to go to sleep, and these poor motherfuckers had to go to work. We divided the world into 'us interesting people' and the rest of middle-class society. We felt superior to most people, like we were on the cutting edge."

While some of Marlon's friends found Darren amusing, others disapproved of the relationship, calling Dublin "a hanger-on type who would follow Marlon like a puppy dog." What few people understood was that the relationship was as real as any Marlon could handle: Dublin's antic, often surreal and outrageous humor served not only to justify Marlon's own high jinks, but Darren could also be trusted and—unlike anyone else on the scene—he knew how to puncture Brando's posturings.

As the year at the Dramatic Workshop went from one production to the next, stories about Marlon's erotic adventures proliferated. Because of the war, there were fewer men around, some of them not necessarily interested in women, and even Jocelyn, perhaps a bit too protectively, acknowledges that "he was screwing everything. . . . Remember, he was shy and unsure of himself. If somebody said, 'Take me to bed,' he'd say, 'Sure.' If it was right there and it was a nice girl and she wasn't gonna hurt him, sure. You're nineteen and at the peak of your sexuality."

More interesting than any number count was Marlon's methodology, which involved a carefully thought out schedule. Dublin says he invested a lot of time, energy, and creativity here. "He had a marvelous game: He'd take a girl out, wine her and dine her, be nice and lovely, and then take her home and say good-night. They would go crazy. He wouldn't call for three weeks, while meanwhile he's seeing someone else. Then by the time he called up, the girl that he had taken out was frantic, you know, so he didn't have to say, 'Let's go to bed.' "

The weakness in this system became apparent when Marlon suffered a dislocated shoulder horsing around during rehearsal for *Doctor Sgana-relle.* Jack Bittner had to take him to the hospital, and in the emergency room he moaned in pain, worrying how he was going to keep his women in place. "He was incapacitated for a few weeks, and the thing he was most upset about was his dates," said Mae Cooper, who later married Bittner. "He asked Jack to fill in for him. He had all these dates lined up with different girls, and he was worried that he wouldn't be able to meet his schedule, so to speak."

Eddie Grove was also under the impression that for Marlon, his dealings with girls were a game: "not so much a sexual drive as a way of dominating a woman, like how to win." In this context he relates a story he heard from Maureen Stapleton, who later lived in the same building with Marlon on Fifty-second Street. Marlon came up to Maureen's apartment laughing, and told her about the girl he had brought home with him: "I gave her the mop and she's cleaning up the whole house! Ha-ha-ha!" He got rid of her once she finished cleaning, says Grove.

Chouteau Dyer, Piscator's assistant, thinks that Marlon was "still a little bit retarded emotionally, still a teenager," a view given credence by classmate Sylvia Gasselle's recollection that Marlon and Darren once placed a microphone under one woman's bed to record her orgasm.

He tended to keep his women apart, which wasn't too difficult since most of them weren't students at the Workshop. Somewhat uncharacteristically, he did brag about his sexual relationship with one of the teachers, talking about it in class, according to Judith Malina, or out in the hallway.

The woman overheard him and slapped him across the face. ("This wasn't Stella," Malina adds. "I can't say who it was.")

One endearing aspect of Marlon's sex life was his attraction to less pretty women—the underdogs. On a social level, the attention he paid to these women was part of his persona, but it was also real. Valerie Judd studied costume design and was part of Marlon's social group. "She was a nice Jewish girl, one of those 'unattractive' types but he *liked* her," said Dublin.

Gasselle remembers a party where he reached out to her instantaneously, responding only to her loneliness. "I was kind of socially backward," she explains, "because I was a teenage war bride, and not free to socialize. In fact, I felt very awkward and out of place. . . . He just chatted with me very nicely, and I remember thinking at the time how extremely kind he was to have come over, to have been so aware."

Joy Thomson brings up another example, that of a dark, big-eyed girl who was a good actress, but "a schizo [who] kept going into the nuthouse." Marlon, Thomson recalls, "had her done, got her an abortion, and he sort of pushed her onto me. . . . He phoned and was in a terrible state, and said, 'Would you look after her?' "

One relationship that was strictly platonic involved sixteen-year-old Elena Patera, a Jewish girl from Brooklyn. Patera was a dance student, and Mae Cooper's sister. (Later, when Marlon was on Broadway in *I Remember Mama,* she was appearing in Agnes De Mille's *Bloomer Girl.*) Cooper describes her sister as a dark, exotic girl—exactly the type Marlon went for. (Even then, he would occasionally say he'd slept with all the white girls he wanted and that his preference had shifted to blacks, Chinese, and Spanish bedmates.)

The two had met when Patera performed in a Children's Theatre production at the New School. Cooper says that Marlon started spending time with her sister because she was "so reserved . . . innocent . . . and sort of respectable, not a theatrical type. . . . She had this amazing aura around her of a respectable Flatbush young girl." The relationship lasted for about a year and was renewed for a few months in 1947.

Patera herself recalls that she and Marlon had an understanding that sex would not be part of their relationship. "Everybody in New York knew about his reputation," she says, "and I think it was probably a relief for him to feel that I was somebody he didn't have to worry about impressing."

Perhaps so, if only because he still had Celia Webb, his first New York girlfriend, on the side. He took Patera to the movies, the theater, the Museum of Modern Art. They would walk through the city, window-shopping, stopping for a yogurt at the health bar on Fifty-seventh Street. They even went roller skating, and Brando came to her dance school to watch her lessons.

Patera's parents were less than happy, however, when Brando would arrive for a Saturday-night date wearing sneakers and a T-shirt. Cooper recalls: "My mother said, 'Doesn't he have any respect? That's no way to come and call for a girl for a date.' " Cooper believes that Marlon felt a little out of place in her parents' middle-class Brooklyn home, and the fact that he dressed that way may have been his way of saying, I'm not intimidated.

Blossom Plumb, a Workshop student, was clearly an exception among Marlon's girls at the time. First, their relationship was relatively long-lived; and second, since the Connecticut-reared Plumb came from an affluent WASP background, she could hardly be considered an underdog. Most people remember her as distinctly special, in fact—"definitely a lady." Her beauty was "very delicate, kind of exotic . . . almost Gabor-y." Maureen Stapleton recalls the first night she met Blossom and Marlon in the cafeteria at the New School: "It was like looking at Mr. and Mrs. Perfect. He was gorgeous, she was gorgeous. You thought, Oh, that's the way it should be." Everybody seems to agree that she was desperately in love with Marlon, even though he was regularly seeing Celia Webb.

Perhaps the most peculiar, troubling story about Brando's dating involves classmate Elaine Stritch. Stritch, who also admits to having been madly in love with him, was then seventeen, the daughter of a rich Catholic industrialist from Detroit. Her parents allowed her to go to New York only because she would live in a convent on Ninety-first Street. Farwell, who remembers her as a very sheltered, very proper girl, says that Elaine once told her that she absolutely would not sleep with a man until she married him. At the Dramatic Workshop, Elaine was clearly among the more talented students, but she was shy and had trouble participating in social life, since she had to return to the uptown convent before the doors closed.

Marlon was intrigued and he decided to try her. On their first and only date, he took her on a long, systematic walking tour of the city's synagogues and churches. After exhausting every denomination, they arrived back in the Village at an Italian restaurant. "I had stars in my eyes," Stritch recalls. "This is a guy who wants to become an artist, an actor, and this is New York City. He doesn't act like the guys at home. But still I just couldn't wait to get a couple of bottles of wine in me so I could relax."

He had promised to take her to a good show, yet after dinner she found herself in a striptease palace, confronted with "the dirtiest floor show I'd ever seen. I was a wreck," she said. "I didn't have the self-possession to say, 'Hey, I don't want to do this, let's do something else.' I don't know how long I sat there, but I think I cried."

She then accepted his invitation to have a drink back at his place on Twelfth Street, across from the New School. It was snowing, and Marlon soon built a fire in the fireplace. "There was a little living room and a sleeping area behind a curtain, and the next thing, he goes behind this curtain and comes out in his pajamas or a robe—I forget which. He didn't smirk or anything. It was simply like nothing was going on, like this was a perfectly normal thing," says Stritch, whose naïveté had now turned to terror. "I told him I wanted to go home. It's now two o'clock in the morning, the convent's doors were always locked at midnight—in fact, there was a rule that you had to get back by twelve o'clock or stay out all night, and remember, I've had a lot of wine. Does he take me home? No, he stays in his pajamas, sees me to the door, and it's 'Good-bye, good-night.' I go down, get on a bus, and get to the convent at quarter to three. I have to ring the doorbell, and of course the poor Reverend Mother has to get her clothes on to answer the door.

"How was I feeling? I'm feeling I'm glad I'm home, which is where I belong. I don't belong in Marlon Brando's apartment. I'm not even mad at Marlon—I was too insecure to be angry. I cried and told the mother superior the whole story, I was that upset. She told me I did the right thing.

"The next Monday I go to school and Marlon does not speak to me. In fact, he does not speak to me the whole rest of the year—including the next summer, when we all went out to do summer theater in Sayville."

By April 1944, Dorothy Brando had left her husband and come to New York. Her Libertyville friend Marian Johnsen remembers that after Marlon Sr. joined AA and stopped drinking, he gave her an ultimatum: "Either straighten up or you get out and don't ever come back." Dodie was not ready to quit drinking yet, so she rented a large ten-room apartment on

West End Avenue in the Seventies. Marlon Sr. moved to downtown Chicago, where he returned to the Lake Shore Club, marking their second major separation in eight years. This one would last more than ten months.

Publicly, the story was that Dodie was in New York to keep house for her kids, who promptly moved in with her. Marlon Sr. was paying the rent, the maid, and all other expenses. Jocelyn now had a three-month-old baby, Davey, and Don was away in the army; Fran was at the Hoffman School while still working part-time for Murray's Space Shoes, whose customized clodhoppers she had started to endorse almost as though they offered spiritual balm as well as dactyl comfort. And Bud, even after more than half a year away from Libertyville, was "still very confused." Another resident in need of attention was Dutchie, the family's Great Dane who was now old and crotchety.

Recollections of the apartment and its inhabitants differ greatly. To Marlon's cronies, the big, sparsely furnished place seemed a gorgeous bohemian paradise—large enough for a party to go on in the living room without disturbing the baby at the far end of the apartment. There was a dining room, a little breakfast nook, and a "marvelous kitchen" with old-style, pull-out cereal and flour bins where Dodie hid her bottles.

To Dick Loving, who was closer to what was going on beneath the surface, the big, empty apartment seemed gloomy, with skimpy, tatty furniture. He says, "The whole place was very minimal and sort of impersonal. It was just a feeling of nothing, in great contrast to the Libertyville place, where there were books and art. There was nothing there—it was just dropped in."

Usually the apartment was swarming with people—"the weirdest people," according to Joy Thomson, who was among the New School group that included not only Darren, Celia, Sara, and Elaine, but also George Bloostein, Adele Dashevsky, and Marcia Mann. Maureen Stapleton and her roommate, another evening student named Janice Mars, came around, too, and of course Dick Loving was usually there. In a typical evening, Thomson recalls, "the whole gang of us would have been somewhere and Marlon would invite us up and we'd get sort of drunk. Dodie was holding court. . . . It was like a salon. She was the floor show. She thought *we* were the floor show, but in fact it was the other way around.

"She was divine," Thomson continues, "absolutely foreign to any mother I'd ever seen." For Darren, she was "like one of the gang, even though she was much older, and you always felt very comfortable around her." Everyone was free to come and go, to use the couch or floor when it was too late to bother with the bus or subway, even to bring over new faces without an invitation. "You never knew how many people would be there for dinner," Jocelyn recalls. "I remember once we fed twelve on one can of tuna fish and a lot of baked potatoes. Just kept cutting celery . . . We had baked potatoes and a very big tuna-flavored celery salad."

What appears so playful in Jocelyn's and Darren's description had a more chaotic, disturbing aspect for Dick Loving: "I remember liquor being smuggled in and Fran being worried, and they'd check to see whether Dodie was eating. People would be dropping in and out all the time. There was no order. People ate at the oddest hours, nobody really cooked, and the dishes piled up despite the appearances of the maid, who did most of the shopping. . . . Bud with his hours—he would be in at odd times, just drop in, then out again. The mother more or less seemed to be the only one there, and I seem to remember her being in bed—usually in the daytime. I can't remember her really functioning, like having friends."

Dodie did, in fact, have a few friends—for example, Bil Baird, the puppeteer, who was living several blocks away, and David and Sylvia Salinger, who came up from Washington, D.C., where they were now living. Perhaps most important, there was also Marty Mann, a former Chicago advertising executive and the founder of the National Council on Alcoholism, who was already laying the groundwork for Dodie to make a genuine commitment to AA. But Marlon's mother really wanted to be accepted by his friends—who adored her and were either blind to her problem (like Dublin, who confesses, "I just didn't want to believe it"), or who found her drinking amusing, even exotic.

Even after she had been in the city for months, most of Marlon's cronies were unaware of the severity of his mother's problem, let alone their shared pain. Edie Van Cleve, Marlon's agent-to-be, recalled how Bud once broke an appointment, with the explanation that his mother drank and he had been out looking for her in bars. A few days later Mrs. Brando called, asking her to lunch. "I couldn't say no," Van Cleve related, "but I was very nervous. I thought, What am I going to do with this lush? So I couldn't have been more surprised when this intelligent, well-groomed, perfectly poised woman arrived. When we went to lunch, the first thing I asked was whether she'd like a cocktail. She said, 'Oh, no!' . . . but there was something in her voice when she refused that drink that made me wonder."

Jocelyn insists that most of the time her mother was able to run the household, do the shopping, even go to the lending library on the corner. "I don't think we were despondent," she says.

Dick Loving, however, continues to have a pretty depressing picture: Jocelyn was, in fact, the one running the household and Dodie had really reached the last agony of her alcoholism. "She would bribe people—the maid or somebody—to smuggle in the bottles," he recalled.

As always, the most difficult, haunting result of the drinking were Dodie's occasional disappearances. Since she didn't have a favorite hangout, it was usually impossible to find her. Thomson recalls that she might take Dutchie for a walk and be found lying facedown in the street. Don Hanmer says he heard from Jocelyn that Dodie "would go out on one of these benders and end up in some flophouse with god-knows-who fucking her." Marian Johnsen later heard the same from Dodie herself at an AA meeting: "She woke up one morning with a one-legged guy in her bed. Where the hell she'd been she didn't know. She'd picked him up in a bar, then the next morning found him there beside her."

Bud and Jocelyn, however, did what they could, which included accompanying Dodie to AA meetings in a small church on Twenty-third Street. It wasn't her first try. She had taken a stab at it back in Libertyville at Marlon Sr.'s insistence, but then, like now, it was just lip service. At the church, Marlon Jr. and his sister would go downstairs to the meetings for children of alcoholics, where the message was that it was up to their mother to quit, that she had to do it for herself. Often, when they'd return upstairs, Dodie was already gone.

The mother-son relationship operated on a plane all its own. Each of their needs was paramount, yet each also guaranteed their bond. "Bud worshiped her, just adored her," recalled Ann Lombard Osborne, one of Dodie's closest confidantes, "and she was the most important person in his life. On the other hand, he was her little boy—she was convinced that he was a genius, and I think at some level she believed that she had a comparable genius."

For each of them, mother and son, the mix was unstable. Even as Marlon lounged around the West End Avenue apartment in Dodie's "ruffly housecoat," whenever she disappeared he would go into a terrible decline, and his feelings of abandonment, resentment, fear—the whole dependency cycle—would snap into place. By the following winter, as she was deciding to return to Chicago, he would urge her to remain in New York. "She told me he wanted to keep her from going back to Marlon [Sr.]," said Kay Phillips Bennett, who, within the next several years, became another one of Dodie's adoptees. "And she had to make a choice. . . . It was very, very oedipal, and of course she was aware of what was going on."

Now, in addition to bringing around his crowd from the Workshop, Marlon had no compunction about spending nights with his girlfriends in his mother's apartment. "It just seemed a little too many," Jocelyn says, "and they were all young and very innocent. Mother wasn't happy about it. But it was Bud, you know."

Rarely would Dodie express her feelings, even when she was furious ("It was the forties, and there were rules to follow in your mother's house," as Jocelyn put it). Sometimes, Dodie's attitude was, Boys will be boys. If it got out of hand, there might be a mild reprimand such as, "Ye gods, Bud, is it necessary to do all that stuff?" For his part, Marlon would say, "I don't think it matters. It's fun—why not?"

As always, he took it to the limit. "Bud not only wanted approval," Kay Phillips Bennett said, "he would badger her, tease her, hector her, and Dodie loved it. He was taking the initiative, testing, pushing. He counted on everyone having manners—everyone except himself, that is."

The testing was somehow his way of showing his love. It also avoided any direct confrontation, something neither of them was ready for. Joy Thomson tells a story that puts the whole tangled skein even more poignantly: "I remember coming to the apartment one night and they all were in a terrible state. Dodie wasn't there at the moment, but the girls were. Marlon had decided he was going to hang outside the window by his fingernails just to show off. Apparently, it was the thing to do, like arm wrestling, only this was a better stage. They were on the eleventh floor or something, and although half the time you didn't pay any attention to them because everyone was always putting you on, now they were really concerned, particularly Fran. 'Oh, is he going to die? There's no way we can get him. . . . What are we going to do?' Then Dodie arrived. She just sort of came into the room very majestically, and said, 'Marlon, that's ridiculous. Come in here at once.' It was absolutely like the goddess had made an entrance and he was waiting for her. He hauled himself back through the window, and I mean immediately."

The Dramatic Workshop students themselves came up with the idea of starting a summer stock theater. *Twelfth Night* had been a great success, and led by Beulah Roth and Sara Farwell, the group approached Piscator at one of the last March of Drama classes. "Please, we want to stay together. Won't you come and be our head, our director?" Piscator agreed, so long as he was spared the bother of having to find a theater or coping with any of the mundane details.

Marlon and Darren were part of the delegation, but the organizers were Roth and Farwell. "Everybody was told to get $100 to cover operating expenses," Farwell recalled, "and with the $2,000 we'd collected we went to look for a theater." They rented a beautiful old, run-down summer theater in Sayville, Long Island, that hadn't been used for years. "The owner charged us $1,000 for the summer's rent—half our money. With the rest, we hired a cook."

The idea was to have the students—now members of the company— "eat, sleep, work, and play as a sort of collective, a commune." The inspiration, no doubt, came from the Group Theatre's first summer rehearsal period (in 1931, in Brookfield Center, Connecticut), which had become a landmark in the history of American acting. When Lee Strasberg, Harold Clurman, and Cheryl Crawford started working with their actors in Connecticut, they set out to revolutionize the American theater through the development of a new kind of acting. Clurman, especially, was adamant about applying their understanding of the Stanislavsky technique to socially committed dramas.

Piscator's students, on the other hand, were too inexperienced to have a theatrical credo of their own. Whatever their enthusiasm, none saw themselves as part of the radical theater movement. Their goals were to spend the next three months together, to learn more about their craft, and to polish their skills and gain additional stage experience. What fascinated them about the Group Theatre, which they all idolized, were the stories about living and working communally, plus the sexual abandon of such legendary couples as Morris Carnovsky and Phoebe Brand, Lee Strasberg and Paula Miller, and Harold Clurman and the grand Stella Adler herself.

Piscator, however, had a different idea about how things were to be run in Sayville. Elaine Stritch, who had also signed on, remembers that strict rules were laid down right from the start: "Everybody was to sleep in their own bed at night, because otherwise the same thing would happen to us that happened to the Group: There'd be affairs and pregnancies, and we'd get thrown out of Sayville. . . . The concern was the local reaction, the townspeople. Remember, it was the 1940s."

In addition to the core group of actors there were a few newcomers. One was dark, reserved, and stood self-consciously apart from the others, looking all the more out of place for his city clothes and slick pompadour. Carlo Fiore had no acting experience and he was on scholarship. Marlon had introduced himself on the train coming out, but he disappeared as soon as they got to the theater. Returning without his luggage, he suggested to Carlo that they bunk together and asked for a hand in moving a few pieces of dilapidated furniture he'd already stacked outside the theater.

As Fiore tells the story in his memoir *Bud: The Brando I Knew,* Brando led him across a meadow to a beat-up old barn. They wrestled the furniture up a ladder and through a trapdoor, until Fiore found himself in a clean, airy attic. With a sweeping gesture at the empty, bright room, Marlon beckoned him to one of the windows.

> I saw a marvelous view of the theater and the bay.
> "From this window," he said, "we can see anybody approaching from the theater." He turned and walked to the window at the opposite end. I followed. "And from this window we can spot anybody coming up the road from town. And if we don't want to see anybody, we can pull up the ladder. There will be times when we'll want privacy. Complete privacy. By the way, one of the girls has already buzzed me about you. She thinks you're sexy."

Fiore was the son of a Sicilian immigrant, a streetwise Brooklyn knockabout who affected blue suede shoes. After a year of high school, he'd gone to work in a factory, steam-pressing men's pants. A close mutual friend would later describe him as another example of Marlon's "good works," since he was not only deeply unsure of himself but had been on drugs—heroin, specifically—ever since high school. Even so, he and Marlon shared certain similarities. Both projected soft-spoken, almost diffident styles, and Carlo, like Marlon, saw himself as an outsider, different from the "artsy" company members who quoted Shakespeare. Sex was another part of their shared agenda. Each defined himself in terms of his ability to "get laid"; unlike most of the middle-class kids in the company, they had both sized up the summer as a turkey shoot, a competitive, score-keeping romp in which they, not Piscator, were going to make the rules.

The twelve-week summer repertoire consisted of ten plays of three performances each, lowbrow balancing highbrow. With the July 4 presentation of *Claudia,* a play they'd begun to rehearse back in New York, the season was under way. Marlon had his first role in the second week, when he appeared again in *Doctor Sganarelle.* This time he had the title role of Sganarelle, the woodcutter who is forced to impersonate a physician in order to cure Argan's daughter of her sudden inability to speak. Described as a "fast-moving musical production that promises a delightful and unusual evening in the theater," the show was well received.

On the following weekend the company presented *Hannele's Way to Heaven,* and here Marlon was in the double role he had played so stunningly in New York; the village schoolteacher who carries the adolescent girl to the almshouse after her suicide attempt and the Christ figure who appears in her dream to drive away her drunken stepfather.

In the audience was Maynard Morris, among the most powerful agents in New York City. Wiry, excitable, and known for his keen interest in new talent, Morris had joined forces with another agent, Edie Van Cleve, only the previous winter to head the theatrical department of MCA, the nation's largest talent agency. He had launched the careers of Gregory Peck, Charlton Heston, and Tyrone Power. Morris had already seen Marlon's *Hannele* performance at the New School, but Stella persuaded him to make the trip to Sayville for another look. What he saw was breathtaking.

"To try to describe Marlon in *Hannele* is almost impossible," recalled Sara Farwell. "He was twenty years old playing Jesus Christ in Hannele's dream, and he came out in this bright raiment. The light was right on him—this young blond god, totally beautiful—then later on he was also an older man, wearing a pair of glasses. He did a complete characterization of both figures, and while the rest of us were striving for that, to get the largeness that Piscator wanted, he just slipped into it almost as though it was waiting for him."

It was pure Brando, intuitive and luminescent—"like nothing you had ever seen," said another student. "It wasn't an actor doing a performance. You suddenly [had] come in contact with genius."

Morris's visit was to prove a turning point for Brando, since the agent started looking for parts for Brando almost as soon as he got back to Manhattan—even though the two were still without a contract. But Piscator wasn't pleased. Part of the problem was his usual difficulty with Marlon's lackadaisical attitude, but on another level he felt betrayed. "It was like he was going to lose his student," said Joy Thomson, pointing out that the moment Morris left, the grapevine was abuzz with the agent's interest in the company's golden boy. The result was that Piscator bore down on the troupe more severely than before. Marlon's response was to mimic the director's accent more blatantly than he had in New York.

Meanwhile, Brando, Darren, and Carlo had become the Three Musketeers. The group effort meant little compared to their self-centered hedonism. But now Marlon did not have the guiding force of a Stella Adler to keep the better part of him working.

"We'd be lying around sunning ourselves," Dublin recalled, "and one of us might make the comment, 'Here we are in the sun, young and healthy, and people are dying.' We'd lie on the beach and think about all these poor motherfuckers in Europe, and we're going, 'Roll over. Am I tan on this side?' I mean, that's the hand that life gives you. Where was responsibility, a sense of obligation? If we'd wanted all that, we would have become policemen."

As the days passed, Marlon indulged in more swimming, trips to Fire Island, late-night bull sessions in the barn about God and fate and other nonsense, as well as runs into town for milk shakes and hamburgers. His top priority remained "screwing all over the place."

Seemingly, it made no difference whom he was sleeping with. On one occasion he and Carlo snared a young runaway whom Brando "was perfectly willing to share." Whole evenings were spent in the barn on locker-room analyses of this one's rear end, that one's boobs, or what could be done under what circumstances with whom. Marlon was "a man in a state of perpetual erection," according to Fiore—a walking, talking *Kamasutra*—and after Celia Webb had come out for a weekend visit, he spent hours going on about how the two of them made love. He would also joke about who had crabs, or the clap, and who had infected whom, as well as which of the girls in the company were still virgins. Characteristically,

Darren listened, laughed, and prompted. For Fiore, this introduction to the real world of the theater was reassuringly familiar, not that removed from the streets of Brooklyn.

As the company prepared *The Petrified Forest,* with Elaine Stritch in the supporting role of Mrs. Chisholm, Stritch became disturbed that Marlon was still not talking to her. Instead, he made a point of using Piscator as an intermediary: "Mr. Piscator, will you tell Elaine that I can't move this way if she's going to . . ." Piscator, ever fearful of a scene—at least a scene created by someone other than himself—went along. No one else objected, either.

Stritch recounted what happened much later that evening:

"I went to bed in my little place off the kitchen and couldn't sleep, so I had candles burning and was saying my rosary. In the middle of the night, about three in the morning, I was still awake, when suddenly the door-knob started to turn. It was Marlon. He didn't say a word. He just came across the room, walked across my bed with me in it, went to the icebox to pour himself a glass of milk, then came back and went out the door. He was dressed in his pajamas and said nothing, just came and went. It was funny. Funny peculiar. Also terrifying.

"The thing is, Marlon considered people's feelings in little ways, but not the deep stuff. I didn't think he was being egotistical. He probably just couldn't handle my reality—as opposed to the chicks he'd hop into bed with."

Twelfth Night opened on July 21, with Marlon as Sebastian, Carlo as Antonio, Darren as Sir Andrew Aguecheek, and Stritch as Feste, the clown. Farwell played Olivia, with one of Marlon's wintertime flings, Valerie Judd, in charge of costumes. According to Fiore, the show was pretty much a disaster because they'd all been goofing off.

The next production was the romantic thriller *Ladies in Retirement.* Marlon, playing the dashing Albert Feather, was again singled out in the local press, this time for the "excellent job [he did] with his cockney accent."

Meanwhile, nothing stayed static at the Brando apartment on West End Avenue. Fran had gone with Dick to Provincetown to continue her painting classes with Hans Hofmann, while Joce and the baby were visiting Don, stationed in Los Angeles. Left alone, Dodie returned to the Chicago area for a spell. But then she was asked to fill in for one of the roles in

Cry Havoc, coming out to Sayville as "just another actress." She arrived in mid-July, more than two weeks before the company's scheduled rehearsals, and in time to catch the opening night debacle of *Twelfth Night.*

Cry Havoc called for a large female cast, and for her fans like Stritch and Joy Thomson, there was nothing surprising about Dodie's participation. "There was a wonderful role for her. She looked terrific: short hair, Katharine Hepburnish, tweedy, and there was nothing more to it than that."

Dodie's motives for coming were actually a little more complex than just filling in. With her usual gregariousness, she mixed with the theater company, even helping with the scenery. But she also laid into Marlon for goofing off. One day, according to Carlo Fiore, Marlon was downcast because Dodie had criticized him for the previous night's performance "and a thousand other things." When Carlo sympathized that this was something mothers always do, Marlon said Dodie had gone further, telling him to grow up and take acting seriously or return to Chicago to go into the limestone business with Marlon Sr.

> "She *knows* I'd never go into business with Pop. . . . This is the first time I've goofed off in a play, the first time, and she cuts out. Just like that."
>
> "Nobody likes a loser," I said. "Nobody."
>
> "That's true," Marlon said. "Not even your own mother. But still . . ." He picked up a stone and angrily pitched it at the trunk of a tree. "Shit!"

What Carlo didn't know was that Dodie was in one of her dry periods and trying to pay attention—emboldened, perhaps, by the theatrical activities once again surrounding her. Marlon did not know how to handle it, and she continued to press, in all likelihood because he was so enormously frustrating for her. Another thing that seemed to make Marlon uncomfortable was that she insisted on total informality with Carlo, just as she had done with Darren and the other friends he brought back to the West End Avenue apartment. According to Fiore, Brando wanted to know if he wanted to sleep with Dodie.

> To deny that I was sexually attracted to Dodie would have been a lie, and Marlon would have seen right through it. There was no way I

could hedge the question, and his anguished expression told me that a great deal depended on my answer.

"Well, would you?" he insisted.

"No," I said. "Never."

"Why not? Suppose Dodie made herself . . . available. Suppose she wanted to. Why not?"

"Because you're my friend. I wouldn't hurt your feelings like that."

He looked into my eyes for a second or two, searching for the lie, then he gave me a curt nod, as if to say he believed me and that was the end of it.

Suddenly his face cracked with a cockeyed grin, and he burst out laughing, leaving me confused again. Maybe he *was* playing the game, and I was taken in again. But I was beginning to understand him now. These lunatic about-face reactions in moments of crisis were his way of coping with his embarrassment, a method he used to ease the tension. . . .

I hadn't lied to him about Dodie. Much as I wanted to sleep with her, I wouldn't have, and later in our relationship I had the chance to prove it, when she gave me the plain invitation and I refused.

It was the dirty little secret all over again. Now, though, their exchange—and Marlon's predictable response—only brought the two barnmates closer: The ups and downs of Dodie's spiraling alcoholism, Marlon Sr.'s philandering, even how Marlon himself had witnessed his father beating his mother, all became the stuff of confession as Marlon uncharacteristically opened up. It may well have been another test, or simply his response to what he perceived as one of his all-but-overwhelming crises, for in addition to these disclosures about his childhood pain, he also revealed how, at "thirteen or fourteen, he had told his father that if he ever touched [her] again, he would kill him."

Cry Havoc opened on August 11, with Dodie playing the role of Doc "wonderfully," according to Elaine Stritch. Marlon, however, was no longer in Sayville: He had been dismissed from the company—or, as Farwell put it, "God had sent Adam out of the Garden of Eden." The angry God was, of course, Erwin Piscator. In the part of Eve was Blossom Plumb, golden-haired, blue-eyed, with peaches-and-cream skin, whose comings and goings the director had been monitoring for weeks. The sin-and-punishment episode was so scandalous that years after the event, it still remained part of the Dramatic Workshop's folklore. This is how Judith Malina heard it a year after Marlon's dismissal:

"He was having a love affair with a young lady who was very poetical, who was enamored with him, and apparently they had spent the night in a garage where Piscator had parked his car, which they were using as a boudoir. In the morning Piscator found the garage locked, knocked on the door, and said, 'Whoever's in there, I hear you! Open the door!' And Brando, in his uninhibited way, said, 'I can't right now, I'm fucking.' "

The car story is, most likely, fiction. The basic plotline however, remains accurate. The episode took place in the barn where Marlon and Carlo had made their bivouac, which also served as Joy Thomson's scenery shop.

"Marlon and Blossom had found this little cozy corner upstairs, their private love nest," Thomson remembers, adding that, weeks before, Piscator had for the umpteenth time already warned Marlon to toe the line. Brando's response was, "He's got no right to have anything to do with what I'm doing. He told me I couldn't fuck Blossom. I'm going to do exactly what I want."

Thomson, ever the loyalist and good sport, had tried to reason with him. "Listen, Marlon, he's the boss. If he says no, don't do it. You're not the boss, dear, are you?" Brando's reply, she says, was, "Oh, drop dead!"

Unbeknownst to many in the company, Piscator had been in the habit of making nightly rounds, and to stymie his snooping, Marlon had been hauling his ladder up into the loft whenever he needed privacy. This time, however, it hadn't worked.

"When Piscator realized what Marlon had done," Thomson explained, "he went into a fit and marched to the stage house to get *another* ladder, which he somehow managed to drag over to the barn. He put it up against the window right where Marlon's bed was. Marlon was screwing Blossom, and later he told me, 'If only I'd had enough presence of mind. I was so fucking scared. Suddenly this face appeared in the window with the white hair glistening like Toscanini with the moonlight behind him, screaming, "Ah so, Mr. Brando!" If I'd pushed him, that would have been the end of it. I could have just shoved the ladder and he would have gone over backward. . . .'

"It was then, about three-thirty in the morning," Thomson adds, "that Piscator yelled *'Out!'* "

At ten o'clock the next morning, the two miscreants trooped into the theater building, where most of the company had assembled, and the clench-jawed Chouteau Dyer, Piscator's assistant, exploded. Marlon's response, she says, was, "You can't fire me, because I'm in the next show. You can't fire Blossom, either, because she has the lead."

"Later in the day, Dodie appeared," Dyer continued, "and I remember her walking into the lobby. 'What's this I hear?' she said, and I filled her in: 'I've told Marlon and Blossom they're out. They're through. They're just defying me and the whole company.' And she said, 'You're dead right. It's too bad, I'm sorry.'"

Piscator's outrage struck Joy Thomson, Sara Farwell, and others as ridiculous, not to say hypocritical, because the director himself was "screwing everything that moved." Thomson explains, "Marlon had Blossom but Piscator was annoyed because *he* wanted her. He told Marlon to stop, so it was sort of an upstaging."

Whether it was Piscator or Chouteau Dyer who kicked him out, the dismissal was felt by everyone, and in a sense it was a letter-perfect replay of what had happened at Shattuck.

"It was outside the theater, in the yard, and he was hauled up kind of in court," recalled Farwell. "We all felt shock because he was our big star. When he left, we were all there to say good-bye. It was terrible. Up until then, it had been a wonderful summer. It was an eye-opener for me, but I didn't have the guts to go to Piscator and say, 'Don't do this.' I wish I had."

Blossom apparently left with him. Back in the city, Stella, too, was upset. A rebel in her own right, she knew that Marlon was incapable of "functioning with continuity and discipline"; nonetheless, she felt that what had taken place was unjust. She set aside her dislike for Piscator and all he stood for, and asked him to give Marlon another chance. She talked to Harold, too. "Stella said that Piscator told her simply—in very typical *deutsche* fashion—that he found Marlon troublesome and did not want him back. That was it. End of discussion."

The irony was that Piscator's ironhandedness had put Marlon in the best possible position to take a role on Broadway, eliminating, as it did, any lesser options. Four weeks had passed since *Hannele's Way to Heaven,* and Maynard Morris's enthusiasm hadn't cooled; with Brando back in the city, the agent started calling.

"Maynard was a dear man who, as an agent, was interested in young people and went to any lengths to see new talent," said Jocelyn, who was taking his calls after her return to the apartment. With the agent pleading, saying that all he needed to know was whether Marlon was "ready to sign," she decided that the only thing to do was to take her brother by the hand to Morris's midtown office.

"Bud just sat there," she recalled. "Maynard waxed on in his sort of gay way, enthusiastic and stuff, but Bud didn't say a word. I was sort of embarrassed because he didn't seem to be giving him any room. He was just sitting there, and after a while we got up to leave. When we reached the door I said, 'Sign with him!' "

News of Marlon's good fortune reached the company almost at once, and no one was surprised when Piscator made it known that he was delighted, as if his hysteria and Marlon's expulsion had never happened. Darren, meanwhile, quit the whole business to accompany Marlon to Cape Cod.

"He called and said, 'We're going to Provincetown. Pack some stuff and meet me at Penn Station,' " Dublin recalled.

The trip was relaxed, Marlon's mood matter-of-fact even though he was now being represented by the best-connected agent in town. Neither of them knew where they were going to stay on the Cape, but as luck would have it, two coeds from Boston took them in the day after their arrival. Without a thought of anything beyond "staying loose," Marlon quickly set out to explore the local art galleries, beach shacks, and weathered piers. "He loved the place right from the start," said Dublin. "In P-town we just played, messed around." After Piscator, it was exactly what Marlon had come for. Within a week and a half, however, he informed Darren that they had to cut short their stay. Maynard Morris had done his job, but all Marlon volunteered was that he had to go back to New York to audition for "some shit Broadway show."

NEW 6 YORK —
PROVINCETOWN

"Some shit Broadway show" was, in fact, *I Remember Mama*. Several weeks earlier Morris had proposed Marlon for John Van Druten's dramatization of Kathryn Forbes's popular collection of short stories, *Mama's Bank Account*. Van Druten, whose *Voice of the Turtle* had been a hit the year before, was also directing his new play; he had already cast Mady Christians and Oscar Homolka in the leads. With the show being produced by Richard Rodgers and Oscar Hammerstein, fresh from their success with *Oklahoma!*, it was the perfect vehicle for any new and unknown actor. Marlon, however, was not enthusiastic.

He took the script home to the West End Avenue apartment to show to Dodie and Jocelyn. The role of Nels, which he was to play, was that of a timid, gentle, fifteen-year-old son of an immigrant Norwegian family in San Francisco. The boy dreams of being a doctor, and grows into manhood in the final scene. The part seemed small and dull, and the family consensus was that the play was no better than *Life with Father* or any of the other escapist schlock filling Broadway's wartime theaters. Only after Stella Adler—who, like Morris, thought it was time for Marlon to test his talent in the professional spotlight—predicted that *Mama* would be a hit did Marlon reluctantly agree to audition.

The tryout took place in Richard Rodgers's office. Instead of sailing through, he stumbled and tripped, and his shyness was so paralyzing that it left everyone in the room uncomfortable. "I was so scared, just one jump ahead of a blood clot," Brando later admitted. For Van Druten, it was the worst reading he had ever heard, but there was also a wonderful intelligence to it, a special "something" beneath the fumbling that caught the director's attention. Lucinda Ballard, the show's costume designer, saw it, too. Recognizing that Marlon looked so much like the play's Nordic teenager, she seconded Van Druten's hunch on the spot, overriding the producers' objection—even when, after the audition had concluded, Brando walked into a closet instead of leaving by the office door.

Fran Heflin, cast as one of Mama's daughters, saw Brando's awkwardness the first day of rehearsals late in September 1944. He was comfortable only when he was on his feet. Many of the actors in the show had had radio experience, but Marlon's sight readings were a disaster. Repeatedly he had to be asked to speak up, and when he'd open his mouth, sometimes nothing came out—literally. Or after a moment or two, there would be a rush, a terrible jumble of words. The second week of rehearsals, he came in late, all beaten up and with a black eye. "He was dirty," said Herbert Kenwith, another junior actor, "his clothing and his hair were disheveled, and when we asked him what happened, he says, 'Why? Nothing.' He was so casual, you had a feeling that you were imagining all of this. It was different from his stumbling. There was concern about his stability, that he might just self-destruct or disappear."

Twice he was nearly fired, and only the intercession of Mady Christians and Fran Heflin saved him. For Heflin, he appeared touchingly absorbed in his own inner world, "the epitome of politeness, never rude or curt or ill-spoken to anyone." Once, she recalled, he was fifteen minutes late and apologized to the group, saying, "It was such a nice day, not too hot, and I went down and sat by the river and just got kind of lost in my own thoughts."

According to theater legend, one of Van Druten's skills as a director had always been his ability to instill a sense of family, yet the family life here was troubled and getting worse as the rehearsals proceeded. More than Marlon, the problem was the self-centered Oscar Homolka, playing the lead role of the lame Uncle Chris. "All he needed was an SS band on his arm," said one cast member, complaining that the old stage-hound who'd had a brilliant career in Europe with *The Emperor Jones* and *King Lear* had a million tricks to upstage his partners. "He never looks in my eyes when he talks to me," Mady Christians complained to the director.

"He's always looking at my forehead, and I get very self-conscious." Onstage he took forever to roll his cigarette, which he positioned in his cigarette holder with agonizing slowness, only to reposition it anew. It was a routine that, coupled with his cavernous pauses and the old ploy of "stepping" on the other actors' lines, eventually added twenty minutes to the show's running time. A martinet and misanthrope, Homolka treated the stagehands "like dirt." Nothing was good enough—not the script, the staging, or his fellow players.

Brando's part was small, and when the play opened to "box-office" reviews on October 19, 1944, most of the critics failed to mention him. Still, among theater aficionados, his performance didn't go unnoticed. Group Theatre alumnus Bobby Lewis thought Brando couldn't be a real actor. "The curtain went up, and there were Mady Christians and Oscar Homolka acting up a storm," he recalled. "Suddenly, in the back, down the stairs comes this kid munching an apple. Here were these two great professionals emoting, and then this kid who really looked like he *lived* upstairs in that house. He started to say his lines, and I said to myself, 'It's a stagehand. Someone's just wandered onstage, or maybe it's an understudy. The fellow that's supposed to play the part isn't here, and this guy, he's not acting.'"

It was as if he'd "come from another planet," Lewis added. He was that "real." Edith Van Cleve, Morris's MCA partner who would shortly take over Brando's representation, had a comparable experience. "Afterward everybody was saying, 'Wasn't Homolka wonderful?' And I'd say, 'Yes, but wasn't the boy good?' 'Wasn't Christians wonderful?' 'Yes, but wasn't the boy good?' And finally someone said, 'What boy? Oh, the one in knee pants who grew up!' The way he listened. He stood on the stage for twenty minutes without a line, and when he did speak it was as if he had been speaking all the time."

Van Cleve, who specialized in movies and already represented Montgomery Clift, asked to meet Brando, who explained that he was happy with Morris and wasn't interested in Hollywood anyway. She explained that she and Morris worked together, that he wasn't yet ready for movies, but that she'd be glad to turn down film offers on his behalf. Six months later Marlon appeared at her office and announced that he had fulfilled his agreement with Maynard Morris and now was ready to switch.

Onstage in *Mama,* he continued to make an impression. What was astounding was the *truth* of what he was doing, "as if he didn't know how to fake, as if he'd never learned." Thinking about his performance afterward, Lewis felt that a lot of it had to do with his phrasing, the way he seemed to ignore the written text while "weighting" its more important emotional core.

According to Kenwith, who was watching from the wings, the same quality of authenticity reached the audience, too. "Marlon's first scene consisted of nothing, really," he explained. "He just stood there, said one line—'Good-night, Mama. Good-night, Papa.'—that was all, then he left. But when he exited, there was this thunderous applause, and the actors were stunned; they couldn't imagine what had happened because it was all behind them. Mady came off and said to me, 'Herbert, what'd he do?' 'Nothing,' I said. 'He did something,' she objected. 'What did he do to get that hand?' I said, 'It probably won't happen again, but watch it tomorrow night.' Of course, the next night it was the same thing: 'Good-night, Mama. Good-night, Papa,' and the same big applause. Van Druten also asked, 'What's he doing? I didn't write anything to get an exit hand there. It's just "Get *off.*" ' "

Marlene Dietrich had attended opening night and during intermission raved about how Marlon was "the most natural boy she'd seen." Like Lewis, what she recognized was the newcomer's ability to relax. Tense and tongue-tied during rehearsals, Brando was able to display the gift of the best actors, like Laurence Olivier and Alfred Lunt—an abundance of inner energy that allowed him complete outer ease. His magnetism seemed to flow from within, and he was startlingly self-assured. "This kid can be intense," Lewis told himself, "but he knows that it has nothing to do with muscular tension."

As Stella Adler and others had predicted, the show settled into a long run of sixteen months, or 714 performances in all, and during this time Van Druten, the English-trained formalist, returned to check up on his actors, in the process retuning everyone's performance. Fran Heflin had left shortly after the opening, then returned three months later in a different part. She was stunned at how Marlon's acting had changed as he "grew, got more involved." His interpretation was so much deeper that she sometimes didn't realize that it was the same boy.

The way he was working was how he would work throughout his career; experimenting, tinkering, always playing at the edge. "He would look at you in a different way or offer a slight change of line reading, maybe a pause that he hadn't taken before," Heflin said, adding that Van Druten noted the adjustments when it came time to prepare his script for publication. He wanted the published text to reflect what was actually being done on the stage, and Brando, he realized, had created numerous "little things" not in the original. "I don't think I've ever seen that kind of development in any other actor in my life," Heflin added. "It was very personal work, very interior."

He had signed a one-year contract for a weekly salary of $200—then the norm for a novice Broadway actor—but by the spring he was becoming bored. Still, Marlon resigned himself to remaining for the run of the play, explaining to Heflin that he had no choice. "He was quite candid about that with me," she said. "He needed the money because he was screwing around a lot. He had to get himself out of a few scrapes with women."

His frustration mounted, and he began to lapse into pranks. In many of the family scenes, Marlon had little to do but wait for incidents to react to, so before one night's performance he added salt to the prop coffeepot. Mady Christians, as Mama, suspected nothing, and poured the coffee for her sisters, who had come to visit. "Ellen Mahar had a mouthful of coffee," recalled one of the stagehands, "and her cheeks were out to here. Ruth Gates, who played Yennie, swallowed the coffee and became nauseous, running offstage in the middle of the scene because she was going to vomit. Mady had the coffee in her mouth and spat it all back in the cup."

Backstage she was livid, and grabbed Marlon by the collar and threw him against the wall. He was undaunted. A week later, Christians brought the coffeepot to the table during the same scene and found that the coffee wouldn't pour at all. She lifted the lid, took a fork off the table and struggled to free the obstruction; what she pulled out was a crumpled shirtsleeve. The audience roared. Marlon wasn't allowed to touch the coffeepot for the rest of the show.

Despite their personal rapport, Christians was turning out to be Marlon's favorite victim. Whenever the script called for her to make an exit, he would hold the doorknob from the back side of the elaborate, three-tiered set, keeping her prisoner onstage. Set designer George Jenkins tried to solve the problem by removing the doorknob so he would have nothing to hold on to, but Marlon hammered a makeshift pull in the form of a nail into the door instead. There was nothing more Jenkins could do, even after he tried to reason with him, and Christians remained on guard. "She watched that door like a hawk," said Kenwith, "and it was as if they mounted a guard."

The one thing Brando couldn't stand was "the horseshit," the ego-driven game playing backstage, and he had already refused to kowtow to Homolka's bullying. Hanging out with the blue-collar technical crew was one response, but so too was the way he dealt with actress Joan Tetzel, Homolka's fiancée and a fellow cast member. She had been barking orders at whoever was within range, and after urging her to "go easy," he took it upon himself to write her a long letter, which he showed to Heflin beforehand.

"It was a little awkward, but genuine and sincere, not angry or recriminatory," Heflin remembers, noting that years later, when people suspected Brando's involvement with the Indian cause was phony, she'd point back to this incident. "Marlon wasn't a good politician," she explains, "never was, never would be. But [Joan] was being terribly imperious and it drove him crazy. What he said was that Joan was hurting people and that this wasn't a part of being in a company with fellow actors."

His reputation expanded when he'd get down on the floor backstage to play with costume designer Lucinda Ballard's two young children. Yet there was also his dark side—mood swings that were unignorable. He could get very low, and then explode in wild exuberance, whooping and running the stairs to his dressing room four steps at a time. "I saw him every single day for over a year and a half," said Kenwith, "and sometimes he wouldn't acknowledge you, wouldn't say hello, wouldn't say goodnight."

On one occasion, he arrived ten minutes before curtain time, agitated to the point of tears. During intermission, he explained to Kenwith that he had found Dodie drunk and lying in the gutter, and that she'd been taken to Bellevue Hospital. He said he was going to visit her after the show, and asked to borrow $75 to buy some flowers.

The next day Kenwith asked about his mother.

"Oh, she's okay," he replied.

"Is she still in the hospital, Marlon?"

"Yes, she'll be there for a while. They have to dry her out. She's a big, big problem."

That very evening, however, Dodie walked in the stage door.

"I thought you were in the hospital," Kenwith said to her.

"For what?"

"Marlon just told me you were taken to Bellevue yesterday," Kenwith said, not wanting to tell her that Marlon had said she was drunk and lying in the gutter. "He told me you had fallen."

"No," she said with anger in her voice, making it clear that she was furious her son had lied, taken advantage of her for his own ends.

Marlon's fable wasn't without precedent. He had already created a false biography for himself for the show's Playbill, claiming he was born in Calcutta, where his father was engaged in "geological research." His personal habits, including hygiene, were just as puzzling.

Onstage he never bothered with makeup or even a shirt, wearing just a collar with a little bib and cuffs under the jacket of his costume. His dressing room was a shambles, with dirty towels, papers, and Kleenex scattered everywhere. When he went to the toilet, he would sometimes leave the door open so he could continue talking to guests, and, according to cast members, he was capable of walking away without using paper. Kenwith recalled that he was stunned when he saw this for the first time, and also remembered the night Brando came to the theater just before curtain time, got undressed, and was wearing girls' lacy underwear. His explanation was that he'd been with "some chick" and just grabbed her panties because he was running late. For Robert Lanum, a Libertyville classmate who had come by to visit, it was equally bizarre when he walked in on Bud playing with a knife. He would hold it by the tip and throw it at the seat of a chair on the other side of the room, twenty to twenty-five feet away.

He didn't bathe and often smelled, something Kenwith and others became inured to. Still, one idiosyncrasy less tolerated was Marlon's habit of fondling himself backstage to get a semierection before making an entrance. The protuberance was visible even out in the audience, since he wore a pair of fairly snug knickerbockers, and it wasn't long before Van Druten noticed it, too. "You've got to talk to him about wearing an athletic supporter," the director instructed Kenwith. "You can see that he has an erection. It's distracting." The actor replied, "If you want to tell him anything like that, you do it. I'm the one who has to be here every night."

Brando's steady stream of female visitors engendered still more gossip. After several months, Kenwith had decided to move out of the top-floor dressing room the two had been sharing, in order to have some privacy. Marlon's girls were often around—usually Eurasian girls and dark-skinned, but any type, it didn't matter. While hardly unheard of in the theatre world, sometimes he'd have sex in between his walk-ons, taking advantage of the twenty-minute break between his entrances.

"Everybody was aware of it—Mady and Mady's secretary, too," said Kenwith. "For him, sex was like eating or going to the bathroom. He wasn't boastful. He might mention a date that he'd set up for after the show—'a fuck date,' as he put it—but he never went into details except when he thought something was funny."

He was still in the habit of going to midnight shows on Forty-second Street, and one night he walked out of the movie theater without his shoes. "He told me about *that*," Kenwith said, laughing, "and he didn't know how he did it. I asked, 'How could you possibly not know you didn't have your shoes on?' He said he took them off because he was screwing this girl he'd picked up, and when they left, he just got up to walk out with her."

Nor did he lock his dressing room, either, which, within New York's tight, incestuous theatre world, led to more gossip about Brando and his mentor Stella Adler. One of the company's actors walked in on them. "Marlon was naked, Stella wasn't," he recalled. "They were on the floor. I'd seen her go into his dressing room beforehand, and when I came in, she turned and saw me. Marlon saw me, too, but it didn't bother him. He just looked up at me, like the time I walked in on him when he was screwing some Eurasian girl and he said, 'Oh, come on in.' "

Most members of the company dismissed the affair with Stella as "a teacher-student fling." Complicatings things, however, was the fact that Ellen, Stella's fifteen-year-old daughter, had also been visiting his dressing room, and in fact she was spotted with Marlon only the night before his episode with Stella.

Marlon's relationship with Ellen would last through each of their many involvements, marriages, children, and divorces. In later years, he would support her, just as she would fantasize that they might finally pass their twilight years together side by side in adjoining rocking chairs. Now, at fifteen, she was striking—not blond like her mother, but a dark gypsy type with coal-black hair, quick eyes, and a sense of presence that many people found disturbingly precocious. Raised by Stella and stepfather Clurman, Ellen had grown into adolescence with a sophistication beyond her years. Regularly exposed to John Garfield, Franchot Tone, Jacques Lipchitz, Irwin Shaw, Aaron Copland, and countless other artists in her parents' apartment, she had attended Dalton and Manumet private schools. At Bard College, the small, offbeat liberal arts school where she'd matriculated weeks before the opening of *Mama,* she studied literature, not drama, and avoided contact with the college's theater students, who worshiped the name Adler.

The conflict for her was palpable, more than a typical teenager's need to go her own way. Standish Thayer, Ellen's boyfriend at Bard, saw it firsthand when he stayed over at the Adler apartment that New Year's Eve. Marlon showed up hours after they welcomed in 1945. "I'd been aware of their relationship." said Thayer, "At first Ellen said he was 'a very good friend.' But I had the sense that there was something between Marlon and Stella, since they seemed to be close, or at least that's the impression I had, third-removed through Ellen.

"Ellen, though, was ambiguous about her relationship with Marlon," he added. "I never really knew, and it was a problem. 'Who will it be, me or him?' I wasn't clear why she'd been going into the city so often, and that night there was some discussion about whether she should introduce me. It was probably about four in the morning when he arrived, and she talked with him until breakfast time. The message Ellen gave me was that he was a very talented student of her mother's who was going to be a world star, but inside he was a gentle little boy whom she had to comfort and help."

At other times Thayer and Ellen had "dated" with Stella and one of her boyfriends, "usually an older guy with a lot of money who would take us out for delicious dinners," he said. "There I was, Ellen's boyfriend, witnessing beautiful Stella being charming to some rather unattractive guy. In effect, because I knew about Marlon, I was being asked to participate in an open infidelity, and I could sense a sort of despair, a discomfort on the part of Ellen."

Stella, no less than her husband, had long made it a habit to go her own way, but the arrangement was a bit surreal for any college student. As Thayer got to know mother and daughter, he realized that Ellen was already assuming Stella's gestures, and her speech. Stella's friend, the composer David Diamond also noticed this and urged her, to no avail, "Ellen, cool it. Knock it off. Stella's Stella. You've got your own personality."

While telling Thayer that Marlon "was just a good friend," Ellen never hid her infatuation. In the apartment, she would sit with Marlon on the living room couch holding hands, or Marlon might be massaging her thigh, caressing the muscles of her calf. She might get up for orange juice or a malted milk, then return and plunk herself down on his lap, "delivering herself as his delight," said Diamond. She loved to do it; but rarely would this go on in Stella's presence. "Marlon," Diamond added, "loved having things done to him, and he always reciprocated. She was so young, she had no basis for comparison, but Ellen spoke of the gentleness of his foreplay, of his hands, and how he loved to do erotic, sensual things before the actual act. The kissing of the entire body. His obsession with the toes, nipples, the neck." She felt she was being adored, even though at the same time Marlon was sleeping with Celia Webb and many others; she was aware of his many girlfriends, but suffered it, just as it seemed that she pretended not to know that there was something between her mother and Marlon.

Stella, for her part, didn't hide her jealousy, although she disguised it with parental disapproval of her daughter's relationship with her protégé. With Marlon in the apartment, there were times when she shrieked at her daughter, *"Shvartzeh,* go in the bedroom." In high dudgeon, she would sweep into the Music Box Theatre, where *Mama* was playing, to search for Ellen as though she were a grade-school truant. Fran Heflin sometimes hid her in her dressing room. "I thought Ellen and Marlon made a terrific couple," Heflin explained, even though, like Stella, she too resented Marlon's tendency "to gravitate toward easy lays. . . . Stella felt Marlon was irresponsible," she added, "and she wanted to break up the relationship. It was the only time in my life I saw her strike a maternal pose, and remember, I'd known Stella for years since Van, my brother, had been in the Group."

Clurman disapproved as well, though his motives were evidently purer. His relationship with Ellen wasn't competitive, and he also recognized that she was "a very spoiled girl who was going to be difficult for any man to put up with."

Clurman, who had adopted Ellen in all but name, was a successful theater and film director and had been hailed as a major intellectual, arguably America's foremost drama critic. Born on the Lower East Side to a Yiddish-speaking family, he had gone to Columbia University, been involved with the Theatre Guild, and was one of the founders of the Group Theatre. He met Stella in Richard Boleslavsky's American Lab Theatre, and they had gotten married twelve years later, in 1943. "If I don't marry Harold, how else can I divorce him?" she had said at the time, and the remark, made to Bobby Lewis, was prophetic. The marriage was tempestuous, punctuated with Stella's dramatic, totally uncompromising *meshugass*.

In one well-known story, which even Marlon liked to retell, Adler and Clurman were having one of their frequent arguments, with Stella screaming, Harold listening. Finally, he shouted back, "Goddamn it, Stella, I can't take it. I'll jump." She walked straight to the French windows, opened them, and yelled, "So jump!"

Another time, Clurman got up in the middle of the night with an anxiety attack, and she asked, "What's the matter?" He said, "You don't understand, I'm $10,000 in debt!" And she exclaimed, "A man of your genius, it should be $100,000! Go back to sleep!"

(When the two finally parted company in the fifties, Stella herself seemed to go out of her way to make sure he was in debt, and the rumor was that the divorce hurt him financially.)

In a world of glamour and poses, there was an earnestness to Clurman. He read constantly, wrote omnivorously, and argued nonstop, all in the service of ideas. Art was his religion. "Harold," his closest friend Aaron Copland once told him, "if you weren't in the theater, you would have been Father Divine." He had little use for psychoanalysis or many of the games often played by actors, which meant that Marlon couldn't manipulate him.

"I can remember Harold repeating Ellen's talk about Marlon-this and Marlon-that," said Juleen J. C. Compton, Clurman's second wife, "and his feeling was that she was a little naive, that she was just parroting Stella, who was drawn to this something that was shiny. He would add, 'I hope he doesn't disappoint Ellen, I hope he doesn't let her down,' and he didn't even feel that Marlon behaved all that well toward Stella, either. He saw Marlon as just sort of an eat-and-run guy, that while he wasn't the conscious opportunist, he seemed to digest everything and assimilate nothing."

Clurman also seemed to be aware that Marlon was sleeping with his wife, but his reaction was that he was "only one of many," a minor blip on the screen of his and Stella's relationship. What mattered to him, Compton added, was that Marlon was "a very spoiled boy who was spoiling himself."

"When I say 'spoiled,'" she clarified, "what Harold perceived was rot, and he saw it back then, early on, a self-destructive kind of rot. Brando lacked moral fiber—and [in] his work, too. Harold didn't see real passion, and for years it bothered him deeply."

• • •

In the spring of 1945, *Mama* was in its seventh month, and Brando found himself drawn to the Katherine Dunham School of Dance. It was an exotic world of conga drums and young black bodies, where nobody questioned anybody about their background, schooling, or plans for the future. In a way far beyond the Dramatic Workshop, the Dunham School was on the cutting edge.

By the end of the war, Dunham herself was already the mighty matriarch of modern dance. Part of her legend was the low-cut costumes, spike heels, and mesh stockings, the island woman swaying among a quadrille of beautifully muscled, dark-skinned men; beyond her reputation as the sexy high priestess of voodoo, though, she had founded America's first professional black dance company and grafted Afro-Caribbean styles onto ballet, demonstrating how American social dances, from the cakewalk to bebop, were indebted to a common African heritage. She had also studied anthropology at the University of Chicago, writing her master's thesis on the dances of Haiti.

More than 65 percent of Dunham's students were black, Haitian, or Spanish. Located between Sixth and Seventh Avenues on Forty-third Street, the school occupied the whole of a floor-through loft except for an individual studio, extra space that had been rented out to Lee Strasberg. Brando had happened on the Dunham School when he had briefly been an auditor in Strasberg's private class in the room next door. Later he would deny studying with Strasberg, but in fact he had shown up a few times, heard the music in the adjoining studio, and wandered down the corridor to discover that he much preferred Dunham's school to the acting class. "He was supposed to be with Lee, but he would play hooky," recalled Lucille Ellis, one of the company's early dancers, explaining that what had drawn him to the dance loft wasn't just the congas, but the drum teacher himself: Henri "Papa" Augustine, the company's *hungan,* or voodoo priest.

The drum teacher, a tall, ebony-black man in his late forties, had come to be called Papa as a sign of respect, "Papa" being the sobriquet Haitians reserve for their gods. Heavyset, with penetrating, all-seeing eyes, he had a reputation among New York's Haitian community as a man who "believed in the better aspects of the gods." He found housing for new arrivals from Port-au-Prince, but more than that, he performed "protective" ceremonies at his Harlem apartment and at the opening of every Dunham show, whether at New York's Belasco Theatre or when the company was out of town on tour.

Marlon had just turned twenty-one, a midwesterner with less than two years of Manhattan under his belt. The drum classes with Augustine exposed him to an exotic and intriguing culture that appealed to him as much as, if not more than, the sophisticated milieu of Stella's apartment.

"The drumming and dancing and the spirits, they are all together," recalled Jean-Léon Destiné, another company dancer, who stressed that Augustine wasn't just a drum teacher and that even the beginners' course in which Marlon was enrolled went beyond technique. Every rhythm had its purpose, "like healing, warding off evil, foretelling the future." Voodoo had its "rules, the specific spirits you have to invoke, the rhythm that goes with the dance for each spirit, the song that goes with each rhythm."

For Brando, it was an exercise made-to-order. His quasi-intellectual search for alternatives, his grounding in Gurdjieff through Dodie and Nana, not to mention the drumming he'd done in high school, all of it made for a one-way ticket: in Augustine he had found a new mentor.

Watching Marlon in the percussion class, Tommy Gomez, one of the school's dance instructors, was struck by how intently he "was trying to find himself." By any number of accounts, he was "very self-contained," "enigmatic and withholding," and also mysterious, as if he "wanted to be invisible." There was "a look in his eye of not knowing where he was going," said Gomez. Yet the drums offered relief. He played for hours on end and became "completely wrapped up in the rhythm." Lucille Ellis observed that he played as if he weren't "going to be alive tomorrow or even the next hour."

Occasionally, he would don a tattered leotard and do dance exercises at the bar in order to "improve his timing." He also took several dance classes, but that seemed more to check out the women than to learn technique. As always, he watched, saying little.

The variety, the *openness* of the place took its cue from Dunham herself, of course, who was known to read palms as well as Tarot cards. Unlike Dunham, Augustine was available and embodied a primitive world apart from anything young Brando had previously experienced. Congas, bongos, it didn't matter—the drums brought Marlon shoulder to shoulder with street-smart Haitians, Harlem blacks, and fiery Latinos. In Augustine's class he practiced so diligently that the skin on his hands would split, and afterward he'd wait for his mentor to take him along to play rhythm for the dance classes. "Yes, you're good," Augustine encouraged him. "But you need to work in order to make yourself better. Work will give you strength. You must work in order to understand what you're doing." The dance school was a place where he could "lose himself," just as he could at the school's *boules blanches,* the once-a-month scholarship fundraisers that drew a mixed crowd of whites and blacks and were among the most talked-about, toniest events in town. Among the regulars were *Vogue*'s Francesco Scavullo, James Agee, jazz musician Teddy Wilson, Stella Brooks, Langston Hughes, James Baldwin, heiress Doris Duke, and Betty Furness. Black, white, straight, gay, rich, poor—it was a mixed group. "We were all going to change the world," said Ellis. And actress and singer Robin Roberts added: "I mean *everything* was going on—second-position turns, shoulder shakings, and rumba—everything." She was describing the dancing out on the floor to the compelling beat of the drummers, who sometimes played for five hours straight.

Here Brando played, too, and although he was one of the few non-blacks among the dozen or so sweaty drummers, he rarely left the stage. He even had his own ritual chant: *"Bow-w-w-w! Harissi! Bow-w-w-w! Harissi! Bow-w-w-w-w!"* "He was a ham," said Jean-Léon Destiné. "He'd get carried away, but he'd also try to show off a little, and people noticed him."

But he still carried his mysterious aura, which only added to his reputation. While many women wanted him, rarely would he make eye contact, said one of the school's students, Joyce Crosbie, adding, "and that was very appealing because everyone else was so loud."

One woman who paid particular attention was Crosbie's closest friend, Julie Robinson. Like so many of Brando's girlfriends, the olive-complected dance student was so dark that people took her for Indian. Actually, she was Jewish. A beauty who wore her long brunette hair parted in the middle, "bohemian style," she was the daughter of well-off Greenwich Village liberals. Robinson had found her way to Dunham's by way of the progressive Little Red Schoolhouse and the High School of Music and Art. Unlike most of Dunham's students, she had been brought up in comfort, a progressive "red-diaper baby" with a fondness for using her mother's charge plate at the city's best stores. Her relationship with Marlon took hold quickly, even though he made no secret of Ellen, Celia, Blossom Plumb, or any of his other women.

"Julie and I went to Mexico with my stepfather," recalled Crosbie, "and Marlon saw her off at the pier. I knew he was driving her nuts. One minute he seemed to be terribly involved, and then she wouldn't hear from him. When we came back at the end of the summer, I think she got involved with him again even though he was still seeing Ellen Adler."

With Julie away over the summer of 1945, and *Mama* on hiatus for the season, Marlon with Darren in tow, took a long vacation himself. Recalling how much he had liked Provincetown the previous year, he had also heard its praises sung among the hip group at Dunham's dance school, especially by Sid Shaw, a homosexual lyricist who, by June, was already settled up at Cape Cod. Provincetown, or "P-town," as it was known to the cognoscenti, now became Marlon's haunt.

Located on the outermost tip of Cape Cod, the town has always deserved its reputation for live-and-let-live bonhomie, and the "underground" word was that this was where the creative scene was happening. Local Portuguese fishermen and Yankee boatbuilders had coexisted there for years, unruffled by the artists in their midst. At the time, the young Jackson Pollock and his wife, Lee Krasner, were in town, along with Peggy Guggenheim and Max Ernst. George Grosz, William Baziotes, and Pollock's fellow abstractionist Adolph Gottlieb, were also around, as was the young Tennessee Williams, laboring on what would be his first major play, *The Glass Menagerie*.

Fritz Bultman, an early student of Hans Hofmann, had been on the scene for several years and came to know Williams in New York through Donald Windham, Williams's collaborator.

"That summer Tennessee lived with us, but eventually we had to throw him out," Bultman's widow, Jean, recalled, describing the close ties among artists who made up Provincetown's social web. "We were building our studio near the old Hawthorne house and had taken an apartment on the water, and Tennessee worked there during the day when we were out. We'd all eat together in the evening, and then Tennessee would go out cruising—seventeen-, eighteen-year-old boys, local kids and sailors. In fact, he got into a little argument with another friend of ours, like, 'Well, I never paid those boys more than two dollars, and here you come to town and you're paying them three! How dare you!'"

Even then, Provincetown's gay scene was open and undisguised, part of the whole crazy quilt of artists, writers, and beach bums whom the locals had learned to live with. "There were a lot of local fellows who were sort of rough trade," Bultman continued, "plus a lot of old-timey queens who came up from New York—mostly guys who ran antique shops. But everything was taken in stride. Straight, gay, rich, poor, it didn't matter. It was, 'We're artists, we're somehow removed.' None of us took anything seriously—'We're never going to sell a painting,' any more than Tennessee was ever going to become the toast of Broadway."

The war was coming to a close (Germany had surrendered in May), but there were no tourists in Provincetown, just painters and writers. It was only a mile and a half's walk from one end of Commercial Street, the town's main thoroughfare, to the other, and with gas rationing and food stamps still in effect, the Atlantic House, or "A-House," was probably the hottest spot in town. Headliners included Ella Fitzgerald and Imogene Coca pulled in a nightly crowd of straights and gays alike. The same mix could be found at the Old Colony, the Fo'c'sle, and Ace of Spades, and more than anything, that was the charm of it. Clayton Snow, a local self-described "queen," was often the center of the scene, drawing people together for after-hours parties. Snow was already a legend, a phenomenon even for Provincetown.

"Claytina," as he was known, tended bar at the New Central House, a small lounge on the beach adjacent to the Provincetown Playhouse. Fast-talking and witty, he had come out of the closet at fifteen while still in high school. Although thin and gangly, he had established himself as the demi-monde's chief impresario, thanks to his shameless flamboyance. "He'd just be flitting all over the place, always playing an act, and it didn't matter where," said one of his admirers. "At Cookie's Tap, there were always a lot of fishermen, very straight guys. One of the older ones was real dark-skinned and not too bright, either, and Clayton would come in and do his routine—'John, you've been out fishing all week and you didn't bring me those silk stockings you promised!' He'd carry on, and these guys would be laughing like hell. They loved him. It was camp before anybody knew what camp was."

The New Central House was his stage, and, in local parlance, he "ran the room." Dame May Whitty was doing *Night Must Fall* at the Playhouse next door, and among the endless procession dropping by were ballet and show business types (real or imagined), as well as such regulars as pianist Gil Evans and his wife, Lila, the theater's production manager. Four others were Victor Bruno, a raven-haired Vitalis model; Parker Tyler, New York editor of *Flair* magazine; Marlon's friend, Sid Shaw, and Shaw's lover, Hugh Shannon. Since the beginning of the summer, all of them had been staying at Clayton's run-down shack—which had a wishing well out front.

Downbeat magazine would later honor Shaw with an award for best musical arrangement of the year (he wrote such songs as "Evil Is 'Live' Spelled Backwards"), but at the time he was principally an aspiring dancer whose credentials consisted of a year's study at the Dunham School. He was small and pixieish, so dark-complexioned as to be occasionally taken for black. Friends still ribbed him for dropping his Jewish family name of Schwartz early in his career, and they also regarded him as the ultimate mooch, "a worm who didn't do a damn thing but hustle."

"Oh, dear, he was horrendous, just impossible," said Clayton Snow years later. "We called him 'the Leprechaun.' Hugh would get at the piano and work for tips, meals at my place, free drinks, you name it, but he was really following in his friend Sid's footsteps."

They also collected people as well as meals. According to Snow, this was how Brando had come to P-town. "I hadn't even known Hugh and Sid were coming," recalled Snow. "But I had the space, so it was mattresses on the floor. Marlon's connection to Sid was that they'd met at Dunham's, then Sid brought him in. What was never clear was whether Sid had known he was coming or if he just appeared, but right away Marlon and Darren were a part of our company downtown as well as at the cottage."

Basically, Marlon was drifting, sometimes alone and sometimes with Darren. There was no structure—no Dodie, no school, no reveille or curtain call. His indifference to social norms, even by P-town standards, struck almost everyone he came into contact with, and no more so than one evening at the Flagship restaurant when he was with a group including Tennessee Williams and his lover, Pancho Rodriguez.

"I noticed Brando because he wasn't ordinarily in the Flagship, since he had no money," recalled Leland Perry, a local who was working in the restaurant as a waiter. "What really caught my attention was that he was staring at me. I returned the look, telling myself, 'This is a straight guy. Fuck him.'

"I knew it was a theatrical crowd, and in those days the theater crowd in P-town was more or less straight, maybe bi-, so I was a little confused. It wasn't a sexual kind of look, but even so, he didn't stop. I took their order and served the first course, then served the next course, but he was still just staring at me. He didn't get personal about it, like say, 'What's your name?' Instead there was this curiosity. Tennessee was loaded, making a hell of a lot of noise yelling at his nice-looking Spanish guy, and meanwhile Brando just kept staring."

It was doubtless another of Marlon's character studies, with the twist that the subject was gay. He showed no discomfort at the gay life that surrounded him in P-town. On the contrary, he and Darren continued to live in Snow's two-room cottage, and sometimes he could be outright campy about his roommates. He was fond of their company, and later even bought Snow a silver ID bracelet that had been on display in a shop window most of the summer. It was a massive piece of custom-made jewelry that had been eyed by many a gay man in town.

Within a week after he had moved into Clayton's cottage in Pumpkin Hollow, Marlon's presence was noticed. If the tall Clayton had often been said to resemble Eleanor Roosevelt, his new friend was compared to Adonis. People talked, and even today old-time Provincetown gays recall that Brando was "just incredibly magnetic," "a sensual beauty," or more vauntingly, "blond, blond, blond, with an earthy sexiness plus a poetic face." Snow had always had the reputation of being on the make—"any guy who wanted to get serviced, all they'd have to do is ask Clayton"—and this promiscuity, coupled with Snow's high social profile, inevitably put Brando center stage in the hothouse of P-town's special world; as usual, he responded to the speculation as to who and what he was with shy indifference.

Harold Norse, a friend of Tennessee Williams, remembered the scuttlebutt quite clearly: "I'd come up at the beginning of the summer and met Clayton through Tennessee. There was still this remoteness about Marlon. I saw him at a party, and I was immediately, violently attracted. But Tennessee was going around saying that Marlon and Clayton were having an affair. Then *everybody* was talking about it—Tennessee kept saying, 'Clayton keeps Marlon on a chain, all locked up, and won't allow anyone near him.' "

Snow, ever the showman, was garnering points right and left, but there was a more personal component to the Brando-Snow relationship that became public knowledge, too.

Clayton's Irish mother adored Marlon. " 'Clayton, he's such a refined young man,' she said after I brought him to her house," Snow recalled. " 'Why can't you be more steady?' Of course, he loved that because she catered to him, making him lunch, telling him to take a nap."

As the question of Marlon's relationship with "Claytina" continued to swirl through P-town's bars, there was also some concern that he was in over his head. Clayton was Clayton, after all, and anyone who knew him realized that whatever he was up to wasn't necessarily so benign.

"Maybe it was just that Marlon admired Clayton, or was interested in watching him," Margaret Roberts, an older, hip habitué of the scene, recalled thinking at the time. "But it was very possible that he wasn't really versed in homosexuality, the routines and all the entrapments and so forth. Remember, for all his craziness, Clayton was one of the smartest people around. He always came toward you wanting to find out a little about you. It was 'Darling, darling,' all that, and then he kind of pulled you in a little after he's told two stories and you've laughed." Another observer mused that Clayton's power stemmed from "the fact that he could read people. He understood the sexual drive thing."

Like Marlon, Clayton Snow was indeed quick, and he had made it his business to get a fix on Darren's role, which he realized was pivotal. "He handled everything," Snow said. "He was like his manager, the hanger-on, close friend, court jester. It was impossible to get a coherent sentence out of him, but he was serious about Marlon's career, I imagine pretending or presuming that it would be his own. And Marlon himself knew *exactly* where he was going. He was measuring his smiles except for when he danced. Afro-Cuban. That's where he found release."

As in New York, there were the same alternating currents of withdrawal and assertion, with the result that sometimes he even dominated the group—including Snow. He was drinking, if not heavily, then often—more than usual, certainly—and on any given evening he might fling himself onto the dance floor at the A-House and hit on a female singer like Marie Music, or the actress Judy Tyler, later to become Princess Summer-Fall-Winter-Spring on the "Howdy Doody Show." If these advances were rejected, he would return to Clayton and the others and fold back into himself, drumming on the edge of the table to the waves of music coming from the bandstand. As for the gays who stood with their backs to the nearby bar and ogled him, with them, too, it seemed as if he couldn't care less. "Marlon was beautiful, yes. But, oh, there were millions of beauties, a thousand other men in Provincetown," Snow recalled happily. "I didn't have to protect him. Besides, I was of the school 'If you're going to hit on him, hit on him.' It was *his* responsibility."

For some locals, however, Brando wasn't so attractive. "A sophisticated asshole who thought his shit was ice cream," was how one fisherman described him, while another saw what he called "a Jekyll and Hyde" when, one evening, Marlon turned violent and got into a drunken fight. Victor Pacellini, the town iceman who had recently returned from the war in the Pacific with two Bronze Stars, found him making passes at his girlfriend, a waitress at the New Central House. He went over to Brando and told him, "Leave the woman alone."

Brando looked at him. "Lay off, soldier boy. I'm not doing anything," he replied, pushing Pacellini away.

"That was when I grabbed him and gave him a lock behind the head," Pacellini said. "Then I pushed him over to the bar and said, 'Why don't you be a good *boy*.' I remember he had lifts on, Cuban heels, and he sort of took a vague swing at me, and I let him have it. I floored him, then picked him up and slammed him up against the wall. My girlfriend told me to get out of there."

Meanwhile the gossip about Marlon's relationship with Snow continued with a patchwork of half-truths and playful inventions underscoring the gay community's need to claim the stunning newcomer as one of their own. One bartender reported that Snow had wandered into the Old Colony, announcing, "I know how big Marlon Brando's dick is." "You do?" joked several customers. "How big?" *"That* big," Snow supposedly replied, opening his mouth as though sucking on a Popsicle, while bystanders broke up laughing.

Queried about the relationship today, Snow waved aside any suggestion that Marlon and he were anything more than "just friends. Anything else you may hear is just embroidery," he insisted. "As for sex between Marlon and other men . . . well, he *was* experimenting around, which was the thing to do in those years if you had any sensitivity or intelligence or curiosity."

If Snow's denial bordered on the coy ("You wouldn't want me to kiss 'n' tell, now, would you?" he added), the waiter from the Flagship, Leland Perry, reported that Clayton gave him a different version after Marlon had returned to New York.

"It was in the late fall when Brando was back on Broadway," Perry said. "Clayton was getting these long, long letters from him. He showed me one, and it was the most unusual letter I'd ever read in my life. There wasn't anything in it about love—he just rambled on about life and God and philosophy and religion and flowers and nature. Rambled and rambled, and I thought, God, this guy must be crazy. There was affection in the letter, but it wasn't like two homosexuals in love. It was like Marlon was lonely and wanted to let loose his feelings, so he was reaching out to Clayton for understanding.

"For Clayton, of course, showing me the letter was boasting, but then he told me what happened. He said that he and Marlon got pretty high one night at a beach party and then wandered back over the dunes to the town water tower behind the Pilgrim Monument. They then started playing, were swinging from the ladder running up the side of the tower, and when they came down, the way Clayton put it was, 'We had sex in the sand.'

"For me there was no doubt that this happened, just the way Clayton described it. Some things I don't believe because Clayton was a famous bullshit artist. If he'd told me he'd had a long affair and Brando was crazy about him, I'd have said, 'Full of shit.' This, though, was different. Clayton used to carry on with local boys quite a bit. Not getting, giving. And when he described what happened, I realized that Marlon had had a few drinks and he let Clayton blow him."

More than a quarter of a century later, Brando himself would address the question of his alleged bisexuality. In 1976 there was widespread speculation over his appearing in drag in *The Missouri Breaks*—while playing a character whose name, interestingly, was Clayton. "Like a large number of men," he said in response, "I too have had homosexual experiences and am not ashamed. I've never paid attention to what people said about me. Deep down I feel ambiguous and I'm not saying that to spite the seven out of ten women who consider me—wrongly perhaps—a sex symbol. According to me, sex is something that lacks precision. Let's say sex is sexless."

For years, rumors linked him with novelist James Baldwin; actors Wally Cox, Christian Marquand, and others; and even Leonard Bernstein and Gore Vidal. Brando's first wife, Anna Kashfi, implied that there were still other male partners. Some of this was tabloid gossip, no question, but even longtime supportive colleagues like Karl Malden and Elia Kazan, as well as members of Marlon's family (Fran and Dick, specifically) had asked themselves whether this was the key to Marlon's always odd, secretive behavior.

Collectively, the suggestion was that Marlon was "experimenting"; several months after he left Provincetown, the assistant stage manager of *I Remember Mama* reported that he started showing up late for curtain call, "dirty and disheveled," straight from the Hudson River docks. It was during this same period that Harold Norse, the poet and friend of Tennessee and William Carlos Williams, ran into Marlon at another party—this one in the Village—where, he claims, he was openly propositioned:

"He didn't remember me from Provincetown," Norse said. "He asked me if I was Italian, a tough Italian from the neighborhood, and he was kind of nervously looking over his shoulder as if somebody was listening. 'What are you doing after the party? Are you busy?' I said, 'Well, Tennessee's asked me to go on somewhere with him.' 'Well, that's hours from now,' he said. 'We could go to my place.'

"I was ill at ease under such conditions in those days. I didn't want anyone to think I was openly gay, so I said, 'I'll think about it.'

" 'Well, I wouldn't think about it too long if I was you,' he said. He was sort of making grunting, macho sounds, and then just walked away, like I'd pushed him too hard and he felt rejected."

In Provincetown the question of Brando and Snow was soon eclipsed by a bigger story: In early September Brando was arrested, and even the diffident *Boston Globe* took notice, running a story with the headline, TOM TOM BOYS BREAK SERENITY OF CAPE TOWN.

Officially, the charge was "drunk and disorderly," a late-night disturbance in the vicinity of St. Peter's Catholic Church. It was a party of Clayton's, and little different from any of the others except that it was now the end of the season, when locals felt they were entitled to a rest. Further, the gathering was larger—close to twenty, and with two Dunham dancers visiting from New York.

"It started with candles burning and listening to classical music," Dublin recalled, describing the scene that began sometime past midnight. Everyone was drunk, having spent hours in the bars. Sid Shaw, "the Leprechaun," was the first to start dancing, and things heated up almost at once as the Dunham girls coaxed Marlon to play the bongos. Clayton then took over with a dance solo, urging the women to join in on the drums; as stragglers arrived one by one from downtown, the volume grew. Soon the din was echoing through the sandy residential hollow like some end-of-the-summer tribal fest, fueled by jugs of cheap Dago Red.

Summoned by irate neighbors, the police came in through the windows as well as the front door. One of them was John Snow, a part-time summer recruit, a cousin of Clayton, and later a town official, whose widow recalled his description of the pandemonium: "He told me there was no place to go," she said. "People tried to scatter anyway, but not Brando. Instead, he tried to refuse the arrest. But he wasn't expecting this hip cop to be able to handle him, so it got a little violent, and John had to subdue him. Brando was drunk, and the next day they found him to be a far different character."

It was not the first time Marlon had been busted, and his attitude when he and the group were led into court the next morning was blasé. Word of the arrest had spread, and the balconied courtroom in the quaint, white-clapboard town hall was packed. Part of the draw was Judge Robert A. Welch, Provincetown's sitting magistrate for decades. Balding, paunchy, and known for his quixotic humor, Welch would later preside over such cases as the so-called "TraLaLa"–*Provincetown Review* obscenity trial, and would also have a drunken Norman Mailer come before him. Now he was confronted with the bedraggled, bisexual crew that had spent the night in jail, and he began the proceedings by directing the hungover Clayton to give the court a sample of his dancing. Marlon was next. The police had seized the offending bongos, and Brando, never one to pass up a joke, happily complied. The spectators, some barefoot, roared. "It was funnier than hell," remembered one of them. "Welch instructed Brando to give him a sample, and then Brando really got into it. Welch had to tell him to stop three times, banging his gavel."

The next day the group left town, ordered by Welch to take a vacation from his jurisdiction. The sentence was hardly binding, since Brando would continue to return in the following summers up until the early fifties, when his buddy Wally Cox, playing a comedy stint at the A-House, got himself arrested as well by riding his Harley-Davidson up the steps of Town Hall. But in 1945 the miscreant group—Hugh Shannon, Victor Bruno, Sid Shaw, as well as Clayton, Marlon, and Darren—rode out of town together, like six musketeers, on the first bus to New York.

• • •

With his return to the city, Brando continued his *Mama* run, his classes at Dunham's dance school, and his complicated relationships with myriad women, including a resumption of his affairs with both Ellen Adler and Julie Robinson.

Ellen was commuting to the city from Bard and continuing to see him despite her mother's objections—and despite the undisguised affair with Robinson. She never made appearances at the *boules blanches,* however, even though Diamond was going regularly with the actor Canada Lee, and sometimes Stella, too. Presumably she stayed away because Robinson was part of the stage show, but she did make arrangements to see Marlon at friends' apartments or at the Park Savoy, the hotel where he now lived. Julie, meanwhile, had been making demands, pressuring him for "a commitment." Soon he segued into another relationship, however—this one with Dunham's part-time secretary, a white dance student.

"He was going through a lot in terms of what to do about Julie, because they really were in love," Dunham insisted. "Perhaps Marlon just wasn't ready for what she wanted—in a sense, there was Julie waiting at the altar—and he broke it up again. At first she couldn't believe it, she was just knocked out by it. Fortunately, Harry came on the scene."

Harry was calypso singer Harry Belafonte, whom Julie married several years later but was then enrolled at the Dramatic Workshop. However, Marlon wouldn't let go completely, even after Julie embarked on a European dance tour with Katherine Dunham's troupe in 1949. "With dogged, self-diminishing determination," as Dunham put it, he showed up in Cannes to see her—and waited three hours outside the recital hall, swinging from a tree. "He kept a lot of women on the string, and he wasn't going to let go," Dunham added. "He was like a cat with a mouse; he was going to hold on, and the more he could get in his mouth, the more he was going to bite."

In the midst of the social whirl that he kept roiling—probably to alleviate his boredom with *Mama*—he made a fateful decision. Although the production was scheduled to run through June 1946, in February he withdrew from the show to join the cast of Maxwell Anderson's *Truckline Café.*

It was with this role—and not with *A Streetcar Named Desire* a year and a half later—that Brando's career decisively turned the corner. *Mama* had been too star-studded, too bland a vehicle, and if *Truckline* was to prove a flop at the box office, it was still the kind of failure that caught the attention of those who counted. And it would showcase Brando's intensity in a way that no one, including his new agent, Edie Van Cleve, could have expected.

As the first offering of the newly established partnership between Clurman and Elia Kazan, *Truckline* was nothing if not a throwback to the Group, a reminder of the turbulent, "fervent years" gone by. Kazan, or "Gadg," as he was known to friends, had started as an actor in Odets's agit-prop *Waiting for Lefty,* and appeared in *Golden Boy* with John Garfield, Morris Carnovsky, Phoebe Brand, and Luther Adler. As a member of the Group's Communist Party faction, he had been deeply involved in the staging of leftist and antifascist plays for the League of Workers theaters before quitting the party in 1936. A year later he began his directing career. His imaginative staging of Thornton Wilder's *The Skin of Our Teeth,* starring Tallulah Bankhead, Florence Eldridge, Fredric March, and the young Montgomery Clift in 1942 catapulted his career to the top. With the release of his first film, a highly acclaimed adaptation of Betty Smith's best-seller, *A Tree Grows in Brooklyn,* only months before *Truckline,* he had established himself as one of the hottest names both on Broadway and in Hollywood.

Unlike Clurman, Kazan was not a prophet but a tough-minded, intuitive director. Here, he was producing and Clurman was directing. Kazan had never liked nor trusted Stella Adler, and now he found that his partner's wife was pushing Marlon for the small but arresting role of Sage MacRae. "You want to get fucked tonight? Hire him," was the gist of what she was supposedly telling Clurman.

Marlon's audition for Clurman and Kazan was as poor as the one he had done for *Mama.* "Gadg said he couldn't believe anybody could give such a bad reading," said actress Thelma Schnee Moss, later a colleague of Brando's at the Actors Studio. Clurman acknowledged as much, also, but insisted that Brando was "peculiarly arresting." The part was small—about six minutes on the stage—but the intense, violently tormented character of Sage suited Brando perfectly, and Clurman convinced Gadg to sign him up.

Another difficulty arose when Marlon's agent brought Kazan the proposed contract in which the actor was demanding $500 a week.

"I thought Kazan would have a heart attack," Edie Van Cleve recalled, "since he was thinking in terms of $125. After a lot of bickering, I got Marlon $275."

Clurman's personality was undoubtedly a factor in convincing Marlon that he should take the role—like Stella, he could be trusted. Clurman had already brought together an extraordinary cast—Karl Malden, Kevin McCarthy, Lou Gilbert, and Richard Waring—but, more, he treated his actors with respect. The custom along Broadway in those days was that during the first five days of rehearsal, an actor could be fired without breach of contract. Clurman told his actors that he did not believe in the five-day clause. "I hired all of you because I wanted you," he announced. "You're the actors for the role, and nothing will happen five days from now to make that any different."

Even so, there were problems from the start. "I'd heard Harold's first talk to the cast," Kazan recalled. "He was at his best, and his analysis of the play and its meaning was brilliant. The cast was dazzled, as all Harold's casts had been, by the man's insights and his eloquence. But then—what had happened? Very little. The play had been an occasion for Harold to perform. . . . As for the rest of the show, it sunk into a slough and remained there. It was damned dull."

Kazan later blamed Clurman for the play's failure, claiming that he had failed to muscle a satisfactory script out of author Maxwell Anderson. The real difficulty, however, was that neither of them had had the savvy to see that even sophisticated New Yorkers weren't yet ready to spend $3 for an evening's reminder of the war. They wanted *Oklahoma!,* which had been dominating Broadway for the past three years.

Kazan came to every rehearsal, sitting five or six rows back. Sometimes he couldn't restrain himself, and jumped in as second director. Later he admitted he was taking perverse pleasure in what was happening onstage.

"I wouldn't have sat by, being brilliant and adored, while the play failed," Kazan said. "I might have even interfered with the rights of the playwright . . . and fussed with the text. Harold had said, when I'd indicated my impatience with the meager extent of Max's rewriting, 'That's the play. It will succeed or fail, but that's it.' This fatalism I found intolerable."

Clurman was stimulating and colorful, but according to Kevin McCarthy, when it came to the staging they all wished that Kazan would step in and take over. Only rarely did he make comments to the actors, and the most notable of his remarks came during the cast's "dress parade," when everyone first appeared in costume for the set and lighting technicians. Marlon showed up in green fatigues that fit him like tights. Kazan yelled from the orchestra, "I know what you're getting at, Mr. Brando, but just one size larger, please."

"Harold was intellectual theater," commented Kenneth Tobey, another actor in the show, "and Gadg was physical theater. He said, 'Do it'; Harold explained what he wanted done."

As it turned out, however, it was Clurman who helped Marlon to deal with—if not completely solve—his problem of mumbling. In the beginning, when Brando was quiet and apprehensive, Harold took him through readings with only Ann Shepherd, who was playing Sage's wife. The other actors watched and listened, sitting in the usual Clurman semicircle. As in *Mama,* there was a general sense that Brando's work began to improve as soon as he found his legs. He was staying faithful to Stella's method of searching, taking one small step at a time. The work was accurate and detailed, but so muted that nobody could hear him beyond the fifth row.

Clurman asked him to speak up. When there was no response, he began to lose patience. "I can't hear you!" he'd scream. "You've got to be bigger!" Kazan put his two cents' worth in, too. Sitting in the back row of the darkened theater, he shouted, "Stop mumbling! If this thing's going to lose money, I want to hear what I'm losing it on." Maxwell Anderson, leery from the start, was equally frustrated and had begun talking about recasting Brando's part.

Clurman, however, continued trying. The difficulty, as he went on to explain in his book *On Directing,* was that Marlon "could not give vent to the deep well of feeling which I sensed in him. He could not overcome some inner resistance: He would not 'open up.' "

Clurman tried a new ploy. He asked all the actors except Marlon to leave. Then he quietly instructed him to *shout* his lines, including his final monologue in which he confesses drowning his unfaithful wife.

"Brando raised his voice," Clurman later recalled. " 'Louder,' I ordered. He complied. 'Still louder,' I insisted. This was repeated several times, and my command for ever greater vocal volume began to exhaust the actor and to rouse him to visible anger. Then I yelled, 'Climb the rope!' as I pointed to a rope which was hanging from a gridiron above the stage.

Without hesitation he began climbing the rope, while I urged him to keep shouting his lines."

The other members of the cast came running onto the stage, drawn by the alarming shouts.

"When Brando let himself down, he looked as if he were ready to hit me. 'Now,' I said quietly, 'run the scene—normally.' He recovered his poise and did as I bid him. He 'spoke up'—effortlessly. In a few days he played the 'moment' beautifully. On opening night—and every night thereafter—his performance was greeted by one of the most thunderous ovations I have heard for an actor in the theater."

In fact, the breakthrough took a bit longer than Clurman reported. David Diamond occasionally dropped in on the rehearsals, and he recalled that these private sessions extended over several days and went on late into the night, with "an awful lot of shouting from Harold." Marlon retaliated with ever lengthening pauses. Sometimes he played dumb, as he had with Piscator. Or he'd inflect his movement with an insolent, catlike roll of the hips when Clurman told him to turn and walk across the stage.

Karl Malden gave up his lunch break one afternoon to watch from the back row, and the anger he saw was definitely two-edged. Clurman was "prying him open, whipping him to get out of that introverted shell he was in," he said. "Marlon was mad, frustrated as hell, and maybe scared, too. Harold was pulling him into a territory he'd never been in before."

Like a psychic geyser, the energy was ready to explode. Even in the intimate scene between Marlon's character and his wife prior to the murder, Clurman wanted Marlon's voice to be heard throughout the theater. "If you've got it, it can be big!" he kept yelling like a drill sergeant. During one session, Marlon was facing the rear wall, his back to the audience, and in sheer frustration he began shouting his lines, bellowing, "I love you! I love you!"

Brando was ready to rehearse the scene with Ann Shepherd now, and Clurman told her not to answer by rote but only when she actually heard him. With the first run-through, nothing. They tried it again, then again, slowly but surely, until Marlon finally returned to his shouting. For Kevin McCarthy, as mesmerized as anyone in the theater, "the change was so incredibly remarkable, I couldn't get over it."

The "murder monologue" was emerging as the centerpiece of the production, and here Kazan offered rare directorial advice to Marlon.

"Before you come out," he told him, "I want you to get yourself out of breath—run in place offstage. Then I'm going to have a bucket of water thrown over you just as you're about to come on." Marlon's contribution was to use his hands. As he told the waitress character that he had shot his wife six times, he banged his fist on the table for each shot. "It was a big, round table," said one of the cast who was watching, "and he broke it in half."

Another bit of inventiveness had to do with his entrance into the roadside café. Richard Waring, the more experienced actor, noticed that Marlon appeared onstage with an "unscripted" handkerchief. "What are you doing?" he asked. Marlon said, "Oh, see, I figured that heading along with the car, I got oil on myself and I'm just rubbing it off."

Brando was equally attentive to detail when he sought Waring's advice after the play's out-of-town opening in Baltimore.

Waring saw Brando pacing outside the dressing rooms in the basement of the Ford Theatre. Sensing that Marlon was upset, Waring asked him what the matter was. "I didn't get a hand on that exit."

His exit, Waring knew, came after he said, "Are you looking for me?" and turned himself over to the police, not an especially opportune moment for applause.

"Are you really worried about that?" Waring asked.

"Yes, I should get a hand."

"Look, Marlon," Waring advised. "In *Romeo and Juliet*, when Mercutio is carried off after he dies, he gets a tremendous hand from the audience. But the greatest compliment is *not* to get a hand. When there's complete silence, it means that the audience is so wrapped up."

"Yeah, yeah," he said, "but I'd still like to get the hand."

"All right," said the veteran, "you know what you're doing wrong? You have a scene where you say what you've done and you hit the table six times, then go to the trooper and say, 'Are you looking for me?' He says, 'Jesus, yes!' Instead of exiting, you should stop and turn around to the waitress and say, 'Thanks for the coffee.' Then say to the trooper, 'Okay, I'm ready,' and go out with him."

The next time he added the line "Thanks for the coffee. Okay, I'm ready," and sure enough, he got his hand.

"He played the scene like that from then on," explained Waring. "What he was doing was deflating himself in order to go properly with the trooper. The point was that he would take anything, any advice that he felt was worthwhile, and it was all the more impressive after the shouting he'd had to go through for Clurman."

After a month of rehearsals and two weeks of tryouts, *Truckline Café* opened at the Belasco Theatre in New York on February 27, 1946. The reviews were so devastating that eight days later the show closed after only ten performances.

Even though the "victory season" of 1945–46 had been inhospitable to war plays, none was criticized as harshly as *Truckline*. John Chapman of the New York *Daily News* wrote that it was the worst play he had seen since becoming a critic, while the *New York Times* announced that "Maxwell Anderson must have written *Truckline Café* with his left hand and . . . in the dark of the moon." *Cue,* in comparison, was positively benign in calling it boring, old-fashioned, and contrived. The notices left the company in a state of shock, all the more so since the opening-night audience had responded with standing ovations.

Neither Clurman nor Kazan had reckoned on such devastating notices. They decided to break the rules by running an ad, addressed "to the theatergoing public," in the pages of the *New York Times.* The critics, they announced, are "more and more acquiring powers which, as a group, they are not qualified to exercise—either by their training or by their taste." Maxwell Anderson followed up with his own broadside in the *Herald Tribune:* "The public is far better qualified to judge plays than the men who write reviews for our dailies. It is an insult to our theater that there should be so many incompetents and irresponsible among them. [They] bring to the theater nothing but their own hopelessness, recklessness, and despair."

The goal was to sway public opinion, and to a certain extent they succeeded; for almost a week afterward the dispute continued in various articles and letters to the editor in the local press, and while the controversy didn't keep the play afloat, it made *Truckline* the talk of the town, with Brando the center of attention. In the theater community—working actors, directors, producers, scenarists, stage managers, and agents, and even the money interests downing martinis at "21"—Marlon was being compared to Montgomery Clift and heralded as one of the hottest new talents around.

"From an actor's point of view," Martin Balsam explained, "what you saw was the elements of truth being done up on that stage. He was being as honest, as close to reality as possible. You knew you were being arrested in midair."

Jessica Tandy, too, had only the highest praise: "He was brilliant. When he came into the café, the whole thing sort of lit up. There was no question, you looked at him and said, 'He's going somewhere.' "

"He came through like a bolt of lightning," recalled Karl Malden. "It was a monologue, a good page of script, why he killed his wife. In fifty years in the business, I've never seen it happen before, and it's never happened since: He stopped the show. Nobody could continue for over a minute and a half, two minutes. The audience shouted, they screamed, they stamped their feet."

An even bigger compliment came from Sarah Adler, the family matriarch, who had not previously been all that impressed. "Marlon," she told him one evening, "if you want, you can change your name to Adler."

Outwardly, he took his success in stride. While the play was still running, he usually needed about five minutes to cool down after his crescendo-like monologue, and he'd go into seclusion offstage, trying to distance himself from his character. "He was drained, he didn't want to talk to anybody." said Kenneth Tobey. "But it was a triumph for him, you could tell. He'd just stand there quietly and grin at you, then challenge you to Indian wrestling."

Like so many other things with Marlon, the playfulness was a deflection, but friends in the inner circle saw what was happening very clearly. One night he came into Sardi's, looking for Stella, who was sitting with David Diamond and Kermit Bloomgarden, the producer. "We were all sitting at this table," Diamond recalled. "Stella saw him and immediately beckoned him over: 'How's my beautiful, wonderful genius? Come here!' Everybody knew who he was, and he took it as though it were the most natural thing in the world. No shifting around, no discomfort as you'd see with Monty. He dragged Blossom over, and embraced Stella. As usual, she had one of her goddamn hats on, and I can still see him getting caught in her veil."

He seemed to adore it because she made him feel that he was part of the great acting world. "Why do you think they were so close?" Diamond insisted. "Because it began with a sexual passion? Nonsense. She put him on a pedestal and kept him there."

He wasn't scanning the casting-call notices in *Actors Cues,* the predecessor of *Backstage,* nor did he make the rounds, trying to sell himself like other young actors. He had Van Cleve, Adler, Clurman, Bobby Lewis, and now the news was out: He was "the actor's actor," and the freedom to resist the need to be liked was the best part of it. "It was like Stella—she's a control freak, too," said one observer. "I mean, if you open your door and people are hanging around like flies, that's gotta tell you something."

He knew what he had by way of allure, and would appear at the Russian Tea Room in Levi's and a white dress shirt that was visibly ripped, once with the collar torn off. Invited to ritzy parties, he might show up wearing sneakers and an old raincoat, and not speak to anybody the entire time. "I don't remember ever having a serious conversation about the theater," said Fred Sadoff, a fellow actor and close friend of Maureen Stapleton and Jocelyn. "There was this quality of something always withheld, so he created this mystique and we didn't really make an effort to crack the shell."

Apparent indifference was his hole card. He knew that he didn't fit into any established category, any designative casting type other than "the poetic," and when he'd touch himself in public, kneading his flesh above the chest, or sometimes on the nape of the neck as though he were a Tuscan model, it only left people more bewildered than before—indeed, more bewitched. Vulnerability, loneliness, inaccessibility, all were part of his appeal, and his fey, injured looks pulled people in, inexorably lending credence to the notion that charisma always demands audience participation.

"It was like when Marilyn came to New York," said Eli Wallach, Monroe's costar and friend. "All the men around her thought, She only looks to me to rescue her and to educate her. Pygmalion-like, I will do it. It wasn't Marlon seeking out these people; these people were magnetized by the whole thing."

Even at Stella's, he'd lapse into one of his Rodin poses, and Diamond would tell him, "Marlon, get your hand off your hip." "He'd always be leaning against something, and if it were the piano, say, he'd sort of lean back, or he'd be caressing his buttock or playing with his ear. Or while he's listening to you, he'd be looking at his fingers."

Once, he asked, "David, do you think I'm what one would call handsome? Do you think I'm as good-looking as Monty?"

Clift was on everyone's tongue since *The Skin of Our Teeth* three and a half years earlier. Kevin McCarthy had already introduced Marlon to him, setting in motion a contest that would last for years until they played opposite each other in *The Young Lions* in 1957. Clift was twenty-six, Marlon four years younger.

"Monty was living in the city at that point," said McCarthy, "and Marlon was aware that he was a big star. Monty was aware that Marlon was somebody to be watchful of. At the heart of it was that Marlon didn't understand the meticulous way Monty worked, which was sort of colder. Monty knew what he was doing at all times—he was much more analytic. Not that he wasn't full of emotion, but it was approached intellectually. Marlon, I think, acted out of some innate understanding. It wasn't studied, it just *happened*—and so he thought that Monty was uptight."

Relying on his intuition, Brando had even said that he felt Stella was too technical, that she made her students self-conscious. He objected to Monty's studied technique, and he told McCarthy that he thought his friend Monty "walks around like he's got a Mixmaster up his ass." "Whenever the two of them appeared at parties, it was really something," said a girl who was on the scene at the time. "You didn't know whom to look at first. Marlon had such basic animal magnetism that he stopped conversation when he entered a group. Monty, meanwhile, was elegance personified."

Even Ellen Adler agreed. "I was around sixteen," she said, "and I think we went to somebody's apartment after the theater for drinks. Monty was there with some other people, and we got to talking. He was so polite and charming, always with the match for the cigarette. Marlon stood it for as long as he could, and then he came barging over and pulled me away. 'She's my Jew, Monty!' he roared. Monty just grinned and shrugged."

Now, however, David Diamond answered Marlon's question about who was the better-looking. "Marlon, there hasn't been anyone on the Broadway stage since Monty," he told him, "and he didn't have the vehicle you've had. What you've got is balls, which Monty doesn't have."

"Marlon looked at me," Diamond added, "and did that jig he had, a way of balancing himself with his hands on his hips. Then he said, 'Tell me more.'"

Even as he maintained his own self-contained isolation, he could also make the best of friends feel as if they were "phony, unreal, untruthful, as if he alone had a lock on the truth," said Fred Sadoff. Sadoff had played Marlon's role of Sage MacRae in the Neighborhood Playhouse production three months after *Truckline* bombed on Broadway; Marlon came to the performance and said nothing, even when the two shared a crosstown cab ride afterward.

"He came because I was a friend and maybe also he was making comparisons," Sadoff explained. "But his whole attitude—and this was before *Streetcar*—was not exactly smug, because he's not a smug man, but self-important. He was so sure of himself. Nobody was as good as he in anything. Never saying a word about my performance, though, was cruel. We were all a little frightened of him, and it was a game he played. He was always controlling. Whatever he needed—if he was lonely, whatever the reason—he would show up as if he was making a guest appearance. If we were having a conversation and he didn't like what we were talking about, he'd leave or change the subject. He'd never involve himself in something where he wasn't the center."

Nevertheless, his acts of kindness, his charming courtesies, continued: He had sent Richard Waring an opening night thank-you note for his help on *Truckline*, and he often visited Kevin McCarthy and his wife to squat on the floor and play with their infant son. He could always be counted on for a handout, either to pals or bums on the street.

As *Truckline* ended its brief run, Marlon started to consider another play. Guthrie McClintic, husband of Katharine Cornell, then the First Lady of the American stage, had been looking for a young actor to cast as Marchbanks in his upcoming revival of Shaw's *Candida*. Originally, McClintic had wanted Richard Waring, Marlon's *Truckline* costar, but once he had seen Brando's Sage MacRae, he became an enthusiastic admirer of the younger actor and actively pursued him.

The Cornell-McClintic team had staged its first and much acclaimed production of *Candida* in 1924. While on an armed forces tour in Europe, Miss Cornell had seen Jean Anouilh's *Antigone,* and she envisioned it as a companion piece to *Candida*. The plan was to play the two alternately, both in New York and on the road, including two weeks in Chicago. In addition to Marchbanks, Marlon would do the small part of the messenger in *Antigone*.

An invitation to play with Cornell was like a membership offer from the most prestigious of clubs. Her past work with Laurence Olivier and Sir Cedric Hardwicke guaranteed the attention of the city's first-string critics.

It was also the kind of role any young actor would give his eyeteeth for—even though the character of Marchbanks, the tortured young poet in love with the married Candida, had been indelibly fixed in the public mind by Burgess Meredith four years earlier. As usual, Marlon's response when he was approached was to prevaricate. What worried him most was that his accent might fail him. He spoke to Stella, to Mady Christians, and to others, including David Diamond. All tried to reassure him. "It was the first time he was intimidated by other actors," Diamond recalled, "specifically Kit Cornell."

He may have been unsure of himself, but when McClintic asked if he would mind auditioning, Marlon replied, "No, not at all, if you wouldn't mind showing me a little bit of your direction." There was no audition, and Brando finally accepted the role.

Just why he agreed to go ahead was unclear, although Edie Van Cleve was certainly pushing him. By now the genteel, almost motherly, mainline Van Cleve had won his confidence. Rumor had it that Clift was interested in the role, but more important (despite Brando's disparagement of acting and his insistent blue-collar brio), he knew that appearing in a Shaw play would stretch him. George Bernard Shaw was "class," and there is also probably no underestimating Dodie's influence, since she had always held Shaw up as one of the great playwrights and had often read aloud from *Man and Superman* and *Heartbreak House* during Marlon's childhood. The fact that Hardwicke, slated for the role of Burgess, was the playwright's personal actor of choice and the foremost proponent of Shavian social and economic values meant something, too.

Rehearsals had started almost at once, within a week of *Truckline*'s demise on March 10, 1946. Now committed, Marlon was on his best behavior. He was punctual, he deferred to his elders, and took tea at the McClintic-Cornell town house on Beekman Place, where he listened to the veterans explain their view of the play. McClintic and Cornell, as well as Mildred Natwick, who was also there, knew that Brando was a different kind of talent. Professionally and otherwise, what they were seeing—indeed, concentrating on—was Marlon's "poetic" half. "Oh, I know what you expect me to say, but it's wrong," Cornell commented when later asked about these preparatory sessions. "He was the gentlest, nicest, hardest-working. He was always wonderful, and I looked forward to seeing what he would do."

Two days after the troupe arrived in Chicago for the first tryout, Brando "just lapsed." Part of it was girls, old standbys like Sheila Petry, who came down from Lake Bluff and Libertyville to see him. Natwick recognized that he was "sort of goofing around mentally," and during one of the last run-throughs Cedric Hardwicke came bounding offstage, fuming at Brando's inattention. McClintic blew up, too, although this was mainly for show. "He saw that Marlon needed a jacking up, so he gave him this big scene of anger," said Natwick, "and it had its intended effect. Marlon pulled himself together and promptly learned his lines."

For the opening in Chicago, Dodie was in the audience, and according to Natwick, a timeless pro, his performance was "just marvelous." Marlon Sr. saw him, too, and voiced his approval, apparently hopeful that his son might yet amount to something.

Even so, this was Shaw, not naturalism, and with the company's return to New York, his performances became uneven again. Somehow he couldn't fill the part. His voice failed to reach even the middle rows of the house. Carlo Fiore recalled sitting with Elaine Stritch, watching him enter "way off the beat. He seemed horrified to find himself onstage," he said. Looking deathly pale, Marlon sat down on a sofa and fidgeted. "He didn't speak for so long that the actors exchanged nervous glances." The prompter could be heard from the wings whispering his lines, then loudly repeating them. Carlo added, "Elaine and I slid down in our seats, held hands, and squeezed hard in agony." No one knew whether Marlon was only acting terrified, for effect, or actually too scared to speak. "Marlon drew in the reins on his scattered concentration, gained more and more confidence, and gradually, almost inch by inch, he slipped into the skin of the character." The crisis passed, and the poet Marchbanks began to emerge.

Afterward, in his dressing room, Stritch asked Brando if he'd been stricken with stage fright, as it appeared.

"I sure was," he said, grinning. "It's a good thing the character was supposed to enter scared shitless. I used my stage fright and incorporated it in the part."

But he still seemed disconnected to the character, the ethereal Marchbanks, and reviewers were evenly divided about his performance. Lewis Nichols of the *Times* wrote, "Marlon Brando gives a Marchbanks which is more weak than poetic, more sniveling than spirited. . . . [He] emphasizes the weakness and banks the fire, the result being a somewhat monoto-nously intoning poet." *Variety* summed up the performance as "remark-able," however, and John Chapman of the *Daily News* claimed that he "managed to make something different, something more understandable out of the trying role of Marchbanks, the baby poet."

Clurman, however, gave the performance a thumbs-down. The voice of Solomon himself, Harold had gone backstage opening night and said, "Good try, Marlon!" For Brando, this dismissal cut deep, amounting as it did to another swipe at his lack of education. Clurman would later feel that Brando never forgave him for the put-down. *Candida* lasted for twenty-four performances.

Finding himself unemployed in June 1946, Brando nonetheless turned down Noel Coward's lighthearted *Present Laughter*, telling the suave British playwright, "Don't you know there are people starving in Europe?" He also added to Broadway lore by reciting "Hickory Dickory Dock" while auditioning before Alfred Lunt and Lynn Fontanne for *O Mistress Mine*. A lot of his erratic behavior was due to fatigue. Since opening in *I Remember Mama* in the fall of 1944, Brando had worked almost nonstop for nearly two years. But Stella had given him a mission, and de-spite his innate laziness, he seemed far more committed to her whole "high-art point of view" than any of his later disparagements of acting would indicate.

Imbued with her leftist values, he had in fact turned down an offer of $3,000 a week from MGM, a seven-year contract personally tendered by Louis B. Mayer himself. There was also an offer from another studio that gave him his pick of scripts—first six, then eight; likewise, he rejected overtures from the famous producer Hal Wallis. Edie Van Cleve had to mollify Lew Wasserman, the emerging power at MCA, explaining that Brando's terms—no giddy comedies, no glitzy romances, no DeMille spec-tacles—"were excessive and premature," but that there was nothing that could be done about it. "I said that if we tried high-pressure tactics," she recalled, "we would assuredly lose him, which we couldn't afford, since some day he'd bring the agency millions."

If movies weren't high enough art and he would remain disinterested, Brando's next role, in *A Flag Is Born*, was swathed in genuine purpose from the start. Even in its early "talking" stages, this propaganda pageant by Ben Hecht had captivated New York's progressive community almost as much as antiwar benefits would galvanize artists, musicians, and students in the late 1960s.

It was now the fall of 1946. With the end of the war, Jews the world over were demanding that the gates of Palestine be opened for Holocaust survivors, while the British government, with its territorial mandate, was impeding immigration. The Haganah—the armed forces of the Jewish Agency—responded by launching an illegal smuggling operation. Often, their small boats were met by the destroyers of the Royal Navy, and passengers were sent to detention camps on the island of Cyprus. With the crematoriums of Auschwitz and Bergen-Belsen barely extinguished, feeling was running high.

As in all fights for national liberation, there was considerable factionalism: The American League for a Free Palestine supported the Irgun Zeva'i Le'ummi, the small but militant anti-British militia headed by Menachem Begin, while the majority of American Zionists sided with the more moderate Haganah. The Irgun's small mission in the United States, headed by Peter Bergson, was now engaged in a bold and imaginative propaganda campaign, and managed to win the support of many antiestablishment Jews as well as non-Jewish politicians and intellectuals. The Adlers—Stella, Luther, and Celia—supported the Bergson group wholeheartedly, as did Billy Rose, Harpo Marx, Will Rogers Jr., Leonard Bernstein, Maxwell Anderson, and even Eleanor Roosevelt. The group's most important recruit was Ben Hecht, Hollywood's best-paid screenwriter, the winner of three Academy Awards, and coauthor with Charles MacArthur of such Broadway hits as *The Front Page* and *Twentieth Century*.

Already Hecht had collaborated with Kurt Weill and Moss Hart on a gigantic memorial pageant for the first 2 million Jewish victims of Nazism, which had been staged in Madison Square Garden with Paul Muni and Edward G. Robinson. Now, with the struggle for independence in Palestine intensifying, the Bergson group's attempts to raise funds for repatriation and the purchase of arms included another Hecht show, *A Flag Is Born*. Weill would contribute the music.

Crudely didactic, the play centers on Tevya and Zelda, survivors of the Treblinka death camp who have lost their ten children to the gas chambers. Wishing to get to Palestine, they stop in a Jewish cemetery, where they meet another survivor, the young David, bitter, cynical, and the exact opposite of Tevya. While Tevya and David argue about their future, they recall Judaism's past glory and watch the biblical kings Saul and Solomon appear as dreamy visions behind a scrim. The play alternates between the past and present, then shifts to the graveyard, where Judaism is being "killed" and where both Tevya and Zelda finally die of exhaustion and despair. David, representing the future of the Jews, is about to commit suicide when he hears the singing of the resistance fighters in Palestine. They call upon him to join in their fight for freedom. Picking up the prayer shawl covering Tevya's dead body, he adds a Star of David in the center, and to the sound of "Hatikvah," the Zionist anthem, he prophetically waves the newborn flag of the Jewish state, heralding the triumph of Israel.

Hecht had chosen Luther Adler to direct *A Flag Is Born*. It was to be his directorial debut, and it was he who brought Marlon into it.

"I'm sure Luther must have approached Marlon about playing the role of David," added Ellen Adler. "People had already taken a great deal of notice of him because of *Truckline*, and everybody in the theater world knew about his talent. Stella was always suggesting Marlon for roles, and when Luther asked, 'Do you think he can play this?' Stella replied, 'He can play anything.' "

The pageant itself was cornball stuff of the highest order, but for the first time in his career, Brando was openly eager to take on an acting assignment. "I knew that this play meant a great deal to him," Ellen explained. "He was always interested in what it is that makes Jewish people what they are. Plus he wanted to do the part because of his extraordinary compassion. And he had already heard these discussions about the Irgun at our apartment."

There was nothing cagey about it, no ploys, no games. He had acknowledged to both Ellen and Stella that he "felt" Jewish, and since most of his friends were Jews—Darren, Igor Tamarin, Sam Gilman, and the comic Milt Kamin, not to mention brother-in-law Dick Loving and Dodie's close friend, David Salinger—it wasn't cultural or political so much as "family." Tevya was to be played by the great technician Paul Muni, who had started his career as Muni Weisenfreund on the Yiddish stage, then set movie marquees ablaze with *Scarface* and *I Am a Fugitive from a Chain Gang*. The part of Zelda was given to Stella's sister, Celia. The narrator was Quentin Reynolds, one of America's most famous war journalists, who would eventually be replaced by Stella herself when the show moved on to Philadelphia.

It was practically the whole *mishpocheh,* and now his talents could be put to work on behalf of a recognizable cause. Yet Brando's own politics were fuzzy, to say the least. He rarely read the newspapers, and compared to the left-wing sophisticates in whose company he often found himself at Stella's, his understanding of the issues was crude, without background or historical context. He had supported the Scottsboro Boys and also backed progressive candidates in Actors' Equity, but according to Earl Hammond, a friend and radio actor who was involved with Bergson in the buying of illegal guns, Marlon really didn't *think.*

His political reactions were like his response to Beethoven or Stravinsky—untutored and instinctual. With the politics of *Flag,* it was the heroism of the resistance fighters in Palestine that fascinated him. Hecht, whose newspaper training had developed his sure gift for narrative, made the stories of Jewish courage sound like tales of the Knights of the Round Table. Marlon had already met Bergson and was taken with how the small, feisty Irgun agent and his six-foot blonde girlfriend had been ducking the FBI. Moved by the fact that Hecht and Weill had announced they were giving up all their royalties, like Luther and Muni, he now agreed to take only the Equity minimum of $60 a week. The receipts of the show were to be used for the purchase of boats to smuggle the dispossessed back into their homeland.

As rehearsals began in the bare studio above Al & Dick's Restaurant on West Fifty-fourth Street, Marlon's usual pattern reasserted itself. He was slow and hesitant, and given the combustible atmosphere of "all these crazy Jews," it wasn't long before his mumbling drove Luther to consult with Hecht and then with Muni, too. Although Stella was often away that summer, Ellen was at rehearsals every day. "I was supposed to be Luther's assistant," she explained, "but that was just a way of being around Marlon. I really don't remember the other actors' performances, because I was young and I was only looking at Marlon all the time. Still, I do remember there were problems with Ben Hecht. He was such a big bossy guy. But the problems with Marlon were because he was a tremendous tease and an extremely playful actor."

As playful as Marlon might have been, even the feisty Hecht was beginning to have doubts about his mumbling and his hesitancies. One afternoon Hecht got up on the stage and acted out a scene himself—in effect, throwing down a challenge. Marlon, unable to hide his low opinion of the performance, replied with a rendition that finally went over the top.

"He was fantastic," Luther later recalled. "Marlon uncorked, and Muni suddenly thought he had a tiger by the tail. Brando was incredible: flash, violence, electricity. My sister Celia has owl eyes, but when she opens them in astonishment, they're like saucers. When Brando started to perform, Celia's eyes became soup bowls. Muni turned scarlet. His lips began to tremble; then he got a kind of foolish grin of approval on his face."

Ellen Adler recalled the moment, too, that Marlon took flight. She had been sitting at her uncle's side when, she said, "I noticed that he was shaking. Then I realized that in fact he was sobbing, because Marlon had released so much and the acting was extraordinary. Then I went back to Marlon's dressing room, and he had locked the door, because he was angry about his performance. He wouldn't let me in, he was so upset. He felt he had let go too much and had lost control."

In later years Marlon would link Muni with Spencer Tracy and Cary Grant as one of the few actors "you can learn from." Observing Marlon, Muni asked, "How the hell can an actor like that come from Omaha, Nebraska?" Muni was already past fifty and had "moments of great warmth and charm," as Luther put it, and his and Marlon's mutual respect continued to grow. "There was none of Marlon's 'fuck you' attitude with Muni, the kind of stuff he reserved for the establishment," said William Allyn, another young actor taking part.

After the play's opening, Brando related how the bearded veteran actor had suggested that he not cover the whole of Tevya's corpse with the prayer shawl, but instead leave the face of the dead Jew exposed for stronger dramatic effect. The next performance, Marlon forgot. He covered Muni completely and began his speech, when suddenly the *talis* began crawling down Muni's forehead, exposing his face inch by inch. "I was afraid I'd break up," he said, recalling that Muni was pulling the prayer shawl down by gathering folds of the cloth in his fist. "I stopped in the middle of the speech, kneeled, pulled the flag away from his face, and tucked it tenderly under his chin. His expression was beatific. Imagine! He was supposed to be dead but he was still acting. If the curtain hadn't come down, he'd have acted out all the stages of rigor mortis setting in."

The play premiered on September 5, 1946, at the Alvin Theatre on Fifty-second Street. Dodie arrived from Chicago and stayed at Stella's so that she could go to the opening. Everybody who was anybody, even Frank Sinatra, was at the party at Toots Shor's afterward. Brooks Atkinson, dean of the city's critics, was ecstatic, expressing "profound gratitude" for Muni's performance, which he called one of the highlights of his career. Celia Adler got raves, too. And Robert Garland of the *Journal American* dubbed Brando the "bright particular star" of the show.

As in *Truckline Café*, he had one earth-shattering speech, where he addressed the audience directly, screaming at the top of his lungs, "You let six million *die!*" The scene was like an electric shock that "just cut through you with true emotion," said Marlon's friend from the New School, Jack Bittner. "The whole audience sort of rose up, en masse. You could feel them reacting."

Jocelyn's response was less articulate, for she fled the Alvin in tears: "Bud was lifting the flag up, his back to the audience.... It was unforgettable. I get a lump right now," she recalled years later. "His back was so expressive that I ran into the subway and cried all the way home."

Even the normally cynical, rambunctious Darren was swept away, so moved that he broke his long-standing silence on the subject of acting and asked Marlon how he'd done it.

"I never knew what inner process he went through in preparation," Darren explained, "but this one performance he was so involved . . . that I asked him afterward, 'What were you thinking about?' Because you know, as an actor you can't relate to six million people whom you don't know, so you take something personal. His answer? 'I was thinking about the police beating up on Negroes around Times Square.' "

Every night Brando stole the show with his emotional, angry monologue. During one performance, when he gave the speech "Where were you when the killing was done?" Ellen Adler recalled that "one Jew got so upset he stood up and called out, 'Where were *you?*' " Each evening brought another standing ovation, and most of the audience was moved to fill out the blank checks that the American League for a Free Palestine had inserted in the program. Once the play's road tour was over, the combined receipts from contributions and ticket sales came to almost $400,000, which went to purchase a small boat in France. The boat, named the SS *Ben Hecht,* was credited with taking some 500 refugees from Europe to Palestine.

The success of *A Flag Is Born* surpassed even the most optimistic expectations, and special arrangements had to be made to extend the run beyond the first month. Muni was scheduled to return to Hollywood, and was replaced by Luther himself. Marlon had been offered a part in Kazan's new film, *Gentleman's Agreement*, but he hesitated, saying, "No, these people are being persecuted, they need help," perhaps unaware that *Gentleman's Agreement* was in fact about Jews and anti-Semitism. But Hecht got wind of his dilemma and sent a cable: "THE JEWS HAVE BEEN PERSECUTED FOR THREE THOUSAND YEARS. THEY LIKE IT. TAKE THE JOB." Marlon left the show and was replaced by Sidney Lumet. The part in Kazan's film, however, went to John Garfield, who would later lose out to Brando for the role of Stanley Kowalski in *Streetcar*.

Marlon's involvement with "the cause" was far from done, though, and he soon found himself in a program that trained actors to raise funds for the Irgun at local synagogues. He was his usual bored, irritating self, but nonetheless shed "real tears," said Bernie Herold, one of program's founders, as some of the more impassioned trainees ran through their routine. Brando's friend Igor Tamarin was in the program, too, and after a week's training the two were assigned a string of synagogues in Brooklyn. Commuting back and forth from the sublet they were now sharing in the Village, they lasted slightly more than a week.

"He was the goy and I was the real Jew," Tamarin said, explaining that their routine consisted of Marlon's coming out first to get the audience "all riled up with the emotional speech," then turning the stage over to his partner for the more extended historical spiel, which was then followed by the collection plate. The evening when things got out of hand, Marlon decided to depart from their script.

"He's doing his number, see, and there are several hundred *alte kochehs* in the audience. As I walked out on stage, though," recalled Tamarin, "he looked at me and sort of smiled, then turned back. 'The dates he's going to give you about Irgun and so on,' he said, 'well, it's all *bullshit*.' I almost died, but I couldn't stop him. 'I mean, he *thinks* he knows but . . .' I tried to save the situation by interrupting and saying to the audience, 'This is no place to joke, but, you know, he's a comic. The facts remain . . .' But these people were scandalized. They were getting up from their seats and walking out, five or ten at a time, so I turned back to Marlon. 'Marlon, please,' I begged him, 'stop 'em. I don't want to lose 'em, not this way, Marlon. Tell them to stay.' 'I ain't gonna tell 'em nothing.' "

Outside, after Marlon had emptied the temple, Tamarin complained that they were going to get fired. "You realize we got no more money?" he said.

"Oh, we'll get it," Marlon replied, now on a manic high. "Fuck 'em. Who cares?"

Brando wasn't unemployed for long. Van Cleve had heard that Tallulah Bankhead was looking for a leading man for her upcoming show, *The Eagle Has Two Heads.* However much the reviews were split over Marlon's lovesick Marchbanks, he had worked with Cornell, and now Tallulah saw him as the perfect Stanislas, the impassioned poet-revolutionary in Jean Cocteau's melodrama of a nineteenth-century queen of Graustarkian ancestry assassinated by her new lover. In a thirty-minute monologue Bankhead, as the queen, was to persuade the handsome poet to fall in love with her. But then when she was to brush off his advances, causing the poet to lose control, he shoots her and then himself.

The script could hardly have appealed to Marlon, but what troubled him even more was Bankhead's temperamental, hard-drinking reputation. Hers was the kind of self-centered, operatic behavior that he detested in women. She had already done *The Little Foxes* and appeared with Clift, Fran Heflin, and Fredric March in Kazan's widely praised *The Skin of Our Teeth.* At forty-three, she had recently broken up with her polished leading man and lover, Donald Cook, and it was rumored that she expected her new costar to fill in as her bedmate.

Marlon's major concern, though, was their professional incompatibility. Tallulah worked in the "star style," as far from the Group tradition as possible. When she spoke, nobody else was to move, yet he liked to live on the stage, to walk around and be part of the room. For Tallulah the stage was a showcase, *her* showcase. "They come to see *me,*" she'd always say, and Bobby Lewis, her friend and neighbor, was not alone in claiming that she "didn't give a fuck" about the play itself.

Genuinely anxious, in November 1946 Marlon took his problem to Lewis, who was at his country house in Pound Ridge, less than a mile down the road from Bankhead's estate, Windows.

He arrived hours late for the lunch meeting, and with Blossom Plumb at his side. His girlfriend eventually disappeared inside the house, and Lewis and Brando sat on the terrace, the latter smoking constantly while he tried to explain his worries.

"We discussed the possible problems Marlon would have acting with Tallulah," Lewis later wrote in his engaging memoirs, *Slings and Arrows.* "Since they employed widely different methods of work, and since they both had unshakable independence of spirit, a clash of personalities was a distinct possibility."

Brando's concern wasn't over "career" so much as how to handle "this bitch, this termagant, this vixen," and Lewis's advice was to insist on a two-week "out" clause that would allow him to leave the show—if necessary, even before it came to New York.

Their talk finished, Lewis drove Marlon over to Tallulah's. At her doorstep, instead of saying hello, Brando queried, "Are you an alcoholic?"

"No, darling, just a heavy drinker," she replied grandiloquently, leading him into the living room. According to Brando's account to Lewis later, it wasn't long before she had her hand inside his jeans. "What did you do?" Lewis asked him. "Well, I was interested in it from an engineering point of view," Brando told him, pointing out that she'd started at the bottom, with his cuff. "I wanted to see if it was possible to get all the way up through that route because usually people unzip your fly. But you know," he added, "it is."

Tallulah wasn't to be deterred by Brando's indifference to her invitation. Back in the city, the never-say-die Tallulah arrived at his apartment a week or so later wrapped in a full-length mink. As she made a grand entrance, she tearfully announced, "Oh, Marlon, my whole life has been one rejection. They use me for what they can, then it's rejection, rejection, rejection." After twenty minutes of "rejection, rejection, rejection," she rose to her feet and dramatically opened the mink to reveal that she wasn't wearing anything underneath. "Now, what should I do?" she asked. Without missing a beat, Marlon gave her a quick glance and then replied, "Well, there's the window. Why don't you commit suicide?"

"He said all kinds of cruel things to her," Lewis conceded, "but with Tallulah there was no way of being honest except by being cruel." When *Eagle* went into rehearsal, Marlon's war with Tallulah only escalated. Bankhead couldn't stand the smell of peanuts, so Brando ate handfuls of peanuts before each of their scenes. She repeatedly phoned him, tracking him down at Maureen Stapleton's apartment, where he would take her long, breathless calls by tucking the telephone receiver in his pocket, every so often pulling it out to say "Uh-huh," then tucking it back in. He dubbed her "Alcohol Breath." He complained constantly, and went around telling everyone from Dick Loving to the show's stagehands, "She lets her dog fuck her, lets him lick her off."

Eagle opened in Washington, D.C., on December 2, 1946. During Tallulah's soliloquy—possibly the longest in the history of drama—Marlon was supposed to stand still, looking at her as he listened. According to Richard Maney, Tallulah's press agent and ghostwriter, "he squirmed. He picked his nose. He adjusted his fly. He leered at the audience. He cased the furniture. He fixed his gaze on an offstage property man instead of his opponent." But these antics were nothing compared to the stunt he pulled at the end. On cue he shot the queen, then watched her pitch headlong down the stairway. The script then called for him to shoot himself and die quickly. But in defiance of Cocteau and everything they had rehearsed, instead of falling to the floor, he staggered about the stage, hamming up a prolonged agony of a dying man.

Playing Cocteau's high melodrama as slapstick, he had the audience in hysterical laughter. Spread-eagled on the stairway, Tallulah was beside herself. "Why wouldn't this misbegotten clown cash in his chips?" the dutiful Maney wrote of the upstaging. "Marlon had been mooning about for a full minute on the apron when suddenly he collapsed as if spiked by an invisible ray. If Tallulah could have gotten her hands on a gun, the coroner would have had a customer then and there."

It continued throughout subsequent performances. Tallulah placed spies out in the audience to report if Marlon was acting or gesturing behind her back in scenes where she couldn't keep her eye on him. To no avail. Several nights later she was coming down the staircase center stage, delivering the line, "What is a queen? A shadow in an evening dress," and he stepped on the train of the evening cloak that was tied at her neck. The grandiose Tallulah did not fall, she just gagged loudly when the neck collar pulled sharply against her throat. Again the audience roared. That same evening there was what came to be known as "the gun episode." The prop man had forgotten to load the assassination weapon with blanks, and when Marlon fired, there was nothing but a long silence. The seconds ticked by, then he improvised: "Snip, snip."

At the end of the Washington run, one night Marlon developed an itch inside his boot during her endless monologue and was heading toward it with his hand very, very slowly. He finally got there and scratched just as the curtain was about to fall. Tallulah turned on him and yelled hysterically, "I suppose if it were your cock, you'd do the same thing!"

As the show moved on to Boston, wags in New York were already dubbing it *The Turkey Has Two Heads*. Van Cleve was getting calls from Marlon almost daily, imploring her to get him released from the contract. Bankhead's opening speech was now clocked at thirty minutes, thanks to her attempt to enliven the scene by taking a fall down the stairs, what the critic John Lardner called "a plunge that I would hesitate to make with football pads." Despite the high comedy, audiences had about had it. After fewer than a dozen performances in Boston, Marlon finally managed to get himself fired. Herb Kenwith, his dressing-room mate from *Mama*, heard the story from Tallulah herself, in what may or may not be the accurate explanation of what had been his ultimate outrage.

"There was a scene at the foot of the stairs," Kenwith explained, "in which she had another long monologue, this one about fifteen minutes long. She held a riding crop in her hand, using it as a prop, just swishing it around as she talks. Marlon was supposed to stand there listening. During rehearsals he'd started scratching himself, moving around and scratching. Tallulah had told him, 'Look, when we're in front of an audience, I don't want you to move. I want you to stand still and listen.' He hadn't paid any attention, and he kept doing it, itching and scratching. Tallulah had been getting very, very provoked, and finally that last night she took the whip and lashed him, hit him on the arm. He looked at her, then grabbed the whip out of her hand and started beating her up onstage. She ran up the stairs with Marlon chasing her and still hitting her. At the top of the steps was a heavy curtain, a backdrop, leading to nowhere, and when they reached the last step, she ran behind the curtain. But there was no place for her to go. She got lost in the darkness and stumbled. As she started to fall back down the steps, she grabbed for the curtain and rolled back down them, pulling the curtain with her. The audience sprang to its feet and shouted bravo. They cheered and cheered, thinking it was part of the play."

N E W   Y O R K :
O F F S T A G E

Despite the crash landing of *Eagle,* 1946 had been a comparatively successful year for Marlon. He had received important critical notices, and unlike most young actors, he had enjoyed a steady income. Yet his personal life had continued in the same chaotic, haphazard way—if anything, growing more conflicted and unfocused. Perhaps it had become even more random and rudderless because his mother, who had been his principal mainstay and support despite her own problems, had left New York. In the fall of 1945 Dodie had announced her decision to commit herself to AA and to try to save her marriage by returning to Chicago. She had spent the summer of 1945 in suburban Rye, New York, and had found herself looking older than her forty-eight years, smoking two packs of Pall Malls a day and still unable to control her drinking.

Bil Baird and David and Sylvia Salinger had been begging her to seek help, and as Jocelyn put it, "she'd finally begun to hear them and was thinking, I'm in a scary place. She had come to the end, hit bottom, and I think she was telling herself that she was sick and tired of getting sick and tired. She never verbalized this to me or anyone else—it was just the battle she'd been fighting inside herself."

Probably just as important was the fact that Dodie had been spending time with Marty Mann, the first woman to achieve lasting sobriety in Alcoholics Anonymous. Although Dodie had already met AA's cofounders, Bill W. and Dr. Bob, Marty Mann was an even more compelling figure for her. She was energetic, progressive, smart, and fiercely independent—qualities that Dodie admired and indeed shared—but more significantly, Mann possessed an inner strength and the resolve to get to the bottom of things. She saw women alcoholics as having to shoulder a "double stigma," and, even more, regarded alcoholism not as a sin but as the genetically and psychologically based disease later medical research would confirm it to be.

It was a crucial turning point for Dodie when Mann supported her decision to return to Chicago and dry out. Dodie showed no signs of a relapse once she sobered up and reunited with Marlon Sr. at the elegant Lake Shore Club, where he had lived since their separation. Her health rebounded; she also joined the nascent Chicago recovery movement, becoming a dynamic, spiritual force.

Within a year of getting sober, she was asked to appear at a massive introductory AA meeting in Chicago's Loop, where the organization invited only its best speakers. With Marlon Sr. in the audience, Dodie stood before more than 300 alcoholics and friends of alcoholics who packed the assembly hall. She looked elegant and poised in her Marshall Fields wool suit and high heels, and exuded confidence and sincerity that reassured the crowd.

"I am Dodie, and I am an alcoholic," she announced. This admission, radical for a woman in 1946, had become her mantra. With its crystal enunciation, her voice cut through the cigarette haze to those who remained skeptical about success in the new program. Her pitch, lasting all of twenty minutes, was mesmerizing.

Marlon Sr. seemed proud of her new role as well. He had joined AA before he and Dodie had separated in 1944, hoping that she would, too. "His drinking," said Leo Knapp, an employee of his, "had not been as bad as hers. He could drink, getting pretty high at times, but the next morning he was on the job."

Dodie took her own room, adjoining her husband's, at the Lake Shore Club. While the place reeked of old money, what with its chandeliers and mahogany wainscoting and the tony membership that Marlon Sr. had always been desperate to impress, the facilities made life easy. Not having to maintain a house, Dodie was comfortable here; she could focus her attention on AA, her friends, and her husband.

The Brando marriage, nearly vitiated by alcohol and infidelities, began to mend. Marlon Sr. appeared enchanted, in fact, by the new woman

Dodie had become. Yet they remained in separate if adjoining rooms, caus-ing friends to wonder if it was a renewed commitment during daylight hours only. Whether they resumed a sexual relationship is not known, but Marlon Sr., despite his new happiness, found it impossible to curb his phi-landering after the first few months of the reunion. Dodie took this in stride—in her special way. Rather than hit the booze as she would have in the past, she went in for payback. One evening, as he was getting ready to go out, her suspicions were aroused by the elaborate care he was putting into his grooming; she checked the jacket pockets of his suit and found a gift-wrapped bottle of expensive perfume, not her brand. "While he was busy in the bathroom," said Phyllis Stewart, a friend, "she took the bottle, dumped out the perfume, peed in it, and put the stopper back on." Re-wrapping it, she then returned it to Marlon's pocket, enjoying the delicious thought of what the other woman would smell later that evening.

By 1947 Marty Mann had founded the National Council on Alcohol-ism while studying at the Yale Summer School of Alcohol Studies. It was Mann who informed Dodie about Yale's then radical approach (which em-braced alcoholism as a disease—an entirely new way of looking at the problem), and suggested her attendance. Dodie headed for New Haven to attend the six-week program that summer. Its effect on her was profound, and she returned to Chicago even more of a crusader than before. She was now back on her feet enough to resume her interests in other causes as well, the NAACP among them.

While Dodie had been thriving, Marlon Sr. had suffered a major pro-fessional setback, so much so that the dynamics of power within the Brando family were about to shift permanently.

During the war, Calcium Carbonate's business had never been better. New products, ranging from putty to automobile tire additives, were being added to the firm's line, and Brando Sr., now general manager, had been doing his best to snag as much of the profit as possible. But by late 1946 there were rumblings of a reorganization at the company. Soon Marlon called Leo Knapp, who had been hired to manage the company while Brando was on the road building up accounts, into his office.

"Before you learn any more about this," said Marlon Sr., "I want you to read this letter."

Knapp skimmed the notice. "Am I reading this right? You're really leaving?" he asked.

"Yes, I'm leaving," he said, almost with a chortle. "I think I'm going to be asked to leave anyway."

Two members of the board of directors then arrived and vanished into Marlon Sr.'s office for a four-hour discussion. When they emerged they announced to Knapp that he had been promoted to general manager, since Marlon "is no longer with us."

The official story was that Marlon Sr. had resigned in order to manage his son's growing career and business affairs. This became the family myth as well, although in reality Pop had been fired when he had been caught double-dealing with the company.

Unbeknownst to his employers, on January 4, 1944, Marlon Sr. had filed the necessary papers with the state of Illinois to form a new corporation called the Chemical Feed Products Company. In its first annual report, for 1945, John Palmer, head of Marblehead Limestone (a competitor of Calcium Carbonate), was listed as president, treasurer, and a director; Marlon Sr. was listed as another director; and Mrs. J. D. Hanmer (Jocelyn's married name) was listed as secretary. The purpose of the company was to manufacture and sell limestone for animal feed, an endeavor that put Brando Sr. in direct conflict of interest with his employer. As general manager of Calcium Carbonate, he was developing the same customers, who needed limestone for their feed mixes.

By happenstance one of Calcium Carbonate's directors had run across a feed bag that bore the same address as his own company. Investigating further, he discovered that just down the hall from Brando's Calcium Carbonate headquarters was a small office leased to the Chemical Feed Company. Brando, it became evident, had been covertly going through his employer's files and ledgers, stealing clients' names for his own Chemical Feed Products, thereby undercutting Calcium Carbonate's market.

When confronted, Knapp recalled, Brando admitted to the double-dealing. Possibly, under different circumstances he could have faced jail time, but he was allowed to quietly resign. Not even Dodie and the children knew the truth, and apparently neither Jocelyn nor Bud had any idea that the Chemical Feed Products company would remain intact for the next several years, listing each of them as directors.

But Marlon Sr.'s ignominious dismissal from Calcium Carbonate didn't quench his thirst for the big score; in future years he would just have more funds to play his games with, in the hope of striking it rich. For his son had begun sending money home for his father to invest, a routine that would continue, and increase in dollar volume, as Bud became more successful.

When Dodie left New York in the fall of 1945, Marlon Jr. had to find his own quarters, and, as usual, things had just fallen into place. Around the time he was fired from *The Eagle Has Two Heads* he and Darren moved into the Park Savoy Hotel, on Fifty-sixth Street just off Seventh Avenue, only two blocks from Stella and Harold's apartment. It was a seedy place, filled with alcoholic pensioners, transient homosexuals, and Broadway hookers, but it catered largely to young actors who'd heard that rooms were available for less than $20 a week. The rent included a communal refrigerator and hot plate on each floor. Leonard Bernstein, Adolph Green, Betty Comden, and Judy Holliday had lived there.

For Marlon, the Park Savoy would be home for close to a year, an eternity compared to his other encampments (by the time he departed for Hollywood in late 1949, he'd lived at ten addresses in less than six years). Even here at the hotel, though, he was hardly settled. From the start, early in 1947, he migrated from room to room since, despite his regular income, he often failed to pay his rent on time. Often, he'd arrive home at one or two in the morning, find that Mrs. Rose, the heavyset Jewish manager in her Minnie Mouse shoes and *shmatteh* dresses, had locked him out. His response was to crash with Darren or one of the other tenants who would let him sleep on the floor. Weather permitting, he also slept on the roof.

The place was an overgrown dormitory. Chaos reigned. At two or three in the morning, the hallways would be pierced by the sounds of squabbling between some homosexual residents. "You could go into the kitchen and somebody would be dyeing their stockings black, I swear to you," said one ex-tenant, "because her husband was going to die any minute. We even had a cat whose name was Pastrami because she'd been stolen from the delicatessen."

It was hard to say who was living in the hotel, because people were in and out constantly. Darren had a room on the seventh floor. Florence Goodman, Darren's redheaded girlfriend, was renting a room there, too, as was Celia Webb, who had her young son with her. Living at the Savoy,

Marlon still had pockets of friends here and there throughout the city, people whom he compartmentalized but many of whom regularly showed up at the Savoy. There were Elaine Stritch and other New School cronies in one group. There was Sam Gilman, a cartoonist who was giving acting lessons out of his bachelor apartment on Sixth Avenue. Carlo Fiore still came around, but he had lapsed back into heroin after a disastrous nose job that was meant to turn him into a leading man. Others in and out of the hotel were the actors Hy Anzell, Earl Hammond, Sidney Armus, and Billy Redfield. Maureen Stapleton and two roommates had their own place on Fifty-second Street, but they were part of Brando's kaleidoscopic cliques as well. All of them kept actors' hours. Most were unemployed, and as on West End Avenue, Marlon was at the center—a role he would play with almost every one of these people for the next forty years.

Among the group as well were the two men who would become Brando's lifelong friends, though in Brando's usual on-again, off-again fashion: Wally Cox, his boyhood pal from Evanston, and Philip Rhodes.

Of all Marlon's friends during this New York period, the most independent—and mysterious—was Wally. It was a kinship that many found strange. Even Brando himself later found it necessary to insist that it was not "an unlikely friendship," explaining that "Wally didn't resemble in the remotest his Mr. Peepers character" but had "the mentality of an ax murderer."

After leaving Evanston, Cox had studied botany at City College in Manhattan at the same time Marlon had been at Shattuck. He and his sister had been dragged from Michigan to Illinois to New York, and both siblings had reportedly held a picnic atop their alcoholic lesbian mother's grave. Happiness had certainly not been a fixture of Cox's life; a self-described "lost soul," he certainly had never dreamed that his future would lie in show business.

It was in the middle of 1944 that Marlon first ran into his old pal in New York. At the time, Marlon had been pushing a shopping cart up Sixth Avenue in the Village and baiting Fran to jump in. Wally just happened to walk by.

"Hello, Bud," Cox said quietly, as if they'd seen each other only yesterday and not nine years before.

"Hi, Wally," Brando replied, equally matter-of-fact about the chance reunion. Without missing a beat, he said, "Wally, I want Franny to take a ride—" But since Fran wouldn't play along, Cox volunteered. As Fran later related to a *Coronet* feature writer, "Wally climbed into the grocer's cart, Marlon pushed him down the street, and they've been in complete rapport ever since."

Living in a coldwater flat on Tenth Avenue, in the same building as the newlyweds Dick and Fran Loving, Wally, more than anyone, was the loner. He had the same pedantic, distracted air as his alter ego, Mr. Peepers, and as his reunion with Marlon unfolded day by day, it was "a meeting of opposites." Each of them drew on the other. "Bud in some way embodied an accepted, conventional sexuality," said Dick Loving, "while with Wally it was a kind of mental strength, a humor and wit, an intellectual fencing.

"Bud had this inheritance of conventional strengths from his father, going to a macho military school and all that, and then Wally had other kinds of strengths that had to do with subtle, verbal exchange. He was no Charles Atlas, but he demonstrated another kind of power, and people listened. Dodie, for example. In Evanston and for years afterward, she looked on Wally as a wonderful original. He was the moralist, and in some way that's what his monologues were all about."

Basic to Wally's laid-back view of life was looking at its viciousness and shrugging. His awareness about the oddballs of the world was deep, all of them outsiders like the kid who was too heavy and couldn't make it over the fence, or the ineffectual Boy Scout leader who couldn't get his troop home after a hike. They were all victims—not the type that would be familiar to New Yorkers so much as the Midwest—and all of them came out of Wally's personal storehouse of pain. "Perhaps," he later wrote, "that is actually the message for us ex-rugged fellows of the twentieth century—to give up gracefully, walk softly, and carry a small twig. Injure a minimum of people."

For most people who saw Brando and Cox together, Wally's role was to make Marlon laugh, to be the comic, to relieve the situation. Yet he was different from Darren. Temperamentally, he wasn't talking for Marlon so much as explaining Marlon, relieving his friend of the responsibility of doing what he couldn't do except onstage. "Marlon told me," said a mutual acquaintance, "that he asked Wally once, 'With your kind of perception, awareness, being who you are in this world, how are you able to hack it? How do you manage?' And Wally answered, 'It's easy. I just look at them all as though they're Martians. They're the interlopers on my planet. I'm not the interloper.' "

To most outsiders, Cox was simply sui generis. He struck New York cops the same way, and they hauled him in routinely because he fit the profile of every psychotic, every rapist, every nutcase. "We used to giggle, 'Thank God he got to be famous, because otherwise he'd spend the rest of his life in night court,' " said one friend.

During this period Philip Rhodes had also become aware of the up-and-coming Brando. Rhodes had been raised in Cincinnati, and he became interested in acting while a member of the University of Cincinnati's mummers group. While completing law school he had presented dramatizations of famous trials. He was extremely well read, with an extensive background in literature, philosophy, and art. During the war years, he studied with Ouspensky, and later even went to Paris to study with Gurdjieff himself. As a result of his interest in painting and sculpting, he became adept with makeup and facial sculpting techniques. Once in New York, working sometimes as an actor, sometimes as a model, he had perfected his talent and earned money doing makeup. His wife, Marie, was an Italian from Boston who had worked as an actress since she was thirteen.

In 1944 a model Rhodes knew had told him about Piscator's Dramatic Workshop and mentioned Brando. Rhodes went down to the class to see if he wanted to take it, but decided he had gone through much of what the younger students were studying when he had taken acting classes in Hollywood during the thirties. Able to get free theater tickets through Actors' Equity, Rhodes had then seen Brando in *Truckline Café*. Several months later, in 1947, a ballet dancer friend brought Brando around to the Rhodes's apartment, and thereafter Marlon kept "coming back and back and back" to listen to Philip talk—about literature, painting, Ouspensky, and the theories of Gurdjieff, even about the theater and acting. "He was a creative listener, even then," said Rhodes. "He could put little questions to you about things, which were to lead you to what he wanted answers about. It was as if he would move you into position and boom, then hit you with what he wanted to hear about. But Marlon always segregated his people," explained Rhodes, "and he was different with each—a comedian with one, a philosopher with another. And he didn't let you know what was going on with him and the other person. When he was with you, that was his life. You weren't allowed to ask about his other lives. He fenced you out and you very quickly found out where the perimeters were. For example, I didn't know that he knew Wally, until several years later. I kept telling him what a wonderful comedian this guy Cox was. But all he'd say was, 'What do you mean, he's funny? What kind of material does he have?' I'd tell him, and he'd say, 'I don't think that's so funny.'

"When Wally and I were allowed to intersect and I finally understood that he was a good friend of Marlon, I realized that while they had been kids together, they really didn't have that much in common. Also, because Wally was not physically attractive to the opposite sex, and Marlon was, that bugged him. He always wanted to be Marlon, even though his real interests weren't the same."

Rhodes would sometimes stop around at the Park Savoy, where two models he also knew lived, as well as Igor Tamarin. Rhodes recalled that Tamarin "was that nice boy who always carried a violin and a fencing foil and danced on tables." But he hadn't realized that Igor, too, was another of Marlon's friends.

It wasn't surprising, though. With Tamarin's verbal skills and ironic quips, he, along with Wally and Darren, was a comedian who punctured pretenses and saw the world darkly. Tamarin had come under Marlon's spell, too, but he refused to be played off against Darren, Sam Gilman, or any of the others whom he quickly came to call "the ass kissers."

More than anyone in Marlon's circle, Tamarin was irrepressible, a bona fide Duchamp, Dalí, and Jack Kerouac rolled into one, and if Brando brought him into the group for his offbeat anarchism, their first meeting was entirely by chance. Tamarin had come down from his home in the Bronx with his violin, bumped into a dancer friend coming out of the Park Savoy, and ended up staying the night. Tamarin recalls: "The next morning the phone rang. I thought it was my mother, but the line went dead, so I went downstairs and there was Brando manning the switchboard.

" 'What the fuck is the idea of disconnecting me?' I yelled. There were millions of plugs, the old kind of plugs on long cords, and he was sitting there crossing all the wires, laughing. He'd taken over for someone, goofed up, and decided to go all the way, so it was like a massive conference call, with everybody talking to each other."

Almost at once, Tamarin moved in to the Park Savoy. In his swimming trunks or Jockey shorts, he'd think nothing of leaping up on someone's bed—his own, Marlon's, Darren's, it didn't matter—to play Bach at two in the morning, and if everyone didn't settle down to listen, the hollow-cheeked mini-Heifetz would yell, "Shut your fucking mouth!" Marlon, smiling, would chorus, "Yeah, if you don't like fucking culture, get out!" The two also played chess, long one of Brando's passions, and Tamarin gave him fencing lessons, too. When they boxed and wrestled, often they wrecked the hotel's furniture, but neither cared. Always, there was their nonstop banter. "You're a Jew and I'm going to tell everybody," Marlon would hiss, holding Tamarin in a half nelson. Unintimidated, the gaunt Russian taunted him: "You're not bored with me, you're bored with yourself. I'm much too intelligent for you, and you fucking well know it!"

One-upmanship had been Marlon's stock-in-trade since grade school, but Igor gave as good as he got. It made no difference that he took Brando's money whenever he was short of cash, that he let Brando pick up the tab whenever they went for bagels or spaghetti. Nothing was off-limits. Tamarin lied, he dissembled, but most of all the rules were not for him. His motto was "The world is my ashtray."

There was also the stealing. Even before moving into the Park Savoy, Marlon had been making a game of shoplifting, and at the hotel Darren Dublin's role was to play staff sergeant and give everyone "assignments": "You go out and steal two oranges. Your job is to steal the paper," and so on, and eventually the group wound up with "service for eight by Horn & Hardart." It was fun stuff, of course, but on his own Marlon was working it almost as an art form: Sauntering into Gristede's supermarket or a bookshop, he'd linger, examine the merchandise and do other busy work, then walk out without paying, relying on his acting skills to make himself "invisible."

Sometimes it worked, sometimes not. One evening he went to the corner drugstore with Igor and Blossom, ostensibly to buy a toothbrush, and tried to stretch his performance. Marlon went to the counter and slipped Igor a huge Hershey bar. Tamarin put it under his coat, but then heard the shopkeeper shout, "Young man!"

Marlon pointed at Igor. "Yes, that's him over there. I saw him take it. It's in his coat."

"Thank you, sir," the owner said.

When the cops arrived, Marlon was still saying, "That's him. I saw it in his coat."

The police were taking Igor away when Blossom stepped in. "No, officers, it wasn't him. It was *him*," she said, pointing at Marlon. "I saw him take the chocolate and give it to the other man, saying it was paid for."

"That's not true!" Marlon said, looking hurt and indignant.

"I'm afraid you'll have to come with us," the cops told Brando. One of them actually grabbed him, while Igor said, "People like that shouldn't be allowed to walk around! It's pretty shabby, particularly when he can afford it." And just to rub it in with the drugstore owner, an old *yidisher,* Igor added, "And you know he's not Jewish!" Marlon started laughing. Finally the cop said, "Just pay for the candy, mister."

But Igor stopped them. "I think I want to press charges."

"Igor," Marlon yelled, "no more money, no more dates, no more nice dinners..."

The police finally walked out, muttering, "My god, these people are all crazy."

A scam at Horn & Hardart on Fifty-seventh Street, which eventually involved the whole group, showed how far the insanity could go. It all began by chance when Igor walked into the automat just before closing time with a beautiful dancer named Tzinta, who was also at the Savoy. Igor and the counterman, who was wrapping up unsold sandwiches, started chatting. Even before they introduced themselves, Igor could tell the other man—a German named Al Bouts—liked Tzinta.

Tamarin knew Horn & Hardart threw out a lot of the food it hadn't sold by the end of the day, so he saw some potential in Bouts's interest in Tzinta. Returning next evening alone, Igor said hello to Bouts, who, as Tamarin recalls, asked, " 'Who's your friend? She's very beautiful.' 'Let me tell you something, Al,' I said. 'She kind of likes you too.' 'Oh, *ja*? What does she do?'

" 'Well, her parents are very wealthy. She lives in the Park Savoy over there with us. She left her parents because she wants to be on her own.'

"He goes, 'Oh, *ja*. I like that very much. You're sure you—' 'No, we're like brother and sister, no problem. Say, what time are you through with work, twelve o'clock? Let's meet, we'll go have a sandwich some-where.' 'No, no, I don't want you to go to any trouble. Here, we throw them out.' "

Bouts gave Igor a package of sandwiches, which he took back to the Savoy and shared with his friends. For the next week, Igor teased Bouts with bits of information about Tzinta, always getting some leftover sandwiches in return—which were, he said, "now feeding everyone in the Savoy, the whole fucking place."

Tzinta, who was from Czechoslovakia, spoke heavily accented English, and was, according to Tamarin, not that bright, agreed to help her hungry friends. She accompanied Igor back to the automat one night, the better to whet Bouts's interest.

After another few days, Igor remembers that Bouts "finally comes out with, 'When am I going to have a date with her?' I tell him, 'It's all arranged. I have to call her father, then I'll put you on the phone with him and you can say hello.' 'Oh, *ja, ja.*'

"I call up Earl Hammond, and Earl's very cool, the best dialectician in the world. He puts on a Czechoslovakian accent that was unbelievable, and I said, 'Al, you're on.' Bouts says, 'Oh, Mr. Tzinta'—he calls him Mr. Tzinta—'I would like to marry your daughter.' He hasn't even been out with her yet!"

The calls between Bouts and Tzinta's "father" continued for a week. The group felt that Igor was leading the German on masterfully, when Marlon decided to up the ante. Igor remembers:

"We're in my room and he announces, 'I'll be the uncle.' I tell him to stay out of it. But no, he gets on the phone with Al Bouts and it's 'I'd like to know what your intentions are . . .'

"Of course Marlon's been eating these sandwiches, too. I've been running this thing to perfection, and the rest of us are furious. We're all in the room whispering at him to shut up, but he goes on. 'What are your intentions?' Finally he says, 'Well, you can fuck her but you can't marry her.'

"We knew that was the end, so as a desperate last stand I said to Tzinta, 'He's going to call you, Tzinta. You're going out with him tonight.' 'No, I'm not,' she said. 'You're going out with him! You've gotta! Play it to the hilt. Say your uncle was drunk.'

"Marlon, meanwhile, is laughing. I tell him to get the fuck out. 'Oh, I'll buy you a sandwich'—that's the consolation he's offering—and I tell him, 'Fuck you, you've wrecked everything.' "

Tzinta finally did go out with Al Bouts, returning to the Savoy at three in the morning and announcing she was in love. (In fact, three months later, they were married.) Igor concludes: "The next day I went back to the automat, thinking, All right, now we can get our sandwiches again. Al Bouts says, 'You're not getting anything. You lied. She doesn't have a rich father. She comes from poor people in Czechoslovakia. You fucks around with me for too long.' "

In the midst of all the lunacy, Brando still had his string of girl-friends—not only Ellen Adler, Blossom Plumb, and Celia Webb, but the frequent one-night stands, the quick seductions. Another woman who became part of his coterie was dancer Sondra Lee. Marlon, she saw, was at the center, the leader, but also capable of protecting those around him.

"I could always call him and say, 'I'm in trouble,' Lee recalled. "We were orphans, abandoned children, abandoned by our families as much as by the structure of society, and that joined us together. He used the word *comfort* a lot, and said things like, 'We drink at the fountain of each other's affection.' It was the womb all over again."

Lee had been only fifteen when she met Marlon in 1945 at Olga Terasava's ballet class, but the two didn't bond until a year later in Washington, D.C., when Brando was on tour with the disastrous *Eagle Has Two Heads*. Lee, who was an underage dancer in a Russian nightclub, had gone backstage at the National Theatre, and soon thereafter the two began taking long walks together. What they talked about wasn't "the usual things like news, politics, and food," so much as questions raised by Marlon in the course of his usual soul-searching—the future, the meaning of fate, what might become of them all.

Within weeks both were back in New York. Marlon had already dubbed the diminutive dancer "Peanuts," and what interested him was her intensity, her energy. Lee was bright, verbal, and imaginative, certainly no ordinary teenager, and his response was to tell her that she had "button hooks in her eyes," meaning that she was *too* sensitive, *too* vulnerable, perhaps too unguardedly smart for her own good. "I had met some kind of force I really followed and trusted," Lee realized, and Brando took her in.

Darren Dublin had seen this sort of thing before, both as a seduction and as part of his friend's endless and genuine curiosity, but the decision to bring Lee into the Park Savoy happened very, very quickly. With Wally and Darren standing by, Marlon simply picked up the phone one night and called her parents in New Jersey, offering to "sponsor" her. A day or two later she moved in, and not long after that their relationship became sexual. Just *how* it became so wasn't clear, least of all to Lee herself.

"We must have been fooling around and it just happened. Marlon, I remember, told me that I didn't have to be frightened." But there was humiliation, too, she said. "We were at Darren's father's in the Bronx and there were other people around—not in the room, but it hadn't been a totally private affair. We used to travel like a pack. We all sort of slept in the same bed together and talked and giggled, so it was like camp that way."

Soon, he began tutoring Lee as if he were a Renaissance scholar. Literature and plays as well as art exhibitions were all part of it. He insisted she see *Brief Encounter,* David Lean's dark drama about a doomed middle-class love affair; after they left the theater, he'd commented, "When you get to be twenty-four, you're going to be a fascinating woman." Since she had already gone to bed with him, Lee didn't feel duped or violated, or that it was just Marlon's need for conquest.

"There was a very special awareness of his, an awareness of someone else's fragility," she said. "He told me about his family and his insecurities, such as being afraid of alcohol, of being taken by women, of being made a fool of, of being a real mama's boy. I don't know whether you'd call it commitment, but he saw that it was his responsibility to understand and include someone else's feelings, their presence."

His talent to understand seemed uncanny, "like a painter who sees to the bones of his subjects," added Lee. Eli Wallach, who'd soon get to know him at the Actors Studio, called this his "X-ray quality," an ability to "decode the mystery of the other person and take away all the insulation." Still, with the exception of his solitary walks, Marlon was rarely alone. Besides the immediate circle of friends, there were the outlying satellite groups—Johnny Fiedler, Hy Anzell, Maureen Stapleton and her roommate, Janice Mars. At the hotel, Monopoly was one of the residents' main diversions, No one could keep a straight face when Marlon was playing because he almost always cheated, much as he had as a kid in Evanston.

"He was always the banker," said Lee. "Or he'd get close to where the banker was sitting, and he'd have money sticking in his socks, between his toes, and I don't remember ever finishing a game because he'd be discovered with thousands and thousands of dollars. We'd just scream with laughter and end up yelling obscenities at each other."

If Marlon was losing at chess, as was often the case when he played Igor Tamarin, he'd knock over the chessboard, announcing, "Ah-h-h-, I'm bored." Yet nobody seriously minded, largely because of his ability to laugh at himself. When he'd lead the group into the bird sanctuary at the Central

Park Zoo, with Wally bringing up the rear. Marlon would continue lecturing in his professorial falsetto. On one such visit, he ignored the zookeeper's warning not to go near the baboon's cage because the ape often spit in people's faces. Marlon assured the group not to worry, since animals got "friendly vibrations" from him. "He stepped right up to the railing and smiled at the glowering beast," said Bob Condon, who was an advertising copywriter at the time, "and Mr. Baboon spit and hit Marlon square in the face. Marlon went to the drinking fountain, wiped his face, filled his mouth with water, and came back and gave the ape 'what for' in exactly the same way." The keeper was furious, but Marlon said, "If more people did that it would teach that damn ape some manners."

Also, Marlon was generous to a fault when it came to money. Having had a fairly regular income the year before, he assumed responsibility for all of them, helping pay for rent and food, even handing out pocket money. Sid Shaw, the songwriter with whom Marlon had spent the summer of 1945 in Provincetown, took the Brando welfare system to an all-time high when he asked for $200. "Two hundred bucks for what?" Marlon asked.

"Because I knocked a girl up," the homosexual Shaw lied.

"Here," Marlon said, howling, "you'll need an extra hundred just in case the abortion doesn't work."

When a friend of Darren had to be institutionalized, he helped pay for her shock therapy. There was also money for Carlo Fiore's heroin. While Marlon had more money than his cronies, he wasn't yet rolling in it. Having asked his father to handle his income, he was living on an allowance, almost like an adolescent. Nevertheless, he helped Celia Webb, too, covering her rent in between her jobs as a freelance window dresser and office worker. "A lot of these people became defined by Marlon," said Sondra Lee, "and they were an entourage."

As is the case with many stars, however, Brando chafed at what was happening, too, wrestling with his recurring anxiety that he was being used. The only way to accommodate the conflict was to redouble his efforts at making himself the nucleus, the giver—the untouchable, mysterious, and all-important center.

"Do you know how I make a friend?" he would later tell Truman Capote. "I go about it very gently, I circle around and around. I circle. Then, gradually, I come nearer. Then I reach out and touch them—ah, so gently. Then I draw back. Wait a while. Make them wonder. At just the right moment, I move in again. Touch them. Circle. They don't know what's happening. Before they realize it, they're all entangled, involved. I have them. And suddenly, sometimes, I'm all *they* have. A lot of them, you see, are people who don't fit anywhere. They're not accepted—they've been hurt, crippled one way or another. But I want to help them, and they can focus on me. I'm the duke, sort of the duke of my domain."

Actually, he was the duke of two domains. Marlon, in effect, had split himself down the middle, intellectually and emotionally. One part of him drew from the richly veined, critical thinking of Clurman and that circle. The other side of him was focused on Darren, Igor, Wally, and the others, all of whom floated day to day, guided by their prebeatnik notion that life was an improvisation, that no one was supposed to judge, and that instinct, not thought, was life's most reliable guide. All of this struck Barbara Grimm, a pianist who met Brando through Igor Tamarin, "like nausea" even then. "I have no doubt that it sounded profound to Marlon," she said. "But who *were* these people? They'd never examined anything. They were limited and shallow, and hoped to get into the theater and thought maybe Marlon could drag them in."

Within the group, Brando's role was becoming dangerously close to that of a guru. With the gang around him, he would still retreat into silence, but now, in the wake of *Truckline,* his silences were taken as profound. "For all we knew, he could have been the dummy of the world, the silent dummy," said Fred Sadoff, who watched from the sidelines. Among his friends, Sadoff noted that Marlon acted as if he were in touch with something "beyond the senses," as if he held "the key to life's deepest secrets." There were his pauses—that faraway, all-knowing look in his eyes—and also the way he had started using the language of psychoanalysis. This included buzzwords from his reading and what he was hearing around town. All of it radiated one message: "We're in it together." That they were all damaged, flawed, in the grip of something bigger than themselves.

Wally and Marlon continued to be the left shoe and the right shoe, a twosome joined at the hip like Siamese twins. Cox continued to have his problems with women, but at parties he had no hesitation in taking advantage of his buddy's rejects. "Was Wally any more discriminating than Marlon? No," said a close mutual friend. "Both of them would hop into the sack with virtually anything."

Dorothy Pennebaker Brando, "Dodie." *Collection Carlo Fiore*

Marlon Brando, "Bud," age two, with his sisters Frances, "Franny," and Jocelyn, "Tiddy." *Archive Photos/Phil Burchman*

Marlon Brando, age eight, in cowbo
outfit, Evanston. *Archive Photos/Ph
Burchman*

Marlon Brando and fellow
cadets, the Dramatic
Association.
Shattuck Yearbook

Ross, President
First Row: BURFORD, BRANDO, DENMAN.
Second Row: HENNINGER, TAYLOR, R.

THE Dramatic Association annually presents two sets of plays: one group b
giving dance, and one before the Commencement dance. This year, three short play

Dorothy Brando, 1948. *Omaha World-Herald*

Marlon Brando and Carmelita
Pope, summer 1942.
Courtesy Carmelita Pope Wood

Marlon Brando and Darren Dub
with fellow Dramatics Works
student, in a Forty-second St
photo booth, 1943–44.
Collection Darren Dublin

Brando in *Truckline Café*, 1946.
The Fred Fehl Theatre Collection,
the Theatre Arts Collection, Harry
Ransom Humanities Research
Center, University of
Texas at Austin

Ellen Adler, age thirteen.
Courtesy David Diamond

Sondra Lee. *Courtesy Sondra Lee*

Brando in *A Flag Is Born*, 1946.
*he Fred Fehl Theatre Collection,
The Theatre Arts Collection,
Harry Ransom Humanities
Research Center, University of
Texas at Austin*

Stella Adler. *Courtesy David Diamond*

Brando at a party for the Hollywood
Ten, New York, 1947.
© *G. Kenneth Vanier*

Marlon Brando, *A Streetcar Named Desire*,
1951. *Photofest*

Igor Tamarin as Nijinsky, performing at a
Greenwich Village party, 1947.
© *G. Kenneth Vanier*

Brando with Vivien Leigh, publicity still, *A Streetcar Named Desire*.
Warner Brothers/Courtesy Kobal Collection

Brando with his mentor, Eli
Kazan, on the set of *Streetc...
Warner Brothers/Courtesy Ko...
Collection*

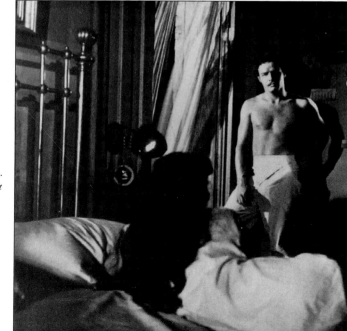

Viva Zapata!, 1952.
Photofest

It is unclear whether Cox participated in the group sex that Marlon was beginning to have an appetite for, just as he may not have known about Brando's contacts with men. There is little question, however, that the two spent hours talking about sex in the most graphic detail, although their main topic of conversation were the great questions of life—death, marriage, loyalty, childhood, whatever. They were "the great dopesters, the great observers of people," noted Everett Greenbaum, a friend of Cox and later a writer for "Mr. Peepers." "They were going to come up with the big answers, and this went on for years."

If it was Wally's dark view of the world that bound him to Brando in the late forties, then Sam Gilman and Philip Rhodes occupied different points on the actor's compass. Gilman was a good-natured *shlub* of a man, and while eager to make it as an actor, he was already worshiping at Brando's shrine. He put on parties at his apartment to provide Marlon with women, ran errands, made phone calls, and would often introduce himself as Brando's "sidekick." In addition, Gilman saw being with Marlon "as his road to the girls," said Philip Rhodes, and afraid to lose the connection, he could be downright fawning. "Marlon once deliberately threw a handkerchief on the floor and Sam went to pick it up," recalled Fred Sadoff. "When Sam picked it up, Marlon asked, 'Why'd you do that?' He obviously meant to embarrass him, and it was a double cruelty—first dropping the handkerchief, then humbling Sam by asking the question."

Sam, however, never got the message, and he'd justify his treatment of him when people would question it. " 'Oh, you don't understand,' he told one mutual acquaintance. " 'You've gotta know Marlon. He doesn't mean it. He really needs me and I'm a lot more important to him than even he realizes.' "

Another one in the shifting Brando circles was William Redfield, a serious if overly cerebral actor who costarred with Paul Scofield in the Broadway production of *A Man for All Seasons* and was later acclaimed for his Guildenstern in John Gielgud's long-running 1964 production of *Hamlet* starring Richard Burton. Redfield would be a founding member of the Actors Studio and an abiding influence, one of the few friends whom Brando could talk to about acting. "We believed him as one believes an eccentric in a subway," Redfield wrote about Brando years later. "Uncomfortable and dangerous, but *there.*"

By the end of the summer of 1947 Marlon decided to leave the Park Savoy, subletting a studio apartment in Maureen Stapleton's building on

Fifty-second Street. Redfield lived several doors down, Blossom was in the neighborhood, and Darren had gone to Fifty-eighth Street and Tenth Avenue with Florence, not far from Wally, Dick, and Fran. Making the exodus complete ("He decided we should all move because he'd gotten fed up with the prices at Gristede's"), Marlon had also rented an apartment downtown for Celia Webb and her young son.

The one large room of his own apartment was furnished with a double mattress on the floor, a few cushions to sit on, his books, a recorder, and his drums. He now indulged himself for the first time, and used some of his earnings to buy a motorcycle—an Indian—allowing him to roam the city and see his friends even more than before. Bob Condon was living a few doors down with Ralph Meeker, and soon realized that his new neighbor was routinely raiding their apartment by coming over the rooftops.

"Marlon had the run of my place whenever he wanted it," Condon remembered. "He liked fresh orange juice but had no squeezer in his room. Not wanting to disturb me, he would go through the fire door onto the terrace and climb through the kitchen window. Then he would carefully and quietly remove two oranges from a paper bag, cut them, squeeze them, drink the juice, and just as quietly clean up and steal away out the window and into the dawn. Several times overnight guests would scream as the window slid open and then stare open-mouthed as Brando crept over the sill."

He was still typecasting women, restricting himself to small, young, dark-skinned girls who, collectively, represented "the opposite" of Dodie, and his sex life was "astonishing," said Everett Greenbaum. It could be a ballet dancer, a model, an aspiring actress; a girl as young as fifteen, or even, occasionally, an older, wealthy socialite. But they all shared the same passive, superficial type of personality. "They were usually plastic," Philip Rhodes explained. "Of course, Marlon could perceive very quickly whether they had any dominance in them, and if they did, you wouldn't see that girl in his company anymore. All he had to do was get a message that they might make some claim or try to control him and that was the end of it."

At the Park Savoy Marlon had already bedded Darren's girlfriend, Flo Goodman (which led Darren to take a swipe at her, not at his pal), and he took women from Carlo Fiore as well. Friends would only shrug when he'd routinely go into the corner drugstore as though on autopilot and proposition salesgirls, or fellow shoppers. Photographer Sam Shaw, another companion, remembered a beautiful, dumb black girl at Hamburger Hall, Marlon's favorite fast-food joint; when the counter girl didn't recognize him, Marlon was "so hot to have her" that he broke down and told her he was an actor.

His usual standbys, however, were still Ellen Adler and Celia Webb; with Celia, he had, at one point, even talked of marriage. Blossom Plumb was around, too, as was Faith Dane, a tall, athletic dancer with a broken Andy Devine voice with whom his relationship was platonic. Still, it was the waitresses who served as his daily fare.

"They were like little naive girls who wore leopard-skin skirts," said Barbara Grimm. "Sort of exotic, sexy girls from B movies who looked like Yvonne DeCarlo or Hedy Lamarr. They had to have dark hair and be vaguely Latin, wear black stockings and zebra stripes. Jungle girls. I don't mean tarts—what I'm trying to say is 'low class.' Hero worshiping, vaguely seedy. Essentially dumb."

Maila Nurmi, an actress who later gained brief fame as television's "Vampira," had her own strange encounter with him, even though he'd made the point that the tall blonde wasn't his type, telling her that he thought she looked like "the woman who guards the ovens at Buchenwald." But one evening she ended up at his apartment.

"We were sitting on the floor," Nurmi recalled. He didn't know me well enough to do any of his whispering, so instead he was saying, 'Here's a book, look at this,' then he was changing the music, then lighting another candle. He was just so gentle, talking in a soft voice and being so easily alarmed, with an intensity that he was trying to hide. He was fascinated that I worked in nightclubs. 'I've never been to a nightclub,' he said. 'Do you go there every night? What's it like?'

"There was no discussion, like 'I want to sleep with you.' It was just bedtime. There was only one bed, so we both fell into it. We necked a little and that's all. No screwing.

"The next morning, we're up at eleven, twelve o'clock, and when we went down for coffee, both of us were walking on eggshells. I'm thinking what a poetic little child he is, how tender. It's the love of my life, the first person I've ever met who's from my own planet.

"Do I see more and more of him? No. I see less and less of him. I was in anguish. I left town because of it, went to California. I thought, I can't be in the same city and see so little of him, it wounds me. . . ."

He was still staggering his dates, as he had done at the New School, and his notion of an outing might be to take a girl to the Vim and Vigor vegetarian restaurant for carrot juice or a health salad, or to his favorite Mexican restaurant near Times Square, or to Chinatown, where he'd insist they eat with chopsticks. A ride through Central Park on his motorcycle. Might be part of it, too. "You know the single biggest cause of motorcycle accidents? Horseshit!" he'd point out (unlike his image from *The Wild One*, he drove the bike with restraint if not outright timidity). Afterward there might be coffee or possibly a walk, browsing the shop windows along Broadway. Sometimes Wally came along, doing most of the talking.

"I was very wary of Marlon," said one out-of-towner who had recently come on the Manhattan scene, later to become one of Broadway's major playwrights. "He had slept with practically everybody I knew. He was very seductive, indiscriminate, and the fact that I was there, it was like the mountain—if it's there, you knock it off.

"I'm not at all what is attractive to Marlon, but nevertheless I existed, so there had to be a *pavane* of some kind. Two or three o'clock one morning, my doorbell rings. In those days one wasn't fearful of anything, so I staggered to the door and there was a little bouquet on the doorstep, which was rather charming, without a card. I hadn't a clue who had left it, or even if it was intended for me, since there were other people living upstairs in my brownstone.

"The next night, the same thing happened. The third night I was waiting for it, actually perched in the hall. The doorbell rang, I opened it, and there was Marlon with the flowers. Alone. Drenched, standing in a downpour. He wasn't going to run away. I think he intended to be caught, but before I could say anything, he said, 'I got them wholesale.' 'Well, come on in and get dry anyway,' I said.

"He came in and asked if he could have something to wear while he dried off, and we had some hot chocolate or something. There was no mention of the two previous nights, just a kind of easing off. Finally he said, 'I want to stay.' 'Okay, you can sleep in the living room,' I said, sidestepping. He said fine, so I made a bed for him and went on back to my room. About five minutes later, he came and got in bed with me. And lay there. He said, 'I won't bother you.' I said okay, neither one of us making a move. And this went on for the next three nights. I wouldn't initiate the move, nor would he. It was a draw, a Mexican standoff."

Everything was a matter of control for the young Brando. He could pin people to the wall with a look, but his favorite strategy was not to speak or even make eye contact until someone came to him. With members of his various cliques, he liked to talk at odd hours, and would phone at two, three in the morning. No one would think of hanging up on him. "What color are you wearing?" he might ask in a low whisper. "Tell me what your clothes feel like against your body." Or, "How would you feel if your throat were full of feathers?" There were accents and false identities, as well as "long-distance calls from Paris." With Barbara Grimm he pretended to be a buddy of Earl Hammond, her boyfriend: "My phone rang," Grimm recalled, "and a voice I didn't know said, 'You don't know me but Earl asked me to call. He's here, helping me with some work in my apartment, putting up some blinds . . . and unfortunately he fell and the broom went up his ass.' I knew it couldn't be true, but it seemed like the kind of thing that would happen to Earl, so I burst out laughing, 'Come on, who is this?' "

It was, Grimm observed, "a form of courtship. . . . It engaged me and certainly disposed of Earl, whom I was seriously in love with."

There was always that enigmatic, challenging part of him, matched only by his neediness and fear of rejection. Brando's own phone was listed under the name Leonard Sloot. He had also begun to monitor his incoming calls by subscribing to an answering service, yet his assumption, as one acquaintance put it, was that when it came to the inner circle, "you were in a way kind of emotionally on call for him." He'd phone and it was "Come play chess," or he'd ask the meaning or spelling of a word in a letter he was supposedly writing. Other times, his calls were "very sweet and comforting," a prelude to his inviting himself over.

"By then I always had clean sheets and nice things to eat and read," Sondra Lee said, "and Marlon liked that. I'd moved out of the Park Savoy into an apartment in the thirties, and it was probably one of those nights when he wandered in from somewhere; we were lying in bed about one or two in the morning with the lights on, chatting away, and he was talking about comfort again—as in the comfort of another person, the comfort of perhaps time going by and our knowing each other in different ways, as the core, really, of what relationships are finally about.

"Then he did it very calmly. Slowly, he poured himself two full tumblers of either vodka or gin, straight. No ice. Then without taking the glass from his lips, he emptied [them], one after another. It had nothing to do with anything that was happening, and I'd never seen him drink before.

"Whether he was testing me, experimenting with me, I don't know, but spontaneously I burst into tears. 'Why are you doing this?' I cried. He turned and said, 'You must remember, both my parents are alcoholics.'

"He then said something about Christian Science, I think, but I wasn't aware enough to ask where he'd been, what was behind this. It was totally out of left field, and the way he did it—there was no face involved, no premeditated point of view—he just drank it down like water."

Elaine Stritch saw his complexity when, again, out of the blue, he tried to make amends for having terrorized her more than two years earlier during their summer in Sayville.

"I got a call one night at nine or ten o'clock," she explained. " 'Come have a drink,' he said, 'I'm at a bar at Sixty-sixth and Lexington.'

"I remember thinking something was askew," she continued. "He ordered a Manhattan, I ordered some wine. He took a sip of his drink, not making eye contact, and then suddenly he crushed the glass. It splintered in his hand and the Manhattan spilled all over the table. He'd cut himself, but he ignored it. He looked at me and said he was sorry for what he'd put me through. I said, 'All right, let's just forget it.' I was shocked and started to cry, and I gave him a napkin to wrap around his hand."

He went out of his way to apologize to Valerie Judd, too, for having described her as one of his "fuck friends." All this penance—and the genuine enough feelings behind it—made no real difference, though. He knew he would be let off the hook. Sam Gilman continued to work parties as his private procurer, coming back always with the stock line, "Marlon, I met this girl. I think you'd like her . . ." No one sought to point out that his promiscuity might just be more complicated than he'd admit, not to mention the inconvenience and contagion of his recurrent bouts of VD.

Even so, when he made love, some of his partners found that sex with Brando could be "seamless." "I knew the skin beneath his hand was mine," said one of his partners, recalling the absence of any posturing or role-playing once he'd committed himself and felt safe with the situation. "You know how sometimes it seems prepared? Well, it doesn't take long to know who the enemy is, but here there weren't any flashes or bolts of lightning. That's what made me captive."

From the "comfort" of his foreplay to his gentle whispers, he gave off something that was almost at one with a female consciousness. "He had a wonderful touch—not only in what he said, but through his hands, through his body," Sondra Lee insisted, echoing others' reports. "He was one of the first men I knew who loved soft fabric, and under his sweater he usually wore a very soft silk shirt."

Bonding, more than appetite, was the dominant emotion, and it moved him to sleep with lesbians because he wanted to "explore." "I never knew him to be vulgar, either verbally or with his body," said one lover. "I remember once he talked about a well-known comedienne and he said something to me on the phone—'You know, she could easily become a lesbian.' I wasn't quite sure what that meant, but of course later she became a notorious lesbian. He spent a night with her. He could have said, 'You know, she's a fucking dyke.' He never did that, anything like it."

Wordlessly, he might reach out and touch a woman's face, or take her hand, caressing the fingertips, or (as he did once in broad daylight on Seventh Avenue) stop on a crowded street to adjust a girlfriend's mussed or windblown hair. When he had met Barbara Grimm for the very first time, in a roomful of people, he'd touched her nose, saying, "It's cold. . . . I wonder if your nipples are cold, too." It was technique, definitely, but the liberties he took were aura-making, and his poise, his slow-time silences, were just as compelling.

Grimm described Marlon's way of inexorably conquering his targets: "What he did was pull you in, and if he paid attention to you, it was to absorb your being, not to leave you without a being. It was as though he wanted to feel what it was to be you."

Even though he might talk barracks talk or have sex atop a bedful of overcoats in someone's back bedroom during a party, the effect was usually the same. Nor were women deterred by tales of the many abortions that supposedly resulted from his carelessness; if anything, the fact that he was ready to take care of his problems, "buying people abortions one after the other," paying "almost unthinkingly," only made him that much more special.

There were "hundreds of them," said Sondra Lee, and while abortions were quite illegal at the time, it was said that he had two doctors who were basically on retainer. One of them, "a real doctor," was in Flushing, Queens, and the other, who walked with a limp, practiced in the Bronx. They both offered anesthetic, and the going rate was reportedly $700.

"The guy in Queens was eventually sent to prison," said one of Marlon's partners, "because there was an embolism and the girl died. Marlon went with me to the clubfooted doctor in the Bronx. I was terrified. The first time I went by myself, then I had to go back because something was wrong. I told him, and he didn't hesitate at all—he went back up there with me."

Like the rest of the group, Brando rarely used birth control. "In those days, if you came prepared it was somehow calculated," Lee explained.

Nobody raised an eyebrow at the prospect of what was dubbed another "spring cleaning." One young actress, a very beautiful, fragile creature who looked like she'd stepped out of a Botticelli, was known to have had four abortions necessitated and arranged for by Marlon. Tamarin knew of three others. When one of the dancers at the Dunham School became pregnant during the winter of 1948, the way the problem was dealt with became the high-water mark of just how casually he took these things.

"The abortion party? I don't know whether I can talk about that," Barbara Grimm said. "It was so shocking, even then."

It was a big party in the Fifty-second Street building, a mob scene. The stairway was right outside the door to his apartment, and inside, Marlon was barefoot, beating on his drums. The door was open and Grimm was sitting with Wally Cox on the landing.

"No one had told me it was a coming-out party for the baby," she recalled. "I think Wally said there had been an abortion and the results of the abortion were in a Dixie cup, and someone was wandering around showing it to people."

It was the woman who had had the abortion that was now herself showcasing the exhibit, greeting guests at the door. "How do you do?" she said, "this is . . . ," pointing at the cup's contents. No one was sure if it was actually a fetus or a piece of raw liver. But no matter. As one guest noted, "These people were knocking their brains out to come up with something outlandish and strange." "I had to ask myself," said another, "if there was any sense of horror, or even inappropriateness. We were all young, of course, but I didn't have a clue as to Marlon's value system, or even if he was a fully formed person."

As it turned out, the party was the end of his affair with this girlfriend. Brando's other rejects, though, sometimes wound up crying on

Maureen Stapleton's shoulder upstairs, often in the middle of the night. It was a regular-enough routine to earn Stapleton the nickname "Aunt Maureen," the resident den mother.

By then Stapleton and Brando had known each other for three years, having met at the New School. Unlike Marlon, however, Maureen was fiercely practical. Originally from upstate New York, she'd had a poverty-stricken childhood, and when she fled to Manhattan with $100 in her pocket, she financed her training not with an allowance from home but "lots of shit jobs." With nothing but her talent to back her—no Maynard Morris and Edie Van Cleve, and no "bankable" looks, either—she landed her first role by phoning Guthrie McClintic in a state of abject terror for an audition for *The Playboy of the Western World*.

The Barretts of Wimpole Street and then *Antony and Cleopatra* followed, marking her as one of the most brilliant young actresses of the day. But rather than her acting talent, it was her street smarts that appealed to Marlon most. In the sprawling family filling the building on Fifty-second Street, they were like brother and sister. Often he'd sprint upstairs for breakfast, rousing the sleepy, protesting Stapleton, "I know, honey, but this is an emergency . . ." Even Dodie, visiting from Chicago, showed up at Stapleton's apartment and Maureen played hostess, putting on what she and roommate Janice Mars, called "little teas." When Marlon Sr. was in town, he came by, too, presenting himself as the fastidiously groomed, successful businessman. Stapleton was delighted with his stiff-upper-lip, pseudo-British charm. "You wanna talk about someone who was sexy?" she recalled. "Marlon's father. *That* was sexy."

There were people in and out of Marlon's place all the time, but Maureen's apartment was the hub, the comfort station. Wally's then girlfriend, a lithe bareback rider from a touring circus company, was bunking on the couch. Helene Franklin, another actress, had taken over the cubbyhole off the living room until she could find a place of her own. Stapleton also held Thanksgiving in her apartment, and the meal (Tastee bread and peanut butter) was so giddily communal that the whole troop—Darren, Wally, the actor David Stewart, Janice, Marlon, and the rest—flung open the windows to yell, "Thanks, God," up and down the street while falling over themselves with laughter. The apartment was also a communal dressing room, the place where non-Equity friends could change before an audition.

"It was a madhouse," said Gail Keith-Jones, another regular, "with everybody doing whatever it was that they were focused on at the moment." Downstairs, Marlon might play his bongos well into the early morning hours, but no one complained; when he ascended to Maureen's, he'd sit on the john with the door open, and Maureen herself thought nothing of walking around in her underwear. Stapleton's other roommate, Jane Fortner, and sometimes a visiting Julie Harris usually held themselves above the fray, but every two weeks Janice Mars was "falling in love." Later, Jane Fortner would literally set the place on fire. "The apartment has been burned," she telephoned Maureen, blithely adding, "Don't go home, because you don't have one."

Eventually everyone had "sort of a nervous breakdown," said Stapleton. The Louise Brooks look-alike Janice Mars fell into heavy drinking. Fortner killed herself, and even Maureen would later come apart. Flo Goodman, by this time Darren Dublin's wife, grabbed a carving knife during brunch one morning and started ranting at Wally's girlfriend, "If you ever speak to my husband again, I'm going to shove this up your ass!" Two of the men in the apartment quickly took the knife away. Janice turned and asked, "Would anyone like some more coffee?" Wally, likewise, pretended nothing had happened.

For Marlon, there was nothing untoward about any of this. When Joe Spery showed up for a visit, he quickly enlisted his old Libertyville pal to help him dump horse turds through the skylight of the noisy nightclub next door. "We were having breakfast at about midnight, upstairs in Maureen's apartment," Spery recalled, "and the place looked down on the skylight of this restaurant, Leon and Eddie's, which Bud told me was *the* place, with big entertainers, 'dancing under the stars.' "

"Then he said, 'Come on,' and we went up to Central Park on his motorcycle, where he scooped up these lovely horse apples with a cardboard lid. Back at the apartment Maureen was looking at us as if we were crazy. But we lobbed them through the skylight. Bud was cracking up. Then he grabbed my arm and we got out of there real quick, and didn't come back until the next morning."

Maureen was more serious about acting than any of them, but nowhere was her basic savvy more apparent than in her attitude toward money. Marlon was chronically borrowing and "I was like always the mean one," Stapleton recalled, "the bag lady. He would borrow because he'd given all his money away, and then no one had the nerve to ask for it back. He was the Golden Boy, remember? So they'd come to me and say, 'Mo, Marlon owes me $5.' I'd tell him, 'You owe her money. Pay her.' It was always little sums, but people were too scared to ask."

The fact that there was nothing physical between Maureen and Marlon made her commands acceptable, just as it allowed for an easiness in their relationship that bypassed a lot of Brando's usual games. After he took her to see *Hamlet*, the two of them wandered around midtown and he goofily pretended to be blind, with Maureen guiding him. Later, when he brought her home and said good-night, she slapped him. "What was that for?" he demanded. "Because you're not even going to ask me to go to bed with you," she replied.

"She was the first girl to make 'fuck' sound funny," said Fred Sadoff, who'd worked with Stapleton at the Neighborhood Playhouse and sometimes came by the apartment. But beneath the humor Maureen and Marlon shared a well-tuned bullshit detector. Equally, they were both especially sensitive to each other's pain, and Maureen, perhaps more than anyone, saw through his veil of silence. "Marlon, oh man, you want to talk about pain," she later acknowledged, pointing out also that he was always there for her, even in the face of Stapleton's growing alcoholism.

"He tried, God knows he tried," she said, recalling how he came to her one afternoon when she was very drunk. "I was in love with an actor who'd left me, I'd been crying for two days, and he said, 'Okay, you want to have another drink?' I said yes. He took me downstairs, we went to a bar, then to another bar. I kept falling down. He kept picking me up. He said, 'Are you ready to go home?' I said, 'Yeah,' and he took me back, dragged me up the four flights of stairs, and threw me down on my bed. 'Are you all right?' he asked. I said no. 'Well, you better be,' he told me, and he covered me up. Janice came in and I heard him say, 'She's so drunk. . . . Will you take over now?'

"But you see, by taking me to every bar and getting me as drunk as I wanted to be, he got me over the hump, broke the back of the pain. He hadn't been drinking with me, he was just waiting for me to fall off the stool. The message was, I'm here. You drink just as much as you want. It's your drunk, it's your life."

Around this time his relationship with Blossom Plumb started to go sour. It started with an altercation. Marlon went into withdrawal, then insisted, "My terms or nothing." Blossom soon ran off with director George Auerbach. Marlon was also increasingly ambivalent about Celia Webb. She was still living in the apartment Marlon had rented for her on MacDougal Street in the Village. But when they were invited together to social evenings, he'd show up with other women and "just pretend Celia wasn't there."

If there was anything emblematic of Brando's confusions, it was his pendulum swings with women—frantic pursuit or defensive withdrawal. It was a clinically overdetermined pattern: a repetition of maternal rejection, a childhood hatred of Dodie as a "whore," and his own adult promiscuity with easy women who became substitutes for the despised yet longed-for mother. Self-loathing lay at the heart of the dilemma, and even the jokey Darren Dublin saw the problem as his friend's inability "to accept love from or trust women, a tendency to destroy the things he loved, to turn on those people who cared about him."

During these months of 1947, in the chaotic frenzy of the New York drama world, Brando was both a whirling dervish and the silent eye of the storm. While he was able to hold the nightmares at bay with his control and manipulation of others, his upcoming role in *A Streetcar Named Desire* would not only bring him unparalleled fame but also leave him more divided than ever, vulnerable to his worst fears and doubts, despite seeking help through psychoanalysis.

STREETCAR AND THE ACTORS STUDIO

1947–49

Brando was not the first choice to play Stanley Kowalski, nor was he expected to steal the show from the play's heroine and turn his character into an American icon. When Tennessee Williams completed *A Streetcar Named Desire* in the summer of 1946, it was still called *The Poker Night,* the story of a lonely, neurotic southern belle, Blanche Du Bois, who has lost her family's estate and is forced to seek refuge in New Orleans with her sister and brutal brother-in-law. The drama of her destruction was clearly Williams's central vision, mirroring the defeat of southern culture by the harshness and vulgarity of the modern world. Yet the loss of Blanche's homestead and sanity was more than an observation of social and historical phenomena: "I draw all my characters from myself," said the shy, embattled playwright. As Williams's biographer, Donald Spoto, has made clear, the protective but destructive Stanley and the spiritual but manipulative sensualist Blanche represent the playwright's own desire for security and his inclination for multiple and casual sexual partners. The conflict between Williams's characters—as well as the conflict within himself—was about to give rise to the most difficult and protracted struggle yet in Marlon's life.

Two years earlier, *The Glass Menagerie*, with the incomparable Laurette Taylor in the lead, had put Williams in the forefront of contemporary dramatists. When it was announced that the producer for his latest work was to be Irene Mayer Selznick, the reaction along Broadway was resentment, then outrage. Many complained that Selznick was a West Coast amateur who stuttered, the daughter of film mogul Louis B. Mayer and the wife of David O. Selznick, producer of *Gone with the Wind*. *Streetcar* was no more than a bauble, a plaything for her to use against her famous husband, from whom she had recently separated (David O. Selznick's affair with leading lady Jennifer Jones was now known). For the thirty-six-year-old Williams and his agent, Audrey Wood, however, this was immaterial. Irene Selznick had connections. Inexperienced or not, she had beaten out more experienced hands in obtaining the rights to the play and, reportedly, she was worth $16 million. She was also ready to invest $25,000 of the play's projected $100,000 budget, with the rest to come from such friends as Cary Grant and John Hay Whitney.

By early summer of 1947, Irene Selznick's first choice to direct was Joshua Logan, Broadway's most successful director. In the meantime, Williams had arrived in New York and seen Arthur Miller's *All My Sons*. Williams decided on Miller's director for his own play—namely, Elia Kazan, who was just finishing editing *Gentleman's Agreement*, a film that would win him his first Academy Award. The two men liked each other instantly, and the intense, thirty-eight-year-old Kazan expressed his willingness to take on the project. But not with Irene Selznick as producer.

In a world of rampant egos and high purpose, what Kazan wanted wasn't unusual: absolute artistic power over all production decisions and the opportunity to produce the play himself. Williams was caught in the middle. He was committed to Selznick, yet he was unwilling to give up Kazan. Negotiations between the producer and the director's lawyer went on for days, with Kazan eventually getting almost everything he wanted: 20 percent of the profits, guaranteed control, and an unprecedented production credit that would read, "Irene Selznick Presents an Elia Kazan Production."

At first, it seemed that two Hollywood stars, Margaret Sullavan and John Garfield, would play the leads. But Sullavan, who was Selznick's choice, failed to win over Williams with her reading. Kazan considered Mary Martin, but only briefly. Garfield was a problem, too. The short, tough-talking Group Theatre alumnus had vowed to return to Broadway after years in Hollywood, and he wanted to work with Kazan on the play, which he very much liked. While contract negotiations were still under way, however, *Body and Soul* had been released, and once again an important star, Garfield was reluctant to make a comeback in less than a guaranteed star vehicle. He asked Williams to do a rewrite and build up the part of Kowalski; Williams refused. Garfield also insisted on the right to leave the show after the first four months; Selznick refused. He also wanted to be guaranteed the movie role. Mrs. Selznick, with considerable embarrassment, was forced to announce to the press that Garfield was not going to star in her show after all.

Meanwhile, the search for Blanche had taken a new turn when the production team was informed of a revival of Williams's early one-act play, *Portrait of a Madonna*, at the Actors' Lab in Los Angeles. The play's protagonist was an early version, a study, of *Streetcar*'s Blanche, and was currently being played by the British actress Jessica Tandy to excellent notices. Tandy's astute husband, Hume Cronyn, was directing, and he had in fact arranged the revival in lieu of a New York audition for *Streetcar*. After traveling to the West Coast, Selznick, Kazan, and Williams unanimously agreed to offer Tandy the role.

It was now mid-August 1947, almost the beginning of the theater season, and next to be cast was Karl Malden, whose work Kazan knew from *Truckline Café*, as Stanley's friend Mitch. Kim Hunter, who had never appeared on Broadway and hadn't quite made it in films, either, was called into the city from upstate New York, where she was doing stock. Although she gave a nervous audition, she was offered the part of Stella. For the all-important role of Stanley, feelers had been sent out to Burt Lancaster, who was otherwise committed, and to Van Heflin, Edmond O'Brien, John Lund, and Gregory Peck. At this point, Kazan got another phone call from Edie Van Cleve, pressing for Marlon.

Brando had already been rejected because he was too young—twenty-three while Williams described Kowalski as thirty. Also deemed too "pretty," Brando looked more like a poet than Williams's beer-drinking mechanic. With the ever persuasive Van Cleve pressing, however, Kazan didn't hang up the phone. A self-described "gambler," he knew from *Truckline* that Marlon had the animal magnetism, and he urged Selznick to reconsider. She had seen Brando in *Mama*, *Candida*, and, more convincingly, watched him bring the house down in *A Flag Is Born*. With yet another phone call, Van Cleve argued that "an audition would prove nothing except that Marlon was a lousy reader," a fact that Kazan already knew.

Marlon himself had already read the play, which left him deeply impressed but equally intimidated. "I finally decided that it was a size too large for me," he later told reporter Bob Thomas, "and called Gadg to tell him so. The line was busy. Had I spoken to him at that moment, I'm certain I wouldn't have played the role. I decided to let it rest for a while, and the next day Gadg called me and said: 'Well, what is it—yes or no?' I gulped and said, 'Yes.'"

Kazan still wanted him to read for Williams, who was up in Provincetown again with his volatile lover, Pancho Rodriguez. Margo Jones and Joanna Albus were visiting from Texas, sitting around the playwright's weathered beach shack discussing the Dallas opening of *Summer and Smoke* when Marlon sauntered in, accompanied by Celia Webb. It was late afternoon, the group was half plastered, and no one seemed to care that the cottage's electricity and plumbing had been out for days. As Williams later recalled, Marlon immediately stuck his hand into the overflowing toilet bowl to unclog it, then tackled the blown fuses using copper pennies. When everything was working again, he began his audition, standing in the center of the tiny, low-ceilinged living room, the tide lapping against the beach only a stone's throw away.

"I had read for about thirty seconds," Brando said later, "when Williams told me to my red face that I showed so much assurance and understanding of his play that he had no doubt I was the right actor for the part. Then he loaned me bus fare to get back to New York to sign the contract in the producer's office."

Unlike Garfield's demand for an "out" clause permitting him to leave the play at any time after the first four months, Brando had committed for two years. The paperwork settled, Marlon proceeded to have his first meeting with Selznick. As she later recalled in her memoirs: "He didn't behave like someone to whom something wonderful had just happened, nor did he try to make an impression; he was too busy assessing me," the producer said. "Whatever he expected, I wasn't it. He seemed wary and at a loss how to classify me. He was wayward one moment, playful the next, volunteering that he had been expelled from school, then grinning provocatively at me. I didn't take the bait. It was easy going after that. He sat up in his chair and turned forthright, earnest, even polite."

Most of the cast, including supporting players Nick Dennis and Rudy Bond, were recruits from the newly formed Actors Studio, which had coalesced under the tutelage of Kazan and Bobby Lewis less than a month before. Among the leads, Tandy was the only nonmember of the Studio. Joe Mielziner, Broadway's leading set designer, had been brought aboard with Lucinda Ballard, the costume designer from *I Remember Mama*. Alex North, husband of the Studio's dance instructor, Anna Sokolow, was to do the play's all-important jazz score. Securing a theater had been problematic, since the feeling up and down Broadway was that *Streetcar* was commercially risky. The three-and-a-half-week rehearsal period began on October 6 in the New Amsterdam Roof Theatre purely on an interim basis. The building was a huge, spooky place—private and silent, just as Kazan liked it.

The director, who was known for his short and intensive rehearsals, devoted the first ten days to exploring the play's "relationships." Sitting in a semicircle on the stage, the actors read individual scenes over and over again while he presented his thoughts on the "spine" of each character: Blanche, he pointed out, wants to "find protection"; Stanley, to "keep things his way"; Stella, to "hold on to Stanley"; and Mitch, he offered, psychoanalytically, "needs to get away from his mother." Brando's Stanley, caught in the nexus of these conflicting desires, fights for the continuation of the status quo despite Blanche's invasion.

Given his background in the Group, not to say his own style, Kazan's method relied heavily on making connections between Williams's script and the actors' personal experiences. To make everything work, he went out of his way to observe the cast members' behavior, interviewing each of them as carefully as possible, usually over a drink in a neighborhood bar. Family, religion, schooling, sexual likes and dislikes, all were fair game for his probing, and he dug very subtly, offering things about his own life in order to draw his actors out.

"It would be like friendship, give and take," Hunter recalled. "But gradually he would lead into things that he just piled up and stored away for when he could go after them. . . . He would sneak into everyone, get to know what keys to press when he wanted this or that . . . [and] he was ruthless in getting whatever he needed. . . . But he also respected his actors. Whatever he'd tell you—and it was often pretty personal stuff that he was drawing out of you—nobody else knew about it except the two of you. Rarely was there the out-loud kind of thing that many directors do with the whole company listening."

Not even Kazan's closest friends, like Harold Clurman or Bobby Lewis, were aware that the director's brother, Avram, was then a practicing psychoanalyst—indeed, an orthodox Freudian—who had invested in the show. Doubtless, Kazan had adopted some of his brother's methods, but even had Marlon known this, it would not have mattered: More than anyone in the cast, he was reluctant to let the short, determined director "sneak in." Kazan, though, had already picked up on this, and while the director's aim was to mine what was beneath the surface, to excavate what he later called Brando's "great underground," he knew he had to work the rim, to proceed "gently." "With other actors, I'd always say just what I want: 'You do this. No, I don't like that, I want you to do it like this,'" he explained. "With Marlon . . . it was more like, 'Listen to this and let's see what you do with it.' . . . I'd heard about his parents, but not from him, and I never asked. I treated him with great delicacy. One reason he got to trust me—as a director—was that I respected his privacy. . . . I was always hoping for a miracle with him, and I often got it."

Nonetheless, it was a slow process. Marlon volunteered little and when Kazan gave directions, he often walked away before the director was finished; not rudely, but to ponder what he was saying. "Look," Kazan recalled, "[Marlon] was always at arm's length and he felt safe there, uninspected, unprobed. How much of the potential penetration was based on my insight, as opposed to stuff I picked up here and there, I don't know. . . . It's my trade, though. I knew where to look, where to put my hand in, what to try to pull out, what to get."

Marlon's anxiety was more than passing, though, and now, as Malden, Hunter, and the veteran Tandy were also struggling with the ambiguities of Williams's play, he kept repeating, "They should have got John Garfield for Stanley, not me." Garfield was beside the point, however. Stanley, as Brando saw him, was "aggressive, unpremeditated, overt, and completely without doubt about himself . . . intolerant and selfish." As he explained, the character whom he had to master was "a man without any sensitivity, without any kind of morality except his own mewling, whimpering insistence on his own way . . . one of those guys who work hard and have lots of flesh with nothing supple about them. They never open their fists, really. They grip a cup like an animal would wrap a paw around it. They're so muscle-bound they can hardly talk."

It was simpler than morals, or even aesthetics, though. Kazan had always cast "experientially": the alcoholic James Dunn as the hard-drinking ne'er-do-well Johnny Nolan in *A Tree Grows in Brooklyn;* later, the neurotic, rebellious James Dean as Cal Trask in *East of Eden,* where Kazan also used Raymond Massey's personal distaste for Dean to step up the tensions between father and son, much as he had unhesitatingly capitalized on the long-standing enmity between Tallulah Bankhead and Florence Eldridge in *The Skin of Our Teeth.* Here, Stanley hit Brando too close to home; given the actor's own bottled-up rage and his paralyzing lack of articulateness, not to mention sexual promiscuity, the character whose skin he had to get comfortable in was akin to a psychological showdown. Kazan sensed and smelled this, and in his inimitably "ruthless" way, he intended to use his conception of Kowalski to force Brando's confrontation with himself: To Kazan, Stanley was not a villain, simply a man determined to protect his home.

In a letter to the director, Williams put it more directly: "There are no 'good' or 'bad' people. Some are a little better or a little worse but all are activated more by misunderstanding than malice. A blindness to what is going on in each other's hearts. Stanley sees Blanche not as a desperate, driven creature, backed into a last corner to make a last desperate stand— but as a calculating bitch with 'round heels.' . . . Nobody sees anybody truly but all through the flaws of their own egos. That is the way we all see each other in life."

Williams had also noted that although Blanche must have the understanding and compassion of the audience, this should not make "a black-dyed villain" of her brother-in-law. Kazan, now working hand in hand with the playwright, agreed. Stanley likes to "keep things his way," he wrote in his notes, "and he does *not* want them upset by a phony, corrupt, sick, destructive woman." Blanche may regard Stanley as her "executioner," but she is the intruder and has put herself in harm's way. *"This makes Stanley right!"* Kazan insisted, adding as an afterthought, "Are we going into the era of Stanley? He may be practical and right . . . but where the hell does it leave us?"

While the ambiguities were enormous, Kazan knew he was dealing with "an actor, an emotional person," not an intellectual, and he continued to leave Brando lots of elbow room. At the end of the first week of rehearsal, Marlon moved a cot into the theater and spent nights hearing the vast silence of the empty hall, still wrestling with the part. By the middle of the second week, it looked as though he were losing the battle. One morning he was very late, pale and unshaven. "He slunk onto the stage," Irene Selznick recalled. "Gadg went over to him. I held my breath. But there was no scene. As Gadg listened, he put his arms around Marlon. It was extraordinary to see so tough a man as Gadg be tender. Gadg gave him some money and sent him out to eat; he hadn't slept either. Lest I be critical of Marlon," she added, "Gadg told me there had been no misbehavior, that Marlon was having a terrible struggle with his role."

The incident was pivotal, even though Selznick didn't see it then. Marlon's dilemma was that he couldn't get a fix on his character because it all had to come from inside. He was working intuitively, more intuitively than the others, and in all likelihood he didn't know quite how he was proceeding. While the other leads were struggling to find their own parts, Kazan let him proceed with just "muttered snatches of his speeches."

It was a "team play," though, and Brando was so intent on his character that sometimes he'd break the tempo completely. The mild-mannered Malden was the first to explode. "We were rehearsing the bathroom scene, the one where I come out and meet Blanche for the first time and Stanley says, 'Hey, Mitch, come on!' Now, as we were working on it, every day would be different. Marlon would come in before you said your line, or way after you said your line, or even before you had anything to say. The beat was all wrong.

"Anyway, it was just beginning to go well for me for the first time— when you think, Oh, my god, this is it—and *boom,* he hit me with one that just upset everything. I said, 'Oh, shit!' and threw something and walked offstage, up into the attic. Kazan said, 'What the hell happened?'

" 'I can't concentrate,' I told him. 'I was going along beautifully and all of a sudden in comes this jarring thing. It throws me. It's impossible.' I was furious and explained that it had been happening regularly. He said, 'Wait.' "

The next day Kazan called a rehearsal just for the four leads. "Let's talk this out right now," he said. "Karl, you have to get used to the way Marlon works. But Marlon, you must remember that there are other people in the cast also."

For the moment, Kazan's authority held sway. Marlon began to focus on his lines instead of wasting the play's flow on "handles"—the antecedent sighs, mumbles, and body movements actors often rely upon as emotional triggers. Nonetheless, his "uh-h-h" sounds still left his partners' timing in shambles, and most affected of all was Tandy. The product of a classical British training with almost twenty years' stage experience, she could not relate to Marlon, especially not to his personal behavior. There were his drums and dumbbells backstage, his cot, and the nights alone in the theater when he'd just crash in his street clothes. It all seemed to be epitomized by the split seam in the back of his trousers, an ordinary tear that had been getting bigger for the past several days until now it extended almost down to his crotch. For Tandy, it was appalling. She spoke to Kazan, who had to tell him to take his pants to the cleaners and have them mended.

This kind of incident, though, only strengthened Marlon's bond with the director, since it gave Kazan further opportunity to show his commitment. "I don't think anyone else was ever in control," said Jay Presson Allen. "Gadg was the only one." If they were both control freaks, Marlon watched the director fend off Selznick daily as she leaned forward to whisper suggestions, smiling as he'd unceremoniously yell, "Get out of my ear!" until he refused to let her sit anywhere near him. What Brando saw was an unwillingness to compromise, an intensity or private "center" that perhaps matched his own. Kazan had *faith,* and if anything, the trust deepened as the director continued making adjustments to his performance, careful always to let his actor find his own way.

"Gadg is a lover when he's directing," said Bobby Lewis, pointing out the delicacy here. "He comes up to you and puts his arm around you and talks into your ear . . . and you feel, This man wants me to be great, I can't let him down. . . . He makes you feel that he's not only talking about what he wants you to do in the play, but that he just loves you more than anybody in the world. It's not only women. Anybody. It's what he wins you with."

In a sense, what Marlon was seeing was a new kind of machismo. Kazan even looked the part. He dressed casually in floppy, unpressed trousers and comported himself like a bantam cock even though he'd attended Williams and Yale. He was tough, instinctively attuned to power, but he was also ready to let his actors make all the mistakes in the world. His message was that they were all searching, every one of them, and he could hand Brando a note onstage, with Tennessee Williams and Irene Selznick and stage manager Bob Downey out front—a change, an idea that had suddenly come to him—and Marlon would nod, murmuring, "Let's try it." There was even the occasional smile. Tandy might be "square," "a joke," or little more than a maiden aunt, but Brando was Kazan's adopted son, and now for the first time he was starting to show signs of working as a team player.

"He needed reassurance or nurturing, and lacked a certain confidence," Kazan recalled, "but he soon felt very at ease with Nick Dennis and Karl Malden and Kim. He'd come to work and he'd be happy in the theater. . . . He'd fool around and box down in the cellar, and you could hear him laughing. You knew that whatever life meant to him, it had to mean this kind of happiness."

To get at what he considered the essential muscularity of the character, Marlon had returned to his daily workout routine at a local gym, working with weights to build up his chest and biceps to "get closer" to Stanley. People who hadn't seen Marlon for a while were amazed at the transformation. Truman Capote actually mistook him for a stagehand when he saw him asleep on a table before rehearsal one morning. "His squat gymnasium physique—the weight lifter's arms, the Charles Atlas chest" was in startling contrast with his features, the writer observed. "It was as if a stranger's head had been attached to the brawny body, as in certain counterfeit photographs."

Another move to get inside the carnivorous Stanley took the form of starving himself. Brando always had a hearty appetite, but one afternoon he ordered himself a burger and fries at a restaurant and just sat there, looking at it. "I was slurping and gobbling everything on my plate," his companion, another actor, said, "but he wouldn't eat. It was an acting assignment he'd given himself, to regard his behavior being hungry, denying himself food in order to see what his juices were."

Lucinda Ballard had done the costumes for Williams's *The Glass Menagerie* as well as *I Remember Mama* and many other shows, but the raw Kowalski was a new challenge. A crew of Con Ed ditch diggers in midtown Manhattan provided the inspiration for the "undesigned" garb that was to become part of Kowalski-the-icon, the new symbol of American maleness.

"Their clothes were so dirty," she recalled, seeing the laborers, "that they had stuck to their bodies. It was sweat, of course, but they looked like statues. I thought, 'That's the look I want . . . the look of animalness.' "

The conventional Hanes T-shirt in those days was worn loose, with sleeves down to the elbows. For Stanley, it would have to cling, so she modified a half-dozen undershirts, dyeing them a faded red, then carefully tearing the right shoulder to suggest that Stella might have scratched Stanley or pulled at him.

Next, she invented the first pair of fitted blue jeans, changing forever not just the face of theater but American fashion. "I thought of them as though they were garments in the time of the Regency in France," she said, "which meant fitting the Levi's wet, pinning them tight. I had seven pair and I washed them in a washing machine for twenty-four hours, then Marlon and I went to the Eaves Costume Company. He was up on a pedestal, looking at himself in the mirror, when he insisted on being fitted without any underwear."

The head tailor, a dignified, old-world Italian accustomed to fitting Barrymore and Lunt in purple velvet, was appalled, but Ballard complied, leaving the dressing room. When she returned, they had finished the basting, and Marlon "almost went crazy." "He was dancing between the glass cases, leaping like a tiger in this costume that outlined his body, literally leaping up off the ground," the designer recalled. The tailor smiled "as one would about a child," but Brando was unfazed, saying, "This is it! This is what I've always wanted!"

During the run of the show, he started wearing the skin-tight Levi's home until the wardrobe mistress got instructions from Selznick to be sure he changed before leaving. Ballard had "painted" the trousers, strategically deepening the blue at the sides to get a straight up-and-down look, to "accent the maleness, the muscles." For the initial fitting, she had removed the interior of the side pockets, which Marlon now pleaded with her not to put back in. When she pointed out that Stanley needed real pockets because he gambled, he countered, "Yes, but the back pocket is where he kept his money." Finally, he confessed: "Well, I think Stanley was like me—very physical. And I think that Stanley would have liked to push his hands in his pockets and feel himself."

He confided in her when it came time to dye his hair, too. Stanley couldn't be blond, but Marlon protested any change. The costume designer wanted his eyebrows and eyelashes darkened, too.

"Where am I going to have it done?" Brando asked, nervously.

"What if I arrange with Charles of the Ritz to do it in the evening so you'll be the only one there?" Ballard offered. "They'll keep the place open an extra hour and a half or something."

"Are you coming with me?"

She agreed. At the last minute, however, he balked, mumbling about how "feminine smelling" the salon was, and Ballard had to "practically drive him in."

He emerged with the dark brown hair that shot him to stardom, and the rehearsals continued. He sucked on cigarettes, cigars, and bottles with a hedonistic gusto, but it was exactly what Kazan meant when he wrote in his preparatory notes, "God and nature gave [Stanley] a fine sensory apparatus . . . he enjoys!" It wasn't just Brando's uncanny absorption in the role that overwhelmed the director. What he was doing was ripping apart the conventional line of dialogue, "discovering a way for scripted words to express the tension in an inarticulate man between what flies out of his mouth and what he can't find words for." Playing a subtext at odds with the written word wasn't anything new, but Marlon was now taking it past *Truckline,* weighting his gestures and silences to the point where they were beginning to eclipse the words.

By mid-October the cast was up to eight hours of work at night, in addition to the two hours of rehearsal each morning. At Williams's insistence, the script was frozen. About a week later Marlon "suddenly shot up," as Selznick's assistant Irving Schneider put it, in a run-through with both Stella Adler and Hume Cronyn in the audience. Afterward Cronyn expressed his concern; his wife, he felt, could do better, and he asked Kazan to keep encouraging her. In fact, what he had intuited was that the meaning of the play had been altered. He foresaw that Brando's performance was beginning to shift the play's balance and would make the young actor the star of the show.

"Perhaps Hume meant," Kazan wrote years later, "that by contrast with Marlon, whose every word seemed not something memorized but the spontaneous expression of an intense inner experience—which is the level of work all actors try to reach—Jessie was what? Expert? Professional? Was that enough for this play? Not for Hume. Hers seemed to be a performance; Marlon was living on stage. Jessie had every moment worked out carefully, with sensitivity and intelligence, and it was all coming together, just as Williams and I had expected and wanted. Marlon, working 'from the inside,' rode his emotion wherever it took him; his performance was full of surprises and exceeded what Williams and I had expected. A performance miracle was in the making."

Days later, the "miracle" was confirmed by the reactions of people who came to the final run-throughs. They raved about Marlon, but had to be asked about Jessica. "Tandy's fine," they said, "just fine."

At the beginning of November, after three and a half weeks in New York, the company went to New Haven for tryouts. The first night was a technical mess. The lighting, like Alex North's jazz score, was very much a part of the overall design and called for a huge array of equipment— "enough to light Radio City Music Hall"—but the complicated cues hadn't been sufficiently rehearsed. Still, the play was well received, and the audience's response was especially warm toward Marlon, which left Kazan worried. "What would I say to Brando? Be less good? Or to Jessie? Get better?" The fact that Williams, also an inveterate worrier, seemed happy puzzled him. When Kazan brought up the subject, the playwright advised him not to take sides. "When you begin to arrange an action to make a thematic point, the fidelity to life will suffer," he cautioned. "Go on working as you are. Marlon is a genius, but she's a worker and she will get better."

After four sold-out performances in New Haven, the company moved on to Boston, everyone wondering if *Streetcar* wasn't too gamey for their blue-blooded audience, which had walked out on an earlier Williams play. But the reception was even warmer than in Connecticut. Cast expectations were running high, and jumped higher still when they went on to Philadelphia. Kazan, fearing that the actors might become overconfident, warned them not to pay attention to what people were saying, to think of their project as no more than "a nice little play." Just before the New York opening, he urged them, "What we've got here is oysters. Not everyone has a taste for oysters. . . . Just do the play and hope for the best."

On December 3, 1947, *Streetcar* opened in New York at the Ethel Barrymore Theatre. Tickets had been at a premium, thanks to all the out-of-town word of mouth, and stars like Paul Muni, Montgomery Clift, and Edward G. Robinson turned out along with Marlon's parents, his sisters, and Dick Loving. Irene Selznick later recalled what happened: "In those days, people stood only for the national anthem. That night was the first time I ever saw an audience get to its feet, and the first time I saw the Shuberts stay for a final curtain . . . round after round, curtain after curtain, until Tennessee took a bow on the stage to bravos."

The audience applauded for a full half hour, in fact, and when Marlon came out, the house caved in. Backstage, after Williams's final ovation, it was a mob scene. Wally Cox and his friend Peter Turgeon had managed to fight their way through the crowds to Marlon's dressing room and found him holding a box of chocolates and several telegrams, standing alone while Malden entertained a throng of well-wishers with champagne. One of the wires read: "TRY NOT TO MAKE AN ASS OF YOURSELF. MOM." Another, from Williams, brought a smile to his face as he showed it to them: "RIDE OUT BOY AND SEND IT SOLID. FROM THE GREASY POLACK YOU WILL SOME DAY ARRIVE AT THE GLOOMY DANE FOR YOU HAVE SOMETHING THAT MAKES THE THEATRE A WORLD OF GREAT POSSIBILITIES."

"You've become a star tonight," Turgeon told him. Marlon just shrugged, "Oh, shit, don't be ridiculous."

The cast had been asked to an after-show party on the top floor of "21" to await the reviews. Louis B. Mayer was there, delighted with his daughter's success, but he still complained that the play needed "a happy ending." Williams himself paced uneasily, downing one champagne after another, haunted with doubt despite his standing ovations. When Marlon walked through the door, the crowd turned and applauded his entrance. Darren was also there, and he watched his pal shyly introduce Dodie, Marlon Sr., and his brother-in-law to Williams, Williams's brother Dakin, and their mother, as well as to Kazan, Kazan's parents, and both Selznicks (Irene's estranged husband, David, had flown in from California for the opening). Shortly after midnight, the show's press agent phoned that the word was good, in fact excellent. By about 1:30, Brando was gone but Kazan rose with the reviews in hand, and as he read them aloud, the room filled with wave after wave of applause and giddy laughter.

The New York critics were nearly unanimous in their praise—better than anyone could have hoped. Brooks Atkinson of the *Times* raved about Williams's writing, Kazan's directing, and Tandy's acting. For Howard Barnes, in the New York *Herald Tribune,* Marlon was "brutally convincing." The *New Yorker* gave Brando full credit for a "brutally effective characterization," while Robert Garland saw "our theater's most memorable young actor at his most memorable." Richard Watts Jr. went so far as to confess in the *New York Post:* "I have hitherto not shared the enthusiasm of most reviewers for Marlon Brando, but his portrayal of the heroine's sullen, violent nemesis is an excellent piece of work."

Although most critics were overflowing in their praise, not one of them saw that Brando's performance was likely to change the face of American acting. But the cognoscenti knew what was happening. "There were no models for Marlon," Robert Whitehead remembered thinking, having dismissed John Garfield as stuck back in the Depression. "His relationship to the sounds and poetic reality of Williams was particularly embracing; what Tennessee wrote, both in relation to the age and Marlon's sensibility, it all worked. . . . That particular kind of reality existed in a way that it hadn't ever before." For Maureen Stapleton, it was simpler still—no actor except Olivier, maybe Gable, Joel McCrea, and Bogart had gotten as close. "It goes well beyond talent," she recognized. "It's *male*. It's talent *plus*." Don Richardson, an actor and contemporary of Brando, had been in the audience with Gary Merrill and a younger, up-and-coming actor named Rex Williams. When the final curtain came down, all three were "overwhelmed. Williams said he was going to quit the theater after seeing Marlon," Richardson recalled. "Merrill told me, 'Well, now I'll only be a second lead.' " Joan Copeland recalls the feelings of everyone at the recently established Actors Studio. "Watching him," she said, "was like being in the eye of the hurricane."

In the rudest sense, he'd knocked the town on its backside. "He'd created not only a standard of acting, but a style," said Bobby Lewis, "which was unfortunate, since everybody after that wanted to act like Marlon Brando."

The obsession with imitating Brando would be abetted by agents and producers for decades to come, and even Ralph Meeker, Marlon's understudy, was about to fall into lockstep. James Dean, Paul Newman, Steve McQueen, Rip Torn, and other Method actors would follow suit. What it amounted to was that Brando's sexuality was something no one had ever seen before—slow, moody, a tapestry of self-doubt. If Clift had introduced a kind of passion that was on the immature side, primarily adolescent, filled with wonder and longing, then, as Billy Redfield observed, Marlon was delivering something that was "uncomfortable and dangerous." Likewise, if Van Johnson spoke for Des Moines, Brando was the future: He'd pried loose something so basic, so ordinary that no one could doubt its authenticity any more than claim comfort from what it seemed to suggest.

Streetcar was a hit, and Brando the hottest star in town. With posters for *Streetcar* everywhere, he was no longer anonymous. He was being paid $550 a week, the equivalent of $7,500 in today's dollars. But the producers could easily afford it. Every show was sold out, and scalpers' tickets had climbed to $50 apiece and more—ten times their face value.

Although Williams was destined to win both the Pulitzer Prize and Drama Critics Circle Award, and Tandy would garner a Tony, it was Marlon who had become the darling of the press: He was young, sexy, a little weird, and as Jocelyn put it, "everybody wanted a piece of him."

With the coaching of Selznick's press agent, Ben Kornzweig, he now offered no more false biographies, and went so far as to differentiate between "legitimate professional promotion" and what he dubbed "the revolting personalized notoriety which passes as publicity in the films, and to a lesser extent, in certain circles of the legitimate stage." *Life, Look,* the *Saturday Evening Post, Vogue, Mademoiselle,* the fan magazines and daily press—all clamored for interviews. Cecil Beaton and lesser lights took his photograph. People pointed him out on the street. Slowly, there emerged a persona.

"The theater to me is just a job. Just like slicing baloney," he told the *New York Post* in an interview titled "Portrait of the Actor as a Young Man." "It's my favorite way of slicing baloney, the pay is better." He talked about the importance of listening to one's own voice, always careful to mention his debt to Adler and Kazan. He explained his attitude to success, at the same time pitching himself as speaking from the heart, which only made him appear more removed: "It's so easy not to live a normal life in the theater—to splash your ego all over Broadway! And if you succumb to all the superfluous temptations that come your way, then you can very easily destroy yourself."

On theater critics: "You can't listen to the reviewers, because they don't know anything about acting. They can only speak in primary terms. The thing that matters is what you think of yourself."

On being an "artist": "It's a word that I don't like to throw around. I really don't know what it means."

On interviews: "They make for a distorted picture of success. . . . People think that as soon as you're successful that you don't bleed when you're cut; you never have any problems. Believe me, it's not true. . . . Why should I lend myself to the distortion?"

Years later, offering a more sanguine appraisal of what was happening, Brando mused: "It took me a long time before I was aware that that's what I was—a big success. I was so absorbed in myself, my own problems, I never looked around, took account. I used to walk in New York, miles and miles, walk in the streets late at night, and never *see* anything. I was never sure about acting, whether that was what I really wanted to do; I'm still not. Then, when I was in *Streetcar*, and it had been running a couple of months, one night—dimly, dimly—I began to hear this roar. It was like I'd been asleep, and I woke up here sitting on a pile of candy."

The roar of acclaim and public celebrity was constant, and it made him uncomfortable. Jocelyn, however, insisted that his overnight success hadn't really changed him. She said, "His attitude was, I opened a play, I was good in it, but am I any different than before? No. He didn't feel any different. He still played his drums, he still had water fights with Wally in the apartment, and he still liked peanut butter sandwiches. He really hadn't changed, but the world around him was being pretty crazy about him."

But while he "didn't feel any different," he sometimes had to escape the burden of sudden success, and over the first few months of *Streetcar*'s run, he would go to see Dodie and Marlon Sr. when time permitted. It was even more a return to his past, because by February 1948 his parents had resettled in Libertyville. Going home thus meant seeing his mother in her recent transformation, "dry" and establishing a new life for herself.

For the previous year, Marlon Sr. and Dodie had lived in a modest one-bedroom apartment on Sedgewick Avenue in Chicago, which she hadn't much liked. Their new Libertyville residence was a gray Victorian farmhouse on five acres of land on St. Mary's Road, just east of the center of town. The house had creaking floorboards, threadbare rugs, a potbellied stove. As soon as Dodie moved in, she had named the place the Little Mohee, asking Dick Loving to paint a plaque of an Eastern goddess to plaster into an inset above the front door. It would supposedly give her new surroundings a spiritual aura.

"When she moved back to the town, it was hard for her at first," said Marian Johnsen, a neighbor whom Dodie soon brought into AA. "Liberty-ville residents had one idea of her, and she had become an entirely different person. But she just said the hell with it, and chose not to worry about what they thought."

Even without booze, Dodie was the same spontaneous and unconventional woman she had always been. She wore smocks and jeans most of the time, took up gardening, painted watercolor landscapes, and then, feeling that she "needed to free herself up a little more," signed up for a once-a-week tap-dancing class in Chicago.

Never a fastidious housekeeper, she usually slept late, and like many sober alcoholics, she drank as many as twenty cups of coffee daily and kept cellophane-wrapped hard candies around the house to satisfy her craving for sweets. She still smoked constantly. Her errands done, she usually retired for the afternoon, taking a book and a giant jar of Marshmallow Fluff up to her bedroom. She also kept a chamber pot in the room so that she wouldn't have to descend to the house's one bathroom.

She was now reading even more intensely about spiritualism, mysticism, and Eastern religions than before; meditation and visualization, fortune-telling and tarot cards, as well as levitation and ESP, were among her interests. She had already met Alan Watts, the philosopher of Zen, at nearby Northwestern University, but what caught her imagination most profoundly were the so-called Betty Books, eight volumes entitled *Excursions into the World of Other-consciousness Made by Betty Between 1919 and 1936,* by Stuart Edward White. In them, White, a widower, reported dialogues with his departed wife in the afterworld. "Dodie came to believe that these books conveyed what life was really all about," said one of her new neighbors, Kay Phillips Bennett, who quickly fell into Dodie's orbit. "They were supposed to tell us what we should all be working toward. Dodie loaned them to me, and we talked about them a great deal."

Psychoanalysis was also central to Dodie's recovery. She had always been receptive to psychiatric theory and while in Chicago in 1945 she had met Dr. Forrest Shufflebarger, an eclectic psychiatrist. They began seeing each other socially, often attending the theater together. Ann Osborne was one of the many friends and family members Dodie urged to seek the care of Dr. Shufflebarger, whom she nicknamed "Shuffie." What Osborne didn't know was that her friend started seeing Shuffie professionally early in 1948, on a twice-weekly basis. He was not a strict Freudian, and his relaxed manner appealed to Dodie, who had studied Jung; it also dovetailed with her interest in spiritualism. One Shuffie nugget that Dodie often repeated was "There are three things in this world that an individual fears: change, rejection, and failure."

"Be good," Shuffie once told Dodie.

"I will if I want to; I may and I may not," she replied.

To Libertyville friends and neighbors, Dodie and Marlon Sr. now seemed like old-fashioned sweethearts, but most of Dodie's attention was still given to her AA work. At the local meetings, she became the star speaker. From her personal experience and her stories, which she told unabashedly, down to the most humiliating detail, she held the others in thrall.

"She always acted as if she was as sure as God," said Marian Johnsen. "I'm sure she must have had self-doubt, but she never let it show. She was controlling in the same ways that Bud was, and the two of them even used some of the same techniques, the pauses, the same air of calmness."

The observation was an acute one, for without realizing it, Dodie inveigled herself into peoples' lives, got "inside their heads." Like Bud, too, her manipulating rested on a cosmic plank, and what she advocated more than anything was a transcendental self-reliance.

"One of the greatest things she imparted to me was that one never really needs to feel sorry for oneself," explained Phillips Bennett, who, though not a member of the group, regarded her in the same light in which Dodie was held by her AA protégés. "She would say, 'Don't let people force you into a corner that you don't want to be in. Realize that you have control of your own life and can make your own decisions.'"

By the time Dr. John Ward, a general practitioner in nearby Lake Bluff, met Dodie, she had become the "mainstay" of AA in the area and "the glue that held everybody together." She was like an alcoholic ambulance, always on call, always on the go. Dick Loving, her son-in-law, would eventually paint a picture that many said best symbolized Dodie's traits as a caregiver: On the canvas was a large ear, presumably Dodie's, the iconography referring to her willingness to listen, even when other alcoholics would call her up in the middle of the night.

Jocelyn, however, objected to this image of Dodie. She said that her mother was just doing what any AA member was expected to do. "That's part of the program. Many do the same thing. If anybody calls you up and says, 'I need your help,' you say, 'I'll be right there.' Was mother a saint? No."

Still, many in Libertyville came to regard Dodie as more than a caring reformed alcoholic. Down the road from Little Mohee lived Bente and Joan Claussen, ages twelve and fifteen. With the girls' parents vacationing in Canada and their grandmother baby-sitting, Dodie went over to see them one morning and discovered that the elderly woman had died in bed. Swinging into gear, she made the funeral arrangements, then took the two youngsters home with her for a barbecue, where they grilled steaks and talked heart to heart.

"It made my grandmother's death so much easier for us," recalled Joan Claussen. "It was so typical of Dodie, and in many ways she was a better mother than my own." Her sister, Bente, agreed: "Dodie gave us permission to talk about my grandmother's death, to grieve and to reminisce. My mother was shocked, but I've always looked back upon that evening as a wonderful way to experience my first death."

In Dodie's Japanese-like garden was a "thinking rock"—no one called it meditation then. "Let's go out and just sit under the tree and talk together," she would say to Bente, whom she soon took under her wing. Or she would just sit in silence, as she often did with Sherry Stewart, who as a teen would also come to regard her as a "spiritual teacher." Stewart recalled that sitting on the rock was Dodie's form of Zen, a way to say, "Get yourself into the present moment. Distance yourself from whatever's going on in your head, the imagination that's driving you nuts. Just be still."

"She had a clever way of seeing the larger picture," added Stewart, who was struggling with an alcoholic mother. "She helped you see how insignificant you and your problems were, and she would reassure me by saying, 'I've been there and I pulled through, so your mother will pull through too.'"

If Dodie was the supporter, the giver, now blessed with a second chance, her regeneration seemed confirmed by Bud's overnight success in *Streetcar*. She had always believed in his talent, and for years had urged him to take himself more seriously. Now it seemed he might be all right. "She was deeply pleased and gratified," said Kay Phillips Bennett. "His success was also a fulfillment of her dreams for herself. Bud was a kind of extension of her in a strange sort of way—the intensity, the tremendous energy. She was wild about him."

To what degree his success would change him she had no way of knowing. But less than a month after the opening of *Streetcar*, he had come home, making a surprise New Year's visit. He also saw old friends, many of whom he hadn't spoken to since getting booted out of Shattuck.

His contemporaries were not ignorant of his success in New York, and few were surprised to find his behavior as strange and inexplicable as they had always thought it to be. Kevin O'Brien, one of Bud's high school classmates, had scheduled a party and then received a call from Bob Hoskins, asking if he could bring "a friend from out of town." When the doorbell rang, there was Bud, dressed in a dapper blue suit, white shirt, and tie, but hanging from the collar of his shirt was a napkin, as if he'd just bolted from the dinner table or was about to play the violin as a strolling minstrel.

"Oh yeah, hi, Bud. How are you?" said O'Brien, who hadn't seen him in years. Brando simply breezed past him with no greeting, leaving O'Brien feeling that the message was Drop dead.

In the upstairs apartment, he sprawled in an overstuffed chair, extending his legs and staring up at the ceiling. Having called attention to himself, he waited as the other guests grew hushed and nervous. "Everyone was thinking, Is this really Bud? And if so, what's going on?" O'Brien recalled.

"Bud, what can I get for you?" the host asked.

"There isn't a goddamn thing you can do for me," he replied, still staring at the ceiling.

"He was just going to make it into a game," said O'Brien. "But with that crack, 'Not a goddamn thing,' I thought, Okay, you just sit there, buddy. No more offers."

Two minutes later Bud followed O'Brien into the kitchen. Then, without a word, he walked out the back door and down the steep flight of stairs. When he got to the bottom, he looked up, as if to peer under the skirt of O'Brien's wife, who was standing on the landing above. "Nice!" he shouted, and disappeared into the night.

To be sure, others noticed his games, too. He could be kind to children and animals, but for the most part he tested, throwing out one-liners or teasing people with rude remarks.

"He had come home, Mr. Hotshot," said Bente Claussen, recalling the day she and her sister met him by chance at his mother's. Both Claussen girls were starry-eyed, but soon, watching Bud's behavior, they weren't so enthralled. He floated into the room wearing a bright T-shirt, looking "stunning and beautiful," said Bente. "That sinuous walk, the whole business." For the rest of the afternoon, though, as he drifted in and out, he playacted, and Dodie only rolled her eyes at his contrivances.

He was "showing off to us two teenage girls, as incredible as that may seem," Bente added. "The most accurate word would be *cocky*. He acted like a major jackass, and Dodie was wonderful—in no way trying to cover up that he was acting like such a jerk. He was ordering her around, 'I'll have a sandwich,' that sort of thing. Dodie's response was 'Just cool your jets, Jack.'"

Kay Phillips Bennett remembered when Dodie brought Bud over to her house for the first time. "He walked right into the kitchen, then started looking around and demanded, 'Got any peanut butter?' " All the while he was ransacking her cupboards, and Phillips Bennett quickly realized that this was one of his manipulative games Dodie had talked about. "I could see that he was taking the initiative, testing, pushing," she explained. "That was the kind of behavior that disturbed Dodie. He was really giving her a message when he did these things but she remained cool as a cucumber."

It wasn't simply that Dodie was trying to ignore Bud; in other ways, she was more than willing to indulge him. For example, no one outside the family could criticize Brando, and Dodie bristled if anyone did so. The official family line was to act as if his behavior was just Bud being his own crazy self—like the times he made such a show of scratching himself in rude places, or when he was discovered urinating in the kitchen sink.

In private it was different, though. "My God, why does he have to do this!" Dodie sometimes exclaimed to Kay, who later recalled how she "got so fed up with some of the things he did, because she thought them so unnecessary. She would talk to me about it with total disgust," Phillips Bennett said. "I think she was also afraid that he was going to blow it. Everything was just falling into his lap, and he was responding in a very unconventional manner."

Added Phillips Bennett, "Bud not only wanted approval, but he also loved his mother very, very deeply. You could feel it. It was in the air. You could also see that his constant teasing was a badgering of love, not hostility. Dodie, clearly, was the central woman in his life."

The complexities were indeed enormous—and much of what Dodie was working on in her therapy with Shufflebarger. If for Bud she was "the central woman in his life," then in equal measure he was the central male figure for her, too. "Bud was the one she really loved," said Jill Johnsen, Marian Johnsen's daughter. "That's why he came home—he returned to Libertyville whenever he felt unloved in the outside world and needed to feel loved by his mother."

"I always had the feeling that both sisters got a certain short end of the stick," Dick Loving confirmed. "Given the constellation of the family, Bud was sort of Dodie's substitute for Marlon Sr."

According to Jill Johnsen, her mother sometimes voiced her suspicion that Bud was "in love" with Dodie. Marian had also sensed an inappropriate intimacy between mother and son the first time she met him. Unaware that Bud had returned for a visit, she and her daughter had gone over to see Dodie. When she opened the front door, they saw him coming down the stairs. Descending casually, he was wearing boxer shorts and a sleeveless T-shirt, but was also flaunting a pink nylon peignoir with ostrich feathers.

"Hello, how are you?" Bud said, momentarily embarrassed. "It's so good to meet you."

"I was a complete stranger to him," said Marian, "and yet there he was walking around in a woman's frilly robe. But he, his mother, even his father, acted as if there was nothing unusual about this show he was putting on."

During his visits home, Bud also managed to "screw everything in sight," including one of his mother's married friends whom she'd introduced at a Lake Forest cocktail party. Dodie didn't close her eyes to this, she just didn't discuss it. Marlon Sr., on the other hand, was more critical of his son's volatile and moody personality, but less clear of his own role. His dominance had been usurped by the son, who was in fact paying Pop from his hefty *Streetcar* earnings. Marlon Sr. would tell people how pleased he was that Bud was finally earning a living and, as he put it, "getting somewhere." "But he would also shake his head," recalled Phillips Bennett, "and then say, 'I'll never understand what this kid is all about.'"

Embarrassment was part of his response to his son's new power, too. When people asked him his name and he responded "Marlon Brando," there would always be the inevitable question, "What? You're not Marlon Brando!" "I'm Marlon Brando's *father*" was his sad retort. "Certainly Bud took his name from him," Jocelyn conceded, "which was always a devastating thing for him. I mean, *he* was Marlon Brando first."

Dodie was perceptive enough to understand that much of her son's eccentric behavior—including his anger and tension, and the anxiety attacks he was now reporting—had its origin in the Brandos' family life. Holding herself responsible, she urged Bud to see a psychiatrist, even to consult her own while still in Chicago.

All Marlon did do on that trip was visit Dr. John Ward, now the family doctor and friend. He was worried about a recurrence of venereal disease, but the new blood test showed no sign of infection. While Dr. Ward noted his previous knee operation and recurrent dislocations of his right shoulder, Bud himself complained of vague pains in his lower back, feelings of panic, fear of heart trouble, insomnia, and gas in the bowel—all symptoms of the stress and anxiety from which he was suffering during the first year of *Streetcar*'s run.

As much as visits home may have helped relax him, back in New York Marlon still had to deal with stardom, and at times it seemed to torture him. One evening, he took Carmelita Pope to Leon and Eddie's nightclub, where he was putting away a string of scotches in order to fortify himself in public. Soon there came an announcement from the bandstand: "Ladies and gentlemen, Marlon Brando!" The spotlight searched the crowded room, going from one table to the next. Instead of rising and taking a bow, he started applauding, pretending he was just another patron looking for Marlon Brando. Similarly, weeks later he was walking down Broadway with Fran and Dick when he stopped at a newsstand and started leafing through a magazine that he quickly tried to put back on the rack. "There was a big picture of him which he didn't want us to see," Loving recalled, "and Fran said, 'Oh, gimme,' and just tore it out of his hand."

Soon, he prevailed on Irene Selznick to limit the press. He also complained to Sondra Lee, mentioning that reporters tried to make him an authority on almost any subject. This was "a new kind of power," Lee said. "I don't think he liked it." Nonetheless, Hy Anzell noted that he was now signing his autograph "*Vote for Henry Wallace,* Marlon Brando."

Writer Helen Lawrensen and her *Mademoiselle* editor Leo Lerman noted the same discomfort. One day they took him to lunch, and he went into his characteristic slouch. "I saw it then," Lerman later recalled. "I looked at that profile and he just seemed to be a boy of enormous talent and enormous beauty. But there seemed to be a doom in it, and I remember sensing this on sheer instinct. Marlon was sitting with his head down, not happy, speaking in monosyllables. We couldn't be sure whether he was putting us on, either. I sat there absolutely fascinated by the look of him, feeling that this was some sort of stage genius. But there was also the echo of other stage geniuses who had either taken to drink or dope, like the Booth family, Keane, all those nineteenth-century titans of the American and English theater. There was the sense not so much of self-destructing, but that he might not fulfill the promise. The need, the drive—something

I couldn't put my finger on—was missing. Even then, I had the feeling that he was a fallen angel."

As the stress and strain increased and Marlon's anxiety attacks worsened, he finally decided to seek professional help. He went to see Dr. Edward Hilpren, a New York psychiatrist who had been counseling Jocelyn and Don Hanmer. But according to Hanmer, he walked out of the first session and refused to pay his bill.

Marlon's initial resistance to the idea of seeing a psychiatrist was strange, given the urgings of his mother and Tid; Fran, too, would soon be in therapy. Further, psychoanalysis was *de rigueur* in New York during these years, especially among people in the theater. The influx of European psychoanalysts who had fled Hitler, the new "dark" plays with psychological themes by playwrights like Arthur Miller, William Inge, and Tennessee Williams—all elevated Freudianism to a shared and common language among artists and intellectuals. At the Actors Studio, psychoanalysis was a given, especially since the Method, with its emphasis on an actor's real-life experiences, depended on it; the goal was to turn trauma into drama, or as Kazan put it, "to make psychology public." Everyone, it seemed, was in analysis. Wally Cox even made a joke of it, telling Maureen Stapleton that she should go into analysis. When she asked why, he quipped, "So you won't be the last one."

As Harold Clurman had also realized, Brando had erected walls of defenses in order not to have to confront and acknowledge his deepest psychic scars. "Brando's mother was a fine, well-bred woman, but [she had been] a hopeless alcoholic," Clurman acknowledged. "He suffered untold misery because of her condition, and the soul-searing pain of his childhood . . . lodged itself in some deep recess of his being. He cannot readily speak of what lies buried there: he hardly knows himself what it is. . . . The nameless 'complex' that possesses him occasionally induces an impenetrable sullenness. He cannot voice the deepest part of himself: it hurts too much. That, in part, is the cause of his 'mumbling.' "

By the end of 1948, Brando was nearly cracking under the strain. As he had reported to Dr. Ward back in Libertyville, he wasn't sleeping and was worried about his heart and his frequent panic attacks. Moreover, as he confessed years later to Maureen Stapleton, during this time "I was terrified I'd kill somebody." "He was so afraid of hurting someone in a rage," she explained. "Physically kill someone, because he knew he was capable of it. But I doubt he knew where the rage was coming from." Sometimes he would walk out of his building on Fifty-second Street and angrily kick his motorcycle. One day a cop stopped him. Marlon shouted, "I can do what I want with it. It's my cycle!"

Although he had had problems with insomnia, his friends noticed that he was now sleeping long hours, almost hiding out at the theater. As Jay Presson Allen surmised, he seemed to be in a deep depression.

He had told the publicist Eddie Jaffe that he had been having more frequent anxiety attacks, some so extreme that he would suddenly fall to the floor and lie there until he caught his breath. Jaffe recalled one episode where he had run all the way from Penn Station to Stella Adler's house. "From my own analysis and experience, I had learned that panic attacks are often symptomatic of homosexual anxiety," Jaffe explained. "Marlon didn't say so outright, but I saw a parallel here, because, aside from his compulsive fucking, he had often made jokes about it. He'd come by my office and leave a note saying something like, 'Sam and I stopped by to see you. He wants to lick your joint.' "

With all these symptoms, he had finally been brought to the breaking point and he approached Kazan for advice. "I didn't have one discussion with him in which he exposed himself or asked for my help," recalled the director. "The last thing you could get him to say was 'I hurt.' What he said to me simply was 'I'd like to talk to somebody.' So I sent him to Mittelmann."

Kazan had begun seeing Dr. Bela Mittelmann, a Hungarian Jewish psychiatrist, when his wife, Molly Day Thatcher, had given him an ultimatum: Either join her for counseling or face divorce. Now that Kazan had "approved" Mittelmann for Marlon, Brando gave up his long resistance to analysis and made an appointment. It was the first step in his decades-long involvement with psychoanalysis. Mittelmann would become the actor's surrogate mother and father for the next ten years, and Brando continued to consult him until the doctor's death in 1959.

Mittelmann's specialty was "motility" and psychosomatic illnesses, especially stomach and digestive problems. By some accounts his research and studies were sometimes silly and inconsequential—like showing movie clips of Hitler's speeches to examine the physical movements of "the totalitarian personality." He had been trained at the New York Psychoanalytic Institute after emigrating from Hungary in the 1920s. In addition to his specialization in psychosomatic illnesses, he initiated a new therapy in which he concurrently treated married couples. He was a short, pudgy man—another psychoanalyst described him as looking "like Moe, one of the Three Stooges," always in a rumpled suit. Although only in his late forties when Marlon entered therapy with him, he seemed older than his years, with his bald head, flabby body, and the pasty complexion of his fleshy face, which some described as having a more feminine than masculine appearance. He also had a heavy Hungarian accent, and according to one colleague, his manners, like his writings, were messy and disorganized.

Mittelmann must have been delighted to have Brando as a patient. Dr. Arthur Weider, a younger analyst who had collaborated with Mittelmann in some research, confirmed, "It would have been personally important to him that he was treating the hottest young actor around. He wasn't a modest man, and he was always dropping names, even though he stopped short of trespassing on confidentiality."

Elia Kazan was aware of what good psychotherapy should be, especially because his brother Avram was an analyst, so he came to regard Mittelmann as little more than "a backslapper": "Old Mittelmann would say to me, 'What are you worried about? You're successful, you're famous. Relax and enjoy.' I finally thought, Why am I paying this son-of-a-bitch $50 an hour to tell me that? I realized that he was no fucking good at all, and later saw a very good analyst."

But for Marlon he seemed perfect, precisely because he was so accepting. "I think Marlon found Mittelmann uncritical enough so that he could talk to him," said Kazan. "That would mean a lot to Brando, to lie back on the sofa and talk without feeling that he was going to be judged." Nevertheless, another psychoanalyst doubted that Brando underwent a traditional analysis. "I'm not sure Brando was healthy enough for that," suggested Dr. Leo Bellak. "Like Marilyn Monroe, he may have needed the less rigid situation in which he could simply rely on Mittelmann and have a more human, less formal relationship."

Whether any analyst could actually have helped Brando by breaking through his deep, dark secrets was a real question. Clinically, it would have been a complicated case, but it would have had to center on Marlon's sexual confusions. Philip Rhodes was convinced that Brando had been sexually molested as a child when he had slept in housekeeper Ermy's bed, both in Omaha and in Evanston. Dick Loving, similarly, recalled that his wife,

Fran, suspected that in her mother's early boozing days, Dodie may also have abused him, although this was something Brando himself never confirmed. The dissociated personality, the manic-depressive mood swings, the anger and resentful rages, the manipulative withdrawals, and the sexual promiscuity were all classic textbook symptoms of anxieties over sexual identity. Moreover, his Shattuck flirtations, his experimentation in Provincetown, and his more recent attraction to Sandy Campbell, a supporting actor backstage at *Streetcar*, had probably heightened his fears about his sexual identity. Yet from what people heard about Mittelmann, he seemed incapable of probing these difficult areas in his patient's psyche. Instead, Marlon seemed glad to have him just to talk to, finding in him the "comfort" that he was always looking for. There was none of the emotional sojourn into self that a full analysis might have required.

Still, Marlon made no secret of the fact that he was seeing a psychiatrist. Indeed, he always wanted one of his pals to escort him to his appointments, and usually it was Darren Dublin who went along. Dublin, who'd been in therapy himself, explained to Marlon that it would be more productive to go alone so that he could be absolutely clear and not have his attention diverted from going deep into himself and recovering memories. But Brando insisted on the support, telling Darren, "Oh no, I have to have someone with me all the time."

"I must have gone with him about fifteen hundred times," Dublin recalled. "As for Mittelmann's letting him get away with things, maybe that just made him a smart analyst. He probably realized that Marlon couldn't have handled any other kind of therapy and probably would have walked out. Even in analysis, Marlon wanted to do it his way."

"Everybody knew that Mittelmann was Marlon's analyst," said Sondra Lee, "and that he was a tremendous force in his life. When something would come up, a problem or question, he'd say, 'I'll have to talk to Mittelmann,' or he'd begin a statement with, 'I talked to Mittelmann' or 'Mittelmann says.' In fact, later on James Dean was so enamored of Marlon that when he heard that Mittelmann was Brando's analyst, he tried to become a patient of his, too."

"I knew Marlon was seeing Mittelmann," added Philip Rhodes. "Not only was he the pet psychiatrist of actors at the time, but he was a fraud. Marlon eventually became a controller of Mittelmann, because the psychiatrist was depending on him for theater tickets, meeting people, like other actors. That was why Marlon liked him. He had him under his control."

• • •

During the run of *Streetcar*, Marlon shared a dressing room with Karl Malden. The door always remained open, and Malden tolerated it, but with little enthusiasm. During a matinee, while Marlon was onstage, Igor Tamarin walked in and started rifling through his friend's pants pockets, not noticing Malden resting on a nearby cot. He was about to leave when Karl stopped him.

"I saw that. Igor, put it back."

"So what?" Tamarin replied.

"It's not yours," Malden said, and told him to wait.

When Marlon came offstage, Karl announced, "I'm not going to have anybody coming up and going through pockets. I don't know what he took, but I leave money here."

"Well, goddamn it, Karl," Brando said. "He's a kleptomaniac and I'm trying to straighten him out." How this would help was unclear, but Malden now mentioned other things that had disappeared, including props. "What about the silver cigarette case that's missing?"

"He took it."

"What'd he do with it?"

"He pawned it. He got fifty cents for the fucking thing."

"There you are. He's not coming up here again."

Brando turned to Tamarin. "Don't you need more?"

Igor shook his head. "No, it's enough," he said, smiling. "I got this date."

Brando looked at him and grinned. "Is she pretty? Maybe I can fuck her."

It was a side of Brando that Malden—a married man with a pregnant wife, and the son of a blue-collar Catholic from Gary, Indiana—had never seen before. "It scared me," Malden conceded. "I had never been that kind of person, even in high school or college. I was square and still am. I didn't want to get too close. For two years we dressed together, and there were days when all we'd say was, 'How are you?' and many days we didn't say anything at all."

Marlon's relationship with Kim Hunter was something else, though, partly because she was the youngest person among the principals after him. Also, Hunter was funny, sensitive, and decent, anything but the young starlet on the make. Like Brando, her personal life was in difficulty, and months into the run she had broken down onstage. David Diamond reported running into her at one of his gay hangouts in the Village. "I don't remember tears, but she seemed very unhappy, and I knew that she was getting involved with a succession of nasty, self-centered men." Brando, always the shepherd and who had just gone into therapy himself, urged her to seek help.

"He was determined to make sure I felt comfortable going to see someone," Hunter explained. "He saw what was happening without my saying a bloody word. So he came into my dressing room and just sat quietly in the corner and started to tell me about his own analysis. What he was saying, in effect, was, 'It's okay. It's all right to admit that you don't have all the answers.' Then he initiated a couple of little meetings to get me in the right frame of mind."

The immensity of *Streetcar*'s success only helped galvanize the cast into a sort of family, and it was usually the crew with whom Marlon was most relaxed at the Barrymore. He also got along well with actors Nick Dennis and Rudy Bond, both easygoing and humorous—and at the opposite end of the spectrum from Selznick and Tandy. At one point he switched dressing rooms with Mehta Klinge so as to spare the aging wardrobe mistress a flight of stairs. When he heard that Lucinda Ballard needed help, he pleaded with her to give the job to a girl he knew and let him pay the salary: The girl, it turned out, had become pregnant by Marlon. He had taken care of the abortion, but she hadn't been well and had lost her job. As Ballard recalled, the girl "worshiped the ground Marlon walked on."

None of this, however, alleviated the problem of the stage-door groupies who lined up every evening at the Barrymore to get a glimpse of the new matinee idol. Sometimes Brando was forced to flee through a rear entrance, then jump fences and cut through side alleys. Years later, he told writer Lawrence Grobel about another woman who "haunted" him for six months.

"She wouldn't tell him her name," Grobel recounted the story, "but said that she made her money by robbing people. She told him she and a friend were into cannibalism and they could take him to a place in New Jersey where they would eat him. That was sufficiently bizarre for him to at least find out who she was, so he told her to come by his place. When she did, he opened the door slightly with the chain in place and told her to put both her hands through the door, where he grabbed them and then frisked her for a gun. When he let her in, she took out a wad of bills and asked if he needed money. Brando said she was into a heavy Jesus trip and he was her Christ. She wanted to wash his feet. Brando agreed, and became aroused when she did. 'I started feeling her body, undressing her, playing with her tits. She got all trembly, started shaking. I got excited and tried to fuck her. I don't remember if I did or not, if I got it in or not, because she was just shaking like a leaf.' "

On the other hand, if he sensed a kinship with a woman, he immediately turned his attention to her, enthralling her with his charm. "It was fascinating to watch," said Jay Presson Allen. "His instincts were extraordinary. He could walk into a room with two hundred people and go straight to the most wounded woman there. The question was, Did he go to them to give them aid and comfort? Sometimes it appeared that he did. He could be enormously sympathetic and had a great ability to make someone like that feel comforted. But Christian fellowship? I doubt it. My perception was that he was drawn to this kind of woman because he saw someone whose needs he could respond to. But then I wondered what would happen to her subsequently if she were left to his tender mercies."

While Marlon kept insisting that success would not spoil him, his friends and his family were aware of how nutty it had all become, and his celebrity affected them, too. Darren recalled thinking, "Shit. Now everybody's gonna know him!" Jocelyn wasn't immune either. She had opened in *Mr. Roberts* with Henry Fonda in mid-January 1948, and although her part was small, she had beaten out Eva Marie Saint for the only female role in the show. There were now two Brandos on Broadway, and the press used her success as yet another peg for profiles on Marlon. "What's it like having Stanley Kowalski for a brother?" reporters asked, directing her to pose for photos astride Marlon's motorcycle. Sometimes she obliged them, taking the middle path by speaking of herself and even her family, but careful not to go into detail about Bud, lest her brother feel violated.

Despite his sessions with his shrink, Marlon still suffered his panics, and the burden of fame was growing. It was in the autumn of the play's second year that William Gibson, then an unknown playwright, came to New York on the advice of his agent to offer Brando the leading part in his new play. Going backstage, he was surprised to find Broadway's hottest star sharing a dressing room that struck him like "an army barracks, a latrine or something." Marlon's outfit astonished Gibson even more: a shirt, sneakers without socks (even though it was almost wintertime), and a pair of jeans held up with a piece of clothesline. "The garb was that of a pan-handler or a Bowery bum," Gibson recalled. "It wasn't high school prep-chic rags," and it made a clear statement, like "I'm not part of this world."

The two went out for a bite at Schrafft's on the corner of Broadway and Forty-fifth Street. Brando was friendly but he said nothing about Gibson's play about young Will Shakespeare. Instead, he talked about how he'd been thinking of going back to school and maybe becoming a history teacher. Gibson, for whom Broadway was still a dream, couldn't believe his ears, thinking, You can't dislike being the toast of Broadway as a boy, making money with your future now practically assured. But Brando went on. "What I really want to be," he said, "is a writer."

"Have you written anything?" asked the lanky, contemplative Gibson.

"Well," Marlon answered, "I've written letters and I keep a diary."

Marlon was absolutely serious. He was talking to himself, lost in rev-erie, as though the future author of *Two for the Seesaw* and *The Miracle Worker* weren't even there.

"His recognition of my existence was nil," Gibson recalled. "I didn't have the feeling that from his point of view the event had happened. It could have been a hallucination. There was a total absence of empathy. In later years I would hear how smart he was. Odets claimed he was as fast as anything, and I'd think, I don't know what you're talking about; I didn't see any of that. In fact, he seemed a little schizy. He seemed to have many questions about who he was, what he was, and he was denying that he wanted to be standing where he was standing, which to me was a very en-viable place to be."

Another sign of Brando's restlessness—not to mention increasing fa-tigue—was his confusion about how to play Stanley Kowalski perform-ance after performance. He'd had problems with the character from the beginning. But the sheer brilliance of his performance had in effect dis-torted the play. As Harold Clurman wisely noted, Marlon had conveyed an inner suffering beneath the "muscle, lumpish sensuality, and crude en-ergy" of Stanley. "For almost two-thirds of the play," Clurman wrote, "the audience identifies itself with [him]. . . . The play becomes the triumph of Stanley Kowalski with the collusion of the audience, which is no longer on the side of the angels."

Now, however, he was not only uncertain but bored, and his rendition varied depending on his mood. On some nights he could be riveting, and on others he just wasn't there. Tandy was trying to keep the show the way they had rehearsed it, and was having one of the hardest times of her life. She had hoped to get top billing with the renewal of her contract, but instead the marquee read: STARRING MARLON BRANDO AND JESSICA TANDY. The reviews and sacks of fan mail, even her Tony, couldn't change the fact that people were coming to see Brando. *Streetcar* was Stanley's show, and Blanche's defeat was becoming more personal with every performance.

"Night after night I had to fight that audience," she recalled. "I had to try to make them be with me, to sit and listen and understand. I went to an analyst. We sat and talked across the desk two or three times and then he invited me to the couch. There was a silence and he said, 'What's uppermost in your mind now?' And I said, 'Failure.' I'd been working since 1927, and had begun to think, Did I really play with Gielgud, with Olivier and Guthrie, or is it an illusion?"

The problem, as Clurman had seen, was that the audience, not just Marlon, was enjoying her humiliation, even laughing at Blanche's most painful moments. However uneven, Brando's performance was brilliant, but he had so sweetened his character that the beast was no longer ambiguous. His costar was helpless. She came down with the flu and continued to tell her psychoanalyst that her professional life was "a mess."

In varying his performance, Brando later claimed he was trying to re-stimulate himself, but the rest of the cast was put in a position where they had to "stand by to catch the ball."

"Marlon was difficult," Tandy once explained. "He didn't have the discipline. When he was tired, as he often was, he played the role tired. When he was bored, and he was often bored, he played the role bored."

But even when he was bored, tired, or just plain "off," it didn't matter. The audience had come to see one actor and they went away thinking he was superb; whatever he did, it was a free ride. "I don't believe in that crap—the show must go on," Brando acknowledged to journalists as the conflict began to leak out to the press. "Some nights it goes easily because I feel the part. Other nights I have to walk up and down thinking of things to make me mad before I can go on." About Tandy he said, "She learns a part and then sets it in. She also thinks you should shave before a day in the country [and] she doesn't like peanut butter."

Tandy later responded to his remark: "If someone has the skin and bones of a character, changes can be made all the time, but it will still be that quintessential character. It will not be, however, if you take the attitude 'I'm going to do this differently because it will have a wonderful effect or make me look like a bloody hero,' or whatever."

Tandy was the lady, chauffeured to her Upper East Side residence after each performance by a driver whom she'd inherited from Judith Anderson. Brando was the brute, taking off after an evening's performance with a girl on the back of his motorcycle. Selznick, too, was appalled by his behavior, commenting, "It just looks terrible to have him out there on the street carrying on at the ticket window." Tandy pointed to his lack of professionalism in smashing the prop telephone night after night despite the prop man's begging him to be more careful. In the birthday scene, she thought he was deliberately rattling the dishes—not as a dramatic touch, but to disturb her whenever she came to her key lines. She talked to him, suggesting that he muffle the noise by "putting a bit of your finger under your cup. Or choose a word that isn't important." He was oblivious. "Was he doing the same things to Kim, or just me?" she began asking herself. "Probably not. It was driving Karl mad, too. But the fact that I was older and had more experience, well, I suppose that made me the enemy."

Worse were his pranks. Marlon planted a story with publicist Eddie Jaffe that Tandy had received death threats from one of her more ardent admirers. Soon the story appeared in the *Daily News*. At the theater, his tactics were less oblique. In the middle of one of her more emotional speeches, Tandy noticed giggling in the audience. Looking back at Brando, she observed him, stone-faced, shoving a cigarette up his nostril.

One night, the chicken in the birthday scene had mistakenly been undercooked by one of the prop assistants. Marlon had gagged onstage, then come off, swearing, "I'd rather have dog shit!" For the next performance, someone left a mound of mock dog droppings on his plate. For weeks afterward he retaliated in kind, leaving joke-store turds onstage in the most unexpected places—in the refrigerator, even in Blanche's trunk. "When any of us found one during a performance we had one hell of a time not breaking up," Hunter recalled, still giggling about it in retrospect.

As Mitch, Malden was supposed to weep as Blanche was led away to the mental hospital, but Marlon had playfully persisted in muttering obscenities in an effort to make him lose his mood. Ordinarily, the two had a ten- to twelve-minute break while the two female leads engaged in lengthy dialogue. The Barrymore Theater wasn't air-conditioned, so whenever the weather permitted they spent the interval outside on Forty-seventh Street.

One night Malden sauntered back into the theater, then rushed back outside, yelling, "Hey, Marlon, you missed your cue!"

Brando raced down the alley and onto the stage. Tandy and Hunter looked at him flabbergasted. He had arrived five minutes early.

"You stupid ass!" Tandy muttered. "What the hell are you doing here?"

Hunter managed to ad-lib, "Oh, Stanley, come back later," and Marlon slunk offstage. Malden, in the wings, was chortling, "I got you, you bastard!"

In their dressing room afterward, Malden told him, "Listen, Marlon, that should be a lesson. Don't clown around. I don't have a big part. I have nineteen sides, you have something like forty-nine. I have to register on all of mine if I want to make an impression. If I throw nine of them away, I got nothing. So please, no more screwing around."

The pranks continued, however, even as Marlon promised to control himself. In the poker game scene, Nick Dennis played one of Stanley's buddies, a "regular guy." In real life he was one of Brando's recruits, and whether or not Marlon actually instigated it, Dennis now started getting up from the table, onstage, with his fly open. Tandy, whom Marlon had dubbed "Mother Hen," asked Dennis to stop the open-fly joke, and when he didn't, she went to Irene Selznick. Even Selznick couldn't impose her control, and eventually it became too much for Tandy. She had begun throwing up between scenes, and finally she asked Kazan to call a disciplinary rehearsal. Brando failed to show up. Another rehearsal was scheduled, and he arrived only after Tandy and Kazan had left. The director demanded that he apologize, and Marlon wrote Tandy a note, to which she replied in a lengthy letter. "I told him how much I admired him," Tandy recalled, "how talented I thought he was, and that he had it in his power to be absolutely preeminent, to occupy the same sort of position that Olivier had at the time, but only if he wanted to."

Tandy got no reply until many months later, when Marlon had gone off to Paris at the close of the show. Then he sent her a note. "His penmanship and writing were like an eight-year-old's," Tandy said. "He mentioned that he'd seen a movie that I had made before *Streetcar, A Woman's Vengeance,* and that he thought it was very good. I had a feeling that it was his way of saying, 'Gee, I'm sorry,' but he didn't say that at all."

What Tandy couldn't, or wouldn't, understand was his fundamental ambivalence about acting. When he did "bummy things," as Bobby Lewis put it, his war with the establishment was his way of keeping himself together. It was a way to convince himself that things hadn't changed, that he was in fact still in control. Kim Hunter saw what was happening more clearly, and she thought it amounted to emotional fatigue, something close to burnout. "Acting was always very painful for Marlon," she said, "because of that incredible sense of truth he had. Karl understood it when he said once, 'Marlon can make wrong choices, bad choices, but I think it's almost impossible for him to be false.' So to drag that kind of reality out of himself every night, in every performance, was really getting to him."

There were numerous signs of his exhaustion. Besides the paralyzing anxiety attacks, which he was trying to chip away at with Dr. Mittelmann, onstage he was mumbling worse than ever. Some nights the balcony audience couldn't hear him, and Edie Van Cleve had to give him a pep talk, urging him to speak up. "Marlon, look, those are the people you care about, not the orchestra crowd. You owe it to them to speak up." Marlon's response was to quip with a laugh, "Some of the lines are so bad I have to mumble them."

He was also having periodic memory loss. More than a year into the run, Hunter was in the middle of the scene in which Stanley tells Stella about Blanche's past, the Hotel Flamingo, and the young men she used to see. Suddenly, almost at the same moment, both of them became aware that he had repeated the same dialogue twice. The audience realized it, too, and burst out laughing.

Brando later described another incident of brain fade. "One night I came to an absolute, complete void," he said. "I just stood there looking out at the audience with a grin on my face. I looked up at the people in the balcony and all over the house, and it seemed terribly amusing. There were fourteen hundred people waiting for me to say something, and I didn't have the slightest notion of what it was supposed to be. Kim Hunter was in the scene with me, and she is inclined to come apart in such situations. Her eyes got as big as saucers, and all she could do was ask me questions like, 'What did you do then?' and 'What did she say?' Somehow we managed to get through it." The same speechlessness came over him when Clark Gable was in the audience.

Another time, he and Hunter started giggling. "We tried to hide it," said Hunter, "but we couldn't stop all the way across stage. We got behind the screen and onto the bed, and we still couldn't stop. Normally, the lights would go down at that point and we'd sit there until the scene with Blanche and Mitch was over and the curtain came down, but the lights were still on the screen and we couldn't tell if the audience could see us. Marlon said, 'How far do we take this realism? What do you wanna do?' The two of us sat there giggling our fool heads off."

With his physical strength and almost feline control over his body, he could handle Hunter with an extraordinary gentleness. "He'd grab, but he didn't break," she said. His most demanding scene came after Stanley is beaten up by his poker pals, when he gives his famous cry "Stella!" which brings his wife back into his arms. During one performance, he lost it completely. A group in the orchestra had giggled nervously, and suddenly, as though something had snapped, he stalked to the footlights and screamed, *"Shut up!"*

In mid-April 1949, less than two months before the end of his contract, he also broke his nose. Marlon had continued boxing bare-fisted in the downstairs boiler room, first with Carmelita Pope, who'd been understudying Hunter, then with one of the stagehands who'd taunted him about boxing "with a girl." He sparred with Karl, too, and when Malden quit, he managed to persuade another stagehand to fill in. Nick Dennis, who was actually a former boxer from St. Louis before Damon Runyon got him into show business, had wisely quit, too, fearing Selznick's wrath. Marlon had continued "doing rounds" at his gym, Stillman's, with Rocky Graziano and others. Now there was a new kid, another stagehand who didn't know what he was doing.

"All of a sudden, he winds up and throws a haymaker from the floor," Brando told Carlo Fiore. "I saw it coming, but I couldn't get out of the way. Next thing I knew, I was flying ass over heels into a pile of wooden crates . . . and I began bleeding from the nose like a stuck pig. The poor guy was afraid he'd killed me, but I told him I was all right and not to worry about getting into trouble. . . .

"I went to my dressing room and put some cold compresses on my beak, but I couldn't stop the bleeding. I heard my cue coming up and ran to make my entrance. . . . I held my nose. But from the break in the bridge, a regular geyser of blood shot about ten feet across the stage."

He whispered to a startled Tandy, "Broke my nose," and she hissed back, "Bloody fool!" When the curtain came down after two more scenes, it was complete chaos. Carmelita Pope and Kim Hunter rushed to administer more cold compresses, holding his head back, and Irene Selznick could be heard shrieking, "No more, this is the end!" Over Marlon's repeated protests, she had him rushed to nearby Roosevelt Hospital. She had mothered him in the past, telling him to bathe or to get a haircut, and even forced him to get new eyeglasses, but now there was the issue of her investment. Brando knew this, just as he was aware that she had publicly implied that there was more between them than just the play, so it was time for a little payback, some fun.

"My nose healed pretty quick," he explained, "and I guess I would've been back in the show practically right away if I hadn't done what I did. . . . When [Irene] wants something, she wants it. And she wanted me back in the play. But when I heard she was coming to the hospital, I went to work with bandages and iodine and mercurochrome, and—Christ!— when she walked in the door, I looked like my head had been cut off. . . . 'Oh, Marlon,' she said, 'you poor, *poor* boy!' And I said, 'Don't you worry about anything, Irene. I'll be back in the show tonight!' And she said, 'Don't you dare! We can manage without you for—for—well, a *few* days more.' 'No, no,' I said. 'I'm *okay*. I want to work. Tell them I'll be back tonight.' So she said, 'You're in no condition, you poor darling. I *forbid* you to come to the theater.' So I stayed in the hospital and had myself a ball."

Unbeknownst to Selznick, that evening Marlon surrounded himself with friends and flowers, entertaining his pals late into the night. "He had the nurses all going gaga," said Sondra Lee, who visited with Blossom and the others. "There was also an Hawaiian tootsie, some stray, who was bringing him sliced pineapple and platters of food. It was like a luau in there." In Marlon's absence, Jack Palance, understudying Anthony Quinn in the Chicago production, was brought in, and he was subsequently replaced by Richard Carlyle.

When Brando was released a week later, he had a different nose. Selznick was aghast, and she urged him to have it broken and reset. Marlon refused, claiming that he liked it the way it was. He wasn't perfect anymore and he looked "rugged, like a fighter." What struck Sam Shaw, among others, was the thought, Jesus, all this time, maybe he always felt he was too pretty.

Despite his celebrity, Marlon still dressed and acted as if nothing had changed, and he still persisted in his boyish pranks. In early 1949 he sublet songwriter Vernon Duke's apartment on West Fifty-seventh Street with Wally Cox, where the two played endlessly with windup toys and held football games with a large industrial sponge. It made no difference that they were in the midst of repainting the place, living with open cans of paint—or wading through the droppings of Marlon's new pet, Russell the raccoon. Eventually, though, Russell became too much for Wally, who moved out.

Oddly enough, by then Cox had achieved something of a name for himself in show business, even though he had always been far less ambitious than Marlon. By the late forties, Joe E. Lewis and Milton Berle were household names, yet the era of the stand-up comic was only beginning. Buster Keaton, Laurel and Hardy, Charlie Chaplin, and Milton Berle had always occupied a special place in Marlon's affections, but Cox's humor was especially appealing to him. Wally was cool, laid-back, his humor anything but physical. His monologues at parties left theater types tickled; still no one had taken notice. Brando supported Wally's talent, but it was Judy Freed, an NBC policy editor, who landed him a job with Max Gordon, the impresario of the nightclub the Village Vanguard.

"I think the party was at Betty Comden's," Freed recalled. "Somebody asked Wally to get up and do his thing, and he did Dufo as well as several other pieces.

"Well, it just flipped me out. His style was so non–New York, so midwestern or wherever the hell he came from, and the stuff was genuine. Afterward, I was sitting next to him on the couch, and Marlon was sitting on the other side of me. I was asking Wally if he had more stuff, and if he would be interested in appearing at the Vanguard, and he just started showing me some of his jewelry. All the time I was ignoring Marlon, and out of the blue he started tapping me on the shoulder. Then he took his jacket and started peeking at me through the buttonhole so I would pay attention to him."

In short order, Freed had Cox booked at the Vanguard, and later at the Blue Angel and Café Society. "It was a shock to every one of us, including Wally," recalled Sondra Lee, who recognized that Cox was fundamentally uneasy in front of an audience. "He was very insecure," said Dick Loving. "He'd come over to our place, saying, 'I want to do this routine.'

Everybody was in analysis at the time, whether it was Karen Horney or whatever, so I remember him trying to develop a routine about taking one's dog to the analyst. He was sort of trying it out on us to see whether we laughed or not."

Marlon, meanwhile, wasn't the only *Streetcar* cast member who had been showing signs of burnout. After the show's first anniversary Kazan was called back to do some "tuning." Although ticket sales hadn't slumped—*Streetcar* had grossed more than $1.4 million the first year alone, giving the director himself a tidy profit of over a quarter-million dollars—the show was getting stale. In addition, there was the Brando-Tandy conflict, and Hunter was wrestling with some personal problems. The road production of *Streetcar*, directed by Harold Clurman, had been playing to full houses in Chicago. Anthony Quinn had the role of Stanley, and he was slated to take over in New York after Brando left in May. Selznick had grown concerned that Quinn's performance was veering dangerously close to Marlon's, while lacking Brando's "shadings." In May, too, Tandy was scheduled to be replaced by Uta Hagen, and Hunter by either Mary Welch or Carmelita Pope, which added to Selznick's concern.

Onstage, Quinn was intense and Selznick had told Carmelita Pope, Hunter's understudy, to watch him carefully. She knew that Pope was more familiar with Marlon and his mannerisms than anyone. "I don't want a pale imitation of Brando," Selznick told her. "There's only one Brando."

Matters were further complicated by Clurman, who insisted that although Brando was the better actor, Quinn served the play better—a critique that dovetailed with his earlier review of the New York premiere. The news eventually reached Marlon, and it could only have echoed Harold's patronizing response to his performance in *Candida,* when he'd gone backstage and quipped, "Nice try, Marlon!" According to Pope, however, Quinn was still set on showing that he could outshine Brando, and with both companies briefly overlapping in New York in preparation for the changeover, the two actors circled each other like "wary animals."

Selznick had been keeping Hunter's understudy on ice, concentrating instead on Mary Welch to fill in as the new Stella. Hunter herself, ever the good egg, was advising Pope. "You know, you'll never get the part when I leave unless they see you do it," she told her understudy. "Thursday night I'm going to be sick. Get yourself ready." When the time came, a hysterical Selznick called Pope in for that evening's performance, and Marlon was particularly supportive.

"He was forever at my side," she recalled, "and what he'd done was change the blocking to move himself closer to me so the audience would be watching. I'd turn to talk to him, going with the original marks, but there he was, right up next to me. 'You'll do it, you're wonderful. Don't worry,' he kept saying. In fact, once he'd carried me to the bed, he wouldn't let me get up. We were supposed to get dressed for the next scene, but he's holding me down, hugging me, saying, 'Oh, you're wonderful.' He'd changed everything that night, even the way he read his lines, all of it to let me know he was there."

Tandy was still at a low point, however, and, with Selznick's prodding, attention shifted to her understudy. A rehearsal was called, and with Pope sitting at Kazan's side, Marlon returned to his usual blocking for the rape scene. After the run-through, the director turned to Pope and said, "You want to see this done better?" He climbed to the stage, whispered something in Marlon's ear, then called out, "Okay, let's do it again."

"Stanley, see, is trying to snare her, trap her," Pope explained. "Only then, Marlon started advancing toward her through the whole scene, relentlessly. She started, then Marlon began swiping at her dress. He was actually trying to pull it off, and she was protesting, 'What are you doing? What's going on here?' He kept backing her into the walls, advancing, advancing, mean and nasty. Nothing like he did in the show—much, much worse."

Kazan said, "How was that? You want to see it better yet?" He got back up on the stage and called out for the stagehand to give him some twine. "He cut it in half with his pocketknife and said to the understudy, 'Kneel. Put your hands behind your back,'" Pope recalled. "He tied her hands, then her ankles. He called Marlon aside and whispered to him again. Bud nodded. They started the scene. Now she was tied and kneeling. She couldn't move, and Bud came over and straddled her, talking down at her. Her face was between his legs, and then he went *slap!* right across the face. She couldn't do anything, and the fear, the anger underneath, was just unbelievable. Then he slapped her again a few lines down and also spit at her—literally a gob of spit across her face—and she just dissolved. Broke down, sobbing."

At the opposite end of Brando's emotional spectrum was Sandy Campbell, a tawny-haired actor who, the previous August, had taken over the small role of the young collector. Very handsome, in his midtwenties, Campbell had started on the stage as a child in *Life with Father*, attended prep schools, and even worked at the *New Yorker*. Privately wealthy, he was literary and had traveled widely, befriending E. M. Forster in England as well as Nora Joyce, James Joyce's widow, with whom he corresponded for years. He was openly homosexual, and Tallulah Bankhead, Tennessee Williams, Maria Britneva, and the young Gore Vidal were among his closest friends.

"He had gotten to know Marlon about halfway through *Streetcar*," said Jean Bultman. She and her husband, Fritz, were intimates of not only Tennessee Williams but also Donald Windham, Campbell's lover. "That's when Marlon asked Sandy. I'm talking about the two of them having an affair. Marlon asked Sandy, more or less, but I don't think Sandy did it.

"Sandy was very attractive and was often approached because he was in the theater," Bultman went on. "He wasn't bisexual. He and Don had started going together at eighteen or something, and stayed together until Sandy died. Marlon was always standing in the wings with Sandy and holding his hand. Of course, Sandy was highly flattered. Sandy also had a long friendship with Monty Clift, although I don't know whether they slept together."

Brando's offer to Campbell was in the guise of a birthday present. "He said, 'I'll give you money, clothes, or *time*,' " Windham confirmed. "It was like, What can I give you? Sandy considered it a pass. Marlon, at that period, was very bisexual anyway. He knew Carl Van Vechten and Truman [Capote], and in a very campy way he went along once when Carl asked him to pose for a photograph with his fly half-unzipped."

No one knows for sure if the relationship went any further than Marlon's "offer," although Truman Capote, in the course of interviewing Brando for the *New Yorker* in 1957, seemed to confirm that it had. In their late-night interview session, a bottle of vodka on the table between them, Capote reminded Brando that he'd gone to bed with "a mutual friend," and Marlon reportedly admitted that, yes, he had. "Brando said he wasn't really homosexual," said Capote's biographer, Gerald Clarke, "but did it because it advanced him as a human being, sort of as an act of kindness."

Clarke's report, based on extensive conversations with Capote, stands as a clear echo of the sort of things Marlon also had to say about his time in Provincetown during the summer's break from *I Remember Mama*. As his relationships with Kim Hunter, Carmelita Pope, and others showed, what mattered was "comfort," not necessarily gender or even sex. It was exactly what David Diamond had seen time and time again, and not just when Marlon would lay his head on the older man's lap. "That's the whole secret of what touched me about Marlon," Diamond said, remembering one night in a restaurant when he was very aware of Brando's struggle to connect with others in a meaningful way. "I noticed in his face . . . that look of his that would be very faraway. Sometimes I had the feeling that there might be tears welling up in his eyes. Because he would speak so little, and when he spoke it was wanting to know so much . . .

"I remember he wanted to know why I was rushing back to Rochester all the time. They had diagnosed that my mother had cancer of the colon. I had told him this incredible story that as far as I could think back my mother was always eating prunes and saying, 'You'll see, *mein Kind,* I'm going to die from cancer.' This is what I grew up with, listening to this horror, and I was telling him how all of it was beginning to drive me nuts, and I remember saying, 'I hope to God I will never be too far away, because if my mother dies and I'm not around, I think I'm not going to make it.' That's when I saw this extraordinary thing happen to his face, like this glazed, teary look. He was absolutely silent, and I called for the check. We walked back very slowly, until I left him at Fifty-seventh Street. But I still see that extraordinary face, the silence, not offering me a word of comfort because he had gotten it, he had felt it. . . . The question I wanted to ask, but never could, was, 'Marlon, am I right that you're so full of pain—maybe worse pain than the pain you sense in me?' "

The same shrouded inner life followed Brando to the Actors Studio, which had been formed only a week before the start of *Streetcar* rehearsals. Despite a great deal written about Brando's involvement, his participation was sporadic, and in later years the actor would joke that he attended only "to get laid." Kazan, of course, was the draw, but in point of fact Marlon and the Actors Studio had very little to do with one another. "He came into the Studio with whatever he had," said fellow founding member Martin Balsam, "and he left the Studio with the same thing." For the gritty-voiced Elaine Stritch, it was simpler still: "Marlon's going to school to learn the Method would have been like sending a tiger to jungle school."

Kazan had founded the workshop with the irrepressible Bobby Lewis. In the seven years that had passed since the demise of the Group Theatre, Lewis had directed and produced a number of shows in New

York and Los Angeles, including the Lerner and Loewe hit musical *Briga-doon,* and also acted in Hollywood movies. Critical and commercial success could not fulfill his need for an artistic home, however, and as Lewis and Kazan both saw it, the Studio would be a place where actors could take chances and explore their talent while ignoring the commercial demands of the trade. Kazan in particular wanted to create a workshop where performers would share the same artistic vocabulary; "a 'farm,' " as Actors Studio historian David Garfield put it, "where he could cultivate a new crop of performers trained in the techniques he had learned in the Group." He envisioned the Studio's purpose, he told actress Lenka Peterson, as developing "a common language among actors, like the one I have with Marlon."

Kazan and Lewis asked Cheryl Crawford, one of the three directors of the Group Theatre, to be the business manager of the new organization. Crawford was also close to Lee Strasberg, and she wanted him involved as well. Kazan and Lewis would not hear of it. Both respected Strasberg for his work with the Group, but they agreed that Lee should not be working with actors "because he's a murderer," as Lewis put it. Kazan even objected to Strasberg's coming in to give the occasional lecture on the tradition of acting. "I wouldn't open a fucking cigar store with him," he allegedly said. "I don't want him near our actors." (Nonetheless, Strasberg was eventually taken in.)

Even before the official announcement of the formation of the Actors Studio was published in the *New York Times* on September 12, 1947, word was out that the Studio was *the* place to be. It became an ideal home, a buzzing hive of energy and community for actors who wanted to be able to work, experiment, and learn. Even today, the Studio is inextricably linked with Method acting—or at least Strasberg's version of Konstantin Stanislavsky's theory, wherein Strasberg emphasized the use of the actor's own past experience to create emotional truth. The Studio also gave focus to a new generation of performers who, as a collection of talents, became an ideal as well as a target in the minds of theater professionals. The list of actors (and directors) associated with the Actors Studio is a Who's Who of American theater at its height.

The first meeting was held on October 5 on West Twenty-ninth Street, and as if to emphasize the organization's links to the Group Theatre, John Garfield, the onetime Group apprentice turned movie star, was put to work greeting people at the door. Other celebrities who agreed to participate were Arthur Miller, Tennessee Williams, and Harold Clurman. Among the twenty-six actors in the beginners class were Joan Copeland, Julie Harris, Cloris Leachman, Nehemiah Persoff, Rudy Bond, and Jocelyn. Marlon was in Bobby Lewis's advanced class with Mildred Dunnock, Herbert Berghof, Montgomery Clift, Maureen Stapleton, Billy Redfield, Eli Wallach, Kevin McCarthy, Sidney Lumet, and others.

For all intents and purposes it was another "family," yet often Marlon was simply a spectator. In class he would slouch in his seat, playing with cigarettes or making little hats from the aluminum foil off the cigarette pack. Vivian Nathan, a fellow inductee, recalled his walking into Gadg's session one day when the director, on leave from *Streetcar,* asked, "How were you last night?" Marlon replied shyly, "All right, I guess." For Anne Jackson, he was "completely unpredictable . . . just a little peculiar." At the Studio's spring picnic in Wilton, Connecticut, he showed up with a hole in the seat of his bathing trunks and whimsically "stuck a daisy up his ass."

Often, he'd sit in Lewis's class, "always next to some girl whom he couldn't keep his hands off," and one afternoon Lewis asked, "Marlon, what'd I just say?" Unfazed, Brando replied, "You stepped in what?" It was meant as a joke, but it reinforced the impression that he wasn't really participating.

After attending the thrice-weekly sessions for several months, Brando was still diffident, but even more than that, he was clearly reluctant to jump into scene work. Lewis laid down the law: "Marlon," he ordered, "you'd better do a scene or you're out."

Karl Malden, who was also a member of the advanced group, suggested a few possibilities, including a scene for the two of them from *Desire Under the Elms,* but Marlon thought Robert Sherwood's *Reunion in Vienna* more interesting. That play, which had been on Broadway in the thirties with the Lunts, was popular teaching fare. It was the story of a Hapsburg family reunion in Vienna after World War I. Marlon was to play Archduke Rudolph Maximilian, a nobleman reduced to driving a cab. When he meets his former lover, now married to a Viennese psychiatrist, he puts on a princely show, pretending to be successful and wealthy in order to seduce her. The key to the scene, as Brando saw it, was pretense; the problem was to show that the well-dressed, well-mannered aristocrat is, in fact, penniless. As Malden recalled, Marlon's solution was brilliant: He would present himself in a beautiful outfit, but after a few seconds would walk to the other side of the room, take off his boot, revealing "the biggest goddamn hole in his sock you ever saw," with a dirty toe sticking out.

Marlon picked Joan Chandler as his partner, and he went to Lucinda Ballard, who put together a beautiful hussar outfit from oddments she found at the Brooks Costume Company. Heeding Lewis's dictum to learn more, Marlon studied Velázquez's portraits of the Hapsburgs for his makeup—particularly the famous Hapsburg lip, over which he drew a thin mustache. As the *pièce de résistance,* he got a record of a Viennese waltz to accompany the scene. Everything was ready. But Marlon kept postponing the performance. "I'll do it next week, because I'm practicing with the monocle and I haven't licked it yet," he'd say, or "I don't have the music. . . . I don't have the record with me." Lewis finally ran out of patience. "You'll have a breakthrough of some kind, or a breakdown, but you have to do it," he said.

The dance studio on East Fifty-ninth Street—where the Actors Studio had moved from the Old Labor Stage at Broadway and West Twenty-ninth Street—had a small stage. When the scene was presented in late February 1948, Karl Malden, the emcee, asked all those assembled, at Marlon's request, to close their eyes until the curtain went up.

When the eager group opened their eyes, they were astounded. Instead of the ruffian from *Streetcar,* they saw a real prince in uniform, replete with a sword and monocle. Marlon's speech was perfect, his Austrian accent absolutely on target, and with his first line he got a big, appreciative laugh that worked like a "blood transfusion," Lewis recalled. "It was as if he realized, Oh, my god, I can really do this. I can be funny."

As Brando picked up momentum, he walked around Chandler, inspected her figure, and then suddenly cracked her across the face, followed by a deep-throated kiss that went on forever. "Have you ever been kissed like that before?" he demanded, heaving her into her chair as everybody let out a howl of laughter. Impulsively and totally unrehearsed, he then poured champagne down her bodice as she screamed bloody murder. It was a seduction unlike any other, and even at the end, amid great applause, he kept in character and bowed deeply from the waist. "He was like young John Barrymore," Lewis realized, "really a light comedian."

Marlon went on to more improvised antics in his next presentation, when Lewis started working on the first act of Chekhov's *Uncle Vanya* and needed someone to play the part of the old professor, Serebryakov, who in the scene says nothing. Marlon volunteered. All he had to do was enter with the others and busy himself with his books, but in fact he stole the show.

"You knew who he was instantly," Vivian Nathan recalled. "He had a lot of books with him, a lot of pencils and a notebook, and he had some kind of pince-nez or glasses on." While the other actors spoke, Marlon fumbled with all his props and conveyed the essence of the old man's absentminded character. Nathan couldn't remember anything about the scene except what Brando was doing. "He was a real person in a real predicament. You knew he had been interrupted and told to get out into the garden. You knew he didn't want to, that he had forgotten something, that he was busy thinking, and that he wanted to make notes. You got all that without him delivering a line."

Marlon was basically "a very benign presence" at the Studio, but a heavy presence, too. His ability to improvise struck everyone as extraordinary, and usually the auditorium would fill whenever he was at work. During another exercise, Eli Wallach played an FBI agent looking for drugs in Marlon's apartment. He had asked Brando to give him a minute to establish the fact that he was in his room surreptitiously, but Marlon was going to do it his own way. He walked onstage, found Wallach rifling the apartment, and demanded, "Who the fuck are you?" Wallach, shocked by the expletive, nonetheless remained in character and mumbled something about the super's telling him the apartment was vacant and available for rent. "The super is a fucking liar!" Marlon snapped. "A cocksucker prick motherfucker." Wallach was speechless. "The fucking super never told you any fucking thing," Marlon continued his offensive. "I'm telling you to get the fuck out!"

Wallach now began to take the insults personally. "Just a minute, watch your language," he protested, but Marlon wouldn't stop. He started pushing Wallach, screaming and cursing.

"Don't tell me to watch my fucking language. I'm telling you . . . to get the fuck out."

Wallach redoubled his lame attempt to defend himself: "Just be careful. Don't put your hands on me."

"Fuck you," Marlon snapped, with more pushing. Now furious, Wallach tried to stick to his character and refused to leave. Marlon picked him up under the arms and carried him across the room. When Wallach charged back through the prop doorway, he found Marlon doubled up with laughter. The whole class was in stitches, too.

In the discussion that followed, Wallach was criticized for not carrying out his objective, but he learned a more important lesson: that Marlon had decided to test him, to challenge him by playing the scene for real.

In many ways the Studio became exactly what Kazan and Lewis had envisioned: a collective in which directors, actors, and playwrights developed a self-defining vocabulary distinctly their own. Most outsiders had difficulties communicating with Studio people. When George Abbott directed a play at the Studio, he asked an actor to cross over to the table and sit down. The actor asked him to explain his motivation for doing so. "It's very simple," Abbott replied. "Your motive is your job." Method acting required more time and preparation than was normally allotted for rehearsal in the commercial theater, and the results of the process were apparent only at the end.

Inside the Studio, there was an excitement and electricity that moved students to reschedule auditions to avoid a conflict with their classes. Money was secondary, the camaraderie unflagging. Marlon responded to this more than to anything. He understood "that actors need each other," as classmate David Pressman put it, and he'd go out of his way to be helpful and encouraging when someone did a rotten scene—much in the same way he'd been supportive of Carmelita Pope at the Barrymore.

Later, the same bonding was apparent after Lee Strasberg took over the Studio in the early fifties, and Brando attended his classes sporadically. Strasberg was delivering his end-of-the-year critique, which could often be cruel. Marlon chose to sit in the front row, reading the *New York Times,* even while Lee was talking to him about his own work. For Vivian Nathan, it was an act of protest. "People thought that was arrogant on his part, not to pay attention to Lee," she said. "Yet somehow I think in some way Marlon was responding, 'You have no right to do this, and this is my criticism of you.' "

Brando was nearing the end of his *Streetcar* run, and he regarded that as a relief. Yet his emotional turmoil seemed just as extreme as it had been the previous year. For all his talk of marrying Celia Webb, in early 1949 she had fled and gone to Paris. Ellen Adler, too, had tried to put some distance between herself and Marlon by departing for Paris as well—eventually becoming involved in another relationship that would last for four years. In a pattern that would continue with women throughout his life, Brando couldn't make a commitment, and became angry when women demanded one; yet once they had bolted, he compulsively pursued them, refusing to let them go.

In the end, his defensiveness was transparent. Afflicted with self-doubt, he continued to build walls and erect fences, forbidding even close and well-meaning friends from trespassing. With his daily performances in *Streetcar* now an exhausting torture, he seemed even more confused about his calling as an actor. The craft of acting had become a tiresome burden, but where his future lay he had no idea.

Most people expected him to leave *Streetcar* after logging over 500 performances—and head directly for Hollywood. Indeed, in 1947 producer Jerry Wald had been exchanging memos with Jack Warner about screenwriter Peter Viertel's treatment for *Rebel Without a Cause*. The story was based on the account by Dr. Robert Lindner of a prison psychiatrist and the juvenile delinquent he helps in prison. Stage actor Sam Wanamaker was eager to play the psychiatrist, and he had been touting Marlon for the role of the delinquent "as the greatest young actor in America today." Wald agreed, and tried to persuade Warner Bros. to try to get Brando for *Rebel* since "these kids grow up fast."

For whatever reason, Warners cooled toward the project, and *Rebel* would not become Brando's debut in pictures. It would, of course, eventually go to James Dean, the young actor who had been so avidly watching Brando and following in his footsteps. Nevertheless, Marlon at least seemed to be considering movies as the next step in his career. Even before he had done *Streetcar,* he had been ready to go to Hollywood to play a slum kid in Nicholas Ray's *Knock on Any Door,* in which Humphrey Bogart was to star. But he had dropped that plan as soon as Williams gave him *Streetcar*'s script and asked him to play Stanley. Now, despite his earlier scorn, he sensed that perhaps acting in front of a camera might be an easier way to make a living than having to muster his energy every night during a long stage run. Kazan had braved the studios, and that fact may have allowed Marlon to think more positively about going into films, too. Money and a sense of his own ranking among contemporary actors may also have been on his mind when he asked Edie Van Cleve, "How much is Clift getting in movies?" and then quipped, "I want a dollar more."

Yet, as with so much in Brando's young life, he was still ambivalent.

Instead of turning toward Hollywood, he put all decisions on hold and took off for Paris. Celia Webb and Ellen Adler were both there, and although he may have been pursuing them, he was also trying to give himself the education that he knew he lacked. It was Brando's version of a student's *Wanderjahre,* and during his months in Paris he was both exposed to a continental world of culture and involved in relationships that would prove central to his sense of identity for the rest of his life.

H O L L Y W O O D

1949–53

Within days of resigning from *Streetcar* in late May, Brando broke camp on Fifty-seventh Street. Leaving what few belongings he had except for his drums, he set off for Europe to meet with the French director Claude Autant-Lara. Autant-Lara paid for his ticket to Paris, supposedly hoping to draw him into a production of Stendhal's *The Red and the Black*.

Once there, though, Brando quickly fell in with a down-and-out, avant-garde actors' cooperative that bore a striking resemblance to the world of the Park Savoy. He stayed up nights listening to his new friends' heated arguments about Sartre and existentialism, and after no more than a week, he took to the streets, doing mime.

He also drifted between his raffish digs and the lovely quai Voltaire apartment Ellen Adler was sharing with her new lover, an American composer. Their relationship had grown serious: she would remain with the man for the next four years, yet for Marlon, with his history of playing Ellen off against her mother, there was the undisguised need to hang on. More than either Autant-Lara or Celia Webb, Ellen had been the one to lure him abroad. Happily enough, David Diamond was on the scene, too. Together, the three (and sometimes four) of them roamed through the French capital, sometimes walking for hours. "It was a tremendous aesthetic experience for him, as if he was discovering ancient Greece," Diamond remembered, recalling how Marlon was just "floating," happy that the French were taking him in stride. He went everywhere and he was more charming, more relaxed, than he had been in years. At the *quartier latin* salon of André Brincourt, a friend of Ellen who would soon head *Le Figaro Littéraire,* he was at his comic best: Putting on a long face as he pretended to be a dour, bona fide expatriate along with other visitors like Richard Wright and James Baldwin.

The Autant-Lara project was delayed (it would not be made until 1954, when it starred Gérard Philipe), but Marlon stayed on in Paris. If he later hedged about his lack of education, even sometimes hinting that he had gone to college, Europe was now his real university. He was soaking up European history and civilization, regularly visiting the Louvre, and he also made a point of meeting people.

One of those he looked up was Hervé Mille, the director of *Paris Match,* the leading weekly magazine in Europe. A self-acknowledged homosexual, the elegant, cultured Mille knew everyone, from Sartre and Cocteau to Aznavour, Piaf, and the renowned photographer Walter Carone. (Earlier in 1949 he had gone to New York, seen *Streetcar* and bought the French rights, intending to stage a production of it in Paris. He had asked his friend Cocteau to adapt the play and wanted the great French actress Arletty to play Blanche, but could not find the right actor for Kowalski.) One evening in early summer, his maid announced, "A gentleman is waiting for you in the lounge." Mille went to the foyer and saw no one. Then he looked out the window into the large garden that fronted the residence. Lying facedown on the grass was a young man, his head pillowed on his arm. Mille approached the sleeping figure quietly, then tapped him on the shoulder. The man awoke and lifted his head. "I had not met him in New York, only seen him onstage," recalled Mille, "but I recognized him immediately and I was quite surprised."

Marlon had a simple explanation for his unannounced visit: "A friend of mine said that if I wanted to have a nice time in Paris, I should go see Hervé Mille's brother."

Mille asked him to stay to dinner and introduced him to his brother, Gérard. "I felt he was a very simple person," said Hervé. "Just the way he invited himself to dinner. And then after dinner, he said, 'Hervé, I would like to know you. If you want, I will be here for lunch tomorrow.' He came for lunch the following day, when my brother and I introduced him to about eight or nine of our friends, including Christian Marquand." Graceful, charming, and full of laughter, Marquand was trying to make his way as a producer in the burgeoning French film industry. He and Marlon hit it off immediately, and from that first lunch at the Milles', Marlon became another one of the brothers' circle.

Hervé Mille soon took him to lunch with Jean Cocteau and another friend, the director of the Théâtre Antoine, who hoped to stage the French version of *Streetcar*. They began to discuss the play, and Marlon was soon speaking "French," but his words were imaginary and made up. "It was a French that doesn't exist," recalled Mille, laughing, "but like a parrot, with all the right pauses, inflection, and accent. And then I realized that he was imitating the way my brother spoke, so much so that it was as if Gérard were actually at the table with us."

After their first lunch, Cocteau often saw Brando at Mille's, and like Hervé, he was struck by the young man's gentleness and simplicity. In Paris Marlon seemed to have shed some of the arrogance that masked his shyness and confusions in New York. Later Cocteau remarked to Hervé, "Marlon is the only man who can make noise without disturbing anybody." "That was the best thing Cocteau said about him," added Mille, "and exactly *au point.*"

Several days later Marlon was at the Milles' for dinner and again announced, "I am coming for lunch tomorrow."

"I'm sorry, Marlon," said Hervé, "but tomorrow my brother and I are going to Biarritz, to Saint-Jean-de-Luz."

"Okay," he replied, "I'm coming with you."

"All right, but you must be here by seven."

The following morning Hervé and Gérard walked out the front door to the waiting, chauffeur-driven automobile. There they found Marlon pacing up and down, half asleep but ready to depart.

Hervé looked at the young man wearing jeans and a jacket but carrying no bags.

"You have no luggage?" asked Hervé.

In reply, Marlon pulled two toothbrushes from his jacket pocket. "One is for the morning, the other for the evening," he said.

Mille found this rather strange, but made no further inquiry as they set off across France. For the first several hours, Marlon dozed in the backseat. Then, as they were nearing Poitiers, he roused himself and uttered his first remark of the drive.

"It's awful, so awful!" he exclaimed.

"What's that, Marlon? What is so awful?" asked Mille.

"It's awful what we do to the Indians."

He fell back asleep and slept for another ten hours, until they pulled into Saint-Jean-de-Luz and proceeded directly to a restaurant.

At midnight, when the Milles were ready to depart to check in at their hotel in nearby Ascain, Marlon was nowhere to be found.

"Mr. Brando asked me to come for him tomorrow at noon," the chauffeur explained. Mille realized that Marlon had left with a girl he had been eyeing all evening.

The following day the chauffeur picked up Marlon and delivered him to Mille, who was lunching in a small village near Ascain.

Marlon sauntered up to the table. "It's too awful, too awful!" he muttered again.

This time, however, he didn't mean the Indians, but the young woman with whom he had spent the previous twelve hours.

"It's a terrible story," he explained to Mille. "I had a very nice time with her, and she made me a wonderful breakfast. I was thinking, Thank God she hasn't asked for anything, but then when I was leaving, she did just that. She said, 'When shall we meet again?' It's too awful—that's what I had been afraid of all along."

Back in Paris, Brando's routine of arriving at the Milles' home unannounced continued for the next month. Marlon was also drawn to Christian Marquand, the tall, handsome Frenchman who was "able to speak to any girl and bring Marlon that girl if he wanted her," according to Mille. Marquand had the reputation of a ladies' man, and already stories about Brando's escapades were rampant, including his Errol Flynn–like conquest of the singer Juliette Greco. For a week or more Greco had rejected his advances, but one night Marlon scaled the outside wall of her apartment and entered through her second-floor bedroom window.

There were also rumors that Marlon's friendship with Marquand included a homosexual affair. Marquand and his other great friend, Roger Vadim, often teased each other about their sexuality, making pointedly gay innuendos and sending each other coy postcards that friends would be sure to see. "But that was all a joke," explained Mille. *Pour épater les bourgeois.* But with Marlon that joke didn't exist. He and Marquand never joked about it, not as Marquand and Vadim did."

By this time Marlon had moved out of the Hôtel Voltaire and into a five-bedroom apartment on the quai d'Orléans shared by Marquand, Vadim, Jean-Paul Faure, and the French actor Daniel Gélin. Gélin was a great fan of American culture, and he and Brando soon became friends as well. (They would be reunited many years later when Gélin's illegitimate daughter, Maria Schneider, costarred in *Last Tango in Paris*.)

When Marlon was at home in the flat, he seemed a voracious reader, pursuing what Gélin recalled as "an interest in the arts. But he had no interest in American culture, except Tennessee Williams, and one time he explained to us the theory behind the Actors Studio. But most of all he was interested in philosophies, the spiritual life, and religions. . . . He was most particularly interested in the German philosophers, particularly Nietzsche, and the Hindu religion. I didn't see it as a game, but a real need for knowledge and a quest for spiritual being."

Sometimes Marlon and Gélin stayed up late in a café, "spending the night in long discussion, trying to rebuild the world," Gélin said.

While most of Paris left Brando alone, journalists, aware of who he was, sometimes hounded him and since Marlon neither could afford nor particularly liked going out to nightclubs, Marquand organized parties in the apartment. Sometimes the evening began with games of charades, and, just as in Libertyville, Marlon liked to act out famous events that the other guests would have to identify. "There were always beautiful women," added Gélin, who himself was recently divorced and enjoying the bachelor's life. "But they never stayed a long time with Marlon. He had the reputation of being a very good fucker and had a lot of success with the girls but nothing permanent."

One evening, the daughter-in-law of a high French government official dropped by. Marlon was lying on the sofa in his jeans, and when Christian introduced the young woman, he did not rise but simply extended his index finger toward her in lieu of a handshake.

"Take my finger," he instructed her and, slightly confused, she complied. "Now *tirez*."

As she pulled on it, Marlon let out a "Wagnerian fart," recalled Gélin. "The woman was so shocked that she left immediately. Marlon just didn't give a shit."

The apartment mates loved the idea of shock, and their camaraderie included schoolboy pranks as well. "We were very infantile. Sometimes we stood at the window and pissed outside. The game was to see who could piss the longest distance."

While never openly raising the question with him, Gélin wondered about Marlon's sexual experimentation because of his spending so much time at the Milles' place. "The Mille brothers were well-known homosexuals," Gélin explained, "and then there was their whole circle of friends, including Cocteau. Cocteau was very attracted to Marlon, not only by his modeled physique but also by his rebellious attitude and his talent. He was the first Frenchman to discover and make Marlon's reputation in Paris. I remember when he came back from New York and announced, 'I saw a play of Tennessee Williams, and there was a beast on the stage'—meaning Marlon, of course."

Hervé Mille and Cocteau were aware that Brando hadn't yet decided what acting project he would do next. "Every day he received a new telegram," Mille recalled. "All from Hollywood, from MGM, from the other studios, asking him to come and do a movie. His attitude was total indifference." Toward the end of his stay, Mille and Cocteau came up with the notion that since he seemed to have no other plans, he ought to stay on in Paris and reprise Kowalski in French.

"You can speak French with a perfect accent," Mille told Brando when he was hesitant to play the part in a foreign language. "You could memorize the French words, and because of your talent for imitation, you would speak it perfectly."

Offering him a "wonderful theater, a beautiful decor, a superb adaptation by Cocteau," said Mille, "I thought I had almost convinced him."

Nevertheless, a few days later Marlon raised the subject again.

"You can't be serious about this idea," he said.

Mille reassured him that he was.

Still, Marlon hesitated. Then he refused. "But I really can't do it," he said. "I have to go back to the States to do my third year."

Mille was confused. In France, "doing one's third year" meant completing one's studies, and as far as Mille knew, Marlon was not in school.

Marlon, however, soon clarified what he was saying. He had to return to complete his third year of psychoanalysis. He added that this was important to him because he was "working out" his problems—that he had conflicting feelings about his sister Jocelyn and "about homosexuality." Then, almost half-apologetically, Marlon mentioned that he might after all go to

Hollywood. Before making that ultimate decision, though, he explained to Mille that he had to take one last trip, this one with Christian to Italy. There, still "floating," as he would later put it to reporters, he lay down in a field of flowers and fell into "a paradisiacal dream" that was "the only moment of perfect happiness I had ever known."

Broke, he returned to Paris several days later, and quite by chance he ran into Maynard Morris one evening. The agent explained that MCA had been searching high and low, trying to find him. Awaiting him among his usual telegrams from California was a six-page outline for a movie from producer Stanley Kramer, along with the promise of a ticket home. The part, Morris advised, was one that he could not afford not to look into.

The Men

As any number of film historians have pointed out, Stanley Kramer's stock in trade was an uneasy compromise between muckraking reportage and kitsch, but *Battle Stripe,* or *The Men,* as it was later retitled, plainly leaned toward the former. Set largely in the paraplegic ward of a VA hospital, the picture presented the difficulties of war veteran Ken Wilochek, a young infantry lieutenant paralyzed from the waist down and wrestling with the nightmare of rehabilitation. Confined to the hospital, Wilochek undergoes depression, rejects his fiancée, and at the order of the chief physician is transferred to an open ward, where the cauterizing camaraderie and black humor of fellow patients force him to cope with his injury.

The idea for the script had come to Kramer when he and Kirk Douglas were showing *Champion,* the film they had made together the year before, to patients at the Birmingham VA hospital in Van Nuys, northwest of Hollywood. One of the doctors suggested they step into the paraplegic ward, where the reception took quite a different turn from the eager questioning on boxing and the glitter of filmmaking they'd been getting from the hospital's general population. Douglas was unprepared for the paraplegics' sarcasm, underscored as it was by their bitter refusal to be impressed with a "movie star." He supposedly left almost at once. Kramer, however, saw the potential for a film.

Carl Foreman, who had scripted two earlier hits for the producer, was asked to write the treatment. With the help of Dr. Ernst Bors, the chief of Birmingham's paraplegic ward, who encouraged his patients to co-operate, Foreman's outline soon included authentic dialogue as well as epi-sodes borrowed freely from the veterans' real-life experiences. Wilochek emerged as a composite, but other figures like Norm, the film's bitter intel-lectual played by Jack Webb, and the abrupt but sensitive Dr. Borck, ren-dered by Everett Sloane, were almost photocopies of actual people. The vets' depression, alcoholism, and sexual struggles, as well as their suicidal car wrecks and cruel but lifesaving joking, further anchored the treatment in reality.

Like almost everyone else, Kramer had seen *Streetcar,* but he first chanced upon Brando backstage after a touring performance of *The Eagle Has Two Heads.* He had overheard Marlon calmly announcing, "You know, Miss Bankhead, I'm going to go to bed with you," to which his tem-pestuous leading lady had answered without a moment's hesitation, "And so you shall, my boy, so you shall." Kramer, who insisted the story was true, later realized that the actor's confrontational "honesty" was a façade, but maybe all the more effective for it. The producer met with Brando in New York within days of the actor's return from France. "Marlon was re-served," Kramer recalled, "but specifically, the idea of working out of a wheelchair and knowing that you are crippled, that you're never going to walk for the rest of your life, that interested him."

There was little question that for Brando the project fell into the cate-gory of "good works," and an added incentive was that Austrian-born Fred Zinnemann, known as a meticulous craftsman, was slated to direct. Zinnemann had just completed *The Search* (1948), which was about the displaced children of postwar Europe. Even more compelling, perhaps, was the fact that *The Search* had starred Montgomery Clift. By the time Kramer returned to the West Coast, Brando's terms were already in place: He was to get top billing and $40,000; the era of slavish seven-year con-tracts was gone and the long-term contract itself was already past its peak, but, taking a cue from Clift, he had refused to sign any sort of option, leav-ing Kramer with a straight one-picture deal.

Marlon, who was still filled with misgivings over selling out, spent his last night in New York with Darren and Flo Dublin. Darren saw him off at the train station (Marlon confessed to his old pal that he was "afraid of flying"). As the train pulled out, Marlon opened his coat like a flasher. "He wanted to show me that he was wearing my pajama top underneath," recalled Dublin. "It was my only pair of pajamas, and I shouted at him, 'You motherfucker!' He thought it was hilarious."

After a brief stopover in Chicago, Marlon arrived in Los Angeles early in September 1949, later joking that he "didn't have the character to turn down such big money." He also confessed to one of his future friends among the hospital's paraplegic population, "I was so drunk I could hardly stand up when I got off the train . . . so worried about coming out here to meet Kramer, and then I got to thinking about you guys, and I wondered if I even wanted to meet you."

Aunt Betty and "Nana" Bessie were waiting as he stepped down from the Super Chief at the old Santa Fe station in downtown Los Angeles. With them was MCA's representative, a young agent named Jay Kanter. There was no studio limousine, no reservation waiting at the Beverly Hills Hotel.

Since Marlon knew practically no one in Hollywood, Kramer invited him to stay at his Beverly Hills apartment for a few days while getting settled. He remained singularly composed at Kramer's, explaining to the producer that he was not interested in meeting starlets or anybody else in "the business," much less going to parties. Subsequently, he told the *New York Times,* "I didn't know where I was or what I was doing. I was confused, . . . nervous and more apprehensive than [I'd] ever been before." Over the next two months Brando would live like a vagabond, camping out in five different places. Even now, at the close of the first week, he was about to shift his base to his aunt's bungalow in the modest suburb of Eagle Rock, fifteen miles from Hollywood.

Kramer's method of operation was based on intense preproduction and thorough rehearsals; the producer had cast forty-five patients in small roles. He also arranged for his actors to spend time at the VA facility, and among them would be supporting players Richard Erdman and Jack Webb. For Marlon, though, this was insufficient. On his own, he checked himself into the thirty-two-bed ward, explaining that he was going to live with the paraplegics day and night; confined to a wheelchair for the three-week rehearsal period, he would undergo the same arduous gym and pool therapy as the disabled patients.

This, at least, was the official story, fanned by the film's busy publicists and still told by almost everybody connected to the film, including Kramer. A different version is told by Pat Grissom, president of the Paralyzed Veterans Association and Brando's closest friend during the shooting. Grissom had been a soldier with the Third Infantry Division as it crossed the Rhine, until a bullet severed his spinal cord; years of rehabilitation at the VA hospital followed, and although he had already been discharged by the time of Brando's arrival, most of Grissom's days were still spent on the ward, as he commuted from a two-bedroom house in Grenada Hills that he shared with two other outpatients. Because Grissom was now the chief liaison between the vets and filmmakers, Zinnemann had asked him to take Marlon on his first tour of the hospital. He spent two hours guiding Brando from bed to bed, but the young actor said almost nothing. Suddenly Grissom found that his charge had disappeared. He checked out the nearby restroom, wheeled himself into the cafeteria, and finally found Brando outside in the hospital's picnic area, stricken with emotion.

" 'I'm trying to take it in,' he recalled Marlon whispering, gazing into the distance. "The next thing he did was ask if he could have a wheelchair for himself, as well as get his thighs and calves measured for a pair of leg braces."

By the end of the first day, Grissom and another patient, "Turk" Behmoiran, the film's model for the ward's resident bookie, insisted he join them at their favorite hangout, the Pump Room. Once they arrived, they mercilessly kidded him as he struggled to unfold his wheelchair getting out of the car. Later Brando managed to get himself jammed in the restaurant doorway. Unfazed by the vets' wisecracks, Brando laughed at his own clumsiness, and once they had finished dinner he asked if he could move in with Grissom and his housemates, having already learned that Grissom had an extra bed in his room. During the course of the rehearsal period, he explained, he'd need only one or two nights in the hospital. What he really wanted was time with the guys outside—especially those at the same stage of rehabilitation as his character. He vowed to live in his wheelchair. "He wasn't making any big deal about it," Grissom said. "He just wanted to do it right."

The vets were moved by the seriousness of his undertaking, and they made Brando their "honorary paraplegic." For his part, Marlon went out of his way to comply with the media's requests for interviews. "Every once in a while I forget and lean down and scratch my ankle," he told one reporter. "A paraplegic never scratches his leg. There is no feeling there."

According to Grissom, the report that Brando was using a urine bag was fiction, but otherwise he was living as a paraplegic. Over and over he would tumble out of his wheelchair as he mounted a curb or got out of bed in the morning. He kept trying, though, and once he began to master the device, he was the old Bud—even at the risk of another fall, when he'd put the wheelchair back on its wheels and race the length of the ward, doing spins and "180s."

Back at the Pump Room one evening, an elderly lady came in off the street, already half-boozed. She spotted the veterans in their wheelchairs and proceeded to extol the healing powers of Christ so that they might walk again. Marlon feigned interest and encouraged the woman to continue. She harangued him with ever mounting fervor. The room fell silent, the other customers unaware that Brando was not a paraplegic. Slowly, he began to clutch at the arms of his wheelchair, then rise. He took a few hesitant steps. Two waiters stood by, ready to catch him should he fall. Then, as the woman stared, speechless, he threw himself into a wild jig up and down the length of the bar to the applause of his comrades, who hooted and howled as the would-be evangelist fled.

Principal photography on *The Men* began in late October, and Brando was slow to start, struggling with his lines as he tried to adjust to the Hollywood practice of doing scenes out of sequence. Equally daunting was the need to relax in front of the camera while gaffers, grips, and sound technicians—along with the usual jungle of booms, cables, and lights—filled the soundstage. "He was under enormous strain," said Zinnemann. The director even phoned Kazan in New York for advice. "I've got Marlon Brando here in *The Men*. What the hell do I do?" Zinnemann asked.

"Leave him alone. Don't do anything," Kazan instructed. "He'll come through, I promise you. Just let him be."

Teresa Wright, who played Ken's fiancée, recalled that Marlon did exactly as he was told, that his attitude was anything but "difficult." One of the first scenes to be shot was their wedding-night sequence, and as the camera dollied in and out, Wright remembered Marlon whispering to her, "What are those guys doing there?" Wright, an experienced film actress, told him that if he was bothered he should say so; the technicians could find another way of getting the shot. Marlon shook his head. "He wanted to be professional," she said, "which meant not asking too many questions."

"When I first started," Brando recalled, "I got there at something like six-thirty, and by nine-thirty, when they were ready to shoot, I had shot my wad. . . . If you do a scene any number of times, you just go dry unless you crank up very slowly."

Unlike most Hollywood film directors, Zinnemann was actor-friendly and had allowed Montgomery Clift to find his way through the shattering concentration-camp material in *The Search*. Now he did the same with Brando. Often he'd call a break and usher Marlon into a corner "to talk," sometimes for thirty minutes or more. Jack Webb, a radio actor for years and accustomed to first takes, began muttering disparagingly about "New York acting." Marlon retaliated by not cuing Webb during their one sustained scene together.

In terms of acting styles, no one could have been more different from Brando than Teresa Wright. Her husband at the time, veteran screen-writer Niven Busch, had urged her to turn down the role. Busch pointed out that Brando had star billing, that all the production values were tipped in favor of his part, and that she was committing professional suicide.

"I just cut my throat," she acknowledged years later, "but I was convinced at the time that I was right, that the film was important."

She could not have been more miscast, and, as has been pointed out, "nothing demonstrate[d] the breakthrough nature of Brando's acting more sharply than the old-fashioned acting of his costar." As with Tandy in *Streetcar,* he was simply overpowering—not by design, but because he was so immersed in his part. More and more he attacked his lines. With half-formed interjections, expressive grunts, and a sense of timing that subsumed syntax, he could dive into the middle of a scripted "emotion," emitting an intensity that was little short of what he'd projected in the Williams play.

The effect was all the greater for the contrast between the paralyzed Ken (or "Bud," as he's nicknamed) and the volcanic eruptiveness of nearly every gesture. His enfeebled, lifeless legs as he climbs the rope in the hospital gym (an improv based on his solitary rope-climbing exercises at Shattuck) or how he struggled to pull himself up into a sitting position with the aid of the bar suspended above his bed, all the while squeezing his eyes shut and shuddering with pain, delighted Zinnemann and, moreover, made it clear that he was playing "from the inside out."

One of the cast members, former child actor Richard Erdman, had a one-bedroom apartment off Hollywood Boulevard, and after several weeks of filming Marlon moved in, sleeping on the living room couch. Erdman's previous roommate had been Luther Adler, but as was his habit of keeping friends separate, Marlon failed to tell Erdman of his closeness to the Adler clan. Push-ups and an incessant stretching routine in the middle of the small living room, it soon became obvious, were part of his routine, just as his diet consisted mainly of junk food, usually take-out Chinese or peanut butter, which he consumed by the jarful; Erdman, a gourmet cook, was even more puzzled by his failure to restock the refrigerator or offer money for expenses, since he knew that the film was paying Brando $40,000 to his own $5,000.

He was "totally unpredictable," and often contentious, too. In the midst of a conversation, Erdman said, he might come up with a question out of nowhere, or make one of his offhand "observations" about anything at all, including his host's driving, smoking, or drinking. Sometimes, even with their early calls, Brando didn't come home at all; on those nights when he returned at four in the morning he'd flop on the couch without bothering to undress.

One evening, when the two were sitting around talking, Erdman pulled out a copy of *Theater Arts* magazine. Marlon glanced at it and suddenly clammed up: In the upper right-hand corner of the page, there was a picture of him as Kowalski. The caption read: "It's his eyes that give him the lie." It was Eric Bentley's review of *A Streetcar Named Desire,* in which the critic implied that Brando was homosexual. For almost two days Marlon said nothing. His simmering anger came to a head the day when the company moved out to the John Ford ranch in San Fernando Valley for location shots in a swimming pool. Physically, Brando was in magnificent shape from weeks of working out with the vets at the VA hospital, and now, without warning, he lunged at Erdman and held him underwater. As the actor thrashed to the surface, screaming, the other members of the company looked on as Marlon switched moods with the deftness of a mime. Responding to his audience's horror, he suddenly became the clown and let out one of his strange high-pitched laughs.

The incident was pivotal, leaving Erdman with the sense that Brando was capable of exploding at any moment, a "dangerous man." Brando had already alluded to his therapy in New York—a reference here, a joke there—but it had come out that since arriving in L.A. he had sought a "second opinion." The name of the mysterious doctor was never divulged (in all likelihood it was Freudian analyst Ralph Greenson, who later treated Marilyn Monroe), but nonetheless he continued to drop hints, playing a cat-and-mouse game that led Erdman to sense that his visits had had to do specifically with the Bentley article.

Gradually Brando began shifting his allegiance to another scene up in the Hollywood hills. Luther Adler, still in town working on a film, was living at the home of Alan Adler, his nephew, and Alan's wife, Mary McNamara. Alan and Mary rented out rooms, and the place was filled with girls—lots of girls. Other tenants included Bobby Abel, an ex–bantamweight boxer trying to break into show business by writing scripts, and Vermelle "Mel" McCarter, a saxophone player from Alabama who was dating Luther. Marlon often dropped by her room to talk. What was mostly on his mind was Dodie.

"It was a love-hate thing," Mel recalled. "He kept saying that his mother was 'a very beautiful woman,' and I began to think that maybe he'd had incestuous feelings for her, that maybe this was what got him so crazy. He didn't say anything about her being smart or being an actress, or even that she was an alcoholic, which I found out about through Luther." What Marlon repeatedly referred to was "her beauty and that she was domineering, controlling," she noted, adding that as he was talking, he also pounded the wall.

"He felt that she was largely to blame for how screwed up he was," Mel continued, "and he was open about it—his anger, his rage, and he used those words specifically. He didn't know how to cope with it, which was how he explained being in analysis. Sometimes I just kept quiet and watched him beat on himself, because he needed the sounding board. You didn't even know how you'd get into these conversations, but he could turn around five seconds later and say, 'Let's go to Benson Fong's to get something to eat.' "

It wasn't long afterward that he took up with a classical pianist who was the live-in girlfriend of Luther Adler's brother, Jay, who had been holding acting classes at the nearby home of Clfford Odets. The move was an opportunistic one, another example of what Carlo Fiore and others described as his "always taking away someone's woman."

There was another Jay on the scene, too: Brando's new MCA representative, Jay Kanter, who was riding the actor's comet. Until recently a

UCLA business student, Kanter had gone to work for MCA in the agency's mailroom. As was customary in Hollywood at the time, he'd been dispatched to pick up Brando when he'd first arrived in Los Angeles, and to chauffeur him around. By the end of his first week in town, Marlon had been summoned to meet with Lew Wasserman, George Chasen, Arthur Parks, Jennings Lang, and all the other senior luminaries at MCA to decide which of them was to handle him. The actor instead decreed that his new agent was to be "the kid" who'd picked him up at the train station. Now, more than a month later, Kanter was often at Alan Adler and Mary McNamara's home in his blue business suit until late in the evening. Affability, decency, even a certain middle-class stability were among Kanter's attributes, along with Marlon's premier requirement of loyalty.

Brando would come to trust him as much as anyone on earth, even in later years when Kanter would rise to the presidency of MGM. At Adler and McNamara's, however, Marlon's attentions were more focused on women. There was Shirley Ballard, a blond actress-model, and he had a brief fling with another boarder, one of Wally Cox's girlfriends from New York. There was also a ripe, Eurasian-looking seventeen-year-old, who asked that she be called Nicki. She got his attention one evening at an all-night party up the hill at the Odets house.

"I was never comfortable around him," Nicki explained. "I don't know if *intimidated* is the right word, but I never felt relaxed [because] he was kind of always 'on,' like onstage. He was constantly toying with me. He told me that he and Monty Clift used to live together and had had an affair, kind of bragging to me. Then he took me with him into a meeting with the people at the studio. I was in ballet slippers and blue jeans, with a bandanna on my head, both of us really scruffy because we'd been hanging out and drinking. He was very considerate of me, very polite, and going to great lengths to introduce me to everyone—me, tongue-tied and seventeen—but it was really 'Fuck you, fuck your decorum, fuck your businessmen's mentality.' I loved it, even though nowadays I can't see it as his so-called rebelling so much as his need for attention."

At other times, Brando talked to the pretty teenager nonstop. Part of his logorrhea was that he was taking diet pills, "little heart-shaped Dexamyls," but Nicki was nonetheless ready to listen, happy to receive him in the middle of the night any time he called. Their sexual encounters were frequent, although "never wham-bam, never rough," she said, pointing to the same easiness noted by Sondra Lee and others in New York. "He was very gentle, always kind of soft when he touched me," she added, "but when I told him I loved him, his response was to tell me not to say that. 'You can't possibly. You just met me,' he said. I remember him looking at my arms and telling me how graceful I was. I'd already admitted to him that I thought I was awkward and a bad dancer, but he said, 'Well, look how graceful your arm is, look how graceful your hand is.'"

This, she felt, "wasn't an act," but since he was also sleeping with several other women at Adler and McNamara's, his attentions were sporadic, even during their short week and a half together. "I didn't even know about one of the other girls in the house and found out only when I discovered her waiting for him on the stoop one evening. What dawned on me was that he was keeping us all separate. It made him feel in control, powerful. New York, for example, was another world completely, and the truth was that he didn't give a shit about me, and because of my insecurity I wasn't able to handle it."

Brando's need to control was overwhelming, and rather than break off the relationship, he would later write her long-winded, abstruse notes from New York, signing off, "Your breasts are always in my mouth." But when Nicki announced she was coming east on borrowed money to be with him, he quickly replied, explaining that he'd talked to his psychiatrist, who had advised against it. As he told her, "You should save your money in a sock." Nine months later, however, he would return to L.A. to film *Streetcar* and pick up where he had left off, underwriting an abortion in the process and even passing Nicki on to Kazan.

Another of Brando's women was Shelley Winters, who brought him into contact with the young Norman Mailer. Mailer had been summoned to L.A. by Sam Goldwyn after the success of his best-selling war novel, *The Naked and the Dead,* and he hoped to follow in F. Scott Fitzgerald's footsteps, having coauthored a script modeled after *Miss Lonelyhearts.* Unlike Brando, Mailer immediately threw himself into the local social whirl; to celebrate his "deal" with Goldwyn, he decided to throw a wingding of a Christmas party, and combed the *Players' Directory* for the addresses of Hollywood's movers and shakers, since nothing less than glitterati would do.

"It was a fiasco of a party," said Winters, who arrived in a blond beaver coat with Brando in the middle of a torrential downpour. "Norman had wanted *everybody* in Hollywood, both left and right, and you didn't do that in 1949. Adolphe Menjou was there snubbing Charlie Chaplin. Bogart was giving Ginger Rogers the fish eye. Monty and Elizabeth Taylor and Marlon were very uncomfortable." John Ford was there, along with Cecil B. DeMille, and throughout the evening the "enemies" continued sniping. Marlon was wearing a tuxedo he'd borrowed from Jay Kanter, and it was too small for him. "There was a black bartender there, and Marlon just stood behind the bar and talked to him in his little suit. I was trying to talk to people, trying to be sexy and everything, but my dress was soaked. Monty was having a fight with somebody. . . ."

Suddenly Brando wanted to leave. The political conversation was too intense, the group too large. " 'This party's making me nervous,' he said," Winters recalled, "but Norman stopped us at the door and said, 'Where are you going? You didn't meet anybody.' That's when Marlon said, 'What the fuck are you doing here, Mailer? You're not a screenwriter. Why aren't you in Vermont writing your next book?' "

Mailer's response was lost in the general confusion. Not only did Winters take Elizabeth Taylor's beaver coat by mistake, but Brando took the coat of a fledging actor, Mickey Knox, whose car was found to be blocking the driveway. Winters added: "Nobody could get out. Hal Wallis, Mickey's boss at Paramount, called me at three A.M. and sent a police car over to retrieve Mickey's keys. . . . Marlon just stayed in bed."

On the set of *The Men,* however, Brando found himself sharing "a tremendous bond" with Erdman, despite their frissons, during the closing week of filming. The norm at the time was to let extras and script clerks cue actors while they were under the camera's eye, but Zinnemann had insisted that everyone play it fully for every take. Erdman had been helping Marlon all along, and now he asked him to return the favor when it came time to do the scene in which Erdman's character, Leo, scores with his horse bet. It was a demanding bit, since the actor had to flop out of bed and race up and down the corridors in a wheelchair. Marlon stayed on the set for close to nine hours straight. Like a true team player, he demanded more with each take. Zinnemann watched, not interfering as the performance grew richer. "When it was over, I couldn't wait," Erdman recalled. "I went over to Marlon and said, 'Goddamn it, I think I love you.' We hugged. It was a real moment, because despite all the other stuff both of us knew we'd done something wonderful."

For the most part Erdman remained confused by Brando's behavior, as did Jack Cooper, the film's middle-aged publicity agent who, with Kramer's partner, George Glass, had been handling Marlon's contacts with the press since the start of rehearsals. Despite all the advance publicity, as well as gentle reminders from Jay Kanter, it was apparent that Brando felt comfortable giving interviews only on his own terms: Sometimes he showed up late, but more often than not he'd take the liberty of co-opting a reporter's questions with queries of his own—sometimes whimsically, sometimes with the deepest seriousness, as when representing his paraplegic pals.

Throughout Hollywood, word was out: Brando refused to play the role of the conventional star. For Kramer and Glass, what was most worrisome was his impression on the two grandes dames of gossip—Louella Parsons and Hedda Hopper. Parsons alone had a circulation of 17.5 million, while the bitchy, jingoistic Hopper appeared in the *Los Angeles Times,* the New York *Daily News,* and the *Chicago Tribune* as well as in some 3,000 small-town dailies and 2,000 weeklies. If Walter Winchell had facetiously suggested honoring Parsons by renaming the town Lollywood, it was common knowledge that either columnist could make or break a film or a performer with ease. Both expected any new arrival to pay court and genuflect before the town's traditions.

But Brando was formidable, too. He had already humiliated Faye Emerson on national TV by pointing out that there was something clinging to the sole of her shoe. Similarly, columnist Sheilah Graham had suffered from his "attentions," when he'd asked backstage during *Streetcar* whether she was Jessica Tandy's mother. When Hedda Hopper finally made her appearance at Kramer's rented headquarters near Cahuenga Boulevard to do her first full-scale story on Brando, he grunted answers to her questions and even made a snide reference to her trademark hats. When she asked if he cared to continue the interview, he said he didn't believe so.

Strangely enough, when Hopper's column finally came out, Brando was "Hollywood's new sensation." His "eccentricity," as she called it, was at one with his disciplined talent, his seriousness and honesty. In her disarmingly daffy prose, her piece dripped with superlatives that promised the biggest sort of stardom for Brando, not to say huge box office for *The Men.* Perhaps Kramer, Cooper, Lew Wasserman, or the majordomos at United Artists, the film's distributor, had greased the skids. If so, the same magic went flat with Parsons, whom Marlon had addressed as "the fat one." The redoubtable lady suggested that if he persisted in being "uncooperative," what did it matter that Brando was potentially the most gifted actor in America? "We Americans," she wrote, "don't even permit our Presidents the luxury of a private life."

On the other hand, *Life* magazine devoted six pages to detailing his lifestyle. Chasen's and the Brown Derby, pink Cadillacs and Roxbury Drive mansions had "no meaning" for the actor, which echoed Hopper's claim that "his integrity is not for sale." The *Life* profile went on: "Brando once told an old friend, 'I put on an act sometimes and people think I'm insensitive. Really, it's like a kind of armor because I'm too sensitive. If there are two hundred people in a room and one of them doesn't like me, I've got to get out!' " On another occasion, as the magazine added, he'd said, "Maybe in another five years I can learn to be happy."

The Men opened in July 1950—unhappily enough, only two weeks after the start of the Korean War. The timing could not have been worse, yet if the picture was destined to fail at the box office, the reviews were predominantly raves:

> A fine and arresting film. . . . Mr. Brando as the veteran . . . is so vividly real, dynamic and sensitive that his illusion is complete. His face, the whole rhythm of his body and especially the strange timbre of his voice, often broken and plaintive and boyish, are articulate in every way. Out of stiff and frozen silences he can lash into a passionate rage with the fearful and flailing frenzy of a taut cable suddenly cut. Or he can show the poignant tenderness of a doctor with a child.
> —Bosley Crowther, *New York Times* (July 21,1950)

> The picture introduces a new and fascinating personality in Marlon Brando . . . unquestionably destined for much attention in the future. . . . *The Men* is indeed worth seeing for its higher values.
> —*Los Angeles Times* (September 30, 1950)

Brando's pleasure—his pride, even—was evident. When *Cue* ran a cover profile, he bought a hundred copies and spent the evening giving them out to everybody he ran into, including waiters and maître d's. Even before the film's release, he hadn't been able to hide his delight at a preview (despite his telling the press he wasn't satisfied with the ending or the souped-up score created by Dmitri Tiomkin). Accompanying him to the screening was Jocelyn, then in the midst of divorcing Don Hanmer and about to marry the writer Eliot Asinof.

"We saw it in a little screening room," she recalled, "eight or nine of us. I was sitting behind him, and the movie started with the soldiers walking across the field, and Bud went down in his chair, slumped way down. Then he appeared on-screen and he turned around to me, whispering, 'That's me,' as he continued to slide down in his seat. It was as if he was saying, 'I'm in that movie, isn't it funny?' There was a grin on his face."

"When I first came to Hollywood," Brando would acknowledge to a reporter, "I had the snobbish idea that movie acting was a pushover, and that screen actors had a plush-lined cinch. All I can say now, after having gone through my first film, is that no stage actor's training can be considered complete until he has first made a picture. It is the toughest form of acting, and anyone who can come through it successfully can call himself an actor for the first time."

For the first time, too, he knew that Zinnemann, Kramer, and the ever politic Lew Wasserman were listening. So was Jack Warner, whose studio was backing the forthcoming production of *Streetcar*; Warner had already offered Brando $50,000 to appear in the film, but with Kanter's counsel, Marlon had started playing the Hollywood game in earnest and was holding out for an additional $25,000.

Whatever hostility and ambivalence Marlon had expressed about Dodie during his drunken confessions while making *The Men,* he still continued to regard the family home as a retreat from both New York and Hollywood. In fact, it had been the financial contribution from his movie earnings that had allowed his parents to buy a new homestead in 1949—forty acres of windswept cornfields in Mundelein, several miles west of Libertyville. Dodie called the spread Penny Poke Farm, a play on her maiden name. Behind the home stood a seventy-foot-long barn, and the residence itself was shielded from the road by a stand of lilacs. It was a typical midwestern farmhouse, with a wide porch, a large living room and small kitchen, one bath, and three small bedrooms upstairs. Like Little Mohee, the Brandos' previous residence in Libertyville, it had a funky, comfortable feel to it, due largely to Dodie's filling the place with books, rocks arranged on the windowsills, and dried herbs and fresh-picked flowers in vases set out in all the rooms.

Dodie also bought an old blue Ford pickup and painted "Penny Poke Farm" in white letters on its side. She was often seen putt-putting into Libertyville to make her rounds to aid her colleagues in AA. She was still the ostensible leader of the AA groups in and around Libertyville, and if one of her followers called for help, she would jump in the truck at any hour.

"The farm," as it came to be called in the Brando family, became a meeting place for all the offspring—including Bud, who, with the release of *The Men* and its attendant publicity, was now being referred to around town as "the movie star." During the times that he returned to the farm, Dodie tried to keep his visits a secret, realizing that if word got out, reporters and fans would make tracks to their door. "If there was any inkling he was in town, all hell would break loose," recalled Dodie's friend Marian Johnsen. "There were all these young girls running out there and hanging on the gate. It was terrible."

While Marlon was staying with his parents after *The Men,* he was still complaining of anxiety attacks. Phyllis Stewart, another friend of Dodie, also suffered from such attacks; one morning Dodie brought Bud over to discuss their shared condition over coffee. "He told me he had these panic attacks, too," Stewart recalled, "and said that when they happened, he just threw himself down wherever he was, on the floor or on the sidewalk, and no one paid any attention to him." The writer Alice Cromie, a Mundelein neighbor, became aware of Bud's nerves when she was asked for a sedative, since the Brandos knew that she had a supply of Librium.

Back in France, Mille and Marlon's apartment mates had noticed that he was usually short of cash. This was, as he had explained to Mille, because he had given all his salary to his father "to buy cows," and with his hefty $40,000 paycheck from *The Men* he had done the same. Marlon Sr. had already decided that his son needed "shelters" to reduce his income taxes. Now, with even more money at his disposal, Marlon Sr. had visions of finally making a killing.

It turned out to be just another one of Brando Sr.'s schemes. A man named Roe Black had an 8,500-acre cattle ranch in northern Nebraska, near Brewster, and he offered just such tax shelters to businessmen who wanted to invest in a hundred or so head of cattle. Marlon Sr. invited Black to the Mundelein farm to discuss the investment. "He told me that he was quitting the Chicago feed business," Black later recalled, "that he wanted to invest all his son's money in my cattle operation, and would make his living out of young Brando's earnings." The two men discussed the idea, with Black making his sales pitch. Then Marlon Sr. turned to Black. "I want to show you something," he said. He produced a recording device that had been concealed in the room and proceeded to play back their entire conversation. It was this side of the Brandos, both *père* and *fils,* that many would remark upon in years to come—something slightly sneaky and shady. Marlon Sr. was enjoying the idea of a hidden tape recorder, a device with which to manipulate and control, and gain power over others. In fact, it was a "toy" that his son had grown fond of as well, when in New York he had hidden recorders under his bed to tape his sexual adventures.

By the spring of 1950 Marlon Sr. had acquired a thousand head of cattle. He and Dodie were in partnership in the operation, calling it Penny Poke Ranch, Inc. But what neither had realized (and what Black hadn't informed them) was that the operation had undergone major financial losses after being brutalized by severe blizzards during the winter of 1949. Black came back to his investor with the deep pockets, and Marlon Sr. offered to help bail him out with another $10,000 investment. In addition, Black took out $200,000 in mortgages and then asked Marlon Sr. if he would like to live on the ranch during the summer and run it while Black tended to his cattle trading in Texas. The idea was appealing, and soon Marlon and Dodie would load their pickup and head out for the spread in the Sand Hills of Nebraska.

For the previous year, Dodie's mother, Bessie, had been living in Illinois with her daughter and son-in-law. Now in her seventies, she couldn't be left alone at the farm for the summer. Fran and Dick Loving came out from New York with their infant daughter, Julie, to stay with her. However, Fran herself was in terrible shape, and she went to Brando family doctor John Ward in July with a litany of disorders. It was during this session that she expressed bitter resentment toward her brother, explaining that with all his wealth, he was neglecting to help her and Dick out of their severe financial straits. "She said by then Marlon was a millionaire," recalled Ward, "and she was rather hurt that he was not of any particular assistance to her."

In all likelihood her animosity had been sparked by a brief visit from Marlon, who had stopped off on his way back to Hollywood to begin shooting the film of *Streetcar*. He recounted his business triumphs, and it seemed to Fran that he was more enthusiastic about the incredible deal he had made than he was about playing his heralded stage role in front of the cameras. But what seemed most upsetting to Fran was her brother's personality. If Dodie had wondered whether Bud, a graduate of Method acting, could ever let go of a role and drop his Kowalski character, it was beside the point; he seemed once again to be stoking his anger in order to revive and energize his previous stage role. There was an upsetting edge and fierceness about him, even when he was supposedly relaxing in the easy climes of Mundelein. With Fran and Dick, he seemed brittle and continued his merciless teasing, remarking on their habits, their gestures, their movements. His stardom, it seemed, was less of a balm than it was a further impetus for him to go to his darker side.

A Streetcar Named Desire

The rights for the film version of *Streetcar* had been purchased by agent-turned-producer Charles Feldman even before *The Men* was completed in early December 1949. Feldman, the founder of the Famous Artists agency, had initiated the coup by skillfully coming to terms with Irene Selznick. Then he'd wooed Kazan to direct after setting up financing through Jack Warner. Far more than Kramer, Feldman was an innovator, widely credited with originating the package deal in which script, actors, and director were presented to a studio as a prearranged entity, endowing stars with unprecedented power. As an agent, his roster included Cary Grant, Claudette Colbert, John Wayne, Lauren Bacall, William Holden, and director George Stevens. Suave and soft-spoken, Feldman had been dubbed "the Jewish Clark Gable," but no less a part of his legend was his phone book filled with the numbers of available starlets, Marilyn Monroe among them—even though he was married to Jean Howard, a former Ziegfeld Follies girl.

On April 10, 1950, the details of Brando's *Streetcar* contract became public: He was to receive almost twice his previous salary; billing on all screen, marquee, and advertising credits "[in] type 100 percent the size of the title"; and veto power over wardrobe fittings, makeup tests, and press interviews during the first week of production. Like his contract with Kramer, there was no multipicture clause, leaving him free to pick and choose future roles.

It was 1950, well into what Hollywood historians would call "the plague years." The industry's in-house censor, the Joseph Breen office, had made it plain that if Williams's account of madness and intrafamily rape had not offended decency on the New York stage, standards for movies were something else altogether. Breen's allies consisted of the American Legion, the Catholic War Veterans, and the Motion Picture Alliance for the Preservation of American Ideals. And they had gone on the alert, too, supported by the likes of columnists George Sokolsky, Victor Riesel, and Walter Winchell. Three years before, in the spring of 1947, the House Un-American Activities Committee (HUAC) had imprisoned the so-called Hollywood Ten. The witch-hunt had moved to Washington, and with blacklisting and censorship unambiguously linked, Breen and his minions had already eviscerated Theodore Dreiser's *Sister Carrie,* blocked production of Nelson Algren's *The Man with the Golden Arm,* and demanded major script changes in *Key Largo* (1948) after Bogart had rallied Hollywood liberals to protest against HUAC.

Feldman and Jack Warner knew what was in the wind, and so did Williams and Kazan, who had chosen to meet the problem head-on by demanding a reading at the Breen office before the film had even been cast. Predictably, the censors insisted that the script's profanity be cut, and Williams also agreed to disguise the homosexuality that was behind the death of Blanche's husband. He drew the line, however, when told to excise the critical rape scene, thus jeopardizing his $350,000 fee for film rights and his services as screenwriter.

"*Streetcar* is an extremely and peculiarly moral play, in the deepest sense of the term," Williams wrote to Breen, whose memos to Jack Warner were filled with references to Blanche's "promiscuity," "gross sex," and "dementia." "The rape of Blanche by Stanley is a pivotal, integral truth in the play, without which the play loses its meaning, which is the ravishment of the tender, the sensitive, the delicate, by the savage and brutal forces of modern society. It is a poetic plea for comprehension."

Breen relented, insisting only that Kowalski be "punished." Williams responded with the solution of having Stella tell her newborn baby that she was not returning home; to the unsophisticated, it would appear that Stanley had destroyed his marriage, while the more urbane moviegoer could conclude that Stella would probably take him back.

It was a less mutilating solution than others, and for the time being,

Kazan and Williams figured they had the problem licked. With Brando cast, Warner and Feldman insisted that Olivia de Havilland play Blanche, because the two-time Oscar winner promised bigger returns at the box office than Jessica Tandy. Kazan soon capitulated; in exchange, the producers "gave" him Malden, Nick Dennis, Rudy Bond, Peg Hillias, and Ann Dere, keeping the New York "family" more or less intact. Although Jack Warner had objected to casting Kim Hunter, saying she had "a negative screen personality," he relented here, too.

However, de Havilland's salary demands, rumored to be $175,000, soon drove Warner and Feldman to approach Vivien Leigh, who had just finished eight months in the London production of *Streetcar,* directed by her husband, Laurence Olivier. If the studio hoped to capitalize on her fame as *Gone with the Wind*'s Scarlett O'Hara, Warner's goal was also to pitch Leigh's exquisite refinement against Brando's Kowalski. The combination was a publicist's dream, cross-casting the beauty and the beast. While Leigh's contract called for $100,000, making her the highest-paid English screen actress of the day, Jack Warner had not blinked; nor was there any of his usual penny-pinching when Kazan, explaining that his leading lady had recently recovered from tuberculosis, insisted that the studio send costume designer Lucinda Ballard across the Atlantic to spare Leigh the rigors of last-minute fittings.

Marlon was happy to be working with Kazan again, and when he arrived in Los Angeles in late July he moved in with Jay Kanter. The large second-floor apartment near the Warner Bros. studio in Burbank was also being shared by two other MCA reps as well as by Tony Curtis, another one of their clients. *Streetcar* was scheduled to begin shooting August 10 and was to completed in thirty-six days; Brando expected his stay in Hollywood to be little more than a stopover.

Leigh arrived four days before Brando and had been accompanied by Kazan on the train from New York. During the journey, Kazan was bracing himself more than usual because the casting of Leigh presented two problems: the London production had presented Blanche as little more than a prostitute, and the English actress had never worked in the Method before. During the run of the play in London, she had supposedly wandered the West End's red-light district, chatting with streetwalkers in the hope of getting tips. According to her friend theater critic Alan Dent, the role had so possessed her that many evenings she had come offstage "shaking like an autumn leaf, her lips trembling." There had been hallucinatory "voices" in the middle of the night, too, almost as if Williams's script had been forcing her to reenact what she feared most: "Blanche is a woman with everything stripped away," she confessed years later. "She is a tragic figure and I understand her. But playing her tipped me into madness."

Leigh, however, was determined to make a go of it, having seen the New York stage production, and a week after her arrival the company assembled at the studio in Burbank. Insiders were claiming that the Method was the hottest thing to hit the film business since the talkies. Leigh herself, through Ballard, had gotten the scoop on Marlon's special relationship with Kazan. To allay her anxieties, the director arranged a get-acquainted lunch in Jack Warner's private dining room.

"Why do you always wear scent?" asked Marlon, arriving in a T-shirt and brown slacks.

"Because I like to smell nice—don't you?"

"Me? I just wash," he said. "In fact, I don't even get in the tub. I just throw a gob of spit in the air and run under it."

Leigh reportedly responded with a deep laugh that turned into malicious delight as Marlon went into a cruelly accurate imitation of Olivier's Agincourt speech from *Henry V* (1944). By the end of lunch, he was also joking about the media, which had already started speculating about what might develop between them, having already heard rumors that Leigh's marriage was crumbling.

On August 14, the first day of shooting, the whole production nearly went up in smoke.

"I requested that Vivien do something we'd done with Jessie in New York," Kazan later wrote, "and she came out with: 'When Larry and I did the production in London . . .' and went on to tell us all what she and Larry had done, which she clearly preferred to what I was asking her to do. Irene had told me about the London production, which she considered misconceived. As Vivien spoke, I became aware of the other actors looking at me. They knew what I knew, that this was a moment not to be allowed to pass unchallenged. 'But you're not making the film with Larry in London now, Vivien,' I said. 'You're making it here with us.' Then, as gently as I could, I insisted on my way."

It was a tense moment, and two weeks would pass before she began to let go of the strained, artificial mannerisms she'd come to rely on. Kazan gentled her. He also laid down the law to Marlon and Kim Hunter, whom he had accused of becoming "a couple of fishwives" late in the New York run. With Brando, he took special pains to press the right buttons, telling him to "get back to basics."

"Okay, this is Stanley's place," he instructed, gesturing at set designer Joe Mielziner's re-creation of the Kowalski apartment. "I want you to go into it and place things around the way Stanley would live." Brando, ignoring the watchful eyes of the assembled company, began rearranging things—a piece of furniture here, a prop there. He tested the bed, then fingered the dirty drapes, and soon went to the nearby prop room, where he found some war medals and a fishing rod and tackle that he thought appropriate to Stanley's character. On the soundstage, he spread newspapers on the Kowalskis' kitchen floor. After a minute or two he stood back and nodded, surveying his handiwork.

"Is that it?" Kazan asked.

"Yeah," he mumbled.

"Okay," the director announced to the crew. "I want everything kept this way. Nothing is to be changed."

As usual, Brando's earnestness extended to his wardrobe. Lucinda Ballard was on hand to oversee Leigh's costumes on a day-to-day basis, and at one point she heard his voice calling out to her piteously from the dark no-man's-land on the far side of the soundstage. "Lucinda, I want to be with you," Marlon wailed, at the same time trying to suppress his laughter. "Wait till you see what I have on." Hollywood tradition dictated that male actors had to be dressed by male wardrobe attendants, a custom dating back to the silents. When Kazan called him over, what stood in front of them was a new Stanley—in "the funniest outfit I ever saw," Ballard recalled. "Sort of fancy black-and-white shoes and a suit like a banker would wear. A suit! Stanley was going to be in a suit!"

This was quickly rectified, but the antagonism between the New York group and union-run studio personnel was bound to grow. Part of the problem was an East Coast–West Coast, stage-screen rivalry. Kazan was also keeping his people apart, which extended to meals in the Warners commissary. Leigh, meanwhile, was being left no practical way to fall back into the safe, standardized reading she had done on the London stage. "Why are you so fucking polite?" Marlon demanded of her at one point, irritated by her lapses into British correctness. Soon he started referring to

Olivier as "Henry the Fifth Larry." The production schedule still hadn't put them together in front of the camera, but he was quietly watching from the sidelines, almost as if lying in wait.

Meanwhile, there were his jokes, nonsense pranks that enlivened the interminable pauses between setups. With equal independence, he ripped the MR. BRANDO sign off his dressing room door and replaced it with a hand-scrawled placard, reading, "Please do not knock. I'm snoozing. —Me." There was also the way he broke the ice with the film's publicity man, Harry Mines, who had been avoiding him assiduously. One afternoon Mines, who was suffering from a hangover, was busy working with Leigh. No sooner had he left her trailer than he came face-to-face with Brando.

"How do you do?" Mines introduced himself, plainly uncomfortable.

"I want to tell you something," Brando announced.

"What's that?"

"One of us is wrong," Marlon answered, pointing out that his reputation for grunting, picking his nose, or scratching his backside in front of reporters was "fallacious." "It's not me," he said. "Someone must get fun out of thinking these stories up."

However specious the stories, Brando was certainly the latest hot topic in the film community. One day Philip Rhodes was on the set. He had been visiting in Los Angeles and dropped by Warners to see not only Marlon but Leigh, too, whom he had known for years. Brando eventually got Rhodes a bit part in the film, but that morning Philip was just waiting behind the sets to say hello. Suddenly, another face peered out of the darkness, looking around the side of a two-by-four scaffolding. Recognizing Humphrey Bogart, another old acquaintance, Philip asked, "Who're you looking for, Bogey?"

"I just want to get a pike at this kid Brando," he said, in his typical tough-guy slang.

It was then that Rhodes realized that Marlon had crossed over into the land of stardom and fame. Not long afterward, he learned that Aldous Huxley had made an appointment to meet Brando. Marlon asked Philip, "Who's this Huxley? The guy wants to have lunch with me."

Marlon's naïveté and ignorance reminded Rhodes of the time in New York when his friend had shown him a fan letter from Clara Bow and asked who she was. Rhodes had explained, then wondered why she was writing him. "Oh, she's typical," Marlon had sneered. "She wants some lint from my navel."

Whatever tension his celebrity was causing him now in Los Angeles, the dominant on-set drama was Leigh. The strain was unrelenting, but slowly she was giving herself over to Kazan's direction, and as she went deeper and deeper into character, it was as if she were feeding on herself. The force of the production came from its compression, from the fact that Blanche was trapped in that small apartment. Marlon continued to watch day after day, wondering when Leigh was going to crack. During one of their scenes together, she came up with a "piece of business" that seemed to evoke Blanche's doomed brio almost to perfection. Because of a technical problem, though, Kazan was forced to call a retake; Marlon waited to see if she could do it again. She did, precisely on cue and with exactly the same emotional coloration as before.

Leigh, according to Kazan, had a "small talent, but the greatest determination to excel of any actress I've ever known," and although her scenes with Brando were fewer than their impact would suggest, they were mainly hers. Tandy's characterization had been more sturdy, not nearly as neurasthenic, and even though Marlon was unable to articulate the differences between the two women, he now played to the wildness in Leigh's fragility. And it opened up something inside himself that no one had seen even on his best nights in New York. Technically, he was working against her "Englishness," but also capitalizing on Harry Stradling's close-ups. Touching himself, fingering his own magnificent flesh while also braying and yelling spittle into Leigh's face, he roamed the confines of Mielziner's set like a caged animal, tearing at her dainty respectability in a way that seemed to turn his rage back on himself. It was almost as if he were choking on the power of Stanley's lust. His hostility was so raw that his silences were, as Kazan put it, "often more eloquent than the lines he had to say." The alchemy was obvious.

At a polar remove from Tandy, Leigh was also oddly familiar with the depths of the Williams play, and it didn't take a genius to see why. Rumors of her affairs with Alexander Korda, Peter Finch, and even a few London taxi drivers had spread throughout the company. Her depressions and smoldering resentment of Olivier, played out in sexual adventurism, were no secret, and for Marlon the echo, ineluctably, was that of Dodie herself. On the verge of a breakdown day after day, Leigh left him weak with pity and contempt.

Even as remote an observer as the *New York Times*'s Bosley Crowther commented on how much more forceful Brando's rendition was than what he'd done previously onstage. Kazan saw it, too, although like others close in, he couldn't quite make the connection to his actor's most private demons. Instead, he talked to Karl Malden, wondering aloud about Brando's sexual confusion.

Marlon may not have understood his intense reaction to Leigh, either. He wrote often to Wally about her " great ass and tits," according to Peter Turgeon, the roommate to whom Wally read the letters aloud. "It was all vulgar, infantile stuff, and what Marlon went on about was wanting to fuck Leigh so badly that his teeth ached, but that her husband was there all the time, like a guard dog."

It was during these weeks that Marlon was seeing Roberta Haynes, the estranged wife of Jay Kanter, who had recently returned from New York and was considering going back to her husband.

"I had been in New York to do *Madwoman of Chaillot,*" the actress recalled. "Jay and I were separated, but he'd been in Manhattan and asked Marlon, who had just finished *The Men,* to meet us at a restaurant. He came in wearing a black motorcycle jacket, and I was just blown away."

Soon after, Marlon had asked her out, and she realized then that Jay had arranged it all. When she had asked Kanter why, he had replied, "I knew you would go for him." Nevertheless, back in California it was apparent to Haynes that Kanter was angry at her, not only for leaving him to return to her theater career but also for the brief affair with Brando that had ensued. The situation was tense and complicated. Kanter now wanted her to stay with him, but she felt she couldn't once she learned that Marlon was also living at the apartment (and letting his pet raccoon sleep in the oven). She stayed with her parents in Encino instead.

"One afternoon Marlon came over," she recalled. "The two of us took a walk out in the country to go swimming. It was hot, the sun was setting, and it was the only truly wonderful sexual experience I had with Marlon, mainly because he wasn't performing. There wasn't even a lot of talk. It was just like falling off a log. There was a vulnerability, an openness on his part instead of the walls he usually put up."

That was the only time in their affair, Haynes said, that she had felt happy. "Sometimes being with him was like basking in sunshine," she added. "It was good, but it wasn't right. There was something emotionally dangerous about him." Perhaps Marlon sensed her misgivings; perhaps the ease and lyricism of the latest encounter unnerved him. Haynes herself had not seen much of a future to their affair, but with an unexpected suddenness, almost as a reflex to their afternoon together, Marlon declared that their relationship was "dead."

Almost at once, he resumed his affair with Nicki, the teenager he'd taken up with during *The Men*, "the only girl who would go out with him anytime he called in the middle of the night," as she herself put it. With her, too, he was anything but straightforward or consistent. Soon she became aware that he was giving out her phone number to friends, among them Kazan and Fredric March. "They were all so peculiar that way," she said. "I wouldn't have been surprised if they were keeping score and bragging to each other."

Another woman who often dropped by to see him always wore a nun's robe with a white starched headdress floating above her head like a giant butterfly. Under the garment, "Sister Beth" was stark naked, and she performed confessions, a ritual that continually amused him. She would kneel on a cushion and in a monotone tell obscene stories while he played father confessor, and at the end of her confession, Brando would solemnly intone, "You have sinned gravely, my child, and I must whip your sinful posterior thirty-three times. Roll up your dress and bend your head down to the floor. Are you ready? The iron rod is in my hand, but before I use it to lash you, I have to dip it in the holy water which is inside you."

Israeli actor Dan Ben-Amotz, one of Brando's close friends at the time, heard about these encounters, and while he never witnessed this "pretty show," he once met Sister Beth at the Kanter apartment. He spoke to her for a long while about the quality of Christian mercy and the suffering of Jesus. She talked in a low voice, almost whispering, and not once did she look into his eyes. "I could not imagine the confession-and-punishment scene [but] I had to believe Marlon's story to me, because suddenly, in the middle of our serious conversation, when I was telling her about Nazareth and Bethlehem, she said, 'Enough already. Let's masturbate!' Marlon and I burst out in laughter," Ben-Amotz recalled. "Afterward we went to a little Italian restaurant, and everybody was staring at us, the two young guys having spaghetti with a beautiful young nun who had finished a bottle of wine with her eyes constantly lowered."

Marlon also passed Nicki on to the Israeli, and she would soon discover that she was pregnant. As always, Marlon supplied the money for an abortion. He also assisted in getting work for Darren Dublin, who had shown up in Hollywood several weeks before the end of *Streetcar*'s shoot. On impulse Darren had driven out from New York with his wife, Flo, yet Marlon's initial response had been anything but welcoming.

"When we pulled up, I recognized the place from his letters," recalled Dublin. "It was about seven or eight in the morning, and all of them were on their way out. Tony Curtis, I remember, was rushing out to do his thing with *The Prince Who Was a Thief,* and I guess Marlon was on his way over to Warners. He was very cool, even upset, and the feeling I got right away, very distinctly, was that he would have preferred we hadn't come out."

Marlon had stayed with the Dublins in their condemned Tenth Avenue apartment in New York after *The Men,* even bringing Jay Kanter with him, but now "everybody was busy and successful," Dublin said. "Me, I had nothing, and he told Jay to get me a job as a favor." In the ensuing days, he made himself scarce, "as if he was worried that we were hanging on him or being too dependent."

By now, Sam Gilman and Carlo Fiore were also in town, and everyone had an assigned place. If Marlon was at first cool toward Darren, another crony recalled that any form of trespass or intrusion was likely to be met with sanctions, which could be both summary and swift.

One acquaintance learned his lesson when he succumbed to the charms of a bit-part actress who was dying to know the star. He brought her to Marlon's place without consulting him first. The moment they entered the studio, Marlon had a cold and hard look in his eyes. Five minutes later he turned to his friend and said in a peremptory voice, "Will you take your guest and buzz off?"

The friend almost had to use force to wrestle the young woman out of the room, and Brando did not forgive what he regarded as a betrayal of his trust. In a lengthy letter—over ten pages long—he described their relationship with honesty, and thanked his friend sincerely for the beautiful hours they had spent together. "But our story is over," he wrote, "and there is no point in trying to revive what is dead."

Darren would eventually meet the same fate, as would Carlo and other friends. The need for control extended to money as well, even though Brando steadfastly refused to discuss the subject. The actor's financial affairs were being structured through MCA, with the agency keeping his bank account, paying his bills, and investing his earnings, albeit in consultation with his father. For the past four years, however, the Nebraska cattle operation, which represented the lion's share of the actor's financial portfolio, had been going from bad to worse, with Roe Black besieged by creditors and Marlon Sr. exacerbating the problems.

In his own quiet way, Marlon Sr. schemed at having it all, thinking up ways to improve Black's ranch and eventually take it over. By now he had acquired 1,400 head of cattle, and to guard his investment, he registered an official Penny Poke Ranch brand under Marlon Jr.'s name. He also bought expensive windmills, and made other capital improvements on the ranch property, fronting the expenditures with his son's money, then billing the absent Black for reimbursement. Bud had visited several times and announced himself in the press as a "partner" with his father in the Penny Poke enterprise, characterizing himself as a plain Nebraska boy grown up to be a simple cattle rancher. By 1951 Marlon Sr. had run up a huge debt in Black's name and he had joined six other investors to sue the ranch owner. They had tried to exercise an option to cash in their cattle, but Black couldn't deliver the funds and was forced to file for bankruptcy; nevertheless, he hung on to his property while he tried to regroup, and for the moment Marlon Sr. was stymied.

The *Streetcar* shoot lasted nearly eight weeks, and by mid-October the movie was finished except for Leigh's remaining three days of location footage in New Orleans. For the second time, the "family" disbanded— but not before Marlon surprised everyone by showing up at the Oliviers' wrap party dressed in a suit and tie, only to strip down to his shorts and jump into the pool as the evening wore on. Leigh, enjoying a little mischief of her own, led her husband to the edge of the swimming pool and said, "Larry, *this* is Marlon." Brando ceremoniously lifted a wet hand out of the water, but Olivier, never to be trumped, remarked, "I hope, old boy, you won't be offended if I don't strip down and join you."

With the editing of the film, the major problems were only beginning—and it wasn't the censorship restrictions that Kazan, Feldman, and Williams figured they'd already beaten. It was Kazan's membership in the Communist Party more than sixteen years before that loomed as a significant threat, especially since Cecil B. DeMille was now seeking to impose a loyalty oath on the entire Directors Guild membership. The Hollywood Ten had long since been packed off to jail. The Dies Committee had already tested the power of "gray-listing," even as the Screen Actors Guild under Ronald Reagan was steadfastly denying the existence of "any such lists." The Directors Guild was going for throats, notably Kazan's, and was also out to get four-time Oscar winner Joseph L. Mankiewicz, the organization's president. The net effect of this was to put Jack Warner on alert, which meant that *Streetcar* itself was in jeopardy.

Mankiewicz, a droll, saturnine man, rushed back to Hollywood from vacation and, with Kazan's help, he stayed up all night drafting an embattled defense of the Guild's traditional principles. At the next day's membership meeting at the Beverly Hills Hotel, he succeeded in quashing De-Mille's *putsch* with the support of John Ford, John Huston, and George Stevens, all of whose politics were anything but left of center. For Kazan and *Streetcar,* however, the damage was done. Kazan had absented himself from the decisive meeting, hoping to keep a low profile, but now it was clear that the time was coming when he wouldn't be able to duck a confrontation with his political past.

While Kazan had already turned his attention to *Viva Zapata!*, which he was scripting "on spec" with John Steinbeck, *Streetcar* was firmly in the hands of the studio. Warners had adroitly maneuvered the early answer print past the Breen office, but the Catholic Legion of Decency stepped in with the threat of a dreaded "C" ("Condemned") rating, which would result in a nationwide boycott at the box office. As a result, *Streetcar*'s release date was postponed, and the studio secretly assigned an editor in New York to cut the film to the Legion's specifications.

Almost eight months had passed since the end of filming, and surprising as it may seem, Kazan caught on to what was happening only because a friend, the composer Alex North, called from the East Coast and told him what he knew of the censoring. The Legion had asked for another screening, and what the churchmen now wanted was a total sanitizing of Stella and Stanley, not Blanche, so that audiences would believe that Williams's couple would "never again be happy together." Kazan went back to Feldman, then to Warner, then to Martin Quigley, the Roman Catholic publisher of motion picture trade papers and Warner's liaison to the head of the Legion. Nothing worked.

The picture had been taken away from him, "secretly, skillfully, without a raised voice," and time had run out, since it was about to be released at Radio City Music Hall on September 29, 1951, less than a month away. In anger and frustration Kazan penned an open letter to the *New York Times,* making good on his promise to Jack Warner that "if someone spits in my face, I will not say it's raining." Twelve cuts, Kazan claimed, had removed some three or four minutes from the film, and these ranged from the trivial to the serious. Even Alex North's jazz score had been tampered with (it allegedly made the marriage "too carnal").

Even so, once *A Streetcar Named Desire* premiered in Los Angeles, it was a huge critical success, just as Kazan had boasted. The New York Film Critics, Screen Writers Guild, and Hollywood Foreign Correspondents Association honored the picture; even the General Federation of Women's Clubs, as well as *Time, Cue,* and *Family Circle*—put it on their "ten best" lists. The *New York Mirror*'s Dick Williams and the *Times*'s Bosley Crowther called it the best film of the year. The film would be nominated for twelve Academy Awards; Malden and Hunter (despite their paltry salaries of $6,250 and $7,500, respectively) walked away with Oscars, as did Leigh, whose performance many reviewers considered the truest of her career. What was no less surprising, at least for insiders familiar with the workings of the Academy, was that Kazan and his iconoclastic golden boy had to be denied—the director for his politics, and first-time nominee Brando because the Hollywood establishment couldn't bring itself to deny its sentimental favorite, Humphrey Bogart in Huston's *The African Queen.* George Stevens would win the direction award for *A Place in the Sun. An American in Paris* was voted best picture.

It is difficult to say how the loss affected Brando. Perhaps he had been afraid of losing when he arranged for Darren Dublin to be on hand to claim his statuette. Perhaps he was simply bored by the Hollywood game. Whatever his reasons, he fled to New York. Earlier he had balked at Charlie Feldman's request to pose in a torn T-shirt for the film's logo. ("He thought it was vulgar," said photographer and friend Sam Shaw, who finally talked him into it.) In addition to leaving Hollywood, he had also announced that he was through professionally, and would be heading back to the New School to devote himself to courses in conversational French and, no less, graphology.

Screen acting, however, would never be the same. More than justifying production costs of nearly $2 million, *Streetcar* was already the second-biggest moneymaker of the season. As ticket receipts continued to soar, Hollywood had no choice but to admit that this film, more than any other, had altered the system as practiced for decades. It was a far cry from the prepackaged, presold three-picture-a-year deals for James Cagney, Robert Taylor, and Tyrone Power—all designed and executed for the stars by full-time studio employees. With *Streetcar,* the actors, the director, cinematographer, art director, costume designer, and composer had been brought from New York on a one-picture basis. Even more, it was all linked to the Method—and the Method, was now virtually synonymous with Brando.

"It's amazing. The character of Stanley fucked them all," said Anthony Quinn, with whom Marlon was about to costar in *Viva Zapata!* "The whole thing up until then, everything was proper. Robert Taylor, Tyrone Power, Van Johnson, and along comes Brando. It was the character, his Napoleonic Code speech—'A man is a king, by the fucking Constitution he's a king!' That statement turned the whole world around. . . . Everybody started behaving like Brando."

Streetcar had made Brando a movie star, limned his reputation in big numbers, and even more, established a momentum that would culminate with *On the Waterfront.* In between, *Viva Zapata!, Julius Caesar,* and *The Wild One* were about to stretch his talent, each of them combining serious intent with high craftsmanship. Taken together, Brando's first six films would establish his indelible, transcendent image as a genius among actors.

Viva Zapata!

Emiliano Zapata, the leader of the 1910 peasant uprising in southern Mexico, had been on Hollywood's agenda years before Kazan began collaborating with novelist John Steinbeck in the fall of 1948. Kazan himself had first started thinking about the project as early as 1944, partly because the mestizo leader's biography was so patently cinematic. He also viewed it as a political polemic, given what he saw as the parallels between Zapata's fate and that of the idealist revolutionaries in Russia purged by Stalin.

Since leaving the Communist Party U.S.A. in 1935, the director had moved toward the liberal anticommunist camp, intent on identifying the totalitarian tendencies of the Left. Much like Sidney Hook, Arthur M. Schlesinger Jr., *New York Post* columnist James Wechsler, and other former New Dealers, trade unionists, and old Popular Front intellectuals, Kazan sought to dissociate himself from his political past. He joined organizations like Americans for Democratic Action and the CIA-funded American Committee for Cultural Freedom, both widely advertised for their commitment to human rights but whose goals, ultimately, were to expose Stalinism. Four years after fastening onto the subject of Zapata, he heard that Steinbeck had been working on a script for a Mexican film company, and found that the novelist's interpretation of Zapata was as anticommunist as his own. Even in the highly charged atmosphere of HUAC's ongoing hearings, he reasoned, the two of them would not have trouble finding backing from one of the major studios.

After a laborious process of writing and rewriting with Kazan at his elbow, Steinbeck completed a draft script. In April 1949 the director passed up Warner Bros. to go to Darryl Zanuck, the volatile, cigar-smoking head of production at Twentieth Century–Fox. Zanuck had already produced John Ford's hugely successful adaptation of Steinbeck's *The Grapes of Wrath* (1940) as well as Kazan's *Gentleman's Agreement* (1947), which had been nominated for eight Academy Awards, won for Best Picture, and brought Kazan his first Oscar for directing. Zanuck's response was not overwhelming, but he was ready to go along. *Viva Zapata!,* as he saw it, was not a political movie at all, just "a big western." Yet, as a good Republican, Zanuck had done what he said he would never do, which was to greenlight a project that pitted a rebel against his government. He had suggestions, however. His most cherished idea for *Zapata!* was that the rebel leader had to have a white horse: "After they shoot him," Zanuck declared, "we should show the horse running free in the mountain . . . a great fade-out."

"Will he fuck her or won't he? Will he catch her or won't he? That's what he said we should always keep uppermost in mind when we were making any film," Kazan said years later. But there were other sides to Zanuck, too. Competitive, volatile, disputatious, and immensely creative, he

poured his energies into every area of production. Beyond his penchant for big-game hunting and polo playing, and a well-deserved reputation for bedding almost every contract starlet in sight, the "last of the great producers" had a keen eye for the unusual. If general wisdom dictated that something couldn't be done, this, and this alone, was usually enough for him to put a project into production.

In agreeing to back *Zapata!,* Zanuck at first refused to accept Brando in the title role. His actor of choice, he insisted, was Tyrone Power, who had made Twentieth Century–Fox a bundle. Kazan was not surprised, but he insisted that it should be Marlon or no one. Reluctantly, the producer agreed to a screen test—and in short order announced that he couldn't understand Brando's "mumbling" and thought that both he and Julie Harris, whom Kazan wanted to play Zapata's bride, were "ridiculous" as Mexicans. Kazan agreed to another trade-off: Marlon for Jean Peters, who was Howard Hughes's girlfriend and a Fox contract player at the time. The matter was settled only after Zanuck finally agreed to MCA's demand of $100,000 for Marlon. The sum struck him as outrageously high, but in return he exacted a multipicture option from Brando.

By late April 1951, with his contract signed, Marlon took off for Sonora, where, alone, he threw himself into researching his role, living among the peasants, and trying (unsuccessfully) to learn some Spanish. He talked directly to old people who had memories of Zapata, studied photographs of the revolutionary's lean, hard-lined face that was so different from his own, and in his own way tried to pick up as much as he could about the region's men and what made them tick.

Kazan, meanwhile, was determined to shoot the film in Zapata's own village of Cuautla, and he joined Steinbeck to scout locations. Then, at an executive meeting in Hollywood, he was presented with transcripts of conversations between Fox emissaries and Mexican censors: The Mexican government wished to see Zapata presented "as a man with communist leanings," and would not accept the script in its present form. Worse, the Mexicans had implied that if the film were made without their approval, it would cause a great wave of anger in their country, resulting in a possible boycott on future Fox productions. In the unlikely event of the censor's approval, the report went on, the script would still have to be approved by the Mexican Defense Department, which had issued a warning that the Indians in the south of Mexico were dangerous. Therefore, without the cooperation of the military, the film crew's safety could not be guaranteed.

It was a serious blow. Kazan had set his sights on two films, and he had already lost the other, Arthur Miller's *The Hook,* because of production problems. He thought that in the prevailing political climate, even Steinbeck's script was daring. Zanuck "was running a business, had to show a profit, or he'd be gone." He figured the project was dead and that he should go back to New York and return to the theater.

Surprisingly, though, the Mexicans had only aroused Zanuck's fighting spirit. In the past he had refused to yield when industry moguls tried to pressure him into canceling *Gentleman's Agreement*. He'd also ignored a statement from the Breen office advising him that the film's heroine could not be a divorcée. Now, as he paced back and forth, swinging his miniature polo mallet, he exclaimed that if the Mexicans did not want *Viva Zapata!,* perhaps Kazan could shoot it on the Texas side of the Rio Grande. But he would need some time "to think about it."

The next day Kazan returned to the producer's office and made a concessionary offer to cut his salary from $162,000 to around $100,000, acknowledging that he expected to be summoned by HUAC and that his appearance in Washington might taint the film. Zanuck remained poker-faced. He turned to his assistant, Ray Klune, and asked, "Do people around the lot think this picture communistic?" When Klune said no, he indicated with a wave of his panatela that the pressure from Washington, like the pressure from Mexico, was not going to interfere with his plans. *Zapata!* was a go. Without further ado, he turned back to Kazan: "About your offer to cut your salary: We accept it. Now the next thing you have to do is take a unit manager, an art director, and a driver and go along our border with Mexico and find a location."

Fearing that Zanuck might have second thoughts, Kazan hastened to complete the casting and scheduled a starting date of May 29, 1951. Anthony Quinn had done *The Ox-Bow Incident* (1943) for Zanuck, and was set for the role of Zapata's brother. There had been talk that the part of the brawling, outspoken Eufemio might go to Jack Palance. As for where to shoot, they soon settled on the Texas towns of McAllen, Del Rio, Laredo, San Ygnacio, and Roma; Roma, in particular, offered a beautiful adobe church and a huge cobblestoned plaza. Town officials there also promised a three-week holiday, which would allow local residents to serve as extras.

Most of Zapata's guerrilla followers, however, were not Mexicans but recruited from the Actors Studio. Among them was Fred Sadoff, who recalled that for a period of three weeks he, Henry Silva, Irving Winter, Lou Gilbert, and one or two others—all of them known as the "Jewish cowboys"—had met in New York's Central Park for riding lessons.

Prior to the ten-week shoot, the cast assembled for two weeks' rehearsal and makeup tests in Los Angeles. Marlon's makeup, in particular, was critical, and for this he turned to his old New York friend, Philip Rhodes, phoning him and telling him to "bring his makeup." Rhodes wanted to work in Hollywood, but for all his experience in theater, he was having a hard time breaking into the West Coast chapter of his union. To get around this, Marlon had his makeup test done in New York, and Rhodes gave him an entirely different face. Inspired by photographs of Zapata as well as by the famous Diego Rivera portrait, Rhodes used liquid latex that, when dried, gave Marlon's eyelids a slant; his nostrils were enlarged with hollow plastic pipe stems inside his nose. A wig was added in order to cover Marlon's already receding hairline. To change the color of the actor's eyes, Rhodes inserted dark contact lenses, which were later lost when Marlon claimed that a female fan on the train from Los Angeles to Texas had stolen them. (According to Anthony Quinn, Marlon had simply broken them.) As it turned out, Brando's makeup was fine without the lenses. The large, bushy mustache he had grown for the role was trimmed, however, to meet leading-man specifications of the time.

It was while Rhodes had been doing Marlon's makeup in New York that he noted that Marlon's nose looked different and that the actor had in fact undergone cosmetic surgery, presumably just before the filming of *Streetcar*. He later ran into the doctor who had performed the operation, who confirmed his hunch. "It wasn't for his sinuses or his mumbling, the doctor said," according to Rhodes. "It was to move cartilage up to the bridge to lengthen it and give him a 'Roman break.' I could see he had gone from a small, rounded parrot beak, like his father's, even though it had been broken, to a Roman profile. The septum had been rebroken by the doctor, who had put a piece of cartilage higher up to give him the curve at the break and a more craggy appearance."

Rhodes had always been aware of Marlon's face because, he said, "it was the kind of face artists are always interested in. . . . It was as if a klieg light had been shoved up his ass and was shining out his pores. The face was androgynous, with the heavy lips and the deep-set eyes that, because he had a way of looking out from underneath his brows, seemed smaller than they were."

Several years later Marlon told other friends that he had never had his teeth capped, either; that falsehood was literally exposed when Marlon went to a stripper bar, and under the black lights of the nightclub, the hollow, cosmetic caps that had been installed to lengthen his teeth showed up red. Someone in Marlon's group noticed it, pointing out the way his own caps appeared, but Marlon refused to acknowledge it himself. "I never called him on it," said the friend, "but it certainly gave new meaning to the phrase 'lying through one's teeth.' "

Viva Zapata! was Brando's first outdoor "action movie," as well as his first film in costume. A thirty-year-old millionaire rancher from southern Texas was to stand in for him in the hard-riding scenes, but the actor was still scheduled to do a lot of the combat footage himself. In one sequence he was to lasso a machine gun, and in another, rescue a peasant being dragged by a rope behind a fast-running horse. In the first weeks of filming, his right knee was seriously injured when his mount rammed him into a wall; he kept to the production schedule nonetheless, using a removable cast that permitted treatment between scenes.

Kazan pointed out that in *Streetcar*, Marlon played a version of himself, whereas here he was faced with creating a characterization, a peasant, a man of another culture. It was more than makeup and costuming, and as the director explained what he was after, Brando listened, staring straight into Kazan's eyes, accepting his suggestions as though they were pilings on which to build. "I told him a peasant does not reveal what he thinks," he recalled. "Things happen to him and he shows no reaction. He knows if he shows reactions he'll be marked 'bad' and may be killed. I told him the goal we had to reach, and before I would finish talking he'd nod and walk away. He had the idea, knew what we had to do, and was, as usual, ahead of me."

The words on peasant psychology couldn't have fallen on more receptive ears, just as Kazan's pointers on Zapata's attitude to his bride, Josefa, struck equally close to home. "Don't be misled by all the shit in the script about how he loves his wife," Kazan said. "He has no need for a special woman. Women are to be used, knocked up, and left. . . . Don't mix it up with love, as we use the word. He loves his *compadres*. They are ready to die for him, and he would do anything for them."

He cautioned Marlon not to play the scenes with Jean Peters in the conventional romantic style but as a peasant, for whom "fucking is not a big deal." Marlon, Kazan recalls with no sense of irony, understood immediately. "He was that way in life. . . . The warmest relations I have seen him involved in have been with men. What I described for the peasant Zapata was very close to the way Marlon lived his life. For both of them, there were deeper needs than 'romance.' "

There seems little doubt that, after hours, Marlon went after Jean Peters, perhaps because Kazan had already tested the waters. Friends like Sam Shaw openly expressed their concern that Howard Hughes might show up with his Mormon bodyguards, but Brando wasn't deterred; he lingered in Peters's dressing room, even as she took calls from her millionaire boyfriend. He also threw pebbles at her window in the middle of the night, and another time, under cover of darkness, climbed a tree to her window to serenade her with his recorder. The same brio extended to Marilyn Monroe, who was also on the set. Hollywood legend has it that the two did not meet until 1955, on the set of *Desirée*, yet *Zapata!* cast members recall that in the early weeks of the production, she'd arrived from L.A. to continue her affair with Kazan. Kazan's family then descended for a visit, and it was left to Marlon to entertain her in Peters's trailer.

But ever present was a Mexican extra somewhere in her early thirties named Movita Castenada, and theirs was no mere dalliance. Older and more experienced than Brando's other girlfriends, it was "Mo" who became his frequent companion, who seemed all-accepting in their on-again, off-again relationship, which would endure for the next fifteen years. Whenever she arrived on the set, the two of them routinely disappeared into Marlon's trailer for hours. She was dark and "vaguely Indian," and as many of Brando's friends were to become well aware, she didn't complicate his life, or so he thought.

While most of the *Zapata!* cast assumed that Brando had simply picked up the Mexican actress when she appeared on the set as an extra, in fact he had met her when he had gone down to Mexico to do his research prior to the shoot. Whether Marlon had made arrangements for her to appear as an extra so that she would be available wasn't clear, but it became evident, said Philip Rhodes, that "he was absolutely smitten with her. He had never met anyone like her. She was like a sexual tuning fork, always aquiver, and she had the mind of a primitive and would believe what anyone said, including Marlon—even when he told her the most incredible stories. He liked the idea of her as primitive, that everything was instinct for her, plus he liked her Mexican nationalism, the way she loved to talk about the Aztecs and how they were the world's earliest civilization."

"She wasn't beautiful in any aristocratic way," added Sondra Lee, who later befriended Movita in New York. "But she was like a stallion, and there was an excitability about her. Her perceptions were gypsylike, a heightened awareness, and she believed in powers. She believed in an animalistic world, that everything is alive and connected, and that's what affected Marlon—that, combined with the fact that she was worldly and had a romantic past."

Movita had already had numerous affairs with leading men, reportedly including Errol Flynn and Clark Gable, whom she met while working on *Mutiny on the Bounty* (1935) and who had nicknamed her "Chili." She had also married Jack Doyle, an Irish heavyweight boxer and singer. She was uneducated in any formal sense, but what she lacked in reading she more than made up for in instinct; part mother, part mistress, for Marlon she was "an equalizer." She would say "feck"—as in "Go *feck* yourself"—and according to Sondra Lee, regularly "beat the shit out of [Marlon] at chess, which just destroyed him."

Few people in the company saw them together—not only because he kept her separate, but also because of the difficulties of the shoot. The June temperatures of 105° to 120°F had turned the production into an ordeal, melting the actors' heavy makeup. Stomach disorders were so commonplace that for two weeks Peters had to be accompanied by a nurse. There were additional riding injuries, and the harsh, overbearing sunlight rendered much of cinematographer Joe MacDonald's equipment useless. There were delays, too, when one of the Mexican extras took it upon himself to use real ammunition instead of blanks during one of the battle scenes. "I'm a good shot. I miss everybody," he said when his live bullets were taken from him.

With less than a quarter of the script shot, the production was beginning to fall behind schedule. With rushes being flown back to L.A., Zanuck started firing off telegrams. What bothered the studio head, above and beyond the anticipated cost overrun, was Brando, whose "mumbling," Zanuck carped after seeing dailies, "I can't understand."

Photographer Sam Shaw, who had done the T-shirt logo for *Streetcar*, was now assigned to do the studio stills and had a chance to observe what was happening at close range. The most difficult scene for Marlon, he recalls, was the one in which the very drunk Zapata is thrown in jail:

"No actor can play a drunk. You've gotta actually be drunk to play drunk," Shaw remembers Brando insisting, preparing himself for the scene by downing "a whole bottle of vodka." Once the cameras started rolling, the acting fell apart, of course, and even though this ended the day's shooting, Marlon couldn't be dissuaded. "Every weekend he'd get stoned," Shaw recalls, "and the thing went on for six weekends—one little scene." During one attempt, he got too drunk to make it back to his dressing room or even to the car waiting to take him back to the hotel. The crew left him lying on the cot where he had dropped. The following morning, the well-connected Shaw got a call from a New York columnist claiming that Brando had been spotted on Madison Avenue.

"It's impossible," the photographer replied. "We left him on the set unconscious. How could he be in Manhattan hours later?" As it turned out, however, Marlon had indeed gotten himself onto a plane and flown east to see a woman. The jail scene was never completed and had to be pieced together from fragments shot before his collapse.

By now, however, he was totally immersed in the part, caught in "the first flight of his instinct," as Kazan put it. He plodded around the set like the slow-thinking, moody Zapata at the end of each day's shooting. Even while he was eating lunch, cast members noticed it as he sat apart, brooding. Rarely was he out of the baggy, white peasant shirt and *huarache* sandals that he wore in front of the camera. It seemed that his only way of getting "out of role" was to indulge himself by setting off locally available fireworks in the lobby of the hotel where everyone was staying. He also enjoyed frolicking with the wide-eyed village kids whom he'd let climb all over him and twirl his mustache. En route to outlying locations at six in the morning, he would hang his head out the window of the studio car as it sped across the desert at 90 mph, letting the wind blow up his cheeks like balloons. "He was scaring the shit out of people," said Shaw. "It was a game with him, and once, he hung himself out of the car upside-down."

Besides his ongoing water fights with the crew, though, Marlon's amusement also took the form of occasional cruelties, like the one he perpetrated against Fred Sadoff. Like any young actor on his first picture, Sadoff had been waiting for the "big moment" Kazan had promised him back in New York. The "Indians" in the film had never been shown a script, so Sadoff had no way of knowing what to expect when the director finally took him aside to explain the "wonderful sequence" in which he was supposed to "save" somebody. "Freddy," Kazan said, pointing off into the distance, "this is it. I want you to go to the top of that mountain there. I'm going to pack you with lots of baggage, and when I give you the signal, you come running down."

As the crew packed bundles and boxes on his back, Marlon murmured, "More, Gadg. He should really be laden down so it looks as if he's burdened." Sadoff agreed to the additional portage, and then, buried under his load, he started climbing, doggedly making his way up through the grass in the terrible heat. He was terrified of the rattlesnakes that, they'd all been warned, lurked in the underbrush. After an hour he reached the top and turned around—only to discover that the crew had taken off.

"They thought it was very funny," he said, "and I was embarrassed. I had revealed my ambition, and my vulnerability had been used to get a laugh. And Marlon had inspired Gadg to do it, no question. Kazan wouldn't have done that unless provoked."

Less than a week later Sadoff found himself driving out to the day's shooting site with Brando, and Marlon asked how much he was being paid. The question was put in that concerned, helpful way of Marlon's, but Sadoff, who was getting $250 a week, resented the condescension. "I thought it was kind of a shitty thing for him to ask, so I lied. I thought $250 was such a small salary, and I said $300. He said, '$300? That's very good.'" As usual, Marlon had to have the last word, and Sadoff, like most others, wasn't about to challenge him.

Not so Anthony Quinn, who was playing Zapata's brother. Quinn had competed with Brando for the role of Kowalski—first in the *Streetcar* road company, then as Marlon's replacement on Broadway. With *Zapata!*, it was rumored that Zanuck had tried to push for Quinn in lieu of Brando for the lead once Kazan had decided against Tyrone Power. Quinn himself denies that he had ever been promised the part, insisting that he was just glad to be cast, "because all of us at the Actors Lab"—the L.A. branch of the Actors Studio—"had been tainted by the gray list, and I really needed the job."

Still, there had been competition from the start, fueled not only by their two titanic egos, but probably by each actor's sense of what the movie had to be.

"The picture was very personal to me," recalled the Irish-Mexican actor, who was born in Mexico three years before the revolutionaries put down their arms in 1918. His parents and other members of his family had fought with Pancho Villa, and as a child, their stories had made a great impression on him. "You always look for a picture that you can identify with," he explained, "and I just thought that a revolutionary picture. . . . I would fit in, absolutely. I mean this was me, this was my background. I was trying to justify my family."

Since Quinn had been brought up as a Hispanic in East Los Angeles, Kazan also asked him to serve as technical adviser. The result was that the actor came up with one of the most impressive bits of directorial input in the picture—the scene in which Zapata is rescued while being taken off to jail. Kazan had planned a "reaction" close-up on Quinn's face, with the actor standing and silently watching, but Quinn objected.

"Mexicans don't stand," he told Kazan. "Mexicans sit on their heels. It's much more dangerous . . . like they're ready to spring." Squatting near a wall, he demonstrated by picking up two small stones and began tapping them together. Hearing the sound, the other actors followed suit, and soon the set was filled with the slow, menacing beat of the peasants preparing themselves for action.

Quinn was also the expert horseman, "*caballero* style," and although Marlon was a passable rider, there was no comparison. "The horse was macho, but Tony was more macho," said Kazan. He dominated, he could whip his mount around in a cloud of dust at full gallop, and the director saw the value of exploiting this, too. Most of all, however, Kazan's goal was to exploit the tensions between his two male leads, and this had started back in Los Angeles when Brando and Quinn had been assigned to share the same train compartment en route to Texas.

"He wanted us to get together and be brothers, and we tried it," Quinn recalled, pointing out that aboard the train to Brownsville, Marlon's only baggage was a little brown bag filled with two T-shirts—though he was also traveling with Russell, his pet raccoon.

"Russell is not only my best friend, he's also my mistress," Brando had boasted back in Los Angeles when a studio spokesman told him the animal would have to be confined to the actor's dressing room. On the train,

Quinn watched as his compartment mate fed the animal with a baby bottle, slept with Russell nestled in the crook of his arm, and even whispered to him in his sleep. It was "strange," Quinn said, and throughout the trip, the two actors hardly talked to each other.

"It was always pretend conversation," Quinn said, "and while he was talking, he was always playing a character. Suddenly he might say, 'I come from Tennessee Williams,' just out of the blue. Or he'd ask these strange . . . very personal questions, like, 'Who gave you that watch?' and it was puzzling, since he was sweet when he'd be asking, so you really thought he was interested."

Quinn, feeling "very self-conscious," tried to spend as little time as possible in the tiny compartment. In the mornings, however, he had little choice. Marlon would wake up at six o'clock and drape a towel dipped in hot water on his head, announcing, "This is very good for not getting bald."

On the set, Brando continued to spend long periods alone, in his trailer or wandering the countryside. "Marlon was a recluse with just about everybody, but Quinn took it so personally and was so jealous," recalled Fred Sadoff, "that it became a joke. . . . Tony was an open free spirit and he just couldn't understand or accept Marlon's refusal to be friendly. He would come to me and the others from New York, the Jewish cowboys that he thought knew Marlon, and keep asking, 'What's with him? Is he queer?' "

Quinn socialized with Sam Shaw, whom he knew from New York; a relaxed, easy guy, Shaw was also friendly with Marlon and tended to serve as an intermediary. Quinn, though, whatever his questions to Sadoff, refused to bow to Brando, especially in front of Kazan. "I'm not going to kiss Marlon Brando's ass," he recalled saying. "He's nine years younger than I am, so what the hell is there to kiss ass about? If God gave him his peculiarities, He gave him peculiarities. He didn't give 'em to me."

Quinn complained that Kazan was giving Marlon more direction, that Brando was his favorite; when the Mexican actor turned "dangerously sulky," the director recalled that he turned to Marlon for help. Quinn, however, failed to remember such camaraderie, recalling instead a certain incident that was recorded on film by Sam Shaw. "Come, let's go to the bushes," Marlon had challenged, playing the good ol' boy, but it wasn't a gesture of reconciliation so much as a contest to determine "who could pee the farthest." Shaw, the judge, was forced to diplomatically declare a draw.

Still, Quinn's resentment lingered. There was the way Marlon wanted to wear the belt with all the bullets thrown over his shoulder. His long, ruminative pauses were another thing: There was no correspondence here to historical fact or to the real Zapata, but even this would not have been a problem if Marlon "hadn't felt that he had his darling friend behind the camera." The pauses, whatever their effectiveness, were scene stealers, and for Quinn his own quick, "kid of the street" acting style was his only defense.

Kazan let Marlon continue, though, trusting always in Brando's "instinct . . . his gifts [that] go beyond his knowledge." At the director's instructions, Joe MacDonald's camera caressed the actor's face, lingering on his form highlighted in shadow. "It was as though Gadg had a son who'd died," Quinn said, "and the only son left was Marlon, so he was putting all the double love on Brando. He'd say, 'You look wonderful. Did you sleep well last night?' Or, 'That was wonderful,' or, 'God, that was good.' Directing him, Gadg let him do a lot of things he wanted to."

In later years Quinn would concede that Brando was "the greatest actor of his time." But as they approached the climactic fight scene between the two Zapata brothers, Kazan upped the ante. Separately, he talked to each of his actors out of earshot of the other. First, he whispered in Marlon's ear, "You know, Tony thinks he was better in *Streetcar*." Then, leaving Marlon to marinate, he did the same with Quinn, provoking him for the sequence about to be shot.

"He was creating animosity between those guys, and I tried to get both of them to go out to dinner," said Shaw, who was hoping to "undo Gadg's work. Back on the set, though, Kazan kept at it. He even told me not to interfere."

Despite Shaw's peace mission, Kazan won out, and with the director's stoking, the fight soon veered dangerously close to the real thing. Quinn was much bigger than Brando but Marlon nevertheless went amok, nearly losing control.

"Every actor is competitive," Quinn explained, "but he pulled my hair, and I could have driven the fucking sword right through him," he added, referring to his prop saber. "He didn't have to go that far. All he had to do was indicate it, and I would have gotten up. I'm an actor. I would have acted it."

Marlon's response was to murmur a threatening "fuck you" to Kazan and walk off the set for three days. Not to be outdone, Quinn stormed off as well, staying incommunicado for the same time.

For Kazan, whose premise was that the end justified the means, the scene was more than he'd hoped for. Quinn's performance was predictably rock-solid, but Brando had simply exploded, improvising even in the face of his fury by doing an abrupt turn and placing Quinn's dead hands beside his own face in an eloquent expression of anguish. "Marlon always gave me more than I asked," the director said years later. "He always gave me more than one hundred percent of himself."

The burden of Zapata, Brando seemed to realize, was that he was a figure in conflict with himself. He is part macho idealist and part peasant with bourgeois leanings, a conflict that had only been latent in Steinbeck's script. Marlon had found that man in himself, and as the shooting progressed, Kazan had let him go completely. On Zapata's wedding night, for example, Marlon took a more or less stock throwaway and asked Jean Peters's Josefa to teach him to read, ad-libbing that after the success of the revolution, "my horse and my rifle won't help me." The same vulnerability and inner heaviness came to the surface as he played off against the hard-edged zealotry enunciated by Joseph Wiseman's commissar-like Fernando. "You're always looking for leaders, strong men without faults," Zapata tells his followers in a voice so weary with fatigue that his later assassination comes as little more than a footnote. "There aren't any," he says. "They change. They desert. They die. There are no leaders but yourselves. A strong people is the only lasting strength."

His portrait, finally, was one of confusion, of defeat and despair, and what elevated it above and beyond the screenplay's historiography was that Brando trusted his own instincts. If the rendition was occasionally muddled by pet mannerisms, ideology had been totally eschewed for material close to home. In the simplest sense, he'd gone beyond anything he'd done in film. Although this was a location shoot and he had to come up with a character from another place and time, what marked the performance was that he had claimed the medium for his own—no longer intimidated by the cameras, the booms, and the sound equipment that had previously dampened the spontaneity of his stage-bred technique.

Viva Zapata! was released in February 1952, and Spyros Skouras, the president of Twentieth Century–Fox, was nervous. He asked all company members to send him letters explaining their politics, which he then shared with Red-baiting columnist George Sokolsky. Rumors, however, were circulating that Kazan had made a closed-session appearance before HUAC in Washington the month before, where he'd been an "uncooperative" witness. Soon, the *Hollywood Reporter* obtained a transcript of the director's testimony and announced that he had "confessed Commie membership but refused to supply any new evidence on his old pals from the Group Theatre days, among them John Garfield."

Most critics, like Bosley Crowther of the *New York Times,* had reservations about the historical accuracy of *Viva Zapata!,* but their focus was not on politics but Brando. Marlon, the *Times* noted, was not at his best in the romantic scenes, but in his moments of anger, there was "power enough in his portrayal to cause the screen to throb." Even Hedda Hopper, the movie colony's rabid anticommunist watchdog, sang the actor's praises. "Not until I saw *Viva Zapata!* was I sold on Brando as an actor," she wrote. "In *Streetcar Named Desire*, he played the part of the brutish Pole so realistically that I confess he revolted me. . . . Here he [has] succeeded in conceiving and sustaining an original characterization."

Time, Newsweek, Variety, and most of the Los Angeles critics all followed suit; the role brought him his second nomination for an Oscar. Marlon himself, however, was dissatisfied. The character of the revolutionary leader, as he had mentally formulated it, was much harsher than his portrayal—and what he told Sam Shaw was that he was "too romantic for the real Zapata, too soft, too sweet."

His instincts were dead-on. He'd reverted to the same poeticism he'd tapped into to do Marchbanks nearly ten years before; it was his ready-made arsenal when faced with "intellectual" problems, a lyricism that was almost feminine at the core. As Quinn had seen, he "didn't know about the Revolution," and thus the film was a reminder of his inadequacies. At twenty-eight, the only option that seemed to be left open was to do a complete flip-flop and take on *Julius Caesar,* which would put him precisely in that territory he feared most.

Julius Caesar

Returning to Los Angeles for postproduction work on *Zapata!* and to nurse his injured knee, Marlon had Movita with him, when after only a month or two he suddenly departed for New York to return to his Fifty-seventh Street apartment. Meanwhile, the apartment where he had been staying in Los Angeles—Jay Kanter's on Bedford Street—made headlines. Kanter had given the key to his fellow MCA agent Jennings Lang, who had been using the residence as a trysting place with his client actress Joan Bennett. On December 13, 1951, Bennett's husband, Walter Wanger, had waited outside, then shot Lang in the groin as he was escorting Bennett to her car. As the story broke and Wanger was arrested, news stories also featured the information that Brando had been living there in the fall. "All of us around here recognized Brando when he stayed here," the landlady announced to the press. "He caused much comment by always appearing with his pet raccoon on a leash. He was in and out a good deal of the time."

Back in New York, Marlon seemed to be "in and out" as well. He took off again for a visit to Paris and a period of decompression—what he called a "good, long schlunk"—with Christian Marquand and his other French pals; Movita was left high and dry. She attempted a reconciliation with her husband, Jack Doyle, but Doyle wasn't allowed to immigrate to America. Her renewed interest in another man was enough, however, to resurrect Marlon's infatuation, and when he returned to Manhattan, the affair resumed anew. Movita was appalled by his living conditions, but, for the time being, she accepted it and began to meet Marlon's family and friends.

Jocelyn had an immediate affectionate feeling toward her brother's new companion. "She was older than Bud and warm and pleasant," she recalled. "She cooked Mexican dinners for us, and I thought, Gee, what a nice girl. I think she loved him and wanted to marry him, and I felt she was sensible, wise—in a nice, womanly way, what I think of as the innate woman-caretaker kind of thing."

Dick Loving also met her during his visit to New York. "She had a certain force and intelligence," he agreed. "She had gone through the ropes; she was strong, and she was smart enough to deal with Bud and all his tricks, anticipating them and ignoring them so she wouldn't get overwhelmed. So she certainly wasn't just some doll hanging around."

For the time being, Brando was maintaining New York as his base. But then he learned that there was another film in the offing, one that simultaneously attracted and frightened him. John Houseman had joined MGM as a staff producer, and he and director Joseph Mankiewicz were developing a new cinematic rendition of *Julius Caesar*. At the last minute, they had come up with a novel idea: cast Brando in a Shakespearean classic.

Shakespeare's historical drama was only the second picture for Houseman at MGM, although his reputation as a man of the theater, not to say culture, had more than preceded him. He had launched the Mercury Theatre with Orson Welles, written radio scripts for Helen Hayes, and directed Leslie Howard's revival of *Hamlet* as well as a much acclaimed, long-running Broadway production of *King Lear*.

The short, feisty Mankiewicz was no less an ideal director for the project. He had won double Academy Awards as writer-director two years in a row, for *A Letter to Three Wives* (1949) and *All About Eve* (1950), and in Houseman's words, "being a writer, he wouldn't distort Shakespeare's text with cinematic devices." Mankiewicz's pride had always been his ability to work with actors, including "difficult" types like Bette Davis, Spencer Tracy, and Rex Harrison.

Both MGM's Dore Schary and Houseman were determined to make *Caesar* as political as possible, with allusions to the recent collapse of Hitler's dictatorship; Mankiewicz, however, was no less resolved to do Shakespeare "pure," even though the relatively tight $1.7 million budget dictated using scenery and costumes from the recently released *Quo Vadis?* The plan was to cast a well-balanced ensemble of American and British actors, starting with John Gielgud as Cassius. For Caesar they had chosen Louis Calhern. James Mason was set as Brutus. Two other Britons, both MGM contract players, were signed: Deborah Kerr as Portia, and Greer Garson as Calpurnia, Caesar's wife. For the small but important part of Casca, the provocateur, Houseman had picked Edmond O'Brien, whose recent tough-guy roles in B sleepers such as *D.O.A.* and *White Heat* had overshadowed the fact that he had played Shakespeare on the stage with Maurice Evans, Gielgud, and Olivier. This left only one major role to be filled.

"Mankiewicz was in London conferring with Gielgud," Houseman later wrote in his autobiography, "[and] he called to say that he was setting up a film test for the rising British stage star Paul Scofield. The day before it was to be made, I cabled and asked him to delay it for a few days. I had just had a mad but brilliant idea: that we seriously consider Marlon Brando for the role of Antony. The first general reaction was one of disbelief."

In later years Mankiewicz would claim that the choice of Brando was his own idea, not Houseman's, and that in his absence the producer and Dore Schary had already chosen MGM contract player Stewart Granger, an idea so objectionable to him that he threatened to drop the project on the spot. "Houseman's story was total bullshit," Mankiewicz recalled. "John wrote books and took credit for a lot of things. And Schary, he wanted to save money. He yanked the whole character of Cinna the poet for length, and I screamed at him and Houseman both: 'For Christ's sake, this isn't Leonard Spiegelgass, this is William Shakespeare you're brutalizing!'"

Schary, of course, was "very offended," Mankiewicz added. Now, before getting on the boat for England, he telephoned Brando to explain that they were doing *Caesar* as "a modern piece." Marc Antony was "as good an opportunity as any" for him to expand his range as an actor.

Brando's response was that he would need time to get used to the idea, since he was apprehensive. But the proposal intrigued him, and he immediately went out and bought recordings of classical actors doing famous soliloquies from the Bard. Dick and Fran Loving were visiting in New York and went over to Bud's apartment on Fifty-seventh Street to see him. Spotting a tape recorder in the living room, Dick flicked it on. "I heard Bud doing the famous 'Friends, Romans, countrymen,'" Loving recalled, "doing it and redoing it and redoing it—giving half the speech and then trying it again with another inflection, then another and another.

"I think I understood him to be saying, 'I am not just Stanley . . .' Nobody wants to be typecast, and at the time there were subtle ways he would react against that, like by dressing up, looking very elegant, sometimes even wearing a homburg, anything to confound people's image of him as Stanley."

When Mankiewicz returned from London, he met with Marlon at the actor's apartment, which reminded him of "the inside of a cage. . . . It was filthy, but it was Marlon. He was comfortable there," Mankiewicz said. No sooner had they gotten past the hellos when Brando explained that he'd "done some tapes." For two hours Mankiewicz listened, realizing that the actor had studied the delivery and accent of every available Shakespeare recording, and come up with an all-too-accurate imitation of classical declamation.

"Marlon, you sound exactly like June Allyson," he finally said, gesturing for him to shut off the tape recorder. "Where are you? You're nowhere. You're trying to copy the goddamn Limeys! Let's work on this together, goddamn it."

Using Brando's phone, Mankiewicz called Hollywood and was able to finagle a few extra days in the already tight schedule. By the end of the week, he had a fresh recording of Marlon, doing Marc Antony's address to the Roman senators after Caesar's assassination. It was now clear, Mankiewicz recalled, that Marlon "wanted to do it," even though he regarded the project as "fucking scary."

Back in Los Angeles, the director headed for Schary's office with Houseman in tow, not yet having told the studio head the name of his new candidate. "I listened [to the tape]," Schary recalled, "liked it, and asked, 'Who is it?' They answered, 'Marlon Brando.' For a moment I thought they were putting me on, and then I played it again and this time I recognized certain sounds that told me it *was* Brando. . . . I was captivated by him."

Brando agreed to a salary of approximately $40,000, and was guaranteed first billing—moved by the prospect of high art as well as the fact that Gielgud was getting only $20,000. (Later he would complain that he'd settled for too little, since his deal didn't include a share of the profits.)

The announcement of his casting in June 1952 was met with predictable sneers, however. "I don't believe the rumor that Marlon Brando will play Marc Antony. His voice just wouldn't blend with the rest of the cast," was Hedda Hopper's unsurprising response, and most other columnists took the same line. On national TV, stand-up comics like Sid Caesar and Jerry Lewis also had their say, treating audiences in Des Moines and Kalamazoo to impersonations of Stanley Kowalski delivering the famous "Friends, Romans, countrymen" speech. Brando's image as "the Neanderthal man," as *Collier's* described it, was more than burned into the national consciousness.

Uncharacteristically, Marlon responded to the press, "I'm sick to death of being thought of as a blue-jeaned slobbermouth." Privately, friends and family knew that it went deeper yet. "For one thing," said Darren Dublin, "he realized he was working with people who knew what they were doing, like Mason and Gielgud, and he didn't want to look like the kid from Nebraska. . . . I mean, everything the columnists were saying was eating at him. He tried to hide it, but it was clear that he needed to prove something."

Dodie was another factor in his decision to take on the part. "You haven't done anything until you've done Shakespeare" was something he had heard for years, and his mother's delight was a foregone conclusion. He had called Dodie with his anxieties about the role a half dozen or more times before signing and his decision "to really go for it" was something that answered not just Dodie's aspirations but her concerns, even her guilt, about where he was headed. "She'd cleaned up her own life," Kay Phillips Bennett said, "and she hoped that he could do the same. All his dumb bimbos and God knows how many times he'd had VD, his infantile self-centeredness and big mouth, she was very aware of these things."

Leaving Movita in New York to fix up his "cage" on Fifty-seventh Street, Marlon soon headed west, stopping in Mundelein to spend more than a week going over the part with his mother. The two of them, with Marlon Sr. accompanying them, ostensibly to check on his cattle, then drove out to the Nebraska ranch, and he even rehearsed the "Friends, Romans, countrymen" oration in the car. At the Brewster spread, reasoning that Antony delivers his speech to a dense crowd, and that the sound of his own voice might rebound off the mob, he felt he could achieve the same effect by shouting the speech into a pillow pressed against his face. At first Dodie was impressed by his ingenuity, but in the close quarters of the Penny Poke Ranch house it got to be too much even for her, and finally she told him to shut up.

"He kept her inside of himself, always," added Phillips Bennett, and by the time he finally reached California, his comments to the press parroted his mother's feelings almost word for word, as though he were sending her a message.

"I accepted this role because I thought it would be good experience for me—and good discipline, too. My kind of acting has always been very free. I always like to be easy and uninhibited in the characterizations I do. But it's a different matter when you do Shakespeare. You immediately have certain bounds and limits beyond which you cannot go."

Part of his preparation included going over the script with Mankiewicz in a monthlong series of sessions. The director was emphasizing a

contemporary approach and preferred to bypass Gielgud and his traditional performance. "Shakespeare had become so overstylized at that time
that it was almost half-ballet, almost as if it was sung," he explained, adding that his request for a three-week rehearsal went unchallenged. The
first cast reading, held during the last week of July 1951, turned into an
unmitigated calamity, and Houseman would later chronicle it in detail:

> Gielgud, who was justly celebrated as the finest reader of verse on the
> English-speaking stage, sailed through the part of Cassius with terrify-
> ing bravura; Mason, depressed and embarrassed by the brilliance of his
> compatriot, chose to read the entire role of Brutus with a pipe clenched
> tightly between his front teeth; Calhern, always at his worst at first
> readings, read Caesar with the meaningless flamboyance of a nine-
> teenth-century provincial ham; O'Brien and Kerr were adequate; Miss
> Garson was very British and ladylike. Brando, who appeared in a
> striped sweatshirt with a rolled umbrella and whom everyone was
> dying to hear, gave a perfect performance as a stuttering bumpkin only
> remotely acquainted with the English language.

The studio's speech coach, Gertrude Fogeler, was brought in, and
Marlon went back to his recordings of Barrymore, Maurice Evans, and
Olivier. On his own, he asked Gielgud to add his voice to his collection of
tapes, specifically as Marc Antony. He was aware day by day that they were
not only eating into the precious little rehearsal time allotted, but that his
biggest problem was staying on top of Shakespeare's long, unbroken lines.
A flawless sound track was essential, and postproduction "looping"—the
standard studio practice of recording dialogue to match actors' on-screen
lip movements—was out of the question. Brando's soliloquies were simply
too elaborate to be broken up into arbitrary fragments.

Perhaps his surest prop was Philip Rhodes, even more than Mankiewicz. Rhodes had still not gotten his union card, and like Darren Dublin, was working on the film as an extra or sometimes as Marlon's stand-in.
He had been a devoted fan of John Barrymore for years, even performing a
one-man show based on the Great Profile's life and roles. Marlon enjoyed
listening to Rhodes's mine of theatrical anecdotes and impersonations.
Philip was literate, enthusiastic, and had a great sense of humor. He even

went along on interviews, where he would often do much of the talking—
"either because Marlon couldn't or wouldn't," according to one of the
makeup man's friends.

Despite objections from the studio's sales department, Mankiewicz
had already settled the issue of shooting in black-and-white. Color would
dilute the film's authenticity, especially that of the forum scene that, as
Houseman himself kept insisting, stood to remind audiences of the mass
Fascist and Nazi rallies in Italy and Germany featured in wartime news-
reels. The recycled sets from *Quo Vadis?* presented another problem: Even
though they had been trimmed and stripped of their elaborate ornamenta-
tion, in color they might easily appear embarrassingly familiar. Costumes,
too, were to be kept subordinate to mood, lest they remind audiences of
Biblical epics like *Samson and Delilah* and *David and Bathsheba*. Other than
Shakespeare, no writer's name was to appear in the screen credits.

While Marlon continued to hide his anxieties and approach the work
at hand with unprecedented diligence, Gielgud was quite open about his
own inhibitions. Cadaverously thin, with the features of a hooded falcon,
he was the ideal Cassius. Still, he had made only one film since 1936, and
he was "terrified" at the possibility that his homosexuality might come
across on the big screen. "I'm afraid," the director recalled him saying,
"sometimes I walk in an exaggerated fashion and I seem to play overelaborately." Mankiewicz reassured him that, as director, he could control those
things. Marlon was less sympathetic. Actor Jack Larson, who was just
starting to play cub reporter Jimmy Olsen on television's "The Adventures
of Superman," was one of Brando's friends during this period. As Larson
recalled, "Marlon seemed baffled by Gielgud, and as with Houseman, also
rather dismissive. I think the word *flit* came up several times."

It was common knowledge that the English actor had brought his
male companion with him to Hollywood. And it had been noted by almost
everyone in the cast that Gielgud often appeared on the set to watch
Brando, sitting off to the side and smoking cigarettes at the end of a long,
elegant Dunhill holder. He was the company's mentor, yet at first, Larson
noted, Marlon made it clear that he found it hard to imagine the flamboyant homosexual—"this effete person in spats"—as a Roman soldier.

"It was rather interesting," Larson said. "When Gielgud finally got
into a breastplate, Marlon was just astonished. It was an education for him.

Gielgud was now the formidable Roman soldier, he'd grown into the part, and as soon as his character began to emerge, Marlon's admiration was boundless."

The script put the two actors together in only one scene—the murder, when Antony confronts the conspirators over Caesar's body. Marlon now asked for Gielgud's opinion of his performance; gracious perhaps to a fault, the British actor walked him through it line by line, showing him where to place his emphasis.

"He thanked me very politely and went away," Gielgud recalls, pointing out that the following morning, when they were ready to shoot the scene, he was "impressed and flattered to find that he had carefully digested my suggestions and spoke the lines exactly as I had envisaged them."

Toward the end of the production, Gielgud would invite Marlon to come to England to costar with Scofield in a classical season that he was planning to direct at Hammersmith. "I do remember begging him to play Hamlet," Gielgud later explained. "He said he had no wish to act in the theater again."

The shooting, which had started on August 8, 1951, was being done in sequence whenever possible. They were still in the midst of shooting the forum speech, Mankiewicz recalls, when Brando nearly came apart, his semicollapse occasioned by the news that Kazan had reappeared before HUAC in Washington and "spilled his guts,"as many put it. The belated report of the director's action had made the front page of that morning's *New York Times,* and its impact was such as to leave Mankiewicz worrying whether Brando would be able to get through the project.

In his first appearance before the committee, in January, Kazan had admitted his membership in the Group's Communist Party cell from the beginning of 1934 to the end of 1935, but he had declined to name his associates. On April 10 he had returned to Washington and acknowledged, "I did wrong to withhold these names before, because secrecy serves the communists, and is exactly what they want." Now he had named eight members of the Group Theatre unit, among them Clifford Odets and actors Art Smith, Morris Carnovsky, Phoebe Brand, J. Edward Bromberg, and Paula Miller (Mrs. Lee Strasberg), and assorted others. His testimony, of course, secured his release from further investigation, and if naming names wasn't bad enough, he'd offered the committee the additional plum of analyzing all his films—*Viva Zapata!* included—as a way of showing that none had "communist content."

If anyone could have resisted the committee's pressure, it was Kazan, and the unforgivable irony was that the director's work had always dealt with problems of conscience and responsibility—even in Hollywood, where he had addressed themes of anti-Semitism, racial discrimination, and the bankruptcy of greed and political power. In the months preceding his testimony, he had told Kermit Bloomgarden, the producer of *Death of a Salesman,* that he "wanted no part of the communists, but if they [HUAC] wanted him to give names, he'd tell them where to get off." Bloomgarden added:

> He told me he'd been to Washington and met with J. Edgar Hoover and Spyros Skouras and they wanted him to give names and he was going to call the people he had to name. Gadg wanted to know what I thought and I said, "Everyone must do what his conscience tells him to do." He said, "I've got to think of my kids." And I said, "This too shall pass, and then you'll be an informer in the eyes of your kids, think of that." We walked down the block and he went his way and I went mine and we didn't see or speak to each other for fifteen years. I immediately called Miller and I said to Arthur that it was ninety-nine percent sure that Gadg was giving names. Miller went over to see Gadg and Molly, and then he and Gadg walked for hours through the woods in Roxbury, Connecticut, where Miller told him he would regret it for the rest of his life and tried to talk him out of what he was going to do. When he couldn't, Gadg went to Washington and Miller went right up to Salem and wrote *The Crucible.*

On both coasts, the theater and film community was sickened. Kazan, who for years had been everyone's mentor, was now "the epitome of a betrayer," a "stool pigeon," a "rat." Until the day he died in 1977, Zero Mostel, who was blacklisted for almost a decade before making it back to Broadway stardom, referred to his old friend as "Looselips." At the Actors Studio, not only was Kazan shunned but a sizable number of members wanted him expelled: "It was just *too* sad," recalled Maureen Stapleton, "and when everyone was ready to throw him out, I said, 'Wait a minute. We can't throw him out, he owns this place. You don't throw him out; *we* get out.' " True to her word, Stapleton gave up the Studio's unique, all-important shelter. Lou Gilbert, one of the Jewish cowboys from *Zapata!,* expressed the feelings of many when he would cross over to the other side of Broadway rather than encounter his mentor face-to-face.

Brando was stricken, although during the morning in question the subject of Kazan did not come up until lunch hour, when he and Mankiewicz left for the studio commissary.

Mankiewicz said later, "We'd been working our ass off, and we were walking along the studio street, and we hadn't gone a hundred yards. He hadn't said a word. We were just walking along, and at one point I looked over at him and there were tears streaming down his face.

" 'Marlon, what's wrong?' I asked. He was staring straight ahead, then in a low voice he said, 'What do I do when I see him?'

"He didn't turn or even break stride, and of course I knew what was bothering him. I didn't know what to tell him, though. My first thought was, How am I gonna get him off this and back onto Marc Antony by the time we get to the stage? He didn't mention Kazan by name once. He just repeated, 'What'll I do when I see him? Do I bust him in the nose or what?' "

For weeks during rehearsals, Marlon had talked about Gadg and the Actors Studio, how they had solved problems together. "Now, though," Mankiewicz realized, "I've gotta get this guy back. He *was* God—Kazan, I mean. Marlon worshiped him."

Over lunch, the director tried to explain the pressures Kazan had been under, the coercion from Skouras, whose Twentieth Century–Fox was having financial trouble. He rationalized. "Try to understand his pain," he said. "He's got to have pain."

"I was full of generalities," Mankiewicz recalled. "I mean, what do you say to somebody whose father has just died?" After about an hour, the two returned to the rehearsal hall. Neither Kazan's name nor what had happened was ever mentioned again.

Marlon, however, was throwing himself into honing individual elements of his forum speech. What was most obvious to Mankiewicz was his ability to restrain himself, to "take measurements" of the emotional road ahead. While Caesar has just been murdered, Marlon's Marc Antony remained composed, even poised as he started "This bleeding piece of flesh . . ." What amazed Mankiewicz was that "he *knew* that the deed is not going to go unpunished, but the rage was being kept in check."

Years before, Brando had learned from Jacob Adler that the key to any dramatic rendition is to "hold back," to resist the urge to discharge energies prematurely. The technique called for the most harrowing kind of self-discipline, a total subjugation of self, and this was no clearer than in the scene after the triumvirate meeting when Marc Antony is left alone and realizes for the first time that he will replace Caesar. Here, what Mankiewicz had done was insist on having a big bust of Caesar placed on the soundstage. As Marlon looked out over Rome, unscripted and without directorial prompting, he slowly turned the statue so it was looking directly at him. Sitting on Caesar's throne, alone with the emperor's bust while silently surveying the city that the mob is burning, Antony has *become* Caesar, just as the future has been made visible in a world gone mad.

Rhodes was on the set and saw Marlon spontaneously improvise the movement. "He had always been very good in that speech in rehearsal," Rhodes recalled, "had captured the venom and anger of 'Let slip the dogs of war.' For the shoot, he came in with his hair combed down and wearing the Roman robes for the first time. He was just standing there, looking at all these statues, these great figures with the sculpted draperies. You could see him become one of the statues, and he began the speech as one of the sculptures. It was evident that he had found the center of the scene, and the rest of it followed, making visual the fact that he was the centerpiece, the king." It may have been little more than a visual gimmick, but for Mankiewicz, what made him "the single greatest acting talent in the English language of this century" and "better than Clift, better than Orson and Burton" was this rare sense of truth: He could move ahead into unknown territory without spooking himself—relaxed, unburdened by the awareness of anything except his inner promptings.

"It's not stripping his skin but just *becoming,* and I'm not even hinting at any of this Stanislavsky shit of Mr. Strasberg's," said Mankiewicz. "With that statue, it was just two silent looks . . . like a passage of exquisite music." Olivier, whom Mankiewicz also directed, was, by comparison, "a giant computer," a huge machine with an arsenal of programmed reactions. Unlike Olivier, too, Marlon wasn't relying on makeup. Rhodes had fashioned a tiny addition to his nose, and also applied body tan all over, but otherwise his physical equipment was unencumbered, mirroring the same "complete absorption."

Nor was he "the slightest bit uncomfortable" being scrutinized by everyone—male and female alike—even with his hair in ringlets, Mankiewicz recalled. "I was looking for that, I wanted him to be a little vain, to show that muscle and how beautiful he was, a Roman ideal. But he used his body to do what he thought he should be doing. The fact that he looked at himself a thousand times mentally . . . well, sure he did; but when he stepped onto the stage and said, 'Good morning, John. Good morning, James,' he was their equal in every way except for the fact they'd look up to him, which they most surely did. They said, 'Holy Jesus!' "

Strategically, the director made himself available "to answer any question, to impart whatever he seemed to be missing," and what he and Brando talked about most often was tempo and pacing, the play's rhythm. " 'It ought to build, Marlon,' I kept saying to him. 'What you're going to do is rise up and build to that, then let fly. I want you to scare *the shit out of me.*' What I got," adds Mankiewicz, "were more surprises."

Mankiewicz didn't know anything about Brando's guarded private life except for bits and pieces via the grapevine, such as the fact that Movita was in the wings even as Marlon flirted with both Deborah Kerr and Greer Garson. In what was an almost letter-perfect replay of what had taken place with Kazan in New York during *Streetcar*, Marlon asked Mankiewicz for a referral to a local psychiatrist. Happily, the director was in a position to comply; he had been seeing Dr. Frederick Hacker, the well-known Menninger-trained Freudian sometimes known as "the shrink to the stars," and Hacker was also treating the director's wife as well as the couple's children. In short order, Marlon made an appointment for himself. Hacker, who would later add Anna Kashfi and the young Christian Brando to his list of patients, recalled, "I saw him about eight or ten times. I was on the set almost every day because of Joe, and Marlon would come to see me three or four times a week, in quick succession.

"You could tell he was troubled," he added, "that this was someone carrying a great burden, and very confused. The occasion for his coming was never really clear, although it had something to do with a woman he was involved with. He wouldn't say anything about his past, or if he would, it was with enormous difficulty, great reluctance. . . . He'd told me he was in treatment in New York, but he wouldn't tell me who it was—namely, Mittelmann. And he'd go to the bathroom two or three times in the course of a single session. Once, he went and stayed for twenty minutes.

I knocked on the door, to ask if he was all right. He came out and said something, very confused, about his reliance on smells and how, through smell, you could know someone and that what he was doing in there was getting to know me. . . .

"He'd said he was coming to see me to 'get a better sense' of his analyst in New York, to get 'a better perspective.' What I realized was that while here was this man celebrated for his masculine strength, in reality he was really quite weak. Then he just stopped coming—first he canceled his appointment, then we didn't hear from him."

Stubbornly—others say devotedly—Movita had followed Marlon from Texas to Los Angeles, to New York, and now back to Hollywood. She wanted him to marry her, and although friends said she "really cared, really looked after Marlon," they also were fighting. "He wanted me to be like in the home and kind of hidden," she told Johnny Brascia, who would later become her live-in lover. Brascia himself observed, "That's why she said they would always fight, because he couldn't control her. She had to wait on him hand and foot. He liked to be catered to, and if he didn't get his way, he'd go crazy, just rant and rave and go to another room or sleep on the sofa and pout all night."

She complained of Brando's sulks and mood swings, the way he would tear out of the house without telling her where he was going, but she always suspected that he was picking up a lot of "floozies." According to Brascia, she said "he had a thing, always wanting to 'fuck down.'"

Movita wasn't unique in her suspicions. It wasn't just floozies, said a number of both New York and Hollywood acquaintances; it was any woman who caught his eye at parties, in restaurants, even on the street. Like the young black woman he pointed out to a friend he ran into, and then he kept on walking. "I'm following her," he had said to the acquaintance, who noted that Brando "didn't seem to think it was strange behavior at all."

Movita, though, was "very street smart," Brascia continued. "She had an intuition about where people were coming from, and another problem was Marlon's friends—not Wally, but the other guys. She was friendly with Philip Rhodes and Marie, but they fought constantly about Gilman and Darren. She was jealous—that was the female part of Movita—and she'd say things to him like, 'Oh, you'll find out. They're just looking for your money or what you can do for them.'"

When Marlon Sr. had halted Movita's renovations of Marlon Jr.'s New York apartment (claiming, according to Rhodes, that they were too expensive), Movita had come to L.A., and she and Marlon soon rented a house in Laurel Canyon. "Marlon had moved out of Jay's," recalled Roberta Haynes, and "one night Jay and I went to pick them up to have dinner. I felt that Marlon had changed—he seemed more open, nicer and more together. She was like his mother, telling him what to do. There was no more dirty laundry lying around. Before, Marlon was a slob, had never dressed like an adult human being. Now Movita was telling him, 'Pick up your clothes, put them in the laundry.' She may have had the reputation of being a fiery Mexican, but my impression was that she was solid and intelligent, not like some of the other tempestuous women he was involved with at the time."

As the tension between them mounted, Marlon started seeing Katy Jurado and also Rita Moreno, then an unknown dancer-actress under contract to MGM. Previously, Moreno had been dating Geordie Hormel, the meat-packing heir and Marlon's former classmate at Shattuck, who had come west to set up a sound-recording studio in Santa Monica. Hormel's lavish parties were legend, attended not only by actors but jazz musicians like Stan Getz and Chet Baker. Despite the fact that Marlon was never much of a partygoer, he fit right in, and then in what seemed a compulsive pattern, he had taken his old classmate's girl away.

While his personal life seemed chaotic, in front of the camera he continued to give the impression of being "very relaxed," even though he was coming up on his real test as a classical actor: the forum scene. His weeks of preparation had been so extensive that he even took the unusual step of reading the scene with Houseman, explaining his discoveries in a state of excitement. Recalled the producer, "Suddenly he had discovered that with a dramatist of Shakespeare's genius and in a speech as brilliantly and elaborately written as Antony's oration, it was not necessary nor even possible to play between the lines, and that having in his own mind created the character and personality of Antony, he must let Shakespeare's words carry the full flood of his own emotion from the beginning to the end of the scene."

It was a denial of Method "subtext," which might well be equated with Mankiewicz's joyous insistence that he was simply doing the job at hand. "I realize now that you've got to *play the text*," Brando had said.

"You can't play under it, or above it, or around it, as we do in contemporary theater. The *text* is everything."

As the scene began, the crowd listened to Mason's Brutus, showing every evidence of being swayed. When Marlon entered from the wings carrying Louis Calhern, six feet five and heavy, he placed the body of Caesar at Brutus's feet. "Friends, Romans, countrymen . . ." he began. The crowd, made up of 250 extras, spontaneously interrupted, not allowing him to go on. He started again, only to be interrupted, and Mankiewicz, who had primed the extras to interfere, now shouted at him, "Get mad!" In his saffron-colored toga, Brando began again.

"Friends, Romans, countrymen, *lend* me your ears," he leaned into it, as the extras fell silent. The speech went on unbroken for its thirty-four lines, Brando's voice rising like a torrent until reaching its climax. With the director's "Cut!" nobody moved. Then from every corner of MGM's stage 24, the crew burst into applause.

"I felt a fucking chill go up my spine," Mankiewicz recalls. "It was the greatest moment I have ever felt as a director. . . . It's what made [my] whole career worthwhile."

By shooting "tight," with alternating close-ups of Marc Antony and individual faces in the mob, Mankiewicz gradually accelerated the rhythm of the suspense. For Gielgud, the strategy seemed senseless, especially when Marlon's voice started to go.

"They would photograph [Marlon] for a couple of days in the taxing speeches of the forum scene," said Gielgud, "and then he would lose his voice and be unable to work. They would fill in time by filming the extras, taking a lot of shots of faces in the crowd responding, then Brando would recover and come down to the studio to do another speech. I imagine that the director hoped he could put it all together in the cutting room, but Shakespeare is too big for that."

Mankiewicz was already off his tight shooting schedule, but even Houseman, who as producer was ultimately responsible for production delays, continued to marvel at Brando's forbearance. "During that long week of shooting," he explained, "he went through his speech over and over, without once losing his energy or his concentration. When he faltered or flubbed a line, he would stop, apologize, compose himself, and start afresh."

• • •

After a troublesome battle scene and postproduction dragging on through the end of 1952, *Julius Caesar* was finally completed and ready to screen. Houseman and Mankiewicz took a united stand in refusing to have their first public viewing at one of the neighborhood movie houses in Pasadena or Inglewood or in the Valley, where sneak previews were usually held. "We did not want it shown in the Los Angeles area, where half the agents in town would drop in to see it," Houseman said. "We wanted a representative, not an illiterate, audience." Pomona was selected instead. Unfortunately, Pomona Junior College was not located in Pomona, as the producer had thought, but in nearby Riverside. Pomona itself turned out to be the home of one of the largest steel mills in the West.

The night of the preview—January 8, 1953—the theater was filled with exactly the kind of audience Houseman had dreaded—teenagers in jeans, parents with quarreling children, strictly a blue-collar crowd. Once, in similar circumstances, Sam Goldwyn had gathered up his film cans from the projection booth and dashed from the theater. Neither Houseman nor Mankiewicz could do the same, since Dore Schary and his *équipe* filled the center aisle, nervously smiling as the lights began to dim.

According to Houseman's account, when the curtain parted on the MGM lion, there was mild applause that "flared into sudden enthusiasm" when Brando's name appeared on-screen. During the first few minutes he was unable to judge the audience's response; the murder of Caesar seemed to work, and so did the forum scene. With the final credits, there was some mild applause but little more. Schary and his staff filed out of the theater, headed for their waiting limousines.

The usual tables had been set up in the lobby with response cards, and when the tabulation was completed the next day, it appeared they were over the top.

First Preview
First Report
"JULIUS CAESAR"

United Artists Theater
Pomona
January 8, 1953

TOTAL NUMBER OF CARDS THIS REPORT — 202

HOW WOULD YOU RATE THIS PICTURE?:

Outstanding	71
Excellent	53
Very Good	36
Good	19
Fair	19
Poor	4

The results were even better at the world premiere on May 8, 1953, in Sydney, Australia, where the word was that audiences were "enthralled." Encouraged, the studio announced the American opening in New York for June 5. "Nothing but regal treatment will be accorded *Julius Caesar* by MGM," *Variety* reported. "It is headed for Broadway's Booth Theatre and on a reserved, two-a-day basis."

Respectability and class, *Caesar* had it all, and by the time the reviewers filed their copy, the film was a certifiable smash: The New York *Daily News* gave it four stars, *Time* called it "the best Shakespeare that Hollywood has yet produced," and the *New York Times* said it was as though Tinseltown had finally come of age with a monument to the Bard that was dramatically superior to Olivier's *Hamlet*.

Gielgud, Calhern, Mason, even Deborah Kerr—all got their due. But out of the something-for-everyone casting, the critics fastened on Brando, "the delight and surprise of the film." "Athletic and bullet-headed," the *Times* claimed, "he looks the realest Roman of them all. . . . Happily, Mr. Brando's diction, which has been guttural and slurred in previous films, is clear and precise in this instance. . . . A major talent has emerged." For the *Saturday Review,* he was "magnificent," "stunning," and "quite clearly, the very best of the younger American actors." "After his amazing success in *Julius Caesar,*" wrote a forgiving Dorothy Kilgallen in the *American Weekly,* "Hollywood knows that Marlon Brando is more than a tight-lipped, beautifully muscled Stanley Kowalski. From now on, he can announce that he is going to play King Lear or Peter Pan and nobody will laugh."

Brando's own muted concession was that he "gained ground as an actor—not so much in end performance." Such modesty notwithstanding, the performance was an event, even if his third Academy Award nomination failed to deliver an Oscar. Proving something to himself, he had also proven something to his mother; according to Ann Lombard Osborne, Dodie told him he had done "a magnificent job."

By this time Dodie and Marlon Sr. were living on the Nebraska ranch year-round, the better to watch over the cattle operation and pursue the claim to ownership. The decision had also been made in part to allow them to turn over the farm in Mundelein to Fran and Dick. Fran was still depressed and drinking heavily, and the thought was that by living the more easygoing rural life, she could begin to straighten herself out. Dr. Ward saw an immediate improvement once Fran followed in her mother's footsteps and joined AA. Even more than Dodie, she was an "earth mother," according to her good friend Bente Claussen. She was becoming a "natural foods" convert, eating "piles of brown rice" and keeping bottles of vitamins everywhere. She also took up her mother's interest in Spiritualism and participated in séances with Dodie's pal Ann Lombard Osborne, who, according to Dick Loving, claimed to be a medium who could put herself into a trance and communicate with the dead through automatic writing.

Marlon was not pleased to learn how much of his income his father had poured into the cattle operation. The Brandos' lawsuit had alleged that Black owed them $213,018—$40,160 to Marlon Sr., and $172,858 to Bud—and argued that if Black was unable to pay, he should be forced to forfeit the property. The claim would eventually go from one court to another, followed by a series of appeals. Throughout the process, Marlon's attitude was as tenacious as his father's.

Whether Marlon Jr. actually understood what all the scheming had been about was doubtful. In fact, during his latest trip he had brought Wally Cox along for a visit to the ranch. Cox was now the star of the "Mr. Peepers" television series, which had debuted as a summer replacement and evolved into a huge success. Although Marlon Sr. had previously failed to enlist Cox as an investor, his son would have more success, and Wally plunked down thousands of dollars on Marlon's encouragement. Neither of them knew anything about the cattle business, and, as "Mr. Peepers" producer Everett Greenbaum recalled, Wally "lost his ass."

By now nothing was simple with Marlon. In *Julius Caesar* he had never worked harder or more freely abandoned that "fragile, shy thing" he called self. As Marc Antony, he had proved himself in a classical role. He chose his next movie because it satisfied his social conscience. And the establishment recoiled.

The Wild One

Brando's decision to make *The Wild One* wasn't immediate. Choosing a project, he knew, was just as important as what you did with it, and even though in the three years since *The Men* he had become Hollywood's most talked-about male star, he seemed content to float. There were screenings at MCA, as well as Charlie Chaplin's parties and Sunday-afternoon tennis games. Meanwhile, he turned down one lucrative script after another, continuing to insist to columnists that if John Wayne, Gene Autry, Roy Rogers, and others "make big business out of movie making," it was all well and good, but he was "not a businessman."

Judith Braun, an actress friend who had chosen to base herself in New York even while under contract to Universal, said, "His sense of being in Hollywood was that he was just there for five minutes. It was always, 'I'm on my way back to Manhattan.' His big anger at the time was that he couldn't walk down the street, that he couldn't go and find the world anymore because the world was trying to break his door down. He had become this fantastically famous person, and he was terribly bitter about it. There was no realistic appraisal, 'I'm a movie star, it makes me a lot of money, I have to pay the price.' "

So disdainful was he that when he discovered that Darren Dublin was keeping a scrapbook of clips of his own (and Marlon's) career, he exclaimed, "What are you keeping all this for? Throw that shit away!" Similarly, if stopped on the street for an autograph, say, he could become incensed and afterward rail, "I hate this, I hate acting."

He had yet to find a new film that interested him when he got a call from Stanley Kramer in September 1952. Kramer explained that after the success of *The Men,* his small independent group had entered into an agreement with Columbia Pictures that put up $25 million in exchange for thirty films, all to be produced with "complete autonomy." Kramer's subsequent pictures, including *Death of a Salesman* (1951), had shown disappointingly small profits, and Harry "the King" Cohn, Columbia's head and the most despotic of studio bosses, was now reining him in. To make matters worse, Carl Foreman, one of Kramer's partners, had run into a HUAC subpoena; he had refused to name names, then fled to England. George Glass, his other partner, had also been subpoenaed, and even though he'd given the Red-baiters what they wanted, the Breen office and columnists like George Sokolsky had targeted Kramer's operation.

Kramer then suggested a project that appealed to Brando's natural tendency to side with the underdog. *The Cyclists' Raid* was based on a *Harper's* magazine article that chronicled the invasion of a small northern California farm town by outlaw motorcyclists over the Fourth of July weekend, 1947. As with *The Men,* most of the script elements were true to fact. Close to three thousand bikers, many of them members of two Los Angeles gangs known as the Booze Fighters and the Nomads, had taken over the sleepy hamlet of Hollister. There, they took turns drag-racing up and down the village's main street while standing spread-eagled on their Harleys, spinning "doughnuts" in the dirt as well as tossing empty beer bottles through storefront windows until they fell down drunk. The bacchanal had continued around the clock, and three neighboring counties sent squads of sheriffs. However, while the town's jail was filled to overflowing, there were no knives, no chains, and no record of rapes or even violence except among the inebriated bikers themselves.

The media had naturally jumped on the story. These road gypsies were a new phenomenon in the postwar years, and all the more frightening for their leather jackets, loud motorcycles, and group bonding. "Juvenile delinquency" had been on everyone's lips for several years already, and the problem had even been addressed in Senate hearings. For Kramer, it was a natural. "It touched my sense of social responsibility," he said. "I wanted Marlon to play Johnny, the leader of one of the gangs."

Moved by Kramer's inimitable salesmanship and his description of his new film, Marlon agreed to come aboard. It made no difference that the Booze Fighters were in fact little more than blue-collar vets cutting loose. He agreed with Kramer that young people were driven to rebellion by the new social pressures in America after World War II. He also insisted that, to make any sense, the film had to show the citizens of Hollister for what they were: drones and Babbitts responding to the leather-jacketed bikers with a hysteria that had driven the group to violence in the first place. In the gray, listless Eisenhower years, the movie was to be about outsiders, what amounted to a rejection of the status quo. Above and beyond Brando's anticipation at riding his own bike in front of the camera, the film promised to be on the cutting edge by showing the townsfolk coming to an understanding of the outlaws, and presenting what Brando was calling even then a "polka dot" world.

Brando agreed to meet with director Laslo Benedek once he returned to Hollywood at the beginning of 1953. Benedek, who was more familiar with Haydn than Harley-Davidsons, later related that Marlon roamed around his living room and never once sat down. He looked at family pictures, picked up objects, and asked personal questions that had little, if anything, to do with the picture. It was a "strange meeting," Benedek recalled, and later Marlon himself would acknowledge that his intuitive approval of the Hungarian director had been a major mistake.

Mary Murphy, a pixie-faced twenty-year-old actress, was suggested by scriptwriter John Paxton for the part of Kathie, Brando's love interest. Then on loan from Paramount, she had little training to speak of, and would have been better cast doing commercials for Wonder Bread than coping with bikers. Yet the project excited her, and when she found herself being auditioned with Brando present, she "just melted."

Within weeks, Brando would be offering the film's stunt coordinator, Cary Loftin, odds as to which of them would be the first to "get in her pants." Now, though, he began preparing for his role by polishing his cycling technique, and soon he took the big, studio-supplied twin-cylinder Triumph (it was not an authentic Harley-Davidson at all, contrary to legend) up to Hollister, a run of well over 250 miles. There he met with Kramer, Benedek, and Paxton, as well as the cycle gang members, some of whom had already been hired to play themselves in the picture. They were also introduced to the gang's loose "mamas," who accepted the premise that to ride with a motorcycle gang meant they had to "put out." Marlon was also struck by the bikers' lingo. It wasn't as stylized as New York jazz jive—and not nearly as easy—but one-liners like "Jus' gotta move, *man*" hung in the air without qualification. When Kramer, ever the serious hands-on producer, asked "Well, what are you rebelling *against*?" one of the bikers made cultural history as well as guaranteed Marlon's attention by replying simply, "Well, what ya got?"

It was clear, Kramer recalled, that this was Marlon's ready-made transit from Gielgud and *Caesar*. What he found most compelling of all was that in the cut-off world of big bikes, long runs, and unarticulated angst, these men were outlaws, coolly scornful of the middle-class comforts of settling down with an unchallenging spouse, dreaming of the ideal life, grouping for an illusory sense of security. "Shit, man," one of them had buttonholed the actor. "Find another little town without a main highway and get that number of bikers together and it could happen again. . . . Yes, sir, we treed Hollister" (*treed* is a term borrowed from Texas trail hands, who traditionally tore apart frontier towns in the course of their cattle drives). It wasn't long after Marlon's Hollister visit that the Breen office fired its opening salvo by calling Paxton's script "antisocial, if not downright communistic."

The specific problem was the suggestion that social pressures and dead-end jobs drove adolescents to violence. There was also the film's ending, where the cyclists were to leave the town unpunished: Here the story was remotely faithful to history, but Sam Goldwyn had always known best when he summarized industry standards with his lisping credo, "Good sentiments must be rewarded. Bad sentiments *must* be punished!" Jack Viszard of the Breen office was less circumspect: "By God," he exclaimed, "if they tried to do that to a town where I lived, I'd shoot 'em first and ask questions later." John Paxton returned to his typewriter, and soon the final scene, which explored the bikers' *raison d'etre,* was cut completely. Brando was furious, and even tried his own hand at a rewrite (the first in his career), although no record exists of what he may actually have written.

The Breen office also demanded that Marlon himself narrate an introduction, as a voice-over, stating that the cyclists' rampage was a single episode that should and (presumably) would never happen again. (At the taping Marlon made faces throughout his monologue.) Then Cohn vetoed the plan to shoot the film on location. Instead, he insisted they use Columbia's ranch in Burbank, where they would be forced to rely on sets used for hundreds of B westerns. He also wanted it shot in black-and-white. In the interest of economy, whole episodes were cut as well. For the first time, Marlon started shooting without rehearsal; Mary Murphy, who would suffer far more, was told that she was being left intentionally unprepared as a way of preserving her "innocence," which, she was reassured, would "get her through" as the film's good-hearted, small-town beauty.

If the production values were now reduced to those of a TV sitcom, Brando nonetheless threw himself into the project wholeheartedly. The first day, while he and Murphy were doing a run-through of the coffee shop scene where Kathie and Johnny meet, the inexperienced actress pretended to be calm and tried to fake it, but Marlon stopped the scene at once. He took her aside, out of camera range. "Extremely perceptive," he understood that Murphy was scared to death, and what he did, she recalled, "wasn't anything more than to chat, like friendly flirtation . . . just to put me at ease. We were sitting at a table, I remember, and as he proceeded to talk to me, he never stopped looking into my eyes."

In short order, they did the scene smoothly, in few takes. What struck Murphy as the camera rolled was the easy, almost seamless transition from what had gone before to the concentration of his delivery of the bikers' credo, "Man, you're too square. I have to straighten you out. . . . You know what I'm talking about? . . . You gotta *wail!*"

The way he delivered the lines seemed to come out of nowhere, and what surprised her even more was when the time came for his character to pay for his coffee. Here, Marlon casually pulled a quarter out of his pocket and began sliding it back and forth across the counter, out of Murphy's reach, playing with her as though he were the proverbial cat toying with a mouse. The move was totally unscripted, a kind of work she'd never seen before.

Next, they argued about one of the bits where Murphy's character asks why the cyclists go on their weekend rampages. The original script called for him to explain the bikers' runs as a release from their deadening, humdrum jobs; the rewrite dictated by censor Jack Vizzard, and keyed to how the "commies would use it in Europe," offered a substitute so watered down that Marlon was having trouble getting the words out of his mouth. "We can't do it the way it's written," he protested. "We've got to explain that these guys are nameless, faceless fry cooks and grease monkeys all week. They've got to break out and *be* somebody. They got to *belong* to something. And when the tensions build up, they do violent things."

Benedek told him to ad-lib it and instructed Murphy to follow him wherever he took her.

Another time, perhaps to bug Benedek, Brando suddenly put up his hand to stop the cameraman just when the actor and Murphy were already in place in the café booth for a setup. Brando asked the taciturn stunt coordinator Cary Loftin how he'd read the lines. Loftin remembers, "I said, 'Oh, hell, I'm a stuntman. It's up to you.' 'Yeah, but how would you read it?' "

The actor copied Loftin's rural drawl exactly, trying to get closer to the tone and style of "real" biker talk. "He was sitting and somebody comes in the door and says, 'Johnny.' In the script his line was 'Yeah'— y-e-a-h,' " said Gil Stratton, another longtime rider who had a small role. "I watched them shoot this thing, and what he did with it, well, he spun around and went, '*Yo!*' And I went, Wow—really neat."

Brando never asked for time to prepare or "get into mood" except once, before the scene where the townspeople beat Johnny up. When Loftin caught him running in place, Brando seemed embarrassed and said, "Hey, I'm a Method actor. I have to be out of breath."

Jocelyn was visiting the set and saw how her brother was working. "He would be talking and laughing with me," she said, "but when he was called, he was right there in the scene, perfect, getting the character's fear and emotions. I was delighted to see how concentrated he was. He wasn't walking through it or sluffing it off, even though I knew he was unhappy with the director."

By the end of the first week, he was deliberately keeping away from Murphy, ostensibly so as not to clutter their relationship on-screen. Most of the time he stayed in his trailer—often with Darren, whom he'd gotten a bit as one of his gang members. Sometimes he'd be with Movita, but she never left the trailer except in his presence. His entourage, Murphy noted, consisted of Sam Gilman and Larry Duran, a Mexican actor he'd met during the *Zapata!* shoot, as well as Darren, and all three struck her as "little guys [who] were just hanging around."

Stuntmen and extras alike were under the impression that Brando had just learned to ride a motorcycle like beginner Lee Marvin, his costar. Prior to filming, both actors had been taken up into the Hollywood hills for instruction. Marlon had impressed no one, but despite his limited skills, he took every opportunity to take some cute little extra for a ride. Loftin, the head stuntman, had earlier seen all this coming. "We had two Triumphs and one Harley, one for Marvin and two for Brando. We [didn't] have insurance, so they'd told me to keep them on the lot. I said, 'Well, it's done.' I'm giving these guys their lessons, and one morning Lee was there an hour early. Brando finally pulls in—I think it was after eleven. He had this girl with him, in an old Pontiac convertible. He didn't say anything about being late, just, 'I'm taking this Triumph and we're going out to lunch.' I said, 'You can't take it off the lot.' So he tells me again what he's going to do and I said, 'Well, apparently you're a little hard-of-hearing. This motorcycle does not go off the lot. That's what they told me and that's what I'll see to.'

"He just got in his car and he blew dust all around and they took off. I don't think he even came back that day."

A week later he still wasn't talking to Loftin when he noticed the stunt coordinator spinning figure eights near the commissary and approached him for pointers.

"He says, 'Hey, champ, could you teach me to do that?' " Loftin recalled. "I says, 'Oh, boy . . .' and I took a long look at him. I said, 'I don't know whether you picked up on it or not, but you really have to be brainy to do that. You gotta know what you're doing.' 'Uh-huh,' he said. 'You think you can teach me?'

"Well, I did. I told him how to spin circles and how not to hurt himself, to keep his leg out of the way. Shortly after that we had lunch at the commissary, and just as we came out we hear a motorcycle going round and round. It's Brando. Kramer and Benedek, none of them are talking to him. They're yelling, 'Cary, you gotta stop him!' Okay. I walked slowly down, he's just breaking it loose and spinning circles. I said, 'Boy, Ace, you really had 'em worried. Now when I teach you to cut back and go into a figure eight, that'll really stand 'em on their heads.' "

Even so, Loftin noted that for all his previous experience, Brando "wasn't too good, especially on the dirt." Later in the week Loftin was having lunch with Gil Stratton when he heard a loud *blam,* then another crash—the unmistakable sounds of an accident.

Loftin explained, "A friend of his—this guy Duran—had come on the lot and he was going to take him for a ride. There was a big limousine parked there, and he's off to the left side and he took off and hit the front fender of this car. He just miscalculated. He ran into it, like he didn't turn enough, then bounced off. Got himself thrown, and almost wound up in the women's john."

Brando's leg was bruised and he had "a big hickey on his hip, like a blister that had to be drained." Kramer immediately imposed a ban on any further riding except in front of the cameras.

Marlon ignored this. He had already started tooling around L.A., occasionally stopping at saloons favored by *pachucos,* the California-Mexican groups of gang bikers. He'd order straight whiskeys, then surreptitiously dump the drink on the floor. One night, reportedly, local police raided the dive and collared the most conspicuous suspects, including Brando. They searched him, examined his arms for needle marks, then let him go, never realizing who he was.

When Brando wasn't cruising East Los Angeles, he was at Darren's place in Laurel Canyon, not far from the rental he had taken for himself and Movita. Despite the proximity to his own address, he was now practically living at Dublin's, and rarely was Mo with him. "Like everyone else, sometimes she'd call," Dublin said. "I'd tell all of 'em, 'He's not here.' MCA, Kramer, Movita, it didn't matter." As he had once done in New York in front of his brother-in-law, Marlon sometimes threw the telephone against the wall when he was exasperated with its ringing. The usual goofy horseplay between Darren and Marlon was as lunatic as any of their best numbers in New York, too. "I dragged the garden hose right into the house once," said Dublin, still laughing about it years later. "Marlon thought it was hysterical." The two sat around for hours, and in between reminiscences, fantasies, and philosophical speculations, Marlon complained not only about Benedek ("He oughta be directing Doris Day movies") but also costar Lee Marvin, who had started dropping by, hoping to establish a friendly relationship.

An ex-marine, a decorated war veteran, and—by most accounts—a guy who liked a good fight, Marvin had been making pictures for three years. Kramer had cast him as a substitute for Keenan Wynn, whom MGM had refused to put on loan after he'd spent weeks in preproduction. Like Wynn, Marvin was loud, gregarious, and blended in easily with the real bikers. He was also a boozer, and it was Kramer's notion to stoke what he saw as the actor's rivalry with Brando, hoping for a carryover in front of the camera.

"Lee was jealous of Marlon and wanted to knock him off his pedestal," Mary Murphy observed, adding that Marvin was threatened by Brando's "sensitivity." Like Quinn on *Zapata!,* Marvin had also become irked by Brando's clout with Benedek, the way he seemed to be taking over the production. Whereas Marlon was quiet and internalized, Marvin's loudmouthed Chino was aptly cast. Most of the real cyclists were assigned to Marvin's gang, the Beatles, but unlike Brando, Marvin had never bothered to research the cyclist culture, perhaps because he was so much like the outlaw bikers himself. When Marvin skinned his nose after dropping his Indian one afternoon, he laughed and told Cary Loftin not to tell Benedek. Even Darren Dublin admitted that "he was a regular guy who you wouldn't know was in show business."

Marvin also wasn't about to keep his ego in check when it came to Brando, especially after he'd been drinking. Things came to a head in front of most of the company when Benedek summoned the two actors to stage their scripted showdown.

The scene called for doubles, of course, but after the stuntmen had worked out the blocking and choreography for the planned close-ups, Benedek changed his mind. Instead of using the stuntmen, he asked the actors to do most of the scene themselves. According to one account, they "started trading barely missed blows . . . rolling in the dirt . . . [and] Brando was the winner, in accordance with the script, but Marvin imposed a grandstanding gesture to compensate in bravado for what he had suffered in physical defeat." The gesture was an upraised index finger.

Professionally, the film was Marvin's biggest break so far, but he nonetheless wore the most bizarre collection of rags, as if to also say "fuck you" to Brando's stylized leathers and silly Buster Bad Ass cap, which some of the extras had already lampooned as the badge of a jerk. Likewise, now everyone recognized that Marvin was playing more to the bikers than to Benedek, trumping his rival with ad-libs and an on-camera drunkenness that made it clear which of the two of them was less uptight, more "cool" and manly.

Marvin would go on to take up motorcycling for real, joining his new buddies on their annual "Big Bear" race across the desert with Keenan Wynn at his side. Moreover, his performance was validated by no one less than Sonny Barger, the founder of the Oakland Hell's Angels, who reportedly purchased the actor's on-screen jersey.

For Marvin and the extras the film was already becoming "the pussycat's version of outlaw bikers," as Chuck Clayton, editor of *Biker* magazine, put it, although from Kramer's perspective, Brando was still intent on making his role "something special." Nonetheless, as the schedule grew more and more intense, often stretching late into the night, the mood further deteriorated—not only between the two stars but also between Brando and Benedek.

Darren Dublin saw the chemistry of what was happening more than anyone: "Benedek was a European gentleman—manners, niceness, decorum, all that—but he had no balls, and here he was dealing with Lee Marvin and the drinking . . . [which] was getting completely out of control."

Benedek couldn't bring himself to use terms like "outlaw" or "hipster." He couldn't tell one black leather jacket from another, and his assistants were just as inept. Aside from how this affected the film's feel, the more pronounced result was that continuity—the all-important matching of one day's footage with that of the next—was all but abandoned.

"It was like going to a party every night," Dublin continued, "and there were all these guys, the actors, the extras. If you happened to be around when they started a scene, it was, 'Okay, you're in.' I remember walking away and then coming back, thinking, Wait a minute, I'm supposed to be in that shot for some matching or something. The assistants just fucked up, Benedek fucked up, and some of the extras wound up with more footage than the actors. Marlon had gone into this thing with the notion that he was going to make a serious movie. He had his own conception of what the part should be, like any actor does, but you know Marlon. If he doesn't feel the director has a good strong conception, he'll just make the guy go get him coffee. If a director disagrees with his conception, he's got to have a good reason. Otherwise it's 'Fuck it.' " One result was that Marlon started directing himself; the more significant outcome was that he stopped taking the picture seriously, becoming discouraged and disgusted. His attitude was "Who gives a shit, let's shoot," and "Ain't we having fun."

With only one woman in the cast except for bit players, Murphy found herself in deep trouble when it came time for the gang-rape scene. There had been time enough only to rehearse the blocking, and since the Columbia ranch lacked the huge cover tarps that allowed for day-for-night shooting (these were only available at more affluent studios like MGM and Paramount), the cast and crew were doing the scene late in the evening when it was actually dark. Without any sense of what was happening, Murphy took her place and quickly realized that she was alone, trapped inside a loud, encircling ring of motorcycles, wondering when—and if— the technical crew would have to come to her rescue. One rider, spinning a doughnut, had his motorcycle come out from under him in the dirt and nearly slid into her. Some of the other extras, not bikers but rodeo riders working for $25 a day, almost plowed into her head-on. "It scared the bejesus out of me," she recalled, "because the whole thing suddenly got very macho. I wasn't worried that I was going to be raped, but the way these guys got carried away with themselves was shocking."

Rumor has it that at the end of the twenty-fourth day of shooting— March 17, 1953—Benedek simply collapsed in tears. The final love scene had been rewritten several times but still didn't work, and weeks of editing, accompanied by extensive looping, didn't help, either. All of this left Kramer's publicity chief, George Glass, with the task of coming up with a new title for the film in the hope of increasing its odds at the box office. *The Cyclists' Raid* gave way to *Frenzy,* which was replaced by *Hot Blood,* a name that was naturally embraced by the Columbia sales department. Here Kramer, who was aware that he had already made irretrievable compromises on the script, drew the line, and in December the film was sold—badly, thanks to Harry Cohn—as *The Wild One*. Even with the Breen office's warnings, the critics' response to its raw violence was more than anyone could have expected:

> The picture's major weakness is that it fails to place the responsibility where it obviously belongs, with the gangs and their leaders, who are not juvenile delinquents but thrill-crazy adults . . . filled with horror and sadism.
> —New York *Daily News* (December 26, 1953)

> The themes of boogie and terror heap up in alternations of juke-yowl and gear-gnash to a climax of violence. . . . The effect of the movie is not to throw light on a public problem but to shoot adrenaline through the moviegoer's veins.
> —*Time* (January 18, 1954)

The film was banned outright in Memphis, Tennessee. In England the furor was so great that the movie would not see release for fifteen more years—until 1968, when it emerged from cold storage with an "X" certificate.

Frustrated and bitter, Marlon publicly agreed that the picture had missed its mark. "We started out to do something worthwhile, to explain the psychology of the hipster," he said, leaning heavily on psychiatrist Robert Lindner's *Rebel Without a Cause*. "But somewhere along the way we went off the track. The result was that instead of finding why young people tend to bunch into groups that seek expression in violence, all that we did was to show the violence."

"[Marlon] was so unhappy with the director," said Jocelyn, "that he began to eat a lot during that movie. That may have been when he began to gain weight, though I don't think it showed on the screen until *The Young Lions,* when his ass looked heavy and he kept having to pull down his jacket."

Kramer himself tried to explain away the picture's failure on the grounds that it was too "radical a departure from the norm." Marlon never worked for Kramer again, even when offered the part opposite Sidney Poitier in *The Defiant Ones* (1958), a film whose late-fifties integrationist theme would seem to have been made to order for him. Brando went further than this, though. After publicly calling *The Wild One* "a sin," he advised the press that he was going to call it quits after making just one more movie, the musical *Pal Joey,* which was beyond the reach of censors. He'd devote himself to the Nebraska ranch and travel, he explained, and despite what he'd told Gielgud, resume his stage career.

Brando's disappointment was greater than he could acknowledge. With *Julius Caesar* he'd thought he could separate himself from "lowlife" and overcome his reputation as the "blue-jeaned slobbermouth." His stint as a classical actor had been designed to quash the insecurity that swept over him every time he wasn't sure he was spelling a word correctly, or found himself in a roomful of educated, "cultured" strangers. In defending himself he'd already lied that he'd been to college, sadly enough telling the *Los Angeles Times* about his desire "to take art, dramatic literature, music, things like that at the New School [because] I didn't take advantage of it when my father was sending me to college," then adding, "I was there physically but not mentally." But, among others, *Time* magazine was still dubbing him a hooligan— "an actor whose sullen face, slurred accents and dream-drugged eyes have made him a supreme portrayer of morose juvenility."

Psychoanalysis had shown him the undercurrent of violence beneath his own defiant nature. He had fought it, thwarting his darker rages by insisting on "loyalty" and "truth" and "sensitivity" to friends, but his anger still dogged him, evident in his drums, his boxing, motorcycles, and pranks. "He had a dread, an absolute fear of physical violence," Igor Tamarin observed after the actor returned east following the shooting of *Viva Zapata!* "But the more successful he became, the pressures only left him all the angrier."

Dr. Mittelmann, no genius to begin with, had lamely urged him to relax, using the Nietzschean mantra "What doesn't kill you will only make you stronger." But without the protection of Kazan or Kazan's substitute in Mankiewicz, without the mantle of good work, Brando was adrift and at loose ends once again, alienated more than ever.

WATERFRONT 10

1953-54

Arms and the Man

When *The Wild One* wrapped, Brando returned once again to New York. This wasn't merely his usual principled disgust with the West Coast, as he had told the press. The film had left him feeling so cold that he talked about "doing a Gauguin" by taking off for the South Pacific or going back to Nebraska. He told reporters, "I have a thousand head of cattle on my ranch which will bring me an income of eighty thousand a year. That will be enough. I'll enjoy life. Any acting I will do will be on the stage." Over the next few years he would announce his retirement every six months or so, more or less whenever it suited him, but now friends observed that his flight eastward was also an escape from domestic turmoil: He and Movita had been fighting more than before, and his answer was to leave her behind in Laurel Canyon.

In Manhattan, he decided to go to Europe with his friend Billy Redfield, but just before he was to sail to Le Havre, he ran into Valerie Judd in Greenwich Village and learned that she, and most of his other cronies, were now out of work and broke. He raced uptown to the MCA offices to visit Edie Van Cleve, the agent whose responsibilities regarding Marlon had been taken over by Jay Kanter. When Van Cleve returned from lunch, she found him lying on the floor of her office leafing through the *Players Guide*. She was thunderstruck when he told her he wanted to do a four-week summer-stock tour with his actor friends and share the profits. The whole idea was to raise money and give his friends some badly needed work. He asked her to take care of all the arrangements, but she refused. "I knew that when word got around that Marlon Brando was going to play the summer circuit, there would be hundreds of offers, and to sift them down to four engagements would take time and tact. To make things more difficult, he was very particular about where he played—he only wanted to appear on a certain part of the eastern seaboard, the Connecticut–Long Island–Cape Cod area. When I promised him I'd find a producer/business manager who'd work for love and just a little money, he agreed." She advised him to see Morton Gottlieb, a casual friend since *Truckline Café* who was now working as a press agent.

"We'd been talking about it," Gottlieb recalled, "just gossiping, and they had already been thinking of doing a Molnár play which wouldn't work. Marlon was also talking about doing a political *Hamlet*. But I suggested *Arms and the Man*."

Gottlieb soon arranged bookings in Massachusetts, Rhode Island, and Connecticut. The George Bernard Shaw play was to start the first week in July. The ever useful Sam Gilman was to be part of the company, along with Philip Rhodes, Carlo Fiore, and Janice Mars, while Valerie Judd was assigned to do costumes. For the all-important parts of Catherine and Raina, Gottlieb turned to "outsiders" Nydia Westman, the well-known actress from film, TV, and radio, and Anne Kimbell. Although Redfield had been prepared to take a leave of absence from his lucrative role on a network TV soap to gallivant around France, he was less enthusiastic about abandoning his job for the small rewards of summer stock. Marlon soon convinced him with an offer of $1,500 a week. According to Gottlieb, the others were to be paid $750 to $1,000, while Marlon himself was going to receive $125.

True to his desire to make the production a showcase for his friends, Marlon elected to play Sergius, the less impressive of the play's two male leads; he gave Bluntschli, the better part, to Redfield, much as Olivier had chosen to do Sergius, with Ralph Richardson doing Bluntschli, in a recent production at London's Old Vic.

"The obvious thing would have been for Marlon to play the more romantic part," Gottlieb recalled, "but he pulled the switch because it was a challenge. If Olivier had been challenged by doing Sergius, why shouldn't

he be challenged? If he's going to do a summer tour with the hope of coming to New York, then his thought was, Well, I might as well try something different and take the audience by surprise."

The plan of "coming to New York," while not at the top of the
agenda, had also been discussed. According to Gottlieb, the idea was
Brando's—namely, that the summer tour would serve as a warm-up for
bringing the show to Broadway, and with the expectation that Harold
Clurman would direct it. Furthermore, if it worked, Marlon would then
make his segue to *Hamlet.*

The tour of *Arms and the Man* opened on July 6, 1953, at the Theatre-
by-the-Sea in Matunuck, Rhode Island. From there the show moved on to
three additional one-week engagements at Falmouth, on Cape Cod; Ivory-
ton, Connecticut; and Framingham, Massachusetts, just outside Boston.
Throughout the run, advance stories in local newspapers were unremit-
ting, and ticket sales were strong enough to guarantee an additional four
weeks. Brando, however, seemed to have lost interest. One night he could
be at the top of his form, but the rest of the time he coasted and Redfield
was bothered by his friend's disinterest.

"Billy was upset because Marlon hadn't learned his lines," said Ellen
Adler. "In fact he told him, 'I'm disappointed in your attitude toward the
theater.' Marlon had a very long monologue in which he was supposed to
deliver the entire point of the play, but he never remembered the lines. So
he just walked to the footlights and delivered a speech that was complete
gibberish, total nonsense. Nevertheless, the audience stood up and shouted,
'Bravo!' Marlon had that ability to stir the audience—like listening to parade music, you forget what war you're for."

But sometimes not even his charisma could disguise his total lack of
preparation from more sophisticated members of the audience. A group of
vacationing Bostonians accosted Redfield in Falmouth and complained,
"Does he think we're deaf and dumb? A bunch of yokels?" When Redfield relayed the criticism, Marlon only laughed. "Man, don't you get it?
This is summer stock!" The apparatchiks were equally casual: Carlo Fiore
spent the time sort of gofering, while Sam struck onlookers as using the
tour to position himself "right at [Brando's] behind, where you would expect him." Marlon was also making magisterial demands on Valerie Judd,
the costume designer—so much so that she would be forced to leave the
company only days before the end of the run.

Day to day, Billy Redfield continued to complain about Marlon's casualness, hoping to juice the company's performance. Marlon's only response was to nail his costar's shoes to the floor backstage just before he was due to go on one night. The real problem, though, was not the two friends' rivalry. Without the guiding hand of a director whom he could trust, Brando could not take the play, or himself, seriously. During one of the performances in Framingham, he climbed up into the rafters above the stage and, visible to the audience, unreeled a fishing line that he bobbed up and down to distract the actors who were in the midst of a scene below.

"I don't want to work, I want to fuck around. . . . I want to leer, wear a mustache, make asides to the audience, like Groucho Marx," he told Carlo.

Since the actors were playing to packed houses, Brando could tell himself that his behavior wasn't alienating audiences. In fact, it was. His attempt at comedy was embarrassing, his timing conspicuously off as he played emotions too broadly. Even though countless friends knew that he could be one of the world's funniest storytellers offstage, his fundamental laziness stood in the way of any emotional shading or subtlety in his role, and resulted in something closer to slapstick than Shaw. The most devastating review came from the *Boston Post*'s Elliott Norton. Norton, who came to Framingham at the beginning of the tour's final week, blasted Brando in a way that he'd never been blasted before, claiming that for a first-rate actor his rendition was "completely ridiculous":

> Marlon Brando, who distinguished himself by his brilliant, brutal performance as Stanley Kowalski in the original production of *A Streetcar Named Desire,* opened here tonight at the Summer Theater in Shaw's *Arms and the Man* and made a fool of himself.
>
> In recent years, no major star, no actor with anything like Brando's reputation has ever given such a completely ridiculous performance. . . .
>
> The part of Sergius is open to fooling. . . . What Marlon Brando does is to burlesque him beyond all resemblance to any human being living or dead—unless it would be one of the Ritz brothers. . . . He strides and struts and overdoes it, suggesting not a man of abnormal vanity—but a ham actor who just doesn't know how to play comedy.

Initially, Marlon had needed the support of trusted intimates to embark on the tour in the first place, but now he announced to his friends as well as Summer Theater owner Lee Falk that he was never going to play the stage again. Even if he'd made a shambles of the production, he was resentful that anyone had dared call him on it.

He was "furious, very, very affected" by the critics, said Falk, who saw that Brando's usual mask of appearing cool fooled no one in the company. Word had gotten back to New York as well. Sid Armus heard that the show was "a laughingstock," "a bomb," and "a disaster." During the final week, consolations from Sam and Carlo didn't help; neither one was able to tell Marlon the truth and probably wouldn't have anyhow, even if such frankness had been permitted.

"I guess I was part of it," Judd acknowledged ruefully. "But I have the feeling that if the show had gone over, he actually might have returned to the theater. He didn't like to be treated badly, though, and he wasn't used to it, since up to then he had been treated miraculously well."

With the end of the play's run in early August, Marlon and Redfield sailed for France—though not before Marlon lost his passport, or, as he insisted, it was stolen. They were expected to remain abroad for two months, maybe longer. Although Zanuck's option hung over his head from *Viva Zapata!* he had no immediate plans and preferred to coast, hanging out in Paris with his friend Christian Marquand. Having turned down a number of projects, he was approached about a new film Elia Kazan was preparing. But he remained sulking in his tent. His antics and withdrawal had left him reluctant to take on anything new. In his inimitable fashion, he almost scuttled the movie that arguably would become the pinnacle of his film career.

On the Waterfront

Despite the inclusion of *On the Waterfront* on virtually every critic's all-time "ten best" list, the production was star-crossed from the beginning. What happened to Brando during the filming and what he achieved in his performance gave new meaning to the Freudian chestnut "Art is a correction of neurosis."

The project had originated in the summer of 1949, when novelist Budd Schulberg was commissioned to write a script about longshoremen and union corruption, based on Malcolm Johnson's Pulitzer Prize–winning news series "Crime on the Waterfront." By 1951, however, Monticello Films, the small, independent company for which Schulberg had been working, was left without backers when the project was deemed too controversial. Unable to let go of the project, Schulberg purchased the rights to his script, as well as its source material, with the intention of developing it further.

At the same time, Elia Kazan and Arthur Miller had been developing *The Hook,* another waterfront story, for Columbia until Miller backed out. The controversy with the Miller script was the same as with the Schulberg screenplay—the studios were afraid of the labor angle but, even more, saw the story as "downbeat and grim." Additionally, after Kazan had named names before HUAC, Miller had stopped talking to him, putting *The Hook* into permanent limbo. Then, in the winter of 1952, Schulberg received a letter from Kazan proposing lunch.

To this day, Kazan, who has been extraordinarily voluble on any number of subjects, has never fully explained why he made the journey to Schulberg's Pennsylvania farm. The two talked late into that first night, and the conversation turned inevitably toward collaboration. Kazan explained what had happened with Columbia's Harry Cohn and *The Hook;* Schulberg countered by hauling out his screenplay, which soon struck the director as "strong, true stuff." For Kazan, the outline story of a waterfront informer was his own story. If in later years critics would excoriate him for having a political agenda, he would also be man enough to acknowledge that the prospect satisfied a desire for revenge: "When critics say that I put . . . my feelings on the screen to justify informing, they are right." Schulberg's commitment wasn't quite so embattled; although he, too, had been a "friendly" witness in Washington, as someone who lived in the country and who was not a man of the theater, he had managed to stay further from the fray. His passion was no less than his colleague's, however, and over the next few months he practically lived on the Hoboken waterfront. Haunting the stevedores' bars, he befriended the dockers and their families and won the trust of local insurgents like Anthony "Tony" De Vincinzo, a former hiring boss. De Vincinzo had stood up to corrupt union officials, testified before the State Crime Commission, and managed to survive. There was Father John Corridan, too, Hoboken's local waterfront priest, and here Schulberg found a sponsor.

"Father John's effect on me was nothing less than to revolutionize my attitude toward the church," he wrote later. "In Father John, a tall, fast-talking, chain-smoking, hardheaded, sometimes profane Kerryman, I found the antidote to the stereotyped Barry Fitzgerald–Bing Crosby *'fah-ther'* so dear to Hollywood hearts."

The New York–New Jersey waterfront, Schulberg discovered, was a self-contained city-state: 750 miles of shoreline, 1,800 piers handling 10,000 oceangoing ships a year, carrying over 35 million tons of cargo with a value of more than $8 billion. The Mob, made up of the Irish and Italian Mafias, controlled it like a private fiefdom, exacting tribute from at least 10 percent of all cargo moving into and out of the harbor. For the 25,000 longshoremen whose livelihoods depended on a baling hook, kickbacks were a way of life.

Even more than Father John himself, the key to Schulberg's acceptance in the waterfront milieu would be one of the priest's most devoted disciples, Arthur "Brownie" Brown. Thugs had once beaten the short, pug-nosed docker senseless before dumping him into the icy Hudson River, leaving him for dead. With his cocky laugh and hearty "dems" and "dose," Brownie gave Schulberg cover by putting out the story that the two had met at Stillman's Gym in Manhattan. For weeks the writer lived with the "sawed-off Lazarus" and his wife in their cold-water flat, scribbling away on their kitchen table. "I wrote down lines I could never make up," he later acknowledged. " 'Ya know what we gotta get rid of—the highocracy! Wait'll I see that bum again—I'll top him off lovely.' And for revenge: 'I'll take it out of their skulls!' "

Schulberg was also growing closer to Kazan. "We became brothers," Kazan later wrote as he looked back on his period of intense collaboration with Schulberg. By May the screenplay was finished and they had a handshake deal with Spyros Skouras, president of Twentieth Century–Fox. Darryl Zanuck then summoned them to a meeting, and as they headed west aboard the Super Chief, Kazan insisted that things had gone too far for their discussion to be about anything besides casting and other production details. Fortified with martinis, he invoked comparisons to *Death of a*

Salesman and *Streetcar*, calling Schulberg's script one of the three best he had ever had to work with.

After the train pulled into downtown Los Angeles, Schulberg noticed there was no studio limo waiting, and his euphoria started to fade. His mood went even flatter when there were no flowers in the suite Fox had booked for them at the Beverly Hills Hotel.

"We're in trouble," said the son of B. P. Schulberg, wise to the ways of his hometown.

"F'christsake, stop worrying. We've got a gutty script. Darryl has guts. He's got to love it."

"I think he hates it."

"Budd, we just got here," Kazan continued. "Give the man a break. He's running a big studio. Wait 'til he sees us."

After an anxious weekend, they called Zanuck's office early Monday morning and were told that the studio head's secretary would get back to them as soon as she could arrange an appointment. "Let's not jump to conclusions," said Kazan, starting to pace their pastel-and-avocado-colored quarters. By midafternoon the call came, but once they arrived at Fox's executive building, they were kept waiting while the producer finished his "conference" with the young actress Bella Darvi (widely rumored to be not just the studio's latest European import but Zanuck's mistress).

When Zanuck finally met with them, he spent the first ten minutes exulting in the invention of Cinerama. This seemed decidedly off the subject, since Kazan had already said that his film was to be in black-and-white. Finally the director asked point blank if Zanuck had read their script.

"Well . . . I read it and boys," he replied. "I'm sorry, but I didn't like a single thing about it."

"You gotta be kidding!" Kazan gasped. "It's unique—something different—it catches the whole spirit of the harbor—the way you caught the Okies in *Grapes*."

"But the Okies came across like American pioneers. Who's going to care about a lot of sweaty longshoremen? . . . What you've written is exactly what the American people don't want to see!"

As Schulberg started for the door, Zanuck wheeled on Kazan. "I blame you for this," he hissed. "Bringing this project in after that goddamn *Zapata!* What the hell's wrong with you?"

Kazan stormed out of the producer's "throne room" to catch up with his partner, who was beside himself with rage. Ever the optimist, he counseled, "Don't worry, Budd. Screw Darryl. I'm still very hot in this town. Every studio in town wants me to do a picture for them."

By the following day, Warner Bros., Paramount, and MGM had all taken a pass, and even Columbia's Harry Cohn, their last resort, messengered the script back. Later that afternoon the *Hollywood Reporter* announced that the project had been rejected by all the majors, and Kazan began wondering if they could take it back to New York and do it as a play. Schulberg wanted only to return to his Bucks County farm and turn it into a novel.

With talk between them now strained, the two men started hitting the bottle more out of boredom than desire. By evening, there was nothing else to do. Instead, they found themselves vying for the attentions of Nicki, Brando's fling from *The Men* and *Streetcar* days, whom they had taxied over to the hotel from the William Morris Agency where she was employed as a typist. The next morning, however, they again set to work on the script. Each of them took turns at the typewriter they had swiped from their office at Fox—tightening, sharpening, and rewriting scenes. "The floor was littered with paper balls of discarded pages," said Schulberg. "Romantics might describe the atmosphere as inspired. Realists would call it manic."

As luck would have it, across the hall there was another gathering—a loud, boozy party that had spilled out into the corridor from the suite of producer Sam Spiegel. With Schulberg and Kazan still banging away at the old Underwood, Spiegel, dressed in an elegant blue blazer and smelling of expensive *eau de toilette,* appeared in their open doorway. He took one look at the disaster and asked the men to join the fun. Champagne and starlets with high cheekbones were in the offing, he promised. Schulberg and Kazan each grabbed him by the arm and poured out their "horror story." Then the rotund, cigar-smoking producer told Schulberg to come by first thing in the morning for "a little chat" before the writer left for the airport as planned.

Spiegel was a master of high risk and chutzpah. As a young man, he had fled Berlin in advance of the Nazis, leaving a trail of bounced checks from Vienna to London. Once he was established in America, beautiful women were constantly at his side, whether at Chasen's, Romanoff's or

"21," and his clothes were nothing but the finest, even when he'd been broke. In Hollywood he once feted a thousand guests at Lucy's, one of the swankiest spots in town, but didn't bother paying his bill until three years later. He had dodged the IRS and mortgaged his house to finance *The African Queen,* and so outrageous were his hustles that he inspired the creation of a new verb; to be *Spiegeled* meant to be soothed, cajoled, or conned.

On the dot of seven the next morning, Schulberg walked through the party debris in the living room to the bedroom, where Spiegel, otherwise known as S. P. Eagle, "lay inert in the splendid bed, as if in state," as he recalled.

"I didn't have much time before catching my plane, so I began . . . haltingly, as it's not easy to talk to a cave of silence. But the muscle of the story began to stir me . . . as I followed Terry Malloy through his waterfront ordeal." When the novelist finished his pitch, there was no response for several long minutes. "Then there was a slight stirring under the blanket. The head managed to raise up a few inches. 'I'll do it,' a murmur rose from the pillow. 'We'll make the picture.' "

Spiegel put together a low-budget financing deal with United Artists on a trip to New York. He also set his sights on Brando. In Los Angeles, Kazan had pointed out that there might be a problem because of Brando's anger about the director's testimony in Washington. But with characteristic brio, the producer had swept this aside: Brando's name on the marquee guaranteed ticket sales, not to say a potentially bigger production budget than the $500,000 guaranteed by UA. Even as Spiegel promised the lead to Frank Sinatra, he pursued Brando relentlessly.

By the time the United Artists financing was in place, Marlon had already sent the script back twice. After the first rejection Schulberg had insisted they send it to him again—only now with tiny slips of paper tucked in between the pages, a trick he claims to have learned in his OSS days. It was returned with the telltale markers still in place, and Kazan quickly approved Sinatra. The singer had recently finished shooting *From Here to Eternity,* in a role that would revive his career, and wanted the Terry Malloy part desperately. As far as Kazan was concerned, "Frank had grown up in Hoboken, spoke perfect Hobokenese, and he'd be simple to work with."

Reenter Spiegel. At three o'clock one morning, the producer found himself at the Stage Delicatessen on New York's Seventh Avenue when Marlon wandered in off the street. Actually the two had already talked several times ("There were these secret dinners," said Schulberg, "where Spiegel specifically didn't want me or Gadg around"), but now, as the producer brought Brando up-to-date, he made his pitch even more pointedly. "Professional is one thing," he argued, "politics is another. Separate them." After twenty minutes he rose and got Kazan on the phone, telling him to come to the deli to make peace.

With Kazan's arrival, Marlon listened, saying little as his mentor reminded him how he had fought to get him the Kowalski role in *A Streetcar Named Desire* when Irene Selznick wanted Garfield. He pointed out, too, that *Waterfront* was an important film, and he added that Schulberg's script, if he would only read it, was "the perfect vehicle" for him. Marlon, poker-faced, agreed to think about it.

For the past week Jay Kanter had also been trying to persuade Brando to do the film. Yet when he finally corralled his client to discuss terms during the last week of October, Marlon was intractable. Kazan was to get 25 percent of the picture's profits, Schulberg 10 percent, and if the project worked, Kanter explained, a similar percentage deal for the actor would be worth considerably more than what they could expect in fixed salary. It was a low-budget picture, he pointed out, so why not compromise? Marlon was adamant, though: What he would settle for was $125,000 in cash, all of it in advance—"no promises, no dickering around with Spiegel." He would agree to do the film, he explained, for one reason. He needed the wherewithal to pay for his four sessions a week with Mittelmann.

It was a business move that he had learned from his father: suspicious, stubborn, a basic take-it-or-leave-it ultimatum. But as usual, Kanter was right. By the end of its sixth month in release, *Waterfront* would gross $4.2 million—Marlon, it turned out, had "really screwed himself." But no matter. Even as the contract was being drawn up, he had another demand: With the film set to be shot in Hoboken, he wanted his afternoons free after four o'clock. When the schedule called for evening work, he would come back out and make himself available, but otherwise his psychoanalysis had to come first.

It was unorthodox, even by Hollywood standards, but Spiegel and Kazan both gave in.

Sinatra, meanwhile, had gotten wind that he was being passed over. He complained bitterly to his agent, Abe Lastfogel, the head of William

Morris, who advised him against a lawsuit. "Do you want the world to know that Hollywood doesn't want you?" As a "softener," Spiegel offered him the supporting role of the priest, Father Barry, which only exacerbated things when Kazan refused to dump Karl Malden, whom he had already cast in the part. Sinatra eventually sued Spiegel for $500,000, but his anger also spilled over to Brando, whom he publicly began calling "Mumbles" and "the most overrated actor in the world."

(Another disappointed party was Paul Newman. Early in the casting process, Kazan, stung more deeply by Marlon's rejection than he would admit, had tested and offered the lead to the newcomer. Newman, another Actors Studio performer, had not yet had a film role, but only recently, in February 1953, he had opened on Broadway in Josh Logan's production of *Picnic*. Once Kanter prevailed, Newman was out.)

With Brando signed, Spiegel forged ahead, jettisoning United Artists to cut a deal with Columbia, which had already turned the picture down twice. Harry Cohn still did not like the project, the contract, or the fact that the film was being made outside the studio. But "Spiegel the Eagle" got his way: The budget shot from $500,000 to $880,000, and the producer snared 50 percent of the profits for himself as well as control over all ancillary rights. "He fought like a tiger for every dime due to him," said Columbia executive Leo Jaffe. The deal was to make Spiegel a very rich man indeed.

The production schedule called for a thirty-five-day shoot, and even with the increased budget, Kazan knew it was going to be exceedingly tight. To compound matters, Spiegel insisted on rewrites. Day after day in his suite at the St. Regis Hotel, where Kazan and Schulberg were holed up, he would command them to revise the script once again, even though they were convinced that they were ready to shoot. One weekend Schulberg's wife was awakened at three in the morning to find her visiting husband shaving and getting dressed. Where was he going? "Into New York." Why? "To kill Sam Spiegel." Spiegel, though, continued to demand more work from the writer. What the story needed was more tension, more movement, more tightening, and as he pointed out, once they were in Hoboken there would be no time for rewrites.

On several occasions Schulberg blew up, screaming that he was quitting. Kazan, treading a more politic line, would remind him they were coming to bat with two outs at the bottom of the ninth. "Let's face it, Sam Spiegel has saved our ass."

Like everything else connected with the production, the cast was decidedly "New York," Kazan having turned to his private talent pool at the Actors Studio. Not only was Malden to play the rebel priest modeled on Father John Corridan, the director also brought in Rod Steiger for Charley, Brando's mobbed-up brother. Lee J. Cobb, Rudy Bond, Martin Balsam, Anne Hegira, and at the last minute, Eva Marie Saint, were also cast. Leif Erickson, playing the head investigator for the Waterfront Commission, had been with the Group Theatre. The crew was also from the East Coast, consisting of cinematographer Boris Kaufman, assistant director Charlie Maguire, costume designer Anna Hill Johnstone, and production manager George Justin. Leonard Bernstein, long a part of the Adler *mishpocheh,* would later be hired to do the musical score.

Cobb, as the corrupt union boss Johnny Friendly, may not have been chosen simply for his talents, but also because he, like Kazan and Schulberg, had named names while under the shadow of HUAC's blacklist. Brando was thus faced not with one but *three* "collaborators," even though he apparently had registered no complaint by the time the cast gathered for rehearsals at the Actors Studio in early November 1953. On the surface it had "all been settled," said Malden. "Kazan had aired everything out, I think. The week before, Marlon had come up to Gadg's office in the ANTA building. They closed the door so you couldn't hear, but I know they talked."

Sam Shaw remembered the situation differently. In the evenings Brando "didn't want to talk about Gadg; it was too painful. He was still his father and he was wrestling with it, and basically I think what was going on was that he just wanted to do the picture."

The same thoroughness for background research that Brando had always practiced came to the fore with the film's boxers. Even though Brando had palled around with Rocky Graziano during *Streetcar*, he had never played a prizefighter before except in an unaired television drama, and pros like "Two-Ton" Tony Galento had been hired to lend the film verisimilitude. Roger Donoghue, a recently retired light heavyweight, was hired as Brando's private tutor. Unlike the other boxers Donoghue was articulate and blessed with more than the usual pug's Runyonesque gift for gab. At Stillman's Gym, at the Actors Studio, and atop Hoboken rooftops he and Marlon practiced combinations, jabs, and hooks as much for fun as anything. Almost immediately, Donoghue picked up on the actor's concentration, his attention to the smallest detail: "Sometimes he'd say, 'Roger, you didn't do it that way before,' " the boxer recalled. "Whenever I'd vary my footwork, he noticed it right away. He enjoyed throwing combinations, and I showed him how to move his left ankle before dragging his right foot so he'd always be on-balance. He was terrific, but I realized he was always studying me."

Another source for Marlon's conceptualization of Terry Malloy was Al Lettieri, a hulking street kid from the Village and a friend of Carlo Fiore who eventually developed into a competent enough character actor to play Sollozzo to Brando's Don Corleone in *The Godfather*. Lettieri would later die of alcoholism at forty-eight, but now his current vice was heroin.

"Al was often brought around with some sort of Mafioso nursemaid, a bodyguard," said Marilyn Sorel, a Village regular at the time. "Carlo and Al had grown up together, and that was the connection to Marlon. Even though Marlon was violently opposed to dope, he was fascinated because Al was the 'real thing.' It was through Al that he got a lot of the 'I could've been a contender' scene. It was sort of based on Al's brother-in-law, a Mafioso, who had put a gun to Al's head, saying, 'You've gotta get off smack. When you're on dope you talk too much, and we're going to have to kill you.' For Marlon the story was like street literature, something to absorb."

Principal photography began on November 17, with the windchill along Hoboken's waterfront well below zero. Kazan assembled his crew and was ready to roll, but Spiegel, swathed in a vicuña overcoat, was grandstanding like a Medici prince. Flanked by Hoboken's mayor and police chief, eager to get into the papers, he was commemorating the start of the film for the benefit of news photographers and reporters.

During the first days the waterfront locals stood around watching. Nobody had shown the script to any of them, the "tough gorillas" who, it turned out, soon became stagestruck. Here and there a docker might be playing with his baling hook, and it was common knowledge that the union "bigs" had planted henchmen to keep an eye on the filming. Kazan had been assigned a bodyguard (the brother of the local police chief), but even though the filmmakers sensed that they were in enemy territory, the danger was more illusory than real.

The cold was something else, though. Using wood scraps foraged off the piers, the crew built fires in metal barrels that glowed cherry-red. And while it was a little easier for the actors, who could retreat to the nearby Grand Hotel during setups, they were often called outside for rehearsals, leaving them exposed to the wind for a half hour or more. In some scenes their breath showed as they spoke, just as the cold brought tears to their eyes. Marlon joked that it was "too cold to overact," later commenting that it was physically "the worst" picture he'd done. Even though he had picked up a heavy, knee-length greatcoat, from time to time he had to be dragged outside. Malden, hatless in his cleric's collar, stoically endured, but Eva Marie Saint resorted to thermal underwear.

Intelligent and college-educated, Saint had already appeared in a number of plays and television dramas. Still, by the end of the first week, she was thoroughly intimidated. "All those people looking at me—the technicians, the crew, the people behind the camera," she recalled. "I realized that this was *a movie.* In my first scene, I was there with Marlon on the rooftop and we were supposed to kiss. Kazan was talking to me as he always talks with his actors, very quietly, telling me, 'Now you're terrified, Eva. You're a Catholic girl, you're not used to seeing men at night.' I was thinking to myself, Gadg, you don't have to tell me a thing about being frightened. I'm so petrified I'm about to run out of here."

The shy and nervous actress had heard "some disquieting things" about Brando, but the audition, a last-minute affair only days before the company was to go to Hoboken, effectively put her doubts to rest. "Gadg gave me a set of circumstances without telling me what he was telling Marlon, and he didn't tell Marlon what he told me," she recalled, pointing to the director's standard bag of tricks. "He explained that I was a very shy girl and that my sister's boyfriend was coming, that my sister wasn't home, so my action was to get rid of this young man. Marlon came in and I tried to tell him to leave, and that's when the sparks started to fly.

"He was very seductive, and I remember ending up dancing with him. In those days we wore full skirts and leather belts, and I remember he took my skirt and went *whoosh,* like spinning me around in order to fan it out after the dance. The hem of the skirt just kind of whipped around. I remember crying, because it was very emotional. Whatever Kazan saw that convinced him to cast me, Marlon had provoked it in me. I would have had to work for weeks with another actor to get what we got, because like Kazan, he knew how to touch certain buttons."

The pace of the shoot was brutal. "You were never reading, writing letters, or calling your agent," Saint explained. "If we were going to do a scene in an hour, and Gadg was working with Karl or Rod Steiger, we wouldn't just sit there talking about life, we'd be going over lines. They would stop shooting and line up for close-ups, and Kazan would come over to listen to us, see what we'd done, make suggestions, and then go back to finish his scene. Rod or Karl would finish, and we'd be up."

Brando and Saint were to become inseparable. Even with his considerably greater experience, Marlon wasn't so much the teacher as a fellow voyager, "searching, exploring, as I was," she said. The two traveled on the subway out to Hoboken together every morning, and his seriousness hit a high-water mark with the "glove episode" during one of their rehearsals with Kazan in the room.

"The glove scene happened," she explained, "because I actually accidentally dropped the glove. When Marlon picked it up and put it on his hand, that became the catalyst for me to stay in the scene. Before, I'd felt awkward, dishonest, wondering why I was talking to him, thinking I ought to just walk off. Once he had the glove, I wanted it back, so there was a reason for me to stay."

His inventiveness did more than provide a rationale for Edie Doyle's lingering. Underscoring Terry's "difficulty" with words, it lent an almost inexpressible tenderness to his teasing, which in turn offered Saint the opportunity to push her character's emergence as a woman. In the bar, as she questions Terry about her brother's death, she elicited the same unspoken gentleness, something so deep, so melancholy and untutored that her openness is the only response possible. Terry's needs—not the church, or the ordinary conundrums she has been brought up with—become her deliverance. Without him, she is headed for spinsterhood, and what made it work in front of the camera was Marlon's understanding that one character's innocence could only be the reciprocal of the other's.

Brando was on a roll, working as much off Saint as she was resonating with him, and the intensity of their work together seemed to allow him "to put aside his ego. With Marlon," Saint recalled, "you felt you were the only person in the world, that you really counted. He was incredibly attractive, of course, but this was not an issue. And I admired Marlon for not making it an issue. Maybe we sensed that each of us was very private. It was as if we were safe *for* each other."

Brando "was involved, which is different from committed," said

Kazan. "But most of it was underneath." His immersion in Terry's half feminine, half "tough guy" character seemed so deep that Kazan sensed that he was "dealing with something that no matter what you did about it—whether you walked away, didn't look at it, treated it gently—it was still there, very strong and emotional."

At no time was this more apparent than with the famous taxicab scene. The morning of the scheduled shoot, things were chaotic: The original plan had been to film a real taxi in traffic, but Spiegel had vetoed this as too expensive. He promised to provide an old taxi shell and rear-projection equipment. Unfortunately, he'd made good only on the car, which forced Kazan and his assistant, Maguire, to improvise.

"Spiegel had really screwed us up, so I said we'll just use 'poor man's process,' " explained Maguire. "That's when you project a background and then put the model of the taxi up in front of it and then rephotograph the two of them to look as if the guy is actually riding in the car. But thanks to Spiegel, we also didn't have the footage to put up on the screen, so we figured, We're shooting in a studio, let's just put a little venetian blind in the back window, like the old DeSotos that had the narrow windows. They're supposed to be driving through the dark streets of Hoboken—there wouldn't be much to see, so we could fake it."

They had crew members shaking the car, and added sticks and brushes in front of the lights so that the electrician could spin them to look like the headlights of an oncoming car, playing shadows across the actors' faces.

With Boris Kaufman shooting tight, straight-on, and in close focus, it worked better than anyone anticipated. But there was the other problem of Brando's four o'clock deadline. By midafternoon most of the scene had been shot, but there were still Steiger's close-ups, which had been saved for last. The fact that the two actors had not been getting along, or that the then relatively unknown Steiger had been "throwing shit fits" for weeks, did not help. Now he was being forced to play his final lines to someone reading Brando's lines off-camera.

Steiger was screaming, 'I've had it with your kissing his ass, indulging him,' " Schulberg explained. "It looked like it was all Brando, and Steiger was lost."

Kazan felt no need to apologize, but did make a concession by stepping in to do the important, off-camera cuing himself. The problem for

Marlon, however, was more than his psychiatrist's appointment or Steiger.

The pressure had been building for weeks. Kazan had been sensitive enough to leave him alone and not to push. Still, Marlon had told Barbara Baxley, a close friend of Jocelyn who was then on Broadway in *Camino Real,* about his growing unhappiness on the set.

"He came up to my West Side apartment one night after they'd finished shooting," she said. "He was cursing Gadg—that the director would go in a warm place and wait for the scene change while the actors were out there freezing. Then he started talking about himself because he was so filled with doubt. 'It gets harder and harder,' he began, then stopped. I asked, 'What?' 'You know, getting it up. I'm scraping the bottom of the barrel.'

"What he meant was using all of yourself to have the emotions of the character. He was saying that he just wasn't picking it up anymore, having it ready and on the button. It was draining away from him, and he felt he was having to go deeper. He was talking about the kind of energy he thought he had left, and he was scared that he wasn't good enough. He kept repeating, 'I don't know how I'm going to do this.' "

He could not afford to express his doubts to either Kazan or Schulberg, and with the latter things had grown increasingly strained. For weeks Marlon had been taking liberties with the script, injecting "tiny details." "He would change the order of words," said Schulberg, "the endings especially, which would flow into the next thing. Like I had 'fellows' and he'd changed it to 'Why don't you two *girls* get lost'—this was when he was doing the scene with Marty Balsam and Leif Erickson, the waterfront investigators. That same scene, also, several things he did physically: They were questioning him, and instead of turning to face them in the most economical way, he took a slow, deliberate turn in the opposite direction, going around slowly in a complete circle, the slowest possible way he could to show his disdain."

Balsam, who was making his film debut, didn't have a clue as to what was happening, and his puzzlement reached a new high when Brando started to ad-lib. Referring to Erickson, who happened to be six feet three, Marlon quipped: "And take your girlfriend with you."

Malden had seen this kind of thing before, but when they'd shot the bar scene, Marlon again had a private agenda—even though they had already done two run-throughs.

"Marlon is seated at the bar," Malden explained. "The camera's behind him, looking at me as I'm coming in. He has the gun in his hand, and I come in and say, 'Put the gun away, kid.' 'No, I won't.' What you see in the picture is his scratching the back of his head, while I'm talking, walking closer and closer and closer. He's stealing the scene from me, but I don't mind it. He had done the same thing in the filming of *Streetcar*. He's watching Vivien and he says, 'Oh, I didn't know you were coming,' and then as he goes to the icebox, he scratches his back as he walks away. Ordinarily the camera would go to Vivien, but it's following him scratching his back. See, he knows where to scratch. That's what's good, that's what I love about him. Other people hate him for it, though, because they see it as hogging the act."

Schulberg grew increasingly anxious as they'd approached the shooting of the taxi scene. "I'd said to Kazan, 'It's one of the best scenes in the movie. I can't understand why he's dissatisfied, and I'd like to talk to him.' 'Well, you might upset him,' Gadg said. Spiegel did the same goddamn thing, always telling me not to talk to him, but finally we were up on the rooftop, not quite at the lunch break, and Brando came out with something about how he didn't like the scene, and Gadg said, 'Look, why don't we stop right now and go down and talk about it.' "

Brando later scoffed, claiming that ten minutes before climbing into the prop taxi, he hadn't known "if I was Mutt, or Jeff, or Falstaff." But downstairs in the little tenement apartment the company had rented for interior shots, Schulberg confronted him directly. "I cannot understand what it is you don't like about it. What is it? I'm proud of it."

"Well—" Marlon started awkwardly. "I just can't do it, I just can't."

"Why?" Schulberg demanded.

"I can't. The scene won't work."

"Why?"

(Pause.)

"Tell me. Why?"

"Well, if someone has a gun, if somebody actually . . . like Charley pulls a gun on me, actually has a gun, I'm not going to say all those things. I can't have all that to say, 'I could have been this or I could have been that.' I can't say all that if somebody is aiming a gun at me."

Kazan said, "Look, why don't you just reach out and put the gun down? Then could you say it?"

Marlon nodded. "Yes, then I could say it fine."

When Marlon finally went in front of the cameras for the critical scene, he stuck with the script word for word. What emerged was one of the most memorable moments in twentieth-century art.

Terry Malloy, Brando's small-time club fighter, has already unwittingly participated in the murder of one of the mobster's opponents, Edie's brother, and has been wrestling with his conscience. Under the influence of the local priest (Malden), Terry moves painfully into opposition with his own brother, Charley, the Mob's lawyer played by Steiger. Charley now finds that he cannot buy Terry's continued cooperation. Terry will eventually testify against the criminals, freeing the docks from Mob control, but now, inside the taxi, he discovers that Charley has given up even the bonds of brotherhood to betray him to the waterfront boss, Johnny Friendly, and his cohorts.

The moment is Terry's turning point, little less than an epiphany, structurally and otherwise. In the scene, Brando, his problem of interpretation solved, had never before been so fluent, so in command of his body. Inside the mock-up cab, he responded to Steiger's weapon with an ensemble of tiny movements consisting of his eyes, the roll of his head, the slope of his shoulders, and even the lift of his lip, all of it mirroring a pain and surprise more telling than the agonized "Wow" that follows.

The body language is inspired, more meaningful than words, and the occasion for an agonized pause before he launches into the unforgettable "contender" lines that subvert the gun, and the threat of Johnny Friendly, to Terry's bigger, more overwhelming crisis: "You don' understand! I coulda been a contender. I coulda had class and been somebody. Real class. Instead of a bum. Let's face it, which is what I am. It was *you*, Charley."

The phrasing was exquisite; the modulation, accent, and pacing all flawless. As any number of witnesses have recalled, he wasn't playing the scene straight into the camera, which was only a half-dozen feet away, or even to Kazan, standing at Kaufman's side. He delivered the lines as if he'd shrunk into himself. Later, with typical complexity, he would complain that the scene took seven takes, but the famous final lines themselves were so brilliant that they were done in a single shot.

The inner coherence of the performance was staggering, so free of false notes that Kazan wound up calling it "the finest thing ever done by an American film actor." For Malden, it was "genius," and almost forty years later Saint remembered watching him at work inside the taxi, setting up his own cadence in response to Steiger's choppy drawl. "I wasn't aware of the specifics of what he was doing—you couldn't be," she said, "but it was such an incredible thing, his little shake of the eyes. Maybe Olivier would work it out more intellectually, but with Marlon it was so spontaneous that if he were to do it again, I'm sure you wouldn't see him moving the same way."

The same private intensity surfaced in the scene when Terry finds his brother's body hanging from a baling hook. Overblown and heavy-handed, the sequence was one of the most wooden in Schulberg's screenplay, scripted as it was to suggest the stations of the cross. But in the grimy, paper-littered alley, Marlon gives it life, first by pausing and saying nothing. Then he throws his arm against the wall to keep from collapsing before taking the corpse into his arms in a gesture of forgiveness. After murmuring, "Charlie," and tenderly lowering the body to the ground, he rises in an animal rage to vow, "I'll take it outta their skulls."

Marlon's animation of Schulberg's script depended precisely on the opposites, the very conflicts that personally confused him. What other actor had ever melded such inner delicacy with the tough-guy trappings of a waterfront heavy? Who had ever hazarded such interiority, such self-exposure? In *Waterfront,* Brando was cutting his own path, in effect finding an antidote to anger, or at least "permission" to package his rage in a way that he had never tried before. Kazan's patience and Schulberg's script were sure ingredients, but it was mainly Saint—or, more properly, her embodiment of a midwestern decency from which he had been fleeing all his life—that was somehow making it possible.

If his cooperativeness, even earnestness was a mark of Kazan's disciplinary magic, the truth was that Marlon was also hiding, using the film as a means of dodging his demons. Psychologically, he was in worse shape than ever. Schulberg had gotten word of "some serious trouble, something with some girl"; Kazan, busy as he was, found himself wondering about the turmoil at the root of which he now suspected, more than ever before, was Brando's conflicts with his bisexuality.

No one knew what was going on, though. No one could, because the company scattered at the end of each workday and Marlon rarely, if ever, talked.

"He would never expose himself," said Kazan. "He didn't ask for my help, and even the thing about going to Mittelmann in the afternoon while we were shooting had been arranged through Spiegel, who'd been the one to tell me Marlon wanted it that way."

Across the river in Manhattan, Brando was having trouble sleeping, even with the aid of tranquilizers, and despite his 6:45 wake-up call, he could often be found on Second Avenue at one or two in the morning, head down against the wind as he tried to walk off his insomnia. There were his middle-of-the-night phone calls. His drums, too, filled the early hours of the morning, sometimes offering greater relief than any phenobarbital or Seconal. When he did socialize, his anxiety at parties was already legend. Surrounded by a roomful of people at Adolph Green's, for example, he would stand in the corner with his back to the wall, wearing the same brown corduroys he'd worn home from Hoboken. While he might engage when someone came over to chat, usually he'd leave early. There was always "too much happening, too many questions." One night at a party at Norman Mailer's loft beneath the Brooklyn Bridge, he sat apart "like a buddha" before making a pass at Mailer's wife even though he'd brought Rita Moreno as his date. He then left before the evening was half over. At Helene and David Stewart's he would "sort of look at people in silence," and on one occasion when James Dean was there, too, he retreated to the corner, opened a book, and pretended to be reading. "The only time Marlon would go up to somebody was to play them a trick," Helene said, "to see how they would react."

Early on Christmas Eve his isolation and discomfort grew so pronounced that he called his friend Judith Braun from a pay phone in a state of obvious neediness.

"It had happened before. He'd often call up and say, 'I've gotta come over, I'm alone,' " recalled Braun, who was living not far from Marlon in the Osborne on Fifty-seventh Street, a Manhattan landmark known for its artistic tenants. "That night I was going to a big theater party downstairs. When he came up, I urged him to come with me, but he didn't want me to go. I told him whose place it was, and I said, 'If you want to, just come down.' Over the next few hours he called down three or four times to ask me to come back, but I said, 'No, I'm having a good time. If you want to come down, come down.' It was a famous person's party—someone he knew, in fact—but he just didn't want to be around people. He was lonely, but at the same time he was isolating himself."

Another time, Sam Shaw ran into him during intermission at a Duke Ellington–Ella Fitzgerald concert at Carnegie Hall. "Everyone was out in the corridor," said Shaw, "and I saw him leaning against the wall. I was about to say, 'Marlon!' But he said, 'Sh-h-h,' so I stopped myself. Nobody recognized him and he'd made himself lost in the crowd, totally invisible."

For all his skill as a chameleon, concerts could be a downright nightmare. One evening he had an anxiety attack while listening to the New York Philharmonic with Blossom Plumb and ran off to the men's room, where he had to lie down on the floor. Like his beloved grandmother, Nana, he had fears of physical disaster, specifically heart trouble. As he had told John Ward in Libertyville, his anxiety over his psychoanalysis sometimes reduced him to a state of paralysis, even on the street. Sometimes he had to run for blocks to get his breathing going again.

The best known of these episodes was the time he ran to Stella Adler's and shrieked her name from the street as though reprising the famous scene from *Streetcar*. The reasons for these attacks were many, but from his sessions with Mittelmann he knew that the immediate problem was Movita. By Christmastime he'd already told Carlo that he was planning their split. Marriage, he pointed out, just wasn't his "bag."

Movita had stubbornly followed him east after *The Wild One,* and despite their friction in California, once in Manhattan she'd set to making a home in the apartment. She cooked, she cleaned, and she even put up with Russell the raccoon. For Marlon the problem was that she was becoming "too intense." He never liked to be held on to, confirmed Jocelyn. "She got very wifey, and it made him very uncomfortable." The greater her efforts, the more he complained—not only to Carlo Fiore, but to Sam Gilman and Wally Cox and even long-distance to Darren Dublin. Movita went to Carlo, too, as well as to Sondra Lee and Judy Balaban, Jay Kanter's new wife, pleading for advice. One of her lines was, "Marlon can't handle a real woman."

Inevitably, Brando turned to Mittelmann. The chubby Hungarian had already intervened in Marlon's life by getting him over the hump after agreeing to do *Waterfront*; Mittelmann had reinforced Kanter's argument that taking the part was "the right thing to do" despite Kazan's Washington testimony. So dependent had his patient become that the doctor offered to counsel Movita, too.

By orthodox Freudian standards it was unthinkable, and in some psychiatric circles even a violation of ethics, for an analyst to mediate between a patient and his spouse. Yet Mittelmann saw Movita privately, then had both of them in together.

Sondra Lee heard Marlon explain that there had been a real "transference" with Mittelmann, yet to the doctor's colleagues, what was going on seemed less like marriage counseling than the psychiatrist's usual endorsement of Marlon's needs and point of view. "Freud would turn over in his grave," said one colleague who knew Mittelmann well, "but I'm sure he would have interceded with Marlon and Movita if Marlon was dragging his tail and wanted confirmation."

During Brando's regular hour of psychoanalysis, Mittelmann delivered his verdict: Marriage was inadvisable because Marlon wasn't ready; his anger toward Dodie was still a long way from resolution, and his therapy itself, now in its sixth year, could well be endangered by so sudden an upset in his living situation.

Darren Dublin, however, thought that the strategy for dumping Movita had been Marlon's idea in the first place. "Marlon was so good at mind-fucking that Mittelmann didn't stand a chance," the old friend explained, indicating that Brando had often been able to choreograph the psychoanalyst's suggestions in the past. Another element of the transaction was that not only did Movita intimidate the analyst but, as a number of insiders realized, she was also perceived as a threat. Kazan's take on the situation was: "Psychoanalysts, I've found them to be quite jealous. Mittelmann was no exception. After all, he couldn't or wouldn't fuck Marlon, so he had to do something else."

"Movita had a kind of strength and power other than Mittelmann's," added Sondra Lee. "Nothing scared her. She'd already had a life, several lives, and if I remember correctly, there was some scuttlebutt about Marlon's having to make a choice between her and the analyst."

Marlon being Marlon, a simple good-bye didn't suffice. Movita was still redecorating, and the apartment was filled with workmen.

"They were coming in to clean, to repair, to paint, and Marlon said it was unlivable and he had to go someplace," recalled Sidney Armus, who was now living with Sondra Lee on Thirty-fourth Street. Armus said Marlon moved in with them while Movita stayed in his apartment. "What better way to get out from under a woman you're living with? He slept on our couch and I don't think he ever went back."

He then rented a sizable studio in the Carnegie Hall building and furnished it as a bohemian "pad." In the living room there were two couches, a television set for watching the fights, two opalescent marble tables, his drums, and a few books. He would occupy the place off and on for the next several years, using it as a base whenever he returned from the West Coast. Neither plants, paintings, nor curtains were ever to find their way into the apartment, and as Jocelyn recalled, the broad, open living room was often used for "football games" when Marlon, Wally, and Sam would toss around a huge hunk of industrial sponge.

Movita's response to Marlon's departure was similar to her reaction in August when the *Arms and the Man* crew had seen him and Billy Redfield off to Europe: Left behind, she had stood on the dock, waving good-bye and weeping. Among the inner circle no one was surprised by Marlon's latest defection. There had always been other women, "many women." The stream of bimbos continued. When Judith Braun dropped by to visit, she usually found him in bed. "He would tease the hell out of me because I'd be embarrassed," she said. "He would announce, 'I'm going to get up now and I'm naked.' The girl with him was always sort of like deadwood, and I don't remember any of them ever saying hello."

He was also scarfing down Mallomars by the boxful, usually accompanied by milk slugged straight out of the carton, but his sexual assignations struck some acquaintances as equally "addictive" and out of control. "I would twit him about it," said one friend, "about being a public toilet. I told him I thought he was bananas. Who'd want to get involved with somebody who fucked everything in sight? He'd laugh, though. His response was to be amused."

It was the usual collection of secretaries, salesgirls, and acting students, but his dates also included Toni Parker, a slim, dark-haired dancer at the Latin Quarter, and Rita Moreno, who was at his beck and call, always ready to fly in from the West Coast. ("Anytime big Marlon calls up, I'll go out with him," Moreno told *Photoplay* magazine in February 1956.) He was also pursuing socialite and fashion designer Anne Ford, whom he had met at Gilman's weeks before his split from Movita. After their first introduction he had phoned her late the next evening from Sam's, and when she told him she had guests and couldn't leave, he instructed her to explain that she had "a sudden need of her ear trumpet and she would have to pick it up." Ford giggled, deserted her friends, and headed straight for the Gilman apartment, where she and Brando ate hot dogs and went to bed.

He would call her in a heavy German accent, saying that he was

"Count Von Heusen." Once he said that he was a crow on his way to Florida for the winter. "I'd like to drop you a postcard," he said, "but these claws make it so difficult to hold a pen." Another time, when she was visiting the set of *Waterfront,* he appeared carrying his "football" sponge, as pleased as a child with a new toy. Ford told him it was beautiful and asked if he was planning to use it to scrub floors. "No, I shall put it under a faucet of warm water and then sit on it for hours," he replied with a grin. He sent her flowers, and wearing the same Buster Bad Ass cap he sported on-screen, he took her to see *The Wild One,* where he covered his eyes with his hands and moaned, "Oh, no! You can't look at this—it's too bad!" During a later scene, he cried, "Look at my fat ass!" explaining that he'd ballooned during the production because of his frustration with director Benedek. The courtship, however, came to an abrupt end when Ford committed the cardinal sin of talking to a writer from *Glamour* about her new boyfriend.

Despite all the other women, he still couldn't let go of Movita. Part of it was sex, as she was reputedly "extremely practical" in bed. Part of her very real hold on him was his investment in her maternal image, which made her indispensable—all the more so for her welcoming open family in Los Angeles, which had given him a sense of acceptance and comfort. Whatever the particulars, a chance encounter with her could throw him into a tailspin, such as happened one evening when he was walking with a date and spotted her, dressed in white, on the far side of Fifty-seventh Street. "I've just got to go across," his date recalled him saying, and he "just bolted."

Movita offered refuge, especially since over that summer of 1953 he had "closed a lot of doors, not only with me but Billy Redfield, too," said Valerie Judd, who was seeing less and less of him. "Marlon made it very hard to feel warm for him, because anything that he felt like doing, he did. And so he spent his time with the people who would just go along and make life easier for him."

Igor Tamarin realized this too—how Marlon's ever loyal pals, Sam Gilman, Darren Dublin, and Carlo Fiore followed him from one coast to the other, and how much he depended on their companionship. "I would have loved to go to California," Tamarin said with perhaps a touch of rationalization, since Marlon rarely saw him during the filming of *Waterfront.* "But then I just rebelled against the idea. 'Oh, no,' I told myself, 'I'm not going to traipse along after anybody.' And then, I suppose, in essence he dumped me."

The entourage worshiped Marlon as the sun god, and they were grateful for his beneficent light. For example, Sam Gilman, a fellow womanizer, was apparently on call at almost any hour and "couldn't see anything wrong if Marlon phoned . . . and told him to go pick up some chick at a dive somewhere and bring her to him." When Harold Clurman's second wife, Juleen Compton, challenged Gilman to explain why he was wasting himself, Sam told her, "You don't understand. Marlon needs me. He really needs me. I'm a lot more important to him than even *he* understands." But for Gilman and others, there were material rewards, too. In Hoboken, Sam was being paid as Brando's part-time dialogue coach, just as he would later have work on *Desirée, The Young Lions, One-Eyed Jacks,* and *The Missouri Breaks.* Carlo, "the leader of the ass-kissers," was also being taken care of, and despite his frequent absences—when he would disappear from the *Waterfront* set to score with his heroin dealer—he was pulling a paycheck as Brando's stand-in.

Brando's arguments and internal debates about whether to remain in Manhattan or to settle in L.A. were confused and futile—so long as he surrounded himself with his flunkies. Somehow convincing himself that with them he could be just "a regular guy," he failed to see that his cronies were so dependent on his success that they would never challenge or question his actions and choices.

"He was waiting for the contrast between the way his friends behaved toward him and the way Hollywood behaved," commented Valerie Judd, "and he expected his old friends in New York to be different. He thought he wanted our straightforward behavior, but being a basically self-indulgent person, it was actually easier for him out in Hollywood. Besides, we were no longer treating him the way we used to treat him so much as imitating the way Hollywood treated him—only we didn't do it as well."

Fred Sadoff saw how relentless Marlon's need for his cronies' trust could be, even when he used it for his prankish manipulations. Weeks before the start of *Waterfront,* the gullible Sadoff had been awakened by a phone call at six in the morning. The caller identified himself as a friend of Marlon.

"I'm producing a documentary in Washington and Marlon was supposed to play the lead. He can't do it, and he says there's only one actor in New York who can do it and that's you. It's an emergency, we're in the middle of filming. Are you available?"

"Yes, yes," Sadoff replied. "When do you want me?"

"Now."

"Okay. What do I—"

"Go to Grand Central—I'll pay you when you get here. Come as soon as you can."

Sadoff packed and immediately set off for the station. "I didn't even know how many days' work it was. It was a job. It was a lead. The caller had said, 'It's a wonderful part.' Who cared what the film was about? It could have been *Deep Throat,* because in those days, hell, it was work."

Halfway to Grand Central, however, he stopped himself, realized the absurdity of such a call at that hour. Marlon was up to his old tricks.

Brando, however, just played dumb when Sadoff phoned him a week later, to complain that he'd been willing to let his friend get on the train and go to Washington. To him it was just a big joke, Sadoff said, "Part of it was his competitiveness, but it also had to do with his disrespect for acting, since the thrust of the whole thing was to point out how ridiculous my own dedication was."

Just after the New Year of 1954, Dodie and Marlon Sr. visited Hoboken, the first time either one of them had seen their son on location. For the past several months they'd been in California, then come to New York before taking a holiday in Mexico. After that, they were planning to return to L.A. to stay with Dodie's half-sister and her husband, Betty and Ollie Lindemeyer. Although Brando Sr. was planning to spend his time south of the border checking out a new business opportunity (this time it was gold mines), he and Dodie were basically homeless (Franny and Dick had taken over the farmhouse in Mundelein), marking time until the weather broke and they could return to the Penny Poke Ranch in Nebraska. Like the forty-acre farm outside Libertyville and the cattle business, their perambulations were being underwritten with their son's money.

The morning of their arrival in Hoboken, it was drizzling and the film crew was shooting up on the rooftops. Carlo, always quick to do duty when he wasn't nodding out, took Brando's parents in tow immediately. With the scene finished, Marlon came down to pose for pictures with his parents as they stood beside a smiling Sam Spiegel. Then he led them to Kazan, to Maguire, to Malden, and ever so gallantly introduced them to Saint. The last time Marlon had seen his mother had been the previous October, when he'd made a trip out to the ranch to confer with Lom Doyle, the family's lawyer, about the ongoing cattle suit. Dodie now looked drawn and older, and he noticed that she was smoking more than ever, too.

To what extent her son sensed her failing health was unclear. She had been on poached chicken and a low-salt diet for the previous month; shortly before Christmas she had had a mild heart flurry—"not a heart attack"—and had already made plans to go into the hospital for a thorough checkup once back in California. Her problem was hypertension, the disease that had killed her mother, Bessie, the year before. The immediate stress, as she confided in Kay Phillips Bennett, centered on how to handle Franny and Bud—"Bud especially," Phillips Bennett recalled, pointing out that she'd been sworn to secrecy. "She felt he was on dangerous ground, like half out of control, pushed by his own intensity, his demons."

After a few days Dodie and Marlon Sr. left for Mexico. Kazan was now rushing to get all of Marlon's scenes filmed because the actor was due in Los Angeles for his next picture, *The Egyptian,* which had been slated to start on January 15. The delay was costing Fox $10,000 a day, and if *Waterfront* took much more time, Spiegel would have to pay a heavy penalty.

Overall it had been a grueling production. Because of Spiegel's prodding, Kazan finally brought the film in on budget, but as editing began, the director didn't suspect that *Waterfront* was destined to become a classic. At Columbia, all Harry Cohn wanted to know was what the picture had cost and, reportedly, he fell asleep during his first private screening.

Kazan, though, rallied after weeks of round-the-clock sessions in the editing room with cutter Gene Milford, and shouted at Spiegel, "Sam, you've finally made a good picture!" Then Kazan organized a preview for his lead actors, including Brando. In this cut, the film was down to length but clumsy and uneven, and also unscored, but it was still a fair indication of what they had. When the last reel was finished, Brando, who had been sitting directly behind Kazan, got up and left the screening room without saying a word.

Malden followed him out, and Marlon looked back at him. "What do you think?" Brando asked.

"It's a damn good movie," he replied. "What do *you* think?"

"In and out," Marlon said, and kept on walking.

" 'In and out' was a phrase we used to use," Malden later explained. "It meant, 'Sometimes I was in the part and sometimes I wasn't.' That's all he said, 'in and out.' He didn't say anything about what he knew the movie was about or that he hated it. But Marlon was too sensitive a guy *not* to know what was going on."

When *Waterfront* opened in July 1954 at New York's Astor Theatre, the lines started forming around the block in the early morning. By the end of the first week, the critics were calling the picture a masterpiece, a certifiable smash whose love scenes and "realism"—and most of all Brando's performance—promised to make it the finest film of the year:

> The sort of galvanic movie we used to get when the Warner Brothers were riding herd on Al Capone. . . . Indeed, I'd give cozy odds that no actor this year is going to match Mr. Brando's performance here.
> —*New Yorker* (July 31, 1954)

> *On the Waterfront* has the substance of full-blown cinema art . . . and by the performance of Marlon Brando, it is a brilliant and moving glimpse into the soul of a poor, enslaved pier worker. . . . A drama of one man's triumph over a bully and over the darkness in his soul.
> —Bosley Crowther, *New York Times* (August 8, 1954)

Marlon received the best reviews of his career, powerful enough to triple his price in the Hollywood bazaar. By the time *Waterfront* was nominated for twelve Academy Awards, it had grossed more than $6 million, won three of the four prizes offered by the New York Film Critics, and received the Gold Cup at the Venice Film Festival.

With Brando's best actor Oscar nomination, Kazan was taking no chances. Schulberg and Roger Donoghue, Marlon's boxing coach, were dispatched to Hollywood to keep him in line. If anyone could ruffle feathers, it was Brando, and the competition was stiff. He was up against two of Hollywood's favorite sons, Bing Crosby for *The Country Girl* and Humphrey Bogart for *The Caine Mutiny*. Kazan wanted his star to play the game this time.

"We went out there to get him to behave," Donoghue recalled, "and we set it up that he'd go to the Foreign Press Awards dinner, the Screen Writers Guild, and also the Directors Guild, where he'd accept an award for Kazan, who'd stayed back in New York. What we were trying to do was get him to keep his mouth shut, not knock the town like he'd done during *Streetcar*.

"Budd [Schulberg] had already straightened him out—'Hey, you'll be hurting a lot of people if you do anything wrong'—still, you could tell Brando wanted that Oscar, because he was making nice. Where he drew the line, though, was when a PR guy from Columbia said, 'Okay, you've been doing great, but there's one more thing you have to do and that's call Louella and Hedda.' Brando said, 'Screw that. I'm not going that far.' "

The evening of the Academy Awards—March 30, 1955—he arrived at the Pantages Theatre on Hollywood Boulevard with an entourage that included Jay Kanter, his secretary, his aunt, his father, and *Life* photographer Phil Stern, whom he had allowed to bird-dog him since early that morning. One columnist described him as "looking somewhat bewildered" when he first lost his father in the crowd, and then before the start of the ceremonies when he was stopped on his way to the bathroom by a security guard because he had left his pass at home.

The set at the Pantages was garish even by Hollywood standards—a three-dimensional painted horizon—and to speed up the TV broadcast, the organizers had eliminated any reading of the nominees before the presentation of each award. Soon after Academy president Charles Brackett introduced Bob Hope, Humphrey Bogart started the *Waterfront* sweep by presenting the Best Black-and-White Cinematography prize to Boris Kaufman. Marlon took the stage to announce that Best Director was Kazan, who appeared on the large-screen TV monitor, making his speech from the NBC Century Theatre in New York. Brando retreated backstage, where he was stopped another time by a second security guard; he had still not done anything about the missing pass, and it took an Academy official to clear up the problem.

Next, Malden, in his role as presenter, announced Schulberg as the winner of the Original Screenplay Award. Frank Sinatra gave *Waterfront* its next prize—its fourth so far—the Oscar for Best Supporting Actress. In New York, Eva Marie Saint, eight months pregnant, dissolved in laughter, gasping, "I think I may have the baby right here."

The next award was for Best Supporting Actor. Rod Steiger, Lee J. Cobb, and Karl Malden had all been nominated, but they had split the vote; the winner was Edmond O'Brien for his work in Mankiewicz's *The Barefoot Contessa*. Richard Day and Gene Milford, however, were soon honored for art direction and editing, upping *Waterfront*'s tally to six.

After the applause died down, Bette Davis arrived to give the Oscar for Best Actor. When she announced, "Marlon Brando for *On the Water-*

front," Marlon removed his chewing gum and ran toward the stage, unabashedly beaming ear to ear. "Thank you very much," he began. "Uh . . . thank you very much . . . uh . . . it's much heavier than I imagined. . . . Uh . . . I . . . uh . . . I had something to say and . . . I can't remember what I . . . uh . . . was going to say, for the life of me. I don't think that . . . uh . . . ever in my life have so many people been so directly responsible for my being so very, very glad. It's a wonderful moment and a rare one and I am certainly indebted. Thank you."

There was little surprise by the time Best Picture went to *Waterfront,* whose total of eight nods tied the record held by *Gone with the Wind* and *From Here to Eternity.*

After the show Marlon posed for pictures backstage with an adulatory Bette Davis. "I have nothing but admiration for your work," she said. "My niece will be so jealous when she finds out I kissed her favorite actor." She then told reporters, "I was thrilled Marlon Brando was the winner. He and I have a lot in common. He, too, is a perfectionist. He, too, has made many enemies."

When she was finished, Brando was taken next to a sobbing Grace Kelly, who had won for Best Actress. He fumbled for a cigarette, then crushed it underfoot when a photographer asked him to put his arm around her. Another cameraman instructed the actress to kiss him, but Kelly insisted, "I think he should kiss me." Marlon complied, kissing her not once but several times until all the photographers were satisfied. Then, so euphoric that he nearly lost his bearings, he started to buss Hedda Hopper until he recognized who she was and shook her hand instead.

While Kelly, Merle Oberon, and Bing Crosby celebrated at Romanoff's, and Jerry Lewis amused the crowd at Chasen's with Marlon Brando imitations, Marlon attended a party at Jay Kanter's home, where he sat on a couch drinking champagne out of a mug. His Oscar stood on the coffee table in front of him; he'd taken off his shoes and loosened his bow tie, and mutely nodded at the congratulations offered by the assembled guests. Instead of sending his own congratulatory telegrams or even calling cast members Malden and Saint, much less Kazan and Schulberg, he refilled his coffee cup with champagne, raised it in a silent toast to the statuette in front of him, and promptly fell asleep.

F L A I L I N G

11

Brando's next project was Darryl Zanuck's $4 million CinemaScope spectacle *The Egyptian,* based on Mika Waltari's best-selling novel and scripted by the well-known Philip Dunne. It boasted a beefcake-and-cheesecake cast of Victor Mature, Gene Tierney, and Jean Simmons, with Brando in the lead as Sinuhe, a young high-minded surgeon who gives up everything for a high-class Mesopotamian whore.

The script was a joke, even as an excuse for as crass a commercial vehicle as this one. Wearing an Egyptian tunic while padding around the Sphinx was hardly a role Brando fans had expected. Worse yet, his love interest was played by none other than Bella Darvi, Zanuck's Jewish-Polish protégée whom the production chief was determined to turn into a star. The middle-aged Zanuck, everyone knew, was besotted. The young actress was born Bella Wegler, and her marquee moniker—Darvi—was a contraction of Darryl and Virginia, the name of Zanuck's long suffering wife (Darvi had actually been living for months in the studio chief's family guest house while Hollywood snickered). And Fox's publicity machine had been told to turn up the heat for the new actress with the high cheekbones—even though her previous picture, *Hell and High Water,* had bombed. Despite the fact that Darvi was talentless, success was assured by the property itself, Zanuck insisted, the millions the studio was investing in elaborate sets and costumes, as well as the casting of Brando and Simmons.

Finding himself in the midst of this ludicrous situation, Marlon's response at the first day's rehearsal in late January was to say nothing. After meeting Michael Curtiz *(Casablanca),* the film's swaggering Hungarian director—who had never been held in high regard for his ability to communicate with actors—he was gone. That night Jay Kanter called Zanuck at home. "Marlon's left for New York," he announced.

"Why?" Zanuck asked.

"He doesn't like Mike Curtiz," he explained. "He doesn't like the role. And he can't stand Bella Darvi."

"He can't do this to me!" Zanuck yelled.

It was no bluff. As Kanter put down the phone, Brando was already en route eastward, having taken the train earlier that afternoon. Three days later, on February 2, a telegram arrived at the studio from Bela Mittelmann: Marlon, the psychoanalyst claimed in his professional role of physician, was "very sick and mentally confused" and would not be able to work for a period of at least ten weeks. Stunned, Zanuck announced a week's postponement on the film. A day later, the studio's spokesman issued the announcement that Twentieth Century–Fox, having already spent "considerable sums" on exterior photography and costumes, was forced to endure additional expenses of "$10,000 a day" because of the delay and was filing a $2 million breach-of-contract suit.

In a lengthy recital of the background of the impasse, Fox declared that Brando had not expressed any dissatisfaction with the script or his role when it had been assigned eight months before. The studio added that the actor, in a private conference with Zanuck, had explained that he had every intention of respecting his contract despite the fact that he was "under a mental strain and facing a personal crisis."

Whether or not Marlon had read the script for *The Egyptian* before entraining from Hollywood was anybody's guess, although the *New York Post* quoted one unnamed intimate as insisting, "Marlon lazied himself into a spot by failing to insist on seeing the finished product." Reviews of *The Egyptian* would later score Darvi's performance as that of "a high-priced harlot who comes off like a five-cent piece," and Edmund Purdom, Brando's eventual replacement, fared no better. Fox, however, had been sitting on its Brando option since *Zapata!,* and with its suit in federal court, the studio upped the ante by pointing out that the ten-week period referred to by Mittelmann coincided exactly with the scheduled completion date of the picture. "Brando was under treatment by the same psychiatrist during filming of *Viva Zapata!* and *Julius Caesar,*" a Fox spokesman commented, "and if he is confused now, he must have been confused then, too, but he made out very well."

Kazan was still finishing *Waterfront* when he was contacted by the press, and he confirmed that Marlon had been under considerable strain during the last days of the film's shoot. But, he added, the actor had never missed a day's work. When Marlon found he could not go on without his therapist, Kazan explained to the reporter, he had returned to New York. "Not because of big-star temperament or a desire to hurt anyone," Kazan was quick to add, "but because he really is a sick boy who needs help. . . . Blame it on the weather. He just finished working twelve to fourteen hours a day in the longest cold spell New York had in five years. He was suffering from cold fatigue. He was exhausted and [is] in no shape for *The Egyptian.*"

Through its legal department, Fox demanded Brando be examined by another psychiatrist and wanted access to his records. An offer was even made to bring Mittelmann west for the filming. With the story making front-page news across the country, Kanter was by now calling around, trying to find his client who, for all intents and purposes, had vanished. "They all wanted to know where he was," Darren Dublin recalled. "MCA was calling us like crazy: 'Haven't you heard from Marlon?' 'No, we don't know where the fuck he is.' We did, of course, and basically he'd gone underground."

Less than a week after he'd taken flight, Fox had process servers scouring Manhattan. Knowing he couldn't return to his Carnegie Hall apartment, Marlon stayed at Wally's, at Sondra Lee's and Janice Mars's, and also camped at Barbara Baxley's tiny studio in Murray Hill like some latter-day fugitive. Once he ran out of hideouts, he registered at a small hotel on the East Side under the name of Dr. Myles Gahan, his great-grandfather. So intense was the legal heat that Baxley remembered him staying at her place for only a single night before a grocer recognized the actor and he was forced to flee.

Brando had spent that evening trying to reassure his friend that he was okay. "He was both agitated and fairly calm as he explained the mess," Baxley said. "He told me that the script was just so bad that it was as if they were trying to kill him. He called it 'sick-making,' as I remember. He said that it was so hateful that he couldn't cope with any more [of their] shit.

What was apparent was that he was really in fear of being destroyed. He didn't have any other choice as far as I could see—it was like sometimes directors will make you do something that's wrong and you know it's wrong. Most people cave in. He wasn't going to, and he was agitated enough to have disappeared and gone into hiding for however long it was going to take."

By the middle of the third week in hiding, his luck had played out. A U.S. marshal who had been on his tail from the beginning caught up with him at his Carnegie Hall studio, to which he'd returned after having no other place to go. The marshal admitted that he had seen Brando in the neighborhood several times. But he had not immediately recognized the actor because Brando was dressed "like a United Nations diplomat," wearing a false mustache and striped trousers, and carrying a cane and briefcase.

All along, the MCA legal staff had been working overtime, meeting with Fox executives in an attempt to keep their client out of court. But Zanuck wasn't budging. The humiliation of Brando's contemptuous dismissal of Darvi—his star-in-the-making—would have been enough, but it was the second headline-making walkout that the mogul had had to suffer in the past year; Marilyn Monroe had disappeared from the set of *Pink Tights* to honeymoon with Joe DiMaggio, wound up in Japan, and from Zanuck's perspective, stuck it to him with every news photo of herself entertaining the troops on furlough from Korea. Now Louella Parsons had got wind of Brando's "capture," and she informed her readers that Fox was some $2 million "in the hole" since the actor first went AWOL.

The columnist's figure was a considerable exaggeration, but this suited Zanuck's purposes just fine when the studio announced that Fox would drop charges only if Brando agreed to pay half the cost for the delay; furthermore, he would fulfill his contractual obligation for two films, beginning with Fox's forthcoming production of *Desirée*, a historical romance based on the best-selling novel by Annemarie Selinko in which he would play Napoleon.

Marlon was appalled. Zanuck's fine, coupled with his cattle losses in Nebraska that were still in litigation, would be enough to wipe out his cash reserves. Yet it was *Desirée* (scheduled to start shooting in June) or a protracted lawsuit, and as the lawyers on both sides began hammering out a settlement late in February, MCA warned him to toe the line. His career was at stake, and no one in Hollywood was going to hire an actor who jeopardized multimillion-dollar productions.

If all this wasn't enough, in the midst of the negotiations Brando got word that Dodie had collapsed at Aunt Betty Lindemeyer's in Pasadena and had been rushed to Huntington Memorial Hospital. As Fran departed from Chicago, he headed west from New York immediately.

"Papa had been there all the time," Jocelyn recalled, "and when Bud arrived, we all stayed at Betty's and went to the hospital in shifts, spelling each other." Marlon Sr. and Fran made up one team, and Joce and Bud the other. This lasted for the better part of two weeks. Dodie was conscious most of the time but slipping in and out of a coma, all the while going lower. She was "handling it beautifully, very calmly," Jocelyn added.

"The feeling in that room was that life wouldn't let her go. She'd take a breath, then she'd breathe out and there'd be sort of a long pause as though this was the last one, and then she'd have to take another, as if she was saying, 'Okay, this is the last one.' We all knew that she wanted to get out, and we were willing to let her go. Bud knew, too, and we were rooting for her because at one point she had opened her eyes and said, 'I'm not scared, and you don't have to be.'"

Soon she started talking as though there were others in the room— Nana, her Evanston radio writer friend Merle Friedell, her father, people in her life who had died and were now "beckoning" her. When she finally passed away, at 5:20 A.M. on March 31, 1954, Bud was on one side of the bed and Jocelyn on the other, each holding one of her hands.

"The nurse and Bud and I all put our arms around each other and cried, just sobbing for the relief."

Back at the Lindemeyers, Marlon Sr. looked out the window but did not weep when Bud and Jocelyn gave him the news. Then the newspapers started calling, and with bulletins on the radio, a line of cars began passing up and down the street, with teenage girls running up on the porch, trying to peer through the windows. Uncle Ollie slipped out to the garage and brought the car around to the next block so that Marlon and his father and Fran could sneak off. Jocelyn and Betty contacted the crematorium.

Later that evening Marlon showed up alone at Darren Dublin's sometime around 1:30 A.M., but was about to drive away when Darren ran outside to tell him that he didn't have company. "The night my mother had died he took me to the Copacabana," Dublin explained, "and afterward, at about four in the morning, we sat on the curb as it started to snow. He was keeping me company, and now the situation was reversed. He stayed a couple of hours. He didn't say much, but he was broken up. Eventually he went back to his aunt's, but he had needed to get away and had been driving around for hours before arriving at my house."

In the days that followed, Marlon's reaction was muted, barely hinting at his turmoil and pain. Condolences poured in from friends in New York, Libertyville, and L.A. Though she was broke, Valerie Judd sent flowers and called from New York, but found him "very guarded" on the phone, with Brando deflecting her sympathy by obsessing about her unnecessary expense for the floral arrangement. Joy Thomson, from the Dramatic Workshop days, was another of those who phoned. "I told him that I was terribly sorry," she said. "I then added something like, 'When Dodie got drunk and did those marvelous things,' and he interrupted me. 'What? My mother never drank,' he insisted. My thought was, Oh, shit, he's in terrible shape, because everybody in the world knew she was an alkie."

Ann Lombard Osborne, Dodie's AA partner, had called only fifteen minutes after Marlon and Jocelyn returned from the hospital, feeling "very strange, sensing that something had happened," and when she got the news from Fran, she'd immediately asked, "How is Bud?" "Oh Ann, demolished," replied Fran. Osborne understood, having realized years before that "he worshiped her. After her death, in fact, he didn't come back here to Libertyville for nearly a year, as if he couldn't bear it."

It was no coincidence that Fox announced its final settlement the very next day after Dodie's death. Notwithstanding Jay Kanter's advice, Marlon was in no condition to go back on his offer to agree to the studio's terms. Only weeks later, he discussed his grief with Maila Nurmi, the spectral, black-clad beatnik and self-described witch who had already made a death pact with James Dean. It was the first time he had ever opened up to her. Nurmi had taken him to see her own mother.

"When we left my mother's," Nurmi recalled, "he told me that his mother had a deathbed conversation with him that was her last utterance. She had said, 'Be more sensible, think about tomorrow, and get your feet on the ground.' She made him promise—and it was very touching, because he said that endeavoring to keep the promise was going to change his life. Only, then he turned on me for taking him to my mother's. 'You didn't have to see your mother. You just brought me there because you wanted to test me.' He also refused to acknowledge that his mother had dried out, and said, 'There was a time when I had so little feeling for her that she could have dropped dead and I would have stepped over her and gone for an ice-cream cone.' "

For the next year Dodie would haunt him, so much so that she was very much with him when he won the Oscar for *Waterfront* on March 30, 1955. The award was something she had always wanted for her son, and in previous years she had despaired that his failure to "play politics" would preclude it. Thus, when he won on that evening, and others noted his muted response, he explained to columnist Sidney Skolsky that "it was just a year ago tonight that [my mother] died and I don't feel too much like celebrating." He later said the same thing to Edward R. Murrow during a "Person to Person" interview, pointing to a large oil portrait of Dodie that hung over his fireplace as he explained his regret that his mother hadn't lived to share his triumph.

Desirée

By the time Marlon Sr. and Fran scattered Dodie's ashes at the Nebraska ranch, Marlon was already shooting *Desirée*. He also had a new girlfriend, a tiny, gamine-faced nineteen-year-old named Josanne Mariani-Berenger. He had met her in February 1954 at a party given by Stella Adler. A former painter's model from the south of France, she had come to America as an *au pair* for the family of a psychiatrist who was a friend of Mittelmann, studied acting in Stella's classes, and with her huge, sad eyes, cropped hairdo, and broken English, she seemed the embodiment of innocence. In his desperate, chaotic state Marlon had glommed on at once, and when he went to California, she followed and moved in with him.

Before the start of the *Desirée* shoot, he had also made sure he was going to be surrounded by friends: Sam Gilman had been hired for the supporting role of Fouché; Darren's wife, Florence, was given the part of one of Napoleon's sisters; Philip Rhodes was brought in as Marlon's personal makeup man, although James Dean had initially asked both him and Darren to work on *East of Eden*. (Dublin had been asked to be Dean's stand-in.) "That was another of Jimmy's attempts to imitate and get close to Marlon," explained Rhodes, adding that Darren had decided to stay with Dean. Marlon had also hired Marie Rhodes as his secretary for the shoot. Perhaps Darren's defection rubbed Marlon the wrong way, but three weeks into the *Desirée* shoot, he flexed muscle with Kazan to get Darren's release from *East of Eden* so that he could join the support group.

It was supposed to be a replay of the best of times, with Marlon surrounded by those who gave him comfort and solace. Unhappily, Darren and Marlon came to an abrupt parting of ways. Their blowup took place in Marlon's trailer, the catalyst being Josanne Mariani-Berenger.

"They were already engaged, although no one knew it because Marlon hadn't told anybody," said Darren, "but apparently she'd gone to him with the story that I'd made a pass at her. I hadn't, but Marlon was furious and he wouldn't listen. . . . I don't want to say what he did. It was worse than not listening to me. I don't want it known publicly because it was too negative, too disgusting."

What Dublin was reluctant to expose, others heard about immediately: Marlon had spat in his old friend's face.

Darren then went to the assistant director and told him that he was quitting. When he asked why, Darren replied, "Because Marlon and I had an argument and maybe it's best if I leave the show."

Later in the day the assistant director returned to Dublin and informed him, "Marlon says you don't have to quit." Darren needed the money, so he stayed on for another three or four weeks.

"But Marlon and I never spoke again," he explained. "Sam, Phil, Marie, no one interceded. Flo continued talking to him, too, but she had to because she had a supporting part. I was very hurt, even though I had seen that Marlon had been changing. They forced him into doing the film and he was bitter."

Later that evening Marlon insisted that it was Darren who had done the spitting. He also complained that Darren had been using him, cadging money on the basis of their friendship. Rhodes perceived that in his vulnerable emotional state Marlon may have felt wounded by Darren's cynical and iconoclastic barbs when they hit too close to home; on the other hand, for years Darren "had been the only one who could get Marlon to laugh," Rhodes said. And, of course Brando was hardly the one to cast the first stone in charging someone with infidelity or making a pass at another man's woman.

Despite what may have been his promise to his dying mother,

Brando's performance on the Fox lot during *Désiree* was calculatedly eccentric. The director was Henry Koster, a genial studio hack whose last project for Zanuck had been *The Robe.* Koster was no Kazan, Mankiewicz, or Zinnemann—or even a Laslo Benedek—and if the director fancied himself something of an amateur Napoleon scholar, Marlon's first act of independence had been to declare himself the expert instead.

He claimed that to prepare for his role, he had read numerous biographies of the French leader. Within the first week he also made it clear he wasn't going to take direction, and when Koster would ask him to take his position, Brando would reply, "Do you really want me to stand over there? I think we should do it over *here.*"

"Yes, Mr. Brando, there."

"Well, what about over here?"

Flummoxed, the director soon abandoned any pretense of authority and began submitting questions: "What do you think? Would this be all right? Are you angry, Marlon? Have I done something?"

Brando believed that Koster didn't understand the script, demanded producer Julian Blaustein's intervention, and increasingly dominated the shaken director with a variety of ploys. Careless in learning his lines, he rarely bothered to rehearse, and on the afternoon of the scene in which Napoleon crowns himself, he started a water pistol fight in front of the film's hundreds of extras. It soon escalated to the point where he was spraying people with one of the studio's fire hoses. At another juncture, Koster found him sitting beside a prop fountain in a pose reminiscent of Rodin's *The Thinker,* refusing to take his position in front of the cameras. Koster pleaded with him, asking what was wrong. Marlon remained silent, and the director, already pushed to the limit, reportedly sank to his knees, begging, "Please, Marlon, please." Finally, in a barely audible whisper, Marlon murmured, "I wish this fountain was full of chocolate ice-cream soda." "Chocolate ice-cream soda?" the distraught Koster asked. "Yeah, yeah, chocolate ice-cream soda!" Marlon exclaimed. "Because I like chocolate ice-cream sodas!"

There was something even more galling for Brando than Koster's ineptitude: Across town, at Warners, Kazan was still working with James Dean on *East of Eden,* and word was already out that Dean was terrific, Hollywood's next big star. Marlon couldn't resist going to see for himself. He arrived on the *Eden* set, posed for publicity pictures with Gadg, Julie Harris, and Dean, but pretended that Dean didn't exist. Later with the film's release all he had to say was, "Mr. Dean appears to be wearing my last year's wardrobe and using my last year's talent."

"It was like Apollo driving the sun chariot," said one of the extras at Warners. "He looks over his shoulder and there's another sun coming up over the horizon. Here Brando was trapped in a very bad picture and Jimmy's working with his best director."

Marlon's competitiveness, though, had been building for some time. In New York, three years earlier, Stella had lectured him about paying Dean too much attention: "You haven't anything in common. He's a little boy." Similarly, at a party at Barbara Baxley's apartment that was filled with Actors Studio people, he'd bumped into Dean, and it was obvious how much the comparisons between the two of them bothered him. "Everybody was imitating him by then and he was very aware of any young actor who got good notices for being 'real,' meaning that they were doing what he did," said Janet Ward, a fellow member of the Studio. "Rod Steiger, Gazzara, anybody. It threatened him. That evening he turned to me and said, 'See that guy who just walked in? You know him?' I said, 'Yes, it's Jimmy.' He said, 'You want to make a bet that he takes off his coat and flings it right on the floor there?'

"Jimmy was saying hello to people. It was winter, and he had a coat on which he was still unbuttoning. I said, 'Why do you say that?' 'Because I do it. Watch him.' And Jimmy did it, which brought a big grin to Marlon's face. I remember he put his hands up. 'See? I told you so.' "

Marlon had played the recorder, and Dean took up the instrument, too. In Hollywood, Dean also sought out Marlon's bongo partner, Jack Costanzo, who recalled that during their several sessions together Dean "asked me, in that broken, hardly understandable way of his, 'How does Marlon play?' and when I told him, 'Great,' all he said was, 'Oh.' " The motorcycles; the copycat Levi's, loafers, and V-neck pullovers; and even Maila Nurmi—all were Brando carryovers.

"Jimmy was so adoring of Marlon that he seemed shrunken and twisted in misery," said Kazan, and even normally blasé Sunset Strip types called it "a weird transference," an obsession that was "just impossible."

Brando refused to use Dean's name in public, instead referring to him as "the kid." To Sondra Lee he confided that Dean was undergoing "some kind of identity crisis." When Jack Costanzo let Brando know that Dean was no good on the drums, he was "tickled. Just sort of smiled and said, 'Oh, really?' "

"Dean . . . had an *idée fixe* about me. Whatever I did, he did," Brando later commented, explaining that he had listened in while the younger actor talked to his answering service, trying to get through. "But I never spoke up. I never called him back."

He also had "a very cute way of imitating Jimmy," said the composer David Diamond. "He envied his lower lip. He'd ask me, 'Do you think he's good-looking?' " Ironically, this was the very question Marlon had asked Diamond about Monty Clift. "Jimmy was terribly self-destructive, like cracking a bottle and threatening to cut his wrists. There were several suicide attempts. Marlon was aware of this. But [Jimmy] was in awe of Marlon. I remember once saying to Jimmy, 'Go over, put your arms around him. He's not going to bite you.' He turned red, like a little girl."

The morning after Marlon's visit to Warners, Dean showed up on the *Desirée* set, still dressed in his *Eden* outfit from the night before. He sat on the sidelines, continuing to watch in awe, studying Brando, trying to find "the secret" even as Marlon blew his lines with utter indifference. No words were exchanged, and a few nights later, at a party for Sammy Davis Jr., they met again; Marlon was in the midst of talking to Mel McCarter, Luther Adler's old girlfriend, when Dean approached and, again, Marlon snubbed him.

"He had his elbow on the mantelpiece," McCarter recalled, "looked around at Dean, then turned his head to the wall. Dean was dying to talk to him, and stood there for a few seconds, then kind of dropped his little head and walked off into the den and started playing bongo drums."

An hour or so later he returned. Brando would insist that Dean had been "throwing himself around, acting the madman," but he took him aside and asked him if he didn't know he was "sick." Soon he had given him Mittelmann's name, suggesting that when he returned to New York he seek out the psychoanalyst to get help.

Back at the *Desirée* shoot, things continued to deteriorate. Producer Julian Blaustein was aware that behind Marlon's contempt, the actor himself was "scared to death that he was going to look like 'all the lunatics in the various institutions' around the country who think they're Napoleon." Marlon had already made a point of not wanting to do "any of the hand-inside-the-jacket stuff," and argued endlessly for his own reading of his character. The production as a whole was listing perilously.

Just as problematic, Blaustein had come to like Brando, largely for the way he'd enthusiastically get down on the floor to play with the kids when he came to the producer's home for dinner. Even so, he had to draw the line, and at one point he went to Brando's dressing room to have a frank discussion. There, he found him half undressed, playing cards with Gilman, Rhodes, and several others.

"I want to talk business with you, Marlon," he announced, "and I would like it if they'd leave."

"Ah, come on. Why can't the guys stay?"

Blaustein turned to Gilman, "Sam, please." After the group had filed out, he turned back to Brando.

"Marlon, you and I are good friends and I value that, but I have a responsibility here," he began. "You know I've asked you more than once, and you've promised more than once. We can't run a production this way. I know you didn't want to do this picture, but you're doing it and we're going to finish [it]. For Christ's sake, don't get into the same trouble you got in before. Forget the lawyers; you don't want lawyers. And I'm gonna tell you, if you don't perform when the assistant calls you, when the set is ready—"

He paused, took a breath, and went on.

"Look, aside from the fact that you're a good liberal and you'll fight for causes, how can you deal with those people out there? Let's forget Jean Simmons and Merle Oberon—they can take care of themselves. They're stars. But those extras who feel like cattle so much of the time, they have children to support. How can you make them feel so demeaned? Let them stand around under hot lights because the big movie star isn't ready?"

Brando was nodding. "Yes," he said, "You're right, you're absolutely right."

"I'm not kidding, Marlon," Blaustein continued. "The next time this happens I'm going to shut the picture down. And it will be a terrible thing for you, because you'll never catch up financially. The company will sue you for every bit of money that's gone into this picture, and I'll tell you exactly how much it is—I'll show you the books. And they will also sue you for profits that they may have made on your production. And what with taxes on your future income, plus paying all this . . . you'll have to go into textiles, Marlon. The movie business will be finished for you, so please, don't do it."

It may have been the bluntest one-on-one warning Brando had had to date. The movie business was nuts and bolts, a matter of "lots of dough" for Blaustein. Recalling the confrontation years later, the producer added that although he felt Brando probably did not believe him, from that point on the actor's behavior was "wonderful"—even if his performance was anything but inspired. For reasons no one dared ask Brando to explain, he'd adopted an English accent modeled on Claude Rains. It seemed all the more bizarre when he would scratch his rear, his nose, or his crotch, complaining aloud that he had crabs or jock rash. He was learning his lines only an hour or so before being called in front of the camera, and only his makeup seemed to interest him. Rejecting help from Rhodes and Harry Maret, Fox's in-house makeup man, he would spend hours working on his fake nose, experimenting with white liner to highlight its bulge, and adding more and more costume stuffing around his middle as Napoleon "aged" in the course of the performance.

In his own quixotic way he was telling the truth when he later boasted, "Most of the time I just let the makeup play the part." Sid Armus visited the set and thought the performance a major "evasion"; Sondra Lee, who was with him, sensed that their old friend and idol was "deeply disturbed.

"I'd thought that Napoleon would have been a very interesting character for him," she added. "But he couldn't remember his lines, which to me always means that an actor disapproves of his work. It comes from hostility, usually, or from insecurity or illness."

Josanne Mariani-Berenger spent the time confined to Marlon's trailer, invisible and behind the scenes even though he was also seeing Rita Moreno and other women. Soon, though, he took steps to exile Josanne from the set. In fact, only a few weeks after she had moved in with him, he announced that she had to live in her own apartment because the studio had rented the Laurel Canyon house for Philip and Marie Rhodes, too. It was another invented excuse, much like the one he'd given Movita when he had moved out of the Fifty-seventh Street apartment because of her redecorating. Josanne dutifully complied, taking an apartment down the hill near Schwab's and moving in with another aspiring actress, blond Isa Childers. Marlon then gave Philip and Marie a new job. "We were supposed to keep her away from the set," Rhodes recalled. "We were babysitting her, not letting her come around. And then on weekends Marlon would say to us, 'Drive her up to San Francisco.' He was definitely trying to get rid of her, even though he was supposed to marry her."

With Josanne kept off the set, Marilyn Monroe visited. For Monroe, it was an opportunity to tweak Zanuck in the aftermath of her walkout on *Pink Tights*. Coyly, she told reporters that she had been receiving sacks of fan mail "from teenagers who adore Marlon, suggesting that I play in a picture with him." In fact Brando and Monroe had resumed their affair, which would peak by the end of the year, when the two would be seen together in public, both serving as ushers at a New York fund-raiser for the Actors Studio. Josanne soon returned to France, apparently at Marlon's suggestion. "He definitely got rid of her," said Rhodes, "and once he did, he got rid of us, too. He told us to move out, so the last two weeks of *Desirée* we had to find an apartment."

Once the Rhodeses departed, Movita returned to the scene. "The impression I got," said Jack Larson "was that he adored her." All the group gathered during the evenings, often either at John Barrymore Jr.'s or at Marlon's on Laurel Drive; Movita was running with a Latino contingent ("a whole bunch of Mexicans—crazy, wonderful people") whom she brought around to mitigate the "suffering, the slings and arrows," as Larson put it, that Marlon was going through while making the film.

When *Desirée* finally wrapped in late September 1954, Brando left for Europe. The purpose of the trip, ostensibly, was to promote the foreign release of *Waterfront* and to discuss a possible role in an Italian production of *War and Peace*. In an earlier interview with James Bacon, AP's Hollywood correspondent, he had made it apparent, though, that he was again fleeing Hollywood.

"A geek is the lowest form of show business—the guy in the carnival who bites the head off live chickens," he'd snarled. "They usually get paid off in cheap whiskey. Press agents made me a geek who gets $150,000 a chicken head. When you reporters are up at midnight thinking about some new phrase that will still mean 'slob,' I'll be over on the Riviera lying on the beach with some beautiful doll who will be dropping grapes in my mouth."

His vitriol said more than enough. In New York he boarded the *Île-de-France,* giving journalists another crack at him when Brando—the star of *Waterfront* and already the well-known liberal—sheepishly crossed striking longshoremen's picket lines. In Paris he spent two weeks with his friend Marquand and with Hervé Mille before heading south to rendezvous with Josanne. Arriving in her hometown, the small fishing village of

Bandol, he found hundreds of photographers and reporters clogging the street in front of the Mariani-Berenger apartment. The next day pictures of the two strolling along the beach in identical striped, boat-necked jerseys appeared in newspapers around the world. More startling by far were the international headlines; the account in *Newsweek* summoned up fairy-tale echoes of a new Brando, of Kowalski tamed:

"On his present European trip, moody, he-man actor Marlon Brando had tarried for two weeks in Paris. Then he slipped off to the little village of Bandol on the French Riviera. There he spent hours touring the area on a rented motor-scooter with Josanne Mariani-Berenger, nineteen-year-old stepdaughter of a local fisherman. . . . Two days after Brando's arrival a brief announcement appeared in a Toulon newspaper: 'Mr. and Mrs. Paul Berenger are happy to announce the engagement of their daughter, Josanne, to Mr. Marlon Brando.' Josanne said Brando proposed to her within two hours of their first meeting. Said Brando: 'Sure, we're engaged— there's no mystery about it.' "

Back in L.A., Rita Moreno responded with one of her rare public statements about Brando, acknowledging surprise and disbelief. "I didn't think he ever wanted to be tied down," she said. "Once on a date he said society wants to tie a person down. He wanted to find some island and live there and do what he wanted. I was amazed to hear he's engaged. But he seemed to be a lost soul, looking for a niche. And apparently he's found it."

Movita admitted that she, too, hadn't thought he was "ready to settle down." She also predicted, "I do not think he will marry her so soon. They probably are engaged, yes. He's very charming, but he was a little immature for me . . . or rather I am a little mature for him. But I think he must be serious about her," she added. "He needs someone so desperately. . . . He isn't the type to walk into something unless he's sure."

In New York, friends were no less skeptical when two days later he fled Bandol alone, bound for Italy. He was leaving, he'd explained angrily to reporters, because he could no longer take their "persecution." Josanne had cleared out as well, pressmen determined—first for Paris and then on to California. "We are still in love with each other," she again insisted, explaining that marriage would not interfere with her plans for a Hollywood career.

Two days later, on November 1, Marlon arrived in Rome aboard the Nice-Rome express. "Spittoon rubbish," he snapped in dismissal of the rumors that he'd abandoned his fiancée. "I love Josie. This is no one-night stand," he claimed. "But we aren't going to get married right away. She has a lot of growing up to do yet. It's not fair to grab her away from her life before it is hardly begun."

The next day he put in a call to Paris, assuring Josanne that she was "the only girl I ever wanted to marry." The young woman responded by publicly proclaiming, "We are still in love with each other. . . . People are saying a lot of things about Marlon—that he is difficult and so forth. It is not true. I know him and I need no special technique to get along with him."

In Bandol, at dawn, Paul Berenger, in hip boots and tattered sweater, was surrounded by reporters as he unloaded his catch. He told them he was fed up. He had no doubt that Brando was going to marry his daughter, he said, adding testily, "He had better."

Neighbors in the small village were not so sure. Josanne, everyone knew, was young but not green, and the door-to-door gossip was that the actor had been furious upon hearing that two years earlier his fiancée had posed nude for Polish-born painter Moïse Kisling. Arriving at the L.A. airport, Josanne, accompanied by her agent, explained that she expected the wedding to take place "perhaps by next June." She was in California, she added, to make her television debut on NBC's "Colgate Comedy Hour" with Gordon MacRae. Pressed for details on her experience as an actress, she admitted in her soft French accent that her only role was a walk-on in an amateur production of *Cyrano de Bergerac*. "But I was very serious," she said.

Two weeks later, on November 26, 1954, Marlon arrived back in New York aboard the *United States,* where he was engulfed by newsmen at the pier. "I do intend to marry the girl," he insisted. Curiously enough, Josanne, who was now in New York, was not there to greet him; he explained this by saying that he had talked to her by ship's telephone and would be seeing her later in the day. En masse, the paparazzi tailed him to his studio in Carnegie Hall and, at a loss for news, the bulldog editions of the city's tabloids uniformly noted that he sent four shirts out to a local dry cleaner.

Josanne finally came to call late in the afternoon, fighting her way through the flashbulbs, and several hours passed before she emerged arm-in-arm with her beau into the narrow corridor outside Brando's apartment. "I will not speak about my private feelings in public," he stressed, then added that the two of them had decided to advance the date to "sometime next month."

Josanne, pert with her carelessly gamine hairdo, looked a trifle moonstruck—but also like "a fisherwoman sure of her catch," as *Newsweek* editorialized on December 6—and with the pack of reporters at their heels, the couple made their way out of the building and on to dinner. That evening they were still being pursued, and in the days that followed, Brando's irritation returned. The "carrion press," as he called newsmen, was everywhere. "The world will not wreck Josanne's and my love. . . . I'm going to get a slouchy hat and a pair of dark glasses and creep up alleys. What a life!" In a somewhat different vein, he was also talking to Sondra Lee, for whom Josanne was "sort of puffy around the eyes—a dip, a nothing." Josanne had been "hacking at him," Lee gathered, about wanting a mink coat; Marlon became so angry that he went out and bought her a mynah bird.

The explanation for what was going on, Lee saw, was simple: "This vapid little French girl, this fucking fishing village . . . suddenly he'd found himself engaged. He makes such mistakes, you can't imagine. You can say he's so rich and famous, how could he be so dumb? But he is that dumb . . . and he just got trapped."

At the Carnegie Hall apartment, they fought. At dinner in Chinatown with Tennessee Williams one evening, Josanne interrupted Williams's boozy singing, turned on Marlon, and bluntly announced, "You and Marquand are lovers." Marlon, of course, responded by saying nothing. "He just ignored it," said Eddie Jaffe, who was at the table. "She wanted him to marry her, and I think she thought this was the way to do it." Here, as elsewhere, Marlon was good at hiding his anger. His grandmother, Bessie, had schooled him in the advantages of putting up a front, of waiting until the time was right, and whenever Josanne would storm out of the apartment, he'd go to her jewel box, where she kept her diaphragm, to see if she was going out to have sex. Carlo, who witnessed such scenes several times, claimed that there was only one thing on his mind, that when she "made a mistake . . . she would be gone."

Guys and Dolls, which Brando had signed to do before *Desirée* had wrapped, was slated to start in less than a month, so in December Josanne was sent to California. Above and beyond the obvious, there was a subtext.

He was aware that the as-yet-unknown Ursula Andress, who had been sharing Josanne's apartment in Manhattan, also had a small, vine-covered bungalow just above Sunset and that, like the cottage, the strikingly beautiful Andress herself was ready and waiting.

"Ursula was delighted," said Maila Nurmi, who was in Hollywood when Josanne and Ursula arrived. Marlon came soon after. "What the arrangement meant was that Brando visited often. Ursula was very like Marlon: She was a conqueror, so she got to see if she could steal her roommate's fiancé. Ursula was a home wrecker, a heart wrecker, and a pretty good one. She followed the little French twerp out to L.A., [where] she got exactly what she wanted."

Marlon was back in his $450-a-month place in Laurel Canyon, this time with Sam Gilman as his housemate, and Andress was only one of his diversions. He had started things up again with Rita Moreno and also brought old girlfriend Celia Webb west to work as his secretary; the fact that he had been engaged to Celia in 1948 made no difference. Plunked down in the middle of L.A. without money or work, Josanne was little more than an appendage. Nurmi, now in her incarnation as TV's campy, sepulchral Vampira, went to dinner with the engaged couple and Celia one evening shortly after Marlon's arrival in L.A. What she saw was that Marlon and Josanne didn't speak. "They were affianced, but not *one word* the whole meal," she insisted, "largely because Marlon had told the two women to be still."

Within days, riled by Nurmi's continued questioning, Brando acknowledged the source of the problem, elaborating his remarks to Sondra Lee back in New York: Josanne, he had believed, was "this untainted virgin—his *private* virgin," as Nurmi recalled his explanation. "Then he had been mortified by her having posed nude for that artist. It was really an idiotic inclination, this totally childish idea of his. I told him, 'This woman you're looking for, this image you're reliving, you're never going to recapture her.' He didn't like that so well. I kept it up, though, and he cut me off for a month or more."

By the spring of 1955 Josanne was still making a pretense of their pending marriage, although she had moved into her own cottage on Havenhurst and was working as a salesgirl to pay her rent. Marlon continued calling, even when she moved in with a young would-be Aznavour, a cabaret singer by the name of André Philippe. Philippe, a Jew born in Brooklyn with the name Everett Cooper, recalled her "pining for him. . . . He was a night caller," Philippe said, referring to Marlon's usual three- or four-in-the-morning telephone calls. "She'd wait for him to phone and then afterward start drinking wine and get depressed. She'd go into the bathroom and then smash glasses against the bathtub. 'That fucker! That son-of-a-*beetch*!' she would yell, always with the accent. She felt that he'd fucked up her life, but she was still waiting."

Years later Josanne would marry someone else, have a child, divorce, and return to L.A. She later became a practicing Sikh, dressing all in white; she gave up meat and lived in the sect's ashram, where she would rise before dawn to recite prayers. Philippe, too, had married and divorced, and later he had a chance encounter with Brando in a San Fernando Valley restaurant. He went over to the actor's table, introduced himself, and mentioned he had lived with Josanne for three years.

Marlon turned, shook his hand, and said, "You have my condolences."

Guys and Dolls and *The Teahouse of the August Moon*

Casting Brando in a musical was the idea of master showman and producer Sam Goldwyn. He had outbid MGM, Paramount, and Columbia for the rights to the long-running Broadway show *Guys and Dolls,* which was based on stories by Damon Runyon, shelling out a record $1 million in the process. The producer had originally thought of Gene Kelly for the leading role, but MGM refused to loan him out. Tony Martin, Kirk Douglas, Robert Mitchum, and Burt Lancaster were other candidates. Bing Crosby and Clark Gable also wanted it, yet the name that kept coming up in casting sessions was Marlon Brando, largely because of Goldwyn's wickedly astute sense of throwing the public a curve: Brando, the moody *enfant terrible,* had never sung on-screen in his life, and the marquee value of this alone promised a megahit.

Director Joseph Mankiewicz had no idea if Marlon could carry a tune, and frankly, he didn't care. Brando was anxious about the proposition from the start, almost as concerned as he had been in approaching Shakespeare. Mankiewicz, on instructions from Goldwyn, cabled him from London: "WANT VERY MUCH TO HAVE YOU PLAY MASTERSON. IN ITS OWN

WAY ROLE AS I WOULD WRITE IT FOR YOU OFFERS CHALLENGE ALMOST EQUAL OF MARC ANTONY. YOU HAVE NEVER DONE A MUSICAL NEITHER HAVE I. WE NEVER DID SHAKESPEARE EITHER. I AM CONFIDENT THIS WOULD BE EXCITING GRATIFY-ING AND REWARDING EXPERIENCE FOR BOTH OF US."

Brando wired back, acknowledging that he would read the play and reconsider. Soon, another cable from Goldwyn arrived on Mankiewicz's desk, urging more campaigning: "BRANDO FEARFUL DETROIT ROLE GREATER THAN HIS. BELIEVE IT ADVISABLE YOU CABLE HIM ASSURANCE MASTERSON IS GREATER AND THAT YOU FEEL THIS VERY STRONGLY AND EXPECT TO TREAT IT ACCORDINGLY IN THE WRITING."

Again Mankiewicz sent off a wire, wooing Brando with his verbal wit: "GOLDWYN TELLS ME YOU FEARFUL ROLE OF DETROIT WILL OVERSHADOW MASTERSON. THIS HARDLY POSSIBLE SINCE I WILL BE WRITING SCRIPT ABOUT LIFE AND LOVE OF SKY WITH DETROIT PLAYING SECONDARY ROLE SINCE AFTER ALL HE OFFERS NOTHING BUT VARIATIONS ON ONE JOKE. FEAR HIM NOT AN-TONY. LET THY NAME BE PRICKED WITH MINE AND LET'S KILL THE PEOPLE. LOVE, JOE."

Mankiewicz's imprimatur would lend greater endorsement to the project, and Marlon also realized that the movie version of the Broadway hit was a sure moneymaker. If the director could go the way of all Holly-wood flesh, so could he, especially since his finances were in a sad state be-cause of the heavy penalty exacted by Zanuck over *The Egyptian*. Besides, he still had to deal with the failing cattle business (and its attendant legal fees), not to mention supporting Movita and sometimes Josanne. *Desirée* had turned him cynical—more and more, he would separate his private passions from his public acting roles—and his attitude with *Guys and Dolls* became one of opportunism at the expense of self-esteem. For the self-loathing that would begin to spread in his soul, he had MCA exact a price of $200,000, one of Hollywood's highest salaries in 1955.

Meanwhile, Mankiewicz was pushing to retain the musical's entire New York cast except for Brando's Sky Masterson character. For the role of Miss Adelaide, however, Goldwyn was pushing for Betty Grable to re-place the showstopping Vivian Blaine. Mankiewicz argued vehemently against America's pinup girl. "I will not direct tits," he told Goldwyn. "Find me a girl with square tits, and I'll make you a million dollars."

Marilyn Monroe then stepped forward, eagerly volunteering for the role. She called Mankiewicz from New York, where she was shooting *The*

Seven Year Itch. "You see, I've become a star," she purred over the phone to the man who had directed her in *All About Eve* six years before. Mankiewicz's response was avuncular but otherwise Runyonesque, side-of-the-mouth patter. "Put on some more clothes, Marilyn," he remembered telling her, "and stop moving your ass so much." When she continued to cajole, he informed her that the part had already been cast.

He had gotten Goldwyn's approval of Blaine, but not without relinquishing the Nathan Detroit role to Frank Sinatra, who had met with him and lobbied for the part. Predicting that there was bound to be tension with Brando, Mankiewicz nevertheless agreed to the popular singer instead of the Broadway actor Sam Levene.

With Sinatra, Blaine, and Jean Simmons (as Brando's "love interest," Sister Sarah Brown) all hired, Brando went into training with Leon Ceparro, MGM's demanding voice coach, several weeks before the start of production. Ceparro claimed that his new student was good enough to "make the Met if he studied hard." He also took dancing lessons from choreographer Michael Kidd, from whom Marlon kept secret his previous dance training with Katherine Dunham and Anna Sokolow. The two liked each other immediately, but once again Brando had to set the terms of the relationship. In another of his twenty-minute, put-on telephone calls to Kidd's home early one Saturday morning, he posed as a bill collector and demanded payment for an overdue account. "He never let on for a moment," Kidd recalled, having been taken in completely. "The whole thing was done in this proper, businesslike voice without any hems and haws—none of the classic Brando mumbling, none of the pauses or anything."

The same kind of testing took place the first day of production. Mankiewicz introduced Sinatra to Brando outside the soundstage building. Brando made the first move. "Frank, I've never done anything like this before," he said, "and I was wondering, maybe I could come to your dressing room and we could just run the dialogue together?" Still smarting over losing the Terry Malloy role in *Waterfront,* Sinatra looked at him hard and replied, "Don't give me any of that Actors Studio shit."

Within days the hostilities escalated, even though in later years Mankiewicz would downplay the bristling tension between the two stars. During the first scene at Mindy's, Damon Runyon's version of Lindy's Delicatessen in New York, Sinatra had to eat cheesecake while listening to

Marlon's Sky Masterson, and whether Brando meant to or not, he began stumbling over his singsong lines. Sinatra, known as a one-take performer, soon lost his temper. After "the thirty-fourth take," according to actor Dan Dayton, he turned on Brando, yelling, "I'm doing this once more. You see that cheesecake? If you don't get it right, I'm going to make you eat the whole thing, every fucking bit of it! Now do it right, goddamn it!"

Brando's response was to take a long, stylized pause, accompanied by a perceptible smirk. This sent Sinatra marching off to his dressing room, followed by his retinue of bodyguards and some of the "street guy" performers from the Broadway company, actors like B. S. Pully and Stubby Kaye who played what Mankiewicz dubbed the "fairy-tale gangsters." Although Mankiewicz persuaded Sinatra to return to the set and finish the troublesome scene, the next morning Marlon couldn't let things rest. He openly complained about Sinatra's work in front of the camera. "He's supposed to sing with a Bronx accent, to clown it up," he said. "But he's singing like a romantic lead. We can't have *two* romantic leads."

Brando's complaints continued, and several days later he asked Mankiewicz to intervene. The director refused, suggesting that Marlon handle the problem on his own, a move that some observers claim affected their relationship for the rest of the shoot.

In the weeks that followed, the two actors studiously avoided each other, with Sinatra holed up with his gang in his dressing room. Brando, as far as Mankiewicz could see, spent his time "screwing half the chorus." He also practiced on his drums, generally with Jack Costanzo, "Mr. Bongo," whom Marlon had gotten a job on the film and who was arguably the best bongo player in the world.

"There was something explosive about Marlon that you knew was there but never had any evidence of," Costanzo said, "mainly because he kept it under control. It was like a volcano inside, but he wasn't going to let it come out. Marlon doesn't explain anything. If you don't agree with him, it's 'Okay, you got your feelings, I got mine. Screw it.' But he talked about the release with drums. 'I'm very happy playing drums, I'm relaxed,' he would say, even though physically he was tearing it up, dripping sweat, the whole bit." The two started playing together at Brando's house in addition to their riffs in the actor's trailer.

While the trouble with Sinatra continued, parallel subplots in the script would put them in few scenes together. Still, Marlon's anxiety over his musical numbers was that whatever he did, good, bad or indifferent, big or small, his efforts were going to be compared to "the wop from Hoboken."

"It was all so strange to him, scary as hell," said Mankiewicz, who likened his state to the way "you'd feel waiting to go over Niagara Falls in a barrel." Understandably, Brando's tension grew as they approached the shooting date of his big number, "Luck, Be a Lady Tonight." When they got to the scene, the set was closed to the press, ostensibly to hype "the miracle" of Brando's singing. But it was even worse than Marlon anticipated. Contrary to the usual practice, the musical numbers were being shot live, so the actors would have to sing, move, and act all at once. After flubbing one take after another—some estimates put the number of retakes at over a hundred—he turned to the visiting Goldwyn, ready to throw in the towel.

"Please, I don't mind," Marlon said. "Get somebody else to sing. I can't cut it the way I think it should be done."

Goldwyn shook his head. "Oh, no," he replied. "When the world sees 'Brando Sings' on the marquee, they're going to flock to the theaters. They'll break the doors down, you'll see."

For Brando, it was more than momentary fatigue. He complained to Costanzo, saying this was "the worst thing that ever happened" to him, and he called the picture "a piece of shit." Over the ensuing days he brooded, and even singing to playback in the privacy of the recording studio, he was out of his depth. The final tracks had to be pieced together out of innumerable takes, edited from some fifteen tapes.

Dance numbers presented less of a problem, largely because Kidd was in agreement that the choreography was best approached in "acting terms." While struggling as he was with "Luck, Be a Lady Tonight," Brando nonetheless pointed out that the staging did not "feel right." His analysis, Kidd quickly realized, was straight Method, totally naturalistic in conception. "He was absolutely right," the choreographer later conceded. "I'd been looking at it technically. In New York I'd put Sky front-center so the audience could hear, which meant I was automatically repeating myself. Marlon came to me and said, 'Look, I wouldn't be doing it with all these people standing around. As Sky, I'd be thinking about my bet in private. I wouldn't expose myself.' "

By then Sinatra felt that he had been put in the same position as so many other Brando costars, playing second fiddle, and he too was bitching to Mankiewicz. Brando, ever competitive, responded. With the company already split into factions—Brando, Mankiewicz, and Jean Simmons as one group, Sinatra and his entourage the other—Marlon continued to put the needle in, making a point of never referring to his costar by name. Yet, as any number of people noted, on the set he was too good an actor to let his antagonism show. Blowing his lines, he would apologize in such sincere tones that Sinatra couldn't say anything without appearing the fool. During a musical number, he might mouth his lyrics to the prerecorded music perfectly until the last line. Feigning absentmindedness, he began scenes with chewing gum in his mouth, repeating this until one of the grips put up a sign reading, "GUM!"

Brando biographer Bob Thomas, then reporting for the New York *Daily News* and the *Hollywood Reporter,* observed how he attempted to upstage Sinatra when Goldwyn arranged for *Vogue* photographer Richard Avedon to come from New York to shoot the two actors together. Avedon had set up his camera outside the studio stage, and David Golding, Goldwyn's publicity chief, went to get Sinatra from his dressing room.

"Where's Marlon?" Sinatra asked.

"In his dressing room. I'm going to get him now."

"When he's there, *then* I'll come."

Golding went to Brando's dressing room. "Where's Frank?" Marlon asked, similarly demanding that Sinatra precede him to the set. Finally the publicity man was told to devise a signal so that both stars would emerge simultaneously.

No one could lay the blame on either one of them completely, if only because both performers were coming from different backgrounds, each with a totally different approach. In due course Sinatra would balk at appearing with Brando and other cast members on Ed Sullivan's "Toast of the Town" for the picture's TV send-off; his explanation was that television was as much of a business for him as movies and that he wanted to be paid. About Sinatra, Brando would only comment, "Frank is the kind of guy, when he dies, he's going to heaven and give God a bad time for making him bald."

By the closing weeks of production, Mankiewicz wasn't the only one pampering Brando. In addition to Brando's $200,000 salary for fourteen weeks' labor, Goldwyn presented him with a surprise thank-you. "Marlon, my boy," the former glove salesman announced, "you have been such a wonderful performer in the role of Sky Masterson that I want to give you a token of my appreciation." Parked outside was a shiny new Ford Thunderbird sportscar, and no sooner had studio photographers snapped the beneficent producer handing over the keys than Marlon jumped in to take a succession of secretaries for a spin around the lot.

There was, however, a catch. When *Guys and Dolls* was about to be released, the producer made clear his expectations: Marlon was to attend the film's premiere in New York, make himself available to the press, and do whatever publicity was asked of him. He hated such exposure, but nonetheless complied.

For Mankiewicz, who had nurtured him through *Julius Caesar,* there was more to it than just a car. "Marlon had never done publicity like this before," he explained, "but maybe he said to himself, 'I've made myself pretty fucking unliked because I pissed on all this stuff. Maybe I want to go through a cure. Maybe I'll be a nice guy and see how it works out.'"

Goldwyn ordered up one of his biggest promotional pushes ever—not only the Sullivan show, but also a Las Vegas tie-in with the Sahara Hotel, an hourlong ABC-TV special, nationwide radio shows, and a Sardi's luncheon to precede the picture's premiere at New York's Capitol Theatre on November 4, 1955. Brando did them all. At the premiere the onlookers were twenty deep on both sides of Times Square, braving the rain as the studio limo carrying the star crawled forward through the crowd.

Brando was awestruck, and the event would be an upsetting revelation to him as well. Margaret Truman was there, along with Mel Ferrer and Audrey Hepburn, Mary Martin, Governor Averell Harriman of New York, Humphrey Bogart, Hume Cronyn, William Holden, and other luminaries too numerous to count. But the throng wanted only Brando. On Fifty-fourth Street fans had crashed through the police barricades and pounded on his car, and one young woman managed to break the windshield before she was pulled off. When Marlon finally arrived at the theater, it took the combined efforts of fifty-two cops plus two mounted policemen pushing back the mob to create a pathway; the resulting melee put several people in the hospital.

"It was the most terrifying experience of my life," Brando said afterward at a party at the Ambassador East Hotel. "It was frightening, like being trapped in a submarine."

Since the premiere was as mainstream as an opening could get, *Guys and Dolls* was guaranteed splash notices from industry publications like *Variety* as well as from the metropolitan dailies. All extolled the film's glossy production values and all-star cast. The project had soaked up $5.5 million in production costs, an astounding sum at the time, but even so, *Time* could only go so far as to say, "Faithful in detail, the picture is false to the original in feeling." The *New Yorker* ran a review entitled, "Sam, You Made the Film Too Long," and scored Brando for singing "through a rather unyielding set of sinuses." It called Jean Simmons's efforts "a half-tone off-pitch," and concluded that the picture might have been "an amusing trifle" if only it weren't so "damnably cute."

Still, middlebrow being middlebrow, and with America stuck in the midfifties, *Guys and Dolls* did more than $13 million in business. It received four Oscar nominations, cited for its score as well as sets, costumes, and cinematography—and *Variety* certified it the top moneymaker of 1956. With domestic ticket sales soaring, Goldwyn sent the Goldwyn Girls on a world tour, from Australia to South America; internationally, the film earned receipts equal to MGM's overseas returns from *Gone with the Wind*. The balding producer was on hand for the film's opening in Japan, and he asked Brando, now shooting *The Teahouse of the August Moon* outside Tokyo, to attend. Marlon refused, saying, "I've done enough for that black Thunderbird."

Summing up his work on *Guys and Dolls,* Brando said, "I wanted to effect a frothy farce style, but I'm heavy-footed with high comedy." All the stranger, then, that for his ninth film he chose *The Teahouse of the August Moon.* But, wearing his businessman's hat, he was certainly aware that *Teahouse,* like *Guys and Dolls,* was another proven commodity. The John Patrick comedy (adapted from a novel) had been a great success on Broadway and promised another major payday—plus, it offered him all the homey comforts of mainstream liberal thinking. In the role of Sakini, the wily interpreter for U.S. Occupation forces in Japan, he would be able to mouth such pithy sentiments as "Pain makes man think, thought makes man wise, wisdom makes life endurable," as well as play out some private fantasy of championing the oppressed citizens of the Third World. *In propria persona,* Brando was beginning to speak of his "recently discovered impulse to try to communicate the things I think are important," and in keeping with his new stance, he had required script approval before the film was to go into production.

In late 1955 the *Independent Film Journal* named Brando Hollywood's top moneymaking star—more popular at the box office than James Stewart, John Wayne, William Holden, or Gary Cooper. Columnist Joe Hyams reported that Brando was also the leader in fan mail, since he was receiving some 4,000 to 6,000 letters a month, a higher number than even Monroe or Clark Gable received. "If Marlon had wanted to play Little Eva, I would have let him," said Dore Schary, the head of production for MGM, which was underwriting *Teahouse.*

Having campaigned for the role, Marlon invested it with high purpose from the start. The script's story line, taken more or less intact from the play, had a group of Okinawan villagers hoodwinking the U.S. government into building a teahouse for local geishas, the implication being that the "Americanization" of foreign cultures was a no-no. However simpleminded, the idea had attracted Brando to the piece in the first place—he claimed he'd seen the play four times and "laughed so hard I almost ended up beating the lady's hat in front of me." And even before leaving for Nara, a small town near Kyoto where the film was to be shot, he had begun reading about Japanese culture, Zen, and even flower arrangement, often bringing conversations to a standstill by quoting aphorisms from ancient Oriental philosophers such as Lao-tzu. Hour after hour he practiced "Japanese" into a tape recorder, refusing all suggestions that his foreign-language bits be dubbed. For his makeup he experimented with studio technicians to make over his Occidental features with a rubber lid around his eyes, protruding teeth, a wig, and layers of yellowish greasepaint. To complete the transformation, he went on a crash diet while in California and shed some thirty pounds. When he did eat, it was often at the Imperial Gardens, an authentic if pricey Japanese restaurant on Sunset where he would sit for hours in the lotus position, studying the posture and mannerisms of the waiters.

Just how he could imbue such a vehicle with the weight of moral sentiment was more than a little puzzling; odder still, he seemed to have overlooked the studio's selection of his costars—specifically Glenn Ford, who was not only the standard studio-bred movie star but a man known within the Hollywood community as anything but a political maverick. Yet that seemed to be a secondary consideration, since Marlon had rationalized the project by exercising the right, granted by his MGM contract, to select the film's director. He had finally chosen Daniel Mann, who was out of Hollywood's mainstream.

Brando had first met Mann at the Actors Studio, and since the director was a friend of Stella as well, he regarded him as an extension of the
New York family. An intense Jew from Brooklyn, Mann had come up
through Sanford Meisner's Neighborhood Playhouse, had even directed
the Actors Studio television series, and had also filled in for Harold Clurman as road-company director of *Streetcar* when Irene Selznick asked
Clurman to come look at the long-running New York production, which
needed a tune-up. Mann had already directed two highly successful movie
adaptations of Broadway plays—William Inge's *Come Back, Little Sheba*,
which he had also directed for the stage, and Tennessee Williams's *The
Rose Tattoo*, with Anna Magnani; *I'll Cry Tomorrow*, the splashy Oscar-
nominated bio pic of actress Lillian Roth's descent into alcoholism, had
also been Mann's.

That Marlon thought the short, voluble director would lend some
weight and seriousness to the flimsy *Teahouse* project was understandable.
But if he assumed that by choosing Mann he would retain the upper hand
during the shoot, he had made a serious miscalculation. Mann was too
shrewd not to have perceived Marlon's propensity for power games during
previous encounters.

Once, at a party held by Stella, Marlon left the room, and a few minutes later Mann and the other guests heard a blood-curdling cry from the
bathroom. "It was like a man getting his balls cut off," Mann said. "An absolutely wild, endless scream with so much intense energy that we all
thought someone was dying, and we rushed to the bathroom."

There Marlon stood in front of the mirror, and having drawn everyone's attention, he simply turned and explained, almost with a shrug, "I
just had this impulse. I wanted to feel what it would be like if someone
were trying to kill me and I was about to die."

"He scared the shit out of all of us," Mann later said, "and that was
another form of testing. With Marlon," the director added, "nothing was
simple. It was as if he had to provoke reactions which he could then remember and save for later use."

Having had forewarning of Brando's psychological patterns, Mann
nevertheless took the job, confident of the financial benefits of directing a
proven winner.

Yet things went downhill almost as soon as *Teahouse* got under way
in early April 1956. The language problem, coupled with the slow-moving

habits of the Japanese crewmen, didn't help. Louis Calhern, who was playing the bumbling Colonel Purdy, died suddenly; Paul Ford, the originator of the role on Broadway, rushed across the Pacific to take over, and Calhern's scenes had to be reshot. Marlon was reportedly upset by Calhern's death, having worked with him in *Caesar*. But there was a far greater source of tension.

Some members of the cast claimed that the rivalry between Brando and Glenn Ford had begun with Marlon's arrival on the Japanese location. Some 300 Nara schoolchildren had mobbed the set to catch a glimpse of him. More important, Ford's trademark mannerisms usually projected middle-class integrity and determination; he had made MGM a bundle with the recently released *Blackboard Jungle*, and like any other mainline star, he was more than a little set in his ways.

Brando detested him—and for reasons that went beyond their differences in technique. What it ultimately came down to was politics. Arriving with Philip and Marie Rhodes, Marlon was bent on indoctrinating everyone within earshot with his recently acquired knowledge of the Orient. He even held forth when Ed Sullivan journeyed to Japan for an interview. All shooting stopped as the star lectured the variety show host on postwar Japanese-American circumstances, questions of economics, Third World sovereignty, and the "new peace." He did the same at packed press conferences: "Of all the countries in the world that suffer from backwardness, America is first," he went on at one such gathering, explaining that Asians "don't strive for success the way we do. They consider the moral development of the inner man equally important." At another, he intoned, "Americans don't even begin to understand the people of Asia. . . . Our understanding of Asians will never improve until we get out of the habit of thinking of the people as short, spindly-legged, buck-teethed little people with strange customs."

The basis for his monologues, aside from his "reading," was that the month before he had logged some 20,000 miles traveling through Southeast Asia. He had gone with Hollywood friends George Englund and Stewart Stern, reconnoitering Indonesia, Borneo, Thailand, Burma, and Pakistan for a "politically correct" film about U.S. intervention overseas. In New York the group had spent days conferring with representatives of Third World countries at the United Nations, held press conferences, and even bamboozled Paramount into underwriting this future film project.

Newly inspired, he never stopped talking. "He was Marlon Brando the star, and he was now working in Japan," Mann observed. "Anybody who wanted to know what was going on, he was going to tell them. Was he equipped to address the problem? In his own mind, I'm sure. In a city of blind people, a man with one eye is a telescope."

His costar, Glenn Ford, was already revealing his irritation. Part of it was ego—Brando was the one getting the attention, not only from the press but from the hundreds of fluttery young Japanese women hired as extras—yet the ex–army man "who subscribed to everything you're supposed to," as Mann put it, also saw that his role as the patriotic, flag-waving Captain Fisby was under attack. When the two were called to do a scene together, it became a toss-up as to which of them would be first on the set. Whether it was a matter of billing or politics, the conflict became a real "pissing match," said Mann.

One of the first sequences shot on the Nara location involved 500 extras, and twenty-eight takes were required, largely because Ford's lines to the assembled Okinawans had to be "translated" into Japanese by Brando's Sakini. During another scene, when Ford's Captain Fisby was to be given gifts by the natives, Brando interrupted the shooting and asked Mann sternly, "Do you see where I am?" The director noted that Ford had gradually moved out of position, forcing Brando to face away from the camera. Ford responded by complaining that Brando was doing the same thing, and over the next few days the upstaging continued.

"It was totally blatant, with neither of them trying to disguise what they were doing," said Mann. "It got to the point where they were literally stepping in front of each other. In some scenes Brando might be half-covered by Ford, or vice versa. Finally I told them, 'Come on, we have to work this out. You're not really doing the scene, you're doing a show about two actors who are trying to fuck each other.' "

Not unlike his response to Sinatra, Brando's moves could also be more covert, and there soon ensued the "battle of the cookies."

"Marlon!" Ford called out one afternoon as Brando was passing his dressing room. "Marlon, did you take some of my cookies?"

"Huh?"

"Did you take some of my cookies from my dressing room?"

"Your cookies?"

"Yes. I have them flown over from the States. If you want some of my cookies, just ask and I'll give them to you. But don't take them without asking."

"Glenn, I didn't take your goddamn cookies. Honest to God, I didn't."

The issue seemed closed—at least until several days later, when Brando walked by Ford's dressing room and noticed on his makeup table a package of cookies fresh from the United States. "Marlon glanced around and noted that no one was watching," reported Brando biographer Bob Thomas. "He entered Glenn's room, carefully strewed the cookies on the floor, and methodically stamped them into crumbs."

Marlon was finding it increasingly difficult to work with Mann, too, and for the director the only thing consistent about the actor was his inconsistency. One minute Brando could be high, earnestly praising the Japanese and their culture; then, suddenly, he would fall into a sulky brooding and so underplay his scenes that he seemed to be sleepwalking. "He was like a kaleidoscope," said Eddie Albert, who played Captain McLean. "That was Marlon. Every day he would turn and make a different design."

For the most part, he kept himself separate from the rest of the company. No one saw him in the communal dining room, and on weekends, which everyone had off, he isolated himself with Philip and Marie Rhodes, or with Machiko Kyo, the fragile Japanese actress who had been recruited to play Lotus Blossom. Day after day, when the company returned to their hotel after work, he would leave the others and slip into a hot bath. "Never," said Mann, "was there so much as a 'see you later,' a 'good-bye,' a 'have a good evening.' "

After close to a month of monsoon rains, the company was forced to return to Culver City, where the whole mess was finally brought to an end. "Marlon was the most distant, difficult individual that I've ever worked with," Mann concluded. For his part, Brando could not have cared less. He dropped in on Edie Van Cleve in New York shortly after *Teahouse* opened at the Radio City Music Hall in November and again waxed lyrical about his stay in Japan. "I can't wait to go back," he told her. "I'd like to live there some day." When he asked her what she thought of the film, she replied tactfully that she thought it "entertaining."

"It's a shame," he said. "I'd hoped that at least some of the magic of the play would have come across on screen."

Reviewers agreed. Bosley Crowther, perhaps Brando's most appreciative and serious-minded champion among national critics, saw his Sakini as "a calculated clown." The *Times* reviewer continued: "He goes his merry way, making gestures with his hands and garbling verbiage with sublime and almost reckless unconcern. . . . Beneath a dark stain, bad eye makeup, and a wig of shiny black hair, you see Mr. Brando enjoying a romp in his own little show. . . . Mr. Ford and Mr. Brando," he concluded, "play their leading roles as if they were out to make Dean Martin and Jerry Lewis look slightly repressed."

Diversions

Throughout the nineteen months separating his Oscar in March 1955 and the premiere of *Teahouse,* Brando had barely looked at scripts. They came to him in batches, often messengered from MCA in large, banded envelopes—two, three, or sometimes a half-dozen at a shot every week. The ostensible reason for turning down projects was his new production company, Pennebaker Inc., a partnership with his father and his friend George Englund that he started up within days of receiving his Academy Award. However, by now his attention was most often diverted by his latest girlfriend, the young starlet Anna Kashfi.

MCA had been the moving force behind Pennebaker In fact, the agency had set up "indies" for any number of its other clients. Charlton Heston, Frank Sinatra, Kirk Douglas, and Burt Lancaster had all established their own independent production companies during the early- and midfifties; the advantages were financial as well as artistic, since a corporate structure qualified as a legitimate tax shelter and provided a bigger piece of a film's profits. Working through his own company a superstar was guaranteed control over his product and received a "package" consisting of himself and a prepurchased property, with distribution and financing coming from the majors. In effect, the actor became his own producer.

On the debit side, anyone running his own production company was faced with the endless minutiae formerly handled by the studios, from casting to promotion. Moreover, because the actor-producer was now playing with his own funds, he couldn't cast himself in anything that was unlikely to turn a profit. Artistic control was one thing, but the picture had to make money, especially if the production company was without a long-term, multipicture deal with one of the studios as its backer. The idea of doing anything edgy, anything avant-garde, as film historian Gary Carey has pointed out, was usually a "delusion."

Pennebaker took its moniker from Dodie's maiden name, and since Marlon Sr. had been put at the helm, it would seem that young Marlon was satisfying obligations all around. George Englund, the other partner, had been a friend for several years; a tall, moderately gifted man, he had slid into the film business through Sydney Chaplin (the son of Charles) and was known to have a wide range of contacts within the industry. Two other partners were soon brought in: George Glass, the former partner of Stanley Kramer and associate producer on *The Men,* and Walter Seltzer, the highly respected publicist and producer who had worked for Hal Wallis, MGM, Warners, Columbia, and the independent Hecht-Lancaster Company. Paramount had pledged to support the company for an "unspecified number" of pictures, giving Brando virtual carte blanche.

"The Paramount deal was a very comfortable one," Seltzer recalled. "Pennebaker would be provided with offices, secretarial help, money to hire staff, including Marlon Sr., George, and myself. 'Senior,' as I referred to him, was drawing probably a thousand dollars a week in the beginning, which was not bad. Marlon was getting a base salary plus the additional salary for acting, and more for directing. It was all negotiated by MCA. Paramount's commitment would be annualized, and the major requirement was that Marlon stay with the studio. Marlon was a big, big star and Paramount wanted to hold on to him for as long as they could."

Soon after Glass and Seltzer got settled, it became clear that nothing was happening and Brando seemed totally disinterested. " 'How can you guys think of making movies at a time when there are millions of Indians dying of starvation?' was his usual excuse. In this case he meant not our Indians, but East Indians," said Seltzer. "Finally George Glass turned to him and said, 'Marlon, the time has come when you've got to stop worrying about a hundred million Indians and start worrying about two Jews—your partners—who are going to starve unless you go to work.' Marlon's response was to laugh." Glass and Seltzer did know a woman on the Indian Film Commission whose job was to promote that country's film industry, one of the biggest in the world. Unfortunately, Indian movies were generally of such poor quality they could not be exported overseas. "We talked to her about Marlon and his interest in the plight of the Indians," explained Seltzer. " 'Gee, what an opportunity,' she said. 'If Marlon would appear as a guest star in an Indian project—his choice—there would be money, first-class transportation, and great treatment, and he could do so much for the Indians by opening up the Indian film industry.' "

Knowing that the plight of India was a genuine concern of Marlon's, Seltzer and Glass presented him with the idea of the project. His response, Seltzer said, was to interrupt them.

"Wait a minute, wait a minute. Does this mean that I would have to go to work?" he asked in a jokey tone. When his partners said yes, he replied, "Ah, fuck it."

Indians of the East weren't Marlon's only concern. As he had told the Mille brothers in France in 1949, he also cared about Native Americans. With the announcement of the formation of the company in the trades, he had explained that Pennebaker's first project would be a western favorable to the American Indian. "Today the Indians are a broken race of people," he said. "The white man took his culture away and destroyed his philosophy of life and morality. We challenged the precepts on which he based his religion and destroyed the very kernels of his existence."

He also spoke of a second film about the kidnapping of United Nations research workers in Southeast Asia, insisting that "there is no more exciting, romantic, and important work being done in the world today than that accomplished by UN technical assistance." By July 1956 the company announced a slate of five pictures. Only one of these, *Shake Hands with the Devil,* would go into production on a timely basis, largely because Marlon had nothing to do with it.

"He'd forget dates and then try to say something diverting and funny," recalled Seltzer. " 'I met Huckleberry Finn' was a favorite one: 'On the way to that interview, I ran into Huckleberry Finn.' . . . I asked him point-blank on one occasion, 'Why are you doing this? What's the purpose of having the company?' And he said, 'It's really something for Pop to do.' That was the only time he claimed that the company was set up for Senior, however, and at the time I just thought he was being a *guten shome*—a good soul—to help out his father. Beyond that I didn't want to analyze the situation."

Brando Sr. was the last person capable of motivating his son, since, even with his title of company president, he was now Marlon's employee. Jocelyn was aware of the problem, realizing that her father was in the office every day meeting people and talking about scripts, "talking money-type talk. He and Bud got along all right." She said, "They didn't fight, though I suppose they argued. Papa said, 'I advise you to do so and so.' Bud would say, 'You do?' I don't think Papa was uncomfortable with this role, not any more than any father who has a famous son. That's a load, but Papa's carriage was always straight. It didn't seem to bow him down any."

Now living in L.A. permanently, Brando Sr. had taken a modest apartment in Hollywood below Sunset, bought himself a stubborn little terrier as well as a green Thunderbird, and continued to wear his Anthony Eden tweeds. Yet if he was an anomaly in this lotusland of palm trees and swimming pools, his qualifications for running a film company were equally implausible. In charge of handling the firm's administrative affairs, he was ultimately taking "a whole lot of crap" off Marlon's back, and, for the most part, he did so with relative equanimity. Only occasionally did he blow up. Seltzer remembered the most heated of these arguments. The Pennebaker partners and secretaries had offices at one end of Paramount's administration building, and the studio's mailroom delivered their letters; one day Marlon Sr. opened an envelope and then realized that it had been misdelivered to him rather than to Marlon Jr. He wrote on the outside, "Bud, I'm sorry. This is obviously for you," and sent it on to his son.

Glass and Seltzer were in their offices several days later when Marlon stormed in.

"I can't have this!" he exclaimed. "I won't have Pop opening my mail."

His two producers laughed. "Come on," said Seltzer in his usually reasonable tone. "Are you really gonna make something of this?"

But Marlon was adamant. "We've gotta do something!"

"Look, why don't you have a talk with the secretary and your dad and get it squared away. It's no big problem."

"You guys come with me," Marlon commanded, and they followed him for the confrontation.

Marlon Sr., who was a pipe smoker, sat and puffed as he listened to his son's complaint.

"Well, what do you want me to do about it?" he asked when Marlon was finished.

"I want you to change your name," Marlon Jr. said without the slightest trace of a smile.

His father sucked on his pipe a few more minutes, then blew it out. "You know, Bud," he said, "I've had the name for about twenty-five years longer than you have. I suggest *you* change your name."

Even in Marlon Sr.'s supposed area of expertise—finances—he was under young Marlon's thumb. The arrangement with Paramount was that the studio's money was being funneled through Kanter's office, which kept its 10 percent, and then the balance was turned over to Pennebaker's accountant, Guy Gadbois. Finally Marlon Sr. would make the day-to-day disbursements; rarely did he balk when his son instructed him to cut a check.

"I'm sure Marlon had an account, I'm sure he had *several* accounts," said Seltzer, "but the source of his money was Pennebaker, and all he had to say was, 'I need $10,000,' or 'I need $5,000.' Senior would seldom ask questions, even though Glass and I constantly wondered where all the money was going."

It was "hundreds of thousands of dollars"—and in the eight-year period of Pennebaker's existence, "a million," the partners reckoned. Since Gadbois was paying the bills for Marlon's living expenses like rent, mortgage, cars, and credit card purchases, most of the money had to be going for "incidentals," what Seltzer became convinced were his giveaways.

"If Sam Gilman needed $50,000 for something, he would probably have gotten it, that kind of money. These disbursements would include women, his children, trips—the bulk of it sheer largesse. I don't remember specifically which friends, but there were a couple of times when he gave cars away. And flowers. We once estimated that his annual flower bill was more than George or I was making in salary.

"We were already speculating about the illegitimate children," said Seltzer, "and by the time Marlon went to Tahiti in 1960, we thought there might be ten or twelve illegitimate kids all over New York, Los Angeles, points west, England, and the islands—particularly the islands, since later there was a Hawaiian girl. But it was all speculation on our part. Neither George nor I ever questioned him about this, for our own sanity. But why the hell else did he have this interest in money? Obviously for girls and his propensity for knocking them up. We would speculate, 'Well, there goes another one.' There were times when it was just a hemorrhage, his increasing cash flow."

Marlon Sr. himself was somewhat split in his response to his son's behavior. He had started dating openly not long after Dodie's death and was reportedly living with the firm's secretary, a young woman in her twenties by the name of Alice Marchak. She had been brought over from Paramount's secretarial pool on a full-time basis. There were other females in his life, too, one of whom he had made pregnant and who, it was reported, he handled with "a payoff." On occasion Marlon Jr.'s peccadilloes amused him; other times he wasn't pleased. By the same token, he realized that it would be useless to argue with him, telling Seltzer, "My son is terribly screwed up and I'm powerless to do anything about it."

"When it's you, it's one thing; when it's your son, it's another," Seltzer explained. "Senior was basically a sensitive man, [and] like any father he was inwardly hurt, wounded, unhappy. Bud himself, I think, enjoyed the complication. Complications kept him from dealing with reality, with going to work, with whatever were the real problems of the day.

"Nor was he at all self-conscious about being thirty-five years old and devoting his life to fucking women—not that I was aware of. He was never what I'd call the most happy fellow, but what he did with ladies, that was no problem. Everything was sort of in the present, and this succession of women, it was *now*. He'd come into the office, and on more than one occasion I can remember us saying, 'Marlon, you'd fuck a snake.' "

In precisely this vein, one afternoon Glass and Seltzer were kidding him and Marlon laughed, demanding to know the name of the person who had told them that his abilities were overrated. "I don't know," Seltzer replied vaguely, protecting his source, "but you remind me of a story about Harpo Marx." He explained that Marx was supposed to be a great but selfish lover, and that legend had it that one of the comedian's sexual partners had once complained, "Jesus, I'm so disappointed, Harpo. This big buildup . . . you don't think about me. Don't you have feelings? Don't you think I need fulfillment?" Marx was supposed to have replied, "Baby, when Harpo fucks, he fucks for Harpo!"

Marlon laughed at this anecdote, but he continued to press for the name of Seltzer's informant. Seltzer, enjoying his newfound leverage, merely explained that a story was circulating that somebody had walked in on a scene in a dressing room at Fox and found him with three women. " 'Marlon,' I said, 'that sounds highly improbable because I understand you can't take care of one, let alone three at a time.' "

In major part it was his self-absorption that led him into a relationship with Anna Kashfi, whom he had first met in the Paramount commissary in November 1955, several months before he was scheduled to leave for Japan for his role in *Teahouse*.

"When I first saw Marlon," Kashfi recalled, "he was sitting with Eva Marie Saint, who was at Paramount doing a film with Bob Hope. I was lunching with Pearl Bailey, and A. C. Lyles, the producer, introduced us. It was no big thing. He just said hello, then called me the next day."

Kashfi was finishing her first movie, *The Mountain*, a totally forgettable B-adventure yarn with Spencer Tracy, E. G. Marshall, and Robert Wagner. She'd gotten the role quite by chance. She was selling saris, scarves, and bangles in an Indian shop near London's Piccadilly Circus when her roommate, a girl who worked at a theatrical agency, persuaded Kashfi to accompany her to Paris to audition for the part. Edward Dmytryk, the director, hired Kashfi on the spot. "She was very quiet. She was wearing a sari to look Hindu," Dmytryk said, "and she even spoke a few words in Pakistani or something to make herself look real."

Philip Rhodes had heard of Kashfi before Marlon met her, since he knew the people who were working on *The Mountain,* including Tracy. "Spence went to the casting director," recalled Rhodes, "and said, 'Look, I gotta carry this girl down the fucking side of a mountain. So don't give me any of your whores with big tits and asses. Get me someone with a good face and no body.' That's why they picked Kashfi, this skinny girl who was passing herself off as an Indian, and then she worked on somebody, which resulted in her being flown to Hollywood. On the plane she sat next to a friend of mine and told him that she was going to meet Marlon Brando. I mean she had set her sights on him, possibly because she'd heard he loved the exotic and was interested in India. He was a setup for her. That's how she ended up in the U.S. and worked that great chess game on Marlon."

Having been brought to Hollywood, she was then living at the Carlton Hotel when Brando called to ask her for dinner. "This is Marlon Brando. I'd like to take you out." He was "very polite," she said, even deferential. Two nights later he arrived to pick her up dressed in a white shirt and white trousers, driving his Thunderbird. When she came down to the lobby, she found him talking to a little boy as he tied the youngster's shoelaces.

At dinner at a Chinese restaurant, she was "tense," she recalled, but he quickly put her at ease. He ordered for the two of them, then asked about India and her acting experience, every now and then interrupting the conversation to ask if she was comfortable. "It wasn't phony," she said. "The only time it was phony, and I could spot it in a flash, was when Marlon started talking with gestures. That night he was charming, and he wasn't coming on hard, either."

Afterward, he took her to his house in the Hollywood hills to show her "the view," then drove her home around 11:30. A week later he called again. Word was already out that they were dating—thanks to the efforts of Paramount publicist Harry Mines, from whom Marlon had originally gotten Kashfi's home phone number. Spencer Tracy took the liberty of warning his costar: "Anna, you're making the biggest mistake of your life."

The two did not have sex, Kashfi insisted, until their third date a week later.

"I was so lonesome. Besides Marlon I knew nobody except Spencer, Katharine Hepburn, A. C. Lyles, Harry Mines, and Harry Towns, all of whom were connected with the movie," she explained. "It started off with holding hands. He was very concerned about me and what my feelings were. Considerate. Nothing kinky, nothing out of the ordinary."

It appeared that Marlon was genuinely smitten, although Kashfi, by her own admission, had little frame of reference by which to gauge his behavior. With the conclusion of *The Mountain*, she was signed for *Battle Hymn* with Rock Hudson, then put under a standard seven-year contract at MGM. She was in the middle of wardrobe fittings for a Dean Martin film, *Ten Thousand Bedrooms,* when late in the spring of 1956 she was diagnosed with tuberculosis and confined to the City of Hope Hospital, where she remained bedridden for the next three months. Once Marlon was back in Los Angeles, after the horrendous *Teahouse* rain-out in Japan, he often drove to the hospital direct from MGM, still in full makeup. "Herro, herro. I am Doctor Meshuggener Moto," he'd clown. "Don't raff. I don't ordinarily make house cawrs." He brought her books, talked endlessly about Zen, about his conflicts with his father, and, most of all, about his regret that Dodie was not alive to meet her. He also charmed the staff and offered to narrate a documentary publicizing the medical progress at the hospital.

"The depth of his sensitivity was extraordinary," Kashfi recalled. "He was very attentive as long as I was in the hospital, as long as I needed him."

Marlon brought her Dodie's favorite pillow, as well as her jewelry and Bible. His visits to the hospital would continue throughout the summer. He phoned her regularly while he was on a trip east, and as soon as he arrived back in L.A., he was at her side every day during her months of treatment.

Kashfi made every attempt to fit in with what Marlon seemed to want. She went out of her way to become friends with Jocelyn, who later agreed, "She wooed me somewhat. She was beautiful, charming, graceful, winsome, really acting her part. She didn't seem phony at all. I suppose it was a campaign."

Whatever it was, she got what she wanted—a proposal of marriage.

"He came at nighttime," Kashfi recalled. "He was allowed in after hours, and it was as if he was drunk or something. He'd already given me Dodie's earrings, and he kept telling me that I reminded him of his mother. Then he started talking about marriage, very hyperactive. Like, 'I want to get this out before I become afraid and close myself off.' "

A silent Fiore, who was with him, kept making faces behind Marlon's back as Brando went on for more than an hour, nervously explaining the complexities of their engagement. " 'There are things that have to be taken care of,' he told me," Anna recalled, " 'like dealing with my father, dealing with the studios. . . . There's also the George Glasses and Walter Seltzers. . . .' What it came down to was the publicity, how he was going to handle it once it became public." For the time being, though, Marlon wanted to keep the engagement secret, especially since he was still seeing Movita. He was, however, at Kashfi's side when she was released from the hospital, and at a family party at Jocelyn's he told his sister that they were engaged. Still nothing was definite when Marlon left Anna in L.A. and returned to Japan to shoot his next film, *Sayonara*.

Sayonara

Near the end of 1955, just around the time Brando had first met Anna, he committed himself to star in Joshua Logan's production of *Sayonara*. Pennebaker Inc. was to serve as the film's coproducer. The script, based on James Michener's sprawling novel, which had been turned into a successful play, was a mix of "travelogue and deep-thinking melodrama," as one critic put it. Although Marlon's immediate response was "I'm just doing it for the money," there was also a political dimension to his decision, just as there had been with *Teahouse*: Set in the closing days of the Korean War, the film's plot turned on the bigotry of U.S. armed forces abroad, specifically in Japan. Here, the drama's archconservative, West Point protagonist falls in love with a local dancer whom he finds himself unable to marry; after considerable soul-searching, Major Gruver concludes that the cultural conflict is insurmountable, the threat to his career too great. Unable to face the difficulties that lie ahead, he returns to his stateside fiancée, despite the loss and self-betrayal.

Whatever the potential financial reward of the film, Brando had initially turned down director Joshua Logan's overtures, feeling that the Broadway-based script reinforced stereotypes, in effect sanctioning an Eisenhower-era notion of the American dream. But in the course of a meeting with Brando, producer William Goetz, one of Hollywood's staunchest backers of Adlai Stevenson, had prevailed on him to reconsider, largely by indicating his flexibility on the story line. Weeks later, at Logan's apartment in New York, Marlon confronted the director on his balcony overlooking the East River.

"I don't like the ending where the major leaves Japan and the dancer goes back to the theater," he said.

"But if he marries her, then it becomes a typical Hollywood happy ending. There's no truth to the story."

"Why not?" Brando insisted. "People of different races are marrying all the time. Why avoid the issue? Face the fact that an American could marry a Japanese girl."

Logan, a southerner from Louisiana, listened as Marlon demanded one additional change: The protagonist, Gruver, would have to be from the South. If anything, this would make the racial conflict all the stronger.

To underscore his seriousness, Brando pointed out that he wanted to use a southern accent modeled on his classmates at military school. "He hated the concept of Anglo-Saxon superiority," Logan later recalled. "His Japanese friends had told him not to do anything that would demean the Japanese race, and he was suspicious the whole time. He talked our heads off all day about the Japanese, about the military and how much he resented it. It was," Logan added, "mostly Marlon bullshit."

Still, Brando would not budge. "I won't do the part unless I can marry the Japanese girl," he insisted, holding off on a commitment.

Logan said they would need to consult with scriptwriter Paul Osborn.

Reached on the phone, Osborn quickly agreed. "The original ending was *Madame Butterfly* all over again," the writer said. "Marlon's suggestion is a wonderful idea."

Goetz, eager to wrap things up, accepted the plot change and offered the additional plum that Brando would be consulted on all major casting decisions. "All right, Marlon," he said, "will you play the part?"

"I'll talk to you tomorrow," he replied, starting to leave. The excitable Logan, however, exploded. "No, Marlon! I can't wait another second!"

Brando paused. "You know, I like you," he said, turning to the director whose Broadway hits *South Pacific* and *Fanny* he had long detested. "I liked the tender way you took dead leaves off that plant out on the terrace. I didn't know you were sensitive enough to care. All right, I'll do it."

Doubtless, he also liked the contract that MCA had hammered out in advance. He was to be paid $300,000 against 10 percent of the gross, which promised to be considerable. Both Michener's novel and its Broadway adaptation had broken records, and there was every reason to believe that the film would turn out to be one of the top moneymakers of 1957–58—an assumption that proved true, as it grossed over $10 million. (Until *The Godfather*, *Sayonara* would be the most lucrative of all Brando's pictures.)

To Edie Van Cleve and others, Marlon had made it clear that he was eager to return to Japan. Carlo Fiore, hired as Brando's dialogue coach, realized that his agenda also accommodated his growing predilection for Asian women. The plan was made to spend a week in Honolulu, where Brando and Fiore would work jointly on the script for the pro-Indian western that Marlon had been talking about doing through Pennebaker. Then the two of them would move on for three months of *Sayonara* in Japan. All of it was being paid for by Warners—"limos, broads, everything," Fiore recalled, "everything first-class."

For *Sayonara* Brando went on a crash diet, living on raw vegetables and taking runs along Waikiki Beach once they arrived in Hawaii. In L.A. he'd had his weight down to 170, but by now it had ballooned up considerably. After a few days in Hawaii, however, his resolve weakened. One morning Fiore found him in a drugstore near their hotel devouring a breakfast of cornflakes with bananas and cream, scrambled eggs, sausages and bacon, and a stack of pancakes slathered with butter and maple syrup.

Arriving in Tokyo on January 12, 1957, Brando and his sidekick were greeted by Josh Logan and several Japanese dignitaries. The next morning

Marlon appeared at a Warners-sponsored press conference, where he delivered another talk addressing the issue of Japanese-American relations. Although privately he doubted the film's sincerity and its chances of amounting to anything more than a sentimental love story, he spoke with genuine clarity on the need for amity and understanding between the two cultures. Logan, who'd been struggling for months to gain permission to photograph the Takarasuka Theatre Company, was delighted with the Japanese response. Brando was the ideal goodwill ambassador. As an embodiment of tolerance, he was someone the Japanese government could trust to handle the sensitive theme of miscegenation.

After a week in Tokyo, the company left for the ancient capital of Kyoto. Marlon settled in at the Miyako Hotel, electing to stay in one of the few suites furnished in the traditional Oriental manner. He wore kimonos and the clogs he'd discovered while making *Teahouse,* and bowed to other guests in the hallway, at times allowing his voice to diminish to a whisper. From his window he had a panoramic view of the city's temples, narrow alleys, gardens, and canals. On the face of it he couldn't be happier. The Japanese, he said after his first trip, "stand at a distance and don't bother you. Often they give you little gifts. . . . The industry, kindness, and courtesy . . . made a terrific impression on me. They seem to incorporate their religion into their daily life."

The local kids made an impression on him more than anything, and he took every opportunity to chat with smiling, uniformed schoolchildren he encountered on the street. He visited a local orphanage, where he extended an open invitation to the set. Fascinated with the stringed-instrument troubadours who roamed downtown Kyoto, he hired two musicians to play on location, and outside the entrance to the Miyako, the crowd always stood at a respectful distance, calling greetings to him as he raced to his limousine.

What dampened his spirit was the weather. While Kyoto was extraordinary, in the first week alone the production lost five days to rain. Logan also had difficulty getting a performance out of twenty-six-year-old Miiko Taka, a $60-a-week L.A. clerk who had been hired as Brando's love interest after Audrey Hepburn had turned down the role (Hepburn claimed that she would be "laughed at" playing an Asian). Red Buttons, who had beaten out John Cassavetes for the supporting part of flier Joe Kelly, was also proving less than inspired, as was Miyoshi Umeki, playing his paramour and co-suicide (though both would eventually win Oscars).

James Garner, who had recently signed a long-term contract with Warners, also had the shakes. "What's the matter?" Marlon asked the strapping Oklahoman, who would later become a star as TV's Bret Maverick and in "The Rockford Files."

"I'm scared," Garner acknowledged.

"What about?"

"This is my first important picture. I'm scared to death."

"Don't be afraid. Relax. You got any problems, just ask me."

He was also coaching the timid Taka, and his sense of responsibility extended to Buttons, too. But what really bothered Brando was Josh Logan. As one of Broadway's most celebrated directors, and a self-acknowledged manic-depressive, Logan was at the top of the heap, even if his celebrated hits tended to be overblown and gaudy. With films like *Picnic* and *Bus Stop*, however, he'd turned comedy-melodrama into vulgar, Technicolor kitsch, which is what he seemed to be doing here. There was also the way he treated people: During the first days of filming, Logan had laid into the frightened Taka when she was late in arriving on the set, lecturing her, "You must never, never be late. *Never!* Not one minute. You must work harder than you've ever worked in your life.... You must carry more than your end or we'll all collapse!"

It was excessive, and all Marlon needed to hear. Later in the week the director decided to shoot Brando's Gruver running to go to the Matsubayashi Theatre in a broad shot with the rock gardens and delicate bamboo kiosks in the rear. As the crew waited, Marlon approached Logan, asking, "Should I be carrying a cigarette or not?"

"Well, it really doesn't matter, Marlon, and we have just so much daylight left."

"But I mean, if he's in this emotional state, if he's feeling this disturbed," Brando pressed, "would he be smoking or wouldn't he?"

"Follow your instincts, Marlon. They've got to be more considered than mine. The audience can't see the cigarette from this distance anyway, so it doesn't really matter. We won't cut into this scene. And this is a scene we'll have to match in Hollywood, so you can have it either way."

Marlon looked at him strangely, and as the director later recalled, almost backed away to his position. The scene was shot, and Brando disappeared without a word, leaving Logan puzzled.

Several days later Marlon was walking across the set with Fiore when he turned and said, "I will not say, 'Look at the carp!' Nor will I say, 'Look at the bridge!' Or 'Look at that cock!' "

"Look at *what* cock? Whose cock?"

"Josh has found a white cock with a tail twenty feet long. For some reason, the Japanese breed these long-tailed cocks. Anyway, he wants a shot of the cock, and he wants me to say, 'Look at that cock!' so he'll have a reason to cut to it. He's seen a bridge he'd like to photograph, too, so he wants me to say, 'Look at that bridge!' As far as I'm concerned, Logan can take the cock and shove it."

Fiore replied by suggesting script changes or giving the lines to Red Buttons or Garner, both of whom, he pointed out, wanted to pad their parts anyhow. On Logan he said, "He may be a craftsman, but an artist? I don't think so."

Marlon said, "I'm going to test him in this next shot."

The scene was with Red Buttons and several Japanese children, with an exterior shot of the house shared by Buttons and his Oriental wife. Gruver is arriving and stops to play with the kids, is met by Buttons's character, and after an exchange of greetings, the two go inside. Brando began by playing it totally "flat," without projecting any emotion at all. Then he suddenly began making faces, which had no apparent rationale at all, waiting for Logan's response. The director let him continue, then ordered the take printed, announcing that he'd been "just marvelous."

Garner later agreed that Logan's refusal to direct Marlon infuriated him. Ironically, while in the past Brando had resented a director's interference, now he claimed to need guidance. "Marlon wanted to be directed or at least have a confrontation about it," said Garner, "but Josh loved everything Marlon did. . . . We would improvise most of it, then we'd go to Josh and he'd say, 'Great.' And that would really make Marlon angry. . . . I said, 'What are you doing this picture for?' 'The money.' 'Okay, do it for the money, but don't kill Josh in the process.' And he would have, he'd have given him a heart attack."

Despite Garner's advice, Marlon put the director permanently in the doghouse and decided to make directorial decisions entirely on his own.

The company was scheduled to move to Osaka at the beginning of February, and over the next two weeks Brando amused himself by frequenting geisha houses, often with Fiore in tow. On the set, he basked in the attentions of the young Japanese extras, as well as Miiko Taka, all of whom left him soporifically happy. "He knows exactly what the effect should be and plays it for all its sexuality," Logan later recalled. "If he came to the set too early, I would introduce him to the group of Japanese girls . . . and two hours later I'd find Marlon still sitting with them, smiling, not saying much, just looking blissful."

The typical young *maiko,* or Japanese maiden, had been trained to make men feel at ease, and Marlon's needs—or simply his self-indulgence—were gargantuan. Jack Warner picked up on what was happening from as far away as Los Angeles, writing Logan on February 5 that "judging from the stills, there must have been jolly good times for Marlon and the geisha girls." Even when Rita Moreno was flown in, accompanied by a horde of photographers, he was unstoppable, going so far as to steal a few women from Fiore.

But it wasn't all "jolly good times." In leaving L.A. for Hawaii at the end of December, he'd departed abruptly, without telling Anna, and now he missed her. Contrite, he'd brought her to Honolulu before moving on to Japan, but they had fought and she left after a day. Aunt Betty, Great Aunt June, Marlon Sr., Celia Webb, and Philip and Marie Rhodes were all on hand in Japan, having been flown into Kyoto after Marlon's own arrival, but there was still a void, no one he felt he could talk to. The rains made it worse. Some nights the geishas took care of his problem; other evenings he spent alone in his suite, writing Anna long, handwritten letters that mirrored his loneliness, his longing for warmth.

Once he claimed that a letter to her that he had left half finished on his desk had been stolen, but for the most part he kept up a steady stream, alternating descriptions of Japan with his wish that he could "fuck your ears off." He congratulated her on her attempts to "make creative order of experience," just as he was trying to do the same thing so that they could both "evolve" in spirit and character; he conceded that he felt he was "such a mess" that he would never "find the way" himself. He reported on Marlon Sr.'s visit, adding that he was sorry that Dodie wasn't alive to see how much "Pop" had begun to open up to experience. And in an attempt to bring Anna into the family, he urged her to phone Jocelyn, because he thought his sister was in need of some loving attention.

In fact, his sister's marriage to Eliot Asinof was growing rockier by the month. But most of the time he was centered on himself, returning to his own labyrinthine search, the difficulties of knowing oneself really well in order to "fully comprehend another." Remarking that even "a trained psychoanalyst" takes years to figure out someone (and perhaps here he was thinking of his own analysis with Mittelmann), he said that he wasn't surprised it was so hard "to determine the proportions of a personality." He had been reading Erich Fromm's "*Psy. and Religion*," as he put it, and urged her to do the same—reassuring her he was still trying to "make some contribution" to himself and others, although, he acknowledged, more often than not he was "never really satisfied" with himself.

The rhetoric was more than felt, more than the product of an actor's sensibility. It was as if he couldn't for a single instant let anything go, or escape the awful weight of his own voice. Worse, his years of psychoanalysis had done nothing to mitigate his misguided faith that big words, like big ideas, would give him "the answer."

His next missive was again filled with abstract words. Here, he seemed to have adopted the role of a writer in his garret, working away on a story that he said he needed to pour onto paper. Feeling fluish and lonely, he told Anna he clasped his pillow at night, thinking of her, and that he loved staring at her brown arms in the photograph propped up on the floor beside him where he slept. He confessed to worrying about her—she had written that she had been "tired and upset" because of dreams she'd been having; he acknowledged that he, too, sometimes had such "compulsive phantasies [*sic*]," but quoting lines from *Teahouse* he philosophized that "Pain makes man think, thought makes man wise and wisdom makes life endurable." Calling her "a very passionate person," he advised her to try to be more temperate since "patience" was necessary to deal with suffering; he then added that he had been reading Radakrishnan on Eastern religions, burying himself more deeply than ever in "philosophical questions." The high-minded tone then gave way to a quick reassurance that he wanted to "fuck [her] fifty different ways" and a request that she put perfume on her stationery when she next wrote.

Throughout his life Brando would crave something akin to book smarts, something that seemed to elude him with his lack of a high school diploma. By turning the quiet, uneducated Anna into his pupil, he was convinced, it seemed, that he could bring himself that much closer. Scribbling another missive, he told her that he had asked Sam Gilman to bring her books that she would "profit" from, and then he shared with her an idea suggested by George Englund: to have a weekly seminar at home in which people could discuss various topics "just for the benefit of learning." They would invite professors from California universities to lecture them on "history, art, sociology, psychology, etc., and then after the lecture we'll have a general discussion period."

It was touching, it was sad. Brilliant as he was as an actor, there was still this gaping hole. In retrospect, it was just this need to embrace, as well as to be embraced by, intellectual respectability that led him to agree to be interviewed by visiting author Truman Capote, who was on assignment for the *New Yorker*. The fact that he had been warned about the writer made no difference. He needed someone to talk to, and the result was a profile that would haunt him for years.

The diminutive Capote was already known for his meticulous, rapierlike pen, and in December both Logan and Goetz had tried to kill the project before they left for Japan. They feared a hatchet job. "I knew from his conversation at many parties that he had it in for Brando and wanted to shatter his powerful image," Logan later commented. After calling the magazine, writing letters through his lawyers, and generally making it clear that Capote would not be welcome on the set, there was nothing more Logan could do. Warner Bros.' publicity staff, after long discussions with the *New Yorker*'s editors, prevailed: The magazine had published Capote's piece "The Muses Are Heard" about the Russian tour of *Porgy and Bess;* it was such a success that everyone was sure Capote would do a favorable article on the big-budget *Sayonara.*

Capote himself had other ideas from the start. Like many writers he was inwardly contemptuous of actors, whom he considered to be overpaid mental midgets. Furthermore, he was gay. For years the stories of Brando's bisexuality had circulated through the New York *demimonde,* and in the same circles there had been much talk about a certain scandalous photograph. Some people claimed to have actually seen it, or to have copies of it—a close-up of Brando, his young profile recognizable, with his lips wrapped around an erect penis. Word had it that this was one of Marlon's backstage pranks during his theater days in New York, but whatever the nature of the joke, it made Brando an even more tantalizing subject.

The more Capote prepared for the interview, the more he realized that the film's theme of intracultural conflict wasn't nearly as interesting as the enigmatic Brando. "A comic novel was . . . what he had in mind," wrote Capote biographer Gerald Clarke, "a Japanese box lacquered in brilliant red, perhaps, and . . . he could see boundless possibilities for his deadpan brand of satire."

Even Logan's vow to keep Capote off the set didn't deter the writer. Arriving in Kyoto on January 23, 1957, with photographer Cecil Beaton, he jumped into the fray. As chance would have it, Logan ran into the pair just as they were checking into the Miyako, and he lifted the small, pudgy Capote in his arms, walked him across the lobby, and dumped him out the front door.

"Now come on, Josh," Capote said in his high, nasal voice. "I'm not going to write anything bad. I just want to talk the teeniest bit to Marlon on the condition of the world. You know how fancy he gets when he pontificates. But really, Cecil Beaton's come with me. We just want to have a nice trip in Japan after my few words with Marlon—a few, that's all. Now, don't try to interfere with it, you hear, or I'll go after you, old friend."

Logan rushed to Brando's suite. "Don't let yourself be left alone with Truman," he warned. "He's after you." Marlon, despite his oft-voiced contempt for the press, soon invited the writer to dinner anyway. "He didn't know I was going to do a whole piece about him," said Capote. "How could he? I didn't know, either."

Fiore was in Brando's room several days later when the desk clerk called to announce that Mr. Capote was on his way up. The two had been working halfheartedly on the script for the Pennebaker western, and after Marlon put the phone down, he explained that he'd forgotten all about the interview.

Carlo said that he'd like to meet the writer.

"Okay, but split soon after. Let's scatter a lot of pages around. Make it look as though we were in the middle of some heavy work and pretend we have to get back to working on the script later tonight. After you leave, call me every hour or so, then I'll have an excuse to cut the interview short if I want to."

When Capote entered, "slim and trim as a boy," he lifted a bottle of vodka nestled in his arm and placed it on the table. Marlon called room service for ice. After Fiore left, the writer got down to business. "What an experience," Capote wrote in his diary later. "And how he loves to talk— and *such* a vocabulary: he sounds like an 'educated Negro'—very anxious to display all the long words he's learned. He talked nonstop, from seven-fifteen until twelve-thirty in the morning."

The booze didn't hinder things, but once Capote saw that he'd hit a mother-lode, he kept mining—trading, as it were, on his own burden of pain. The fact that the writer stood all of five feet two didn't hurt, either. On the surface he looked as dangerous as a chipmunk.

"The secret to the art of interviewing—and it is an art—is to let the other person think he's interviewing you," he later said. "You tell him about yourself, and slowly you spin your web so that he tells you everything. That's how I trapped Marlon." Later, Brando would agree. "The little bastard spent half the night telling me all about his problems. I figured it was the least I could do to tell him a few of mine."

The irony was that Capote's modus operandi wasn't all that different from the manipulative games Marlon himself had been playing for years. No topic was off-limits. Capote mentioned one of their mutual friends—most likely Sandy Campbell, Donald Windham's lover and an actor Marlon had known during *Streetcar*—who, Capote said, had bragged that Marlon had gone to bed with him. "I asked Marlon and he admitted it. He said he went to bed with lots of other men, too, but that he didn't consider himself a homosexual. He said they were all so attracted to him: 'I just thought that I was doing them a favor.'"

Acting, Hollywood, Broadway fame, money, performers like John Gielgud, Gérard Philipe, and Jean-Louis Barrault, director Logan, and the "hearts-and-flowers nonsense" of *Sayonara*—all were covered. Marlon also included his ruminations on love and his years of psychoanalysis, and his conviction that his telephone was tapped.

Monologuist that he was, Brando even spoke about Dodie. Fiore called up to the room several times as instructed, and Logan phoned, too, but Brando was unstoppable. The next morning he shared his enthusiasm with Philip Rhodes, but Rhodes immediately sensed that Marlon would soon regret the evening. "He told too many secrets to Capote," he later explained. "Not just about his mother being an alcoholic, but also about how he regarded his friends—how he was 'duke of his domain' and even when people were miffed, all he had to do was reach out and put his hand on their shoulders, a little touch of Marlon in the night, and he'd reel them back in. Then the hints of homosexuality, and Capote going around New York talking about gay friends they had in common."

Meanwhile, Capote knew that he was sitting on top of a scoop, and two days later he couldn't contain his excitement at dinner with Beaton, Logan, Logan's wife, Nedda, and the Goetzes.

"Oh, you were so wrong about Marlon not being gossippy," he taunted Logan. "No matter what you say, he talks. I couldn't stop him. His mother's drinking, his father, his uncles, aunts, cronies, everything. He talked his head off."

"I don't believe it, Truman. You must be leaving something out. He just doesn't reveal intimate or personal things."

"He did with me."

"Now, come on, Truman. How did you trick him into revealing secrets about his family?"

Capote, according to Logan, giggled. "I didn't trick him. We simply swapped stories. . . . He began to feel sorry for me and told me his to make me feel better. Fair exchange."

"Truman, please don't write this story. It's going to hurt him where he is tender. I can smell it. And it belittles the picture, too."

"Oh, don't feel sorry for Marlon, Josh. He doesn't feel very sorry for you."

"What does that mean?"

"You'll find out."

It took a while—exactly how long is unclear—but belatedly Marlon realized that he had been had, and on May 16, long after everyone had left Japan, he finally woke up.

"Here, of course, is the inevitable communication," he wrote to the writer, masking his anger in bombast. "It is indeed discomforting to have the network of one's innards guy-wired and festooned with harlequin streamers for public musing, but perhaps it will entertain. . . ." Trust alone had moved him to talk so freely, he explained. He had assumed that their conversation in Kyoto was "off the record," that they were merely exchanging private confidences, that as an artist and honorable man, Capote should have understood this. "In closing let me just say," he wrote, "I am sorry, in a way, that you didn't complete your plans for the full travesty you had planned to do, because it has come full upon me that there are few who are as well equipped as yourself to write, indeed, the comedy of manners."

Capote's piece, "The Duke in His Domain," was published in the *New Yorker* the following November, and it "caused every bit as much comment as Truman had hoped it would," according to Capote biographer Gerald Clarke. Never had a writer been able to get so close, and if Brando had been worried, now his innermost secrets had become public property. Here are some samples of Marlon's words to Capote:

> The last eight, nine years of my life have been a mess. Maybe the last two have been a little better. Less rolling in the trough of the wave. Have you ever been analyzed? I was afraid of it at first. Afraid it might destroy the impulses that made me creative, an artist. A sensitive person receives fifty impressions where somebody else may only get seven. Sensitive people are so vulnerable; they're so easily brutalized and hurt because they *are* sensitive. The more sensitive you are, the more certain you are to be brutalized, develop scabs. Never evolve. Never allow yourself to feel anything, because you always feel too much. Analysis helps. It helped me. But, still, the last eight, nine years I've been pretty mixed up, a mess pretty much. . . .

> I'd like to be married. I want to have children. . . . You've got to have love. There's no other reason for living. . . . That has been my main trouble. My inability to love anyone. . . . I can't. Love anyone. I can't trust anyone enough to give myself to them. But I'm ready. I want it. And I may, I'm almost on the point, I've really got to. . . . Because— well, what else is there? That's all it's about. To love somebody.

> Anyway, I have *friends*. No, no, I don't. . . . Oh, sure I do. I have a great many friends. Some I don't hold out on. I let them know what's happening. You have to trust somebody. Well, not all the way. There's nobody I rely on to tell *me* what to do. . . . Oh, Jay [Kanter]. Jay does what I tell *him* to do. I'm alone like that. . . . Do you know how I make a friend? . . . I go about it very gently. I circle around and around. I circle. Then, gradually, I come nearer. Then I reach out and touch them—ah, so gently. . . . Then I draw back. Wait awhile. Make them wonder. At just the right moment, I move in again. Touch them. Circle. . . . They don't know what's happening. Before they realize it, they're all entangled, involved. I have them. And suddenly, sometimes, I'm all *they* have. A lot of them, you see, are people who don't fit anywhere; they're not accepted, they've been hurt, crippled one way or another. But I want to help them, and they can focus on me; I'm the duke. Sort of the duke of my domain.

There was an account, as well, of his self-absorption at the time of *Streetcar*, his ambivalence about acting and the burdens of fame, and for the average *New Yorker* reader it was moving, confused, heartfelt, and also nonsensical, adding up to a portrait of the actor as a troubled young man. For Marlon himself, however, what hurt the most were his disclosures about his mother—the loss, the abandonment, the vulnerability and pain.

> My father was indifferent to me. Nothing I could do interested him, or pleased him. . . . But my mother was everything to me. A whole world. I tried so hard. I used to come home from school. . . . There wouldn't be anybody home. Nothing in the ice box. Then the telephone would ring. Somebody calling from some bar. And they'd say, "We've got a lady down here. You better come get her."

In presenting the memory, Capote, the master craftsman, had noted how Brando suddenly fell silent as "the picture faded, or, rather, became fixed," then shoved his narrative forward in time to New York and the West End Avenue apartment where, as his subject explained, it had all come crashing in.

> I thought if she loved me enough, trusted me enough, I thought, then we can be together. . . . We'll live together and I'll take care of her. Once, later on, that really happened. She left my father and came to live with me. In New York, when I was in a play. I tried so hard. But my love wasn't enough. She couldn't care enough. She went back. And one day . . . I didn't care any more. She was there. In a room. Holding on to me. And I let her fall. Because I couldn't take it any more— watch her breaking apart, in front of me, like a piece of porcelain. I stepped right over her, I walked right out. I was indifferent. Since then, I've been indifferent.

Despite the reams of copy previously written about Brando, never before had the elusive actor been so plumbed in print. Friends were astonished that he had been so candid, while Jocelyn called the article "a well-written, bitchy hatchet job." Logan, whom Marlon called screaming that he was going "to kill" the writer, pointed out that it was too late. "You should have killed him before you invited him to dinner," Logan said.

Dodie's friends in Libertyville had a different response, something bordering on outrage that Bud had so trashed their idol. "It was the same self-absorbed, self-dramatizing Bud," said Kay Phillips Bennett. "It gave a totally untrue picture of Dodie, and I was furious. She wasn't fragile, she didn't shatter when he 'stepped over her.' In fact, she left him, decided to go back to Chicago, and I guess he was still angry that she had refused to stay with him in New York. But it was a dirty trick for him to say that in public." Dodie's other close friend was equally astonished and angry at Bud's remarks. "Dodie wasn't any 'piece of porcelain,'" objected Ann Lombard Osborne. "She was a tough, serious woman who'd come to grips with her problem almost ten years before she died. It was Bud's problem. He hadn't grown up."

Although Marlon denigrated Dodie in talking with Capote, it still seemed at times that his mother was very much with him. Late in 1956, he and photographer Sam Shaw had gone to see Sidney Lumet's production of O'Neill's *Long Day's Journey into Night*. Before the first intermission, Brando whispered to his friend, "Let's get out of here." Shaw felt that Marlon couldn't take the portrayal of the mother in the play, the alcoholic drug fiend Mary Tyrone. "He was emotionally shattered that night," recalled Shaw. "Afterward he didn't talk about his mother, he was silent, but I could see that the play had thrown him for a loop. Maybe that's why he later refused Lumet's offer to do the film version."

In the immediate aftermath of the publication of Capote's article, Marlon went to Walter Seltzer and George Glass to try to initiate a lawsuit. Neither man thought much of his chances. Seltzer, an experienced press agent, was able to see the whole affair in context. "He came back all excited about having had a marvelous time in Japan," Seltzer recalled. "Then he told us of meeting with a very nice guy who, he was surprised to find, was so kind and sympathetic, and, of course, it was Capote. A couple of months later all that euphoria was shattered when the piece appeared and I said to him, 'Marlon, did you tell him all these things?' He said, 'Yeah. I didn't think of him as the press. I thought of him as a friend. He sandbagged me.' I asked what he meant, and he explained that Capote had told him about his own mother and his problems, all that *meshugass*. 'Well, Marlon,' I said, 'you've got no reason to be upset.' 'No, no,' he insisted, 'I didn't tell him for publication.' I said, 'Did you say, "You're not going to write a story about this?"' 'No,' he said, and then he just walked away." Like many other Brando threats, the lawsuit never materialized.

• • •

In mid-March of 1957 the *Sayonara* company had packed up and left Japan, the production fairly close to schedule. But there were still the interiors to finish back in Hollywood, and for weeks now Brando had vowed to "walk through" them as though in a coma. It made no difference that on April 3 the crew celebrated Marlon's thirty-third birthday with a gala party featuring a three-tiered birthday cake with greetings in Japanese.

On the soundstage at Warners he and Logan were locked in battle over his character and the deficiencies of the script. Before the end of the production, the two had several shouting matches. The major one occurred during the penultimate scene in which Gruver announces his intention of defying his parents to marry Hana-ogi, Miiko Taka's character. The young woman is in her bridal costume backstage at the opera house when Gruver bursts in, impatient to see her. The scene had been rewritten per Brando's dictates, but after considering the changes—"We had studied it and weighed it very carefully"—Logan decided to return to Paul Osborn's original because it was smoother and not as "loud" as the revision.

Marlon began the rehearsal by charging into the room, grabbing Taka and shouting his intentions to marry her. "He was so tough with her," Logan recalled, "that I didn't think anyone would be able to imagine them getting married." He put up his hand to stop the run-through, walking across the set to speak with Brando quietly so that Edie Goetz, the producer's wife, on the set with a group of her friends, and the crew itself wouldn't hear.

"Marlon, you're confusing me. I don't understand your attitude."

"What the hell do you mean, I'm confusing you?" Marlon shouted. "Who do you think you are? I've got this thing worked out and I'm going to play it this way."

"If you do, it's going to be our ruin and yours, too."

"I don't give a damn about you or your picture. I give a damn about myself. I've got one strong scene; they expect it of me."

"But it's not strong—it's loud. You're the one who's being hurt by playing it this way. You're throwing your whole performance in the ash can."

"You don't know what you're talking about. I have instincts, and I trust them more than I trust you. This is the right way to play it. I've had to do one tough scene in every picture I've made. They want it."

"Well, this isn't the time to do it!"

Logan was shouting now, too, and as the director later recalled, "people were ashen-faced, turning their heads away." He suggested that they repair to the privacy of Marlon's dressing room. There, even though the cellutex walls were so flimsy that the room "bounced," the screaming escalated.

"You can't end the picture as an incomplete man," the director insisted. "You can't end on this childish note."

"What do you mean, childish?"

"You're supposed to be an adult by this point—no longer an air force Boy Scout. But you're like a three-year-old."

Logan went on, pointing out that Gruver could be strong but also contained. "An adult can have the same strong feelings but he should be in control of them. Not hysterical. Know what you feel. But don't yell your head off." Marlon, ready with a hundred comebacks, suddenly nodded, making one of his abrupt withdrawals: Saying nothing, he walked past the director, out onto the set, and almost before Logan could catch up with him, played the scene as a compromise between his own reading and the director's.

"He just played the shit out of it," Logan recalled later. "I never could have told him how to read those lines, and I realized afterward that the son-of-a-bitch made me get mad at him so he could figure out how to play it. . . . He needed the direction. He needed it badly, and it was as if he'd been milking me the whole time."

As the shooting neared its completion, the pace was so frantic that everyone in the cast and crew "were like fire horses who had smelled smoke." Logan's description wasn't entirely fanciful. Although smoke did not envelop the Warners soundstage, Marlon's closing number created "a fire" in everything but fact.

Seltzer and Glass had driven to the studio that day to meet with Marlon to discuss Pennebaker business over lunch. "Marlon didn't want to eat," Seltzer recalled. "Instead he wanted to go sit in the sun on the soundstage roof. We got up there, we were talking, and partway through the hour he said, 'I'm thirsty, I want a drink of water.' " Seltzer suggested they all climb back down the ladder, but Marlon, who was nearsighted but rarely wore glasses, insisted there was a drinking fountain up on the roof. Seltzer continued, "So he went over to the 'drinking fountain,' leaned over, and pulled something. Suddenly there was a deafening clatter of bells. The drinking fountain was the fire alarm—for the entire studio." They soon heard the sirens of the Burbank fire department racing to Warner Brothers, but Marlon remained calm. "We got down off the roof, and George and I made a beeline for the studio security office to report it as a false alarm. Too late—eight fire engines had already arrived. The head of security knew the ropes in Burbank, and he suppressed the story. Soon we heard that it was worse, though. One of the fire engines was hit by a freight train on its way across town. A fireman on the back was very seriously injured. The studio then made a settlement—not niggardly but certainly not generous. They called it a 'contribution.' There was never a suit from the fireman's family that I knew of, nor did the true story ever get out."

But that wasn't the only consequence, Seltzer explained, because when the alarm went off, work had to stop throughout Warners, affecting three films in progress and hundreds of employees. Eventually the bells were cut off and people went back to work, but at great expense in time and money. "But Marlon was apparently unperturbed by it," added Seltzer. "There was no discussion about what had happened, nor did he seem to feel any serious guilt about the fireman. If he did, he said nothing."

If Logan knew what had taken place, he never said anything about it either. With only four days left to shoot, he picked up the pace, trying to make up the lost time. The fact that he was manic-depressive did not help. The morning after "the fire," he arrived on the set to find Brando sitting in a chair, looking forlorn, his right arm in a sling. Panicked, he demanded to know what had happened.

"Now, don't blame him. It wasn't his fault," Marlon said apologetically.

"*Who? Whose fault?*" he shouted.

"It was my stand-in," he gestured at Fiore, who stood nearby. "But don't blame him. We were just pretending to box and he was only going to take a fake crack at me—only he hit my arm. I think maybe it's just out of joint. I can be in some scenes, don't worry about that. At least I can say my lines offscreen if you want me to."

"*Offscreen!*" yelled Logan, aware that he was in most of the shots that were left. "Don't make any more moves—anybody," he screamed at the cameramen setting up the next shot.

"Can you move your fingers?" he turned back to Brando.

"Oh sure. Yeah."

He looked as Marlon tentatively bent his index finger, then his thumb. "Oh, that's not so bad, then," he sighed.

"The only thing is, I can't do *this,"* Brando said, suddenly shooting his clenched fist up in the air as he slapped himself on the arm. "Can't possibly!" he yelled.

By the time Marlon finished his work on the production on April 25, he earned a hefty $60,000 for the two additional weeks they'd run over.

Released in late November in time for the Christmas season, *Sayonara* was an immediate hit—and with his 10 percent of the gross, Brando would eventually clear in excess of $1 million. Whether the money had any direct bearing, Logan received a note from him months after the picture's release, explaining that he had talked to Japanese friends who had congratulated him on "the first breakthrough film about Orientals." He was proud of the two of them, he said. Even though he had thought the director "a blithering idiot," now that he had seen their movie on the screen, he was wrong and wanted to apologize.

Reviewers, however, weren't so enthusiastic, even as *Sayonara* was packing movie houses coast to coast. It was true that Bosley Crowther at the *New York Times* gave the film a thumbs-up, applauding Brando's acting in "a conventional role that spins what could be a routine romance into a lively and tense dramatic show." But on the other side of the fence, opined *Newsweek,* "Brando and his girl . . . spend most of two and one-half hours frozen in a dreadful standstill. . . . [A] dull tale of the meeting of the twain."

Good, bad, or middling, what none of the reviews commented on was the politics that Brando thought the picture conveyed. Truth, he believed, had the power to save. With each successive film after *Sayonara*—among them *The Ugly American, Mutiny on the Bounty, Morituri,* and *The Appaloosa*—he figured he was treading God's little acre, returning again and again, almost reflexively, to the notion that he could "contribute in a telling way to the achievement of a peaceful world."

The same impulse lay behind his visit to the UN in September 1956 and the tour of Asia he had made six months earlier with George Englund and writer Stewart Stern, and it was about to have a significant effect on *The Young Lions,* due to start production in early June 1957, less than two months away. In the meantime, at Pennebaker virtually nothing was getting done save for vague and amorphous discussions with Harry Belafonte and Edmond O'Brien. Both men wanted nothing more than to work with the master, though Marlon himself never came to meetings. He "simply didn't give a shit," said Seltzer. The atmosphere in the office took an even darker turn when the usually cooperative producer was called upon to pick up the pieces with regard to Jocelyn, who was being victimized by Hollywood's Red-baiters.

Now thirty-seven, in years gone by, she had helped sponsor the Waldorf Peace Conference, signed the Willie McGee petition and Stockholm Peace Pledge, supposedly attended a conference of the American Labor Party, and lent her support to an allegedly pro-Communist meeting in Mexico City—all of which had made her highly suspect. Though Jocelyn had played a leading role in *The Big Heat,* appeared in several other films, and starred with Henry Fonda on Broadway, she was now effectively shut out of further film and TV work. Marlon Sr., middle-of-the-roader that he'd always been, was aware that his daughter was seriously unhappy, but he refused to believe it was anyone's fault but her own. Bud knew better; he called upon Jay Kanter to use MCA's clout to get his sister work. When Kanter refused, he turned to Seltzer, ready to fire his friend and agent as well as quit MCA altogether.

Seltzer recalled, "It was one of the few times, maybe the only time, I'd ever seen him openly angry with Jay, and he came to George and me saying, 'We've gotta get rid of MCA. I mean it, they won't get Jocelyn a job. I've asked Jay, and they won't cooperate.' "

Glass and Seltzer confronted Kanter, who told them that Jocelyn had essentially been blacklisted. Seltzer recalled that he pointed out that "there were ways of working these things out, but he still said, 'No, we don't get into that.' I next told Senior that there were ways to take care of it. I said, 'It's harrowing, it's demeaning, but it's the only way.' "

What Seltzer, the longtime Hollywood insider, was referring to was a short, cigar-chomping Nebraskan by the name of Roy M. Brewer. He had originally been brought west in the midforties to help clean up the racket-infested International Alliance of Theatrical Stage Employees. An ally of Ronald Reagan during the latter's tenure as head of the Screen Actors Guild, Brewer quickly became one of the film community's most vocal anticommunists and, for the past half-dozen years or so, his job had been to "separate the sheep from the goats." Perhaps more than anyone in town, he had the power to hold confessionals as well as grant absolution.

"They were after her on two counts: her being married to Ellie Asinof, who was on the blacklist, too; then the fact that she had signed those petitions," Seltzer continued. "Brewer had set up a clearing apparatus. He was at the time working for Allied Artists as an exhibitor-relations specialist. If you were in trouble, he was the man to see. Money, generally penny-ante, personal gifts, clothes, etc., changed hands somewhere along the line. Somebody would get in touch with *Red Channels* and a guy in New York was ultimately the one who cleared the accused."

Seltzer drafted a letter for Jocelyn's signature, but she balked at signing it. "Finally I told her, 'Jocelyn, you want to work—this is what you do, or forget it. It's your choice.' It took months, but finally she signed.

"The letter was along the line of 'I didn't know what I was doing, I was foolish,'" added Seltzer, "and it did not involve naming names. It was just, 'I'm sorry. I was young, stupid, idealistic,' a *mea culpa*. Senior did not like it at all, but he had told me, 'Do whatever you have to.' Marlon said the same thing. He didn't know about Brewer and the kind of machinations that went on. I just told him, 'She's going to have to go through a lot of shit,' and he said, 'Well, whatever she has to go through, do it.'"

Over the next weeks, Marlon kept probing. "It was, 'What's happening? What are you doing?' He was interested and concerned," Seltzer recalled, "as opposed to a lot of stuff that he would start and then disappear from. But he never asked *how* I was getting it done. Whether he was talking to Jocelyn, I didn't know, but I was pressuring her to move quickly."

Within a month, Seltzer was able to tell Jay Kanter that Jocelyn was off the blacklist. Kanter quickly got her a job on a TV show.

There had been more to it than just Jocelyn's letter of contrition. Whether Marlon was aware of the specifics of his sister's "clearance," in fact money had changed hands—precisely, a Pennebaker-issued gift certificate in the amount of $200 for use at a local department store. Brewer himself recalls:

"Now in that case, I probably made a mistake [but] I did it as a matter of convenience because it was so small a sum, and also because Seltzer had come to me. But I did not think that Jocelyn Brando was a communist in the sense that she was in any way participating [in] any of these things. She had just gone along with the crowd. Kim Hunter did the same thing. As for her brother, Marlon was too emotional a guy, too much of a loner, and we never took him seriously as someone whom the Reds could direct."

In years to come, Brando would secure Jocelyn roles in projects of his own, such as *The Ugly American* and *The Chase*. He also helped her purchase a cottage in Santa Monica in 1958 after her marriage to Eliot Asinof broke up. Doubtless, too, he contributed to the cost of her psychoanalysis.

"It was very simple," said Fred Sadoff. "Marlon related to Jocelyn. Whatever it was, there was a deep emotional connection. He might disappear out of her life and then suddenly reappear when there was a need, *his* need. But whatever the estrangement between them—which I think may have come from her behavior, not his—he went out of his way to help. My sense was that obviously Jocelyn was the replica of the mother, and it was Marlon's need for Mommy that always brought him back to her."

Seltzer put it more directly: "He was protective and concerned. He loved his sister very, very deeply."

The Young Lions

In *The Young Lions* Brando was again donning military fatigues, albeit as a German officer in the big-budget adaptation of Irwin Shaw's best-seller. The shoot would return him to Paris, and even though he was back at Fox, working off his multipicture obligation to Zanuck, he was both professional and engaged.

Edward Dmytryk, the director, had indirectly figured in Brando's life, having been the one to "discover" Kashfi and bring her to Hollywood. Nevertheless, at this point, only Marlon's closest friends knew of his relationship with the actress. Indeed, he may have kept his engagement hidden not only because of "problems" with publicity but also because, unbeknownst to Kashfi, he was still profoundly ambivalent. In the previous few months, he had been unwilling to forgo the array of women who passed through his home in Laurel Canyon, often brought around by his pals.

One woman Carlo Fiore showed up with was Nan Morris, then a seventeen-year-old recent arrival in Hollywood who sometimes had dinner with Carlo because "he was very nice and seemed lonely." Having heard that he was Brando's "best friend," she teased that she would no longer go out with him unless he introduced her to her hero. Carlo just laughed, but late one night he picked her up, and without a word drove her up to Marlon's. Grinning, he took her into a darkened bedroom, closed the door, and locked it.

"Pretty soon the doorknob started rattling," Morris recalled, "and there was a knocking, too, and a voice calling, 'Who's in there? Let me in!' Carlo was giggling, like it was a game, and finally let Marlon in. I couldn't see him very well, but he came over and sat on the edge of the bed."

Morris reached for a cigarette and Marlon lit it, holding the match to see her face and meanwhile telling her that smoking would spoil her "beautiful teeth." He chatted with her, asking her where she was from, what she did. Then, abruptly, he said, "Take off your top."

"No, I won't."

"Come on," he insisted, "I want to see what you look like."

"No," Morris repeated, now aware that Brando was wearing only Jockey briefs.

With Morris's adamant refusal, Marlon began to laugh. "I don't believe it, Freddie," he said, turning to Fiore. "She's the first woman here in three years who hasn't dropped her clothes and bounced her ass across the room."

Then, as if the pressure were off, Marlon invited them down to the kitchen to get something to eat. There they raided the refrigerator, with Marlon and Carlo stopping a few times to shadowbox. Morris soon became aware that Marlon had a woman in his bedroom, but he seemed in no rush to return to her. Indeed, after Carlo went to bed, Marlon gave her a tour of the house. He eventually brought her to a room downstairs, one enlivened by wallpaper in a black jungle motif with tigers. This was where Marlon kept his drums. He played for an hour or so and then retired to his bedroom, but Morris was too keyed up to sleep.

On the tour of the house, Marlon had not shown her a top-floor room, a sort of cupola, saying there was nothing in there. She now "made a beeline" for it and found it empty, although its windows afforded a spectacular view of the sunrise over the city. As Morris leaned out into the morning air, she noticed a black book lying on the nearby roof. She scrambled out and retrieved it, discovering "it was Marlon's telephone book, filled with names and numbers, a lot of them in New York."

When he came down later for breakfast, she gave it to him, and he was delighted. It seemed that a "jealous woman" had thrown it out the window and he hadn't been able to find it for three months. Soon "the red-headed bimbo" emerged from his bedroom, scowling to find Morris there. Carlo was still asleep, and Marlon asked Morris to "stay and play" while he drove his date home. But Morris asked to be dropped off, too, and when Marlon drove her home, just down the hill to her boardinghouse near Googie's and Schwab's, he told her to "drop by the house anytime."

A few weeks later she and Carlo did drop in at Marlon's, but they didn't stay. She heard a whispered conversation in the kitchen, with Carlo complaining, "But I thought you wanted me to bring her up."

"I do—I mean I did," hissed Marlon. "But *she's* here, upstairs, and she would really throw a fit."

As Morris later recalled, "I kind of had my feelings hurt. Afterward Carlo explained that 'she' was Kashfi, who would fly into rages of jealousy if other women were around and that she was 'a very difficult lady.' "

At this time Kashfi claimed she was with Marlon almost every night, and thus had no idea when and how he found time to be with other women. But in January 1957 she realized that he was still carrying on with Rita Moreno.

One night she and Marlon were lying in bed at his house when they heard a banging on the door. "It's me, Rita! R-I-T-A," came the voice from outside.

Kashfi said, "Okay, Marlon, go see to it. You either choose her or me."

Before he returned to their bed ten minutes later, Kashfi had already fled the house. When he telephoned the next day, "I told him, 'I don't want to get involved with a sick person like you,' and hung up." She returned his mother's earrings and other gifts. He brought them back the next day. They talked, and "as usual," she recalled, "we ended with mutual pledges of devotion."

Several weeks later, Kashfi found a heavy black wig draped over the endpost of his headboard. "Oh my God," Brando stammered. "It's Rita's . . . it was my fault—I shouldn't have gotten involved," he said.

"No, Marlon, it's my fault—my fault to be involved with you," Kashfi said.

Nevertheless, being naive and not terribly strong, Kashfi allowed him to reel her back in, thinking that she had won the battle. Yet Movita was still in the picture, too, though, predictably, Marlon had not told her about his so-called engagement. In the late spring of 1957, he even showed up at a party with the Mexican at the Bel Air mansion of Geordie Hormel, where dancer Johnny Brascia noted that the two were arguing all evening. Sometime after midnight Brascia encountered Movita, alone, outside in the parking lot.

"She was pretty upset, crying," he said, "and I told her she shouldn't drive." Brascia took Movita out for coffee, where she told him that she and Marlon "fought a lot." But when Brascia asked her for a date, she refused. "Marlon's my fiancé," she said, "and I can't do that."

Two weeks later, however, she called Brascia to ask if he would escort her to another party. During this date she explained that she was tired of waiting for Brando and that she didn't see any future there. "They were always fighting," Brascia reported. "They'd break up, then he'd come back with all kinds of offers: 'I'll buy you a home and we'll live together and we'll have your [proper kind of] life.'

"From what she told me," Brascia added, "she really loved him, but wasn't *in* love with Marlon. . . . She had a lot of respect for him as a human being, because he was a man of honesty and integrity, but she said he wanted to control her and they would fight—when she refused to let him have his way. Then he would rant and rave, go to sleep on the sofa and pout all night."

Whether or not Brando had told her about Kashfi, he was still unwilling to let go, and he once tried to use Movita's mother to get back into her good graces. He was sleeping at the mother's house in Silver Lake occasionally and would sometimes take the mother and Movita's two sisters to drive-in movies. When Brando heard that Brascia was dating Movita, he made inquiries to find out more about the young man. "[Marlon's] ego was hit right in the middle because I was a nobody," Brascia said, "no money, no star—and he couldn't understand why she left him for me." Movita's intractability was, in fact, what kept Marlon coming back for more.

His jealousy surfaced again when he asked Fiore to travel to New York with him for "business reasons." The "business" was to check up on *another* of his lovers, France Nuyen, who was starring in the Broadway production of *The World of Suzie Wong.* Nuyen and Brando had also broken up, but when he heard that she might marry a psychiatrist, he told Fiore, "I guess it's my vanity. I still want to believe I'm top man. . . . With women, I've got a long bamboo pole with a leather loop on the end of it. I slip the loop around their necks so that they can't get away or come too close. Like catching snakes."

Marlon was in generally good spirits as *The Young Lions* shoot neared. His bases seemed covered, since he had won over Kashfi, whatever her fits of jealousy. "Love," he told her, "is the absence of anxiety, the absence of personal defenses. It's spontaneous. Above all, it's honest."

Like so many other major film properties, *The Young Lions* had kicked around Hollywood for years, ever since the publication of Irwin Shaw's novel in 1948. Fox had outbid Warner Bros. for the rights to the book but Dmytryk hadn't liked Shaw's adaptation, which had centered on the American GI character, a Broadway playboy and coward. Instead, the more complex Jewish soldier Noah intrigued the director. As a result Edward Anhalt, the tough, burly screenwriter who had already won an Oscar for *Panic in the Streets* (1950), was brought in to script another screenplay, a move that infuriated Shaw.

Despite the bidding war to get *Lions,* Fox was not completely enthusiastic. "Fox decided to make the film rather cheaply for $2 million and [with] what I call a second-rate cast—all contract players and no stars at all," said Dmytryk, who had just finished directing *Raintree County.* "I don't know whether they thought the story was outdated or whether they just didn't have any faith in Lichtman, their head of distribution who was going to produce. Then, just by accident, I got Marlon Brando."

On April 8, 1957, shortly before he finished *Sayonara,* the trades announced Brando's signing. With the disclosure several weeks later of Montgomery Clift's participation, suddenly *Lions* had gone from a B picture to a major production. Unacknowledged in *Variety* or the *Hollywood Reporter,* however, was the fact that Marlon was still eating crow for his *Egyptian* walkout and was forced to accept a $50,000 salary, less than half of what he had received for *Waterfront* three years before. Clift was rumored to be earning approximately $750,000, and even Maximilian Schell, making his first Hollywood film, was being paid close to $200,000. Zanuck, however, had Marlon over a barrel.

The news that Brando was to be teamed up with Clift, his most respected rival, sparked the imagination of those who hoped for a Method-acting duel. Yet if the Fox studio publicists were excited by the Clift-Brando teaming, Dmytryk was worried. In his meeting with Brando he had been "scared to death." Despite Marlon's altogether cordial behavior, afterward the director had called all over town, wanting to check out the mounting horror stories about his star's on-set behavior. Fred Zinnemann told him that Brando once needed seventy-one takes just to look out a window. Daniel Mann, still in paroxysms over *Teahouse,* reported that Glenn Ford had lost his focus because of the repeated takes forced by Brando, and that overall, the production had been the worst of his career.

"I can tell you right now that if I had ever had Montgomery Clift and Brando in the same scene, that would have been the end of the picture," Dmytryk explained later, "because their way of working was completely opposite. I knew that Monty was good for one or two takes and after that he got mechanical."

But the director reassured himself that the two stars were scripted to appear in only one scene together, and even then, they would exchange not a single word of dialogue.

Dmytryk had different qualms about Clift, with whom he had worked on *Raintree County.* "I liked him very much as a person," he said. "But I had sworn I'd never work with him again because of the booze and drugs. He was never nasty. He just fell apart."

In the years since they'd met in New York in the late 1940s Clift and Brando had followed parallel career paths and watched each other's growth carefully. It was no secret in the New York theater community that Clift admired Brando's work in *Streetcar,* while Marlon felt the same about Clift's in *The Seagull.* Despite their mutual respect, however, the two never really hit it off. Clift, more literate and more refined, thought Brando clownish; Marlon found his rival to be overly "serious" and "intense."

Their differences had been apparent at the Actors Studio, where Clift was analytical, always "talking out" a scene. But Marlon, as Bobby Lewis put it, "was not a writer or director—you gave him a part and he understood it partly out of his brains and partly out of his instinct."

For actor Kevin McCarthy, one of Clift's closest friends, the Brando-Clift relationship was made up of equal parts respect, rivalry, and fear—on both sides. "By the time of *A Place in the Sun,* Monty was this sort of massive star and Marlon was coming on fast," he said. "Marlon was aware that Monty was a big star, yet I don't think he understood the meticulous way Monty worked. Monty knew what he was doing at all times—not that he wasn't full of emotion and feeling, but it was approached intellectually. Marlon acted out of some innate emotive force. It wasn't studied, it just happened."

After Clift's success in *From Here to Eternity*, Brando got in the habit of calling him for his reaction to Brando's performances. About *Guys and Dolls*, Monty said hesitantly, "Well, I was watching the picture and . . . you know what I saw? . . . This big, big, *big*, fat ass!" Marlon reportedly had a fit. It was Clift's way, according to biographer Robert LaGuardia, "of telling Brando that he had given a mediocre performance in a mediocre film."

The balance of power between the two rivals had shifted by the time of *The Young Lions*, however. Brando was at the height of his box-office power. Moreover, only the year before, Clift had destroyed his face in an auto accident, driving into a telephone pole after a dinner party at Elizabeth Taylor's, nearly killing himself in the process. Although plastic surgeons had tried to repair the damage, the results were Frankenstein-like. Clift was left with hideous scars, and half his face looked paralyzed. Largely because of his closeness to Taylor, he returned to work, but then had gone into a depression that was accompanied by an increase in his already suicidal drinking.

Marlon, tapping into his better half, had tried to help. It was on a weekend, just before Clift's return to the set of *Raintree County*, and Brando had sent Billy Redfield ahead to announce that he wanted to visit.

Jack Larson, another close friend of Clift, recalled: "Monty was a little bit offended and he said to me, 'He wants to see how I am, whether to come up or not, so he sent somebody to reconnoiter . . . to see if I'm drunk, worth talking to.'

When Brando himself arrived, Larson left the two men alone to talk privately. The discussion went on for several hours. "I had a feeling that Marlon was giving Monty a vote of confidence," said Larson. "It was Good Samaritan time."

With Brando's departure, Larson drove Clift to his orthopedist's office. In the car, Clift had tears in his eyes. "Monty was very moved," his friend later explained. "He said that I should never tell this to anybody because it wouldn't reflect well on him. But what Brando had come to say, essentially, was that he had always admired him, that he'd been rooting for Monty to win the Oscar for *A Place in the Sun* the same year he was up for

Streetcar. He also said he'd always been jealous of Monty, always envious—that he'd go to see his movies and say, 'How can he do that? How can he be that good?'

"As Monty related it, Marlon ended up telling him, 'You're what I challenge myself against. Take care of yourself for me so that you can keep challenging me because you're all I have.'"

Years later, Marlon himself retold the story to Maureen Stapleton, adding that he had begged Clift to join AA and had even offered to go with him and help dry him out. Monty kept saying how moved he was by the offer but denied having a drinking problem, even though all the while he was downing double vodkas.

The casting of the third major part for *Lions* was a bit unusual. Edward Anhalt was displeased with the idea of Tony Randall in the role. He claimed that a bar owner friend suggested Dean Martin instead—an idea he found so right that he immediately took it to the head of Twentieth Century–Fox, Buddy Adler. At first, Anhalt's suggestion was greeted with dead silence, but then Adler said, "That's a brilliant idea."

When Dmytryk told Clift they were thinking of Martin, Clift reacted tepidly, but went off to see Randall in a movie with Ginger Rogers. The next morning he called and said, "Take Dean Martin." Martin, who was widely considered to be career-dead after his recent split from Jerry Lewis, was overjoyed to be cast, even though he was being paid only $25,000.

As the company's departure for Europe approached, Marlon met several more times with Dmytryk, who turned out to be well read in Eastern religions. The recurrent issue was Brando's role as a Nazi, and while he had indicated he wanted to do "something interesting" with the part, what he talked about was Krishnamurti, covertly probing the director's mettle.

As with Kazan, Brando might have been expected to have problems with Dmytryk's politics. One of the original Hollywood Ten, he had served a prison term for refusing to testify and then left for exile in England. But, in 1951 in the second round of HUAC's investigation of the entertainment industry, he had cooperated with the committee and given them the names of twenty-six "communists." Brando, however, never raised the issue of Dmytryk's past. "We never talked politics of any kind," Dmytryk said. "Brando may have gotten some heat from his friends for working with Gadg, but of course once he worked with Gadg, that was over and done with, and he could work with me more easily."

In June 1957 Marlon departed for France, where the film was to begin shooting. From Paris he phoned Kashfi regularly. She rarely went out, although a few times she had dinner with the character actor Curt Jurgens, whom she had known for two years, and often Jurgens sent flowers. The relationship was completely innocent, she said, yet Marlon became furious after he was tipped off by his father, who was living in the same West Hollywood complex as Anna. This proximity to each other was made all the more troublesome when Kashfi overheard his girlfriend Alice Marchak screaming from across the courtyard one afternoon, "threatening to expose Marlon Sr. and to commit suicide in his apartment."

Marchak, the Pennebaker secretary, had become hysterical when he announced that he was breaking off the affair. "He wanted to marry Anichka," Kashfi recalled, referring to Anna Frenke Paramore, a young woman in her late twenties and the daughter of producer Eugene Frenke. "Alice was saying, 'I'm going to kill myself, really expose you. This is wrong.' To shut her up, Pop got Alice the job as his son's personal secretary."

While Kashfi stewed under Marlon Sr.'s censorious gaze—he always regarded Anna as a blatant gold digger—Marlon was enjoying himself in Paris, even plunging into his role with enthusiasm. He was working hard at perfecting the German accent he'd picked up from his old pal, Earl Hammond, an actor who specialized in dialects. "He told me, 'I'm going to do your Nazi,'" recalled Hammond. "Well, it wasn't mine, but he was very pleased that he was going to do a German."

Philip Rhodes was the makeup man on *The Young Lions,* and in Paris with Marlon he saw how the actor was digging deeper into the characterization by recalling a German movie he had once seen.

"I've forgotten the German actor's name," said Rhodes, "but Marlon had seen him in that old film and was struck by his appearance. Sometimes he would fall in love with a face, and he did with that German boy. He was blond, with a very good nose, and Marlon wanted to look like him, so I gave him the closest thing he ever had to a Barrymore nose. But he was also remembering how the German had played the character of a boy in the army breaking the rules to get a pass to go home and see his father. He identified with that role because it showed the Germans as trapped in the war and what a prison Germany had been. He thought Shaw and Dmytryk saw it too much in black-and-white, so he changed the script. There was that dichotomy throughout the picture, with Dmytryk directing it one way, Marlon playing the character his way."

It was just this issue that would elicit heated, partisan debate from Shaw and, eventually, from movie audiences worldwide. In the novel Christian Diestl begins as a harmless, womanizing ski instructor who is transformed into a devout follower of Hitler and then eagerly guns down Clift's Noah, the sensitive American Jewish GI. In the film, however, Diestl becomes disillusioned by Nazism and is often at odds with his superior, Hardenberg, played with cold relish by Maximilian Schell. His disenchantment reaches its peak when he chances upon the true nature and purpose of the Reich's SS-operated death camps.

Climactically, the character as played by Brando doesn't ambush Clift's Jew. Instead, he smashes his machine gun and walks into American crossfire. After he is fatally shot, he somersaults into a shallow, symbolic puddle. Brando declaims his lines as if he were giving an oration, turning his Nazi into a saintly martyr.

The abiding question for critics and viewers alike was whether Brando had dictated this interpretation of Diestl's character. Fiore, invited on the shoot as Marlon's dialogue coach, agreed with Rhodes that this had been Marlon's intention from the outset. Brando, he claimed, had told him at the beginning of the shoot, "I'm changing the Nazi heel into a kind of tragic hero. I'm gonna do a complete about-face in the interpretation of the character, and it'll be a lot of work." *Life* magazine reported that he then delivered a fifteen-hour lecture to Dmytryk, producer Al Lichtman, and Anhalt in which he gave a detailed analysis, replete with humanistic exegesis.

"That's not true," Dmytryk argued years later. "*Life* got me into a lot of trouble.... *Time* said this, too, but when I went up to talk to Marlon, the writer wasn't with me and we just discussed the character. We didn't even have a script.... Anhalt and I already had these ideas about the character, and I explained them to Marlon."

Anhalt agreed, saying that the decision to soften the Nazi character was made by the director and himself, partially because they felt that if they didn't, "no Hollywood star" would take the role. "We were going to give Marlon the script and I remember saying, 'He'll never play the part because it goes downhill. There's no conversion, no change.' Cagney played heavies, but he always loved his mother.... Remember, actors want to be loved—it's their disease. It takes a very special kind of performer to play a genuine heavy."

Despite Dmytryk and Anhalt's denials, it seemed evident that this time Brando in fact went beyond his usual habit of tampering with his lines. That he diverged from the original conception of the character was proved, conspicuously, by Clift, who was completely versed in the shooting script and registered his complaints about Marlon's changes in several arguments and furious exchanges with Dmytryk.

Brando's summer in Paris and Berlin, the two European shooting sites, was marred by continual interference by his fans, who were often provoked when the actors walked through the streets in their Nazi uniforms. On June 15 in Paris, Brando was mobbed at a benefit for World War II veterans being held in the Tuileries. The police were called after demonstrators tore off his coat and ripped his shirt, and at least three persons were reported to have suffered injuries.

During preproduction on July 2, Brando, tired of fiddling with wigs, decided to have his hair bleached. Every three days he had it rinsed, but sometimes it came out more green than blond. At dinner he would lapse into Hammond's accent, often stopping himself in midsentence to repeat hissing sibilants or rephrase his *v*s, and even his usual loping stride underwent a change.

Photography on *The Young Lions* began late in the first week of July near Chantilly, thirty miles north of Paris. In the first scene, French partisans surrender to Diestl's unit, who keep firing despite Diestl's screams for his men to desist. Dmytryk was impressed, but Fiore thought that Marlon was grandstanding, using his character as a mouthpiece.

"I was disturbed," he later explained. "Brando was no longer speaking as an actor but rather he was declaiming to the world when he spoke his lines. . . . With lines like 'You cannot remake the world from the basement of a dirty little police station,' Marlon's commitment to social causes was beginning to show in his acting." It went along with everything he'd put in motion with *Sayonara*. Several nights later at dinner Marlon told Parley Baer, a character actor: "I don't want to do any pictures from now on that don't have social significance, or a social message."

While in France, Brando visited writer Irwin Shaw in his Paris home and asked him, "If you were writing it today, would you show Diestl the same way?"

SHAW: I wouldn't change it that much. This is the breed that killed twenty million people and the people they killed are still dead.

BRANDO: But the world can't spend its life looking over its shoulder and nursing hatreds. There would be no progress that way. No nation is all good. There are Nazis and men of goodwill in every country. If we continue to say that all Germans are bad, we would add to the Nazis' argument that all Jews are bad.

The debate went public when David Schoenbrun of CBS television set up an interview between Shaw and Brando. It would prove a far from harmonious session. Shaw accused Brando of wanting to change the role because he wished to appear sympathetic on-screen; Brando replied that Shaw "knew nothing about the character."

"It's my character!" the author replied.

"Nobody creates a character but an actor," Brando countered. "I play the role; now he exists. He is my creation."

Shaw called Brando "stupid," going so far as to voice the popular view that stars suffer from a lack of formal education. "An actor is an empty fucking inkpot. You have to pour ink into the goddamn fool to get anything out of him."

For director Dmytryk the main problem was not Brando's character but the weather. The beautiful French spring had quickly turned into a rainy summer, and before anyone knew it thirty-five days had been lost.

As the delay lengthened, Dmytryk was deluged by cables from Fox. Left to his own devices, Marlon couldn't have been happier. He had Philip Rhodes and Sam Gilman to keep him company, as well as Carlo Fiore, who had recently broken up with his wife. Christian Marquand and his contingent were on the scene, and Marlon had also reunited with his old Village friend Marilyn Sorel, whom he hadn't seen since *Waterfront*.

Sorel had recently moved to Paris, and as a self-described "Proust freak," she made her home in a "crappy hotel—a transformed male brothel" that was run by the novelist's former maid. Now penniless, she was wearing a stolen mink coat and, to make ends meet, she was churning out pornography for Maurice Girodias's famed Olympia Press, publishers of Henry Miller, Terry Southern, and Vladimir Nabokov.

The connection was one Marlon was certain to relish. The short, fast-talking Sorel presented a hip alternative to "the bullshit" of the production.

Marlon soon had her hired as an extra, and the two began having hours of intense conversation in his trailer.

"He was very curious about people who led lives that he couldn't fathom," she recalled. "I fit into that category. . . . I was what he considered a 'genuine' person. He was at the height of his stardom, very lonely and neurotic, and it was a nightmare for him. He would open the trailer door and people would be trying to get in. Very conventional, beautiful women, who would stare at me. 'What's *she* doing here?' Why was he with someone like me?"

Early in the shoot, Dmytryk had brought Brando, Clift, and Schell together for dinner at a Middle Eastern restaurant on the Left Bank. At the table Marlon held back as always, listening to Clift's avalanche of talk, and as Dmytryk recalled, his first substantive contribution was to suggest that his costar needed a psychiatrist.

Clift got his digs in, though. "Marlon was trying to speak in French, and doing quite well," said Dmytryk, "but Monty, who had gone to school in Switzerland, started speaking to the waiter in perfectly grammatical French but with the goddamnedest American accent you can imagine— just putting it on, to taunt Marlon, I think. Just his way of saying, 'I think you're pretty damned pretentious.' "

Mostly Brando fraternized with Christian Marquand. Hervé Mille, the *Paris Match* executive, was in and out, though generally too busy running his magazine to stay up through the night. There was also the lovely Liliane Montevecchi, the actress playing a Parisian prostitute whose partisan loyalties interfere with her feelings for Brando's Diestl. Initially, her attitude toward Brando was very clear.

"I didn't want to meet Marlon, I just wanted to work with him," she later said in her still fractured English. "Because his reputation, you know. He knows he's a big star and he knows that the girl is going to fall in love or whatever, and I'm completely against all this."

Brando had nonetheless masterminded a rendezvous, having twisted Dmytryk's arm to send Montevecchi a bogus dinner invitation. Feeling obliged to meet with her director, she found Brando alone in the limo.

Dinner started out amiably, with Marlon leading the conversation, largely about the theater. After closing the bistro they walked for hours, still chatting, until both of them fell asleep on the grass beneath the Eiffel Tower. At daybreak, the police woke them and sent them home.

" 'I want to be your friend, because I don't think you have as much friends as you have women in your bed,' I told him," she recalled. "And oh, he loved that. He was interested. . . . I have dark eyes, and you know Marlon always in his life the women had a certain look which is all the same—Rita Moreno, Anna Kashfi—all with dark, sort of passionate eyes.

"But we had a great friendship," she added, "because I didn't want to be seduced. I was not easy to get, and I didn't want to be gotten."

As he had in Japan, Marlon was writing Anna regularly, using her as his sounding board. Reassuring her that he was on his best behavior and keeping his "noble tool" in his pants, he claimed that he was actually enjoying the work. While admitting that he was still "smoking a little too much," he announced that he had managed to shed excess pounds and was also trying to give "some meaning" to his idle hours rather than wasting his life with "all that running around."

However much he was distorting his own "good" behavior, the letter reflected as much of an emotional commitment as he had ever been able to make. His list of self-improvements sounded like the promises he had made at Dodie's hospital bedside: self-conscious, dutiful, almost those of a Boy Scout. He needed Kashfi's approval, even when she was 6,000 miles away and still under Marlon Sr.'s watchful eyes.

On July 11, during one of the many rain-outs, Marlon received permission to leave for a few days. He, Montevecchi, and Gilman drove to Madrid, where they hopped a train to Torres Molinos. "Brando had not a shirt on him anymore," the French actress said with a laugh. "All the girls in the train raped him."

They rented an unfurnished castle that had no water and electricity but was near the beach where they walked, swam, and relaxed. They also took a side trip to Barcelona and at one point ended up in a hotel where Montevecchi watched Brando quickly service a bothersome fan. "It was so funny. The maid came by constantly, 'Marlon, please, please, *por favor.*' So Marlon said, 'Liliane, would you mind to go out for five minutes?' I was in the corridor and he does what he has to do with the maid and the maid is very happy. She comes out smiling."

Yet she also saw his sullen side at a local bank when a teller refused to cash his check. "Don't you know who I am?" he demanded. "Don't you recognize me?" In Spain, as in Paris, she saw his violent reaction to autograph hounds. "He punched people in the nose quite a few times. . . . That first dinner date, a fan comes, Marlon said quietly, 'I do not want to be disturbed, I'm having dinner.' And they still come, and he punches them in the nose."

Once the weather finally cleared, even more shooting time was lost because of an accident on July 28 that made headlines around the world. "Brando Scalds Balls at Prince de Galles" was the joke version proffered by Kashfi. It was around two in the afternoon, and Marlon and Liliane were eating in the restaurant of the swank hotel.

"Dean Martin came in and I, of course, jumped up very extravagant," recalled Montevecchi. "I went to kiss him, and I pulled the table up with me and the teapot went into Marlon's lap. He took off his pants in front of everybody. He was just screaming."

The reaction of the crowd was "marvelous," said Patti Page, who happened to be staying at the hotel and had nothing to do with the film. Everybody was hysterical, laughing as Marlon stripped and doused himself from a nearby soda-water siphon.

It was no laughing matter, though. Brando was in the hospital for a week with second-degree burns, his body shaved and placed in a diaper. Montevecchi and Marquand visited him daily, bringing books, while Marlon lamented, "This would have to happen to me now in the middle of Paris in spring, with my prick in a sling."

While Montevecchi enjoyed Brando's company, she also attributed her personal growth as an actress to working with him. Throughout *Lions* he shared his skills, forcing her to go deeper and become more serious, almost with missionary zeal.

"Before, I thought I was just a pretty girl reading a script," she explained. "He said, 'That's not what it's about. You have to go inside your character—why did you do this? What did your parents have to do with who you are, what could you have done?'

"I worked before with big stars. They were so bad. They were vain, always their beauty. Marlon said, 'This is not what it is at all. It's a serious thing, acting. You have to make believe that you *are* this character. You just don't read a script.'"

Basically he was directing her, schooling her in his version of the Method. One afternoon he stopped the cameraman during one of their scenes together in an indoor café, taking her outside while the crew waited more than an hour.

"He made me an actress and I was never an actress before, just a puppet. Here, I became this woman, this prostitute. . . . Back inside the café, I started to cry and was uncontrollable. I had to leave the set. I had never felt that before, and only he can do it. When he looks at you it's the truth. It's not bullshit. It's not a lie. He had this power of putting an imaginary wall around, and it became this instant. . . . this intense *vérité*."

Other cast members felt his power rubbing off, too. Because he'd heard stories that Brando was difficult to get along with, Parley Baer had gone into *Lions* with the same apprehension as Montevecchi. Instead, he found him "extremely courteous . . . one of the most considerate of the big stars I've worked with. He was willing to rehearse, and he gave as much in a rehearsal as he did in a performance.

"Most of all there was his controlled action. He never used two gestures if one would do it, as opposed to many actors who just gesticulate with their hands. Many times I saw that if I'd known that, if there had been a paucity of gesture, it would have been better."

For the love scene between Brando and Montevecchi, where Diestl decides to return to the army, Anhalt had written three pages of dialogue. They rehearsed it, and afterward Marlon said, "It doesn't work. I don't know what's wrong, but you don't need it." Instead, he wanted to use a prop, a little toy lit by candle heat that twirls and makes noise. "I'll make up my mind while I'm looking at this thing," he said. "She knows it, and I know it and the audience will know it, so when I go to bed with her, they know it's the last time. You don't have to say anything."

Anhalt thought the solution was "brilliant." "He used to call the script pages 'the jokes,' " the scriptwriter said. "We were going to do the three pages that day, so he'd say to me, 'Have you got the jokes?' The implication was that he was contemptuous of the script.

"The only time I had a problem," Anhalt added, "was in the scene with Mai Britt, where he insisted on drinking real vodka. I said, 'What are you doing that for?' He said, 'I'm going to play it drunk.' The scene was wonderful. He wasn't acting, he was just drunk."

"There was no rush to Brando," added Baer. "I don't think Zanuck himself could have caused him to hurry. It was his theory that a scene didn't really get good until about the fifth or sixth take, and he definitely got better as it went along. You had to keep your eye on him, because his performance was variable."

Dmytryk, who considered him at once careless, charming, and gifted, was growing worried, too. "Brando would appear in costume but didn't know what scene was going to be shot that day," he recalled. "He'd glance over the script girl's shoulder for clues. I'd call for more takes. After a ridiculous number of false starts and incompetent renditions, Marlon finally said, 'Oh, *that's* what the scene is about!' as if making a discovery. It went on like this for days, and then Marlon began to develop a real interest in the project and the part.

"Why had it gotten better? He rather quickly, thank God, made up his mind that we had a hell of a picture. His attitude at the beginning was 'Oh, shit, this is just another film.' "

During off-hours, Christian Marquand was constantly at Brando's side, trying to win favor. "He courted Marlon," said Marilyn Sorel, "and they had a lot of practical jokes together. They were involved." The French actor was so obsessed with Brando's celebrity that he supposedly hoped the actor would marry into his family. He "schlepped his aunt, his sister, a cousin, anybody," Sorel added, "in the hope that Marlon might fancy the person. Marquand didn't want anybody else to be around to distract Marlon, so Phil [Rhodes] and I would leave."

Dmytryk also felt Marquand was parasitic and "trying to make something" out of the friendship. "It was a feeling, that's all. I didn't particularly care for him. I just didn't like the type. Possibly a gay or a switch-hitter, which I didn't like, either. Brando said to me that he himself had homosexual tendencies and that's why he went to the shrink."

Montevecchi dismissed such talk of homosexuality as nonsense, yet she acknowledged that she, Brando, and Marquand were "like the Three Musketeers. . . . We went all over France, we ate together, sometimes we slept together like brothers and sister," often in Marquand's untidy apartment, which was unfurnished except for one mattress. "It was a very wonderful, exciting relationship because here we were three beautiful things and people started talking, and we liked that," she added.

Whatever the innuendos about Brando, the talk about Montgomery Clift was explicit. Clift had a male lover with him on the set, and even more than in his early years, his homosexuality seemed to be wrenching him apart. "There was a good deal of discussion among members of the company," said Duke Calahan, a cameraman. "The theory was that when he was sober he fought it, but when drunk he submitted to it." For Dmytryk, Clift was just plain sick: "The women on the film wanted to meet both Marlon and Monty, but about Monty they'd say, 'I can help him.' Which was a great mistake. Nobody could help him."

Despite his increasingly professed contempt for acting, Marlon himself was occasionally caught lurking behind the camera, watching Clift at work. "Tell Marlon he doesn't have to hide his face when he's watching me act," Clift whispered to Dmytryk one day. After watching Brando do two takes, he commented, "He's using about one-tenth of his talent." Monty went on to tell Jack Larson that he found Marlon's character "dim-witted and dumb" and the rendition "slow and ponderous."

Clift himself was working in a fog of pills and liquor, however. One evening a crew member saw him go "momentarily berserk." As biographer Patricia Bosworth reported it, "He hadn't had that much to drink but suddenly he crawled on top of a car right outside the Georges V Hotel. He stood on top of it and did a little dance—jiggling and twitching like a paralytic. Then he collapsed on the hood. He had to be lifted off."

Two or three times Clift disappeared from the production completely, and Dmytryk, with cinematographer Joe MacDonald, found that he had duplicate passports so he could travel without the press (or anyone else) knowing. One time he vanished and was found in southern Italy at a third-rate brothel, dead drunk. On the set his eyes were "like pinholes," wrote Robert LaGuardia, "and he'd pretend that it was just juice he was drinking from his thermos." In fact, Anhalt discovered that it was a mixture of bourbon, crushed Demerol, and fruit juice. Duke Calahan, the cameraman, recalled that "they used to try to get finished with Monty before lunch. By afternoon, he was starting to giggle and treating the whole film as a joke. He would crouch in corners, rolled into a ball; use his hands like monkey-paws."

While Clift guzzled his pill-and-booze brew, Brando fought his usual battles with food, and his weight fluctuated wildly. Dieting helped, but often, Montevecchi said, he'd get "fed up." This led to further difficulties when he needed to be stuffed into his military uniform.

He also took every opportunity to explain his "good" Nazi—even in Berlin, where he went to shoot two scenes with Mai Britt. "Irwin Shaw wrote his book while war hatreds were still white-hot," he offered sagely at a packed press conference. "We hope they have cooled. The picture will try to show that Nazism is a matter of mind, not geography;

that there are Nazis—and people of goodwill—in every country."

He carried the same message with him when the production returned to California in late August. Borrego Springs, not far from Palm Springs, was to represent Rommel's North Africa. There, Dmytryk planned to shoot the scene in which an exhausted Diestl is riding a motorcycle with his superior, Hardenberg, on the back. Brando's character is struggling to stay awake, but his superior is disintegrating in the face of the Nazi retreat, telling him to keep talking, to sing—anything to prevent him from passing out. For Marlon it was a ready-made opportunity for additional "significance."

Dmytryk suggested that he try to write out his ideas, and Marlon dutifully returned with ten typewritten pages filled with Zen koans, as well as a speech on race relations. He had also put in Diestl's mouth a discourse on the Scottsboro Boys and the American Indians.

Keeping a straight face, Dmytryk said, "This thing about the Scottsboro Boys. That's a worthwhile cause, but you can't do it in two pages. Make a whole film. Zen Buddhism, I've been reading it for several years and still don't understand it. How the hell are you going to make people understand it in two pages?"

Brando looked at him for a moment, and before turning away tore the pages up "with a wry smile," not saying a word. This left the director to wonder what had happened—whether Brando had been serious or was just covering his tracks in the face of an obvious blunder.

The next scene on the schedule was the Nazi assault on a company of bivouacked British soldiers—a turning point, of sorts, in Diestl's growing consciousness. The early-morning sneak attack works because Brando's character, still unaware of the extent of Hardenberg's cruelty, suggests that the assault be postponed until the rising sun blinds their adversaries. For Diestl the strategy is a tactical one, yet once it is under way Hardenberg refuses to halt his machine guns, turning the desert basin into a charnel house. Again the audience is asked to accept Brando's dismayed Nazi.

"Brando refused to play the character as written," Walter Seltzer complained, "and I remember we said, 'Marlon, for Christ's sake, there were no nice Nazis.' He said—I'll never forget the line—'It's *a polka-dot world.'* What he meant was that there are no nice guys, no bad guys, just 'polka-dot' guys. It wasn't an isolated conversation. He genuinely considered the world to be what he said—polka dots."

The week before *The Young Lions* wrapped in October 1957, Clift,

Martin, and Brando convened at Charlton Flats just off Angeles Crest Highway to film the long awaited climactic meeting of Shaw's three main characters. Marlon, still bent on his humanistic revisionism, had ideas for this, too. Despite his precarious state, Clift put his foot down, openly refusing to sanction Brando's polka-dot Nazi.

"When Brando's character dies, he came up with the notion that Monty should pick him up and carry him into the sunset," Jack Larson said. "Monty's response was 'I don't know how he's going to get his ass down the road, but my character's not going to carry him.' "

To Dmytryk, Brando also suggested that he go out on a bundle of barbed wire, spread-eagled like a Christ symbol. Here, too, Clift was outraged. "If Marlon's allowed to do that," he said, "I'll walk off the picture." In the filmed finale, however, Brando ended up facedown in a puddle of dirty water and actually dislocated his right shoulder rolling down a hillside.

Back in Borrego Springs Marlon's good spirits had initially been buoyed by Kashfi, who bent over backward to please him, determined to keep their engagement in place. He philosophized, even as they played water tag in the hotel pool under desert heat. He talked about psychiatry and philosophy, telling her, she recalled, "Sit down and quietly reflect, reflect inside, know yourself. Self-knowledge. Balance."

Dutifully, compliantly, she listened, playing Eliza Doolittle to his Professor Higgins, and she would also make herself available whenever he wanted sex. Soon she "wasn't letting him out of her sight," recalled Fiore, "and . . . we ate together nearly every night. This sociable behavior, which Marlon and I had enjoyed together for so long, roused Anna's ever-ready jealousy."

It had all the ingredients of a Darren-Josanne replay, and soon Kashfi struck, telling Marlon that Carlo, behind his back, had offered to work for Joshua Logan and was only using him to further his own career. Unlike Dublin, Fiore convinced Brando that the story was baseless. The next day, he warned Brando against marrying Kashfi. "If you do, she'll fuck you up, that's for certain."

Brando, though, was a sitting duck. Only six weeks earlier, in Paris, Marilyn Sorel had seen that he was upset. "He'd never been married," she explained, "and he kept asking me, 'Can I trust her?' He felt caught, that her desire to be married to him was moving him into it."

There was more to it than simple indecision or ambivalence about Kashfi as the ideal mate. "It was really that he couldn't be involved with a woman," Sorel added. "He had this terrible burden of being a 'cocksman' when he wasn't—of being a sex symbol, which he was—and then having women relate to him in this prescribed fashion. He was preoccupied by gender. He could be very funny, but if you had a particular masculine movement and you were a woman, he'd interrupt and say, 'Do you know how masculine it is to smoke a cigarette that way?' He was very into body behavior, and the key to Marlon was to understand his sensitivity here. When somebody who was kind of simple like Anna Kashfi expected him to behave like a man, it was naturally going to create tremendous conflicts from which to act out his own neuroses."

Circumstance, however, stripped him of indecision. In September Anna informed him that she was pregnant, and his first response was, "Let's get married." Fiore still disapproved of the union and was bold enough to say as much. "Let her have anything," he argued, "only don't marry her."

"But it's going to be my child too," said Marlon, ruling out the possibility of an abortion.

When Marlon repeated his feelings back at Pennebaker, Seltzer could only conclude that he'd gotten "a bad case of being an honorable man." Even Anna realized that for him it was "a big step," in all likelihood an attempt to live up to his promise to Dodie, possibly also to free himself from his ghosts.

Now that they were to be married, Kashfi reiterated her demands that he stop seeing other women—delivering what was, in effect, an ultimatum. "I questioned him about our relationship and what was going on," she later explained, admitting that she then lost her temper, as did Marlon. When she stormed out of his house, he chased her, she said, and "hit me very hard. He was pounding my head on the stone pathway. I was frightened out of my mind, and the only thing that stopped him was that I said, 'Marlon, keep on doing this. I don't give a damn.' He wasn't yelling, just very red in the face, and finally I ran." A week later he phoned her at her apartment to apologize. "I lost my temper," he said. "Do you think we could go out for dinner tonight?" At one of his favorite Italian restaurants, he was "charming," and neither of them spoke of the incident again.

The wedding was set for October 11. Marlon wanted a small, low-key ceremony, but contrary to his desire for secrecy, it was reported that he had gone to Pasadena "to purchase a wedding ring—dressed in a flowing Hindu robe."

Seltzer and Glass were enlisted to make the arrangements; the idea was to file for the license in nearby Riverside through a court reporter who would delay making it a matter of public record so as to stall the press. On the drive down, Brando sat in front with Glass, and Kashfi rode with Seltzer in back. No one spoke through the whole hour-and-a-half trip.

The wedding took place at the Eagle Rock home of Marlon's aunt, Betty Lindemeyer, as scheduled. Present for the nondenominational rite were Marlon Sr.; Jocelyn and her husband, Eliot Asinof; Marlon's great-aunt, June, and cousins Mr. and Mrs. Allen Pardee; and Kashfi's friends, Peter Berneis, his wife, and Louis and Kathy L'Amour. As usual, Anna wore a sari, this one pale-green and embroidered in gold.

With typical casualness, Marlon hadn't bothered to make honeymoon plans, so the newlyweds proceeded to drive around L.A. for more than an hour before deciding to visit Jay Kanter and his wife, Judy. Though the Kanters hadn't attended the wedding, they quickly offered their Beverly Hills home for the night.

"There was no sex," Kashfi said. "There was mostly concern from Marlon, about what Jay and his wife were saying about me. There was a certain awkwardness on both our parts. I was awkward because I thought, Oh, God, what do we do?"

The maid brought breakfast in the morning and, again, the couple took to the streets, tooling around Beverly Hills in Brando's Thunderbird convertible, not knowing what to do with themselves. Eventually Anna suggested they visit her friends the L'Amours down in La Quinta, outside of Palm Springs. Over the next week they lounged about, watching television and strolling in the desert. L'Amour, America's most prolific writer of westerns since Zane Grey, spent several hours each day with Marlon shooting at tin cans while Anna and Kathy cooked and cleaned the house.

Back in Hollywood, Anna moved her belongings into Brando's Laurel Canyon residence. The place, which had been leased by MCA all these years, was still furnished with rented French provincial furniture, cellophane-wrapped lampshades, and pastel draperies. Marlon's only possessions, she recalled, were his clothes, drums, books, and a black mother-of-pearl-inlaid Oriental coffee table somebody had given him after *Sayonara*.

The honeymoon was truly over as soon as the two found themselves alone, and Anna noticed the change in Marlon immediately. He'd withdrawn, largely because only two days after the ceremony, while they were still in Palm Desert, he had heard some distressing news: William Patrick O'Callaghan, a Welsh factory worker, had told reporters that Anna was his daughter. She had apparently changed her name to Kashfi in order to advance her film career, he explained. Anna had indeed been raised in Calcutta, where O'Callaghan had worked as a traffic superintendent for the Indian State Railway, but as O'Callaghan was quick to point out, "There is no Indian blood in our family."

The media in Los Angeles and England were having a field day; on October 18 Edward Dmytryk got into the act, stating that he knew Kashfi's real name was Irish but assumed she was Anglo-Indian.

With the press blizzard still building, Brando asked Glass and Seltzer to investigate and determine the truth. The two Pennebaker executives turned up, unannounced, at Brando's house.

"Senior didn't like her. He thought she was a fake, and after the story started to break, Junior dispatched me and Glass to grill her," Seltzer recalled. "Marlon was very, very shook, and he wanted us to get to the bottom of it. His frustration was that he didn't want to be victimized. It was a question of control."

Seltzer and Glass found Kashfi alone in the living room, Marlon having retreated to his drum room in the basement. "She was all tears and hysteria," Seltzer continued, "crying, 'Marlon put you up to this—I told him the truth.' We never got the same story twice from her. Very defensive. Totally schizy and obviously lying. I think she was quite ill, sufficiently as to raise questions as to whether she was mentally competent. I felt sorry for her."

Jocelyn thought she understood why Kashfi had become so unbalanced and distraught when Seltzer and Glass confronted her. "She had this *idée fixe,* and she had really come to believe her own story," said Marlon's sister. "She had adopted that identity—that she was Indian from Darjeeling. When the news got out, suddenly she wasn't who she thought she was and that caused a breakdown. It was crazy and delusional and very sad."

Glass was less sympathetic in his response when he announced to Marlon in private: "She's as Indian as Paddy's pig." Marlon raised the possibility of an annulment, citing Kashfi's giving false information on the marriage license as the cause. But later he refused to talk things out directly with Anna. Instead, "he looked at me very hard," she said, "no anger, no nothing," and withdrew.

The withdrawal continued for days, his anger exacerbated by the press coverage. Sometimes he came home in the evening, sometimes not.

On October 17, 1957, the *Los Angeles Examiner* reported that Brando was suffering "intellectual boredom" because his wife "just can't keep up with him mentally." Kashfi, the article added, was repelled by his "beatnik hangouts," but had gamely enrolled in classes at USC to "better discuss philosophy" with him.

Soon Marlon Sr. got in on the act, too. Anna had fired Marlon's long-time cook, complained to the Pennebaker office about repairing the steps to the hillside house, and had also gone on a Rodeo Drive mink-shopping spree with her friend Pearl Bailey.

"I got into a big, big argument with Marlon Senior, who came to the house and gave me hell," she later explained. " 'You're spending too much money. All these clothes you're buying!' What clothes? I bought some maternity dresses," she said, forgetting the mink and other extravagances such as designer gowns. Marlon Sr. even asked her to produce the sales slips from the grocery store, which he then "audited with the scrupulousness of a bank examiner."

A few days later, Esme Chandler, a publicist at Paramount, called and heard her crying. Soon Anna was talking about her unhappiness, Marlon's withdrawal, and an incident when, she claimed, she had fallen down the stairs in the hillside house. Chandler rushed over to console her. It wasn't more than an hour before the publicist called Hedda Hopper, handing the phone to the distraught Kashfi sitting beside her.

The next day, November 14, Hopper ran a weepy column that read, "My heart aches for this little girl. . . . She doesn't deserve this rough treatment." Brando, she stated, "is . . . a nonconformist, a law unto himself without regard for anyone's feelings. His friends tell me he's under a great mental strain, but can't say what caused it. . . . But I hope if he does love her, as his friends claim, he'll have enough sense to prove it by staying home and trying to make her happy."

Marlon was incensed. He'd already told Kashfi, "Reporters are all scum. Hired buffoons. Scribblers. Assassins." Now, more ominously, he fell into "passive coldness."

Variety's Army Archerd announced on December 12, 1957, that the actor and his wife had separated, and Sam Gilman was called upon to deny the claim. Hopper, too, jumped in the next day, armed with more information from Anna. In a column headlined, "Brando Walks Out on the Bride," she rehashed the sad melodrama, casting Kashfi as the abused heroine, with Marlon "rude" and self-serving. Within days Anna checked herself into Cedars of Lebanon Hospital, fearing a "miscarriage," which resulted in an item from Dorothy Kilgallen wrongly announcing that she had lost her baby.

Three months later things were no better, and on April 2, 1958, *The Young Lions* premiered at the newly renovated Paramount Theatre in New York. Brando did not make an appearance, even though the show was a benefit for the Actors Studio, with Lee Strasberg, Cheryl Crawford, and Elia Kazan all in attendance. He remained in Los Angeles, but after Kashfi, now eight months pregnant, kept carping about the dangers of the Laurel Canyon stairs, he moved the two of them into a single-level, two-bedroom Japanese-style home at 12900 Mulholland Drive.

Within weeks he fell in love with their new residence. Originally built for Howard Hughes, it wasn't regal but offered what he wanted most: privacy. It sat on four acres atop the crest of the then undeveloped San Fernando hills, at the end of a long private drive. It also commanded a panoramic view of both Beverly Hills and the Valley to the north. Its current owner, a show-biz-loving wine columnist, interior decorator, restaurateur, and part-time Buddhist monk, had agreed to rent it—Oriental furnishings and all—for $1,500 a month. Teak floors and white carpets, chairs in orange Thai silk, Chinese missionary chests, wall hangings, a seventeenth-century Japanese shoji screen, and a carefully maintained water garden were all part of the deal. There was a swimming pool, too, but most appealing was that it was named Ryoanji, for the famous rock-garden Japanese temple. Reportedly, one of the first things Brando did upon moving in was to post a sign on the gate: UNLESS YOU HAVE AN APPOINTMENT, UNDER NO CIRCUMSTANCES DISTURB THE OCCUPANT.

After the premiere of *Lions,* reviews were mixed. Bosley Crowther noted that Shaw's "unregenerative Nazi is changed to a very nice young man who never embraces Nazism with any apparent zeal. Indeed, he regards the whole business with sadness and disgust that become increasingly depressing as time and disasters pile up." While Brando had a few defenders, most critics were negative about his performance. The *New*

Yorker took a snide view, claiming that his Diestl "is really just a poor, mixed-up skier who wishes that he didn't have to go around shooting people and longs for the day when amity will reign among the nations on earth." *Time* added, "Brando underplays to the point where . . . only a telepathist could hope to tell what he's thinking."

But few reviewers were as upset about the movie as Maureen Stapleton, who took Marlon to task so firmly that she could re-create their conversation almost thirty years later. When the film was released she was in Los Angeles, working on *Lonelyhearts,* her first movie. One night she went to dinner with Marlon and Sam Gilman.

"I said, 'How could you do that? How could you play a Nazi like Jesus Christ?'" she explained. "He got very defensive, and said, 'Did you read the book? The Nazis were only ten percent human in the book. I tried to make them eighty percent.' I said, 'Marlon, he's a *Nazi;* that's already not a human being! Maximilian Schell played a Nazi, you played Jesus Christ!' I was starting to scream at him. 'Take it easy,' he told me, but I kept screaming at him, 'How could you!'

"Gilman was just sitting there as usual, and Marlon turned to him. 'Sam, do you agree with her?' Of course Sam wasn't going to agree with me, so I started yelling again, 'Why the fuck didn't somebody stop you?'

"That's when he jumped up, real mad, screaming back, 'Because they don't know anything! Only Gadg would know! They don't know anything!'"

The Young Lions would mark the end of a busy, successful, and commercial era for Brando. (*Sayonara* was proving to be a blockbuster at the box office and Brando was named one of the ten biggest box-office attractions in the business.) But two years would pass before the release of his next film, *The Fugitive Kind.* Meanwhile, *One-Eyed Jacks,* his directorial debut to be produced at Pennebaker, was bogged down with script rewrites.

With the birth of Christian Devi Brando on May 16, 1958—Marlon insisted on naming him after Christian Marquand—his relationship with Kashfi worsened. He was "overwhelmed" by his new son and would hold the baby with tears in his eyes, but now, more than ever, he was looking to escape from Anna—and tried to resurrect his relationship with Movita.

"He used to call a lot but disguise his voice, sounding like a woman," recalled Johnny Brascia, who was by then living with Movita in New York.

"He'd call her a couple of times a week, and she would tell him to quit calling. A month would go by, but then he'd start phoning again."

Fiore was worried about his friend's emotional state. Nan Morris saw Marlon a few times during the summer of 1958, and she agreed with Carlo that Marlon "was very disturbed, restless, and on a bummer." Fiore laid the blame for Marlon's bad mood entirely on Kashfi, Morris added. "Carlo used to say that she was the meanest bitch he'd ever met in his life, that 'she won't stop until she's made everyone around her miserable.'"

It was a prognostication that would hold true for more than a decade.

TURNING A CORNER

One-Eyed Jacks

Kashfi wasn't the only reason for Marlon's unhappiness during these months. By 1958 Pennebaker Inc. was a production company in name only. Paramount was becoming impatient after paying Brando's expenses for years with no results, largely because Marlon wouldn't make any decisions. The IRS had begun to take an interest in Pennebaker and similar companies that MCA and other agencies had set up for their movie star clients. Pennebaker was already in the midst of a major audit, and something needed to be done, fast. To bridge the gap Seltzer and Glass had announced a trio of non-Brando vehicles under the Pennebaker flag, all to be shot overseas: *Shake Hands with the Devil* with James Cagney; *The Naked Edge,* a London-based murder mystery with Gary Cooper; and *Paris Blues,* slated to star Paul Newman and Sidney Poitier.

Still, in order for the production company to justify maximum tax benefits for Brando, he himself had to be put in a film and bring in some income.

"He liked money and wanted money," Seltzer said, puncturing the myth of Brando's indifference to lucre by pointing out that Marlon was extravagant in his own way, like frequently sending friends flowers, the bills for which were adding up to thousands of dollars yearly. "He never splurged on clothes or cars," Seltzer added. "But he liked to think of himself as a righter of wrongs on a personal level; if he saw an abuse happening, he became the guy that flies around—Superman. A girl who got knocked up and needed an abortion, he'd pay for it. There was also eating well. Three or four times a week, he'd be at expensive restaurants."

For the Pennebaker braintrust, the answer seemed to be a western. *The Searchers*, *Shane*, and *High Noon* had made a bundle. The project Pennebaker undertook was *One-Eyed Jacks,* whose genesis went back to 1956, when Pennebaker had optioned Louis L'Amour's *To Tame a Land*. Novelist Niven Busch, author of *Duel in the Sun* and an experienced scripter of westerns, was hired to pen an adaptation. Busch, the husband of Teresa Wright, worked for six weeks at $30,000, commuting from his ranch southeast of San Francisco for regular story meetings with George Englund, who was serving as cowriter, producer, and Brando go-between.

"I only got to Marlon through Englund," said Busch, "although Marlon would come into the meetings sometimes and sit on this window seat in George's office, where he'd put his feet up."

As far as the writer could tell, Brando hadn't read the L'Amour book, a typical cattlemen-versus-sodbusters melodrama, but rather seemed enamored with its title, *To Tame a Land,* as a visual motif. He kept stressing ways to capture "the beauty of nature."

"He said, 'I think we ought to have . . . the rivers and the woods, the beautiful hills. And the wildlife.' That was his main contribution," added Busch. "You had to keep a straight face, which was very hard because this was just a hard-boiled western."

As the conferences dragged on, it also became obvious that he had "no structural sense whatsoever." If the discussion veered toward technical matters, it was, "Well, you guys do it." Englund, acting more "like the senior partner who had been empowered to keep a less experienced partner on the right track," was unable to sustain Brando's focus.

The few times Busch ran into the actor in the Paramount commissary, he would start talking Zen. Marlon had already bought hundreds of copies of *Zen and the Art of Archery;* from the cartons of paperbacks purchased wholesale, he doled out copies to almost everyone he came in contact with.

"He was usually alone and had the book with him," said Busch. "This stuff was just getting fashionable, and he'd give me quite a long exposition about what it ought to mean to me. I'd say, 'Well, that's very interesting,' because it was all rather incoherent, which only took me back to the idea that this was a guy who shouldn't be messing with production unless he'd hired a real producer, which Englund was not."

Then Marlon began voicing disappointment with Busch's conventionally styled treatment, and the result was that two or three weeks after being hired, the writer was fired. Englund forged ahead on his own with the screenplay, which soon underwent several changes of title in lieu of anything more substantive. These included *Guns Up, Ride, Comanchero,* and *A Burst of Vermilion*—all during the filming of *Sayonara* and *The Young Lions.* Englund and Brando had been friends since the early fifties, so their writing sessions tended to be social. By now over $500,000 in expenses had been put on the studio's tab, but the western was still floundering.

In the summer of 1957, almost a year after Busch's departure, independent producer Frank P. Rosenberg (a former national publicity and advertising director of Columbia Pictures) inadvertently revived the project when he read a *New Yorker* review of a novel called *The Authentic Death of Hendry Jones.* Rosenberg, who had produced one of Zanuck's Cinema-Scope blockbusters, *King of the Khyber Rifles,* soon met with the book's author, Charles Neider, who agreed to sell the rights for $25,000.

Rosenberg was taking a flier, and after working briefly on an adaptation with Rod Serling, he had encountered and become friends with dialogue director Sam Peckinpah while producing a television pilot on the Pony Express. At the time Peckinpah was accumulating a list of writing credits for TV westerns, but had never done a feature. Still, he impressed Rosenberg with his eagerness to pick up where Serling had left off. The producer therefore agreed to let him have a crack at it, paying the feisty Peckinpah $3,000, which was then scale, out of his own pocket.

Not long afterward, George Chasen, Rosenberg's agent at MCA, who was well aware of Brando's problems in getting a film off the ground, took the Peckinpah script to Jay Kanter. Marlon received it on a Thursday, and both Rosenberg and Chasen went into shock when word came back two days later that he wanted to do it.

The deal was in place before Rosenberg ever met Brando, but the producer was invited to an icebreaker at Seltzer's house in Sherman Oaks later the following week. When he arrived, Rosenberg recalled, Brando was sitting in the backyard under Seltzer's orange trees, wearing "very, very black" sunglasses. "He had these shades on. It was the way he wanted it.

He could see me but I couldn't see him, so I knew immediately he wanted to have the edge."

Rosenberg had come with the usual preconceptions about Hollywood's most notorious rebel, but no sooner had Seltzer gotten past the introductions when Marlon announced that the script was "great," insisting that even though it was the first draft, he was perfectly happy with it.

"Well, Marlon, I think it needs about six weeks' work," Rosenberg countered as Seltzer watched, saying nothing.

"Oh, I don't know about that," Brando enthused.

Rosenberg disagreed, Seltzer still said nothing, and after a moment Marlon nodded his okay. As things turned out, some eight months would be spent revising the screenplay.

"Brando was pliable, reasonable, pleasant," the producer insisted, and on April 25, 1958, Pennebaker formally purchased the script for $150,000, while Rosenberg retained the property. As Seltzer saw it, Kanter's influence was mainly responsible for finally bringing Marlon down to earth. "Jay had always known how to handle Marlon whenever there was a problem and when it was time to consider doing something. MCA had a financial interest in the project too, of course."

For Seltzer and Glass, it was "hats-in-the-air time." The budget was planned at $1.8 million, not including Marlon's salary. At least the $500,000 already blown on the L'Amour adaptation as well as Busch's salary and other expenses had all been figured in. Rosenberg would produce, with George Glass and Seltzer as executive producers. Though Pennebaker was coproducing, it was a Paramount picture and Paramount put up the money.

When it was time to choose a director, a prominent name on the short list was Stanley Kubrick, who had exploded on the scene only two years before with *The Killing*, a tense heist yarn starring Sterling Hayden. More impressive yet, he'd gone on to make his authoritative World War I drama *Paths of Glory*, which was already being talked about as the work of an outsider genius.

Brando, Rosenberg said, was aware of Kubrick's name when it came up during meetings. But Carlo Fiore, who was then on Pennebaker's payroll, claimed that Marlon had never heard of him. According to Fiore, Brando set up a screening of the two Kubrick pictures at MCA's office in Beverly Hills and loved both of them, wondering why the obscure *Killing* had never been rereleased. Several weeks later, at a Mexican restaurant, he told Fiore that he'd been seeing "a buddy . . . Stanley Kubrick," and asked, "Do you know him?"

"I'm the guy who brought him to your attention, remember?" Fiore said.

"Well, I've decided to let him direct the Western. . . . He doesn't want *you* on the picture."

When Carlo said he was willing to step aside, Marlon shook his head, insisting, "Uh-uh. This is *my* picture. My toy. And nobody's going to tell me who works in it and who doesn't."

On May 12, 1958, Kubrick was formally hired both to revise the Peckinpah script and to direct. Meanwhile, Pennebaker was coming under increasing pressure from Paramount executive Y. Frank Freeman, who wanted something to show for years of paying overhead and salaries.

Kubrick and Brando rented cheap digs in the bowels of Hollywood near Gower and Melrose to avoid distractions while they got to work. Instead, they drank, played dominoes and chess, and did whatever else Marlon could think of to keep from writing.

Seltzer, Glass, and Brando Sr. eyed Kubrick suspiciously. "Kubrick was not being honest: He agreed to shoot the script we had, then three weeks in, he and Marlon were saying that the material was wanting," Seltzer claimed. "Marlon was being charmed by Kubrick the artist and Kubrick the con artist, since Kubrick in addition to being the very, very effective director was the other kind of artist as well."

After six weeks of rewriting, Kubrick suggested that his friend, novelist Calder Willingham, be brought in to help. Willingham had collaborated on *Paths of Glory,* but possibly more impressive to Brando, he was the author of *End as a Man,* a scathing *roman à clef* dealing with the brutal climate of a military school not unlike Shattuck. Marlon then informed Peckinpah that he was fired. The news was "devastating" to him and, his wife later recalled, it would give him his first glimpse of Hollywood back-stabbing. Neither Seltzer nor Rosenberg was thrilled that Peckinpah's "perfect" script was now being trashed. They were even less pleased when the nucleus quickly became Brando, Kubrick, and Willingham to the exclusion of everyone else.

Over the summer of 1958, script meetings shifted to Marlon's Mulholland house, where because of the teakwood floors, no one was allowed to wear shoes. Kubrick, for some reason, routinely took off his pants as well and worked in only his underwear and dress shirt. "Brando sat cross-legged on the floor within easy reach of a Chinese gong," Rosenberg recalled, "and when the discussions became too emotional, he would hit it."

The gong was some four feet across, and when struck with its heavy leather-headed clapper, it sounded thunderously throughout the house, even causing dishes to rattle in the nearby galley kitchen.

Kubrick and Willingham had produced a new story outline that was so problematic that Rosenberg told Brando and his collaborators that he didn't see how they could proceed to a shooting script. Willingham, a rather laid-back southerner, responded with "one of the most imperishable lines since the invention of the printing press," said Rosenberg. He slapped his book of matches down on the coffee table and drawled, "You've gotta have faith in ma God-given gifts as a writer."

When Rosenberg still voiced his dismay, Marlon took the producer behind a nearby Chinese screen. "Why don't we give them a chance and see what they can do?" he said. Rosenberg reluctantly agreed, but after a few weeks Kubrick and Willingham only made it to page 52 before deciding the script wasn't working.

In the meantime preproduction work had already started. In August Rosenberg traveled alone to Mexico to find an actress for the role of Louisa, Brando's pivotal love interest. Legend has it that Marlon instructed him to hire "a flat-chested woman," as opposed to a voluptuous costar who might detract from the script's hoped-for lyricism. "We were looking for somebody who was virginal-looking," Rosenberg said, "an innocent Mexican."

The winner was Pina Pellicer, an elfin, doe-eyed, five-foot-one-inch actress of twenty-two who had appeared in the Mexican television version of *The Diary of Anne Frank*. The *Los Angeles Mirror* later dubbed Pellicer "Hollywood's newest Cinderella, a tiny, black-haired Mexican girl who looks like Audrey Hepburn." She spoke only halting English and was a troubled, frightened girl whose fears bordered on the neurotic. So shy was she that upon arriving at the L.A. airport, she burst into tears when the immigration officials routinely asked what she would be doing in the United States.

For the other women's roles, Brando did much of the interviewing himself. He was searching for actresses with emotional rawness, those whose passions were "on the surface," as he put it. Fiore was with him one afternoon when he auditioned a girl named Nina Martinez for the supporting role of Margarita.

"Have you ever had a producer ask you to raise your skirt?" Marlon asked.

"Yes," she admitted.

"Who?"

She pointed to Rosenberg, who flushed with embarrassment.

"Are you a virgin?"

"No," she said matter-of-factly.

"Do you have a family back home? Someone you're especially fond of?"

"Yes, I do," she answered, naming an eight-year-old niece.

Marlon responded by concocting a scenario of the niece struck by a truck, her bloody body strewn across the highway, and as he piled detail atop detail, the young actress began to cry and soon became hysterical. "Okay," Marlon said. "You get the part."

The starting date was pushed back again, to September 15, since Kubrick and Brando increasingly began to disagree. Marlon had been drawn to the director as the class-act artist, but for the very reasons he had been hired in the first place, Kubrick was refusing to play the yes-man. Carlo tended to side with the director, which only made Marlon cagier.

One disagreement centered on the role of the two-faced Dad Longworth; Kubrick wanted Spencer Tracy, Brando wanted Karl Malden. "Malden usually plays losers," Kubrick insisted. "Let's put two champions in the arena." When Brando explained that Malden had been promised the part, Kubrick suggested paying him off. Brando laughed. "I'm sorry, fellers, but the final decision is mine. Tracy is a fine actor, but I mean to keep my promise to Karl."

Some of Kubrick's objections to Malden may nonetheless have struck a chord. Covering his flanks, Brando had put out feelers to Henry Fonda, who'd asked to read the script. Malden, however, was not complaining about the indecision. Principal photography was already three months behind schedule, and since Malden had already been signed to start earlier, he was now drawing a salary. "I didn't do anything and got paid," he said, gesturing at the gracious West Los Angeles home he still lives in, a smile on his face. "This is the house *Jacks* built. I bought this place off that loot." Seltzer later recalled that the payout amounted to as much as $400,000, since Malden had been hired for four consecutive ten-week periods.

If Kubrick was becoming odd man out, Willingham was almost gone. During story conferences he grew increasingly quiet as his ideas were shot down, one after another. While he would later claim to have resigned, Fiore said that Brando took him for a night on the town, fed him a good dinner, and "by the time he had finished his lamb chops, he was fired. As a parting gift, Marlon gave him an expensive, inlaid rosewood chess table."

By November the script was still not finished. Frank Rosenberg considered rehiring Peckinpah but finally brought in Guy Trosper, who seemed to hit it off with Brando at once. The result was that the new writer was to remain on the project throughout the lumbering shoot, rewriting dialogue day by day. With the new December 1958 starting date for what was now titled *One-Eyed Jacks* edging closer, Kubrick's situation was becoming more tenuous, and it was not long before he followed Willingham out the door.

Here, too, Brando claimed that Kubrick quit, although once again the story had its streak of *Rashomon*.

Brando's version: "Just before we were to start, Stanley said, 'Marlon, I don't know what the picture's about.' I said, 'I'll tell you what it's about. It's about $300,000 that I've already paid Karl Malden.' He said, 'Well, if that's what it's about, I'm in the wrong picture.' So that was the end of it. I ran around, asked Sidney Lumet, Gadg, and, I don't know, four or five people, nobody wanted to direct it. There wasn't anything for me to do except to direct it or go to the poorhouse."

Rosenberg's version: "At a meeting, Brando had been urging that we put a Chinese story into the script, with a Chinese girl. He wanted his Rio character to romance a Chinese girl, since there was a sizable Chinese population in the Monterey area during the script's 1880s time frame. I was resistant. Kubrick said, 'Who could play this?' Marlon said, 'What do you think of France Nuyen for the part?' 'France Nuyen?' Kubrick came back. 'She can't act.' At that point Marlon kind of looked at me, and being the great actor he is—he doesn't do very much—he excused himself and went into the kitchen. The eye contact he made with me indicated he wanted me to follow him, so I did. We stood there in his long, narrow kitchen and he was patting his stomach. 'We've gotta get rid of Kubrick,' he said. That's an exact quote. I don't know if I said anything by the time he got to the next sentence. 'I'd like to direct the picture myself.' "

Rosenberg was skeptical and suggested that he consider postponing his directorial debut for a smaller-budget picture he wasn't acting in. Brando urged him to help him through the process; a good cameraman and editor, both with an understanding of the story, would make it possible. "Look," he said, "if you don't go any further away from me than you are now, I can direct the picture. Just help me."

Rosenberg acquiesced, but not without some trepidation.

On November 21, 1958, Seltzer brought Kubrick to the Pennebaker offices at Paramount and fired him. "Marlon had changed rapidly from being a fan, an admirer, to saying, 'This guy is a fake,'" he recalled. "I sat with Kubrick and said, 'This isn't working, Stanley.' And he was very happy to get lost. Marlon, of course, was nowhere to be found."

Kubrick claimed that his contract forbade him from talking to the press, but issued a statement that he had resigned "with deep regret because of my respect and admiration for one of the world's foremost artists, Marlon Brando. Mr. Brando and his assistants have been most understanding of [my] desire . . . to commence work on *Lolita*."

Insiders recognized this as window dressing, and Kubrick stepped in to helm *Spartacus* instead. He also told Carlo Fiore that he was relieved to hear Marlon was directing: "If he had hired another director, it might have appeared that I was lacking in talent, or temperament, or something. But if Marlon directs it, it gets me off the hook."

Had directing *One-Eyed Jacks* been Brando's plan all along? "My feeling, unsupported by anything but my gut, was that Marlon always intended to direct it," said Seltzer. "Through legerdemain he had arranged it so that he would both control production and direct—by using Jay as an ally he achieved just that. He'd always talked about directing; he was smart, he'd starred in a number of pictures, and if given a script and a scene, he could probably get fine performances. The only problem was that he had to mess around with any script he went near."

In all likelihood, the true scenario was that Brando had brought Kubrick aboard in the hope of directing Kubrick's direction of himself. In this way he could tap the renegade director's talent while maintaining ultimate control—plus have the added benefit of a built-in fallback. If the film failed, he could always blame someone else. Whatever his original agenda, the actor approached his new job with an air of insouciance, even brio.

"I usually direct myself anyway, so it's not much of a problem," he told Joe Hyams of the *Los Angeles Times,* "and I'd never direct myself in a part that was hard to play. We couldn't get anyone else to take over who was worth his salt. No good director would go in with only a week's preparation, and since I worked constantly on the film, I took over. It was a matter of expediency."

He also took the occasion to dismiss acting with a statement that would be quoted for decades to come: "I have no respect for acting," he said. "Acting by and large is the expression of a neurotic impulse. I've never in my life met an actor who was not neurotic—not that it's bad to be neurotic, it's just not satisfying. . . . Acting is a bum's life, in that it leads to perfect self-indulgence," he went on. "You get paid for doing nothing, and it all adds up to nothing. Acting is fundamentally a childish thing to pursue. Quitting acting—that is the mark of maturity."

He could not have picked a worse time to tackle the challenges of directing as far as his personal life was concerned. Anna was growing angrier—more demonstrative and hysterical by the week. One day she accosted Marlon on the street, outside the rented bungalow, where he and Rosenberg were meeting. She had suddenly appeared, leaped out of her car, and rushed at Marlon, talons extended, and started to claw him in front of the producer. Another afternoon their landlord, Robert Balzer, arrived with Cambodia's Prince Sihanouk, who had requested a tour of the house. Anna slammed the door in their faces.

In September, the Brandos' Japanese maid had accidentally drowned in their swimming pool, and a week later Kashfi moved out, taking four-month-old Christian with her to her new apartment. Later that month, Jay Kanter called Anna with the news that Marlon had overdosed on sleeping pills, although whether he had done so on purpose was unclear. She thought it was another "vaudeville act," a bid for attention. The upshot was that Kashfi filed for divorce on September 30, eleven days shy of their first wedding anniversary, charging Marlon with "grievous mental suffering, distress and injury." It was a one-and-a-half page complaint, one of the shortest ever filed in Santa Monica Superior Court.

Years later Marlon himself would clumsily explain that he had known the marriage was over a month after their wedding, and that he had actually gone through with the ceremony only because "I didn't want Christian to be internationally known as an illegitimate child. . . . Finally it just fell apart. I told her, 'It is not going to work out.' "

At the time the complaint was filed, however, he wasn't quite so matter-of-fact. Behind the scenes he approached O'Melveny and Myers, one of the largest law firms on the West Coast, which had been doing work for Pennebaker for years, to determine if its attorneys could find a way to trim the amount of alimony the court would order him to pay. Seltzer, as always, was caught in the middle. "They had been the company's lawyer since the beginning," he said. "They told him they did not handle divorces but would find the best divorce lawyer in the area. Marlon said, 'Fuck 'em. If they won't handle my divorce, I don't want them to handle anything else,' and he fired the firm." To little avail. His new attorney informed him that Kashfi had him hamstrung and that all his cries of "unfair" would do little good now.

Kashfi was anxious to justify herself, and in Hedda Hopper's syndicated column she again complained of his nocturnal absences, social misbehavior, indifference to her health problems, and the parade of fawning cronies. To friends she spoke even more bluntly, particularly about Brando's relationship with Christian Marquand, who was their son's godfather. With Marquand, she was convinced, her husband had "something sexual." The handsome French actor and their pal Roger Vadim had stayed with the Brandos in Los Angeles after the completion of *The Young Lions*. Both struck her as "the queerest, the closest to Marlon in temperament." Both shared his philosophy of making no judgments, but Marquand in particular, she felt, displayed an affection toward Marlon that overstepped the usual expressions of friendship. "Just the way Marlon was talking to him, squirming like a woman," she later insisted. Equally lurid, she insisted, were the stories Vadim loved to tell about a Parisian brothel called Le Canard bleu that "specialized in supplying ducks for sexual intercourse." Marlon, she claimed, "enjoyed listening to Vadim recount the story, probably for the fiftieth time. Brando's favorite expletive," she added, "was 'up your cloaca!' "

Brando now had even more distractions: Producer Aaron Rosenberg (no relation to Frank P. Rosenberg) was already holding preliminary discussions with him about a remake of *Mutiny on the Bounty*. At the same time, the actor had been drawn into negotiations for *The Fugitive Kind,* based on Tennessee Williams's play *Orpheus Descending*. In the midst of all this, he was about to embark on *Jacks,* one of his most personal films. But since it was a project that he deeply cared about, there was none of his usual sloughing off, and he made it clear that he was taking the job seriously. "I have the obligation and opportunity . . . to try to communicate the things I think are important," he said. "I want to make a frontal assault on the temple of clichés."

The outcome would temper his feelings about the industry forever, if only because the picture's basic story line, set in the Pacific Northwest of the 1880s, was built around his cherished values of loyalty and revenge. The film's title was meant to refer to people who don't reveal their true natures, who, like their namesake in poker, operate as wild cards in a world populated by outlaws. "Our early-day heroes were not brave one hundred percent of the time, nor were they good one hundred percent of the time," Brando explained. "My part is that of a man who is intuitive and suspicious, prideful and searching. He has a touch of the vain and a childish and disproportionate sense of virtue and manly ethics. He is lonely and generally distrustful of human contacts."

The two-faced nature of the characters is a recurring theme, plainly autobiographical in intent but also hardly something to cheer the conventional studio executive's heart. It was the late 1950s, the era of *Gigi, Ben-Hur, The Nun's Story,* and Doris Day vehicles such as *Pillow Talk.* In contrast, Brando's bank robber, Rio, is not above using a stolen ring claimed to be his mother's to seduce a wealthy *señorita,* then coldly yanking it from her finger when his gang arrives, pursued by *federales.* Suspicious of everyone, he is loyal only to his hard-living partner, Malden's Dad Longworth, yet it is Dad who betrays him, leaving him to rot in a Sonora prison. When Rio finally escapes, accompanied by Modesto, an amiable Mexican who suggests that he start life anew, he cannot be swayed from revenge. In his initial meeting with his former partner, now the Monterey sheriff, Rio hears Dad explain that he has become a new man because of his wife, Maria, and stepdaughter, Louisa; Rio, coolly Janus-faced, stays for supper, plotting his payback that will consist of stealing Louisa's virtue, robbing the bank, and finally murder.

On December 2, 1958, the company arrived in Monterey to begin the shoot. In addition to longtime colleague Malden, the cast included at least two of Brando's former romantic interests—Katy Jurado and Joan "Gina" Petrone—as well as his Actors Studio friend Miriam Colón. As usual, Sam Gilman was on hand, playing Harvey, one of the "scum bucket" bank robbers. Another apparatchik was Larry Duran, the Mexican extra Marlon had met on *Zapata!*, who was graduating to a dramatic role as Rio's side-kick, Modesto. Other friends were Philip Rhodes, who was doing the makeup not only for Marlon but for the entire cast, including all the simu-lated wounds and blood spilling; Sam Shaw, who was doing the stills; and of course Carlo Fiore, Marlon having given him the title "assistant to the producer." Alice Marchak was in attendance for her first location shoot since being promoted from the Pennebaker office staff to Marlon's full-time personal assistant.

The cast also included a former cowboy, Ben Johnson, in the role of Bob, the character who is to become the most important single influence on Rio; although Johnson had initially been hired by Kubrick, Brando was happy to keep him in the cast. He had actually worked as a range hand, then had been recruited by John Ford for such westerns as *She Wore a Yel-low Ribbon*, *Wagonmaster*, and *Rio Grande*. For weeks prior to the move to Monterey, Brando had been studying the actor's mannerisms and accent, often sitting in restaurants quizzing him at length, usually with Marchak in attendance, taking notes. He was the real thing, and whenever Johnson himself asked Brando for advice, Marlon would answer, "How would Ben Johnson play it?"

Brando's eventual cowboy impersonation was to receive high marks from Johnson, who thought his boss an able rider and only differed with his insistence on choosing a horse with an unusual tail and gait. (No real bandit would ride such an easily recognizable animal, he said.) Like Brando, Johnson had also come from a broken home, hadn't finished high school, and had spent all of his young adulthood angry and undirected. Very much a man's man, he knew about guns, horses, stoicism and gener-osity, and he too had had a fair amount of experience with women. They swapped tales incessantly.

"Marlon was so bitter toward his father's drinking and what it had cost the family . . . well, he just laid everything on his old man," Johnson explained, recalling their talks. "He had such a bad childhood—all his life he grew to hate authority figures, and this sort of started to come out."

One night at a restaurant, Johnson had his first taste of Brando's toughness. "If you get in a situation, a bar fight or whatever, you'd want him on your side," the cowboy-actor said. "He unloaded on some locals, and it didn't last very long, I'll tell you. Wasn't no chairs, just a few fists, one thing and another, and these two fellas who'd been botherin' him got the shit kicked out of 'em."

The script of *One-Eyed Jacks* was still unfinished at the start of principal photography, and Marlon had already spent $1.25 million, leaving Rosenberg's $1.8 million budget as little more than a pipe dream. "Would you believe that . . . we're five days behind schedule?" the producer moaned to Fiore, noting that they had only shot one-half page of the three pages of script that were supposed to have been completed the first day. Brando, meanwhile, had tossed his own script aside and mumbled to his actors, "Let's improvise," letting the cameras roll while the actors ad-libbed. "There is nothing so unusual about improvising before a camera," he told the gathered press, defending his methodology. "During the silent movies, they used to do it all the time. Actors are much freer in improvisation than when they are restricted by a script." He wasn't wrong—some of the film's best lines came out of his improvs with Johnson, lines like "Harv, you're 'bout t' lose yourself a handful of brains" or, better, the unforgettable "You scum-sucking pig," one of the nastiest put-downs on celluloid.

Brando had already announced to Paramount that he was "making a film, not a schedule," and felt more than a bit vindicated when Johnson told him that John Ford had often worked in the same way. "Yep," added Johnson. "On *Rio Grande* a studio representative visited the set and told Ford, 'Jack, we're behind schedule.' Ford said, 'Are we?' Then he got the script and he tore a page out, then another one, tearing every page until there were only about twelve pages left. He closed it up and said, 'Now we're on schedule.' "

The actors were often stymied, however, by the lack of blocking, and when they asked what to do with their hands, Marlon told them, "Well, just scratch your ear. Scratch your shoulder," recalled Sam Shaw, who was covering the shoot for *Life*. Five days into production, a worried Frank Freeman called Rosenberg from Paramount. The unit manager had been following standard procedure and filing daily reports on footage as well as the number of setups and scenes completed, but he had smelled trouble early on. Two weeks later Freeman reportedly pleaded with the producer in his thick Georgia drawl, "Ah had my first heart attack on *The Buccaneer,* my second on *The Ten Commandments,* and ah may have my third attack on this one."

Seltzer, meanwhile, had returned from Ireland, where he'd been supervising postproduction on *Shake Hands with the Devil,* and he found a letter waiting for him from George Glass describing the *Jacks* shoot as "chaos." The defining incident referred to by Glass would soon pass into

Hollywood lore as emblematic of the tyro director's self-indulgence.

One morning around eleven A.M., Rosenberg found Brando seated on a rock staring at a necklace and thinking about Pellicer's character, Louisa. The producer could see that Marlon needed to be alone, so he drove into Carmel, got himself a haircut, and, still killing time, did some shopping. When he returned to the set hours later, Marlon was in the same position, still staring out to sea. "I'm waiting for a wave," he said.

"What do you mean, 'a wave'?"

"The perfect wave," he replied, explaining that he needed the frothing surf as background for his contemplated shot.

Soon Malden arrived and Rosenberg said, "Jesus Christ, let's go and shoot something else."

"No," Marlon replied, "find out what the weather will be."

Dutifully, Rosenberg went off to get the report. When he returned with the news that the afternoon tide was likely to bring bigger waves, Marlon nodded. "Good, we'll sit here and wait."

He continued looking across the water, at "the little piddly, bubbly things coming up, no white," as Malden put it. Soon Chico Day, the assistant director, arrived and quickly realized what was happening. He also saw another problem. "Marlon," he said gently, "you're looking through the wrong end of the range finder."

Brando laughed. "Holy shit, no wonder I'm a week late."

A similar incident occurred when he spent over half the day pulling petals off a wild rosebush, still thinking of Louisa. At last an assistant meekly asked, "Mr. Brando, don't you think we should get this shot?" Brando turned to Johnson, hollering, "Ben, go anywhere you want for three or four days, 'cause I'm gonna be sittin' on this rock."

Expenses were now running more than $50,000 a day. The format was 70-millimeter VistaVision, the most expensive film of the time, but of the average 11,000 feet Brando exposed in the course of a day, only 270 would wind up in the finished film. The problem was not just his need for covering shots. When Chico Day would call out his warning that they were coming to the end of a magazine with, say, 150 feet left, Brando's usual response, whether he needed the coverage or not, was to tell him to let the film run out."

Rosenberg cautioned Brando, but it didn't help. Perhaps it was Malden who perceived what was happening more clearly than anyone. "I don't know if anyone told him outright," he said, "but Chico Day and [cinematographer] Charlie Lang tried to help by advising him, 'Marlon, it would be faster if you shot this, you can save time if you did this.' Only he wouldn't listen. 'We'll do it this way. This is the way I've set my mind to it, and this is the way we're going to do it.' In other words, he never said, 'Fuck the time, fuck the money'—not in so many words—but you realized after a week of this, Why waste your breath? He's going to do it his way anyhow."

While Paramount executives writhed, the shoot was proving to be a busman's holiday for the actors, with the prospect of fat overtime bonuses. The feeling of goodwill grew when Brando insisted on sending the entire company home for Christmas. The production schedule called for work until 4:30 P.M. on Christmas Eve, but Marlon intervened—and because of a Pacific Southwest strike then in progress, he chartered cars, a train, and several planes, insisting that all 120 members of the cast and crew stay home for several days even though they had been working less than three weeks. While Paramount was paying everyone's salary, Brando, reportedly, went to New York to see France Nuyen.

Delays aside, Malden still trusted him more than anyone, even in his new role as director. "Karl, I want the makeup man to work on you," Marlon had said. "I see you with a bushy mane like a lion." Soon fitted with a hairpiece, Malden realized that the choice was "brilliant." "I trusted his eyes," said the experienced actor. "Anything in front of the cameras I can handle, but I didn't know a goddamn thing about behind the camera. Marlon knew lighting and how to frame a shot pictorially, he knew what he was doing."

Rosenberg had also taken the unusual step of bringing along film editor Archie Marchek to ensure they were getting sufficient coverage. But Brando himself must be credited with the near painterly sweep of *One-Eyed Jacks*. Niven Busch may have grown disgusted with his ramblings about the "beauty of nature," but he had plainly given thought to the visualization of his ideas: The crashing waves off the rocky Monterey coast, he told Malden, Seltzer, and others, was to serve as the central metaphor for the changing faces of his characters. "It was Marlon's idea to film by the sea . . . and it was something distinctly visual for him. There was no esoteric connection; he saw it as novel," explained Seltzer. The spectacular scenery, lovingly captured by cinematographer Charles Lang, would win kudos even from the film's most vehement detractors. Yet the most telling footnote to the whole process came from brother-in-law Dick Loving, whom

Brando had visited at the family farm in Mundelein just before the shoot. There, he practiced using a movie camera, putting himself through a dry run. "We went out into a field," Loving recalled, "and we did verticals, horizontals, all the while looking through the viewfinder. His thing was figuring out the compositional dynamics of space. He didn't talk about color. What interested him was what the diagonals were, the near vision, the middle range; he was trying to sensitize himself to landscape."

He had never talked this way with his brother-in-law before, even though he'd posed for several of Dick's portraits. Now, on location, he was behind the viewfinder "setting up absolutely every shot." Masters, pans, close-ups, and two-shots, he was composing with the utmost care, shooting from every conceivable angle. To help himself visualize his character in upcoming scenes, he had hired Steve Marlo, a stage and film actor, to "play" Rio by not only wearing his costume and standing in the right place, but by also delivering his lines and gestures. Philip Rhodes's wife, Marie, was also called upon to stand in for the blocking and setups. The rationale was simple: He wanted more, or as Miriam Colón put it, "He just wouldn't settle for quick results. He had to believe in his own mind that it was right."

"It's been trying," said Brando after Christmas. "The first few weeks were very difficult, but it improves as we go along. I work fourteen hours a day. Directing by itself is hard enough. But I've found that there are no divisional lines between an actor becoming a director. Things are so subtly interlaced it is hard to know where one begins and the other ends."

Some scenes were lifted whole cloth from the life of the western outlaw Billy the Kid, several of whose bios Brando had consulted before coming to Monterey. As he worked with his actors, though, it was straight Method improv. For the sadistic whipping-post scene, which would become one of the movie's best-remembered episodes, Malden was positioned far enough back so he'd miss Brando by two feet, and was told to go at it until the sweat poured off his face. Given the risk of injury from the genuine twelve-foot bullwhip he was using, Malden started tentatively. With the line "Have you had enough?," Brando was supposed to collapse, but once, after several takes, Marlon wheeled and extemporaneously spat in Karl's face. "I mean, he put a real glob there," Malden recalled. "I wiped it off and ad-libbed, 'Guess you haven't had enough,' and went back to the whipping. Later he said he thought I was really going to let him have it. But he got the scene exactly as he wanted."

Malden was the old pro, and Sam Shaw saw that together "they just knew. There were no hurdles to jump over, no inner struggle to get at other things," like Marlon's last-minute decision to have Malden smash his hand to a pulp with his gun butt. The sequence was singled out by critics as unusually violent—Penn's *Bonnie and Clyde,* like Peckinpah's bloody *The Wild Bunch,* was still years away—but here Marlon was letting his instincts run free.

With Gilman, who had never been on a horse before, Marlon spent hours giving lessons in riding, as well as in pantomiming quick draws with a six-gun. He used even more direct means to get a performance out of the inexperienced Larry Duran. When the Mexican couldn't come up with the reaction he wanted, Brando grabbed him, then cracked him across the face with the back of his hand. "It was done pretty briskly," said Johnson. "That's the only thing I saw Marlon do I didn't approve of. He'd done that with me, hell, the fight would have been on. Ol' Larry never said a word."

No one proved as challenging as Pina Pellicer, who, though she brought a poignant vulnerability to the role of Louisa, was so anxious and uncertain that as early as the second week Marlon had nicknamed her "Pigeon."

"I am still afraid when I go on the set, but I try to do the best I can. Mr. Brando is very kind and patient with me," she told a reporter.

Although she was often effective in rehearsal, her biggest problem was that she'd freeze during takes. To loosen her up, Brando tried firing a gun in the air without warning. In the difficult, emotionally charged scene where Louisa tells her mother, played by Katy Jurado, that she's pregnant, he had rehearsed her repeatedly; now, getting close to a solid performance, he signaled Lang to start filming without the telltale slate. "Marlon was rotating his finger behind his back," recalled Rosenberg. "He got a tremendous performance out of her. Then he said, 'Cut, print.' Charley said, 'Print what?' He hadn't seen the finger."

Brando tried to help her in other ways, too, and while there was a Svengali component to it, just as there often is between directors and their young actresses, it led inevitably to an affair. It was no secret that he had been sleeping with Jurado, and as the shoot progressed, he began juggling the two of them while also hitting on Colón. France Nuyen made an appearance on the set, too, and soon a new woman was added to the menu: She was Lisa Lu, a young Chinese woman who had interviewed him for her school newspaper when he had been in Hawaii two years before.

Brando had become infatuated with her—despite her refusal to have an affair because, she told him, she was happily married. "He had a thing about trying to make it with her," said Rhodes, adding that Brando offered her the small role of the waitress who brings him food when he's drunk and lying in bed with his hand smashed. (Even though his previous idea for a subplot of a Chinese woman had been rejected, he still had a ploy for getting his latest obsession on the set.)

Lu agreed to do the scene, though not before acquiring an agent who demanded and received a guarantee of a week's salary. As usual, Marlon intended to play being drunk by getting drunk. He thus scheduled the scene for a Friday so he wouldn't have to work the next day with a hangover.

"So Lisa Lu brought in the food as instructed," recalled Rhodes, "but by then Marlon was so drunk he couldn't say his lines. The scene was put off another week, and the next Friday he was again too drunk. She stayed for so many weeks, all the while with the company having to pay her salary, that we heard she got a restaurant out of it."

Ironically, though, if Marlon was using this ploy to keep her around and "trying to make her," added Rhodes, this time it didn't work. "Marlon was on fire at the time," he noted. "He was having an affair with anybody who would stand still. But the weekend he was going to fuck her, Movita showed up on the set, so I don't think it happened."

Whether or not Movita realized that Marlon was, as Rhodes and other friends commented, "fucking everyone in sight," she had succumbed to his months of pleading and returned to Los Angeles. In their tempestuous, on-again, off-again affair, she was now telling her family and friends that she expected Marlon to marry her after his divorce was final. But in the overheated atmosphere of the *Jacks* set, Marlon seemed to have little interest in that kind of commitment, and he made little attempt to disguise the sexual bouillabaisse he had concocted.

Pellicer, though, was hardly stable enough to accept the bizarre situation. Talking to costume designer Yvonne Wood one afternoon about another actress who had recently committed suicide, she peeled back her cuffs to display wrists welted with scar tissue. She had slashed herself a few years before, when only seventeen. "She told me that was not the only time that she had tried it," the costume designer recalled. "The subject just came out of nowhere, and she was upset with herself since she was Catholic. 'This is very bad. Your soul is taken,' she kept saying."

According to any number of sources, Brando then began playing "some dangerous mind games."

"Obviously, there were discussions about suicide vis-à-vis Pina," said Seltzer. "The rumor around was that Marlon had many discussions with her on the advisability of suicide as a concept—a general concept, mind you, but as it turned out, for Pina it was tragic. I don't think he told her to go kill herself, but there may have been an idea planted," he added. "The gossip was that he encouraged it. Not by simple suggestion but overtly— 'There is a way out.' "

Seltzer's suggestion was not as far-fetched as it may have seemed. As early as the 1940s Marlon had discussed suicide with David Diamond, his sometime alter-ego and confidant in New York. "There was a lot of talk about death as an abstraction," composer Diamond recalled. "I told him he should read Paul Valéry's essay on suicide."

Gia Scala, Pier Angeli, and his onetime secretary Susan Slade—all were Brando dates over the years, all suicides. Kashfi would soon take a crack at it herself. Dodie had made at least one attempt at taking her life, and apparently, so too would Rita Moreno.

Pellicer, however, was not so fortunate. Sam Shaw believed that her death stemmed from a lesbian relationship with a beautiful, older Mexican woman who visited the set. Whatever her reasons, after the *Jacks* shoot the beautiful, birdlike Pellicer returned to Mexico, made two movies there, and took her life in December 1964.

Brando's compulsive womanizing on location was undoubtedly a diversion not only from the pressures of the production itself, but from those back home. Jocelyn and Eliot Asinof were still in the throes of their difficult divorce, which had done nothing to lessen his sister's drinking. In February Kashfi was hospitalized for hepatitis, giving her a strategic advantage when she formally filed for divorce on March 16 after six months' separation. She was awarded a half-million-dollar settlement, plus $1,000 a month in child support, at the end of April. The Nebraska ranch suit had finally come to court, too—with no satisfactory resolution.

The collective burden was huge, and as much as he tried to hide it, it exacerbated his usual tendency toward mood swings.

"I didn't understand it emotionally, though intellectually I did," explained Seltzer, who was now visiting the set often to do what he could to speed things up. "He was two guys. He was always either very exhilarated or down in the dumps. There was always a crisis, and if he had to, he could perform. . . . But there was some deep emotional disturbance. He would show it through not smiling, not answering, not responding to a joke—or conversely, through overresponding to a joke by being a buffoon."

Back at the Pennebaker offices, Marlon Sr. had started talking about his son's mood swings, and when he'd get off the phone to Monterey, it wasn't unusual for him to announce, "Bud's low today," or, simply, "There's no problem." What he wasn't aware of—and this was certainly minor in relation to other things—was that Marlon was packing on weight, compulsively overeating in a way he hadn't during *Desirée* and *The Young Lions.* All the principals were staying at the Tickled Pink Motel outside Carmel, where the management had futilely tried to accommodate him with a low-fat diet. Even the ministrations and reminders from girl friday Alice Marchak failed. "Suddenly, we're eating and there it goes," Malden recalled. "Two steaks, potatoes, two apple pies à la mode, a quart of milk. I don't know what did it. Aggravation during the day maybe, but before you knew it, they'd have to go out and make another outfit for him. He'd just bloat up."

Costume designer Yvonne Wood was forced to make his trousers and even his tops out of elasticized material. Yet even with the "multisize" costumes, he still split his pants. Wood reported that she had to make him eighteen pairs, running up a budget that was actually queried by the front office. "They kept saying, 'Yvonne, you're just picking the wrong fabric.' When they saw what I was using, they said, 'My God, how in the world is he splitting that?' "

Sam Shaw had to lend a hand, too, and soon began serving as a sort of "fat coach" whenever Brando was in front of the camera. "I'd point to my chin, telling him to keep his head up so there wouldn't be a double chin," he explained. "Or I'd point to my belly button to remind him to suck in his stomach." Cast members, prompted by Marchak, posted a sign announcing, DON'T FEED THE DIRECTOR.

As usual, Marlon drank little except when the onscreen action called for it. He put away half a bottle of vodka for the "scum bucket" barroom scene with Johnson, Duran, and Gilman. He was so drunk then, too, that Fiore bet him that he couldn't walk the thirty feet to the set—and indeed watched him pass out, face first. Later, at two A.M., he woke up calling,

"Where is everybody?" Carlo helped him to the bathroom to vomit, later recalling that he hugged the bowl and bawled like an infant. "This reminds me of my mother," he reputedly cried. "I don't know why." It was the same foolish stunt he'd tried on *Zapata!*

Unfortunately, chores like shepherding Brando to the bathroom wouldn't spell job security for Fiore, who had maintained contact with Kubrick by bringing to the director's attention the early Vladimir Nabokov novel *Laughter in the Dark*. Kubrick had never heard of the brilliant black comedy, but saw the need to protect his upcoming production of *Lolita;* he'd quickly optioned the book, proposing that Carlo try his hand at turning the story into a screenplay. Meanwhile, Marlon had just signed to star in Sidney Lumet's upcoming film, *The Fugitive Kind,* soon to start shooting in upstate New York. When Fiore told his boss that because of his chance to work with Kubrick, he wouldn't be able to join him on location, Brando became enraged. Unable to endure such a defection, he soon fired Fiore from *One-Eyed Jacks.*

"He was blocking the gun-dueling scene with Malden," Fiore recalled. "When it was set, the cameraman took over and Marlon came to me, took me aside, and said, 'Freddie, I'm letting you go. I'm way over budget and I can't carry you anymore.'

"*Carry* me? That's a hell of a way to put it."

"Take it any way you like," Marlon said, "but you're fired."

"As of when?"

"As of now."

"Don't you think there's a lot of hostility in the *way* you're firing me?"

"M-m-m-m—nope. I don't feel any hostility toward you. As a matter of fact, I'm still going to give you that single-card screen credit I promised you. Your old Brooklyn buddies will be impressed when they see it."

In April 1959, after four months of filming including several weeks of location work in Death Valley, Brando moved the production to Paramount's back lot in Hollywood. No longer able to hide in the desert, he was now within striking distance of executives like Frank Freeman, whose concern over the film's spiraling budget was approaching apoplexy. Brando didn't seem to care. On weekends, he'd fly to Manhattan for a quick rendezvous with France Nuyen, leaving Rosenberg and others to stew.

Freeman was ready to draw the line. He was tired of supervising a production initiated by Paramount president Barney Balaban, Jay Kanter's father-in-law, and he had even told Rosenberg he might resign his position at the studio in protest. Rosenberg took the news to Brando, who was putting on his makeup; he just laughed and said, "It's my money, my film."

Freeman quickly set up a meeting between the actor and Jack Karp, the overseer of the studio's finances. Brando told Rosenberg that he wasn't fazed in the least. "They're going to complain about this picture," he said beforehand, "then somebody's going to say, 'Would you make another picture for Paramount?' and the meeting will be over."

At the meeting, Karp ("very uncomfortably," according to Rosenberg) "kept telling us that all the footage was great. Soon he got around to the fact that we were four zillion dollars over budget, five months over schedule, etc., but still, 'The stuff is great, Marlon.' Finally, he said, 'We're sure looking forward to you making another picture for us.' So it happened exactly as Marlon had said it would. He has the shrewdness that I describe as the instincts of a jungle animal."

The same scenario repeated itself several weeks later when the huge fiesta scene was dragging on with no end in sight. Freeman, the unit manager, had already confronted Seltzer: "You know that whole sequence ain't gonna run more than two minutes, Walter, but he claims he's got twenty pages [about twenty minutes] to shoot. You're goin' out there and you're gonna tell him that come Friday, ah'm personally gonna pull the plug."

The threat—as old as the movie business itself—meant he was ready to cut the electricity that fed cameras, lighting, and sound equipment, but the warning brought only a laugh from Brando. "Freeman's full of crap," he said.

"Marlon, I got an idea," Seltzer urged. "Freeman's really steamed up about this, and I've gotta agree with him. You're not going to use all this footage in the sequence. You've got your scriptwriter Trosper sitting right here. You and he go over the remaining twenty pages, cut it down to bare essentials. Don't sacrifice anything. I'm not telling you to throw out stuff that you need, but you know there's an awful lot of crap, and we can finish it in one afternoon."

"Tell him to go fuck himself," Brando instructed Seltzer, who went back to the producer and relayed the message in more diplomatic terms.

Angry, Freeman headed for the back lot at once, with Seltzer bringing up the rear.

"Marlon, who has eyes in the back of his head, saw us coming," Seltzer recalled. "He peeled off from what he was doing and greeted Freeman with a beatific smile. Y. Frank put his arm around him, and said, 'I've seen the rushes of the last couple of days' work. It's just beautiful.' He watched for thirty seconds, then he said to me, 'Okay, let's go.' We walked away. As we're heading back to the front office, I turned around and Marlon was thumbing his nose at me. Paramount was letting it go so long because Marlon was still hot, still a big star, and they thought that if they did something to displease him, he wouldn't make any more pictures for them. Marlon knew exactly what was up all along."

One-Eyed Jacks had started with a script without an ending, and even now there was still no conclusion the director was happy with. "Marlon, who dies today? You or me?" Malden kept joshing him, and a stumped Brando even held a vote so that the actors could choose the story line of their choice.

For the final confrontation, Malden suggested using the well set. "Suddenly Marlon invented the shooting," said Malden. "And then he jumped across, did that leap that he made. It was part of the technique—he'd think these things up and not tell you ahead of time."

In due course, Brando also came up with a narrative frame for the film's last movement. In Brando's anything-but-clichéd finale, which was filmed but never incorporated in the studio's release print, Rio and Louisa escape on horseback while the dying Dad gets off one last shot, hitting his stepdaughter in the back. Rio sees Louisa bleeding, and, broken, decides to stop running. "I've had it, I've run long enough," he declares, and she dies in his arms.

Brando had to help Pellicer through her death scene, and he played Harry Belafonte's haunting recording of "Shenandoah" to bring tears to his eyes. The story ends with Rio riding back to town with Louisa's body, but Paramount, Malden lamented, insisted that it "had to end with him as the hero. They cut the part where he sees the blood on her, and added that I'll-come-back ending, which was a lot of crap. In fact, in the original ending all three of us are finished. When he takes her back into the town in his arms, the townspeople come out and presumably it's the end for him, too."

The shoot concluded officially in June 1959, although the studio forced Brando and Malden to return on October 14 to make the alternate ending. By the close of principal photography, more than a million feet of film had been exposed—six times as much as for the ordinary feature—

and 250,000 feet printed, a new Hollywood record. The budget had gone from $1.6 to over $6 million, though Paramount had stopped keeping a running cost sheet in an effort to hide the mounting cost from the media. "We've got the Brando name in a class western. We feel that is worth the four- to four-and-a-half million this picture will cost," a studio flack lied. "It will be our blockbuster of 1960."

At a raucous wrap party in the Paramount commissary, Marlon played drums and met guests in a top hat and tails, wielding a cane. "He was pretty loaded," said one of the participants. He was also exhausted. Comedian Mort Sahl, the emcee, announced, "I want to notify you officially that this picture is completed because we ran out of money." The food arrived late but, as Sahl added, "Why shouldn't it? Everything's been late about this movie."

Brando dove into the lavish buffet with abandon. "He must have eaten four pieces of cake," Yvonne Wood recalled. "Then he leaned back, patted his stomach, and called out, 'Well, bring on the derrick.' " The crew awarded him with a western belt with a card saying, "Hope it fits."

Brando could have used some time off before beginning the process of editing but, instead, he had to leave the next day for New York to report for *The Fugitive Kind*. During that shoot, he had to attend to postproduction work on *Jacks,* flying back to L.A. each weekend. What he had waiting for him at Paramount was literally 200 miles of film.

The sheer bulk of the footage was partly the studio's fault, at least as Johnson saw things. "They would say, 'We're over budget, we're behind schedule . . .' so he'd just put another load on them, shoot another ten thousand feet. If they'd left him alone, this thing would have come in half what it cost."

This argument is no more credible than another often heard excuse: that the million feet of film had offered him "coverage" in the face of his anxieties as a first-time director. "I can cut any kind of picture out of this I want," was what he'd told Johnson, which in fact was roughly how he proceeded. Working with cutter Archie Marchek during the weekend sessions, he viewed raw footage, then told the editor, "I want this line from this take, I want that line from this one," mixing frames as though he were melding tracks in a recording studio. "Jesus Christ," moaned Marchek, "it will take me four years to put it together this way."

He was not too far wrong. Postproduction crawled from June 1959 to March 1961 as Brando kept shuttling between New York and L.A., editing on the run while Paramount trucked the film from one coast to the other. He even set up a temporary editing facility in Chicago. He cared about the project, certainly, but the meticulous process of poring over stock frame by frame was bound to take its toll. Unlike the "real time" work of directing, postproduction was something else again: Brando was now trapped in a tiny room with only Marchek, a Moviola, and thousands of strips of unconnected celluloid. The editing called for a decisive awareness of structure, hardly Brando's strong suit. "For months nothing was done," said Seltzer. "Marchek was the only one looking in the Moviola."

In later years Brando would attempt to write several screenplays, as well as his autobiography, with similar results. What marked them all was his refusal to cede authority. He was "in over his head," Malden realized, but "maybe he was ashamed to go to a good cutter and say, 'Please, I'm up a creek. Will you come when nobody's around and tell me what to do?' "

At one point even Fiore got a call at three A.M. "I'm down at Paramount, wearing out my eyeballs in the cutting room," Brando moaned. "I can't see the forest for the trees. Why don't you come down and help me?" Fiore, still smarting from being bounced from the film, refused. Several nights later he received another call, and Marlon asked how many Seconals Fiore had ever taken at once, explaining that he had just taken six. For more than an hour he rambled on and on in a barely audible whisper. Finally he passed out in midsentence, leaving Carlo with his slow, heavy breathing at the other end. "He got in the habit of calling me often, at two or three o'clock in the morning, his voice fogged with the pills he was taking," Fiore said. "What he wanted me to do was listen while he talked himself to sleep."

After several passes he finally arrived at an eight-hour cut that Seltzer watched with Marchek. "Even in the eight-hour version, there was a fascination with story, character, and incident," Seltzer explained. "He had no intention of releasing an eight-hour picture; but basically his attitude was 'For my masterpiece they'll stand in line.' He wasn't concerned with the exhibitors' problems. But it wasn't something called vision or artistic commitment—it was ego. E-g-o," Seltzer stressed. "When we'd tell him the print was too long, he'd mumble, 'I don't think so.' That or a vague promise, 'I'll do something about it.' "

Finally, Brando edited it to a 4½-hour "director's cut," which he then screened for Rosenberg. When the lights came up, the producer let Brando sweat. Embarrassed, Marlon asked, "Where we going to eat? Chianti?" In the car, he kept giving Rosenberg sidelong glances, and it was not until they were well into their meal that he finally broke down and asked directly, "Well, what do you think of the picture?"

"Picture?" Rosenberg replied. "That's not a picture. That's just an assemblage of footage."

Brando then brought the cut down to a three-hour version, but by then Paramount had finally run out of patience. The man who wrenched control of the film away from Marlon was D. A. Doran, one of the studio's senior executives. Seltzer became aware of the move beforehand, but kept the information to himself.

"One day Doran came in," he said, "and bang, the print was no longer the property of Marlon to play with, no longer his toy store. The minute Doran took over, Marlon lost interest. He didn't fight it. He didn't say, 'Shit, no, you can't do that. I'll start work on Monday.' It was by default as much as anything else, and I think he was totally relieved. This was an albatross he'd been carrying around for a couple of years, and now he was free of it."

The three-hour *One-Eyed Jacks* might have been the definitive statement that he was hoping for. Sam Shaw, one of the few to see the longer version, called it "a masterpiece, one of the most romantic westerns ever made." Unfortunately, Shaw's assessment can't be validated, since the excised hours of *One-Eyed Jacks* were destroyed by Paramount—according to a studio spokesman, for the negative's valuable nitrate.

Publicly, Brando reacted to Paramount's sanctioned 141-minute version with disdain. "Now, it's a good picture for them, but it's not the picture I made," he stated. "In my film, everybody lied, even the girl. The only one who told the truth was the Karl Malden character. Paramount made him out to be the heavy, a liar. . . . Hypocrisy is not necessarily evil, and the audience understands this. How often does a mother lie to a father to protect her child? Now the characters in the film are black and white, not gray and human as I planned them."

In the presence of friends the actor could not hide the fact that he was deeply hurt, that Paramount had "broken his heart," as Sam Shaw put it. Even the frustrated Seltzer agreed. "Granted, Bud got every possible break," he said, "but this was going to be a statement. It was going to prove that he could produce, direct, and star in a movie that was superior, correct, and ethically mature. And he came close to doing it, so he was hurt. Number one, there was the hurt that he couldn't accomplish it himself, but number two, the reason that he didn't accomplish the cutting was that boredom had set in. All he had to do . . . was step in and go to work."

Philip Rhodes agreed. "Marlon had so much energy on that film," he said, "and I don't mean just his sexual energy. He was into everything—the cameras, the lighting, the wardrobe, the makeup. He was working on the script, he had writers coming in and helping. He was even going to rushes, which he had never done before. He was on a roll, so when they yanked it, he was hurt. It wasn't his swan song as far as his energy was concerned, but on *Jacks* it reached a peak and never appeared again in that force."

If *Jacks* left him embittered, his continuing problems with Anna Kashfi were draining him even further. Between August 1959 and the studio's final cut, Marlon's relationship with Anna had turned into a bitter custody fight over Christian that included physical violence, alleged break-ins, and five hearings in a Santa Monica courtroom. To complicate things, he'd started a relationship with actress Barbara Luna, ended the affair with France Nuyen, and was still seeing Movita, behavior that did not win him any points from the judges in the court proceedings.

One-Eyed Jacks was previewed in Sacramento, Denver, and St. Louis, and received favorable responses. The official premiere was March 30, 1961, but Brando didn't attend. Having finished *The Fugitive Kind,* he was already on location shooting *Mutiny on the Bounty* in French Polynesia. Nonetheless, he managed to make his feelings known in *Newsweek:* "*One-Eyed Jacks* is a potboiler," he declared with contempt. "I think it is quite conventional. I took a long time on it . . . six months to shoot. After a while, I got an attachment to it. It's like spending two years building a chicken coop. When you're finished, you want to feel you've done something with your time.

"It is not an artistic success. I'm a businessman," he repeated with sneering self-mockery. "I'm a captain of industry—nothing less than that. Any pretension I've sometimes had of being artistic is now just a long, chilly hope. *One-Eyed Jacks* is a product, just like . . . a news item. News makes money, not art. Movies are not art."

After seeing the film, Sam Peckinpah was just as disillusioned, though he, still angry about his firing and the destruction of the script, laid the blame completely on Marlon. "He screwed it up," he said later. "He's a hell of an actor, but in those days he had to end up a hero, and that's not the point of the story."

The critics were kinder to *Jacks* than its director had been. The New York *Daily News* gave it four stars, calling the film "stunning," just as *Time,* the *New York Post,* and the *New Yorker* used words like "startlingly beautiful," "top-hole, forceful, and lively," and "spectacular . . . graphic and sickening." *Hollywood Reporter* reviewer Jim Henagahn began with an admonishing attack on Brando. "I truthfully went to see the great multitalented genius, Marlon Brando, tumble on his rump in Technicolor. I don't like Brando personally. I think him a poseur, a doubtful asset to the community in which he lives, a self-centered, willful hedonist." But having gotten that off his chest, Henagahn, a pal of Eddie Jaffe, lavished his praise: "I think it might be the best western ever made, and surely a classic that will stand with most of the all-time great motion pictures; for it has taken the bones of cliché drama and superbly enhanced them with daring innovation. . . . Brando must, indeed, be honored as the father of this achievement."

Despite the furor at Paramount over the huge cost overrun, *One-Eyed Jacks* was never on par with later disasters such as *Heaven's Gate.* Still, it proved a loser. Business was brisk from the start, and over the years the film has grossed $10 to $12 million, but with advertising, interest, and distribution costs, this put it nowhere near breakeven.

Like Erich von Stroheim's *Greed, One-Eyed Jacks* is a maddening tease, a staple of art houses and a continuing subject of debate among film buffs; it is a touchstone in any argument about Hollywood's trampling of "artists." The film bounces back and forth between being a pastoral and an advertisement for Brando's scabrous, macho violence. Its underlying romanticism is as hokey as can be, but even the yearning tone mirrors its director's anger, reflecting the personal impulses behind his picture's creation. *Jacks* is Brando at his most vulnerable—his frankest and most revealing statement since the botched *Wild One.*

It was a project he had needed to do, "a passion that he wanted to fulfill," as Karl Malden put it. Years later Malden still kept a photo of the two of them, given to him not long after the shoot, with an inscription that reads: "In remembrance of things that will never be past. We had the very best of one another. That's a lot for our life. With love and respect and friendship, Marlon."

The Fugitive Kind

Battle of Angels was the first play by Tennessee Williams to be produced professionally. The story of a tragic love affair between a married, middle-aged shopkeeper and an ex-gigolo in a southern town, it opened for tryouts in Boston in 1940 but was so badly received that it never played in New York. Sixteen years later, with two Pulitzer Prizes behind him, Williams rewrote the play, naming it *Orpheus Descending.*

For the leading roles in the Broadway production, the playwright had wanted Brando and Anna Magnani. Brando was, in his opinion, "probably the greatest living actor . . . greater than Olivier," but he deplored the "crummy movies" that Marlon was making, obviously only for the money. However, Williams's new play failed to bring Marlon back to the stage; although the actor thought it had some of the playwright's best writing, he saw that it belonged to the leading lady. "The Magnani part is great," he said. "She stands for something, you can understand her—and she would wipe me off the stage."

Williams rewrote the part several times, but Marlon was never satisfied. "I had no intention of walking out on any stage with Magnani," he added. "Not in that part. They'd have to mop me up."

Magnani, the earthy, raven-haired Italian star, was one of Williams's favorite actresses—and a close friend. She had won the admiration of American critics and film viewers with her passionate performances in Roberto Rossellini's *Open City* and in Jean Renoir's *The Golden Coach.* The French director described her as the world's greatest actress, and Williams had been so inspired by the screen persona she was establishing that he created the role of Serafina in *The Rose Tattoo* for her. At that time, however, Magnani felt that her poor command of English would not allow her to perform the role on the stage, so in February 1951 *The Rose Tattoo* opened with Maureen Stapleton as the passionate, memory-haunted widow. Magnani did play the part in the 1955 film version, for which she won the best actress Oscar. (Brando had also been considered for the film, but the male lead went to Burt Lancaster.)

A year later in Rome, Williams asked Magnani to do *Orpheus De-*

scending on Broadway. Still frightened at the prospect of speaking English onstage, she refused, but was willing to commit herself to the film version, where her dialogue could be rehearsed and recorded in small pieces. As a result, Hal Wallis, the producer of *The Rose Tattoo,* hastened to take an option on the screen rights for her. Yet, when the play opened in New York in March 1957, it proved a critical and commercial fiasco. Even the immensely gifted Stapleton—once again in a part written for Magnani—could not save *Orpheus Descending* from failure. This did nothing for Williams's reputation in Hollywood—especially since *Baby Doll,* with Kazan at the helm, had foundered only months earlier.

Although there was no reason to believe that a play that had failed twice on the stage would succeed as a motion picture, Williams insisted on adapting it for the screen. After Wallis had dropped his option, the rights were sold to the neophyte production team of Martin Jurow and Richard Shepherd, whose low bid was accompanied by a commitment to Magnani (not a surprising outcome, since Jurow had been her agent).

Naturally, the producers turned to Brando. Shepherd called Jay Kanter, his best friend at MCA, only to hear what Marlon had said previously: The play was a vehicle for the leading actress and he was not interested. The producers, who in the meantime received backing from United Artists, offered the part to Anthony Franciosa. Williams approved of the choice, and Magnani, who was a silent partner in the film, was extremely enthusiastic: Franciosa had been her real-life as well as on-screen lover in *Wild Is the Wind,* although he had subsequently returned to Shelley Winters, his wife at the time. Arthur Krim and Bob Benjamin, the heads of United Artists, also gave their consent. Soon Franciosa signed a contract for $75,000, with additional "back money" pending the film's success.

Meade Roberts, a young playwright, was chosen by Williams to collaborate with him on the screenplay, and Sidney Lumet was soon signed to direct the film. Magnani had suggested him to the producers after seeing *Twelve Angry Men* (1957), the highly acclaimed courtroom drama that was his debut film. Lumet had gained a considerable reputation for staging live plays on television, and as a Group Theatre veteran he was an obvious choice to do Tennessee Williams. The management at United Artists was equally happy to have him, since *Twelve Angry Men,* a UA film, not only made money but had been nominated for three Oscars.

Using a final draft that Williams renamed *The Fugitive Kind* (the title was borrowed from a play he had produced while in college), the Williams-Roberts script was essentially faithful to the original stage play. It is the story of Val Xavier, a tarnished, knockabout New Orleans blues player who decides to go "straight." Wearing his trademark snakeskin jacket and carrying his guitar—his "best companion"—Val wanders into a small, vicious southern town where Vee, the wife of the corrupt local sheriff, gives him shelter and arranges for him to work as a clerk at the general store, which is owned by a bedridden bigot and managed by his neglected Italian wife, Lady Torrance. The middle-aged Lady is hungry for love and throws herself at the stranger.

Val is also being frantically pursued by another desperate woman, Carol Cutrere, the outcast member of an old plantation family. Catastrophe seems inevitable: Lady's jealous husband rises from his deathbed to set her new outdoor "confectionary" on fire and fatally shoots her after she reveals that she is carrying Val's baby; as Val tries to escape from the burning store he's beaten back into the flames by the hose-wielding sheriff and his sadistic deputies. His snakeskin jacket—the only thing that has not been consumed by the flames—is picked up by Carol, who flees the hate-filled town.

By autumn 1958 the script was complete, when there was a new snag. Hal Wallis may have lost his option on *The Fugitive Kind,* but he also had an option on Franciosa's services; now he told producers Jurow and Shepherd that because the actor was needed for Wallis's own picture, *Career,* he might not be available to do the Williams adaptation after all.

In December Shepherd received a surprising call from Kanter, reporting that Marlon had changed his mind and was now interested in the part if it was still available. Kanter explained that in addition to the expenses of *One-Eyed Jacks,* which he had just begun to shoot, Brando was going through a difficult and expensive divorce. For the first time in his career, the agent said, he felt compelled to take on another film quickly. Shepherd replied that although they had already committed to Franciosa, he had little doubt that UA would prefer to have Brando if it could be worked out.

With Marlon home for Christmas from the Monterey shoot, Jurow and Shepherd went to see him at his house high atop Mulholland Drive; they listened as the actor reiterated his reasons for having rejected the part. As Shepherd noted, he was equally candid about his reasons for changing his mind. Even more, the producer was struck by what he saw as his "conscientiousness" with regard to Franciosa: Under no circumstances would he take the part, he insisted, unless Franciosa "was emotionally and financially satisfied" to step aside, and he insisted that the producers go to the actor and "explain it to him in just those terms."

There was no talk of money—"I never knew Marlon to talk of money," said Shepherd. "That was always left to Jay"—and soon Kanter presented Marlon's financial demands: a flat $1 million. This unprecedented salary (unmatched until Elizabeth Taylor signed to do *Cleopatra* a year later) constituted almost half the film's overall $2.3 million budget. By comparison, Magnani and Lumet were each being paid approximately $125,000 (with an additional partnership percentage).

Nevertheless, UA president Arthur Krim quickly approved this deal since a Brando-Magnani combination was sure to have great box-office appeal both in America and abroad. In addition, Williams had suddenly reemerged as one of Hollywood's most bankable writers: His *Cat on a Hot Tin Roof* had just been released with stunning success and would soon become the fifth-highest-grossing film in MGM's history. His new play, *Suddenly, Last Summer,* was also doing well, both on Broadway and in London; the screen rights had been sold to Sam Spiegel, who had announced he was casting Taylor and Montgomery Clift.

Publicly, Brando's salary was announced in the trades as $750,000, but in fact that was only the "front money," which was to be complemented by another $250,000 in percentage arrangements, tax breaks, and partnership benefits for Marlon's production company.

Brando, however, was not overwhelmed by this windfall. On the contrary, after Jurow and Shepherd had left his home, Frank P. Rosenberg arrived to discuss the problems that had cropped up on the *One-Eyed Jacks* shoot and saw that he was "depressed at having sold his soul." According to the producer, he lamented, "I just decided to make a picture for a million bucks with Magnani. Why? So I can pay my alimony."

For Magnani, the prospect of working with Brando more than offset Franciosa's departure. As early as 1951, when Magnani had been in New York to do publicity for Luchino Visconti's *Bellissima,* she had asked her translator, Natalia Danesi Murray, to arrange a meeting with Marlon, whom she had admired in *Streetcar.* The admiration was mutual, since Brando had long been a fan of Italian neorealist cinema. When he arrived at Magnani's suite at the St. Regis, he came bearing a single long-stemmed rose and quickly proposed that he take her on a tour of the city. Murray, who accompanied them, recalled that after dinner at Brando's favorite restaurant in Chinatown—reached by subway, not by Magnani's limo—he took them to Staten Island to see the lights of lower Manhattan from the ferry. Trying not to intrude, Murray observed from a distance the two stars looking out over the rail, saying little—although in a patois of pidgin English and broken French, Brando was doing most of the talking. "Anna was fascinated," Murray said. "When we got to Staten Island, we turned around and got another boat coming back, again seeing the spectacle of the city, and Anna, I think, had probably some idea that perhaps they could have an affair." Indeed, after her Academy Award for *The Rose Tattoo,* she flirtatiously announced to the press, "I want Marlon Brando to come to Rome and bring me my Oscar personally."

Several years later, when Marlon had first turned down the role, Magnani wrote Williams from Rome, asking him to expand Val's role so that the two of them would have "equal" parts. Audrey Wood, Williams's agent, told Murray that she had never heard of a star asking to have her part diminished so that her partner's role would be enlarged. Magnani, however, was that eager to have Brando as her leading man. It wasn't long before word reached New York that she had been making bets up and down the Via Veneto that she would have him as her lover.

In the meantime, Jurow and Shepherd completed the casting. For the part of Carol Cutrere, they took Joanne Woodward, who had won an Academy Award the year before for her performance in *The Three Faces of Eve* (on loan from Fox, Woodward was paid $30,000). This made *The Fugitive Kind* the first film in Hollywood history whose three stars had all won best-acting Oscars, and the studio's publicity department was already taking full advantage of it. Maureen Stapleton was offered the small part of Vee, the sheriff's wife.

In May 1959, "La Lupa" (the "she-wolf," as Magnani was nicknamed) arrived in New York, where she was put up in a luxurious suite in the Sherry Netherland Hotel, overlooking Central Park. A few days later screenwriter Meade Roberts found her "a nervous wreck." She had wanted to show Boris Kaufman, the cinematographer, how she could look "like Gina Lollobrigida . . . or maybe Sophia Loren," and had brought a reel of footage to prove it. She then walked into the UA screening room wearing tight black slacks, gold hoop earrings, big dark glasses, and, according to Roberts, makeup "like you couldn't believe." After the screening, she strolled with the young screenwriter up Broadway to the producers' office, commenting that she was afraid people might recognize her. Roberts recalled, "I wanted to say, 'Anna, you're unrecognizable on this street. You look like every other hooker on Broadway.' "

The two-week rehearsal period was set to begin in early June. Woodward had just had a baby. For Brando, too, it was bad timing. The difficulties with Kashfi had escalated after she'd recently gone amok up at Mulholland, resulting in legal complications. And he also had to finish shooting *One-Eyed Jacks*. His contract with Shepherd and Jurow stipulated that the shooting of *The Fugitive Kind* was to take no longer than nine weeks, so that he could return to Hollywood and the cutting room. (He did not inform them that he would be flying back to California almost every weekend to work on the editing.) He had hardly looked at Williams's latest script, but even so, he had made suggestions to Lumet when they'd met in L.A. None of Brando's more sweeping ideas had been adopted, but one of his requests, stemming from his long-standing unhappiness with the weakness of his character, had led Roberts to create the film's famous courtroom prologue. Here, Val, after a night in jail, delivers a monologue that many critics have commended as the best scene in the film.

The night before the first day's rehearsal was a sleepless one for Roberts, who kept telling himself, "Tomorrow morning I have to face Marlon Brando, Anna Magnani, Tennessee Williams. Ah-h-h-h!" The rehearsal was scheduled for eleven A.M., and at 8:30 the young writer went for coffee in the drugstore beneath the Palladium Ballroom on Fifty-third Street and Broadway. There he came upon Joanne Woodward sitting by herself at the counter. "What are you doing here so early?" he asked.

"I couldn't sleep last night," she replied. "I thought, Tomorrow, I have to face . . ."

Rehearsals were to begin in the Palladium, one of Brando's old drumming haunts and still a dingy, depressing place. Lumet and the producers arrived at about quarter to eleven. A few minutes later they received a message from Marlon: He had missed his red-eye flight, then rescheduled one for a 10:30 landing, and he would be coming directly from the airport.

Roberts recalled that it was 11:20 when Magnani made her grand entrance, with Tennessee Williams on one arm and Williams's lover, Frank Merlo, on the other, plus a small entourage trailing behind. Again, she was dressed like "a Times Square hooker," and as soon as she walked in, she stopped dead. "Where is Marlon?" she demanded, rolling her *r*'s thickly. When told that he had missed his flight, her face fell. "She didn't believe it," Roberts said. "Already La Lupa was convinced that he was upstaging her, because the star always enters last."

It wasn't until 11:45 that Marlon appeared at the door. He was alone, out of breath, and gave everybody a "shy, little boy grin." With his small shoulder bag and casual summer clothes, he looked anything but prepossessing, but this upset Magnani more than if he had arrived with an entourage. When he walked over to her and "in the most gentlemanly fashion" told Magnani how honored he was to be working with her, she only nodded, broadcasting the message that things were definitely not going to be easy.

The tension in the room grew steadily as the reading got under way. Lumet had placed everyone at the table, and Brando started going through his lines cautiously. With his elbow on the table, his chin cupped in his hand, and his palm covering half his mouth, his voice was hardly audible. Woodward tried to enliven things, but to no avail, and soon she too flattened her reading. Magnani, looking nervously at her script, kept comparing it with the Italian translation that lay alongside.

Finally, when Magnani had her first line, she whispered so softly that no one could hear her. "If Marlon and Joanne were going to do it that way, she was going to do them one better," Roberts realized, trying not to burst out in laughter. Williams, who finally could take it no longer, yelled, "I need radar equipment to hear what you're saying! If I can't hear my fucking dialogue, I'm going home!" There was a long silence. Marlon and Anna looked at Williams. "It's the only moment I remember when Marlon and Anna were in concert," Roberts said. "They smiled, and went right back to trying to outwhisper each other."

The first week took its toll on everyone. Williams turned his frustration against Roberts, demanding at one point that he leave the rehearsal and screaming, "I don't like sharing the spotlight," even though both he and Lumet had specifically requested Roberts's presence for on-the-spot rewrites. Even Woodward was irritable. Once, when Cokes were brought in, Marlon blew the paper cover of his straw at her and she lost her temper. Then, when Roberts tried to appease her by passing it off as a joke, she looked away, muttering, "I don't think it's funny."

The paranoia, as Roberts put it, "was flying," so much so that when

Magnani saw Brando massaging Roberts's back one afternoon, she labeled the writer "Marlon's spy." There was also the basic incompatibility between the two stars' approaches to acting. Brando had always worked himself into a role slowly as he searched out connections; Magnani, on the other hand, was straight-ahead, according to the Italian director Luchino Visconti, "like a racehorse who you must always let go."

In the second week Maureen Stapleton and Victor Jory joined the rehearsals. Stapleton's casting was a sore point for everybody except Stapleton herself. "I think it took tremendous guts on her part to play that little part," producer Shepherd agreed, recalling his embarrassment when he first approached her with the secondary role, a "demotion" from the lead she'd played on Broadway. Prior to her arrival it had been unanimously agreed not to refer to the stage version of *Orpheus* under any circumstances. One afternoon, though, there was a problem with a scene between Anna and Marlon at the end of act 1; after endless discussion there was still no solution—until Williams called out, "Maureen, honey, what'd we do here onstage?" Roberts, who related the story, did not see Stapleton's immediate reaction "because my head went under the table." He then heard her say, "Oh, Tenn, I don't remember."

Brando's response to the incident was to invite both Magnani and Stapleton to have lunch with him, leaving everyone back in the rehearsal hall anxiously wondering if they would still have a cast later in the afternoon. After forty-five minutes, he came back alone, saying that he had left the two women at Woolworth's. "Maureen likes tchotchkes," he explained, "and Anna's never seen a five-and-dime before." Ten minutes later Stapleton and Magnani came in, arm in arm.

Brando's mumbling continued. When they finished reading the first act, Stapleton, who could be as blunt as a fishwife, wasn't afraid to announce, "I only know my cue is coming up when somebody's mouth doesn't move anymore. But I can't hear anything, and I'm too young to be deaf." Everybody laughed, including Magnani, who said, "I love you." That night, Williams dropped by Stapleton's house to express his admiration, and she confronted him about his passivity. "You're the muscle," she told him. "Why don't you do something?"

"Oh, hon," Williams replied, "they'll just say I'm an old faggot."

Shooting began on June 22 in Milton, a blue-collar hamlet on the Hudson River about eighty miles north of New York City. Since the interiors were to be shot in the Bronx, economically it made sense not to travel south for the location work. Milton was almost ideal, requiring only minimal cosmetic work to resemble the backcountry Mississippi town called for in Williams's narrative.

Cast and crew were put in a hotel across the river in Poughkeepsie. Despite a downpour the first day of filming, Marlon's car was mobbed by fans at dawn; the police proved powerless to stop them as they hung on the limo and started rocking it violently. "It was scary," Stapleton recalled. "I'm not a very brave woman, and I finally said, 'Marlon, this kind of adulation is terrifying.' " Marlon was calm. For him, the crowd was responding to a movie star, not to him personally. "You know, they feel about me the way you and I feel about Adlai Stevenson," he said.

"Yes," she answered, "but they don't try to kill him."

The relationship between Marlon and Anna continued to deteriorate. Magnani, who was notorious for her stormy affairs with her leading men as well as her directors in the past, was now offended at Marlon's courtesy, which had become obsequious to the point of parody. He opened doors, allowed her to go first whenever they entered or left a set. Yet, when they were not in front of the cameras, he preferred a book or a ballgame with the electricians to her company. For Shepherd, growing more anxious by the day, the two stars were "hydrogen bombs waiting to explode."

Not surprisingly, Brando was testing her the way he tested everyone. "Here were these two giant energies coming together," Shepherd explained, "and I think the script had a very painful effect on both of them. For the play to be really effective on the big screen, you have to feel that there is a physical attraction in spite of the disparity in their ages." Shepherd remembered that Magnani, who was fifty-one, "was pressing Marlon, trying to be attractive to him, emotionally and physically, [and] it put a demand on him that I think he was uncomfortable with." Stapleton said, "She wasn't a Barbie doll, but she was still a great-looking lady. The bottom line was that in those days *everybody* wanted to hump Marlon. Magnani wasn't after his ass any more than anybody else."

The love scenes were especially difficult. "Why can't she use Nair?" he complained, referring to Magnani's furry upper lip. "Why doesn't she take a shave?"

The insult of being so flatly rejected hit her where she was most vulnerable, and the film itself, with its theme of an older woman's need for a younger man, could only have reminded her of her own dilemma.

"She'd tell the cameraman she wanted every line in her face to show on film," said Joanne Woodward. "Yet she was very vain, and it was touching—she hid her neck with scarves and was constantly pushing them closer to her chinline." To make matters worse, the makeup department was trying to conceal her more obvious wrinkles with tape. One makeup man was insensitive enough to suggest using a clamp—literally, a small woodworker's C-clamp—on the back of her neck "to tuck her up." The idea was quickly dismissed, but word got back to the Italian star, who threw a temper tantrum and demanded to have the man fired.

Magnani's age also posed a serious problem in terms of the narrative. Namely, "Why would Val Xavier go to bed with Anna Magnani and not Joanne Woodward?" To justify Val's choice, the filmmakers exaggerated the physical unattractiveness and bizarre qualities of Woodward's character. Costumed in a baggy trench coat, her hair dyed blond and looking dirty and stringy, her face smeared with white makeup and eyes rimmed with kohl, Woodward looked like a lunatic.

For his part, Marlon admitted only to feeling drained by Magnani. "She's like a vacuum cleaner," he complained to Sam Gilman, during a late-night call to his pal in California. "Like she's just sucking me dry."

Lumet had not done much to ease the tension, either, and his own relationship with Magnani was also strained. She found him "too technical," limited by his background in live television. When she saw the floor marks on the set one morning, Murray recalled, she erupted. "What are these signs on the floor?" she yelled. "I have to move where the signs are? I can't act this way, I'm not used to it. You must let me breathe," she implored, "you must let me act the way I *feel* the scene. . . . Then if you don't like it, I'll do it your way. But first time, my way, *please.*" Like so many others, she also complained that Brando was getting the lion's share of directorial attention, which was probably true.

Yet Lumet called Brando "a very suspicious man. In the first two days . . . he will do two takes that may seem identical, but one is full and the other is only technical. Then he will watch which one you decide to print, and on that decision relies your whole subsequent relationship with him, because if you don't know your job as well as he knows his, you've had it. In those performances where you have seen him just walk through a film, he made the test and the director flunked it."

Lumet passed the test, apparently, even if Marlon saw him as "maybe a little sophomoric, maybe a little overzealous." When it came to handling the problem with Magnani, he seemed intimidated, though—almost indecisive. Trying to avoid conflict, he tended not to discuss or interpret scenes but simply shoot them, and when there was a disagreement between his two stars, he'd go with Brando. Stapleton, once again caught in the middle, saw it clearly. "Marlon was treated with sort of kid gloves."

It was inevitable that the difficulties between Magnani and Brando would reach the press, and one story making the rounds was that whenever the actress did a scene she seemed happy with, Brando would intentionally blow his lines and ask for another take, which led her to call him "a sadistic egocentric" in print. Both actors were using the tricks of their trade, and surprisingly the results could be intriguing. In the scene when Val comes to the store to ask Lady for a job, and she in turn asks him for references, the two actors had rehearsed the exchange several times. But when Lumet yelled "Action!" Marlon reached into the pocket of his snakeskin jacket. "He started searching through his pants pockets, sort of shit-kicking smile on his face," Shepherd said, "just milking it. Finally he took the envelope out, and it was all wadded up. He smoothed it out and handed it to her, and she was just standing there glaring at him. Marlon had set the whole thing up, and it was a brilliant acting decision, but he was also grabbing the screen time for himself."

Lumet cried, "Cut! Let's try it again." Marlon did the same thing on the next take, but when he handed Magnani the wadded-up letter this time, she had to "smooth it out . . . more . . . and . . . more, and the camera was just filling up with Anna while she took her time reading what it said."

The acting duels and delay tactics did nothing to keep the film on budget, and whatever her competitiveness, Magnani began to feel increasingly isolated, partly because she couldn't explain herself in English. She was constantly on the phone, worrying about the numerous cats and dogs she had left at her villa in Rome. Maureen and Joanne were playing cards with the cast, Marlon was with the crew, and Anna was "alone, brooding." Even Williams, her great admirer, did not offer his support.

Finally, Magnani's translator, Natalia Murray, went to Marlon's dressing room to talk to him about her conflict. She asked him to be less hard on Anna, less aloof. She tried to explain the difficulty of being a foreign actor ("How would you feel if you were doing a part in an Italian film without speaking Italian?"). She pleaded with him to give in on what had become a fight over their billings in the credits. Marlon said nothing in response to Murray, but within a few days Magnani received a large bouquet of red roses. Quietly, in his own fashion, he also agreed to a compromise and gave Magnani top billing in Italy.

A few days later, however, Magnani was as moody and capricious as ever. "You never knew what was going to happen," Roberts recalled. "Some mornings you'd say, 'Good morning, Anna,' and she'd just stare at you. At other times you'd say, 'Good morning,' and she'd go *'Ffft.'* She spat. I mean literally, on the floor, in front of you. . . . But other times it would be *'Caro!'* and she'd bite your ear."

Marlon's moods were equally mercurial, but he went out of his way to be friendly to the crew and the townspeople. One resident, overhearing him complain of the heat, invited him to use the family swimming pool. Marlon often retreated there, a book in hand, to withdraw from the curious onlookers and the tempestuous flare-ups on the set. After the shoot was over, he sent the wife of the pool's owner a bouquet of five dozen red roses.

Maureen Stapleton was also more popular, and among some of the locals employed as extras, she was even considered a better actor than the feuding stars. When she delivered her monologue describing her "divine revelation," she received a standing ovation, but the scene was eventually cut. For years the scuttlebutt in Milton was that the scene was dropped "because she did too good a job and outdid Brando."

By the time the company moved to the Bronx for a few weeks to shoot interiors, Magnani had managed to alienate most of the cast and the entire crew. She had already demanded the firing of Boris Kaufman and several technicians, and when Jurow warned her that she was turning everyone against her, she responded, according to Roberts, "I'm a queen, and the queen rules and her subjects love her. If she loves them, whips them, kicks them, kills them, they still give her loyalty." To this the producer angrily replied, "This is the United States. We have a democracy here!"

For several weeks the production remained in New York, and Marlon began seeing Marilyn Sorel, who had moved back from Paris. Sorel soon realized that his encounter with Magnani could not have come at a worse time or been anything but threatening.

"He had a lot of distrust for women," Sorel observed. "People in general, but especially women." And especially strong women. Domination was key. Hardened by Kashfi, he was "insisting on his space," which carried over as open hostility toward fans and often manifested itself when he got into lengthy arguments with people asking for his autograph. Often, he would launch into absurd five-minute disquisitions when a simple no or a quick scrawl would have ended it; he refused to oblige anyone older than seventeen, and whenever a petitioner tried the line, "This is for my child," he'd snap, "How do I know that's true?"

His suspiciousness—or at least his self-righteousness—was rampant. Locked into the notion that he was being perceived as a myth, "not a person," he began to distrust his friends, too. He also worried that they were using him for money, influence, or status. Rhodes was doing his makeup and Marie was now Magnani's stand-in, and they too realized how paranoid he was becoming about money. "But it was always with people like Marie and me, the 'small' people, not the 'big' people. The small people became suspect because we didn't have money, so we must always be looking out to steal it or make it from knowing him. So he was tremendously suspicious of any below-the-line people, which is what we were to him. He was convinced that such friends could be dangerous, because they knew things [about him]. He would stop thinking rationally. On the surface he was like an iceberg, but below the ice was pure terror."

For Rhodes the suspiciousness and "terror" behind the frozen expression went all the way back to *Viva Zapata!* Yet with Sorel, Brando seemed to have achieved a form of trust, if only because he perceived her as fitting into a special category, just as she had during their Paris escapades while making *Young Lions.* "He had an idea that it was like some rite of passage to fuck me," she said. "He knew that I'd lived with various sorts of subculture heroes, and that might have activated his imagination. Like somehow I was 'authentic.'"

Their sexual relationship was indeed "natural and uninhibited," just as Marlon still liked to do shocking things in public, like hiking her dress up so it was barely covering her. "He felt he could do anything, because of who he was," said Sorel.

He took her to private screenings that had been arranged for him—personal bar service included—at MCA's office on Madison Avenue. "You could see him get kind of uptight if you uttered a word," she recalled, "even in the presence of the Moviola operator." In private he would never censor her, but in the company of others she was expected to remain silent. "I'm going to have to think of you as a man," he told her, making it clear that talking in public was decidedly "unfeminine." The clear message was, "If you remain silent, you can stay with me." The rule of silence struck her as particularly odious insofar as he was surrounding himself with drones at the same time he was trying to relate to her as a free spirit. Likewise, while he fumed over his lack of "privacy," his own cadre allowed him no privacy whatsoever, she said, citing as an example that while the two of them were still in bed one morning, the woman who was coordinating his travel arrangements walked right in, unannounced.

One evening he and Sorel went to a restaurant in the East Fifties with an old friend of his, Jeff Brown. Brando received the usual star treatment—the owners greeted him effusively, later refused to let him pay, and other diners lined up for his autograph. The friends weren't hungry, so only Marlon was eating—gorging himself, according to Sorel. Meanwhile she was chatting with Brown. After a moment or two Brando seemed upset, and he got up from the banquette. "All right," he said. "I'm going to leave you two to talk. You have so much to say, good-bye."

Sorel decided to try to appease him.

"I babied him and cajoled him to sit down," she explained, "like 'Yes, we were being rude, don't leave.'" For the moment it worked, and he rejoined them. After dinner, however, once the three of them climbed into a taxi, Brando told her that they were going to drop her off and continue to a party without her.

It was "punishment for my transgression," as she put it. When they arrived at her apartment, Marlon walked her to the stoop and began to talk, leaving Brown in the taxi. After about forty minutes he finally told the friend to drive on without him; then he returned to the stoop, where he talked to Sorel for another three hours, until early morning. "He poured his heart out again about Anna Kashfi and her tricks, how she would try to trap him, and how he didn't know what to do about the situation. I began to sense the fragmentation of a person."

The Fugitive Kind reached its sixth week of filming and then moved back to Milton, where tensions between Marlon and Magnani did not ease one bit. Roberts, who returned after a quick trip to Europe, noticed that Magnani was wearing the same tight slacks and hoop earrings she had worn to rehearsals. It appeared that she had not changed her clothes for the past month and a half despite the muggy New York summer. "My analysis," he said, only half-humorously, "was that she didn't change deliberately so that she'd stink like a skunk. Everybody was the enemy, and she was putting out a protective smell to keep us away."

The set was an armed camp and basically the only cast members siding with Magnani were Stapleton and Joanne Woodward, who later informed journalists that "she was very kind to me, very gentle in her own strange way." Woodward's own history with Brando went back to 1953, when they had met through Jay Kanter and dated for about a month. Woodward had also dated Paul Newman, but he was still married to his first wife. A close friend once said that although Brando wasn't her type, she "may have given up on Paul. Marlon may have come on to her and she said, 'Why not?'" She may also have been trying to make Newman jealous, since "at the time Paul was very competitive with Marlon," opined an Actors Studio colleague who was privy to what was happening. "Like all of us, she had to grow up. We all had round heels, we all fucked a lot of people we shouldn't have fucked."

Six years later, when Woodward met Brando again on the set of *The Fugitive Kind,* she was an Oscar winner as well as Newman's wife. Newman, the star of *The Long Hot Summer,* was still grappling with his image as a Brando clone, for not only did he resemble Brando physically, dressing like him in sweatshirts and jeans, he had also built his career doing Williams—the film of *Cat on a Hot Tin Roof* was soon followed by *Sweet Bird of Youth*, then running on Broadway—as well as a decidedly Brandoesque reprise of Rocky Graziano in *Somebody Up There Likes Me.* For Woodward, all this was a sort of subtext for what she saw as Brando's mistreatment of Magnani.

Her complaints, however, were professional as well as personal. "I hated working with Marlon," she said with uncharacteristic bluntness years later, "because he was *not* there, he was somewhere else. There was nothing to reach on to. The only way I'd work with Marlon Brando is if he were in rear projection."

Even his old pal Stapleton was finding him difficult. After several run-throughs of a scene in which he was taking pauses that were long even by Brando standards, she exploded. "Marlon, you're a genius; I'm not. I can't fill those pauses," she yelled. "I could make a dinner in all that space.

Could you go a little faster?" The next time around he wound himself up like a mechanical doll, running through his lines so quickly that Lumet and the crew burst out laughing. "That fast enough for you?" he asked.

"Yeah, perfect," she replied dryly, thinking, Gimme a break, will ya!

On weekends Marlon continued to fly to California in secret, nominally to work on *Jacks* and see his young son; in fact, he was carrying on with Rita Moreno. Shepherd recalled that twice he was late returning to the Milton set, and the result was more postponements in shooting. Brando had stipulated in his contract that he did not have to work past six P.M. One night, when the shooting was still going at 6:15, he announced he was about to depart, but Shepherd protested. "We waited for you four hours last Monday, Marlon. You'll stay here at least till ten o'clock." Brando grinned and returned to the set.

In fact, when it came time to shoot Val's monologue about the bird that keeps flying without ever touching the ground—Williams's all-important metaphor for personal freedom—Brando postponed his weekend trip. It was a challenging two-page monologue in which Val describes himself, by inference, as soaring aloft and never lighting on earth until death. Lumet was shooting with the camera dollying closer and closer to Brando's face while also circling. At the same time, Kaufman had a bright, cathedral-like light coming through a window at the rear. As Brando spoke, the light dimmed gradually as the camera moved in for its extreme close-up; it continued to highlight his eyes until the end of his reverie, when the lighting reverted back to its original mood. The technicalities were complex, calling for multiple takes, and as the afternoon wore on, Lumet made it clear that if Marlon left before they finished, they'd never be able to pick up where they left off. Brando agreed to stay. They worked for an extra seven hours—well into the night—and it was Marlon who kept asking for additional takes until he, not the director, was satisfied. He would complete thirty-nine takes in all.

"I don't know any actor that could have done it any quicker," Shepherd observed, and Charlie Maguire, on loan from Kazan, was struck by Marlon's apology to the crew when he again arrived late one day from Los Angeles. They were behind schedule, with everybody waiting, and Lumet had been screaming at Maguire, "Where's Brando? I want to shoot, I want to shoot!" Marlon's immediate response when he jumped out of the cab was to ask Maguire to assemble the entire crew.

"I want to apologize for being late," he announced, standing in the middle of the soundstage. "I know you guys are docked for being late and it affects your paycheck, and that should happen to me but it probably won't. But I'm sorry. I'll go down to makeup and be back up as soon as I can."

It was the kind of gesture that won Brando the admiration of technical people throughout his career. In fact, however, as on *One-Eyed Jacks,* the crew wasn't being docked for his delays, they were being paid. "There was no way of understanding his thinking on something like this," said Walter Seltzer. "Studio money didn't matter. He just couldn't make the connection."

On the last—the fifty-second—day of shooting, Anna and Marlon finally exploded. What initially ignited their fuses was unclear. But the set reverberated with screaming and name-calling. The producers, who could no longer deny the rumors about the actors' animosity, tried to play it down with the press. The flare-up, they told the *Los Angeles Examiner,* was the exception, insisting that the shoot as a whole had been extraordinarily productive. They commended Marlon for his cooperation, saying little about Magnani. Back in California, Seltzer got word of what had been happening all along: Magnani's fury at Marlon for scorning her sexual invitations. "I thought to myself, If he turned her down, she's the first creature from snake to goat to human that he's ever rejected."

In early December 1959 a preview of *The Fugitive Kind* was held in Manhattan. As Meade Roberts saw it, the evening was a disaster. The film was greeted with guffaws that began when Woodward, in the cemetery scene, announced that she had "fragile arms and a birdlike body," then the laughter escalated to boos a few minutes later as she sank to her knees with her head out of frame—but somewhere in the vicinity of Marlon's crotch. After that, there was too much noise to hear the dialogue on the screen. On his way out, Williams refused to speak to Lumet and later commented that watching the film was like "having an iceberg roll slowly over you." As a result of its reception, the picture was extensively recut and shortened by twenty-five minutes. The editing left so many gaps in the narrative that the *New Yorker* reviewer would eventually call the convolutions of the plot "endless . . . beyond my grasp."

With all the time taken up in recutting, the Academy's deadline came and went for the 1959 Oscar nominations. The film would not be released until April 1960, to almost uniformly empty houses. With a few scattered exceptions, the reviews were terrible. The *Los Angeles Examiner* exclaimed, "Too much is too much, even from Tennessee Williams!" and labeled the characters as "psychologically sick or just plain ugly." "Sordid" and "repelling," chided the *Los Angeles Times,* while *Variety* described Brando as "mumbling with marbles in his mouth."

By the end of its first month in release, the film's grosses were abysmal, a fraction of the amount earned by *Cat on a Hot Tin Roof* over a comparable period. Whatever the chemistry between Brando and Magnani, it simply did not spell sex the way Elizabeth Taylor and Paul Newman did. Throughout the 1950s Brando had frequently made the lists of the ten top-grossing stars, but now it seemed that everyone was bored by Magnani's earth-mother realism—and even more bored by Brando. *The Fugitive Kind* was the first Brando picture to lose money.

Marlon himself said little, although Seltzer saw that it was "a wound to his ego." Early in the shooting, Brando had made a comment about Magnani: "This explosive woman is the type I like to play opposite. She is real. Of course, she is crazy like me and we have our differences. But actors have a way of understanding these things. We forget very quickly." This, though, he quickly amended, saying that he would work with her again "only with a rock in my fist." But his last word one-upped Williams's usually nimble wit. After the Hollywood premiere he had offered the playwright a ride in his limo. Williams had started to inveigh against Brando's behavior to his close friend, Magnani. "But I haven't got enough time to tell you exactly what I think," Williams snapped.

Marlon turned to the chauffeur and said, "Mr. Williams wants a longer ride."

Mutiny on the Bounty

Even while Marlon had fussed, fretted, and ultimately turned bitter with *One-Eyed Jacks,* he was already signed for his next project, *Mutiny on the Bounty.* Not surprisingly, his cynical disillusionment with Hollywood would come to the fore with this picture, turning the experience into a nightmare for all concerned. MGM's remake of *Mutiny* is often linked with Twentieth Century–Fox's *Cleopatra,* as the one-two punch that irrevocably brought down the Hollywood star system. Originally budgeted at the then staggering figure of $12 million, *Mutiny* ultimately cost more than $25 million—and bring the studio to its knees.

It also marked the pinnacle of Brando's self-indulgence, which, after *One-Eyed Jacks,* took on a mean-spirited edge. During the laborious thirteen-month shoot, Brando outdid himself with time-wasting tantrums, on-the-set script doctoring, and flagrantly irresponsible behavior. But if *Mutiny* represented a turning point in his personal and professional life, it was no less important that the film introduced him to Tahiti, the Edenic paradise that would become his refuge from Hollywood and the symbol of his hopes for the future.

In 1959 MGM executives had chosen to dust off James Norman Hall and Charles Nordhoff's novel *Mutiny on the Bounty,* largely because big-screen "location" spectaculars, long the studio's specialty, were still profitable. In the wake of Dore Schary's departure, the company had suffered the first net losses in its history, and only the highly successful remake of *Ben-Hur* had saved it from a worse fate. Although *Mutiny* had already been made in 1935 with Clark Gable as Fletcher Christian and Charles Laughton as Captain Bligh (in one of his most memorable performances), producer Aaron Rosenberg was only slightly concerned about unfavorable comparisons. Rosenberg had recently arrived from Universal, where he'd produced projects like *The Benny Goodman Story,* to oversee an epic western, *How the West Was Won.* But that project had been snatched away from him at the last moment, and to placate him the MGM hierarchy offered him the new *Mutiny.*

The abiding premise was that only the biggest stars would do, and who else was a better candidate than Brando? Even with the abject failure of *The Fugitive Kind,* his star was at its zenith, and if anyone was bankable, it was he. When Marlon was approached, however, he turned Rosenberg down cold despite his ongoing financial crisis.

Soon, however, he had second thoughts; according to his later comments, he reconsidered his decision because he had been reading about the little-known epilogue to the true-life *Mutiny* saga: The escaped mutineers who tried to establish their utopian settlement on Pitcairn Island ended up destroying one another instead, and a second generation was left to grow up under the spiritual guidance of one of the few adult survivors.

Brando then contacted Kanter, instructing him, "Tell MGM I'll do the picture—as long as it's not just a remake of the old one. I want to investigate what happened to the sailors *after* the mutiny. Why did they go to Pitcairn Island and within two years kill each other off? What is there in human nature that makes men violent, even in an island paradise? *That's* what would interest me."

A meeting with Rosenberg and Sol Siegel, Dore Schary's replacement as MGM's production boss, soon followed. By the end of the discussion there was no consensus, but Rosenberg finally agreed to assign mystery writer Eric Ambler to begin on a script; the producer had been spurred by Paramount's announcement in October that James Clavell would write, produce, and direct a project based on the adventures of the mutineers' lives after the *Bounty* episode. This was the same material that had piqued Brando's interest.

Brando, however, wasn't yet ready to make a full commitment to Rosenberg. He had already embarked on a series of ugly court battles with Anna, and on November 18, 1959, the two had been in Santa Monica Superior Court, contesting visitation rights to Christian. The *Los Angeles Times,* capitalizing on the soap opera quality of the hearing, quoted heavily from Brando's testimony in open court: "I slapped her twice, once on the face and once on the shoulder, and started to spank her. Our child began to cry and I stopped," Brando reportedly conceded. "[She] followed me to the kitchen [and] on my way out, picked up a knife and started to come at me.

"I had told her to go ahead if it would make her happy. She threw the knife on the floor and came at me again and grabbed my hair. I freed myself and left."

Their most violent quarrel had taken place at about one A.M. on August 15, Brando explained.

"I was asleep in my own house. The door burst open and the plaintiff flung herself into the room and . . . slapped me and bit me three times. I got her out of the house . . . and locked the door.

"She threw a log through one of the windows and came through the window. I held her down on the bed and tied her with a sash from my dressing robe. I then called the police and asked them to escort her home."

Kashfi claimed the arguments were "caused and provoked" not by herself but by his lawlessness and out-of-control behavior, which she described as "very harmful to the mental, physical, and emotional well-being of said child and his mother."

Judge Mervyn A. Aggeler put off permanent action until January 13, 1960, but he restricted Marlon's visitation rights to two and a half hours each Monday, Wednesday, and Friday, predicated on two hours' advance notice. A week later, an exposé appeared under Kashfi's byline in *Redbook*, in which she claimed that Marlon's friends had contributed to their quarrels. "They are leeches," she wrote. "None of them can stand on his own two feet. They are all sort of merged into his personality . . . and, of course, they resented me." Wally Cox, Sam Gilman, and Carlo Fiore were all cited by name.

In December 1959 Anna took Christian on a trip to London after refusing two requests by Brando to visit the boy. After she rebuffed his attempt to visit on Christmas Eve and again on Christmas Day, he was back in court on January 7. Kashfi met his complaint by acknowledging the Christmas lockout, but blamed it on the actor's decision to turn up with "an unidentified woman." Marlon, in turn, charged that she "heaped vilification" upon him and his companion.

Judge Allen T. Lynch reiterated Brando's right to visit and impressed on both of them "the necessity of good faith in carrying out the court's order." Marlon responded by returning to his peripatetic love life—Rita Moreno in Los Angeles, France Nuyen in New York. He then brought Nuyen back for a Los Angeles visit. In March he dumped her for actress Barbara Luna, which caused the distraught Nuyen to gain so much weight that she was fired from *The World of Suzie Wong*. Some sources said that she was in fact pregnant, and the rumors were rampant when she fled to Europe, only to hook up with Brando again in New York after her return.

At the same time, script work had continued on *Mutiny,* and by mid-January 1960, Ambler's first draft was submitted to Kanter in the hope that Brando would reconsider. Again he said no, still treading water with the editing of *Jacks*. Meanwhile, U.S. State Department officials were deciding whether to lend support to his long-standing "political" project, the U.N. kidnapping story (which would later evolve into *The Ugly American*).

Brando was also contemplating the starring role in *Lawrence of Arabia,* but he had reservations about it as well. "I'll be damned if I'll spend two years of my life out in the desert on some fucking camel!" he said angrily, expressing his irritation at producer Sam Spiegel for having jumped the gun and announcing his participation. Soon, deciding that beach sand was preferable to the desert, he told Kanter to negotiate the contract for *Mutiny*. The deal, as it was drawn up, promised him $500,000—plus 10 percent of the gross receipts, $5,000 for every day the film went over schedule, and $10,000 a week in expenses. Given just how protracted the shoot turned out to be, the extra stipulations would prove a bonanza: His total pay broke the $1.25 million mark.

With Brando aboard, Rosenberg's budget was virtually unlimited. Marlon's salary, however, was the least of the producer's concerns. The deal also included an all important clause guaranteeing the actor "consultation rights." In the past Marlon had taken license with scripts, but with this clause he had been given a free hand to make changes at will, a privilege that he exercised from the beginning. He was already insisting on an ending that would include a long sequence about the Pitcairn settlement— fully one-third of the film's running time. This part of the story, he announced, "presents a microcosm of man's situation throughout history: the struggle of black versus white, of good versus evil, of the urge to create and the urge to destroy." In a similar vein, he also insisted that all background natives had to be "*real* natives."

The MGM publicity department started trumpeting *Mutiny* as the studio's *Ben-Hur* of 1961. Sir Carol Reed, the cultured British filmmaker responsible for two classic thrillers, *The Third Man* and *Odd Man Out,* was signed to direct. Unlike the original 1935 version filmed mainly on Catalina Island, 95 percent of the photography for the new film would be shot on the then primitive island of Tahiti. The film, which was dedicated to total realism and "historical accuracy," would feature not only an international cast but also a 350-ton, three-masted replica of the original ship, the *Bounty,* already under construction in Nova Scotia.

In his initial meetings with the newly hired Reed, Marlon barely gave *Mutiny* a passing mention. Instead he discussed the film he really wished to make instead: the story of Caryl Chessman, the convicted California rapist whose recent execution had been the occasion for protest from anti–capital punishment groups. In fact, Brando and Shirley MacLaine had stood vigil outside San Quentin the night Chessman went to the gas chamber.

October 15, 1960, was announced as the starting date for *Mutiny on the Bounty.* This gave the studio eight months in which to complete a final script, finish its replica of the *Bounty,* and tend to all the details of preproduction, which were made more complicated by the shooting's remote locale. For its technical adviser, MGM turned to Bengt Danielsson, a dour, bewhiskered Swedish anthropologist and longtime resident of Tahiti who first arrived in French Polynesia in 1947 as a member of Thor Heyerdahl's famed *Kon Tiki* expedition. An expert on the *Bounty* mutiny, Danielsson was writing a book on the subject, but when MGM asked him to consult, he put his manuscript aside to fly to Los Angeles and lend authenticity to costumes, weapons, and artifacts.

Danielsson met Brando in Culver City to discuss the project. Rather than talk about *Mutiny,* however, the actor again had the Caryl Chessman idea on his mind because, he explained, "the only films that interest me are those with a deeper meaning." *Mutiny* was not what he actually wanted to do, but he had agreed to it, he said, because "I need the dough. I lost a pile not long ago on a ranch, and my divorce is going to cost me a hell of a packet. . . . Whatever you do, boy, beware of cows—and women!"

In the spring of 1960 Rosenberg, Reed, Brando, and Robert Surtees, the cinematographer who had just won his third Oscar for *Ben-Hur,* flew to Tahiti to scout locations. They were accompanied by a dozen film technicians and production aides.

After the group was given a welcoming festival by local natives, they traveled to Matavai Bay, some twelve kilometers north of Papeete. It was here that Captain James Cook, the first explorer in Tahiti, had anchored his ship on June 26, 1769, and where Captain Bligh had also dropped anchor. The site was a natural amphitheater, a vast, sleepy lagoon sheltered by sheer hillsides of lush green, but Rosenberg was shocked. "The goddamn beach is black!" he roared.

"It's black lava from extinct volcanoes," explained Danielsson, adding that nothing could be done about it.

"That's what you think," said the producer, who summoned the production manager and instructed him to see how much white sand and how many trucks were available on the island.

These early physical setbacks didn't weigh heavily on Rosenberg's mind. The Matavai Bay visit, Danielsson said, "was the first and last time [they] surveyed a shooting site; I saw Aaron and Marlon only a few more times, mostly in a whirl of undulating Tahitian hula-hula girls, drunken seamen, and sweating tourists." Reed scouted a few more locations with cinematographer Surtees, but he was in no shape for rain-forest treks and hikes up Mount Orohena's 7,000-foot slope. Finally he retired to his bungalow to make extensive script notes.

On May 31, 1960, Rosenberg and Reed flew to England to test British actors. For the pivotal role of Captain Bligh, they cast Trevor Howard; Richard Harris, the flamboyant Irish stage actor, was assigned the role of John Mills, a manipulative mutineer, and veteran character actor Hugh Griffith was signed for the role of seaman Smith.

While Reed and Rosenberg were in London, Brando returned to Los Angeles, infatuated with his memories of Tahiti. The purple hills, blue-green waters, lush vegetation, and orange-pink sunsets had captured his imagination. Doubtless, the island seemed an escape from his chaotic domestic life and his restless swings between New York and L.A.; yet the lure of the exotic could be traced back to his school days in Libertyville. At twelve, confined to afternoon study hall, he had read back issues of *National Geographic,* poring over illustrations of Polynesian coastlines, shoals, and tropical waterfalls, as well as the bare-breasted natives. "I always felt an affinity to these islands," he said years later. "Then in 1960, I came down here and it just sort of confirmed what I'd always known."

Brando's summer in L.A. was as stressful as ever. In addition to Rita Moreno and Barbara Luna, there was another Asian actress, Nancy Kwan, as well as Movita, who now informed him that she was pregnant. Earlier, she had become so fed up with him that she had refused his proposal of marriage. "She said he was pounding on her door, pleading with her," recalled Maila Nurmi, who had heard the details from Movita. "She finally came to the door, and he tried to give her an engagement ring. But she threw the ring back at him, threatened to call the police, and then slammed the door in his face."

But now she had changed her tune or at least her story, though whether she was actually pregnant with Marlon's child—and whether the secret wedding on June 4, 1960, confirmed a legal marriage—remained shrouded in mystery. By October 1960 Movita had an infant son. For unspecified reasons, Marlon chose to honor Christian Marquand's brother Serge by calling his second son Sergio, although the boy would later become known by his nickname, Miko. But the marriage itself was not announced for over a year, prompting much speculation in the Pennebaker office, as well as among Brando's friends, that either Marlon had married Movita, as he had Anna, simply to do his parental duty, or that Movita had staged the pregnancy, disappearing into Mexico to adopt a child in order to rope Marlon in for financial gain.

Lending credence to the story about an adoption through a Mexican orphanage was Movita's age of somewhere in her forties (though no one knew her exact birth date). Nevertheless, Marlon soon bought Movita a house in Coldwater Canyon, near the home his father had moved into with his recent bride, Anna Paramore.

Nan Morris, Carlo Fiore's friend, heard that it was France Nuyen who had actually given birth to Marlon's baby and that an "adoption" deal was then supposedly arranged with Movita, followed by the secret wedding ceremony in Mexico. Kashfi was also certain that Miko was Nuyen's child. In the last months of her marriage to Brando, the actor had brought the Eurasian actress to the house. "She was very pregnant at the time," noted Kashfi, who also claimed that several months later Marlon called her at two in the morning from Guadalajara, where he had gone with Nuyen to arrange for the birth of the child discreetly and out of public view. An infant boy had been delivered the previous day. "Would you like to adopt him?" she later insisted Marlon had asked in a reasonable tone. Still half-asleep, Kashfi said she had mumbled, "I'll see. Let me think it over."

Marlon, however, left no telephone number in Mexico, and he would never pose the question again. As Walter Seltzer ruminated time after time, "the possibilities" as to what was real and what was true were "endless."

Marlon locked horns with Kashfi in court once more in October 1960, renewing his charge that she had denied him his visitation rights on ten separate occasions. At that time unaware of the marriage to Movita or the birth of a son Marlon claimed as his own, Anna countersued, insisting on assurances that her ex-husband and his friends "conduct themselves with appropriate decorum" whenever Christian was brought to the actor's house. Two-and-a-half-year-old Christian-Devi, she declared, had already "acquired such phrases as 'go to hell' and 'fuck you.'"

Judge Benjamin Landis, denying Brando's charges of contempt, informed him, "You are a great artist, and have a right to your eccentricities. I know you want to have a secure, healthy child. You are not going to have one if this bitterness continues."

During this time preproduction on *Mutiny* had progressed slowly. In June, Danielsson returned to Culver City, where MGM's workshop continued to turn out "Tahitian" artifacts and costumes as if from an assembly line. A thousand plastic breadfruit were ordered at $25 apiece, and four hundred wigs for natives were produced at $200 each—even though Danielsson pointed out that Tahitian men were rarely bald and that native women wore their hair down to their waist. In the wardrobe department, he was shown a Roman toga designed by the artist who did costumes for *Ben-Hur,* as well as a *Suzie Wong* skirt with a Melanesian pattern. When he complained to Rosenberg about the lack of authenticity, the producer said, "The picture's got to be spectacular. Don't forget *Spartacus* and *Cleopatra* are going to be released at [about] the same time." Finally Danielsson resigned in exasperation and returned to Tahiti, where, like most of the island's expatriate community, he would follow the *Mutiny* shoot from the sidelines as an amused, and sometimes critical, observer.

The building of the *Bounty* replica was proving to be the most troublesome detail of all. Its construction in Nova Scotia had already been delayed the previous year when a lumber shipment from New Jersey was halted by a snowstorm, and the ship's projected $500,000 cost was already over budget by 50 percent. Then, on its sail to Tahiti the engine caught fire after it passed through the Panama Canal, and the crew was almost forced to abandon ship. A few days later a second fire broke out on board. Top-heavy with its modern diesel engine and elaborate camera mounts, the *Bounty* proved so difficult to sail that it didn't reach Tahiti until December 4, nearly two months after the film's scheduled start date.

Nevertheless, cast and crew alike had begun drawing salaries on October 15, as their contracts stipulated. For Brando the clock had started ticking six months earlier, putting him that much closer to his $5,000 daily overtime. Even as the company prepared to depart for their three-month stay in French Polynesia, the script was still unfinished—or at least not yet approved by its star, despite the intense efforts of several writers over the summer.

The Ambler version bore practically no resemblance to historical fact, and worse, the description of Tahiti and native life had struck Danielsson and others as little less than bizarre. Borden Chase, a well-known scripter of westerns, had started placing contemporary slang in the mouths of eighteenth-century mariners and actually wondered aloud, "What about putting in a scene with a crowd of murderous cannibals chasing the *Bounty?* Or could I have Captain Bligh chase the mutineers?"

Arriving on Tahiti in late fall 1960, Brando rejected the stately manor provided by MGM in favor of a traditional thatched *fare* next to Danielsson's home. He also began wearing a free-flowing pareu (the multicolored Tahitian sarong), and adopted the native custom of wearing a frangipani blossom behind his ear. "I love it down here. I'm not Brando the star, I'm Brando the man," he told assistant director Ridgeway Callow after a week. "I can go around barefoot, stripped to the waist, wear anything that I want and nobody pays attention. Here, one is judged by local standards."

But to Tahitians who met the actor, Brando's search seemed to be deeper than the escapism of a harried man. Like many other newcomers to Tahiti, he was losing himself to the island, something that was obvious not only to his anthropologist neighbor but also any number of other longtime residents. Journalist Al Prince saw it and drew the analogy to the Tahitian sojourns of Gauguin, Melville, Maugham, and the poet Rupert Brooke. For Prince, Brando also seemed to be infatuated with the myth of the noble savage, which had been part of the colonial European perception, he explained, ever since "Cook brought a Tahitian to London in the 1700s and made him a public spectacle, parading him as the pure, unspoiled primitive. Likewise, Brando fell for that image of the Polynesian native—hook, line, and sinker."

Almost from the beginning, Alec Ata sensed what was at work. Of Chinese and Polynesian descent, he was a Tahitian insider and a figure of political influence, serving as director general of tourism. Slight of build, fastidious, and prone to wearing custom-tailored linen puttees, he was Harvard-educated, and because of his literary and philosophical bent, Brando often sought him out for late-night discussions.

"He never mentioned anything about himself," Ata said, "although he told me that he never, ever watched one of his films." Instead they talked about literature, "a smattering of Keats, a little Shakespeare." But what remained clearest was Ata's impression that Brando was intent on losing himself to the sublime beauty of his new surroundings.

"He was really floating," he observed. "In the middle of breakfast or lunch, or even when they were filming, he might leave and go out to the reef alone in a canoe, maybe with a ten-pound box of ice cream. He would talk to the birds and sometimes not come back until sunset." The desire for privacy and isolation was nothing new to the reclusive actor, who had long steeped himself in Buddhism and found comfort in nature.

"Unconsciously, he seemed desperately trying to discover something," added Ata, "as if he had a great uncertainty. It was in his eyes. He was looking at you, but he was not *seeing* you. Even in the middle of a party, with all sorts of things happening around him, he seemed not to be there."

Jimmy Taylor, *Mutiny*'s costume designer and the brother of actor Robert Taylor, noticed the same moodiness and self-isolation as soon as the shoot commenced on November 28. "When people would walk toward the camera," recalled Taylor, "he'd say, 'Jimmy, who is that coming in?' I would go find out, then tell him it's a pastor from such-and-such an organization. Usually it was someone like that, but he'd say, 'Tell him it's a closed set. I don't want anybody around.' "

To insulate himself further he had brought his secretary, Alice Marchak, along with, as usual, Sam Gilman, actor Larry Duran, now working as a stuntman, and Philip and Marie Rhodes. All of them were on MGM's payroll. Rhodes had initially turned down the job of makeup man; when going on long location shoots, he always wanted his wife with him, but he was expected to pay her way. When Brando insisted that he work on the film, it was Jay Kanter who came up with the solution: Having worked as Magnani's stand-in on *Fugitive*, Marie would now be hired as *Marlon's* stand-in, testing setups, camera angles, and lights. This arrangement—having a woman serving as a male actor's stand-in—was unprecedented but it ensured Rhodes's presence on the set. Bob Hoskins, Marlon's pal from Libertyville, was on hand, too, put on salary as Marlon's "voice coach"—even though he had never worked in show business before.

Removing himself from the cast and crew, Brando liked to hold gatherings at his *fare* in the evenings. Marchak would bring in local musicians whose chests, backs, and arms were covered with traditional ink-black Polynesian tattoos. Brando would reportedly play drums into the night with them, sweat pouring down his forehead, his face expressionless. "The Tahitians were impressed by his staying power," recalled Danielsson, pointing out that the local drummers were a world apart from Hollywood, and that only during these parties did Brando seem to unwind and relax. To entertain him further the Tahitian men usually brought with them a retinue of willing *vahines,* voluptuous beauties, some no more than sixteen. Early explorers like Bougainville's crew had been confused by the natives' hospitality, which included offering the seamen their daughters, but Marlon wasn't fazed in the least. Nothing more fully embodied the sweet ease of Polynesia than the Tahitian girls' faces, bodies, motions, and perfumes.

All were at one with uninhibited passivity, a sexuality that was in no way complicated or entangling. Merely a look could prompt a stroll to the nearby beach, and it didn't matter who was married, who was whose girlfriend. Adultery was tolerated—almost expected—and was the subject of good-humored gossip. "Tahiti is very little, very small," explained one local resident. "Everybody knows what everybody said and did the night before. We call it coconut radio."

While Marlon didn't go out that much, he occasionally fraternized with Papeete's conservative elite of wealthy and social expatriates, politicos, and bureaucrats. Some had been hired as advisers on *Mutiny,* essentially as liaisons to grease the way with permits and cut through the endless French paperwork. Among them were Nick Rutgers, the scion of the Johnson and Johnson pharmaceutical dynasty, who would be hired as an assistant director, and his wife, Nancy, the daughter of James Norman Hall, coauthor of the original *Mutiny* trilogy.

Heimata "Charlie" Hirshon was another American expatriate and local businessman whom producer Rosenberg had enlisted to help with the notoriously slow local bureaucracy. Brando befriended him early on, just as he took to Leo Langomazino, a native Tahitian who was city engineer for Papeete's street department. He was also recruited, and for a year he worked for city hall and MGM both, in the latter capacity as de facto production manager. Langomazino was handsome, with "a big beautiful smile," said Hirshon, "and Marlon liked him right away. Leo treated him not like the biggest actor but like the gardener, and Marlon loved him because he was such a pure man."

Hirshon often had Marlon and Leo for dinner, but sometimes they went out to restaurants. One evening they were dining at a café along Papeete's waterfront. Having put away four vodkas, Marlon let loose, holding the other diners spellbound. "Suddenly he got up on the table," said Hirshon. "Then he gave a 'Heil Hitler' salute and went on in a heavy German accent, playing his role in *The Young Lions.* For Brando to do that in public was unbelievable. You pay him ten million dollars to do that. Everyone was gaga."

Another close friend was Carlos Pallacio, a Chilean diplomat in his seventies who had worked for the United Nations Information Service before retiring alone to Tahiti. Small-boned and contemplative, he had come to the South Seas convinced it was a paradise. Like Ata he was well read, and the draw for Marlon was obvious: The two could sit and talk about almost any subject: politics, Tahitian culture, archaeology, anything and everything but Hollywood or the film. Brando, always looking for expertise, soaked in the older man's knowledge and experience.

A pillar of the French community not directly involved with the *Mutiny* production was Jacques-Denis Drollet, a third-generation Tahitian whose grandfather had been a friend of Paul Gauguin. A sometime minister of tourism as well as the minister of education and a member of the Territorial Assembly, Drollet, like Pallacio, was looked upon as one of the island's most cultured figures. The half-brother of Leo Langomazino, he was Jewish by birth and had fought with the Free French during World War II; after earning the Croix de Guerre, Drollet had then gone to Palestine to fight with the Irgun.

According to some observers, he "looked down on" Brando almost from the start. And unlike some of the other locals, Drollet was not dependent on the actor for employment, amusement, or status.

On December 4, Reed shot his first major scene on Bora Bora, some 150 miles northwest of Papeete, utilizing nearly all of the island's 1,000 residents. Each was paid $10 a day, with double pay for those with canoes. Eight hundred canoes showed up, and almost all appeared in the famed stone-fishing scene in which hundreds of native women wade through shallow waters, thrashing the sea by hand to drive fish into the waiting nets.

While the crew nervously watched for sharks, grinning natives pointed out that barracudas were a far greater danger. The teenage girls seemed especially happy in their work. Side by side with the cast and crew members in the chest-deep water, they grabbed at the men's genitals, causing both assistant director Callow and actor Noel Purcell to leap out of the placid lagoon as though struck by an electric eel. Richard Harris didn't mind, nor did Brando. "They got hold of Marlon, took off all his clothes, and threw him into the water for laughs," Callow said.

Around Christmas the crew returned from Bora Bora to Tahiti, where another major scene was to be shot—the arrival of the *Bounty* at Matavai Bay. For that scene 7,000 extras were hired—all under the supervision of Leo Langomazino, who was issuing instructions in Tahitian. That morning it had rained, a harbinger of disastrous weather to come, but a bigger problem was the clash between authenticity and what Reed could expect from the censors. The director wanted the women to appear bare-chested. Soon the offending breasts were camouflaged by leis and surgical "nipple covers," much to the amusement of the girls themselves. "It was a little piece of brown material with glue on it," said Jimmy Taylor, "but it still looked too much as if they were nude."

Since the necessary leis wilted in the humid heat, each had to be discarded after a single day's use. "A woman, Fifi Clark, who was supplying them made a fortune from the film," said Taylor. "But over the weeks the damn leis kept getting shorter. I said, 'Fifi, if you make them any shorter, they're going to wear them as bracelets.' 'There are no flowers left. I've cleaned Tahiti out,' she told me." Taylor ordered a dump truck and told the woman to hire a staff of fifty to comb the countryside, even the inland slopes of Mount Orohena. His requirement was a thousand leis every morning.

Once the Tahitian *vahines* were properly clothed with leis, and their nipples covered, there remained the problem of their teeth—which were heavily stained and filled with cavities. "If a European man falls in love with a Polynesian woman or wants to seduce her, his best gift is a set of teeth," said Danielsson. The production staff prepared 5,000 sets of false teeth for the stock girls and extras. These partial plates, uppers and lowers, were "a kind of universal fitting," Al Prince said. "But they weren't permanent, so you couldn't eat with them."

During the first week some of the extras were given their teeth, and they never returned. From then on, every morning an MGM employee distributed the teeth when the extras arrived, and when the shooting was over for the day he collected them. Meanwhile, Rosenberg, still obsessed with white sand, had had tons of it trucked in from a nonvolcanic beach on the other side of the island.

In December the *Chase* script was still unfinished and, riddled with cowboy slang, it was far from satisfactory to Brando, who felt it lacked "a social or philosophical message." Not surprisingly, the actor complained to his neighbor, Danielsson, delivering what the anthropologist called "a short lecture rich in references to Zen texts and recent psychoanalytical and sociological studies. 'Take a look at what's going on in the Congo and other places in Africa right now,' Brando said. 'That's the lesson I want to put over.'"

The studio had now assigned Charles Lederer to complete the script, and he was locked in his quarters under strict instructions "to give birth to a thrilling adventure-story with a profound message." As he dutifully turned out pages, he was being yanked in three different directions. MGM preferred a safe approximation of the classic version of *Mutiny;* Reed wanted a Captain Bligh who was a less one-dimensional villain; Brando, despite what everyone was starting to see as his inability to articulate what he truly wanted, continued to insist on "significance."

Nevertheless, Brando "was always completely sincere in his hopeless endeavor to give the *Bounty* mutiny an idealistic slant," said Danielsson. Lederer was trying to achieve this. "It was nothing short of pathetic," Danielsson added, "to see how he suffered each time he gave Marlon a few more sheets of script. Lederer produced a few pages every night, and then, the following day on location, Brando would sit down under the palm trees, have breakfast, and read the pages very carefully. If he didn't like the script, he tore it up and said, 'No good.' "

On such occasions there was no shooting the rest of the day. If he approved, photography began at once. The crew had no problem with the delays, happy to have the free time—pay and all. Many had already taken *concubines,* and the company was rife with stories of nubile girls walking into crew members' hotel rooms unannounced, grinning ear to ear.

"Brando stalled on this and that," added Jimmy Taylor, "and he was milking it. Every day the more people got employed, the more they loved him. The Tahitians are not above fleecing you, and if they figure they can get money and do it legitimately and you'll help them do it, they'll always stick by you."

Since *Mutiny* was being shot in Panavision 70, Brando's penchant for multiple takes was extraordinarily expensive. But, although production costs ran around $50,000 a day, Rosenberg made no attempt to rein him in. On the contrary, he indulged him, even organizing a Christmas party at Brando's home by flying in an L.A.-based charter plane filled with turkeys, hams, and cases of booze.

Such elaborate preparations paled in comparison to Charlie Hirshon's wedding celebration. When he married a local dancer, Anna Toomaru, toward the end of the production, everything was charged to MGM. Moss Mabry, a costume designer for the studio, was told to design the wedding dress; lighting and set people were pulled off their regular assignments and instructed to decorate Rosenberg's home; and, to no one's surprise, another plane flew in from California with more food and champagne. "Can you imagine?" Hirshon exclaimed, still smiling at the memory years later. "A movie company organizing the most beautiful wedding that Tahiti had ever seen? At the party Marlon was so drunk he was sitting on the grass telling my new wife, 'Why don't you sleep with me tonight? I want to fuck you.' Trevor Howard was there, Hugh Griffith, and both were also bombed out of their gourd. You multiply that $50,000 day rate by twenty, thirty, fifty—there went another couple of million dollars."

It was like a disease, as if Tahiti's slow pace had infected everyone, and the producer's willingness to take orders from Brando was deeply entrenched when just after Christmas Brando announced he wanted to ditch his role as Fletcher Christian to play seaman John Adams, a minor role that he felt might solve the problem of "significance." Allowing Brando to change roles would have required a massive script overhaul, but Rosenberg actually flew back to Hollywood with the proposal. The idea was too ludicrous even for MGM, and for once the studio took a stand. A memo was fired back and Brando was told to resume playing Christian. Yet he would slowly, and in complete defiance of the script, turn the character of the mutineer into an effete, aristocratic fop.

Besides script problems, what no one had calculated was the so-called Tahiti factor—namely, just how extreme and flagrant the visitors' behavior with the local women was becoming. "It was very confusing, and out of control," said one staffer. "You had girls getting pregnant and having to leave the cast, so they had to bring in new girls and shoot the scene again for continuity."

To the crew's amazement and delight, the *vahines* weren't after money or husbands but merely romance. Old, fat, thin, alcoholic, or infirm, women continued to invade male cast members' apartments, sometimes naked. "You would come home and find one in your bedroom with another woman, performing," said Taylor. "They didn't mind you watching. There you were, wondering what the hell they were doing in your house."

"Sex to a Tahitian is merely an uncomplicated part of their way of life," Ridgeway Callow explained. "I've known girls who would be living with a man for a couple of weeks or a month, go to the Tahiti Hotel, and after seeing a man at another table they liked, immediately dump the man they were with and leave with the new fellow." Callow rented an apartment for five crewmen and was invited for drinks the day after they got settled. "There were five *vahines* already moved in. Practically everybody in the troop had their own girl."

For Brando, sexual partners had never been a problem, but what he found particularly attractive about the local women, aside from their extraordinary skin, was that by and large they "made no attempt whatever to exploit him or tie him down," said Danielsson. After the combative Kashfi, the stubborn Movita, and the clinging, sometimes hysterical Rita Moreno, Tahitian women were a relief.

"He was screwing like mad," said Hirshon, who in many quarters was regarded as an accomplished playboy himself. "He was trying to fuck as much as he could—local products." The word Marlon used in describing them was "sincere," by which he also meant "easy." So enthusiastic were many of the local teenagers that he was forced to post a guard at his *fare*; his "pool" consisted of the film's dancers and extras, but nothing was really off-limits—including, said Taylor, "the most awful wharf rats in town, just plain little *pufias* as they say down here. Little whores. His goons would pick them up and bring them to his house."

While Brando's coterie of Hoskins, Gilman, and Duran loved the action, the married Rhodes withdrew, happy to remain separate from all the partying. Although perfectly willing to sit with Marlon and discuss what was on his mind, he had by now noticed that his friend had "immersed himself in a sexual Shangri-la and freedom he'd never known before." So out of hand had it become that it amounted to "a free-for-all," and it was turning into "the main part of his life," Rhodes added. "It was like, 'I can't talk to you until I get somebody over to give me a blow job.' "

Most of the Tahitian women cast in the film had minor, nonspeaking parts, but there was one role of substance: Maimiti, the chief's daughter and Fletcher Christian's lover. Reed, Rosenberg, and Brando auditioned a hundred candidates, finally choosing nineteen-year-old Tarita Tumi Teriipaia, a dishwasher at the restaurant Les Tropiques. Part Chinese, part Polynesian, Tarita was also a dancer in the floor show at the restaurant, which was managed by her Danish lover, John Christiansen.

Hirshon, Tarita's former boyfriend, had brought her by three times before Reed and Brando made up their minds; they'd been more interested in Anna Toomaru, then Hirshon's fiancée. Marlon himself had first lobbied for Anna Gobray, another dancer at Les Tropiques with whom he was having an affair. Then he turned to Vaea Benet, a fifteen-year-old who danced in the same floor show. But Tarita had finally caught his eye.

"Tarita was a marvelous dancer, which is why she finally got the part," said Ridgeway Callow. During the Matavai Bay scene, as the native women performed, Brando had watched her closely, calling out, "Put that girl up in the front row. I want to see more of her, let the camera get her. She's got beautiful gestures." Tarita claimed that she had no idea who Brando was. She was also far from thrilled when offered the role, and at first was reluctant to accept it. "She was saying, 'I don't like it, no,' " said Jimmy Taylor. "The Tahitian people cry easily, and so the tears would come and she would say she wasn't going to do it." After much persuasion she finally agreed, and was signed to a long-term MGM contract.

To overcome her fears, Brando took it on himself to coach her. As with Pina Pellicer, he became Svengali.

"Tarita was extremely gullible," Taylor noted. "The girl wasn't conceited, she wasn't selfish. She didn't think she was anything special, and she didn't know why everyone was going to so much trouble to do all these things for her. Therefore, Brando could say . . . 'I'm teaching her to be Maimiti—she is my product,' that sort of thing."

One problem was that she couldn't remember her lines, so there were "miles of film" that had to be junked. As to the question of her acting, this was secondary, since her role as Fletcher Christian's pliant maiden was so undemanding that she could almost do it *in propria persona.*

"She wasn't too intelligent," recalled John Christiansen, her boyfriend, who had been hired as a cook for the *Mutiny* crew to keep him from interfering with her tutorial sessions. Hirshon, who had first met Tarita when she was fourteen and subsequently lived with her for nearly two years, agreed. "She had a terrible blank up in the head. If you had a five-minute conversation with her, it was the end of the world."

Still, her beauty was overwhelming—a vision of voluptuous, innocent South Seas languor. Taylor, who was charged with the responsibility of dressing her day to day, appreciated this as much as anyone.

"She had a beautiful little butt, with these little dimples high up," he said. "Also a very prominent mound of Venus—flesh, not hair—which was visible when she was wearing a *pareu,* and her breasts were bountiful, full and lush. When she walked, that pretty derriere went from one side to the other. The one other girl I saw do that was Marilyn [Monroe] but she did it with intention. Tarita's only flaw, a common one among Polynesians, was her feet. They were as big as a camel's."

It reportedly took Brando six months to seduce her, largely because the nineteen-year-old thought he was "a terrible man." Another problem was that he had invested Tarita with his Rousseauesque notions of purity, casting her as the madonna among his many one-night stands. While he had several other girls servicing him in what basically was a turnstile arrangement, he would "never go to bed with her," said Nick Rutgers. "He would sleep on the floor and she'd sleep on the bed. They'd hold hands, that kind of thing."

Once the affair with Tarita was consummated, however, Brando rekindled his romance with Anna Gobray and juggled the two women. Tarita played a similar game, moving back and forth between Marlon and the familiar arms of Christiansen. Yet Brando did not limit his interests to Tarita and Anna. There was also another local woman, who, like Tarita, worked on *Mutiny* and eventually had a daughter, Liliane, who today is in her early thirties and a pop singer in Tahiti and Australia; according to Guy Roche of Manuiti Studios, for years Liliane's boss and her record-album producer, the singer would later speak openly among Tahitians of Brando as her father. Hugh Kelley, another American expatriate and a hotel developer on the island, was under the same impression, just as Tarita herself told people that Liliane was Marlon's offspring.

Brando had also returned to dancer Vaea Benet. At the time she was called "the Brigitte Bardot of Tahiti," Jimmy Taylor recalled, "very beautiful and with the eyes of Elizabeth Taylor." They were all beautiful, as were his many other women; the "coconut radio" grapevine claimed that Brando got one of them pregnant, too. The problem was reportedly handled by secretary Alice Marchak, who convinced the girl to have an abortion—paying her off, so the gossip went, with a Vespa motor scooter.

Brando, like many of the crew, paid the price for womanizing and suffered the so-called MGM flu, as gonorrhea swept the island. The problem had not taken long to present itself, and soon a local physician who claimed to have huge stocks of antibiotics on hand was put on salary. According to Jimmy Taylor, the doctor was lying. "It was nothing more than an antiseptic iodine ointment that he painted patients with." The ointment was totally ineffective, and soon Brando's private physician, Dr. Robert J. Kositchek, was flown in from Beverly Hills at a cost of $10,000 to handle a case of "indigestion." Rex Kennemer, one of the movie industry's premier doctors, was also brought in for a second opinion, reportedly at Marlon's insistence. It was not Brando's first experience with the clap, certainly, and after ten days of injections the actor was able to return to the cameras. "Everybody knew he had the clap," said Taylor, "so I couldn't understand why anybody still wanted to sleep with him." In short order, Tarita was infected, and she passed it on to Christiansen. Like Brando, she had to undergo treatment.

With the loss of valuable production time, costs continued to mount and Brando, apparently, added to the problem by nickel-and-diming MGM with personal expenses. He required a personal, radio-equipped speedboat to ferry him back and forth to the *Bounty,* which was moored far out to sea. He also got a special delivery of the Sunday *New York Times,* flown in each week at a cost of $27.94 a copy. He then used the film crew to decorate his rented house, including wall hangings and curtains, and then started sending bags of shells back to Los Angeles, reportedly billing MGM $1,700 for shipping. Taylor, who was trying to outfit the thousands of extras as well as the principals, was asked by Brando to do his personal tailoring, too—specifically, to cut down ten double-breasted blue serge suits into single-breasted models.

Perhaps word of Brando's professional reputation had also spread, since the British actors were already on guard against his upstaging. His relationships with both Trevor Howard (the group's unofficial point man) and Richard Harris were constantly on the verge of flaring into open hostility.

By now the company had broken into essentially two factions: Brando, MGM exec J. J. Cohn, producer Aaron Rosenberg, production manager Ruby Rosenberg, and cinematographer Robert Surtees went their own way; while Howard, Harris, Hugh Griffith, Noel Purcell, and the other British actors kept apart, pursuing their heavy drinking at Quinn's Bar along the waterfront. With Papeete's mandatory last call at two A.M., the English group usually wound up at the Lafayette, an after-hours club beyond town limits, described as a "tin shack with a big hall, lots of good-looking women dancing on the tables, drinking, hanky-panky on the beach. Total bedlam."

When sober, Richard Harris tried to do his work, but it was not long into the picture before Marlon's habit of forcing multiple takes pushed him past the breaking point. In one scene, according to Taylor, Brando was especially flat and finally said, "I don't know if it's going to work or not." Harris blew up. "Damn you! Look at me! Act! Who the hell do you think you are?"

It was the same with Trevor Howard. "Brando never knew his lines. He just made them up as he went along and always to his own advantage," said Hirshon. "There was one scene when Marlon asked for a retake maybe eighteen times because in seventeen of the takes Trevor was better."

Howard complained, "He's a great politician, and as a politician he could destroy my work. . . . He's constantly demanding that scenes be rewritten. You never know where the hell you are—you don't know for ten minutes what you're playing because the next scene contradicts it."

A typical scenario unfolded when the veteran British actor was facing a scene that entailed five pages of dialogue. "Every time Trevor hit his lines, Brando fluffed," reported Vivienne Knight, Howard's official biographer. "They went on for eight takes, an unheard-of number for Trevor. Then, when Brando felt that Trevor might be off-key, he threw his line back. It was one of the oldest and dirtiest tricks in the actor's manual."

Sometimes Howard would blow a line just to make Brando repeat himself, hoping that he would pick up his tempo. The rivalry grew, and Brando began using some of the young boys on Taylor's costuming staff— sycophants all—to keep an eye on his British counterpart. Keester Sweeney, MGM's makeup man, was enlisted, too. "Has Trevor got his wig on? Is he ready?" Marlon would ask. More often than not, Sweeney's reply was, "He's waiting for you to put on yours."

With forced restraint, Howard later commented, "I can't honestly say that I got to *like* Brando. I didn't hate him, either. I just didn't get to know him. No one ever does. The only thing I *could* feel for the fellow was pity. . . . He hasn't a friend in the world. He never speaks to anyone unless it's someone smaller or younger."

Director Carol Reed was becoming as annoyed at Charles Lederer's one-dimensional depiction of Bligh as he was at Brando. Howard had his own idea about the character, and Reed agreed by refusing to film scenes that presented Bligh as an abject villain.

For Bengt Danielsson, who was still being consulted even though he had officially left the production, Reed and Howard were on the right track. The real Bligh was dictatorial but multifaceted. He provisioned vitamin C foods to defeat scurvy, made sure his ship's forecastle was regularly washed with disinfectant to kill roaches and lice, and provided a fiddler for his men as well as a canvas awning so they could play cards on deck. Yet the Bligh in the script was Simon Legree in a navy uniform.

If script problems and Brando's showboating weren't sufficiently trying, the film's crew then had to contend with the rains. The monsoon season had arrived, and in January 1961 there was a downpour that lasted for seventeen consecutive days. Rosenberg had been forewarned of the problem, but Brando had pushed for starting the shoot before the rainy season passed, reassuring MGM executives that they could film around the weather when, and if, it materialized.

In February, with only one-third of the *Mutiny* footage shot, the cast and crew gave up and departed for Los Angeles. Only the replica of the *Bounty* remained behind, docked in Papeete harbor for the winter. During the rain-out period, filming continued at MGM's Culver City studios and Marlon was once again distracted by women. As might be expected, Los Angeles was even more complicated than Tahiti, if only because by now Tarita had learned to impose her will.

When Brando's love interest and the other *Mutiny* dancers were lined up to board the plane for Los Angeles, she noticed that Vaea Benet was among them, and dug in her heels. "If Vaea gets on that plane, I don't get on," she announced. Fully aware that Marlon had continued his affair with Benet, she apparently was not nearly as indifferent as she had led others to believe.

"Tarita showed power that once and won," recalled one observer, "which was unfortunate because of any of those dancers, Vaea was the most lovely. She was really set on getting to America or to Europe, and she probably could have made it in movies, but she wasn't allowed to make the trip."

Anna Gobray, however, did join the other dancers, and Marlon continued his affair with both women once they were installed at the Hotel Bel-Air with Leo Langomazino as their "chaperon." According to Leo's wife, Andrée, when Gobray spotted Marlon with Tarita at one of his favorite restaurants, she quit in anger and flew to Honolulu, even though, according to some accounts, she may have been pregnant with Brando's child.

Making her movie debut, Tarita was now subjected to Hollywood hype, with the press describing her as a primitive who had "never worn shoes." Ultimately, however, she was a pawn in the hands of Brando and MGM. When she returned from one quick shuttle between Tahiti and Los Angeles, Tahitian photographer Gérard Pugin asked, "You've been plenty of places?" She replied, "No, Marlon don't want I see people."

Another dancer had also made the trip to L.A., and he was having a fling with her, too, while also seeing Movita. Kashfi, getting wind of all this, was already drawing up more papers to force him back into court.

In March 1961 second-unit photographers returned to Tahiti, and the cast was scheduled to regroup there the third week of April. But Brando was delayed because on April 19, just days before his scheduled return, Rita Moreno suddenly reentered his life by trying to take her own.

"The peppery Puerto Rican actress was rushed to a hospital from the home of Marlon Brando Wednesday after she took an overdose of sleeping pills," stated a front-page L.A. news story. "Moreno swallowed the pills at the home of Alice Marchak, secretary to Brando, and then begged to be taken to the actor's home at 12900 Mulholland Drive, police said. Brando was not home when they arrived, but a phone call from Miss Marchak brought him on the run."

Moreno became unconscious and Brando's physician, Dr. Kositchek, now back from Tahiti himself, was called in. Kositchek ordered her removed to St. John's Hospital, the actor's hospital of choice in nearby Santa Monica. Barraged by reporters, Marlon said he didn't know anything about the suicide attempt.

Kashfi heard the news while getting Christian ready for a visit to his father. Harrison Carroll, the columnist, had phoned to say, "Don't send your son up to Marlon's. Rita Moreno's there and she's taken an OD of sleeping pills. . . . They're pumping her stomach." To protect Brando, the Pennebaker-issued statement placed the attempted suicide at the home of Alice Marchak.

Only a few days later, however, Brando was winging his way to Tahiti. Soon afterward, he telephoned Kashfi for the first time in three months, letting her in on the secret he'd managed to keep for nearly a year.

"He told me he had married Movita the previous summer and that he wanted their son, Miko, to be a brother to Devi," she recalled, using Christian's middle name, which she favored. "He suggested that I and Devi should move to Tahiti to live. He said it would be better for Christian as well. 'I don't like the racial prejudice in the States and Christian will experience that prejudice because of your Indian blood.' " Kashfi then wondered, "Had he forgotten France Nuyen and the phone calls from Guadalajara?" She had no intention of going to Tahiti, and if Marlon thought the phone call would appease her, he was sorely mistaken. Instead she took him back to court.

During the L.A. hiatus, the troubled nature of the production had become one of the worst-kept secrets in Hollywood. "The multimillion dollar epic is about one-third completed amid laments from MGM that costs have soared far beyond the budget," Hedda Hopper had warned in the *Los Angeles Times*. MGM stock had dropped drastically and studio executives were preparing to delegate the blame. Because of the delay on *One-Eyed Jacks,* Brando's reputation as a troublemaker made him "the prime candidate as scapegoat," according to film historian Gary Carey. But while Brando could be fingered and even set up, he couldn't be fired. Instead director Carol Reed, who was in failing health as well, took the fall.

Back in Culver City during the rain-out, Reed clashed with production head Sol Siegel over the depiction of Bligh and the more pressing matter of how badly the film was falling behind schedule. Reed's slow, methodical approach had been questioned, and he offered to resign. Siegel refused.

"Ray Klune, an MGM vice president, asked me to make an honest schedule of the estimated time to finish the picture based on my experience of shooting to date," said Ridgeway Callow, a devout supporter of Reed. As requested, he drew up a schedule for an additional 139 shooting days; Klune asked him to pare it down to a hundred.

"The schedule was presented to Carol," he continued, "and they asked if he would guarantee to finish the picture in that length of time. He told them absolutely not. That's when he was removed from the picture. He was absolutely taken aback by the whole setup, completely brokenhearted."

On February 26, 1961, Reed was fired. While his replacement, Lewis Milestone, would claim that virtually nothing had been accomplished during the British director's tenure, Reed had in fact shot most of the spectacular, epic sequences that would eventually garner most of the film's meager praise. His dismissal caused an uproar among the cast, particularly among the British actors, who refused to go on with the shooting until he was reinstated.

In the face of the sudden publicity, Brando called a meeting of the cast and announced, "I don't give a damn what the press says about me concerning this matter, but I do care about what you people think. My loyalties are torn. . . . I'm fond of Carol, but the argument doesn't concern me, and I had nothing to do with it."

Despite the protest, on March 1 Milestone stepped behind the cameras. The sixty-five-year-old director was a stubborn, salty veteran who'd worked on such classics as *All Quiet on the Western Front* (1930) and *Of Mice and Men* (1939). During the first two weeks he was on the job, Brando behaved himself, but soon after, noticing him talking privately to the cameraman, Milestone realized that the actor was undercutting his authority. The director signaled the cameraman to start, but he waited for Brando. Another time, Milestone didn't say "Cut!" yet the camera was turned off anyway—when Brando nodded that he was done. No one even asked Milestone if the scene was a print.

Marlon had reverted to his old "Are you asking me or telling me?" line. Milestone's position was, "I'm trying to make this scene work." Brando's response, reportedly, was, "No, let's go back to the beginning. I won't do that; I'm going to do it this way."

The demoralized director was next seen sitting on the sidelines reading the *Hollywood Reporter*. Rosenberg asked if he wasn't going to participate. "What for?" he replied. "When the picture's finished, I'll watch the whole bloody mess in a theater." Later Milestone told Siegel, "Sol, this Brando is going to ruin you."

Unlike Henry Koster or Daniel Mann, Milestone was ready to go public, if only because he was too old, too fed up to care. "Did you ever hear of an actor who put plugs in his ears so he couldn't listen to the director or other actors?" the director told reporters. Brando, he said, "rallied to his side every punk extra who claimed he was a Method actor. If I raised my voice to one of them, Brando would complain to Rosenberg. It got so bad, some eighteen-year-old punk walked off the set when I refused to reshoot a scene in which he 'emotionally felt' his performance was not quite right. I said, 'Okay, walk. But don't come back.' Like his master, he sulked for a while—but he came back."

By the spring of 1961, Brando was barely speaking to Milestone, who he regarded as stilted and rigid, even worse than Edward Dmytryk on *The Young Lions*. If he objected to something, he'd argue it out with Rosenberg or Lederer, sometimes haggling over a single line for an hour. If they reached a stalemate, the trio voted: Brando had one vote and Rosenberg and Lederer a half each. "The arguments went on until His Highness had won either Rosenberg or Lederer over to his side," Milestone commented.

It was usually Rosenberg who gave in. "Brando could convince anyone that the moon was made of green cheese," said Taylor. "He had that ability to pull the bullshit over somebody's eyes. Aaron didn't have that much on the ball to begin with, but it got so bad that you would have thought Brando had something on him."

Another problem was Marlon's waistline, which was again expanding as a result of his love for ice cream. "I'd say, 'Suck in. I've got to button you up,' " recalled Jimmy Taylor. "So he'd hold it in, but when he'd let go, his stomach just hung right over the top. God, it was awful."

Brando, however, was more concerned with his height. "I found homemade elevators on the inside of his square toes," said the costumer. "The shoes were authentic, with buckles, but I found cork elevators, half an inch. He'd done it on his own—I knew nothing about it. There was no reason for it. He just wanted to be taller."

He had also demanded tight breeches, and somehow managed to go through fifty-two pairs of them in the course of the shoot, often splitting them when he fell from the stilts some of the men made. "Brando and [actor] Tim Seely were always playing on them," said Taylor. "Then he would land on his big fat butt and *boom,* the pants'd rip. He'd say to me, 'Pin it up. Hide my back.' "

Often, when Callow told him they were done for the day, Brando would jump into the water—uniform, baldric, hat, full coat, and all. "His attitude was 'Who gives a damn?' " added Taylor. "The hat would be ruined, and all I could do was get one of my boys to jump over and retrieve the coat. No matter how much you rinsed it out, though, you could just watch it shrink in front of your eyes."

Refitting Marlon was an ordeal in itself, not only because of his changing waistline but also because he didn't like underwear.

"I'd be ready to fit him and he would drop his pants," said Taylor. "There he was, all hanging out. I offered him a pair of brand-new Jockey shorts, but he said, 'I don't wear them,' and that's all there was to it.

"I had to make these knickers for him," added Taylor, "and I made them with a fullness on the left side to hold the genitals. When he tried them on, he said something about it, telling me, 'You have to tighten the crotch a little bit—it's too loose. I don't want restriction, I want protuberance,' so protuberance is what he got."

On June 29, 1961, Marlon left Tahiti for a thirty-hour visit to L.A. to battle Kashfi in court in Santa Monica. The issue once again was Christian—specifically, that a crazed Kashfi had barred the actor from seeing his three-year-old son that April. In the course of the proceedings, Marlon for the first time publicly announced his marriage to Movita and the birth of Miko.

During the hearing, Brando admitted that he had telephoned Kashfi to tell her about his marriage. Calmly, with his hair pulled back in a pigtail in the manner of British seamen of the time of *Mutiny,* he told the court, "Yes, she was jealous of the woman to whom I am married—Maria [Movita] Castaneda. Then we discussed the relationship of the little boy I have by the other woman, and Christian. I thought it would be fair, honest, and considerate for me to tell her rather than for her to find out through gossip. But she screamed, railed, and raved at me."

Movita was present in the courtroom, and at one point was reprimanded by the judge for making faces at Anna while the latter testified. Brando also declared that Miko was Movita's son and that she had been pregnant at the time of the marriage. "But I've had no sexual relations with her since the baby was conceived," he then added, "and I've never lived with her since." Why this was important or why he'd kept the marriage secret for a year, he didn't explain.

He was equally vague about whether the marriage was legal. Asked for details about the ceremony, he testified that the union had taken place in Mexico, that the presiding justice of the peace had been pledged to secrecy, and that the marriage certificate was not officially registered but was "hidden away in a box."

Kashfi had countered Brando's complaint about lack of visitation rights with accusations of her own, including her allegation that he continually harassed her with late-night phone calls and that because of his string of girlfriends he was "a morally unfit father." She did not, however, include in her declaration any reference to Rita Moreno's suicide attempt only two months before, since, she later explained, "it would have been gratuitously cruel . . . to publicize it further."

Even without that incident before him, Judge pro tem Eric Auerbach was hardly impressed by either spouse's behavior. At the close of the hearing he lectured the two of them to "minimize this turmoil . . . because this case is becoming a vendetta, and the child is becoming an instrument of vengeance."

The news of Brando's Mexican wedding was flashed in headlines around the world. Several weeks later, from a London studio apartment, Jack Doyle, the Irish tenor and boxer, announced, "She couldn't have married Brando. She's still married to me." He cited a 1938 civil ceremony in California and a Catholic church wedding in Dublin in 1942, adding that he had later refused Movita's request for a divorce on the grounds that they were Catholics. He said he intended to sue Brando for "alienation of affection," that it would be "a fight to the bitter end," and that he "want[ed] his wife back—after all, marriage is marriage." No one paid much attention to Doyle's complaint, at least not at that time.

Immediately after the hearing Brando left for Tahiti, but he stopped en route in Hawaii to visit Anna Gobray. Back on location, he continued his relationships with Tarita and other women. A few weeks later an exhausted Brando left Tahiti again, returning to Los Angeles for treatment of what was announced as a "bladder infection."

When he reappeared, the production had encountered new problems. On July 25 the second unit, under assistant director James Haven, was filming a canoe chase, the scene in which Bligh orders some runaway mutineers to be run down and captured. Four canoes were to give chase, with a camera crew following them in a motorboat to film the sequence. As the sea grew rougher, the first canoe was thrown against the reef and the men were jettisoned overboard. One Tahitian was killed, and other actors and extras were severely wounded.

The incident cast a pall over the production. Surprisingly, the Tahitians weren't angry about the accident. What rankled more was that the duration of the shoot had taxed their patience, and according to Danielsson, even additional money couldn't persuade them to get to work on time. The July 14 holiday made matters worse, when the Bastille Day party continued for more than two weeks and no one reported to the set. MGM sent executives from Los Angeles to Tahiti to confront Rosenberg about the skyrocketing budget, and a few days later word leaked out that the studio was worried that it could no longer afford Brando's guaranteed fee, especially now that his overtime rate was about to kick in.

Rosenberg responded by turning to his wife, who was well connected in Arizona banking circles. Together the couple decided to refinance *Mutiny* by initiating a coproduction deal. "Aaron went to Cohn," Ridgeway Callow recalled. "He said, 'Look, J. J., I got hot troubles right now. If you're willing, we're going to take MGM off the hook. We'll call it Arcola—the credit can read, 'An Arcola production presented by MGM.' "

On August 1, with only half the film shot, Brando's $5,000-per-day overtime fee went into effect. There was also "forfeiture overtime," double his regular rate, then "golden time," which amounted to triple his daily salary for extra overtime. The sum would eventually reach $750,000 above and beyond his $500,000 base pay and per-diem rate. Brando's lack of interest in the usual Hollywood trappings of wealth as well as his lackadaisical approach to investing was one thing, but as Seltzer had seen day to day at Pennebaker, the actor viewed his salary competitively, as an emblem of stature and clout.

"You figure which salary bracket a Hollywood actor is in by the kind of smile he gets," Brando explained. "When I first came here I got $40,000 a picture. The smiles people gave me showed me two teeth. Now, I'm paid around $125,000 and more, I get both upper and lowers. But they are locked together. The mouth goes up at the corners but the teeth are set. I'll never get the big fat grins that go with $250,000 a picture; they only pay that kind of money to cowboy stars."

But no one was smiling now at MGM, especially while Brando was being quoted in the press as saying that the movie "was a bore." In the meantime his behavior in front of the camera worsened.

Sometimes Brando stumbled onto the set bleary-eyed, searching for cue cards to remember his lines. At other times he would storm off and lock himself in his dressing room without explanation. While claiming to be rewriting the script, he might nod off, weary from his nocturnal revels.

"Aaron didn't attempt to knock on the door and say, 'Come on Mar, let's go,' " said Taylor, "though before, there were times when Aaron would talk to him like that, as if he was a football coach." Charlie Hirshon was also struck by Marlon's shows of temper. "He'd just go, 'Oh, fucking shit!' and just take his costume off and walk off. It happened for any reason—either he was fed up with the directing or the stuntman wasn't doing something correctly; someone made eye contact when he was saying his lines; or he was too hot; or he wanted to go home and screw. Whatever it was, he'd walk off at ten in the morning and we couldn't shoot anymore that day."

The only thing that interested him besides his women was Tetiaroa, a coral atoll that he had first spotted during location scouting for the Pitcairn sequences. Situated some thirty-five miles north of Papeete, Tetiaroa was composed of twelve small *motu,* or single reef islets, enclosing a central lagoon. Its bone-white beaches fringed with abundant coconut palms were breathtaking, both for their beauty and their tranquility, but equally beguiling to Brando was what he had read and heard about the atoll's history. Tetiaroa had been used in ancient times by the royal Tahitian Pomare rulers as a sacred meeting place for their pagan *tabuas.* The property was not for sale, Brando learned, but he asked both Rutgers and Leo Langomazino to look into the possibility of his buying it.

Obviously more financially secure with his growing overtime pay, Brando was characteristically charitable with money; he often made generous, impulsive gestures, such as underwriting the expenses for surgery and transportation to L.A. for the clubfooted child of one of the extras. Yet he also claimed to be "traveling light," often hitting up friends and crew for pocket money. Some, like Taylor, became so leery that they pretended to be broke whenever he asked. Langomazino, on the other hand, was willing to oblige him, even though he could scarcely afford it. Brando would say, "Leo, I hate to have money on me. Can you just be my bank? When I need money, you give it to me and then I'll pay you back. Now I need ten thousand francs." Nick Rutgers saw trouble ahead and warned him, "For Christ's sake, Leo, when he does that, please have him sign a note for it."

By summer's end, MGM had had enough. Fed up with the production's unprecedented expenses, the studio recalled the company to Culver City while industry columnists continued to lay the blame on Brando, openly calling him irresponsible, inconsiderate, and careless of other people's money.

In September 1961 Marlon felt compelled to reply.

"I'll tell you why it cost so much," he told UPI's Hollywood reporter, Vernon Scott. "They started shooting without a completed script and eventually had seven scripts for the picture. The studio sent the entire cast and crew on location to Tahiti, where it cost them $32,000 a day—and we were out there six months!"

Wall Street was less concerned with the reasons than with the studio's bottom line. On October 3, 1961, MGM stock plummeted ten points because of the production delays. Sol Siegel, MGM's production chief, threatened to sue Brando for "throwing" his performance and trying to force his ending on the picture. He also claimed that Brando was trying to sabotage the production by adding homosexual overtones to the role of Fletcher Christian.

The latter assertion was ridiculous and, in the climate of 1961, little short of craven. Although Brando's foppish portrayal of the aristocrat was possibly part of his rebellion, it was more likely that the actor had seized on this interpretation in earnest, hoping to "deepen" the role, especially since his performance would invariably be compared to Gable's. Arguably, it was a wrong choice; nevertheless, he'd put a brave spin on the character, reverting as always to his notions of class, politics, and gender.

Still, Brando's foppish portrayal annoyed Richard Harris, particularly during a scene in which Brando was supposed to slap Harris in the face. Brando merely flicked his wrist. Harris, taking the gesture as an insult, responded by kissing Brando on the cheek. On the next take, Brando tapped him again. "Shall we dance?" Harris exploded, and stomped off the set. The next day Brando stubbornly played the scene the same way, and Harris once again took his leave, this time refusing to reappear for three days. Harris later told the American press that when he finally returned, Brando approached him and said, "Dick, you shouldn't have done it. I'd like you to know this: I'm the star of this picture and you're opposing me. Remember that, please."

The same controversy had even erupted at the Pennebaker offices. "George and I felt he was playing Fletcher Christian as an obvious, campy gay, and we told him so," recalled Seltzer. "It was a very serious argument. Marlon's comeback was, 'I did not play the character as a faggot. You don't know how to read it. Obviously, your artistic judgment is inferior to mine. That's the way the director has accepted it—Fletcher as a fop.'

"That was the director whom he had been pissing on," added Seltzer wryly, "but now he was citing him as the last word. You didn't win arguments with Marlon; he invoked a kind of poetic mantle—that we didn't understand what he was doing but that the audience would."

Script trouble continued as well, since Brando was still insisting on a Pitcairn sequence that he couldn't articulate. Exasperated, Rosenberg asked him to write his own ending, which he actually did. In Marlon's script, which resembled a vague version of Plato's *Republic,* Fletcher sits in a cave and contemplates man's inhumanity to man while seeing the shadows of the *Bounty* sailors outside, raping, looting, and murdering the Pitcairn natives. Marlon had effectively written himself out of the action, and Rosenberg turned it down.

"You're making the biggest mistake of your life," Brando responded. "You've made nothing but mistakes since this picture started. Okay. This is what you want; this is what you're going to get. I'll just do anything I'm told."

While the threat may have been exactly what Rosenberg most wanted to hear, Marlon wasn't about to make it simple. Feigning inability even to read his cue cards, he stopped speaking to Rosenberg, and on December 7 Hedda Hopper publicly came to the producer's defense.

"For six weeks [Brando] sabotaged the production," she wrote. "He'd show up on the set when called and ask, 'Where shall I stand and what do I say?' Then he'd speak his lines in meaningless monotone. In the scenes where the mumbling would have been all right, he played it brisk and British. But if the great Brando doesn't like it, he won't act. A million words have been written about what's wrong with Hollywood. Well, here's the answer."

By early 1962 Rosenberg assembled a rough cut of *Mutiny* and despaired. Brando's response was, "That's a pretty damn good picture—but the ending is lousy." Again, he proposed they put together a new, brief Pitcairn sequence and offered to forgo his usual $25,000-a-week salary for a fortnight's shooting in Culver City. But with no satisfactory final scenes written, the film languished for another several months. Oddly enough, after all the writers who had struggled with the ending, it was German-born writer/director Billy Wilder who came up with the climax in May, fifteen months after the film was supposed to be finished.

Wilder suggested that Brando's Fletcher Christian propose that the mutineers return to England and face justice. His companions don't agree, and they burn the *Bounty,* killing him in the process. Christian would live long enough to struggle through a farewell speech to Maimiti and the seamen.

In August 1962 Tarita returned to Los Angeles along with several of the cast's mutineers for the final days of the shoot. Milestone stayed on for appearance' sake, but refused to go near the camera or Brando. George Seaton, an MGM contract director, was nominally in charge but, aware of the stigma attached to the project, he had agreed to take the assignment without pay and only on the condition that his participation not be publicized or credited. Essentially Brando directed himself, and his death scene, shot on the MGM lot, was more bizarre than anything he'd done to date.

"He was lying there naked," said Jimmy Taylor. "The makeup man had put burns on his exposed flesh, and I had this fabric with simulated burn marks that I was going to paste on his skin to cover up his genitals. Then he asked, 'Why doesn't my crotch burn?' I said, 'Well, I can't do that, Marlon. We've got a censor problem. Maybe we can use makeup to blend this in with the pants.' 'No, no. If the pants are going to burn, so is the cock. You've got to show it.'

"I then got to Rosenberg and explained what Marlon was demanding. Aaron's reply? 'Well, he's shown his cock to everybody else, now he wants to show it to the American public. Don't worry, I'll put a tarp over him.'

"I'd never seen anything like it in my fifty-year career," Taylor added. "An actor, a star who is prepared to lie out in the middle of the stage with his cock hanging out. The whole crew was there—we had firemen, extras—there must have been sixty or more people standing around, and he had no embarrassment."

To help Brando prepare for the scene, Seaton told him that when a person is severely burned, the loss of body fluids leaves him in a state similar to that of being frozen. "Get me a couple of hundred pounds of cracked ice," the actor ordered. "Spread it out and throw a sheet over it."

After Callow brought out the ice, Brando lay down on it for forty-five minutes. "I want to get the death tremors," he announced, as his skin turned blue. Through chattering teeth he gave an enormously effective rendition, even though he couldn't remember his lines. This time, a human cue card in the person of Tarita was utilized. The camera was shooting over the back of her head, and Marlon was supposed to murmur a couple of words in Tahitian as he died. As Ridgeway Callow recalled, "We got a grease pencil and wrote the words on Tarita's forehead."

Three more days of work were then lost when Marlon came down with a cold as a result of his ice experiment. Yet after twenty-two months of filming, the mood was strangely upbeat with the end in sight. "I am amazed that everything is so amicable after all the name-calling and back-biting and shit that has gone on," Brando himself marveled.

With the burning of the *Bounty,* the movie finally wrapped. But it was decided that one more Dionysian party of the survivors should be shot. Since the British cast was long gone and Milestone was off-salary, Callow was given the chance to direct the last scene, in which Marlon and another sailor were to come ashore and dance with the native girls in a drunken orgy.

Brando arrived with a couple of bottles of Jack Daniel's under his arm. "Everybody says I'm supposed to be a Method actor," he announced. "Well, by God, I'm supposed to be drunk today and I'm going to be drunk. And so is everybody else."

Worried, Callow notified the production office. "We won't inter-fere," he was instructed. "Do the best you can."

Marlon was already "passing the bottles around and everybody was getting crocked," said Callow. "He came over to me and insisted that I have a drink with them. I tried to fake it by gurgling and giving the bottle back but he said, 'No, you can't fool me that way. You swallow it.' So I swallowed a little. Meanwhile, they were getting drunker and drunker."

In a repetition of what had happened on *Viva Zapata!, The Young Lions,* and *One-Eyed Jacks,* Marlon soon became so drunk in the course of the four setups that he had to be held up. By eleven in the morning, the other actor had passed out cold and was dragged off the set. As Callow, with typical understatement, put it, "Naturally, the scene was never used."

The long simmering controversy over who-did-what-to-whom-for-how-much finally erupted when the *Saturday Evening Post* ran its cover story, "Six Million Dollars Down the Drain: The Mutiny of Marlon Brando." Brando "cost the production at least $6 million and months of extra work," the always candid Milestone told the magazine.

"I can only say that the movie industry has come to a sorry state when a thing like this can happen, but maybe this experience will bring our exec-utives back to their senses. They deserve what they get when they give a ham actor, a petulant child, complete control over an expensive picture."

Richard Harris joined in: "The whole picture was just a large dreadful nightmare for me, and Brando was just a large dreadful nightmare for me, and I'd prefer to forget both as soon as my nerves recover from the ordeal."

Brando, the article asserted even more broadly, was responsible for far more than squandering MGM's money. Director-producer Robert Wise, flush from his recent Oscar-winning success with *West Side Story,* delivered the coup de grâce: "I think the *Mutiny* problems with Brando, plus the problems with Elizabeth Taylor on *Cleopatra,* might well mark the end of the star system as it exists in Hollywood today. The big-star monopoly—the monster that we created ourselves out of fear of television—has now become such an expensive luxury and so loaded with trouble that it's just not worth it. . . . Brando's behavior has made us realize how far out of hand the situation has gotten."

For the first time since the Capote interview, Brando was openly outraged by what had been written about him. Walter Seltzer was one of the first people he phoned. "I was summoned to Brando's house up on the hill," Seltzer recalled. "Jay Kanter was already there. Other than the time when he had confronted his father for opening the forbidden letter, I'd never seen Marlon so angry. He had a copy of the magazine and was pacing, furious. Jay wasn't saying very much, since his approach was always calm and considered; he never shot from the hip."

Seltzer, however, jumped in. "I don't understand," he said. "All the years that I've been with you, you refused to look at stuff, even when I would try to get you steamed up about some bitchy untruth or distortion. Remember how you'd put your hand over your eyes, like, 'It's nothing, it's unimportant'? How come all of a sudden you're upset by this story by Bill Davidson, who's got a hard-on for you anyhow because you didn't approve the earlier piece he did? Explain to me why all of a sudden this is important, whereas for years it didn't matter."

Marlon paused for a minute, then replied, "My kids are now going to school and I don't want the other kids to say, 'Your father's a kook.' "

"I accepted that," Seltzer later explained. "I had begun to realize that his kids had become the source of a kind of normalcy for him. He had begun to see that things that he did reflected on them."

With that explanation, Brando demanded, "Who is the head of MGM?"

"The head of the studio is Sol Siegel," Seltzer said.

"No, not the studio, the head of the whole company."

When Seltzer told him that it was Joseph Vogel in New York, he commanded, "Get him on the phone."

"Marlon, it's about seven-thirty in New York, Friday night," Seltzer reminded him. "Where the hell am I going to get him now?"

"Find out."

Through his many contacts, Seltzer tracked down Vogel at home in Connecticut and passed the telephone to Brando.

"Mr. Vogel, I want to come to New York tomorrow morning," the actor said in a peremptory tone. "Meet me in your office at eight o'clock."

Later that evening, Brando, Kanter, and Seltzer caught the red-eye to New York, where they checked into the Plaza, shaved, showered, and raced off to Vogel's office for the early-morning meeting. There they encountered not only Vogel but also his vice president in charge of advertising and publicity.

"Obviously Vogel sensed what this was all about, even though Marlon hadn't told him on the phone," added Seltzer, "and obviously the Marlon magic was still working, despite this horrific experience that they'd had with him. The picture wasn't out yet, so they didn't know what the result was going to be, nor did they realize that they were almost going to lose the studio because of it."

Instead of standing firm, Vogel stroked Marlon from the outset. "You have no responsibility for the cost overrun," he told him. "You did a beautiful job."

"Okay, I want something done about it," Marlon demanded.

After a brief moment of internal struggle, Vogel asked, "What is that?"

"I want you to issue a statement," Marlon said. "I want you to incorporate what you've just said, that my conduct was beautiful and that I didn't cost the company any money; that there were production problems that had nothing to do with me—the weather, the ship not working, that it was the studio's decision to change directors. I want you to say all that."

When Vogel agreed, Seltzer drafted the two-paragraph statement—"this nonsense totally exculpating Marlon," said Seltzer, which Vogel signed.

While Marlon hadn't mentioned legal action, Seltzer was certain he was "setting MGM up to give himself ammunition to file a suit against the magazine. This signed vindication would box MGM in from becoming an ally of the *Post*."

On the plane home several hours later, Marlon and Seltzer sat side by side in first class. "Marlon had a copy of the magazine on his lap, and he was looking at me slyly," Seltzer recalled. "After a moment he murmured, 'How do you like that—"Brando Wasted Six Million Dollars During *Mutiny*." Actually, I'd say it was four million, *maybe*.' Then with a grin, he patted his breast pocket where he had the signed piece of paper."

On June 25 Vogel, as promised, issued a statement to the Screen Actors Guild as well as to the press, announcing that it was "gravely unfair" to blame Brando, who "performed throughout the entire production in a professional manner and to the fullest limit of his capabilities, resulting . . . in the finest portrayal of his brilliant career."

Instead he attributed the film's huge overrun to the delay of the *Bounty* replica, the shipboard fires, the weather, clashes between directors and cast, as well as the resignation of the first director, Sir Carol Reed.

"Marlon the marvelous manipulator," mused Seltzer later. "Within the industry it came down to one important thing—executive abdication, a corporate failure. It didn't use to be a problem with the Louis Mayers and the Jack Warners, when it was one strong guy running the studio. Louis Mayer would have eaten Marlon for breakfast and spit him out."

Marlon, flush with victory, continued to plot while justifying his behavior. Inevitably, there was the question of Brando's mental state. Marlon Sr. had recently spoken to Kay Phillips Bennett, who was visiting from Lake Bluff. She had asked him how Bud was holding up with all the negative publicity. "He looked at me very seriously," recalled Bennett, "and said, 'Kay, I think Bud is one of the most miserable people alive today.' "

Seltzer, aware that after Mittelmann's death in 1959 Marlon had found a new analyst, probably Gerald Aronson, was again struck by Marlon's impractical and extravagant self-indulgence, not to mention the energized paranoia. "I considered him emotionally unstable," Seltzer explained, "constantly convoluted and locked in. Of course, I was aware of his history with psychoanalysis, but I was also aware that he was anxious about being seen as a fraud, chiefly in connection with the *Post* piece. One classic measure of intelligence is a person's ability to learn from the mistakes of the past, and Marlon is certainly deficient in this area. At times like this, he had absolutely no sense of responsibility and seemed out of control—this was the usual pattern of a manic-depressive."

Marlon now took to calling friends late at night in a frantic effort not only to unburden himself but also to cover his flanks and elicit their support. In a motherly tone Maureen Stapleton lectured him after hearing his long complaint about the *Post* article. "Marlon, you mustn't waste other people's money!"

"Wait a minute, wait a minute," he objected. "I wasn't wasting money! They were laying off their expenses on me." Philip Rhodes also realized what was happening, but continued to keep his counsel. Sondra Lee dealt with Brando by simply listening, while telling herself that he seemed to have become a "control freak." For Seltzer, though, the setbacks on *Mutiny* were reminiscent of the agonizing *Jacks* shoot, only on a grander scale, and were similar to the self-delusion Marlon had demonstrated through years of waffling about doing only "important films" at Pennebaker.

Mutiny on the Bounty was released in November 1962, two full years after the cast and crew first hit Tahitian shores. The studio's publicity apparatus had started cranking in advance trying, desperately at times, to plant stories that would take the edge off the indignant articles about the movie's inflated cost. Gossip columnists had already linked the twenty-one-year-old Tarita to Brando, which suited MGM's interests fine except that the Tahitian woman was now denying that she had any feelings for her actor-mentor.

Mutiny premiered at the famed Egyptian Theatre in Hollywood and then New York's Loew's State. Brando attended the star-studded, $100-a-ticket benefit opening in Los Angeles with Movita, but refused to be photographed with director Milestone. Rosenberg escorted Tarita, who seemed indifferent to the presence of Marlon and Movita. Marlon then made an appearance at the New York premiere, where die-hard film buffs booed his performance. After fifteen more agonizing minutes he left.

Reviews of the film were mixed: While Richard Harris and Trevor Howard were invariably praised, as was Tahiti's scenery, Brando took it on the chin: "There is so much in this picture that is stirring and beautiful that it is painful to note and call attention to the fact that it also has faults," stated Bosley Crowther in the *New York Times*. "But it has, and the most obvious of them is the way Marlon Brando makes Fletcher Christian an eccentric who dominates the entire dramatic scheme. . . . Brando puts tinsel and cold cream into Christian's oddly foppish frame, setting him up as more of a dandy than a formidable ship's officer. . . ."

The high-toned *New Republic*'s Stanley Kauffmann asked somewhat rhetorically, "Is it all a talented actor's revenge on a big studio for snaring him inside an empty spectacular film? Only in a few moments of fury does life touch the part and Brando burn through. The rest is like an All-American halfback imitating Leslie Howard as the Scarlet Pimpernel."

Even Pauline Kael, who sometimes praised Brando for refusing to play by the rules, insisted that his performance was "more eccentric than heroic . . . like a short, flabby tenor wandering around the stage and not singing."

Around Christmas Marlon, hit hard by the uniformly hostile reaction, volunteered to make an appearance at the premiere in Tokyo—although there were other motives at work as well. While en route he stopped in Honolulu, probably to revisit Anna Gobray, but he had also arranged to meet up with Tarita in Japan. She was by then four months pregnant, and he had asked the wife of one of his Tahitian friends to accompany her, hoping that the two of them could persuade her to have an abortion.

"He told me, 'I have so many problems with my two wives, I don't want that kid. I have too many. You ask her, you are a woman,' " the friend recalled him pleading.

The abortion was scheduled, but Tarita refused to go through with it. "When we flew there," her escort added, "Marlon told Tarita, 'It is time now because soon is Christmas coming and I have to go home to be with all my kids,' so he asked her, 'Say yes or no.' Tarita then told me, 'I say no.' " Realizing he couldn't prevail, Marlon abruptly left and returned to Los Angeles, instructing Alice Marchak to break the news of his departure to the women as well as to the press.

After the birth of a son on May 30, 1963, in Tahiti, Tarita told her friend, "I had my baby and Marlon was very mad after me."

The baby was named Teihotu, but he was not given the Brando name. Marlon reportedly demanded a blood test to verify that the infant was in fact really his. Later he would blame his reluctance to acknowledge paternity on the complications of his ongoing legal problems with Kashfi; at the same time, he probably did not want to upset Movita, either.

There was another legal maneuver on his agenda as well. After his return from Tokyo he filed a libel suit against the *Saturday Evening Post*. His attorney, Allen E. Susman, asked for $4 million in general and special damages, and $1 million in exemplary and punitive damages. Both Seltzer and Kanter had tried to dissuade the actor, but it was obvious that the suit had dictated his actions for some time. His willingness to oblige MGM by attending the film's premieres in Hollywood, New York, and Japan, his generous offer to reshoot the ending, and the letter he'd finessed out of Vogel were all among his preparations.

Conniving and calculating, locked into what one of his personal assistants later called "his James Bond mode," he took other measures, too.

He had tried to enlist Trevor Howard. In October the British actor had received a long letter from his costar expressing dismay at Howard's depiction of him in the *Post* piece as "unprofessional and absolutely ridiculous." As far as he knew, Marlon claimed, he'd never been criticized by another actor before.

Howard, no doubt, wished he'd seen the last of Marlon; however, he was soon asked by Brando as well as producer Aaron Rosenberg to appear in another project, a World War II drama called *The Saboteur: Code Name Morituri*. The part was small but promised a big salary. Howard, who needed quick money after several auto accidents, agreed to take the offer, and unsuspectingly helped build Brando's suit against the *Post* because the article had alleged that after *Mutiny* no British actor of stature would ever work with Brando again.

In his 1979 *Playboy* interview, Brando would claim that he couldn't recall what eventually happened in the case, but thought "the *Post* settled and gave me some money." In fact, the suit was dropped.

While he couldn't remember the outcome, he certainly elaborated on his reasons for initiating the litigation, and in the intervening years he had become no less vindictive against the MGM publicist who had arranged for the *Post* article in the first place.

"He was Sam Spiegel's public relations man, Bill-something, who later got hit by a taxi. Serves him right," Marlon said. "As it turns out, MGM was paying him off! He was telling the head of the studio everything I told him."

"Bill-something" was in fact Bill Blowitz, a publicist who had worked for Stanley Kramer and Twentieth Century–Fox and was a close friend of both Walter Seltzer and George Glass. Glass was so irate at Marlon's comments that he fired off a letter:

April 17, 1979

Dear Brando, you pious fake.

I just read your interview in Playboy. *I am outraged and disappointed.*

Let me tell you why:

You profess concern for mankind, for the Indians, for the children, and all who are dispossessed. Yet you have the callousness, the savagery, the cruelty, to say "served him right" when you talk of Bill, your press agent killed by a New York taxicab. You couldn't even recall his last name.

Well, I'll tell you, his name was Bill Blowitz. He was one of the best, both as a professional and as a human being. You said he ratted on you to MGM. I say, having known Bill for twenty-five years, that was absolutely impossible. No man in the motion picture industry practiced higher ethics. He was incapable of ratting on you or anyone else.

Another thing about the Playboy *interview, the disappointment you express because, you say, Jewish movie moguls are not so concerned as you about the human condition. They come from a persecuted minority, so they should be sensitized, in your opinion. Let me add to your education on this point: Persecution desensitizes as often as it sensitizes. . . .*

Come, come, Brando, I could forgive you for your own peculiar brand of anti-Semitism, unwitting though it may be, but about Bill Blowitz, never, unless you tender a public apology to his family and friends—after you've finished your next walk on the water, that is.

And here's something else to paste on your mirror—who does not care about one man cares for no one, Indian, child, or anyone else.

Sincerely,

George Glass

In the year following its release, *Mutiny on the Bounty* earned only about $10 million in the United States and the same amount abroad—a disastrous take, given the fact that it needed to make $60 million to recoup its $30 million total cost. As a result, in April 1963 MGM reported a $3.39 per share stock loss. A clean sweep of the executive offices followed. Studio head Sol Siegel was removed from his job, and Joe Vogel, the chairman of the board and the man who had been intimidated into signing Brando's letter of exoneration, was soon to follow. (Angry stockholders cited the letter itself as the reason for voting him out.)

Mutiny could very well have closed the studio. "It's just by magic that it didn't. It was a huge, huge failure," concluded one industry analyst.

Though Brando couldn't have cared less about the chaos the film left in its wake, the production also changed the face of his beloved Tahiti. What had first appeared a windfall had driven up prices to the point where the island paradise was on the brink of being commercialized forever.

Homer Morgan, manager of Les Tropiques, had foreseen the problem when, during *Mutiny*'s location shoot, he told *Variety,* "MGM is making it difficult for local tradesmen and residents; they're offering higher prices than prevailing for whatever they see and want. They are not subtle. They will knock our economy for a loop."

"Every house that was available in Tahiti was rented. People even moved out," agreed Hirshon. "Places were renting for $3,000 a month that would ordinarily go for $200."

During the production the Bank of Indochina, then the only bank in Tahiti, had even run out of money because MGM was picking up $40,000 or $50,000 every night to pay the hundreds of extras. Eventually Rosenberg had to summon a plane from New Caledonia to bring in extra cash.

The movie also whetted the Tahitians' appetite for *la bonne vie.* "They had been watching Americans being Americans, throwing their loot around," said Al Prince, the editor of the *Tahiti Sun-Press,* the island's English-language newspaper. "When the movie people left, the locals wanted the same prices. People said, 'That's ridiculous.' The Tahitians said, 'Well, tough.'"

The film put the economy "on a rocket." Up until *Mutiny,* Tahiti was "a sleepy, backwater, South Pacific–quaint, Somerset Maugham–type dump," added Prince. "Now suddenly it had been put on the map." On his return trips Brando would complain bitterly about the crowds and the diesel fumes that polluted the waterfront. Still, he kept coming back. Tahiti, he claimed, was his reality check from the confusions of Los Angeles, his other life where he could undertake his private journey and inner quest.

THE SIXTIES (I)

1962–68

Although Marlon made public appearances with Movita, by 1961 their marriage was in name only. She and Miko continued to live in the large Mediterranean-style home in Coldwater Canyon that he had purchased for her and the baby. He often visited there, and the residence was only a five-minute walk from the cul-de-sac where Marlon's father and his second wife, Anna, and Anna's father, Gene Frenke, all lived. For the next several years Marlon paid many visits to the Frenke-Brando enclave, where a near incestuous soap opera would be played out.

Brando Sr. had married Anna (or Anichka, meaning "Little Anna") in 1958. At the time of their wedding, Anichka was thirty years younger than the sixty-three-year old Brando Sr. But that seemed to be her pattern in marriage. Her first husband, Edward Paramore, a severely alcoholic screenwriter who had died in a freak elevator accident several years before, had been at least twenty years older than she.

Anichka was a petite, attractive blonde—a Tippi Hedren type who even bore some resemblance to the young Dodie. She had a model's high cheekbones, and a Dutch boy haircut framed her strong Slavic features. She, too, had a severe drinking problem, which friends attributed to her complicated and unhappy relationship with her father. Frenke's secretary, Louise Monaco, diagnosed it as "a real Electra complex, a sick obsession."

Gene Frenke was a wealthy businessman, a real estate investor, and a well-known Hollywood figure who produced films such as *The Barbarian and the Geisha*. Very much the man about town, he had known everyone from Garbo to Chaplin, and his second wife had been actress Anna Sten. Anichka had always felt neglected by her hospitable father. She often told people how much she had hated her stepmother, Sten, and still blamed her father for sending her away to boarding school and paying little attention to her while she was growing up. Although Frenke and Sten were no longer together, even as a grown woman Anichka harbored resentments and seemed to seek in her marriages the father that she felt she had never had.

Brando Sr. must have been the perfect candidate, courting her as he did with old-world gallantry and flowers. "I think Senior married Anna for companionship," said Walter Seltzer, who traveled with the couple on their honeymoon to London—which happened to dovetail with the premiere of the Pennebaker production *Shake Hands with the Devil*. "He was also taken with her exotic background. She was traditional in some ways, but also unconventional and often unpredictable. She cared about literature, and her interest in art was genuine."

Despite Anichka's own tempestuous love-hate relationship with her father, she and Marlon Sr. had moved into a house that Frenke bought for them, located directly opposite Frenke's own home on a short driveway they shared in Coldwater Canyon. Diagonally across from Frenke, at the end of the private cul-de-sac, was Frenke's young protégé, producer-writer Harold Nebenzal and his Korean wife, Dorothy. Dorothy was close to Anichka and also a friend of Fred Ishimoto, Hollywood's leading agent for Asian actresses, many of whom dated both Frenke and Marlon Jr.

The living arrangement was by all accounts "a compound" of relatives and friends. Frenke often played tennis with Marlon Sr. and Walter Seltzer on the shared court; the Nebenzals frequently had dinner with Anichka and Marlon Sr.; and Movita was also a friend of Anichka, who was on good terms with Marlon Jr.'s retinue, especially Wally Cox. Marlon eventually brought Philip and Marie Rhodes as well as Sam Gilman and his wife-to-be, Lis Hush, to visit. As Nebenzal recalled, "We were constantly in and out of each other's houses, the kind of situation where you'd go next door to borrow a head of lettuce. And Marlon and his friends were there quite often, either just dropping by or coming to Anichka's holiday soirees."

At least once a month Marlon also went to the compound, not so much to see his father and Anichka but to visit Gene Frenke, who represented a combination alter ego, soul mate, and surrogate father.

In contrast to Marlon Sr., who struck Nebenzal as "ramrod-straight and remote and reserved," Frenke was a *bon vivant* and delightful sophisticate whose motto was "Seize the day, live for the moment." Most of all he was a notorious Lothario. With his self-styled aristocratic bearing and European finesse, his piercing dark eyes and trim physique, he was proud of his reputation as one of Hollywood's most accomplished ladies' men. "He was in his late sixties at this time," said a business associate, "and he was still what I would call a stud's stud. He and Marlo had many private conservations. I was sure I knew what the basis for their relationship was during these years. Pure and simple—it was pussy. I'm sure they were comparing notes about all the Asian women they knew."

While doing military service in the Orient, Nebenzal had become deeply immersed in Asian culture. Frenke, too, considered himself an expert after producing a movie in Japan, although his passion was less for the culture than for the women. With his own attraction to Asians—who were termed "exotic" women in those days—Brando fit right in. According to friends of both, the two were sharing their women. "Marlon got what we used to call a wet dick," said one observer. "I think Gene got a charge out of sleeping with a woman, then passing her on to Marlon."

Before Frenke, Brando had already developed his fondness for Eurasian and Asian girlfriends. But Frenke, with his wide range of contacts, was a bonanza, introducing him to even more young women, many of whom were aspiring actresses and had heard that he was the man to contact when they arrived in Hollywood hoping to make it in show biz.

"All these Asian women knew that Frenke was an easy touch," said Philip Rhodes, who had met Frenke during his early days in Los Angeles. "He was a lovely, generous man and always helped these girls when they came here. Most of them were on the make."

Among them was a beautiful young dancer from the Philippines, Marie Cui. She had become one of Frenke's coterie when she had first hit town, and "the story was that she had been a peasant girl," added Rhodes. "She'd supposedly come down out of the mountains to sell baskets, and she was so gorgeous that she was discovered and brought to Hollywood to be in movies. She became one of Frenke's girlfriends, and then Gene introduced her to Marlon." According to acquaintances who knew Frenke, Brando, and Cui, she had a continuing relationship with both men, al-

though it was Marlon whom she naively fantasized about marrying someday.

While Marlon Sr. continued to work as the nominal manager of Pennebaker, from 1961 onward the production company was slowly dying. In
the past seven years only *One-Eyed Jacks* had emerged specifically to give
Marlon Jr. the freedom to follow his muse. Among its bona fide productions, Pennebaker had released *Shake Hands with the Devil, Paris Blues,* and
The Naked Edge, featuring talent like James Cagney, Gary Cooper, and
Sidney Poitier. Marlon Jr., however, didn't bother to see them or even
come to meetings, according to Seltzer. His involvement with the 1961
Paris Blues had amounted to nothing more than a cablegram to his father,
Glass, and Seltzer, who were on location in Paris to begin shooting the picture. "He sent it to us from Beverly Hills," said Seltzer. "He was con-
gratulating us on the start of production, and he wired, 'Dear George,
Walter, and Pop. I kiss you all on all twelve cheeks. Mazeltov.' Very jokey,
typical Marlon, and of course the twelve cheeks referred to the cheeks of
our ass as well as face. That was the only communication I had from him
about the movie." George Glass had finally quit in October 1961 to join
Universal-International; the studio had been bought by MCA for the purpose of packaging television shows for the agency's clients.

MCA had by now become so powerful that even Brando was impressed; the actor who proclaimed his support for the little guy had also put
himself in the legal hands of the same powerful Beverly Hills firm of
Rosenfeld, Meyer & Susman that represented MCA. Allen Susman handled the custody petitions against Kashfi, while Norman Garey, Susman's
wunderkind and protégé, became one of the most powerful entertainment
lawyers in town and Marlon's trusted adviser. Over the next two decades
Garey would negotiate both the purchase of Tetiaroa and the actor's most
lucrative movie deals, including *Superman.*

When Glass left Pennebaker, Seltzer remained on board, the only experienced hand left to run the company. Soon, however, he was tipped off
by a lawyer friend who had been handling Pennebaker's affairs that Marlon Jr. was now talking about folding the business. The lawyer said that
the actor was feeling a financial pinch, might have been having personal
problems with his father, and no longer wanted the responsibility of a company. Seltzer soon decided to quit, but on the day of his scheduled depar-

ture, he received a phone call from Marlon Jr. at five in the morning. The time of the call didn't startle him, since Seltzer knew he was keeping "peculiar hours," but the tone of indignation was surprising.

"What is this bullshit about your leaving me?" Marlon demanded.

Seltzer noted that the emphasis was on "leaving *me,*" not Pennebaker, but he replied, "It's not bullshit. I've heard you're going to close the company. I have a family to support, and as a matter of fact I have a new job."

"I don't know where you got this ridiculous idea," said Brando. "Maybe I was kidding around with our lawyer, but I didn't mean it. I want to continue the company. I need it, I want it, and I want you with me."

Feeling himself drawn in by loyalty, and even though Brando was not offering to raise his salary, Seltzer spelled out the conditions for his return. "I told him that he had to join me and his father in operating the company," he recalled. "I wanted him to be involved in any outside picture we made, and that he had to consider doing a film for Pennebaker. Marlon said, 'I can't promise that I'll run out and do a picture, but I will involve myself and you can count on it.' Three days later I couldn't get him on the phone," Seltzer said. "It was phaseout time."

In 1962 Marlon agreed to a buyout of Pennebaker by Universal for a reported $1 million. Under the terms of the agreement, the studio assumed ownership of the company's films and provided a pension for Marlon Sr. as well as an undisclosed amount of MCA stock. In return, Marlon Jr. gave Universal commitments for five films at $270,000 each. Jay Kanter, now a highly placed production executive at Universal, helped close the deal by eliciting the studio's pledge to cover the Pennebaker budget for *The Ugly American,* Brando's long delayed "political" movie, which was about to go into production.

Despite Kanter's sweetener, the contract was a disaster. Given the fact that Brando had cracked the $1 million barrier with *The Fugitive Kind* and made at least $1.3 million on *Mutiny,* not only was $270,000 per picture ridiculously low, but it would force him to muddle through a lost decade of pictures that looked, as one film historian put it, as if they were "churned out of a subway photo booth." Even worse, the actor would be stuck in a situation that left him vulnerable to the industry's titans and their attempts to cut him down to size.

It must have been quite apparent to Lew Wasserman, the MCA executive now running Universal, that the bloom was off Brando. There was no ignoring how poor the returns had been from *Mutiny, One-Eyed Jacks,* and *The Fugitive Kind,* and Wasserman would have realized that Universal had the upper hand; Brando would have to accede to the studio's demands in order to make the money that he now needed.

"Part of the reason he made the deal," said Seltzer, was that, despite his reassurances the year before, "he'd come to the conclusion that he didn't want the bullshit of having a company and having to live by certain rules. But the main reason was that he was financially strapped, so his attitude toward the studio became 'This is what they want me to do, I'll do it.' It was a mentality altogether different from the one he'd had before. He'd lost his cachet and he knew it, so he was in no position to be selective. That's why he had to do those clunkers during these years—he had to play things short just to be able to make money."

Brando's cash squeeze had indeed become acute. The divorce from Kashfi, the continuing court battles, his extravagant spending, and his new obligations to Movita and Miko continued to drain him. Sloppy and inattentive financial planning in the past had left him without any real capital or any income from investments, and he was now sliding into the red.

Seltzer, who had long seen the crisis coming, said this state of affairs bothered him. "But not as it would bother most of us. When we talked to him about money, he would get jokey, as if it hadn't really sunk in."

For all his jokes about money, Marlon insisted that he was seriously concerned about his children's future. In an attempt to give them some stability, in 1962 he hired a middle-aged Belgian couple, Raymond and Cécile Ruysseveldt, to help Movita at the Coldwater Canyon house. Ray was nominally the chauffeur and butler, Cécile the cook and housekeeper, but during their nine-month stay the couple attempted to lend some normalcy to the household, having witnessed firsthand the eccentricities and mood swings of their employer.

Along with the Ruysseveldts, several young Mexican women had been hired to take care of Miko. Brando couldn't keep his eyes off them. "He always looked at their legs, giving them the once-over," said Ray. "I would catch him doing that when they turned around. Always the roving eye, you know?"

With Movita, meanwhile, Marlon seemed more cordial than passionate. "The two of them were always kind of distant, but it was more him," recalled Ray. "He never really showed a lot of emotion. He was nice, but he put a kind of a wall in-between and was always on his guard. He didn't want to play big boss with us, and at the swimming pool he'd even invite me to join him, but we could never really have a conversation."

The Ugly American and Bedtime Story

In the spring of 1962, Brando finally began work on *The Ugly American,* which had been long delayed by the still unfinished *Mutiny.* The new film was an indirect conceptual spinoff from a 1956 UNESCO project in which Brando had wanted to tell the story of the kidnapping of United Nations research workers. Now he seemed even more serious about making an "important" picture that would examine the role of emerging Third World nations, the needs of "unaligned" peoples, and America's Cold War arrogance.

Having made enthusiastic statements (including denunciations of American foreign policy) to the press about the anticipated film, Marlon could only have been heartened when on March 24, 1962, Senator J. William Fulbright, chairman of the Senate Foreign Relations Committee, condemned the project as too controversial and even unpatriotic. Brando counterattacked, announcing that nothing was going to stop him. "There are few countries left where a picture like this could be made," he told reporters. "It certainly couldn't be done in France, the one-time citadel of freedom. Certainly not in Russia. Only America, England, and Sweden and a few other countries would permit such self-criticism."

But the political significance of the film was already undermined by Brando's unfortunate choice of director—his buddy and former Pennebaker partner, George Englund. Although Englund had previously traveled to Asia with Brando and writer Stewart Stern to research the aborted UNESCO picture, he had never directed a movie before. He was basically a promoter and businessman known for his svelte suits, social contacts with the likes of Paul Newman and producer John Foreman, and his marriage to actress Cloris Leachman. Stern, who adapted Eugene Burdick and William J. Lederer's best-selling novel, could at least lay claim to having scripted the hip James Dean success, *Rebel Without a Cause* (1955). Like Englund, however, Stern was basically controlled by Brando, which didn't bode well for making good and hard decisions.

While the actor approached *The Ugly American* as a groundbreaking venture, Universal, which in the Pennebaker buyout had agreed to finance the film, saw it quite differently. The Burdick-Lederer book was little more than a thinly disguised polemic; whether the studio's skepticism stemmed from an accurate, nonpartisan assessment of the source material or just cold feet, once production got under way, word came down that the picture was not to be filmed on location. Brando took this in stride. He kept to a regular and prompt schedule, every morning driving to the Universal soundstage, arriving early enough for Philip Rhodes to apply his makeup at a leisurely pace. His behavior on the set was equally measured, although in the usual Brando style he called for endless retakes. Director Englund complied because, as he explained to a *Paris Match* reporter, "it is the job of the director to help the actor to find himself." Justifying his method of directing Brando in the role of the American ambassador, Englund added, "I've let him play him waiting for the right moment and not pressing or pushing him, because he is the finest actor in the world. But no actor is at his best all the time. . . . Even he has his moments. He may well prove at his greatest in this one because the subject means so much to him." Allowed his freedom on the set, Marlon couldn't possibly rail against his pal Englund, who bore the title of the film's producer as well as director.

Marlon had cast his sister, Jocelyn, in the small role of the manager of the film's UNESCO-like children's hospital. Although she had gotten off the blacklist, her acting career was again stalled. She was living alone with her two sons in Santa Monica, seeing a therapist, and though attending AA meetings, still drinking. "Bud helped me by putting me in that movie," she acknowledged. "I needed the money. The kids were growing up and I wasn't getting that many jobs."

With brother and sister in the same picture, the press smelled a story, and Marlon used the opportunity to go after MCA for what he claimed was the former agency's role in derailing Jocelyn's career. Conveniently, he chose not to mention the agency by name.

"You know," he told one interviewer, "she was one of the many performers in Hollywood who were blackballed by the agents because they had innocently joined some reform organization that later was infiltrated by communists and found themselves unable to get a job. If a producer wanted the services of a player whose name was on one of the blacklists, he'd fix it with an agent, and that was all there was to it. But that was done mainly for the stars and well-known players, while the others were just dropped from the lists of available performers. . . . I fixed that."

In another problematic bit of casting, the film's production consultant, Kukrit Pramoj, who was a Thai publisher and future Parliament member, was persuaded to make his acting debut by playing the prime minister in the film. Universal, already stung by Fulbright's denunciation, became even more worried about the "pinkish" hue of the cast and imposed a press blackout, banning all publicity until the film's release date. Brando again refused to be riled. Instead he announced calmly, if cryptically, to reporters that "children are the most satisfying thing."

For all the actor's stated concern about his own children and his extended visitation rights, the Ruysseveldts recalled that he was actually seeing his offspring in the Coldwater Canyon home no more than twice a week. During these afternoon visits he would arrive and swim in the pool with Miko and Christian, whom Kashfi would drop off for the visit. Often he brought the two boys expensive miniature toy cars and other presents, but the pattern was always to see the two kids at the same time, leading Ray, the chauffeur, to conclude that "maybe he wanted to kill two birds with one stone."

According to Kashfi, Brando referred to these gatherings as "group therapy sessions," at which she was initially present until Movita had her banned from the house. During one visit Marlon instructed Christian to "kiss your little brother, kiss the baby." Christian's response was to punch Miko in the nose.

The nights Marlon stayed at Movita's home, he would leave at five or six in the morning and "just disappear," Ray added, although it was apparent that the two kept separate bedrooms. Whatever the arrangement, he was also flying Tarita in for visits. Lisa Lu, the Hawaiian he'd brought to the *Jacks* set, had been hired as his "dialogue coach" for *The Ugly American,* and she was often with him, reading his lines aloud, since, as he explained, that was the only way he could remember them. He also continued to see Marie Cui, and when word of his affair with the young Filipino woman reached Kashfi, Anna again went amok.

"She could have no logical claim to him," wrote Brando biographer Charles Higham, "yet she responded with the passionate anger of an offended lover. . . . She arrived unannounced at Marlon's house. . . . Unable to raise anybody when she rang the bell, she discovered a door open at the side of the building and walked into the entrance hall. . . . [She] made her way upstairs to the master bedroom, where she found Marlon in bed with Marie Cui, who was naked. Furious at Anna's sudden invasion, Marie flung a lamp at her. Anna fled down the stairs. She alleged later that Marlon ran after her and threw her to the ground, beating her head against it as she burst into hysterical laughter."

In her own account of this incident, Kashfi insisted that her actions were not motivated by jealousy but because she wanted to confront him about his latest "jolly sport." She said that she had driven to Marlon's newly rented home on Tower Road above Beverly Hills (he had briefly relinquished his lease on the Mulholland home and was now renting the lavishly furnished estate of John Barrymore) because her ex-husband had repeatedly entered her home in her absence and poked holes in her diaphragm with an ice pick. When she burst into Brando's bedroom, Kashfi said she had been hysterical with laughter because of Marlon's evident embarrassment—pulling the sheet up to his neck—but that his embarrassment turned to fury when he "tackled me on the front lawn and proceeded to knock my head against the curbstone." Then he bound her hands and feet, and she was not released until the police, summoned by a neighbor, arrived on the scene.

At the same time that Brando and Elizabeth Taylor were being excoriated for enormous cost overruns, another major Hollywood star—and an old friend of Brando—was taking a similar beating for what the studio charged were repeated absences and an "underwater," lackluster performance. Marilyn Monroe, with whom Brando had had an affair in 1955, was making *Something's Got to Give* for George Cukor and Twentieth Century–Fox. Cukor was so frustrated with her that on June 1, 1962, her thirty-sixth birthday, he had refused to throw a party on the set for her. Outraged by her absence from the set the following week, Fox executives fired her from the picture on June 8, filing suit for half a million dollars. During the following weeks Monroe made a series of public appearances and gave several interviews in an attempt to restore her image. For the most part, however, she retreated to her bedroom where, like Brando in the midst of his depressions, she made contact with the outside world only by telephone in long, late-night, insomniac conversations with friends.

According to her masseur, Ralph Roberts, one of the callers she frequently spoke to during the final weeks of her life was Brando, and their conversations lasted for hours. Brando seemed to cheer her up with jokes, but given the length of their conversations, in all likelihood he was also playing psychiatrist, talking her through her dark hours of despair and hopelessness. The bond was real, given their long intimacy as well as Marlon's own morose periods of withdrawal when his personal demons would keep him droning for hours.

Once filming of *The Ugly American* was completed at the end of July 1962, Brando left town for a two-week vacation in Tahiti. It was there that he heard the news of Monroe's death in the early-morning hours of August 5. Contacted by the press, he refused to say a word.

Rita Moreno, too, had followed up her overdose of sleeping pills in April 1961 with two other self-destructive incidents the following year: On one occasion she arrived at Marlon's house in a seething rage and persuaded him to go for a ride to discuss their tortuous relationship. During their drive through the Hollywood hills, she became so distraught that he lost control of the car, which spun off the road. Moreno's face struck the dashboard, requiring treatment at the hospital. "When I got to the emergency room, I was bloody and hysterical," she later said, by way of explaining her tantrum in the emergency room. "A bunch of photographers surged into the cubicle, shouting questions, popping flashbulbs. I was screaming, fighting them out of the room." Only a few days later she and Marlon had another angry quarrel, and this time she slashed her wrists, was again rushed to the hospital, and for several weeks appeared around town wearing bandages.

Not long after Marilyn's death, another woman in Brando's life attempted suicide. It was reported that Brando had been in Rome when, on October 20, 1962, eighteen-year-old Vaea Benet, the Tahitian dancer, was rushed to the emergency room bleeding from a wrist wound and suffering from an overdose of sleeping pills. Friends reportedly explained the suicide attempt by saying that she was "in love with . . . Marlon Brando, who has been in Rome recently." Whether he had been in Rome on business or to visit Vaea the press never determined, although Benet's suicide attempt seemed to follow the usual pattern: Brando was often attracted to emotionally fragile women, then after drawing them in, he would resent their dependency and break with them. Realizing that their affair would never lead to marriage, much less any kind of commitment, his women seemed bent either on ending it all or recapturing his attention by any means at their disposal.

As the release date of *The Ugly American* approached, Brando went on the offensive. Still smarting from the adverse criticism of *Mutiny,* he now made himself available to the press—not only available, but unable to stop talking, as if he needed to win people over with a "kinder, gentler" Brando. Perhaps that was the point, since even greater public antagonism was expected once *The Ugly American* was released.

In fact, the film was not nearly as incendiary as Senator Fulbright and Universal's executives had feared or the actor himself had predicted. Brando's role was that of Harrison Carter MacWhite, a Waspish former newspaper editor appointed ambassador to the fictional Southeast Asian country of Sarkhan who suddenly awakened to the folly of U.S. foreign policy. But what Brando the pundit had promised as strong statements against America's mindless anticommunism became muted and fuzzy in the characterization. "If the Cold War disappeared right now," MacWhite lectures, "the American people would still be in the fight against ignorance and hunger and disease, because it's right. It's right." The message was standard liberal pap; nowhere did the script have any real bite to it, since the politics of the early sixties was reduced to his character's vague slogan "Live and let live. Help your brothers because . . . it is *right.*"

As part of his campaign for the film, on April 9, 1963, Brando taped "Open End" with David Susskind, where he further established his political credentials by challenging southern senators James Eastland, Russell Long, and Strom Thurmond to discuss race relations. *Ugly American* co-writer Burdick was with him, as was Englund, both supplying their plugs for the film, which had its New York premiere on April 11. Marlon then embarked on a rare and extensive worldwide publicity tour, hitting Hong Kong, Tokyo, Honolulu, Boston, Chicago, and Washington, D.C., as well. "The amazing odyssey of Marlon Brando," wrote one Hollywood columnist, "is the town's most talked-about about-face since Garbo clammed up. The heretofore inaccessible Mr. Brando . . . is concerned about his children . . . sensitive to the many problems of the world, and feels that as a member of the human race he has a right to speak out."

During the grueling trip Marlon repeatedly railed against the *Saturday Evening Post* and also jousted with reporters as he demanded that they use the forum to pose "relevant" questions. On Irv Kupcinet's late-night show in Chicago, he claimed he would be quitting acting in two years, a bizarre enough assertion under ordinary circumstances and doubly so in light of his Universal contract. But again, no one challenged him. "Directing interests me a great deal," he told syndicated columnist Bob Thomas. "Also, I scribble. My briefcases are bulging, and I should do something with what's inside."

Not surprisingly, he continued to target the press. "If you don't kowtow," he told NBC's Hugh Downs, "when you presume to keep some vestige of self-respect and independence, you are considered an enemy of the people by Hollywood columnists and people like Dorothy Kilgallen." Gossipmongering and tabloidism, by which he also meant an avoidance of "real issues," was the enemy, he insisted, calling the tabs a "multimilliondollar industrial complex."

The strategy was clever, artful even, as the actor commingled his "new image" with the political message of *The Ugly American* and at the same time justified his ongoing libel suit.

However well intentioned, *The Ugly American* caused barely a ripple of response. Unlike anything Brando had done to date, the film was consistently bad, as dim-witted as *Teahouse* but more ponderous. Its demise at the box office may well have been hastened by its *auteur*'s outspokenness on civil rights, which in turn prompted many southern theaters to cancel bookings; nonetheless, the homilies that lay at its core contributed to its failure. Self-righteousness all but smothered the film's imagery. Visually it was a mess—anemic, academic, and worst of all, boring.

Even so, by the start of the sixties, liberals had little doubt that American foreign policy was bankrupt, and so the picture was "correct." The Berlin Wall, the Cuban missile crisis, the fact that Vice President Richard Nixon had been nearly trampled by angry demonstrators in Venezuela and Peru during a goodwill tour of South America in 1958—none of this could be ignored, just as the U.S. government had backed despots like "Papa Doc" Duvalier and Juan Perón.

All of this, then, like Brando's imminent involvement in civil rights, put the actor on the side of the angels, at least for any number of critics fed up with Doris Day and John Wayne. The reviews were anything but mixed, so fawningly supportive as to buttress the conservative canard that a left-wing conspiracy exists in the media.

"Whatever professional dishonor he may have suffered for his *Bounty* role should be wiped out by the solidness and vigor of the performance he gives," wrote Bosley Crowther in the *New York Times*. "Brando is at the top of his form when the script and George Englund's direction are most firm and plausible." "One of his best performances," chorused the New York *Daily News*. Even while conceding that *The Ugly American* was flawed by "stylized, mannered, and artificial acting," the *New York Morning Telegraph*'s reviewer, Leo Mishkin, urged his readers not to miss it.

More than a decade would pass before columnist Shana Alexander capped the lovefest by asserting that no American had done more "to reduce injustice in this world." At the time, only Andrew Sarris caught a whiff of what was happening, at least with the film itself. Sarris wrote that the entire film was "designed to make Brando the center of attention at all times." Second- and third-rate actors had been cast so as to offer no competition. Sandra Church, Broadway's original *Gypsy,* could be eclipsed on-screen, he observed, simply by Brando's "breathing," while the Japanese actor Eiji Okada, in the key role of Sarkhan's indigenous revolutionary, was so deficient in his command of English that he was hardly able to get through his lines.

The implications of Sarris's read were significant. In the past there had been Brando's upstaging of Frank Sinatra, Glenn Ford, Anna Magnani, Richard Harris, and even Anthony Quinn in *Zapata!,* but this was different. Here, his overshadowing of minor players amounted to domination, even bullying, far more than a simple ego trip. It was so blatant that it mirrored the very imperialism and colonial mentality he had loftily set out to expose in the film itself.

In explaining his arduous publicity tour as well as his libel suit against *The Saturday Evening Post* to Art Buchwald, Marlon had added a second rationale to his new accessibility: "I have kids growing up now. . . . The children made me realize I have a duty to perform."

How many children, exactly, he did not say; nor was it clear what duties as a father he actively did "perform."

Marlon simply came and went, making irregular visits to Coldwater Canyon to see his sons. Kashfi would drop Christian off, but since Brando was frequently a no-show the Ruysseveldts found themselves having to baby-sit the five-year-old, who struck them as a disturbed, hyperactive "little devil" who rarely took orders. Often he broke apart cigarettes and strewed tobacco all over the floor. Starved for attention, he stalked the kitchen, pinching Cécile or nibbling the centers of deviled eggs and leaving the half-chewed egg whites scattered on the counter.

"We thought he was a little brat," Cécile admitted, "and also cruel. We had to hide the dog whenever he came over. He had a toy bow and arrow, not the kind with suction cups but pointed plastic arrows, and he'd try to shoot him, a Saint Bernard named Toto." Ray agreed that Christian was unruly and spoiled. If Ray tried to discipline him when Marlon was visiting, the boy would simply whine for his father: "I would tell him, 'You do that again, kid, and I break your bow, I break your arrow. You understand?' " Ray recalled. "And then he'd cry, *'Daddy!'* so Marlon would come to see what was happening. I would explain and all he would say to Christian was, 'You cannot do this,' in a very nice voice."

Movita, Ray added, took no real interest in Christian but she made sure that Miko toed the line. "Miko was the center of her life," said Ray. "She insisted on discipline. Marlon didn't interfere."

Along with baby-sitting, the Ruysseveldts also had to keep the refrigerator stocked—a full-time job in itself, since whenever Marlon arrived he often headed straight for the kitchen and "stuffed himself," sometimes eating half a cheesecake, a pint of ice cream, or both in a single setting. So uncontrolled was his intake that the Ruysseveldts had come to the conclusion that one explanation for his irregular appearances was that he was trying to keep himself acceptably thin for the camera. His threshold, they knew, was 200 pounds. Many times, however, Ray guessed that he weighed over 240.

"Movita was telling us to put locks on everything, including the refrigerator," added Ray, who one morning was horrified to find huge chunks ripped out of the center of a fresh round of Brie. Thinking that the rodentlike teeth marks meant that either vermin or the young Christian had chomped away at it, he went to Movita, who had another explanation. "That's Marlon," she said. "He comes at night. He's a night raider."

Marlon often borrowed Ray's 1951 Pontiac and donned his "big Onassis sunglasses" and a large floppy hat. The attempted disguise had precisely the opposite effect. So strange did he look that the outfit only drew more attention to himself and his forays were usually disrupted by avid gawkers. Still, his appetite overcame his desire for anonymity, and in his ridiculous getup he often drove off for late-night snacks with Movita at his side. "They would go to a little stand somewhere—East Hollywood, maybe near the freeway," Ray recalled. "Movita would come back fuming. 'Marlon did it again!' she would say. 'He ate six hot dogs!' "

The phone orders to Hazen's, the market that catered to the stars, reportedly amounted to $3,000 a month, which Brando's accountants, Gadbois Management, paid directly. They also dispensed Movita's monthly allowance of $5,000. "That check, though," recalled Cécile, "went right into her savings account. I think what she was doing was putting the money away for the day that they would split."

She was also helping out her own family, said Philip Rhodes, who, along with Marie, stayed in the guest house while looking for a place to live. "Often she ordered food from Hazen's and had it delivered to her mother and sisters in the barrio," he explained. "She knew all along that the house, with the maid and butler, was transitory—that it was all a front to allow Marlon to tell the court he had a stable home to bring Christian to. So she was getting what she could get out of it while she could."

While Kashfi continued to keep her distance from Coldwater Canyon, she would often phone looking for Marlon, sometimes yelling, "This is Anna Kashfi. Get that son-of-a-bitch over here!" If he happened to be around, Brando would take the call in his private bedroom, while Movita, at poolside or in the kitchen, would turn to the Ruysseveldts and tell them that Kashfi was "crazy" and that she was drinking.

For all Marlon's eccentricities, however, Ray and Cécile found him to be a cordial, undemanding boss who could take a practical joke, even those lampooning his weight. He had been equally good-natured the afternoon he nearly sliced off his big toe with a hatchet while playing gentleman farmer. "He had some trees that he wanted to cut down," recalled Ray. "So he bought hundreds of dollars worth of tools, more than he was paying us in a month. Then he went whistling into the yard. Five minutes later he came back in, white and pale. In French he politely told Cécile to call for a doctor. All the while he was bleeding on the floor."

He had shown neither emotion nor pain, but never touched the tools again, Ray added. The incident had been caused by his nearsightedness, which had now become progressively worse, so that he would stumble around like Mr. Magoo if he didn't bother to use his contacts. Once Cécile played a practical joke and had him blindly biting into a piece of plastic cheese that she had set out on the counter.

• • •

While juggling his busy personal life during the spring and early summer of 1963, Brando was also back at work filming the ironically titled *Bedtime Story*. Even though the project seemed absolutely wrong for Brando, he really had no other choice. Not only was Universal insistent that he honor his five-picture contract, he also needed the money. Besides, when Brando had signed on, the studio had offered another inducement: In addition to the actor's $270,000 salary, Pennebaker was to receive 10 percent of the profits, a modification of the original Universal contract that would also be extended to the remaining three films he owed the studio.

Given the palpable vulgarity of Stanley Shapiro's script, this is the most likely (if not the only) rationale for his agreement to attach himself to such farcical material. While some Brandophiles like Stanley Kauffmann defended Marlon's performance, and even Bosley Crowther called him a "first-rate farceur," most critics dismissed Brando as a comic actor. As Molly Haskell pointed out years later, there was only one interesting and "significant" scene in the movie, and that was when Brando's character tries to seduce a young woman by telling her that he is paralyzed from the waist down. His rival, played by David Niven, beats his legs with a cane while Brando sits and smiles, registering no pain. Noting that "here is the screen's great masochist," Haskell added, "Brando's unflinching submission to physical assault" was the comic equivalent of the scene in *One-Eyed Jacks* where his hands are smashed and he refuses to cry out."

Still, such intentional self-parody would hardly lift the movie from its inept and stumbling pace. Originally titled *King of the Mountain,* the project was also produced by Shapiro, who had brought Universal a string of profitable light comedies including *Pillow Talk*. Here, collaborating with writer Paul Henning, the producer had put together a script about two Riviera gigolos who join forces to con rich widows and divorcées. Before production began, Shapiro had reportedly sat Brando down for a talk. "I've heard some wild stories about you," said the producer. "I don't know whether they're true or not. But when we work together I'd like to have an understanding: one, that you'll be on the set on time; two, that you'll know your lines." Brando was not offended. "Look, a lot of what you've heard was not true," he said. "A lot of what you heard may be true—but I had my reasons. You don't have to worry."

Brando forgot a few lines but basically cooperated. For the most part he horsed around with costar David Niven and even appeared to immerse himself in his brainless character. The only explanation was that it was easy—that light comedy allowed him to save his energies for the more meaningful work of civil rights in which he was more and more involved and which was probably the real reason for his unusual courtship of the press throughout the shoot.

"If an actor can be influential selling deodorants, he can be just as useful selling ideas," Brando explained, adding that at least as an actor he had a ready audience for the messages he wanted to convey. His old image, he conceded, was the result of his "to-hell-with-it attitude" in the past, but the time had come to set things straight. "I haven't changed a bit," he insisted. "It's just that I go on television and be myself—and let people form their own judgments of me. I call it the true image of Marlon Brando. . . . Strangers tell me after a television appearance that I am entirely different than they had imagined."

What many newsmen overlooked was that this was more than film promotion or self-promotion. He was already becoming involved in civil rights protests and with the guidance of his old friend Harry Belafonte, was starting to organize Hollywood's liberals to travel with him in August to join Martin Luther King's March on Washington. Brando's involvement was real; spotty and inconsistent like most of his commitments, but undeniably sincere. He had already suffered from the southern boycott of *The Ugly American,* and his outspokenness would do nothing to help *Bedtime Story's* box office when it was released nearly a year later in June 1964.

In the midst of completing the movie, however, Marlon was also busy putting out another fire in his personal life. The previous summer Marie Cui had still been in Los Angeles, a frequent visitor at Frenke's and also continuing her affair with Brando. As she later told her friend, Mallory Jones Danaher, she and Marlon had decided to have a baby and she had gotten pregnant deliberately. Brando had been happy, Cui insisted, and even paid for obstetrical care by his own physician. She gave birth to a daughter on February 27, 1963, and after registering her name as Maya Gabriella Cui Brando, Cui then went to the Philippines to be with her family for several months. But hearing nothing from Brando and receiving no financial support, she flew back to Los Angeles with the baby.

On the flight back she made a stopover in Hong Kong and ran into a few friends at a restaurant. Catching up with one another's news, she told them that she just had a child. Before she could finish her announcement, the friends remarked on the coincidence that another friend of theirs had just had a baby, too. "And guess who the father is?" they added innocently. "Marlon Brando!"

Cui had no idea who the other woman was. It could have been one of the Tahitian dancers from *Mutiny,* or even Tarita, whose son, Teihotu, had been born on May 30. But whoever the new mother was, Cui was furious and immediately boarded the next plane to Los Angeles. As she later told Danaher, she "took a taxi directly from the airport to Marlon's, walked into the house, and slapped him in the face." Since the actor refused to acknowledge the child or give her financial support, on July 19, 1963, Cui had him served with a court subpoena while he was in St. John's Hospital in Santa Monica suffering from an alleged case of "acute pyelonephritis, a kidney and pelvic infection."

Marlon's first reaction to the publicity and lawsuit was to blame Philip Rhodes. In the first of several disputes—periods when the actor routinely banished his friend and makeup artist—he accused him of talking to the press about Cui, leaking information that "only [they] could know." Because Philip and Marie now lived on the same street as Cui, and because Philip was also a friend of Frenke, Marlon took the two facts as indisputable proof of betrayal. Yet, "in fact, it was Frenke who got his own lawyer to sue for Cui," Rhodes later insisted, pointing out that Frenke had planned the arrangement as a stratagem for getting "inside information" that would ultimately be to the actor's advantage. Marlon was eventually convinced that Rhodes had nothing to do with prompting Cui to sue, but he remained suspicious. One night he dropped by Movita's to find the Rhodeses there for dinner. Once again he started to complain about the misinformation he thought Philip had passed on to the writer of the piece.

"I thought he reported it very well," Movita piped up, a grin on her face. "It was beautifully done, just the way I told him."

"Marlon looked at her in amazement," added Rhodes, "as if a monkey had just typed out *Hamlet.* He couldn't believe that she had done it. After that we were on good terms again, but he never apologized to me or said he was sorry for causing all the trouble."

Nevertheless, Brando still had Cui's lawsuit to contend with. On August 1, 1963, he reported to court in Santa Monica before Judge Edward Brand (by now a familiar face, since he had presided over several of the Brando-Kashfi custody hearings). Cui was seeking temporary support of

$775 a month for herself and her daughter until the case was decided. In her petition she alleged that Brando's doctor had delivered the baby, that the actor had paid all costs for the delivery and prenatal care, and that Brando had once remarked in her home before witnesses that "the child is probably mine."

On August 6 Judge Brand dismissed the suit after blood tests indicated that Brando was not the father. The furor refused to die, however, when Cui's lawyer provided the press with details of a relationship stretching back over the past seven years, including the dates of meetings in Manila, Kyoto, and Los Angeles as well as an account of the actor's strange nocturnal phone habits. Pointing out that Cui "wasn't intimate with any other man during the period of conception," her attorney left further room for speculation, stressing that it was California law to accept blood tests as accurate and conclusive, even though "Miss Cui still insists vehemently that no other man could be the father of her child."

In spite of the suit, Brando and Cui's on-and-off love affair continued throughout the following years. Danaher also insisted that Cui regularly received checks from Marlon's accountants and that Maya "was raised to believe that Marlon was her father." In 1981, Danaher added, Brando paid for Maya's schooling in Paris and told her that "she was now allowed to use his name."

His largesse, in and of itself, proved nothing, but friends noted that this, too, conformed to his usual pattern. When forced to do something, Marlon's immediate response was to dig in his heels. Given the opportunity to show generosity, kindness, and charity on his own and without duress, Brando could be the most responsible man in the world.

With the close of the paternity hearing, however, the headlines had once again broadcast his philandering reputation. Movita took it all in stride. Day to day her relationship with Brando was calm but aloof. They would sometimes sit outside in the garden, and at best their conversations were flat and listless. "As husband and wife Ray and I would fight, make love, fight again," Cécile explained. "But with them they were more like couples who have stayed together for thirty years, maybe because of the children. That was why when I first came to work, I thought they'd been together a long time. I didn't know that they just had gotten married."

Ray, more direct, called it a marriage of convenience, necessitated by the arrival of Miko. There were some infrequent and unpredictable nights when Brando showed up and would insistently knock on her bedroom door, but she usually refused to let him in. "She'd tell us, 'He was at my door banging again,' " recalled Ray, adding that her usual explanation was, "I had a headache."

The sexual coolness between the two was apparent not only to the Ruysseveldts but also to friends and intimates. One acquaintance had remarked that in the early days of their relationship, the couple's sexual passion had been like "two trucks colliding," but now it was more like two ships passing in the night. Movita seemed to accept the situation with equanimity, and even raised no fuss about Tarita, whom Marlon was now flying back and forth from Tahiti on a fairly regular basis. Still, the irony of the arrangement did not escape her, and she jokingly referred to having played the Tahitian girl in the 1935 *Mutiny on the Bounty* with Clark Gable. "Movita was the first Tarita, and she was replaced by the other Tarita, and she laughed about it," said Ray. "She could have a bad temper, that Mexican temper, but about this she would just roll her eyes and shrug."

In any case Movita had her own outside romance. She had taken up with an Irish actor, "a good-looking guy who drank like a fish," said Ray, explaining that even when the couple stayed out until four, five, six o'clock in the morning, upon their return the Irishman would demand, "Gimme a whiskey." Having seen photographs of Movita's first husband, Jack Doyle, Ruysseveldt and his wife found it uncanny that the new man in her life was the spitting image of the Irish boxer.

During the autumn of 1963, Ray and Cécile decided that their increased workload merited a raise. (With Marlon often failing to visit and with Movita out on the town, they frequently found themselves baby-sitting both Christian and Miko.) They had already approached their contact at Gadbois Management, but had been turned down cold; when they broached the question with Marlon directly, he too refused, explaining only that he was sorry to see them go. He seemed to respond to them with the same aggrieved sense of being "taken advantage of" that Philip Rhodes and others had noticed in the past. The same thing had been evident when he had rejected a Pennebaker secretary's request for a raise of $5 a week.

According to Ray, however, Marlon's refusal of their request might have been prompted by another motive. Ray felt that their employer seemed to be looking for a reason to let them go, since "he was jealous of our closeness to Miko." More and more the three-year-old had become dependent on the Ruysseveldts—especially Ray, who at times seemed to have assumed the importance of a surrogate father. Despite the language barrier (Miko spoke only Spanish at this point), the boy gravitated to Ray, and Brando's long absences made it more pronounced. The couple would usually retreat to their room to watch TV after working hours, but characteristically Miko tapped on their door, wanting to stay with them. Even if Marlon was in the house, he still clung to the Belgian couple. "It was kind of embarrassing," said Ray. "When Brando finally got around to picking him up, I almost felt like saying, 'Gee, thank you.' "

The situation was getting too complicated for Cécile as well. "Miko needed a father, but Marlon didn't come too often, and at the end he was coming less and less," she explained. "We had no children and I was getting very fond of the boy, too."

In fact, the day the Ruysseveldts left, Miko wanted to go with them. "Bye, Mommy," he said to Cécile with tears running down his face. Movita was crying, too, as the couple pulled out of the driveway.

If the setup at Movita's house lacked a semblance of family unity, Anichka sometimes tried to make up for it, apparently enjoying the opportunity to play the role of matriarch—despite her ambivalent feelings about her "stepson," Marlon Jr. Given her family background and her competitiveness with her well-known father, she seemed to take a certain delight in her connection to Brando celebrity. Once, she and Brando Sr. were in an elevator, both uncharacteristically dressed in leather motorcycle jackets. Another passenger wisecracked, "Who do you think you are, Marlon Brando?" A look of triumph crossed Anichka's face, and pointing to Marlon Sr., she replied, "Well, yes, actually he is." Although she undeniably had reservations about Marlon Jr., she went on to become friends with Jocelyn. She also cultivated a friendship with Movita and took a great deal of interest in Christian and Miko. "She was especially close to Miko," observed Louise Monaco, Frenke's secretary, "and part of that was because she disparaged Marlon as a proper father, that he was miserable to his kids and didn't treat them right."

According to Monaco, Anichka often said that Marlon Jr. was doing with his children what he did with his wives and the other women in his life. Either they were "in" or "out," and it was a form of manipulation never to let them know when they were in his favor. "With his children,"

Monaco added, "it took the form of whether they were going to be allowed to come and stay with him. Or sometimes he would send them lots of presents, but other times he wouldn't do anything and just disappear. That was why Anichka was very concerned, especially as Miko got older. She thought he was going to be a fucked-up kid."

For all her disparagement, she made her annual Christmas and New Year's Eve parties into family affairs, inviting the entire Brando clan. However, she and Monaco, who handled the invitations, soon realized that if Marlon were explicitly invited, he would fail to show up, but if his name was left off the guest list, he was sure to make an appearance. "Definite pattern, that was the joke," recalled Monaco. When Marlon did decide to come, he would also invite "his satellites," as Nebenzal put it, including Wally Cox, Sam Gilman, and Lis Hush. But on these occasions Marlon himself usually arrived alone, and then, after a brief tour of the party, he'd take off, leaving Gilman and the others to hold down the fort. Anichka seemed particularly aware of Marlon's moods. One Christmas she told one of her friends, "You've got to be prepared. If Marlon's quiet, he's dangerous. Watch out. As long as he's saying, 'Fuck this, fuck that,' he's fine."

Even more striking was the difference between Marlon Sr. and his son, and the obvious strain between them when they were in the same room. At Anichka's gatherings they remained cordial but distant, either circling each other warily or staking out opposite corners of the room. The father was still heard to remark that his son "seemed the most unhappy person in the world," and Bud continued to make his contempt for his father quite evident.

It seemed clear that even at this late date, their differences hadn't been resolved. Probably more important, neither father nor son recognized their similarities, especially the primitive, childhood sense of loneliness and betrayal that each had felt in his own way. Jocelyn sensed that her father was mellowing with age. "When he was over sixty he began to realize that he was getting old," she said. "I think he wanted to get close to us, but by then it was really too late. By that time we didn't care. . . . [There was] too much water under the bridge, especially with Bud, because Papa had been much sterner with him."

Marlon Jr. still had not been able to get over his deep resentments, yet his father, in his own fashion, was equally guilty. Perhaps defensive that he had to depend on his son for a job, the elder Brando continually tried to prove his superiority by hitting the jackpot with various "investment schemes." His past disasters in cattle and land investment seemed not to matter at all, nor did his recent failures in gold mines as well as a cannery business in Mexico. Still grasping for the brass ring, he was searching "to find a place for himself," said Seltzer.

On one occasion he introduced Harold Nebenzal to a man who could supposedly help Frenke and Nebenzal market a silicone serum invented by a mutual friend in Japan for use in breast enlargements. Another scheme involved launching a shrimp-farming operation in South America, a so-called opportunity in which Marlon Sr. uncharacteristically invested "$5,000 or $8,000" of his own money. Similar projects included reopening abandoned mines in the Rockies and developing a diagnostic "black box," a device that when passed over the body was supposed to vibrate in the presence of disease or malignancy.

If Marlon Sr.'s pie-in-the-sky hopes for financial success seemed naive, so did Marlon Jr.'s attitude toward his own career. Marlon was still stuck with having to make three more films for Universal. No alternative offers were coming his way. "After *Mutiny, Ugly American* and *Bedtime Story,* his record was a disaster," said Seltzer. "The talk around town was that he caused films to go way over budget, and even worse than that, he was no longer considered box-office magic. The luster was gone. He was out of gas, and it was evident to him as well as everyone else."

Morituri

During the early months of 1964, Marlon returned to Tahiti several times to see Tarita and their son as well as to check on the continuing negotiations for his purchase of the twelve-islet atoll of Tetiaroa. The hope of a new life in the South Pacific did not buoy his spirits, however, burdened as he was by his lingering film commitments and the failures of his recent productions. Even before he could begin to fulfill his contract with Universal, he had another "command performance" to make: As the final installment of his decade-old debt to Zanuck and Twentieth Century–Fox, incurred when he had walked off *The Egyptian,* he had been forced to sign on for *Morituri.* That film was scheduled to begin production in the summer of 1964.

The Saboteur: Code Name Morituri, as the movie was originally called, should have been a brisk, lightweight World War II thriller; instead, the simple cloak-and-dagger adventure yarn set aboard a Nazi steamship became a drab vehicle burdened by waterlogged direction and an incongruously heavy subplot, and not even Brando's German accent kept it from a watery grave. Film historians would laud it for Conrad Hall's photography, and little else.

When Brando had originally agreed to do the film, it was widely assumed that he was chasing an easy paycheck. As he himself conceded, "I need the money. . . . I have three households to support and I pay alimony to two women." Yet *Morituri*'s screenwriter Daniel Taradash sensed that Brando wanted it to have more significance.

"He phoned me, impersonating character actor Akim Tamiroff," Taradash recalled. "He said something like, 'This is terrific!' He was actually anxious to make the picture, because he saw it as some great attack on anti-Semitism, an important statement for the Jews."

This theme was somewhat in the original script, but ultimately that "wasn't the reason to make it," said Taradash. "It wasn't a message picture, it was an adventure story. Marlon, though, took it seriously for a long time. Whether he was taking it seriously once the picture got under way— well, that was something else."

Unbeknownst to the screenwriter, *Morituri*'s added attraction for Brando was the producer Aaron Rosenberg. Rosenberg's compliance on *Mutiny* had already shown that when push came to shove, Brando held sway.

The plot of *Morituri* revolves around Brando's character, Robert Crain, a self-indulgent German pacifist who has been hiding from the war in far-off India. Confronted by Trevor Howard, a British intelligence agent, Brando's layabout initially refuses to be recruited. But eventually drawn into the fray, Crain accepts an undercover assignment: He is to impersonate an SS agent, board a freighter transporting a valuable cargo of wartime rubber, and working alone, deliver the ship into Allied hands by defusing its scuttling charges. Crain the outsider finds a heavy-drinking soul mate in Yul Brynner, the ship's German captain, who is also skeptical about the war. Their bonding is odd, even "metaphysical." It is further complicated by a fleeing Jewish refugee, played by Janet Margolin, who is under constant threat of being violated by the low-life crew.

Brando, Taradash knew, had been heartened by the choice of German director Bernhard Wicki, a follower of Max Reinhardt, whose lean, documentary-like antiwar film *The Bridge* (1959) suggested intelligence and artistry beyond the usual Hollywood style. As their script conferences continued, however, the screenwriter noted a change in Brando's attitude. For several weeks they had been meeting at Brando's home, starting usually around eleven o'clock or noon, often with Rosenberg present. While the arrangement ensured Marlon's attendance, he was often late and had taken to wandering in aimlessly, only to curl up on the couch "in a fetal position," said Taradash. Occasionally he might interject, "Oh, I don't like that line," but more often than not he'd just shrug. Knowing that Brynner was slated for the other lead, he also insisted on playing his part bald: "Let Brynner wear a wig," he threw out during one conference, expressionless as he held Rosenberg's incredulous stare.

"Was he kidding? I was never totally sure," said Taradash. "No, I think he really meant it."

Although Brynner had dubbed Fox "Sixteenth-Century Fucks," he had nevertheless agreed to do the film because he needed the money as much as Brando. He did not even carp about taking second billing to the star with whom he had crossed paths at least once before—in the forties, when Brynner's then-wife, Virginia Gilmore, had appeared with Marlon in *Truckline Café*. Whatever their exchanges or contacts at the time, or during the intervening years, the two had long since decided never to lock horns, "even if," as Brynner's son put it, "they were not close friends."

There were rumors, however, of anticipated friction between two strong egos. At the studio's inaugural press conference, the actors entered from doors at opposite ends of the room, and then fifty feet apart stopped and angrily glared at each other. After a dramatic pause, they roared with laughter, embraced, and did a little jig together.

Only once did Brynner flex muscle during *Morituri*'s production. Since almost all of the film's scenes take place aboard ship, a 10,000-ton World War II freighter had been rented in Nagoya, Japan, and sailed to Catalina Island, where the first month of principal photography was to start in September 1964. Brynner then demanded that a landing pad be built on the ship's fantail so that he could helicopter to shore after each day's shoot. Brando became equally adamant that he have the same perk.

"Both of them had it in their contracts that at six P.M., whether they were in the middle of a take or not, the helicopter would arrive and they could leave," cinematographer Conrad Hall explained. "The crew became annoyed, because even if the light was perfect, Brynner would get in his helicopter and leave." The on-set scuttlebutt, according to Hall, was that Brando was also sticking to this hard-and-fast schedule as his way of getting back at Fox for "shitting on him in the past."

The six-week location shoot consisted mostly of straightforward action scenes, but even so, once they got going, Brando soon sank into one of his "moods." In between takes he would retreat to his cabin dressing room and bury his face in a pillow. One afternoon he ran amok and trashed his quarters. On the set he barely disguised his mounting irritation with Wicki. The short, rotund director, who affected a walrus mustache, seemed more a meticulous technician than the artist Brando had hoped for. Furthermore, Marlon's relationship with young costar Janet Margolin was also tense and growing progressively worse, largely because, as Margolin herself conceded, her inexperience as a film actress and her tentative personality were no match for Brando's willfulness.

The casting of the dark-haired twenty-two-year-old had been a miscalculation from the start. Embraced by highbrow critics and the public alike for her performance as a disturbed adolescent in *David and Lisa,* Margolin had never done a full-scale Hollywood production before. When she had first read the *Morituri* script, she had thought it was "awful, stilted, and uninteresting." Rosenberg and Fox had nevertheless pressed for her— she was "New York," she represented sophistication and class—and the studio flew her to California, where Rosenberg and screenwriter Taradash wooed her with promises of the highest production values, including script rewrites. Her own agent brought his powers of persuasion to bear, too, urging her to consider "the boost" of starring alongside Brando and Brynner. The two-day campaign to win her over, she recalled, "was like that line, 'Can I put it in a little way?' It was as if I'd already spread my legs. There was no way back."

Initially Brando himself had joined in the courtship and lavished star treatment on her. Arriving at the Beverly Hills Hotel, she found that her would-be leading man had sent an extravagant bouquet, and the next evening he took her to dinner at his favorite sushi place, the Imperial Gardens on Sunset.

"I was deeply uncomfortable," she said. "Marlon had an uncanny knack for knowing exactly what one was thinking, and he responded to that in different ways, depending on what kind of mood he was in."

His first observation was that she was blushing, and more specifically, that her skin changed color as she ate. In a kinder tone, he told her about the film, but then turned more aggressive. "Women with intellects are bad fucks," he murmured. "I can tell you wouldn't be any good because you're much too uptight, too neurotic. You think too much."

Although he complained, too, that she was neither "Oriental nor Tahitian," with her dark, Semitic good looks, Margolin was not all that removed from other women in his life. Marlon himself made the leap, several times likening her to former girlfriend Ellen Adler.

Margolin became even more tense and rattled as he continued to stare at her "and said things like, 'You feel this,' or 'You want this,' or, 'You're uncomfortable, you're shy.' It was a total stripping away, and at the same time he was reassuring me—telling me about the script, telling me not to worry. That, of course, was only freaking me out more, because I knew I'd gotten the job on his approval. This was friendly, as friendly as he gets. He was capable of controlling just about anybody, any way he chose, and I wasn't quick enough for him. Me, I was small potatoes, and in way over my head."

After a few weeks of shooting on Catalina, Margolin found that Brando was only one of several problems she had to face. Although she was playing the young Jewish refugee, she was incongruously expected to wear a push-up bra under her ragged costume. Also, like her character, she was the lone woman on the remote production site except for "a drunk costume designer"; Rosenberg had told the crew to stay away from her, but his warnings went unheeded. Alone and isolated, Margolin then fell into liaisons "with people I didn't like or respect, and who made me feel even crappier than before." Miserable and lonely, she languished in the motel where she listened to Bach cantatas on her tape recorder.

During the off-hours, Brando also kept to himself, growing more remote as he confined himself to his clique of compadres consisting of Sam Gilman, Philip and Marie Rhodes, Billy Redfield, and Wally Cox, all of whom he had gotten work on the production. Rhodes was doing the actor's makeup, Gilman served as his "dialogue coach," while Redfield was on-screen in a minor role as an American POW. As for Cox, Marlon had procured him the role of an alcoholic doctor, an assignment meant to deliver a message to his old friend. After the demise of "Mr. Peepers," Wally was now unhappily married and drinking heavily. Marlon had been urging him to join AA, but Wally would have none of it and according to Cox's friends, the part was really intended as a humiliating reminder of his failure to take himself in hand.

Nevertheless, Cox's drinking only escalated on location, with Brando sometimes joining in. He shared his rented villa with Cox and Redfield, and every day the group gathered to tinker with the script, usually finishing with an afternoon of cocktails.

Margolin, meanwhile, was repeatedly thrown off balance by Brando's changing demeanor. He was "like quicksilver," she said, "one moment incredibly seductive, adorable, funny, gentle and ten minutes later vicious, insulting, frightening."

Brando's antics were not confined to her, however. Doing a scene with Brynner, he tried to see how many hard-boiled eggs he could stuff in his mouth and still get through his dialogue. He was more and more open in his contempt for director Bernhard Wicki, even while he himself was unprepared and had to resort to cue cards. In the middle of one scene with Brynner, Marlon inexplicably turned away and walked over to the porthole and looked out. "We didn't know what the hell he was doing, because this wasn't in the script," explained Taradash. "Then we realized that he was looking out at a blackboard he'd set up with his lines on it, that the porthole was just an excuse. From one day to the next, nobody knew where the hell he was going to put the cue cards. It became a joke."

As the shoot dragged on through the fall of 1964, Brando continued with his "rewrites," and there were days when he'd tear apart scenes only hours before everyone was to go before the cameras. As invariably happens, word of *Morituri*'s problems leaked out, and the *Hollywood Reporter* broke its story during the first week in November: "Fox denied weekend column reports that *Morituri* was $1 million over budget and a month behind schedule. Instead, the studio said, 'The picture . . . is only $162,000 over budget and seven days behind schedule—the latter due to inclement weather on location off Catalina Island and the breakdown four times of a 10,000-ton freighter on which the picture was filming.' "

Brando adopted his usual blasé attitude toward delays and cost overruns. "It's like pushing a prune pit with my nose from here to Cucamonga," he told columnist-turned-ally Bob Thomas. "Of course, if this picture is good, all the grief will be forgotten. But when a picture is bad, all you can do is stick a lampshade on your head and stand real still and hope nobody notices you."

In fact, Wicki was down to shooting an eighth of a page of dialogue daily, and Brando, whatever the high seriousness that he had initially professed to Taradash, did not seem to care. His relationship with the director deteriorated. Once Brynner finished his scenes and departed and the production returned to the Fox lot for final shooting, his mood was poisonous. One afternoon he even manhandled Wicki during an argument in front of the cast and crew, seeming to snap completely.

Second-unit director Charlie Maguire, who was working with Steve McQueen on *The Sand Pebbles,* happened on that scene. Elia Kazan had asked Maguire to give a tour of the studio to a prominent Polish director who was visiting the United States as part of a State Department cultural exchange; upon meeting Maguire, the Polish director had expressed his desire to see Brando, whom he had heard was on the lot. While Maguire was aware that there were continuing problems with the production, he nevertheless escorted the visiting director to stage 5, where a mock-up of the ship deck had been built. Just as they rounded the corner of the set, they saw Marlon. "He had grabbed Bernhard Wicki by the back of the collar and seat of the pants," Maguire recalled, "and he was literally throwing Wicki off the stage. At the same time he was screaming at the crafts service guy: 'As soon as he's out, close the stage door and let's roll it. Let's shoot it.' I looked at this Polish director and I knew he was thinking, This is the way American stars treat their directors?"

The next day, and the day after, no one on the set remarked on the fact that Brando could give his director "the bum's rush" without so much as a reprimand from either producer Rosenberg or from the studio's front office. Now, with Wicki gone, Marlon's behavior became even more excessive, and Margolin in particular felt the full force of his antagonism. The majority of her scenes with him had been scheduled for last, including the one in which Brando's character was to establish his Nazi credentials in front of the crew by hitting Margolin. Brando had gone to elaborate lengths to instruct her in the ABCs of taking a slap, a process that was supposed to have her "rolling with the fake blows." She was to remain calm, and then at a timed moment he would slap her, pulling the punch as she mimed her reflex. "But when we did the scene for real," said Margolin, "he whacked me a beat before he was supposed to, and he slapped me hard. I mean *hard,* and not just once." Her jaw, Margolin added, was "numb for a day, and I felt tricked. He could have said, 'Look, I'll try not to slap you so hard. Let's work on it together.' Back in New York I'd done a play with Rip Torn, but as much of an amateur as I was, he wanted to work with me and we were very much in it together. There was no together with Marlon. The slapping thing was a setup."

Although there were streams of women in and out of Brando's dressing room, he still insisted to Margolin that he was giving his full attention to rewriting and improving their scenes together "to really make them right." But then he abruptly announced that within the week he was leaving for Tahiti. " 'My contract time is up,' he said," Margolin explained. "What he was doing was forcing us to accept his rewrites even though nobody liked them."

The revisions in question were, by wide consensus, "far worse" than Taradash's original script, and one rewritten episode was particularly bizarre. In this new scene Brando had Margolin's character inciting the prisoners to overthrow the ship, but then, already raped by the Nazis, she was to be attacked by the internees as well. As a result she would become so unhinged that she would be left a latter-day Ophelia, a wandering, babbling sylph trapped in the hold of the creaking World War II freighter.

"I was so beaten down," Margolin conceded, "that I didn't even have the wherewithal to call my agents and say, 'Look, I'm not going back until something gets changed.' I didn't have a shred of self-esteem left." In fact, by the end of the picture, the actress added, she was "as close to committing suicide as I've ever been in my life, and I was driven into psychoanalysis."

The sequence was eventually cut in the editing room to a single view of Margolin's face, but looking back at the experience, the actress concluded that the episode was representative of Brando's attitude: added to the continual and often silly rewrites, his eruption with Wicki, his competitiveness with Brynner despite their public detente, and his reclusive bonding with Cox and other buddies, it later led Margolin to believe that throughout "what he'd really wanted was for us all to fail, for the movie to drown with him. At the time, though, I was too scared to be sure of that," she added. "Now I realize that there was this intense self-loathing on his part, something so bottomless that you could just feel it. He was tortured and miserable."

Marlon's intimates knew that with the completion of *Morituri* his mood was as black and embattled as it had ever been. At age forty the actor seemed on a downhill slide, and in a November 1964 interview with the *New York Times,* he was candid enough to acknowledge his past mistakes, at the same time deflecting his self-contempt to complaints about Hollywood and acting in general: "Looking back, I guess there are a lot of things I might have done differently," he said. "I've spent almost no time reading scripts—to my disadvantage. Sometimes, I've had to grab what's at hand at the last minute—instead of taking pains to choose something better. . . . I have a contract to finish some pictures for Universal, and some other projects in mind. After that, in six or seven years, who knows? . . . I'll have to do something . . . but I don't know if it will be acting . . ."

He went on to say that with the completion of *Morituri,* he intended to make an adaptation of Jean Genet's *Forbidden Dreams,* directed by Tony Richardson, and then appear in *The Deputy* for Anatole Litvak. "I don't care if *The Deputy* doesn't make a penny," he insisted. "I'd do it for nothing."

Whatever his hopes for doing more meaningful films (and both these projects eventually came to naught), his pessimism about *Morituri* seemed warranted. Within two weeks of its release in August 1965, the movie sank from sight, buried by notices that were devastating. Mainstream publications like *Newsweek,* ordinarily content to review films as entertainment products and little more, scored Brando for his self-indulgence by pointing out that while he "has his pick of directors and scripts [and] can make a picture as he pleases . . . he contents himself with patent claptrap." Pauline Kael was even more trenchant: "Like many another great actor who has become fortune's fool," she wrote, "he plays the great ham . . . as pleased with the lines as if he'd just thought them up."

While such remarks may have exceeded the bounds of standard film reviewing, they were directed less at the movie itself than at the star whose talents and standards seemed to be fading. Although Brando had tried to explain the conflicts of his art-versus-Hollywood thesis in his interview the previous November, critics perceived something deeper—not simply "artistic differences," but rather a seismic shift in his attitude that had been evident ever since *Mutiny.*

Marlon responded by flying to New York to give more interviews, starting with a press conference. To reporters' questions he replied by asking questions of his own, substituting self-deprecatory jibes and puckish digressions for anything resembling straightforward responses. With an attractive but overwhelmed female television reporter from Boston, he threw aside all restraint and took over the interview entirely. After questioning her about her age and ascertaining that she was only twenty-one, he toyed with her as she repeatedly asked to hear something from him about the making of *Morituri*:

BRANDO: Excuse me, I didn't mean to touch your ankle. What can I tell you about it?

REPORTER: Oh, if you'd like to tell us something about, oh, behind the scenes while you were making the picture, or . . .

BRANDO: How far behind the scenes?

REPORTER: Oh, just some interesting things our audience would like to hear about.

BRANDO: Well . . . Bernie Wicki smokes the worst cigars of anyone I ever knew. I hate his cigars. And . . . he smokes cigars that were made of— they got some shoes from Italian fishermen, with rope soles, rope-soled sandals, they crushed them up and mashed them around and sent them to Vladivostok. [*Publicist hands Brando a note.*] She was Miss U.S.A.! Is that a fact?

REPORTER: Yes, it is.

BRANDO: Well, I . . . I could have guessed.

REPORTER: That's very sweet of you.

BRANDO: Well, you know, it's unusual to find somebody as beautiful as you who is also a college graduate, and seriously interested in world affairs and studying law.

REPORTER: Well, I enjoyed being Miss U.S.A.

BRANDO: What year was that?

REPORTER: In '64.

BRANDO (*to other reporters*): In 1964 she was Miss U.S.A. I asked her if she was pretty and she said—well, that was a subjective opinion and she didn't really know.

REPORTER: Well, there were only six judges who decided, so I don't think that's very decisive.

BRANDO: Yes, but you went through several stages to finally arrive at the title, didn't you? So it was really more than six judges?

REPORTER: Well, six here and six there . . . and I was very honored. But Mr. Brando! Thank you so much for being our guest.

BRANDO: Good night, folks. Smoke Optima cigars.

While the farcical press conference did nothing to help the foundering *Morituri,* his sarcastic jibes were tolerated as charming Brando antics. Even Margolin herself could not let go. Having returned to Manhattan, she was aware that he was in town and she telephoned, ready to shoulder responsibility for the film's failure. Exactly *why* she called was unclear—compassion, her lingering need for approval, even unacknowledged attraction, all were possible motives—but when Marlon answered the phone, he claimed not to know who she was. "Two minutes. Totally abortive. Silence," Margolin said. "And there I was, willing to take the rap."

Either he was pulling one last ploy or he had actually managed to repress the entire experience, but eventually he apologized to Margolin, explaining that he was befuddled, and then quickly hung up. This only left the impression that the moodiness he had shown during the shoot had worsened during the intervening months.

If Anna Kashfi had been difficult in the past, during the previous year she had turned implacable, and Christian, then six, was again caught in the crossfire of his parents' war. At three he had been enrolled in a Montessori school, but in his second year he was pulled out. Shuttled back and forth between Mulholland and Anna's rented bungalow on the flats below, cared for by a succession of nannies, maids, and baby-sitters, he had been left disoriented and confused. The courts' seesaw custody decisions during the eighteen months of *Mutiny* had not helped either, and Brando himself was now aware that his firstborn son was nervous, insecure, and scared.

"We all saw what a terrible situation it had become," said Jocelyn. "Anna was always flying into temper tantrums and firing the latest nanny. It had gotten to the point where Christian never looked at anybody's face, he just went to the person wearing a white dress if he needed something. The custody battle went on and on because Bud really felt he had to save Christian's life. Anna was sick, she had an epilepsy problem . . . Still, she wasn't trying to help Christian, she was trying to get back at Bud."

In the fall of 1964, however, Kashfi and Brando had reached a short-lived truce when she did not object to his court petition for temporary custody to take Christian to Tahiti for a vacation. The trip was a sound enough idea, but then Brando made another miscalculation: Returning home afterward, he brought Tarita and their eighteen-month-old son, Teihotu, back to Los Angeles.

During her own visit to Tahiti the year before, Kashfi had actually met Tarita, but now her fury was at an all-time high when she heard that Tarita and the baby were installed at Mulholland. Once again the unstable former wife went over the edge. On December 7, 1964, she was found comatose from an overdose of barbiturates and was rushed to the UCLA Medical Center.

Brando was immediately awarded temporary custody of Christian, and left him at home with secretary Alice Marchak, while he went off to the *Morituri* set at Fox. Later that afternoon, according to Brando's subsequent court declaration, Kashfi discharged herself from the hospital, "broke into [my] house, assaulted and struck my secretary, threw a table through the plate glass window, and ran off with our son." Soon Brando arrived with his attorney, Allen Susman, and two private detectives at the swank Bel Air Sands Hotel, where she had taken the boy. As they removed Christian from the suite, Kashfi ran after them in her nightgown and robe, barefoot and screaming. Confronted with the court order for the boy's return, she lost control in the hotel lobby and slapped three people, including a policeman, until she was subdued and arrested for assault. On December 9 she was ordered to return to court. Her admission that she had attempted suicide prompted the judge to rule that she could see her son only in the presence of an attorney. Sobbing in the courthouse corridor, she gave an impromptu press conference to assembled reporters.

"I've spent six years alone in this country fighting studios and fighting Mr. Brando," she said. "I have been beaten. I have been knocked on the head in front of my child. . . . If you're stymied, you almost go out of your mind. . . . Above all I want my child back. . . . In fact, the other night when he was taken from me by four men who burst into my room, my son screamed, 'I don't want to go, I don't want to go.' "

In his petition for custody, Brando had already claimed that Kashfi kept a loaded revolver in her home and was "capable of doing great physical harm to herself and our son." In the next hearings—in January and February 1965—the battle heated up and the latest chapters of the Brando melodrama were narrated in detail in newspapers and tabloids coast to coast.

Marlon Brando during rehearsals for *Julius Caesar*, 1953. *Courtesy Mrs. Joseph Mankiewicz*

Brando, in an overstylized publicity still for *The Wild One*. *Photofest*

Brando and his parents, with Sam Spiegel (*second from left*), *On the Waterfront*. *Archive Photos*

Brando in *Teahouse of the August Moon*. *Photofest*

Marlon Brando and Anna Kashfi. *Photofest*

Marlon and Christian Marquand, Paris. *Paris Match*

Marlon Brando mugging for the camera, Hollywood, 1958.

Marlon Brando and Marlon Brando, Sr., arm in arm, Hollywood, 1958.

Brando with Anna Magnani, *The Fugitive Kind*, 1960. *Photofest*

Marlon Brando and Walter Seltzer, on the set of
One-Eyed Jacks.

Rita Moreno. *Photofest*

Wally Cox with Marlon Brando on the *Morituri* set. *Collection Pat Cox*

Jocelyn Brando with her brother, between takes of
The Ugly American. Photofest

Brando with Alice Marchak at Los Angeles Airport, returning from *Mutiny on the Bounty*. *Photofest*

Brando in *Candy*. *Photofest*

Marlon Brando as the Godfather. *Photofest*

Marlon Brando, Pat Quinn, and Bob Dylan on the *Appaloosa* set. *Courtesy Pat Quinn*

Alice Marchak was called to the stand and stated that the nearly two-year-old Teihotu was Brando's son born out of wedlock. Dr. Gerald Labiner, Kashfi's physician, testified that he had diagnosed her as an epileptic with "a wide, swinging personality—episodes of deep depression to normal elation, all with hysterical overtones." Further medical detail was provided by Brando's doctor, Robert Kositchek, who said he had treated Kashfi on five occasions at her home, when she appeared to be "confused." A former tutor for the boy added that she had often heard Anna threaten suicide as far back as 1959, and once, the witness said, Kashfi gave a Seconal pill to Christian, "but I told him to spit it out."

Other bizarre scraps of information came directly from Brando's testimony, including his explanation that he married Kashfi "with the primary purpose of getting divorced within a year."

At the end of the proceedings, Superior Court Judge Laurence Rittenband ordered that Christian be put in the care of Brando's sister, Fran, for a six-month "cooling off" period. Kashfi, he ruled, was to undergo treatment with a neurologist and see a psychologist appointed by the court, and he warned that any further violation of Brando's temporary custody would cost her whatever chance she had for custody in the future.

Kashfi recalled storming out into the corridor and exclaiming to the assembled press that her son was "being given away to a woman I don't even know." She fired her attorney, whom she suspected of collusion with Marlon, then hired and fired two other lawyers within a month. But all of her petitions to overturn Judge Rittenband's decision were rejected, and Christian was sent to stay with Fran and Dick Loving.

On March 6, 1965, Marlon and Alice Marchak brought Christian to the Brando family farm in Mundelein, Illinois, to live with the Lovings and their three daughters. "Like Marlon, Fran and I thought of the farm as a sort of haven," Richard Loving explained. "Fran was teaching elementary school, we were low-key, living in the country, and into this structure came this little bolt of dynamite. Christian was almost seven and an absolutely wild child. He was incredibly aggressive and a real manipulator, in every situation sizing up who had the power, which person he had to win over. He wasn't destructive of property but he was very rebellious, and I think he got into some fights at school."

Fran wrote regular letters to Judge Rittenband to report on Christian's progress, both in school and in the family environment. She conceded to the judge that neither she nor Dick had "anticipate[d] the degree of Christian's emotional disturbance, nor the amount of disruption that it would cause in our ordinarily calm household." Their daughters were at first upset by the boy's "gratuitous hostility" and "to be spit at and kicked and called names and have their hair pulled out was almost too much."

The boy seemed most surprised, Fran explained, that "we like the people we know (our friends, the teachers, shopkeepers, household help, carpenters, etc.), that we don't hate any of them, haven't fired any of them, or gone to see lawyers." Christian spent the first several weeks "testing . . . to see how angry we would get with him, with the other children, and with each other" and was "visibly relieved" when situations passed "without fighting, screaming, or throwing things—all of which, he told us, happened around him before." He finally asked Fran and Dick if they ever fought, and they explained that the most fighting they did was to become annoyed occasionally. According to Fran's account, Christian said, "That's *good*—I hate fighting."

In Fran's letter to the judge of July 24, 1965, she put her finger on what seemed to be his basic problem: "He has been subjected to a great deal of arbitrariness and whim in his short life—probably an inevitable result of constantly changing hired help." He still had difficulties relating to his classmates, she added, coming on too rough or aggressive, sometimes physically hurting them or making them cry with taunts like, 'God is going to kill you!' or 'You're going to get put in jail.' "

In exchange for the Lovings' surrogate parenting, Marlon financed the construction of an addition to their small Illinois farmhouse, at the same time having buddy Bob Hoskins oversee the construction. (Later, Marlon had a room built in the barn, where he would stay when he came to visit the family.) During Christian's six-month stay, however, he made only a few appearances, although he phoned regularly.

"Much as I love Bud, in certain ways he was kind of an incompetent father," Loving added. "The nature of his position and his own personal stresses made it very, very difficult for him to be a father. The life he was living, the number of women—there was no constancy there. Kashfi wasn't very steady, either, so Christian was deprived of any stability."

By necessity Brando's travels to the farm had to be scheduled around the shooting of *The Chase,* Marlon's next movie, which was being filmed during the spring and summer of 1965. During his sporadic visits, he often slept long hours and, according to Loving, seemed "very depressed." Joining the others in the family living room, he would take "the most comfortable chair, or make himself more comfortable with an assortment of pillows." He was also eating huge quantities of food—two chickens at a sitting, and going through bags of Pepperidge Farm cookies—while at the same time constantly joking about extra poundage, not only his own but also that of his sister Fran. Once, while driving back from town, he insisted that his brother-in-law get out of the car and pose for a snapshot in front of a roadside sign. "The sign read, LOAD LIMIT FIVE TONS," Loving recalled. "He had me get on my knees, supplicating. The picture was for Fran, this image of her husband begging her to stop gaining weight. The irony was that Marlon had already had to wear corsets for a couple of films."

On one of his visits Marlon showed up with Tarita, but within three hours of their arrival, Brando was on the phone, rounding up Bob Hoskins for a night on the town in Chicago.

"It was sort of appalling," Loving said. "Bob came out with his car and the two of them drove off to eat a 'proper meal' and pick up some women. Tarita was just left there. I remember her standing out in the field bordering the house, watching the sun go down—her back, her long hair, gorgeous, silhouetted against the sunset, an almost painterly vision of a sad, wistful girl." On another visit Marlon brought Rita Moreno for a few days; the two of them stayed at a nearby motel instead of the house. Moreno seemed eager to be involved in family activities. At the dinner table she was affable and gregarious—in dramatic contrast to Tarita, who sat through meals without saying a word. "I sensed that Moreno was much more social and overt," recalled Loving. "Tarita seemed more withdrawn, like a displaced person going through traumas."

Although Marlon had won the previous round in court, the fight for permanent custody of Christian was far from finished. In July 1965 Brando had been called by the prosecution as a material witness in Kashfi's trial for her December assault on the policeman. (Initially Marlon had ducked the subpoena, Kashfi recalled, siccing his Saint Bernards on the marshals who had arrived with the summons, but eventually he was required to appear.) He testified that he knew Kashfi suffered from "psychoneuroses, which at times caused hysterical blindness . . . [and] a psychological and physical addiction to barbiturates, alcohol, and [from] tuberculosis." The jury found Kashfi guilty, and she was fined $200.

At the end of the required six-month stay, the boy returned to California, noticeably calmer and less disturbed, although he apparently made up a story of the Lovings' burying an effigy of Kashfi while telling the boy, "Your mother is wicked. She has to be buried deep down," an event that on the face of it seemed highly unlikely. Kashfi herself seemed to have stabilized, and in October 1965, at the couple's next hearing, she regained full custody of Christian. While she had been on her best behavior, Brando was still married to Movita and living with common-law wife Tarita, an arrangement not conducive to court approval.

Now it was Marlon's turn to erupt. He accused Judge Scott of courting publicity and pandering to the press, calling the decision "barbarous." Kashfi, he inveighed, was "cruel" and "violent," and dependent on drugs. To close friends and relatives like Fran, who had been at his side in court, his pain at losing Christian was palpable.

The Chase

If Brando seemed depressed during his visits to the Mundelein farm in the summer of 1965, his mood was no better on the set of Arthur Penn's *The Chase*. He had begun the picture in the spring with ample reason to hope it would pull him out of his downward spiral, but his high expectations were soon thwarted. He had signed up for the film in April 1964, happy at the prospect of working with *Waterfront* producer Sam Spiegel, with whom he'd always had a boyish, macho rapport; the cast, too, was solid, made up of Robert Redford, Jane Fonda, Robert Duvall, Actors Studio alumni Janice Rule and E. G. Marshall, Angie Dickinson, and James Fox. Jocelyn was to have a part as well, thanks to Marlon's direct request to Spiegel. (Spiegel had Marlon bring Jocelyn to his office, where he offered her the choice of two roles. Later Marlon told her that she'd selected the wrong part, because she would "end up on the cutting-room floor.")

The biggest draw had been director Penn himself, largely because he was anything but mainstream Hollywood. Well regarded for his Broadway productions of William Gibson's Tony-winning *The Miracle Worker* and *Two for the Seesaw,* the short, wiry New Yorker was known as a director who *liked* actors. Kim Stanley, Mildred Dunnock, Anne Bancroft, Howard da Silva—he had, he said, "collaborated" with them all. Different from Hollywood's stock-in-trade technicians, Penn thought of actors in almost existential terms: courageous and gutsy, ready to strip themselves of inner feelings in order to deliver authentic emotion.

For Brando *The Chase* also held every promise of being a meaningful picture because of Lillian Hellman, whose politics had lent the script a cutting-edge slant: JFK had been assassinated only two years before, and now in the summer of 1965, as the actors were about to stage mock mayhem in a Hollywood back-lot reconstruction of a racist Texas town, the real thing was destined to explode in Watts but fifteen miles away.

Unhappily, for all its talent *The Chase* would prove chaotic to its core—a blend of *Peyton Place* and *High Noon* whose bits and pieces never jibed. "Schizoid . . . a potter's field of banalities," *Newsweek* claimed after its release in early 1966, while Bosley Crowther and Pauline Kael, respectively, called it "a phony, tasteless movie" and "a liberal sadomasochistic fantasy."

The sources of the problems were many, but for the most part, Penn laid the blame on producer Sam Spiegel. Prior to starting the film, Penn had told Spiegel that because he had a commitment to direct on Broadway after the production wrapped, he hoped to do the editing in New York. But while the director was on the East Coast, the high-flying, always-on-the-make Spiegel snatched Penn's footage and edited it on his own in England.

"What happened was that the center of the film moved out of my hands and clearly into Sam Spiegel's hands," Penn claimed years later. "By that point Spiegel and I were speaking mostly through the editor, but I was a babe in the woods. I didn't know from fancy Hollywood fucking. When I came to London from New York, I saw eight reels of the picture, finished and scored. It was the performance Marlon had given, but stripped of all his improvisation. It was like, 'You want the scene? Here it is, as written. This is the dialogue.' "

For all the responsibility laid at Spiegel's door, both for the rewrites and later editing, the shooting of *The Chase* had its own problems, exacerbated by the dynamics that were established among the actors and in response to Brando's presence. During the early days of production, which extended through June 1965 and included two weeks' night work, Marlon remained on best behavior. Significantly, he had told Penn that he was determined to reverse the damage done to his reputation by *Mutiny*. "He didn't want it to be taken as a representative experience," the director recalled, "and as he reported it to me, what had happened was that he'd been stiffed by the studio, absolutely screwed. Knowing Brando, I would say that this would be the most dangerous thing to do to him—to promise, then to lie, not to keep your faith. The probable outcome would be a war, with a kind of savagery."

Penn himself would suffer exactly the same kind of retribution at Brando's hands ten years down the road with *The Missouri Breaks*. Yet now Marlon's "genius" kept the director spellbound. As the decent southern sheriff going against type, Brando had arrived on the set and slowly made it his own, calling to mind the same sort of inner preparation Kazan had seen on *Waterfront*. "He'd move this here and that there, and pretty soon it was *his* place, *his* environment," said Penn. "The other actors—actors of no small accomplishment themselves—stood around literally in awe while he worked."

Penn remembered a particular scene in which Brando and Jane Fonda were to have an exchange: "We'd done the two-shot in which both of them were on camera. Marlon was there off camera, feeding back to her the lines that he'd already performed, and in the middle of the take he came up with a new idea, something so extraordinary that Jane stopped in the middle of her take, looked at him, and exclaimed, 'You're the best fucking actor in the world!' "

All Brando had done was change the rhythm and inflection of his lines, and by ordinary standards, his affect was "inappropriate," Penn added, "like laughing at something serious, the kind of thing we all do in life but none of us dare to do with dialogue."

At the root of Brando's spontaneity was his refusal to be daunted by the camera, the director said: "I know of no other actor who doesn't concern himself with the mechanics here, but he had this bravery, like, 'I'll just do what I need to. I'm not concerned whether it's usable or consistent.' It was like unleashing a jungle creature in a confined place." Because Penn recognized that Marlon's capabilities were there at all times, he set up two cameras—one close-up, the other to do a wider shot—and filmed with both of them at the same time. "That liberated him," added Penn. "It allowed him to rely on his sense of play without boundaries."

One offshoot of this *kinderspiel* was the actor's gusto in the staging of what now seemed the requisite beat-up-Brando scene. But this version pushed movie bloodletting traditions even further than his whipping in *One-Eyed Jacks*. Brando came to Penn with his ideas for the shoot. "Have you ever been in a fight?" he asked the director. "You remember how bloody and startling it was? Let's put a fist in my face but shoot it ever so slightly faster, then faster until we find the right speed. Then we'll know how to perform it."

The technique was to speed up the camera so that upon playback, fewer frames were exposed for each second of elapsed action. The effect was a slow-mo, but one that had never been used with this result before. Penn would later be criticized for the graphic violence in *Bonnie and Clyde,* but the style, as well as the thinking behind it, started here. Brando's position, according to the director, was "If we're going to show this kind of beating, it's got to be the objective correlative of the film as a whole. We're mirroring a complete reversal of authority, the beginning of mob rule."

Critics would later take Brando to task for his blood lust, pointing to how he insisted on more and more makeup from Philip Rhodes. But his fascination with the beating scene wasn't simply excessive. He was trying to deal with what he considered a significant problem in the interpretation of his role.

His character's actions, as originally conceived, are meant to reverse those of the stereotypical sheriff in traditional westerns. Instead of re-storing order to a lawless town, the character's choice in *The Chase* is to withdraw from the conflict. Yet Marlon was well aware that the fires were already burning in the streets of Watts. *Real* social battles were being fought, ones from which he felt he, like any responsible, concerned citizen, could not withdraw. His role in *The Chase* had caught him in a dilemma: Acting, as he pointed out to Penn, was ultimately "irrelevant and nonfunc-tional"; in contrast, he felt that as a man of conscience, he was compelled to engage in the civil rights issues of the day, even while he was playing a character whose message was contrary to his own beliefs.

With political activism dominating the national consciousness in the mid-1960s, the split between acting and activism was bound to deepen for Brando. He had already marched on Washington with Martin Luther King and participated in local California pickets to end discrimination, and now he attended a number of fund-raisers at Penn's house and at the Newmans'. He also appeared at public meetings under the auspices of CORE and the Southern Christian Leadership Conference. Yet the dilemma in which he felt trapped would grow into something much deeper than politics, much broader than the traditional conflict between art and social consciousness.

Brando's problems worsened as Spiegel continued to tamper with the shooting script, inserting what many in the company (including Penn) regarded as rewrites of his own intended to goose the movie at the box office but which served in fact to destroy the story's original spine. In response to Brando's complaints, the producer only derided the actor's need "to pseudo-torture himself to function." For Brando, however, the money-versus-art issue raised by Spiegel's interference was classic. "Fuck 'em," was his response not only to Spiegel but to the studio. "If they're going to be so stupid, I'll just take the money, do what they want, and get out."

On the set the change in attitude was immediately apparent. Rather than continuing as before, he started to "casual it," creating delays during setups by turning from his makeup mirror and, with the production staff waiting, bantering with Philip Rhodes. "Five to go yet—at least," he remarked one day, clapping both hands across his burgeoning gut. Rhodes, in a Shakespearean baritone, replied, "Oh, that this, too, too solid flesh would melt!"

"It won't!" Brando said, burning up more of Spiegel's budget with a grin.

Yet there was also "a kind of liveliness and cunning," Penn said, that could come over him when he and the director had long discussions about how to play a particular scene. In such circumstances he could turn meditative, serious, analytic. "Our discussions could go on for two hours," explained Penn. "He had a lot of passion about it, going at it from different angles, trying to show me what a scene would look like. It was a pretty good con job, but it was intended as a con job, and Marlon is one of the best con artists in the world." Penn himself recalled Marlon's observation of this. "One afternoon he said to me, 'You know what I see as your characteristic gesture? Raising your shoulder, shrugging in a gesture of helplessness.' And I said, 'Really? That's a terrific gesture for a director.' It was jive, but it stayed with me," Penn added.

The director may have been more vulnerable than most others, since actors would continue to notice a laxity about him, even a vacillating temperament when it came to making decisions on the set. Later, when Penn directed *Bonnie and Clyde,* it was generally accepted that it took Warren

Beatty's decisiveness to bring out the best of Penn's talent. Brando, however, did not have that toughness, and indeed seemed to be playing off of Penn's passivity for his own reasons.

Unhappiness with the film and his working conditions seemed only the half of it, however. Extended discussions about his role may also have been a sign that he was worried about his own abilities as an actor. Psychoanalyst Margaret Brenman-Gibson became aware of just how rampant and unfocused Brando's dissatisfactions were when she visited the set to interview the actor for her biography of Clifford Odets.

Odets, the celebrated playwright of the proletariat, had been at the center of the Group Theatre circle and friends of his like Harold Clurman, Stella Adler, and Bobby Lewis had helped launch Brando's acting career in New York. However, Marlon had never really known Odets during that period, and it was only later, when Odets moved to Hollywood, dismissed by serious theater people for having "sold out" to do hack work in movies and television, that the two spent much time together. He had always admired Brando and was genuinely pleased when the actor called him or came by for a visit.

After Odets was stricken with cancer, Marlon had spent an evening with him and Elia Kazan in January 1963. Kazan felt that Odets's evident suffering and imminent death seemed to affect the actor profoundly. During their visit Brando had suddenly opened up, confessing his own despair and hopelessness: "Here I am, a balding, middle-aged failure. . . . I feel a fraud when I act. . . . I've tried everything . . . fucking, drinking, work. None of them mean anything. Why can't we just be like—like the Tahitians?"

Brenman-Gibson, a psychoanalyst at Harvard Medical School, had known Odets through her husband, playwright William Gibson (Penn's frequent collaborator). She had also become the executor of Odets's literary estate. Never having met the actor before, Brenman-Gibson went to Brando's trailer, where he greeted her half-undressed—shirtless, and in his underwear.

"Were you and Clifford lovers?" he asked her almost immediately.

She told him no, and he asked, "Why not?"

"Well, I wasn't that attracted to him, nor I guess he to me," she replied.

"Well, do you find me more attractive than Clifford?"

Brenman-Gibson concluded that Marlon "had started to make his move," and, she conceded, "like any other woman in her right mind, I was attracted to this man. Not unqualifiedly, though, because I sensed that I was at the very end of a very long line of women who all had let him know, 'Hey, just say the word.' I don't go for that too well.

"There are casual lady-killers and serious lady-killers," she continued. "The casual lady-killer is a person who doesn't try to involve you in a relationship but seeks to get you only by the magnetism of his sexuality. A serious lady-killer has much more imagination and tries to capture you in more intricate ways—meaning that he involves you with his ideas, his thinking. The seduction is much more complicated—only then, he has more trouble because women inevitably fall in love with him."

Brenman-Gibson soon found that Marlon was a combination of both: casual because he had moved so fast, but serious when he began to speak at length about Odets. "He gave me one of the most beautiful, literary interviews," she recalled. "It was literary in the sense that his gift for language was marvelous. He said something like, 'Clifford gave me the feeling that life at the end is just a question of nasty fluids going out.' There was a lot of stuff like that, and it just bowled me over. It was what I was looking for, and it felt very original, although it may have been the language that was so original and not the ideas.

"In any case, there was a big bed in the trailer, and I couldn't concentrate: One, I was aware that this was Marlon Brando, and, secondly, because he was so good at seduction. Given the halfway compliant audience that I was, I was complicit in getting him off the track."

The seductive atmosphere of the trailer was just for openers. Later in the week, after running into Brando at a large party where he was surrounded by Movita, Philip and Marie Rhodes, and Wally Cox, she was invited to dinner at Mulholland. This would turn out to be a smaller gathering of "six or eight," including Arthur and Peggy Penn, Judith Bernstein (the wife of screenwriter Walter Bernstein), Christian Marquand, and, as the psychoanalyst recalled, "a redhead, a friend of the Penns, who was courting Marlon madly."

They were sitting around drinking, while Marlon was sending out flirtatious signals to both the redhead and Brenman-Gibson. "Everybody had gotten quite looped," she said, "and the next thing I knew, I found myself alone with Marlon in his bedroom. Then, suddenly, he asked, 'By the way, how's Bill?' "

Marlon had already expressed his admiration for *Two for the Seesaw* and *The Miracle Worker*. But his abrupt remark, Brenman-Gibson said, "was a little number. He was saying, in effect, 'Hey, sister, you're about to betray your husband. Aren't you ashamed?'"

"Well, that wasn't really what I had in mind but I was also angry," she said. "Because it was a very unfriendly thing to do, to pursue it to that point, to set it up and then go *whoosh!*, even though he then asked if I didn't want to stay the night. I realized then that this little boy *had* to be extraordinarily charming, funny, seductive, energetic, and lively so that he could establish control. Anybody who needs to be that controlling must have felt very early on that he was on the receiving end. So the victim becomes the victimizer, the abandoned one the abandoner whose security depends on controlling every interaction."

They then returned to the dinner table, but Brando continued his games.

"How many people in this crowd consider themselves liberated?" he asked his guests.

Hearing unanimous assent from the group, he announced, "Well, let me tell you what we're going to do. We're all going to take our clothes off for dinner."

He turned to each of his guests for their agreement, but Brenman-Gibson shook her head. "Count me out," she said.

"It didn't have to do with modesty, it was vanity," she explained. "I didn't feel like sitting naked next to Judith Bernstein, who had an exquisite body, or Peggy Penn, who's also lovely, slender, and young. Plus, there was the redhead."

Her refusal seemed to spur Brando on.

"Oh, come on, Margaret!" he said with withering sarcasm. "You call yourself a free soul?"

"Well, yes, but I don't think this has to do with my lack of freedom," she objected. "It feels potentially humiliating."

By then everyone except Margaret and Peggy was undressed. Marlon still wasn't satisfied and continued to tease Brenman-Gibson, taunting her for being an intellectual snob, and having two houses in Massachusetts (one in Stockbridge, the other on Cape Cod, in Truro) and living only among artists, writers, composers, and psychoanalysts.

Several times the other guests interrupted trying to deflect him, but he was relentless, and Margaret grew increasingly upset. "It was ridiculous," she said. "Here I was, a grown woman, a psychoanalyst, and he had reduced me to tears."

With Brenman-Gibson weeping, Marlon rose from the table. He was stark naked, and he now grabbed a lily from a nearby vase. The last thing his guests saw as he grandly left the room was the lily sticking out of his bare ass.

Brenman-Gibson didn't meet Marlon again for many years, until she encountered him at an antinuclear fund-raiser in Manhattan. There she found him surrounded as usual by a drove of admirers, but when she went to him to say hello, he pulled her down on his lap.

"You know something, Margaret, I still love you," he said, giving her what she felt was "a friendly, nonpredatory kiss." Then he whispered in her ear, "I would have been in better shape if you'd been my analyst."

Brenman-Gibson had been aware of Marlon's unhappiness while filming *The Chase*. Fellow cast members, however, were so intimidated by the Brando legend that they seemed to play right into his hands. Jane Fonda was among his chief conquests. She remained in awe of his technical mastery, but even more captivating was his political intensity, the anger and righteousness with which he infused his role. Although Fonda had not yet made her controversial trip to Hanoi, at twenty-seven she was already emerging as one of Hollywood's most vocal politicos. America's involvement in the war in Southeast Asia, civil rights, and the plight of Native Americans—all were on her agenda. In a sense, Brando was her role model, the definitive *artiste engagé*. There was their family connection, too, and if the echoes of Omaha were not enough, they had the additional tie of Jane's recent marriage to French director Roger Vadim, one of Christian Marquand's oldest and closest friends and once Brando's roommate in Paris.

Janice Rule, also an Actors Studio alumna and old New York friend, was another Brando loyalist. The East Coast cast as a whole had by now taken an us-versus-them stance in relation to Spiegel and Columbia, and Rule's fidelity to Marlon was reinforced by her marriage to Ben Gazzara, another Lee Strasberg protégé. Penn was aware of these connections and also smart enough to use the constellation of loyalty and enthusiasm, in effect to build a pyramid with Brando at the top. Even Celia Webb, Marlon's former fiancée who had suddenly popped up in L.A., was on the payroll as his personal secretary.

Nobody blinked an eye at the visits to his trailer by female cast members as well as girlfriends of cast members and the usual array of groupies. It was standard star stuff, predictable and unworthy of note, but a more serious and indeed telling encounter involved Pat Quinn, a twenty-eight-year-old actress then living with cast member Richard Bradford. Half-Irish, half-Colombian, Quinn had accompanied Bradford from New York after Penn had cast him as the redneck mob leader who beats Sheriff Calder nearly to death. But she was more than an appendage; Quinn had studied with Stella Adler and Lee Strasberg and had appeared in several plays on and off Broadway—and Penn had offered her a small part in *The Chase* as well. Still, it was neither Bradford nor the job that had brought Quinn to California so much as being "on a mission," as she explained. "At fourteen I'd seen *The Men,* which for me was the Truth. It was real, it haunted me. I determined at that time that I was going to be the one to push Marlon Brando around in his wheelchair."

In May 1965, when Penn brought his actors together for their first run-through and Quinn confronted Brando face-to-face, she found herself torn between her idealized, adolescent fantasy and her sense of a man on the make. Penn went around the table, introducing everyone, but skipped right past Quinn. "Arthur and I had known each other from CBS when I was doing typing for him and Fred Coe on 'Playhouse 90,'" said Quinn, "so *why* he wasn't introducing me, I didn't know. Maybe he was playing, maybe it was just an oversight. But suddenly somebody put their hand on my head, which forced him to say, 'And this is Pat Quinn.' The hand, of course, belonged to Marlon."

As the reading proceeded, Quinn, reading lines for an absent Angie Dickinson, soon came to a Greek name that she had trouble pronouncing. She repeated it carefully, sounding it out syllable by syllable, only to be interrupted by loud laughter. As the hand had been Brando's, so too the guffawing. "There I was, very nervous, and here he was, laughing, and I do mean *loudly,"* she recalled.

This was just the opening round, and over the next three weeks his campaign escalated. He was "constantly coming on to me," Quinn said. "He was flirting but he was also overt, asking me to go home with him, wanting to fuck me. And already Philip [Rhodes] was calling me 'Princess Pat,' and I was telling Richard that it was getting really hard for me to keep turning Marlon down.

"Marlon puts you on, he puts everyone on," Quinn summarized. "It's a smile, it's a look—he knows exactly what he's doing and exactly what effect he's having. We're talking the king of control here. He uses people like chess pieces."

Marlon had set his sights on taking Quinn away from Bradford, and as the days rolled by, he was "pouring on" the sex appeal. "It was looks, laughs, pauses, the whole thing," she said. But each time he made an overture, Quinn told him, "Forget it."

Five or six weeks into the shoot, however, when they were filming an evening scene, he came up to her and said bluntly, "What about tonight?" This time Quinn replied, "I have to think about it." She walked around the square in front of the set's courthouse several times, then returned to him.

"Of course," she said simply.

After everyone had been let go for the evening, she followed his directions and around midnight drove up to Mulholland. Arriving at his house, she was surprised to find him drinking in his bedroom with the columnist Bob Thomas, who was out from New York to stay with the actor while researching his biography. The first few minutes seemed "very pleasant," but suddenly Brando turned to her and said, "You know, you're going to have to fuck us both."

Thomas's mouth dropped open. Without a word Quinn went out to her car. Marlon came running after, apologizing. "It was just a joke," he insisted. "Please come back in."

She followed him inside. "My big mistake, right there," she said later with a laugh.

Thomas had already retreated to the guest quarters. Brando led her back to his bedroom, where there was a roaring fire in the fireplace. From the phono came the romantic strains of the Jackie Gleason Orchestra, with soaring instrumentals like "Shangri-La."

"He was a very, very sensual man, a very giving partner," Quinn recalled. "I felt I was with somebody who really cared about my enjoyment, and also he was obviously experienced. I did not feel I was being used. It was a shared experience."

Nevertheless, after they had made love, Marlon turned to her and said, "Do me a favor. Go tell Bob that you were in on the joke."

She dutifully complied, but returning to Brando's room, she refused his request to spend the night. She felt that the evening's events compelled her to tell Bradford what had happened. Arriving home, she found him waiting and explained where she had been.

"I'm a one-man woman," she said, "and I feel I have to move out."

"No, you don't have to leave," she recalled him saying. "I understand. All actors want to fuck Marlon, even if they don't admit it."

Quinn moved anyway, and began receiving Brando's telephone calls; when she was out he'd leave messages, tagged with his code name, "Martin Bumby." Their routine often included driving Philip Rhodes home from the set of *The Chase,* then stopping for milk shakes en route to Mulholland Drive, where she frequently spent the night. In his bedroom she noticed a framed photo of Dodie atop his bureau, and repeatedly he told her that she reminded him of his mother and also of his sister, Jocelyn. Equally beguiling, he spoke of his days at Shattuck, boasting that he had burned the school's bell tower. This was fiction, but it had the effect of drawing her in further. Indeed, Brando was soon urging her to move in with him.

"I thought he felt about me the way I felt about him," Quinn said, "but I soon realized there was another girl, someone by the name of Florine. He called us 'Hoé' and 'Pitou'—Tahitian for One and Two, and he wanted both of us up there with him. Besides Tarita in Tahiti, he wanted Hoé and Pitou in the Mulholland house which wasn't my idea of heaven. I was hurt, but I kept it to myself."

On a later occasion she found him at the house with yet another woman, "a blonde who was somebody else's girlfriend." Quinn donned a kimono, made tea, and shuffled into the bedroom like a little Japanese housekeeper while he was romancing the new woman in front of the fireplace. Brando started laughing. "I don't think she can handle this," he said aloud to Quinn, who left immediately.

"I didn't see him for a while, even though he kept calling," Quinn said. "My part in the film was over, but by then I'd discovered that he was also making it with everybody in his trailer—people in the cast, whatever. More conquests, like me. What I hadn't understood is that Marlon has his own theory of morality—that it's just a set of rules imposed by others."

Quinn's insight was further confirmed several weeks later at a party Jane Fonda gave for *The Chase* cast. Christian Marquand, who had been in town for several months to find backers for his film of Terry Southern's cult novel, *Candy,* was there. "That's when I realized that it was open season," said Quinn. "Marlon wasn't paying attention to me and Christian was, so I went home and slept with him. But it didn't bug Marlon. The two of them had been swapping women anyway. That was their game."

While aware of the two men's sexual competition, she was in the dark about the extent and nature of their friendship. Although their behavior might not have seemed unique in the sexually liberated sixties, their relationship and "games" went back fifteen years. Marlon considered Christian one of his loyalists, even though the stylish Frenchman could sometimes be snide about Marlon behind his back, telling Quinn that he considered his good friend "a peasant in silk stockings."

When *The Chase* had finally finished, Brando seemed to be even more withdrawn and depressed. His weight was fluctuating, sometimes by as much as twenty pounds, and he was having trouble sleeping despite what his friends were describing as a growing dependence on Valium.

Even with Marquand's presence, Brando needed more attention. In the same vein he used Christian, he turned back to Quinn, calling her nightly for "the news along the rialto"—by which he meant not industry gossip so much as debriefings on the action he was missing along Sunset Strip.

"I was doing shows like 'Gunsmoke,'" Quinn recalled, "and also seeing a lot of other actors and actresses, listening to Motown, to the Byrds. Jim Morrison was playing at the Whiskey. I was hanging out, and he needed to know what was happening. I was his pipeline to the street, so he would check in late at night. But he also used the calls to fall asleep," she added. "We'd talk for two hours or so, sometimes longer, while he wound down, and finally I'd hear him snoring into the phone."

Marlon's depressed mood, his anxiety-driven insomnia, and his withdrawal to his bedroom were understandable: Not only had *The Chase* drained and disappointed him, but also his father had died a few months before. Early in June 1965, Marlon Sr. had been diagnosed with a melanoma on the back of his hand. Both Marlon Jr. and his father knew that despite radium treatments, the cancer was terminal and inoperable. When Marlon Sr. checked into the hospital for the last time, he was "stoical," but his son himself was "visibly shaken and concerned," said Walter Seltzer. "It was the most compassionate I'd ever seen him be. He was subdued and attentive—there were frequent phone calls, visits, flowers, and he and Anichka formed a closeness that hadn't existed before." Marlon Sr. died six weeks later, on July 18, 1965, in St. Vincent's Hospital in Santa Monica. In his obituary he was described as "a successful businessman" whose "one regret was that he gave his name to his famous actor son."

As his father had instructed, there was no funeral. The body was cremated, and Brando reportedly scattered the ashes over the fields at the Mundelein farm. He had initially told Fran and Dick Loving, "Poor Pop has cancer," but hadn't seemed "that upset when he was originally diagnosed," said Loving. Then Brando had kept them informed of his decline. "He used to phone and say, 'Pop's very sick, Pop's real bad,'" Loving added. "There was a kind of matter-of-factness about it, until finally it was, 'Pop's going,' then it was 'Pop's gone.'"

Making the arrangements to send Marlon Sr.'s ashes to the farm, Marlon encountered the California law that prohibited private citizens from shipping ashes out of state to anything but a cemetery. His answer was to address the ashes to "Penny Poke Cemetery," Mundelein. "We thought that was slightly amusing," said Loving. "I remember going out to our little rural mailbox one day, and there was the box of ashes. I shook the box and thought, 'Here is Marlon, coming home.' About three weeks later Bud showed up. After our usual big dinner, he pulled back from the table and said, 'Well, I think I'll go out and spread Pop's ashes around.'"

When Loving had shaken the box, he had heard slight rattles and realized that among the ashes were the remnants of his father-in-law's bones. When Marlon picked up the box to take the ashes outside, he heard them, too, and both he and Dick "did a double take." At the time, the Lovings had a collie that would bolt for the door whenever anyone went out. "Suddenly we had this vision of the dog going after Pop's bones and chewing on them," added Loving with a laugh. "So I held the collie back while Bud went out and sprinkled the ashes in the field."

The atmosphere had been neither solemn nor grieving, as Loving recalled. "There was a kind of dumb animal sympathy for his father," he explained, "but I don't think Bud was touched that deeply. What I remember most of all about our conversation that evening was that Bud was worried about his own chances of getting cancer."

Anichka and Marlon remained on friendly terms as she mourned the death. "For a while she played the grieving widow," recalled Louise Monaco. "But then she went into a period when she was really drinking again. Then she finally admitted to me that she was glad he had died, that she thought both Marlon Sr. and his son were 'shits.' She was receiving some kind of yearly income from the Pennebaker pension, maybe ten or twelve grand a year. But she was unhappy with Marlon Jr., because she felt she wasn't getting the money that had been agreed to."

Brando himself never spoke about his father's death, even to close friends. Still, the event must have deepened his sense of loss and hopelessness during these months. When *The Chase* was released, it was reviewed as an interesting attempt that not even Brando, this time surrounded by interesting actors, could elevate from its redneck sensationalism. To make matters worse, he was already mired in two more Universal projects, *The Appaloosa* and Chaplin's *A Countess from Hong Kong*, films that would only accelerate his fall.

The Appaloosa

With Marlon Sr. gone, Brando must have viewed his commitment to Universal as all the more ironic, since it had in part been structured to provide his father with a secure income. *The Appaloosa* was Marlon's third picture for the studio, and more than confirmed Bob Thomas's prognostication that with the Universal contract Marlon "had climbed in bed with his one-time agents, men with an obviously greater regard for commerce than art."

His experiences in his previous two movies had only increased his disdain for studio moneymen and hacks. Still, he was in no position to argue with Universal executives, and it was no wonder that he approached *The Appaloosa* with antagonism. His mood had been apparent when he summoned the picture's screenwriter, James Bridges, to his home in early May. Bridges had been writing for Alfred Hitchcock's TV show, but this was to be his first feature film, and he drove up to Mulholland with some trepidation.

"I was twenty-eight years old and scared to death," Bridges explained. "At Universal I had been told that he wanted to do the movie and that he liked the script. But in fact he hadn't read it. There had also been talk that he had to fulfill a certain commitment that he had at Universal, so I think I had been set up. But he was very friendly to me, I must say, except he was also very rough on the script, basically telling me that I didn't know anything about American Indians and that he would never kill an Indian in any film that he was in. 'Politically immoral' was the term he used. He gave me forty books to read on the Indians that he had stacked up, saying, 'Read this before you do any more writing.'

"He was playing with me, just as he always tries to see if he can get your back up," Bridges continued. "He was testing me to see if I had any smarts about the movies, if I was a total sellout already. Then, as we walked out to my car, he said something to the effect of, 'I haven't said anything nice about your script, but if I didn't like it, you wouldn't be here.' "

Confused, Bridges wrote to his friend and mentor, Salka Viertel: "I have had only one meeting with him and found him snakishly clever, totally vague about what changes he wanted in the script . . . and in a dim way, brilliant. . . . But Salka, I am scared to death of him. . . . He made certain suggestions, demanded certain things, mainly *messages . . .*"

Producer Alan Miller told Bridges that Brando had wanted Kazan to direct, but apparently Kazan was not returning phone calls. George Stevens had been interested but was now too ill to handle the assignment. After studying movies then in release, Marlon settled on Canadian-born Sidney J. Furie, whose espionage thriller *The Ipcress File* had made a star of Michael Caine.

Drawn by the Brando magnet, Furie signed on even though he, too, wasn't thrilled with the script. "There are very few scripts that are terrific ever," said Furie, "but here it was a deal at Universal put together by Jay Kanter, and they said Brando went along with it. The script was good conceptually, but in terms of action and structure it wasn't exciting enough. James Bridges was ready to go to work on it, though, and so was I."

The story line follows Matt Fletcher who, after his Indian wife is murdered, pursues the Mexican bandit who has stolen his horse. The story was no *Bicycle Thief,* but Furie, then thirty-two years old, had seen every picture Brando had ever made and was willing to gamble in order to work with the actor he so admired.

At their first meeting at Universal, Furie initially found himself in awe of the man he considered America's number one star. He also noticed that the actor looked heavy and "not in very good shape."

"Why do you want to do *this*?" Brando asked abruptly, referring to the project in a derogatory tone.

"Because I want to work with you," replied Furie.

"Don't give me that fucking bullshit," said Brando with a cynical laugh.

In retrospect, Furie acknowledged that he probably should have taken a different tack: "It was as if he couldn't believe that I'd be thrilled to work with him. So maybe I should have said, 'Look, I know this isn't great material, but it's a western, it's got a good core, it's got you, and we'll make it into something.' That, or I should have just left. He couldn't have respected me for agreeing to work on such material."

Buttering up Brando wasn't the key to winning him over either, as Bridges would also learn from director Sydney Pollack in an anecdote that made Marlon's self-contempt explicit. "Sydney told me that he and [director] Mark Rydell and Marlon were playing pool at somebody's house," recalled Bridges. "Rydell put up the cue stick and said, 'I have to go home.' Marlon said, 'Why?' Mark said, 'I'm directing a television show and I've gotta go prepare.' Marlon said, 'Why?' Mark said, 'Because I want it to be good.' And Marlon said, 'Why?' Mark replied, 'Because I want to be a success like you.' Marlon then said, 'Lemme tell you something, Mark. There's *nothing* up here.' "

Even this early in the script process of *The Appaloosa,* it was clear that the production would be troubled. As with *Morituri,* its star had script approval, and his power already had the others intimidated. At script conferences, Furie said, "it wasn't a positive 'Okay, let's try to do this. What if the character did this?' Instead, it was like, 'What can we get by Brando? What'll he buy?' And before Jim Bridges, Alan Miller, or I knew it, we were worried more about what he'd accept than the right thing to do."

Brando remained adamant about including his "messages." When Lew Wasserman and Universal tried to change the title to *Southwest to Sonora,* Brando had become "incensed," insisting that the studio keep the original title. "Marlon, I was told, hired some mariachi players," said Bridges. "They wrote a song called 'Southwest to Sonora' and strolled around Universal singing it until the studio said, 'Okay, for Christ's sake, okay, we'll change it back to *The Appaloosa.*' "

More troublesome to Brando than the material was the bland, Pollyanna outlook of producer Alan Miller, a former MCA agent turned independent producer in the Universal buyout to whom the studio had assigned *The Appaloosa*, his first feature. Seltzer had already warned Miller to "be careful," that Marlon could be "difficult," but Miller had announced confidently, "Don't tell me about Marlon. I know how to handle him."

"Alan made the mistake of trying to pump Marlon full of happy times," said James Bridges. "He was one of the sweetest, clumsiest men you've ever met, and this picture almost destroyed him. *The Appaloosa* was the last film he ever produced, because he was made so unhappy by the way the studio, and Brando, treated him."

The actor had his entourage surrounding him, and here, too, he exercised his clout. Not only was Marquand in attendance, but Brando wanted Marquand's wife to play the slain girl, and she was tested for the part. Similarly, Miriam Colón, the Puerto Rican actress from his New York days whom he had cast in *One-Eyed Jacks,* was hired, along with friend Rafael Compos. Naturally, Philip and Marie Rhodes were also aboard, which, indirectly, led to a heightening of tensions when Rhodes started experimenting with Brando's makeup during the first few days of shooting.

"He was supposed to be Mexican," said Rhodes. "So I made him up the way he thought a Mexican should look. I was always one for prosthetics, artificial teeth, artificial eyelashes, suck his cheeks in, bring his cheekbones out. I thought he looked fantastic. But he also wanted a mustache, which unfortunately made him look like Charlie Chaplin."

The next day Rhodes received a call from a Universal executive.

"What the fuck did you do to Marlon?"

"It's not my fault. I just take my directions from him," said Rhodes. "That's what he wanted, and he's fallen in love with how he looks."

"Well, now it's your job to talk him out of it."

But neither Rhodes nor the studio could prevail on Marlon to change how he wanted to appear in the role.

"The studio thought his face had gotten lost," added Rhodes, "so they changed the script—turning his character into an American in Mexico. That way the studio could control the makeup."

"The studio said he looked like Genghis Khan," agreed Bridges. "He had a big mustache, which was his vision of what he wanted this half-breed character to look like, and they told him he couldn't wear it. Marlon was so pissed off that he then threatened not to wear any makeup at all."

Brando also nixed Furie's suggestion that Pat Quinn play the female lead, which Anjanette Comer was slated to have. He told the director that he would back out if Furie persisted in the idea, claiming, "I won't work with anyone I'm emotionally involved with."

"When he told me that, I was so angry I kicked him in the shins," Quinn said. In a rage she left town to visit her parents in Panama but soon returned with a peace offering, an ocelot that she gave to Marlon to add to his growing menagerie of dogs and cats up on the hill.

But soon enough her relationship with Brando became complicated again. She was staying at a hotel on Sunset when a friend, the son of a famous acting teacher, visited. He was "high on acid, freaking out, and then walked through a plate-glass window," said Quinn. Police were summoned, but discovering a bottle of pills in her room, they arrested her. "In Panama I'd been driven to the airport by a friend," she explained. "He had very tight pants on, and he had asked me to hold this bottle of Dexamyls, which down there are legal." After she was released by the cops that night, Marlon called, again playing general.

"Don't talk to the press, whatever you do!" he barked into the phone. "Just come up here as soon as possible."

When she arrived, he was out by the pool on the far side of the house. He abruptly picked her up and threw her in, clothes and all. His explanation—that she was in "a state of shock."

Quinn's response was characteristically divided. "I thought he was showing me the way, like a teacher," she said, "but I also knew it was just another number." Even so, several days later she agreed to accompany him to the hospital to visit Wally Cox: Cox had recently returned home to find his wife with her lover, who beat him so badly that he had suffered a concussion. By visiting Cox, Quinn realized, she had once again become entangled in Brando's life, and she pulled back again. Late that summer she decided not to drive to Utah to visit him on location and instead remained in Hollywood.

Upon first meeting director Furie, Marlon had promised to shed twenty pounds, and as a result of disciplined dieting, he was fairly trim in August when he and the crew assembled at Burbank Airport to leave for location. On the commercial flight to Las Vegas, from where they were to drive to St. George, Utah, however, his strict regimen went to pieces.

The flight attendant came down the aisle with bread and butter on a tray. Marlon reached for a slice, then stopped and pulled his hand back.

"Atta boy, Marlon! Atta boy!" exclaimed Miller. "Stay out of the bread and butter."

Marlon looked at Miller, then called the attendant back, taking several slices and telling her to bring him more. During the flight he continued to shove one slice after another into his mouth, each time turning back to Miller and Bridges to show them what he was doing.

After the plane landed, Bridges, elated by the prospect of beginning production, struck up an effusive conversation with Brando. "Marlon

Brando in my first film! Marlon, I can't tell you how excited I am," he exclaimed.

"You won't be," Brando said with a smile.

Just as Marlon had found allies in Fonda and Penn on *The Chase*, Bridges became the anointed one on this set. No sooner had the group arrived in St. George than Bridges received a phone call from Alice Marchak, inviting him to Marlon's for dinner. This was only the first of many such invitations—he ended up eating with Brando almost nightly—but he soon realized that a pattern was being established from the outset: Miller and Furie were to be excluded from the gatherings, which often included Philip and Marie Rhodes, Marchak, and Paul Baxley, a stuntman who was Alice's boyfriend.

Bridges later described his sense of a developing relationship with Brando in a letter to Montgomery Clift's close friend, Jack Larson:

> *Marlon never talks about the script or the picture, but last night I got a bit drunk and we had a serious talk. He said that I was the only one on the picture who hadn't bullshitted him. Thinks Alan is a fool because he keeps coming around trying to inject enthusiasm in him, and that Sidney, who he hates, is talented, because word has filtered through a stuntman, Paul Baxley, that their stuff is really good and that Sidney knows what he's doing. . . . I really like the man. He's just so goddamned unhappy that it just doesn't seem true or possible. Like Monty, like Monroe . . . I told him he lit up the screen [in the rushes], then stopped because of the look on his face. . . . He laughed a lot and ruffled my hair. You know, con, con.*

To keep himself amused, Brando had started flying in women by private plane. "They were exotic types," Bridges noted. "We were constantly rewriting over at his house, so we'd meet them. It was one at a time, but serially—one would leave, another would come in."

Not even his harem was enough to keep Brando happy, however. He had already refused to work on Saturdays and Sundays (on location, actors and crew often shoot straight through the weekend to make the most use of their time away from the studio). Brando sometimes hired a private plane to fly him back to Los Angeles on Fridays, which—besides forcing the production to shut down for two days—had the company worried that they might lose their star in a plane crash, since he flew no matter what the weather. "The mail couldn't get through, birds wouldn't be flying, but

Marlon would go anyway," added Seltzer. "It was executive abdication again. The studio didn't like it, but they gave in to him because they felt they had to keep their relationship with him, even if it meant spending extra money or getting behind schedule."

For the first few days of the shoot, however, Bridges insisted that Marlon had been "marvelous, saying all the right words and believing in himself," and that the dailies had left everybody "very excited." The atmosphere then changed when Brando became ill. Local doctors diagnosed his condition as swollen lymph glands, but he insisted (as he had during *Mutiny*) that his personal physician be brought in from L.A. Soon it was discovered that he'd been scratched on the neck by his ocelot, the gift from Pat Quinn. The infection was lanced and drained, with packs put on his head and neck. Filming was delayed for a week. During the downtime, Marlon not only convalesced, he again put on weight.

To make up for lost time, Furie tried shooting around his absent star, using his double and including over-the-shoulder shots very much in the style of *The Ipcress File*. When Brando got wind of this, he demanded to see the dailies, then refused to do whatever covers were needed to complete the scenes. The result was that Furie had to refilm them from the beginning.

Bridges had been serving as a buffer between Brando and the director, but by this time the writer had returned to Los Angeles. "I got an hysterical call from Alan," he explained, "and I rushed back to the set. I was met at the plane by Alan and Sidney; they told me that Marlon was now refusing to play any of the scenes as written. He was just going crazy. Part of the problem was his weight—he didn't want to take off his shirt, as it was written in this one scene. Alan and Sidney said, 'This is the scene we shoot tomorrow and you've gotta rewrite it,' and they gave me notes."

Bridges went to his hotel room and wrote deep into the night, preparing three different versions of Marlon's homecoming scene. Furie and Miller picked one version the following morning.

"Jim has just done this brilliant scene," Miller began by announcing. "You've gotta read this, Marlon."

Marlon read it, then looked at Miller. "What do you want me to do, Alan? You want me to play this scene exactly as it's written?"

Unaware that Marlon was testing him, Miller persisted. "Oh, it's brilliant, Marlon, it's brilliant."

"Well, I don't think it's brilliant, Alan," Marlon said flatly, refusing to play it.

While Furie was lining up and lighting the shot, he asked Marlon to work with Bridges on the scene. The two of them went to Marlon's trailer.

"God, Marlon, I'm lost on this scene," Bridges said. "Why don't you just sort of improvise while you're putting on your makeup?" Bridges then typed as Marlon talked, continuing to take down the dialogue verbatim.

The two then went back out to the set, and Bridges handed him the sheets with the new script. Marlon read them through, then looked up and announced that he was unhappy with this version, too.

"Marlon, I didn't write that," exclaimed Bridges. *"You* wrote it. It's exactly what you said."

Brando's response was to throw the script in the air. Exasperated, Bridges announced that he was giving up and going back to L.A. Brando, in turn, resorted to the same number he'd pulled on *Morituri* director Wicki: He grabbed Bridges by the collar and the hem of his coat and walked him to the door.

"Then he gave me a little shove with his foot in the ass," said Bridges. "It wasn't violent, but I was really pissed. I turned, looked back at him, and was about to say something when he interrupted, 'You're the only one here with any integrity.' "

Bridges returned to L.A., but within days Brando made it known that he wanted him back. The writer had already begun another project, however, and besides, as he told Miller when he phoned, "This is not for me. You need to get a stenographer or a hack." The studio issued a press release claiming that Bridges was to be replaced by screenwriter Roland Kibbee "due to weaknesses in the script." As soon as Kibbee arrived on location, he too saw that the production was in shambles.

Meanwhile, the war between Furie and Brando escalated. Furie had his own competitive streak. "When I make a movie, I'm the fucking star," he stated flatly. "I don't give a damn about the stars. And there are *always* games going on with stars. As for Brando, he loves chaos. He has no discipline. He's a procrastinator. Every day he had another complaint—his tummy ached, his head ached."

He certainly wasn't worried about keeping up to speed with costar John Saxon, whose role was ever expanding because of all of the rewrites. One day Saxon remarked to Brando, "You know I've got a lot of things going for me now. I might steal this picture."

"Be my guest," replied Brando.

With his weight still ballooning, he no longer protested the use of

Paul Baxley as his double. "We established Marlon's body as Paul's body," said Furie. "I would stage a scene so Paul could do it, and then when Marlon would show up the next morning, I'd pop him into it."

"His heart, it bleeds for the masses / But the people he works with / get kicked in the asses," wrote Alan Miller in a jingle that swept the set. Unperturbed, Brando continued to make his antagonism toward Furie evident. At one last location, filming a snowy scene in Wrightsville, California, their tension finally erupted in a full-scale shouting match.

According to press reports, Brando and the director began yelling at each other in front of the assembled crew. Giving vent to his long-standing frustrations, Brando lashed out, "What the hell do *you* know?" Embarrassed, Furie shouted back, "You may be the star, but you're full of crap!" In fact, as the director later explained, he had been the one to start the argument. "I told him, 'You think you're such a big star, but you're a failure as a human being.' I said that because he didn't treat people well. His response was to laugh in my face."

Looking back at the production, Furie tried to analyze the source of the problem: "To me and everybody else in that movie, he was still the great Marlon Brando," he said. "We weren't a bunch of scumbags who had read the grosses of his last three movies and decided, 'Oh, he's down and out now, who cares about him.' He was a hero to us. Everybody on that set had great respect for him, but he had no respect for himself. . . . And in a strange way, it encapsulated what was wrong with the whole contract star system—Brando was a thoroughbred, and they were racing him at a state fair. It wasn't fair to him, and it wasn't fair to any of us."

However sympathetic Furie was to Brando's predicament in retrospect, he had a different reaction when he ran into him in London several years after the movie. Brando was surprisingly friendly. "It takes me a long time to get to know people," Furie recalled the actor saying. "I thought you were a phony, a liar, a dirty double-crosser. I discovered you've got the great visual sense of good directors. Let's do another film."

"Never!" Furie told him.

"Basically, he is kind of a son-of-a-bitch," Furie elaborated, "but also a good little boy. When he does something or says something that's out of his own needs, he tries to make up for it."

As an example, Furie described Brando showing up at the wrap party for *The Appaloosa*. The production had finished in Antelope Valley without the actor, but Marlon flew in on a chopper, introduced himself to everyone, and danced with everybody's wife. "It was as if he had this thing about wanting to be liked. After putting the crew through all this shit, he came to the party almost as if he had to make amends."

Having subsequently followed Brando's career, Furie said that his experience with the actor had taught him one important lesson: "I learned from him that you should never give up. Because that's what he did—he really gave up. Maybe it happened right after *One-Eyed Jacks,* but once he found he wasn't where he should have been [in his career], he somehow gave up. And the fact that later he insisted on doing only one or two weeks' work for any picture was proof that he didn't care anymore. Acting became just a way to earn a living to pay for his life. It's almost like Dorian Gray—if I can't remain young, then I don't want to compete with myself ever again. I'll just take the money and become a character actor."

When *The Appaloosa* was released in September 1966, reviewers like Philip Scheuer in the *Los Angeles Times* took aim both at Furie's stylized direction and Brando's mumbled, "somnambulistic" performance. "Poor Marlon Brando!" Pauline Kael exclaimed in her *New Yorker* review: "Here he is trapped inside still another dog of a movie. . . . Failure was guaranteed by Mr. Brando's weird interpretation of the hero and by Sidney J. Furie's equally weird direction. Not for the first time, Mr. Brando gives us a heavy-lidded, adenoidally openmouthed caricature of the inarticulate, stalwart loner. If he is trapped, it is not by others but by himself."

Yet in a more extended essay that year, "Marlon Brando: An American Hero," Kael probed deeper to explain why "our most powerful young screen actor . . . , the major protagonist of contemporary American themes in the fifties, is already a self-parodying comedian." She laid the blame on mediocre Hollywood movies, "trashy assignments," and what she described as the studios' large-scale campaigns to cut a "big star . . . down to an easier-to-deal-with size." In Brando's case, she concluded, the result was that "he became an eccentric, which in this country means a clown, possibly the only way left to preserve some kind of difference. It's as if [his] hidden reserves of power have been turned to irony. Earlier, when his roles were absurd, there was a dash of irony; now it's taken over: the nonconformist with no roles to play plays *with* his roles. Brando is still the most exciting American actor on the screen. The roles may not be classic, but the actor's dilemma is."

During the making of *The Appaloosa,* Brando seemed again to deflect his artistic dilemma with game-playing in his personal life. He had continued his relationship with Quinn, who, having moved to a place of her own in Laurel Canyon, had decided to adopt a more nonchalant attitude toward Marlon and his other women. One night when she was at his house and another woman appeared on the scene, she took it in stride. According to Quinn, when he could not incite a jealous tantrum from her, Brando had exclaimed, "What is it about you! I've tried to destroy you, and I can't do it."

As a way of further asserting her independence, she had begun seeing other men as well. Brando's phone calls became more frequent. "He was always checking up on me. What was I doing? Who was I seeing?" Quinn explained. His competitiveness became even more extreme when the special target of his one-upmanship turned out to be none other than Bob Dylan.

At the time, Dylan was performing at the Hollywood Bowl and Quinn asked Marlon to accompany her to the postconcert party. He refused. When she arrived at the party, however, she found him already there, having come with Christian Marquand and his new wife, the daughter of Jean-Pierre Aumont. "He was getting high," Quinn recalled, "and all these girls, music groupies, were hanging on him. As soon as he saw me, he sort of pulled me over and announced to these hippies that they were phonies, that I was the real thing."

When Dylan arrived, he met Quinn and Brando simultaneously, and what quickly became clear was that Dylan knew how to play the game as well as Brando. Unabashedly, he cast an eye on the shapely Quinn, dressed in cowboy boots and tight polka-dot hip huggers, and his attentions left the actor less than happy.

"Dylan adores, idolizes, and maybe, for all I know, even lusts after Marlon," said Quinn. "But at that moment he turned his attention on me, so Marlon began to talk to Miles Davis's wife, Frances, who was really gorgeous. An hour or two later Bob left and I went to sit with Marlon. He then turned to me and announced, 'I'm going home with the black bitch.' Those were his exact words. Me, I left and drove over to the Château Marmont and knocked on Dylan's door. I said, 'Well, here I am' and spent the night with him."

Brando did indeed take Frances Davis home that night. Weeks before

the Dylan party, the wife of the great jazz genius (and friend of Julie Belafonte, with whom she had danced in the Dunham troupe) had fled Manhattan, panic-stricken by her husband's out-of-control drug habit.
Brando's attentions the night of the party seemed to offer solace. Once in
his bedroom, however, he showed her little affection but instead put dirty
movies on his projector.

"I was there, like a little toy," she recalled, still pained by the memory
years later. "We were lying together on the bed, but then he got up to
watch my reactions. It was very strange—he was just watching me and
saying nothing. I didn't have my glasses on, so I wasn't reacting at all to the
movies, which made him kind of wonder. Then I got embarrassed and he
turned it off. I don't remember if I was in tears, but I know he kept asking
me, 'Why are you upset? What's bothering you?' It was as if he was trying
to get inside my head."

After Quinn's night with Dylan, the singer invited her to accompany
him to his Hell's Angels concert in Berkeley. Four days later, when they
were flying back to L.A. on a chartered plane, Dylan told her, "I'd love to
see Marlon again." Quinn contacted Brando, who was then doing the final
shooting of *The Appaloosa,* and he left passes for them at the gate at Universal. A few days later Quinn and Dylan went to his trailer.

"The first thing Marlon did was take this thing from around his neck
and put it around mine," recalled Quinn. "I looked down and it was a
scalp, a real human scalp. Possession is nine-tenths of the law—he was
claiming me." When Dylan asked for a Coke, and the bottles arrived with
no opener, Marlon then proceeded to uncap them with his teeth. When
they left the trailer, Dylan confided in Quinn, "You know when I knew he
was straight? When he opened the bottles that way."

What he meant, exactly, Quinn wasn't sure, although it was no secret
that "he was terribly attracted to Marlon," she said. "I never saw anything,
but the word going around then was that Dylan was swinging both ways."

During the visit in the trailer, Brando and Dylan had agreed to get
together that evening at Quinn's Laurel Canyon home. "The mood that
night at my place was strange, too, like this was guys only," said Quinn. "It
was almost like a summit. Dylan was the new boy in town. He was twenty-
four, Marlon was forty-one, but even though Bob was coming on a little
cocky, he was also idolizing Marlon, so it was like two living legends eyeing each other."

Dylan brought a couple of members of The Band with him, and at one point Quinn tried to join in the conversation. "Bob's response was very brusque," added Quinn, "indicating that I needn't be there, that I should take a powder. Marlon said, 'Oh, no, I want her right here,' and he reached out and put his arm around me."

According to Quinn, Dylan saw Brando a few times after that, but whether in a social group or just the two of them, she couldn't be sure. "Still, Christian Marquand told me they were meeting each other," she said, "so I'm sure there was something there, and I think it involved Christian, too."

Whatever their competition over Quinn, the usually taciturn poet-rocker talked about the actor for weeks afterward, telling his biographer as well as friends in New York that he'd encountered a soul mate, a life force. "I hung out with Marlon Brando so much," he boasted. "We talked . . . about four or five hours. He came to a concert and he called me. . . . Marlon Brando's a friend of mine . . . I love him. Somehow, [he] pulled through all the bullshit he had from the press and the public."

Quinn was aware of Brando's manipulations and no longer quite so vulnerable after his return from the *Appaloosa* shoot. Although he persistently tried to argue her into therapy by asserting that she was "crazy," she refused. She sensed the deep scar left by someone, probably his father, telling him that "he was such a bad person that no one could love him."

Things remained calm between Quinn and Brando during the latter part of 1965, until Dylan called again, asking her to bring the actor to the concert he was giving in L.A. Marlon and Quinn, along with one of her girlfriends and Christian Marquand, attended and then went to the Château Marmont. There, when Brando saw the limos and the crowd of Dylan groupies in front of the hotel, he drove directly up to Mulholland for what he may or may not have planned as a party of his own.

Waiting outside Brando's door, suitcase in hand, was Reiko Sato, one of Marlon's girlfriends from Japan and another newly arrived Hollywood hopeful. "She had just come from the airport," said Quinn. " 'Reiko!' Marlon exclaimed, and picked her up. I said to myself, 'Okay, it's Reiko's night.' "

As Quinn and her own friend started to leave, Brando again asked her to stay, but she refused.

"Who knows what would have happened?" added Quinn. "But all

five of us together wasn't my scene. So my girlfriend and I left Christian behind and went back to the Château Marmont party. I spent the night with Dylan."

Brando wasn't pleased. Despite his apparent indifference, he was bothered by her refusal to show anger or jealousy. "If you didn't want to stab the other woman," observed Quinn, "Marlon thought you didn't love him or really care about him." Accordingly, into the better part of the following year, he sought to turn the incident into a sign of her rejection: Quinn was the betrayer, not he. Whenever he phoned her, his first words were always, "How's your pal, Bob Dylan?"

An American Star in Europe: *Countess* and *Reflections*

Brando was soon to leave for London to begin shooting *A Countess from Hong Kong*. While others might consider the film yet another of what Pauline Kael had dubbed his "trashy assignments," with this third Universal project no one had to twist his arm, and he had agreed to do it with great enthusiasm. In fact, during the last days of the *Appaloosa* shoot, Furie had overheard Brando on the phone talking with excitement about working with an idol of his own—Charlie Chaplin.

Brando had met Chaplin in the fifties, when he and Darren Dublin had played tennis at the great comic's private court. The acquaintance had been renewed through Brando's and Chaplin's mutual friend, Gene Frenke, as well as through Philip Rhodes. But beyond the social ties, Brando had long been a fan of silent screen comedy; and even though he had expressed a personal dislike of Chaplin (Brando found his monologues tedious and boring, said Rhodes), he thought him a genius. Brando was so eager to work with Chaplin that he did not even bother to read the script. He also promised to lose weight, just as the master demanded.

Countess ranks as one of Brando's worst failures and is the sad swan song of Chaplin's career. Originally written in the 1930s as a vehicle for Chaplin and Paulette Goddard, the production creaked like the timbers of its ship-bound set.

Arriving in London to begin shooting at Pinewood Studio in January 1966, Marlon was apprehensive—"terrified" even—at the prospect of doing comedy, or at least doing it "for real." At seventy-seven, Chaplin wasn't able to reassure him, however, since a strain of flu then sweeping London had left him weak and gaunt, alternately sleepy and impatient. Brando soon became ill himself, which caused further postponements and prompted the usual gossip that he was sabotaging the movie's budget. (Indeed, because of Brando's reputation for delays on films, he made a point of having his personal physician, Dr. Robert Kositchek, announce to the press that his absences were due to an attack of appendicitis.)

Since the director was such a venerable institution, Brando remained courteous to Chaplin. With costar Sophia Loren, however, he dispensed with decorum altogether within weeks of the company's coming together, and taunted the actress whenever he could. When she walked into Trader Vic's one night while he was dining there, he called out loudly, "There goes Soviet Loren!" During his first kissing scene with the Italian star, he whispered in her ear, "Do you know, you have black hairs growing out of your nose?"

Recently wed to Carlo Ponti and considered the queen of Italian films, Loren was appalled by Brando's gaucherie. Playing a Hong Kong dance-hall girl who stows away in the stateroom of a dull ambassador to Saudi Arabia, played by Brando, she had demanded first billing. Although Chaplin had refused, acceding to Brando's insistence that his name appear first, she still remained his strongest advocate on the set, and as Brando began to chafe against his direction, she took sides—and worse. "You must tell him off," she urged Chaplin. "You mustn't let him get away with this behavior." Chaplin took the advice, and when Brando showed up late one morning, he grabbed him by the arm. "Listen, you son-of-a-bitch, you're working for Charlie Chaplin now," he shouted. "If you think you're slumming, take the next plane back to Hollywood. We don't need you."

It was diplomatic of Brando not to counterattack either directly or by talking to the press. This time he reportedly fell into line like a "little boy," thereafter dressing in his limo as it sped toward the studio. Even if he had been up all night carousing with Christian Marquand, he tried to get to work on time. And when Chaplin again told him to lose weight, he did not sulk or rage.

Nevertheless, the acting styles of Chaplin and Brando were utterly incompatible. As always, Brando needed space; Chaplin was a choreographer, telling him where to stand, how many steps to take, and how many beats to take before turning. Brando might appreciate Chaplin's virtuosity as the director acted out how *he* would play a scene, but his own performance was leaden and lifeless.

Writer Ron Moseley visited the *Countess* set one day and watched Chaplin directing Brando and Loren. "Chaplin wanted everything precise and exactly how he planned it," recalled Moseley. "When they didn't understand what he wanted, he'd say, 'Watch me.' First he mimed and mouthed Marlon, as if in a mirror. Then in turn he did Sophia's lines and movements in response. Here was this great comic acting out their characters, and he was much better at them than they were. Brando was obviously in terror of having to imitate exactly how Chaplin played the scene."

As shooting progressed, however, Brando muted his discomfort when he described to interviewers what it was like to work with Chaplin. "I feel content just to be an animated marionette," he told one reporter, adding that he considered Chaplin "a genius. . . . Whatever I do on the screen . . . is really Mr. Chaplin plotting, moving, talking. He says whether I tug my ear, or fold my arms, or cross my legs. . . . I really feel as if I've gone back to school again." Brando then asserted that "only about one in five films is successful for almost any movie actor," almost apologetically conceding, "I don't know whether this one is going to be a success or my swan song."

After Chaplin's death in 1977, however, Brando would be far more scathing, as he talked at length about his frustrations with the director, his analysis not only reliable but unusually candid: "My style of acting has always been sort of, well, *roomy*," he conceded, pointing to his creative need for freedom. "This is different. It's a mosaic. Mosaic acting, with each tiny piece honed and polished and put into place. . . . With Charlie, it's chess; chess at ninety miles an hour.

"He was a mean man, Chaplin," the actor later asserted. "Sadistic. I saw him torture his son. Humiliating him, insulting him, making him feel ridiculous, incompetent. He [Sydney Chaplin] played a small part in the movie and the things Chaplin would say. . . . I said, 'Why do you take that?' His hands were sweating. He said, 'Well, the old man is old and nervous, it's all right.' That's no excuse. Chaplin reminded me of what Churchill said about the Germans, either at your feet or at your throat.

"He tried to do some shit with me. I said, 'Don't you *ever* speak to me in that tone of voice.' God, he really made me mad. I was late one day, he started to make a big to-do about it. I told him he could take his film and stick it up his ass, frame by frame.

"That was after I realized it was a complete fiasco. He wasn't a man who could direct anybody. He probably could when he was young. With Chaplin's talent you had to give him the benefit of the doubt. But you always have to separate the man from his talent. A remarkable talent but a monster of a man."

Even if *Countess* was another ordeal, Brando seemed to enjoy London, then the hip epicenter of the sixties youth culture. Skirts were up; working-class accents were fashionable, and there were discos, drugs, and parties nightly.

Lew Wasserman, the head of Universal, had put Brando's former agent and friend Jay Kanter in charge of the studio's London offices. Kanter was living high in an elegant home in Chester Square, chauffeured about town in a Rolls-Royce, and partying or hitting the gambling clubs almost nightly. "There is such a thing as a charmed life," David Chasman, the head of United Artists in London at the time, observed. "Jay has always had his protectors. First it was Marlon, who took him under his wing and made his career at MCA. Then it was Lew Wasserman at Universal. It was Wasserman who sent Jay to London to get Universal in on some of the film money gravy. Because of tax advantages offered by the British government, all the studios had set up offices in England. Jay presided over the London operation and blew $60 million of Universal's money."

Kanter had in fact brought Marlon into *Countess*. Although the two men saw each other often while shooting the film, Brando usually avoided the posh parties that Kanter and his third wife, Kit, liked to throw. Jerry Epstein, *Countess*'s producer and a friend of Kanter, was also part of this social scene. So, too, was executive producer Elliott Kastner, who had worked with Kanter as an agent at MCA. "Elliott and Jay were pals in the early fifties," recalled Roberta Haynes, Kanter's former wife. "Elliott was very successful because his attitude was 'There is a buyer for every property.' Then he became a producer and, like Jay, went to London when that was where so many movies were being made."

With Christian Marquand at his side, Brando was more social than he'd been in a long time. He even seemed to enjoy the cachet of being a superstar in Europe, helping to organize a televised gala benefit for UNICEF that celebrities and the elite of European society, including Madame Pompidou, attended. With other stars he provided the entertainment, and wearing jeans and a flower in his hair, he brought down the house by dancing barefoot with a Tahitian dance group. He also enlisted Pat Quinn, who had become a follower of the Maharishi Mahesh Yogi and now worked for his transcendental meditation center in Los Angeles, to arrange for the Maharishi and the Beatles to attend the event as well. (Marlon later made a point of telling Quinn that "your friend the Maharishi was wearing thermal electric underwear beneath his robes." Quinn took this as another one of his typical put-downs of someone important to her, his competitiveness subsuming his usual interest in matters spiritual.)

Friends saw what was happening, that here in London he was moving with the elite, and though he might deny it, he was relieved that his losing track record hadn't caught up with him across the Atlantic. One evening he arrived boozed at Kathleen and Kenneth Tynan's flat for a party to celebrate the Labour Party's electoral victory earlier in the day. Other guests included such literary and film heavyweights as Gore Vidal, Richard Harris, and Michelangelo Antonioni, and in their midst Marlon loudly dared his drama critic host to accompany him into the bathroom for a full-on-the-mouth kiss "as proof of their friendship." Rumors later circulated that Brando and Vidal had a brief affair.

Residing in London during this same period was Igor Tamarin, Marlon's zany, anarchic friend and onetime roommate from New York. One morning Tamarin was awakened by a phone call and was startled to hear the voice at the other end reciting Yiddish-sounding gibberish.

Since Tamarin had taught Brando such nonsense, he knew immediately who was calling. Brando told him he was at the Savoy and asked him to come right over.

"Oh, for Christ's sake, Marlon, it's eight-thirty in the morning," he complained. "I'm tired and sleepy. Can I call you later?"

Soon Tamarin's doorbell rang. It was Brando's chauffeur, instructed to bring him back to the hotel; since he was already awake, Tamarin pulled on his clothes and went to Brando's suite.

"Marlon's door was ajar, so I walked right in," he said. "There was no one in sight, but I could hear a shower running, so I followed my ear to the bathroom. There, through the translucent glass shower door, I saw the fattest ass I've ever seen in my life. Well, I wanted a shower myself, so I got undressed and hauled off and gave him a kick. He whirled around, and without a single word, we wrestled like the old days, full nelson and all."

At the end of their horseplay, Brando looked his friend over. "My God, you're still thin!"

"Not you!" Tamarin taunted. "What happened to you?"

The enormous breakfast they then ate seemed explanation enough. Later they were chauffeured to Jay Kanter's, and on the drive over they caught up on old times, including what had happened to mutual friends. Most of all, Igor wanted to know about Wally Cox and Darren Dublin. In fact, Marlon hadn't seen Dublin for many years, except once during the previous summer: In the midst of rewrite sessions on *The Appaloosa,* Dublin and his new wife, Sandy, had dropped by to see him on the Universal lot. Marlon had then given his former sidekick a dry, dismissive greeting, leaving Dublin to think that he "should have known better" than to try to resurrect the "good old days" and repair their broken friendship.

But now with Tamarin, Brando had more to say. "You know, Darren's really sick," he announced.

"When I heard that," recalled Tamarin, "I thought to myself, Hey, this is really the pot calling the kettle black."

After their initial reunion at the Savoy, Brando soon moved to an elegant town house in Belgravia, and when Tamarin made his first visit, it was Christian Marquand, not Brando, who greeted him.

"Marlon's just come back and he's very tired," Christian said. "Let's not disturb him."

"He's expecting me," Tamarin replied, brushing past Marquand and up the stairs. He had never met Marquand before, although he had heard, he said, that the Frenchman "was a friend of Brando's and was, in fact, procuring for him. But I didn't pay attention to those kinds of things."

Tamarin found Marlon in his bedroom, lying down on the bed. Marquand then came in and lay down beside him.

"Hello, Igor," Brando said in a quiet, bored voice. "What can I do for you?"

"Somebody told me I had an appointment to come up here," said Tamarin, all the while feeling that this attitude was what he had always hated about Marlon. "Besides, I'm hungry."

Marquand tried to shush him.

"Fuck you," said Tamarin.

Brando began to laugh—an affected laugh to Tamarin's ear. Then he said, "Igor, you're intelligent. Why don't you join the Peace Corps?"

"No, Marlon, I can't afford it. You join the Peace Corps. I want to go back to New York to visit my mother. I'm broke." Marquand again made little gestures of disapproval. Tamarin turned on him. "My God, I heard you were an actor, Christian," he said. "So why don't you do the mummy's hand or something."

Brando said nothing. He just lay with his hands behind his head, staring up at the ceiling. Then, after a minute or two, with Marquand still lying beside him, he gestured toward the nearby night table and sighed, "You'll find it in the drawer, Igor. Take what you need."

Despite his sense of betrayal, Tamarin did not cut off contact. Each time that he returned, however, he was irritated by Brando's entourage. "It was as if they were all under a death sentence," Tamarin recalled. "They all jumped when he came in, like he was an electric shock. I hated that bullshit of Marlon's, and the only one there who didn't take it, either, was Phil Rhodes."

Marlon's new girlfriend, whom Tamarin had noticed as a constant presence in the new house, was Esther Anderson, a twenty-two-year-old from Jamaica. She had studied with Stella Adler in New York, then gone to London, where she had been involved with the Blackwell scion of the Cross and Blackwell company, and she knew both Marquand and Al Lettieri (who was now working for Kastner in London). She had also been given a bit part in *Countess*. Meanwhile, Tarita had arrived in town halfway through the film, and struck Tamarin as anything but "a spiritual beauty" or a "primitive Gauguin creature." "That's nonsense," he said. "She knew exactly what she was doing. She was obviously a very shrewd gal. Marlon humored her."

Adding to the complicated arrangement, Movita also showed up with Miko in March 1966. That September she was to announce the birth of her daughter, Rebecca, although she didn't show any signs of pregnancy during this London visit, and no friends commented on a pregnancy during the intervening months. Leading to later speculation about the baby's parentage was the fact that Movita was then nearly fifty and that Brando had already left Los Angeles in December 1965, the month of the presumed conception.

Actress Sondra Lee, Movita's good friend in New York, doubted that Marlon had fathered Miko, let alone Rebecca. While Louise Monaco had thought that Miko could have been Marlon's child, she added, "But about Rebecca, there was some dispute." One of Marlon's employees confirmed that the actor claimed the child was definitely not his, even though she had his name. Rebecca herself would later tell her siblings that she did not regard Brando as her biological father, either.

During this period Marlon's philandering was so flagrant that gossip columnists took even more notice than usual. As Hollywood reporter Joe Hyams commented in an extended story about Marlon's women, "It requires a statistician rather than a reporter to get Marlon's private affairs in some kind of perspective and order." He then proceeded to give a "rundown" of Marlon's "romances for the past ten years," and even though he omitted several along the way, he felt justified in headlining the article, "Brando—As a Great Lover He Seems to Be Without Equal in Contemporary Film History."

Hyams seemed unaware, however, of the string of Filipino and other Asian women whom Brando continued to see once he was back in Los Angeles in the summer of 1966. Not only were Marie Cui and the Asian actresses he had met through Gene Frenke still current, but also Brando was infatuated with Anita Kong. "Kong was an interesting woman," said one of the actor's inner circle. "She had an incredible story of how she escaped from China with her five daughters, and then she married a very wealthy physician whose name was Wiley, from an old California family. Marlon enjoyed her competitiveness and feistiness, and they carried on their affair for years, even though the husband was aware of it and hated Marlon for it."

During these months Brando also continued to see Pat Quinn, although they were no longer lovers. "Marlon knew that my feelings about him were conjugal," explained Quinn, "but he always bolted from that. In fact, one day he repeated the line 'You know, we're never going to stroll hand in hand down the lane like Hansel and Gretel' three times. I later told this to the psychoanalyst that we shared, who said, 'Weren't Hansel and Gretel brother and sister?' In fact, when he came back from London, we were more like brother and sister and just very good friends."

In the autumn, after Brando left to shoot his next picture, Quinn had a brief affair with Baird Bryant, a noted cinematographer, and became pregnant. She chose to have the baby but decided not to marry the father. Although friends were certain that Brando was the father of her son, born in June 1967, Quinn maintained that this was not the case. "I didn't marry my son's real father because I was in love with Marlon," she said. "Years later, when Baird was talking to Marlon about a film he had made about a

Tibetan spiritual leader, he happened to mention that he was Caleb's father. Marlon immediately called me and demanded to know if this was in fact true. So maybe all those years he did have a fantasy that *he* was actually the father. Still, Marlon was Caleb's godfather and has always been very good to him. I was working for Jim Coburn—recommended by Marlon— as his secretary at the time I got pregnant, but I didn't have much money. Marlon sent over cribs and layettes, baby stuff that had been Christian's, and even said he was willing to acknowledge Caleb as his own, but I didn't want him to. When Marlon offered to do this, even though it was obvious he was not the father, it was only because he was feeling paternal and benevolent."

Having survived the tedium of working with Chaplin, Brando could at least look forward to a more compatible director in John Huston, who was slated to direct his next film, *Reflections in a Golden Eye,* in the fall of 1966. Not only did Huston have a distinguished movie career, he was a man's man whose macho reputation and bold, confrontational style appealed as well. Thus, instead of knocking off his last remaining Universal commitment, Brando now grabbed hold of a project that at least had the potential of reviving his talents.

There was a large emotional component in his decision to make *Reflections in a Golden Eye,* the long delayed and controversial adaptation of Carson McCullers's novel. Almost two years before, he had turned down the picture for the same reason that other actors had—concern about appearing in a role with explicit homosexual themes. Elizabeth Taylor, who had already signed for the female lead, then persuaded the ailing Montgomery Clift, her lifelong friend, to join her and enlisted Huston to direct. The production was repeatedly postponed, however, largely because studio executives were uncertain that the alcoholic Clift could be counted on to see the project through. In an attempt to force the film into production, Taylor went public, announcing to the press that she and Clift were set to costar for the first time since *Suddenly, Last Summer* in 1959. Unmoved, the studio again reminded her that Clift was uninsurable. Since Taylor felt that her friend's life might well depend on his going back to work (at this point he hadn't appeared on-screen since *Freud* in 1962), she paid the insurance bond out of her pocket.

Nevertheless, the studio had continued to drag its feet. While Clift did complete *The Defector* in the meantime, *Reflections* still did not have a starting date. In the summer of 1966, they were inching closer to a production schedule, but then the studio's waiting game worked: Clift was found dead of a heart attack in his Manhattan brownstone on July 23, 1966.

Richard Burton and Lee Marvin were among those first considered to replace him, but they were still wary of the story's homosexuality. Brando, as well, was cautious. Nevertheless, he still felt a special bond with Clift, his old rival and Actors Studio compatriot. In addition to their shared past, into the early 1960s, Clift had expressed his faith in Brando's talent. Hearing the negative remarks that followed *Bedtime Story,* Clift had defended him: "Marlon's not finished yet. He's just resting up. He'll be back—bigger than ever."

Before making a decision on *Reflections*, however, Brando flew to Huston's estate in Ireland to discuss the project. "He wasn't sure about the part," Huston wrote. "He had read the book but doubted his suitability. As we were talking about it, the final screenplay was being typed, so I suggested that he wait and read it. Marlon did so, then took a long walk in a thunderstorm. When he came back, he said simply, 'I want to do it.' "

The decision was a brave one. He was risking further damage to his stature, already diminished in so many eyes—not only because *Reflections* was the first Hollywood film to deal openly with homosexuality, but also because Warner Bros. wasn't going to fully support the project. Once Brando had made a commitment, Warner Bros. executives issued an internal studio directive that he receive no more than $1 million in salary, the same as Elizabeth Taylor; unwittingly, they were giving him a substantial raise from the pittance he was receiving under the Universal contract. Brando readily agreed to the terms and also accepted the studio's decision to shoot most of the film in Italy. Despite the fact that the story was set on an army base in the American South, Warners had settled on the Rome location ostensibly to accommodate Liz Taylor and Huston, who wanted to work abroad "for tax reasons." Still, it was no secret that the studio was about to benefit from low production costs by using Italian crews and extras.

Thus, after spending September supporting Indian fish-ins in Washington State (all but ignoring the New York premiere of *The Appaloosa*), Brando completed the one week of preliminary photography on *Reflections* in Mineola, Long Island. In late October 1966 the production moved to the

Dino De Laurentiis studio in Rome for the ten-week shoot.

In Rome, as in London, Brando again was treated as America's top star and badgered by paparazzi. Each morning Alice Marchak would bring him his wake-up coffee and provide a report on the crowds gathered below his rented apartment. One stormy day, he was nearly beside himself when she pointed out that a photographer was perched in a tree outside his window. Nevertheless, he enjoyed Rome. Christian Marquand was at his side, as were Philip and Marie, and an added bonus were the Burtons, whom he was starting to see regularly.

It was Burton's habit to pick up Taylor from the set, and in what seemed a tribute to Brando, he often came early enough to watch him work. Rumors flew that the Welsh actor was jealous, that he was in competition with Brando, perhaps even leery that something might be going on between him and his wife. Nothing could have been further from the truth, judging from Burton's diaries:

> *1966—Nov. 3:* Marlon's immorality, his attitude to it, is honest and clean. He is a genuinely good man I suspect and he is intelligent. He has depth. It's no accident that he is such a compelling actor. He puts on acts of course and pretends to be vaguer than he is. Very little misses him as I've noticed.

The tacit connection between Burton and Brando was understandable—in many ways the two were cut of similar cloth. Burton had made his own fair share of screen trash, and although he had not forsaken the stage, Brando's withdrawal from the theater was not something he would criticize. Likewise, Brando and Huston seemed to have a strong alliance. Just as the actor was now trying to make a comeback, Huston had recently directed a string of bombs, including *The Bible*. And although *Reflections* would eventually be neglected at the box office, it was a serious work that both men could consider more worthy of their talents than their previous films.

In the movie Brando plays Major Weldon Penderton, an army officer who wrestles with his repressed homosexuality and eventually kills a sexually ambiguous young soldier who's given to sneaking into the bedroom of Brando's wife to fondle her underwear. The wife, played by Taylor, is neurotic in her promiscuity, her love of horses, and her sadomasochistic interest in whips. She flaunts her affair with another officer (Brian Keith), whose own wife (Julie Harris) is unstable and preternaturally sensitive.

According to Lawrence Grobel, Huston's biographer, the director characteristically tried to control his actors "as little as possible," and Brando relished the freedom. "He gives you about twenty-five feet," Brando later explained. "He's out in the background. He listens. Some guys listen, some guys are auditory; some guys are visual. He's an auditory guy and he can tell by the tone of your voice whether you're cracking or not. But he leaves you alone pretty good."

Huston would later try to sign Brando for the director's comeback film, *Fat City,* because of the way the two of them had now started to click. In contrast to Taylor's perfect preparation and one-shot takes, Brando often repeated a scene. But when he did so, "it was *never* the same," and wisely enough, Huston gave him whatever slack he wanted.

"If you remember the scene where he talks about the army, standing at the mantlepiece, it's a long speech and he fiddles with a candle," Huston recalled. "Well, after the first time I could have said, 'That's it,' as I often do; but knowing Marlon and the way he works, I said, 'Let's do it again.' We did it three times, and each time was different; any of them could have been used. . . . I've never seen any other actor do that."

Huston was also struck by what seemed to be Marlon's identification with his character. During their initial meeting in Ireland, the director had asked Marlon if he could ride a horse, since several scenes would require it. Marlon had given him the oblique (if inaccurate) reassurance that he had grown up on a horse ranch. "Later, during the filming of the movie," Huston wrote, "I noticed that he exhibited such a fear of horses that presently Elizabeth Taylor, who is a good horsewoman, began to be afraid also. I wondered then, as now, if Marlon got his fear because he had so immersed himself in his role. The character he played had a fear of horses."

Julie Harris was equally impressed with Marlon's immersion in his role. "He'd just be having fun, squeezing you and leching around and wisecracking," she said. "Then they'd call, 'We're ready,' and it was as if he'd transform himself. You'd watch him and think, Where'd Marlon go? It was beautiful, like instant magic."

The characterization he had to capture was no piece of cake—the complexity of Major Penderton's repressed homosexuality, replete with smoldering anger and violence. Harris watched transfixed as he found subtle movements of his hands, or as he created a scene alone in front of a mirror, cold-creaming his face and giving a quick pat to his hair. They were the perfect private gestures to convey his character's secret infatuation, the crosscurrents of his fascination with the young soldier who is about to arrive at his home.

"He seemed to love the part," Harris added, "and you felt he had a great deal of empathy for this man. There was nothing campy about it. He was taking the role seriously, almost as if he was exploring his own sexuality, or his own inner torment.

"Perhaps playing the part was an escape for him," Harris continued. "He never held back in giving you the character." As an example, she cited the scene in which her own character was to walk down the stairs and, distraught, confront him: "Do you realize your wife is carrying on with my husband?" He was to smile and try to calm her down. "It was a difficult scene," she explained, "because I found myself becoming actually quite agitated. Other actors might have said, 'Oh, look at her, she's carrying on.' He didn't do that. He used it to act a real confrontation. I had to make him realize what I was feeling, and he was absolutely fearless in being there and responding to me in character."

In contrast to his delays and latenesses on other movies, Brando never caused similar problems for Huston, even if the actor was still "trying to screw everyone around." He was so "like a male nymphomaniac, propositioning everybody," said Bill Hamilton, Huston's assistant, "that Brian Keith eventually made a crack about it. The English nanny taking care of Keith's children back in California had begged him to get her an autographed picture of Brando. Keith quipped to Hamilton, "If I'd known he was like this, I would have brought her over here and just picked up her skirt and got him to service her. Much better than an autographed picture."

Harris, too, saw this side of Brando. She visited him and his entourage at his apartment occasionally, and his life seemed chaotic. In his well-appointed quarters, surrounded by his women and his toadies, he "had everything, but nothing was channeled," she said. "He was innately brilliant but it was all scattered, almost as if he'd been told early on that he was nothing and worthless. Yet his work was so beautiful and so pure that there was no explaining where it came from. He still didn't love acting, he didn't love the theater and he didn't respect his own talent, but his gift was so great he couldn't defile it. He could put on pounds, he could say that it was all shit, but he still couldn't destroy it."

Huston called *Reflections* "one of my best pictures . . . scene by scene, pretty hard to fault," but critics gave it a surprisingly cool reception when it was released in October 1967. Typical was Bosley Crowther of the *New York Times,* who found it "anticlimactic and banal." Although he praised Brian Keith, Crowther gave Brando only mediocre marks, despite what had been the finest sustained performance he'd delivered in years. The movie bombed terribly, and producer Ray Stark blamed it on the film's subject matter. "People weren't willing to understand or accept homosexuality at the time," he said, adding, "It's a picture I'm very proud of."

Reflections was a cut above the dreck that had preceded and would follow it. For the first time in years, Brando seemed to touch an interior part of himself and to be willing to go to "the bottom of the barrel," whereas his stylish artifice and the self-parodies of previous films had only gloomily suggested escape and evasion. Here he seemed to have been able to return to the Method, at least in his better scenes. What Molly Haskell has insightfully analyzed as his vulnerability masked by toughness, his androgynous mix of masculine and feminine elements, was once again in play. Sadly, this was not to last. *Candy*, his next film, would be his greatest self-betrayal yet.

"Marlon went out of his way to get that stupid movie going and bring Burton into it," recalled Rhodes, shaking his head. "He was sending Burton presents, which even included shipping him one of the first video cameras ever made when Burton was in Africa. When Marlon really wanted something, he would go all out, and finally he convinced him." The movie was to be shot quickly in Rome starting late in 1967, and Marlon's cameo appearance would be squeezed into the midst of his next picture, *The Night of the Following Day.*

Candy and *The Night of the Following Day*

Perhaps the only explanation for Brando's involvement in such a piece of patent junk as *Candy* was that he felt an obligation to Christian Marquand, who—with his brother, Serge—had helped overcome local resistance to his purchase of Tetiaroa. The crux of the Tahitian authorities' position was that for centuries the atoll had been the private gateway of Tahiti's royal family, and it was now of inestimable value to the region's burgeoning tourist trade. Brando, though, had persevered. Dealing with the opposition in the Tahitian Territorial Assembly—headed by Jacques-Denis Drollet, whose murdered son would later figure so prominently in the actor's troubles—he insisted that he had only the purest motives. It was Marquand who made the transaction happen. Thanks to the well-connected Frenchman's interventions in Paris, French Polynesia governor Jean Sicurani received a letter from Georges Pompidou, then the premier of France, asking Sicurani to tell Drollet that he and others must give up their opposition. As Drollet recalled, the governor said, "I cannot refuse the premier of the French Republic."

The first part of the sale was concluded in October 1966, when Marlon was allowed to buy 438 hectares (acreage comprising several islands in the atoll) for $200,000. The rest of Tetiaroa would be purchased in January 1967 for $70,000. Brando's new Beverly Hills lawyer, Norman Garey, was instrumental in completing the yearlong negotiations, too, and while Marlon was to become increasingly dependent on Garey's legal acumen, he remained most of all grateful to Marquand, who was the prime mover behind the *Candy* project from the start. On the face of it the film itself was not without promise, either. A bizarre sex farce, *Candy* had plenty of hip credentials: Terry Southern, who had been a screenwriter on *Dr. Strangelove,* had penned the best-selling book with Mason Hoffenberg, and Buck Henry, hot off *The Graduate,* had adapted it for the screen. The lead was to be played by an unknown, Ewa Aulin, a pouty-lipped seventeen-year-old blond Scandinavian, but *Candy*'s gimmick wasn't Aulin so much as its slew of star cameos: James Coburn, Walter Matthau, John Huston, Charles Aznavour, Ringo Starr, Sugar Ray Robinson, and even Anita Pallenberg, the wife of Rolling Stones guitarist Keith Richards, in addition to Burton and Brando.

Like the "rat pack" films that Sinatra and his friends did, *Candy* brought its players together mainly to make money. Its stars were to be paid $50,000 for a week's work, and Burton, Starr, Brando, and Coburn also had "points." Brando had been the catalyst for the others, having signed his letter of intent early on; once Burton was enlisted, Coburn and the others had quickly followed suit. It didn't seem to matter that Marquand's only other directorial effort, *Le Grand Chemin,* had been a disaster;

whatever his deficiencies, it was thought that the colorful array of celebrities would more than compensate. ABC-TV, hoping to cash in on the burgeoning youth market, had put big money behind the project, budgeting it at $3 million.

Coburn had signed on with the expectation that the production might also be fun and imaginative, even somewhat subversive. "We were all kind of gathered around the idea of doing a sixties movie," he recalled. "Our attitude was 'Let's see if we can do it.' Nudity was beginning to come in, fucking on-screen, and it was all much freer. Also, everybody would have a say, and we knew we'd be inventing as we went along, with Buck Henry there all the time altering whatever came out. It was supposed to be a total collaborative effort."

There was nothing that unified the project thematically or even politically; nevertheless, Marquand managed to keep the production under control for the first several weeks of shooting during the winter of 1967–68 as the players came and went for their seven-day shoots. As planned, the actors' appearances were in serial, with none of their stints overlapping. Starr had done his week, Brando followed, and Coburn was set to appear after him, although when the tall, infinitely cool actor arrived in Rome, he learned that things had gone haywire the week before. "Everybody had done their stuff, boom—one week, and out," he explained. "I came in on the day I was supposed to, but Christian met me at the airport and said, 'Well, there's been a little problem. We'll probably have to close down for a week or at least until we can do some shooting that Ewa isn't in.' "

Aulin, it seemed, had been so rattled by Brando's antics that she was no longer able to do their scenes together. Instead she burst into out-of-control laughter. To stem the rampant hysteria, she was given a "rest cure." It was decided, Coburn learned, "that she had to be put to sleep out in a little resort town on the coast, Taormina."

It was not long before Coburn heard the full story behind Aulin's problems and the strange solution that had been invented.

"She was this young, naive thing," he said. "Nobody was banging her but everybody, of course, had been hitting on her. She had a wonderful ass, man, and Marlon just couldn't resist. He'd started coming on to her pretty strong, turning on his great charm, even during their scenes together." As he had with Janet Margolin on *Morituri,* Brando had been using all the weapons in his arsenal, playing any number of different roles to get a response from the vulnerable teenager. "He tried everything," added Coburn, "being the father, the psychiatrist, the stern disciplinarian. She was so besieged and befuddled that all she did was laugh and laugh, so uncontrollably that she couldn't get through her lines."

For his wacky role of the Great Guru Grindl, Brando was outfitted with Indian robes and a stringy wig that made him all the more ridiculous. A prominent caste mark stood out on his forehead. "She would look at him in this fright wig," said Coburn, "and just get hysterical. He was so funny and ingratiating to begin with—only now he wanted to fuck her, so that was the icing on the cake. It was overwhelming. She just went over the edge."

During the sixties, stylish clinics had started using drug-induced sleep cures developed in Switzerland to help patients stop smoking, drinking, or overeating as well as to lessen anxiety. The *Candy* production team in Rome was nothing if not trendy and created its own version of the treatment by removing the teenager to a coastal hotel and giving her shots to keep her asleep. (The story was so incredible, however, that according to Pat Quinn, rumors reached Hollywood that the girl had been "kept high just for the fun of it." After the movie she was never heard from again.)

Brando had to hang around while Aulin underwent her "sleep cure," and with the interruption, he and Coburn were able to get to know each other. One day he took Coburn by surprise when he walked into the latter's dressing room, plunked himself down, and began to talk.

"I don't know," Marlon said. "The last ten years have been like smoke, so vague I can hardly remember anything that's happened."

"He was trying to remember his past but couldn't," Coburn explained. "He described the last ten years, from '57 to '67, like a fog, as if *everything* was hazy."

Coburn was also surprised when Marlon then began to discuss his children and his anxiety "that the women were ripping his kids away from him." Marlon may have been particularly upset at this time because in June of that year, Movita had filed for divorce, charging him with mental cruelty and demanding custody of her two children. Perhaps he anticipated the same kind of grueling legal battles he'd had for years with Kashfi. Indeed, his conversation with Coburn seemed to center on his worries about his son Christian. "Marlon told me he hoped that his son wouldn't be destroyed by the weirdness of the mother," Coburn said. "As he went on, I had the feeling that he liked kids and was very fond of his own and concerned about them."

Marlon then asked Coburn if he had children as well.

"Yes, two kids," replied Coburn, "but I don't get a chance to see them too much."

"I don't either, and I don't know how they're going to grow up," Marlon said with a note of sadness.

During their conversation Marlon appeared to be "in a reverie," said Coburn. "There's always a bottom for everybody, and I had the impression that this was what was happening here, and why he was looking for my friendship."

Subsequently, on several occasions Coburn dined with him and Marquand. Grass and drunken conversation filled the air, and women were in abundance, including Esther Anderson, whom Marlon had brought over from London. Brando was always the center of attention, and he had his audience mesmerized with his practiced charm. It was as if he was "trying to draw everyone into his nucleus," said Coburn. What also seemed evident over the ensuing days was that he repeatedly drew a line between those who were inside his domain and those who were outside. "He seemed to think that people were out to get him," Coburn remarked. "It was very, very strange—if you were describing a character like this the first thing you might say was that he was a real paranoid. It seemed that all of his tests were performed on people he didn't know or trust."

The set's freedom didn't translate into the freewheeling comedy all had anticipated. Marquand had neither directorial control nor the sense of comic timing to suture together anything coherent or funny. When the *New York Times* review leveled charges of "ugly racialism" and "arrested development," some doubts were raised about his taste and political awareness. But it was Brando's reputation that suffered most when *Newsweek* and other mainstream publications caught the whiff of filthy lucre behind the whole dreadful enterprise: "For sheer ignominious ineptitude, *Candy* takes the cake," wrote the magazine's reviewer. "What this shabby European production is really about is money: a whole bunch of actors getting rich in Rome, an American television network footing the bill in hopes of cashing in on some sexy stuff they can't put on the air. Marlon Brando has a few funny moments as a guru in a trailer truck . . . but he winds up playing Peter Sellers playing Quilty in *Lolita*."

• • •

If an emotional fog had shrouded Brando's last ten years, others re-membered them all too well. They suspected—as Brando may have him-self—that, with the exception of *Reflections,* he had so cut himself off from authentic emotions that he would never again be able to reach down and come up with the intense and electrifying performances of his past. His masks and manipulations, it seemed, had replaced any inner core, very much as if he were lost. As Philip Rhodes so aptly put it, having witnessed the changes in his friend during these years: "Marlon has multiple identi-ties. These are images that constantly shift, merge, and finally dissolve. There was no essential core except for a hazy emotional vortex. No one central figure in the carpet."

His string of tacky, meaningless movies and his announced contempt for acting—as well as for reviewers and audiences—only seemed to mirror his self-contempt. In her long essay "Marlon Brando: An American Hero," Pauline Kael cited Emerson's description of the artist's way of life: "Thou must pass for a fool for a long season." But she redefined that "long season" not as youth, when artists prove their talents, but as the time after recogni-tion, when artists suffer "the degradation after success."

Stella Adler, Marlon's mentor and surrogate mother, took his down-hill slide as a personal rejection and seemed dismayed by what was hap-pening. Coburn, among others, saw her during this period, and he soon realized that she became upset whenever Brando's name was mentioned. "If you asked about Marlon," he recalled, "she would say, 'Marlon . . . ahhh . . .' and quickly go on to something else. I think she was very disap-pointed that he had become more of a character than an actor."

Fellow actors, too, were beginning to remark on his deterioration. While Burton had expressed admiration for Brando's work in *Reflections,* his feelings soon soured. "Marlon has yet to learn to speak," he com-plained. "Christ knows how often I've watched Marlon ruin his perfor-mance by under-articulation. . . . The worst thing that ever happened to him was Gadg Kazan, the Actors Studio, and fantastic over-publicity when he was a baby. . . . I long to take him in my teeth and shake enthusi-asm into him."

Even one of Marlon's inner circle, Billy Redfield, felt compelled to publicly assess what had happened. Redfield was fiercely committed to the theater; after playing Guildenstern to Burton's Hamlet in the long-running Broadway production, he wrote about the experience in *Letters from an Actor*. In it he included his own analysis of Brando's career, which was excerpted in the *New York Times* on January 15, 1967. Between the lines the personal pain of a long devoted friend was evident. "Brando was the American challenge to the English-speaking tradition in the classic roles . . . an artistic, spiritual, and specifically American leader," Redfield wrote. As a pioneer Marlon was "not only truthful but passionate—not only Greek handsome but unconventional" and he "promised vindication of the American conviction and style. . . . He was like a prizefighter: brutal, but strangely graceful; illiterate, but unaccountably sophisticated."

But by 1953, Redfield asserted, "he no longer cared—which is the last stop on the streetcar. To try may be to die, but not to care is to never be born. . . . He is a movie star. . . . Brando is not to be blamed, merely regretted. The money he commands is irresistible, while important roles alarm him. As an actor, Brando must be either forgotten or fondly remembered."

Despite their previous debates about the theater versus movies, Marlon took Redfield's book and the *Times* excerpt as the ultimate disloyalty, no matter how insightful or accurate his friend's observations. What he failed to understand was that Redfield and Rhodes, the most intellectual figures in his circle (as well as others he ostracized) most of all *cared*. This, however, made no difference. Redfield's wife, Betsy, recalled that there was never an explicit break. "Marlon was like somebody who blacklists people," she said. "You didn't know you'd been blacklisted, but as time went by, you just became aware that was what he had done."

Brando might have been heartened by the storm of letters to the *Times* protesting Redfield's comments. Reputations, certainly the reputations of icons, die hard. Molly Haskell would wait five years before penning her seminal critique, "A Myth Steps Down to a Soapbox," and yet Brando's next movie would only reconfirm Redfield's conclusion, underscoring the bewildered disappointment felt by so many other colleagues, as well as serious film devotees.

The Night of the Following Day, a low-budget thriller, had been announced in mid-September 1967 and quickly put into production four weeks later. Revolving around the kidnapping of a young heiress (played by British actress Pamela Franklin), the film features Richard Boone as a sadistic gang member, Rita Moreno as a drugged-out accomplice, and

Brando, in a blond wig and black T-shirt, in the role of a kidnapper who undergoes a last-minute moral conversion and rescues the gang's victim. Thirty-six-year-old Hubert Cornfield, son of Albert Cornfield, head of Twentieth Century–Fox's European operations, and the director of such B movies as *Lure of the Swamp* and *Plunder Road,* wrote the script and was slated to produce and direct. With someone young and relatively inexperienced at the helm, there were bound to be problems, and Brando's own mood could only exacerbate the confused, chaotic production.

The deal had been put together by Jay Kanter, Jerry Gershwin, and executive producer Elliott Kastner of Gina Films; Gershwin, a regular on the London scene, had coproduced *Countess,* and Kastner, who would go on to produce both *The Nightcomers* and *The Missouri Breaks,* were both content to sign Marlon and walk away, leaving the actor unconstrained by the usual producer's supervision.

"It was a very low budget picture," explained Marion Rosenberg, who, as Kastner's personal assistant, became the film's de facto line producer. "Marlon was always short of money. Let's say that he was paid a couple of hundred thousand dollars, which was not his market price. As head of Universal in London, Kanter's position allowed him to green-light any project he wanted, and his attitude was 'Let's get this picture done so that Marlon can work off his commitment.' That was everybody's point of view—doing a quick, cheap, low-budget film was the easiest way to take care of Marlon's obligation to Universal."

Translation: No one much cared about the project, especially Kastner, who was already famous for his extraordinary hustles and deal making. Some acquaintances joked that he himself seemed to realize how unsavory his deal making was when he took to wiping off the telephone mouthpiece with a eucalyptus-scented disinfectant. Kastner, however, seemed to revel in his dubious reputation. "He loved the fact that everybody loathed and despised him," Rosenberg said. "He took the attitude 'As long as they're talking about me, it means I'm important.'"

The only allure of the film was the eerie backdrop of the barren dunes along the northern coast of Brittany, where the company settled in for its shoot in October 1967. The sixty-member cast and crew (small by Hollywood standards) was bivouacked in the nearby vacation town of Le Touquet. Only the Hôtel Bristol was open to the off-season guests, and the production company virtually had the run of the few restaurants, the nightclub, and grocery store in the all-but-deserted summer resort. Marlon chose to stay apart from the others, some twenty kilometers away, at the nineteenth-century Château de Montreuil—*"un ravissant hôtel,"* as it billed itself.

For the first time in a long while, he looked svelte and trim. Physically, he would remain in good shape throughout the shoot, thanks largely to Jan Lettieri, the wife of Al, who was still Kastner's right-hand man. Jan kept Brando to his new regimen of drinking a glass of lemon juice mixed with hot water at every meal. But Marlon grew more dissatisfied and unhappy as the production limped along. While by the end of the first week, Cornfield and his French crew had struck him as incompetent, more problematic was the day-in, day-out presence of Rita Moreno, who inevitably brought her complicated history with Brando to the set.

In his own strange way the actor had never been one to let go of his past conquests, and it was he who had insisted that Moreno be hired because she was "down on her luck." Two years earlier, at age thirty-three, Moreno had married Dr. Leonard Gordon, a cardiologist from New York; she brought him and their baby with her. But as everyone in the company realized, she was still carrying the torch.

"With Moreno back on the scene, things got crazy," said Rhodes. "She may have been there with Lenny and her kid, but Marlon was fucking her again. With Marlon, it isn't over until it's over."

Marion Rosenberg, who saw the couple throughout the shoot, said, "The strain for Rita was all the greater because he was shipping in his various dusky maidens. I don't think Marlon meant to torture her, but just seeing him with all these other women . . . well, it must have opened up a lot of heartache."

The tension between Moreno and Brando erupted during a scene they were doing together in the third week of the shoot. The locale was a small villa in the dunes where Moreno's character was supposed to have been snorting cocaine or taking heroin, and Brando's character was to become angry at her and begin to quarrel. "With the cameras rolling, Marlon broke off the top of a bottle and handed it to her to hit him with," recalled Rosenberg. "Suddenly their scripted fight became a real fight. Things were flying around, and she started to grab at his hair. They were hurling accusations at each other, and all her pent-up anger and frustration just came pouring out—and this with Lenny and the child on the sidelines watching. The room where we were shooting was so tiny that the camera-man was sort of plastered against the wall trying to get some depth to the picture. Some of it remained in the film, because even though she lost the script, she stayed in character."

In fact, much of the melee would be left in the movie, and reviewers would point to this scene as one of the few moments in the film that showed a spark of emotion. After the emotional free-for-all the crew departed, muttering among themselves in disbelief. Acting as if nothing untoward had happened, Moreno calmly left the set with her husband and child and returned to the hotel for dinner. Marlon, however, wasn't nearly as composed. Instead of taking off for the château, he lingered in town, where Jan Lettieri encountered him in the Bristol's bar, still embarrassed, even shaken.

"Jesus Christ, I can't figure this out with Rita," he said. "Why'd she do that to me?" Noting his naïveté, Jan, a worldly enough woman, muttered, "This is too much."

His solipsism extended to Lettieri herself. Despite the presence of her husband, Al, whose physical bulk would have allowed him to snap Brando in two with ease, the actor still made overtures to her. Regularly, he phoned and "pretended to be other people with all these different voices," Jan recalled. "He was always flirting with me, and once he pressed me up against a wall. When Al was out, he'd drop by my room at night and just lie on the bed with me. Al found out, but like a lot of actors he was totally crazy about Marlon and never said a word."

Soon Brando, in his typical fashion, had pulled both the Lettieris into his circle. On their first free weekend, the three of them took the train to Paris. "There was this wonderful little incident," Jan recalled fondly. "Marlon loved to fart. We were in this compartment on the train and he kept farting to get the other people out. He was being naughty and funny."

Marlon soon began traveling to Paris almost every weekend. Sometimes he even forgot to return on time for Monday's shoot, and according to reports, his secretary had to track him down and hire airplanes to speed him back to Le Touquet. As the days dragged on, he also took every opportunity to taunt Cornfield, addressing him as "Herbert," not Hubert, which left the young director terrified.

"Marlon just trod on him like an ant," said Rosenberg. "The one thing that Marlon can do, like all movie stars, is sniff out people who are intimidated. Marlon in particular knows when someone is afraid, and he uses it and then despises that person for his fear."

Cornfield later insisted that Brando regarded with him contempt because "neither he nor Richard Boone could stand being directed by someone younger than themselves." From the beginning, he added, Marlon had tried to impose his version of the screenplay and resented being contradicted. In retrospect and "in an effort to clear my good name," the director described what he called Marlon's "betrayals," his efforts to sabotage the production and undermine his authority.

Cornfield had envisioned the film as a premonitional dream about the kidnapping of the heiress. In his original script Marlon was supposed to fall in love with his captive. "But when the time came to shoot the seduction scene," the director recalled, "Marlon told me he did not want to play anything romantic between himself and the girl." When Cornfield tried to explain how important the scenes were, Brando simply said, "I don't care to discuss it."

To sustain the dreamlike atmosphere, Cornfield's script did not give any of the characters names; Marlon stubbornly continued to assign names to the cast, almost randomly and for no apparent reason (although he called himself by his own family nickname, Bud). Cornfield didn't stop him, he said, because "I knew I could remove the names in the editing." But again, Marlon seemed to take this as a sign of weakness. (The names in fact reappeared in the film when Universal decided that its running time was a few minutes short, and added the cut sequences to "gain seconds," said Cornfield.)

In the scene in which Brando was to wait at a private airport to be picked up by Moreno and then watch as the cops moved slowly toward him, he wanted to hail the police car as if it were a taxi. "*Your* character would never do that," objected Cornfield, "while *you* probably would, being a crazy son-of-a-bitch." "That was the end of the honeymoon," explained Cornfield, adding that when Marlon objected to the script's final scene and wanted to substitute his own idea, Kastner intervened, taking Cornfield aside and persuading him to shoot Brando's version with the assurance that it would never be used. The director complied—even though it gave Marlon more reason to believe that Cornfield could be "stepped on."

Soon Brando was complaining again to Kastner, demanding that the veteran actor Richard Boone take over the direction. Once again Kastner capitulated, but even with Boone lending a forceful presence, Marlon put little effort into his work. Finally Boone himself exploded, "Hey, asshole, don't pull that shit on me! Quit phoning in your lines."

The antagonism between Cornfield and Brando hadn't been the only difficulty. There were still problems with the script; to remedy them and try to finish the shoot as quickly as possible (the desolation of the resort town seemed to be driving everyone crazy), Al Lettieri was assigned to do a rewrite. Plied with brandy, he worked long into the night trying to restructure scenes for the next day's shoot. But even as Lettieri wrote, Marlon improvised, clowned around, and grimaced into the camera in almost every scene, delaying things further.

Marlon's games weren't limited to the movie set. Sometimes in the evening he donned a black velvet Pierre Cardin jacket and held forth in the dining room of the Château de Montreuil. According to the *Paris Match* reporter covering the shoot, he came downstairs looking very much like a "romantic prince" and at dinner played the role of lord of the manor—slapping the servants on their rear ends, throwing his knife and fork loudly onto his plate, and laughing heartily. Any woman in the dining room who took his fancy was fair game: He sat down at her table and conducted an inquisition, brazenly asking her one personal question after another until she felt backed into a corner.

Marlon seemed so out of control that he finally managed to alienate Esther Anderson, the Jamaican girlfriend whom he had installed in his hotel, just as he had during the location shoots of *Reflections* and *Candy*.

"He was crazy about Esther," recalled Jan, who had known Anderson since *Countess* days in London. "She was wild and fiery, not in the least subservient, and very sexual. They used to lie in bed and see who could fart the loudest. She was also a big hash and pot smoker."

Whether she did dope with Brando, Lettieri could not say. She had never seen him use the stuff. What was obvious, however, was that in Le Touquet he was "treating her like shit" and finally she had enough.

"He was making fun of her in public, harassing her and even trying to put butter up her nose," Jan said, recalling an evening they were all at dinner in the Bristol dining room. Finally he drove her to the breaking point. She picked up a bowl of spaghetti and dumped it on his head, then got up and walked out. He kind of laughed it off, and we went on with dinner. But by the time we finished, she was already out of the hotel and on a flight back to London."

At first Brando was "devastated" by her departure, recalled Jan. "He told me, 'Jesus Christ, it's like losing my right arm,' and I think he even begged her to return. But Esther refused. She had too much pride to let herself be put down by him again."

Brando's grief was apparently short-lived. Fay Sparks, who had played the role of a black maid in *Reflections,* was soon imported to Le Touquet. For about a week the two were seen taking bicycle rides together along the coast, but then Fay disappeared as well, either fed up with Marlon or ordered to make herself scarce because of his next anticipated visitor—Tarita, who was bringing their son, Teihotu.

After several more weeks the company moved to Paris, where Marlon, Tarita, and their four-year-old moved into the Hôtel Raphael. Tarita was gone every afternoon because she was supposedly having extensive dental work done. "But *every* afternoon—that was the funniest thing," said Jan. "Finally Marlon got suspicious and had her followed. It turned out she was having an affair. I don't know who the guy was, but she had this wonderful little liaison going. Marlon was dumbfounded."

The complications of Marlon's domestic life multiplied. Although she had filed for divorce several months before, Movita also turned up, bringing with her to Marlon's hotel her mother and two children (now seven and one, respectively). Even with his children on hand, however, Marlon flirted and tried to conquer any female who crossed his path. "I don't remember a single woman he didn't try to pinch or grab," said Marion Rosenberg. "He was always touching somebody's tits or bottom—mostly, I think, just to see what the reaction would be. He was incapable of not touching. In fact, the very first time I had met him, he put his hand in my sweater and kept it on my breast for as long as he possibly could."

Given the discord and craziness that had dominated the making of the film, it was inevitable that the *Night of the Following Day* production would finish on the same chaotic note on which it had begun. Shooting continued through the end of 1967 (there was a hiatus of a few weeks while Marlon did his brief stint in *Candy*). With the footage finally in the can, an editor was brought in from London to try to make something of the reels of disjointed scenes. "It was amateur night. Nobody knew what they were doing," recalled Rosenberg. "We sat and looked at about two or three

hours of film and just did the best we could to end up with a final cut."
Even Kastner was displeased by the outcome. "I saw him practically strangle Cornfield because he was cutting it all wrong," said Rhodes. "It was the first time I ever saw Elliott go crazy. On the other hand, I figured Elliott deserved what he got in that mess of a picture."

Critics agreed that it was a disaster when it was finally released in January 1969. As the *Los Angeles Examiner* complained, "The dialogue . . . leaves the viewer with the impression that it was improvised on the spot. . . . The acting is almost uniformly bad." Pauline Kael saw the film as yet another downward step in Brando's decline, noting that he had "never been worse or less interesting, not even in *A Countess from Hong Kong.*"

The movie's senselessness had serious consequences for him: Finally, he had really hit bottom and no Hollywood studio would cast him in an important picture, even at a reduced salary. Not only was *The Night of the Following Day* his eleventh commercial failure, it also seemed to confirm that he had all but thrown in the towel.

THE 14 SIXTIES
(II)

1963–71

Although Brando had threatened to retire when his long servitude to Universal had run its course, in early 1968, he seemed to catch a second wind. In the same way he had grabbed for the lifeline of Huston's *Reflections in a Golden Eye,* he signed for two film assignments outside the Hollywood system: Gillo Pontecorvo's *Burn!* and Elia Kazan's adaptation of his autobiographical novel, *The Arrangement.*

With *Burn!* he was pursuing a long deferred dream: to make a politically significant picture. He hadn't reached for this lofty goal for several years, not since his muddled attempt in *The Ugly American.* But *Burn!* appeared to have both the political meaning he was looking for and a director whose radical credentials seemed to guarantee that the message would not be sacrificed to the medium. Brando had admired Pontecorvo's *Battle of Algiers,* the highly praised depiction of urban guerrilla revolt that won an Oscar nomination for best foreign film of 1966, and he had told the director he would be interested in working with him someday.

Pontecorvo was now proposing a picture that would be an indictment of colonialism, international big business, and slavery, one that would "join the romantic adventure and the film of ideas." At first, though, Marlon had hesitated, leaving Pontecorvo to inquire if James Coburn might be interested in the role. Not wanting to step on Marlon's toes, Coburn talked to Brando about it, asking what he thought of the director. "I don't know, but I kind of like him," Marlon said. "He's got those blue, sincere eyes, so I guess he must be sincere." Marlon seemed then to talk himself into it and returned to Pontecorvo to accept the job.

Originally called *Queimada,* the movie was eventually retitled *Burn!* in the United States in an allusion to the Watts riots and the catchphrase "Burn, baby, burn!" (While the radical lingo hardly matched Pontecorvo's narrative, United Artists, the film's distributor, knew that revolution was in the air and cynically set out to exploit it in its marketing strategy.)

Brando had a less jaded attitude when he agreed to undertake the role of the white colonist. The project, he acknowledged, was a direct link to his continuing involvement in civil rights, and announcing that he'd signed to shoot the movie in the fall of 1968, he explained that it was only the explicit connection between his political commitment and the film's subject matter that had persuaded him to step before the cameras again.

During the previous year he had passed up opportunities to work with Paul Newman, David Lean, and others in order to devote himself full-time to the civil rights struggle, and he was doing the film, he said, at a reduced salary. This was not the case, however. According to producer Alberto Grimaldi, Brando was being paid well to make *Burn!*—$750,000, by anyone's estimate a hefty chunk of change in 1969. Still, he was returning to material of substance and, more, he used the announcement of his new role as the occasion to articulate his views on the civil rights struggle. During the years that he had been churning out some of his worst pictures he had clung to political activism as the one authentic value in the otherwise meaningless and tawdry world of Hollywood, and friends attributed his desire to change the world to his own self-doubts. As Harold Clurman commented, "Because he is not sure he can ever be as good as he would like to be, he wants to help others." His commitment, "whether sound or not," Clurman added, was "always thoroughly sincere" precisely because of his "hunger for purification."

Brando's complex feelings about the civil rights struggle undoubtedly had their roots in his mother's social activism. The state of the world and the welfare of the have-nots, the poor, and the working class had been of central concern to Dodie, and Marlon had grown up voicing his allegiance to the "underdog" as much as his mother. His attention had been focused on the state of race relations in the United States since the early sixties, even though he chided himself for coming late to an awareness of the issues. "I guess everybody came late to them," he acknowledged. "I could have been involved in the social aspects of this country twenty years ago, but I ducked them."

Despite his own self-criticism, Brando in fact had entered into a new phase of social involvement early in the decade, when he'd been ticking off his contractual obligations in meaningless movies. Looked at from another perspective, Brando had been finding significance in a different world from Hollywood schlock.

He had first become aware of "the country's problems" when he followed Martin Luther King Jr.'s mounting struggle to integrate the South and became one of the first white celebrities in America to support the movement. While filming *Bedtime Story,* he and other actors such as Paul Newman and Burt Lancaster organized Hollywood backing for King's Southern Christian Leadership Conference (SCLC). Their efforts culminated in May 1963 in a star-studded rally at the old Wrigley Field in Los Angeles, followed by a private fund-raiser at Lancaster's home. California Governor Edmund G. Brown had sent out the invitations, and King himself was in attendance. When a Hollywood lawyer announced that it took $1,000 in hard cash to run the SCLC each day, Newman, Polly Bergen, and Anthony Franciosa all wrote checks, followed by John Forsythe and Lloyd Bridges. Brando, according to Taylor Branch's history of the civil rights struggle, "mumbled a warning against 'what-have-we-doneism' and bought a week of the movement for $5,000." Meeting King that evening only strengthened Marlon's commitment, especially since his old friend Harry Belafonte was now the civil rights leader's point man and organizer within the film community.

With Medgar Evers's murder on June 12, 1963, and the rioting it sparked throughout the South, King stepped up his efforts to bring President Kennedy's attention to the worsening situation, although JFK still procrastinated. Undaunted, King told his advisers Stanley Levison and Clarence Jones, "We are on a breakthrough. We need a mass protest." What he had in mind was a march of perhaps 100,000 people on Washington in an effort to get Kennedy to give full support to civil rights legislation. He reportedly told his advisers that both Brando and Paul Newman "had offered to help."

As preparations for King's March on Washington began to gather momentum in Atlanta, Brando traveled to Sacramento with Newman for a CORE sit-down on the state capitol steps. Here, and over the next several weeks of the summer, as reporters increasingly quizzed him, he would repeat his usual complaints against show business. He stressed that acting was not merely child's play but irrelevant when judged against the more important issues of the day. King, Roy Wilkins, and James Baldwin, he explained, were his touchstones to the movement.

For those few who were familiar with the actor's personal history, his mention of Baldwin would have been especially telling. Brando had first encountered the writer at the New School for Social Research—according to Baldwin's own recollection, as early as 1944. "I had never met any white man like Marlon," Baldwin said. "He was obviously immensely talented—a real creative force—and totally unconventional and independent, a beautiful cat. Race truly meant nothing to him, just society labels—he was contemptuous of anyone who discriminated in any way."

The two became good friends, and later, in 1953, when Baldwin was finishing *Go Tell It on the Mountain,* the book that would make him famous, Brando provided $500 to settle the writer's Paris hotel bill so that he could return to New York to meet with editors. Several years later Brando was approached to play David, the American with homosexual secrets, in an Actors Studio dramatization of Baldwin's later novel *Giovanni's Room;* Paul Newman and Montgomery Clift were also asked, the idea being that a big star would carry the play to Broadway. But Baldwin was surprised and pleased that it was only Marlon who had replied, prefiguring the courage he would later demonstrate in doing *Reflections in a Golden Eye.* When the two became reacquainted at civil rights events during the early sixties, they seemed completely at ease in each other's company. With Baldwin in one corner and the charismatic Harry Belafonte in the other, Brando was energized by their intensity, their sense of purpose. During the early summer of 1963, Brando continued to provide cash, and in July, two months after meeting King, he joined other show-biz notables, among them Newman, Lancaster, Franciosa, Charlton Heston, and James Whitmore, to press for reform in the television and movie business.

"They speak of prejudice in motion pictures—it is there," Brando announced. "A studio head [has] said he wouldn't advocate any story with miscegenation in it. I've seen people refuse to hire Negroes [in the movie industry]. We will lose forty percent of the market, they say. We have a moral obligation to the banker, they claim. . . . [But] all of us . . . can do something. We must do something. This is not a Negro movement. It's a democratic movement."

Driving home his point, he threatened to refuse to work unless the industry accepted "a fair representation of Negroes," and the following week, as the last scenes of *Bedtime Story* were being shot, he upped the ante by pledging to travel to Cambridge, Maryland, where for more than a month the Maryland National Guard had been brutalizing civil rights workers in an attempt to break their voter registration drive.

As fate would have it, a kidney infection landed Brando in the hospital instead. Marie Cui had also filed her paternity suit, which required both a blood test and his presence at a court hearing. With the tabloids filled with gossip about Cui and their affair, he kept talking to the press, but only about civil rights.

In a far-reaching interview with the *New York Post,* he weighed in on a number of issues, singling out Rosa Parks, the black domestic whose refusal to accept segregated public transportation had triggered the 1955 Montgomery bus boycott. "She was tired. She was worn out. She just said, 'I don't want to sit in the back any more,' " Marlon explained. "It sparked someone else to be inspired—and as the result, many are now making a contribution. . . . I think this country needs, in addition to a good five-cent cigar, a little five-cent investment in tolerance for the expression of individuality. . . . I got a peculiar note from some Negro organization when I decided to go to Maryland that 'we don't want Marlon Brando there,' that I was exploiting myself personally. My answer was that it's not a Negro cause—it's mine as well as everybody else's."

At the end of July, he joined a civil rights protest against all-white housing in nearby Torrance, a suburb of L.A., where forty demonstrators had already been arrested. Still weak from his hospitalization, he fell into step with some 125 other picketers but spent much of the afternoon once again answering reporters' questions. One homeowner protested that photographers and pressmen had trampled over his lawn and shrubbery, and Brando replied, "I'm sure some of the flowers are being stepped on today, but so are some people's human rights."

Choosing not to be arrested later in the day with picketers, who refused police orders to disperse, he prepared for a much more dangerous undertaking. With Newman, Franciosa, and the young actor Virgil Frye, he made plans to go to Gadsden, Alabama, a factory town not far from Birmingham where more than 500 CORE picketers had been arrested since June for demonstrating against local discriminatory hiring practices.

Frye had been working on the upcoming March on Washington with NAACP Los Angeles president Tom Newsome when he met Brando at an organizational meeting at the home of Charlton Heston. He was the least known of the many figures in the room, and Brando's casual invite took him altogether by surprise.

"It was, 'Hey, Virgil, I'm going up to Gadsden. Wanna come?' and it just knocked me for a loop," recalled Frye. "This was just before the March on Washington. We were trying to work out a liaison between blacks and whites so that black people would get more jobs. Gadsden was one of the centers of protest, because a lot of different factories were located there—Goodyear and so on."

The Gadsden trip was a brave venture. Although the lynching of a well-known movie star wasn't likely, violence couldn't be ruled out completely. Gadsden, everyone was aware, was Klan country. Gadsden mayor Lesly Gilliland had already denounced the actors' visit, accusing them of "rabble-rousing" even before the group, using assumed names, flew into Birmingham on August 22, 1963. Governor George Wallace was on hand for their arrival—scrutinizing them, Frye said, from behind a waiting-room window as they stepped off the plane and were met by CORE field-workers. Brando was "very relaxed" and immediately assumed the role of spokesman, trying to deflect the mayor's criticism. "We are here as devoted and peaceful representatives of good will, not as agitators, interlopers or interferers," he announced. "While no one can deny that Negroes have not achieved racial equality in the South, we have trouble in New York, in the West, the East, and the South. Too long has the South been accused as the sole source of friction and trouble between the races. They are just as much to blame in the North, the East, and the West."

After a rally and meetings in Birmingham, the group went on to Gadsden by bus. There, the four actors were escorted from gathering to gathering, rally to rally; along the way Marlon talked to locals, visiting with the rank and file just as he continued to give interviews to reporters. "I was scared, but Marlon was cool all the way through," said Frye. "Several locals from the NAACP were taking us around, but it was just the four of us and we all thought the chance of our getting blown away was very strong. I'd cut my hair. We wore ties, and, I remember, when we walked into this all-black church and got up on the stage to speak, Marlon turned to me and whispered, 'Now remember, don't lick your lips because there are photographers, and they like to catch you with your tongue out.'"

At each stop Brando was equally impressive as he spoke to various groups. He was fully prepared on the issues, articulate as well as caring, leaving the young actor as well as Newman and Franciosa hanging on his every word.

"Mainly, Brando was searching," Frye continued. "He'd talk to the black taxi driver or anyone else we ran into, asking questions like, 'How does it make you feel that you're treated like this? That you're given lesser jobs? How does it affect your kids?' He was concerned with how people *felt* about the situation, not so much their politics or ideas."

After a nonstop day of activity, the group finally retired to the Mary Sue Motel, but even there, at four in the morning, Brando continued with his statements to the press.

"This is another world," he announced to a *New York Post* reporter, adding that civil rights workers had revealed their scars from beatings and told him what it felt like to be jabbed with a cattle prod. "All of us were shocked," he said. "We turned [the cattle prod] on ourselves. When you're stuck with these things, you can't control your emotions. . . . What they do down here, Colonel Al Lingo and his state troopers, is to hold you somewhere, in jail or somewhere, and press it into your flesh until the flesh becomes scarified. And it's all been designed by Governor George Wallace."

Soon after Gadsden came the famed March on Washington on August 28, 1963, the defining moment in the sixties civil rights movement. Earlier, Brando and Newman were among 2,000 who attended an Apollo Theatre benefit in New York to raise money for the event, and the two then traveled to Washington, where they joined a delegation of some ninety entertainment celebrities led by Belafonte.

A quarter of a million people marched peaceably to the Lincoln Memorial to hear Dr. King's memorable "I have a dream" speech, which transformed the day from an outing into a crusade. Among the notables were Burt Lancaster, James Baldwin, and Josephine Baker, who had flown from Paris with a petition of support signed by 1,500 Americans in Europe. From New York came Sidney Poitier, Diahann Carroll, and Tony Curtis, and among the Hollywood group were Dick Gregory, Ossie Davis, Sammy Davis Jr., Lena Horne, Charlton Heston, and James Garner. During the march Brando carried the cattle prod that he had been given in Gadsden.

"I was sitting next to Dorothy Dandrige, with Tony Franciosa and Paul Newman," recalled Joe Mankiewicz, who had directed Brando in *Ju-*

lius Caesar. "He told me he had picked it up in Alabama, and he had brought it to Washington to show what they were using on the blacks down there. When I wasn't looking, he poked me in the ass with it. I must have jumped fifteen feet." On television later that day, Brando appeared alongside Baldwin, Heston, Poitier, and Belafonte, and he again carried his souvenir from Gadsden to demonstrate to the public.

Despite the attention that his celebrity prompted, Brando still insisted to the media that he participated in the march not as a star but in "the role of Mr. Citizen, as if I were a dentist from Duluth." From the perspective of the leaders of the civil rights movement, however, his fame and stardom were precisely what mattered, and his commitment had helped turn the march into one of the most momentous political events of the decade.

Attorney Clarence Jones, the special counsel to the SCLC and, along with Stanley Levison, one of Dr. King's principal advisers since 1960, had assisted in coordinating the celebrity delegation. "My own opinion was that the support for the movement in Hollywood was at best a slim reed, and I also thought that Brando was less consistent in his involvement than some of the others. For example, Burt Lancaster evidenced a depth of commitment that was matched only by Charlton Heston, who was then very vocal and very articulate in spite of his subsequent turn to the right. But Harry felt that it was his relationship with Marlon that was the foundation for building broad-based support in the movie industry."

Longtime activist Harry Belafonte had forged links among all factions of the movement, from nonviolent moderates to radicals, and used his credibility to help negotiate between King and Stokely Carmichael's more militant Student Nonviolent Coordinating Committee (SNCC). His engagement was total, a model of the ways in which a celebrity could initiate meaningful social change. Belafonte had made Brando his L.A. satellite, drawing on their long-standing relationship and Brando's reputation as one of the most outspoken people in town. For his part Brando took up the role with enthusiasm, but also needed and welcomed Belafonte's guidance.

"Harry felt more comfortable reaching out to Marlon than to Sidney Poitier," said Jones. "He'd just pick up the phone and tell him, 'Marlon, you didn't do this, do it,' or 'You're supposed be at such and such event, I'm counting on you.' He knew that it mattered to Marlon that he had a close connection to King, that it gave him authenticity in Marlon's eyes, and that allowed Harry to exert direction over him."

Brando, though, was not alone among actors who found it difficult to reconcile their commitment to King's goals with their own careers in an industry that was as retrograde in racial matters as the Deep South. Following the summer of unrest, Hollywood liberals, led by Marlon, threatened to boycott the studios unless blacks were given greater opportunities. When the studios turned a deaf ear and made little change in policy, stars who had rallied to Washington never marched on MGM or walked away from a production. For Clarence Jones and others in King's camp, the message was clear: It was "probably easier" for an actor to travel to Washington "than to deal with the institutional racism in the industry."

Marlon was hardly in a position to stage a boycott either, faced as he was with his still unfulfilled obligation to Universal as well as his ten-year-old debt to Fox, which would force him to begin shooting *Morituri* in April 1964. More important was the way he had always approached things and even now, in connection with something that unquestionably mattered to him, he fell back into had habits. An issue or incident would grab him emotionally, lead to sweeping pronouncements for change, but then, more often than not, he would fail to hang around for the detail work. Part of it was his limited attention span. There was also plain irascibility and impatience—organizing, even on behalf of Martin Luther King, was neither spontaneous nor immediately gratifying.

Typical of this impulsive behavior was when, in February 1964, he declared that he was going to pull his films from "color-bar" theaters. In London ostensibly to check out the film possibilities for the stage play *Oh! What a Lovely War,* he spoke at an antiapartheid meeting at Central Hall and announced that he and the eleven other signers of a petition he carried would henceforth insist on a clause in their contracts that barred their films from segregated theaters in South Africa and in the American South. His sincerity was not at issue, but since he was still locked into the Universal contract and had little or no control over his films' distribution, he could hardly live up to such a pledge. The journalists peppered him with questions, not simply about the practicality of the pledge but about the nature of his relationship with Christian Marquand, who was at his side and introduced as one of the group's organizers.

"There had always been gossip about them and their secret assignations at the Savoy," recalled Roy Moseley, author of *The Gang,* an account of Moseley's exploits as a celebrity autograph hound during this period.

"Marlon wanted to talk only about South Africa, and when one reporter asked another insensitive personal question, he ran from the room in tears. I followed him and called after him. 'Why are you stopping me? Can't you see I'm crying?' he said. He was shaking and in a highly emotional state. 'Didn't you hear what they were saying in there?' "

"We accepted the person as he was," explained Clarence Jones, echoing the views of others in the higher echelons of the civil rights movement. "We would rather have had a Marlon Brando with all his inconsistency and craziness than not have him. Belafonte was special, but in terms of stature, Marlon was a legend. Dr. King was pleased to have him. He was valuable, a special kind of person, and he delivered whenever he showed up. So it was a pragmatic, political judgment of what was good for the cause."

During the early months of 1964, Marlon's attention wavered because another cause had sparked his imagination: the burgeoning Indian movement. He would eventually become spokesman, tour guide, and guru, with his name more prominently linked to the rights of Native Americans than to black Americans. Although his most famous involvement with the American Indian Movement (AIM) would not come until the mid-1970s, Brando began working with Indian activists as early as 1964.

Back in 1949, while on his first trip to Paris, Brando had told friends that although he had signed for *The Men,* the film he really wanted to do would be "about Indians." The same goal was voiced in his instructions to screenwriter Niven Busch, hired by Pennebaker to draft *A Burst of Vermilion* five years later. With *One-Eyed Jacks* he got closer yet. A California Indian by the name of Red Arrow had been hired as a technical adviser on *Jacks* and instructed him in the Indian way of life and beliefs; he also introduced him to Yeffe Kimbel, a painter and early Indian activist, who heightened Marlon's awareness of the government's denial of rights to Indians and the repeated breaking of treaties. During location shooting of *One-Eyed Jacks* in Death Valley, Brando also visited a nearby settlement of Native Americans several times and talked to actor Ben Johnson, himself part Cheyenne, about making an Indian movie. But it wasn't until early 1964 that Brando publicly began to announce his support for Indian rights.

It wasn't as if he had forsaken SCLC and Dr. King; in some ways, he saw the two causes as related, though he seemed to jump into the Indian movement with renewed energy. On January 17, 1964, he was in Washington, D.C., for the executive council meeting of the National Congress of American Indians. There he announced, "Most people in this country don't know that United States treaties with the American Indians have been broken. They don't know the Indian has been blackmailed into keeping quiet. The Bureau of Indian Affairs of the Interior Department has followed a nearly consistent policy to obliterate the Indians. The bureau hit its depths during President Eisenhower's administration. . . . The Indian has five more years to win a battle of understanding or he faces extinction." At the close of the speech, he made his first public (and often repeated) promise to produce and act in "a movie that would tell the story of the misery of the American Indian today."

Surprisingly, whether as a result of the Indians' own lobbying, Brando's support, or for more intangible reasons, on January 21 the *New York Times* reported President Johnson's pledge to the National Congress of American Indians to help. Brando's response was to announce that he, writer Eugene Burdick, Mel Thom of the Paiute tribe of Nevada, Bruce Wilkie of Washington State's Makati tribe, and Clyde Warrior of Oklahoma's Ponca tribe were initiating "a campaign of awareness" to inform the American public of past injustices against the Indian.

Five weeks later, he moved from words to deeds and—as he had in Gadsden—put his body on the line by going to two Indian "fish-ins" in the State of Washington. The purpose of the demonstrations was to dramatize violations of the 1854 Medicine Creek Treaty, signed in the state's territorial days, which gave Indians the right to fish with nets off-reservation.

"There were two rivers primarily—the Puyallup, which runs through Tacoma, and the Quillayute, which flows into the Pacific about 110 miles from Tacoma," explained Jack Tanner, a black lawyer in Tacoma and member of the board of directors of the NAACP, who was representing six Indians recently arrested for fishing off-reservation. "The Indians had always fished there, but once the restraining order came down, there was the usual police brutality, the game agents' brutality, and as things evolved, it was just as emotional on a local level as school desegregation in the South."

With the courts on every level in the state deciding against the Indians' right to fish, and with arrests and protests making the news, Dick Gregory, then performing in Seattle, had phoned Tanner to ask if he could join "his clients on the battlefield." At the next fish-in at Quillayute, "Gregory took his coat off," recalled Tanner, "sat right down, and said, 'I'm home. I'm staying here.' He and Lil, his wife, were both arrested that day."

It was in the aftermath of the massive publicity surrounding Gregory's arrest that Brando came to Washington State for the fish-ins. His first stop, on March 1, 1964, was Olympia, where he spoke before several thousand demonstrators at the state capitol building. Afterward, he attended a six-hour session with Indian leaders, where he met with Tanner and several key Native American activists, including Bob Satiacum, a Puyallup from nearby Fife, and Hank Adams, who filled him in on the reasons for the protest. Although Satiacum and Tanner had their own conflicts with Adams, later to come to a head in the midseventies, Adams's knowledge of Indian treaty history so impressed Marlon that he would stay in touch with him and help support him financially throughout the next decade.

On March 2, Tanner took Brando, who was hung over from drinking vodka until five that morning, to Frank's Landing, where, inside a store, another leader, Janet McCloud, and thirty-five Indians were discussing strategy while Bureau of Indian Affairs personnel, local police, and sheriff's deputies lined the nearby riverbanks. Although the temperature was near zero, Tanner recalled that Brando wore " 'pimp' shoes with very thin soles" and a "light leather jacket."

At the protest site, multicultural egos erupted. Bob Satiacum and Marlon were both eager to be the first protestor arrested, while McCloud had already decided that Brando was posturing as though he were Zapata, displaying a "real pitying attitude." Tanner told the group that the actor had paid his dues by going south with the civil rights movement. "But the problem was," he later explained, "they mistrusted all outsiders, and the issue was, Who was going to get the publicity that day, Satiacum or Marlon?"

There was still a good deal of grumbling, and Brando's answer to the conflict was, reportedly, to offer McCloud and her group $500 to "let me fish before you do." McCloud and the others were not to be bought so readily, and the final compromise was that Satiacum and Marlon would both go out on the rivers.

For all their prolonged strategy session, Marlon in fact led the fish-in in a canoe shared with Reverend John Yaryan, canon of Grace Episcopal Church in San Francisco. Neither Tanner nor the priest noticed any anxiety on Brando's part in anticipation of an arrest. In fact, the reverend was more worried by the way Marlon handled their boat. "I tried to tell him you can't stand up and paddle a canoe," he reported. "I thought we were going to have a total immersion baptism. Marlon just grinned and advised me, 'This is the way we do it in Tahiti.'"

Brando and Yaryan were soon arrested and charged with casting a net and catching two "illegal" fish. As the actor had predicted, his own arrest unleashed pandemonium. The news spread that he had been taken to the Pierce County Jail, and the courthouse parking lot was soon jammed with cars, with gawkers abandoning their vehicles in the middle of the street to catch a glimpse of him. Brando's response was to do the unthinkable, for him, and sign autographs while announcing that he would sit in his cell and write a press release every day.

"The hell he will," said the local sheriff as he and the local prosecutor quickly dropped the charges so as to avoid further publicity. "I don't see any purpose in allowing Brando to make a martyr out of himself. This was done for show only and we are not going to make a mockery out of the law or our own office."

The day after his release Marlon proceeded to the Quillayute River, near Lapush. Here he would join Satiacum for a fish-in where the river flowed into the open sea. The treacherous currents were even rougher than usual because of a blinding rainstorm, but sharing a dugout canoe, the two set out, Brando still underdressed but determined to paddle past the waiting Fish and Game agents.

While Janet McCloud dismissed Brando's contribution, *Tacoma News Tribune* reporter Don Hannula credited him with focusing national attention on the issue, even if this last demonstration ended inconclusively. "He elevated public consciousness," the journalist said. "After Brando's visit, Jane Fonda came up, apparently at his urging. I used to be the only person who would cover these things, but he, and then Fonda, brought a lot more media coverage."

The fish-ins didn't mean that Brando was throwing aside his role as spokesperson for racial integration. Almost immediately after his Washington State visit, he flew to the nation's capital to confront Republican Everett Dirksen, the Senate minority leader, who had been opposing President Johnson's pending civil rights bill. Likewise, on March 11, 1964, he joined singer Miriam Makeba, Diahann Carroll, Sidney Poitier, and Harry Belafonte to sponsor a benefit for the Student Aid Association of South Africans, held at Basin Street East in New York.

Despite public pronouncements about institutional racism in Hollywood, Brando still had little control over what material he could use in his movies. His meddling with scripts during this period (worrying about his characterization of the white sheriff in *The Chase,* for example, or handing *Appaloosa* scriptwriter James Bridges a stack of books to learn about Indians) was one response to the problem; another was that he had several times explored the possibility of making a movie with a civil rights theme. At one point he met at James Baldwin's New York apartment to discuss a script in which he would play a prejudiced sheriff. Stokely Carmichael and James Foreman were present and "they eyed Brando skeptically," reported Baldwin's biographer. "Baldwin was a fussy host obviously wanting the two young Freedom Riders to like his old friend. But they were clearly going to make up their own minds. Carmichael was chuckling when Brando did his southern sheriff act. . . . Brando, recognizing his power, suggested that Stokely might play himself in the movie. Stokely thought about it but didn't commit himself, at least he didn't laugh at the prospect of being a movie star. . . . Brando did seem deadly serious—talking about schedules, when he would be free to make the film."

In the meantime, the movement itself was changing. The murders of CORE organizers Michael Schwerner, Andrew Goodman, and James Chaney near Philadelphia, Mississippi, in June 1964 and the subsequent killing of civil rights activists Reverend James Reeb and Viola Liuzzo had prompted calls for militant action. And then in the summer of 1965, while Marlon had been shooting *The Chase* only several miles away, Watts burst into flames, marking a significant turning point for many young activists who had begun to feel that King's nonviolent teachings were inadequate. For groups like RAM (Revolutionary Action Movement), the Black Muslims, and even the Student Nonviolent Coordinating Committee (SNCC), desegregation was now a bourgeois business at best; with Johnson in the White House and ghetto poverty exacerbated by his hawkish obsession with Vietnam, black separatism and militancy were becoming the order of the day.

For Brando, as for many in the Hollywood community, there was a lag between what was happening in the streets and the entertainment community's understanding of exactly what these events signified. While finishing *The Chase,* he was approached by writer Budd Schulberg to participate in the community workshop Schulberg and others had set up in Watts in the hope of keeping Los Angeles from erupting again. Despite the fact that Schulberg was one of the few people in "the business" he could trust, Brando chose to look the other way. Schulberg sent him an angry letter. "I complained to him about his lack of support," the writer recalled. "I wrote about a combination of his doing shit movies and talking a big game about the blacks but not really helping me by sending money or coming to Watts." Brando then telephoned Schulberg and said, "Budd, that letter really gave me nightmares." "I accepted that remark, 'gave me nightmares,' as a mea culpa," Schulberg explained. "I took it that he basically agreed with me but in some unspoken way seemed helpless to do anything about it." Again it seemed that Brando's own ambivalence—the unrealized contradictory impulses of his personality—had paralyzed him. "Look, he's not a thinker," added Schulberg. "I was sure he felt strongly about the blacks, there was no question about that, but something was missing."

During the summer of 1966 the various factions of the civil rights movement were united to march across Mississippi. James Meredith had been shot by a sniper, and though still convalescing, he was to lead the protestors from Tougaloo College into Jackson on June 25, 1966, along with King, Ralph Abernathy, and Stokely Carmichael. Sammy Davis Jr. organized a Hollywood contingent; only recently back from making *A Countess from Hong Kong* in London, Marlon agreed to join the 10,000-strong march.

His participation was important, Dick Gregory later explained. "In the South black folks had been dominated by powerful white folks, so when Marlon came in, it was like telling the black folks, 'White folks said it's okay.' I mean this was Brando. Nobody in the history of the movement made a difference like that."

Brando himself was impressed with all that Gregory had done for the struggle, and while in Jackson the comedian and his wife visited him in his hotel room, where Gregory was struck by how genuine and how transformed Marlon seemed. There was no question that Brando was by now under government scrutiny—by the FBI and the Los Angeles Police Department's "Red Squad," and presumably the army's Domestic Intelligence group as well. Still, insisted Gregory, he chose not to show his anxiety. His soon-to-be established links to the Black Panthers would alter his attitude considerably.

As soon as Huey Newton and Bobby Seale cofounded the Black Panther Party for Self-Defense in 1966, patrolling the Oakland ghetto in black leather jackets and berets while openly carrying shotguns, the group became synonymous with the forces of revolution in the United States. When thirty Panthers marched into the state capitol in Sacramento on May 2, 1967, openly displaying arms to protest a bill that would make it illegal to carry unconcealed weapons, the street-smart, disciplined cadre simultaneously frightened and intrigued the public with its iconography of black power, resistance, and revolutionary "purity." It was Newton's arrest on murder charges in October 1967, just a week after Oakland's Stop the Draft demonstration, however, that put the Black Panthers in the vanguard of the radical movement.

Although Brando himself had not had any prior contact with the Panthers, in early 1968 he suddenly took an interest. On one level, he was prompted by *Burn!,* the film about a fictional nineteenth-century black uprising that he had just signed to do with Pontecorvo. Needing to prepare himself, he sought out Panther leader Bobby Seale. The combination of Brando and Pontecorvo—whose *Battle of Algiers* was considered a film textbook on revolution by both the white and black Left—was enough to persuade the usually secretive Panthers to let Brando in.

"I had always admired Marlon from the time I was sixteen and saw *The Wild One*," Seale said, adding that he had continued to follow Brando's acting career and also identified with his character in *Waterfront*. "I knew from media information that he had this rebellious streak in him, too. I normally didn't buy gossip magazines, but anything about Brando I would read. So I was extremely receptive to him coming up to see us."

A few days after Brando's call, Seale picked up the actor at the San Francisco airport and took him on a quick tour of the Panthers' sandbag-fortified headquarters in Oakland. But Marlon most wanted to meet Eldridge Cleaver, the volatile and dogmatic best-selling author who had become the Panthers' high-profile and outspoken leader while Newton remained in jail. Seale and Brando drove back to Cleaver's apartment in San Francisco's Haight-Ashbury district about lunchtime and joined Cleaver and several other Panthers—all large, intimidating men—at the Cleavers' round oak dining table.

Kathleen Cleaver, then Eldridge's wife and the Panthers' communications secretary, was also present and recalled that the meeting was "intense" as they sat and talked almost until dawn. "What sticks in my mind was that Brando couldn't take his eyes off Eldridge," she said. "It was as if he was just glued to him, trying to absorb everything about him all at once."

As the conversation went on, Brando explained the reason for his sojourn on Panther turf—that he was making "this new movie" and really wanted "to hang around a bit and talk with you guys." "He was carrying the script for the movie," recalled Seale, "and he told us that it was about black revolutionaries in the islands somewhere. He said he needed to understand how real revolutionaries felt, reacted to, viewed the white power structure because he was playing this white oppressor."

At one point Seale was outlining the Panthers' political program when Brando interrupted him. "Wow, I'd really love to put that on-screen," he said to the Panther, "just the way you've been expressing yourself for the last five or ten minutes. I'd love to put that in context."

Above all he wanted Eldridge to read the script for *Burn!* and advise him. But Cleaver was neither as enthusiastic nor as starstruck as Seale. "Eldridge was very cool about the visit," Kathleen said. "He was probably awed by Brando but didn't show it, because in general Eldridge was a very unemotional and in-control-type person."

Seale concurred. "I don't think Eldridge ever read the script for him," he said. "After Marlon's visit, Eldridge began to reject him. It was the usual egotistical shit that Eldridge Cleaver usually went through."

In February Seale was arrested on an illegal weapons charge and was due in court for a preliminary hearing a week after Marlon's visit. Brando returned to accompany him as a show of support. As Seale recalled, he seemed more interested in Seale's feelings as "a revolutionary" than in the inner dynamics of the Panthers or the group's basic political programs, including their position on self-defense and violence. "He wanted to know what had caused us to be revolutionaries," said Seale. "He would ask questions like, 'What makes you go out there and take a chance that you may get killed?' "

The impulse was no different from Brando's riding the New York subways as an acting student to study body language. But his involvement soon went beyond research. He seemed inspired by strength and militancy—after all, the Hell's Angels had once appealed to him because they were a gang of outsiders, both anti-establishment and bonded in brother-hood, and the Panthers, even down to their black leather jackets, followed in the same tradition, with the added excitement of Third World politics.

By the end of the day Brando had given Seale his home telephone number, telling him to call anytime he needed help. Seale soon took him up on his offer. "A few more Panthers were busted, and I needed money to get them bailed out," he explained, "so I called and he sent a check for $2,500. About a week later I called again and I think he sent me another $2,000, and there were a few more donations, like maybe for $1,000 or $1,500 each time. I know that the money was a piss in the ocean to him, but it proved that his interest was real, that he was not a fake."

(Although the checks were sent directly to Seale, they did not bear either Brando's name or signature but were issued by one of Brando's private foundations—in all likelihood the sentimentally named Pennebaker Foundation, a "public benefit corporation" registered in California in December 1962.)

In Los Angeles, Marlon's house became a sort of hangout for privileged activists. According to those who came to these evenings, Brando obviously liked being accepted as someone "who could help."

The actor had already met Giselle Fermine, a statuesque Trinidadian, through Esther Anderson, his former Jamaican girlfriend. At the time, he was not aware that Fermine was really a Hollywood call girl with big-name clients, but her looks as well as her knowledge of voodoo intrigued him. Repeatedly, he tried to see her but she had been too busy. Then one night in March 1968, shortly after his visit to the Panthers, he told her, "Either come tonight or you'll never come."

When she arrived, she found him with James Baldwin and some black militants whom Fermine called a "bunch of funky niggers. . . . I thought they were phonies, though Marlon didn't think so," she commented. "They didn't approve of me because I didn't think like they did." She told Brando she was going to leave, but he explained: "These people need me, they know that I'm going to help them. They're black, I'm a white man, and they think you're getting too close to me."

"I wasn't sure what he meant—maybe that they might feel funny that a black woman was getting close to him and not to them, but he also told me I should go stay in the back room until the meeting was over." Instead, Fermine left. Later that night, Marlon phoned, upset that she had not hung around. Explaining that the others had departed, he requested she return. She spent the night with him and over the next several years, even as his interest in the militants dwindled, he continued his relationship with her as a paying client, setting her up in an apartment and paying for her clothes.

In addition to the gatherings at his house, Marlon also turned his attention to another movie project, which he believed he could finish before the start-up of the Pontecorvo film. Having completed his Universal contract, the timing could not have been better when Elia Kazan, despite the many years of strain between them, approached him to star in the film version of his own best-selling novel, *The Arrangement*.

"I was convinced that Marlon was the perfect person for the film," Kazan wrote in his autobiography. "[He was] the best actor in the country and the actor with whom I once had the closest relationship. He'd alienated himself from me after my testimony but consented to work with me in *On the Waterfront*. . . . I saw him rarely after that; it was obvious he felt reluctant about any friendly connection because of what he heard from friends: that I was a reactionary bastard."

Marlon's response to Kazan's call was a noncommittal "Well, I might take a stab at it." Irritated by the offhanded reply, Kazan sent Marlon a deeply personal, candid letter:

> I was meeting with Warners [about The Arrangement] and they urged me to see Countess from Hong Kong *and* Reflections in a Golden Eye. *Their point was not about your talent but two other things, first that you'd become terribly heavy and second that you were just "going through the motions" now. . . . I saw the Chaplin film and they were right . . .*
>
> You said to me on the phone, "Well, I might take a stab at it." And I thought, "Fuck him!" I'm too old now to pump up an actor I'm working with. . . .
>
> Then I saw Reflections in a Golden Eye. *And I admired you. Without any real help from Huston (he directs to make everyone a "character," thus, in a subtle way, patronizing them) you were bold and daring and made a difficult part moving and human. I admired you. But what I said about your looks in* Countess from Hong Kong *was even more true here. . . .*
>
> I don't want [the protagonist] plump.
>
> I'm not trifling with this picture. That's why there's a chance it might be a good one. But just as I'm not kidding in this letter, don't kid me now. If you tell

me, "I don't really want to bust my balls acting any more," I'll admire you for telling the truth. I want you to do this film but I only want you if you're genuinely enthusiastic about it and only if you will come to me ten months from now at the weight you were at during On the Waterfront. *Be a good friend and don't kid me. If you really want to, you can be a blazing actor again. The wanting is the hard part.*

The director did not get an immediate response from Brando and "never in the plain language I was asking for." Instead, Marlon's agent simply began negotiating for him to take the role. With the deal in place on March 1, 1968, Marlon called Kazan; the two talked about the hairpieces he wanted ordered from a master wig-maker in Rome, and over the next few weeks there was the usual exchange of information on the script and scheduling.

On April 4, Martin Luther King Jr. was assassinated. Marlon was at home when he heard the news, and by friends' accounts he was devastated. In addition to talking to many people over the next several hours, Brando telephoned Kazan, and according to the director he sounded "distressed" when he summoned him to the Mulholland Drive house.

When Kazan arrived, Marlon was waiting for him in the parking area, and right away he launched into a long, rambling speech about what a terrible state the country was in, what King's death signified, and what it meant for the future.

"He was so intense and so convincing that I didn't realize he'd walked me back to my car and opened the door to help me in," Kazan recalled. "Before I got behind the wheel, he informed me he simply couldn't do the part in my movie. At which he kissed me and looked so sorry I didn't ask any questions but drove away, planning to call him in a few days. I saw the man in the rearview mirror, walking to his house and going in; he looked desolate."

Several hours passed before Kazan was able to regain his composure and remind himself that Brando was "one hell of an actor." Although he sensed that Brando's "feeling about King was certainly sincere, the depth of emotion he projected came as much from his talent as from his sense of tragedy," he noted. *The Arrangement* was made *sans* Brando, and with Kirk Douglas in the lead, it proved a major disappointment.

According to Charles Maguire, Kazan's longtime assistant director,

Kazan had gone "out on a limb" and fought to get Marlon for *The Arrange-ment.* "That was in the period before *The Godfather,* when Brando couldn't get himself arrested," Maguire recalled. "I had spent several weeks talking to Marlon about wardrobe and scheduling, stuff like that. And then he called Gadg and just walked out on the picture."

Whatever the bad timing, there could be no doubt that Brando was genuinely moved by King's death. Pat Quinn, having driven from Santa Fe, where she had been living with her son, arrived at Mulholland early in the afternoon, presumably not long after Kazan's departure, and found him in bed, "overcome with sadness." In the days that followed, he was on the phone almost nonstop, talking to his sisters, to Judy Balaban, and to other Hollywood friends who had supported the civil rights leader, among them Jimmy Baldwin and Belafonte.

His phone conversations, his need to talk, were his attempt to under-stand King's assassination, why it happened, how American society had fostered such violence and hatred. Over the years he would come to sub-scribe to conspiracy theories put forward by Gregory and others. In his 1979 *Playboy* interview he theorized that King and Robert Kennedy, but especially King, had been eliminated because of their stand against the Vietnam War. As he explained, "J. Edgar Hoover hated black people, hated Martin Luther King. If he stayed in the civil rights area, fine. Let the civil rights bill pass so we can deal with the Africans and get their raw ma-terials. . . . But when he got on the issue of the Vietnam War, he was talk-ing to twenty-three million people who were pretty willing to go down the road he told them to go down. That was too heavy. He upped the ante and they didn't want to go that high."

Brando, like many people, seemed to be radicalized by King's assassi-nation, the process spurred by a phone call several days after the killing from Bobby Seale, who wanted to know if Marlon could help him get to King's funeral in Atlanta. Brando's immediate response was to send airline tickets and to make hotel arrangements not only for Seale but also for Rev-erend Earl Niel, the Panthers' minister of religion, and for a third Panther, a woman with the title of Captain of the Sisters.

In Atlanta, Brando shared a room with Anthony Franciosa, who re-called that during the day Brando seemed "absolutely shattered by King's death." Following the service, Marlon brought Seale back to his hotel suite where Franciosa, Peter Lawford, Sidney Poitier, Eartha Kitt, Sammy Davis Jr., Belafonte, Baldwin, and others were gathered to share their grief. "But even with everybody else there," Seale said, "Marlon wanted to offer me comfort and wanted me to talk about why I was so depressed. I told him that it wasn't only Martin but Bobby Hutton that I was thinking about."

Only two nights after King's death, "Little Bobby" Hutton, the Panthers' seventeen-year-old treasurer, had been killed by police bullets outside party headquarters in Oakland. Seale described how the police had raided the building, forced the Panthers to walk out naked, and then gunned down Hutton, wounding Cleaver and arresting eight others in the process. Marlon's response was to tell Seale that he wanted to attend Hutton's funeral, which was to be held later in the week in Oakland.

On April 12, 1968, Brando joined 800 mourners at the two-hour service, which was widely covered in the press. In his brief eulogy, he warmly trumpeted his identification with the militants when he announced that Hutton "could be my own son." He also promised to help raise money and to make people aware of what the police were doing to the group.

"Brando's speech was a creditable performance," recalled Peter Collier, then the editor of the Bay Area–based radical magazine *Ramparts*. "But what struck me was that he was obviously very much taken by the radical imagery of the Panthers. Until then I had never realized that he actually understood the kind of role that he had played in our society in the fifties. Tom Hayden has said this, too—that the first, political gesture we remember, the first one that had a real resonance for us, was the Brando of *The Wild One* in that scene when he's asked, 'What are you rebelling against?' and he replies, 'What have you got?'"

When Bobby Seale requested that Marlon give a television interview about Hutton's death, he readily agreed, appearing on "The Joey Bishop Show": "I knew he didn't usually do television interviews," added Seale, "but he did this one, and he talked about the shoot-out and how the Oakland police had murdered Bobby. He got sued by the cops for saying that, but just by doing the interview, he brought us a lot of support."

The lawsuit in question, asking for $6 million in damages, was based on the actor's public statement that the seventeen-year-old Panther "came out of the house with his hands up . . . , was told to run . . . , and was shot down in front of any number of witnesses." The case dragged on for three years, and not until Brando appealed to the U.S. Supreme Court was he free of it.

In the next few weeks Brando's speeches back in Los Angeles took on a feverish, militant cast. Feelings among the Hollywood Left were running high in general—bewilderment and grief, fear and anger, a mixture of emotions so pervasive that people seemed harder hit by King's death than that of John Kennedy. A fund-raiser for the Poor People's Campaign, started by King before his death, was soon organized at the home of movie producer Edward Lewis, and brought out almost everyone of liberal persuasion in town. Screenwriter and producer Abby Mann, an active supporter and friend of King, witnessed Marlon's bizarre, seemingly out-of-control behavior.

"We all had the feeling that we should try to continue what King had done on the basis of nonviolence," Mann explained. "But Marlon was going on and on in angry, radical terms, saying 'Now's the time to *do* something.' He was very militant and got up and said, 'I want the name of everybody who isn't here and I'm going to put the names in the trades.' He kept calling the no-show liberals 'shallow.' "

Mann had taken actress Jean Seberg to the event. She was an early Panther supporter, more radical than most of the other guests, yet all the while Marlon was speaking, Seberg was whispering in Mann's ear, "What is this, a take-a-nigger-out-to-lunch meeting? He's the biggest pile of shit I've ever heard."

Marlon droned on. Others continued their own conversations until he finally exploded: "Who's that talking in the bar? I want him *here*," he shouted. The guilty party turned out to be James Baldwin, and Seberg burst out laughing. Brando wasn't amused. "He just glared at Jean," said Mann. "He was so pissed off that he wasn't being taken seriously."

In the April 29 issue of *Newsweek,* he announced again that he was leaving acting to dedicate his life to civil rights. Soon afterward the magazine reported the next Brando rumor—that he would dye his skin and live like a black man, adopting the *Black Like Me* gambit to understand oppression from the inside.

Los Angeles civil rights lawyer Luke McKissick, who was defending several Panthers during this period, was uncertain that Brando was "all that deep into it." "I think the stories of his contributions were largely overinflated to match the public perception of his personality. He could get set off on something, as he did at Eddie Lewis's, and act it out. But then if you saw him the next week, there wouldn't be any meaningful follow-up."

During the months Marlon made his visits to the Bay Area, Gene

Frenke also had contact with the Panthers through his secretary, Louise Monaco, who was serving as the California coordinator of Eldridge Cleaver's 1968 presidential campaign on the Peace and Freedom Party ticket. Frenke, she felt, in his own quirky way of loving "the action," was more consistent than Marlon. He arranged fund-raisers, but she recalled that it was rare that Marlon attended. When he did come, bringing Tarita if she was visiting from Tahiti, he seemed bored.

"I thought Marlon was a dilettante," she explained. "I was also aware that for all his talk, the black radicals thought he was a jerk who didn't know his ass from a hole in the ground. The sense of people in the movement was that he would get emotionally charged for half an hour, come and do something, then somebody else would talk to him and he'd back off. . . . He was persuaded by whatever emotional response he had at the moment, and that made him very fickle, which was typical of everything else in his life."

From the outside it may have looked as if Brando was letting his attention wander. In fact, by late May he had privately broken with the Panthers, and at issue was the group's militancy. It would seem that during his visits to the Bay Area he had scarcely taken in the implications of the Panthers' revolutionary rhetoric. Now he was quizzing Seale about the goals of the group's "revolution." "He was asking, 'What do you mean about driving the white man out?'" Seale recalled. "I told him, 'Wait a minute. Our revolution is about putting political and economic power back into the hands of the people.' Marlon said, 'I've been getting a different reading about what you guys are about.'"

Brando's misgivings were brought to a head at the end of May when Cleaver published a party communiqué called "The Catechism of a Revolutionary." Officially endorsed with the party symbol on the cover, the pamphlet was based on the writings of Bakunin, the nineteenth-century anarchist, and it posited that true revolutionaries should be willing to kill even their parents if such were necessary to achieve their goals.

Marlon read the publication and called Seale.

"Bobby, I really like you guys," he said, "but I'm going to be honest. I can't roll with this Bakunin stuff, saying that a revolutionary has to kill his mother and father for the sake of the struggle."

Seale recalled that at the time he hadn't yet read the manifesto, but when he did, he didn't like it, either. He told Marlon he agreed with his objection and added, "I'll get back to you." It was not uncommon for Seale, Newton, and especially Cleaver to take divergent positions, but the Panther organization required that such disputes be resolved internally. Seale expressed his dissatisfaction with Cleaver's "Catechism" before the Central Committee, but the group outvoted him.

"And that was the end of my relationship with Marlon," added Seale. "We didn't talk from that time on. I wanted to, but I never had the chance."

Ten years later, in his *Playboy* interview, Brando obliquely acknowledged the contradictory responses to Bobby Seale, the Panthers, and guns, although he himself did not explicitly indicate into which camp he fell. "There's a tendency for people to mythologize everybody, evil or good," he said. "Bobby Seale, for some people, is a vicious, pernicious symbol of something that is destructive in our society . . . , a man from whom no good can emanate. To other people, he's a poet, an aristocratic spirit."

In retrospect Brando seemed to have more sympathy for the militants' position on violence than he had at the time of his conversation with Seale. "Understanding prejudice is much more helpful than just condemning it out of hand," he added. "There is a point, however, where you can understand so much and then you've got to take a gun out and say, 'I'm not gonna let you do this to me anymore; if you do that, I'm gonna kill you.' "

Ramparts editor Peter Collier saw Brando's break with the Panthers as "very canny. . . . It was at this point that the Panthers had gone into their maximalist phase," he said. "This was before they were concentrating on their neighborhood school and breakfast programs, and they were really into violent rhetoric and action. After his first endorsement, I think Brando realized that he shouldn't get in over his head. . . . It was probably smart to withdraw and not plunge wholeheartedly into that quagmire of Oakland and Berkeley and the Panthers' murderous activities. At least he didn't go whole [hog] like Jane Fonda and Bert Schneider, who eventually got fleeced by the Panthers."

While Brando never publicly denounced the Panthers, his turnabout was decisive. He gave over monies he had raised for them to Coretta Scott King and the Center for the Study of Nonviolence. "Brando acted with his heart," Kathleen Cleaver summed up her interpretation of the actor's fling with the Panthers. "He was a big softy, more like a kid who doesn't have a strong understanding of what he's doing. He wants to help somebody, but then other people will come along and tell him what they think, and he responds to them."

Fanned by self-righteous columnists, the public continued to identify Brando with the Panthers, but he reasserted his full commitment to the late Martin Luther King, his organization, and its philosophy of nonviolence. On the "Tonight" show he told Johnny Carson he was pledging a tenth of his earnings to the SCLC and appealed to the American public to join him in his support by contributing 1 percent of their incomes.

On the evening of the California primary, Robert Kennedy was assassinated. Kennedy's death, coming just two months after King's, culminated a year when American society seemed to be falling apart. In direct contradiction to the Panthers' position on a citizen's right to bear arms, Marlon now joined Candice Bergen, Shelley Winters, Robert Wise, Hugh O'Brian, and others to form a film industry committee lobbying for gun control.

Then, throughout the summer of 1968, he seemed to retreat from public activism in general. King adviser Clarence Jones wasn't surprised. "It's been his demon," he said. "Listening to him, you think, God, this guy is so committed. Then nothing happens. That forces you to ask, 'What intervened between the depth of that commitment and its execution?' I think it was obviously his crazy personal life."

The point was well taken. In fact, when Movita had filed for divorce the previous year, she demanded separate maintenance for herself, Miko, and Rebecca, and in July 1968 Brando responded by demanding blood tests for the children and then successfully petitioned Judge Edward R. Brand (who had also heard many of the Kashfi custody battles and the Cui paternity suit) to hold the divorce proceedings behind closed doors.

After the proceedings it was simply announced to the press that the marriage to Movita had been annulled on the grounds that, just as Jack Doyle had claimed, she'd still been married to the Irish boxer at the time of her alleged wedding to Brando. The terms of the settlement—and whatever testimony and evidence was presented to determine the children's true biological parents—became unavailable, since the records disappeared from the courthouse (the Los Angeles County Archives noted "File missing when microfilming").

Movita reportedly had sued for $8 million, but Sondra Lee had doubts about this figure. "I don't think she got anything like that," she said. "Marlon would pay for the kids' education, but I'm sure she wasn't getting shit because she had to move in with her mother." Philip Rhodes agreed: "As soon as the divorce was declared, Marlon put her Coldwater house on the market, since he'd always kept it in his name. . . . The scenery for the possible home for Christian was dismantled like a movie set and then sold."

Whatever personal and family crises deflected his attention from civil rights during the summer, he was thrown back into the welter of politics once he started making *Burn!* in December 1968. Although he had rejected the Panthers, he was about to embark on a film that would extol the necessity of violent rebellion, just as he would now be working with a director who had made the ultimate cinematic endorsement of guerrilla warfare. Thus, despite his earlier enthusiasm for the project—a movie with a nearly all-black cast and a theme that was supposed to have a significant contemporary relevance—he would begin shooting *Burn!* with as much ambivalence as he had brought to his other pictures.

Alberto Grimaldi, *Burn!*'s producer, had already been alarmed that Marlon might not see the project through. When it was announced that he had withdrawn from *The Arrangement* to concentrate on civil rights, press accounts suggested that Marlon would not be making any more movies at all. Grimaldi had cabled him, asking for a clarification of his commitment. By return cable Brando reassured him, "I AM IMPATIENT TO INITIATE MY PARTICIPATION IN THE FILM."

When push came to shove, however, Marlon seemed more reluctant than impatient when he pulled an impulsive stunt upon boarding his plane to fly to the film's location in Cartagena, Colombia. Pontecorvo had begun shooting on November 4, but Brando had put off his arrival. Then sporting long, dyed blond hair and a full beard in preparation for his role, he boarded his plane at Los Angeles International Airport on December 6.

"Are you sure this is the plane to Havana?" he flippantly inquired of the stewardess as he took his seat.

The flight attendant stared at him, the smile disappearing from her face.

"Get him off the flight!" the captain yelled, having heard the remark, and the attendant threatened to call in the FBI unless Brando deplaned.

He was forced to return to the terminal, all the while apologizing. As the plane taxied away from the gate, an airline representative learned who he was and offered profuse apologies.

"That's all right," Marlon said agreeably. "Maybe with the crew that nervous about skyjackers, I shouldn't go anyhow." He then beat a fast retreat, and ignoring the representative's pleas to wait, exited the airport and headed for home.

The "hijacking" incident was only the first of many setbacks that would plague the production. For all his enthusiasm, and despite asking Eldridge Cleaver to comment on the *Burn!* script, Marlon himself had not actually read the half-completed screenplay, nor, apparently, had he given much thought to the narrative's politics. The irony was that he was unprepared for Pontecorvo's historical sophistication. A complex man, the short, balding Italian was more than anything a political director uncompromisingly drawn to subjects that interested him and reflected his commitments. *Burn!* promised to be a cold, dark work, its exploration of revolution more deliberate, complicated, and cynical than *The Battle of Algiers*.

Brando was to play William Walker, an eighteenth-century British *agent provocateur* who had been sent to foment insurrection among the natives of a Portuguese colony in the Caribbean and thus ensure English control of the island's sugar trade. Successful in his mission and leaving behind a black army led by his disciple, José Dolores, Walker is then reactivated and sent back to the island ten years later when Dolores bolts and leads an insurrection against the English colonial forces. Walker undertakes a search-and-destroy mission that brings about the capture of his former ally, now turned freedom fighter. Dolores, however, chooses martyrdom rather than Walker's belated offer of escape, and after the revolutionary's death Walker is stabbed by another young black, who represents another potential guerrilla leader.

For all Marlon's proclaimed interest in films of contemporary relevance, Pontecorvo would soon discover that his biggest challenge was not solving the many technical problems of shooting in Cartagena, but keeping his star interested once he finally arrived. For the first few weeks the actor and director got on well, despite torrential rains that required the Colombian navy to rescue the company from its washed-out location on a nearby island. As shooting progressed and Pontecorvo demanded more and more retakes, Brando bristled; the fact that there was a language barrier did not help.

Producer Grimaldi soon realized that his star and his director were on a collision course. Somewhat like Charlie Chaplin, Pontecorvo was directing with a firm hand. "He was very demanding, very meticulous," said Grimaldi. "The script was the script, and there were discussions, but there was certainly no freedom. At a certain point Marlon didn't like that, so the friction started. Marlon began to think that Gillo was out to break him."

At the same time, the heat and humidity of the Colombian locale had pushed most of the company to the point of overload. Marlon soon began taking off, using a private plane to fly to Miami, so that he could spend weekends in Los Angeles. "The rest of us were all stuck," said Philip Rhodes. "Because the government was so worried about hijackings to Cuba, it would take two weeks to have our papers processed. But Marlon secretly had this plane and would just walk off whenever he felt like it."

The actor's escapes did nothing to alleviate his unhappiness, however. In addition to bugs and the unbearable heat, food brought to location sites was unrefrigerated and rotten; the sets were usually swarming with crowds and noise, not only because of the extras but also because of the armed guards who surrounded the campsite.

"The working conditions were worse than I've ever seen," Rhodes agreed. "There were all these bandits around, who came out of the hills to steal everything from the production, even costumes. We had to go to the flea market to buy them back after they were stolen. It got so bad that we couldn't take a leak without an armed guard going with us to make sure we weren't robbed."

Marlon solved the problem of the noise and the chaos by using earplugs, but he was still distracted by all the movement around the set and equally resentful of Pontecorvo's repeated takes. "If he wanted a purple smile," said Brando, "and I gave him a mauve smile, he continued to [reshoot] until he got exactly what he wanted, even if I got a dislocated jaw in the meantime."

The situation was made worse by the rampant drug use on the set; the crew, including some of the cameramen, were stoned half the time. Marlon withdrew, angry and suffering, but he expressed his personal dissatisfaction in knee-jerk political terms. Pontecorvo, he charged, was exploiting and mistreating his native cast. He was especially derisive about Pontecorvo's superstitiousness. For all his cool calm and meticulous intellect, the director had his "good-luck fetishes" (his Italian crew openly joked about these, claiming that every day Pontecorvo put on the same jockstrap that he had worn while shooting *The Battle of Algiers*). Hearing about the director's primitive beliefs, Marlon took the opportunity to sneak up behind him one afternoon, carrying a mirror and a hammer, and break the mirror with a loud crash as if to hex the production. Pontecorvo flew into a rage and, according to cast and crew members, began stalking up and down the hotel, muttering, "I'll kill that cocksucker, I'll kill him."

"It was awful, yet sort of funny in its way," added Rhodes. "At that point Pontecorvo started carrying a gun."

Marlon was furious, even more so when Sam Gilman, hoping that he might land a job with Grimaldi's production company, sided with Pontecorvo. Marlon told Philip, "Sam will do anything for a job," and stopped speaking to him for a while.

Brando also had to deal with a more physical irritation: He came down with a rash on his face that required treatment between every take. A flu epidemic hit, and like so many of the company, Brando also succumbed. Then came the final straw: Pontecorvo had him stand in the sun in front of a burning sugarcane field while insisting on forty takes of a single scene. Without further ado and not bothering to tell anyone, the actor fled Cartagena and returned home.

"The forty takes," Pontecorvo conceded later, "were probably my fault. I shouldn't have been so stubborn. I should have realized that Marlon was not in the mood and put the scene off another day."

Officially, the reason for his decampment was the skin problem. Producer Grimaldi, then working in Europe, heard another story—he was advised that Brando felt compelled to leave because of "death threats." This unofficial reason for Marlon's abrupt departure presented an ironclad alibi that couldn't be challenged.

"I doubt he was in jeopardy," conceded Rhodes. "If he was referring to Pontecorvo, it made no sense. Pontecorvo was carrying a gun because he had to make that gesture, since everybody else was armed on the set. It didn't have to do with Marlon. All of us were scared of the armed robbers whenever we left the set, but Marlon never went anywhere, so he had very little to worry about."

With Marlon in Los Angeles, Pontecorvo carried on. Hot, dirty, and tired, and with his son bedridden with dysentery, the director scouted locations against the day when his star would return, which could be a week, a month, or longer. Openly conceding that the film was seriously behind schedule and in financial trouble, Pontecorvo remained undaunted, and persisted in his vision. His unwavering hope for *Burn!,* he told a visiting journalist, was that his picture would transform itself into "a call for revolution." In words that might have appealed to Marlon if the actor hadn't been so antagonistic, Pontecorvo added, "What I would prefer for people to discover is something that is in *all* my films—a certain kind of tenderness for man, an affection which grows from the fragility of the human condition."

If anything, the walkout left Brando feeling tenderness for no one. He took to his Mulholland bedroom with Christian Marquand, George Englund, and Wally Cox in attendance. Often he slept until noon. He roamed the house, refusing to take phone calls even from Norton Brown, his accountant. In the evenings, when he was not staring at the flickering TV at the end of his bed, he would make his late-night calls to the women in his life, sometimes summoning them to the house. But for the most part he was alone, exiling himself from all but a handful of friends.

One person who saw him during this time was Marie Cui's close friend, Mallory Jones Danaher. The younger sister of feminist Kate Millett, she had arrived the previous year from the Philippines. Recently divorced and with a young baby, Danaher had met Cui through mutual Philippine acquaintances; she was soon drawn into the fray, which was still ongoing despite Cui's recent marriage.

Danaher's friendship with Marlon had started when she met him during Christmas 1968; Marlon had asked Marie to come up and help decorate his Christmas tree, and she brought Danaher along. After Christian Marquand had tried to pull Danaher down on his lap, she retreated alone to the couch until Marlon moved to the adjacent armchair. Brando soon learned that she had been living for several years in the Philippines and had steeped herself in Eastern religions, and he then began to ask her about Buddhism. "His form of conversation was to shoot question after question at me," she said. "There were weird questions thrown in, too, ones that shocked me, like 'Do you ever masturbate?' I was trying so hard to answer right, because I was only twenty-four and defensive and wanted to impress this big man, Marlon Brando." Despite his power, Marlon refrained from making a pass, which, by the time she went home several hours later, left her all the more impressed.

Over the next several months Marlon often tried to contact Cui, and if she wasn't home he would telephone Danaher to find out if she was there. "He would call me at midnight, three in the morning," Danaher explained. "Marlon never says, 'Hi, this is Marlon.' He just breathes into the phone, as if you've been interrupted in the middle of your lifelong conversation. That's how you know it's he, and I would say, 'Marlon?' Then he'd be screaming, 'Where is Marie?'"

Their phone calls "went on for hours," she explained, recalling his two-month hiatus from *Burn!* "He would call at ten at night, and sometimes we'd stay on till ten the next morning—talking, talking, talking our brains out about metaphysics, men, women, love, all very autobiographical, but more about his psyche and his soul than anything informational about his life. What I soon realized was that he was an extremely unhappy man. Fame had driven him crazy, and he was in a terrible, terrible state."

During these weeks it was not unusual for Danaher to receive frantic phone calls from Cui as well. Cui, described as an expert manipulator in her own right, was again playing hard to get, making herself unavailable when Marlon wanted her. Reaching Danaher late at night, she'd plead with her: "You have to go up to Marlon's house and sit through the night with him." Sometimes it was, "He's got a bottle of vodka up there, and he says he's going to kill himself. He's all alone, so please, *please,* go up."

"I was such a kid, I didn't think twice about it," said Danaher. "I would get dressed and drive up to his house."

Looking back, Danaher conceded that she should have been more alarmed about Brando's state of mind. "At the time I thought he was just being weird," she said. "He wasn't leaving his bedroom. I'd see him on a Monday, then go back up on Thursday, and he was still wearing the same clothes. He was also keeping his new raccoon, Emma, in his bathroom and letting her shit all over the floor."

Every day he wore the same ragged red serape from *One-Eyed Jacks*, and he looked like a bum," she recalled. "His personal hygiene was terrible, he wasn't taking care of himself, and he was going on eating jags, too."

It would seem that the underpinnings of Marlon's belief system had been kicked out from under him. While he was fed up with his career, his hope that the Pontecorvo film would, in the broadest sense, legitimize both his acting and his sense of himself as politically engaged had all but turned to dust.

Although Brando's therapy at the time was an on-again, off-again proposition, reportedly involving occasional sessions with not one but several psychoanalysts, he now contacted Thelma Schnee Moss, a UCLA psychologist and former actress whom he had known at the Actors Studio. Marlon struck her as "brilliant but tightly wrapped," simmering with the volatile anger of his early roles. "He was so goddamn angry with his mother," said Moss, "that any woman who encroached on his life would take on that aspect of his mother and he would become furious."

As a psychologist, Moss specialized in parapsychology and other phenomena, not personality development. By the late sixties she was appearing on talk shows to discuss her latest book, a study of LSD therapy, and what had occasioned Marlon's call at her UCLA office was his need to talk about the "paranormal"—LSD, life on other planets, ESP, all of which he had suddenly taken an interest in. Most particularly he wanted to talk about his experiences with acid; not only had he accidentally taken a trip, he explained, but since then he had purposefully tried hallucinogens on two other occasions. The mystical and religious visions had continued to haunt him. Moss, who had experienced similar visions herself, understood why they were so upsetting.

"I saw the same kind of visions that he was describing," said Moss. "Religious figures, biblical or archetypal, Buddha, Jesus, wise old men, as if they are real, as if you're with them when it's happening. It comes as a shock to anybody who has not put any faith in something like that before."

The key, as Moss was well aware, was that Brando had been in Freudian analysis for years, and hearing him go on, she was alerted to how disturbing the nonrational, drug-induced experience had been for him. In the early years of their acquaintance, she remembered, he had told her that through therapy he had found ways of "holding in his anger, his love and hate for his mother, his fury at his father, his sexual confusions—all those forces that could be called neuroses or psychoses." Now those defining structures seemed to have been blasted. Quite simply, his questions seemed a cry for help.

"He described feeling a surge of power or energy that just obliterated him," explained Moss. "I knew exactly what he was talking about, because with that kind of experience it's as if you lose your whole personal identity and your ego totally disappears. You feel as if you're in a fountain of ecstasy, fireworks in the sky, but you *are* the fireworks, [caught] inside this totally consuming fire. I knew his analysis of many years had probably convinced him that there was no such thing as God. That must have been the rock that he clung to, because it reinforced his cynicism. Then he had these visions, and he began to think, What was I believing in? Has it been there all the time when I was just laughing at it and acting as if it wasn't real?"

Over the next few weeks, he continued to telephone, randomly, always keeping himself at a distance. Invariably, the calls were framed by an explanation that he had *read* about such experiences, not undergone them himself. "I had always thought he could go crazy," she said, "especially because he always had this need to control everyone and everything in his environment. I realized that what he really needed to control was himself. He was so scattered, so undisciplined, that if he was left on his own with no appointments to keep, he would either never get out of bed or eat himself into oblivion. He developed extraordinary self-discipline to control that lack of discipline. He was like a pendulum back and forth—drinking bouts, then long periods on the wagon, then his constant battle with overeating. His years of therapy had helped him come to that sense of control before, but his phone calls suggested to me that he had lost faith in all those controls."

Whether it was the acid trips, the disillusionment with the Panthers and with politics in general, or his disappointment in Pontecorvo and the "meaningful" film, he seemed to be falling apart—so shattered that he seemed to have no recognition of what was happening.

Talking with Danaher, however, it was different. Perhaps because she was open to such nonrational cosmic speculation herself, or perhaps just because of her youth, she was permitted greater entrée. That spring the young woman continued visiting the isolated hilltop two or three times a week. She soon realized that Marlon was sleeping a great deal of the time and always ate in his bedroom, usually Chinese food he had had delivered. What struck her, too, was the routine he'd adopted with the phone. He might let it ring more than fifty times as she sat beside his bed, listening to him talk. Other times he'd lift the receiver, then drop it back into its cradle. When he did pick it up and listen, friends like Englund or Cox knew enough to shout, "Marlon, it's me, it's me, take this call." Still, as often as not he might ignore them, or if he chose to exert himself, he answered with a desultory, "Oh, hi."

Despite Cui's alarm about his drinking, Danaher didn't think that he was abusing alcohol or drugs, with the possible exception of Valium and sleeping pills. In fact, deeply disconcerted by his acid trip, he usually disparaged drugs. The few times that Christian Marquand, who was often a house guest, wandered in, he usually brought his hash pipe and passed it to Danaher. "Marquand was doing a lot of drugs," she said. "But when Marlon saw Christian and me smoking hash, he'd laugh and say, 'Oh, you two still do those childish things! How silly of you!' "

As much as she wanted to be a good friend to Marlon, Danaher found their relationship complicated by the fact that she had begun having an intense affair with George Englund. No one knew except Brando and Cui, because Englund was still married to Cloris Leachman. He was "extraordinarily handsome and witty, a universal hunk," Danaher said. "He came from a wealthy family and was always immaculately dressed. I always had this image of him with a cashmere sweater draped over his shoulders. He couldn't have been more different from Marlon, and sometimes I was amazed that they were such old friends, because George seemed exactly the kind of upper-crust guy that Marlon wouldn't like. Still, I was madly in love with George, and at the time I believed it was a serious relationship."

Just as Pat Quinn had noticed Marlon's and Christian's sexual rivalry, Danaher was aware of what was going on between Brando and Englund. She even suspected that sometimes George was at Mulholland, listening in on the extension, when Marlon phoned for late-night conversations. One day when she was leaving after a marathon talk session, Marlon put his arms around her in what seemed a more sexual way.

Danaher stopped him.

"Why?" asked Marlon.

"What do you mean, 'why?' " she said. "Because I'm having an affair with your best friend, and I really care about him. And you're sleeping with a close friend of mine. I just don't do things like that."

"Oh, don't be silly . . . ," Marlon started to say, but Danaher waved any more discussion aside.

"I knew it was some sort of test," she later explained. "I was perceptive enough about these guys and their locker room games to know that if I'd given even the slightest indication of being interested in Marlon that way, he would have been on the phone telling George. Also, I realized that sex with Marlon would be the end of our friendship. If I were to go to bed with him, he would no longer regard me as an intellectual equal, which was how he had been treating me during these months."

While fond of her friend Marie Cui, Danaher perceived her as another potential problem. Marlon had acknowledged that Marie "was disruptive," and as he and Danaher grew closer, they agreed that she was probably incapable of understanding their nonsexual intimacy. Not only did Cui throw plates and dishes, but she was already starting to tell lies about them behind their backs. "Marlon and I made a pact," Danaher recalled. "We said to each other, 'Let's be alert to Marie's personality—that she may try to damage our relationship.' We then touched hands and vowed, 'We will not allow Marie to destroy our friendship.' "

It was not Marlon's habit to discuss the women in his life with anyone, but with Danaher he sometimes complained in general, fuming, "Women are nuts," or "Women are crazy." From what Danaher could see, most of the females in his life "*were* pretty nutty, and a bunch of bimbos, too." As Kate Millett's sister, she had no illusions that Brando was anything but "a terrible male chauvinist.

"I had been struck with how much Marlon and Kate looked like each other," she added. "I often talked to him about her, telling him that he and Kate were practically identical, not only in looks but in personality. He would ask me more about her, and I told him, 'You'll soon hear about her, she's going to become world-famous.' In his cynicism he'd just say, 'Yeah, yeah.' I'd insist that she would be, but of course, I didn't go on to say that she would become famous as an anti–male chauvinist and that his personality was exactly what she would be attacking."

Depression is often a sign of anger turned inward, and there seemed to be no rescuing him from his self-hatred. Sycophants like Marquand and Gilman weren't going to confront him, and Philip Rhodes had gone to Paris with his wife while awaiting the resumption of the *Burn!* shoot. As for Wally, his drinking problems had escalated acutely during the past three years and he was in no shape to help anyone. "They were all so used to seeing the big, rich Marlon Brando and were so scared of incurring his disfavor that they refused to recognize that this was a dying person," said Danaher. "George may have seen that he was in deep shit—after all, he and Marlon had a profound bond. But if he did, he never—and wouldn't have—talked to me about it. Later George would just make dumb jokes. I'd ask him, 'How's Marlon,' and he'd say, 'He's fine. He's eating California and gaining a pound a minute.' "

Pat Quinn also realized that Marlon was failing. During the previous year they had not been in contact. She had been east, starring in *Alice's Restaurant* for Arthur Penn, and she had also taken up with a Cuban filmmaker, whom she would marry in New York after the shoot. He was the father of her second son, Chance, and extremely jealous, so when Marlon had telephoned a few times, she couldn't really talk. "His name was Octavio, but Marlon would always refer to him as Rodrigo, in a condescending way," Quinn said. "Still, Marlon soon got the picture—that I was living in a Latin prison—and never forced the issue."

When Quinn returned to Los Angeles in the spring of 1969, she realized that he had virtually barricaded himself inside the house. He wouldn't answer the phone and was regularly changing his number, just as he let it be known that he didn't want anyone coming up upexpectedly. One evening Quinn was shocked to find how out of hand his fears had become. Unannounced, she had driven up to Mulholland, "just to surprise him," she recalled. The security gate was open as she turned up the driveway. She thought perhaps he had been expecting someone, but when she pulled up in front of the house, he came outside on the run.

"You almost got yourself killed," he told her. "Do you know that there are guns pointed at you this very moment?"

Quinn was aghast. "Well, in that case I'm leaving," she said, and got in her car and drove home.

During this period of barricading himself against the outside world, Marlon was also paradoxically capable of inviting friends over on the spur of the moment.

One night he asked Carlo Fiore, then living in L.A., over to a small gathering. Relations had been strained between the two ever since Brando had fired Fiore from *One-Eyed Jacks,* so the invitation, on the face of it, was strange. Carlo brought along a friend and surrogate daughter, Diane Ivarson. A tall, blond actress, Ivarson had heard so many stories from Carlo about her idol that she had long been wanting to meet him.

The other guests—James Baldwin, the young actor Billy Dee Williams, Wally Cox and his new wife, Pat, and Christian Marquand, among others—were all in the den when Ivarson and Fiore arrived. Brando came to greet them, still wearing his ratty red serape. Nervous at seeing his old friend, Carlo resorted to teasing and lifted the serape to see how much weight Marlon had gained. Fiore and Ivarson were not lovers, but she sensed some of Marlon's competitiveness when she was introduced to him and she offered only two fingers for him to shake. "It must have felt like a dick," recalled Ivarson, "and he was fascinated that I would give him that kind of handshake. He was looking at me as if I didn't have anything on." Just before she left that night he made a quick pass, "lifting my skirt from behind." Ivarson fended off the play and later recalled what Carlo had told her was Marlon's description of loneliness: " 'It's like being out on a limb,' he said, 'and none of the other birds will talk to you.' "

During this period it was not uncommon for Brando, on the spur of the moment, to arrange for one of his several women to service him. If Cui was unavailable, he'd return to the group of Asian women he shared with Gene Frenke. Anita Kong was still on the scene as well. But if he didn't want to bother with preliminaries or arrange clandestine trysts with married women, he summoned Giselle Fermine, the Trinidadian call girl, for whom he had rented an apartment and agreed to pay her shopping bills.

In return, he expected Fermine to be on call whenever he was in town. He admitted that pills and alcohol sometimes interfered with his "performance," but being with her, Fermine noted, seemed more his way of fending off his feelings of loneliness than of fulfilling sexual needs. "I was happy just to be with him," she said. "He was intelligent and I liked talking to him."

What Marlon most liked to discuss with her, until all hours of the morning, was Fermine's experience with voodoo. At first he had said to her, "That stuff doesn't work," but then he wanted to know more about her grandmother (who was a voodoo priestess), *obeah* rituals, and her knowledge of female and male witches. He was also intrigued by her self-announced ability to guess people's signs.

Brando sometimes complained about the money he was giving her, and a few times he exploded at the bills for her more expensive shopping sprees. Fermine recalled, "Once he called me, 'Nigger bitch,' and I screamed at him, 'Don't you *ever* call me that!' Then he sort of smirked at me, as if he was happy I'd responded like that." Another time, when he warned her that he was an "egomaniac," she laughed and pointed at his wrinkled shirt, which was not tucked in. "If you had an ego, honey," she said, "you wouldn't go around looking the way you do."

Often, she claimed, he would call her to ask, "Are you coming over to suck my cock?" Fermine reported, "I'd say yes, and then he would want me to repeat why I was coming over. I'd say, 'I'm coming over to suck your cock,' and then he'd ask me, 'Why do you like sucking my cock?' I'd reply, 'Just because I love to suck your cock.' Then he would accuse me of lying. I'd say, 'If you think I'm lying, why do you ask me all those questions?' He said he just liked to hear me say it, which I think he did. I think he got off on it."

The aimless, time-killing desultoriness of his routine, as well as the same need for comfort, also seemed evident the morning she arrived at the house as scheduled to find Brando asleep in bed with James Baldwin. "They weren't making it, though it was obvious he had spent the night," she said. "I just turned around and left. I knew Baldwin was gay, and Marlon always said that they were *very, very* good friends, but he never let on to me that he had had an affair with him."

Fermine was aware of the several other women whom Brando was involved with; besides Cui and Kong, she said, there was Lisa Lu and Reiko Sato and other Asians whose names she didn't know. While they may have offered comfort and solace in his bleaker moments, he still was mired in a depression and remained in brooding withdrawal as he contemplated having to return to *Burn!*

On June 16, 1969, Brando had delivered an ultimatum to Pontecorvo: transfer the shoot from Cartagena to a more humane location or he would never finish the film, even though he was needed for only three more scenes and ten days of shooting.

"The conflict basically stems from fatigue after seven consecutive months of doing exteriors in a hostile, primitive region, cut off from the niceties of civilization," reported *Variety*. "At least one *Queimada* [*Burn!*] production source tended to side with Brando in the dispute, mainly as a result of the almost insufferable climate and facilities, and estimated that 50 percent of the unit was either hospitalized or threw in the sponge at one time or another."

Brando himself later conceded that the threat of deserting the production was a ploy to force Pontecorvo's hand. "I did not want to blow the picture, because it was an important picture," he explained. "I really felt that it could have been a wonderful picture. But I had to give the very strong impression that I didn't give a fuck and I was willing to blow it all."

Producer Grimaldi had a different take on Marlon's motivation. "I think *Burn!* was important for him politically," he said. "But, in my opinion, he knew it was not going to be a commercial success, and that's why he had risked walking out."

With the film only days from completion, Grimaldi had no choice but to comply with Brando's demand, although more than a month would pass before a "matching" location could be found. The choice, eventually, was Morocco, and the move added some $700,000 to the film's budget, with the shortfall landing squarely on the producer's shoulders. Grimaldi would later sue Brando for the money, but then settle because he wanted the actor for *Last Tango in Paris*.

Although Grimaldi complied with the change of location, he was not willing to remove Pontecorvo, the other source of the actor's complaints. "Even if I had wanted to, I couldn't fire the director," the producer explained. "It wasn't a commercial movie, it was a special movie. If Pontecorvo didn't direct it, there was no movie."

Once the company had moved to Morocco and Marlon had installed himself there, neither his relationship with Pontecorvo nor his mood seemed to improve. The director's perfectionism continued to drive him crazy. New York playwright Josh Greenfield visited the production to interview Brando; in the course of his questioning he asked the actor if he had ever wanted to kill anybody.

"I've spent ten years on the couch and I still don't know what to do with the urge to kill," Brando replied. "Right now I want to kill Gillo. I really want to kill him . . . because he has no fucking feeling for people. . . . I once tried to kill my father. Really . . . I always used to imagine I was killing him by pulling out his corneas."

Marlon's pent-up fury, the inner aggression that so often plagued and frightened him, came spilling out. He launched into his favorite litany of criticisms against acting, movies, Hollywood stardom. Although he refused to discuss the film "until I see . . . whether certain ideas that I have about it are in it or not," he adopted his usual stance of self-effacement. "A movie star is nothing important," he insisted. "Freud. Gandhi. Marx. These people are important. But movie acting is just dull, boring, childish work."

At bottom, he seemed to be saying that he had no identity other than what was projected on the screen. "People *create* me," he said emphatically. "So who I really am is of no importance. It's so easy to forget that, and to begin thinking that you are what you are up on the screen and carry that notion over into life. That was Marilyn Monroe's mistake."

In the midst of his ramblings, he did, however, concede that being a movie star allowed him to meet anyone he wanted, like "senators and politicians." To make his point he added, "And it does do away with the necessity of a lot of preliminaries socially. There's no chick I can't have if I program it and time it right. They all fall for the movie star bit."

Greenfield was interviewing Brando in a local nightclub, and now, as if to prove his point to the writer, Marlon scanned the dance floor and proposed that they pick out their favorite girls. Soon he was demonstrating his technique by approaching a young German woman. "Would you like to make love with me tonight? You don't seem to understand. . . . Tonight's beautiful. There's a full moon. Let's not each allow this moment of beauty to pass separately and alone."

When *Burn!* was released in Europe and America in late 1969 (in the United States, 20 minutes had been cut from the original running time), critics hungry for political significance were less than satisfied. Having seen the uncut 132-minute version, Italian reviewers were more sympathetic to Pontecorvo's far-reaching ambition than to the film itself or to Brando, whom they described as "too intellectual" and "playing the classic film hero with his godlike attitudes." Likewise, there was grumbling over Marlon's failure to attend the film's premiere, even though he had not made a movie "in some two years" and had announced that he had returned to acting "because of [the film's] antiracist theme."

The American reviews were just as mixed, although reactions were slightly more favorable to Brando than to the movie, which was considered "simplistically Marxist." Kevin Thomas of the *Los Angeles Times* called it "one of Brando's finest performances," while *Playboy*'s reviewer saw "many unhappy and unsatisfactory compromises" as well as "Brando's rudderless performance."

In retrospect and despite his lingering bitterness, Brando went on to call it "a wonderful picture." Even more puzzling, he would continue to extol *Burn!* as his best picture ever, and then, in 1974–75, try to enlist Pontecorvo to direct his long promised movie about Native Americans. But the renowned director of *The Battle of Algiers* did not make another full-length film after *Burn!;* instead, he joined the ranks of directors, producers, and studio heads whose careers crashed after working with Brando. Pontecorvo returned to Italy, produced commercials, and became head of the

Venice Film Festival; although *Burn!* seemed to spell the end of his career, in his spartan living quarters in Rome he continued to keep a photo of Brando propped up on the mantelpiece.

From 1967 on, Brando had been using both Tahiti and Tetiaroa, his private atoll, as his respite from Hollywood as well as his personal demons. Whenever he went for a week or two, he would stay with Tarita and their son, Teihotu, in the waterside compound he had bought for them in the wealthy Punaauia section, not far from Faaa Airport. But often he would make the two-hour voyage across open seas to Tetiaroa to wander the bone-white beaches of the atoll alone, contemplating his dreams for his private paradise.

The twelve *motu* constituting the atoll were formed from coral accretions on the remnants of an extinct volcano. The outer perimeter of the atoll was surrounded by a barrier reef that could be crossed only at high tide. The American from whom Brando had purchased the island had not maintained either the wharf built out over the reef or any of the small huts. Thus, by the time Brando took charge, the atoll was a tabula rasa on which he could inscribe his personal visions. Conditions were so primitive that any visitor had to bring not only food but also drinking water.

Initially Brando had joked to John Rosenthal, a Tahitian acquaintance, "I want my own island, and I want to be king." But for the first few years of his ownership he didn't formulate a definite plan, merely discussing some vague notions with Tahitian friends whom he brought out to tour Tetiaroa in his Boston whaler.

Hugh Kelley was one of the first guests whom Brando ferried to the atoll. The American expatriate owned several island resorts, both on Tahiti and the neighboring island of Mooréa. After crossing the treacherous reef, Marlon took Kelley around the various *motu*, stopping to point out features of each islet, all the while telling him how he envisioned his atoll. "I'm going to build a colony where intellectual people from all over the world can come, converse and trade ideas," he said. "They will be artistic, scientific, literary people, famous people. And they will all come and stay here for free." But since Brando had bought the atoll for privacy and solitude in the first place, he said he would build himself a residence on a separate *motu*. Kelley was not impressed with Marlon's vision.

Brando began to talk to developers and others with experience in

Polynesia, and although nothing came of these consultations, he kept fantasizing. Whenever he was in Tahiti he would stop by the office of Alec Ata, director general of tourism whom he had met during the making of *Mutiny,* carrying designs for an atoll community. "Always he had these plans and color sketches," recalled Ata, who was invariably asked to comment.

"Very nice, very nice," Ata would reply, having already seen myriad versions. "But when, Marlon, *when?*"

"Oh, let me dream first," Marlon replied.

While Tahiti continued to offer him solace and Tetiaroa the chance to dream, nevertheless his serene moods sometimes gave way to outbursts and eccentric dismissal of social conventions, with an almost regal assumption that he could do as he pleased. Dave Cave, a prominent real estate developer, said that the actor frequently arrived at his house unannounced and then stayed long enough to wangle invitations to dinner. Similarly, Nick Rutgers, the American who had first shown Brando the atoll during the *Mutiny* shoot, recalled his childish behavior about food. "He would often come to our house at lunchtime," he said. "But he would refuse our offer of food, saying, 'Oh, I'm not going to eat, I'm on a diet.' Then he'd say something like, 'Hey, look at that bird,' or 'See that airplane?' While you were turning to see what it was, he'd grab a fork and stab some food, practically clean your plate while you weren't looking."

When Brando visited Tahiti he sometimes brought family and friends. One time he persuaded Alice Marchak and Jocelyn to make the trip out to Tetiaroa, along with a group of Tahitian friends including expatriate Dolly Higgins.

The party set sail with enough supplies to stay several days. After riding irregular six-foot waves crashing in front of them, they crossed the reef and reached the lagoon. Their campsite on Onetahi, the largest *motu,* consisted of a main *fare* (badly in need of repair), a kitchen *fare* with a sand floor, an outhouse, and rain barrels to collect water. Marchak and Jocelyn set up their camp beds in the deteriorating *fare;* Marlon, hacking away at pandanus trees, built a rough A-frame for himself and the other men. The Tahitian women pitched tents on the beach. He then created a "shower" by poking the eyes from a coconut husk, taking delight in his invention. He relished the feast, including bananas flambé and a rum punch, that Dolly and her cousin prepared.

During the visit, it did seem that all that Marlon had been saying about the atoll was true: It was an extraordinarily lovely and pristine place. Equally evident was the way Marlon became a different person when he was there, reveling in the natural beauty, energized by the adventure, and, like a young boy, amusing himself with "roughing it" outdoors.

During these years, even at his lowest ebb, Marlon insisted that interviewers focus their questions on his politics and Tahiti, and he often described his dream of establishing a utopian, ecologically balanced community on Tetiaroa. Although he still had no definite plans for the atoll, he had employed a few workers from Mooréa who were now assigned to repair the dilapidated *fares*.

The job went slowly, and Brando sometimes complained that Tahitians were "not workers." Tiring of the rough conditions on Tetiaroa, the men would often return to Mooréa or Papeete for a few days off.

In Marlon's absence Dolly Higgins agreed to check on the construction. Like Hugh Kelley, she had seen firsthand how difficult it was to get people and supplies onto the atoll, and she knew that any building there was going to be a complex task. She also became aware of another overriding problem when, during one visit, she realized that the workmen repairing the roofs were not putting the usual layer of tin beneath the thatched palm leaves. The foreman of the work crew explained to her that this was what "the white man told us to do."

"But you know better," Higgins objected.

"Yes," the workman agreed, "but he won't listen."

When she asked Marlon why he wasn't repairing the roof in the tried-and-true manner, he mentioned that it was prettier to look up at the leaves instead of the tin underlayer.

"But in a few months the rain will come through."

Brando only shrugged. "I'm paying for it. I'll do it my way."

He also asked Carlos Pallacio and Leo Langomazino, his two associates from *Mutiny* days, to handle the payment of bills and manage other business matters in his absence. John Rosenthal had the impression that Pallacio was on Brando's payroll, "and he was expected to order and make payments for supplies and the workmen on Tetiaroa," just as he also handled household matters for Tarita.

Langomazino, the half-brother of Jacques-Denis Drollet, took care of Marlon's business affairs in Tahiti, too, but as a friend rather than an employee. He had been subjected to Marlon's vagueness about money, even his stinginess, ever since the *Mutiny* days—Brando would routinely forget to carry cash with him and often asked Leo for money. Leo's friends had reminded him "to keep a record," and Nancy Rutgers, Nick's wife, had gone so far as to predict, "One of these days, Leo, you'll ask Marlon for the money he owes, and he's going to tell you that you're a thief." But Leo continued to accommodate him, even paying overdue bills out of his own pocket, then expecting repayment from Brando on his next visit to Tahiti.

But as Marlon's depression worsened his attitude changed from simple absentmindedness to miserliness and suspicion.

One time when Leo presented Marlon with a receipted bill for roughly $750, Marlon gave his old friend a stony stare. "You didn't have my authorization to pay that."

"I was just trying to keep your credit good," Leo insisted. "After all we're friends, and I don't want you to get a bad reputation."

Brando refused to repay Leo, and it was the end of their friendship. (Pallacio had similar problems, but merely complained to Rosenthal in private and kept his job.)

More than any other woman in Brando's life, Tarita seemed to accept the terms that he imposed on her. She would be there when he needed her and rarely made any demands, but she also had her freedom. Affairs were common in the Tahitian social milieu, but, according to her friends, Tarita made it clear that her first loyalty was to Marlon. He kept her in the style to which she had grown accustomed: her waterside house, a swimming pool, and a Mercedes, as well as financial security. "With Tahitian women, it's a competition to see who can get the biggest fish," one American expatriate said, "and with Brando Tarita had caught one of the biggest fish of all."

Whatever the sporadic nature of their union, Brando did spend a fair amount of time with her in 1969. Tarita became pregnant again, and on February 20, 1970, Tarita Zumi Cheyenne was born. (Like her brother, Teihotu, her last name was listed as Teriipaia on her birth certificate; the Brando name was not added until February 12, 1973.) Her brother's name was a Tahitian word meaning "the natural spirit of growth, the force from which life blossoms." With his new daughter Brando affixed the name "Cheyenne" to acknowledge his evolving interest in Native American culture—and, as she grew up, she became known as Cheyenne almost exclusively.

Late in April 1970 Brando received word that Carlos Pallacio was near death. "I was in Paris when I heard he was dying," he said. "I took the first plane I could, but I didn't get back in time."

The funeral was held May 1, a traditional Tahitian affair with mourners drawn from the French elite, expatriate American community, and the native-born Tahitians.

Most at the funeral were struck by Brando himself. There had been the traditional procession of mourners who lined up to pass by the coffin; Brando, however, broke ranks, waiting until they had all filed past and taken their seats again. "Then he walked up to the coffin alone," recalled John Rosenthal. "That was a very vivid image for me because he made such a big scene of it. He stood over the coffin alone, then dropped a flower on it."

Carlos's death deeply affected him, and exhausted by the previous year, Marlon seemed especially morose that summer. He joined Elizabeth Taylor and Richard Burton on their yacht in the Mediterranean, but his sullen moods hardly made him a fit traveling companion, and he ended the cruise in a shoving match with Burton. He then returned to Tahiti, deciding this time he would stay a longer period for "decompression."

He was again absorbed by his plans for Tetiaroa. He wanted to develop part of it as a resort but also to set up experiments to convert waste products into energy, explore the use of solar and wind power, and to learn how to develop native-grown products as food. During his stay, he began to talk much more seriously about dropping out of moviemaking altogether.

Stopping in to see Hugh Kelley, he announced that he had decided to "give up Hollywood. My life is going to be this island," he said. "I just have to find a way for Tetiaroa to sustain itself and support me, too."

Ever the realist, Kelley got down to brass tacks: How much would Brando need to profit from a Tetiaroa resort in order to support himself? Brando told Kelley that with all his alimony payments and other family responsibilities, he had to make "about one million dollars a year."

"My God, Marlon," Kelley exclaimed. "You're talking about getting out of a business that's the easiest way in the world to make money and going into a business that's the hardest way to make money—the hotel business."

Still, Brando said he wanted to give it a try. In fact, Marlon's accountant, Norton Brown, mindful of Marlon's declining income over the past decade, had been urging his client to consider a resort and condominiums on the atoll.

Kelley suggested that he discuss the idea with a friend of his, one of the biggest developers of Lake Tahoe. Despite his own doubts, Kelley contacted the man, who was enthusiastic. The following week the developer came to Tahiti and outlined what would be needed to get the ball rolling. He and Kelley then accompanied Brando on a flight over the atoll to photograph it, preparatory to further discussion.

The developer was undertaking the first steps "on spec" and he spent the next three weeks drawing up his designs and projections. By the time he was done, Marlon had returned to Los Angeles. But when Kelley's friend tracked him down there and called the Mulholland Drive house he couldn't get through. He tried repeatedly for several days more, but Marlon never took his phone calls.

"Marlon just seemed to have lost interest," said Kelley. "He never got back in touch with the guy."

Brando then entered into long discussions with Bernard Judge, an architect who was living in Papeete while designing and building a hotel in Mooréa. In 1965 Judge had formed Environmental Systems Group, a progressive consortium of architects, engineers, designers, and ecological experts, which adopted a "systems approach" to their projects.

"The word *systems* was new in those days," Judge explained. "The 'systems approach' was to address a problem by bringing in lots of knowledge all at once, analyze it and come together with a solution that was not premeditated. That had always been my goal, but I didn't always get clients that were able to let me loose on a project that involved that sort of thinking."

Brando and the ecology-minded architect found themselves very much in synch (even sharing Christian Science forebears) as they discussed their visions for sustaining the natural state of Tetiaroa. As a result, Brando contracted with him to develop a master plan for Tetiaroa.

Over the course of the next year Judge developed the proposal that would, as he stated in its introduction, embody Brando's vision of making the atoll "a haven for artists, scientists, and intellectuals . . . a natural living laboratory for insight into the interdependent relationship between the animal world, of which man is a part, the ocean, and a coral atoll. For it is the objective of the Master Plan," he explained, "to establish on Tetiaroa a self-supporting community, a blending of research and training, nutriculture, aquaculture and tourism within sound ecological constraints for the particular benefit of all." Native Tahitians would also be included in the community so that, as Judge put it, they could "live their lives in their own various ways."

Most important, Brando and Judge were committed to "creating a community that would be nonpolluting and would not upset the lagoon ecology."

Marlon announced that he was finally going ahead with his long-range visions for his atoll as he enthusiastically presented the first draft of the master plan, taking the inch-thick, stylishly produced proposal to friends and local government officials alike, among them Alec Ata. Ata was less than taken by it. The plan was too abstract, a compendium of elaborate sketches that had little basis in reality. "I could draw a grandiose sketch in a minute, too," he said, "but that wouldn't mean it was ever going to happen." Knowing Brando and how much he guarded his privacy, the head of Tahiti's tourist board also doubted whether Marlon would in fact be able to tolerate living in a community where he would be surrounded by visitors.

The initial plan called for successive stages of development on the atoll's main *motu,* beginning with construction of four bungalows and sixteen "overnight 'A' frame huts," where the island's first paying visitors would be able to stay. Unaware that the actor was no longer receiving the huge salaries that he implied were collateral and persuaded that paying guests would soon be providing the funds for more development, a bank granted a large loan in 1971.

Operating the village at a loss for the first few years "wasn't part of the scheme," Judge conceded. "As soon as we got the plan going, we hoped to have people who paid to be there. And that meant we had to have a water system and an electrical system." Marlon burnt up the telephone wires, calling one expert after another. "Because of Marlon's persona," added Judge, "he could pick up the phone and get advice from some of the best experts in the world about all the things we were trying for the first time."

But from the outset the implementation of the plan faced one major obstacle. As virtually everyone who had been to Tetiaroa realized, the barrier reef made it very difficult to bring in the necessary supplies and equipment. "We had to get trucks and graders in, as well as fuel and supplies," recalled Judge.

Judge and Brando vetoed the idea of blasting a passageway in the reef on the grounds that this might upset the ecological balance of the atoll's all-important lagoon. Instead, the answer was deemed to be the construction of a small airstrip on Onetahi, the site of the proposed village. This, though, presented its own dilemma: How could they build the airstrip without heavy equipment, and without an airstrip how could they bring in that equipment? Carrying heavy earth-movers over the reef in a boat would be treacherous, since only small boats with shallow drafts could be lifted by waves over the coral.

Judge's solution was as wacky as it was effective. Marlon brought his considerable clout into play and, despite his accountant's dismay, he leased a World War II landing supply transport (LST) from the Tahitian navy, onto which Judge loaded the largest Caterpillar tractor they could buy, then sailed for Tetiaroa. The LST crew tied the shallow draft vessel up at the dilapidated nineteenth-century wharf, Judge then dropped the landing craft's loading door directly onto the reef's balcony, and looking much like a tank commando invading on D-Day, he drove the bulldozer directly onto the coral. With water lapping at its treads, the big Cat lumbered across the reef, then up onto the sandy beach. Successful with their first attempt, Brando and Judge soon brought a grader and an enormous front-end loader onto the atoll in the same manner.

Judge anticipated that the 660-meter-long airstrip would take about four months to complete. Assuming that this construction, as well as that of the bungalows, would require his constant presence, the architect pitched a tent on the beach and brought his wife and their young daughter out to stay. It was not long before he realized that the proposed site of the airstrip would have to be shifted, however.

Judge's decision had been prompted by an archaeological survey of Tetiaroa, another of Brando's ideas. For this, he had hired Yosihiko Sinoto, a well-known anthropologist from the Bernice P. Bishop Museum in Honolulu who had been working in Polynesia for years; Sinoto had discovered some fishhooks and some pottery shards, leading him to conclude that there were possibly two archaeological sites, one of which lay directly in the path of the airstrip. As a result Judge resurveyed his runway to avoid disturbing the location of what would become a future dig. "Brando wasn't even aware of the revision," said Judge, "because he was away making *The Nightcomers* in England."

Upon his return Marlon was greeted by scant progress. "The problems were unbelievable," observed Judge. "The Tahitian work crews would rather fish than work." Brando decided to impose some rules on his workmen.

Much like a nineteenth-century plantation master, he routinely gathered the crew on the beach and lectured them about their work habits, beer-drinking, and long weekends in Papeete. Nick and Nancy Rutgers sometimes ferried Marlon out to the island for these inspections, and they were amazed by his rambling lectures as he stood before the crews. "He would go on and on, telling them that they were going to have their own village, including a school and a church," Nick said. "Then he would tell them again that they couldn't have any beer on the island, and that they weren't allowed to go over to Tahiti. Sometimes I'd interrupt him and say, 'Listen, Marlon, we gotta go, the sun's going down.' But he'd just keep talking. I couldn't possibly figure out why he would go through this rigmarole, but he did it every time we went out there. It was as if he was insisting that they had to be in Marlon's monastery."

"He kept saying they were not to leave the island until the work was done," Nancy added. "You can't do that to a native. You can't do that to anybody, it's just inhuman."

Seemingly oblivious of the natives' disinterest in his utopian vision, Brando tried to persuade the laborers to bring their families from Papeete to live on Tetiaroa, offering them a lifetime tenancy in exchange for five years' of service. For the ever loyal Judge, the suggestions seemed quite in keeping with the idea of creating a new world. "That was *exactly* what we were trying to do," the architect said, ignoring the fact that there really wasn't all that much difference between the Tahitian's servitude to tourism (which he and Brando often criticized) and a lengthy servitude to Brando and Tetiaroa.

The workmen themselves were not entranced. Nor did they step up their efforts, and the construction of the airstrip and the overnight units dragged on. Like Dolly Higgins before them, Nancy and Nick Rutgers were also dismayed that in building the A-frame *fares* out of coconut palms cleared from the landing strip, the workmen were sinking the posts directly into the wet sand. The Rutgerses wondered why they weren't using cement blocks. Brando and Judge insisted that they wanted to build in a purely Tahitian style, which meant no cement in the postholes to which to bolt the frames. Nancy Rutgers quipped, "Sometimes you have to fake Tahitian style if you want a house that lasts." Her prediction was that with the first big tropical storm the posts would topple and the huts collapse.

Brando and Judge chose to go their own way. In retrospect, Judge insisted that their methods showed neither poor judgment nor ignorance, but were in keeping with their overriding philosophy. "We knew that these buildings wouldn't last for more than five or six years," he explained. "Our philosophy was that the Tahitians we would have living there would continue to redo the bungalows as they needed it. So it would be a continuing process, as it is in all island life. These things don't last—it's a process, a natural cycle."

Wood preservatives and insecticides were banned, as well. With the accumulation of standing water and garbage from the workmen living there, the atoll was overrun by both mosquitoes and *no-nos,* Tahiti's killer sand gnats.

Although both Judge and Brando intended that the atoll would ultimately support itself, during the first two years of development, money was only pouring out. This put Brando, who remained in financial straits, in a difficult position. His accountants were clamoring for a hotel to be opened as quickly as possible. To attract guests, Marlon decided to publicize the island retreat. At the time there was a series of television travelogues featuring celebrities, like "Sophia Loren's Rome." Marlon lined up producer Ray Stark to supply the seed money and on spec enlisted Conrad Hall, cinematographer on *Mutiny* and Nancy Rutgers's brother. Hall organized a camera crew, and they set sail from Papeete in two boats.

After Marlon's gala traditional cookout, the following morning he wanted them to shoot the arrival of the first vehicle on the island, a Chevrolet pickup that Judge was bringing over the reef on the LST. But the truck became stuck on the reef and the camera crew had to pitch in to help get it out of the coral potholes. Marlon, who had been supervising the operation from the beach, then suddenly announced he was leaving, that he had bronchitis and was taking the one remaining boat back to Tahiti to get penicillin. "Wrap a *pareu* around your soundman," he instructed Hall. "Shoot him long-range. He's white, no one will know it's not me. I'll be back in a day or so."

Ten days passed, and still no Marlon and no boat. They were running out of food and had been eaten alive by the *no-nos*. Finally Hall and his crew were rescued by Nancy and Nick Rutgers, who realized that they should have heard from them several days earlier.

"The film crew was just a bunch of sad sacks by the time we picked them up, and the movie was never made," added Nick. "As for Marlon, I don't think he could endure the rigors of that primitive living situation, which was why he'd left immediately."

From the outset Judge and Brando had been exploring other ways to make Tetiaroa a self-sufficient, profitable venture—especially in these early phases of development when paying guests could not possibly be a source of revenue. They were particularly interested in finding a project that could enhance the atoll's natural food supply.

Through Brando's many contacts, he was put in touch with Taylor "Tap" Pryor. A scientist who combined his ecological interests with entrepreneurial enterprise, Pryor had started a marine park on Oahu and was currently engaged in various aquaculture experiments. He had several long brainstorming sessions with the two men, as they considered a range of possibilities, from pearl harvesting (which the Tahitian government had previously favored) to raising turtles or *cavao,* the local coconut crab.

But what Brando and Judge were most enthusiastic about was Pryor's idea for a lobster farm, much like one he had been experimenting with in Hawaii. Although he had yet to do any extensive studies, Pryor concluded that growing lobsters in Tetiaroa's lagoon offered the best way to give the island a profit-earning operation without jeopardizing the natural habitat.

While work on the airstrip groaned on, Brando jetted to Hawaii several times to check with Pryor, but he still took no practical steps to initiate the lobster project; instead, as before, he talked—and talked—about his dreams for an ecological paradise. Most of his talk was abstract, larded with high-tech buzz words, and none of it, according to his family, lifted his depression. In late 1969 he visited Dick Loving and his sister Fran at the Mundelein farm. Since the new private room in the barn had been built, he usually regarded it as his solitary retreat, much like Tahiti. But this time he was concerned because Fran and Dick were separating. At Fran's request, he arrived to discuss the situation, and he and Dick took a walk together. He questioned his brother-in-law about the impending split, asking him if he was serious about leaving.

The discussion lasted about twenty minutes, and the two men "philosophized to a certain extent about the problems of marriage, fidelity, long-term relationships," said Loving. "He wanted to know whether Fran and I still fucked, whether I had a girlfriend (which I did), and whether that had been going on for a long time. I wasn't taken to task, it was more an attitude of 'this is the way life is.' "

What struck Loving most forcefully was that his brother-in-law seemed to grasp what these changes meant in terms of being an artist. "At one point he looked at me and said, 'This is going to be your time,' " Loving recalled. "He wasn't just talking about my leaving the marriage but about my painting and my career." At the same time there was resignation and sadness in his tone.

Even while Marlon was showing his care and his concern for his family, he was wistful, almost as if the thought of his brother-in-law's moving on and changing his life reminded him of his own inertia. "I thought he seemed diminished," said Loving. "It wasn't just that he was overweight. I sensed a real loss of focus and intensity in him. He seemed depressed, and I didn't feel the concentration and energy I'd seen in him before."

1970–73

"I'm all washed up," was the message Brando delivered to *Godfather* author Mario Puzo in a 1970 phone call. "I don't have a chance of playing Don Corleone. The studios would never take me on."

Hanging up, he turned to Pat Quinn, who was up at Mulholland with him, and shrugged.

"This guy wants me to play an old man," he said. "I can't play a sixty-year-old man."

"Well, take a look in the mirror, Mar," Quinn joked.

Brando gave her such a dirty look that she hurriedly added, "Besides, with Phil's help you can do anything."

Brando's pessimism suggested that he was deeply aware of the damage done by the previous decade of terrible movies and his emotional disengagement. Depressed and rudderless, he was also in financial straits, and by November 1970 he was forced to accept a comparatively modest fee—a reported $50,000 for a month's work—to appear in yet another low-budget, second-rate movie, *The Nightcomers,* a kinky psychological thriller to be directed by Michael Winner.

Puzo, though, wasn't dissuaded. He was struck by the actor's honesty, even his courtesy, as Brando acknowledged his unbankability and diminished draw. The problems and failures of *Burn!* had put the finishing touches on his reputation as troublesome and uncooperative, but Puzo, an outsider to the movie world, had nevertheless written him a letter of admiration, telling him that he could think of no one better to play his Mafia don. In fact, while writing his novel, Puzo had often imagined Brando as a way of bringing his character alive in his mind. In 1965 Puzo had submitted to publishers a ten-page proposal for a projected novel about the Mob that he envisioned as big, sprawling, and above all moneymaking. Hardly a literary doyen, the workaday writer hoped that his attempt at marketable pulp fiction would solve his economic woes. With a large family to support as well as a self-admitted gambling habit, he accepted a $5,000 advance from Putnam. But after completing only 100 pages, he was again short of cash, and when Paramount had offered $12,000 for an option on the film rights (with a total payment of $50,000 if the option were exercised), he overruled his agents' objections and took the offer.

With its hardcover publication in 1969, *The Godfather* quickly hit the *New York Times* best-seller list and remained there for sixty-seven weeks, eventually selling more than 1 million hardcover and 6 million paperback copies in the United States alone. Paramount was euphoric that its bargain-basement property was proving to be the hottest novel since Jacqueline Susann's *Valley of the Dolls,* and on September 12, 1969, Robert Evans, the studio's senior worldwide production VP, announced that *The Godfather* was being put into production, adding that it would have an "authentic" cast of "unknowns rather than big-name actors and actresses."

Fearing that Don Corleone would become a caricature if the studio typecast the mobster, Puzo, who was writing the screenplay himself, raised the possibility of Brando with producer Al Ruddy. The predictable reaction of the Paramount brass was, "No way. Who needs a guy with a string of failures?" Instead, they were looking at George C. Scott, among others. Meanwhile, in December 1970, Evans hired thirty-one-year-old Francis Ford Coppola to direct the picture.

The decision to go with Coppola was made only after Ruddy had scoured the ranks of the *Hollywood Directory,* approaching Arthur Penn, Fred Zinnemann, Franklin Schaffner, Peter Yates, Richard Lester, Richard Brooks, and even Costa-Gavras before settling on the young director who had begun his career in 1960 with Roger Corman. Coming up through the ranks, Coppola's credits were less than overwhelming, but he had proven that he had a way with scripts by writing the screenplay for *Patton,* which would eventually win him an Oscar. Since Paramount was lukewarm about Puzo's first draft, Evans was swayed by the thought that

Coppola could salvage the script. Furthermore, Evans explained, "He was the only Italian director in Hollywood. I wanted to smell the spaghetti."

From the outset Coppola made it clear that he wouldn't be pushed around by studio executives, and even as Paramount proceeded with its low-budget mind-set, he insisted that he would undertake the rewriting and directing of *The Godfather* only if it was made on location in New York. His second condition—that it be cast with "unknown, authentic" types—was something that Evans agreed with, although gossip columns were already announcing that Laurence Olivier and famed Italian producer Carlo Ponti were being seriously considered for the Corleone role.

Once Coppola came aboard, Puzo met with him in Los Angeles and immediately raised the possibility of Brando. As another anti-Hollywood maverick, Coppola was intrigued. He had already established contact with the actor, having sent him the script for *The Conversation* the previous year. Now Coppola and Ruddy sent out feelers. Brando's response was low-key, and he told Ruddy that he'd heard it was cheap fiction in the Harold Robbins tradition. At Ruddy's insistence, he agreed at least to read the novel before making a decision, and Ruddy delivered a copy.

Three days later Brando announced that he now wanted to play the aging don. Just as he had been persuaded to undertake other film projects because of their political "messages," he agreed with Coppola that *The Godfather* was really about American capitalism more than the Mafia. The story, he felt, revealed why America permitted organized crime to flourish—it was another form of private enterprise, and inextricably entwined with the nation's corporate interests.

With Brando committed to the role, Coppola set out to overcome Paramount's resistance. "Al Ruddy said that Francis was the greatest salesman he ever saw," said Puzo, "and I want to emphasize that, too. The success of *The Godfather* was due to Coppola's willingness to fight for Brando." Stanley Jaffe, the studio's president, was unbudging: "I assure you that Marlon Brando will never appear in this motion picture, and furthermore, as president of the company, I will no longer allow you to discuss it."

Coppola, moved by forces that many have called manic, pulled out the stops. First he argued that Brando would attract other actors to the cast with his "mystique." Then he argued that Brando was the only actor up to the part. When his arguments failed, he fell to the floor, apparently so distraught by Jaffe's refusal that he collapsed, hyperventilating as he clutched his stomach, writhing. Dumbstruck, Jaffe agreed to Brando but only under three conditions: that the actor make the film for no up-front money; that he put up a bond to cover overages caused by his well-known penchant for delays and difficult behavior; and finally, that he agree to a screen test, his first since *Julius Caesar*.

Ruddy and Coppola were in a bind. How could they ask Marlon Brando to take a screen test without humiliating him? Much to their surprise, Brando agreed to the conditions. Not only was he fascinated by the idea of playing with makeup to portray an old man (just as makeup, wigs, costumes, and disguises had always piqued his interest), he now spoke of being struck by the themes of family and honor, power and control that he saw in the character of the don. He even acknowledged being broke, to journalists as well as Coppola: "The women [have been] . . . ruining me. I've never known how to say no . . . never hesitated to pay a fortune in order to have the woman who pleases me. Then one fine day I had to surrender to the evidence that I was ruined."

In late 1970 he and Coppola, already sensing a bond in the iconoclastic, antistudio outlook they shared, arranged for the screen test to take place privately at Marlon's home. Coppola arrived with actor Salvatore Corsitto and a video-cam operator in tow. Instructing Corsitto to wait outside, the director went in to set up the session. Marlon was still asleep, but when he finally appeared in a long, flowing caftan, he had Philip Rhodes at his side. They had already darkened his hair and combed it straight back, and then added shadows under his eyes to make him look older. After Coppola described his old Italian uncle's thin mustache, Rhodes quickly penciled one in on Marlon's upper lip. Then he wadded toilet tissue into Marlon's upper and lower gums to give him heavy jowls. "It was easy to give him that jowly look," recalled the makeup artist, "because he was heavier at the time and didn't have a definite jawline." The transformation complete, Marlon changed into an old shirt and tie and a threadbare sport coat while Coppola set out a plate of apples and cheese and a small espresso cup.

As the camera rolled, Coppola called actor Corsitto inside and without giving Brando any warning, introduced him as one of the don's minions. Without missing a beat, Brando fell into the character of Corleone and the two actors played an impromptu scene. Afterward, Coppola played the tape of the session on a monitor, and Brando liked what he saw.

As he described it, it was "the face of a bulldog. Mean-looking, but warm underneath."

While Puzo believed that the required screen test was a "face-saving measure" by Paramount executives so that they wouldn't appear to be "caving in too easily," the session actually did seem to convince them that Brando was right for the role. Without identifying the actor, Coppola ran the tape for Evans and Jaffe. Evans said, "He looks Italian, fine. But who is he?" As soon as the name Brando was mentioned, Charles Bluhdorn, whose Gulf + Western owned Paramount, started to walk out, but was persuaded to watch the entire scene. At its close, he too had to admit that Marlon's rendition of the aging Mafia don was persuasive.

Nevertheless, Paramount still held back on making a final decision. With the film and its cast "up in the air," in mid-January 1971 Brando left for England for the scheduled shoot of *The Nightcomers*. Arriving in London, he rented Al and Jan Lettieri's flat on Mount Street, near the Dorchester Hotel and across the street from Mick Jagger's home. Al and Jan had split up that year, Jan having moved to another flat, and the Mount Street residence was in the heart of swinging London. On her own initiative, Jan quickly began giving parties for Brando and for his *Nightcomers* boss, Elliott Kastner—large fetes attended by the "beautiful people" like Joan Collins and Michael Caine, as well as an assortment of dark-haired, Eurasian "bimbos" who, she knew, would appeal to Brando. Marlon repaid her hospitality, she recalled, by eventually stiffing her for the huge quarterly phone bill he ran up while living in the apartment.

It was not long after the actor had left London for the *Nightcomers* location, an estate outside Cambridge, when on January 28, Paramount announced that Brando would play the godfather. Although studio executives dropped their demand for the actor's bond against losses, they pegged his salary at a meager $50,000, with $10,000 a week in expenses during his contracted six weeks on the shoot. But he was also to receive one percentage point of the gross after the first $10 million, escalating to a maximum of five points for a $60 million gross. "He's on the incentive plan," Evans confirmed when he announced the casting. "If the picture is a success, it will make him a fortune."

Brando was pleased. He also knew that the studio would be closely watching his behavior, and thus he stepped into *Nightcomers* with a more cooperative attitude than anyone could recall in years.

The Nightcomers

Created as a "prequel" to narrate what had happened to the evil children before the story told in Henry James's *Turn of the Screw, The Nightcomers* was a low-budget, dreary psychological thriller put together by Brando's old pals Elliott Kastner, Jay Kanter, and Alan Ladd Jr., now production partners.

While Brando seemed to give little thought to playing Quint, the brooding Victorian butler, much less to learning his lines, British director Michael Winner, known as a tough director and star handler, did not seem to mind. More famous for crude box-office pleasers than subtle directing talents (he would later make the vigilante *Death Wish* pictures), Winner knew he had Brando over a barrel. In fact, according to the actor's costar, twenty-one-year-old English actress Stephanie Beacham, Winner seemed to take a blackmailer's delight in the situation, knowing full well that Brando needed a "clean bill of health" in order to qualify for insurance on *The Godfather.*

Of all those on location at the walled-off, security-guarded estate, Beacham was in an ideal position to gauge Brando's mood. Besides their many scenes together, she was classically trained at the Royal Shakespeare Company and was educated, but, even more, her strong, sensible strain combined with a bohemian outlook set her apart from the needy women who frequently threw themselves at Brando and paid dearly for it. The first day of shooting began with a small confrontation between the two. As they strolled in the estate's gardens, Beacham picked a rosebud from a nearby bush and handed it to him.

"Thank you," he said, but then began to tear off the petals.

"That was your present!" she exclaimed, her tone filled with hurt. He stopped in his tracks and stared at her, so piercingly that Beacham felt as if she were being X-rayed. Then he led her back to the rosebush.

"Is there another one?" he asked quietly.

"Yes," she conceded, and plucked a second bud. He slipped this one into the lapel of his costume's jacket, where it remained throughout the shoot.

After finishing her first scene with him on January 28, Beacham noted in her diary: "A marvelous, complex, simple, muddled, anarchistic, amazing talent. . . . Marlon has drawn a picture in my script and written something in Japanese which I hardly want to have translated because I imagine it as many things as I want. The fact that he can't spell just melts me. Unfortunately, so do quite a few other things he does. I must immunize myself quickly or it's going to be unbearable when he goes."

There was a little-boy quality to his poor spelling and inept, childish handwriting in the notes she received from him. "He'd write something about his 'thoughts,' only he would spell it *thouts,*" she said, adding that his evident embarrassment made her feel protective, even maternal. The possibility of an affair was ripe, obviously, but Beacham, whatever her feelings, had ruled this out as "tantamount to giving up one's power. Besides," she added, "I knew that if I got involved with Marlon, I'd be done for."

The two had already begun to talk earnestly ("a bit of Gurdjieff, existentialism, and Buckminster Fuller—that kind of 'where are you coming from?' late-sixties talk"), and on one occasion Beacham went through a list of his credits. "What is this *Candy* business? This rubbish?" she confronted him.

Brando went down the list, one by one: "Pain. Pain. Pain. Pain," he said when he came to each "good" film he'd made. As he came to each of the trashier endeavors, he muttered either "alimony" or "Indians." It was his way of telling her that the negligible movies had been made simply for the money.

"How can you call the good ones 'pain' when you were so brilliant?" she countered.

"Those were all so painful," he replied, as if to say that in his best performances he had exposed the deepest part of himself. Explained Beacham, "I knew what he was talking about, because I was into that, too. To do good work, we actors have to tear the scabs off the wounds."

Brando's part in *The Nightcomers* was Quint, the coarse groundskeeper who introduces Beacham's repressed governess to sexuality. The script gave him every opportunity to play his customary sexual games, and while in many scenes he had his hands all over Beacham's body, he often broke the tension—and gained control—with practical jokes. For a run-through of their bondage scene, "he trussed me up like a chicken. Then he simply winked and strolled off to lunch." Even the property master couldn't untie the ropes. Finally Brando had to be summoned to release her from the bonds. "He knew very well that he'd have to be called back to untie me. He was being the naughty boy, having a ball," she said.

He also insisted that in their explicit sex scenes she appear nude only from the waist up. Of course, his demand may have originated in his own self-consciousness about the fifteen pounds he had put on before arriving in England, since he too refused to appear nude from the waist down, even in long shots when he was to have been photographed from behind. Beacham was aware of his self-consciousness when she watched him trying to do up the buttons on his dress shirt "with his pudgy little fingers." As she wrote in her diary, "Heavens, the sight of Oliver Hardy, as Marlon thinks of himself, in [Jockey shorts] and Wellington boots just made me die."

Without realizing it, Beacham had in fact tumbled to the one feature about which Brando had always been self-conscious. As Philip Rhodes confirmed, "Marlon never liked his hands. They were small and stubby." At one point Rhodes contacted an orthopedic plastics designer who made gloves for badly burned soldiers and considered having a pair made for Marlon. "That way the gloves would have extended his fingers," added Rhodes. "They would have looked real on camera, but I never did it. It was just an idea because I knew how he hated his hands."

Brando's anxiety about his girth also changed the way certain scenes were shot, such that the original "straight" sex episodes were reblocked so Marlon would appear to be taking her from behind. This was not a forerunner of *Last Tango*'s sodomy scene, but a strategy that allowed his body to be hidden by Beacham's. "I was actually fronting to cover his pot," she explained, "and he joked about it." Sometimes he was more serious about the problem and insisted to her that he had to lose weight. "I must," he told her, "I can't fuck anymore. It's really interfering." And at the end of the month's shoot, when they were saying their good-byes, he was still joking about his bulk, telling her, "We are but ships that pass in the night—or in my case, a tug."

Marlon used jokes and bantering to ease the tension of their explicit sex scenes as well, often causing her to burst out laughing. In the midst of one scene, she told Marlon, "I'm going to giggle." Marlon replied, "It's okay if you giggle, providing you don't fart. You're still a lady." Flatulence was a source of amusement for Marlon throughout the years, and with Beacham it was no different. "He was so anal," she confirmed. "I've never known anyone except a four-year-old boy to be as anal as he was, always talking about farting."

Beacham sometimes was startled by the sexual explicitness of the dialogue, but she managed to hide her innocence behind wisecracks. During one scene in which Marlon had his legs completely entwined with hers and was squeezing her nipples, she quipped, "So what are we doing after filming?" The crew roared with laughter. Several times, when she noticed that Brando had actually become aroused, she teased, "Got you there! Teehee." When he again had her tied up, he retaliated by dropping his pants and threatening to urinate right there.

"Marlon, don't you dare!" she shouted. "You do your bloody trousers up this minute!"

The line between Brando's domination and that of his character was sometimes blurred. Already hinting at the psychic compulsions that would infuse his character in *Last Tango in Paris,* he tried to engage Beacham in improvisational games during the bondage scenes. In one sequence he had her in a half nelson and demanded, "Say you're a dog, a bitch in the street." When she refused, he increased the strength of his hold. Finally Beacham had no choice but to repeat, "I'm a bitch in the street."

When she recalled the incident, Beacham rationalized that it wasn't Brando indulging in his own S-and-M fantasies but rather his playing the character to the fullest so that she could be true to her own role. "It wasn't me who said those words," she explained. "By being so Quint, Marlon helped me to be as much Miss Jessel as I was capable of. That's what made it such an extraordinary acting experience."

One of Brando's on-set eccentricities was his attitude toward his costume and his makeup. Once the actor put on his gamekeeper's shirt, he refused to relinquish it. It was his way of getting into his character, he told Beacham, even as the costume became grungier and ranker as the shoot wore on. Finally the wardrobe mistress made two more identical shirts so that she could sneak into his dressing room and substitute a clean one without Marlon realizing that the switch had been made.

One reason Brando's shirts were so dirty was his obsession with putting on his own makeup. "Philip Rhodes used to sit there reading poems while Marlon would be putting his makeup on himself," Beacham explained. "He's one of the few macho figures I've ever known who didn't abhor makeup but was actually fascinated with it. I think he liked the ritual of it, like an actor preparing to get into character."

Brando sometimes evidenced his dislike and distrust of director Michael Winner, who had the reputation for throwing temper tantrums and shouting at actors in crude language. "I'm very fond of Michael," Beacham later said, "but he can be a terrible bully. On the set he did a lot of yelling. He never did that to Marlon himself, but he did it enough to others in front of Marlon that Marlon would ask, 'Does he think I'm deaf?' " Brando's response was to make a point of going to lunch with the person at whom Winner had yelled the loudest during the morning takes.

Although Beacham recalled a few times when Brando seemed ready to storm off the set, he always reined himself in, ever mindful of the need to be on his best behavior. The nearest he came to overt rebellion was his imitation of Winner as "mein Führer." Winner was Jewish, and one day Brando lost his temper and shouted, "Thank God you were on the other side. If Hitler had you on his side, he would have won." Still, *The Godfather,* and the issue of his insurability, was paramount.

The Godfather

On February 16 he didn't show up on the set of the *The Nightcomers,* however. What kept him away was a visit from Francis Ford Coppola, who had flown to England and come to Cambridge to consult with his lead actor about the script and the Corleone role. For the previous several weeks, preparations for *The Godfather* had been in chaos, with the movie's cast and locations still largely undecided. While shooting was officially scheduled to begin March 1, so as to have the film ready for a Christmas 1971 release, the production was already behind schedule, with Robert Evans countermanding some of Coppola's proposals and insisting that he would personally keep a tight rein on the director's more flamboyant ideas (such as re-creating the old smoke-blowing sign for Camel cigarettes in Times Square).

Coppola seemed unconcerned as he spent several days with Brando going over the rough-draft script. Because Marlon wanted some background on the "real" Mafiosi, the two of them listened to tapes of mobster Frank Costello testifying before the Kefauver Senate hearings on organized crime. Costello's voice was surprisingly high-pitched, and Brando was taken with its light, wheezy quality; Coppola agreed, saying, "Powerful people don't need to shout." Brando, for whom the notion of power and control was almost second nature, concluded that this would be the guiding trait of his characterization.

After Coppola departed for Rome to cast the small roles for the Sicilian sequence, Brando's preparations for his part continued. With Philip Rhodes, he spent a day experimenting with how to create the heavy-jowled look that had been so compelling during the first Los Angeles screen test, and Dick Smith, the makeup artist who had aged Dustin Hoffman to 120 years in *Little Big Man,* was hired to help. He came up with a device to enhance the massive jowls that Rhodes had created with toilet paper. It was a triangular mouthpiece made of plastic that did not interfere with speech but pushed out his lips, jutted out his jaw, and accentuated the sag of his cheeks.

Working with Brando in London, Rhodes and Smith also developed the method for aging Brando's skin. "I pulled and stretched his skin out," Rhodes explained, "then Dick painted rubber on it. When the rubber was dry, I let the skin fall back into its relaxed position, and the rubber wrinkled up so that we could highlight and shadow the wrinkles." They then experimented with Brando's hair, again emphasizing the heavy forehead by combing the strands straight back. "He had been losing his hair, so he'd begun to comb it forward," added Rhodes. "Now we brushed it up and back and darkened it. This worked because even though he was balding, he had a good skull."

On February 25 Marlon flew home from England to Los Angeles, reassuring both Coppola and Evans that he was immersed in the part and could handle it easily. Privately, though, he had his doubts, or so he said later: "I've always felt that you can't ever play a part that's either bigger than you are in personality or so far a reach for you that you fall on your face. I had no frame of reference to play a sixty-five-year-old Italian."

Brando stayed in California as the start-up date still was undetermined and the part of the don's son, Michael Corleone, remained uncast. Several big-name actors had lobbied for the role, including Rod Steiger (improbably wanting to play a twenty-five-year-old), but Coppola much preferred Italian-American Al Pacino, whose only screen appearance to date was as a junkie in the highly regarded *Panic in Needle Park.* Paramount wanted Warren Beatty, Jack Nicholson, Robert Redford, or Frank Langella. Coppola insisted that Pacino be recalled for a second screen test. The first one had proven to be a disaster, and in fact, Coppola had labeled

Pacino a "self-destructive bastard" because he'd turned up without bothering to learn his lines. The second test wasn't much better, with Pacino again blowing his lines, and once again he was rejected.

Still, Coppola remained convinced that he was right for the part, and Brando himself called Evans to argue for Pacino in the role of his son. "Listen to me, Bob," he said. "He's a brooder. And if he's my son, that's what you need, because I'm a brooder." It was Brando's "insight," Evans later conceded, that finally convinced him, and on March 4 the studio agreed to sign him. Now the casting was almost complete: In addition to Diane Keaton as Michael's wife, James Caan was to play his older brother, Sonny; Robert Duvall was chosen for the role of the stoic Irish-German consigliere, Tom Hagen; and John Cazale would play the fragile middle son, Fredo. Talia Shire, Coppola's sister, had been hired to do Michael's sister, Connie. Because of his long friendship with Brando—and having met producer Al Ruddy through Elliott Kastner—Al Lettieri was cast as Virgil Sollozzo, the drug-running turk who touches off a Mob war.

With most of the cast in place, Coppola scheduled more makeup and costume tests in New York. Marlon's habitual weight fluctuations now became an issue, for having complained about being overweight during *The Nightcomers* he had shed almost twenty pounds during the previous two weeks in California. "Evans phoned me," Rhodes recalled. "He said, 'We're in trouble. Marlon's lost too much weight. The makeup and costumes don't look right.' So they brought me in to New York, and I padded him up to give him the big stomach and the bulk." Rhodes also applied the latex wrinkles and inserted the mouthpiece to jut out his jaws; ten-pound weights were added to his shoes to slow down his movement.

For the makeup test, Coppola's plan was to have cinematographer Gordon Willis shoot Brando drinking wine and peeling and eating oranges while singing along to Italian folk music. Willis had been handpicked by Coppola because he wanted to give the film the look of old period photographs. Most of the features Willis had shot had been done in New York, but nonetheless he had heard all the stories of Brando's misbehavior on other sets. To his surprise, he found the actor to be anything but difficult. "He was entirely cooperative. His concern—and rightly so—was that with all that age makeup on, he had to be lighted properly or it would look like shit. I knew that if I simply put light directly in front of him, the effect of the makeup would be neutralized. So I had to come up with the kind of lighting that would not only be right for him, but also right for the rest of the movie. I explained this and he immediately understood. He seemed to have an intuitive grasp of what had to be done technically and how to function within those limitations."

Before each take, Brando even asked Willis which lens would be used and how much of his body would be appearing in the frame. "He was aware of having to determine how big or small the field size of the screen would be," said Willis, "and he adjusted his movements accordingly. From that first makeup and lighting test, I saw that he had a very attuned sense of visual containment."

The only real problem during this session was that Brando sometimes had to have Coppola and Willis repeat their instructions because of the flesh-colored earplugs he was using to silence outside noise and force himself to concentrate. In between takes he relaxed and chatted with the crew, but throughout he remained in character, never relinquishing the persona of the aging but powerful don.

At the first full rehearsal it became clear just how much the role suited him. Chairs had been arranged to suggest the meeting in the godfather's study in the opening scene, and Duvall, Caan, Pacino, and Frank Puglia (playing the character who beseeches the don to avenge his daughter's beating) were seated when Brando walked in. "They had been talking and joking," said producer Ruddy, "but when Marlon arrived, everyone turned to stone."

It was as if by joining an almost exclusively male cast, a group of players who revered and honored him, Brando had in fact become the real godfather. To the younger men he was "like a god," Puzo confirmed. "He was the one guy with whom they all had wanted to act, and here was their chance. Even the director and the producer were in awe of his talent."

Coppola perhaps most of all; to the others it appeared clear that Brando and the director had reached a solid, indeed trusting relationship. What seemed to concern Brando most was the question of when he should begin to suggest the godfather's evil side. Coppola wanted some hint of it in the opening scene; Brando argued that such revelations should come later. At first the others simply hung back, afraid to say anything. Then Caan began nervously to joke while Pacino retreated into a morose silence. Duvall, having worked with Brando on *The Chase,* was not as intimidated. Behind Marlon's back he began to make faces and ape his gestures. His pals stifled their laughter, terrified that the legend would catch them laughing as he and Coppola droned on in their intense analysis of the scene.

"Keep talking, Marlon," Duvall finally called out. "None of us want to work, either."

The joke broke the tension, and a clear pattern of male bonding was establishing itself. It was this masculine camaraderie that would take the edge off Marlon's usual twitchiness throughout the shoot.

Although principal photography began on March 24, Brando's first scene wasn't scheduled for another three weeks, so he returned to California. While he was away, the production began to be plagued by conflicts. Resenting the interference of Evans and Paramount, Coppola drew a faction of the crew around him for support, mainly his associates from San Francisco. Most of the cast was left to exchange rumors about delays and tensions.

On April 12, at 7:30 A.M., everyone assembled at the New York Eye and Ear Hospital to film the scene of the godfather being brought to a hospital after being shot. By midmorning Coppola received word that Brando had missed the red-eye, which would have reached New York in time for his 8:00 A.M. set call. There were murmurs among the cast and crew about Brando's notorious troublemaking.

Brando finally showed up in costume for the hospital scene the following afternoon. Once again he seemed to be making an effort to be "one of the guys" as he shook hands with the assembled production staff. Then he climbed into the hospital bed, where he was to lie motionless—prop IVs and tubing attached—for an hour and a half before the take was completed. He played the critically wounded don without complaint, despite a constant stream of curious hospital staffers who wandered in to catch a glimpse of the star.

The next day, April 14, was Brando's first full shoot on location, a loft in Little Italy where a set had been built to represent the Genco Olive Oil Company. His scene, the meeting with Al Lettieri's Sollozzo, went sluggishly, and he suggested to Coppola that they have more rehearsal. Already under fire for schedule delays (it was estimated that he had been losing two days a week), Coppola refused. But several days later he was quickly shaken to hear that the front office had hated the rushes of the Brando-Sollozzo scene, calling it boring and undramatic. Coppola now decided that the scene had to be reshot, with the result that his vacillation caused studio executives to doubt him even more. Talk escalated among the crew that Paramount was ready to replace him with Elia Kazan or Aram Avakian; so relentless were the rumors that Coppola began to have dreams of Kazan stepping in.

When the talk reached Brando, his position was clear and unequivocal: "If they fire you, I'll quit," he told Coppola.

"Brando saved my neck," the director later confirmed. "The next morning I scrapped the shooting schedule and told Brando, 'Let's do it again. They're going to fire me.' He came through."

Whether the studio had been swayed by Marlon's threat or whether the cost of replacing any director in midproduction had determined their decision, Coppola was allowed to hang on. (Later Evans would confirm that during the course of the shoot Paramount came close to firing Coppola four times.) The following Monday, April 19, the crew again gathered on Mott Street in Little Italy to shoot the scene in which Corleone is mowed down by Sollozzo's thugs. The street was roped off, crowds had gathered, and a horde of reporters and photographers pressed against the barricades, trying to get a view of Brando as the aging don. When Brando appeared in the street, his fans went wild, one woman screaming, "I touched him! I touched him!" as he passed by.

In his persona of the godfather, Marlon didn't give the woman a glance, concentrating on the job at hand. After an initial staging, Coppola called for multiple retakes. Each time, a spray of gunfire sent Brando running across the street, wounded in the throat, writhing against a parked car until he fell and lay motionless. With each performance the crowd gave Brando a loud ovation, sometimes ruining the take by clapping before the scene was over. After these bursts of applause, Brando picked himself up off the pavement and with a flourish bowed low to the throngs on the street, who sent up further cheers and shouts.

Despite the crowd's approval, the shoot that morning did not go smoothly. The sun was too bright and because of high winds it was difficult to string up the tarps necessary to modulate the lighting. As Willis and his crew struggled to get it right, Marlon ambled over and suggested solutions. Willis gave him a long, stony look without saying a word.

Brando stared back, then with a faint smile, he added: "I know—just shut up and act, right?"

"You got it," Willis replied.

The pressure wreaked havoc with Coppola's emotions as well. Not only were the rushes of the retakes of the Sollozzo scene disappointing, but he had also learned that the film lab had underdeveloped the last batch of footage, thereby losing another day's shoot. He admitted that he wasn't sleeping (the studio's doctor finally prescribed sleeping pills), but he overcompensated with maniacal attempts to speed up the schedule. Once he screamed angrily that "just for once" he'd like complete quiet on the set. He even took his anxiety out on his own sister, neophyte actress Talia Shire, whom he threatened to fire, shouting "Tallie's too pretty for the part."

Roger Donoghue, the former middleweight boxer who had been Brando's coach in *On the Waterfront* and now worked as a Rheingold sales executive, was checking on the delivery and placement of the beer for the wedding scenes. Between takes Brando was telling Donoghue about one of the young company members from *Waterfront,* who had been imprisoned for theft but whom Brando was now trying to help get paroled.

"Hey!" Coppola yelled, angrily marching into their conversation. "We got a ton of people here! Let's get a move on."

"This is my friend Roger," Brando said quietly, ignoring the director's outburst. "We're talking Hoboken."

"I don't give a fuck what you're talking, you gotta get to work!"

Even in the face of such an outburst, Brando kept his cool. However, he continued to delay Monday-morning shoots by returning late from weekends in Los Angeles. Ostensibly he was making the 6,000-mile journey for female comfort, but the real reason was Christian. In a January court hearing he and Kashfi had been awarded joint custody, but after hearing psychiatrists' evaluations of the twelve-year-old, the judge had ordered that the boy be enrolled in the Ojai Valley School. In addition to his emotional problems, he was starting to drink and take drugs.

Marlon continued to miss the Sunday-night red-eye that would get him back to New York for Monday's call. To justify his lateness, he fell back on his old habit of trying to deflect any responsibility by complaining to Coppola about the script. Soon the director was well aware of the pattern: When Brando was half an hour late, he complained about a specific line. An hour late and he claimed not to understand a scene. If half a day late, the explanation became, "I don't like this scene at all."

Still, what perplexed Coppola the most was the actor's inability to memorize his lines, particularly since Brando had made *The Godfather* a rare exception and had actually studied the script. Brando's cheat sheets and cue cards again found their way onto the set, turning up pasted on cameras, to desks, and even on fruit in a bowl on Don Vito Corleone's table.

"He had his lines written all over the place," Willis recalled with a laugh. "Sometimes he even wrote them on his hands or on his sleeves. Sometimes I think that's where all that famous Brando style came from— the dramatic pauses, looking around before he spoke. I always found it hysterically funny that he was doing all that just so that he could come up with a way to read the lines he'd written on his hand."

Brando's fellow cast members found his cue cards disconcerting as well, and once they were less in awe of his legendary reputation, they decided to make a point of it. Caan persuaded former wrestler Lenny Montana, playing the thug Luca Brasi, to try a stunt. On May 3 Montana was to shoot his one major scene with Brando. With the cameras rolling, Brando began his cue-card shtick, this time using an envelope he was supposed to hand to Montana in the midst of his first speech, but which he held on to so that he could read his lines from it.

Cued to reply to Brando's speech, Montana simply opened his mouth and stuck out his tongue. At the tip of it was a strip of surgical tape on which was written, "Fuck you, Marlon." Brando convulsed with laughter, and Coppola, too, cracked up. After a break, they started to reshoot the scene. This time instead of giving his speech, Brando stuck out his tongue. There was another piece of tape, this one reading, "Fuck you, too."

For all the joking around, Coppola couldn't shake his annoyance over Brando's resistance to learning lines. On those occasions when Marlon blew his dialogue repeatedly, such as his speech to other Mafia leaders declaring a truce, Coppola tried to calm him down as they repeated the scene again and again. One day he confronted him, demanding to know what the problem was.

Brando denied that it was a matter of loss of memory or failure to concentrate. Instead he claimed it was a necessary part of his naturalistic acting style. "You said you liked me in *Waterfront*—right?" Brando argued. "Well, I'm doing the same thing now that I did then. Real people don't know what they're going to say. Their words often come as a surprise to them. That's the way it should be in a movie." Later Brando elaborated, "If you know your lines, very often most of the time it sounds like 'Mary had a little lamb . . .' And people intuit, they unconsciously know that you have planned that speech."

Just how cue cards made for spontaneity, he didn't explain, and the problem was exacerbated by frequent last-minute script revisions. In response Coppola dealt with his anxieties by often consulting with the actors about their lines, ordering more and more takes if he thought a different version of a scene worth trying. Like Brando, the other members of the cast appreciated such freedom, and Dean Tavoularis, the film's production designer, confirmed, "Actors like Coppola a lot. They're not props. He involves them, asks them what they think."

Coppola was especially amenable to spontaneous ideas from Brando, even in the middle of shooting a scene. "I could understand how he got his reputation, because his ideas were so bizarre, so apparently crazy," said Coppola. "Yet without exception every one of his crazy ideas I used turned out to be a terrific moment."

Throughout the shoot, Coppola and cinematographer Gordon Willis would have a number of fights; Willis argued that the issue was not his alleged antipathy toward actors, but Coppola's lack of technical knowledge. "At that point in his career Francis didn't realize that you can't get art without craft. He knows it now, but he didn't know it then. You can't just arbitrarily block a scene and forget the fact that you're making a movie. The blocking has to be basically comfortable for the actors and it has to function for the director, and then finally it has to work for the camera. If the scene doesn't fit in that little hole that you're looking through, then it's all irrelevant. Unless a director can transpose his feelings and interpretation into a visual structure, they're meaningless."

The major blowup between Willis and Coppola occurred when they were shooting on the interior set representing the don's home. According to Willis, Coppola hadn't blocked the scene but instead began to discuss whether Brando should have his suspenders up or down. Brando tried them up, pulled them down, then snapped them back up again.

Coppola then stepped back and called to Willis, "Shoot."

"Shoot what?" Willis replied.

Coppola ignored the question and shouted "Action!" a second time. Willis again refused to roll, arguing that because there had been no blocking, the lighting wasn't adequate. To shoot now would be a waste of film. When Coppola blew up, Willis simply walked off the set, muttering about directors who throw "temper tantrums." All the while, Brando had been snapping his suspenders as if to punctuate the argument, and now he burst out laughing.

Nevertheless, Coppola's basic approach continued to generate a good working atmosphere, and Brando seemed to relax more on this set than he had on any other in a long time. "The meeting of their minds was probably a good thing for both of them," Willis conceded. "If Marlon feels there's one controlling factor on the set, he won't screw around. Where he gets out of hand is if no one is in charge. It's as if he's seen the hole in the boat and he panics."

Philip Rhodes saw how important the picture was to his friend and also realized that Coppola was allowing him to flourish. "Marlon was *really* involved in his performance," he said, "and Coppola went with him completely. The other director who had done that was John Huston, and that was the secret of Huston's success—get good actors and let them take off. Coppola was doing the same thing. He was in love with Marlon's performance, because he saw how Marlon could make a scene work better than anyone."

Brando's directorial role sometimes extended to the other actors, too. One scene that dissatisfied Coppola and that he'd been continually rewriting was the one in which Al Martino, playing the singer Johnny Fontaine, comes to the godfather to complain about his stalled career and to ask him to intervene. Martino was unhappy with his rewritten lines, but Coppola saw the problem as more in the acting than in the dialogue, especially when several takes hadn't improved anything. "It was at that point that Brando saved the day," recalled Willis. "He had the idea of having the godfather slap the singer to 'bring him to his senses.' Naturally, Martino's reaction finally looked real, because he was actually dazed by the slap."

Of course Brando's slap was among the actor's usual bag of tricks, but Al Ruddy was similarly impressed, especially with those improvised turns that lent the powerful and ruthless don a gentler side. "It's in those little shticks of the godfather that you get the totality of the film as well as the character," the producer explained. "It was Brando who came up with them. Like stopping to smell a rose between the first part of his line, 'After all, we're not murderers,' and the second, 'whatever that undertaker thinks.' Plus all the stuff with the cat in the beginning. That was never in the script. A cat happened to be in the studio, and Brando started stroking it during the scene. I had never watched a genius at work before in Hollywood. The stuff he did was mind-boggling. The guy's a certifiable genius."

Paramount executives, however, saw less than genius in the dailies as Brando continued to mumble his way through lines, and Charles Bluhdorn, Gulf + Western's chairman, continued to subject Coppola to his complaints.

Willis interpreted the mumbling as a subtle strategy on Marlon's part, a code for evading lines in the script that displeased him. "There were occasions when he didn't want to say the lines as written," Willis explained. "It was then that he mumbled, basically so that no one could understand him." Coppola would call, 'Cut,' he and Brando would huddle, and generally there would be a rewrite."

Even when he liked the script, though, Brando still mumbled, and the effect became more problematic after the don was shot in the throat and his voice was to become more raspy. Finally Al Ruddy, put on notice by Paramount that almost all of Brando's dialogue might have to be dubbed, visited the actor in his dressing room. He tiptoed around the problem until he informed the actor that many of his lines were hard to hear.

"Why didn't anyone tell me?" Brando replied. "It's no problem. Just tell me, and I'll speak more clearly."

As the shoot progressed, the younger actors' initial awe had given way to a kind of fraternity house atmosphere, and it was Caan and Duvall who broke the ice. One morning in late April, bored by the delays as Coppola rehearsed Brando upstairs, the two of them sneaked onto the soundstage and hid behind some flats of scenery. Then, with a silent signal, in unison they leaped out, whirled around, and dropped their trousers and shorts to moon everyone. According to one witness, Coppola reacted with only the faintest smile and Brando looked "positively disapproving." Duvall and Caan, failing to distract them from their work, crept away.

Despite Brando's apparent disapproval, mooning soon became a competition between him and the team of Duvall and Caan. The latter two achieved their "height" of success the day that Brando looked up into the rafters of the studio to see their two bare behinds hanging over him. On another day after shooting was finished, Duvall, his wife, and Caan were being driven in a limo up Third Avenue; in front of them were Brando and secretary Alice Marchak in their own limo. Realizing that the opportunity was too good to miss, they had their driver overtake Brando's car. Caan then dropped his pants and pressed his backside into the rear window. Marchak reminded her boss that mooning in public during rush hour would be hard to beat. Marlon smiled and bided his time, waiting for the moment to achieve the perfect moon.

That opportunity didn't present itself until one of his last days on the set. On May 26 the wedding reception was to be filmed at a mall with over 500 extras, including 50 children. Part of the scene was the Corleone family posing for a formal portrait. As the cast lined up, Brando turned, quickly undid his tuxedo pants, and mooned the assembled cast, crew, and extras, including the children. A roar went up from the crowd, and Duvall followed suit, dropping his trousers as well. Some mothers registered complaints, but their chagrin only added to the consensus that Brando had won the competition hands down.

However infantile these jokes were, they eased the tension and provided respite from the intense conflicts that still surrounded the production. On the day following another heated blowup between Willis and Coppola, Brando contrived a different kind of prank. The scheduled scene was the one in which the godfather, brought home from the hospital, was carried on a stretcher upstairs to his bedroom. Brando took his position on the stretcher, and two extras playing orderlies grunted and groaned through their first attempt to hoist the heavy star. Seeing their evident strain, Coppola then replaced the extras, costuming two hefty grips in white coats and trousers to perform the task. Each weighed more than 200 pounds and had the muscular physique of a weight lifter. But even they strained and pulled and broke into sweats, their veins bulging. At the landing of the first flight of stairs, they were forced to set the supine Brando down. Embarrassed by their failure, the two grips were even more upset when the assembled cast and crew burst out in jeering whoops, and the actor, giggling, rolled off the stretcher.

It was all his doing, he finally admitted. While the grips had been changing into costume, he and members of the crew had hidden six 50-pound sandbags used as boom weights underneath the bedding on the stretcher. The grips had been trying to lift both Brando and 300 extra pounds up the stairs. No one took offense at Brando's shenanigans, unlike the resentment that his stunts on other films had usually provoked. As with his mooning, it only earned him points among his macho colleagues, and apparently not even Coppola objected, despite the fact that the stretcher number cost the production an estimated $5,000.

Marlon, like Jimmy Caan and any number of others involved in the project, was drawn to real-life Mafiosi, many of whom were hanging around the set as unofficial "supervisors." Rhodes saw that Brando often watched them, quietly absorbing their movements and gestures: "I've seen Marlon pick up a characterization a minute before he starts a scene. On *Guys and Dolls* we had an opening street scene in New York in which all these people were around, including real-life pitchmen, the kind of guys who hawk ties on the street. Marlon saw one of these guys doing his spiel, and that was it—one glimpse, and the pitchman became the basis for Sky Masterson."

But Rhodes knew that it had been a long time since a role had grabbed Brando enough to engage him fully and prompt such attention to detail. "A good artist takes from everyone and everywhere," added Rhodes, "and that was Marlon's great talent. Everything was grist for his mill, but what was important was the use he made of it, how he improved on the original. I could see that this part really mattered to him—not just for the money, not just to put him back at the top, both of which he needed, of course—but because he loved the character of the aging don. And that was undoubtedly why he was watching these guys on the set and picking things up from them."

During the shoot Al Lettieri, who had connections with New Jersey mobsters, was another source, and he went so far as to plan a dinner so that Brando could get the feel of a real gathering of authentic "family" members. He had limos pick up Brando, Rhodes, and the other cast members to drive them out to his sister's large suburban home. The guests were escorted to the basement—referred to in old-fashioned parlance as "the bar downstairs"—an elaborately decorated room.

"These people obviously had money," said Rhodes. "About forty people were there, and it was great food and a lot of servants. No question, Lettieri's connection helped Marlon get to know some of them and he was struck by their courtesy and manners. Al's brother-in-law, who was in the Mafia, apparently left town that evening. Officially the Mob wasn't happy about the picture for suggesting there was such a thing as the Mafia."

On May 14, the company moved to Staten Island to begin shooting the exteriors for the wedding sequence, but a violent rainstorm again jeopardized the schedule. Worse, the storm destroyed the tomato patch that Coppola had been carefully cultivating for the godfather's death scene. The director had insisted that for authenticity the garden had to be planted with Italian plum tomatoes, and now the plants had been leveled by the high winds and rain. Brando, however, had only two days left on his contract; after the deadline, he would have to be paid overtime. Worried about the estimated $100,000 cost of keeping him until both the storm was over and a new tomato patch could be brought in, Al Ruddy visited Brando in his hotel room.

"Look, Marlon, this is the deal," Ruddy announced. "Francis was growing this tomato patch for your last scene. He wanted only Italian plum tomatoes, and now this storm has wiped the garden out. He's very unhappy that his tomatoes have vanished, but I tell you frankly that if you insist tomorrow is your last day, I'm going to glue plastic tomatoes on those vines and do the scene that way. I need to keep this picture at a certain budget. But if you'll go home for a week or so and let me call you back when the tomatoes are ready without charging me, we'll do it the way Francis wants. It's up to you."

Brando's response was immediate. "If Francis cares that much about the tomatoes, we'll do it that way," he replied. "I'll leave, and when you want me I'll come back and I won't charge you."

True to his word, he didn't charge Ruddy "an extra nickel." With Coppola estimating that it would be another week to ten days before the last scenes could be filmed, the actor made plans to fly to Tahiti, where he would await his summons back to New York.

For all Brando's spirit of cooperation, he may have agreed to Ruddy's suggestion because he needed a respite. Those who knew him better than the cast and crew did could sense a real split between his public persona of Mr. Good Guy and the private worries that still beset him. By and large he'd kept to himself off the set, retiring to his hotel, the Elysée, at night and usually seeing only Philip and Marie and secretary Alice.

One old friend, however, did look him up. Pat Quinn, who had been with Marlon when he had first talked to Puzo about the role, was in town and she dropped by to see him. "We spent the evening just talking and catching up," she said. "It was then that I realized Marlon had changed.

The previous years had been a pretty down and cynical time, and that night he seemed much older and much more tired, literally exhausted and without much energy."

Brando was weighed down by a plethora of pressures, all coming at him from different directions. In the first place, he was still at war with Anna Kashfi. Dismayed by her drinking and her evident self-destructive mood after her petition for a new custody hearing had been denied, he sensed more trouble brewing. Christian was in terrible shape—emotionally disturbed and already involved in substance abuse. Brando's financial worries were also exacerbated by mounting legal costs, not only from his continuing battles with Kashfi but also from other lawsuits. The suit by three Oakland cops (stemming from his 1968 comments on "The Joey Bishop Show," about the Bobby Hutton case) had been dismissed, only to be reinstated by the California Court of Appeals; rather than settle out of court, on April 28, 1971, Marlon had his lawyers appeal the decision, petitioning the U.S. Supreme Court to widen its free speech rulings to include talk shows.

Brando had also been sued by producer Alberto Grimaldi, who was demanding $700,000 in damages in connection with the making of *Burn!* Alleging that Brando had shown "incomprehensible attitudes" and "open hostility" toward director Gillo Pontecorvo, the suit rehashed the problems with the shoot, including its star's perpetual lateness and his bolt from Colombia, which had forced the production to move to Morocco. There, Brando still allegedly caused repeated delays, driving up costs even further. Although Grimaldi conceded that he had signed a preproduction agreement assuring that he would not seek damages from Brando, the suit asserted that the actor had broken the terms of the contract with his outrageous behavior. Moreover, although he had said he would not charge for dubbing the film into English, Brando submitted a bill for over $195,000.

During his weekends in Los Angeles, he had also been checking on his sister Jocelyn's welfare. She had gone through a difficult period, and after a time of estrangement in previous years, the two had now reached a rapprochement and openly grown closer. Fred Sadoff, Jocelyn's close friend, soon became aware of their renewed affection, having just returned to Los Angeles in 1971 after a decade of living in London. "It had been very difficult for Jocelyn to talk about Marlon in those earlier years," he explained. "But [by the time] I came back, obviously something had happened in their relationship to cement it. She now talked about him with great love. She had never exposed that kind of feeling about him before, and it was more like family."

"We've always been supportive of each other, whatever was going on," Jocelyn herself later insisted, resisting the suggestion of hostility or coolness between her and Marlon during the sixties. "If one of us was going through a hard time, we'd say, 'All right, I'm with you.' We don't take sides, but we've always been frank with one another, and if one of us seems to be doing something nonproductive, then it's, 'That seems pretty dumb, but I love you anyway. I'll try not to act superior to you, even though I think you're acting like a horse's ass.' "

The Brando offspring, said Jocelyn, had always bonded together to help one another, much as "we united against Mother and Papa. But none of us imposes our approach or our choices. It's what our grandmother called 'Jamie's goat'—we gave each other that kind of freedom. Like all brothers and sisters we've had good fights, but let anybody else get into it, and we're right back together, a sort of 'I'll cover your back, and you'll cover mine.' "

But what most preoccupied Brando at the time was Tahiti. With his ten-day respite, he was also able to make a quick visit to the island to see his two Tahitian offspring, and to check on the progress of the long delayed airstrip. The delays had only added to his financial woes, so he now hoped to appeal to the French government for funding in the form of low-interest loans.

The trip seemed to rejuvenate him, and when he returned to New York the morning of May 26, he was attentive while shooting the wedding interiors. By late afternoon, another storm was threatening, and Willis knew that the dark clouds would ruin the lighting for the exterior shots. Jack Ballard, calling from Paramount's Manhattan offices, ordered Coppola to continue shooting despite the weather. By the time the scenes had been relit, it was too dark to continue and everyone threw in the towel for the weekend. On Tuesday, after the Memorial Day holiday, Coppola ran into the same lighting problems late in the day and left the location convinced that the wedding scenes would have to be reshot in their entirety, since none of the footage would match.

Willis ultimately solved the problem by inventing the qualities of light for which the film would eventually be praised.

"We ended up shooting the wedding party outside in a kind of bright

Kodachrome with a 1940s feeling," Willis explained. "I introduced the yellow-red of those scenes, which gave it an orangy period look. I made that particular sequence much brighter so that we cut from there to the dark interior of the study where Brando was handing out favors, and then bang, you cut back outside to the wedding, in that orangy color."

When the studio executives saw the rushes, they complained that the lighting was too dark. "They kept saying people wouldn't be able to see the movie at drive-ins," added Willis. "I said, 'Well, I don't really give a damn about the drive-ins.' In fact I ultimately changed the way lighting is done in American films in general. It was all overhead lighting, which was necessary because of Brando's makeup. That wasn't new per se, but the way we used it brought a tone of reality to the film that hadn't been seen before."

On June 2, the day after the wedding scene was finished, there were problems and, for the first time, it was Brando who caused the delay. Coppola wanted a sequence that more clearly showed the emotional bond between the godfather and his son Michael. While Coppola thought that Pacino had done exemplary work in his only previous scene with Brando (the one in which he watched over his father in the hospital), the director wrote another to make their relationship as well as the passing of power from father to son more explicit. Brando, however, remained in his dressing room throughout the morning, resorting to his usual habit of sending excuses through a second assistant director that "he wasn't ready."

Discounting *Reflections in a Golden Eye,* this was the one film that Brando had taken seriously in the last decade, and he did have sincere reservations about the prospective rewrite. Finally, Coppola persuaded him to come out and shoot immediately because the light was "perfect," but at the same time he offered a compromise: He would photograph him and Pacino walking around the garden in long shots while the two actors improvised a conversation. Later the scene would be dubbed with rewritten lines. Meanwhile, Coppola called in screenwriter Robert Towne to revise the script that evening.

The solution seemed to suit Brando; he and Pacino were wired with mikes and took their walk through the garden as the cameras rolled from a distance. Only the soundmen listening through earphones were aware that instead of improvising dialogue appropriate to the scene, Brando was whispering obscenities and dirty jokes into Pacino's ear.

How Pacino managed to keep a straight face was nothing short of miraculous. Later, when asked about doing his one major scene with The Legend, Pacino merely replied, "Have you any idea what it was like to be doing a scene with him?" But when asked what he had learned from working with Brando, he quipped, "From Brando I learned to come late."

That evening, Towne, Coppola, and Brando met in the actor's dressing room to discuss the scene's revisions. Brando argued that in Towne's latest version the godfather seemed too manipulative and controlling of his son. "Just once, I would like to see this man *not* inarticulate," Brando said. "I would like to see him express himself well." His point was that the don's love for power had to be subsumed by his feelings for his son, who is about to take over the empire. When Vito Corleone asks his son how he is going to handle the other five families, Michael, he said, ought to resist telling him about the arrangements he has already made and instead talk about the don's grandchildren. With the theme of the family resurrected, the godfather can then express his remorse that Michael has been drawn into the "business" instead of going on to become "Senator Corleone" or some other mainstream public figure.

The touchstone obviously was depth, a rounding out of the film's central figure. Friday, June 4, was Brando's last scene, and at the Staten Island shooting site, he became inspired with an idea of how to portray the godfather as he suffers a stroke while playing with one of his grandchildren. Philip Rhodes had once described one of his father's favorite tricks—cutting up the rind of an orange to make it look like fangs and inserting it in his mouth to play a monster. Rhodes had also told him that his father had in fact died while playing this "monster" game with a grandchild. "Marlon is a creative rememberer," Rhodes added, "and he used that as the don's death scene."

The episode would become arguably the most famous in the movie, and deservedly so. Through the improvised "game" with the grandson, Brando was able to capture the complexity of the godfather's contradictory sides—the monster with a heart, the affectionate grandfather and mortal old man inside the massive shell of power and control.

The death scene marked Brando's final day on the set, and even those actors not on call that day showed up for his farewell party. When Brando emerged from his dressing room—his makeup removed and in black jeans and a leather jacket—he looked even younger than his forty-seven years.

Women from the production company offices immediately swarmed him, giving him affectionate hugs and asking him for autographs. Al Ruddy, always the expansive personality, presented him with a new drum, and Caan and Duvall awarded him a silver belt buckle inscribed "Mighty Moon Champion." Charming, jocular, and gracious as he was in accepting praise for his work, the actor talked about the previous weeks' toil in what was finally a dismissive tone.

"Give me the negative so I can burn it," he called to Gordon Willis in the midst of the compliments.

It was a stance he had often adopted in the past—not only a sort of false humility, but denigration of himself and his talent. "It seemed to me that he had contempt for everybody and everything in general terms, and for himself in particular," Willis added. "I had never understood the reason for that, but I heard it in his remark that last day."

Still, the quip may also have signaled Brando's tendency to protect himself. The negative reactions by assistant directors, the doubts expressed by the rough-cut editors, and the general snide gossip about Coppola's incompetence as a director had presumably reached him. At this point he may also have had real doubts whether Coppola in his editing would be able to surmount the problems that were apparent both during the shoot and in the rough cuts. It would be another several months before Coppola and Evans, cutting and recutting over 500,000 feet of film, would know what they had.

Although Brando had anticipated a long respite from moviemaking after *The Godfather,* during his last several days of the shoot events conspired to compel him to change his mind. One night at the hotel, Alice was awakened by a long-distance call from Rome. It was Luigi Luraschi, with whom she had become friends when they had both worked at Paramount. Luraschi now ran Paramount's office in Italy and was producing his first film, to be directed by the young Italian director Bernardo Bertolucci, who had recently won extraordinary critical acclaim for his third feature, *The Conformist.*

Both Luraschi and Bertolucci wanted to interest Brando in the director's next project. Marlon rejected the idea out of hand, telling Marchak what she already knew—he explained that he was going to Europe to see French government officials about his Tetiaroa plans, then planned on returning to the atoll. Nevertheless, Luraschi called back, this time saying that Bertolucci was so eager to work with Brando that he would create a script especially for him and would go anywhere—even to Tahiti—to discuss it.

That same day Brando's frantic business manager in Los Angeles called: In pursuing his lawsuit, Grimaldi had succeeded in freezing all of the actor's assets except for "living expenses." Brando became exasperated. It was absolutely necessary for him to pursue the financing of his Tetiaroa projects with the French government, he told Marchak. His peremptory command was, "Figure something out, Alice."

Her solution was to get back to Luraschi and negotiate a European trip for Brando. In exchange for his meeting with Bertolucci and Luraschi in Paris, they would pay all Marlon's expenses, not only for the few days when he would be meeting with French government officials, but also for a vacation in the south of France.

Bertolucci had seen his first Brando movie, *Viva Zapata!,* at the age of eleven, and when he met the actor in Paris he felt shy, overawed for one of the first times in his life. He was even more disconcerted when Brando sat silently staring at him for all of fifteen minutes before he asked the Italian to talk. The designated subject: Brando. Bertolucci deflected him by describing the character he had in mind.

Bertolucci had just gone to an exhibition of paintings by the British artist Francis Bacon, and one in particular had moved him deeply. It was of a man "in great despair," and he told Brando that this was what he wanted to capture in his film. "In Bacon you see people virtually throwing up their guts and then doing a makeup job on themselves with their own vomit," he said later, adding, "I found this same kind of appeal in Marlon."

He showed Brando the Bacon picture in the exhibition catalog he had brought along. Brando was drawn to the intellectual and literary director, perhaps most of all to his intuitive, fearless understanding of despair. The two shook hands in general agreement, but Marlon didn't give him a definite commitment. He said he wanted to see a script, and then left Paris for his vacation in Provence.

Last Tango in Paris

After his French holiday, Brando returned to Los Angeles and then made several trips to Tahiti, crisscrossing the Pacific as if he were a commuter. He began to take off the weight he had gained during *The Godfather,* which he sometimes joked was Coppola's fault. "He made me into the pig I am today," he said. "He makes the most delicious spaghetti in the world." Although he was officially finished with the picture, he was still preoccupied with it, and in a rare exception to his rule of never seeing his own films, even in their finished form, he visited Coppola in San Francisco to view the director's early rough cut.

In public he announced his enthusiasm, calling *The Godfather* "one of the most powerful statements ever made about America," adding that his favorite scene was when Diane Keaton says, "Senators don't have people killed," and Pacino responds, "Don't be naive."

In private, though, Brando may not have been convinced that Coppola had made the hit that everyone was expecting. Perhaps he heard as much from Robert Evans, who had been so dismayed by Coppola's rough assembly that he deemed it "unreleasable." "He'd taken out all the texture," Evans later insisted. "The picture was supposed to open that Christmas and I went to the Paramount hierarchy and said we couldn't open it then. I almost lost my job over it. They pushed the release back and we added fifty minutes to the picture."

Whether Brando was actually pessimistic about the movie's eventual profits or whether his worsening financial crisis prompted the ill-advised decision, over the summer of 1971, his lawyer phoned Evans to ask for a renegotiation of the actor's *Godfather* contract and a cash advance. "Marlon was desperately in need of $100,000," Evans explained, adding that he then conferred with Charlie Bluhdorn about the proposal. In his tough businessman's style, the CEO agreed to Brando's request but told Evans, "Get the points back." Foolishly, Brando took the check and returned his points. As a result, the quick money fix during the summer eventually cost him an estimated $11 million; later, when Brando realized how much the film was grossing and how much he had lost, he called Evans, demanding his deal back. "He went crazy, and I don't blame him," added Evans. Brando even offered to appear in *The Great Gatsby,* a movie Paramount then had in development, but Evans refused, insisting that "one picture had nothing to do with the other."

The actor's money problems had indeed worsened that summer; the Grimaldi lawsuit was still keeping his assets frozen, and despite the projects that he already had under way on Tetiaroa, the French government hadn't approved his loans. The only answer was to sign on for another film. But with *The Godfather* not yet released, his stock was low, and he agreed to make *Child's Play* for director Sidney Lumet. The movie, Broadway maven David Merrick's debut as a film producer, was scheduled to begin shooting in early November.

Brando had also taken another step to save money. He'd always resented the alimony he'd been ordered to pay Movita at the time of their annulment, and now hearing that she was in the midst of an affair, he abruptly stopped sending her the monthly $1,400 payment in June. Movita promptly filed suit, and another legal struggle loomed during the following year, with Norman Garey, his lawyer, having to fight on this front as well. Again, this seemed shortsighted on Brando's part, since Garey's notoriously high fees may well have cost as much as the alimony payments themselves.

The situation with Kashfi was no better, either. Christian was home from school and staying with her in the apartment complex on Havenhurst Drive where she had moved two years before. The boy had become friends with a neighbor, Virginia Hardy, and the two of them spent at least a few hours a day together. Often he arrived at her apartment for breakfast when Kashfi hadn't awakened from an all-night drinking binge; over the summer Hardy saw that Kashfi's behavior had worsened. She was taking huge amounts of pills and drinking heavily, and when she was intoxicated she often screamed at Christian—so loudly that Hardy was sometimes awakened by the hysterical outbursts.

"She would get up in the middle of the night," Hardy recalled, "and rush into his bedroom and snatch him up from a deep sleep and slap him . . . and yell at times hysterically for him to apologize. . . . He kept saying, 'Well, Mommy, I would, but I don't know what I am apologizing for.' She said, 'You just apologize to me.' And then he would say, 'Okay, Mommy, I apologize, I apologize.' And then she would scream at him, 'What are you apologizing for? What did you do?'"

Sometimes Hardy was concerned enough to intercede, and she later recalled the thirteen-year-old boy helping to calm his mother down so they could get her back to bed. At other times Kashfi would become so enraged that she locked the boy out of the apartment; Hardy would hear him banging on the door, begging to be let back in. One day Kashfi locked him out in a raging thunderstorm, and he went next door to ask the neighbor for money for a taxi.

"What do you want a taxi for?" she asked.

"I want to go up to my dad's because my mother won't let me in the house," he replied.

In the joint-custody arrangement, Brando would have Christian up at Mulholland a few afternoons a week and on weekends. But the actor's routine hardly betokened a stable home life, either. Brando came and went, and Christian was often left to his own devices.

Sadly, Brando saw that neither Christian's school and its psychological counseling nor the AA meetings the boy had been ordered to attend were helping. The father's anxiety and anger only mounted when he realized that the boy was still sneaking alcohol and smoking pot on the sly. As Brando later explained, "I found bottles of Jack Daniel's and other liquor bottles under the furniture in his room. I said, 'If you are going to smoke pot and you are going to drink, do it at home. . . . I don't approve of it, but if you are going to do it, I want you to do it in front of me." Once again Brando asked his lawyer to set in motion the legal steps to obtain sole custody, but neither his schedule nor his temperamental predilections made his plan realistic. He was due in New York that autumn to begin filming *Child's Play,* and he would also have to spend time looping his scenes in *The Godfather.* Besides, Brando's attention span was short, even when it came to his own son, and his worry and anxiety also gave way to aloof withdrawals when he'd retreat to his bedroom to ponder his own concerns about money and the Tahitian projects.

By that summer Marlon had renewed his friendship with Wally Cox, who was in worse shape than ever. His career had continued to languish and he had been forced to become a regular, along with Paul Lynde and Jim Backus, on the game show "The Hollywood Squares." Backus, among others, realized that Lynde and Cox were drinking throughout the tapings of the shows. "They would go across the street from the studio to a bar," he said, "and both would come back loaded. I don't think viewers ever realized that they were blind drunk, but they'd do the show absolutely loaded."

To make matters worse, Cox had become involved in shaky financial deals and been fleeced by one of his investment partners. Brando had heard reports from Jocelyn, Fred Sadoff, and Philip Rhodes, and during the summer of 1971 Wally's friend Everett Greenbaum was sometimes around when Cox and Brando began to spend time together again. According to Greenbaum, their "bullshit" was astonishing. "They were doping out life's mysteries—sex, marriage, work," Greenbaum explained. "They had great rapport and they were feeding each other, sometimes quoting writers, or in Wally's case, citing some article in *Scientific American*. They were both outside normal relationships, but loved to spin out all these great theories."

Throughout 1971, Brando continued seeing Marie Cui, and also maintained his relationship with Anita Kong. Through her and Gene Frenke, he met a new arrival from the Philippines, Caroline Barrett, an aspiring dancer/actress who had been James Clavell's mistress, bearing the British novelist a child, Petra.

As for Gene Frenke, he had taken one particular Japanese immigrant under his wing. Yachiyo Tsubaki was a young, long-haired, petite woman with large black eyes and a fragile passivity to her, and even more appealing was her accommodating silence (she couldn't speak much English). Brando was struck by her beauty as well as her background—his interest piqued by the fact that her father was a Zen master whom Frenke had brought to the United States to establish a religious center in Hollywood. Marlon remained so attentive to her that when Frenke felt his own powers failing in the late seventies he turned her over to him.

As complicated, as emotionally lawless as all this was, Brando added another woman to his array of girlfriends, one so different from his usual type—and in many ways so much like Dodie—that she aroused and defined his most intense emotional conflicts during these years. He had met Jill Banner when she was only twenty-one and had a bit part in *Candy*. A petite Irish Catholic from Iowa who wanted to succeed as an actress, she was, as one friend put it, "too proper" to hustle in the Hollywood game. When the affair with Marlon became more serious, she dropped her career. She allowed him to pay for her apartment even though she was "ashamed" of her dependence, just as she was reportedly mortified that she had permitted him to talk her into an abortion. Her friends, more than a little leery on the subject, said that Marlon's lack of commitment led to angry arguments that sometimes involved physical violence.

"She didn't talk about that very often, and I don't want to get into it, either," said one intimate. "She knew she was just another number on Marlon's list, and realized she shouldn't put up with it. But neither one of them could let go."

Marlon also had a new neighbor who seemed to offer more female adventures, or at least challenges. In August 1971 Jack Nicholson bought the adjacent property on the other side of Marlon's shared driveway and the two "started sharing women as well," said Pat Quinn. "Once Jack moved in next door, Marlon was going after his women, and it became another Hollywood game."

In the fall of 1971 Brando flew to New York to begin shooting *Child's Play.* Whether he thought that he could hold sway over Lumet as he had during the making of *The Fugitive Kind,* he gave up any pretense to the cooperative, good-guy role he had adopted during *The Godfather.* Arriving in New York to begin rehearsals for his portrayal of one of two rival masters at a boys' school (the other lead was to be played by James Mason), Brando asked Lumet to cast Wally Cox as a schoolteacher. Brando informed Cox that he was hired, so Wally flew to New York, where he discovered Lumet wanted to *audition* him. "Lumet told him, 'The part is an alcoholic schoolteacher,'" recalled Everett Greenbaum. "'You used to play Mr. Peepers, a schoolteacher, and Marlon says that you're also an alcoholic, so you should be just right for this role.' Wally was furious at Marlon for this."

Wally, in fact, didn't get the part because in the first few days of the shoot Brando had reverted to his aggressive on-set behavior, demanding script revisions and location changes even before he put one foot in front of the camera. David Merrick, the flamboyant producer, wouldn't have any of it. Hearing about Brando's demands and delays, he took immediate action and replaced him with Robert Preston. Asked about the "disagreement" that had prompted the firing, Merrick replied: "Disagreement? There was no disagreement. I simply threw Mr. Brando out of my film. He wanted to make basic changes in the story and I could not accept that."

Once Brando was gone, there was no need to accommodate Cox, and with Wally blaming Marlon for his humiliation as well as for the loss of a job, the rupture was so bad that Cox didn't speak to Brando for a good part of the following year. Their falling out—and Wally's withdrawal from the close circle of friends on whom Brando depended—may have contributed to Marlon's emotional storm, which had been gathering since the summer.

Brando himself had reached some sort of "critical mass," as Philip Rhodes termed it, which more than likely underlay the extraordinary isolation and loneliness of the character he was about to portray in *Last Tango in Paris.*

Brando's agreement to work with Bertolucci wasn't confirmed until November 1971, after the director and Franco Arcalli, his collaborator and editor on *The Conformist,* had pulled together a draft of a script and also brought Alberto Grimaldi on board to produce, a step that would eventually help persuade Marlon to make *Tango.*

Grimaldi knew that Brando's finances were in disarray. Not only was he pressing his own lawsuit, but through his contacts at Paramount he had probably heard about Brando's renegotiated *Godfather* deal. Agreeing with Bertolucci to pursue Brando, the producer came up with an added inducement. "I very much wanted him for *Tango,* so I phoned his agent and told him that I'd settle the case if he would do the Bertolucci movie. I also offered him $250,000 plus ten percent of the gross after we broke even," Grimaldi later recalled.

Thus, when Bertolucci appeared in Los Angeles in November with his screenplay, it was in Brando's interest to give the project more than casual consideration. The actor had already done his brain-picking, surveying Rhodes and others about *The Conformist,* and when Bertolucci arrived at the house, he asked him to talk more about the character of Paul. Bertolucci spent the first half hour describing the personality he envisioned for his main character, then stopped abruptly and said, "Let's talk about ourselves—our lives, our loves, about sex. That's what the film is going to be about."

The meeting turned into a two-week psychoanalytic session, with Bertolucci arriving every day for long discussions of sexual identity and family background, as well as the passions and obsessions that the two men discovered in each other. "I tried to develop a pre-rational relationship with him," Bertolucci said, having penetrated Brando's usual defenses to discover the uncontrolled, darker forces that only a few of the actor's closest friends had seen. "There is an element of wild, irrational violence in him. If you can enter into his universe and harness this intuition and violence, then he becomes incredibly intelligent."

While Bertolucci gave Brando the script to read, he emphasized that he wanted much of the movie to be improvised. "Finished scripts are only necessary to impress producers," the Italian director said. "The script serves only as a guide to the mood I hope to get from my actors." Wanting to explore questions of isolation, despair, and sexual obsession through Brando's character, he asked the actor about his memories of his childhood, his feelings about his parents, his deepest sexual fantasies. Remarkably, Brando seemed to open up to him, recalling his early years in Libertyville, including his father's strictness, his mother's drinking. He told him about his love for the drums and waxed lyrical about his retreat in Tahiti. Bertolucci listened carefully, and indeed many of the details were to eventually find their way into the movie itself.

As usual, Brando's moods seemed to fluctuate between emotional openness and defensive aloofness, and this Bertolucci picked up as well. "An angel as a man and a monster as an actor," the director later said. "He is all instinct, but at the same time he is a complex man: On one side he needs to be loved by all; on another he is a machine incessantly producing charm; on still another he has the wisdom of an Indian sage."

In due course both acknowledged their experience with Freudian analysis, and as much as anything this became another touchstone. As the director explained, "It was a great synchronization. I wanted him to forget [the character of] Paul and remember himself and what was inside him. For him it was a completely new method. He was fascinated by the risk, and afraid of the sense of violation of his privacy."

"He was so wonderful," Bertolucci later added. "I always fall in love with my actors and actresses, but especially with Marlon." The director was infatuated with Brando, not only for his smoldering volcanolike inner life but also because he found him so physically attractive. Holding a photograph of Brando, he once exclaimed, "Isn't he beautiful? Just look at that face." He then brought the picture to his lips and kissed it. "Oh, Marlon," he said, "you are good enough to eat."

It was, indeed, a very special meeting of kindred sensibilities. After the two weeks, Brando committed to the film without even reading the script that had sat on his bureau since Bertolucci's arrival.

With Brando's go-ahead, Grimaldi then took the project to Paramount. In later recollections, Robert Evans insisted that he was very enthusiastic and that he himself had persuaded Marlon to take the role. Yet Paramount wouldn't make the deal because *Tango* clearly promised to be an X-rated picture. After the studio decided to nix the project, Robert Littman, MGM's production chief in London, was approached, but his studio's executives rejected it, too. Grimaldi then went to David Chasman, head of United Artists in London, with whom he had worked before. "The sexual scenes as Bertolucci described them were even more candid than in the actual film," said Chasman. "He didn't talk about butt-fucking, but he conveyed that it would be very explicit. From what he said, I thought we were going to get a look at Brando's balls."

Once United Artists agreed to distribute *Tango*—and Grimaldi's company, PEA, signed a coproduction deal—the film was budgeted at $1.4 million and scheduled to begin in Paris in February 1972.

Before turning his attention to the new film, however, Brando was asked to dub many of his scenes in *The Godfather*. He completed the looping on Christmas Eve 1971, and receiving a check from Paramount for $12,000, he told Evans, "That's four thousand dollars too much. I didn't actually work the first day. Where can I send back the difference?" Evans thought he was "a strange guy." Ironically, Brando's hours at the soundstage and his additional compensation would prove pointless anyway. Preview audiences soon confirmed that his delivery had been perfectly understandable in the scenes as originally shot. As a result, the redubbed dialogue was never used.

Bertolucci anticipated a seven-week shoot, and entrepreneur Bernie Cornfield offered Brando his apartment, a suite of rooms near the Arc de Triomphe, one of several originally designed by Napoleon for his generals. Brando arrived early so that he could diet before stepping in front of the cameras.

Bertolucci and his cinematographer, Vittorio Storaro, began to shoot on February 12. From the beginning the director acknowledged that his conceptual influences were Céline, Bataille, Henry Miller, and even his own psychoanalysis, and in a sense he was asking the actor to do what Brando had often done in his early, best performances with Kazan—namely, in an almost clinical way, to "act out" and explore. He hoped that Brando, by tapping into his emotional reservoirs and spontaneously recreating "hidden" moments, could convey the psychosexual pain and existential dilemma of the protagonist.

In outline, Brando's character is a world-weary, desperately lonely, and disillusioned man who, after the suicide of his wife, becomes obsessed by Jeanne, a beautiful twenty-year-old woman. During their three-day anonymous sexual orgy in an empty apartment, he dominates and subdues her, prohibits the use of names and references to their pasts or the outside world, expresses his misogyny and his tenderness, and in effect uses sex as a weapon to vent his anger and revenge on social conventions. While *Tango* would later provoke controversy because of its sexual explicitness, the themes that Bertolucci—and Brando—had set out to explore had much more to do with pain, grief, and loneliness than erotica.

Still, the sexual scenes he had written were so explicit that Alice Marchak, who had accompanied Marlon to Paris, was appalled. It was her custom to retype Marlon's dialogue without descriptions and directorial explanations (so that they could be put onto Brando's cue cards), and during the first week she had begun to transcribe the screenplay. She was shocked by the "pornography" of what her boss was expected to say and do on-screen, and she registered her dismay. Brando reassured her, explaining that his scenes with Jeanne, played by Maria Schneider, would not be filmed as written.

For the moment Alice relaxed, and Marlon duly arrived for his first day of shooting, delivered by his assigned driver. It was a cold morning, and he was already wearing the clothes he had chosen as his costume, a cashmere coat over a V-neck sweater. He was in makeup, completed by Philip Rhodes, whom the crew immediately recognized as Brando's "friend, adviser, confidant, and psychoanalyst." But in truth it was Bertolucci who would become Brando's therapist during these weeks, drawing from him his most authentic performance since *On the Waterfront*.

In the film's opening scene, in which Brando was to appear standing under the Bir-Hakeim Bridge while the Métro roars by overhead, Bertolucci chose to shoot the actor's back as he clamped his hands over his ears. After fifteen minutes of rehearsal Brando complained to Jean-David Lefebvre, the second assistant director. "I can't believe this," said Brando. "Bernardo is completely crazy. He wants me to play this with my back to the camera." However, he went along and did the director one better. With the camera rolling, Brando not only put his hands over his ears but also erupted in a heart-piercing scream. "I was shocked," said the director. "He started at such a violent pitch that I said to myself, 'Maybe I cannot work at the level of this actor.' I was very scared."

He continued to be spellbound for the next several scenes. As he confessed to his longtime first assistant director, Fernand Moskowitz, "I'm a catastrophe as his director. I don't know what to tell him, he's so brilliant."

Brando and Bertolucci began to develop a pattern. Each day they huddled privately for several hours to discuss what they'd been thinking about, what feelings would work where and why, and what the consequences of such expressions might be. Typically the talks evolved into a sort of mutual psychotherapy session. With both men deeply immersed in these questions, each seemed to energize the other. Risk taking, it seemed, was the order of the day. Brando appeared to be more alive, more concentrated than he'd been in decades. "He was really riding high," commented Philip Rhodes, who perhaps more than anyone was in a position to know. "He had *Godfather* behind him, and this was going to be the real thing."

Even though Bertolucci called for many takes as they tried variants of the opening scenes, Brando was cooperative, establishing easy rapport with the crew, who teased him about his Americanized French. When he checked in with friends long-distance, he told them how well the film was going, how much he was enjoying the shoot. Marion Rosenberg, who had become acquainted with Marlon when she was the de facto line producer on *The Night of the Following Day,* was surprised to receive his phone call. "He'd just begun making *Tango,"* she said. "He told me it was the most exciting experience he'd had in years, the most thrilling relationship he'd ever had with a director. It was an odd revelation for Marlon to make, because it was the only time he ever discussed his work with me."

With Bertolucci's interest in improvisation, he was allowing Brando the freedom to experiment and test in ways that many of his recent directors had dismissed as the actor's eccentric self-indulgence. Yet it went beyond that. With their shared commitment to psychoanalysis, Bertolucci was encouraging Brando to do what he had never done before—confront and express his deep reservoir of pain and anger. "I make documentaries on actors," he explained. "All my films are documentaries on my actors. I follow them. I let them do what they want." It was exactly the kind of open form that would allow Brando to flourish, but it went further still, because Bertolucci was creating a safe place—not only a closed set, but a supportive dialogue that seemed to relax Brando's habitual defenses.

Several days into the shoot he finally met Maria Schneider, the actress chosen to play the young Frenchwoman with whom his character becomes obsessed. Bertolucci may not have realized it, but they had a prior connection. Schneider was the illegitimate daughter of French stage actor Daniel

Gélin, one of Brando's apartment mates from the summer of 1949. Now Brando was to enact on film an obsessive, sadomasochistic affair with his old friend's daughter.

Schneider was not yet twenty when she was chosen at the last minute to replace Dominique Sanda, Bertolucci's original choice, who had become pregnant. The director interviewed more than 100 actresses, and although Schneider had little acting experience—she'd left home at age fifteen, danced in a French stage comedy, worked as Brigitte Bardot's stand-in, and appeared in two small movie roles—Bertolucci thought she was the personification of the hip but bourgeois student. "She was a Lolita, but more perverse," he explained, adding that when he had asked her to take her clothes off during the screen test, "she became much more natural."

Schneider had led a wild and freewheeling life in Paris, consciously adopting a rebellious, *épater les bourgeois* philosophy to explain her marijuana smoking, belief in "free love," and bisexuality. With her shoulder-length, wavy reddish brown hair, huge green eyes, and voluptuous figure, she had an attractive, overripe, even decadent insouciance.

The first day Marlon and she were introduced, he had tried to shock her—knowing full well that she was the daughter of an old friend.

"Let's go for a walk, Maria," he said, leading her away to nearby café. "You're going to have to put your finger up my ass, so let's get to know each other."

On the way to the café, Brando asked her what her sign was, then confessed that like her, he too was an Aries. Inside, they sat down and Marlon stared at her in silence.

"Is it difficult for you to look someone in the eye for a long time?" he asked.

"Sometimes," she replied.

"Don't talk," he instructed her. "Just look me in the eye as hard as you can."

Beneath her ingenue exterior, Schneider wasn't easily intimidated and she seemed to have passed the test, because that evening a bouquet of flowers arrived from him at her hotel. The card was inscribed with Chinese characters.

"What do those characters mean?" she asked him the next morning on the set.

"I'm not going to tell you," he teased, adopting the same guru stance he had taken with Stephanie Beacham.

From then on he was "like Daddy," Schneider later recalled.

For all her inexperience in acting (or perhaps because of it), Schneider claimed to be looking forward to Bertolucci's improvisational approach. "He knows what he wants to achieve, but leaves it to you to get the feeling and to express it. He provokes response." In fact, however, the crew shortly realized that Schneider was finding the situation difficult. Like many others working on the movie, she saw that Brando and Bertolucci had formed an exclusive club, with the result that she often was left in the dark about what impromptu changes they had made in a scene after probing each other's psyche. Another problem was that during the first weeks, Brando stuck to his contractual schedule, insisting that he be able to leave the set by eight every evening. He would usually meet Christian Marquand and other friends for dinner afterward. Schneider had neither the clout nor the contract to escape. Bertolucci insisted that she stay on the set to do cover shots and backup shots, sometimes keeping her until midnight.

"With Marlon, Bertolucci was more relaxed," Fernand Moskowitz explained. "With Maria he was very bossy. We would rehearse in the Italian way—technical rehearsals, not real ones—but then the scenes would be modified after Bernardo and Brando spoke. Brando and Maria had an excellent relationship, though. He was helping Maria in the scenes she found difficult to do, like the one when she was supposed to masturbate him. She didn't want to, and he helped her."

Despite Bertolucci's attempts to keep a tight schedule, Schneider soon grew casual about appearing promptly on the set each morning. Because Philip and Marie Rhodes always arrived at work early (Philip on makeup, Marie as Marlon's stand-in for the lighting setups), they were often sent to find Schneider and bring her in their cab to the shoot.

"We started out early, and our daily routine was to go and make the rounds looking for the leading lady," recalled Rhodes. "You never knew where she was. She could be with some guys or some girls, and when we'd finally find her, she would always get into the cab and open up her tin of marijuana and light up a joint as big as a cigar. She let the ashes fall all over the cab, burning the seats, but finally we'd deliver her to the set."

Brando wasn't very prompt himself, however. For all his interest in the film, he still required someone to rouse him and deliver him to the day's location. "Nearly every morning someone has to go and find him," Schneider claimed. "Without that, he [would] never arrive for work."

Later there would be much speculation about whether Schneider and

Brando actually had an affair. Schneider confided to her father that she and Marlon had indeed begun one. "Nobody was allowed on the set," recalled Daniel Gélin. "Every time I saw Maria she was upset, because it wasn't easy for her to do this movie. She wasn't a virgin, but she was young, so she was finding some of the scenes difficult. But she told me that Marlon treated her with great tenderness. It was while they were talking so much together that they began to have their affair. And afterward she followed him to spend a few weeks with him on vacation."

It would seem that there was some residual bitterness, however, because later Schneider was quite outspoken about Marlon's age and flabbiness. "I never felt any sexual attraction to Brando," she said. "He's almost fifty, and he is only beautiful to here," she added gesturing to her neck. "He was very uptight about his weight; he kept pulling curtains whenever he changed clothes."

From the start Bertolucci had made it clear that he expected *Tango*'s erotic scenes to be explicit. "I decided that to suggest and allude instead of saying it outright would create an unhealthy climate for the spectator," he explained. But once the shoot had progressed to the empty apartment where the three-day encounter was to be filmed, Brando was startled to hear that the director expected him and Schneider to strip. Schneider was willing, but Brando demurred and later confessed to Marchak how deeply upset he was by Bertolucci's insistence on nudity. Marchak's response was abrupt and emphatic; she advised her boss to drop out of the film immediately.

"I can't," Marlon replied, Grimaldi's previous lawsuit apparently having taught him a lesson. "The picture is half-done. They'll sue for millions."

Brando came up with a compromise. He wore either his clothes or an overcoat during most of the sex scenes, an affectation that was later seen as a symptom of his character's disengagement. The idea originated not in his sense of decorum but in his desire to hide his bulk from the camera, much as he had in *The Nightcomers*. But Bertolucci still insisted that there be scenes in which the actors would appear nude. "Marlon was still on his diet," recalled first assistant director Moskowitz. "He was always asking to put off those scenes in which he had to appear naked. 'We have to wait a bit longer, I'm not thin enough yet,' he would say." Finally, cinematographer Vittorio Storaro blurred the shots of Brando's backside, never shooting him totally nude (Schneider's body was fully revealed from all angles and was often positioned to hide Brando's waistline and hips).

Bertolucci claimed that keeping Brando clothed much of the time was actually his idea and that the actor had had no objection to being filmed nude. "I wanted to show it as essentially an oedipal relationship," he said. "Her nakedness makes her more childlike, his clothes make him more fatherly." He then said that in fact he did shoot one scene that showed Brando's genitals, but he added, "I finally cut it out to shorten the film." Perhaps Bertolucci was simply enjoying his castration puns, but he speculated further: It is also possible that I had so identified myself with Brando that I cut it out of shame for myself. To show him naked would have been like showing myself naked."

As they proceeded to rehearse the sex scenes, Bertolucci made what Brando regarded as an even more outrageous request.

"I want you to screw Maria on-screen," he told the actor.

"That's impossible," was Brando's immediate response. "If that happens, our sex organs become the centerpiece of the film."

Bertolucci kept pushing, however, locked into what he later called his own Freudian hang-ups, and describing the film as his personal cathartic. The sadomasochistic scenes, he insisted, had to be developed enough to suggest modern man's despair and disillusionment, and he took Brando to look at more Bacon paintings. Still, as the days of shooting lasted long into the evening, there was an increasing sense of the director's confusions. One day he conceded as much to his assistant director. "What are we doing here?" he asked plaintively. "What is this movie about?"

During rehearsal on another day he watched Brando with Schneider, still urging them to become more sexually explicit.

"You are the embodiment of my prick," he told Marlon. "You are its symbol."

Later Brando would diminish the importance of the movie by exclaiming, "What the fuck does that mean? I don't think Bertolucci knew what the film was about. He went around telling everybody it was about his prick!" Just what the director's conflicts were Brando did not explain, and Bertolucci himself did nothing to clarify things when he himself announced, "Actresses and actors, I fall in love with all; they are the prolongation of my penis. Yes, my *penis*. Like Pinocchio's nose, my penis grows."

Then he paused for effect and added, "Please understand, this is not a declaration of my bisexuality."

Schneider, meanwhile, claimed that she understood what was happening, since she shared the same sexual proclivities that both Brando and Bertolucci were rumored to have. In her usual unflinching way, she announced that she and Brando got along together because "we're both bisexual and it's beautiful." The sexual scenes, she added, were a way of "acting out Bernardo's sex problems. [He is] more intellectual than Brando or me. We are more animals . . . , really more simple. . . . It's Bernardo's problems. It's in his head."

Interestingly enough, after the film's release director Ingmar Bergman posited that *Tango* was really a movie about homosexuals, that Brando and Bertolucci had really wanted to make it that way but then "got worried about taboos. . . . There is much hatred of women in this film, but if you see it as being about a man who loves a boy, you can understand it." Later, when asked about Bergman's remark that Bertolucci hadn't had the nerve to cast a boy in Schneider's role, Brando said, "Well, he came as close to it as he can get. I mean she's a professed . . . homosexual."

Although much of the film was improvised and a minimal amount of line-learning required, Brando again relied on cue cards hidden in inventive places on the set or on his person. One day he came up with a new idea for the scene in which Schneider was to arrive with a record player and dance while Brando's Paul sat on the floor and watched.

"How about I take off my shoe and play with it?" he suggested.

"Yes, that's perfect," said Bertolucci.

But the assistant director was aware of what Brando was up to. "His goal was to read his lines which were written on the sole of his shoe," said Moskowitz. "The only problem was that he had to walk across the floor before he sat down. He was afraid that this would erase the lines on the bottom of his shoe, so he limped in the first take."

"Why are you limping?" asked Bertolucci. Brando simply shrugged and proceeded to read his lines off his shoe.

On the day that Brando was to give his monologue over the body of his dead wife, Bertolucci saw new and extraordinary depths in his affect. As scripted, it was a genuinely moving and painful episode, but afterward Brando acknowledged that the scene brought him to real tears and anguish, because, as Daniel Gélin recalled, "he was remembering the death of his mother." Dodie had tried to commit suicide at least once, and there was also the love and grief mixed with anger and a sense of betrayal in his character that paralleled Marlon's own ambivalence toward his mother. All of it pushed him beyond anything he'd ever done before. In front of the camera his pain, grief, and indignation were extraordinary, as if the inner Brando, propelled by a spring, had jumped out of a box. There was his intonation, his agonized pauses, but far more, as he gave his speech he rolled his eyes upward, spiritually moved and profoundly repentant.

Later he would mock what viewers had regarded as a brilliant moment, diminishing the scene and thereby denying his own depth of emotion. The soulful look toward heaven, he asserted, was only his cover for reading his lines off the cue card posted high on the wall behind the coffin.

There was no doubt that Brando was using the cue cards; he had even, in another context, suggested writing his prompts on Schneider's rear end. Yet no one on the set had any illusions that Brando had very much taken to heart Bertolucci's instructions about how he wanted his actor to approach his role. "Instead of entering the character," the director said, "I asked him to superimpose himself on it. I didn't ask him to become anything but himself."

Philip Rhodes had utterly no doubt about what was happening. "I had often told him," said Rhodes, " 'You've made all the money in the world. Why don't you do something in a film, work something out that helps you in your own life?' I knew that he had done all those terrible films in the sixties strictly for the money, but I kept saying, 'Why don't you really let it all hang out, explore what your problems are, just as Shakespeare did with *Hamlet*?' Bertolucci was basically saying the same thing—'Make use of the role for yourself.' And that's why *Tango* mattered to him."

Likewise, Christian Marquand put it even more simply. "Forty years of Brando's life experiences went into the film," he later explained. "It is Brando talking about himself, being himself. His relations with his mother, father, children, lovers, friends—all come out in his performance as Paul."

Brando's introspection the preceding summer and fall had prepared him to undertake the task set by Bertolucci. But during his first month of shooting *Tango,* another personal crisis forced him to confront the complicated questions of father, children, and family in his own life.

While he was in Paris, Kashfi had become even more aggressive in her demands to reclaim custody of Christian. In a strange series of coincidences, she had become friendly with Giselle Fermine, the Hollywood hooker who had been set up by Brando in an apartment (she had since broken things off with him). Two years later, in 1971, a friend of Fermine, who was also Kashfi's lover, asked if she could help get sleeping pills to help Anna with her insomnia. Fermine was receiving prescriptions from both her personal doctor and the UCLA Medical Center, where she was being treated for an aneurysm. Thus, she always had a vast supply of pills available.

She picked up a prescription for sleeping pills and delivered them, as requested, to Kashfi's home on Havenhurst.

"Oh, you're that voodoo lady," Kashfi said when Fermine arrived. "I've been hearing about you from a lot of different people."

Kashfi and Fermine began spending evenings together, long hours filled with Kashfi's drinking, pill-popping, and nonstop complaining about Brando, his attorney, Norman Garey, and his private investigator, Jimmy Briscoe.

"She was really fucked up during this time," recalled Fermine. Kashfi continued to rail, claiming that she had to chase a snoopy Briscoe away from her house one night with a shillelagh. She also charged that attorney Garey had once beaten her with a log after he had been summoned by Brando. She said that she had driven up to Mulholland unannounced, walked into Brando's bedroom, where he was having dinner with Marie Cui, and demanded to see Christian. Incredibly enough, she reported that when she went outside, followed by Brando, the lawyer "was suddenly there and picked up a log from the woodpile and beat the hell out of me— my shoulders, my back, my hips. I was screaming, 'Help me, Marlon!' but he just stood there and watched." Claiming that Garey and Brando were conspiring to keep Christian away from her, she alleged that one night when the boy had finally come to stay with her, attorney Garey had sneaked in during the early-morning hours and spirited Christian away.

Fermine listened to all the stories, finding most of them unbelievable, and even asked Briscoe, whom she knew slightly, if Brando had really hired him. "This is getting crazier and crazier," Fermine recalled the detective saying as he denied Kashfi's allegations. "Anna had all these black-and-blue marks on her," said Fermine. "It looked as if she was being beaten, but in fact it was because she was always falling down when she was drunk and stoned."

In February 1972, after Brando had left for Paris, Kashfi had moved out of her apartment and gone to stay with Fermine. "I couldn't handle her," said Fermine, no stranger to substance abuse but overwhelmed by Kashfi's behavior. "She always had a gallon open and another fifth stashed." Kashfi's presence also interfered with visits from Fermine's clients, so she made arrangements to move her to the apartment of a friend who actually needed a housemate.

During that same month, the Ojai Valley School informed both Kashfi and Brando that Christian had set fire to his dorm. Kashfi was distraught, certain that Christian was emulating his father's much beloved but apocryphal story of having been kicked out of Shattuck for setting the school's bell tower on fire. "Devi, it was evident, was being drawn under by his father's twisted wake," she insisted. "I resolved to extricate him from the vortex. I drove to the Ojai Valley School to collect Devi for the weekend, promising to return him by Monday."

She did not bring Christian back as promised because, she said, he had bronchitis. Then she asked James Wooster, a friend of the woman she was living with, to drive her and Christian to Mexico. A doctor had advised her, she said, that the boy needed a warm, dry climate in which to recover.

All hell broke loose. Notified by the school that Kashfi had kept Christian, attorney Norman Garey requested a court hearing to discuss Kashfi's latest violation of the custody orders. He also sent Briscoe, the private investigator, up to Mulholland to find out if Reiko Sato had heard from Kashfi about what was going on. Sato, one of Brando's old girlfriends and now working for him as a secretary and caretaker while he was gone, had indeed been contacted and was perplexed. First she had received a phone call from Kashfi's housemate, complaining that Anna was drunk and was becoming loud and obnoxious. A few hours later a blond man driving a blue pickup had arrived with Christian, who gathered up some clothes from his bedroom and left.

Briscoe reported this to Garey who made plans to take the custody violation to court. But at five the following morning, with Kashfi still drunk and raging, her housemate put Christian in a cab and sent him back up to Mulholland. Once Kashfi realized that Christian was gone, she jumped in her car, shouting that she was going to bring him back. Unsure what to do, the housemate telephoned Fermine.

"I don't want Anna living with me," she announced. "I can't handle her. She's very drunk and screaming because Christian has gone back up to his father's. And now she's gone after him."

Fermine then telephoned Reiko to find out if the boy had arrived and to warn her of Kashfi's intent. Having been instructed by Brando never to let Anna into the house, Reiko again summoned Norman Garey, who, on reaching Mulholland, found Kashfi sitting in her car in the driveway. Garey went inside to talk to Christian and concluded that the boy preferred to stay as far away from his mother as possible. In later court testimony Garey insisted that Kashfi then broke in through the back door and tried to drag Christian out to her car. The police were called, and in the ensuing commotion Christian agreed to go with his mother so that she would calm down, but said that he would return that evening.

The following day, March 7, Kashfi had Wooster drive her and Christian to Baja California. Perhaps the March 9 court hearing on her failure to return Christian to school prompted her action, but whatever her thinking, after arriving in Baja she left the thirteen-year-old with Wooster and returned alone to Los Angeles. Her housemate, afraid that Christian had been kidnapped, phoned Fermine again. A few hours later Kashfi herself contacted Fermine.

"Your housemate just called and she's saying that Christian has been kidnapped," said Fermine.

"Devi is just going on a fishing trip with some friends of mine," Kashfi insisted. "You know, James Wooster, that friend of yours who helped me move. I'm going down to Mexico to meet him and Christian tomorrow."

Fermine was astonished. Fed up with Kashfi's recklessness she telephoned Jimmy Briscoe, then called Kashfi back to ask if she could go along on the fishing trip. Kashfi agreed. Wooster's friends arrived at four in the morning to pick up the two women, but at the border Fermine realized that she did not have any ID. They quickly devised a new plan: Wooster's friends would cross the Mexican border, retrieve Christian, and bring him back to El Centro, the border town where the women would wait.

Fermine and Kashfi sat in a bar all day downing drinks as Kashfi became more and more agitated. A screaming brawl between the two women ensued, with the inevitable result that when the police were called, a photographer got wind that Brando's ex-wife was in town. Kashfi ensured their arrest by slugging the photographer and breaking his camera, but

Fermine managed to talk the police captain into letting them go with the promise that they would be on the next bus out of town.

Learning that Kashfi was returning to Los Angeles without Christian, Garey phoned Brando in Paris to advise him that not only had she spirited the boy away to Mexico, but had now lost track of him altogether. Brando had Briscoe enlist Jay J. Armes, the well-known detective who had lost both hands and used hooklike prosthetic devices, to search for Christian. On the set of *Tango* it was clear to all that the actor was "very upset," said assistant director Moskowitz. "He said his son had disappeared. He was crying. That day he left immediately and was absent for several days." Officially Brando was granted a week off from *Tango* to attend the New York premiere of *The Godfather* on March 14. Instead he headed for Los Angeles, all the while insisting that there had been no kidnapping and that Christian was safe and on a scuba-diving vacation with friends in Mexico.

Meanwhile, Fermine and Kashfi had been wending their way back to L.A. by bus. Despite her frantic concern about Christian, and despite having to appear the following day at her court hearing, Kashfi continued drinking and created such a fracas that the driver threw them off the bus in the small California town of Salton City. There the police arrested her and Fermine on a drunk and disorderly charge. They were kept in jail overnight until the morning of March 9, when the secretary of Kashfi's attorney arrived to bail them out.

The three women then headed for the San Diego Airport to catch a plane back to Los Angeles in time for the court hearing. Before their flight, however, they stopped off in the lounge for a drink. Soon Fermine was regaling the other two with tales of her sex life with Brando, and one drink turned to several. They missed each succeeding flight to Los Angeles, and as a result Kashfi wasn't in court when Brando's lawyers were asking that he be given sole custody of Christian. Accusing Kashfi of kidnapping, they also requested a restraining order prohibiting her from setting foot inside Brando's home. Kashfi's lawyers denied the allegations and repeated the story that Christian was merely on a fishing trip. The judge scheduled another hearing for March 13, at which time he expected to see father, mother, and son in court.

Even as Kashfi's lawyers were dismissing the kidnapping story, detective Armes was searching for Brando's son, crisscrossing Baja by helicopter. On March 10 he spotted a blue pickup at an encampment. Landing in a nearby town, he rounded up a posse of *federales* and raided the campsite, where they found Wooster with four other bearded, long-haired men, an older woman, and a young girl. There was no sign of the boy.

The *federales* lined up the scruffy group at gunpoint.

"Where's Christian?" Armes demanded.

"What Christian?" Wooster replied.

But one of his companions was intimidated enough to point to a nearby tent.

Armes marched to the tent and pulled the flap aside. There he found the tall, gangly teenager hiding under a pile of clothes. Christian tried to make a run for it, but Armes caught him.

"Okay, okay," Wooster now confessed. "Anna promised us ten thousand to heist the boy for a while."

Indeed, the rest of the group agreed that they had expected $10,000 from Kashfi for hiding Christian in Baja. Armes also confirmed that there were several months of supplies at the campsite, as if they had prepared for an extended stay.

Three days later, on March 13, Brando and Kashfi appeared in a Santa Monica courtroom before Judge Rittenband. Kashfi denied that she had anything to do with the kidnapping plot, but Jay J. Armes testified that James Wooster had confessed to accepting Kashfi's offer of $10,000 to keep Christian out of sight. The judge postponed the hearing on Brando's petition for sole custody for another month, but gave him permission to take the boy to Paris until he finished making *Last Tango*.

Kashfi's abduction of Christian was the final straw for Brando. The incident clearly traumatized the teenager, who years later would recount incidents of abuse during his stay. One friend attributed his "paranoia" and purchase of guns to his being "very, very afraid of being kidnapped again." Christian told another friend that the experience had been a nightmare. "He never really liked to go into that too much," the high school classmate said a few years later. "He did say that his mom took him away, and then this guy that Marlon hired had come to get him. He always had this image of being in the tent and then, out of a bad dream, these two hooks came through the flap. He said the guy that Marlon hired was a bad-ass dude. I could see that the experience definitely left a scar and real psychological problems."

Brando was later informed by police that one of the abductors had tried to force Christian to give him a blow job. Christian himself didn't mention the incident and even said that he had been having a good time in Mexico, but Brando blamed Kashfi for putting their son in such jeopardy.

In the midst of this difficult personal crisis, Brando's career was revived with the release of *The Godfather*. Long delayed in the editing process, the movie had already shown early signs of extraordinary success, and word of mouth was generating much excitement. A *London Express* reporter had sneaked into Paramount's private screening, and on February 25, 1972, the *New York Post* scooped everyone with a guerrilla review based on the spy's report. Finally, on March 8, when film critics were given an advance viewing, *Variety* ignited the publicity storm with a rave review; soon the movie's premiere, its New York Boys' Club benefit at "21," followed by a party at the St. Regis on March 11, became the hottest event of the social season. (In fact, it was reported that many real-life Mafiosi were upset when they weren't invited to the gala. As a member of the Genovese crime family complained, "If the movie was about the military, they'd turn out the generals. So when they do one about us, we should be there too."

Calling *The Godfather* "one of the most brutal and moving chronicles of American life ever designed within the limits of popular entertainment," Vincent Canby of the *New York Times* summarized the importance of the role to Brando's career: "After a very long time in too many indifferent or half-realized movies . . . Marlon Brando has finally connected with a character and a film that need not embarrass America's most idiosyncratic film actor, nor those critics who have wondered, in bossy print, whatever happened to him. . . . His performance . . . is true and flamboyant and, at unexpected moments, immensely moving. This is not only because the emotions, if surcharged, are genuine and fundamental, but also because we're watching a fine actor exercise his talent for what looks like the great joy of it, because, after all, it's there."

Pauline Kael also pulled out all the stops, delighting in Coppola's direction as well as Pacino's talents, but saving her most lavish praise for Brando. Analyzing what made the performance so special, she wrote: "The role of Don Vito Corleone . . . allows him to release more of the gentleness that was so seductive and unsettling in his braggart roles. . . . Brando's acting has mellowed in recent years; it is less immediately exciting than it used to be, because there's not the sudden, violent discharge of emotion."

One correspondent to the *New York Times* explained why the public was so mesmerized by Brando's performance; it was, he said, his "redemption" and was "enhanced by our knowledge of what has come before. . . . It's all the scandal and arrogance and temperamental surliness that surround the Brando genius; it's the legend. That's why those last scenes are so touching; we realize suddenly that the legend is an old man, a grandpa playing with children in his backyard, and there is a sad dignity in watching a legend behave with such humanity."

As the laudatory reviews poured in, most critics were similarly relieved that America's most famous and talented actor had come alive again. This time Brando actually seemed to care that the critics loved him. During the *Godfather* publicity blitz, he made himself more available to the media than he had since his whirlwind tour touting *The Ugly American*. In this case, too, he was intent on making political pronouncements in the guise of explaining the movie. Shana Alexander, a personal friend and one of his most ardent fans, interviewed him for *Life* magazine in Paris. She breathlessly announced, "Brando's heresy is that he refuses to worship at the altar of himself." She also quoted him at length on the meaning of *The Godfather*: "I felt the picture made a useful commentary on the corporate thinking in this country. If Cosa Nostra had been black or socialist, Corleone would have been dead or in jail. But because the Mafia patterned itself so closely on the corporation, and dealt in a hard-nosed way with money, and with politics, it prospered. The Mafia is so . . . *American.* To me, a key phrase in the story is that whenever they wanted to kill somebody . . . they told him: 'Just business. Nothing personal.' When I read that, McNamara, Johnson, and Rusk flashed before my eyes."

Lolling on a sofa in a kimono and "looking more handsome than ever," Brando, maintaining his pontifical tone, turned to Tahiti. "Being in Tahiti gives me a sense of the one-to-one ratio of things," he said, explaining that he was establishing a "research station" on Tetiaroa to explore the possibilities of solar and wind energy as well as nutrients in seawater. "The three factors that concern us all are pollution, overpopulation, and aggression, and they're interlocked. If we don't solve all three problems, we can't really look to the future." When Alexander congratulated him on convincing a "certain tycoon" to fund his project for extracting protein from seawater, Brando shrugged. "Wasn't hard," he said with a cynical grin and evident contempt. "All I had to do was rub his hump with yak butter, and suck on his earlobe a little."

One thing that Brando wasn't forthcoming about—not even to his closest friends—was that he had given back his percentage points the previous summer for a quick $100,000 in cash. "He was putting on an act, and I was bamboozled," Philip Rhodes acknowledged years later. "I guess he couldn't stand to tell me that he'd screwed these things up, so he was stringing me along, and I believed him. Now looking back, it was all part of the way Marlon played the game.

"I've found that what people dislike in other people is something that is in themselves," Rhodes added. "Marlon has always made a big point of hating liars, but of course he's one of the great fabricators of all time. He changes the rules. He also has compartments that he keeps secret from everyone—psychological doors—so that he says even to his friends, 'I close the gates on you.' "

As friends and family well knew, Brando's attitudes toward money were strange, secretive, and compulsive. While obsessed with it in private, in public he made light of the wealth that had come with his success, dismissing the notion that fame and fortune meant anything to him. As he commented to *Newsweek*, "Success has made my life more convenient because I've been able to make some dough and pay my debts and alimony and things like that." But in fact "some dough" wasn't enough to cover the mounting Tahitian debts or his alimony and child support payments, and he certainly wasn't going to admit that he did not stand to earn the millions that everyone expected him to from *The Godfather*.

With the public primed for a history-making film, Paramount had taken the then extraordinary step of running the movie in five New York Loew's theaters simultaneously, and even with the total seating capacity of 4,700, every show was sold out. The following days the price of tickets was raised from $3.50 to $4, with scalpers getting as much as $50 a ticket in Miami. In the first twenty-six days of release, *The Godfather,* which had cost $6.2 million to make, moved over $26 million in ticket sales—a rate of $1 million a day. "No other film has grossed so much in so short a time," gloated Paramount executives as Gulf + Western stock soared in value.

Because of the extraordinary box office, there was much supposedly knowledgeable discussion about Brando's "take." *Variety* calculated, "He could wind up with $1.5 million as his share," a figure that was often repeated among Brando's friends and in press accounts. Adding to the obfuscation was Frank Yablans, the head of Paramount, who bragged that with the legions of Americans clamoring to see the movie, *Godfather* profits had become a certain "annuity" for the star. In fact, while *The Godfather* marked his comeback, it in no way solved his ongoing financial woes. It was *Tango,* instead, that would help defray the costs of wives, children, and ecological projects.

Upon returning to Paris with Christian and basking in the success of *The Godfather,* his improvisations in *Tango* took on a new energy. "Little by little he gave the movie an intensity that no one would have predicted," said Fernand Moskowitz. "He became totally invested in his role, and it was sometimes difficult to separate him from his character. And that got stronger and stronger toward the end, when we had to finish the shooting very quickly because we had gone past the schedule."

It was as if Brando could finally express his self-contempt and all his anger. In the scene from *Tango* in which he visits his mother-in-law and becomes infuriated at her and her religion, he spontaneously erupted and punched the door. The blow was so hard that he actually cracked the door and hurt his hand. He went to the hospital, and Bertolucci assumed that the shoot would have to be delayed. The next day, however, Brando appeared on the set, dismissing the severity of the wound and ready to go to work.

"I'm crazy," he told the crew. "Why did I do that?"

But much of his motivation seemed to be a general letting go of his past demons, including his war with Kashfi and his animosity toward women in general—all expressed through his character.

For the scene in which Paul sodomizes Jeanne, the butter was Bertolucci's idea. "Get the butter!" Marlon commands as he mounts Schneider from behind and forces her to repeat vile epithets against convention, religion, and the idea of family. "I'm going to tell you about the family. . . . Repeat it after me. . . . 'Holy family, church of good citizens . . .' Say it! 'The children are tortured until they tell their first lie. . . . The world is broken by repression. . . . And freedom is assassinated. . . . Family . . . you fucking, you fucking family," he rants in an orgasmic gasp as Schneider sobs out the black litany until he falls spent on top of her.

The butter, which would become the joke that would haunt Schneider for several years, was just the start, however. Two scenes later, in the bathroom, Brando's vision was even bleaker.

"You're alone, you're all alone, and you won't be able to be free of that feeling of being alone until you look death in the face," he proclaims, resisting Schneider's attempts at intimacy. "I mean that sounds like bullshit, some romantic crap. Until you go right up into the ass of death, right up in his ass, till you find the womb of fear . . ." he continues, suddenly adding, "I want you to put your fingers up my ass."

Bertolucci pushed Brando even harder when it came to the monologue in which his character was to reveal his past and cry with bitter revulsion. Here in the movie's climactic scene, the enthusiast of psychoanalysis was asking his actor to go straight to the Freudian core with memories of his parents. His father, the emotional problems of his mother—both were to be dealt with head-on as the source of his dialogue. The night before the scene was to be shot, Brando went to Bertolucci and acknowledged what he had often feared but rarely expressed—that he could no longer reach such deep and authentic expressions of feeling on camera, that he found it too costly, too gut-wrenching.

"I don't know how to do it," he conceded.

The director's response was immediate, as if he were Brando's psychiatrist.

"Think of the nightmare about your children," he instructed, reminding Brando of a frightening dream he had related to the director several days before.

Brando stared at him in stark fury.

"For a second I thought he wanted to kill me," Bertolucci later explained. "I knew I had asked him to violate his intimate self."

Bertolucci was ready to relent when Brando turned back to him.

"Okay, I'll do it," he said, and the next day he appeared on the set, ready to try to meet the director's expectations.

He was sailing closer to the wind than he had ever done before, and the scene took almost two days, which belied any argument that his performance was spur-of-the-moment or impulsive. "Bertolucci was pushing him, but once he started, the gates opened," Rhodes said. "Once you've scarred yourself over a period of time, and you know what you're doing, it's very easy to improvise."

Rhodes had seen Brando use his hostility toward his father in a film only once before, when George Englund had urged him to base his portrayal of the ambassador in *The Ugly American* on "Pop."

"George pushed him into it," explained Rhodes, "and once he started doing it, Marlon continued with that portrayal, even though he hated himself for doing it. It was the same here. He got caught up in how much he hated his father, and even though he felt invaded, he continued the performance."

Brando was to lie on the bed playing a harmonica while Schneider's character tried to tell him about her own father and his military service in Algeria.

"All uniforms are bullshit," Brando announced. "Everything outside this room is bullshit. . . . Why don't you stop talking about things that don't matter here. What the hell's the difference?"

Schneider replied, "Okay. So what do I have to say, what do I have to do?"

Brando singsonged the tune, "Come on the Good Ship Lollipop," then returned to playing the harmonica.

It was at this point that Bertolucci interrupted the loosely scripted dialogue. He had already included details about Brando's own life in the character, like his playing the bongo drums and living in Tahiti. Some details of Paul's background were obviously meant as reminders of Brando's film career, like his having been a boxer (as in *Waterfront*) or a Mexican revolutionary (as in *Viva Zapata!*). But now Bertolucci wanted more—and more directly from the actor himself.

"Give me some reminiscences about your youth," the director instructed him, and then told Storaro to load 900 feet of film in the camera. "The scene was completely improvised, and Marlon was *truly* naked at that moment," he later explained. "I had no idea of how long it was going to last."

As Brando later explained, when Bertolucci made his request, "that made me think about milking a cow, my mother's getting drunk, one thing and another." His explanation was typically understated and dismissive, as if to insist that the scene wasn't nearly as intense or as revelatory as it was for everyone who viewed it. But what he actually created was a complex speech that exposed not only the spiritual isolation of his character but also the still painful scars of his own life; in a halting and haunting voice, he talked about his parents and the years in the house in Libertyville, with the stable out back. It was as open and as truthful an utterance as he had ever made in public, or even in private to his closest friends.

The improvisation was framed by Schneider's question, "Why don't you go back in America?"

"I don't know—bad memories, I guess," Brando said.

After Schneider asked, "Of what?" Brando took a long pause and rubbed one of his eyes, as if he were going into a self-induced meditation.

"Oh," he said with a sigh, "my father was a drunk, tough whore-fucker, bar-fighter, supermasculine, and he was tough. My mother was very, very poetic, and also a drunk. And uh-h . . . All my memories of when I was a kid was of her being arrested, nude. We lived in this small town, a farming community." He paused again, giving a small cough as if to cover his emotional discomfort. "We lived on a farm. . . . I'd come home after school. . . . She'd be gone, in jail or something. Uh . . . and then I used to have to milk a cow every morning and every night, and I liked that. But I remember one time I was all dressed up to go out and take this girl to a basketball game. And I started to go out, and my father said, 'You have to milk the cow.' I asked him, 'Would you please milk it for me?' And he said, 'No. Get your ass out there.' I went out and I was in a hurry, didn't have time to change my shoes, and I had cow shit all over my shoes."

He paused, shaking his head slightly, as if he were still smelling the manure, then continued. "On the way to the basketball game, it smelled in the car, and . . ." He stopped, as if blocked. "I don't know, I can't remember very many good things."

Schneider urged him on. "Not one?" she asked.

"Yeah, some," he mumbled, and then began to describe another image from his troubled boyhood—the summer he was thrown out of Shattuck and returned home in shame, totally at the mercy of his father's stern discipline. The person he described was not his father but the old man with whom he had toiled that summer, laying drainage pipes.

"There was a farmer, a very nice guy, old guy, poor, worked real hard," he recalled. "I used to work in a ditch draining land for farming, and he wore overalls and he smoked a clay pipe. Half the time he wouldn't put tobacco in it. And I hated the work. It was hot and dirty and broke my back, and all day long I'd watch his spit, which would run down the pipe stem and hang on the bowl of the pipe. And I used to make bets with myself about when it was going to fall off. And I always lost. I never saw it fall off. I'd just look around, and it would be gone, and then a new one would be there."

Brando was remembering an actual figure from his past, a man he worked with who had lived in Libertyville. But now, in contrast to earlier scenes in which he had faked his sobs, real tears welled in his eyes. Not surprisingly, it was talking about Dodie that prompted the emotion.

"Well, my mother taught me to love nature," he continued, "and I guess that was the most she could do. And, um, in front of our house we had this big field, meadow. It was a mustard field in the summer, and we had a big black dog named Dutchie, and she used to hunt for rabbits in that field . . ."

His voice faded away. It was not another "bit of business." Mentioning his mother and the dog, who had been his beloved youthful companion, he was unable to go on. In the silence Bertolucci exclaimed, "Wonderful, wonderful."

Brando rose from the bed, and giving the director a strange, fierce look, he left the room.

"I had the feeling that maybe the next day he would not appear on the set," Bertolucci later explained. "I think what he was feeling was the intense horror—and *fascination*—of the intrusion upon his intimacy."

But Brando did return. Despite the intense psychic pain that the improvisation must have caused, he was still willing to go on, and voluntarily he extended his working hours, overlooking his 8:00 P.M. deadline.

The production was now approaching 12½ weeks, well over what had been anticipated. The final days were devoted to the wonderfully choreographed, stylized scene in the musty tango palace. Bertolucci had already introduced his actors to the locale, the Salle Wagram, an old-fashioned Parisian dance hall on a backstreet near the Étoile, squeezed between a horse-meat butcher and a *triperie*. It was here that Brando celebrated his forty-eighth birthday on April 4, as Bertolucci staged the scene.

In the background a band of accordionists played a tango. Brando arrived with a smile on his face and tossed the glass he was carrying to a technician, who caught it and gave the actor a friendly wave. Schneider walked in licking an ice-cream cone, and Marlon planted a welcoming kiss on her cheek. He then embraced Simone Signoret, who was visiting the set to see her daughter play a small role.

As the band struck up another tango and Bertolucci ordered his dancers into their ritualized poses, Schneider shook her head at the scene.

"It's very strange," she exclaimed. "It's for old-fashioned people. I was born in 1952. I've never heard of the tango."

Brando, however, was delighted with the music, and off to the side he began to dance around a pillar, making up his own impromptu steps as he whirled to the tango slides, much as he had improvised a soft-shoe routine entering the apartment from the rain.

"Very snazzy," a bystander complimented him, winning a smile from the actor.

With Bertolucci's command that all take their places, Brando got down to work. Against the background of the tango competition, the actor played at a parody, mimicking a whimsical Cary Grant formality. "I'm awfully sorry to intrude," he said to Schneider, "but I was so struck with your beauty that I thought I could offer you a glass of champagne. Is this seat taken?"

He was having fun with his dialogue, and now the whole business became more playful as he proposed a life together in a "house in the country."

"You're a nature lover?" asked Schneider.

"Oh ho, nature boy," he giggled. "Can't you see me with the cow and the chicken shit all over me?"

"I'll be your cow."

"And listen, I'll get to milk you twice a day," Brando exclaimed with a silly, leering grin.

On the dance floor, Brando and Schneider were to disrupt the last tango of the competition with their drunken shenanigans. The organizer of the contest, a matronly lady, was to chase them off the floor. But Bertolucci was disappointed in the first few takes and suggested, "Marlon, I want you to do something outlandish!"

"Camera! Action!" he called.

Chased by the tango matron, Brando reached for his belt and in one fell swoop dropped his trousers, pulled down his Jockeys, and bending over, pushed his bare buttocks into the woman's face. "Kiss this, kiss this!" he called to her. The matron's gasps were real as he called over his shoulder, "Farewell, my peach blossom," and then, pulling up his pants, scampered away with Schneider.

The champion mooner had topped his *Godfather* wedding stunt and just as the crew had given him an ovation during the previous shoot, the assembled crowds did so now.

The incident lightened the mood of the final days of the production. This was an illusion, however, for in filming his death scene, Brando once again reverted to his darker half, adding his own strange final gesture. After Schneider shoots him, he stumbles toward the balcony, intoning, "Our children, our children will remember." Then he removes a wad of chewing gum from his mouth and sticks it to the balcony railing. Before crumpling to the floor in a fetal position, he ad-libs again—a barely audible and unintelligible word.

Bertolucci later asked him what he said. Brando told him it was a Tahitian word, but refused to tell him what it meant. It was the last gesture of the master controller. While the director had been able to invade the actor's most intimate self, Brando could still withhold one last secret, somehow keep his barricades in place.

Shortly after the company's wrap party at Régine's, the actor confessed that he felt that Bertolucci had forced him to go too far. "I will never make another film like that one," he said. "For the first time, I have felt a violation of my innermost self. It should be the last time." Later, however, he would dismiss further talk about the emotional toll the movie had taken. "Na-a-ah," he sneered at an interviewer. "As soon as they let go of your leg, then it's out to Tahiti or the desert."

In mid-April 1972 Brando returned to court with Christian to settle the custody dispute. Kashfi did not show up, apparently resigned to the fact that the kidnapping caper meant that she would lose. After a series of psychiatric tests for Christian, the court reconfirmed that it would be best for the boy to remain with his father. On May 9 Brando and Kashfi reached an out-of-court settlement giving him sole custody and allowing her visitation rights every other weekend and one month during the summer.

Brando enrolled Christian the following autumn at Fernauld, a private school run by UCLA that specialized in learning disabilities. Kashfi took her revenge by talking to the press. Painting herself as the victim of Brando's merciless moves to deprive her of her son, she claimed that it was his habit to act out in real life his last part, and now that he had played *The Godfather,* her former husband had decided to take control of his family as the fictional don did in the movie.

After one last court hurdle, in which he was ordered to resume his monthly alimony and child support checks to Movita, Brando fled Los Angeles with Christian, intent upon catching up with his projects on Tetiaroa.

In mid-July Alice Marchak, who had been left in charge of the Mulholland house, received a frantic call from Alberto Grimaldi in Rome. *Tango* was scheduled to premiere at the New York Film Festival, and for the film to be completed in time, Brando would have to loop his lines by August 1.

"We need him in Rome right away," Grimaldi said.

Well aware that her boss's contract with Grimaldi guaranteed he would have the summer free, Marchak objected.

Grimaldi reasoned with her. For *Tango* to receive a "seal of approval," it had to open at a film festival and be classified as an "art picture." If it didn't open at the New York festival, it would have to wait until Cannes in the spring, which was much too long to hold the picture.

Marchak saw the logic of his argument and left messages at all of Brando's possible locations, and waited for him to be in touch. At first the actor refused to return to Europe, but when Marchak pointed out the financial benefits—namely, that he had gross points in the picture—he agreed to do the looping, but in Los Angeles, not Rome.

Brando's last-minute looping in August allowed Grimaldi to present *Last Tango* on the final night of the trendy, all important New York Film Festival on October 14, 1972. Unlike any of the other pictures on the program, *Tango* had no advance screenings because Grimaldi and Bertolucci had already run into problems caused by the film's explicit sexuality. Since the picture was a joint French-Italian production, they were required to submit it to the Italian censorship board. To circumvent the censors, they flew in a single print in a diplomat's pouch from Italy; they also offered no advance screenings for reviewers and showed it only once (on October 14), then immediately returned it to Italy. Because of the controversy and secrecy surrounding the movie, *Last Tango* played to a sold-out crowd and left them gasping.

Pauline Kael registered the shock of the audience by announcing that *Tango* was "the most powerfully erotic film ever made, and it may turn out to be the most liberating." Predicting that people would be arguing about this movie for years to come, she asserted that the date of the screening "should become a landmark in movie history comparable to May 29, 1913—the night *Le Sacre du printemps* was first performed—in music history. . . . Bertolucci and Brando have altered the face of an art form."

Noting the improvised script (including Brando's self-revealing monologue) within the framework of the story supplied by Bertolucci, Kael went on to say that Brando had dug deeper and fused more with the role than any other actor would be capable of, as if he had "a direct pipeline to the mystery of character. . . . Paul feels so 'real' and the character is brought so close that a new dimension in screen acting has been reached." But even as she explained the movie and trumpeted its great achievement, she was riveted by Brando himself, by the resonances between the on-screen portrayal and what the public had been permitted to know about the legendary actor throughout the years. "We are watching *Brando* throughout this movie, with all the feedback that that implies," she wrote. "His willingness to run the full course with a study of the aggression in masculine sexuality, and how the physical strength of men lends credence to the insanity that grows out of it, gives the film a larger, tragic dignity."

Vincent Canby was also enthusiastic, though with some reservations. In the context of the sexual liberation of the early 1970s and X-rated movies like *Deep Throat* and *I Am Curious (Yellow)*, he assured his readers that while *Tango* had its "sometimes brave, sometimes wildly foolish-looking Lawrentian gestures of an intense sexual fashion," it was "anything but pornographic." Calling it an "invasion of self-assuring, middle-class privacy," he, too, focused on Brando's performance, calling it "courageous," since the actor had "pulled out all the stops without fear of looking absurd."

The advance notices whetted the public's appetite, but the movie was delayed for general release until February 1, 1973, because Italian magistrates were filing obscenity charges against Grimaldi, Bertolucci, Brando, and Schneider. This only heightened audience anticipation, with the case going to trial in Bologna in late January 1973 and Bertolucci scheduled to testify before flying to New York for the film's American opening.

The controversy surrounding the film from the very beginning had resulted in an extraordinary pre-release swell of interest; advance-seating ticket sales in New York alone amounted to more than $100,000. And once the movie was in general release, the debate grew only more heated and extreme. Some critics and viewers condemned it as pornographic; others, comparing it to "real" hard-core porn, called it a yawn. Feminist critics were especially scornful: Grace Glueck, for example, condemned it as "the perfect macho soap opera" and contended that "Brando's and Bertolucci's dislike of women is intense."

Bertolucci, Brando, and *Last Tango*, it seemed, had ushered in porno chic in the name of sexual liberation. Admission to the film was the hottest ticket in town. One didn't dare attend a society dinner party without having seen the movie, and even Princess Lee Radziwill, the sister of Jacqueline Kennedy Onassis, was begging for a ticket. The most heated debate on the cocktail circuit was not simply about whether the sex was too explicit; the all consuming question was whether Brando and Schneider had actually "done it" on camera.

But beyond all the controversy about whether *Tango* was great art and a filmic "breakthrough" was the obsession with Brando. Both *Time* and *Newsweek* ran cover stories. Bertolucci and Schneider were willing to tell interviewers a lot about Marlon. Schneider, in her youth and in her bid for notoriety, fueled the gossip about Brando by telling the press that they had one thing in common—their bisexuality—and she cheerfully explained that his hang-up about nudity meant that he was less free than she. So outspoken was Schneider that Rod Steiger, not one of Brando's usual defenders, wrote indignantly to the *New York Times* to complain of the actress's "unnecessary revelations concerning Marlon Brando's private life, choice, vanities, physique, or what have you."

While Bertolucci himself was calling the making of the movie a "psychoanalytic" adventure, Brando was mostly silent except to deflect all those who were analyzing his private self on the basis of his character. "If you ask me about the fact that *Tango* seems to expose more of me than my previous roles," he said, "the operative word is *seems*. . . . Each part demands something of you. You either maximize yourself or minimize it—to whatever extent seems necessary." But unlike his round of publicity for *The Godfather*, Brando chose to say comparatively little about *Tango*. By and large he seemed to feel that critics had invested too much meaning in it. "I have no idea what that picture was about," he insisted several years later.

Last Tango would prove to be a true gold mine for Brando, "the big turnaround that put millions into his coffers," as United Artists executive David Chasman described it—since with this picture, he would actually earn a percentage of the gross. "It cost about $1.4 million to produce and its breakeven was about $3 million," Grimaldi explained. "The movie grossed more than $45 million, and it was still making money twenty years later. I would guess that Marlon earned at least $4 million from it, probably more."

Most of that money, Brando said, would be devoted to his Tahitian projects. Sadly, while he was back in Polynesia at the time the film went into general release in February 1973, Wally Cox died at the age of forty-eight. Cox's body was found dressed in his shirt, pants, and slippers and slumped over on the pillows of his bed. On the bedside table was a nearly empty bottle of prescription sleeping pills. Many friends speculated about suicide, but Dr. Thomas Noguchi, chief medical examiner of the Los Angeles County coroner's office, issued a preliminary report attributing Cox's death to a massive coronary, noting that "traces of a drug found in his body were not a high level."

There was more to it, however.

While there had always been rumors that Cox and Brando had had a homosexual relationship, people close to both men always vehemently denied it. "I'm sure they didn't have one," insisted Sondra Lee, "because I knew each of them separately. But what shocked me was that Wally had aberrated sexual needs that erupted or returned years later." Cox had made no secret of his penchant for kinky sex with hookers. Rhodes, for one, had been aware of his difficulties as well as his self-confessed sexual interests for some time. On the night of February 14, around midnight, he was surprised by a phone call from Cox.

"You know the girls I like," Wally said. "The ones with leather and whips and all that stuff. Do you know any I could get in touch with?"

"It's kind of late, Wally," Rhodes said.

Nevertheless, he could hear in his friend's voice that he'd been drinking, and he gathered that his wife, Pat, was out, so he stayed on the line when Cox changed the subject. Long fascinated with electronic devices, Cox asked Rhodes about his collection of old telephones, adding that he'd like to buy some of them.

"I'll give them to you, Wally," he said, "if you'll rout the doors of this bookcase I'm making."

Cox agreed that Rhodes could bring the doors over the next day. The following morning Rhodes strapped the eight doors, each six feet long, onto the roof of his Volkswagen and drove out to Cox's home on Roscomare Road in Bel Air. When he arrived, the driveway was filled with television crews as well as police and paramedics from the fire department. The emergency squads had been called by the private security patrol, who had themselves been summoned to the residence when Pat, away visiting a friend, had been unable to get an answer to her early-morning phone calls.

Just as Rhodes pulled up to the house, he saw the paramedics carrying a stretcher out the door, the body completely covered by a sheet.

"I knew it was Wally and I knew he was dead," Rhodes later explained. "What I figured was that Pat wasn't there and Wally couldn't find any contacts for getting his type of girls, so he got drunk. Then he was tired and wanted to go to sleep, so he started taking pills, washing them down the quick way, with liquor."

Pat Cox denied the radio reports that a suicide note had been found near the bottle of pills, although she did concede that her husband "had been despondent recently." This still did not end the gossip, and Wally's friends began calling one another to ask what any of them had heard about the suicide rumors.

Darren Dublin, Sondra Lee, Everett Greenbaum, Peter Turgeon, Billy Redfield—all refused to believe that Wally had intentionally killed himself. It was Philip Rhodes, though, who may have understood the tragedy most clearly. "The way I look at it, it doesn't much matter if that particular night he meant to kill himself," Rhodes later commented. "I've gone through a lot of suicides, and it seems to me that suicide is like an artwork with them. They're working on it for a long time, so that when they actually die it's as if it's the last brushstroke of the painting. They don't even think about it. It's like finishing a Roman arch, putting in that last inevitable stone. So in the strictest sense, I don't think Wally meant to kill himself that day. He just wasn't all that interested in living anymore. I don't think Pat or anyone could have saved him. The scenario had been written by then, and he just completed the last page of the script."

Wally was to be cremated, and as the *New York Times* reported, a memorial service was to be held "if the family is able to reach his closest friend, Marlon Brando, who is in Tahiti." As soon as Brando heard the news, he flew back to Los Angeles. There he helped Pat Cox make arrangements for the cremation and even volunteered to scatter the ashes in the woods near his Mulholland home, where he and Wally had so often walked.

Because there was to be no formal memorial service, Pat held a reception following the cremation. The gathering was really more like an Irish wake than a funeral service, with friends honoring their old pal with stories of his wit and humor and reminiscing about his special gifts of talent and sensitivity. Brando, however, kept to himself, refusing to join in. He sat off in the corner of the room, the expression on his face more angry and sour than sad and grieving.

"There were a lot of people there who were saying how fond they'd been of Wally," recalled Rhodes. "They were all showing their love for him. But Marlon would have nothing to do with it, and he seemed very put out by the gathering. At one point he said, 'These people weren't Wally's friends. *I* was his *only* friend.' It was his incredible possessiveness—he had to own people. So even in Wally's death, he had to be the *only* friend."

During the next several years Brando would create a hagiography for Cox, often announcing how much he missed him and insisting that Wally was the only person he'd ever been able to talk to. In reality, though, he had often treated the comic with patronizing irony, like a naive little brother who didn't know the ropes. Of all the acolytes who had surrounded Brando, Cox had been his own person, and yet even with Cox, Brando had often reached what Philip Rhodes called "critical mass," the point at which a friendship or a closeness became too threatening to endure. He had cut his friend off several times. With their ruptures Brando had also overlooked or simply denied that his own needs might have brutalized Cox and that he might have paid closer attention to him and his problems during this final year.

But after his death Cox was elevated to the repository of wisdom, and Brando placed his friend's photograph in the most honored position: next to that of his mother. In a similar vein Brando told a *Time* magazine reporter, "He was my brother. I can't tell you how much I miss and love that man. I have Wally's ashes in my house. I talk to him all the time."

In the months that followed Cox's death, Philip Rhodes had the impression that Brando never came to terms with what the relationship really meant to him. "He just couldn't believe that Wally was gone," said Rhodes. "He was always reminiscing about their walks together through the woods below his house on Mulholland. He loved Wally, but he talked about his feelings for him in the same way he sometimes talked about old girlfriends, even his ex-whores. He would say, 'I could have married her and been happy with her because we laughed a lot.' And that's how he talked about Wally. It was the same sense of mourning someone after the fact—crying about what could have been and never was."

Perhaps the making of *Tango* and Cox's death together had carried with them intimations of mortality for Brando. Still, his immediate response to the loss of his friend was to retreat to Tetiaroa and immerse himself in his projects, in effect give himself over to what Cox had called his "healer" role. If he couldn't save his best friend, he would save the world. Now Brando seemed to be looking for a source of authenticity simultaneously in Polynesian natives and Native Americans. But even in these efforts, he would be as unreliable and wavering in his attention as he had so often been with his old friend during their many years together. The pity was, he'd arrived at a point where he didn't know any other way.

16

THE AMERICAN INDIAN MOVEMENT

On March 27, 1973, toward the end of the customary long evening of less than sparkling wit and rambling speeches, Liv Ullmann and Roger Moore stood onstage at the annual Academy Awards ceremony and announced the nominees for best actor: Marlon Brando for *The Godfather,* Michael Caine and Laurence Olivier for *Sleuth,* Peter O'Toole for *The Ruling Class,* and Paul Winfield for *Sounder.* There was an expectant hush as Liv Ullmann opened the envelope: "The winner is . . . Marlon Brando!"

Brando had come to the ceremony once before, to pick up his Oscar for *On the Waterfront.* While Hollywood was now feting his career comeback in *The Godfather,* this time Brando had chosen not to attend. Although George C. Scott had snubbed the Academy's honor two years before by refusing his award for *Patton,* Brando sent a photogenic Apache woman in his place. As the celebrity-studded audience broke into thunderous applause with the announcement of Brando's name, she made her way to the podium. Moore waited, about to offer her the gold statuette, but she held up her hand to signal "stop." The clapping dwindled away into gasps of surprise and audible groans when she moved to the microphone to address the gathering.

Dressed in traditional clothes, with braided hair and a buckskin dress, Sacheen Littlefeather had arrived at the Dorothy Chandler Pavilion only minutes before the best actor nominees were read. An usher smelled trouble as soon as she appeared, clutching Brando's tickets in one hand, a sheaf of papers in the other, and accompanied by Brando's secretary, Alice Marchak. Howard Koch, producer of the Academy of Motion Picture Arts and Sciences event, was immediately informed.

Koch had assumed that *Godfather* producer Robert Evans would serve as the actor's stand-in. For weeks Paramount had no idea whether Brando would attend, and like Koch, had heard that the star of their blockbuster epic had recently taken off to Tahiti. Around six in the evening, after rehearsals for the evening's program, Koch was taking a shower in his dressing room when there was a knock on the shower door from *Variety* columnist Army Archerd, who'd been a contact of Brando's for years. "Archerd yelled through the glass," Koch recalled. " 'The Indians are coming! Marlon's not coming, but the Indians are coming!' And he left. I knew Marlon was into this Indian thing, but I didn't know about the girl."

Alerted by the usher of Littlefeather's intention, Koch now held an emergency meeting backstage to consider whether to confiscate her tickets—a tricky move, since other stars often used proxies. He decided to confront her head-on.

Meeting her backstage, he announced that she wouldn't be able to read from the lengthy typewritten speech she was carrying because the show, as usual, was running late. Sacheen shook her head. If Marlon won, she would proceed to read the text that the actor himself had composed.

"If you try, I'll cut you off the air," Koch repeated.

Standing in front of the cameras five minutes later, she discarded Brando's lecture and instead spoke extemporaneously. "I'm Apache and I am the president of the National Native American Affirmative Image Committee," she said. "I'm representing Marlon Brando this evening and he has asked me to tell you, in a very long speech which I cannot share with you presently because of time but I will be glad to share with the press afterward, that he very regretfully cannot accept this very generous award. And the reasons for this are the treatment of American Indians today by the film industry and in television reruns.

"I beg at this time that I have not intruded upon this evening and that we will, in the future, in our hearts and our understanding meet with love and generosity. Thank you on behalf of Marlon Brando." Then she quoted from the conclusion of Brando's written statement: " 'I would have been here myself tonight but I thought I could do more good at Wounded Knee.' "

The spurned Oscar would accidentally be taken to Mexico by Roger

Moore and end up in the Academy vaults. The presenters who followed, rankled by Brando's hijacking of the ceremony to lecture about the Indians, ad-libbed their disapproval with pointed gibes. Rock Hudson, still the untarnished matinee idol for Middle America, remarked smugly, "Often to be eloquent is to be silent," while best actress copresenter Raquel Welch, after reading the nominees, added, "I hope they haven't got a cause." Clint Eastwood wondered aloud if the best picture award should not be presented "on behalf of all the cowboys shot in John Ford westerns over the years."

Meanwhile, as the broadcast's closing credits rolled across millions of TV screens, Littlefeather handed the press copies of Brando's full fifteen-page statement scorning America and the film business alike for their treatment of Native Americans. She also confirmed that Marlon would soon be on his way to Wounded Knee, South Dakota, to support the American Indian Movement (AIM) protestors who had been under siege there for four weeks.

Brando's prepared statement about the plight of the Indians was his usual long, heartfelt, kind of speech:

> For two hundred years, we have lied to them, cheated them out of their lands . . . , starved them into signing fraudulent agreements that we call treaties that we never kept. We turned them into beggars on a continent that gave them life for as long as life can remember. And by my interpretation of history, however twisted, we did not do right. . . .
>
> It would seem that the respect for principle and the love of one's neighbors has become disfunctional in this country of ours. . . . I think . . . the motion picture community has been as responsible as any for degrading the Indian and making a mockery of his character.
>
> Describing him as hostile, savage and evil. It's hard enough for children to grow up in this world—when Indian children watch television and they watch films and they see their race depicted as they are in films, their minds become injured in ways we can never know. . . . I do not [therefore] feel that I can as a citizen of the United States accept an award tonight. . . . I thought perhaps I could have been of better use if I went to Wounded Knee.

The basic reaction to his rejection of the Oscar was righteous indignation, made all the more extreme by the fact that after ten years of bad-mouthing Brando, Hollywood had gone all out to welcome him back to its fold. Rona Barrett led the attack. Why, she asked, if he "wanted to tell the world how he feels about the Black Panthers, or the Indians, or whatever," had he sent "an alleged Indian princess?" The implication was cowardice, and more, that Brando had misused Hollywood's most sacred institution. "Rudeness," editorialized *Variety*.

Andrew Sarris, hardly an extension of the Hollywood establishment, took the affair more seriously. Conceding that Brando was "as sincere as anyone in the . . . fields of show biz, politics, and the pulpit," the *Village Voice* critic referred to the evening as "a night that will live in infamy for its sordid spectacle of unbridled ego, bad taste, and worse timing." He then took on the question of Brando's "courage and judgment" raised by the actor's refusal to appear and make the statement himself. "It was a classic example of his being damned if he did and damned if he didn't," Sarris concluded. "I suspect that what was at work here was a multilayered murkiness of self-hatred."

Marlon's snub of Hollywood was also interpreted by some as an expression of years-old ambivalence toward the movie business and the studios; it also seemed symptomatic of his insecurity, his political statement simply a rationalization for his anxiety that he would look stupid if he attended and the Oscar went to someone else. As a close Brando associate told *New York Post* critic Jerry Tallmer, "The simple answer is that he wasn't there because he wasn't sure he was going to win—whatever the odds in his favor. And if he wasn't going to win, he'd just have to sit there. It all comes down to fear."

That he had sent Sacheen Littlefeather to deliver the message seemed to undermine his desire to make a statement. Rather than focus on what was happening at Wounded Knee and the issues involved in the American Indian Movement's protest, the media clamored to know, "Who is this Indian princess?" Digging into her background, reporters sneered that she was "an actress, chosen Miss American Vampire of 1970." This announcement barely scratched the surface.

Twenty-six years old at the time she appeared at the Chandler Pavilion, Sacheen had been born into squalor on a reservation outside Tucson. That she was named Maria Louise Cruz wasn't unusual, since many Indians near the Mexican border carried Hispanic names, but news reports included this bit of "evidence" to prove she wasn't a "real" Indian. Her part-

Apache, part-Yaqui father was the child of "hard-core" alcoholics and had grown up in foster homes. He was abusive to her mother, Littlefeather claimed, and also beat and sexually molested her. At the age of nine she had tried to kill herself by jumping in front of a car. Her mother, a white art student, had then given Sacheen up to be raised in the Salinas Valley by Caucasian grandparents, who were obsessed with making her "white." Her assimilation included a perm and a nose job.

After college and a stay in a mental institution, she took part in the nascent Indian movement's occupation of Alcatraz Island from November 1969 through June 1971. For her it felt "like going back into the blanket . . . finding your heritage," she said. "For the first time I began to feel that maybe there was some hope."

She was given the tribal name of Littlefeather, which she retained partly out of pride and partly because she was already dabbling in a modeling and acting career (her agent told her that it was a more marketable name than Cruz). To earn a living, she took a full-time job as public service director for a San Francisco rock station.

At the same time, she became involved with the Native American Action Committee, a San Francisco group headed by Lee Brightman, a Sioux who was also a leader of AIM. In the dense, interconnected political climate of the Bay Area, she networked easily and solicited support from movie figures like Anthony Quinn, Jon Voight, Jane Fonda, and Sidney Poitier, all of whom showed interest in the Native American cause. She also wrote to Brando, knowing of his involvement with the Tacoma Puyallups, and she enclosed one of her modeling photos.

Eight months later, in the spring of 1972, Brando called her at the radio station. They spoke for nearly three hours, and he called several times more over the next few weeks. Littlefeather sent him information about the Indian group's project on affirmative image, and she accepted Brando's invitation to meet him and be his guest at his home.

When she arrived she was given the guest room, where she spent the night, much to her relief, alone. (Both Littlefeather and other Indian activists insist that she did not have an affair with Brando. In fact, during his years of working for the Indians, Brando never made overtures to Indian women, almost as if he needed to maintain the "purity" of the Native Americans and their cause by abstaining from any sexual involvement with them.)

Late the next morning Sacheen and Brando began to talk, "It was private, just the two of us," she said. "He told me that if anyone asked about the two of us together—our relationship—I should say that it was just based on mutual interest and that was it." At one point "tears came to his eyes," she added, "and what struck me was his sense of our real oppression, his feeling for our people." She was asked back to Mulholland several times during the fall and winter of 1972–73, with Marchak always reimbursing her for the airfare from San Francisco.

Their talks continued, although during some of her visits he spent most of his time in his bedroom speaking to her on a phone line in the guest room. She was told that she had free run of the premises, but that his bedroom was off-limits. Young Christian was often around, as was Marchak and Brando's current number one girlfriend, Jill Banner, whom he had met while making *Candy*.

"I thought it was unhealthy," said Littlefeather, referring to the atmosphere in the house and, specifically, to Banner. "She kept getting rejected and kept going back. It was an abusive relationship, emotionally and mentally; she seemed depressed and had all these mood swings." Marchak frequently dropped hints to Littlefeather about the girlfriend's instability and referred to an attempted suicide from a drug overdose.

"There was an element of anger that was like an undertow," Littlefeather explained. "Jill couldn't separate herself. Marlon needed to have her around—he was like the agitator. There were storms and clouds, name-calling and constant turmoil."

The week before the Oscar ceremony, Littlefeather had visited Brando again and he interrupted their conversation about the Wounded Knee protest to mention the Oscar nomination. "If I get this award I'm not going to accept it myself," he told her. "I won't even be there, but I'd like you to go up and make a speech on my behalf. But you can't tell anybody about this. You must be sworn to secrecy."

He said nothing about actually turning down the Oscar, but instead went on with a word of warning.

"People are going to lie to you," he instructed. "They'll print things that are untrue and there'll probably be a lot of flack about who you are or why you did it. People are likely to dig into your private life, into your family. You have to be ready for that."

She was already feeling "like a sacrificial lamb," but took his words as "very fatherly advice. I may have been manipulated," she added, "but perhaps he knew there was a little girl within me seeking exactly that—some sort of father figure."

The night before the ceremony, she flew from San Francisco and arrived at Mulholland Drive to find Marlon and his son Christian making up the guest bedroom for her. Brando then retreated to his own room until early the next afternoon, when he reemerged to outline his plan: Marchak would accompany her to the Chandler Pavilion; if he won, Sacheen was to refuse the Oscar and read a speech on his behalf.

By Hollywood standards it is a gross breach of etiquette to enter the Chandler Pavilion after 6:30 on Oscar night, but neither Littlefeather nor Marchak had any hope of arriving on time. At seven P.M., with the ceremony already under way, Marlon was still dictating his speech, still revising. Alice, in her evening gown, typed feverishly, trying to keep up with him and simultaneously edit the overlong text. Marlon then inspected Sacheen's makeup and her antique Indian buckskin dress, "as if he was a director," she recalled. (Later press reports to the contrary, she was not, she insisted, wearing "$5,000 worth of Navajo turquoise.") Brando's nephew, Marty Asinof, Jocelyn's twenty-year-old son from her marriage to Eliot Asinof, stood ready to chauffeur the two women in Marchak's Cadillac. A buddy of his, who had come by earlier to practice guitar, joked about going along to "ride shotgun."

Already late and then getting lost in downtown traffic, they arrived just fifteen minutes before the show was to end. Marchak managed to talk their way into the lobby as one of the startled guards scurried off to warn Koch.

With the best actor award only minutes away, and after jousting with the Academy president, the two women took their seats near James Caan. Caan, Marlon's mooning buddy, leaned over and grabbed Alice's hand. "He's gonna win, Alice, he's gonna win!" When Brando's name was announced, Sacheen found herself, half in a daze, standing at the podium and giving her own brief impromptu version of Brando's statement.

Outside the stage door a group of blacks and Chicanos cheered, "Right on, girl! Right on, you really spoke it." No sooner did Littlefeather reach the parking lot, though, when she was surrounded by hecklers shouting mock Indian war whoops. "Where's your tomahawk!" she heard one of them yell. The security guards on either side pressed in on her more protectively, but were useless as the mob seemed to swell by the minute.

"There were all these flashbulbs going off in my face, television cameras, people screaming and yelling," she recalled. "When I got inside the car, people were already starting to rock it. We were surrounded."

Marty Asinof started to let the Cadillac inch forward, shouting, "Fuck me, man! What's going on?" In a scene out of *The Day of the Locust,* people were hanging on to the door handles, climbing on top of, then sliding off the hood, and it was only when they reached the comparative safety of the freeway that he could joke about having had to leave Alice Marchak behind.

Back at Mulholland, Marlon was "delighted," Sacheen reported. "He gave me a hug and told me, 'That was very good. You spoke eloquently!' " Christian and Miko were sprawled on the floor, both watching the two or three TV sets that had been arranged in Brando's bedroom, each tuned to a different channel. With Marchak's arrival, they all settled in to watch the reports. Whether it was network or local, every broadcast was filled with interviews, commentary, and Brando film clips going back to *Streetcar,* as well as footage of the scene outside the Chandler Pavilion. Brando's latest exploit, following *Last Tango*'s release the month before, had cast the actor as the most discussed and controversial man in America.

Within less than a year Brando would concede, "If I had to do it all over again, I'd probably handle it differently." Yet at 2:30 that morning no one could read his impassive face as he sat slumped in front of the flickering screens, still watching. Neither Christian Marquand's arrival nor Jack Nicholson's congratulatory telephone call could rouse him. Finally he got up to get dressed and packed a small overnight bag, supposedly headed for South Dakota to join his Native American brothers at the barricades.

At Wounded Knee, Littlefeather's speech and the announcement that Brando was on his way was treated like the Second Coming. "At the time, none of us knew Brando personally," AIM leader Dennis Banks later explained. But they had heard about his involvement in the Washington State fish-ins in 1964 through their contact with Hank Adams. Adams had spent some time instructing Brando on the fishing treaty issues, and he had always praised him. "But still, that night as far as we were concerned, the Academy Awards ceremony was the last thing on our minds.

"We'd been up against armed personnel carriers, with rounds coming in constantly," Banks continued. "Now, suddenly, with just this three-minute statement from Brando, people all over the world would be watching. It was the biggest exposure we'd had for the month we'd been under siege in our bunkers. At that moment it was like the war was over. Total euphoria. People ran outside into the snow to fire off their rifles, yelling. We just couldn't believe it."

It was what Brando had intended—using his Oscar to call attention to the Indians' cause. After participating with Dick Gregory in the 1964 fish-ins in northern Washington, he had made no direct contact with the growing, high-profile American Indian Movement and its two charismatic leaders, Dennis Banks and Russell Means. Mostly, he'd devoted himself to black civil rights. Yet AIM's rhetoric, stressing the Indians' traditional faith in *ina maku*, or Mother Earth, offered an alternative, had grabbed him in a way that went beyond the secular issue of justice or merely writing checks. On-screen, in *Tango*, he'd acknowledged his mother's love of nature, and with his own feelings equally strong, he was drawn to the AIM members' attachment to the land as well as their tribal bonding. Both, for Brando, were profoundly compelling.

By early 1973 AIM had become a household word, its leaders idolized by young Indians as well as white campus radicals coast to coast. The FBI, through its still secret COINTELPRO program, had targeted Means, Banks, and others as "key extremists." Banks, who had come to spearhead the movement, was AIM's most vocal spokesperson. An Ojibwa Chippewa from Leech Lake, Minnesota, he had spent his youth in white-run Bureau of Indian Affairs (BIA) boarding schools. When he was sent to jail for five years on burglary charges, he discovered his cultural identity behind bars; Indians, he had come to realize, had to repudiate government supervision and assimilation if they were to survive. Existing Native American rights groups such as the National Congress of American Indians and the all-Indian National Indian Youth Council were too urban in perspective, too pacifist. With George Mitchell, Clyde and Vernon Bellecourt, and Eddie Benton-Banai, an Ojibwa medicine man, Banks had founded AIM in July 1968, more than a year before the celebrated occupation of Alcatraz.

Though not a founding member, the strapping six-foot-one, 190-pound Russell Means would become the organization's other major figure. An uncompromising, sometimes intimidating Oglala Sioux, Means was born in Porcupine, South Dakota, on the Pine Ridge reservation, had grown up in Oakland, California, and was also a college graduate. Twice married with four kids by the time he became involved in the movement in 1970, he was deeply, personally embittered over white racism. Outspoken and relentless, he became a visible target and over the next decade eight attempts would be made on his life.

Other young lights in the organization included John Trudell (a Santee Sioux), Leonard Crow Dog, Pedro Bissonnette, and the soft-spoken Leonard Peltier. Peltier's cousins Steve and Bob Robideau were closely involved, too. Steve had participated in the early Washington fishing-rights demonstrations with Hank Adams, and also had become close to Means.

All of these AIM activists had converged on Wounded Knee to participate in the occupation that began February 27, 1973. The location had been chosen for its symbolic importance: It was in the hamlet of Wounded Knee that some 350 Lakota men, women, and children were massacred in 1890 by U.S. Army troops, and the present takeover was meant to dramatize not only the years of destruction wreaked on the surrounding coal- and uranium-rich Black Hills, the Indians' sacred *Paha-Sapa*, but also the ongoing, devasting problem of corruption in the tribal government.

For more than a decade, the reservation had been under the thumb of a BIA puppet, tribal council president Richard "Dick" Wilson, who reigned like a Tammany Hall boss, allegedly lining his pockets by dipping into federal funds earmarked for the reservation's emergency medical program. He stuffed tribal ballot boxes, and his private police force (the "goon squad") put down opposition at will, often brutally. Beatings, drive-by shootings, car rammings, and random acts of arson were commonplace, often with the tacit support of federal law enforcement personnel who had no legal jurisdiction on the reservation. "It was literally a reign of terror," said John Trudell, later AIM's cochairman. Concomitantly, the rates of alcoholism, poverty, crime, and suicide on the 3-million-acre reservation were at an all-time high—statistically, the worst of any ghetto in the nation.

Seizing the Wounded Knee trading post, which was located on the south quarter of the Pine Ridge reservation, the AIM activists then took over the adjacent church and tourist museum ("WOUNDED KNEE MASSACRE SITE. MASS BURIAL GRAVE. ALL CREDIT CARDS ACCEPTED"). The activists demanded a reexamination of the Fort Laramie Treaty of 1868 and an independent federal investigation of the BIA and its complicity in Wilson's tribal government. Means announced, "We have high-powered rifles, shotguns, explosives, and fourteen hand grenades. The government has two choices: Either they attack and wipe us out, or negotiate."

In response, the feds mustered their troops. By February 28, the day after the takeover, the Indians found themselves loosely surrounded by 300 U.S. marshals and FBI agents. Reinforced by Wilson's tribal police and BIA personnel, the high-tech "task force" would soon swell to more than 1,000. Night after night, as small-arms gunfire escalated, the Indians' supporters, arriving from as far away as Los Angeles, Seattle, Denver, St. Paul, and upstate New York, slipped around the government's roadblocks. U.S. marshals, using their armed personnel carriers as bunkers, positioned themselves on the hills overlooking the village; at the Rapid City municipal airport, seventy miles away, federal C-130 transports flew in and out, delivering additional personnel, jeeps, and half-tracks, as well as pallets of ammunition and supplies.

On March 16, after three hours' firing, one of AIM's volunteer medics was wounded in the stomach. Believing they were now facing "another massacre," the AIM leadership called upon their resident medicine man, thirty-one-year-old Leonard Crow Dog, to conduct a ceremony for the determined braves. As each man stepped forward, Crow Dog applied a single stripe of red paint below his eyes and across the bridge of the nose. "It wasn't war paint," Means explained, correcting the slanted press reports of the time. "What it signified was that we were willing to spill our blood." Some warriors, reportedly, made flesh offerings by cutting pieces of skin from their arms, just as Sitting Bull had done in 1876 a few days before defeating Custer. Crow Dog even revived the long outlawed Ghost Dance, which lasted for four days in the freezing snow.

The barren, butte-broken terrain offered the Indians scant shelter. At night, strobe light–equipped helicopters bore snipers aloft, shooting at anything that moved within the AIM perimeter. Trip-wire flares saturated the surrounding no-man's-land, bathing the landscape in a strange ghostlike light if anyone stepped on the trigger wires. Militarily, AIM's position was indefensible, "like Dien Bien Phu," said one of the AIM activists, a Vietnam vet. "You can't hold this against a superior force on the outside."

Indian sympathizers continued to pour through the government's gauntlet, nonetheless. One especially determined West Coast supporter engineered an "airlift" with his private Cessna, restocking AIM's dwindling ammunition supplies. Another flew in food, also by small aircraft, paid for by donations from Jonathan Winters, Carroll O'Connor, Troy Donahue, Jane Fonda, Brando, and others. Sammy Davis Jr. helped with the medical supplies.

Journalists also made their way through the sievelike war zone even as the authorities tried to impose a press blackout. With such support and with Brando supposedly on his way on March 28, the AIM militants were more optimistic. But one day passed, then another, then a third. There was still no sign of Brando, nor any communication from him. Disappointed as the Indians might have been by the actor's no-show, they were heartened by a nationwide Louis Harris poll showing that 60 percent of the Americans surveyed thought Indians were being treated poorly.

Still, the authorities weren't about to be dissuaded. On April 17 violence flared again as more than 5,000 rounds of ammunition, laced with fiery government tracers, were exchanged in a single night. Over the next two weeks the situation deteriorated rapidly. Two Indians were killed, twelve wounded. A shortage of good water as well as three blizzards added to their hardship. The Watergate scandal had begun to take over the front page, siphoning off liberal support for their continued protest.

On May 8 the occupiers finally surrendered, having been promised a hearing with a White House delegation to negotiate the issues in conflict. In place of serious discussions, however, over the next eighteen months AIM members would be tried in such far-flung places as Lincoln, Nebraska; Pierre and Sioux Falls, South Dakota; St. Paul; and Rapid City, Iowa.

"The 1868 treaty was never seriously discussed," author Peter Matthiessen pointed out, "nor was corruption in the BIA investigated; hearings held in June by the Senate Subcommittee on Indian Affairs accomplished nothing. . . . Neither Richard Wilson nor his goons were ever prosecuted. Instead more than 500 traditional people were indicted by the FBI in connection with Wounded Knee, and 185 were subsequently indicted by federal grand juries on charges of arson, theft, assault, and 'interfering with federal officers.' "

What had happened to Brando?

The actor himself had no explanation until almost three months later, when he appeared on Dick Cavett's television show on June 12 and acknowledged that he hadn't even tried to get to the reservation.

"Wounded Knee was surrounded by federal marshals, state policemen, deputized ranchers, any whites who wanted to hold a gun," he said. "All I needed was to go to Wounded Knee and be arrested by them and give them an excuse to say I was part of a plot to make headlines. So I wasn't able to go."

(From a public relations point of view the Cavett show was a disaster anyway, with Brando droning on in vague platitudes. The fiasco was capped outside the studio when Brando broke paparazzo Ron Galella's jaw; Galella sued for $250,000, and a settlement was later arranged.)

Brando's failure to appear at Wounded Knee still wasn't adequately explained, and during the following winter the actor would have a slightly different rationale when he was confronted by the Indians at the St. Paul trial of both Means and Banks. Surrounded by AIM leaders, he insisted that he had been on his way to the siege when he was halted by marshals at the Denver airport and was turned back. "That's what he told me—that he left L.A. but was stopped by the marshals and the FBI," recalled Russell Means. "How do you stop someone in Denver? I have no idea."

According to Anna Kashfi, however, when Brando and Christian Marquand left Mulholland the morning after the Academy Awards, they had driven to Trona, California, near Death Valley, and checked into a motel, registering under the names "Mr. Marquara" and "Mr. Christian." The following day, Marlon flew to Tetiaroa, where on March 30 his hotel, consisting of sixteen roughly built bungalows, was scheduled to open for a trial run of ten days. Over the next few weeks Brando regularly made the eight-hour flight between Tahiti and Los Angeles, hopscotching the Pacific, ensconced in Qantas first-class, and it was this that had accounted for his conspicuous absence from AIM's struggle until the St. Paul trials.

After Brando's departure Littlefeather had lingered for a day or two at Mulholland; but, hearing no news of his anticipated arrival at Wounded Knee, she returned to the Bay Area, where she went into hiding—feeling, as she put it, "totally abandoned." She was hounded by the FBI and even, she claims, shot at. With therapy she was eventually able to rethink her feelings about what she had gotten herself into.

"I saw Marlon as a man who was caught up in all his money and ego and fame," she explained. "He can't go down to the corner drugstore and buy some cough drops without having hundreds of fans, local radio, and TV there, so what kind of perspective could he have? I was a victim of my own stereotype—naive and too trusting.

"I don't think he meant to exploit me or hurt me," she added. "It just happened. What he does is bring people into his drama and into his pain. That is the way he hurts people, because after he brings people closer, he then goes far away. Then he hurts himself, whipping himself over and over with this masochism."

The grosses for *The Godfather* were breaking all records, and Paramount was wooing Brando to make a brief appearance (in a flashback) in the film's sequel. Still furious about the loss of his points, however, Brando demanded $500,000, plus 10 percent of the gross for *Godfather II*. Paramount was equally adamant about rejecting his terms, although the actor continued to schmooze Coppola, hoping that the director would be able to persuade studio "suits" to give in to his multimillion-dollar demands.

During the summer and fall Brando again seemed to be drifting; he announced that he was dismissing his agent because he expected to be doing little acting while he concentrated his energies on Tetiaroa and the plight of the American Indian. None of the AIM leaders, however, recalled seeing him during this period.

Instead, in July 1973 Brando took a trip to the Midwest, which was perhaps best explained by his need to reexamine his roots after his wrenching revelations in *Last Tango*. Brando took local residents by surprise when he arrived at Omaha's Eppley Airfield dressed in a denim jacket, jeans, and cowboy boots and climbed into a Checker cab, directing the driver to South Thirty-second Street, the site of his early childhood home. En route, he noted the leafy, overarching elms, well-trimmed lawns, and broad front porches, and he told the cabby that he hadn't been back to Omaha in twenty years. He reminisced about seeing monkeys in cages at the Hanscom Park Zoo when he was a boy, but volunteered little information about why he was in town. When he arrived at what had formerly been his grandmother's house, he told the driver to wait, then had a short conversation with the present resident, asking if the home was for sale. Back in the taxi, he directed the driver to the Field Club School, where he had attended kindergarten. After a slow cruise by the building, he asked to go back to the airport.

There he bought two magazines, and in the coffee shop he ordered an open-faced minute steak sandwich and a large chef's salad. When a kid came in and tried to buy a twenty-cent piece of pie but only had fifteen cents, Marlon told the waitress, "Give the boy a piece of pie, and he's got to have a glass of milk to go with it."

At the airport Brando was waiting for Jill Banner—"a mystery woman," as the local Omaha paper described her. The two of them, ticketed as "Mr. Brando and Ms. Malumby," then flew to Chicago to visit Fran on the family farm in Mundelein, the last leg of his "look homeward" pilgrimage.

After this brief visit Brando returned to Tahiti and his family there, his sojourn allowing him to duck the problems that had surfaced during the previous months. Kashfi had again been stirring up trouble. Several times she denounced Brando in the press, complaining bitterly about losing custody of Christian: "He has been taken from me and is with a man I honestly think cannot relate to reality." After denigrating the actor's reputation as a lover ("just plain clumsy"), she worried about the effect of his "insecurity" on Christian. "I don't want [Christian] growing up thinking that every girl he sees he has to jump into bed with just to prove he is a man." When Brando had turned down the Oscar, Kashfi reminded the press that she, too, was "Indian" and sneered, "I agree 100 percent [that] Indians are mistreated in this country—and Marlon's the worst offender."

Caught in their usual dance, neither could let go of the other or cease their warfare over Christian. After Anna announced her engagement to James Hannaford, a salesman more than fifteen years her senior, Brando had him followed for several weeks by his private detective, Jay Armes.

When Hannaford and Kashfi married in Las Vegas on January 12, 1974, Christian gave his mother away. Soon after the ceremony, Kashfi, hoping to impress the court with her newfound stability, once again renewed her petition for custody and alleged that Brando was refusing her access to the boy. She claimed that during a skiing trip to Sun Valley the previous winter, Brando had thrown a just showered, towel-clad Christian onto the terrace, then locked the door, keeping the boy outside in 15°F weather. When Christian demanded to be let in, she alleged, Brando "dropped his pants, pressed his buttocks to the glass, and yelled, 'Here, climb into this!' "

Eventually she was advised by her new lawyer, Marvin Mitchelson (later to achieve notoriety as the plaintiff's attorney in the Lee Marvin "palimony" trial), that her petition was bound to fail, and she relinquished her suit. Ironically, once Kashfi stopped making her demands, Christian and Marlon began to have difficulties, and the teenager let his mother know. With Alice Marchak virtually running the Mulholland household, he complained, "Mom, I can't live up there. I can't stand Alice."

During the summer of 1973, Marlon had taken Christian to Tahiti. The boy seemed happier there, enjoying the water and the sea life and becoming interested in the scientific consultants' work on the atoll. But back in Los Angeles that fall, the teenager reverted to abusing alcohol and smoked pot. When Marlon was around he would alternate between stern lectures and affectionate overtures, but a friend who saw Christian at home during this period recalled that it was "usually Alice who dealt with Christian and who handled the day-to-day stuff. Marlon was the absentee father, gone a lot of the time," he explained. "Alice was very tightly wound, very repressed and remote. I also think she was scared of Christian. She was so fixated on Marlon and his demands that she seemed to ignore Chris's basic emotional needs and the way he was screaming out for attention."

Now fifteen, Christian was going through adolescence with a vengeance; any teenager would have problems sorting out an identity, but with a famous father like Marlon Brando and his contradictory messages, Christian seemed to suffer enormously from confusions about who he was, who he could be, and whether or not he could win his father's approval. According to a schoolmate and friend, the boy often felt "manipulated" by his father, since Brando "manipulates so well that you don't really see it. He can set the pieces up like a player on a chessboard." Christian's own behavior did not help. Whenever Marlon "would try to bridge the gap, make overtures of friendship," the friend recalled, "Christian dismissed it. He always had the suspicion that when Marlon was nice, there was a reason for it, that it was a precursor to being rebuffed."

At one point Christian ran away from home, showing up at his mother's again. Kashfi recalled, "He said to me, 'I can't stand that man, I want to come home to you.' He was in a state of complete confusion." Because of the court order, Christian couldn't live at Kashfi's, so another solution was worked out: The teenager agreed to go and stay with family friend Joanne Torres in Vancouver. The thought was that if Christian had a new environment, he might calm down, focus his attention on school, and set some goals for himself.

• • •

During the early months of 1974, Brando was away from Mulholland even more frequently than usual. Although he had failed to bear witness at Wounded Knee, he did appear at the Wounded Knee trials, which opened in St. Paul on January 8. Dennis Banks and Russell Means were the first of the 130 defendants to be tried on felony charges ranging from conspiracy to assaulting a federal officer. "If convicted we were looking at 250 years in prison," explained Banks, "plus I had already been convicted of a felony in South Dakota." Banks was being represented by Mark Lane, the early critic of the Warren Commission report and an attorney known for his meticulous preparation; Kenneth Tilsen, a Twin Cities lawyer and the founder of the Wounded Knee Defense Offense Committee (WKDOC); and Larry Leventhal, another AIM advocate from San Francisco. Means also had three lawyers: activist and master courtroom showman William Kunstler (who had recently won an acquittal for Abbie Hoffman, Tom Hayden, and others of the Chicago Seven), Doug Hall, and Ramon Robideau, a Sioux attorney from Rapid City.

Among the many supporters were Indians in traditional dress from the Pacific Northwest, New York, New Mexico, California, and points in between. Some of the elders spoke no English; some had been "born free" in the last century, before America's native peoples were herded onto reservations. A few had even been born before the original Wounded Knee Massacre in 1890.

Despite the overflow attendance during the opening of the trials, there had been a conspicuous lack of media attention. On January 25 this changed abruptly when Brando turned up with screenwriter Abby Mann, best known for his work on *Judgment at Nuremberg*. Neither Banks nor Means had ever met Brando, but they realized that the effect of his presence was "just immediate." Other celebrities, including Harry Belafonte, would visit the trials, too, but none drew the press more than Brando, who proved unusually cooperative with reporters. The day of his arrival, he spoke quietly on the courthouse steps, announcing that he was there to call attention to the proceedings as well as the plight of the American Indian in general. "I came to give my support to Dennis and Russell," he said, "and to give my hopes that they will get a fair trial and perhaps to say that on trial here really are the American people." He added that he also "wanted to meet the prosecutors. I'd like to find out how their minds work."

Besides working the media, Brando's charisma wasn't lost on the jurors. During a recess he went to the front of the courtroom and embraced Banks and Means, a gesture that also caught the attention of attorney Mark Lane.

"He identified with the defendants, and that was very, very important," said Lane. "It probably played as much a part as anything we had going for us in those nine months of trial. Everybody wanted to meet Marlon—even the judge, who wanted an autograph."

While Brando was in St. Paul to offer moral support, Mann had another agenda. Long active in liberal politics, the screenwriter had both an Emmy and an Oscar to his credit, and the previous September Brando had contacted him about their collaboration on a script about Wounded Knee. Now he had accompanied Brando to take a firsthand look at the trial and to meet the AIM leaders.

Mann was excited. Brando was one of the few actors he found "really compelling"; however, at their earlier meeting to discuss Brando's idea to do an Indian film, the actor had been vague. On the one hand he wanted to play "some kind of American military figure who had treated the Indians harshly," said Mann. "Then he entertained the idea of doing Kit Carson." Mann argued for a contemporary scenario. Their sessions, always at Mulholland, had turned into endless script conferences resembling those the actor had carried on during the making of *One-Eyed Jacks* and *Mutiny*.

"He had a compulsion to talk about Indian history," recalled Mann. "He'd studied a great deal and would talk about the Indians' problems endlessly. But every time we actually got down to specifics of the characters or plot, he looked as if he was going to throw up."

Finally, it was the scriptwriter himself who proposed Wounded Knee as the subject of the film. Mark Lane and William Kunstler, Mann pointed out, were both close friends, and somehow this seemed to tip the balance and make for some progress in their discussions. Columbia Pictures then gave them a development deal that required no contract to deliver a script, no delivery deadline, and $250,000 in seed money. "That's how badly they wanted Brando," said Mann.

During the first months of the trials, the two worked intensively and visited St. Paul often, staying at a hotel near the Federal Building. The lawyers were soon sucked into the project as well, despite the fact that they were regularly staying up until one and two in the morning to plan the next day's court strategy. One evening Lane joined Banks and Means in

Brando's suite for a script conference. Lane noted Brando's frequent interruptions—he launched into vague descriptions of his vision for the film—and the attorney sensed that little was getting accomplished. When he tried to bring the conversation back to the details of Wounded Knee, Marlon interjected, "No, I see a much greater aperture. I see the struggle of the Indian people from the beginning."

It was during one of these sessions that Brando announced, "I can't play an Indian. I have to play a white rancher or a marshal."

"But everybody will love you and hate the Indians just because of who you are," objected Lane.

"I have to think about that," Brando muttered, as if Lane's observation surprised him.

Impressed by Brando's ability to captivate reporters, Lane suggested that the actor do the "Today" show with Banks and Means. The arrangements were made, then a day before the scheduled TV appearance, Lane received an "emergency" phone call in the middle of the night, asking him to join a meeting already in progress in Brando's suite.

"Abby was there, Dennis, and other Indians," recalled the lawyer. "Marlon had summoned everybody because he was thinking about the best way for him to do the show."

Lane was due in court the following morning, and as the discussion progressed he became edgy, since he felt that the session was becoming "incoherent."

"Well, Mark, say we have four and a half minutes. I can make thirteen or sixteen points—maybe seventeen," Brando was arguing. "But you could make twenty-one points because you talk faster, so you should be on the show instead of me."

"Look, Marlon," said Lane, "the reason the 'Today' show is even presenting this is because of you."

"Well, we could drop one of the Indians," Brando countered.

The meeting dragged on until dawn, with Marlon, Banks, and Means making their appearance the following day. The actor talked briefly at the beginning, then forced the interviewer to question Banks and Means directly. The host complied, although he kept mixing up the AIM leaders' names.

Over the next several months, while Marlon commuted back and forth between L.A. and St. Paul, he kept his hotel suite, with Columbia footing all expenses. When he was absent, he would turn his quarters over to Indians and their supporters, sometimes whole families straight off the reservation. It was a much appreciated kindness; in the meantime he had quietly donated $25,000 to the WKDOC.

"An Indian family moved into his suite," recalled Mann. "They kept saying to me, 'When is Marlo Brandon coming back?' *Marlo Brandon!* I mean, they didn't even know his name!"

At one point Mann had to inform the Indians in residence that Brando was expected back the next day, leaving the family downcast at the thought of losing their quarters. When Brando returned, he insisted that they stay. "He had a terrible cold and he was carrying around a box of Kleenex," said Mann, "but he didn't want the Indians to move. Instead, he moved into the bedroom, and they lived in the parlor. This family had the virtual run of his suite, and he was living in a cubbyhole."

By the middle of the trial, Mann was making real progress on the treatment, and despite his many distractions Brando was warming to it. They took road trips to South Dakota for tribal functions, usually staying at austere motels. Mann observed that Brando could sometimes become so moody that he seemed "a manic depressive. Suddenly he would just be tremendously depressed," Mann noted, adding that he'd sometimes hear his partner fretting about his weight, then dismissing his concern with the offhand remark, "Look, Orson Welles can't diet and underneath all that blubber it's still Welles."

He also continued to vacillate over his role in their script—one day it would be a judge; the next day it would be an Indian; and the following day the "opportunistic lawyer" Mann envisioned as the protagonist.

"Whatever role I do," Brando said, "people are just going to see someone in despair."

Part of his despair may have been due to his sense of invaded privacy. Attracted by Brando's comeback, a number of Brando biographies had been published during 1974, including one by his old friend Carlo Fiore. Brando viewed the publication of Fiore's sometimes bitter account of their friendship as the ultimate act of disloyalty. His penchant for secrecy, already heightened by the revelations coaxed from him in *Tango,* prompted him to adopt a Tahitian phrase as his favorite motto: "Leave no footprints in the sand."

Despite his detestation of celebrity, he was still willing to appear in public to publicize the Indians' cause. Toward the end of May he flew to New York for a round of interviews and a fund-raiser for Hank Adams's American Indian Development Association (AIDA). Following a quick jaunt to Tahiti he met up with Mann, who was still urging him to take the role of a fictional sixties AIM lawyer who had done jail time; jaded and cynical, the lawyer would go to Wounded Knee with the suspect motive of cashing in, either by writing a book or by soliciting clients. But witnessing the siege and coming to know the Indians, the lawyer would undergo a re-awakening of his leftist-humanist principles and end up siding with the AIM activists.

Mann should have guessed that this character choice would never fly with Brando, since the actor, contrary to his public reputation, was openly skeptical of leftists. When the screenwriter disputed this simplistic, "knee-jerk" anticommunism, Brando woodenly defended his view by quoting articles. "He would instruct me," Mann said, " 'If you read this, it explains it all,' or 'If you read this book . . .' The lecturing never stopped."

Whatever Brando's feelings about Kunstler, though, the lawyer and the rest of the legal team seemed to be working well. Throughout the first months of the trial, Judge Frederick Nichol had appeared to be siding with the prosecution, often erupting in altercations with the defense attorneys. On one occasion he threatened to jail Kunstler for contempt of court. Yet as the weeks rolled by the magistrate began to show a growing irritation with the FBI, especially when Justice Department lawyers had stalled in producing their files. In mid-August, after the defense rested its case, the prosecutors called a surprise witness: twenty-two-year-old Louis Moves Camp. His testimony was meant to buttress the FBI's contention that AIM was part of "the international communist conspiracy." In Tilsen's words, he "filled in every gap in the government's case." Camp claimed to have been present at both Wounded Knee and the first meeting of the AIM-sponsored International Indian Treaty Council in June 1974 on the Standing Rock reservation where, he testified, he had seen agents from Russia, China, and Czechoslovakia in attendance.

After listening to this improbable scenario, defense attorney Mark Lane spent two days arduously researching the testimony, only to discover that this key government witness had been in California the very day he and the prosecutors claimed he was witnessing AIM mayhem at Wounded Knee. (His mother, Ellen Moves Camp, an AIM supporter, was willing to testify that her son was lying.) Furthermore, news reports of his testimony had elicited a phone call from a deputy sheriff in nearby Wisconsin who advised Lane that a rape charge against Moves Camp had been filed three nights before the opening of the trial; and, as it turned out, the FBI had gotten him off the hook in exchange for his testimony. Filing a motion for prosecutorial misconduct, the defense charged not only that the prosecution's witness had committed perjury but also that the Justice Department had "developed" Moves Camp for six weeks without ever bothering to check his story.

Although Judge Nichol dismissed some of the charges, the case soon went to the jury, with Brando back in St. Paul to await the verdict. On September 14, 1974, he and Mann invited Judge Nichol and his wife to lunch at the St. Paul Hilton. Later Nichol would insist that the trial was not discussed. Nevertheless, Brando did seem to be trying to charm the judge on behalf of the defendants, since he complimented him for running an open, relaxed courtroom and said that other judges he had come across were cold and rigid. Then, with winning panache, he added that his experience was limited to divorce courts.

That was not the whole of the conversation, however. As Mann recalled, by the time they arrived at the dessert course, the judge's wife was feeling relaxed enough under the flattering attentions of Brando that she took the liberty of scolding him for making *Last Tango*. "She was saying things like, 'God, how disgusting,' and 'How dare you do that!' " said Mann. "Marlon then became very apologetic. Obviously he wanted to do anything he could for the defendants, and he said, 'You're right. Forgive me.' He was almost fawning, but at the same time I knew he also felt that way—he really didn't like the film."

Neither Brando's charm nor his apologies were necessary. That Monday, following additional legal maneuvering when an ill juror had to be excused, Judge Nichol dismissed the charges and, because of the blatant manipulation of Moves Camp, he expressed his shock that "the FBI, which I have revered for so long, has stooped so low."

After the dismissal Brando did not join in the Indians' celebration at a nearby Holiday Inn, nor did he issue any press statements. As important as his shared sense of AIM's triumph was, his more personal connection was with Dennis Banks, established during the preceding weeks.

At Brando's invitation Banks and his young wife, Kamook, traveled with him to New York, where they saw a play in which Rita Moreno was starring, and then returned with him to Los Angeles. En route, the two men rendezvoused with Mann in Minneapolis and drove to the White Earth reservation west of Duluth. There they all participated in the authentic Indian ritual of a sweat lodge, this one led by wise man and tribal elder Eddie Benton-Banai, one of AIM's founding members.

"Marlon was a very different and more real person in the sweat lodge than he was outside," said Benton-Banai. Pressed for details, the medicine man refused to elaborate until told that Clyde Bellecourt, another participant, had already revealed some of the experience.

"I heard a little boy speaking," Benton-Banai then recalled. "Probably nine, ten, somewhere in there. At the beginning a frightened boy. And then someone growing into maturity. Then a man who appreciated sitting on the bare ground next to the Mother Earth with this understanding that he did not know existed, which he explained was something he'd thought could only be found in basilicas and cathedrals.

"He was truly speaking from somewhere he hadn't spoken before. He said, 'I've traveled all over the world and this is the first time in my life I've felt close to anyone as a people—to the earth as Mother.'

"He wasn't articulating all that he was feeling—I remember sensing that. He didn't say the word *mother,* referring to his own mother, but it was there. . . . It may not be important, but he talked about a military school near Minneapolis. What he was saying was definitely autobiographical."

There were "some very deep emotions," Benton-Banai noted, "violence and pain."

At the end of the ritual, with tears of gratitude on his cheeks, Brando pledged some of his land holdings to AIM, an oblation true and deeply felt.

"You don't have to give us anything. All we want is your faith and your love," replied Banks.

Over the next half-year, Banks consulted with Mann and Brando on the script, and he, his wife, and their infant child moved into the Mulholland Drive house, where they lived in the bedroom across the hall from Brando's.

Banks noted the frequent friction between the father and his rebellious son Christian. Sometimes Brando asked his new friend for advice about how to deal with the boy when he wouldn't do his chores or his homework, and worse yet, lied or made lame excuses. Having returned from Vancouver, Christian was enrolled at Cal Prep, a private school in Encino, and it was no secret that he was still having problems in his classes and that his late-night carousing on Sunset Strip was adding to his repeated absences from school.

Brando's worst suspicions were confirmed on October 28, 1974, when Christian was arrested for possession of marijuana. Called down to the police station to bail him out, Brando lectured the boy in front of the detective for a full fifteen minutes. As Christian stood before him, his head bowed, his father preached the need for responsibility. His voice was stern and angry as he advised the teenager that he had better shape up, that he was screwing up his life with his pot smoking, and at one point he turned to the policeman standing by and said, "You tell him, officer."

"He was genuinely trying to maintain a home, have a semblance of being head of the household," said Banks, who pointed out that there were times when Brando would take his long-haired son aside "to talk, maybe for half an hour, about the direction he had to go in."

Still, Brando's attempts to create a unified, stable family were undermined by the multiple women in his life. Bunking so near Marlon's bedroom, Banks became aware of the girlfriends who coasted in and out of the house.

First there was Jill Banner. Yachiyo Tsubaki, Gene Frenke's protégée, was often around, too. The other woman who had become more central to both Brando and Christian's life was Caroline Barrett. She had joined Brando's old girlfriend Reiko Sato and Alice Marchak in organizing the household and handling his correspondence and phone calls.

Another visitor was the sweat lodge leader, Eddie Benton-Banai, whom Marlon summoned from Minneapolis for more spiritual counseling. His first evening there, however, his host ate dinner with him in the TV room, then retired to his bedroom with a quick "See ya." For the following three days the medicine man found himself alone, waiting for the actor to come forward and talk. It was almost a week before Marlon joined Benton-Banai one noon at the outside picnic table and indicated he was ready for serious conversation.

As he had with Banks before, he began by seeking advice from the Indian spiritual leader about what to do about Christian's drinking and drug problems. "What I heard was the breach, the distance between them,

and I empathized," said Benton-Banai. "As a father, I could see his struggle, trying to do something for his son and at the same time being at a complete loss. His key phrase was, 'Whatever he is, he's still my son.' That's
when I wanted to say, 'Yes, Marlon. Maybe you're understanding it a little
more.' But I also wanted to point out that our children don't belong to us.
They are our responsibility, but we cannot expect repayment."

Marlon, however, did most of the talking for two hours, and still
didn't break off his soliloquy to ask for Benton-Banai's response. Then he
abruptly changed the subject to talk about the death of Wally Cox.

"His feelings had been going from high to low when he spoke about
his son. Then he suddenly was telling me about his friend, and the energy
field became very, very sad. No confusion, just affection, loyalty; a sense of
loss, with disappointment and some guilt, too."

At one point Marlon paused and pointed to a tree nearby. "Wally's
ashes are buried near where we're sitting," he said. Then he added, "The
son of a gun left me here.

"Do you think he hears me?" he asked, in almost a plaintive tone.

"Of course he can hear," replied Benton-Banai.

After Brandon's outpouring, Benton-Banai sensed that the actor
needed to talk for "three or four days," not just a few hours. But Brando
made himself scarce after that afternoon. A few days later, the wise man
returned to Minnesota and Brando never contacted him again.

Despite Brando's efforts and concern, Christian was still sneaking out
of the house. When the teenager brought friends back to the hilltop, they
sequestered themselves in his room for long hours at a stretch. Brando was
again finding empty liquor bottles under the furniture and in the closet.

When Brando tried to discipline Christian by withholding money for
drugs and liquor, the boy simply found other ways to get it, and he went so
far as to steal pot from neighbor Jack Nicholson's stash. "One time Jack
caught him," said a friend. "Christian laughed when he imitated Jack
scolding him in the voice of his character in *Chinatown:* 'You do that again
and I'll break your fucking fingers, man.' "

Concerned about what Christian and his friends were doing behind
closed doors, Brando took the extraordinary step of having the teenager's
quarters "wired" with a sound-activated tape recorder. Eventually Christian came to him one evening and said, "Dad, for God's sake, will you turn

the tape recorder off? Every time it clicks on, I hear it, and I can't get any sleep." Why the tape recorder should be activated when Christian was asleep was unclear, but as Brando himself later acknowledged, he "tore the wall out" to remove the listening device, adding almost ruefully, "I thought I was so very clever, but I was not so clever."

Christian's new school, Cal Prep, was a small private academy for children from wealthy families, and the teenager generally hung out with the "wild" groups: the fast drivers, the beer drinkers, the pot smokers. Classmates recalled a young man with two sides: There was the quiet, sensitive Christian who loved nature, animals and his dogs; and there was the very macho Christian, a "tough, cool guy" about whom it was said that he had "kicked an older guy's butt" on a camping trip and was capable of great anger and physical roughness.

One of Christian's best friends at school was Steve Hunio. Spending as much time as he did up at Mulholland, Hunio came to see how unsettling Christian's home life actually was and how it was mirrored in his friend's contradictions: His kindness and gentleness often gave way to explosive rage and fits of temper. "I think a lot of his anger was directed against himself," the schoolmate said. "I think what was really going on was that he didn't know who he was because of his problems with his father."

There were times when Brando became the strict disciplinarian, laying down the law to Christian; if he came home and found his son smoking dope with his friends, he "would kick them all out of the house." When Christian continued to receive bad reports from school, Brando would become "quite upset," added Hunio. "Ten minutes before, he had been the nicest guy in the world, then he would deliver a diatribe, sternly telling Christian, 'You better get it in gear, and *do it now!*' "

Although he was unaware of the resemblance himself, Brando's lectures were like those of his own father—the "get your ass in the saddle" routine that Marlon had recalled in *Last Tango* and which he had long resented. But when Christian continued to fail classes, Brando gave him an ultimatum: Do better in school or go to work in a gas station. "Marlon liked to scare, and in this case he wanted to scare Christian good," Hunio said.

Sometimes Yachiyo was around, sometimes Jill Banner. "It was all very chaotic," conceded Hunio, "and that was hard for Christian to reconcile himself to. I think he wanted a more stable home life, which was why he liked visiting my home. It was as if he came over to soak up a little bit of family atmosphere by osmosis."

Hunio noticed as well that sometimes Caroline's friend Anita Kong and her husband, Dr. Wiley, acted as surrogate parents. Christian was probably unaware that the nice, fatherly Dr. Wiley continued to suffer with the knowledge that his wife and Brando were still carrying on their long-term affair—or as Philip Rhodes insisted, the doctor "hated Marlon because he knew he was fucking his wife." Again, like so many instances in Brando's life, the cast of characters was complicated, the situation verging on the incestuous.

Jill Banner and Christian had a more heartfelt connection than Christian had with either Marchak, Caroline Barrett, Yachiyo, or Anita Kong. Perhaps they bonded out of a shared sense of needing more than what Marlon could ever give. Christian did have one girlfriend to whom he turned for comfort and solace: Mary McKenna. They had practically grown up together and called themselves "Laurel Canyon brats" as they scrambled around the hillsides behind Marlon's house; when life had been too chaotic at either his father's or his mother's, Christian had sometimes also retreated to Mary's home, where her mother, a warm, hospitable Greek, often let him stay for dinner and even overnight.

Now, as teenagers, they were still buddies, but gradually they developed a romantic attachment as well. Nevertheless, Christian continued to cruise the Strip, sometimes openly, otherwise on the sly. While this was the usual adolescent sexual experimentation, Hunio also felt that Marlon's lawless sex life had significantly affected the way Christian viewed the opposite sex. "If there had been one woman as counterpoint to Marlon, it might have helped," said Hunio. "Instead, there was almost a competitiveness between Christian and his father about women. And while it didn't give him a real good role model to see how to treat a woman, he still admired his father's success and gallant charm. Marlon's a womanizer, and Christian became one too.

"But at the same time," Hunio explained, "he saw that his father could also be loyal and supportive toward the women in his life and it seemed a contradiction in terms. He couldn't figure out which he should be—a womanizer or caring and generous. Marlon never tried to hide all the stuff with women—it was pretty blatant and brutally honest. His attitude was 'Fuck you—if you don't like it, get out of my face.' In one way that attitude was refreshing and healthy. In other ways it only made things more complicated for Christian.

"Marlon was more like an eccentric big brother than a father," added Hunio. "He and Christian were like two people in bubble suits—they wanted to get close but their suits didn't allow them to touch. They were both very guarded and waiting for the other to make the first move. Christian loved Marlon, wanted desperately to win his approval, but he didn't have a clue how to do it."

As Dennis Banks had noticed, Christian kept himself apart both from the guests in the house and from his brother, Miko, who often stayed there, preferring the freedom of Mulholland to the discipline Movita imposed in her Cheviot Hills apartment. There had always been "underlying resentment," said Hunio. While Christian, like everyone else among family and friends, "suspected that Miko wasn't really Marlon's son," he also disliked Miko's "glad-handing, bluff, hearty, hail-fellow-well-met personality."

When Tarita and her children visited, Christian seemed fonder of them. He was affectionate toward Cheyenne, a smiling four-year-old who always had a flower tucked into her long, black hair. Perhaps the visits from Brando's Tahitian family revived Christian's pleasant memories of his summers on the island, when he was at his most relaxed and untroubled. In fact, the one time schoolmates recalled Christian excelling in his English class was the day he gave an oral report about Tahiti.

During the latter part of 1974, Brando's attention was less on his own family than on Native American causes. He and Dennis Banks attended several fund-raisers, including a gala in New York City. Organized by Lucy Saroyan, daughter of Brando's friend, Carol Matthau, and her former husband, author William Saroyan, the celebrity-studded gathering raised money for Hank Adams's American Indian Development Association (AIDA).

On December 28, 1974, following up on the pledge he'd made in Benton-Banai's sweat lodge, Brando announced he was deeding all his property holdings to Adams's AIDA, starting with forty acres of land in Liberty Canyon near Calabasas. "I think giving up all my land here in America will entitle me to ask others to make a contribution, too," he said, offering apologies for "being four hundred years too late." Although he did not include Tetiaroa, the properties he listed were his Los Angeles home, an apartment complex in Anaheim on a half-acre of land, plus the Mundelein family farm.

" 'Over my dead body,' said Mrs. Richard Loving of Mundelein, Illinois," reported the *Los Angeles Times,* "referring to the family homestead." Mrs. Loving said, 'We are not giving this land away—there is no question about it.' "

A little back-peddling was in order, and that night the telephone lines between Mundelein and Mulholland burned. The next day Brando announced that his sister would continue to live on the Illinois farm while supporting his choice to give up his one-third share. (In fact, though, Marlon never did turn over this asset to the Indians.)

The donation of the forty acres in Liberty Canyon was not without problems either. KABC-TV, the local network affiliate, reported that the land had a $318,000 lien against it, which the Indians were now obliged to pay by the end of the year. Brando's attorney confirmed the report, adding that arrangements would be made and that "it's safe to assume that the Indians will not be called upon to make the payment."

The only immediate explanation was that Brando's enthusiasm had again run away with him after attending the opening rounds of the so-called Wounded Knee nonleadership trials in Lincoln, Nebraska, two weeks before. Nearly one hundred of these cases were on the docket of U.S. District Court Judge Warren K. Urbom, and they would run for almost a year. Dennis Banks had persuaded Brando that his appearance in Lincoln was important for its publicity value, and on December 17, 1974, they hurried from an appearance at the Lincoln courthouse to a fund-raising cocktail party, and then went on to an AIM-sponsored powwow at the University of Nebraska student union. There, the defendants and their tribal supporters embraced Brando and presented him with a peace pipe symbolizing the spiritual blood bond that occurs with the making of a new relative.

"I don't believe in honors of any kind," he told the assembled audience of 700. "It puts people in some kind of condescension. This is not so much an honor as an inspiration. It humbles me. This is worth more to me than the Nobel Peace Prize, more than any silly Academy Award, because it reaffirms me as a person."

It was heady stuff. With this welcome and ceremonial adoption as a brother, he was being brought "inside," and with the exception of AIM lawyers such as William Kunstler and Ken Tilsen, he was now the Indians' main man. It was the acceptance he had long yearned for, all the more beguiling when the AIM leaders designated him *kola,* or friend.

Back in his seat on the dais, Brando turned to Gladys Bissonnette whose son Pedro, head of the Oglala Sioux Civil Rights Organization, had been shotgunned to death by Pine Ridge police while "resisting arrest" in October; he showered the elderly woman with his attention, chatting, joking, deferring to every word. When the weathered life-long resident of the reservation warned him that he'd better not leave his coat unattended or she'd snatch it, he tossed the expensive, heavy shearling garment across her shoulders, insisting that she accept it as a gift.

A few days later Brando returned to California and handed over the quitclaim to the forty acres promised to Hank Adams. On January 2, 1975, he flew back to Nebraska to attend another AIM fund-raiser, this one at the Omaha home of Douglas County Supervisor Lou Lamberty. He arrived at 11:15, five hours late, flanked by Banks and Means, and quickly apologized: "I forgot the time difference from California." He recommended to the 200 guests that they read the Federalist Papers and two books, *Bury My Heart at Wounded Knee* and *Custer Died for Your Sins,* the latter written by his friend Vine Deloria Jr. He also announced that he would soon start filming his Indian movie about Wounded Knee.

In these intervening weeks, Judge Urbom was dismissing and reducing many of the charges against the Indians in the nonleadership trials, marking significant victories for AIM. At the same time, however, another struggle erupted. During the first hours of 1975, forty-five Menominee Indians who called themselves the Warrior Society occupied an Alexian abbey in the sleepy Wisconsin town of Gresham, an hour-and-a-half drive northwest of Green Bay.

The takeover began with the general feeling that the Menominees were being cheated and financially broken by the Restoration Act. This piece of legislation from the Eisenhower years had laid the basis for returning land taken from Indians in the nineteenth century; to regain their land, however, the Menominees had been "terminated," or removed from federal ward status, with an automatic reduction in federal subsidies. The process called for ratification by the Indians themselves, which resulted in fierce tribal factionalism.

One side, about 4,500 Menominees, backed an "assimilated," college-educated Native American leader named Ada Deer, and wanted to return the tribe to federal control.

Buddy Chevalier, the charismatic leader of the Menominee Warrior Society, found this group "too white," and he argued that the women were in fact "the feds' salespeople to the reservation." With AIM's research help, Chevalier and his fellow insurgents—many of them Vietnam Vets, some with criminal records—had uncovered an obscure law allowing any abandoned religious property to be claimed by tribes able to show previous ownership of the land. They chose the abandoned sixty-four-room, Renaissance-style novitiate less than a half-mile from the reservation as the symbolic center for their protest.

The takeover by the Indians began shortly before midnight on January 1. In response, law enforcement units were called in from Appleton, Green Bay, Menasha, Wausau, and towns as far away as seventy-five miles. The telephone lines to the abbey were cut, and its electricity disconnected. Within several days local vigilantes, some on snowmobiles, had started shooting. "It wasn't as bad as the Indians say," said Gary Ehman, a local reporter, "but there were definitely people around here who were all for going in and killing them."

After a week the National Guard replaced the 250 local law enforcement officers, but the guardsmen were not issued bullets and the locals didn't trust them. The Guard's commander made an impassioned plea for calm and was determined that Gresham not become "another Wounded Knee." Aggravating the locals further, Chevalier had set up a pirate radio station in Keshena that was airing "Fidel Castro style broadcasts," complete with tom-toms and singing in the background.

Inside the novitiate, the defending force had swollen to more than a hundred, including women and children who were subsisting on smuggled food and bomb shelter rations found in the basement. To keep the building's fireplaces burning, they broke up pews, tables, and chairs. Since most of the windows were already shattered by the snowmobilers' bullets, every water main in the building had burst in the subzero cold, and long icicles hung from the ceilings. Morale remained high, nevertheless. Drinking wasn't tolerated, although marijuana was.

By midmonth, the National Guard still hadn't made a move, but there was another development: Forty members of AIM arrived, led by Dennis Banks, Russell Means, and Darryl Butler.

"AIM saw this as another national event, and when they came in the flavor changed at once," said newsman Ehman, referring to the print and TV reporters who then set up camp in nearby Keshena. "Suddenly we weren't writing about local issues, we were writing about national issues."

AIM leaders seemed to overlook what Chevalier had wanted to accomplish, and it wasn't long before Means generated outright ire by diminishing the Menominee local concerns as unimportant, then instructing Chevalier to have his troops shovel out a "landing strip" in front of the novitiate so that AIM leaders could come and go by airplane. "They thought they were going to run the show," said Robert Chevalier, Buddy's younger brother. "But it was our operation and we didn't care what they wanted."

Because of the conflicts, Means stayed only a short time, but Banks had to be dealt with more delicately since he had promised to deliver Brando. "AIM was operating without any resources," said Chevalier. "I had been at Wounded Knee, so I knew that AIM was using Brando financially. They had buttered him up by saying that he was a red brother."

Brando arrived on January 31, and according to Ken Fish, one of the more temperate members of the Warrior Society, "he seemed lost, looking for somebody to tell him what was happening."

Louis Hawpetoss, assigned to be the actor's watchdog, was equally perplexed. "We were about thirty days into the occupation. There's the Guard, the goddamn rednecks, but Brando didn't know that the shooting was actually here. He also didn't know about the Ada Deer conflict. He told me he admired our struggle, but it was as if he been only half-briefed on the situation."

Marlon was as ill equipped for the Wisconsin weather as he had been for the Washington fish-ins ten years before. Now wearing only oxfords, not boots, he had also skipped long underwear, a necessity in the frigid cold. Because he was so unprepared for the weather, the Indians drove him out to the area of the abbey in a station wagon, and when they pulled up at the National Guard checkpoint, he got out of the car and stood silently, listening to the drum ceremony of a group of supporters who themselves had trudged the several miles in the snow. Then, as the chanting died down, he announced that he would hold fund-raisers in California to raise the $750,000 the Alexians had been demanding for the Indians to buy the novitiate and its 225-acre tract.

The question on everybody's mind was whether Brando would join the militants inside the abbey. Beyond the Guard's forwardmost emplacement lay the beginning of no-man's-land, the corn-stubbled, snow-patched acreage that sloped across an open valley, at the bottom of which stood the novitiate, partially obscured by a stand of tall tamarack cedar. In the hard crystalline light the building's three-story bell tower loomed as if framed through a high-power telescope.

This wasn't the hard butte-broken plains of the South Dakota Badlands but dairy country that in summertime was lush with fields of alfalfa and timothy; in winter it was bleak and unwelcoming, and it must have taken resolve for Brando to decide to climb into the pickup waiting to drive toward the besieged Warriors. "Let's face it," said Hawpetoss, "it was an armed conflict. Those local snowmobilers were using 30.06s, 7mms." Riding with them was Reverend James Groppi, a maverick clergyman from Milwaukee known for his civil rights and antiwar work, who had already made it known that he was going into the novitiate to stay. Banks was to remain outside to handle damage control, necessitated by fringe activists.

The ride took only several minutes, and when the truck entered the grounds, Vietnam vets Donny Waukechon and Paul Tender (the latter carrying a derringer pistol, as he did at all times) ordered the newcomers to be spreadeagled and searched.

Brando's wallet and watch were confiscated. Then the Indian sentries motioned him and Groppi inside.

In the building's crowded cafeteria, the actor seemed to confirm the group's worst suspicions. The crowd heard Father Groppi speak briefly and to the point, pledging to support the weary Indians to the fullest. Then Brando took the floor. Almost immediately, he prompted resentment by insisting that the building was not worth "anyone's life."

Hawpetoss recalled, "He kept repeating, 'Is the building worth it? Is it worth it when it can be bought? We can do it a different way.' "

One warrior in the back of the crowd yelled, "If you're so sure there's another way, why're they shooting at us?"

"I want to be you, I want to be part of you," Marlon responded softly. "I wish I had your ancestral background because Indians have always been spiritually closer to the Creator than most races, closer to Mother Earth."

He then continued with a long speech recounting abuses against the

Indians. Several times he had to bow his head, overcome by emotion, and the gathered Indians noted that he nervously touched himself on the collar, patting his hair. Toward the end he was so moved by his own reflections that he broke into tears. For a moment the room filled with silence; then someone muttered, "Fuck, this guy's just acting." From the rear came a few titters, then a wave of laughter. Brando shrugged and walked into the nearby kitchen, where he sank into a chair.

When the leaders joined him, Brando asked, "Is there a chance we'll get attacked?"

The Indians were dumbfounded. "We looked at him like, 'What the hell you talking about, man?'" recalled Don Waukechon. "Christ, everybody knew what was going down. The Guard had been threatening to shell the place with 105s."

As if he sensed their disapproval, Brando seemed to want to reaffirm his resilience by asking to be taken up to the abbey's bell tower "to have a look around." Waukechon, a seasoned helicopter waist gunner in Vietnam, vehemently objected. The bell tower was the snowmobilers' prime target, they explained; he might be exposed to gunfire, especially since it was now dark.

"I want to see where the action is," he argued.

"It was like the fucker didn't believe us or something," said Waukechon. "So we finally agreed to show him."

The campanile offered a view of the surrounding countryside all the way to the Guard checkpoints. Waukechon and Ken Fish, with two or three others, led the way to the steel-rung ladder that was upstairs in the attic; again they cautioned Brando, emphasizing that a climber's head became vulnerable to gunfire at the second step from the top.

"When you get up there, stay down," Fish instructed as the first warrior, Paul Tender, climbed the ladder and crouched low.

Ignoring their warnings, Brando stood straight up when he reached the top of the ladder and started to walk across the parapet to the waist-high outer wall. "It was as if he still thought it was a game," said Fish.

Suddenly shots rang out.

"I threw him on the ground and lay across him," recalled Waukechon. "I had to because he was kicking and yelling. He'd just lost it, man."

"Those are real bullets!" Brando exclaimed. "I gotta get out of here!"

The Indians dragged him back toward the ladder, still struggling and screaming. Then, with two of them handling him, they carried him down.

Once again Brando's recollection of the event put a different spin on what the warriors remembered. Four years later, Brando wouldn't admit to what the Indians viewed as his uncontrollable terror when he described the event in *Playboy:*

BRANDO: I was up on the roof one time and bullets start whizzing by me, wheew, wheew, sounds very funny. The bullets came by before you hear the gun.

PLAYBOY: Were you scared?

BRANDO: No. [But] it was unbelievable, people going out with guns and ammunition, lying in the snow and firing at 2:30 in the morning; everybody sleeping, huddled, trying to get warm, bullets flying around."

"Everybody just laughed when they read that," commented Waukechon. "I mean it was total bullshit."

Despite the experience, Marlon rallied later that evening. Downstairs he delivered a second speech that was no more in sync with what was happening than his first. He argued that if the Indians were unwilling to surrender, as he had proposed, they should gather their forces and go down against the vastly superior Guard in a glorious, Kiplingesque charge.

"He just went into a different act," recalled Fish with disgust. "All of a sudden he wanted to go out there and take 'em on—three hundred fifty National Guardsmen with machine guns!"

Afterward, the Warriors continued to torment Marlon. Two days earlier, a horse had wandered onto the abbey grounds, the Indians had slaughtered it for meat, and in a grisly reprise of *The Godfather,* later that night they stuffed the animal's bloody, severed head inside the actor's sleeping bag.

"He didn't think it was too funny," said Chevalier dryly.

His tormentors still weren't satisfied. Brando's wallet, stripped of cash, turned up in Reverend Groppi's pocket, and one of the Indians was openly flaunting his Rolex. Another had publicly suggested they switch shirts, leaving him no alternative but to agree. "They were just kind of playing with his head," said Fish, who tried to get the others to lay off. "It became so bad that Brando looked like he was in a trance. He didn't want to talk to anybody, not even Groppi."

The next morning the conflict escalated. The governor ordered the novitiate sealed off, and the National Guard contingent ballooned from 350 to more than twice that number. Fourteen APCs were deployed along the outer perimeter, and Chevalier's scouts claimed to have spotted four M-60 tanks hidden in the woods. That evening, February 1, a sixty-six-year-old white farmer was shot while standing on his porch not far from one of the National Guard's checkpoint three miles from the abbey.

The Menominee command group gave the order to seed the novitiate courtyard with improvised mines as well as plant dynamite throughout the building.

On February 2, after Marlon had spent two nights at the abbey, the Alexian Brothers offered to sell the building to the Indians for "$1 and other valuable considerations." Two hours of shooting took place later in the day. With time running out, the Indians told Brando to leave. Hours after he was driven back across no-man's land, the siege ended with the Menominees' surrender.

Brando had been inside the novitiate for forty-eight hours but in his later *Playboy* interview he conjured up a scenario of "about a week":

> They were shooting bullets twice a day, in the afternoon and at night. Dog soldiers came and they were fighting it out for over a month. . . . There were contingent plans to go in with percussion bombs and gas. That would have killed a lot of people, because the Indians wouldn't have surrendered. The expression on their arm bands was Deed or Death.
> They finally got the deed, and then those goddamn Alexian Brothers, the group of priests who owned the property, took it back after everything died down. Those lying bastards! I was right there in the room where they were negotiating.

Not only had he not been present, but the land, once offered to the tribe's strife-torn "assimilated" leadership, was voluntarily returned to the Alexian Brothers, who then sold it.

The question of Brando lingered, though, leaving the Menominees divided. Some felt his presence was pointless; others insisted that his arrival had sparked needed media attention and possibly even saved lives. Dennis Banks did not want to discuss the bell tower incident, except to concede,

"Yeah, they gave him a hard time." Yet the experience was more meaningful to Brando than the Menominees realized. "The incident at Gresham," Banks said, "earned Marlon that stripe he was looking for. It was the only stripe he ever wanted—I mean as a man."

The Wisconsin episode, Brando's most radical involvement to date, was also his most disillusioning. Yet was bravery the issue, as Banks insisted? At age fifty, now back in Los Angeles, the actor had a swimming pool, owned a private atoll in the South Pacific, and as much as anyone alive, had access to the world's cultural and political elite. But he wanted more, driven between his soft "spiritual" impulses and the need to "run with the boys." Interestingly, these two drives were personified by the two rival leaders of AIM, Russell Means and Dennis Banks.

Standing behind Means despite their long-standing differences, Brando posted a $30,000 cash bond when Means was charged with murder in a Scenic, South Dakota, bar shooting; he plunked down another $20,000 for Means's codefendant.

Stylistically, there was a huge barrier. The tall, toweringly handsome Means had never been shy about "chicing it up for the media," as he might joke. For him, grabbing the spotlight was something that came naturally. In 1970 he had led 200 militants in burying Plymouth Rock under a ton of sand, a "symbolic burial of the white man's conquest." At Wounded Knee he'd been mesmerizing. "You're going to have to kill us!" he yelled. "I'm not going to die in some barroom brawl. I'm not going to die in a car wreck on some lonely road . . . because I've been drinking to escape the oppression of this goddamn society. . . . I'm going to die fighting for my treaty rights. Period!"

On the other hand, Banks could influence Marlon subtly, calmly. "He's both charismatic and manipulative," said Michelle Vignes, AIM's San Francisco–based photographer. "It wasn't that he was opportunistic. He's like a coyote—he just goes with the wind."

Still, there was a limit even to Banks's abilities, and in the aftermath of Gresham he noted that Brando seemed to be "rambling" even more than before. With Mann, Banks, and Means moving full steam ahead on the Wounded Knee film, there was now only one obstacle: Marlon himself.

The moral of the story is that hope truly springs eternal. When Mann had come aboard, writer-historian Vine Deloria Jr., who had been involved in a previous incarnation of Brando's "Indian" movie, had given

Mann some sobering advice. "Vine told me, 'He'll never do it,' " Mann conceded. "He warned me, 'It's like *Young Man with a Horn*—Bix Beider-becke trying to find a note in his trumpet that didn't exist.' To Brando the film was going to be all encompassing, so nothing was ever good enough or right."

As things evolved, the two had already had "some terrible fights. . . . He'd get furious and then I would walk out on him. I was doing that constantly, and that is something you don't do to Marlon. In fact, he told me that once: 'Never walk out on me,' and he said it in a real quiet voice," said Mann.

The AIM leaders were caught squarely in the middle, juggling personal interest with the potential political gains of getting a film about Wounded Knee made with Hollywood's most famous actor. Nevertheless, even Banks's patience was wearing thin. "I began to dread talking about this movie," he explained. "I didn't dread talking about it with Abby, but I dreaded being in the room with him and Marlon because the discussion would go nowhere."

Banks went so far as to enlist the help of AIM's resident medicine man, Leonard Crow Dog.

"Dennis and I kind of set this up," Mann confessed. "The problem was that the conflict between Marlon and me, or rather *his* notion of the conflict, had hardened. So Dennis brought in the medicine man to adjudicate the conflict. He had all the paraphernalia, bones, feathers, what have you. We were in Marlon's living room, and he started the ceremony. He was chanting, '*Woo pu tu tu tu,*' then, 'Abby Mann? Marlon Brando?' " It was no surprise when Crow Dog intoned, *"Abby Mann!"*

"Dennis was smart that way," added the screenwriter, still chuckling years later. Naturally, Brando agreed with Crow Dog's "vision" and that won the battle, at least for the moment.

During these months Brando had been talking to San Francisco rock impresario Bill Graham about putting on benefits on behalf of Indians. In January 1975 Graham had called him about a fundraiser to help raise money for San Francisco schools, which at the time were undergoing drastic budget cuts. Graham had personally enlisted the help of such stars as the Grateful Dead, Bob Dylan and The Band, Santana, Neil Young, and he then phoned Brando. Not surprisingly, Marlon not only donated $5,000 but agreed to fly up to speak at the benefit.

When Graham introduced "another friend of ours, and certainly a friend of yours, *Marlon Brando,*" the crowds in Kezar Stadium went wild. "It was like Zeus had just walked out on that stage," Graham later said. *"Royalty.* True royalty, on the highest level. . . . It was awesome."

Dressed in a bush jacket "with big pockets to cover up some of his girth," Brando was bearded, Graham recalled. He had that "all powerful presence" when he "rapped to the kids," telling them, "Be strong but listen to the people who can teach you. The American Indians were here before us and we have to respect them as we respect one another."

After he finished his talk, he left the stage and stood alone, as if he were in a trance when the tumultuous applause washed over him. Graham rushed to his side, asking, "Are you all right?" Brando simply shook his head. Graham brought him some water and Brando sat down, then clutched Graham's arms and looked into his eyes. "You know something?" the actor said. "Thems not *extras* out there."

Hearing the story later from Graham, Elia Kazan had a similar interpretation. He noted that Brando had "become very suspicious of adulation, having had so much of it and seen it fade like yesterday's rainbow. On the other hand, his self-esteem was starved." And why was his self-esteem starved, so shortly after his comeback in *The Godfather?* Kazan attributed it to the fact that now he was again "being offered parts for a lot of money, which when he accepted them, further reduced people's respect for him."

Still hating to go in front of the cameras but needing to bring in money to support his families, to fund Tetiaroa, to underwrite the Indians' cause as well as his envisioned Indian film, he now signed to make two new movies. The first was Arthur Penn's *The Missouri Breaks,* which would eventually earn him about $16.5 million. The second was *Superman,* which would generate a reported $15 million for all of fifteen minutes' combined on-screen and voice-over time.

During these months when Mann had been working with Means and Banks, the only actor, besides Brando, ever linked to the Indian film was George C. Scott, who had offered his services for scale. Before casting, though, Brando and Mann had had to find a director. They considered William Friedkin and Franklin Schaffner, but in May 1975, Brando suggested Gillo Pontecorvo. In the years since making it, Brando had come to consider *Burn!* his favorite movie. He frequently ran it for Banks, Means, and any other visiting Indians, largely because, as Pat Quinn realized, "That's how he saw himself, as the freedom fighter, the mythological hero coming to the rescue."

When the Italian director arrived at Mulholland, carrying a briefcase and a still camera, he asked to take photographs of Brando and Banks. Marlon agreed and went to his bedroom to don a kimono. Back on the patio he told Gillo he would allow him only one shot. The director posed them, then as he counted to three Brando whipped around and lifted his kimono to expose an expanse of bare ass. "That's the only picture you're going to get of me," he announced, laughing.

Still, over the next three days and nights the group hunkered down, trying to resolve the script. Pontecorvo had changes but seemed ready to bend: "I'll make it the way you guys want it, but if you don't answer my calls, how can I get it done?" Marlon, sensing Mann's interference, pushed for further rewrites—"major rewrites," added Mann, who later insisted that although not yet polished, the script was already more than solid in terms of plotline. During one of their sessions, Pontecorvo asked Banks about his parents, both dead, his childhood, and his years in BIA boarding schools.

"I hadn't talked about this in years, not ever, really," said Banks. "In the midst of this, suddenly Marlon blurted out, 'That's what I want out of this film, this kind of emotion, so that it hits people!' "

If it seemed they'd hit bedrock, this was another illusion. The next afternoon Pontecorvo proposed that he visit the Pine Ridge reservation, and Banks made the arrangements. But soon after arriving at the reservation, Pontecorvo disappeared back to Italy. Brando seemed to put the blame on the AIM leaders. "They scared the shit out of him," he claimed. "Indians are very strange folks until you understand them."

With Pontecorvo gone, Martin Scorsese was the next candidate. The young director was distinctly "New York," not Hollywood, and Brando liked his richly textured *Mean Streets*. The group's first meeting took place at Abby Mann's house, although at the last minute Brando bowed out and sent Banks and Means alone. "You guys check him out," he told them.

After a few hours of conference, Means suggested they visit a bar. Neither Mann, Scorsese, nor Banks wanted to go but Mann's wife and Scorsese's girlfriend insisted.

"We were there for about only twenty minutes when I was ready to leave," Banks recalled. "Russ and this girl who was with Scorsese were talking, so Russ said, 'Look, why don't you deadheads go on home. I'll bring your car back . . . in about an hour.' " The girl stayed behind with Means, and the others left, with Banks taking a cab back to Brando's.

"The next morning Abby called me," Banks added. "He asked me if Russ was up there, and I said no. He said, 'Jesus, you know, Martin's here, and Russell didn't come back with either the car *or* his girlfriend.' "

A few hours later, when Banks checked back with Mann, Scorsese had left for New York.

When he heard the news, Brando laughed. "He said, 'Oh, shit, maybe I should call him,' " Banks said. "That's when we knew it was all over with Scorsese."

Scorsese himself disputed the rumor that he and Marlon had quarreled: "There were political problems between me and the Indians involved." But as Banks laughed about it later, the politics came down to a woman and a car.

They had now been working on the project for nine months, when Brando and Banks flew to New York on the red-eye to meet producer John Foreman, responsible for *The Life and Times of Judge Roy Bean* and the soon-to-be-released *The Man Who Would Be King.* Foreman was not at home when they let themselves into his plush wall-to-wall carpeted East Side town house. Brando got him on the phone.

"John? Yes, Marlon . . . John, you know Dennis Banks? He's here with me. I told him he wasn't supposed to have any animals here but he's got this great big German Shepherd. . . . John, I don't know what to say. . . . No, I told him. But the dog is shitting all over the carpets. Oh, Jesus! Now he's pissing! Look, I'll call you right back."

He hung up, barely able to contain himself. Several minutes later he redialed.

"John, listen, we got the dog out. No, no, it's okay. But he really pissed all over the place. I think the poor dog is sick. He threw up, too."

Again, he hung up, then took the receiver off the hook. An unamused Foreman soon arrived to find that, like Pontecorvo, like Scorsese, he'd been "had."

The straw that broke Mann's back occurred several weeks later on a flight from New York to Los Angeles when Mann tried reading Brando the script out loud. "I was saying, 'Listen to me,' " Mann recalled. "I was shouting at him. He was again muttering things like, 'Well, maybe we'll set it in another period.' Or he'd say, 'I have to think about it,' but it was more like total boredom with the project."

Not surprisingly Mann soon went off to work on another script, trying to make a graceful exit. "Columbia's response to my withdrawal," said Mann, "was 'Well, this is a typical Brando adventure. It was worth the shot, he's an enormous star, but it just didn't work out.' "

The Indian movie never died a formal death, and over the next several years Marlon would continue to try to revive it in one form or another, but it remained more fantasy and fiction than a realized effort. Of course, Marlon's rationalization was that prejudice in Hollywood made funding impossible. Those close to the project, however, insisted that the problem was never funding but the actor's resistance to moving past abstract discussions and endless research.

Marlon, Banks realized, was so locked into himself that he could not "let it happen. . . . He never said no, he just put up obstacles. Maybe he was afraid that it might be a colossal flop."

The relationship between Banks and Brando nonetheless grew stronger as a result of the June 1975 shoot-out involving an AIM group headed by Leonard Peltier at Oglala, South Dakota, a town within the Pine Ridge reservation. Just before the event, Banks had returned to "the res," concerned because violence had escalated on the reservation during the winter and spring of 1975. At least seven Indians, two of them children, had been gunned down by Dick Wilson's BIA-backed goon squads in the month of March alone. Many tribe members had then begun to shoot back. The FBI responded by assigning more personnel in the Pine Ridge reservation, and an additional thousand National Guard troops were deployed in the nearby Black Hills. On June 26, the firefight that everyone had been expecting started sometime around 10:30 A.M.

When the seventeen or so members of the Peltier group found themselves under fire, they began to shoot back while Peltier tried to organize his people to escape over a nearby ridge. As the shooting escalated, more law enforcement vehicles, one a green-and-white BIA patrol car, poured in off the two-lane blacktop. One of Peltier's group was killed, shot in the head, and in the meadow below, two FBI agents lay dead.

By late afternoon SWAT teams had arrived from as far away as Philadelphia, New York City, Denver, and Minneapolis. After disappearing into the vast acreage of the reservation for a couple of months, Peltier, Banks, and other Indians fled in a four-car caravan headed for Colorado as police helicopters continued to scour Pine Ridge in what turned into the

FBI's most extensive manhunt in history. "We couldn't hang together," Banks said. "Peltier and I were the feds' number one priority. Finally we decided some of the people would go back to Arizona, others to Rapid City, and Leonard and I would get help from Marlon. I told Leonard, 'I know Marlon's house, the people know me there, so let's go. It'll be safe.' "

At the time, Brando was away filming *The Missouri Breaks* in Montana. Because of his newfound bankability after *The Godfather* and *Last Tango in Paris,* he could have picked almost any role. Instead, nearly three years after *Tango* the actor had again turned to Elliott Kastner and Jay Kanter in a United Artists deal involving a large paycheck. Kastner had commissioned author Thomas McGuane to write a script—another off-key western, like his previous *Rancho Deluxe.* The producer then played a shell game, wooing director Arthur Penn by implying that Brando and Jack Nicholson had already signed up. Penn, hot off *Bonnie and Clyde* and *Little Big Man,* was then used to lure the two superstars.

Brando had attorney Norman Garey negotiate his contract before he agreed to do the movie. During months of deal-mongering by Garey, the attorney finessed another turning point in Brando's reputation: No longer was he the has-been slouching through parodies of himself in the kind of movies he'd done during sixties; instead he would become known as a fast-buck cameo man.

Brando finally signed on for a salary in excess of $1.25 million plus a percentage, and with the delays over contracts resolved, *The Missouri Breaks* had to be rushed into production. To hasten the process, Penn utilized standing sets from *Little Big Man,* including a modified reproduction of the frontier town Virginia City. Cinematographer Michael Butler and his brother, cameraman David Butler, lined up their crews almost overnight; all was ready to go by mid-June 1975 on the location shoot outside Billings, Montana.

In the attempt to speed things up, however, little attention had been given to the still flawed screenplay, a fact that Penn would later cite as the real source for the difficulties with the production. "It was potentially a very strong script," agreed associate producer Marion Rosenberg, "but we never really got to the point where it worked, although God knows we tried, getting Robert Towne to rewrite the ending when Tom wasn't available."

Brando's first day was to be July 4, two weeks after the start of principal photography. No one had heard a word from him, and on the morning of the fourth, the cast and crew gathered early, eager to see if he would actually show up. In the distance a large vehicle, leaving a cloud of dust in its wake, was sighted—a mobile home. When it came over the next rise, the observers saw that Brando was indeed at the wheel, making his timely though dramatic entrance.

He parked the Winnebago, climbed out, and looked around at the gathered cast and crew.

"How do you do?" he said as he went from one person to the next, as if moving down a receiving line. "I'm Marlon Brando."

"His attitude was sort of 'Why should they know who I am?' " noted Rosenberg, "which was rather silly, since obviously everybody knew who he was."

There seemed to be some snag in the terms of his contract, however, so Jay Kanter and Elliott Kastner, attorneys, and studio people flew in the next morning, only to spend almost the entire day in negotiations. One of the sticking points was Brando's contract stipulation that Kastner had to be on location every day Brando was. Having experienced the chaos created by Kastner's many absences while making *The Night of the Following Day,* the actor was making sure that Kastner would be present on the set. (It was also the ideal way to get Kastner's goat. The producer was irritated while imprisoned in Montana, and he let everyone know it.)

The following day, Brando initiated long discussions with Penn about the script, suggesting that Nicholson play his role as an Indian. Then he wanted to make his own character an Indian, "fantasizing," as Penn put it, "that we would change the script—lock, stock, and barrel."

From the first day Marion Rosenberg saw that Brando "had decided to push the limits. Like his dumb Irish accent. That came out when he said his first line. Once he established it, he had to keep using it, but nobody had the courage to say, 'Hey, wait a minute, what are you doing?' And it went on from there. Behind his back people were saying, 'Is he crazy? We can't use this shot!' But nobody stood up to him."

When Brando was not in a scene he usually retreated to his Winnebago, which he had parked under a grove of trees on the nearby riverbank. Inside he had his congas and meditation tapes, as well as his books on Tahiti, solar energy, and Indian history. He was also trying to lose weight and had embarked on a new diet of cold turkey breast and Tab. When reporters were allowed admission, Brando would talk into the night about his voluminous "master plan" for Tetiaroa, his acknowledged reason for making this picture. "I've sunk millions in this project," he told an interviewer. "So, from my point of view, *The Missouri Breaks* is simply Bucks and Company."

While Brando proved unusually cooperative once he had granted an interview, he seemed much more resistant to photographers taking stills of him—perhaps because of his weight. In his usual way of "keeping it all in the family," he had brought neophyte photographer Stefani Kong, daughter of Anita Kong, having told United Artists, "She's the daughter of a personal friend." When the studio's publicity department objected, he made it clear that he would not cooperate with anyone else attempting to take pictures of him.

Brando seemed to be withdrawn at night, but he was fully engaged during the day. "He'd go out and buy rubber spiders," said one of the film's production coordinators, "then leave them in your bed. Or he'd buy rubber plastic fried eggs and put them on your plate at breakfast. Real stupid, childish jokes. And then, he was mooning all the time during the shoot."

One morning the camera crew watched in amazement when he interrupted the shot to pluck a live frog from the river. He took a large bite out of it and threw it back in the water. On another occasion, when Brando's character was to fire at Nicholson in his garden, he took pot shots at passing grasshoppers instead; when he decided that the scene wasn't going to work, he climbed onto his red Honda trail bike and drove off into the prairie. "Oh well," shrugged Nicholson. "Another day, another twenty-one grand."

To Rosenberg, director Penn seemed to have no handle on Brando and could only sit back and watch the film sink around him. In retrospect, Penn insisted that the actor's pranks were not a sign of contempt so much as his attempt to revitalize the chaotic script and invent scenes to give the film a better story line. Day after day, however, crew members stood around the set, as if in a ghost town; in the boiling heat, a few of them fainted. During one two-hour wait, while Brando was pondering how he wanted to play his next scene, an anonymous voice came over the company's walkie-talkie. "Has God's gift to the world appeared yet?"

Penn tolerated Brando's behavior, allowing him his experimentation not only with accents but also with his costumes, including the bizarre Mother Hubbard dress and bonnet the actor cooked up for the climactic scene with Nicholson. Some in the company thought that he was simply trying to conceal his excess weight, but Brando defended his choice as "fitting" for his "preposterous" character. Penn went along, even when Brando mounted his horse in the ludicrous outfit, then instructed the director, "Don't say 'Action.' Say 'Marlon.' "

To be fair, many of the endless discussions about Brando's characterizations and scenes were needed because of defects in the script, especially the ending. Initially, McGuane called Marlon "learned, human . . . a *really neat* man." But over the course of the script conferences, his enthusiasm diminished. "Brando could sell refrigerators to Eskimos. I watched him manipulate the whole company for a long time. First, he wanted his two dogs in the movie. Then, he wanted his role changed to an Indian good guy. Now how do you make a former Confederate border-ruffian-turned-contract-killer into an Indian good guy?"

McGuane eventually decamped, claiming that Nicholson (as well as Brando) "was absolutely full of it." Yet his original script had only one scene in which the leads appeared together (when Brando's character was to track down Nicholson and finally kill him). With two superstars the movie needed more confrontations between them. Brando, Nicholson, and Penn brainstormed, soon coming up with the scene in which Brando lies in a bathtub like a child, playing with soap bubbles. Nicholson, the rustler with a heart of gold, sneaks into his room but is unable to shoot him, moved as he is by his enemy's childlike vulnerability.

The bathtub scene was one of Brando's larks that worked, if only because he camped it up with no reservations about being photographed nude. Another of his contributions was the film's exotic weaponry, such as the idea of using a throwing stick apparatus made out of a tire lug wrench with the tips sharpened.

It was a glorified ninja "star," what Brando later dubbed a combination "harpoon and mace." "I always wondered why in the history of lethal weapons no one invented that particular one," he explained. "It appealed to me because I used to be very expert at knife throwing."

Inventiveness was the keynote for his character's murder scenes, too. "He chose the most perverse moments for the killings," said Penn. "I would pose the problem, 'We've got these four or five killings. How do we do them so that they're not repetitive?' And he and I would come up with ideas." One scene had Brando shooting someone in an outhouse; a second murder, prompted by Penn's suggestion that the killings ought to be "ignominious," was of a man in the midst of making love.

In another scene, Randy Quaid, one of the rustlers, was supposed to be sleeping, his mouth open in a loud snore, when Brando, dressed as a minister, was to wake him with a line of dialogue. Instead, Brando crept up on him, picked up a grasshopper and dropped it into Quaid's mouth. "Randy nearly choked on it," said Rosenberg, "and as I remember, he got very angry." He may have been upset, but it was decided that this was such a clever invention that it had to be repeated several times. Quaid ended up with a sore tongue from the insects, but Brando's prank was so effective that even McGuane conceded that it was one of the best variations on his screenplay.

For all Penn's tolerance of Brando's antics and praise of his creativity, the director didn't realize that Marlon seemed to hold him in contempt for not exerting directorial control, much the way children will simultaneously exploit their parents' lack of discipline and disparage them for their weakness. "It was clear to me," said Pat Quinn, who had played the title role in Penn's 1969 *Alice's Restaurant,* that after Marlon returned from the shoot, "he didn't have any respect for Arthur. He told me that he thought Arthur had one foot in each door—the establishment and the non-establishment," recalled Quinn. "He criticized him for wanting to be both commercial and artistic at the same time." *The Missouri Breaks* was arguably the last of Brando's films to reveal his originality and brilliance, but most critics weren't taken. Vincent Canby labeled the performance "out-of-control," observing that after his delayed entrance, Brando "spends the rest of the movie upstaging the writer, the director and the other actors." The film "too often seems like camp," the critic observed, because Brando's turns and larks seemed to have no "apparent connection to the movie that surrounds him."

What had been billed as a major box-office draw failed both artistically and commercially. Penn's following films did no better, and he would join the list of distinguished directors—Elia Kazan, Bernhard Wicki, and Gillo Pontecorvo—who never seemed to recover from the experience of making a picture with Brando.

With Bernardo Bertolucci on the set of *Last Tango in Paris*. *Paris Match*

Charlton Heston, Harry Belafonte, Jar
Baldwin, and Brando at the March
Washington, 1963. *AP Wide World*

Brando with Dennis Banks, AIM fund-
raiser, San Francisco. © *Michelle Vignes*

Brando in Tahiti. *Paris Match*

Brando and Martin Sheen
in *Apocalypse Now*.
Photofest

Philip Rhodes.

Brando outside a
Hungarian restaurant, Los
Angeles, 1980s.
© *Ramey Photo Agency*

Brando in Tahiti, presenting his family. *Paris Match*

(*Above*) Police investigator's photograph of Dag Drollet, Mulholland Drive, Los Angeles, the evening of May 16, 1990.

Cheyenne with Dag Drollet; happier times in Tahiti. *Jacques-Denis Drollet*

Marlon Brando testifying in tears, at his son Christian's sentencing hearing, 1991.
© *Ramey Photo Agency*

cques-Denis Drollet and Lisette LeCaill at
hristian Brando's sentencing hearing.
Ramey Photo Agency

pposite) The Brandos—Christian, Jocelyn, Marlon,
iko—at the sentencing hearing.
Ramey Photo Agency

ight) Christian Brando in handcuffs.
Ramey Photo Agency

Cheyenne Brando, Berkeley, California, 1993.
© *Phil Ramey for* Paris Match

• • •

During the shoot, his Indian movie and AIM's struggle had certainly been on Brando's mind. To the press, he explained that he had been eager to turn *The Missouri Breaks* into a vehicle for the Indians' cause, since he had "thus far failed to find American financing for his long projected film, *Wounded Knee*." No one bothered to check the facts; Columbia had after all put up a quarter of a million dollars in development money, and the project would have gotten a green light if Brando himself had ever given the go-ahead.

Still, whatever his fudging Brando was keenly aware that the violent confrontation just a few months before on the Pine Ridge reservation had had dramatic consequences for his friends. While on location for *Missouri Breaks*, he had been visited by two FBI agents and interrogated for hours about the whereabouts of Banks and Peltier. Later he assured *Rolling Stone* writer Chris Hodenfield that he and the agents had had a "nice, long talk."

What this meant in terms of how he intended to deal with the FBI's unprecedented search for his Indian compatriots was unclear. Still, he adopted a more "philosophical" attitude toward his conversation with the agents when he subsequently described the visit in greater detail, calling them "nice men." Despite his bravado, the encounter seemed to heighten his paranoia, undoubtedly for very good reason. "They're probably monitoring the phones," he said, "bugging the trailer, stuff like that. They're always around."

Brando was still away from his L.A. home when Banks and Peltier showed up unannounced. Three days later, around eleven in the morning, the actor returned, accompanied by Jill Banner, and found Peltier sleeping in his TV room.

Brando shouted to Jill, "Get my gun!" Hearing the commotion, Banks hurried out of the rear bedroom to greet Brando. As the two men hugged, Marlon blurted, "Shit, who is this guy? I thought somebody had broken in!"

"He had never met Leonard, and he didn't know the name Peltier," recalled Banks, "so he wasn't making the connection. I told him that there was a warrant out for Leonard, just like there was for me. He accepted it, he didn't question why we were there."

"Well, do you need some lawyers?" Brando asked.

Banks and Peltier didn't want legal help; they waned to head back to Pine Ridge in anticipation of "the blood bath" now that the BIA cops, goon squads, and federal agents had descended on the reservation. In their frantic search for the AIM leaders, the government forces were randomly and frequently firing on the residents.

"Marlon realized that we had already made our decision," said Banks. "He knew we were on the run and his major concern became our safety."

Banks and Brando stayed up talking that night, first in the living room, then outside on the patio (the actor suspected that "there might be a listening device," said Banks).

"Marlon was very collected, very concrete, completely down-to-earth. He wanted to help and was willing to be more specific, since he realized support was needed immediately." The next morning, when he saw the car the Indians were driving, Brando said, "Dennis, you can't take that jalopy—it'll never make it. Take my motor home. If anybody asks, tell them I lent it to you months ago and you just never returned it."

Banks accepted. Brando then asked how much money he had.

"Couple hundred dollars," replied Banks, "enough to get back on."

"No," said Brando. "You'll need more."

He sent for $10,000 from the bank. Perhaps unaware that the money was going to be used for weaponry (a felony that would subject him to arrest if the authorities could prove complicity), he handed the cash to Banks. The evening of their heart-to-heart, though, he had told Dennis that he "would welcome an indictment for aiding and abetting. . . . He was very serious," recalled Banks. "He said, 'You know what? I'm kind of hoping they indict me so I can say why I believe in helping you people.' "

The next day, as Brando bid the Indians good-bye, he became very emotional.

"I know they're going to be out looking for you guys hard," he said. "If they find you, they may not ask questions. They may shoot first."

Tears welled up in Brando's eyes. "I might never see you again," he added in a choked-up voice as he embraced Banks. "Be careful. Tell Kamook I love her and the kids, and keep in touch as much as you can."

Banks and Peltier met up with Banks's wife and baby girl, along with other associates in South Dakota. After conferring with tribal elders, they drove to Seattle to pick up rifles, ammunition, and dynamite. Already Bob

Robideau and several others from the original Peltier group had been arrested in Kansas, and state police there claimed to have found a .308 rifle belonging to one of the dead FBI agents after a search of the Indians' car. An AR-15 was also recovered and this would later be offered into evidence as the gun that had killed the two agents.

On November 14, 1975, Brando's motor home, loaded with armaments, was stopped by Oregon state troopers on Interstate 84, not far from the Idaho line. When the troopers insisted that everyone "get on the ground" (including Kamook, who was seven or eight months pregnant), Banks made a run for it, hoping to ditch the motor home and its incriminating cargo.

About a quarter of a mile up the highway, he jumped from the still moving van and disappeared into the woods. Peltier, meanwhile, had been shot in the shoulder while sprinting across a field at the side of the roadblock. He spent the night hiding in a haystack, bleeding profusely.

According to police and FBI bulletins, Brando's vehicle was found to contain seven boxes of dynamite, nine hand grenades, and fourteen firearms, among them a .357 Magnum revolver taken from the body of one of the two FBI agents. Also inventoried were several Brando credit cards and airline tickets charged to the actor.

Peltier made the FBI's Ten Most Wanted List while hiding out in Canada. Within weeks of the Oregon intercept, Banks was arrested in El Cerrito, California, and at his arraignment he made it clear to the court that if he was returned to South Dakota he would probably "be killed." He was held in a jail cell in San Francisco's federal courthouse, where three days later Brando arrived with Vine Deloria Jr., the historian and writer.

With bail money provided by the Inter-Tribal Friendship House in Oakland, Banks returned to Los Angeles to ponder his fate. The major consideration was his extradition from Oregon, since that was the jurisdiction from which he had fled arrest. When Jack Nicholson had been on location in Oregon to make *One Flew over the Cuckoo's Nest,* he had become friendly with the state's governor, and with Marlon's prodding, calls were made. Likewise, California Governor Jerry Brown was contacted by Brando and also by Abby Mann, who had contacts within Brown's inner circle.

Contrary to liberal mythology, Brown dragged his feet on the decision to give Banks sanctuary. Worried by the delay, the AIM activist finally put it to Brando: "The decision may come down in the next couple of weeks. I'd rather be out of the country," he said, suggesting that the ideal place for him to go would be Tahiti.

It was early in 1976 that Banks made the journey, although many of the details of Brando's help still remain unknown. "It's extremely important to Marlon that information about how I got there not be released," Banks later explained. "Let's just say I was moving around from plane to plane, then private plane, and I did make it to Tahiti."

When Banks arrived in Papeete, he was met by Tarita, who came to the airport with five-year-old Cheyenne. "At first I was just a guy without a passport," he added. "I told the officials who I was and that I had an invitation to be the guest of Marlon Brando, and then, after two or three hours, the officials came out of their office and said, 'Enjoy your stay at Tetiaroa.' "

Plainly, the fix had been put in—possibly through Brando's Tahiti government connections. He had in fact told Banks that such arrangements could be made when reassuring him about the trip. After customs officers bid Banks a good holiday, he was immediately taken to the adjacent terminal for the next plane to Tetiaroa. On the atoll he was greeted by Reiko Sato, Brando's former girlfriend, who was now managing the island.

"She asked me to tell her all about Wounded Knee and why so many people were interested in my whereabouts," Banks recalled. "After I told her, she said, 'Well, this is your home now. We're having dinner tonight, so we'll come and get you. There'll be about six people, friends of Marlon's. A French scientist, somebody from the French government, all of them involved in the development of the island.' "

Soon Marlon himself arrived for a four-day visit. According to Banks, they spent only a single evening together, talking about Brando's plans for a university, his solar- and wind-power experiments, and the research that he had done on fish hatcheries as a source for "Third World self-sufficiency." The rest of the time Brando kept to himself or huddled with the visiting scientists, leaving Banks free to fly into Papeete, where Tarita "showed me around and gave me a car."

Later gossip about the Indian leader's stay reported that he was "going crazy" surrounded by the open ocean. In truth, Banks insisted, he "loved it on the island. . . . But my head was mostly wondering what was going on with Governor Brown. How were my wife and kids? The other part of the plan had been that if Brown made an adverse decision, then Kamook and the kid would come and join me on the island. That was the plan Marlon had initiated."

After nearly two months in Polynesia, Banks returned to the United States and surrendered to authorities. Brando and Abby Mann visited him in the San Francisco jail. Mann continued to lobby Jerry Brown to grant Banks asylum, going so far as to meet with him in Sacramento.

With violence on the Pine ridge reservation continuing, Governor Brown finally granted Banks asylum for nine years, until 1985. Dennis then enrolled at the University of California at Davis, where he soon appointed himself chancellor of D-Q, the Indian-chicano study center established after the occupation of Alcatraz.

During 1976 Brando's involvement with AIM eventually cooled, even though on April 9 he made his wish known to do a *Black Like Me*–style documentary in which he would travel the country in "redface," testing America's racism. When he turned down the Hollywood NAACP's annual Humanitarian Award with the words "No white man . . . can know what the black experience is," columnist Liz Smith attacked him as boring. "Even sympathetic liberals who get Brando's calls find themselves desperate to hang up after the first fifteen or twenty minutes of his endless monologues. ZZZzzz, pardon me, I just dozed off myself."

But other concerns were also drawing his attention, leeching his energy. The death from leukemia of his old but banished friend, actor and writer Billy Redfield, was another saddening event, especially since Marlon himself was now being warned that his obesity was a serious health hazard. Soon afterward, Christian announced that he was dropping out of high school. His father was disappointed, since he had still tried to impose some discipline, even forbidding Christian's purchase of a motorcycle. Sometimes Marlon complained to Pat Quinn about Christian's rebellions and his drinking and drugs. She countered: "After all, you were drunk and disorderly, you drove a motorcycle, you were an outlaw. Those are the same things you come down on Christian for. Isn't it hypocritical?"

"I'm stopping him from committing the same mistakes," he insisted, adding that his child-raising philosophy was simple: Do as I say, not as I do.

Complicating life further at Mulholland during that spring was

Brando's disintegrating relationship with Jill Banner. Jill was upset by the gossip about other women in Brando's life, including a nonsensical tabloid item about his being "engaged" to Lucy Saroyan, who had organized the New York fund-raiser for AIDA, and a new girlfriend, an airline stewardess whom he reportedly had met at a political rally after the Menominee abbey siege.

Onetime teen idol Bobby Sherman had been a friend of Banner for years, and he thought that Banner and Brando "were equally guilty" for perpetuating the destructive relationship. "It was just uncontrollable warfare," he said. "All of a sudden out of nowhere there would be a new manufactured problem and another fight."

During the previous year, one of the more evident problems was Banner's attitude toward Brando's AIM friends. "All she talked about was their horrible behavior, like urinating in front of people," said a friend. "She was sickened by the way they acted, and she saw it as this whole male-bonding thing. Marlon was giving them money, and she thought they were just stepping all over him."

But most of all, she felt that Brando could be cruel, manipulative, and selfish to those who loved him and those he supposedly loved. "What she always wondered about," said her friend, "was how he could be so virtuous on the outside when at the same time he was so self-centered and such a mess inside himself."

Perhaps Jill and Christian were united in their feeling that Brando gave more attention to his Indian pals than he did to them. Or perhaps they both felt wounded by his abrupt withdrawals of affection. Whatever it was, the two eventually embarked on a clandestine love affair. "I think it was a year or two later that Christian and Jill started sleeping together," said Pat Quinn. "She was still sleeping with Marlon, too, so it seemed a bit incestuous to me. It was also as if Marlon had been visited by the old ghost of suspecting Carlo Fiore of sleeping with Dodie."

Steve Hunio, Christian's friend, became aware of the affair, even though it wasn't discussed openly or directly. "I doubt Christian was trying to compete with his father. He didn't talk all that much to me about Jill, but I gathered he had a lot of feeling for her. And then there was a huge brouhaha when Marlon found out about it."

In early July Brando contacted Dick Gregory and asked him to join him in Cedar Rapids, Iowa, for the trial of Darryl Butler and Bob Robideau. Butler and Robideau had been charged with the murder of the two FBI agents in Oglala; Peltier, also charged with the killings, was to be tried separately.

"It was late when Marlon phoned," Gregory recalled. "He began by telling me how beautiful I was, and he was crying."

The two arranged to rendezvous in Des Moines. But Brando mistakenly flew to St. Louis. A day later he hooked up with Gregory. "I almost didn't know who he was," said the black activist-comedian. "He'd gained so much weight and had sunglasses and some kind of costume on, like he was hiding. He walked up and said, 'Dick, I'm sorry about last night. Jesus Christ, how'd I get to St. Louis?' "

In Cedar Rapids it seemed apparent that the Justice Department and the FBI intended to use the Robideau-Butler case as an anvil on which to break AIM's back. Federal lawyers had already bent every rule in the book to extradite Peltier from Canada, including their use of testimony that was later recanted and acknowledged as coerced. Now the Justice Department had posted a highly visible contingent of armed guards around the Cedar Rapids courthouse, scaring the local citizenry. In addition, incriminating information about the defendants was reportedly leaked to the press.

The deaths of the two FBI agents at Oglala, argued Kunstler and co-counsel John Lowe, were the result not of radical blood lust but the Indians' legitimate, justifiable need for self-defense. The government's case was "circumstantial," "replete with inconsistencies and kill-a-cop-a-day rhetoric," insupportable as to specifically *who* had gone down into the meadow at the base of the Jumping Bull compound to finish off the agents at close range. But it was the defendants' own testimony, along with that of their supporters, that soon left the jury and Judge Edward McManus sympathetic. On July 16, 1976, in what has been called a "historic verdict," the defendants were found innocent on all counts, a virtually unprecedented victory in shooting cases involving Indians and lawmen.

Little of the credit could be claimed by Brando, though. He had been present at the trial for less than two days, and what was most apparent to the defense team and AIM leadership alike was that he was "very much aware of his own safety."

Arriving late as usual, his first move after greeting Kunstler had been to go with the lawyer to meet the defendants in jail, a stopover that lasted ten minutes. The next morning in the courtroom and in plain sight of the jury, he reached out and attempted to shake the defendants' hands as they were brought into the room in shackles. The gesture was similar to his embrace of Banks and Means at the St. Paul trial; what reporters missed, however, was his exchange with defense attorney Bruce Ellison during the lunch recess.

"He asked me something to the effect, 'How many people have actually died on Pine Ridge?' Ellison recalled. " 'Was it three hundred and fifty?' I said, 'Well, no. We know for sure it was a little over sixty, but we've heard as high as two hundred.' 'Oh,' he nodded, 'so four hundred fifty people, okay.'

"He then went out and gave a press conference using his own figures. I don't know what the problem was—either just his personality or his intense self-absorption. My impression was that the guy was just not all there."

The day's news reports also had the actor complaining that Judge McManus had refused to let him take the stand. This, too, was a fabrication. That afternoon the Indians had wanted Brando to testify about why he had supported Peltier and Banks, giving them money and his motor home at a time when both men were known fugitives. This would show people in conservative Cedar Rapids that the defendants weren't "just a bunch of wide-eyed radicals going around killing FBI agents," said defense attorney Ellison. "Brando, because of his reputation, could have gone a long way toward making that bridge."

John Trudell, AIM's national chairman, had consulted the defense lawyers, who agreed that Brando would not be at risk if he were to testify. But the actor absolutely refused, convinced as he was that the Justice Department was watching him, waiting to make its move. Internal FBI documents in the agency's "RESMURS" file obtained by the WKDOC revealed that Bureau informants had erroneously placed him at the August sundance at Leonard Crow Dog's Paradise on Rosebud. The FBI's inventory of Brando's confiscated motor home listed his credit card receipts: one piece of paper noting various names, addresses, and telephone numbers, beginning with "Rita Moreno" and including the message "Please call Dick Gregory"; a letter dated May 14, 1975, to Harry Belafonte from Banks; a Master Charge receipt with "three pages of itemized room charges, all in name of Brando, M"; and a piece of AIM stationery bearing the notation: "MARLONS island called Tetiaroa, TAY-TEE-ARO-A."

Reports from the FBI's identification division also revealed that the

Bureau had been trying to match Brando's fingerprints with those lifted from the motor home and from a United Artists "booklet" and American Airlines ticket coupon found inside the vehicle.

Nevertheless, the attempt to bag Brando had gone no further than this. The reason was apparent in the FBI's own advisories: Although the actor's dossier was proof that the government had put him on its "enemies list," within hours of stopping Banks and Peltier and identifying the motor home, the FBI also issued a confidential memo to all agents and to all regional bureaus. It cautioned that the actor's name and "such information not be sent by teletype in view of possible publicity."

In short, the FBI was wary of taking on the world's most famous movie star. The Indians knew it and the lawyers knew it; everyone knew it except Marlon.

The morning after being approached to testify, Brando left Cedar Rapids. "My personal opinion," said Bob Robideau, "was that . . . he really got scared out." Six months later, in January 1977, not even Banks could persuade him to attend Leonard Peltier's trial, which was being held in the highly charged atmosphere of Fargo, North Dakota, where the government was determined to make up for its losses in the Robideau-Butler case. Peltier was found guilty on April 18, and on June 1, the day before his sentencing, the thirty-two-year-old Sioux addressed the court:

> No, I am not the guilty one here; I'm not the one who should be called a criminal—white racist America is the criminal for the destruction of our lands and my people; to hide your guilt from the decent human beings in America and around the world, you will sentence me to two consecutive life terms without any hesitation.

Judge Paul Benson, a Nixon appointee, could hardly control his rage at the defendant. The next day he handed down the harshest possible sentence: two consecutive life terms. In future years the Archbishop of Canterbury, South African bishop Desmond Tutu, Amnesty International, and some sixty Republican and Democrat congressmen would all petition for a retrial. Brando was conspicuous for his absence from the Peltier support team; in contrast, others such as Robert Redford and writer Peter Matthiessen have crusaded for a decade for his pardon.

In private, AIM was reassessing Brando and his seeming withdrawal in both the Robideau-Butler and Peltier trials. Said Ellison, "In Cedar Rapids it was hard to know whether he was even dealing with the reality of the situation. I just listened to him explain his reasons, and it was almost like jabbering. He'd come to support the defendants but exactly how or why was unclear to me, and certainly I didn't perceive that he understood what the facts of the case were, or even knew in any great detail what had been going on in Pine Ridge."

Bob Robideau said, "I think that being in Wisconsin, being under fire, he started realizing what he'd gotten himself into. I'm not saying Marlon's a coward, but after the incident with the motor home, all this became a reality."

Banks agreed but saw it a little more clearly: "He had earned his stripe, from his point of view, at least, and that was as far as he was going to go. Wounded Knee, the shooting at Gresham, the activity surrounding the Oglala incident—I believe that all of those things made him realize that the type of physical activity he wanted to be involved in was not the Dennis Banks or Russell Means type."

To make matters worse, the rumors of AIM's misuse of funds bothered him enormously, especially after he had given so much—and so unstintingly—whenever his Indian friends had come to him. As Christian was wont to complain to his friends, "The Indians really took Pop for a ride. They really soaked him."

"He put in over a half-million dollars," conceded Means. "So he thought he'd been nickel-and-dimed to death by Indian people and he never saw any tangible results."

While Banks still had some sense of Brando's spiritual quest and the importance of the Indians in his private journey, Means was more cynical. "Victim junkie," he called Brando. "That meant that we were supposed to be his redeemer. But Marlon has always been somewhat naive. He had wanted results, and when he didn't see any, he became too frustrated. . . . It was the whole ball of wax—cynicism, despair, 'I'm throwing in the towel, fuck it' kind of attitude. I asked him, 'How come you never checked out anything?' I pressed him, but he had no answer."

The sense of wasted money, futile investments of cash for a cause, was a problem common to the adventure of radical politics in the sixties and early seventies. Suddenly, after so much time and energy given, hopes raised, and expectations dashed, the excitement was gone and history was taking a different course. But what Brando was searching for, no one had the power to bring about—not AIM, not the UN. He had asked for too much; he had never defined his own priorities, and every time he tried he was blocked by his own defenses. Eddie Benton-Banai, in his quiet wisdom, had perceived Brando's problem from the beginning.

"It never occurred to him to try to separate the two things he was looking for. On the one hand, he was asking the American Indian Movement for acceptance and recognition, not as a movie star but as a man, a conscientious person who cared. On the other, he was asking for something that was spiritual. In the sweat lodge he discovered that he was sitting in this pitch-black, comfortable place—as he said, 'I'm sitting here with my brothers, on the lap of my Mother Earth whom I have never known.'

"But the sweat lodge is not about politics," Benton-Banai continued. "It's not about treaty rights. It's about the connection between you and the Creator. He could have had both the spirituality *and* the politics, but only by asking for them in their distinctive differences. In AIM, though, he insisted on seeing all of it.

"He had the ability to make the distinction but he didn't spend enough time, not with me, not with anybody. He was so close to something that he desired, so close that he could touch it, but he didn't know it was there."

17
TAHITI

At the same time that Brando was most actively involved in the American Indian Movement, his attention was often diverted by his scientific and ecological projects on Tetiaroa. From 1972 to 1983, just as he was searching for spiritual meaning through Native Americans, his development of the atoll represented another attempt to exorcise his personal demons and find something approaching a private peace.

In September 1972 he had asked aquaculture consultant Tap Pryor to organize a "think tank" of experts to discuss the feasibility of a lobster farm and other projects on the atoll. Those invited were Wallace Heath, an aquaculturist who had worked with the Lummi Indians in Washington State; Carl Hodges of the Environmental Research Laboratory, whose specialty was raising vegetables; and John Hughes of the Massachusetts State Lobster Hatchery on Martha's Vineyard.

The group was brought to Tetiaroa for three days. Touring the lagoon with Brando at the helm of a sixteen-foot Boston whaler, John Hughes noted that the boat had been banged up against the coral reef so often that the hull was completely scraped away on one side. Brando seemed oblivious of his guests' anxiety as he steered them through the churning surf, absorbed in explaining his plan. Each specialist, he instructed, should feel free to roam on his own, take samples, and then report back with his conclusions. Hughes's summary was unequivocal: The atoll was not the place for a lobster hatchery. Undaunted, Brando said he would like to be able to call Hughes after the marine biologist's return to the United States.

"He wanted to be able to phone me at any time," said Hughes, "and he asked how much that would cost. I said I was getting $225 a day for consulting, so I would charge him $225 a month. For five months Marlon sent me a check and called often, sometimes in the middle of the night. I still considered him a pioneer in his attempt to use the sea to produce food, even though the idea of a lobster hatchery on Tetiaroa just wasn't practical—the water was too warm and you would have to construct an insulated building with complicated water recirculation, which would require a stable supply of electricity. If you were going to do that," Hughes added, "you might as well raise lobsters in the Bronx."

Tap Pryor remained enthusiastic, however. By the end of 1972, and with approximately $15,000 put up by Brando, Pryor had created Mona Mona Products in Honolulu to explore the possibility of raising lobsters in tanks built under a roof at the edge of Tetiaroa's lagoon. Brando seemed pleased and explained that the French government offered long-term, low-interest loans to support such projects. Pryor, an experienced fund-raiser, advised that in order to pursue French financing, they would have to make a presentation in Paris.

A few weeks later Brando phoned Pryor and said that he had to be in Paris "for some stupid reason." He asked Pryor to meet him there, accompanied by any other experts who could help make the presentation.

The "stupid reason" that brought Brando to Paris was the French premiere of *The Godfather*. Because the film was receiving a great deal of attention, Pryor had an easy time attracting an audience for Brando's presentation—"not only significant figures in the French overseas loan bureaucracy but also the most glittering of current society, government and filmdom." After Pryor showed slides of the atoll, Brando spoke. As Pryor recalled, "Marlon rose to the occasion with an impassioned plea in French for Tetiaroa, the Polynesian way of life, the future of children everywhere, and above all, for the glory of France. He received a standing ovation. Even the government types had tears in their eyes."

Afterward Brando was filled with enthusiasm, but Pryor cautioned him that the follow-through was equally important. He suggested hiring an attorney in Paris to steer the proposal through the French bureaucracy. Brando agreed, and Pryor quickly found a suitable lawyer to meet them over lunch. The attorney was doing a good job explaining how to guide matters through official channels, but Pryor said, "Marlon was becoming more and more paranoid. The lunch turned into a disaster, and I'll never know why. Perhaps it was because Marlon has never trusted lawyers. Perhaps he thought that the follow-through was unnecessary, or maybe he was beginning to feel the heat of reality. He did not retain anyone, and then, having spent about $15,000 on the successful lobster trial in Hawaii, he stopped funding the project without explanation."

Erratic behavior was nothing new in the actor's life, yet his vacillation and indecision were resulting in mounting costs. Tetiaroa was continuing to drain his resources, although after the airstrip had finally been completed, he insisted that he would be present to open the sixteen new bungalows as a hotel at the end of March 1973, just after the Academy Award ceremony.

While the hotel was getting under way, Brando continued to chase other experts, even after he dropped Pryor. As his sister Jocelyn confirmed, anytime an idea came into his head, "he went straight to the top. . . . He'd call up and say, 'I'm Marlon Brando,' " she explained. "He talked to anybody and everybody about whatever was on his mind. He just wanted to get the best information, as well as the best people, and he'd bring these experts to the island."

In the middle of March, he flew in F. R. Fosberg and M.-H. Sachet of the Smithsonian Institution to study the ecological effects of the proposed hotel development, largely by cataloguing the flora and fauna of each *motu,* but he then cut short their visit and failed to give them the promised aerial photographs necessary to complete their survey. Instead he returned to Los Angeles to prepare the speech that Littlefeather delivered at the Academy Awards on March 27. Then, while the Indians at Wounded Knee waited for his arrival, he returned to Tetiaroa for the March 30 opening of the hotel, staying for about ten days. Before leaving Tahiti he made a loan application to Bank-Socredo and Caisse Central for 10,000,000 Pacific francs to fund his next project.

Brando and business associate Bernie Judge had also reinitiated the proposal with Yosihiko Sinoto, the anthropologist at the Bernice P. Bishop Museum in Honolulu, to undertake another archaeological survey of the atoll; throughout 1973, Sinoto and his associate, Patrick C. McCoy, brought undergraduates from the University of Hawaii and six students from the

Ecole Normale in Papeete to do the research. Whether they found anything of real significance was questionable. Nevertheless, Brando was intent upon uncovering and preserving the early history of his island and its
indigenous peoples, and he continued to fund the archaeological project
and field school.

Meanwhile, Norton Brown of Brown and Kraft, Marlon's Hollywood accountants, was still hoping that the hotel would bring in the necessary funds to underwrite the actor's continuing scientific studies. But
Brando then turned his attention to other things, and in his absence he left
Bernie Judge (now officially designated as "manager and construction supervisor") and Reiko Sato in charge. He had also opened an office at the
Papeete's Faaa Airport to handle reservations and book the small airplanes
needed to fly tourists to Tetiaroa and hired an office manager to run it. Yet
the resort operated at a loss throughout the year.

Even so, he soon announced that twenty more bungalows would be
ready in November 1973. Monitoring the financial hemorrhage, Brown
and Kraft now insisted that their client employ an experienced hotel manager to handle the mounting problems, and in 1974 Henry Rittmeister
agreed to come aboard. A native of Germany, Rittmeister had managed
successful hotels, both in Hawaii and Tahiti. He saw at once that Brando
was being pushed by his California accountants to reopen the new hotel as
quickly as possible.

"That was largely for tax reasons," explained Rittmeister, "because by
then not all the huts had been completed. The others were still under construction, and the kitchen and dining room were still unfinished, too. The
place was staffed with a large crew of local people, and morale was very
bad. Fights were commonplace, mainly because of all the drinking."

He also became aware of Brando's visionary bent and despite his
pragmatism found himself intrigued with the idea of a turtle farm on the
atoll, using scraps from the hotel restaurant to feed the animals. He joined
with a few more experts Marlon flew in to build an enclosure in the lagoon,
but neither he nor the experts had taken into account the strong tidal currents and the turtle farm was washed away. Brando then came up with the
idea of redigging the enclosure farther away from the reef and the tides.
"He loved to play with his bulldozer," recalled Rittmeister. "So he went
out and dug this deep hole for a new lagoon." Water rose in the hole, as
expected, and a new turtle colony was lodged there. A few days later

Brando left again; in his absence the lagoon became stagnant, the turtles died, and the mosquitoes thrived. Without consulting Brando, Rittmeister simply had the hole filled in.

Instead of finding immediate down-to-earth solutions, Marlon continued to make his phone calls to his experts. "All kinds of studies were done," said Rittmeister, "on insects, on flies, on how people live together on an atoll that was once uninhabited, what happens to the mind and the souls of people who work there. He was constantly into this idea or that. We had problems with the *no-nos,* so he brought a man to Tetiaroa to make an extensive study of the feasibility of controlling the bugs. Then there was the water problem, and that was researched for a long, long time, too."

One problem that Rittmeister immediately perceived was the construction of the new bungalows according to Judge's design. The thatched roofs were modeled not after the traditional Polynesian *fares,* but African huts with rounded, domed roofs. "The design of Polynesian thatched roofs has been proven for centuries," Rittmeister argued. "But Judge thought the African roofs looked better, even though the pandanus or palm leaves he was using for the thatch are flat and unlike the African straw didn't fit onto the dome shape."

Rittmeister soon discovered that tourists weren't all that enamored with the remote quiet of the island and its primitive conditions. The accommodations were similar to those of a summer camp, palatable only to guests who shared Brando's love for roughing it or were lured by the hope of catching a glimpse of the star himself—which they rarely did, since he often withdrew to his bungalow whenever he was on the atoll.

(In fact, his self-isolation seemed to have become extreme. Now when he regularly crossed the Pacific from Los Angeles to Faaa Airport, he would buy the surrounding first-class seats to ensure his privacy; he would then refuse to deplane in Tahiti until everyone else had left. On one trip, a UTA–Air France purser found him lying on the floor, unwilling to get off even though the cleanup crew was waiting to board. Spotting the workmen on the Tarmac, Brando insisted, "Not until everyone down there has gone." Finally he left the plane, wearing a huge sombrero to hide his face, a disguise that drew more attention than ever.)

But when Brando was feeling more sociable he would invite friends to Tetiaroa with promises of a week in paradise. Marquand came, along with Roger Vadim, some other French friends, and a few Hollywood pals like Quincy Jones. Yet, either out of maliciousness or inattention, Brando ignored his guests' comfort. "For example, he once brought Norty Brown, who was far better off staying in Beverly Hills than trying to enjoy an atoll," said Rittmeister. Perhaps accountant Brown had insisted on the stay in order to check up personally on how the hotel was doing. But his first night there, his *fare* was invaded with *no-nos*. He went to Brando the following morning.

"I must get out of here," he said.

"Sorry," said Brando. "I don't have a plane."

Whether this was payback for Brown's insistence on seeing the hotel, Rittmeister couldn't be sure, but he knew that in fact a plane was available and he guessed that Marlon was just "giving him a hard time, making that poor bugger suffer for a week."

Hotel Tetiaroa was still not attracting a crowd of tourists and in 1975, even Brando was conceding that it was not yet successful. While he wasn't calling it a "complete bust," the *National Tattler* noted, "those who travel in the right financial circle are calling it just that." It was estimated that Brando had poured $5 million into the project, but much of that, the *Tattler* snidely added, had been used "to make the island 'modern free'— without electricity and a host of other conveniences many have come to feel are necessities."

In April 1975 Marlon had signed on to make *Superman* for $3 million, making it explicit that he was taking the job simply for the money. That fall he also agreed to appear in Francis Ford Coppola's *Apocalypse Now* for $3.5 million—again, he said, because he needed the cash to fund his experiments. By then Judge had already left the island, and there was continuing deterioration of the facilities.

With the anticipated influx of new income, his visionary enthusiasm was revived and in October he summoned Stewart Brand and Jay Baldwin of *The Whole Earth Catalogue* to Mulholland to discuss establishing a reliable, nonpolluting energy source.

A graduate of Stanford with a degree in biology, Brand was a well-known player in the sixties counterculture, having been one of Ken Kesey's Merry Pranksters and also the compiler of the original *Whole Earth Catalogue* in 1968, which was intended to help kindred spirits to live independent of the establishment, defy the status quo, and try to preserve the planet. A design and alternative-energy specialist, in previous years Baldwin had worked with Buckminster Fuller.

"We had no intention of asking for money," said Baldwin, referring to Brando's phone call summoning him and Brand to Los Angeles. "It was a chance for an adventure, and a gold mine of possible information and future articles." Over lunch Brando elaborated his ambitions for Tetiaroa and tape-recorded the dialogue. He now had a new idea for raising more money—a television series about Tetiaroa and ecological advancements. As a way to frame the TV project, the actor envisioned a "farce, fun and games" on the atoll to hype viewer interest.

As Brando explained it, he and his friend, producer George Englund, had come up with the idea of a "game show format" in which contestants would win trips to "Marlon Brando's honeymoon island in the South Pacific." Then they would film skits of the visit there, with farcical episodes that would simultaneously explain serious ecological innovations. As an example he described a proposed scene in which the contestant-visitor to the island would be told that toilets there were "flushed with oil" and that one had to "flush it just right because it was a delicate operation." But the contestant would push the wrong button, Brando narrated, "and we have compression valves that open up and a sound like whale flatulence comes out and takes the roof off in the flushing." Then the audience would be told that in fact ecologically innovative toilets are flushed with oil, and the serious message would be conveyed.

"It's such a pleasure to me to figure out a way to make a pencil sharpener more efficient," Brando went on. "I could spend a whole afternoon doing that. And then I just get overwhelmed. I get calls from Indian people I know. They say, 'Marlon, I need $25,000. Six guys got shot, ten are in jail.' You just can't reach over and switch the world off. It'd be nice if you [could] do it, but it just keeps invading you. You've got to deal with the large issues."

After several hours of conversation ranging from methane generators to perpetual motion machines, Marlon suddenly paused.

"God, you've never seen any place like it," he exclaimed. "You've got to come. What are you doing tomorrow? I'll have Alice get you tickets and I'll meet you there."

It was an impetuous but perfectly serious suggestion. Brand and Baldwin found themselves flying back to San Francisco to pick up their passports, then returning to the airport to catch the next plane to Tahiti. "I didn't even have a damn suitcase with me," Baldwin said.

After ten hours on the plane Brand and Baldwin arrived in Papeete expecting to meet Brando, who was supposed to have left directly from L.A. Instead, an elegant Frenchwoman introduced herself as the manager of Tetiaroa's flight office, and advised them that the actor had been delayed. She escorted them to a small private plane that was to fly them to the island, adding that Brando would be on the next flight.

The trip from Papeete to Tetiaroa took about twenty minutes, and when they reached the atoll, the pilot buzzed the landing area to alert workers to clear the strip of fallen coconut shells. When they circled the island, Baldwin realized that the narrow airstrip began and ended at the water's edge on either side of the narrow *motu* and was about a hundred yards shorter than he thought safe.

"Everything is fine, *monsieur*," the pilot reassured him. "I land here all the time."

The pilot set them down exactly between the trees, and applying the brakes instantly, he brought them to a hard stop, with the plane's nose hanging out over the water. When they stepped onto the coral runway, they were met by "a tall, beautiful Polynesian woman," recalled Baldwin. "She introduced herself as Tarita and then disappeared."

They were told that she was "one of Marlon's wives," and they didn't see her again until they had lunch in the dining room, where she sat apart from them at a table with other women.

It wasn't until six days later that Brando arrived, full of abject apologies; he then proceeded to give Brand and Baldwin their first tour. As they followed him around the facilities, he explained that he had had a famous architect design the hotel and the bungalows.

"What do you think?" he repeatedly asked. "Isn't this great?"

While struck by the natural beauty of the atoll, neither man was particularly impressed with the *fares,* which included such recent compromises as cement floors and chicken wire covering the thatched roofs to hold the uncooperative palm fronds in place. "It was awful-looking," said Baldwin, "but I suppose practical, since Marlon no longer wanted to go with the natural cycle of replacing the roof every year after the annual typhoon season."

As they continued on their walk, Brand and Baldwin became aware of Marlon's physical discomfort. He seemed short of breath at every incline, and after climbing the ten-foot ladder to demonstrate the solar collector he had installed on the beach, he was breathing even more heavily.

"I'm whuffing like a walrus," he conceded with a smile.

He told them that he had just made *The Missouri Breaks* and had been so overweight during the shoot that he had decided to wear a dress. "He said it like a joke," recalled Baldwin. "It was, 'Ha-ha-ha, I did these scenes in drag because I couldn't lose weight fast enough and I didn't want to ruin my hunk reputation. Ha-ha-ha.' "

For all his attempts to joke about it, the guests soon realized that their host's weight and health were a real issue for him. "He fussed a lot about his health," Baldwin added. "He was always talking about the pills he was taking and the doctors he was seeing."

Nevertheless, much of their conversation seemed to revolve around food. At one point Brando stopped during their walk on the beach.

"You like Mounds bars," he asked.

"Sure," they replied.

"Have you ever tried a real one?"

"What are you talking about?" Baldwin asked.

In response Brando called to a Tahitian boy and pointed up into the palm. The kid shimmied up into the tree and brought down a coconut. Brando cut open the shell, then produced a piece of raw chocolate, melted it in the sun, and stirred it into the coconut's center.

Before lunch they toured the kitchen, and Brando asked them, "Do you like bread?" Once again they replied, "Sure," and Brando instructed one of the women to make them a fresh *baguette,* which she brought to their table. Baldwin conceded that the food was wonderful: "The fish was so fresh, I suppose they had just gone out and batted it on the head five minutes before. Red snapper, and cut so thin you could read newsprint through it. No gourmet would have complained."

Over lunch Brando continued to explain his utopian vision for Tetiaroa. While Baldwin felt his host was sincere, he was also aware of his concomitant naïveté. "He was really emphatic that he was going to 'do it right, by God!' " recalled Baldwin. "It was as if he wanted to make the island into a symbol of righteousness in a world that is generally fucked."

After a few more days of exploring the island, a badly sunburned Brand departed, but at Marlon's request, Baldwin stayed to consult with him further. Baldwin took altitude, temperature, and wind measurements and noted the plants and animals on the island. He made detailed notes as Brando kept asking, "What should I do?"

Baldwin had no ready-made, quick answer. Brando, though, continued to prod him. "Look, I can have a whole bunch of those solar things sent out here right away," he told the hip futurist, impatient for action.

"Hold on, Marlon," Baldwin said. "It isn't so simple."

One day Baldwin came upon the Caterpillar tractor that Brando and Judge had brought over to the island on the navy landing craft. It was sitting unused and in the moist tropical air, it had practically rusted away. "It was almost a pile of crumbs," said Baldwin. "So every time he brought up another idea, I kept telling him, 'Marlon, Marlon, *corrosion.*' So he started joking, 'You come here and I'll appoint you minister of corrosion!' "

The joke had a serious side, however. "I think he knew that he couldn't handle all the forces of nature in order to maintain the island," added Baldwin. "So he needed to find someone who could. He was hoping I might know someone, or even be that person. But it was only when all the equipment he'd brought in for the hotel, like heaters, generators, diesel tanks, began to fall to ruin that he became aware of the problem."

As the two continued their discussions, Baldwin sensed not only Brando's romantic naïveté but also an abiding sadness. One morning they started out on a walk together to look at coconut crabs. He had told Baldwin they were beautiful but that they were radioactive as a result of the French nuclear bomb tests in the South Pacific. (This had become one of his principal concerns in the last several years, and he had even banned the serving of lobster at the hotel because he was sure it was radioactive—just as he had earlier told Brand and Baldwin that he had milk from Tahitian cows tested for radioactivity, too.) As they started toward the lagoon, Brando excused himself.

"You don't need a guide every minute," he said. "Go look at the crabs and I'll meet you at noon."

On the way back, Baldwin spotted Brando, sitting on the beach alone. "I was about to call out to him," said Baldwin, "but then I saw that he was staring out over the water and looked as if he were about to cry."

In the distance, Baldwin saw an incredible sea bird and now, approaching the actor, he hoped that his enthusiastic description of the way the creature was building its nest would spark his enthusiasm.

"Yes, isn't it wonderful?" Brando began, for a moment starting to open up. But just as quickly he stopped himself, then adopted the formal, aloof pose of the innkeeper. "I notice you're eating a lot of bread at breakfast," he prattled. "You really like that bread, don't you? Here, let me get you some more bread."

As Baldwin's stay drew to an end, he became aware of Marlon's primary dilemma: He seemed unable to recognize that by keeping the hotel small, "primitive," and ecologically correct, it had no real financial future. "It wasn't making money because it wasn't flashy enough," said Baldwin. "It didn't have the pool or the shuffleboard or the golf or the horses or the speedboats that people expect as the luxuries of the big resorts. By its very nature, a resort that would be profitable was going to wreck the island."

Over the next several months Baldwin would have to dampen Brando's enthusiasm for each new fad or each new attempt to woo him to another kind of solar or wind equipment. "I was Marlon's debunker of alternative-energy hype," he added. "He kept calling me. I think I saved him from wasting a horrendous amount of money."

By the spring of 1976, the lack of maintenance had given way to the ravages of nature. The facilities had been so damaged by the latest typhoon season that Rittmeister was told to close the hotel for three months for renovations. It was anticipated that the necessary work would not be completed until July.

At this time, surprisingly enough, Brando gave several interviews. In the first, published in a French film magazine, he announced, "I, too, have had homosexual experiences, and I am not ashamed. Homosexuality is so much in fashion, it no longer makes news." His admission, however, made headlines.

The second interview, conducted on Tetiaroa, was oddly enough for his old nemesis, *Time* magazine. Brando was cooperating with the press to publicize the May 1976 opening of *The Missouri Breaks,* but he required anyone who wished to speak to him to fly the 10,000 miles to his island.

For most of the interview, he concentrated on his two usual themes: Tetiaroa and the American Indians, yet he focused less on his ecology experiments than on providing a future for his children, a subject that seemed to preoccupy him even more than in the past. "I am convinced the world is doomed," he said. "The end is near. I wanted a place where my family and I could be self-sufficient and survive." It was one of the first times that Brando had described the island as a form of bomb shelter, but with his many allusions to French nuclear testing in Polynesia, the *Time* reporter described Brando's sense of the "abysmal state of the human condition" as an "obsession."

In early 1976, Rittmeister departed, having come to the end of his two-year contract. "It was by mutual consent," he claimed, although he conceded that the "accumulation" of problems leading to his departure had to do with the ideas for Tetiaroa's development. Yet, later that summer, Brando's attention was more focused on losing weight than on Tetiaroa. In signing with Francis Ford Coppola to appear in *Apocalypse Now,* he had agreed to shed his excess pounds before going in front of the cameras. Coppola's shooting schedule in the Philippines had been disrupted by typhoons, but he had now resumed filming. Brando was notified that he would be needed in late August, and after returning to Los Angeles from the FBI murder trial in Cedar Rapids, he checked himself into St. John's Hospital. Pat Quinn, recruited to work for him part-time, found that beyond her secretarial and research duties, she was expected to help Alice Marchak squeeze gallons of vegetable and fruit juices to supplement the hospital's weight loss diet.

Quinn also became aware of Marlon's increasing ambivalence toward the Indian movement. One day the two women heard the gate buzzer sound, announcing an unexpected visitor. Marchak answered it in her office, and then went to Quinn.

"It's Dennis Banks," she said. "He and his wife and baby are down there and want to stay tonight. I don't want them here—the dirty diapers, the apple cores stuffed behind pillows. Those Indians are a mess."

"I'm not going to turn them away," Quinn replied.

Marchak wheeled from the room, but a few minutes later she called Quinn to the phone to speak to Brando, whom she had reached in his room at the hospital.

Marlon issued instructions: "Tell Dennis and his wife that I'm out of town and you're not allowed to let them in."

Ten days later Marlon checked himself out of the hospital, but just before leaving for the Philippines, he asked Quinn to house-sit.

"I've kicked Christian out of the house," he told her, adding that he had finally laid down the law because the teenager was still staying out all hours and not getting up until late in the morning. "I don't want you to let him come here while I'm away."

Quinn was shocked. She was fond of Christian and felt this was a strange way to handle him, since it meant that he would be at even more loose ends. She moved into the house with her two children, Marlon left for *Apocalypse,* and she promptly disobeyed his instructions. "I just didn't have the heart to keep Christian out," she said. "I let him come up in the evening, but he still refused to sleep there." Instead, he crashed at friends'—usually either at Steve Hunio's or at the home of his on-and-off girlfriend and childhood playmate, Mary McKenna, whose mother still welcomed him.

Apocalypse Now

Apocalypse Now had originally been conceived by screenwriter John Milius in 1969 as both an adaptation of Conrad's *Heart of Darkness* and a prowar testament to the career of Robert Rheault, a Green Beret officer in charge of Special Forces who had been forced to resign from the army for executing a double agent. But then Coppola entered the picture. "I've got to do this movie," he told Milius. "I consider it the most important picture I will ever make. If I die making it, you'll take it over. If you die, George Lucas will take over." Having worked out a deal with United Artists, he then spent almost all of 1975 revising its basic themes and trying to find a cast.

Coppola had decided that the movie should have an antiwar motif and changed the focus from Rheault (renamed Kilgore in the final script and played by Robert Duvall) to Kurtz, a man so consumed by his thirst for power that he withdraws and establishes his own mini-kingdom in the jungle. The theme of battling against the civilized world might well have appealed to Brando; but the actor didn't return his calls, and he had his attorney tell the director that he wasn't interested.

Coppola spent several months trying to cast the key roles of Kurtz and Willard, the army officer assigned to track Kurtz and "terminate him with extreme prejudice." The prospect of seventeen weeks of jungle shooting was making the Willard role unappealing to any number of actors—even those who claimed to love the script. Redford, Nicholson, and Caan all took a pass. Steve McQueen wanted $3 million to play Willard, then said he'd play the much smaller role of Kurtz for the same price (Coppola went looking elsewhere). When Pacino turned down the Willard role, too, Coppola, in a rage of frustration, threw his five Oscars out the window of his San Francisco town house (only one survived). Finally, Harvey Keitel agreed to do it.

In the midst of the casting shuffle, Norman Garey contacted Coppola again and informed him that Marlon would consider the role. In early February 1976, Brando's contract was finalized—as was his habit now, he drove a hard bargain. He was to receive $3.5 million for four weeks on location. The figure was even higher than what McQueen had demanded, and furthermore, Brando had won Coppola's concession that his summer on Tahiti with his children would not be interrupted. In addition to losing weight, he was asked to read *Heart of Darkness* to get a sense of the script's underlying themes and his character, the American colonel who establishes his own montagnard army across the Cambodian border and becomes a great white god to his native followers.

After his experience with Paramount on *The Godfather,* Coppola was also determined to retain as much creative control as possible. His team at his production company, American Zoetrope, had raised $8 million by pre-selling the distribution rights abroad to add to the $7.5 million from United Artists. With the film budgeted at $12 to $14 million, production costs seemed to be covered. The only hitch was that while Coppola retained ownership and control, he would also assume full financial responsibility in the event the film went over budget, an arrangement that left him in an extremely vulnerable position.

The shoot had begun on March 20, 1976, on location in Baler, a six-hour drive from Manila on rough country roads. Within the first week, Coppola, dissatisfied with the early rushes, fired Harvey Keitel and hired Martin Sheen, who finally did not arrive in the Philippines until May 1.

Throughout the spring the problems continued. Having built a facsimile Vietnamese village in Baler, Coppola rented helicopters from President Ferdinand Marcos's air force, but in the middle of crucial scenes, the Philippine government found it necessary to call them away to fight insurgents in the country's ongoing civil war. Costs were rising, too, as the cast and crew, including Coppola himself, continued to spend money for their private luxuries while ignoring "petty" details. The director, for example, had rented a house in the wealthiest section of Manila for himself and his family, as well as his San Francisco entourage. When cinematographer Vittorio Storaro's crew insisted on pasta imported from Italy, a tax of $8,000 was mistakenly levied by Philippine customs and the management of the film paid the bill without batting an eye.

Similarly, equipment, props, and stuntmen's asbestos safety suits were lost when special-effects fires spread and incinerated storage sheds. The humid heat was stifling, sometimes so bad that people fainted, including Sheen. Even worse, Coppola had begun filming in the middle of the Philippines' rainy season—against the advice of his mentor, Roger Corman. On May 25, 1976, a typhoon swept the islands, flattening the recently constructed sets in the coastal town of Iba. Coppola closed down the production for six weeks while the sets were built at their next location, Pagsanjan. There he was greeted with the news that Zoetrope's accountants reckoned that the production had already blown $7 million and was $3 million over budget. Given Coppola's personal liability, the Philippine nightmare was nearly bankrupting him—and he was literally losing sleep over the script, feeling that he didn't know where the story was going or how it should end.

Coppola returned to his home in Napa and called Brando several times before he got down to what had been on his mind all along—namely, money. Coppola was pushed to the limit. The film's overrun and the promise of more delays made it imperative that Brando agree to a cut in salary in exchange for points. Never forgetting his huge loss when he sold back his *Godfather* points, Brando said that for his good friend he would be glad to accept $1 million for five weeks' work instead of $3.5 million for four weeks—as long as he was given points. In exchange, good friend Coppola coughed up a whopping 11.3 percent of *Apocalypse*'s adjusted gross profits. In addition, if the adjusted gross surpassed $8.8 million, Brando would stand to make 34 cents for each and every $6 ticket sold. Coppola had no alternative but to accept these extraordinary terms. (When there were further delays to resuming location work, good friend Brando, however, threatened to take the money and run, arguing that the postponed shooting date was in violation of his contract. With a few more frantic phone calls, Coppola managed to persuade Brando to show up on location at the end of August.)

With that settled, the two of them went on to discuss Brando's character. Coppola insisted the ending should grow out of the Kurtz portrayed in *Heart of Darkness,* and suggested that Brando also take a look at T. S. Eliot's bleak poem "The Wasteland." Brando agreed that he perceived Kurtz in the same way, and he reassured Coppola that having just read the novel, he was getting deeper into his character.

Back in the Philippines, members of the cast and crew soon became aware that Coppola was making up his movie as he went along. Word started to get back to Hollywood that many of the crew were turning to drugs—usually grass, but also cocaine, speed, and readily available, over-the-counter quaaludes. Late-night partying was routine as well. Into this confused situation came Brando early in the morning on August 31, 1976.

The director was counting on the actor's talent to fill in many of the details of Kurtz's character as well as the concluding scenes of the film, decisions he was still wrestling with. What he hadn't counted on was Brando's elephantine proportions: He weighed over 250 pounds.

From the beginning, Coppola and the actor disagreed about how to handle the weight. Brando wanted to shoot scenes in ways that would camouflage his obesity; Coppola was interested in exploiting it, presenting the Kurtz character as overindulgent and eating all the time. Then the two men compromised: They would shoot the scenes as though Brando were six foot five, thereby creating a character of mythic proportions.

One afternoon Marlon emerged from his dressing room, full of new ideas about his character, and explained to Coppola his latest conception of the role.

"I think he should be more like Kurtz in the book."

"That's what I've been trying to tell you," Coppola replied. "Don't you remember last spring, before you took the part, when you read *Heart of Darkness,* and we talked."

"I lied," said Marlon. "I never read it."

Given the short duration that Brando was contracted to be on the set, Coppola decided to start filming the final scenes. Even though script problems still weren't solved, he was hoping that the actor's talent for improvisation would provide the answers. But on the morning of Brando's first scenes, when he was due on the set at eight, he didn't show. When he finally arrived at ten, he wanted another script discussion. Coppola followed him into his houseboat dressing room, where they remained until seven that evening, discussing "motivation," with Brando repeatedly querying his character's every action, like "Why did he go up the river? Why there?"

"It was laughable," said Philip Rhodes, who was on the scene to do makeup and accompanied Brando to script conferences. "We sat in that houseboat for hours in that tropical heat trying to figure out his part. I was amazed he didn't walk out, which he could have done, since Coppola wasn't shooting him according to the schedule in the contract."

Brando, however, tolerated the delay and further discussions ensued. A few days later, still with no ending and no footage in the can, he even threw a huge party at his hilltop resort, as if to reassure the cast and crew that he was Mr. Good Guy. Four hundred people attended, including the Ifugaos natives who served as extras and whose priests had held an all-night ceremony on the set. (At one point the priests chanted, "Coppola, Coppola, Coppola," and the next morning they ritually killed pigs and a carabao.) There were disco singers, magic acts, acrobats, and a finale of fireworks set off by the film's special-effects crew. Like the phantom Kurtz, Marlon was nowhere to be seen.

Brando and Coppola continued to hold nightly script conferences. The director envisioned Kurtz as a hulking wildman, a Gauguin-like jungle recluse gone to seed and madness. The actor saw the character as a Daniel Berrigan type, dressed in black Vietcong pajamas and expressing guilt over the war. "Hey, Marlon," Coppola objected, "I may not know everything about this movie, but one thing I know it's not about is *our guilt!*"

After many hours Brando came up with a new idea: He would shave his head. The goal was to find the symbolic key both men were looking for, but in the light of day, Kurtz with a bald head did not alleviate the problems. The next morning on location Brando was late again because Coppola hadn't been able to write a scene that satisfied him.

The cinematographer, Vittorio Storaro, saved the day by creating a strange aura of light and smoke inside the ruined temple where Brando's scene was to be shot. The star was prevailed upon to give it a go by improvising. Coppola was revived by the talent of his actor, and the mere inspiration of actually filming him after three weeks of endless conversation seemed to lift his spirits and suggest ways to move from one scene to another.

But the ending was still unresolved, and Coppola summoned Dennis Jakob from California to help him work out the ending. Jakob was Coppola's self-described naysayer, whose "brain could be picked whenever Francis was in trouble." Jakob arrived in Pagsanjan bearing vegetables and fruit from Napa as well as definite ideas about what his boss should do with the final scenes. "By the time I got there he had run out of emotional gas," said Jakob. "The typhoon killed him; he was taking dope and his mind was like jelly.

"I thought Francis was in way over his depth," Jakob continued.

"He'd decided to do *Apocalypse* almost on a dare. About a year before his older brother had called him a 'hack' in the middle of an argument, so he almost had to do this movie to prove that he really was an artist."

The first question Coppola asked Jakob was whether Kurtz should die in the end.

"He has to die," was the intellectual's immediate response.

"Why?" asked Coppola.

Jakob explained that he interpreted Conrad's story as a version of "The Fisher King," in which the king is killed every year in order that crops will grow. Realizing that he needed to give Coppola a reason to believe in a death scene, he thrust at him a copy of *The Golden Bough*, Frazier's compendium of myths, as well as *From Ritual To Romance*, T. S. Eliot's acknowledged source for "The Wasteland."

Jakob met with Coppola and Brando for hours, immersing them in discussions of the myths to justify why Kurtz had to die. It was exactly the kind of rambling, high-minded discursiveness that Brando loved. The newly arrived script doctor wasn't all that convinced that improvisation was the way to do it. "Initially I found Coppola's reliance on Brando as a writer dubious," Jakob said. "But then I understood that it was necessary for Brando himself to create the script because Coppola was just floating. Brando was in terrible shape physically, very overweight, but his mind was active and alert."

Coppola then turned the scene over to Brando's spontaneity. During the improvs, Marlon did invent some extraordinary lines, many of which were not included in the final cut. Years later the film's soundman, Jack Jacobsen, played a tape recording of Brando's full improvised speech for Meade Roberts, Tennessee Williams's coscreenwriter on *The Fugitive Kind*. "It was eighteen minutes long, from which only about two minutes were included in the final cut," Roberts recalled. "Some of it was incoherent, but I thought most of it brilliant. You could hear how hard Marlon was trying, and at the end, Marlon said, 'Francis, I've gone as far as I can go. If you need more, you can get another actor.' "

In the scene that was eventually used, Kurtz is hacked to pieces by Martin Sheen's Willard, his death juxtaposed with the agonizingly slow, chop-by-chop ritual slaughter of a bellowing bull. What seemed to make the scene work was not Marlon's brilliant though random associations, but the surrounding violence and gore. While the underlying theme was meant to be fertility renewed by death, Brando's final words heightened the sense of doom and foreboding. Just as in *Last Tango,* when Bertolucci's psychological probing had unleashed something in him, here he seemed to release the pessimism and loathing that had been building inside him for months, not only about himself but the human condition in general. Kurtz's famous last words, "The horror, the horror," were a fitting coda— the theme for *Apocalypse,* the theme for the production problems, and finally the capstone to Brando's bleak vision of the future.

Brando finished his work on October 8, 1976, and departed for Tahiti. It wouldn't be until mid-May of 1977 that *Apocalypse* finally wrapped after 238 days of shooting. When the dust cleared, the picture had cost nearly $27 million, and Coppola needed another $10 million for post-production. Two more years would pass before a "work print" of *Apocalypse Now,* distilled from 1.5 million feet of film, was shown at the Cannes Festival where it shared the grand prize with Volker Schlöndorff's *The Tin Drum.*

When the movie opened officially in the United States in August 1979, critics found it difficult to separate the work from the accumulated scuttlebutt, and while a good number of reviews were fair to positive, many complained about the movie's confused theme and weak ending. Vincent Canby, in his *New York Times* review, praised the film's evocation of the disastrous and senseless Vietnam War, but concluded that it suffered from "delusions of grandeur" while Brando's performance was filled with "foolish pretensions." The usually hip David Denby of *New York* magazine was openly dismayed by Marlon's overripe performance: "This man has become so ponderous, so absurdly imposing, that he's virtually unusable. How can anyone *act* with him? The only thing you can do is render him homage."

Brando's toughest review came from Tennessee Williams. As he exited a New York screening of the film, a friend asked him what he thought of Brando's $3.5 million fee for the role. "Gee, I don't know," responded Tennessee. "I think they paid him by the pound."

For all the rumors of wild spending and directorial ego, *Apocalypse* actually made money; the tally for domestic rentals exceeded $40 million, and worldwide revenues topped $100 million. "I know," laughed Coppola, "because we pay Brando on percentage!" Coppola's laughter would eventually dissolve to tears when Brando decided that his "good friend" wasn't paying him enough.

• • •

With all the publicity about the high salary Brando was receiving for what many people regarded as a cameo role, the actor found himself having to justify his salary demands. "I have a right to the money I get," he said. "First of all, because I'm not forcing anyone to give it to me. Secondly, I've gained a lot of experience over the years and I don't need the same kind of coaching a newcomer does—I use my rage, my entire catalog of human emotions." But most of all he defended himself by insisting that the money he was paid would go to good causes: both the scientific experiments on Tetiaroa and the development of a "Roots"-like television miniseries about the Indians—yet another version of his much heralded "Indian movie" now that the Wounded Knee project had all but disappeared.

Actually, Brando was doing little about either his atoll projects or the Indian pic. Despite his renewed interest and the Brand-Baldwin visit, he hadn't initiated any further ecological endeavors and the facilities were rapidly deteriorating. When he returned to the atoll, he spent most of his time alone, retreating to his private *fare* to read and play his drums. Late at night, he stayed up talking on his ham radio to strangers either on other islands or on ships at sea. Murmuring into his microphone beneath a canopy of mosquite netting, he usually identified himself as "Mike," "Martine," or "Martin Bumby," and further disguised himself with a variety of masterly accents, usually French and German but also Japanese.

Brando had become obsessed with radio communication the previous year. (When French filmmaker Roger Vadim, Brando's old friend from Paris days, would visit the actor on Tetiaroa, he commented, "All he does now is play with his ham radio.") Most amateur operators used portable equipment on the islands, but Brando's was "top of the line," a permanent installation with each of the radio's dials carefully labeled with Dymo marker strips, providing him with detailed instructions on how to use it. This was necessary because Marlon seemed to have a difficult time remembering how to broadcast and receive and had problems passing his ham licensing test as well. He explored the possibility of getting a license in Panama through a friend of Pat Quinn, a congresswoman there, but in 1977, he still hadn't become "official." Nevertheless, that January, his signal from Tetiaroa was picked up by four American tourists.

Brothers Peter and Mike Metzger and their friend Bradley Collins and his sister were vacationing in Moaréa. One evening they were manning their radio when they heard a voice identifying himself as "Martine," call letters "FO Zero MB."

"Where are you calling from?" Peter Metzger asked.

"Onetahi Atoll," said Martine.

They exchanged a few remarks, with Metzger explaining that he was on Mooréa and asking the other's address. The man seemed clipped and terse, as if he were unwilling to reply to questions. He spoke in a strange combination of accents: first a little French, then a little German.

"You seem to have a slight accent," said Metzger. "Where are you from?"

"I'm from all over," the voice replied wearily.

"You sound like you come from the States."

"I'm from Omaha."

As their conversation continued for a few more minutes, Metzger was again struck by the omission of standard ham's terminology and protocols that would confirm an operator as knowledgeable. He also seemed suspicious and was in a rush to sign off. Once he did, Metzger entered the call in his log: "Martine, FO zero MB." Then he remarked to his brother and friend, "That guy I was just talking to was bogus. I bet he's a bootlegger."

An evening or two later they were in the bar at Mooréa's Club Med when a young man introduced himself to the group as Marty Asinof. Metzger soon mentioned his talk with Martine.

"Oh, that's my uncle," Asinof said. "He's a ham around here."

"Really? Who is he?" asked Peter Metzger.

"It's Marlon Brando," he replied, "He doesn't like people to know who he really is or where he lives."

Collins then mentioned that he would very much like to see Tetiaroa and since he was a pilot he could fly out.

"I'll give you a story that will be like a password to get you in," volunteered Asinof. "That way Marlon will know that you're a friend of mine and could only have gotten this from me. His nickname is 'Bud,' and the story is that a cow shat on his shoes before a school dance at the age of fourteen."

A few days later Collins rented a small plane and made the twenty-minute flight to Tetiaroa. As he approached the landing strip, he saw a woman waving at him frantically. When he set the plane down and climbed out, she introduced herself as Reiko Sato, the manager of Tetiaroa. She needed help, she explained. Brando had departed several days before and had forgotten to order supplies. This was not uncommon, the woman said, but now she was running out of food and neither had she been able to get the radio to work.

She took Collins to Brando's bungalow to show him the radio. Collins immediately discovered that the problem was simple—the radio was unplugged. Just as revealing was the refrigerator in the bungalow—it had a massive chain around it and was padlocked closed. At Reiko's invitation Collins stayed the night and the following morning he flew her to Papeete.

Brando was next scheduled to appear in *Superman* for another huge salary. Oddly enough, he had been brought the project by his old girlfriend Marie Cui. She was now the live-in aide for the aging Hollywood agent Kurt Frings, and through him she had met the father-and-son team of European filmmakers Alexander and Ilya Salkind. The Salkinds had made a splash with their *Musketeer* movies and were now trying to go big time in Hollywood. "Cui factored the *Superman* project for them and got it to Marlon," confirmed one of the actor's friends. "But at the time he wasn't aware that she was receiving $30,000 for putting the Salkinds in touch with him. When he found out, it pissed him off that she had made money off of him. Still, he agreed to do the movie."

When Brando first signed on, he had bragged to the Indians then visiting him at Mulholland that he had just made $3 million. In fact, the deal that Norman Garey finally cut in December 1976 was worth much more. For twelve days' filming in the two *Superman* movies (they were to be shot simultaneously), he was to receive $3.7 million, plus 11.3 percent of domestic and 5.65 percent of foreign grosses, with a minimum guarantee of $1.7 million.

Due on the set of *Superman* at London's Shepperton Studios on March 23, 1977, Marlon arrived a week early, hoping to raise money for a proposed thirteen-part "Roots"-type series on Indians. He had also intentionally delayed his scheduled flight by one day to avoid dealing with the studio executives' official welcoming committee.

Appearing on the set for his first day of work, he was in a foul mood, however, swathed in sweaters and scarves, and complaining about flu and jet lag. Veteran director Richard Donner, who had made his name and fortune with *The Omen,* did not know quite what to expect from the eccentric star. Brando had already tweaked him by suggesting that his costumed character, Jor-El, looked "like a bagel" and by relaying the message that he expected to play Jor-El as a "green suitcase." Already Donner had phoned Coppola to ask for insight into Brando's personality; Jay Kanter had told him Brando didn't like to work, and Coppola seconded this assessment.

Nevertheless, that first day Brando seemed willing to cooperate. Ready to rehearse his opening scene, he suggested to Donner that they roll the cameras during the rehearsal. "Who knows?" he said. "We might get lucky."

Costumed in a long, flowing robe that effectively hid his bulk, he looked like a pagan priest, and his hair was left silver and slightly long, much like a stentorian southern senator. He took his marks and began his opening monologue in which he was to lament having to send his infant son to earth. While camping it up as Superman's father might have been appropriate, he chose to play it straight, and delivered the Polonius-like adages much the way a Shakespearean actor might soliloquize. "When he finished, there was stunned, respectful silence," said Donner. "The first take became the one that was in the picture."

Over the next twelve days, stories spread in the British tabloids that Brando was temperamental, vain, and eccentric, although these negative reports probably had more to do with indignation at his salary than with his actual behavior on the set. Donner insisted that the actor hadn't been difficult, just ill with flu, and had completed his scenes nearly on schedule. "In fact, Brando was wonderful," confirmed Tom Mankiewicz, who had been called in as "creative consultant" to doctor the script. "By the time we were finished we had more than an hour of usable footage for both [*Superman I* and *II*]."

Two days into the shoot, Brando was still feeling sick and asked to go home early. Donner nearly had a heart attack, having counted every minute of the tight, twelve-day schedule that Brando had insisted on. "I had even been figuring out what it cost every time he went to the bathroom," the director explained. "But I said the only thing I could say: 'You're Marlon Brando. How can I stop you?' "

Brando replied, "Tell you what, I'll give you an extra day. How about that?"

Brando was offering to do for free what would ordinarily have cost $250,000, and Donner was reassured that he would get everything he needed for the actor's scenes. "So I sent him home happily," he recalled.

The production would be besieged by later troubles, but these were not Brando's responsibility. While continuing to note Brando's income for his brief appearance in *Superman,* critics actually praised his performance when the movie was released on December 15, 1978. Still, Andrew Sarris got it right when he likened his "solemn intonations" to "an Old Vic actor compelled to declaim in a Khyber Pass movie."

Superman was an immediate blockbuster at the box office, grossing $64,423,042 in just thirty-three days. But Brando, Donner, and the original scriptwriter, Mario Puzo, were all unhappy, charging that the Salkinds were cheating them out of their expected percentages of the profits. Just two days after the movie's opening, Brando filed suit for $50 million. He also petitioned the Los Angeles Superior Court for an injunction against Warners' distribution of the film or the use of his "name, acts, poses, appearances, performances, image, likeness, voice and/or other personal attributes." On December 26, the court refused to issue a temporary restraining order, concluding that there was no evidence of injury. Nevertheless, Norman Garey would pursue the case for the next several years. The Salkinds, meanwhile, removed Donner as director of *Superman II,* replacing him with British director Richard Lester, and excised all of Brando's scenes from the sequel.

After the release of *Superman* and *Apocalypse Now,* Jack Swan, a Libertyville friend, asked Fran Loving why her brother was taking so much money for such brief appearances on the screen. She quipped, "Well, he had better make a lot of money because he's supporting half the South Pacific."

But to Marlon it was no joke. Returning to Tetiaroa from the *Superman* shoot, he told reporters that among his ecological projects, he had a new scheme of scooping algae out of the lagoon and processing it into a protein supplement to feed the hungry of the Third World. He had also said that the income from *Superman* would allow him to take two years off to concentrate full-time on Tetiaroa and his Indian miniseries. But only a few months later he was evidently feeling the need for more cash. In September 1977 it was announced that he had signed to do another film for a hefty paycheck: *The Formula* (originally called *Opium*). "I didn't have any money," he explained, "and I did it for the bucks. Ten days for three million bucks." Granted, there would be a long delay before *The Formula* would go into production; still, it was astounding that within a half-year of shooting *Superman,* Brando was complaining that he needed another paycheck. As several people wondered aloud, where was all the money going?

Back in Los Angeles in the fall of 1977, his thoughts were again on family. Christian still seemed aimless and confused, and at one point Marlon suggested opening up a club or a coffeehouse for him to manage. "That was bandied about for about fifteen minutes," said Christian's friend, Steve Hunio. "As usual, Christian just pushed Marlon away."

Other ideas included Marlon and Christian learning how to weld. Brando's notion was that the skill would also be useful to him in keeping up with "corrosion" on Tetiaroa, and he enlisted his and Wally Cox's old friend, producer Everett Greenbaum, to give lessons. The actor soon dropped the project, although it did serve the purpose of getting his son interested in working with metal, such that Christian would later take a full-fledged course and get himself set up in business as a welder. Now, however, almost as a last resort, Christian fastened on the plan of going to the Pacific Northwest and working as a fisherman. Out from under Marlon's dominance and Anna's renewed demands for visitation, he could perhaps forge his own identity.

In addition to Marlon's continuing concerns about Christian, he again became involved in the career of his sister Jocelyn. Often she insisted that she would rather be a recluse than schlep downtown to read for a five-line part. She had repeatedly claimed that acting meant nothing to her, although her good friend Fred Sadoff once again perceived that her maternal, "Florence Nightingale" role in Marlon's circle was hardly fulfilling. In late 1977 Sadoff prevailed upon her to return to acting in his latest Actors Studio West Production—"a sort of *"Chorus Line* for actors," as he described it.

As a ploy to persuade Jocelyn to participate, Sadoff asked her to prepare a scene for him. He needed an episode, he told her, in which an actress was to be confronted with the question of what acting meant to her. "For dramatic purposes," he urged her, "I want you to ask, 'Am I happy in that little house in the Canyon, living as a recluse?' Then I want you to create an emotional moment and say, 'No, I care. I really care.' I want you to do that moment for me."

The scene that he cajoled her into presenting was included in the performance as the climactic moment that Sadoff had envisioned. Watching from the wings during the presentation, he spotted Marlon sitting up front. Jocelyn delivered the lines she had written, and when she proclaimed, "I care, I really care," she broke into tears. Brando was visibly moved. The monologue that Jocelyn delivered was so close to her own situation, so self-revelatory, that Marlon seemed to perceive something in their relationship that he had never realized before.

"The pain that went across his face at that moment," recalled Sadoff, "wasn't an actor's pain. He dissolved and his eyes really filled and he seemed to feel Jocelyn's anguish. When you're Marlon Brando, it's easy to say, 'I don't care,' and dismiss acting. When you're Jocelyn, or me, it's much harder to say, 'I don't care'—especially because as actors, we really *do* care. It was an absolutely cathartic moment. And I think Marlon felt a lot of guilt. He realized then and there that she had been hurt by his success."

After the performance Brando offered to bankroll Sadoff's show and put it on the road. That never came about, but the performance did seem to inspire Jocelyn to return to acting for a brief spell. Sadoff helped her find an agent, and in late November 1977 it was announced that she had been cast in director Stanley Donen's *Double Feature,* later released as *Movie Movie.*

After this film, however, Jocelyn did not pursue her acting career. Instead, she became interested in the therapeutic technique known as "dialoguing," and like her mother and grandmother, became much more involved as a lay healer, running workshops out of her home in a studio that Marlon built for her.

Brando himself spent the first half of 1978 at home in Los Angeles, doing little and lapsing into one of his depressed, withdrawn periods. One day out of the blue, he phoned Everett Greenbaum. "Why don't you ever call me?" Marlon asked plaintively. "Why don't I ever see you?"

Greenbaum countered, "I don't know if I'd be comfortable around anyone who makes a million dollars a day."

"Ah, come on," he replied. "You know that's Monopoly money, that I'm never going to see it. I'm the same guy I always was. I just happened to be walking down the street when a brick fell off a building and hit me and not some other person."

Once again, after making a quick trip to New Mexico with Jocelyn, Jill Banner, and Alice Marchak to see Maureen Stapleton perform in Beckett's *Waiting for Godot,* Brando went into retreat. He was still alternating between Yachiyo and Jill, demanding that each give him her full attention. Neither woman could lift his depression and only rarely could either one induce him to leave Mulholland. The few times he did go out he resorted to outlandish disguises. Bobby Sherman's wife was training Tennessee walking horses and entering them at an annual horse show. Jill persuaded Marlon to accompany her, but as they walked in to meet the Shermans, Bobby was astonished.

"Marlon had completely wrapped his head in gauze," Sherman recalled, "like Claude Rains in *The Invisible Man.* He had glasses on over the slits for his eyes, and he'd left only a tiny opening for his mouth. At first I didn't realize who it was, and then I recognized his height and weight, and my first reaction was, 'Oh, my God, what happened to you?'"

On the surface, it was another one of Marlon's pranks. He had asked Philip Rhodes to do the bandaging, and spent the afternoon watching others' reactions to him. Claiming to yearn for the days when people hadn't stared at him, his imitation of the Invisible Man all but guaranteed that people gaped. For the most part Marlon simply stared back, anonymous behind his mask, but sometimes he could hardly control his laughter. Then, to make the disguise even more ludicrous, he bought a hot dog, but the concoction was too large to fit through the small slit in the bandage, and soon the gauze was emblazoned with large smears of mustard and relish.

"It was really disgusting," said Sherman, "which made people stare at him harder. He really seemed to enjoy grossing them out. I think he was getting off on the fact that all these people were looking at him and weren't realizing that they were actually looking at Marlon Brando. Jill was upset," he added, "and thought he was being ridiculous."

During this time Brando had agreed to give an interview to *Playboy,* nominally in exchange for $50,000 Hugh Hefner contributed—or lent—to the bail fund for Russell Means. After months of negotiations and postponements, the actor and Lawrence Grobel, *Playboy*'s ace interviewer, spent ten days together on Tetiaroa in June 1978. With the tape running, he did everything possible to rewrite his recent past, including his "weeklong" stay with the Menominees and even his explanation that he had beaten the draft in World War II by being declared "psychoneurotic. . . . When I filled in their forms, under race I wrote 'human.' Under color I wrote, 'It varies.' " (In fact, he had been exempted because of his knee surgery, according to both Jocelyn and his family doctor.)

Another distortion was his assertion that the Wounded Knee film hadn't been made because there wasn't funding and Abby Mann's scripts were "really bad."

At dinner, Grobel realized that all of the tables in the dining room were empty. He and Marlon were joined only by Caroline Barrett and her eight-year-old daughter, Petra. A few days later Cheyenne and Teihotu arrived from Papeete to celebrate Father's Day. But besides the family there were no guests. As Grobel swatted at flies, Marlon insisted, "I could open this up for tourism and make a million dollars, but why spoil it?"

After a few more days of taping, Grobel returned to Los Angeles and was editing the interview when he received a phone call from Brando. The actor was nervous, it seemed, that Grobel might tell others what he had seen during his ten days on Tetiaroa. He was charming and affable, but the message was clear: "Friends don't talk about friends in public."

In addition, it seemed he had already flexed his muscle with the man at the top. The magazine's reliable and experienced fact-checker had noticed inconsistencies and problems with some of Brando's statements in the completed piece and queried his account of some of the AIM events. But soon she got instructions from on high. "The word was, 'Don't challenge Brando,' " she recalled. " 'I was told, 'Just go with what he says.' "

The Brando interview was published in January 1979. Grobel received a three-page, typewritten letter from Brando on January 18 in which the actor seemed to feel that Grobel or his editors had "arbitrarily" omitted remarks he had made that were "vital in respect to Indian matters." Conceding his "obsessive personality," he asked to have the complete transcript of their tapes so that he could use them for future articles. He then added a postscript: "Fuck the press. Unless you know them, and trust them and know them not to be at the mercy of the editors. It's the same old story."

Before flying to Tetiaroa to meet with Grobel, Brando had called Alex Haley and asked to do a bit part in "Roots: The Next Generation." He had declared that "the success of 'Roots' shows that the American people are ready to see a fresh perspective of themselves historically."

He told Haley that "he didn't want to play a nice guy," and then contacted Stan Margulies, the producer of the sequel. Margulies came up with the idea of his playing George Lincoln Rockwell, the American Nazi leader whom Haley had interviewed for *Playboy*. Rockwell had begun the interview by taking a gun from a desk drawer and placing it on top of the desk.

"Sounds good to me," Brando said after hearing this. "Get it to me as soon as you can."

Margulies and his writer, Ernie Kanowe, scripted a seven-page scene—a day's work in television production—and sent it to Mulholland. A few days later Brando asked Margulies up to the house to discuss it with him. He told the producer that he was interested in playing a character like Rockwell, a man with strong views that he did not share. He also liked the idea of being cast against type. "An actor only has so many shots. I don't want to look like the same box of Wheaties all the time."

He then stopped to analyze the dynamics of their discussion. He pointed out that for the past hour they had been interrupting one another, overlapping, veering off into another thought when an idea suddenly occurred to them. This, it turned out, was a prolonged rationalization for Brando's needing cue cards on the set. "If an actor knows his lines, he has to fight glibness," he declared, adding that he would place the cards wherever it was conceivable for him to look during the scene. "I might put my hands behind my head and lean back in the chair, so it would be good if I had my lines on the ceiling. I might search for something in the desk drawer, and if I have some lines in there, that would help."

Margulies found it strange that Brando was going on at such length to justify his request, but he agreed to the cue cards. He also explained that the scene would be shot in one day, on a date of the actor's choosing (within a certain time frame). Brando told him he was going to Tahiti but would be back for the scheduled shoot. At the end he referred him to Norman Garey to settle the salary question; he also recommended that Margulies read Hannah Arendt.

When contacted, Garey was unenthusiastic. "You really have me over a barrel," he told the producer. "Marlon really wants to do this, so there's really nothing to negotiate. Besides, it's television, and I know he's not going to get a million dollars. What can you do for me that makes it sound reasonable?"

Since Henry Fonda, who had a major role in the sequel, was to be paid $250,000, Margulies impulsively came up with the equivalent of one day's salary for Fonda.

"$25,000," he offered.

"Deal," Garey said, much to Margulies's astonishment.

Because Marlon had already told him that he would be giving the money "to charity," Margulies suggested that the check be made out directly to the American Indian Movement. Garey demurred and told him the check should be sent to him to disburse per Marlon's wishes. Garey added that he hoped that Margulies and ABC would keep Brando's salary quiet. "Obviously," Margulies later explained, "Norman did not want anyone to know that Marlon was so much as sticking his head out his door for only $25,000."

On a Saturday in December 1978 Brando reported for rehearsal to a deserted Warner Bros. soundstage to meet with Margulies, James Earl Jones, who was playing Haley, and the cameraman who would be shooting the scene the following Monday. They read the scene through once, then Brando raised an objection.

"Stan, there are things in the original interview that aren't in the scene," he said. "I think we're missing a bet by not having them."

"Like what?" asked Margulies.

Brando pulled out a copy of Haley's interview with Rockwell, in which he had underlined passages that he thought should be added.

"I'll include some of them," Margulies agreed, "but not all, because that would require two days of filming. It would also throw the rest of the schedule out of kilter."

"That's not a good reason," argued Brando. "Don't these additions enrich what we're doing?"

"Sure, and I'll use a few of them as long as the shoot is kept to one day. Two days is impossible."

They went back and forth: two days, one day, two days, one day. James Earl Jones and the cameraman sat watching this tennis match as Brando grew increasingly stern and unmovable.

"Look, Marlon," Margulies said, adopting a reasonable tone, "this isn't a motion picture. Even though you're Marlon Brando, they're not going to give me an extra day to shoot. I think the script is good. It has the essence of the scene, and after all, this was only a short, single episode in Haley's life."

Brando still refused to "give an inch," recalled Margulies, "not one inch. The confrontation was becoming unbearable, and I could hear the silence of the empty stage set roaring in my ears."

"I have to have two days to do this properly," Brando said flatly, staring angrily.

Margulies stared back at him. "Marlon, we are going to do this scene in *one* day."

Brando leaned back in his chair. He looked down at his shoes. He looked at Jones, then the cameraman, then at Margulies.

"That was the longest pause," recalled Margulies. "I was *kerplotzing*. I had told myself, 'It's okay to say no to Brando, because it's just a game. And then I'd watch him and think, Uh-oh, this is not a game. I just had to remember that Marlon is a terrific actor offstage as well as on."

Finally, after another long pause and a piercing stare, Brando's scowl turned into an impish grin. "What time do I show up on Monday?" he asked Margulies in a light, casual voice.

Margulies thought to himself, I guess that was my big test, and I have just passed.

Brando was due at the studio Monday morning at 7:30 for makeup so that the shoot could begin at eight. He arrived exactly on time, but first he went around to the assembled cast and crew, and in his usual "regular Joe" routine, introduced himself.

He then conceded to the producer and cameramen that he was self-conscious about his size. "He was about three hundred pounds then," recalled Margulies, "and he asked if there was anything we could do to deemphasize it. We suggested filming the scene with him seated behind the desk the entire scene."

Brando's requested cue cards were hung around the set as well as tucked in the desk drawer. The shoot went smoothly and wrapped about 6:30 in the evening. Brando then cheerfully posed for photographs with the crew.

As they were leaving the studio, he turned to Margulies and complimented him on filming the scene in such a short period.

"I've never done seven pages of script in one day in my life before," he said. "You guys made it so easy. I wonder why it isn't done this way all the time."

Brando again retreated to Mulholland to read and meditate, and friends heard that he was depressed and having a difficult time. Karl Malden hadn't seen much of Brando since *One-Eyed Jacks,* but during this period he had heard some disconcerting stories about his being drunk in public. Knowing Brando's family history with alcohol (they had discussed it during the Broadway run of *Streetcar*) and how much he "hated booze," Malden had always disputed such rumors. But one time when he did so, his informant objected, "I was there, and I saw it happen." That evening Malden called Brando's home, and Alice Marchak answered. She told him Marlon was out, so—knowing they were close—Malden spoke openly to her.

"I've now heard rumors that Marlon was drunk," he said. "I ridiculed them and said they weren't true . . ."

"Oh, I know, that's the old story about Marlon on a plane," Marchak interrupted. "Some stewardess was making a play for him and kept feeding him vodka. He was being very macho and kept drinking and I had to help him off the plane. That's how that came about."

"Will you tell him for me," Malden said, "that if there's a curse on the Brando name, it's alcohol—his mother, his father, and Jocey. It's a curse, and he's strong enough to be able to fight it."

"I'll tell him what you said," said Marchak.

In 1979 Malden was filming *The Meteor* with Sean Connery, who expressed interest in meeting Brando. Malden offered to set up a dinner party; besides the Connerys, the Richard Widmarks were invited.

Brando arrived with flowers and "this gorgeous woman"—Malden wasn't sure who—and drinks were served to the guests; Brando asked for vodka on ice. At dinner white wine was poured (although Malden himself doesn't drink, nor does Widmark). Connery's wife requested red wine, however, and a bottle of that was placed on the table as well. Brando was drinking glasses of white wine, then downed some red as well. The conversation was pleasant and spirited, Malden's guests were enjoying themselves, and after dinner Karl brought out a tray of cordials. Connery asked for Courvoisier, and Brando, according to Malden, said, "Me, too."

A while later Connery pointed to another bottle on the liquor tray, asking what it was. Malden told him it was Slivovitz, a Yugoslavian liqueur, and poured him some in a glass for him to taste.

"I want some, too," said Marlon.

"You still have some Courvoisier," objected Malden.

"Put it in there," he demanded, indicating his glass. He mixed the Slivovitz with the Courvoisier and continued drinking. Malden knew that

Brando had really put away the liquor that evening, and before the actor left, he made sure that Brando's date would be driving him home.

Only after the party did Malden perceive that Brando was putting him in his place that evening. "He was out to make a statement," said Malden. "It was as if he was announcing, 'It's none of your business about alcoholism in my family.' To this day I'm not sure whether I had been right to make that phone call to Alice. It's just that I love Marlon so much for his talent. That night he was out to show me that I'd better mind my own business. I suppose he was right in a way, though I was sad that he was pissing his life away."

The past was catching up with Brando in 1979 in other ways. Much to his dismay, in August Anna Kashfi's kiss-and-tell memoir, *Brando for Breakfast,* was published. During her publicity tour with husband Hannaford at her side, she called Brando "neurotic, a bisexual, a bigot, a lousy lover, who had no class and no communication." She claimed to have written the book simply to set the record straight so that Christian might realize that she had been telling the truth about his father all along. Nevertheless, she had to admit that Christian was "quite perturbed about the book," and it was later reported that he had retreated to his Oregon cottage and had the phone taken out so that she couldn't call him.

Brando had been on Tetiaroa when the book came out and at the end of October, he returned to Los Angeles. In November, with his weight at a reported 243 pounds, he again checked into St. John's Hospital to diet, as he had before *Apocalypse Now.* He knew he'd be self-conscious about his bulk when he stepped before the cameras with George C. Scott in *The Formula,* which after long delays was finally to begin shooting the following month.

Steve Shagan (who wrote the novel, adapted it into a screenplay, and was producing the movie) had criticized the major oil companies in *The Formula,* a theme not without appeal to Brando. After all, the actor had been saying some of the same things that Shagan had pronounced on talk shows—that America wouldn't have an energy problem were it not for the oil cartels—and the attacks on the writer from the oil companies had made the script even more attractive. Before signing, Brando had summoned Shagan and director John Avildsen (who'd done *Rocky*) up to Mulholland Drive. There, Shagan later recalled, they were greeted by two Dobermans and two bodyguards; then Brando appeared, presenting both the writer and the director with bouquets, which he explained were "Tahitian flowers" that he grew in California. They talked until midnight about politics, ecology, and the plight of the American Indian. All along, Shagan said, he was conscious that Brando was testing them. Toward the end of the evening the actor began to pace and presented his spiel that any film he did had to have a message. He added that perhaps "portraying the energy cartel in the form of a mystery might be interesting." But most of his comments were so negative that Shagan became sure that Brando would turn down the role. But then there was Marlon's impish grin as he suddenly interrupted his doubting remarks. "But you've sold me," he said simply.

For *The Formula* Brando would receive the extraordinary salary of $3 million for two weeks of work; he had also demanded 11 percent of the gross, from which he stood to make an estimated $2 million more—a total of $5 million for what would eventually amount to three scenes in the final release. He was also being paired with George C. Scott, an actor whose reputation for authenticity and power was close to that of Brando's, but who had sustained a real commitment to acting; still, both were notorious mavericks, having rejected Oscars in scene-stealing ways. As Shagan quipped, "It was Patton meets the godfather."

Contracted to appear for only ten days, Brando, as always, dragged each day's shooting longer and longer by halting scenes to discuss the dialogue. He had invented his costume to appear as an aging, fat oil baron, complete with ill-fitting polyester suits, granny glasses, and a few strings of gray hair arranged over a bald pate. Moreover, he had come up with the idea of wearing a hearing aid to complete his image. In actuality, the hearing aid was a radio transmitter designed to feed him his lines, replacing his usual cue cards.

One day after several takes, with Marlon inventing and reinventing his lines, Scott took his marks opposite him.

"What are you going to say this time, Marlon?" he asked in all good humor.

"What difference does it make?" Brando replied. "You know a cue when you hear one?"

Having pushed the cast and crew to finish Brando's scenes within the allotted ten days, Shagan was then amazed when Brando proposed to "donate" an extra day or two to film a scene in which he could make his ecological message more pointed. He asked the writer to create a specific episode: His character would rescue a frog that was dying from the chlorine in his swimming pool. "I think it's poison," Brando told Shagan, "and people are swimming in it." Shagan agreed, willing to have Brando for filming free of charge. Since Brando was portraying an oil baron supposedly indifferent to such ecological concerns, the quickly cobbled-up episode made no sense whatsoever.

The Formula debuted a year later, on December 15, 1980, the release having been delayed because of disputes over the editing. Many of Brando's improvised speeches, including the frog scene, were left on the cutting-room floor, and critics were sufficiently unimpressed with his inventiveness to point out that none of his three scenes was worth $1 million apiece. The general consensus was that the movie was murky, silly, confusing, and boring. *Variety* also couldn't resist a swipe at Brando's size: "Appearing grotesquely fat and ridiculous, Brando apparently thinks he's making some visual comment on the nature of his character. But it's so overdone, those seeing it are more likely to be so taken by how big Brando has gotten, they'll never think about the corporate fat cats at all."

Despite all the money Brando was raking in, the one abiding theme behind his vision of his island was that it represented his children's future; this was probably very much on his mind when, after returning to Tahiti in 1979, he made arrangements to divide the atoll into shares for Cheyenne and sons Teihotu and Christian, while assigning the remaining shares to Tarita; to his Tahitian lawyer, Claude Girard; and to Los Angeles accountant Norton Brown. (Perhaps significantly, given the controversy over Miko and Rebecca's parentage during his "divorce" from Movita, Brando did not include these two children in the division of island shares.) The Tetiaroa hotel had finally reopened and ten-day tours of Tahiti, including a five-day stay on the atoll, were now being offered by travel agents for $1,450 per person plus airfare. Those affluent few who came conceded that the island was beautiful but still found the *fare* living primitive and the *nonos* impossible.

Acquaintances in Tahiti began to notice Brando's waning enthusiasm. Alex Ata, who was now an assistant to the governor, had lunch in Papeete one day with Marlon and his son Teihotu and sensed the actor's growing disillusionment.

"All the plans for the island, two stories high by then, never materialized," said Ata. "That day he didn't talk anymore about doing anything significant in the South Pacific. It was always a mystery to me what he was trying to find in Tahiti. I don't think he really knew either, and that's why he failed."

Although Marlon had used some of his new income to buy a condo on Bora Bora, next door to one purchased by Jack Nicholson, in early 1980 he made an initial contact with new advisers—John and Nancy Todd, biologists from Falmouth, Massachusetts, but did nothing further about proposed aquaculture projects for the next year.

If Tetiaroa had come to represent simply his children's future, he again was stymied by Christian's problems. His son had returned to Los Angeles in the fall of 1980 and taken up residence at Mulholland. He soon went to work as a tree trimmer, becoming more expert when he became friends with Bill Cable, twelve years his senior, who supported himself between acting and modeling stints as a tree surgeon. "Christian had the natural instincts for climbing," Cable said, "but I taught him the finetuning. We met through a friend in Hollywood, and instantly we just clicked."

Christian also took up with his sometime girlfriend, Mary McKenna, who had become a makeup artist, working in a cosmetics store on La Cienega in Los Angeles. Soon they decided to get married, and Brando was enthusiastic about the idea, feeling that Mary could be a stabilizing influence. As a wedding gift he presented Mary with $17,000 to allow her to buy the cosmetics store. She and Christian were married on January 28, 1981, and for the first several months lived with Brando at the Mulholland house.

After the wedding, Brando's attention shifted back to Tahiti, and he again contacted John and Nancy Todd in Massachusetts. The Todds were in the vanguard of food and energy experiments; in the glassed-in atrium of their living room, they had created a perfect example of a solar-powered, self-sufficient ecosystem in microcosm, exactly what Brando had been talking about for years.

Summoned by Marlon to discuss experiments in island food production, the Todds flew to Tetiaroa in mid-February 1981, but Brando felt no need to make a timely appearance. For nearly a week the couple explored the lagoon, sailed, and scuba dived. Then one afternoon, Nancy saw a female figure walking through the palms on a nearby path. "She was wearing a red-and-white flowered sarong [and] a long-sleeved white shirt tied at the waist for coolness," she recalled. "I could see saggy breasts, and the body was pasty and pale and heavy. It was a careful walk, not a casual walk. I stopped and stared, because I wondered how I could have been on this tiny island for five days and not have met this old white woman, obviously a commanding presence. This person then just glanced at me and continued along the path to the schoolteachers' house."

It was only later at lunch when Brando came over to their table and introduced himself that Nancy realized that the old woman and the actor were one and the same. She was flying off the island the next day. After meeting Brando, she was struck by how her earlier impression was contradicted by what she described as Brando's "personal magnetism, personal power."

For John Todd, events grew stranger after his wife left as he became aware of the complex cast of characters on the island. Among Brando's guests was former girlfriend Ellen Adler. But Brando often locked himself in his room, leaving Todd to dine with Adler alone. When their host did join them, more often than not he became a "malicious mimic," at one point mocking a German tourist who was sitting at another table. (He also did a wicked takeoff of Carl Sagan, whose "Cosmos" TV series he'd been watching on tape as a model for the American Indian series he still insisted he was going to make.)

Marlon seemed to have little to do with Tarita, who usually sat with other Tahitian women at a separate table. "I came to feel that Tarita and Marlon were two opposing camps on the island," said Todd. "She knew more about the island and what she was doing there than he could have dreamed possible. I thought she dealt in a psychic realm that he didn't have any experience with."

At eleven every morning, Todd and Brando met to exchange ideas. After talking biology for about twenty minutes or half an hour, though, Brando would excuse himself and disappear—or change the subject altogether, often returning to his weight problem. Still more surprising was his fixation on money. While Todd outlined the costs of his proposed models for an experimental "food chain," Brando interrupted: "Why should I respect your ideas? You're not rich."

On March 9, a typhoon hit. Todd was in his bungalow, "just hanging on to keep from being blown away," he recalled. "When it was finally over the next morning, I was grateful to be alive. Everything had been flattened, the gardens flooded. My response was 'Let's start to rebuild.' Marlon had the absolute shit scared out of him, though, and was still in a panic. He ordered everybody off the island. Tarita stayed, but the rest of us were flown to Papeete, where he holed up in a hotel room.''

That was the last Todd saw of Brando; disillusioned, he returned home to Massachusetts. Yet within weeks Brando started phoning, repeating the same pattern he had played out with John Hughes, Jay Baldwin, and Stewart Brand. "He never said yes, he never said no," explained Todd. "Brando may be a visionary, but he lacks the courage to spend money. Looking back, if I had had the confidence, I would have said to him, 'I don't think this island matters a rat's ass to you. What I'm interested in is why this issue of weight matters to you. Is it sexual power? And with money, is it a loss of control?' Because these two issues were overriding," Todd continued. "He was reading Ruth Benedict and trying to understand Polynesia. But he hadn't sorted out his priorities—plus, he didn't have Tarita's authority or power. In fact, the bartender who had lived on Tetiaroa for a long time, said, 'Anything Marlon attempts on this island will be destroyed.' " Todd agreed that "all his plans were doomed."

Brando's response to the typhoon damage was to get back in touch with Bernard Judge to revive the original master plan for a major and elaborate resort, a plan that would enlarge the existing hotel to fifty-five bungalows.

The idea was to offer the island on a long-term lease to a resort management company: The sum being sought was $7 million plus rent, but ownership of the atoll would remain with Brando.

Meanwhile, Brando hired Cynthia Garbutt, a graduate of the University of Hawaii, to manage the tourism business as well as handle household and financial matters for Tarita and the children out of the office at the airport. Also recruited was a new manager and his wife from San Francisco. The manager had never seen an atoll before, but once in place the couple immediately reorganized things. First on their agenda was to hire two receptionists and a wine steward, as well as gardeners to take care of the coconuts and pandanus that had been growing wild for ages. The staff, now forbidden to joke with customers, was tripled in number. More absurd was the island's new dress code, which required male guests to wear long pants and jackets at dinner. For all the couple's efforts, Tetiaroa lost more than half a million dollars in 1982.

Brando was removed from all of this, even though he spent October through December on the atoll, withdrawing even further from outside contact. He had a wind-powered generator installed so he could stay up late with his radio, well after the power to the hotel had been turned off. He also called Al Prince, the editor of Tahiti's only English-language newspaper, the *Tahiti Sun Press,* to complain about a recent political article Prince had published. After the long phone conversation, Brando agreed to an interview on Tetiaroa. Prince was flown over in the afternoon, given a bungalow, and like so many other guests before him, he waited. Finally, about ten or eleven that night, Brando summoned him to his own bungalow, where they played a game or two of chess. The scene Prince recalled was so reminiscent of *Apocalypse Now* that it struck him as both strange and depressing: a huge Brando draped in a flowing white caftan, sitting in the semidarkness, with the primitive, thatched-walled room lit only by a single sixty-watt bulb. The actor's quarters were dominated by a king-size bed, his extensive radio equipment, and books. Half in shadow atop a nearby bureau stood a framed photo of his mother. Most of all, though, there was Brando's voice, the wheezing million-dollar tenor that drifted out of the shadows as the two men sat talking until three in the morning.

"He was massive," said Prince. "All that was left from the young Brando were the eyes, plus the charisma and the charm. He was mimicking other guests, and when he told his stories he played all the roles, including the women. He ate fruit continually and explained it was because someone told him fruit would help control his weight. He had bongo drums in the bathroom, and whenever he went to take a piss, before he came out he would tap on them, do a little riff, before coming out. After our talk he walked me back to my bungalow because I didn't have a flashlight and would have been lost. But I found it all weird. He gave me the impression that the only time he felt secure in that place was at night when nobody was visible. He was almost a phantom, wandering around in the dark."

By now any number of people were aware that Brown and Kraft had basically taken over by insisting that the only way to justify Tetiaroa was as a tax write-off. But whatever Brando's lingering dreams, all plans were dashed in April 1983 by another typhoon. It was the worst yet—with tidal waves washing over the atoll from the north, Brando's private *fare* was leveled, although the cement walls of the new home he was building at the other side of the islet remained standing, like some Polynesian Stonehenge. One *motu* was left without a single tree, and on the others more than 500 palms were down. The usually crystal-clear lagoon was carpeted with dead birds. Brando, who was in L.A., was described as sickened by photographs of the damage. His response was to send Christian (already separated from Mary) to the atoll with his pal, Bill Cable, to clean up the mess.

After another series of damaging storms, in 1987 Brando wrote to Alex DuPrel, a journalist with hands-on know-how as a licensed civil engineer and land surveyor, for advice. DuPrel now suggested a first-class operation consisting of the fourteen remaining (but totally refurbished) bungalows and six new ones, all solidly built and easy to maintain. It would be solar powered, low maintenance, and ecologically in balance with its natural environment, and it would be designed to attract the same exclusive clientele as Malcolm Forbes's retreat on Fiji, where rooms were booked for $800 to $900 a day. "We agreed that between $500,000 and $750,000 would do the job of renovating properly along these lines," said DuPrel. "That would give him something proper to pass on to his children. We shook hands on it."

Between DuPrel's competent management, and public relations skills, the hotel broke even for the first time in several years. Despite its primitive accommodations, it attracted celebrity guests such as Bo Derek, Jean-Paul Belmondo, the director Claude Lelouch, and Robert De Niro, who, according to DuPrel, enjoyed playing a waiter, tossing a napkin over his arm and taking orders from the other guests at dinner. Even Quincy Jones returned, spending thirty-one days in prayer and meditation, to recover from a nervous breakdown.

Club Med arranged day trips to Tetiaroa for its guests, luring them with the possibility of seeing the star. One day a group of forty Italian tourists arrived for a day's excursion, but were forced to stay overnight by a sudden tropical squall. Since all the bungalows were already occupied, DuPrel arranged for them to stay for free in the "university building," a roughly built, unfinished structure a half-mile away. Although the building featured camp beds and fresh linen, it had no mosquito netting. The group complained loudly. "They were forty screaming Italians," said DuPrel, deciding on the spur of the moment that the only way to mollify them was to give them a guided tour of his employer's private *fare.*

Leading them through the bungalow, DuPrel pointed to the three-by-four cubicle at the rear. " 'This is Marlon's toilet,' I told them and everything changed instantly," DuPrel recalled. "They almost kneeled in front of that toilet and made signs to Mecca. For Italians, Marlon is a god."

Despite the upswing in business, DuPrel was growing increasingly frustrated, largely because his boss had not yet come through with the funds promised to set the facility right. Often pouches of mail were delivered by the morning plane, including overnight deliveries from Federal Express, and one day Brando opened a package, and there was a script from yet another producer eager to sign him up for a film.

He scanned the covering letter.

"Okay," he said, "three weeks filming, $1.5 million."

"Great!" exclaimed DuPrel. "There's the money we need to get this place in shape."

Marlon then began to read the script, one, two, three pages. He was soon scowling.

"I'm not going to do this kind of crap," he said, tossing the script like a basketball into the waste basket.

"That was always the way it was," DuPrel later explained. "Offers coming in for $3 million, and he just threw them away."

Refusing to go back into harness, Brando again looked for other options. At one point he offered the atoll to the Cousteau Society as a research station. When Cousteau's people failed to show enthusiasm, the next plan was to turn Tetiaroa into a habitat for gorillas. Primate scientist Penny Patterson, who had done the famous experiments with Koko, approached Marlon, who invited her to the island.

DuPrel recalled the visit: "I got the message that she was arriving as a special guest and I was to take care of her. In the evening I took her out on sunset cruises in the motorboat. She sat in the back, always under an umbrella, with a big hat on—very much the lady of the manor. I was trying to explain to her about an atoll, which is only two feet above water, with very fragile trees. It's a bird sanctuary, and I couldn't see gorillas swinging in the trees.

"She said, 'No, I'll protect the birds. I'll put up electric fences.' She kept insisting she was so in love with the island.

"Finally, I said, 'If you persist in this crazy idea, I'll put out an ugly press story about you putting hundreds of apes in danger just because you want to play queen of the island.' At last she left. I suppose Marlon had a lot of fun watching me fight with her."

One problem that was growing worse were the poachers invading the lagoon. Most of Tahiti's coastal waters had been seriously fished out, and hearing that there was still a good supply of fish on Tetiaroa, fishermen began coming across the reef in canoes. DuPrel, Tarita, and Cheyenne were furious, but the government would do nothing about it—despite the fact that by landing their canoes on the beach, the fishermen were actually trespassing. Indeed, when Tarita destroyed boats belonging to turtle thieves, the police required her to pay 300,000 Pacific francs (roughly $3,000) to replace the canoes. "When I told Marlon about such things," DuPrel added, "he just shook his head and said, 'I'm amazed,' as if he couldn't believe that the law would not be obeyed and our pleas to save the fish wouldn't be respected."

Still, Brando did nothing to provide the lump sum of cash promised to refurbish the atoll, and after twelve months DuPrel quit, as exasperated with his seemingly pointless assignment as his predecessors had been. "As long as he is on Tetiaroa, he has Tetiaroa and Tahiti in mind," DuPrel explained. "But the moment Marlon goes back to Mulholland Drive, he goes back into his world of isolation. He forgets. So I finally resigned in 1988 after being there just over a year. I wrote him, 'I'm tired of being the keeper of the most exclusive slum in the South Pacific.'"

Apparently so was Brando. By the end of the eighties his utopian visions for Tetiaroa were reduced to the merest flicker. He spent less and less time there. Tarita, Cheyenne, and Teihotu were more often in Papeete, all of them preferring the cosmopolitan life in French Polynesia's capital and only returning to the atoll for holidays or weekend parties with friends. The property continued to deteriorate. One day a group of elderly schoolteachers were so disappointed with their Tetiaroa day tour that one of them registered her complaints with Tarita in the gift shop.

"I happen to know Marlon Brando," the woman announced indignantly. "And when I get back I'm going to tell him that his island is not being run the way it should be."

Tarita stared back at her. "You know something?" she said in a quiet voice. "Marlon Brando doesn't give a shit."

• • •

But it wasn't that Brando no longer cared. He had to do something more, to search for something, just as he always had, and if anything ran through his life, it was the refrain driving him onward in a quest for purity and authenticity. Yet what the medicine man Eddie Benton-Banai had so insightfully described about Brando and the Indians was equally applicable to the actor's long but dwindling involvement with Tetiaroa. He was so close to what he desired that he could touch it. But neither with the Indians nor his atoll did he know it was there.

In this decade of his life, Brando had earned tens of millions of dollars, yet he seemed to be disappearing in both his professional and his personal life, retreating even further into his private world at Mulholland. There he indulged himself, playing out his obsessions—talking, talking, talking to friends about the films he wanted to write while sliding into a withdrawal that would further separate him from reality. "Everybody's looking for the one who will tell the Truth," he stated glumly. "So you read Lao-Tzu, Konrad Lorenz, Melville, Kenneth Patchen, somebody you think is not a bullshitter. Somebody who has the eyes of a saint and the perceptions of a ghost. They're gonna tell us the way . . . [but] they never really do, and we run around being cheap imitations of all those influences."

T H E 18 T I E S

1982–89

Having done little during the first two years of the decade, in 1982
Brando became reenergized by a new project. While spending
one of his longest extended periods on Tetiaroa, he invited an
old acquaintance, director Donald Cammell, to work on an original
screenplay that promised to provide the actor with his first respectable role
in years. The idea for the film had come from Brando himself and drew
on, as Cammell put it, his need to wrestle with the "myth" of the adventurer "driven by metaphysics and angst in search of true love."

The film was to be called *Fan Tan*. Set in the 1920s, Brando was to
play a fisherman-smuggler traveling from Polynesia to the South China
Sea. An ex-jailbird with pretensions to being a writer, he joins forces with a
band of Chinese female pirates, steals the pirates' pearls, falls in love with a
waiflike innocent only to be jilted, and finally, filled with guilt, settles
down with his wife and children back on his remote Polynesian isle. Much
of the action, not surprisingly, would be shot on and around Tetiaroa.

Brando and Cammell had talked off and on for several months in Los
Angeles before flying to Tahiti, and the collaboration made sense. The two
had met more than twenty-five years before in Paris at the time of *The
Young Lions*. Cammell, a Scotsman and a friend of Christian Marquand,
had started out as a painter and later moved into films and directed *Performance* (starring his friend Mick Jagger). Brando first reestablished contact in the mid-1970s, although not as an overture of friendship. At the

time, Cammell was having an affair with a young woman under the accepted age for matrimony, and she happened to be China, the younger daughter of Anita Kong, Brando's own longtime lover, as well as the sister of Stefani Kong, the actor's "official photographer" on *The Missouri Breaks* and, later, *Superman.* It did not affect Brando's righteous indignation that he had frequently visited the girl's mother at her nearby Mulholland home, nor even that he continued his liaison with Anita herself despite her husband's discomfort. Brando's attitude toward Cammell, the director recalled, was nothing less than that of the censorious grandee. As self-anointed paterfamilias, Brando made threats on behalf of the family, and only later, when Donald and China were married, did he apologize.

Brando's friendly phone call to Cammell in early 1982 had been occasioned by the rerelease of *Performance,* and in the course of expressing his admiration for the film he asked the director to work with him on *Fan Tan,* explaining that he needed both a writer to help him and a director he could trust. For Cammell it was "a very enticing premise." The proposed arrangement was that Cammell would do the actual writing while Marlon dictated, sometimes into a tape recorder. "He felt completely happy and enthusiastic working like that," Cammell explained. "With Marlon it's a matter of keeping him up and going in the same direction."

After a month and a half on Tetiaroa, Cammell had a 150-page outline, which he then showed to one of the major studios back in L.A. "It knocked their socks off," said the writer. But with the go-ahead to put the film into production, Brando began to waffle. After several weeks during which Cammell had trouble getting his partner on the phone, the actor announced he wanted the script withdrawn.

"He changed his mind for reasons related to his general problems in executing material he's created himself," explained Cammell, who, ultimately, had no say in the matter. "The excuses he used were the expense of the picture, the fact that it had to be a studio movie, that he wanted to produce it independently to keep control. That nothing could be done through the Hollywood majors. It was one of those burdens he invents for himself."

The excuses were the same ones Abby Mann had heard repeatedly in connection with the Wounded Knee film. Brando also seemed concerned that his character—one of his own creation—might be perceived as autobiographical. He was still unable to let go, however, and then suggested to Cammell that they repackage their material in the form of a best-selling novel. A book, he argued, would serve as a launching pad that would allow them to finance the picture independently.

Cammell was dubious but agreed, clinging to the hope that the project might still be salvaged. But then with the novel half completed, Marlon balked again. Calling a halt to the publication, he refused to return the publisher's advance. When another publisher weighed in with an even larger advance, trying to save the day with a comprehensive buyout, he invented another evasion.

"He maintained that he couldn't read it because he hadn't written it himself," said Cammell. "He had a crisis of conscience, that he couldn't claim coauthorship. He maintains he's never read it. I don't know if that's true. He's not a very truthful man. But then artists and actors seldom are."

In 1982 Brando turned fifty-eight; he was grossly overweight and recognizing his depression he returned to therapy. But his unhappiness soon deepened as he faced the loss of several close friends. That summer, Sam Gilman was diagnosed with cancer and was now undergoing chemotherapy but the prognosis for recovery was poor. Then Reiko Sato, who had returned to work as Brando's part-time assistant in Los Angeles, suffered a mysterious and fatal seizure. Brando went to her funeral and gave a tearful eulogy.

"It was very strange," recalled another mourner. "He said, 'I hadn't seen Reiko in a while, but I got this message she had phoned. So I went to her house and she was lying there, having this seizure. So I called my psychiatrist to ask what to do.' I was thinking, Why is he telling this story? It was as if he didn't understand that if the girl is having a seizure, you call an ambulance, not a psychiatrist. I guess the psychiatrist told him to do just that, because she was taken to a hospital but died there."

In August 1982 Jill Banner's Toyota was rammed by a truck on the Ventura Freeway. Banner was thrown from the car; an ambulance rushed her unconscious to Riverside Hospital in North Hollywood, but she never regained consciousness and died at three in the morning.

Marlon was genuinely distraught. Christian, too, was very moved. After his own brief affair with her, they had remained close. "He couldn't mention her name without getting real misty-eyed and teary," recalled Christian's friend Steve Hunio. "After she died, he also told me that his dad was feeling so bad that all he could do was lie in bed, miserable with grief and crying."

An additional blow to Brando's equilibrium came only two weeks later when Norman Garey, the actor's trusted friend, dealmaker, and attorney, put a .38 to his head and killed himself. He was forty-six. Throughout Hollywood explanations for the high-profile lawyer's suicide, covered widely in the press, ran the gamut from financial overload to the pressures of studio politics, to talk of stomach cancer. In the harsh afternoon sunlight of the funeral, Marlon stood silently beside Garey's law partner, Allen Susman, and at the end of the service, he broke down sobbing.

It was a terrible, burdensome period, made all the worse by Christian's drinking and ever escalating flare-ups with his estranged wife, Mary. But rather than accept his anger, grief, and guilt, Marlon again handled his pain by externalizing it—specifically by becoming obsessed with lawsuits, pursuing the two he had already initiated and plunging into a new one.

The wheels had been set in motion years before. In 1981, with the release of *Superman II,* Norman Garey had renewed the long-standing 1978 suit against producers Alexander and Ilya Salkind, which amounted to $50 million. On April 6, 1982, the suit was quietly settled out of court when the producers and Warner Bros. agreed to pay Brando a share of both *Superman* films' earnings, estimated at between $10 and $15 million. Brando, wrote one columnist, "made more money in the courtroom . . . than he did on screen." While no dollar figures were confirmed, Brando later told Lawrence Grobel, his *Playboy* interviewer, "I got fourteen million dollars. They had to defer it until this year. After taxes it's about seven or eight million." When Grobel congratulated him, joking, "Not bad for a couple of weeks' work," Brando corrected him. It had been only twelve days, he said, adding laughingly, "It's so ridiculous. Absurd."

Large as that sum was, the settlement did not slake his need for "payback." Three weeks later, on May 1, 1982, he had gone back into court to file against Francis Ford Coppola, his former protector and champion. The issue was his 11.3 percent of the adjusted gross from *Apocalypse Now.* Brando claimed that in addition to $8 million in residuals, he was due $40 million in punitive damages.

Strategically, Brando's timing could not have been better. Coppola was broke, and his film company, American Zoetrope, was bankrupt. After Garey's death Brando had asked the attorney's partners, Allen Susman and Marvin Meyer, to take over the suit. The besieged director had already agreed in principle to pay Marlon, but when—and how much—

could be determined only upon the settlement of Zoetrope's mortgages. Brando spent hours counting Coppola's assets as well as his ties to people in the industry who might be prevailed upon to cover the director's debts. He talked endlessly with his attorneys on the phone, plotting strategy as well as psychoanalyzing Coppola, trying to anticipate his future moves.

Philip Rhodes and the few others who were aware of what was happening could only remind themselves that Brando, once he set his mind to it, had always been capable of all-out war. Yet even Rhodes did not know the half of it. Prior to filing his suit against Coppola (and the amended action against the Salkinds), Brando had asked his lawyers and accountant to quietly reorganize and/or file applications for four "blind" California corporations: Pipestone Corp.; Penny Poke Farms, Ltd.; Marlon Inc.; and PPF Properties, Inc. The last two of these entities were registered on the same day, just four weeks before the Salkind settlement. With the Coppola suit promising another settlement, there would be more corporations, some renamed after being suspended, some created anew, plus a raft of Delaware-registered entities with names like Brand of California, Brand of Michigan, Brand of Kalamazoo and Brand of West Virginia, Inc. Some were listed on official documents as public benefit corporations and were undoubtedly meant to maximize the tax benefits of Brando's many charitable contributions, but their sheer number suggested something beyond charity alone.

Just as telling, were Brando's real estate purchases. Until the early 1980s the actor's holdings had been limited to his homes in Beverly Hills and Tahiti, as well as some acreage on Maui. For the two-year period of 1984–85, however, California state records show that he acquired five additional properties, including a four-story commercial building in San Diego assessed at more than $2.5 million. There were also three private bungalows in a condominium complex in Bora Bora and a flat in London, in addition to a reported land purchase in New Mexico.

In December 1982, Brando became involved with his third lawsuit. His target here was novelist James Clavell. The accusation? That the British writer, whom Brando had neither met nor ever done business with, was guilty of neglecting his offspring.

Strangely the $15 million action, filed in Los Angeles, was almost completely ignored by the American press, although Fleet Street raised a storm even as details of the case were put under seal at Brando's insistence.

"A former actress has filed a £7 million 'palimony' suit against *Shogun* author James Clavell," reported the *London Daily Mail* in a headline story on December 20, 1982. "Caroline Naylen claims she lived with Clavell for sixteen years and that he is the father of her daughter Petra, ten. . . . The author had agreed to pay the ex-actress £40,000, together with £800 a month for Petra. Now Miss Naylen wants half of the author's estimated £14 million assets instead. She claims she was emotionally ill when the original settlement was made."

Caroline Naylen was in fact Caroline Barrett. The suit, it seemed, had also been encouraged, financed, or perhaps even engineered by Marlon, whose rationale was the welfare of Petra, two years younger than Cheyenne, "a very bright, very attractive girl." At Petra's birth Clavell had tried to keep the affair quiet since he had a family back in England, and now Barrett and Brando were claiming that the Clavell name should be on the birth certificate so that when Clavell died, she would have equal claim to his estate.

"I have no idea why all of a sudden Marlon had it in for this man," Philip Rhodes said. "They wanted to get Petra recognized as Clavell's legal heir so she'd inherit with his other children, but they were also suing for damages so they wouldn't have to pay taxes on whatever money they collected. Marlon had lawyers, private investigators running all over England. He was so fascinated with the law, I never saw such preparation. In fact he had never prepared for a picture or for a play as much as he did with that case—not *ever.*"

As Brando and Caroline pursued this suit through 1983 and 1984, Pat Quinn, Brando's former assistant, was back, working part-time for Marlon, and he had her running across town to do research at the UCLA Law School for the case.

"He really loved Petra, no question," added Quinn. "He was taking care of her, putting her through private school. But the other motive was that Marlon didn't want to work again, so they worked it out among themselves—five million dollars apiece. He'd get five, Caroline five, and the little girl five."

There was also more than a note of hypocrisy at work, given the fact that Marlon had several unacknowledged offspring of his own—one of whom, a local guy in his twenties by the name of Bobby, Quinn knew to be one of Christian's friends. In a sense, though, the assault on Clavell was no different from his earlier attack on Donald Cammell's involvement with China Kong. In both situations, Brando cast himself in his favorite role of child protector.

During these years Quinn became aware that Marlon's self-mythologizing had become overwhelming. One favored persona was the freedom fighter from *Burn!* The other was that of the grand patriarch. For example, when Tarita visited from Tahiti bringing Cheyenne as well as her two young children (fathered by her latest Tahitian boyfriend, Jean-Claude Munrovier). Brando sent them all off to see Yul Brynner in a revival of *The King and I*. It was "part of their indoctrination," Quinn said, "as if he were announcing, 'This is who Daddy is—the King.' He didn't want people, even his own kids, to know that he was just an ordinary man."

Even his relationship with Yachiyo, based from the start on the young woman's traditional Japanese readiness to bend, to defer, to cater, seemed to exist wholly on his terms. Yachiyo would have liked to marry and have a child, but he refused, prompting many arguments between them. When she angrily stormed out of the house, Marlon made repeated phone calls to her, punctuated by his sullen sighs or angry gibes. But then a few days later she would meekly return.

"He just didn't want what she wanted," said Quinn, who was treated to a number of these displays. "Once, when they had an argument about her having children, Marlon called me and said, 'I want you to come up here and get rid of her.' He wanted me to take all her things out of the house. Did he ever apologize to her? Never. I've never seen him be anything but omnipotent. I called him a Zen master. He had that sort of attitude, 'Smack you back, that's the lesson.' "

Brando's real difficulty, however, remained Christian. Now separated from Mary and living at Mulholland, he had again been in trouble with the police.

On December 3, 1983, he was arrested for shooting at an abandoned government missile silo on Mulholland Drive. With him were two companions, one of whom was his purported half-brother, Bobby, who managed to elude the police. But Christian was brought to the station house. "He phoned me instead of Marlon when they were ready to release him on his own recognizance," Quinn recalled. "He said, 'I can't tell my dad, so you gotta come get me.' " As she arrived at the station, the officers reached Brando. "I got on the phone with him," Quinn continued, "and he told me, 'Let him stay there.' I told Marlon I couldn't do that. Outside, Christian said, 'Don't take me back up to the house. He'll kill me.' I told him I had to: I had promised to bring him home. When we got to the gate, Christian pleaded, 'Just go inside and let me out, because he'll kill me.' From things Christian had said before, I gathered that Marlon used to really slug him. When I drove him back to the house, he was terrified, and inside the gate he jumped out and ran off into the night."

He had been busted before, in 1974, for possession of marijuana, but nevertheless he continued to smoke pot almost daily and sometimes also dabbled in LSD, PCP, and magic mushrooms. His drinking had escalated also—friends referred to "the Christian Brando breakfast," meaning a slice of jalapeño cheese and a couple of cans of Colt .45 high-octane beer. He had started to experience blackouts, and his father tried to address the problem by enrolling him in a treatment program at St. John's Hospital. After three days, according to official documents, he was kicked out for "noncompliance"—meaning that he was caught smuggling in liquor.

Christian's tenth-grade education had left him unprepared for nine-to-five jobs, let alone a career, and if he was living under the shadow of his father, his real mentor during this period was Bill Cable, who had taken Christian under his wing in the tree surgery business. Brando tried to help by calling friends like Jane Fonda and Jack Nicholson to offer the team's services. He also had the pair working up at Mulholland and also bought his son the necessary tools. (At the same time, however, he forbade Christian to work at Universal Studios as a set carpenter. "Christian very much wanted to do that," said Quinn, "but Marlon wouldn't hear of it.")

Brando laid out $14,000 in cash for a 1984 Camaro, paid Christian's laundry, transportation, and medical, dental, and insurance bills. He gave him monthly expense money as well. While the actor continued to run hot and cold—just as Steve Hunio, Christian's buddy, had observed—Brando the father could be sentimentally affectionate, sometimes leaving his son spur-of-the-moment mash notes. On one occasion he had welcomed Christian back to Mulholland with a scrawled card left on his pillow: "My Loving Son—I'm very glad to have you home. You make the house feel good. Sleep well—Please don't play the getto [*sic*] blaster to [*sic*] loud. Big hug— Love Da Da." Later, when Christian had become interested in wood carving, he presented him with a knife, again accompanied by a note reading, "Here's a little touch of Dad on a windy day—For no reason in particular except I love you. Dad."

But at other times, he could still turn into the relentless taskmaster. If Christian didn't perform according to Marlon's wishes, Marlon was likely to erupt, "What do you think this is, a fucking hotel?" When his father came at him "like a freight train," as Christian put it to friends, the son danced across the lawn, out of Marlon's lumbering range, chanting, "Fuck you, Fats! Fuck you, Fats!" Then he would jump in his truck and tear down the driveway.

Christian continued to roam the underside of Hollywood, drifting deeper into drugs. He wrecked a number of cars, and his auto insurance rose to $3,500 a year. His world became populated by dopers, hangers-on, and dumb bimbos, most of whom were one-time hits or lasted a week at most. There were "a lot of mad husbands and boyfriends," as one of his acquaintances put it, which only added to his growing paranoia.

Brando had once told Pat Quinn, "I have spent a lifetime trying to become less crazy." Several times a week he was now meeting with G. L. Harrington, a therapist he saw off and on from 1981 until the therapist's death in 1988. As Fred Sadoff recalled, when Brando first went to see Harrington, he was acutely ready for help. "He was nearly sixty, and was asking, 'What is my life?' " said Sadoff. "He had to talk to somebody . . . express his feelings about being lonely, or just ask 'Why am I manipulative?' 'Why do I behave this way?' 'What am I doing with the Indians?' 'What am I doing with my son?'—things he could not express to others." One of Harrington's greatest virtues, added Sadoff, was his directness in telling patients they were equivocating. "He would just point out very simply, without making you feel defensive, that what you were saying was bullshit."

As the problems with Christian had escalated, Brando arranged for his son to see Harrington as well. His sessions with the therapist were apparently less successful. "Christian felt very manipulated by the situation," said Steve Hunio. "He suspected that the doctor was reporting everything he said to Marlon, and he was probably right. So the experience left Christian with a severe distrust of all psychologists, of anyone who might actually help him deal with his feelings of self-worth and identity, his anxiety that he couldn't make something of himself. I'm sure Marlon was genuinely worried about Christian's problems as well as his drug use," Hunio added. "Unfortunately, the doctor you're sending your son to shouldn't be reporting back everything he says."

● ● ●

In March 1983, only three months after Brando had mounted the first phase of his legal assault against Clavell, the actor tried to get organized by hiring yet another assistant—someone to run things at Mulholland, including construction, security, and other projects he had in mind. This time he turned to Tom Papke, a middle-aged "techie" with a background in films, computers, and electronics whom he met through Sam Gilman. Papke remained in Brando's employ for the next fourteen months, after which he would work for the actor on individual projects for more than six years. What struck Papke the first day he reported for work was the inspired craziness of the actor's lifestyle.

"The first thing Marlon asked was, 'Do you have lock picks?'" Papke recalled. "I didn't, but I improvised, and he led me outside to the building where he kept his motorcycles, the welding gear, and tools. It took me only a minute—two steel doors. Then we went on to some giant master padlocks that you couldn't blow apart with a .357 Magnum. Once I'd done those he had me working on all the locks on the property. Some I couldn't open, but most I did, and he loved it."

After a few hours of lock picking, Brando proceeded to his next area of interest—biofeedback. "He had a biofeedback device in his bedroom," said Papke, "that could control your blood pressure, temperature, and thought patterns. He hooked me to this thing, and I was able to lower the tone right away. 'That's remarkable,' he said. I mentioned that I'd taken a course at UCLA's pain control unit, where I learned how to control pain without anesthetic to have teeth removed, so he demanded that I prove it. So I poked myself with the pin; what he liked best was that when I pulled the needle out, there was no blood."

Papke was exactly Brando's kind of guy—bright, loyal, eager to please, but also unconventional and sometimes zany. Brando was most fascinated with Papke's computer expertise. "Throughout our relationship, what he wanted to do was use technology to make lots of money," Papke explained. "It was 'Let's start a company—let's get something rolling . . . ' Money, though, wasn't ultimately what was pushing him," Papke added. "What motivated Marlon was that he wanted to do a high-technology project that would gain him the respect of the world as someone of intellect, not just some actor. Later, quite often he'd say, 'What people see of me on the screen is not me. I'd like to be remembered for something other than being another person.'"

Brando would lose interest in the computer business the two of them discussed, but Papke threw himself into his job as the actor's personal assistant, a general factotum who served as the liaison between Brando and the world at large, keeping the day-to-day workings of the estate as self-contained as possible. Although Brando had seemed ordered, even meticulous, in outlining the on-site building projects he had in mind, when Papke asked where he was to begin, the actor suddenly became vague, turning away with the words, "Well, do anything you want. You're in charge. We'll talk about it later."

Papke was immediately struck by Brando's living situation and the layout of the estate on top of the hill. First there was the side building, whose walls were made of one-foot-thick steel-reinforced concrete with a slab floor, no windows, and the heavy plate-steel doors. Its nickname, "the Bunker," was more than a joke—Brando had already had Pat Quinn make arrangements with a helicopter service to be on call at a moment's notice; in the event of disaster, an earthquake, or riot—whatever Marlon envisioned as Armageddon—the helicopter had a standing order to pick up Pat, Jocelyn, Christian, Philip and Marie Rhodes, and anyone else Marlon chose to add to the list, and deliver them to Mulholland, so that they could be safe in the Bunker.

Equally unique was the ham radio equipment in Brando's bedroom, which was hooked up to a huge beam antenna mounted atop a fifty-foot tower in the backyard. Then what caught Papke's attention was the padlocked refrigerator in the kitchen, a two-door, side-by-side model. Brando explained that every night he had Yachiyo lock it up by looping a length of chain through the door handles. Then he gave Papke one of his first tasks: He was to give his employer lock-picking lessons on the sly. "At night the refrigerator was padlocked to keep Marlon from snacking. The next morning the chain would still be in place, but the fridge would be half-empty. Marlon would say, 'But the thing was locked!' "

The same sneaky impulses seemed to be behind the time sheets that Brando insisted Papke fill out daily, recording other employees' activities hour by hour, including any petty cash expenditures and job-related auto mileage. Also to be logged were incoming and outgoing phone calls, appointments, orders with outside contractors and suppliers, and even the elapsed time of the maid's expeditions to the supermarket.

Perhaps the biggest eye-opener for Papke was his next principal assignment—organizing the Bunker. There he found an astounding surplus of supplies: half-pallets of lumber mixed with electrical conduit, an array of power tools worthy of a professional shop, and four Apple computers, some in their original cartons. It became obvious that Brando would acquire things and promptly forget about them. (The actor's penchant for forgetting things was nothing new, and in the months to come Papke would be asked to computerize the actor's telephone book so Marlon could have a copy in virtually every room of the house. Similarly, Pat Quinn had been required to catalog the library by assigning bookcase row and shelf numbers to every title; she was also to compile a master list of everything by subject categories.)

Papke's task of organizing the Bunker was complicated. Everything in the storage shed had to be labeled, assigned a number and a specific shelf space, and then photographed, with the Polaroids themselves cataloged and keyed to a master inventory so that Marlon could spot-check. With Papke being paid $50 an hour, the job took weeks.

By Hollywood standards the actor was not living opulently. The main house, often described in the press as a "sprawling Beverly Hills estate," was in fact quite modest—3,000 square feet of open, whitewashed, Japanese-style space. His vehicles consisted of a pickup truck and a several-years-old, leased Mercedes. Yet as Papke was beginning to see, his boss' impulse spending could be disastrous. On the weekends spur-of-the-moment, he was capable of sending Yachiyo down the hill to pick up $2,000 worth of tape recorders. With cameras, radio equipment, and tools, he was unstoppable. What most fascinated him were gadgets, like the home blood-pressure/anxiety meters he bought for himself and Jocelyn, or the seven brass kaleidoscopes Papke found tucked away at the bottom of a closet.

"I could be browsing somewhere," recalled Papke, "then come back to Mulholland and say, 'Gee, Marlon, I saw this device which I think is pretty nifty.' He'd ask, 'What's the phone number?' and grab the phone. I'd plead with him, 'Marlon, it's no big deal,' but he'd already be punching the buttons."

His most outrageous purchase was fifty bags of sand, which he had flown in from Tahiti at a cost of $18,000. "He wanted it for his saltwater fish tank," said Papke. "We could have gotten white sand locally for a couple dollars a bag, but he insisted, and so he brought bags of it in the passenger seats that he purchased on a flight from Tahiti. Even he admitted it was excessive."

The actor's impulsiveness was driving Papke to distraction, and Marlon's accountants were equally upset. Between the calls from Brown and Kraft—who begged Papke to try to curtail the spending—and some elementary calculations, the assistant concluded that his boss was shelling out several hundred thousand dollars a year just on staff and food. "He was just pissing it away," he said. "I'd been hired to monitor and control costs, to tell him when he was going overboard, but he was his own worst enemy."

Brando's financial situation, however, was not nearly as dire as Papke assumed, or as Marlon and Norty Brown seemed to want him to believe. Like most people in Brando's galaxy, Papke was not allowed to see the whole picture. Brando might cry poor, citing his burden of supporting Tarita, Movita, and his various offspring, or complain about the costs of Tetiaroa and his legal bills, and even intimate that he was subsidizing Jocelyn as well as Fran, still on the family farm in Illinois. In fact, he was sitting on assets far greater than he was willing to acknowledge. Over the past ten years he had grossed, at the minimum, $35.2 million from his film work and related lawsuits. *The Missouri Breaks* alone, though a critical bomb, had brought him an astounding $16.5 million. The take for *Superman* was almost the same, and counting the $3 to $5 million from *Tango*—plus revenues from *Apocalypse Now* and an additional $2.7 million generated by *The Formula*—some industry estimates pegged Brando's income for the past decade at $47.2 million, or roughly $5 million a year. This huge sum excluded profits from his investments as made by Norty Brown or the double-digit appreciation of his real estate holdings.

If Papke found his boss's sense of values frustrating, he was also taking undisguised pleasure in other aspects of the job. The access to Brando's hardware delighted him, as did their frequent, often entertaining conversations. At Brando's request, he might stay as late as ten as they kibitzed their way through dinners of prime rib or New York sirloin; regularly, they would burn up the better part of the afternoon with Marlon propped up in his king-size bed surrounded by books and memo pads, issuing instructions for Tom to look something up in the encyclopedia or log into some computer data bank. The topics of conversation could be history, philosophy, electronics, medicine, music, astronomy, "everything and anything, really," said Papke. Sometimes they would do nothing more than challenge each to remember the lyrics of Broadway show tunes or reconstruct the Spassky-Fisher matches, replaying the games over and over again on the actor's electronic chessboard.

Much of it, Papke later admitted, was plain "bullshitting," but there was a personal dimension to their conversations, too. Marlon was surprisingly open in talking about his kids, especially Christian who he readily acknowledged was becoming more mired in drugs. Yet Marlon was worried about all his children. Teihotu had no use for the United States and just wanted to be a masseur. "He was concerned about Cheyenne, too. She was then a young teenager and he worried about her because she had gotten into modeling in Tahiti," Papke recalled. "He talked about Miko and Rebecca, but Miko basically came and went, because he was always running around with Quincy Jones and Michael Jackson. He liked the Hollywood scene."

The staple of their chats, however, was technology, much of it Marlon's interest in the ecological and experimental equipment that he had researched for Tetiaroa and was now attempting to apply to his bivouac in Beverly Hills. Papke's job was to prime him whenever they were scheduled to meet with a contractor so that he wouldn't make the same mistake twice, "to supply buzz words so he wouldn't make a fool of himself." During this period Brando's other major fascination was with security. Already he'd had plans drawn up for a TV-surveillance system for Tetiaroa, and Pat Quinn was often present when he enlisted Papke in discussions of what could be done atop Mulholland. His "obsession" with fortifying the hilltop, she felt, had to do with the continuing Clavell lawsuit, for which he had already hired detectives.

Brando not only wanted to record telephone conversations, he also told Papke he wanted "to have a special recorder hooked up to all the extensions. . . . He said, 'I'm working on this screenplay, and I want to be able to pick up the telephone in any room in the house and punch in a number so that then I can speak into it and my thoughts will be recorded.'" It was a setup that was made all the more complicated by the added requirement that Brando be able to activate the tape deck in his bedroom while using the intercom line, too.

Marlon also instructed Papke to modify his answering machine; here the parameters were that whenever someone called, they would not get a recorded message, a beep, or even a ring: Insiders would know not to wait for a signal but just to start talking; strangers, on the other hand, would hang up, thinking they had reached a nonworking number.

Naturally, Brando's four or five numbers were all unlisted, but somehow calls from outsiders got through. When Brando decided that too many people had his phone numbers (and Christian was free with the information, much to Marlon's irritation), he had his call-forwarding service direct everyone to the numbers of either Air France or the Los Angeles County sewage department. Then he would fiddle with the phone lines so that he could overhear his callers' befuddlement.

Because of his reluctance to have strangers on the hill, Brando relied more and more on Papke to take care of electronic modifications. The door to his bedroom was fitted with a combination lock, and the large windows on the north side of the room, were shuttered with "blackout blinds" of the type commonly found on inner-city storefronts. The shutters could be rolled up and down electronically at the touch of a button. To one side of the king-size bed and the two couches separated by a cocktail table, he had a small safe installed next to the built-in TV. Under his bed he kept a loaded .38 pistol and 12-gauge riot shotgun.

The Manson killings in nearby Coldwater Canyon had spooked him years before, but even worse was the more recent incident when Brando had awakened one night to find a black man holding a zucchini in his bedroom. "The black guy says, 'Hey man, you're Marlon Brando. I got this zucchini for you,'" Christian had told Bill Cable. "Marlon pulled his gun out, cracked off a round, and said, 'Get the fuck out of here.'"

The fortification of 12900 Mulholland Drive that Brando asked Papke to do proceeded in stages. The first plans, quickly discarded, included a series of Rube Goldberg contraptions—from heavy electromagnets buried beneath the drive and designed to "freeze" intruding vehicles, to laser beams that would "fry" trespassers (he actually ordered giant Fresnel lenses for this purpose). Brando also considered mounting television cameras on model helicopters flown around the hilltop. Another concept was to hook TV cameras and lights to self-inflating balloons that would go straight up on a cable from the roof of the house, with the cameras rotating to scan the whole property. For the driveway he was briefly intrigued with the idea of "pneumatically driven spikes," but settled for planting 300 bamboo trees along the property's perimeter, which were then laced with concertina wire sprayed green, Vietnam camouflage–style.

The next bizarre idea? Electric eels, to generate cost-free power.

After Papke undertook a massive research effort on the current and amperage output of tropical fish, two eels were purchased that Brando, always the joker, quickly dubbed Redi and Kilowatt.

"They were ugly fuckers two or three feet long," said Papke. "Dirty greenish gray, disgusting, with beady little eyes. They just lay there and you wouldn't dare put your finger in the tank because you'd get thrown across the room. The plan was to have them charge huge storage battery banks that we could then draw down, convert the lighting in the house to twelve volts or twenty-four-volt aircraft. He even hired an aquarium keeper. The whole thing was costing enough to light half of Beverly Hills, but that didn't matter."

The experiment went on for months. If provoked, Redi and Kilowatt could blast as much as 600 volts of pulsating DC current, and several times the aquarium man was bounced off the walls of the workshop. One balmy Saturday the eelkeeper was performing his periodic tank cleaning. As part of his routine, he put the eels in the swimming pool, the only place they could stay while he attended to the tanks. He hadn't realized, however, that Christian had invited one of his girlfriends up for a swim.

"She was one of Russ Meyer's so-called vixens," recalled Papke, who heard the story from Brando two days later. "She was like a 44D or something, what I used to call Christian's mussy-tufted, large-breasted pad thrashers. She walked out to the pool and jumped in naked. Ten or fifteen seconds later, Redi and Kilowatt let go with one of their mighty blasts and she went out of the pool like she'd been shot out of a cannon." She was yelling and screaming. Marlon came outside to see what the commotion was, and then burst into peals of laughter. "Of course, that story could have been bullshit," said Papke, "because often he'd make up this stuff. But when he told me the story on Monday, he was still laughing so hard he was falling off the bed. He thought it was hilarious, giving that girl a six-hundred-volt whack from an electric eel."

Ultimately, the eel project proved to be no more than a joke. One project that did not fizzle was the construction of a several-thousand-pound gate at the foot of the driveway that took the better part of the winter and spring of 1984 to bring to completion. Up until that time entry to the hilltop had been unimpeded. The drive came in off Mulholland, wound up the hill for several hundred feet, then split into a Y, with Jack Nicholson's and his friend Helena Kallianiotas's homes on the right fork and Brando's on the left. Brando's chief requirements for the complex design were a drive motor, actuating arms, and an electronic control box on the inside in order to ensure security. The final configuration, involving a complex series of offset arms, weighed so much that the gate required specialized bearings that could literally support a railroad car.

The bearings were only half the battle. Brando also wanted a number pad at the entry that was programmed with two codes—a master code for staff and friends and a private override that only he had access to. "That way," Papke pointed out, "he could change it. If someone fell out of favor, they would no longer have access."

With the gate completed, Marlon was ever more the king of the hill. Papke saw it, Rhodes saw it, and so, too, Marlon himself. "Brando accepted himself as overly suspicious," Papke said. "He absolutely trusted only one person in the world, and that was Jay Kanter. Maybe Alice, too. But everybody else at Mulholland he checked up on, monitoring the work done and the money spent by any of us."

Papke himself felt Brando's sting in March 1984, when Gene Frenke died. The actor questioned his report that the florist did not have a full four dozen long-stemmed roses and even called Hollywood Famous Florists to verify this in Papke's presence. Shaken, Papke felt driven to phone the floral shop himself to ask them to messenger over a note confirming his explanation.

Later that day Papke left the florist's handwritten confirmation along with a note to Brando:

> *Once again, I am accused of lying. . . . I, however, cannot work effectively when, like the sword of Damocles, your suspicion, distrust, and apparent lack of belief in me hangs over every single action I perform on your behalf . . .*
>
> *Either trust me or fire me. It is as simple as that. I want to continue to work for you. . . . Please do not make it impossible for me to do so.*

The next afternoon, Marlon merely shrugged, then said, "Well, it appears that you were telling the truth." After that, he never mentioned the incident again.

When Brando's suspiciousness nonetheless continued, the frustrated Papke finally erupted. Brando advised his assistant to schedule himself an appointment with his own therapist, G. L. Harrington, the bill for which would be "taken care of."

Rattled, Papke went off to see Harrington, whose interpretation of the problem was less psychological than straightforward common sense. "He said, 'Tell Marlon to go fuck himself,' " Papke recalled. "Tell him you don't need this harassment. If he stops, fine. If he doesn't, look for another job.' "

Upon hearing Harrington's recommendation, Brando seemed unimpressed. "Well, everybody's entitled to an opinion," he muttered.

Papke nonetheless hung in at Mulholland. At $1,000 a week, the pay was good, and irreducibly, like so many others in Brando's orbit, he'd been won over. If Marlon could be a bastard, he could also be sympathetic, generous, hip, charmingly wicked, and lots of fun, as was never more evident than the afternoon Papke took a call from the Reagan White House. Brando's response was enough to offset the other irritations.

"The caller said he wanted Marlon to be one of the presenters at the Katherine Dunham honorary something or other," Papke explained. "At first I thought it was a joke. 'No, no, this is really the President,' he insisted, and then I recognized the voice. I said, 'Mr. President, Mr. Brando is currently still in bed, but I'll be glad to tell him.' Later I gave Marlon the message. He told me to call him back. I said, 'What should I say?' He replied, 'Tell him to take a flying fuck at a rolling doughnut.' "

This was Brando's favorite expression, used in *Last Tango,* and Papke revelled in it, much as he was amused by Brando's easy scatology, his willingness to joke about "pussy" or about some of his own women. "Funny stuff," Papke said, like the fact that he'd turned down Elizabeth Taylor at the time of *Reflections in a Golden Eye* because "her ass was too small," or that he couldn't stand Sophia Loren because her breath was "worse than that of a dinosaur."

Just for effect, Marlon liked to dribble food out of his mouth while eating. Like a musician challenging his audience, he might also let loose long, rippling, glissando explosions of gas in the middle of a conversation, waiting for the other person's reaction. Nor had he given up his pleasure in mooning, as Papke would discover one afternoon when coming up the drive. There, he found himself staring at three bare behinds protruding from the bushes. The one in the center was of "monumental proportions," said Papke, explaining that the other two belonged to Brando's full-time engineer and his assistant.

The apotheosis of Brando's humor was called "Dial-a-Fart."

The actor and Papke were sitting around one day, thinking of something to do with 976 numbers, a local variant of commercial 900 numbers that were then an emerging technology. "Why not Dial-a-Fart?" said eleven-year-old Petra, wandering into Brando's bedroom. "You'd have to identify famous movie stars' farts."

Brando came unglued. "Why," he said, "I'll call up Charlton Heston and see if he'll fart for us. I'll call up Jack. There are dozens of people."

Petra, in another coup, thought of having people contribute their own noises. "We rig it up so people would fart into the phone and there's another contest there," said Brando, excited. "We'll call it Fart of the Week, Fart of the Month, Fart of the Year. And we could give a big prize."

Dial-a-Fart was a recurrent topic of conversation for weeks. Brando thought of sending a safari to Africa to record elephants. Then it turned into a zoological expedition, a "gas menagerie" on tape. This, said Papke, degenerated into talk of the creature with the smallest audible wind—a mouse, perhaps. Finally, with the solemnity of someone negotiating a film deal, Marlon called Allen Susman, his attorney.

"Here are our ideas," he told Susman, running down Dial-a-Fart from A to Z. "What are the liabilities? The federal laws here, and the local ones? . . . "

Soon the attorney was laughing, said Papke, who was on the extension. "Finally he said, 'Marlon, if you'll excuse the expression, if anyone gets wind of this you're finished in Hollywood.' And then, click, he hung up the phone."

An equally zany scene occurred when Marlon, in one of his frequent attempts at losing weight, decided to try the current fad of hanging from the ceiling. He had already purchased a rotating hoop-frame device and special hooked boots, but because of his girth, he found that he was unable to flip himself over in the frame. He sent Papke and two other assistants out to the garage for a winch that had been mounted on his truck, then had them bolt it to the ceiling of his bathroom.

"In the meantime," Papke recalled, "Yachiyo had come over to cheer him on. She was all in favor of it, since she'd been making him all kinds of salads and the Thanksgiving before had even prepared a tofu turkey. But all along he'd been paying employees from McDonald's in the Valley to come up on the sly and toss him food over the fence. So by then Yachiyo was looking for anything that would help him lose the weight."

After six hours had been spent locating the jousts in the ceiling and setting up a twelve-volt power supply for an on/off switch, the homemade apparatus was in place and the mounting had been tested.

Soon, using the shoes from the discarded store-bought machine, Marlon was hanging in the air. A new problem quickly became apparent, though. "He was hanging head down," Papke explained, "and because of his weight, the blubber started to roll forward, almost choking him. He was coughing and muttering, unable to speak."

They immediately lowered him to the floor. Brando, however, was determined to stretch, and the solution he proposed was to try to use the winch and frame horizontally. The assistants fixed another heavy screw eye into the wall of the bathroom opposite the doorway, and once again, Marlon readied himself. "He wanted Yachiyo to straddle the doorway and hold on to his hands while the winch pulled from the opposite direction," said Papke.

"The winch was so strong that she couldn't hold on. But Marlon wasn't letting go, either, so Yachiyo was being pulled through the door into an almost inverted position. When he finally released her, she popped through the doorway like a cork, and the whole megillah collapsed."

The episode was laughingly referred to as "Brando in Bondage," but more and more the hilltop was becoming Brando's "little universe," his "private domain"—already he had told Papke, "You know, I'm going to die up here." But he occasionally ventured down the hill to his favorite restaurants, usually lured out of the house by Yachiyo. One night he happened upon the Budapest Restaurant on Fairfax, in the heart of L.A.'s traditional Hasidic neighborhood. Not chic, the Jewish-style Hungarian restaurant was nonetheless a popular spot in Hollywood because of its chopped liver, roast goose, stuffed chicken, and Wiener schnitzel. Russell Friedman, the owner, was more than willing to cater to Brando's whims.

The first time Brando appeared at the restaurant, Friedman recognized the actor immediately. "We were tremendously busy," he said, "and they just walked in off the street with no reservation. He asked for a table for two, and the Asian woman he was with added, 'Do you have anything a little bit private?' By some miracle, there happened to be one free table and it was around a corner, somewhat out of the way. I kind of guarded them to let them have dinner in peace."

While Brando and Yachiyo were dining, Friedman went to his office. Later the hostess rang to tell him Brando wanted to speak to him. Returning to the floor, he greeted the actor, who had risen from his seat.

"Mr. Friedman, you're making a very, very big mistake here," said the stern Brando, who had evidently made a point of finding out the owner's name.

"I started quaking and I said, 'Yes sir, what is that?' "

Brando said, "You don't charge enough for your food."

When Friedman cracked up, Brando joined in, a loud guffaw. "He set me up real good," the proprietor recalled.

Thereafter Brando returned to the Budapest regularly. "He tipped absolutely gloriously," Friedman added. "If his bill was forty-two dollars for two, he'd leave a twenty-five-dollar tip. He appreciated being left alone, and I always kept people from going to his table."

Another night Brando called the restaurant and asked Friedman if they delivered. The restauranteur said no but offered to make an exception, taking Brando's order for chopped liver, blintzes, and goose. After Marlon explained how to reach the house, Friedman asked if he should add something to the charge slip for the busboy who would be delivering the food. Brando said, "Yes, Fifty dollars."

"I said, 'Fifteen dollars?' He said, 'No, Fifty. Five-zero.' " Friedman sent the busboy on the twenty-minute drive to Mulholland. When he got there, Marlon gave him another twenty dollars in cash.

Brando wasn't the only one eating well; when it came to his 200-pound mastiff, Schlubber, the actor's feeding routine was to open a can of Alpo top and bottom and then *whoosh,* blow the whole can of food directly into the animal's mouth. His favorite dog, however, was a German shepherd that had to be put down during the winter of 1984. Marlon sobbed as he waited for the vet. He and Christian built the coffin themselves, put the dog in the box, nailed it shut, then lowered the box into the grave, not far from the tree where Wally Cox's ashes were buried. "It was the one time I think Chris and Marlon were very close," Papke added. "No complications, no nothing."

Equally touching—at least on the face of it—was Brando's attempt to reach out to his son with a proposal that the two of them, together, get their high school diplomas. Brando had never finished at Shattuck, and Christian, now twenty-five, had gotten only as far as the tenth grade. Unfortunately, it was Marlon himself who after only several weeks sank the program by refusing to apply himself in their joint tutoring lessons, which were conducted by Papke's girlfriend.

During the mideighties, the actor continued his lawsuits. One afternoon Papke found himself speaking to the lawyers on the telephone and relaying messages to and from Brando; the attorneys asked if Brando wanted to file a motion that would signal an escalation of the suit against Clavell. Papke relayed the question, then waited. After a moment, Marlon made a quick thumbs-down gesture, snapping, "Waste 'im."

In his crusade against the novelist, he stopped at nothing, contacting the IRS to get them to investigate Clavell's finances and even reeling in a United Artists executive as his ally. Caroline Barrett referred Marlon to the producer, who had previously worked with Clavell. Now Brando stroked the executive with promises of doing a film together in exchange for evidence on Clavell. Although the executive could supply no real documentation as Marlon had wished, Brando still thought the executive's testimony might be useful to coordinate a strategy against Clavell.

Marlon continued to diddle the executive with the spurious film project while the lawsuit progressed. Clavell wasn't the only target of his litigious fervor. Mr. Liberal, who was so willing to cozy up to the IRS to achieve his ends, still kept "old friend" Francis Coppola in his sights, again sounding like a real-life godfather in phone conversations held in front of employees. Whether he was parodying his Coppola role or had come to believe in his tough-guy routine, no one was sure. But his threats in the Coppola case were as astonishing to friends and staff as his willingness to bring in the IRS.

Throughout the first half of 1984, Marvin Meyer, Allen Susman's law partner, had been trying to reach a settlement with Coppola's representatives on the *Apocalypse* lawsuit. He succeeded in getting Marlon priority on all foreign receipts from the film up to $2.5 million, and Coppola was to pay Brando $250,000 every three months. In the event of a missed payment, he agreed to turn over control of the foreign distribution of *Apocalypse*. Irritated that Coppola had sent him a letter that showed no signs of contrition, Brando sighed, agreeing with a grin to his assistant that "two mil in two years" wouldn't be too bad, if he actually received it. But, he warned, if Coppola didn't come through, "I promise to break both his ankles with a baseball bat."

The telephone was his lifeline during the mideighties, and Marlon was constantly on the phone with those closest to him: Jocelyn, Caroline Barrett, Philip Rhodes, Alice Marchak, Pat Quinn, Yachiyo Tsubaki, and Tom Papke, as well as the writer Vine Deloria Jr., the dying Sam Gilman, accountants George Pakala and Norton Brown, and Christian Marquand in Paris. His sessions with Harrington seemed to have prompted him to think about his past, especially his grief over the loss of Jill Banner, and he now was able to express his sense of self-entrapment.

"It wasn't until Jill's death that I could begin to love," he acknowledged one night. "I could have loved her had she lived. I was beginning to be close to her. . . . It was as though I was forgiving my culture, forgiving my past, forgiving my people, because she was unlike any other girl that was ever in my life because she was midwestern, born a hundred miles from where I was born. So I rejected those kind of women all my life. But then she died and now I'll never know. But I now feel much more comfortable with myself about that. . . .

"And I am convinced that the answers are within you," he went on. "They are not external circumstances that conspire against you. They are just things in your mind that you—out of fear and anguish, or dread or habit, or whatever it is that determines the habits you have of thinking in certain ways about your relationships with people, or relationship with yourself. . . .

"Although I pretended to study my feelings and went through psychoanalysis and all that, I really was avoiding certain realizations that didn't come to me until I was willing to experience pain. And so I've learned a lot in the past five years, I guess, and I had a very good experience with this doctor I saw. I went to see him for a couple of years and he helped me enormously, but he couldn't have helped me unless I was ready. And now I'm doing many, many things that I never thought I could do before."

The "many, many things" Marlon claimed to be doing were in fact few and far between. The "Roots"-like miniseries on the American Indian still languished. In 1981 he had interested Adrian Malone, producer of the acclaimed PBS series "The Ascent of Man." But again he waffled, claiming that they had differences in their conceptions of the series. "I've never quite understood what our differences were," Malone admitted later. The essential problem seemed to be Brando's deep discomfort with collaboration, and in 1984 Malone gave up. The latest version of Marlon's repeatedly cited Indian movie was dead.

Marlon did, however, have something else to preoccupy him by then, having embarked on an extraordinary new venture: giving acting lessons to Michael Jackson. The combination of Brando and the young, waiflike pop superstar was odd to say the least, but never had the actor sounded so committed, passionate, and purposeful about acting since his early days with Kazan.

Brando had met the singer through Quincy Jones, whom he had known since the late sixties. In the eighties he stayed in touch with Jones, "probably because he wanted to take his kids to Michael Jackson's concerts," said Pat Quinn, "especially when Cheyenne was visiting from Tahiti." Through Jones, as well, Jackson hired Miko as a bodyguard. In January 1984 Miko saved the singer when his hair caught on fire during the filming of a Pepsi commercial. It was not unusual for Miko to bring Jackson up to Mulholland. And it appeared that Brando's interest in Jackson had deepened during this time, while the young singer himself came to regard Brando as a father figure and an idol. At one point the actor enticed Martin Scorsese to write an outline for a film in which Brando was supposed to play God and Jackson the devil.

"Marlon wants to preserve a certain public identity," Pat Quinn noted. "And this was what he was teaching Michael."

Yet, more than the art of being famous, Brando was also tutoring the singer in the art of acting, and Jackson taped their sessions. Brando, always referring to himself in the third person, told Jackson of a time when he had to do a scene onstage in which he had to cry:

"He would have to cry and feel deeply sad, and he said all day long he would prepare to become the part, listening to music that would stimulate sadness, pain. He was at the height of feeling the part truly, but his mistake, he said, was preparing too far in advance, and he spilled his guts out backstage. In the dressing room he wept—pain—and he was in deep agony, and when he hit the stage he was dry; there was no truth because he wasted his performance backstage. He said he learned to reserve, to hold back the part.

"He said this pertains also to making a movie. He said reserve and reserve—hold back until the time is perfect, until technically the camera is on a close-up of you. He said all the other takes they do of you of the same part, do it good but reserve. But spill your guts when the camera is close up and all is perfect."

Another session, which he called "Truth," plainly referred to *One-Eyed Jacks*:

"While directing a movie, he said he couldn't get this certain Mexican actor to get angry. . . . The same thing happened to a girl he was directing, and she just wasn't doing the part with truth, so Brando walked up to her and told her, 'You're awful. I should have never hired you for this part. You are the worst, you are fired.' The girl cried and cried, bursting into tears, but without her knowing Brando was filming her all the while, even while he was insulting her, and finally again he got Truth. He then told her what he did. Now after he built her emotions to the truth he told her to do it again but this time with words and to hold back a bit, and she did and all worked perfectly in *Truth.*

"But everything he did to them they should have done themselves, within themselves. You must live the part, you must dig and dig and touch upon deep past truths, become stimulated to the highest possible level, then spill your guts to the camera at the proper time. Build and build, then reserve."

The tutorials even included a poem, "Marlon Brando to Michael Jackson." Here, he again stressed the need to trust one's muse, to "play on what has touched you deeply." Following the verse, in capital letters, appeared the words "BRANDO TOLD YOU."

In another session, Brando's message was "Please the truth. Don't please the people, please the truth. Example: If you're dancing and a choreographer gives you set steps, you do them but if you don't feel certain about the movement and feel by instinct you should be doing something else, then do it. Act on truth by feeling and instinct. You know when to spin, when to freeze, turn your head, put your hand in your pocket.

"Don't fight feeling and instinct. *Truth.* Please the truth. Let things create themselves."

The message was straight Zen, with a bit of Keats and Allen Ginsberg wrapped around Stanislavsky. In light of Brando's work over the past ten years, it might well have been a sign that his fires were not completely banked. But Jackson was hardly a budding stage genius, and probes for truth might yield strange consequences, given the singer's eccentricities. Even Brando himself would have to acknowledge this in 1985, when he took Pat Quinn over to Jackson's to discuss the possibility of a job for her.

After her most recent stint assisting Brando, Quinn had been told that he had to let her go. The reason, she later discovered, was that Yachiyo had become jealous. When she had been hired this time, Marlon instructed her

not to tell Yachiyo about their past relationship and Quinn had been extremely careful. "But she found out, and even though I was an *ex*-lover,"
said Quinn, "she hit the roof. She was giving him a hard time and he decided to let me go, under the guise of not enough work." Brando then arranged for her to work for Jackson and brought her over to the singer's
family enclave in Encino.

When they arrived Michael greeted them at the door dressed in a Pinocchio outfit, complete with long nose. "It was quite surreal," said Quinn.
"He was standing there like a character out of a Disneyland parade, and he
spent the entire meeting in that getup. We were both nonplussed, it was so
extraordinary. Marlon's idea was that since Michael was starting a production company, I could get in on the ground floor. But after six weeks I
couldn't bear it any longer. I was in Michael's bedroom, with him looking
over my shoulder as I, doing what he requested, was changing his chimp's
diapers. That's when I asked myself, 'What am I doing here?' and I left.
Marlon was furious at my decision. He was sure I could have had this wonderful career in Jackson's film company."

Even while Marlon was instructing Jackson to "please the truth," he
himself was loath to return to acting in a serious or authentic way.

During the mideighties Joe Mankiewicz, who had directed Brando in
Julius Caesar thirty years before, bumped into Marlon in New York, on the
corner of Fifty-seventh Street and Madison Avenue. Mankiewicz stopped
him as he shambled along, seemingly lost in his own thoughts. The two
men hugged, then took a few steps backward to appraise each other.

"You look great," Mankiewicz lied, taking in Brando's weight.

"What're you doin', old stud?" Brando quipped.

"Well, do you think you can get yourself into shape for one more
fight, champ? Think you can make it?"

"What do you mean, 'make it'?" Brando asked, looking at him expec-
tantly.

"Well . . . physically."

He looked down at his girth, then back at the director. "Whaddaya
got in mind?"

"I want to do *Macbeth* with you and Maggie Smith. What do you
think?"

It was one of the busiest intersections in town, Mankiewicz recalled,
and neither of them moved or said a word. Then Brando grinned.

"Nah. Couldn't make it," he said, turning away. "See ya, pal."

For Mankiewicz it was a moment of honesty, signaling some real self-appraisal on Brando's part. "When he was standing there, looking at me, it was about whether he was any good or not," he later said. "I don't believe he was thinking about *Macbeth* but whether or not he could deliver a performance. Period."

Between 1981 and 1983 Brando had already turned down several films and huge salaries: a whopping $4 million plus 50 percent of the profits to play Picasso, then another $5 million for two weeks' work as Al Capone, and an undisclosed sum to appear in a bio pic based on the life of Karl Marx. Throughout the spring of 1984 he had also been negotiating with British director Adrian Lyne to do a costume comedy with Laurence Olivier. Instead of accepting any of these assignments, he was nonetheless again talking about writing several other original screenplays of his own (despite never following through and completing either *Fan Tan* or the Indian miniseries).

Brando's latest idea was *Jericho,* a high-concept shoot-'em-up focusing on the U.S. government's involvement in the Latin American dope trade. For this he sought out Frank Snepp, the young former CIA operative who had served as Saigon station chief during the closing years of the Vietnam War. Snepp, whose book-length exposé of the agency's dirty tricks, *Decent Interval,* had created a firestorm with its publication in 1977, was to serve as consultant as well as be the model for the film's main character (to be played by Brando), a rogue agent bent on exposing America's covert operations abroad. Snepp visited Mulholland several times to discuss the project, and Brando led him to believe that he was serious about making the picture "correctly," by which he meant without compromise.

Their meetings stretched throughout the spring of 1984, sometimes with George Englund present and Pat Quinn taking notes. Marlon talked at great length about the hypocrisy of American foreign policy in Vietnam, about the Green Beret training programs at Fort Bragg, medical experiments at Auschwitz, the psychology of violence and killing. Snepp, like so many others before him, listened enthusiastically, hoping for validation of his own experience through a film with Brando. But Brando's attention to *Jericho* would waiver over the next several years, with many others drawn into the project each time he decided to revive the idea.

Despite the actor's disparagement of acting and his career, he still showed glimmers of delight in performing—but only in the privacy of his bedroom. Sometimes during his epic conversations with Tom Papke, he launched into renditions of his own best film roles. Startlingly enough, he generally seemed to remember his lines word-perfect.

" 'Tom, I was just thinking . . . do you have a moment?' That's how it usually began," said Papke. "Then he would go through an entire scene of *Julius Caesar* or *Streetcar* or *On the Waterfront*. Word for word he would reenact it. He could be lying in bed, he could be sitting, playing chess. All of a sudden he would become that character again—the inflections, body movements, totally. Before my eyes it was no longer Brando, the fat sloppy guy who was giving me a lot of grief. All of a sudden it was Marc Antony or Kowalski or Terry Malloy."

While Papke was entranced, he knew that a sad and defeated aura surrounded Brando's miniperformances. "One of the most amazing of these was when he did the scene in the back of the taxi with Rod Steiger from *Waterfront*," added Papke. "He said, 'I kind of wish I had done it this way,' then he launched into it.

"He had thought about playing the scene by grabbing the gun or grabbing Charley, and he said, 'Tom, you be the character here and I'll do this. You don't have to do a thing . . .' Then he did his run-throughs, two or three of them, each with different inflections—more violent, more passive. It wasn't that he was trying to do the scene right. It was a question of how it could have been done *differently*."

One day Brando gave Papke his revised rendition of *Caesar*. "He was loud—full-volume Shakespearean theatrics," said Papke. "Once he'd get himself in role, he never lapsed. His favorite picture was *Burn!*, and he brought it up so often that I finally had to go out and rent it. He loved the English accent. All of a sudden he was on the horse, I mean he was *there*. Then when he'd wind down, it was just chop, cut. Scene's over. It was that abrupt, totally professional."

While Brando was talking to Snepp and supposedly reading as preparation for writing *Jericho*, he also assigned Pat Quinn and Lis Hush to research yet another Indian film that he had in mind, *The Sand Creek Massacre*. "He said he was going to do it for free and also ask people like Redford and Newman to participate," said Quinn.

The Sand Creek Massacre was to be based on a nineteenth-century frontier incident of the same name. After a treaty had been signed, a group of Cheyenne and Arapaho had agreed to move their encampment with about 200 warriors and 500 women and children forty miles away to Sand Creek, Colorado. On November 29, 1864, roughly 750 U.S. cavalrymen led by Colonel John M. Chivington made a surprise attack on the Indians at dawn. Estimates of the number slain, including women and children, ranged from 150 to Chivington's figure of 500. Initially the soldiers were hailed as heroes, but the colonel was later discredited in investigations by Congress, a military commission, and the commissioner of Indian Affairs. Marlon wanted to play John Smith, the translator-trader for the Cheyenne.

He dispatched Quinn to the Los Angeles Public Library to study the incident and the period. Quinn made the surprising discovery that every white person of rank involved with Sand Creek, from the president on down, had been a Mason, a fact that seemed to please Brando greatly—although just why Pat was not able to fathom. The explanation in all likelihood was simple: Marlon Sr. had himself been a Mason and had risen to the order's highest ranks before his death.

Lis Hush, wife of the dying Sam Gilman, was also turning up the kinds of details Brando was avid for. Chief among her discoveries was that scalping, although it may have originated with Indians, was practiced by U.S. soldiers to the extent that they unintentionally taught it to tribes among whom the practice was unknown. Following the massacre, the soldiers marched through Denver carrying scalps, supposedly collected from the Indians' belongings but which in fact were the product of their own butchery.

In May 1985, Brando told Quinn to take her draft of the treatment to Sydney Pollack, the director of *Tootsie.*

Two weeks later Pollack called. "Pat," he said, "it's too much. I don't know how to put this picture together."

"When I told Marlon," Quinn recalled, "he said 'Bullshit.' That was the end of the discussion."

Brando tried a German producer, Thomas Schuhly, who was willing to go ahead on the basis of the loosely organized material. Schuhly arranged financing with an Italian producer. "But then Marlon stopped taking his calls," said Quinn. "That's when he said, 'I'm done with it.' "

So ended the last incarnation of Marlon's much heralded Indian project. His ambivalence and his inability to move toward a coherent, finished script had driven the last of many collaborators away. Philip Rhodes said of this dream of Marlon's: "All that went back some thirty years. It was like an old tune played over and over without much variation."

In the autumn of 1985, six months before the end of the line for *The Sand Creek Massacre,* Brando found it necessary to pursue another project, his so-called Irish movie, *The Last King.* It was based on a screenplay he'd first commissioned in the 1950s, but now he needed to give the appearance of seriously wanting to make the picture as a ploy to keep the United Artists executive on his side in the still ongoing suit against Clavell. With United Artists forging ahead with what they thought was a real project, Eoghan Harris, a journalist and former left-wing member of the Irish Parliament, was assigned to take a crack at rewriting the script. On the morning he was to meet with Brando to discuss the screenplay, Harris received a modest floral bouquet. The card read, "Welcome to the City of Angels, you won't find any, Marlon." At Mulholland, Harris, as a dedicated communist, was first struck by Brando's unpatronizing relations with his staff and commented, "You're the kind of fucker that gives communism a bad name. How do we organize against guys like you?" Brando laughed, loving the familiarity. Having immediately dismissed the "suits," the week of script conferences that followed was typical; Brando wouldn't work, and he soon made his preference for antics evident when he asked Harris one evening, "You okay for women?"

"I'm okay . . . I could always do for a woman."

"Don't worry," said Brando. "I'll fix that."

He then picked up the phone and dialed Harris's hotel, the swank Beverly Wilshire.

"This is Marlon Brando. Could I speak to Joachim."

"Marlon, please . . . " Harris whispered.

"Joachim, I have this guest here, Eoghan Harris. He's an Irish guy and, you know, he hasn't been around sex a lot. I want him to be happy . . . "

" . . . No, Joachim," Brando went on, "I can't accept that. I gave strict instructions he was to have a whore sent up to his room . . . "

Pause.

"What do you mean you don't have whores? You don't have anything else in your hotel. What the fuck good are you?"

"Please Marlon, don't. Please—" Harris whispered several times.

"Fuck you, too," Brando shouted into the phone. "Don't give me that shit. Don't tell me you don't have hundred-dollar whores. You have fifty-dollar whores all over your hotel."

By then he was roaring. "What? You're going to put the guy out on the street? You can't do this to him. . . . *Don't you hang up on me!*"

Brando put his head down, looked up and said to Harris, "Don't worry, I think I can get you a place to stay tonight."

"Marlon, couldn't you kind of ring back and apologize for this?" Harris pleaded.

Brando burst out laughing. It had all been a one-person call—a practical joke at Harris's expense.

Yet when Harris returned to his hotel one or two evenings later, he was greeted at the reception desk by an irate manager who complained about a supposed call from Harris requesting women to perform kinky acts.

"Oh, sweet Jesus!" Harris exclaimed. "He's at it again!"

Brando, Harris said, was a perfect mimic. "To do me," he added, "he had to do a Cork accent mixed with a brogue mixed with a touch of County Roscommon, and he was one hundred percent perfect. That's why he fooled the Beverly Wilshire with his voice."

Over the next three or four days Brando made it clear that he thought the proposed film was a crazy project and that he wasn't serious about it at all. Nevertheless, he seemed to like his long conversations with the screenwriter, often hoping to establish a bond by announcing, "I'm Irish like you are." Harris added, "He told me that several times, but he didn't share my class background or my working-class beliefs. He was a radical bohemian—a person without barriers, frontiers or boundaries, who has no sense of history nor of his class. Such declassed people are capable of anything."

Their discussions were all over the map. Brando would start talking about Greek philosophy, then switch the role of a zen master or a guru "like the fucking Maharishi," said Harris. "There would be twenty key buzz words that were going to unlock the secrets of the universe." At one point Brando even turned to his visitor and, like some overpraised college freshman, actually popped the question, "Who do you prefer, Plato or Aristotle?"

One afternoon Harris was talking to Brando and noticed some movement in the surveillance monitor of the front gate, above the actor's head. It was "a manic young guy in a T-shirt and jeans. He was waving and making faces."

Brando glanced at the screen. "Don't worry about it. That's my son. . . . He wants to get in."

"Well, why don't you let him in?"

"He just wants money," said Brando.

"What kind of money?"

"A hundred bucks."

"Well, give it to him," said Harris. "If you don't, I'll give it to him."

Said Brando, "This disturbing you?

"Well, it is," said Harris. "He's jumping up and down at your gate."

"Okay," said Brando, and "as a courtesy," he flicked off the monitor. Then, very movingly, he told Harris about his son—about how Christian wanted money for drugs; how if he gave him money, he'd be busted by the police. "It's the same story," he lamented. "It's happened again and again and again." He added that while he was very wealthy and famous, he really had nothing because he didn't have his son.

But Harris felt that "it seemed all histrionics. I had the sense with Brando that there was an inner commentary going on, that this was a performance rather than a felt experience. It was as if he were quoting lines and seeing himself in a play or movie of his own life.

"The problem with Brando was that he didn't seem able to distinguish between drama and real life. The pain of what was happening to his son was masked by the fact that he was playing a role, that he was constantly working through his part. To feel genuine pain is to join the world as a social animal. Marlon couldn't do that because he had withdrawn."

Brando's only genuine effusion, and his ultimate performance, during Harris's visit took place after a conversation about fathers. Harris had been talking about Jonathan Miller, the English medical doctor, astronomy buff, author, director of theater, opera, and film, and comic. What spurred Miller, said Harris, was his belief that nothing he did was worth anything compared to the work of his father—a brilliant surgeon famous for his contributions to medical science. "Jonathan Miller would give up everything else in his life if he could have been the discoverer of one planet," Harris told Brando. "He feels that all of his theatrical and film accomplishments are shit."

Brando responded by launching into a diatribe about the worthlessness of his own life. Nothing he had done was of any value, he told Harris. All his films were "shit, too" every last one, and then he went through the list chronologically. "It was sheer rant," added Harris, describing Brando's two hours of invective against the mendacity, the uselessness and meaninglessness of movies. He railed against his own films and the movie business in general.

At that point Harris became angry. "What about *Citizen Kane, On the Waterfront?*" he asked, arguing that films are an "art form."

Brando gave him a cold look. Then he went to his bookcase and opened a volume to a picture of the Sistine Chapel. "Don't talk about movies and art in the same breath. *This* is art," he said, stabbing his finger at the photo. "Michelangelo is an artist. This"—he swept his arm around his hilltop and L.A. beyond—"is just shit. These people out there, they're all making shit.

"I am not an artist," he continued. "I *hate* when people say I'm an artist. If I could have done a little bit of what he did . . ." He pointed again at Michelangelo's masterpiece. "I won't last, nothing I've done will last. The whole film business is evanescent, a passing chimera.

"Thousands of years from now," he concluded, "the Sistine Chapel will last. Even these pictures of it will last."

After he left Brando's that week, Harris never heard from him again, and he soon became aware that Brando's film and the United Artists deal were all a setup.

Nevertheless, the emptiness Brando had exposed to the Irishman was also revealed to his old acting comrade, Anthony Quinn, who had recently received attention in his second career as a painter. After not seeing each other for many years, Quinn had run into Brando in Hawaii, and Brando surprised him by suggesting they have dinner. Quinn and his wife were expected at his gallery owner's that evening, but asked Brando to join them. He agreed.

Arriving at the gallery owner's house, Quinn introduced Brando to the other guests, but Marlon immediately pulled him aside. "I want to talk to you, Tony." The two men retreated to the far side of the room and sat alone on a sofa.

"You still care, don't you?" Marlon began abruptly. "You're still in there punching, huh?"

"What else is there?" Quinn replied. "I like to paint, I like to sculpt."

"Jesus, I just like to look at fish. I stand there on my island and put my finger in and play with them. The water is so green, sometimes it's blue. That's all I like to do."

"Oh, yes, you've got a hotel . . . ," commented Quinn, not really sure what he should say.

Marlon continued, repeatedly returning to Quinn's commitment to his work as if he found it incomprehensible. After another five minutes Quinn's wife called them to the table, and as Quinn began to rise, Brando looked up at him.

"Do we have to?" he asked.

"Yes, I think we should, Marlon," Quinn said. "They're exhibiting my stuff. It's sort of expected."

Over dinner Marlon seemed to withdraw again, retreating into either silence or pseudo-Chinese conversations with his date.

"As for his seriousness in asking me whether I was 'still plugging away,' who knows?" added Quinn later. "Does anyone know when Marlon is serious? I must say he's always fascinated me, but at that dinner I had no idea why he needed to ask me this."

Whether Brando was playing with Quinn or reassessing how he lived his life, he didn't drastically alter his habits. He was deeply saddened when Sam Gilman lost his long battle to cancer on December 3, 1985. He had been generous and attentive during the months of his friend's steady decline. "Marlon went over to see him every few days," recalled Pat Quinn. "He truly loved Sam, and even though he had a poor relationship with Lis, he wanted to make sure that Sam had everything to make his final days more comfortable." According to Papke, Marlon paid bills for Gilman, and even after his death he continued to support Lis and their son.

Marlon's attitude toward helping his own son, Christian, was more ambivalent. As screenwriter Harris saw, Brando had again gone into a "tough-love" approach, after trying to help his son get on with his life.

Only a few months before the gate incident he had bought Christian a small run-down cottage for $200,000, on Wonderland Drive in Laurel Canyon. The property was deeded in Marlon's name, the arrangement being that Christian was to repay his father for the purchase when he came into his trust fund at the age of thirty in 1988.

In 1985 and 1986, Marlon tended his hilltop. He decided that he needed another inventory of his possessions, and in addition to surveying the house and the bunker, he also sent Papke down to a Beacons storage locker he had rented in Culver City to take photographs and make another list. Then he had Tom computerize the outbuilding he had constructed as an office for his secretaries—be they Quinn, Aiko (a friend of Yachiyo whom he had hired as a temp), or Barrett. When the Macs, modems, and printers were all in place, he decided to landscape the grounds outside the building with bamboo and a lawn. Next, he came up with the notion of building what he called "a Japanese studio," a low-slung, glass-walled outbuilding by the far side of the pool, to serve as a guest house.

With his real estate experience Papke felt that the land on which Marlon had built his storage shed and office and where he now planned to build the studio was in fact beyond the surveyed boundaries of the property, which amounted to only about 1.5 acres. He warned him that his deed, as filed with both the Building Department and the Registrar of Deeds, might indicate that he was encroaching on neighboring property, and he urged him to reconsider the new construction site.

Marlon's attitude was, reportedly, "Fuck 'em."

"So as before," said Papke, "he just went ahead with the Japanese studio and assumed that no one would stop him. He figured he'd grandfather it through. It was all part of his love for games. The same as his saying to me, 'Tom, I'm the sneakiest man I know after you.' "

During this time, Papke found Marlon even more irritating in his need to double-check on everything he did, and while Brando focused on his inventories and time sheets, it was evident to Papke that his involvement with the Indians had dwindled. Through her work on the *Sand Creek Massacre* project, Pat Quinn had become involved in the Indians' cause, most particularly in Leonard Peltier's defense fund, and she too saw the way he cut himself off from the Indians. "Marlon gave every indication that he supported the group," said Quinn. "I was organizing a number of benefits, but he'd just grumble, 'Yeah, yeah, use my name.' "

The Indians weren't the only ones he suspected of cheating him. He habitually complained about money, and while accountant Norty Brown was nominally his friend he was "very suspicious" of Brown, too, Papke said. "He once remarked, 'You know, Tom, any time Norty suggests a deal with me, I know he's making more money on it than I am.' "

Nevertheless, because Brown was worried about Marlon's dipping into principal he was still urging him to sell off property above and beyond

Tetiaroa. Brando, though, "thought he knew better." When he received an offer well over the $2.5 million he had paid for the San Diego industrial complex he had bought several years earlier, Marlon dug in his heels and refused to sell. "It was a very good offer," Papke confirmed. "But Marlon just wouldn't do it, figuring he would eventually get a higher price. Of course, those were the go-go years, and eventually he lost out. Norty was furious, and he called me again, saying, 'Tom, please, either have Marlon sell something or make him stop spending money.' "

What neither Brown nor Papke seemed to realize was that Marlon's need to hold on to and to itemize all his possessions was in a sense a reversion to his midwestern roots: just as he was constantly redoing and redesigning his hilltop retreat, he would not let go of his property. Like any Nebraskan farmer he seemed to view land and family as inextricably connected: his holdings were both a sanctuary for the family and a way of sanctifying it.

Perhaps as an extension of this, during 1986 Brando was taking an active interest in his son's disputed divorce settlement. Mary had simply had enough of Christian's repeated drug and alcohol abuse, their violent and angry arguments, and the many women who were either phoning or leaving notes on his windshield. The final straw, she said, was discovering Christian in bed with another woman earlier that year. Mary was then living in her own small apartment in West Hollywood and continuing to run her cosmetic business. Christian's cocaine habit was costing up to $500 a day, some friends said, and he had started to dip into both her business's profits as well as her small inheritance from her family. But it was Christian who had filed for the divorce.

Mary later claimed that her father-in-law hadn't wanted the divorce and that Brando had said that he would disinherit his son if he went through with it. In June Mary filed for an injunctive order that attempted to restrain Christian from hiding or transferring his properties and assets; it was also meant to keep him away from her apartment and her place of work, and to forbid what she described as harassing phone calls. She declared that in March 1986 Christian had told her, "My dad's lawyers are pressuring me to get it over with. They want you to sign some papers." When Mary disagreed, he then went "into a rage and said, 'You better call the police or get out of the house, because I'm going to kill you if it's the last thing I do. . . . Even after the divorce you better look behind your door.' "

Determining the value of the couple's assets in order to divide up the community property was extremely difficult, since most of Christian's assets, including the Laurel Canyon house, were in his father's name. Even his trust fund would not be available to him until he turned thirty, which was two years hence. Complicating things further, Mary's business bookkeeping was being done by Brown and Kraft, Marlon's accountants, and they knew where their loyalties lay. Mary hired famed "palimony" lawyer Marvin Mitchelson to argue her side of the case, but when the divorce was finalized in March 1987, she received monthly support of only $400 through that year—plus $1 a month for four months thereafter.

As 1986 had blurred into 1987, Marlon's only activity seemed to be Christian's divorce and the Clavell lawsuit. Pat Quinn noticed that he seemed to be increasingly withdrawn and that he spent almost all of his time in his bedroom in his Japanese robes. His lifeline remained the telephone, and often all he would talk about were his children, old times, mutual friends. It was during one of these conversations that the name of one of Marlon's old girlfriends came up—an actress whom Quinn also knew from New York. She had gotten pregnant by Marlon, had an abortion, then stuck her head in an oven when Brando broke up with her. Marlon had found her and "saved her life," as she later informed Quinn, but she said that she had never told Marlon that her suicide attempt was over him. "I mentioned that to Marlon in 1986," explained Quinn. "He was absolutely dumbfounded but didn't show any more affect than that. He just didn't seem to feel anything during those years."

"I saw increasing weight, increasing paranoia, decreasing vitality and a lack of interest in things," agreed Papke. "When I had first gone to work for him he had been vigorous. He had actually walked up and down the hillside. Now he wouldn't walk at all. He had a hard time just moving."

Marlon was not unaware of his depression or at least his lethargy. As he did with his weight problem, he made defensive jokes, sometimes calling himself a "couch potato" and even drew a cartoon of himself watching television: the T-shirt logo read "Peace and Quiet." Above his head was a trail of z-z-z-z's. The girl standing behind says, "Is it a bird? Is it a plane? No, it's Passive Man!"

Brando was stirred from his lethargy in early 1987 by news accounts of Eugene Hasenfus, a CIA cargo handler detained for weeks by the Sandinistas after his supply plane was shot down over Nicaragua. According

to a *New York Times* report, Brando had been among several interested celebrities calling Hasenfus for the rights to his story about running guns to
the contras. Frank Snepp, the former CIA agent, had also been talking to
Hasenfus. Brando rehired Pat Quinn to work on the project and got back
in touch with Snepp to suggest resurrecting the screenplay for *Jericho,* in-
corporating some of Hasenfus's story.

Marlon held four- and five-hour meetings with Quinn, Snepp, and
others throughout May and June. Finally, after six weeks, Brando threw
up his hands in exasperation. He told all concerned parties to write their
own treatments, but then decided that his version was best and that he
himself would finish the script. "Nobody's done anything on this but me,"
he announced. "I'm the one who's written this thing, so I'm the only one
taking credit."

Brando's screenplay was a strange mixture of supposed revelations of
the CIA's dirty tricks interwoven with his own personal obsessions: The
former CIA agent Jericho, a combination of Snepp and Brando, has retreated to his isolated lair, an underground den in Baja California. He is
haunted by memories of his missions as a government assassin, chiefly in
Vietnam, and his only companion is his longtime girlfriend. He is putting
together a documentary about his experiences in Vietnam, but also experimenting with biofeedback and meditation. His isolation is ensured by a
twelve-foot-high chain-link fence topped with razor wire; a gaggle of
geese within the compound, whose squawks will warn him against intrud-
ers; a surveillance camera and monitor; a large, black rottweiler; and a
half-ton, four-wheel-drive truck, loaded on a hydraulic hoist for quick and
secret getaways.

In the story the CIA tries to recruit its former agent for one last hit,
but Jericho refuses to take the job. He tells the agent he is "really interested
in butterfly migrations." The agent offers a lot of money, but Jericho re-
torts, "I'm on a permanent kickback. Besides, I just planted some rhubarb
and I want to watch it come up."

What was most intriguing about Brando's screenplay was the glimpse
it offered of an obsessive frame of mind and its unconscious associations,
even down to the smallest details, so that the whole construct became a self-
referential jigsaw puzzle. For example, he selected "Billy Harrington" as
Jericho's real name, in homage to G. L. Harrington, his psychiatrist.
(Before Harrington died in 1988, Quinn told the therapist that in the script,
Brando was crediting him "for saving his life.")

Brando was also intent on presenting an antidrug message; he blamed the CIA and the government for allowing drugs into the United States and corrupting the nation's youth. "He was very antidrug at that point, because only a year or so before he had put Christian back into St. John's for chemical dependency," Quinn recalled. As a further impetus, George Englund's son had recently died, which the press had attributed to a possible overdose.

Even more suggestive in the actor's script was a subplot involving an adopted daughter. The development of the idea coincided with the war he was still waging with Caroline Barrett against Clavell, and his own decision to adopt her daughter, Petra. If the idea of including an adopted daughter was strikingly close to the real-life Petra, it was even more disturbing that the girl in the movie was to be presented, finally, as a mate for Jericho.

Brando and Quinn finished a draft of *Jericho* in July 1987, and Brando's old friend Elliott Kastner made the project public by giving the scoop to New York gossip columnist Suzy, announcing himself as producer. Emily Lloyd, Cathy Moriarty, and Meryl Streep were discussed for the part of the daughter. Rita Moreno also wanted to be cast. She had reappeared after many, many years, and Quinn (much to her dismay) became the go-between, identifying herself as "Rosie" on the phone to make sure Moreno's husband didn't discover the trysts they were arranging.

In fact, Brando seemed to be generously promising parts to everyone. "He wanted all his friends in the movie," recalled Quinn. "Quincy Jones was going to be a black CIA agent, and he was also writing a part for Jocelyn. He then said, 'You want a part in the movie?' I said, 'What part, the daughter or the black singer? Give me a break. Let's not be funny here.'"

Sadly, another person swept into the chaos was Christian. Having taken an interest in modeling and acting, he was assigned the role of Biff, the young CIA agent. While Christian had previously insisted on trying to make it on his own, he was ecstatic about the part, hoping that working with his father would bring new harmony to their relationship.

"I'm making a movie with my dad," he told Steve Hunio with great delight. "It amazed me," Hunio later commented, "because that was the first time Marlon had made an overture like that. I think for one of the first times in his life Christian felt very close to his father."

Christian very much needed this boost, having fallen from a tree on one of his trimming jobs. He had smashed his knee so badly that he could no longer work with Cable, and the injury was "a major turning point," said Hunio. "He was sedated for quite a while because he had a lot of pain, and that gave him another excuse to lie around all day. He was on Percodan, then he would drink. He just got more and more depressed, and after that he began to use drugs again."

Although Christian still did some welding jobs, he had agreed to appear on Skip E. Lowe's Hollywood cable program—Lowe was a local celebrity hound and gossip columnist—and soon Lowe was booking him on shows in Spain and Italy as well as serving as his connection to starlets. He introduced Christian to Nan Morris Robinson, Carlo Fiore's old friend who had since become a Hollywood manager. She agreed to help Christian with his budding career. "Acting was very much what he wanted to do by then," said Robinson. "But he was also worried about whether his father would permit him to go into pictures. I was enthusiastic, yet I wanted to be sure that anything he did was on the up-and-up and had Marlon's approval."

Christian apparently also wanted his father's approval, and on more than one occasion he told Lowe, "If I find out you're giving items to the tabloids about me . . . " "He was joking, but it was that imitation macho, that impression of his father that he loved to do," Lowe recalled. When a good part finally came along and Christian didn't take it, however, some friends thought his father had nixed the project, while others blamed his new girlfriend, Laurene Landon, the "roommate" listed in Christian's divorce filings. Introduced to Christian by Lowe after his television appearance, the Love's Barbeque waitress and aspiring actress (her credits were almost exclusively grade B violent exploitation films) had set her sights on him. Hearing that Christian needed a new chain saw, she had bought him one for $1,600. "That obligated him to her," commented Robinson, "and Christian became dependent on her." By the time his divorce from Mary was final, Christian had moved Laurene into his Wonderland Avenue house and was depending on both his father and her to support them. When Laurene discovered she was pregnant, Christian was ecstatic—he was going to present his father with a grandchild. She lost the baby, however, and, according to Robinson, she almost died. "That's when she committed herself even more to him," the agent added. "She made out a will, leaving him everything she had."

In August 1987, with *Jericho* taking longer than expected, a film offer finally came Christian's way. Carmine De Benedittis, an Italian TV executive who was making his first feature, *The Issue at Stake,* approached the younger Brando. Christian tentatively agreed, provided that both Bill Cable and his wife, Shirley Cumpanas, were also cast and sent to Italy with him.

For the first few weeks things seemed to go smoothly on the set in Apulia, until it appeared that De Benedittis was reneging on his verbal agreement when it came time to put everything in writing. Christian, perhaps tutored by Marlon, announced he was flying back to the States to have his attorneys draw up contracts; he was going to ask for double the money, and insisted that De Benedittis accompany him to Los Angeles for a meeting with Marlon.

"Christian later told me that Carmine was like a child going up to Marlon's," said Cable. "He had a big statue to give to Marlon, almost as an offering, but Marlon looked at it like 'What the fuck is this?' and threw it in the closet. At one point Marlon took Christian aside and said, 'Who the fuck is this dago?' From then on it was a different story with Carmine. We all got our money."

On February 2, 1988, *Variety* reported amazingly that *Fan Tan* cowriter Donald Cammell would direct as well as cowrite *Jericho*. Both Cammell and Brando were supposedly already at work cutting the actor's script. At the same time, it was announced that Brando had signed for a cameo in *A Dry White Season,* an adaptation of André Brink's novel about a white South African waking up to the injustices of apartheid, which was scheduled to be shot in the fall of 1988.

That August, Brando decided to spend several weeks in Tahiti, intent upon losing weight for his appearances in both *A Dry White Season* and *Jericho*. Papke recalled, "He had to take off maybe thirty or forty pounds. During that period Marlon was never the three-hundred-pound blubber ball the tabloids liked to picture him as. He was a big guy, but he was only about forty or fifty pounds overweight. If he lost that, he would have been in top shape."

Soon enough, though, the *Jericho* production was faltering, with raging arguments between Elliott Kastner and Brando because of the latter's refusal to schedule a shooting date. Brando was supposedly completing his script revision, but once again making himself unavailable to his collaborator, Donald Cammell. At this point, Pat Quinn was once more advised by

Brown and Kraft that her services were no longer needed and she was given notice. Quinn never knew if Marlon took this step because he didn't want her to realize that he really wasn't revising the *Jericho* script, or because he sensed her disapproval of the affair he was having with his Guatemalan maid, Cristina Ruiz. "He told me to take all my research and notes to Donald Cammell, and that was the end of my involvement. I was very upset because he would not give me any credit for the work I'd done on the script. Maybe that's why he wanted me gone, too."

Cammell found Brando's lackadaisical rewrite almost unusable. "It was one hundred forty pages long and only two-thirds there," he later recalled. "Marlon had tried to cut it in a week, having procrastinated for months. He fucked it up completely. Left out all the good parts. It really became incoherent. But he wouldn't let anyone help him."

At the time, though, Brando had a built-in excuse for not working on the script: He was due in London to film his scenes for *A Dry White Season,* which would mark his first appearance before the cameras in almost nine years.

Martinican film director Euzhan Palcy had won international acclaim for her *Sugar Cane Alley,* but it took an enormous amount of effort to launch *A Dry White Season.* Donald Sutherland and Susan Sarandon had signed on, along with South African actor Zakes Mokae. Brando was on Palcy's and producer Paula Weinstein's wish list to play their cynical, battle-weary, antiapartheid barrister. They mentioned this fantasy to Jay Kanter, who as MGM's production president asked Brando to read the script. Then Kanter put the young director in touch with the star. At a meeting at Mulholland, Palcy told Brando that her $9 million budget did not permit big salaries. He replied, "I'll do it for nothing." He wanted his scale salary (about $4,000) donated to an antiapartheid organization and explained that "a movie like this shouldn't cost a lot of money."

Perhaps Brando was trying to make amends for all the bad press about the obscene piles of money he had made doing his earlier cameos. Undoubtedly, he was also attracted by the combination of a strong political message and a nonmainstream director who intended to make a film "from a black perspective." Meanwhile, Brando had been relatively unsuccessful in his attempt to lose weight in preparation for his return to the screen. His inability to finish the revisions of the *Jericho* script also seemed to trouble him, and he flew to London in a sullen mood and again ill with the flu.

The morning he arrived at the studio, he gave his usual reception-line performance, introducing himself to the waiting cast and crew. Palcy and Weinstein were still revising the script for his scenes, and he now added his own interpretations of the old barrister, changing him to an English attorney with a limp. Constantly sucking on lozenges for his flu, Brando had decided that his character also suffered from allergies.

As they ran through the actor's first rehearsal, there was awed silence. "Nobody was talking," recalled director Palcy. "It was magical, the myth was there. At the end of the first shot, he did something very funny: He said, 'And now I'm going to pee.' Everybody laughed, realizing he was a human being."

Donald Sutherland was equally enthusiastic. "As a fellow actor, he is blissful and so sharing," he later exclaimed. "He makes you feel so secure. I'm fifty-four, and to work with this man that I used to see in movie theaters . . . was incredibly intimidating."

However, members of the sound crew were astonished to discover that Brando's lines were being fed to him through a tiny radio in his ear. At the other end of the transmitter was Caroline Barrett, his assistant, who sat in his dressing room.

Caroline was with Marlon on the set every day. Philip and Marie Rhodes, who were also working on *A Dry White Season,* were excluded as Marlon and Barrett sequestered themselves, both at the studio and their elegant hotel. Although Marlon had been putting on his genial face with the company, Rhodes realized that he was in terrible shape; not only was he vastly overweight, but he seemed irrationally antagonistic toward old friend Sondra Lee, whom the producer had brought to London as a script and acting consultant.

When Marlon caught sight of Lee on his first day on the set, he asked Rhodes what was going on.

"They brought her in as a troubleshooter," Rhodes replied. "She's saving the show."

"What the fuck does she know!" he said angrily.

A little later, Sutherland made the mistake of telling Brando how happy he was that Sondra had been helping him. Marlon again disparaged Lee, and according to Rhodes, Sutherland then changed his tune: "For the rest of the shoot he wouldn't even say hello to Sondra." Rhodes added, "Sondra was a lovely girl, an old friend and old lover, but Marlon just cold-shouldered her. It was weird, and nobody could understand why. Of course, Marie and I had had had this done to us before, so we just said, 'Well, Marlon's gone off again.' "

Lee's response was simpler: "That person [whom I used to know] didn't exist anymore. I realize Marlon's capable of the most extraordinary cruelty—very lethal, precisely because it's so quiet and so gentle. I'd rather preserve my old image; I don't want to say that I hate him—that he's a shit and a manipulator—because that gets me nowhere."

Nothing about *A Dry White Season* alleviated Brandon's inertia and moodiness, however, nor was he about to go back to work on *Jericho* once he returned to L.A. At first the actor's resistance took the form of withholding—simply not discussing the project and refusing to take phone calls. Having been left on hold repeatedly, and not getting a return call from Brando in more than a month, Papke, who had also been promised a job on the project, finally reached him and asked, "What's new with *Jericho?*" Brando's response was abrupt: "Nothing. I fired Elliott and I fired Don Cammell."

Donald Cammell made it clear that he was absolutely finished with the man this time. "I don't need Brando to make more films," the director announced. "I'd be a sucker to fall for it again. He can always find someone else. There are plenty of suckers out there."

If anyone was disappointed by Brando's abandonment of the project, it was Christian. "All of a sudden I heard that there wasn't going to be this movie," Hunio recalled. "Christian told me it was the CIA that stepped in and pulled the plug, that they were pressuring his dad, and that it was too 'dangerous.' I don't know whether he really believed that. It could have been a way to vent his frustrations, and he may have been hiding that he knew it was Marlon himself who stopped the project."

"Whatever happened, it was a terrible blow for Christian, it really upset him," said another acquaintance, aware of how much he was looking forward to his role in the film. "He couldn't really get it together after that. I think it was then that he tried to parlay the money from his trust fund into bigger money by dealing, and that put him into the fast lane with a lot of undesirable people. And he again had a $500-a-day cocaine habit—freebasing—to support."

During the early months of 1989, Marlon went through another series of attempts to lose weight, spending a few weeks at an Australian health farm; but he returned to Los Angeles with no weight loss and in an even worse emotional state. Michael Jackson reportedly tried to help by bringing him fresh vegetables from his organic garden.

His failure to lose weight (along with the renewed suspect rumor that he was also drinking heavily) was reported by the tabloids as the reason for Yachiyo's storming out of the house during the spring of 1989, after devoting her life to Brando for seven years. But more than likely it was the culmination of many disputes and Brando's increasing interest in his housekeeper, Cristina Ruiz.

When Cristina had arrived from Guatemala as a teenager, Brando had hired her, and pleased with her quiet, unquestioning ways, he had had Quinn train her in housekeeping, "how to do things the way Marlon wanted them done. . . . Marlon is a stickler for cleanliness and order," Quinn explained. "He is very concerned about germs. All employees have to wash their hands with hospital antiseptic soap before they prepare his meals. The bathrooms have to be sparkling clean. Even the bottom of the refrigerator, where the grid collects dust, has to be scrubbed. All of this I had to teach Cristina.

"He actually whistled for her to come," Quinn continued. "At age sixty-three he got himself a slave—and sadly, that was probably all he really wanted anyway. He had his sisters as women to talk to, but I don't think he ever wanted a man-woman, equal-love relationship."

When Cristina became pregnant, whether Brando wanted the child or not, there was no question of an abortion for the young Catholic woman. Brando summoned Tom Papke and in very vague, enigmatic terms told him to locate a house in the San Fernando Valley to buy, and to work out the financial and legal arrangements. Just then, Cristina, her condition quite apparent, entered Marlon's bedroom, where they were talking, to serve Coca-Cola.

After she left, Tom asked, "How did this happen?"

"Oh, you know," Brando replied, laughing. "Those cold winter nights on the hill."

On May 13, 1989, Brando accompanied Cristina to St. John's Hospital in Santa Monica, where he watched her give birth to a daughter named Ninna Priscilla Brando. Publicly, he chose to present himself as the proud papa. "I can't believe I can feel all this love at my age," he reportedly announced, adding, "I'm going to take care of my baby. I'll do the right thing." What wasn't made public was that he had no intention of living with the twenty-one-year old mother and child, and he immediately moved them into the new $450,000 home in the San Fernando Valley.

Brando would provide Cristina with a maid of her own, a car, and a cellular telephone; once she was out of the way, he started seeing Yachiyo all over again.

Despite having given up *Jericho,* Brando was still committed to making a movie in June 1989, this one featuring a more extended role than his *Dry White Season* cameo. For all the anticipated projects, all the writing of screenplays, all the discussion of films that were to have important political themes, what he chose to appear in for his nominal "comeback" was writer-director Andrew Bergman's *The Freshman.* It was hardly a socially relevant or important picture; indeed, Brando's role was a lighthearted parody of his own performance in *The Godfather,* thus diminishing his achievement in Coppola's epic.

Why he had fastened onto this movie was a mystery to those closest to him, but according to Bergman, Brando himself had initiated everything by calling the director "out of the blue" to tell him how much he admired Bergman's script for *The In-laws.* He said that he had always enjoyed Jewish stand-up comedy, adding that he also liked Jackie Mason. A year later Bergman sent Brando the draft of his screenplay for *The Freshman,* which featured a gangster-businessman named Sabatini who "adopts" a naive Vermont kid attending film school in New York. Three weeks after receiving the script, Brando called. "I'm sorry it took so long," he said to Bergman. "Why don't you guys come to Tahiti?" By late August Brando had signed with TriStar to do the project—for a reported $3.3 million, plus 11 percent of the gross. (Brando's part of the deal was another promise to lose weight.) Bergman soon revised the script, inserting references to *The Godfather* in the form of actual movie clips to be shown in a film school class. He also introduced details that were highly suggestive of Don Corleone; although the godfather's name was never mentioned, characters remarked on Sabatini's resemblance to Brando's Mafia overlord.

The shoot finally began in New York on June 12, 1989. Brando was on the scene for twelve days and he seemed relaxed, even enjoying his reunion with Maximilian Schell, who had worked with him in *The Young Lions* thirty-two years before. More than a month later, Brando rejoined the production in Toronto for another month of shooting. Here, however, he would turn on his old friend Philip Rhodes with unprecedented fury, and Rhodes came to believe that the actor was undergoing some sort of breakdown.

Rhodes and Brando had parted angrily after *A Dry White Season,* where the Rhodeses had criticized Marlon for his treatment of Sondra Lee. When TriStar approached Rhodes to do the actor's makeup for *The Freshman,* Philip had argued about the proposed salary. Again Brando failed to stand up for him, reportedly telling the studio, 'Get another makeup man.' Hearing this, Rhodes decided to retract his demands, thinking sentimentally that since this was supposed to be Marlon's last picture, he would do it for scale. After only a few days of the Toronto shoot, the actor tore into Rhodes for leaking "something" about his personal life to the press. Just what it was that Rhodes had divulged was not made clear, but this time Brando went into a full-scale tantrum.

"He had never turned on me like that," said Rhodes. "It was frightening, and then he refused to talk to me throughout the rest of the picture. He froze me out, just ignored me. But this outburst of his really affected me. My health went to hell, and that's when I realized I couldn't live with somebody like him. I came to understand that he had decided that people like me, who know about his life, are dangerous, and then he stops thinking and has these irrational blowups. So after *The Freshman* we didn't speak for at least a year and a half."

Anxiety and tension between him and his children were probably part of what was bothering Brando. Christian was telling friends that he was supposed to join his father in Canada, giving them the impression that he was hoping his father's pull would lead to a small part in the movie. Brando nixed that idea, however, prompting an argument; as loath as always to have one of his children anywhere near a film set, he seemed unaware of Christian's disappointment.

He reacted the same way when Cheyenne called him on August 3 from Tahiti, telling him she was coming to Toronto as well. When Brando emphatically turned her down, Cheyenne took his refusal as another rejection. "He had deceived me," Cheyenne later insisted. "He had said I could visit, and made arrangements for me to come to Toronto. I wanted to see how movies were made and also see my father act, which I never had before. But most of all I just wanted to be with him. But then he started playing his foolish games and then that night he told me I couldn't come. I got so mad at him, that's when I had my accident."

Storming out of the house, she careened down the road in her brother

Teihotu's Jeep at speeds nearing 100 mph, and ended up rolling it into a ditch. The result was massive head and face injuries, and Brando had her flown to Los Angeles to be treated by specialists. He rushed from the set in Toronto and kept a vigil at her bedside after she had seven metal plates inserted in her skull and underwent extensive plastic surgery.

When he returned to Toronto he was in pieces, although he managed to hide this from the cast and crew for the next two weeks. Bergman had been able to shoot around him during his absence and had nothing but praise for his star, telling *Variety,* "He is the best—the only one left of that stature (now that Olivier is gone). He contributes constantly to the movie, and he will make you laugh." A few days before the end of the shoot, Brando threw a party, laying on an extravagant feast and showering everyone with gifts. On the evening of the movie's wrap, he went out to dinner with many of the cast and crew; he joked and laughed and lobbed matches at costar Matthew Broderick at a nearby table. But unbeknownst to any of them, he had already given a reporter from the *Toronto Globe and Mail* an exclusive interview in which he had trashed the entire production.

The story appeared the following morning, August 31, shocking everybody with Brando's blatant contempt for the movie. "It's horrible," he was reported as saying. "It's going to be a flop, but after this I'm retiring. I'm so fed up. This picture, except for the Canadian crew, was an extremely unpleasant experience. I wish I hadn't finished with a stinker."

What was stranger yet was that Brando himself had initiated the interview by calling the newspaper. He told the managing editor that he was impressed with the paper's seriousness in treating Indian issues and asked the editor to send a reporter—not an entertainment writer, but a news or political reporter—out to see him at the day's shooting location.

As it turned out, one of Brando's reasons for making his remarks was to exact retribution from TriStar. Through his London lawyer, Belinda Frixou, Brando had objected to working an extra day and claimed it should be billed as overtime. When a low-level TriStar functionary refused to pay the $50,000, Brando went ballistic and picked up the phone.

"After all that brouhaha over the interview," Papke recalled, "I asked him, 'Marlon, why did you say something so dumb about the movie?' He replied, 'The usual, those fuckers didn't want to pay me.' 'That's a strange way of getting your money,' I told him. He said, 'It worked, didn't it?' "

Despite the actor's notion that he had won the battle, his remarks were widely interpreted as mean-spirited, petty, cruel, and vindictive. Even the *Omaha World-Herald* felt compelled to scold its hometown boy in an editorial, noting that Brando "did not give much back," in contrast to Robert Redford.

But Brando soon retracted his words because it dawned on him that the movie might be a success; by bad-mouthing it, he was cutting into his own potential profits. "He had forgotten that he had a share of the gross, a piece of the action," said Sondra Lee. "He had hurt a lot of feelings, so then he had to go around saying, 'Oh, I didn't mean you.' "

First he left long messages on Matthew Broderick's answering machine, but the young actor had been so stung by Brando's disparaging comments that he refused to return the calls. When they at last did talk, Brando insisted that the feelings he had expressed in the newspaper were not his real ones. "A phone call was very nice, but nobody else hears that," Broderick later quipped.

Once the actor had gotten the $50,000 out of TriStar, he showed up to do his looping with no complaints and had the industry's heavy-hitting publicist, Pat Kingsley, and her firm, PMK, issue a statement of contrition.

It was a 1½-page combination of Academy Award thank-you list, mea culpa, and his usual self-aggrandizing statements about the state of modern society. Acknowledging that his comments "have led to painful misunderstandings on the part of a number of people," Brando blamed personal difficulties, then thanked Bergman for "a screamingly funny script," young fellow actors Broderick and Penelope Ann Miller for their "wonderfully comedic portrayals," and Bruno Kirby, "who, I'm afraid, will steal the show out from under us all."

Then he addressed the derogatory remarks he had made about the film: "Clearly, I was wrong about the quality of the picture," he averred. Slyly playing off his reputation, Brando recalled telling Broderick that his first reaction to Kazan's *On the Waterfront* was to be "convinced that I had failed. I was astounded that people thought enough of the picture to have made it a picture worthy of remembering."

Now having seen "most of *The Freshman*," he had decided that "the movie contains moments of high comedy that will be remembered for decades to come." He also insisted that if there were to be a sequel, he would be happy to appear in it. "There is no substitute for laughter in this frightened and endlessly twisting world," he intoned, and concluded by again offering his "sincere apologies for any discomforts I may have caused."

When the film opened in July 1990, reviewers were for the most part charmed by his self-spoofing godfather character. Janet Maslin praised him as "an unexpectedly deft comic actor . . . , presenting himself quite matter-of-factly as a character any filmgoer of the last twenty years will recognize." What Maslin and all the other critics seemed to ignore in their rush to flatter him for spoofing his *Godfather* role was the actor's own underlying contempt, not only for Hollywood but for himself.

The film was only a middling success, and if critics had hoped to woo Brando back to the screen with their accommodating praise of his "light comic" touch, he couldn't have cared less. Only a month after his Toronto interview he had pulled the same godfather number with MGM just before *A Dry White Season* was due to be released. Incensed that several of his long speeches had been edited out, the actor called an executive at MGM, Jeff Barbakow, demanding that the scenes be restored. When the executive refused, Brando exploded in such a rage that Barbakow filed a report with the police, alleging that the actor had threatened "to kill him and his children." Brando then contacted *Variety*'s Army Archerd to deny he had made the threat but, as with *The Freshman,* he was out to publicize his gripes about the present film and coerce the studio into meeting his demands.

"I swear on my children that I did not [threaten Barbakow]," he told Archerd. "I have never done anything physical except to a couple of paparazzi." He then proceeded with his beef against the studio: "I want this picture to succeed," he added, claiming that he had written "twenty-one pages—my courtroom scenes with Donald [Sutherland]—and I eventually directed myself as I usually do anyway. . . . They cut the climactic scene where I am confronting the judge and dragged out of court. The dramaturgy is ruined. This picture is critically important."

Brando claimed that the studio had cut the scenes for commercial reasons, although that seemed unlikely since he was the film's major box-office attraction. MGM still refused to reedit, and with the picture's release the critics were less worried about the missing bits than bent on praising Brando's "brief exquisite characterization."

Not getting his way, he took the attack one step further by agreeing to a TV interview with Connie Chung, apparently unconcerned that his public bashing might hurt the movie's chances of drawing large audiences to hear the antiapartheid message. Chung, unhappily, let him set the terms, and the show's opening teaser had Brando putting her on the defensive. When Chung asked, "What were you thinking about?" he replied, "I was thinking about what I would do if I were interviewing you, how I would get you excited, how I would steer you and manipulate you. See, that's what you're doing to me. You're manipulating me."

After a clip from *A Dry White Season,* Brando's remarks were so confusing that it was difficult to understand just exactly what had sparked his wrath. First he insisted that he was not complaining just because his time on the screen had been reduced, but because MGM and studio executive Jeff Barbakow had reneged on promises to present the picture in a certain way. His accusation seemed to be that by cutting the speeches he wrote, MGM had diluted the antiapartheid message in order to make the movie acceptable enough to be shown in South Africa.

Then, he insisted that he had donated all his salary to an antiapartheid organization on the understanding that the studio would make an equally significant contribution. Asked by Chung what his salary was, he replied: "It's hard to tell because my salary up front is $3.3 million. . . . But then I have 11.3 percent of the gross. . . . But if this picture—and as many pictures are doing today— making $100 million, I probably could stand to make maybe $10 million." He was either confusing the facts with his *Freshman* salary or intentionally distorting, since at his own insistence he had been paid scale, or approximately $4,000, making it possible for the low-budget filmmakers to hire him.

Chung then asked what the studio's reaction had been to his complaints. Brando explained that Barbakow had called the police and alleged that the actor had said, "I'm going to shoot him and I'm going to blow up his family." Brando denied all this, adding, "What would be the point of it? I mean, I've got nine children. Why would I want to jeopardize their lives and—I mean, it's unthinkable. The only thing that I can figure out is they wanted to get a jump on me because they wanted to portray me as some sort of unbalanced fanatical person who really didn't deserve the time to be listened to. But they're mistaken, because I'm not going to go away. This is life and death. We're talking about human relations, we're talking about human rights. We're addressing ourselves to racial issues and that's why I care, because it's not the money, for Christ's sake."

Chung used this rambling comment as a springboard to the logical question of why Brando didn't make his own movies to convey the message he wanted to express. "You are making me really angry now," he said, as if scolding a schoolgirl, "because I want to tell you in simple chapter and verse that I have tried to get on before the American public, before the world, a movie about the American Indians and the manner in which we committed, as a country, genocide upon those people. And I have been told to go take a flying you-know-what at a rolling doughnut."

"Is that true?" asked Chung, meekly.

"That's absolutely true," insisted Brando. "For ten years, I've tried to do it. I've written so many scripts. I have gone with so many networks, to so many studios with this tale. They don't want to hear about it."

At one point in the interview Brando insisted, "You can't act unless you are what you are and who you are." But that seemed the problem for him in his sixty-fifth year: He had donned so many masks and worn so many disguises that he no longer seemed to have a core. What struck many people who had been closest to Brando during much of his career was his ability to distort and apparently believe in his own self-sustaining fictions. For example, Walter Seltzer, the actor's old business associate in Pennebaker Inc., had watched the broadcast in amazement and then sent Brando a letter:

> Dear Bud,
>
> I was delighted to see you on Connie Chung's show. I must inform you, however, with regard to your statements about being unable to get your Indian movie project off the ground after years and years of trying to persuade "the establishment," that with over forty years of experience in this town as a producer, I would be delighted to arrange financing for your project within a single week.

During the interview Brando had described himself as staring at ants and becoming a couch potato for the past nine years. When Chung expressed her dismay, he came up with one of his most disingenuous answers: "No, I've been doing a lot of things," he told her. "I've got nine children, don't forget, and that takes quite a bit of doing."

This left everyone who knew him reeling. How could he possibly claim *nine* children? Obviously, there were Christian, Teihotu, and Cheyenne. Although his "marriage" to Movita and the births of Miko and Rebecca had always been questioned, he was evidently counting them as well. There was the last baby with Cristina Ruiz.

He had adopted Caroline Barrett's daughter, Petra; then there was the contested daughter of Marie Cui, officially named Maya Ryan, whom he had supported early on. By the mideighties Brando had given Maya permission to use the Brando name, even though at the time of her birth, he had denied that he was her father, and Chi's paternity suit had long been dismissed.

That brought the count to eight. Who was the remaining one? Possibly one of the two children that Tarita had had with her lover (Brando now claimed to be contributing to their support)? But names of other illegitimate children were floating around as well, such as Bobby, whom Christian referred to as his half-brother. Possibly he was also including in his family long ago rumored offspring such as his alleged child with Anna Gobray in Hawaii; or Liliane, the daughter of the Tahitian dancer from *Mutiny* days. And then there was the vague suggestion that he still entertained the fantasy that Pat Quinn's firstborn son, Caleb, was his as well, even though Quinn had always denied it. Nevertheless, since Brando had employed both Quinn and Caleb, perhaps he had come to believe that he had been supporting this boy, making Caleb another one of the clan.

By 1989 there was very little else in Brando's life except this notion of family, even though most of his offspring were by now young adults. He had lost friends to death, he had cut others out of his life, and as a result he had severely narrowed the number of people he was close to. Even his most loyal confidants had felt the sting of his anger. After turning against Philip Rhodes, Brando lashed out at Pat Quinn. Following the *Jericho* fiasco she had been unemployed for several months, and she called the actor to ask for a loan of $880 to help her cover arrears on her rent. There was a long pause at the other end of the line. Then he growled, "Eight hundred eighty, huh? Why don't you go down to Sunset Strip and suck somebody's cock for the rent?"

A few months later he phoned and left a song on her answering machine, either forgetting his previous remark or failing to realize how hurtful he had been. "I suppose he was getting bored and wanted somebody to talk to," added Quinn. "But he had gone too far. That was always his problem. He didn't know any limits and he was always crude, as if that was his way of proving no one could really love him."

Quinn didn't return the repeated messages from him. Then Christina phoned with a message from Brando, practically accusing Quinn's son, Caleb, of taking one of his tape recorders. Quinn wrote him a letter, which although she never sent it, was a way of coming to terms with her disappointment:

> *I have never met such a sad little boy. My heart goes out to that little boy . . . His god-given gifts, his astonishing physical beauty and extraordinary reflection of being, his amazing talent—all provided him with opportunities others can barely dream of. Yet he chose to mistreat friends and relatives and to play God with their lives, and worst of all to be a hypocritical teacher. It's no wonder to me that he chooses to hide from people, intimates, and the public. He wants to keep his own myth alive. I was one of the lucky ones who didn't choose to throw herself on the altar of this insatiable greed, the living energy given over to satisfy his needs. I guess I have my ancestors to thank for that. Maybe in an afterlife we'll meet again. If he doesn't change his ways, I'll turn and walk in the other direction and never look back.*

THE S19OOTING

1990–94

Two hours after Marlon Brando reported a shooting at his home on Mulholland Drive on the night of May 16, 1990, homicide detectives Lee Kingsford and A. R. Monsue arrived at the house. Uniformed officers had already "perimetered" the property and paramedics had pronounced the victim dead of a single .45-caliber gunshot wound to the face. Christian Brando, the thirty-two-year-old son of the world's most famous actor, had been handcuffed and was on his way down to the station for questioning; he had spontaneously blurted out to the police that he'd accidentally killed his pregnant half-sister's Tahitian boyfriend. "Man, I didn't mean to shoot him," he had said, according to the police report. "He fought for the gun. . . . We were rolling around on the couch. . . . I told him to let go. He had my hands, then *bloom!* Jesus, man, it wasn't murder. . . . Please believe me, I wouldn't do it in my father's house."

Kingsford and Monsue surveyed the small TV den where the victim lay. Around a coffee table were three white couches, and sprawled on the center one was six-foot-five Dag Drollet, barefoot, in blue surfer shorts, looking as if he'd dozed off watching television. His eyes were closed, his head leaned back against the sofa, and a blanket was draped across his legs. His left hand clenched a Bic lighter, a pouch of tobacco, and a packet of cigarette papers. Next to his right hand lay the TV's remote control. Monsue studied the fatal wound: a half-dollar-size charcoal circle on the victim's left cheek. It was discolored by gunpowder blown into the skin from perhaps as close as an inch away, and this bull's-eyed with the glistening entry wound. At the base of the neck, the bullet's exit had left only a modest trickle of blood on the sofa's armrest.

"As soon as I walked into the den and saw the guy on the couch, I said to myself, 'Something's not kosher here,' " Monsue recalled. "Nothing indicated to me that there was any big fight or ruckus. I got the impression that in fact there was a lot of history involved in this incident—that what had happened was something more than a spur-of-the-moment-type thing."

After making his preliminary walk-through of the house, Monsue found himself in Brando's bedroom, where the actor motioned for him to take a seat on one of the couches. Brando then spoke of the difficulties of raising children. "He told me he has nine children, four of whom are adopted," Monsue said. "Myself, I have three adopted children, so that gave us something in common. He talked about how we ought to apply moral standards in general, broad terms—how each of us had tried to do this with our own children. But I had the distinct impression that he felt he could have done a better job.

"Sad, very humble, very meek, he was like a tired old man," Monsue summed up his impressions, pointing out that the actor had referred to Hinduism and mystical Eastern religions. "There was a sense of being beaten about him, and he cried several times—sometimes tears, sometimes sobs. In this business, in this town, I've seen lots of hard people, but Brando's reaction was not unlike a guy who's been in prison for sixty years and comes out. Especially when he talked about his children."

Brando explained that Cheyenne, her mother, Tarita, and her boyfriend, Drollet, had been living in the house at his invitation. Cheyenne had been having severe psychological problems for the past year, owing to the automobile crash and subsequent plastic surgery. The actor had brought the girl from Tahiti over a week earlier for prenatal care in Beverly Hills as well as to see a psychiatrist. "She carries seven plates where her skull was crushed," he explained, adding that he had asked Tarita and Drollet to come along for support.

That evening Christian had visited the house for two reasons, Brando explained: to bring his pistol to Mulholland for safekeeping and to take his sister Cheyenne out to dinner. The two of them had returned from dinner around nine or ten, he said, adding that he "never keeps track of time" when he is at home. About fifteen minutes after their return, he became aware that they were in the living room, so he left his bedroom to see what was going on. He had not heard the shot, but in the living room he found Christian holding a large handgun, and his son told him that he had just shot and killed Dag. He told Christian to unload the gun and give it to him, whereupon Christian ejected an empty casing from the semiautomatic and it landed on the end table next to the couch. He then handed his father the weapon. The odor of gunpowder was plain, Brando said, and he put the gun under the cushions of the sofa in the nearby computer room. Christian, highly agitated, said that he hadn't intended to shoot Dag, but that Dag had grabbed for the gun, which had gone off.

At first he hadn't believed his son, Brando said, but when he went into the den, he found Dag lying on the sofa. He felt for a pulse and immediately called 911. He attempted to give Dag CPR but soon realized that it was too late. He said, according to the police report, that at first Christian had wanted to run, but he told him to sit down and wait for the police.

Brando added that he had instructed his son to bring his weapons to the house, because California had virtually outlawed assault rifles and he was concerned that his son still had such guns. Christian, he said, had met the victim only once or twice, but he was angry with him because Cheyenne had said that Dag had beaten her up. That was not true, Brando said. Dag had been extremely nice to his daughter—"a polite, low-key, fine young man." In recent months Cheyenne had often been irrational, her father reiterated, and she had made untrue allegations against family members in order to stir up trouble.

When Monsue asked him about Christian, Brando replied that his son had always been flighty and had a bad temper, that he exploded violently when he became angry. The actor also said that his son had always been overprotective of his baby sister.

"I think Marlon believed what his son told him," Monsue said, "but he wasn't attempting to justify Christian's actions. Although I tried not to let my own skepticism show, I think he picked up on it. I wasn't questioning what he was telling me his son said; I was wondering why certain things didn't gibe. But I think way down deep he knew that what his son had said wasn't all the truth. He kept saying, 'I don't know what happened, because I wasn't in the room when it happened.' "

Meanwhile, Detective Kingsford, the soft-spoken lead homicide detective for the West L.A. division, had interviewed Cheyenne, who told him that she and Christian had gone out for dinner at about seven. Among other things, she said, "we talked about my relationship with my father. After dinner, we stopped by his girlfriend's house, then we came back home. Christian was really upset with Dag and he went in to talk to him. I went into another room. After a few minutes I walked into the TV room where they were to see what was happening. Christian was holding a gun in his right hand and he and Dag were talking. I thought they were just playing. I went back into the other room and sat down. Moments thereafter, I heard a bang. Then Christian walked into the room and told me that he had shot Dag. I don't know who called the paramedics or the police."

Tarita, in turn, had been interviewed by Detective John Rockford. She told him that she was in her bedroom watching TV when Christian and Cheyenne returned from dinner. Cheyenne had come into her room and, in a good mood, talked about the evening. About five minutes after her daughter had left the room, she heard the shot, she said, and went into the kitchen to ask Cheyenne what had happened. Cheyenne told her not to go into the den, which she did anyway. On the couch she saw Dag. Christian and his father were in the living room, and Brando told her to be calm. He and Christian then went into the room where Dag was, but she stayed behind in the living room.

At about 2:30 in the morning, after giving his version of the night's events, Brando asked if he could contact his attorney. Monsue and Kingsford stayed in the room as he called his secretary.

"Get me Bill Kunstler *now*," he demanded. "Not five minutes from now. *Now.* Not ten minutes from now. *Now!*"

The tie between the Brando and Drollet families went back thirty years, to when Jacques Drollet, a member of the Tahitian Territorial Assembly, had led the opposition to the sale of Tetiaroa to a foreigner. Jacques had also known Brando's "Polynesian" children, as he called them, when they had been students at the Tipaerui School, where he was principal.

Cheyenne had grown from a spoiled little girl into an astonishingly beautiful young woman who dabbled in mysticism and spent her evenings at discos along Papeete's waterfront. It was in one of these discos that she met Drollet's son, then twenty-three, in May 1987, and for four years the two had been lovers. Dag, as his father would tell American authorities, "grew up well." After finishing his schooling in Tahiti, he had gone on to study in France and then undertaken a course in technical skills to prepare him to go into the construction business with his stepfather, Albert LeCaill. Sports were a major part of the young Drollet's life, too—spear fishing, sailing, and surfing, and he was also a champion motorcycle racer. With his own hands he had built a wooden house in the Polynesian style for Cheyenne and himself. It faced a lagoon on the same property as the home of his mother and stepfather, with whom he had lived since the age of four.

Cheyenne had dropped out of high school the year before. She also had drug problems, and was reportedly using both LSD and PCP, or "angel dust." Her recent favorite, according to Tetiaroa's manager, Cynthia Garbutt, was MMDA, or "ecstasy," a mild hallucinogen reputed to create a sense of love and intimacy. In 1988, when Dag went to Mooréa on business, he took Cheyenne with him to "get her away from drugs," and when she was in withdrawal, wild and screaming, he'd slapped her. There was also the issue of other women. Cheyenne would admit to reproaching Drollet over a fling with a local girl by the name of Valérie Duguet, but she also resented Tituana Degage, the mother of Dag's four-and-a-half-year-old daughter, Tiairani.

"I am the most beautiful girl in Polynesia, the most intelligent and also the richest because of my father," Cheyenne was said to have boasted, and it may have been true. As Brando's daughter, she was also the number one subject of island gossip. Unfortunately, she shared the deep insecurity of other beautiful, rich girls who felt rejected by their fathers. "She was morbidly jealous," said Jacques Drollet. "She would go to the schools of Dag's ex-girlfriends and fight with them. . . . She threw cakes in Tituana's face at the *pâtisserie*." Although intelligent and surprisingly well read, Cheyenne lacked any purpose or ambition and seemed unable to make a life for herself.

"When I met Cheyenne, I thought she was very aloof," said Christian's friend Bill Cable, who was introduced to her during his stay on Tetiaroa in 1984. "I'd walk up to her and her girlfriend and say hi, and they would just move away from me. One time Christian saw me looking at her, and he said, 'Hey, Cabe, you better watch it. That's Pop's pride and joy.' "

Nevertheless, Brando had been an intermittent father at best, and even before her accident Cheyenne felt deeply bitter toward him. Teihotu had pulled away to have a life of his own—he was now married with two children—but Cheyenne had remained in her father's orbit, where she was constantly reminded of her mother's and her own secondary position in his life. Her father's new baby, Ninna, born to housemaid Cristina Ruiz, was another blow, all complicated by her own pregnancy.

After her Jeep accident and extensive surgery in August 1989, Cheyenne had recuperated in Los Angeles and then returned to Tahiti, where she was reunited with Dag in October and soon became pregnant. Hearing the news of her pregnancy, Brando arranged to hire Dag to supervise construction on Tetiaroa in January 1990.

Brando had often told Christian that he wanted to become a grandfather, and now that Cheyenne was pregnant, he was reportedly thrilled and wanted to do anything he could to make the young couple happy. But Cheyenne and Dag were growing increasingly estranged from each other, and she was becoming even more emotionally unstable.

"Dag and Cheyenne lived like two scorpions in a glass," said Jacques Drollet, who had been watching the relationship deteriorate. "They were looking at each other suspiciously, they were jealous of each other, they were having fights and slapping each other." Marlon was equally concerned, and in mid-March 1990 in Papeete, he and Jacques discussed the problem of their children's drug use. Jacques, however, said later that he had advised his son to find some way to end the relationship. "Otherwise you will be hurt," he told his son. "Your life smells of tragedy."

Cheyenne had undergone brief psychiatric treatment that April at Tahiti's military hospital. The twenty-year-old's symptoms, according to medical records, were "aggression and instability . . . , sleeping problems that seem to be accompanied by episodes of vacillating contact with reality, the result of drugs," coupled with a failure to "understand or recognize the existence of these problems."

Brando then decided that she should return to Los Angeles, so he removed her from the hospital and made plans to bring her to Mulholland. He wanted her put in the care of American professionals, and he also thought it would be better for her to give birth in the United States. Dag had decided to break up with her, but with Cheyenne's trip to Los Angeles already planned, he'd told his father that he felt it was his last responsibility to accompany her to Brando's house and help her get settled there.

In the first week in May, Cheyenne, Tarita, and Dag flew to the United States and moved in at Mulholland. Cheyenne saw psychiatrists at once, but her mood did not improve; part of the problem was her reluctance and sometimes her refusal to stay on schedule with her psychotropic medication. According to Detective Monsue, "she was supposed to be seeing a doctor and taking medication, but she was fighting her father about this, refusing to take the medication. He had thought if he brought her to his house along with her mother and boyfriend, then she might do what she was supposed to. I didn't speak with her directly, but I did see her, and she definitely had some problems. She was obviously not all there."

Cheyenne became especially agitated and depressed after Dag informed her that he was pulling out of the relationship. He said he would stay only a few more days because he had to be back in Tahiti on May 20 to stand trial for a car accident that he'd been involved in. Dag phoned Cynthia Garbutt, Brando's office manager in Tahiti, and in the course of working out his travel arrangements, he told her that Cheyenne was trying to keep him from leaving by hiding his passport.

This was the least of it, though. Cheyenne's emotional state worsened over the next few days; she was popping tranquilizers and smoking non-stop, and one afternoon, in another raging argument with Dag, she declared that he was not the father of her baby. By May 16 the atmosphere inside the house was tense, even though Brando had reportedly phoned Jay Kanter in one of his oversentimental moods to tell him that it was "wonderful having the family all together."

If Cheyenne's problems were disconcerting, Christian had been in an even worse state the previous year, his downward slide escalating with every passing month. He had pulled back from his father, fearful of Brando's wrath and disapproval, and several times when Marlon had phoned to invite him up to the house for dinner, he had declined with vague excuses that he was "too busy." Although he pretended to get a kick out of Cristina Ruiz's new baby ("Hey, guess what," he told friends. "Pop knocked up the little Mexican maid, but don't tell anyone"), he never mentioned the birth of his new half-sister thereafter.

He had repeatedly told friends, however, that he was very concerned about Cheyenne after her accident. "He said, 'My baby sister has had a bad wreck,' " his friend Bill Cable recalled. "He always referred to her as 'my baby sister,' and he said that her injuries had just freaked his father out."

Though Christian tried to hide from Marlon the chaotic and self-destructive life he was leading, ironically, he had tried reestablishing contact with his mother. Skip E. Lowe had been in touch with Anna Kashfi when her second husband, Jim Hannaford, died, and he passed along the information that she was destitute, on government assistance, and staying at a friend's home in a small town east of San Diego. He also relayed the message to Christian that his mother was begging to see him. Finally Christian relented—he phoned and made arrangements to have his mother stay with him at the Wonderland Avenue house.

Anticipating the visit, Christian seemed excited and even told friends that the reason his mother was in such a desperate state was that, following their divorce, Brando had blackballed her in Hollywood. Steve Hunio was skeptical about Christian's newfound sympathy, having heard the many horror stories about his childhood. He thought that Christian's problems with alcohol had started when he was a baby and Kashfi had allegedly spiked his bottle with whiskey to keep him quiet. "I told him that I thought the idea of his mother's visit was absolutely lunatic," Hunio recalled. "But he really wanted to say, 'Oh, Mom, welcome back!' and he went ahead with it."

In preparation for his mother's arrival, he bought a new bed for her and told Cable, "I'm going to take care of my mom. She's so down and out, I'm going to give her some money and have her stay with me." Cable realized that it would be a tense situation, but encouraged his friend. "I know you've had a tough time with her," he said, "but I wish you luck." Like Hunio, he had heard Christian recall the terrible things he claimed Kashfi had done to him when she was drunk and on pills; yet he still thought it was commendable of Christian to want to assist her.

When Marlon got wind of the visit, he phoned Christian and angrily demanded an explanation. Said Cable, "Christian told me that he had tried to explain how down and out Anna was and that he just wanted to help her. Marlon said, 'Get her a fucking shopping cart,' and hung up, like 'Fuck her, she's a street person.' "

Whether Brando's disapproval put the kibosh on Christian's attempt to reconnect with his mother, or he simply found Kashfi too difficult as a housemate, their reconciliation lasted only two days. "He was really trying to be a good boy," said Skip E. Lowe, "but something happened—I don't know what—and Anna left soon after she arrived." Hunio thought Kashfi's swift departure had less to do with Brando's angry reaction than with Christian's realization that he still harbored angry feelings toward her. As he later told Cable, "My mom is gone. Boy, she's such a mess."

There was, however, one other member of the Brando clan with whom Christian kept up a close relationship—his half-brother Bobby, his cohort at the time he and another friend had been picked up for shooting at the government missile installation up on Mulholland.

Although Brando had refused to recognize him as a son, Bobby sometimes visited at the Wonderland Avenue house and Christian openly introduced him as "my little brother," said Cable, adding that Christian explained that Bobby "lived with his mother, who had married some rich guy who had died and left him around twenty million." None of Christian's friends knew the full story behind the handsome young Asian or who his mother was or even his last name. "He never visited when Christian lived at Mulholland," Cable added, "but when Christian had his own place, he would often come by. He was half-Oriental, a little younger than Christian. He had long black hair and was into kung fu and that sort of stuff. He didn't do drugs or drink, only had juice when he visited because he was clean as a whistle—a sensitive, sweet kid. Christian liked having him around, even though apparently Marlon never wanted to see him."

While Christian made a point of saying Bobby was his "little brother" and Cheyenne his "baby sister," he went out of his way to explain to friends that Miko was in fact "adopted." He never even mentioned Miko's sister, Rebecca, who was then a student at the University of Arizona. While he claimed great love for Cheyenne, he often expressed resentment toward Teihotu and his life on Tahiti, complaining, according to Cable, that "I'm busting my fucking ass, and Teihotu's over there surfing, with my dad paying the bills." Christian evidently liked the idea of being the firstborn and favored son, the child whom Brando considered truly his own, but he seemed to feel that more was expected of him than any of the actor's other offspring—which, according to Pat Quinn, was exactly the case.

Perhaps it was for this very reason that Christian had remained more aloof from his father during the year or so preceding the shooting; he was desperate to create a persona. It was as if he had to prove that he was as tough as his father, because, said Hunio, "there had been competitiveness between them for years." Cable agreed. "He liked to tell the story of when he was a kid, wading in the lagoon on Tetiaroa, and a reef shark, three or four feet long, swam by. He said Marlon shouted 'Motherfucker!' and hauled off and socked the shark in the snout. Christian always talked about this to show how macho-tough his father was. He'd say, 'Shit, Pop will duke it out with anybody.' " Part of his father's macho image, too, was his having guns and being willing to use them, and Christian often told Cable the story of the intruder breaking into Mulholland and Brando's pulling his .38 on him. Christian's own interest in guns seemed to be part of his attempt to measure up, and in fact, with a $75,000 paycheck from the Italian movie in his pocket, one of his first purchases had been an expensive Beretta shotgun.

On the other hand, he was afraid of his father and feared disappointing him. Christian had come into his trust fund in 1988, and it was being paid out in installments of about $2,000 a month, tax-free. But during 1989 and the early months of 1990, he had been running through his funds as if there were no tomorrow. Instead of repaying his father, as promised, for the Wonderland house, or using the money to try to get his life in order, it had all gone for dope, a $9,000 motorcycle, and more guns, along with gifts and handouts to friends. As his guilt and self-hatred accelerated, so too did his substance abuse and out-of-control behavior.

His old girlfriend, Laurene Landon, had tried to get him to stop drinking, but Christian's reply was, "Fuck you, leave me alone. You're not my mother." Their relationship had further deteriorated after Laurene's failed pregnancy. "That tore him up," recalled Cable. "Marlon kept telling Christian how much he wanted a grandchild, how much he hoped Laurene and he would have a baby." Christian continued to drink and pick up other women for one-night stands, and finally he and Laurene broke up.

Christian then spent most of his time with the ragtag band of a half-dozen or so bikers, dopers, and bottom-of-the-barrel bums he had hooked up with in Laurel Canyon—the "Down Boys," as he called them. Several had arrest records. Christian still supplied the beer and the dope, and the Wonderland house became a crash pad, filled with these hangers-on who could become violent when crossed. One especially dangerous member of the group was a thirty-five-year-old mountain of a man known as Big Bad Frank, who was evidently Christian's main drug connection. "It was like Frank was his bat man," explained Hunio. "He had a ready-made drug dealer on the premises, somebody he could tell to go make the dope runs for him, so of course he was not going to throw him out." The house was always in squalor, with dirty clothes and beer cans strewn around the living room. Whenever friends like Cable or Steve Hunio suggested that he clean up the mess, he'd yell at them, "Fuck you! If you don't like it, go home," and he still continued to down a six-pack of Colt .45 by noon.

"Getting his trust fund in 1988 was like getting the means to his own downfall," said Hunio. "He didn't have to worry about what he would do for money, and if he sometimes ran short at the end of the month, he'd just go to Brown and Kraft and give them some song and dance and hit them up for an advance on the monthly payment. He was doing nothing about his life, just hanging out with these leeches, staying up all night, waking up at two in the afternoon. He knew that I felt he was destroying himself, and maybe he stayed away from me for fear of being rejected. He was very concerned about it, scared that he was on a roller coaster, but he still never kept those guys out of his home. They were real scum—put twenty of them together and you still wouldn't have a human being."

Although Hunio absented himself from the scene, Christian maintained his friendship with Bill Cable throughout most of 1989. Cable lived in Studio City, and because of his interest in bodybuilding, his bedroom walls were covered with photographs of shirtless men, including himself. Resting on long-horned racks were two saddles that he used in his stunt riding. Bullwhips, hunting bows and barbed arrows, and an extensive knife collection were also on display. But more noticeable than anything else were Cable's guns. In one corner of the room stood two .22s, two shotguns, and a 7mm Mauser high-powered rifle, while draped over the door to the clothes closet were bandoliers filled with 12-gauge 00 buckshot and slug shells; in the drawer of the nightstand there were several handguns.

Cable and Christian had always shared an interest in guns, but during 1989 Cable realized that Christian's attitude had changed. "He said he was getting phone calls," recalled Cable, "someone threatening, 'We're going to kill you and your whole family.' Sometimes I stayed with him when my wife and I were having fights, and one day I answered the phone and heard the same threat. Christian didn't want his father to know about them, but he asked me, 'Do you think these people mean it?' I said, 'I don't know, but there are crazy people out there.' But this really added to his paranoia, and he was amped out anyway."

It was at this point that Christian said that he wanted to get "a handgun for self-defense," Cable explained. Cable, a former cop, suggested that they go browse at B&B Gun Sales, a firearms dealer in the Valley. "It was like someone taking a little kid to a candy store," Cable recalled. "I was supposed to help him choose."

The Sig-Sauer .45 was the Porsche of handguns, and even though it cost over $800, Cable bought one as well, dubbing the pair the "sister Sigs." "But you have to promise me, Christian," he said fifteen days later, when they left the store with their new guns, "This is not a toy. You have to be careful with it."

"Okay, okay, I promise," said Christian. "I'll get a gun safe for it."

Christian always kept the Sig-Sauer next to his bed, and just as Cable instructed him, he kept the gun loaded. Since it had a double-action trigger, Cable also taught him his own routine—keeping the ammunition clip in place, with a round in the chamber. "That way if someone breaks into the house," added Cable, "you don't even have to pull the hammer back."

But having the .45 wasn't enough to give Christian peace of mind. A few months later he bought Cable's MAC-10, another semiautomatic and the favored weapon of Miami drug dealers. Like other assault weapons marketed to civilians, it featured a large-capacity magazine and could, with a few modifications, be turned into a full-fledged submachine gun. Christian then bought another gun—a Springfield Armory M-14, a standard-issue military weapon.

In addition to his guns, Christian had also been collecting an array of women, usually one-night stands. "It was basically just for sex," recalled Cable. "There were all these chicks around. He'd have this one, then that one, and then a couple more on the side, just like his dad." One of the women among Christian's long line of conquests was a stripper described as a "wannabe starlet" by a former boyfriend. She moved into the Wonderland house for a few weeks, becoming familiar with the Down Boys as she, too, began to drink and use cocaine more heavily. Several people reported seeing Christian treating her badly, hitting her at parties.

In the fall of 1989 Cable and his wife, Shirley Cumpanas, were having difficulties, and when she told him she was leaving him, he went to Hawaii for several weeks to cool off. In his absence Shirley dropped in at Wonderland, and that evening she and Christian began an affair. Hunio had been present when Shirley stopped by, and he was, as he put it, "underwhelmed. . . . She was fondling Christian in front of everyone, and I realized that she was going to go with Christian into his bedroom, which didn't even have a door on it and, inside, there was only a mattress with a torn blanket. All the time I was thinking how sad it was, because I knew that this didn't mean anything to Christian. I thought he also enjoyed putting the digs into Bill Cable."

Whatever his delight at besting his surrogate older brother, Christian was also afraid of his friend's wrath. "Bill walked in on us one night when he got home from Hawaii," Cumpanas later explained. "We were on the bed, and he said, 'Well, isn't this a cozy scene?' We tried to convince him that nothing had happened, but in fact it had. We were together for several months after that, and during that time Christian was scared to death of Bill. Bill had all his guns; he was a big guy and had a reputation for being 'bad.' I was frightened, too, because I had seen him get angry and then take out his guns and play with them."

Taken together, the conflict with Cable and the various run-ins with dopers heightened Christian's paranoia, so much so that he had then hired Big Bad Frank, the old-time Down Boy and sometime drug procurer, as his "bodyguard."

"Frank was one of the cleanest of the bunch," said Cumpanas, "but he was also one of the baddest. He was the one who could handle Bill if he walked in with a gun, and he became Christian's best friend, now that he didn't have Bill. He used to stand guard outside the house, always on the lookout."

Whether Cable was actually threatening his former "brother" was unclear, but Christian had evidently reached a crisis level. He soon took the strange step of renting another shack in Laurel Canyon, an even more dilapidated one located deep in the canyon's brush. He rationalized the move by explaining that he could rent the Wonderland Avenue house to bring in money "to repay his dad," as he told Cumpanas; it also seemed that he thought he could escape the amorphous threats posed by Cable, the Down Boys, and anyone else he was afraid of. Certainly none of his friends and family could reach him there, because he had his phone disconnected.

During the fall of 1989 Christian worked at odd welding jobs, but he also made a few halfhearted attempts to continue his acting career. In September he went to read for Henry Rakin, a casting director working as an associate producer, for a role as a heavy in a film.

"He came into the interview and told us, 'You'll have to excuse me,

I'm a little bit shook up,' " said Rakin. "He explained that his girlfriend's ex-husband had broken into the apartment with a gun that morning. He said that he almost hadn't come because of the incident, but that would be 'unprofessional' and he wanted to impress us as being 'together.' "

The Rakin project was postponed; Christian missed meetings with his agent, Don Gurler, or he'd show up directly from a welding job wearing dirty jeans. Then he dropped out of sight, and Gurler recalled that he heard through a couple of his friends that "he was partying."

Gurler phoned Christian at Wonderland, but to no avail. Later Christian told friends that he had moved out of his home because it was haunted. One night, he claimed, he'd heard a woman's screams coming from the bathroom. He told Cumpanas the same thing. "I never heard or saw anything peculiar," she added, "but he insisted."

Perhaps Christian was now having full-scale drug hallucinations or DTs. His friends claimed that he had finally moved out of the Wonderland house completely, even though he hadn't found a renter. Instead, he paid Frank to stay there to guard the place and his possessions. The rented shack, which cost $1,300 a month, was built into the side of the hill and had a cavelike quality, and Christian furnished the place with only a futon in one bedroom and his welding equipment in the other. Friends suspected that the new hideaway wasn't just to escape the Down Boys and Bill, but also served as his secret place where he could hide his guns and/or carry out drug deals. Some people who knew Christian also claimed that he had tried to make money as a dealer, but he then used the coke himself and often didn't have the cash to pay his suppliers. "He used to say, 'I'm Marlon Brando's son, I'm good for it,' " recalled a Sunset Strip regular familiar with the crowd Christian was running with. "But these guys don't give a shit about Marlon Brando, and they started leaning on him."

Paranoia, hallucinations, alcohol, and cocaine were bound to be lethal when combined with guns. But having the guns raised another fear—that the Down Boys would try to steal them. Now Christian purchased a large lockable cabinet. Even that did not quell his anxieties, so it may have come as a relief, strangely enough, when in January 1990 California passed a law banning assault weapons. His father ordered him to bring all his guns up to Mulholland, intending, he later told the police, to turn them over to authorities.

Whether Brando had actually meant to do so was questionable, since neither Christian nor his friends had the impression that Brando was doing anything but holding the guns for his son at Mulholland. Not all of his guns, however. Christian retained the Sig-Sauer .45, which he kept with him wherever he was living.

During the first few months of 1990, Christian was again on the move, staying often at the apartment of Jocelyne Lew, an Asian model and aspiring actress whom he had also met through Skip E. Lowe. With Lew he seemed less belligerent but often spoke of the conflicts he was having with his father, who was now insisting that Christian go to Tetiaroa to work. Marlon had also criticized him for his continued drinking and smoking, despite the fact that his nicotine habit paled in comparison to his coke addiction. "He said that whenever his father saw that he had a cigarette in his hand, he would take it, break it in half, and spit on it," said Lew. "Which he thought was ironic because it had been Marlon who got him smoking in the first place when he was only thirteen. He said that he was living in Paris with him while his father made *Last Tango,* and they used to sit in the sidewalk cafés and smoke." Lew neither smoked nor drank, and she had the feeling that Christian's interest in her was part of his attempt to "get back to more wholesome friends. . . . He told me," she added, " 'I feel like I have to be so good around you all the time.' " Nevertheless, it was soon obvious that Christian always needed a drink—not to get drunk, but to get through the day. When he and Lew went out for breakfast, he often ordered a couple of Irish coffees. When she commented that this was not a good idea, he'd laugh and tell her about his grandfather, Anna's father, who he said was "Irish" and still alive in his nineties, even though he drank a bottle of Bushmills every day.

By the beginning of May, Christian was seeing Lew less frequently and had resumed his relationship with Laurene Landon. "We had been together for almost six years before that," Laurene insisted, "and then we broke up for a period of two months and two months only. We were back together in May and we were very much in love with each other."

Laurene had seen the desperate straits Christian had fallen into and she set out not only to reconcile with her old boyfriend but also to help him. According to Bill Cable, she continued to encourage Christian to join AA and dry out. Hunio felt, however, that Laurene also provided Christian with excuses, rationalizing his drunkenness and accepting his behavior so as not to risk losing him again.

Whatever her motives, she did seem to provide some stability in the midst of his whirling passage. He began to stay at her apartment, which she shared with her mother. Often the two even went out shopping, and Christian began to buy himself new Levi's and work boots to replace the threadbare outfits he'd been living in during the previous months.

Bill Cable was now reunited with Cumpanas, and while he was still upset about the affair with Shirley, he also missed seeing his old friend. "He said, 'I'm still hurt. I've never gotten over this,' " Shirley explained. "I calmed him down and told him, 'Billy, Christian really loves you. He's cried many times about you.' " Her words seemed to have a soothing effect, and Bill phoned Christian on May 14 and they made plans to "get together for a few drinks." Hence, one day before the shooting, Christian had reconciled with his "big brother."

During the afternoon of May 16, Christian went up to Mulholland to see his father, who summoned him to his bedroom, where they held a private conversation. What they talked about later became a matter of dispute—whether or not Marlon told him that Cheyenne said that Dag had been beating her—but Brando apparently at least let Christian know that his little sister was depressed and asked him to cheer her up by taking her out to dinner. Christian agreed, and then Brando made another "request," one that his son apparently took as an order: He was to bring his last gun, the Sig-Sauer .45, up to the house when he returned with Cheyenne from the restaurant.

The interrogation room where Christian was taken after Dag Drollet's shooting was not much bigger than a walk-in closet, and shortly after midnight he was read his Miranda rights. He waived the presence of a lawyer, and with Detective Steve Osti and uniformed officer Steve Cunningham across the table from him, he talked and chain-smoked, his voice rising in odd intervals of contralto panic and macho bluster. Early on in the session, he was very controlled.

DETECTIVE: Okay. Officer Cunningham has told me that apparently this guy is the father of your sister's kid?

CHRISTIAN: Yes, sir, that's quite correct. . . . We got in a struggle and the gun went off in his face. I didn't want to hurt him. I didn't want to kill him.

DETECTIVE: No man wants to kill anybody.

CHRISTIAN: I know. You know, we got in a struggle. I said, "Let go," and I'd been drinking, you know. I had about three gin and tonics. I didn't I mean, go up to him and go *boom!* in my dad's house. If I was going to do that, I'd take him down the road and knock him off.

The detective tried to take him back to earlier that evening.

DETECTIVE: So you and your sister went out. What happened with you and your sister. What did you talk about?

CHRISTIAN: Oh, how's life.

DETECTIVE: So that was at dinner. Okay, when you came back from dinner, back to your dad's house, what happened?

CHRISTIAN: I had that thing under there—I put it under there and I went in the other room and I went back. He's lying there on the couch. I said, "Get your fucking ass off the goddamned couch. I want my—" You know, I couldn't get at it. I'd wanted to pull it out, and I was going to put it in the old man's room, all right, with the rest of my—you know, my $2,000 shotguns and that stuff. We got in an argument and he grabbed the gun.

DETECTIVE: Tell me about the argument, what was that about? . . . Did you argue about your sister being pregnant?

CHRISTIAN: No. No, sir, that wasn't . . .

DETECTIVE: So it was more or less just the fact that he was sitting on the couch and—

CHRISTIAN: I just said, "Get up, I want to take it in the other room." And we started struggling with the gun, and there was one in the chamber. It was cocked. There was a round in the chamber, and—

They questioned him about Cheyenne.

CHRISTIAN: My sister's been going through a lot of emotional stress.

DETECTIVE: What did she tell you tonight?

CHRISTIAN: I don't know. She took acid, was smoking pot, and then she—I guess Pop told her she'd been driving everybody nuts. She did a bunch of tranquilizers and throwing up blood and stuff, and they had to rush her down to the hospital with the baby inside of her. Drinking.

Partway through the interrogation, the officers came upon a discrepancy.

DETECTIVE: I know I've been out of the room for a while and you've been talking to Officer Cunningham, and apparently you told him the gun wasn't really where you told me it was.

CHRISTIAN: In the couch?

DETECTIVE: Yeah.

CHRISTIAN: Underneath the couch.

DETECTIVE: But there's some . . . When you left wherever you and your sister were having dinner at, you went to your girlfriend's house and . . . ?

CHRISTIAN: Oh yeah, I went over there to get it, because that's how I got there.

DETECTIVE: That was tonight?

CHRISTIAN: Yeah. That was—yeah.

DETECTIVE: So the gun was at your girlfriend's house? You picked up the gun there?

CHRISTIAN: Yeah.

The officers asked more questions about the stop at Laurene Landon's house.

DETECTIVE: And then you went up to Laurene's apartment and got Laurene?

CHRISTIAN: I went up to Laurene's.

DETECTIVE: When you came down—that's when you went upstairs and then you came downstairs back to your car—that's when you picked up the gun?

CHRISTIAN: Yeah. When I came downstairs, right.

DETECTIVE: Which was after dinner, before you got to your dad's house?

CHRISTIAN: Right.

DETECTIVE: [That] is when you got the gun, okay. What did you say to Laurene?

CHRISTIAN: I don't know. I was all pissed off or something, I said, "I'll be back." I said, "Come down and meet her. She's pregnant, and this guy's giving her a bunch of gruff." And I—I don't remember what I said really, honestly. I can't tell you.

DETECTIVE: What did Cheyenne say about the relationship that she wanted with this guy? Did she talk to you about, she wanted it to continue, or what were her thoughts on this guy?

CHRISTIAN: Well, she wasn't too happy. You know, he's a leech, you know?

DETECTIVE: Does your dad know that she's pregnant?

CHRISTIAN: Oh hell, yeah. Her belly's out to here. Of course he knows. I love her to death, so much, and I just, I wouldn't go that far to . . . if I was going to do something devious like this, I mean, I would have: "Hey, let's go out, you know, check out the mine shafts on the Mojave." You know, or something like that. Whoops! He fell down a hole. Couldn't help it. "See you later, sucker." You know, I mean, all delicately laid—take him out to Death Valley, no clothes on, and give him three gallons of water. "Get a suntan."

As Christian continued to undergo questioning at the police station, his father was forced to deal with the consequences of his son's act. With the police combing the house and the forensics technicians photographing the crime scene, the coroner's office personnel arrived and prepared to take Dag away in a maroon body bag. As the assistants recalled, they were carrying the bag through the kitchen to the side door when Brando stopped them and asked that the bag be unzipped so that he could take one last look at Dag. Finally the investigative teams left and he retreated to his bedroom, apparently shattered, because he did nothing more for about an hour except fumble for his Valium. Then, he phoned Cynthia Garbutt, his office manager in Papeete, to tell her of Dag's death and ask for the telephone numbers of the young man's parents.

As Brando would later confirm in court, he had been able to reach Jacques Drollet three years before to comfort him when his daughter died in a Pan Am jet that had crashed while taking off from Papeete's Faaa Airport. But now, for whatever reason, he seemed incapable of making contact. At 8:45 A.M. Drollet was at breakfast when word reached him through his nephew's office that someone in the United States was trying to contact him about Dag's "having problems with the police in Los Angeles." Drollet took the number and made the call from his bedside phone. He reached an unknown voice at the other end and the man identified himself as a Mr. Monsky, executive producer of "Hard Copy." He asked if he could tape-record their conversation. Immediately wary, Drollet asked what he was up to, thinking that someone "might be trying to frame Marlon."

"Don't you know your son has been shot dead by Christian Brando in Marlon's house?" the producer replied.

Drollet sat down on the bed, stunned. All he could say was, "Are you kidding?"

Monsky replied, "No, I'm not kidding. I never kid . . ."

"Oh my God," said Jacques. "Oh my God."

"What was Dag like?" the producer asked, still intent on carrying out an interview.

Drollet abruptly ended the conversation and tried to reach Brando. But when he phoned, it was "as if someone picked up, and I would say, 'Marlon, it's Jacques-Denis Drollet. Can I talk to you?' Five times I did that, and there was a click and a disconnection."

Cynthia Garbutt tried several more times herself to reach Brando for Drollet. "Finally I got through," she said, "and he told me, 'There will be a call.'" Garbutt repeated this to Drollet, advising him to wait at his home. Later, however, she shifted gears and insisted that Brando had been trying to reach Drollet "all night."

Brando finally telephoned Jacques not at his own home but at the home of Dag's mother, Lisette, and her husband, Albert LeCaill. His message was that Dag had been shot by Christian "in an accident"—a brawl, he termed it. "I didn't know the word—I had to look in the dictionary," Drollet recalled. "Marlon said, 'Dag is dead, there is nothing we can do about it.' I asked him how he got shot and he said, 'Christian was told by Cheyenne that Dag was beating her, and that was totally untrue.' That was his word, *untrue*. And then he was sobbing." The conversation, lasting only two or three minutes, was the last private communication that Drollet and Brando would ever have.

In the days following the death of Dag Drollet, reporters gathered around the heavy steel gate at the foot of the Mulholland driveway, searching for scraps of information. Some resorted to sifting through trash in a bin outside the compound, but they found only fan letters addressed to Jack Nicholson. Helicopters carrying photographers circled overhead. Worldwide, the headlines were all similar: BRANDO SON HELD AFTER MURDER, MURDER IN BRANDO MANSION, DEATH IN THE HOUSE OF BRANDO.

Christian had been in jail for three days before his father finally went to see him. His visit earned him more coverage: BRANDO IN TEARFUL VISIT TO SON, and THE GOOD FATHER, the press painting him as the loving patriarch. Reporters had it wrong, however, or at least were covering what was happening only superficially. Brando was in fact working his own agenda, playing amateur detective: Not only was he questioning Cheyenne, but he was also trying to reconstruct the crime scene, and once again he had called on the man upon whom he had often relied for scientific and technical knowledge in the past: his on-again, off-again assistant, Tom Papke.

Papke arrived at Mulholland the day after the killing, around noon, just as a team of LAPD investigators were about to leave after reinspecting the TV room. "Marlon was very pale and very, very quiet," he recalled. "Not his usual self. A little bit ratty."

The police had been trying to find the spent .45-caliber bullet. The furniture had all been removed, the couch stored in the bunker, and the white carpeting showed a blood stain slightly less than a yard wide. Marlon asked Papke to proofread a long, convoluted letter he'd written to the paramedics and police, thanking them for their consideration.

"Marlon, don't send this," Papke advised him. "This is ridiculous. You don't send letters like this. It's off the wall."

"I knew he wanted to be a good guy about this," Papke explained later, "but he was just absolutely torn to shreds, and he wasn't functioning."

Soon, though, Brando would go right ahead and send the letter, full of his usual misspellings:

> *Dear Sgt. Walker,*
>
> *The fact that we lost the chance to have cristian back home with us, out on bail and relitivly free, does not diminish in the slightest degree my appreciation of the maner in which you and all of the other detectives, ploice officers and para-medics conducted themselves at my home last Tuesday in addition to those officers who came on successive days. I was greatly assisted by those who counseled me because I thought I was going to lose my mind three or four times. I was fight to control myself sometimes it it felt like I was going mad. It still seems as though I am actually living a dream that I can't wake up from. I guess, some times you just have to scrap it out to the end. I was especially greatful because my daughter is pregnant and she as well, had had a very serious car accident that produced severe damange to her head and face witch left her with deep emotional problems and behavioral disorders plus other things that are appalling, on top of everything else. The conduct of all the officers was exemplary. The sensitivity shown by all the officers in this dreadful time will be remembered by me and the family. We've lost our boy for the now but we will remember all of you and the kindness you*

extended to our family, given the constraints of your professional obligations. You will be rememberd in our prayers for Dag, Christian, and Dag's family.

For the next several days Marlon brought Papke up to the house to photograph the murder room as well as the couch in the bunker. Police investigators seemed to have given up on finding the bullet, but since they hadn't sealed off the crime scene, Brando continued searching himself. After a day or two, Papke got another phone call.

"Come up," Brando said with some urgency. "And bring your camera again."

"What's happening?"

"I'll tell you when you get here."

When Papke pulled into the parking area, he saw Brando with an assistant on the front steps. "They were standing there," he recalled, "like a couple of fat and happy cats."

Papke walked over to them. "What's going on?" he asked.

With a grin Brando held out a clenched hand, then slowly uncurled his fingers. In his open palm, like an iridescent pearl, lay the bullet.

"Where'd you find it?" Papke asked.

"I was walking around barefoot in the room," Brando replied, "and I stepped on it."

The bullet was flattened on one side but otherwise intact. Whether it was bent from where it had hit the concrete floor under the TV room's carpeting or whether it had been distorted by Brando's weight, Papke couldn't be sure. For his part, however, Brando was excited, convinced that the flattening would prove that the police were inaccurate in their ballistic analyses. What they had to do at once, he explained, was reconstruct the crime scene themselves. Key to the exercise was analyzing the angle of the shot, starting with where he said he had found the bullet.

Soon, back inside the TV room with the couch in place, Brando had the two men down on the floor, probing the carpet with a pencil for the bullet's point of entry. Next, they positioned another pencil where Brando had found the projectile. Then they cut a line through the rug between the two, peeling back the carpeting and the padding underneath to reveal an approximately ten-foot-long skid mark where the bullet had skated along the concrete after passing through Dag Drollet's skull.

Next, they strung lengths of yarn back to the couch, simulating several possible angles of the shot. Papke took hundreds of pictures. "We even moved all the furniture out again to get a clearer view of the strings and took more photos," he said, adding with a touch of pride, "It was really quite nice, certainly better than what the cops had done."

What Brando seemed intent on proving, he later explained, "was that Chris just didn't walk in and blast him lying on the couch, but that there was some sort of confrontation."

In order to verify this theory, Brando now decided to reenact the killing itself. The furniture was moved back into the room, and Brando turned from detective to stage director, assigning Papke and the assistant to play the roles of Christian and Dag according to several different scripts. Taking turns lying on the couch, the three of them reenacted the crime— not with guns, but with more pencils. "We were just walking through it," recalled Papke, "and Marlon was saying, 'Okay, move into the line of fire.' Marlon was really enjoying the role of detective. He had found the bullet when the stupid cops couldn't, and now he was going to prove that there had been this struggle."

Having walked through various scenarios, the three men left the room as it was, with Brando dismissing Papke's suggestion that perhaps he should hire someone to clean it up. Unbeknownst to them, Cheyenne crept into the room afterward and, distraught that she could still see Dag's blood, tried to wash the dark stain from the rug.

For the next several days Brando and Papke continued to discuss the possible scenarios of the killing. Like all obsessed people, Marlon remained self-absorbed as he endlessly reran the same events through his mind. Papke sometimes interrupted and gave him what he considered to be reasonable explanations. "Knowing Christian's macho character," Papke proposed, "I think that maybe he had come around behind Dag, talking at him and intending to hit him with the fucking gun. I don't think he intended to shoot him, although I'd heard he was pretty trigger-happy. Christian himself never explained what really happened, so it's possible that he didn't even know. He was probably so boozed that he couldn't remember what exactly occurred."

As they conjectured, Brando got around to wondering aloud, "Do you think we should not say anything about this and just not turn the bullet in?" Papke replied, "Marlon, don't be ridiculous."

Papke's common sense prevailed, although Brando waited several days before giving the bullet to the police, and then only with a vague explanation of how and when it had been found. (He described himself moving about in the room for the purpose of lighting candles and setting up a "shrine" to the slain Drollet.) By the time detectives tried to analyze the scene for themselves, the room had been so rummaged through, the carpet in such disarray, that they could not verify the exact point of entry, let alone the angle of the shot and the precise positioning of the furniture. Brando had tampered with the crime scene, although later he would insist that it had been the police who had so drastically cut up the carpeting.

Nevertheless, he was convinced that his reconstruction proved the police forensic and ballistic experts wrong—"that there had been a confrontation, that Christian and Dag were having a fight," as he explained it to Papke—so he insisted on a reautopsy of Dag's body by his own privately hired coroner, Dr. Michael Baden. The famed New York City medical examiner had been a consultant to the 1975 House Select Committee on the assassinations of John F. Kennedy and Martin Luther King Jr. Baden took a set of photographs—about fifty shots in all—during the second autopsy, and Papke was asked to get them developed "quietly."

Brando was also considering another move. He proposed to hire Papke at $500 a day and send him to Tahiti to nose around, presumably to dig up stories about Dag that would help Christian's defense. More than likely, what he had in mind was confirmation that Dag had been abusing Cheyenne.

Meanwhile, the actor continued to isolate himself. Friends from all over were trying to reach him to express their condolences and offer their support, but he neither read his mail nor answered the phone. "During those days Jay Kanter kept phoning," Papke recalled. "Kanter knows about the phone devices, that you just have to keep talking until Marlon picks up. We were sitting in the bedroom, and he'd just listen to Jay's voice trying to get through and never would answer."

Six days after the shooting, Brando sat stony-faced in the first row of division 91 of West Los Angeles Municipal Court. To his left, holding his hand, sat Tarita, then Teihotu; on his right, Rebecca and Miko. His hair was gray and he was balding; he wore light-gray trousers and a blue sport jacket. More massive and strong than hopelessly fat, he closed his eyes, lost in meditation, as photographers pushed forward, their cameras' automatic winders whining like gnats. The famous face was pale and frozen, beyond perplexity or humiliation.

The district attorney's office had charged Christian with first-degree murder, and Brando was faced with a situation—perhaps the first one in his life—that he couldn't laugh away, run from, or immediately manipulate to his own ends. His firstborn son sat no more than a dozen feet away, clad in L.A. County prison denims and looking dazed. He was flanked by attorney William Kunstler, who had flown out at Brando's personal request, bringing two assistants.

The purpose of the hearing was to determine bail. "This is going to come down to a tragic accident," Kunstler began, "a confrontation over an alleged attack on Mr. Brando's daughter Cheyenne by the deceased, and a confrontation and accidental discharge of a firearm." He added that all the firearms possessed by the defendant and by Mr. Brando himself had been turned over to the police. He pointed out that the defendant had made no attempt to flee the crime scene, that he had waited for the police after his father had called 911, and that he'd "cooperated with the police one hundred percent." Lastly, Kunstler said that since there had been rumors of Christian's jumping bail for Tahiti, the young man was ready to surrender his passport.

Acknowledging that Christian did have a trust fund, Kunstler portrayed him as an ordinary young man of modest means who earned his living at ordinary jobs, as a fisherman in Alaska, as a tree trimmer, and most recently as a welder, and "rented" his home from his father. Citing the results of Christian's 2:30 A.M. blood-alcohol test—0.19 percent, or twice the California limit for drunk driving—Kunstler tried to pull an ace from his sleeve. Turning to Judge Rosemary Shumsky, a black woman, he announced earnestly, "I knew [Christian] when he was fourteen years of age, when I first met his father in the civil rights movement, and I have been a friend of his father in that civil rights movement since 1972 or 1973." There were several more references to the movement, and the judge, who for the past forty minutes had listened to the proceedings impassively, now allowed herself an ironic smile.

Declarations from eighteen friends and neighbors were read: Bill Cable, Shirley Cumpanas, Alice Marchak, Laurene Landon, Fran Loving, and even Jack Nicholson and Helena Kallianiotas were among those who supplied endorsements of Christian's character. Unacknowledged was that ten of the eighteen had been, or were still, on Brando's payroll. With the testimonials completed, Kunstler asked his assistant Ron Kuby to step in. "We primarily handle civil rights matters, and we spend a lot of time trying . . . to prevent poor and oppressed people from being chewed up by the system because they're anonymous," Kuby said. "Here we find ourselves in the most ironic position of trying to defend a man who has a famous last name. Famous people are often dealt with more harshly than regular people. But Christian Brando is not a famous person. He's a person who happens to have a famous father. He's a person who has made his own way in the world." Kuby closed by asking the judge to treat him "as if he were any other defendant . . . without the Brando name."

Steven Barshop, the deputy district attorney assigned to the case, didn't mince his words: Christian Brando, he pointed out, had gone to his girlfriend's house to get the murder weapon on the way back from dinner, en route to his father's house; the wound to Drollet's left cheek was a contact wound at an angle of 45 degrees, indicating that the victim was shot while seated; the deceased was still holding a Bic lighter, cigarette papers, and a small pouch of tobacco in one hand and a TV remote control in the other, negating any theory of a struggle. (In Marlon's own police statements he had muddied the waters by insisting that he had picked up the remote control after the shooting to turn off the television, and that Drollet's one hand had been free to strike at Christian. Barshop's response was that up until that point, he hadn't realized that Brando was willing to lie for his son; that realization had persuaded him to pursue the strongest possible indictment.) "This case, for the purposes of this bail motion and at the present time, is a first-degree murder," he concluded.

At 2:40 Judge Shumsky announced her decision, matter-of-factly and without explanation: "The court finds no basis for setting bail in this case."

Christian, who had remained motionless in his chair, now slumped. His father's eyes closed, but only briefly. With the photographers swarming, he moved to the defense table. Then, with the rest of the family, he quickly exited through the rear of the courtroom to face the press.

It was almost hallucinatory, as if a landmass had suddenly shifted. The man who had dodged interviews for the past forty years—who had so often walked into courthouses as well as restaurants with his eyes closed so photographers couldn't capture his emotion—now stood before a mob of them, giving even tabloid newsmen his full attention, speaking evenly, generously. Tears came when one of them asked, "What are you going through right now?"

"There's no way to describe it to you unless you've gone through it in your life . . . ," he said. Another reporter commented, "You seem very strong, sir. How do you find that spiritual strength?" This proved too difficult for him, and again tears welled in his eyes. He shrugged and gave a wan smile.

With Tarita at his side, Brando told reporters: "The messenger of misery has come to my house, and has also come to the house of Mr. Jack Drollet in Tahiti. To those people who have known these kinds of tragic circumstances in the world, no explanation is necessary. To those people who do not know the nature of this acute misery that both our families suffer, no explanation is possible. We must just be strong, and I think that the family, with love and supporting each other, will prevail."

Kunstler implied that political pressure affected the loss of bail. In fact, though, if politics were involved, they would have worked more to Brando's advantage, since his name and power certainly influenced how the DA's office was approaching the case. "We were told, 'Whatever you do, be careful,'" Assistant District Attorney William Clark later confirmed. "His name and his reputation accorded him that kind of treatment. We were advised to give him no quarter, and if he was the problem, then to deal with him. But it was, 'Don't cast stones unless you absolutely know.' Of course, we suspected that he was taking an active role through his attorneys to limit our ability to prosecute the case, but we didn't make that public."

On the same day that Dag Drollet was buried in Tahiti—May 27, 1990—Christian was transferred to a small cell in the hospital unit of the Los Angeles County Jail, placed there for his own protection after other prisoners allegedly threatened to kill him.

A swarm of visitors soon descended on him. Laurene Landon was there every day, monopolizing his visiting time, according to some friends. Anna Kashfi, according to Skip E. Lowe, came up from the San Diego area and tried to visit, but Christian refused to see her. Brother Miko and Christian's former wife, Mary McKenna Brando, also visited, and despite the acrimonious allegations in her divorce, she announced her unwavering affection. Hollywood being Hollywood, people were also cashing in.

Kashfi reportedly sold her story to the tabloids for $20,000; Shirley Cumpanas was peddling photographs of herself to *Penthouse* and *Playboy;* up and down the Strip, "friends" of Christian were selling tidbits to the gossip columnists and grabbing the limelight in front of TV cameras.

Cheyenne, in the immediate aftermath of the shooting, remained sequestered in her father's house, speaking to no one. A week after the killing, Helena Kallianiotas had come by and found her in the kitchen, licking Comet kitchen cleanser off her hands. Already Kunstler had been replaced by Los Angeles defense attorney Robert L. Shapiro, who had told the press that while it was "a little premature" to hold plea bargain talks, he hoped to settle the case without a preliminary hearing or a trial. Finally, on June 12, at Steven Barshop's insistence, Shapiro allowed Detective A. R. Monsue into the house on Mulholland Drive to question Cheyenne.

What she told the detective was woefully simple. Christian, she said, had indeed retrieved his pistol as well as a knife on the way back to their father's house after dinner, had repeatedly vowed on their drive home to "bust on" Drollet (a threat she could not take seriously, she insisted), and had shot her Tahitian lover within minutes of parking the truck and following her into the den. According to the detective's report, she said, "Christian just walked in and killed Dag." And then she told Monsue, "It's murder, in case you don't know it."

Shapiro, who was hovering nearby, quickly terminated the interview. With word from Monsue that the questioning had been closed down, Barshop immediately went to work preparing a motion for a "conditional examination," in which a witness is present with his or her attorney and testimony is taken in open court. Barshop's instructions to Monsue were to go back to Mulholland and serve Cheyenne with a subpoena.

The following morning, when the detective tried to reenter the Brando estate, he received no answer on the gate's intercom. From a nearby pay phone he tried the three numbers listed on the police report—without results. Back at the gate he tried the buzzer again and waited. Again, no sound came from the speaker box.

On Thursday, he tried again. Each time he called any of Brando's numbers, the phones did nothing but ring and ring. He then drove to the address, where again no one responded on the intercom. Back at his office at the West Hollywood homicide division's headquarters, he tried several more times, continuing to phone throughout the day whenever he got the chance. Nothing. On Friday, June 15, both Monsue and Detective Lee Kingsford made another attempt to get inside the estate but to no avail. This is annoying, they thought, but they still remained confident that time was on their side.

What they had not counted on was that Brando had called Rosetta Valenti, his longtime friend and ticket agent, within a few hours after Detective Monsue's interview with Cheyenne three days before. Valenti had known the actor for thirty years and often handled the family's travel arrangements; she was also a coinvestor in the Bora Bora condominium complex where Brando and Jack Nicholson owned units. As she later acknowledged to investigators from the DA's office, Brando had phoned and said that he needed "tickets to Tahiti." He had explained to her that "he wanted a ticket on the next flight to Tahiti for Cheyenne" because "Cheyenne wanted to go back to Tahiti to have her baby." When confirming the flight plans with Garbutt in Tahiti, Valenti learned that Cheyenne "was very upset with her father," "that they had been fighting," and that "Cheyenne would not listen to Marlon and didn't want any of his advice." As instructed by Brando, though, Valenti made a reservation for Cheyenne on an 11:15 A.M. Qantas flight on Friday, under an assumed name. She then made a second reservation on a different flight to "throw off the news media, especially 'Hard Copy.'" Cheyenne's ticket read "C. Brand," so that if the police were watching for such a move, it could be attributed to a typo instead of a deliberate attempt to escape official scrutiny.

Stunned by the news that his star witness had fled, Assistant District Attorney Barshop reassessed his options. The prosecutor had first viewed the case as an involuntary manslaughter. "When you take a look at a .19," he said early on, referring to Christian's alcohol reading the night of the killing, "what you're looking at is just a stupid guy." Based on his taped confession, things didn't look too bad for Christian: "A lot of it was babble and unintelligible and made no sense, but the bottom line was there was no intent to kill. That seemed clear, and I've been around a long time." But after Cheyenne's statement and her clandestine flight out of the country, that had changed: "Now," Barshop said, "I'm looking at murder one."

Back in Tahiti, apparently pushed over the edge by Dag's killing, Cheyenne was reported to be consuming hallucinogenic drugs by the handful. Several days later she was hospitalized for psychiatric observation;

Tarita, having returned from Los Angeles two days after Cheyenne, was also hospitalized, reportedly suffering from exhaustion. On June 26, three weeks before she was due, Cheyenne gave birth to a son, Tuki, who was allegedly addicted to drugs.

Jacques Drollet, the victim's father, had remained in Tahiti but kept a close watch on both the Los Angeles district attorney's handling of the case and on Cheyenne. Almost from the start he had little doubt that Brando was manipulating the situation. Albert LeCaill, Dag's stepfather, and Drollet's other son, Bjarn, had flown to L.A. to retrieve Dag's body and had asked for a meeting at the Brando house to go over what had actually happened. Through his assistant, Brando sent word that he wanted no meeting. "His message to Cynthia Garbutt was very clear," said Drollet. "He said, 'I don't know what to talk to them about.' He refused to sit down in the Polynesian way and discuss what had happened as a family matter. If it was an accident, he could have explained how it happened. But he didn't want to see us, and that made me start to question if maybe it wasn't an accident. I also realized he hadn't cared enough about Dag to give him protection. He may have been grieving, but for whom? His aura, his ego. After all, he's a great actor."

Later Drollet explained his frustration to the DA. "Can you imagine that?" he asked Barshop. "Refusing to see Albert and my son, Dag's brother."

"Jacques, don't forget—there's a war on," said Barshop.

On July 2 Drollet filed a civil suit in Tahiti, charging Cheyenne with murder and complicity in murder. It was an understandable tactic by the grieving father: He wanted answers about how and why his son had been killed. Since the American prosecutors might be stymied in their attempt to bring Cheyenne to a Los Angeles trial, this suit would at least prompt the French authorities in Tahiti to initiate an investigation of their own.

Four days after Drollet brought the suit, Cheyenne's physician noted her "maladapted behavior" and "barely coherent talk" and requested that she receive further psychiatric treatment. She was moved to the locked isolation unit at Vaiami Hospital and confined to a tiny first-floor room with bars on the windows. Teihotu visited her there and later told reporters, "She cut off all her hair in a fit of rage, and now she looks like a boy. We fear she'll kill herself. They've taken all sharp objects away from her."

Despite her reportedly serious condition, on July 17 magistrate Max

Gatti compelled Cheyenne to give her first extended statement about the shooting. The interview lasted four hours, and she began by repeating that the death of Dag Drollet was a murder, adding that after the shooting, Christian came to her and said, "It's done. I killed him." She also implied some sort of incestuous motive to the event by telling Gatti that Christian didn't see her as a sister but as a "young woman." When Gatti asked her about the baby, she said it was born at term, that he weighed 2.87 kilograms and measured 49.5 centimeters. "But for me," she declared, "he was born on the nineteenth of August, as I noted in my personal calendar." She went on to explain that since June 16, the day she returned to Papeete, there had been a difference between the dates of the newspaper and those in "my calendar."

Tarita had already given her deposition three days before, and she confirmed that she had been in her room when Cheyenne and Christian returned from dinner. "A little later," she said, she heard noise and someone calling her. She had gone into the television room, seen Dag lying on the couch, and tried to rouse him, thinking he was asleep. When she saw the wound and realized that Dag wasn't breathing, she had called Marlon and gone to the living room, where the actor told her to "calm down."

Tarita also stated that she had become aware that Dag sometimes "hit" Cheyenne because he was "jealous." Then, in what seemed to be becoming the official Brando line, she added that Cheyenne had accused Dag not only of beating her but also of getting her hooked on drugs. When confronted with Brando's statement that Cheyenne had lied about the beatings, however, Tarita clammed up. "I don't want to answer you," she said. When asked if Cheyenne had warned Dag, she replied, "I have nothing to say."

On July 19, Judge Gatti took a further deposition, this one from Cynthia Garbutt. Brando's office manager confirmed Cheyenne's drug use, claiming that she had been taking hallucinogenic drugs with Dag on their trip to Mooréa.

Judge Gatti concluded that Cheyenne's own deposition was enough to warrant bringing an indictment charging her with complicity in Dag's death. According to the magistrate, she had "inculpated" herself. Under French law, someone who knows that a serious crime is about to occur has an obligation to do what can be done to thwart it—short of endangering oneself—or he or she will be charged with complicity. Although Cheyenne claimed she had not taken Christian's threats seriously, she admitted that her brother had said repeatedly during the evening that he wanted to kill Drollet; moreover, she had done nothing to warn Dag, or to try to stop Christian. The magistrate seized her passport and Cheyenne was then forbidden to leave Tahiti—an order that would further complicate matters for the prosecutors back in Los Angeles.

Jacques Drollet remained unsatisfied and worried about a possible cover-up. "The reality is that my son has been taken from me under the most suspicious of circumstances," he told reporters. The media had flocked to Tahiti from all quarters of the globe and were present when he tossed white petals on Dag's grave. "I'm a simple man, from simple, family traditions. Unfortunately, my son fell for a girl who had been brought up in that pseudocelluloid cinema world. He loved her with all his heart, and in the end it was that love which killed him. Please do not regard me as being filled with bitterness or hatred for Cheyenne. The truth is, I feel nothing for her at all. My feelings are dead, just as they are for Marlon Brando."

Meanwhile Deputy DA Bill Clark continued to research ways of bringing Cheyenne back to Los Angeles to testify at Christian's pretrial hearing.

Jacques Drollet, accompanied by Albert and Lisette LeCaill and other family members, flew to Los Angeles, planning to present themselves *en famille* at the preliminary hearing. On July 20 Drollet met with Steven Barshop and Bill Clark in Barshop's office. Since the French Foreign Ministry had given the DA's office permission to exchange information directly with the magistrate in Papeete, Barshop, Clark, and Drollet phoned Judge Gatti in Tahiti. When Barshop asked him point-blank whether he would allow Cheyenne to travel to the United States for the purpose of testifying, Gatti confirmed previous reports that she didn't seem well enough to travel. In any case, he added, he would want some guarantee that Cheyenne would be returned to French Polynesia at the end of the hearing.

Clark left the room to confer with officials of the U.S. Department of Justice. "We all came to the consensus that such a guarantee [was] not possible because of Cheyenne's U.S. citizenship," Clark explained. "No judge in the country would have the power to deport Cheyenne. Extradition might work, but if we did not believe that Cheyenne's conduct rose to a level of a crime under U.S. law, we probably would not extradite her."

Barshop had come up empty, and on Monday, July 23, 1990, the preliminary hearing began as scheduled, but without the principal witness. Since early morning, crowds had been gathering outside the Los Angeles Municipal Court, and as might be expected it was a media circus. Members of the press were seated in the jury box, and once the 200-odd spectators' seats were filled, the remaining unlucky throngs clustered a half-dozen deep around the television monitors set up in the courthouse hallway.

Ten minutes before the start of the proceedings, Brando arrived, a massive figure moving through the spectators like Moses parting the Red Sea. A hushed silence came over the hallway as he made his way toward the courtroom's double doors wearing a tight-fitting blue blazer, white shirt, and red tie with baggy slacks. His face was ashen and pasty as he stared straight ahead, seeming to focus on nothing. He was accompanied by Miko, Tom Papke, and a bodyguard. The wife of defense attorney Robert Shapiro was also at the actor's side, glancing bright-eyed at the crowd as the entourage swept into the courtroom. They took the front row of reserved seats directly behind the defense table, where Christian sat with Shapiro.

His hair neatly cut, wearing a crisp white dress shirt, tie, and slacks, Christian looked like an all-American college kid. He seemed thinner, and his complexion was jailhouse white. He kept his head bowed, not even acknowledging his father or any of his other supporters as they took their seats behind him. The Drollet family, dressed in black, sat in the first two rows of the left section of the spectators' area, behind the prosecutors' table.

If the Brandos and the Drollets were a study in contrasts, so, too, were Robert Shapiro and Steven Barshop, the key spokesmen in the drama. During the weeks preceding the preliminary hearing, their legal skirmishing had provided the press with more than a few clues as to each man's distinctive style. Shapiro, known as the "stealth defense lawyer" for his low-profile work in high-profile cases, wore an apricot-colored Armani suit and tasseled loafers. His receding black hair slicked back from his forehead, he was tanned and smiling and was soon dubbed "the Jewish Cesar Romero." He had most recently represented Hollywood producer Robert Evans in his refusal to testify in the Cotton Club murder case. His other clients had included Johnny Carson, Linda Lovelace, and fellow attorney F. Lee Bailey. Over the years in private practice, he had acquired a reputation for presenting a well-focused and methodical defense. Instead of blasting his adversaries with a scattershot approach, he picked off the targets he knew he could win, and among his colleagues at the bar he was often described as "a sniper."

On the other side of the room stood Assistant District Attorney Steven Barshop, inspecting his notes through heavy-rimmed glasses, wearing plain Jane Brooks Brothers. Barshop had prosecuted fifty-six homicide cases. Determined and tough-talking, he was known as an indefatigable worker; ultimately fed up with the perks of the rich and politically connected, rarely did he allow himself a decent night's sleep while trying a case. On the table in front of him lay Christian's guns, including the murder weapon, which were to be introduced as evidence. While Christian stole a few glances in their direction, he seemed less the macho blusterer than zoned-out zombie, which several of the journalists in the press box chalked up to Prozac.

Late in the morning, Detective Steve Osti was called and the interrogation tape was played, which left the courtroom totally hushed. Shapiro had evidently been lying in wait and now jumped on the fact that Osti had failed to read the last line of the usual Miranda warning—that if Christian could not afford a lawyer, one would be appointed for him. The detective countered lamely by saying that he had thought that this was not applicable to the son of Marlon Brando. When Shapiro moved that the entire interrogation be withdrawn from evidence, Miko leaned toward his father, whispering, and the two exchanged brief smiles.

Tom Papke had already become aware of how much Marlon had tried to assert his will in conferences with Shapiro. Just as he had devoured law books while marshaling his suit against James Clavell, he was demanding copies of every document Shapiro had. He argued with the attorney so often that Shapiro finally had to put his foot down and let Brando know who was running the defense.

While Marlon sometimes seemed depressed, most of the time he was in his manic mode, confident that he could win. Today was similar. When court reconvened after lunch, the judge ruled against the prosecution on the Miranda issue, and Shapiro grinned in triumph. Brando lifted his head to stare with mocking eyes at the detective as he left the courtroom. But Brando's hope that Osti's error would bring a quick dismissal was in vain, and as the day progressed, with one witness after another, Brando's complexion grew more pale, his lips frighteningly bluish against the whiteness of his skin.

When the medical examiner appeared to explain his autopsy findings, a Styrofoam head was set on the rail of the witness stand, supposedly to represent Dag as the coroner began to demonstrate the site of the wound and the bullet's trajectory. It was a grotesque sight, and Dag's mother, Lisette, dabbed at her eyes as the examiner inserted a knitting needle into the Styrofoam, slowly pushing it through the mannequin until it came out the opposite side.

Christian had remained unmoved and inattentive throughout, but now as Detective Monsue took the stand to identify the guns taken from the scene, the young man suddenly became interested. Marlon himself was more attentive to the detective's description of finding Dag's body and the position of the television remote control.

After court recessed that afternoon, Brando returned to Mulholland, and sitting on the overlook with its view of the Valley, Papke tried to cheer him up.

"Yeah, it's really great," Brando sighed. "My son is in jail for murder, my daughter's a drug addict. . . . My son has killed my only grandchild's father."

He continued to ventilate, in a sense excusing his reactions that others had considered strange. "If I giggle inanely," he said, "it's only because if I don't, I'll lose it."

He then paused. "You know," he added, "everyone thinks I'm acting. I'm not. I'm just a father. I'm not manipulating."

As the preliminary hearing opened for the second day, Brando took the same seat as before, directly behind Christian, then looked across at the reporters in the jury box. Shirley Cumpanas again took a front-row seat, relishing the attention of tabloid reporters whose questions she now referred to her "new agent."

When the police ballistics expert testified, the Drollets were now subject to more heartrending testimony as huge color blowups of Dag's body were introduced. Among the photos placed on the easel in front of the courtroom were several close-ups of the deceased's face, clearly revealing the bullet hole on his cheek. When the expert testified that Dag had been shot at such close range that bits of his flesh had stuck to the top of the Sig-Sauer's barrel, Lisette covered her face and wept silently. Jacques looked stricken. Brando had turned sideways in his seat, however, chatting with Miko as if to ignore both the photographs and the testimony.

Later in the day, he seemed to pay more attention, assiduously taking notes, sometimes passing slips of paper down the row to Papke. These were not the crucial messages to his assistant that they appeared to be. Instead he was writing little bits of Brando nonsense like "The shortest distance between two points is not a straight line espicially [*sic*] in a court of law. Almost in all cases."

After the midafternoon recess there were no more witnesses to be called and Shapiro asked the judge to reduce the charge to manslaughter, arguing that Christian had been drinking. The other mitigating factor, he pointed out, was that the defendant had been upset to hear that Dag had been abusive to his pregnant sister. But Judge Larry Fidler disagreed: The district attorney's evidence "supported the strong suspicion" that Drollet's death was indeed murder, and it met the criteria required in a preliminary hearing to proceed to trial. Barshop now argued that Christian should not be granted bail, given what had happened with Cheyenne. Here Fidler seemed to take a middle position and set bail at $10 million, which was believed to be the highest ever set in Los Angeles County. He also ordered Christian to surrender his passport.

Since Shapiro and Brando had been giving statements to the press, Jacques Drollet and Albert LeCaill decided to air their dissatisfactions in an extended interview. They were poised and dignified, but most of all, Dag's father and stepfather were joined in their intense desire to get to the bottom of what had happened. With a reporter and a tape recorder facing them across the conference table in the office of an L.A. lawyer they hired to file a civil suit, they talked for more than two hours:

REPORTER: How much do you think Cheyenne had to do with it?

DROLLET: I think Cheyenne pushed Christian into it because she was losing Dag.

LECAILL: She had been with men, going out with them, since she was thirteen, and that was very young for a girl of that social bracket. She had had four or five boyfriends before Dag, and each time she was the one to throw them out. But this time, Dag was leaving *her*.

REPORTER: Why was Dag going to leave Cheyenne?

DROLLET: He told me she was too difficult, impossible to live with. She was morbidly jealous and egoistic. Dag probably used marijuana, cocaine perhaps, but he thought she was deeply addicted and wanted to get her away from her friends who were addicts.

REPORTER: Cheyenne supposedly told Dag that the child was not his. Do you have any doubt that Dag was not the father?

DROLLET: I can't say who I think the father is. But Dag told us the child was his, even though she had said after the baby was born that Dag didn't believe that he was the father. To clear everything up, I have asked for blood and genetic analysis. Samples of Dag's blood are still with the coroner and it would be possible to do the tests.

REPORTER: Did Marlon offer to pay any of the expenses of transporting Dag's body back to Tahiti?

DROLLET: It's paid for by the state, but we have never gotten any offers either from Brando directly or through Cynthia. We asked her, as well as Barshop and Detective Monsue, to help us get Dag's belongings back—his passport, his clothing, his wristwatch, and about $1,400 in cash. Monsue said he hadn't been able to get into the house to search for these things, and then Cynthia told us that Cheyenne had burned them.

REPORTER: You regard Cheyenne as an accomplice in this?

DROLLET: Yes, after her declaration, and according to French law, and what she told Detective Monsue in her statement. Dag was only supposed to stay one week, but he told Cynthia that he hadn't been able to leave because Cheyenne had hidden his passport and his ticket. That day he said he would be returning on the next Sunday. . . . Then Cheyenne declared that after they stopped at Christian's girlfriend's after dinner, they went to the market, where Christian bought some beer, and then they stopped along the roadside and Christian went off alone and drank a bottle. She said she picked up the gun and was surprised that it felt very light, because the only other gun she has ever touched was Marlon's gun in his house. Then they went to the house, and she walked inside ahead of Christian. She declared that all night Christian had been saying, "I'm gonna kill him." But she said she was very relaxed, and she took Dag back to Tarita to say good-night and got her little cocker, Bill. Then Dag went back to the den and she went back to the kitchen with her dog. It was then she heard the shot. And Christian then came to her. He was barefoot and he said, "It is done." But she had never warned Dag, "Be careful, Christian is very upset, he has a weapon." We think that Christian was probably hiding in the den, waiting for Dag to come back in.

REPORTER: What was your reaction to the allegation that Cheyenne had said Dag was slapping her around, but Marlon told the police he hadn't believed her.

DROLLET: As we understand it, Dag had slapped her sometimes, but not since she was pregnant. It happened in 1988 when he realized she was addicted and he took her with him on his business trip to Mooréa to get her off the habit. She began to interrupt conferences and make trouble for him, and since she was without her drugs . . . , one night she went wild and was screaming and slapping him. He said he had to slap her twice and put her under the shower to try to calm her down. But then she ran away and stayed at a little hotel at the airport. . . .

REPORTER: What was Marlon's relationship with Dag?

DROLLET: In the beginning Marlon didn't like him. He was jealous that Dag was taking his daughter away from him, and also he seemed to think that because I was a retired schoolteacher and not a rich man, Dag wasn't good enough for Cheyenne. Cheyenne herself was a bottomless pit when it came to spending money. . . . Then he came to Tahiti in March, and I saw him. He said he liked Dag, but that he knew he and Cheyenne were having problems. The only thing bad he said about Dag was that he didn't like that he and Cheyenne had taken LSD together, that Dag shouldn't have done that. But he told me at the same time, "Since we're going to be grandfathers of the same child, I have decided to hire Dag to work on Tetiaroa." I didn't like that, I didn't think it was good for Dag because he was being put in a subservient position. He seemed to be doing whatever Marlon and Cheyenne wanted, and I told him so. Marlon also made Dag sign a confession—we don't know what it was about—but he had tears in his eyes when he told me. Maybe it was a confidentiality agreement when he agreed to work for him. We don't know because Marlon still has it.

REPORTER: Today the judge set bail for Christian. How do you feel about his getting out of jail?

DROLLET: I have great respect for American justice, but I still think that with Marlon's money he can buy many situations and maneuver things. Marlon Brando is a master of manipulation, of controlling other people . . .

REPORTER: Are you satisfied you know what happened the night of the shooting, that Christian killed Dag?

DROLLET: Not necessarily. There were only four people at the house that night: Marlon, Christian, Cheyenne, and Tarita. Among them one is the murderer. It seemed to me from how Dag was shot that a left-handed person would have done it, and the only left-handed person among them was Cheyenne, so I had those suspicions. But then I thought of Christian, with no shoes on, hidden behind the couch, creeping up behind Dag, and *boom,* one shot, a very professional killing . . .

REPORTER: And what about Marlon's responsibility?

DROLLET: It reminds me of the story of Cain and Abel. When Cain assassinated his brother Abel, he couldn't sleep a wink because he felt there was an eye looking at him. That was his conscience, the community's conscience, too. And I think that will be Marlon Brando's fate, to have that eye always staring at him. And as long as we can breathe, we will put pressure on him.

A few days later a $100 million wrongful-death suit against both Christian and Marlon was filed. It was part of Drollet and LeCaill's two-pronged attack—pressing charges against Cheyenne in Papeete while tightening the screws with a civil action in America. Again Drollet made a statement to the press to explain their actions. "How can you shoot someone who is lying down on the couch watching television?" he asked reporters. "I loathe Christian Brando and his family for what they have done. My beloved son was killed Mafia-style. He was shot practically in the eye from point-blank range. It was a very nasty death."

When Brando heard about the two men's suit, he snapped to Papke, "They're becoming bothersome." He paused, and in his godfather style added, "But I've got that covered."

Even after bail had been set, Christian remained in the county jail, presumably because his passport had yet to be found. Papke then received a phone call from Shapiro. "Do you know where Christian's passport is?" the lawyer asked. Papke said he had a pretty good idea where it might be, but Shapiro, according to Papke, interrupted him. "Don't tell me," he warned. "I don't want to know. I want to be able to say to the press that we can't find it, and if you tell me where it is, I can't honestly make that statement. But I want you to go get it and make sure it's safe until I need it."

Nobody had decided to "find" the missing passport for several reasons, Papke claimed. In the first place Brando insisted that it would be too difficult to make the $10 million bail; yet he didn't want the public to know that he couldn't—or wouldn't—pay the money to release his son. "But he also didn't want Christian out," added Papke. "He thought it would be better for him to stay in the jail hospital and detox. He didn't trust what Christian might do if he were released, and if he took off, all that bail would be forfeited."

On August 1 Brando phoned Papke to announce in an angry voice that he was on his way over to Tom's condominium. Papke assumed that the actor was coming by to pick up the passport. Miko drove him in a new Lincoln, its side bashed in from a recent accident. Marlon strode into the living room, his eyes glaring and his mouth thin with anger. Without bothering to greet Papke, he began to yell. Even at his angriest Brando rarely shouted, choosing instead to retain control with smoldering, low-pitched tones. But now he thundered in a totally uncharacteristic fashion.

"How dare you talk to Skip Lowe?" he ranted. "I saw you at the hearing. You're telling him things!"

"What do you mean?" Papke replied. "All I said was hello, since I've seen Skip and Christian together at the Roosevelt Hotel many times. What's the big deal?"

Brando brushed aside his response. "I can't trust you anymore!" he shouted. "Give me Christian's passport."

Papke handed him the passport. Without a word of thanks, the actor raved on, absolutely certain that his former employee was a threat to him. "You're dangerous to me!" he stormed. "You know I'll do anything to protect my family. I'm richer and more powerful than you, so watch out!"

"I wish you'd stay for a moment so we could talk about this," Papke said, trying to calm him down.

"Oh, you're sweet!" he said and slammed out the door. Papke followed and watched from above as he stomped down the stairs. Miko waved from the car, apparently unaware that his father had just written Papke out of his life.

"I'll talk to you down the line," Brando called over his shoulder in a menacing voice. "Bet on it."

The threat was not an idle one. For the past year Papke and Brando had been involved in a Las Vegas real estate deal, and now, with their partnership agreement expired, the actor was obligated to return Papke's $100,000 seed money. When Papke realized that Brando was refusing to relinquish the money, he began writing letters to Norty Brown, then calling him directly. "I was getting nowhere," said Papke, "and then one day I called Norty again and this cold secretarial voice announced, 'Mr. Brando has instructed us not to take any more calls from you.' *Click.*"

Papke then phoned Marlon's old friends, thinking that they might prevail on Brando's sense of fairness. He reached Philip Rhodes, only to be told that Rhodes had been placed on Brando's blacklist as well, as Caroline Barrett had been only too happy to confirm. "When I asked Caroline about this," Rhodes told Papke, "she said [Marlon] thought we had both been talking to reporters. That's why I've given up on him. I have lived through more than forty years of his suspicions. It's like original sin—he can't wipe it out of his mind. He's been suspicious of everyone, and that's why it has been so easy for him to drop people."

Yet in some sense Rhodes felt relieved to be removed from Brando's web. "Only when you're completely on the outs with him," he said, "can you take a deep breath and realize that you were never on the inside with him, you were out all the time. And this time I'm completely out."

After six months of effort and considerable expense, Papke was eventually able to receive the money via Marlon's London lawyer. Brando's willingness to hurt his longtime associate was the final straw for Papke, just as exiling Rhodes had ended that relationship. Additionally, Brando now rang down the curtain of impenetrable silence on others, including his old friend Ellen Adler. After Christian's arrest, Brando had noticed that she hadn't phoned. Several weeks later it was reported that he phoned her, outraged that she hadn't been in touch. Wailing and weeping about his plight and her abandonment, he ended by telling her that after all their years of affection, he did not wish to see her ever again.

The only insiders left were George Englund (who seemed to be living up to his reputation as, in Sondra Lee's words, "a professional stick-arounder"), Caroline Barrett, Alice Marchak, and Cristina Ruiz, who was about to give birth to another Brando baby.

The week of Christian's preliminary hearing, Cheyenne had finally been released from Vaiami Hospital's locked isolation unit, where she had been since July 6. On July 30 she was again interrogated by Gatti, and she told the court that she wanted to make a correction to her earlier statement. Accompanied by her lawyer, Marie Léou, she seemed to have been tutored on her responses, since she was covering exactly the facts that the DA considered most pertinent to the murder charge. She claimed that she had used the word *murder* only because it was the word her questioners had used, and she now insisted, "Dag was killed by Christian, but without pre-meditation. . . . Personally, as I have already said, I thought that Christian simply wanted to scare Dag by showing him his weapons." Under further questioning, though, she undercut what seemed a rehearsal of her father's version of the event by again insisting "that there was not any struggle, and there were no blows exchanged between them."

Back in Tahiti, Drollet gave another graveside interview and vowed to haunt Brando, explaining that he had ordered a large supply of the police photos showing Dag's face in close-up with the bullet hole, which he intended to distribute to the press as well as send to Brando. "Marlon Brando will always remember what happened at his house," he added. "He is as much responsible for my son's death as Christian Brando. I want him to feel the shock and agony that still runs through my veins."

Cheyenne then made a series of phone calls, one to Albert LeCaill: "She said that she hoped to see us soon, to see Lisette and Tiairani [Dag's four-year-old] and to introduce us to Tuki," LeCaill reported. "She said that Tuki was the son of Dag, that he looked like him—he had his nose—and that he behaved well and was handsome."

When LeCaill asked if she was sure that Tuki was the child of Dag, she asserted that she was because she had never been unfaithful to Dag. The following morning Cheyenne called Lisette and demanded, "You have to come over so that I can tell you everything that has happened." Lisette refused, but Cheyenne pressed her to come. Lisette again refused, telling her simply that she must speak the truth to Judge Gatti. "It is not possible, because I must defend my half-brother," Cheyenne replied.

Later in the day Cheyenne went to see Maeva Bonno, a close friend she had known for eight years. When Maeva asked why she had done nothing to prevent Dag's death, Cheyenne became upset. "But why didn't he do anything to defend himself?" she argued. "He was a lot bigger and stronger than my brother Christian." Before leaving she lifted her dress to show Maeva the bruises on her legs, which she blamed on her brother Teihotu. "He pulled my hair and kicked me," she told her friend. "He was trying to keep me from going out."

That same day, August 7, Christian appeared for his arraignment. He entered his plea of Not Guilty, and for reasons thoroughly puzzling to the prosecution, the judge slashed his bail to $2 million. The following day Brando was sworn in and declared to the judge that it would be a "privilege" to put up the house on Mulholland as security for his son's bail. After handing over his son's passport, he patted Christian on the back and bent to kiss him on the top of his head.

Brando then walked up to Barshop and grabbed his arm.

"Mr. Barshop," he demanded, "I want to know if you've changed your mind."

"About what?" asked the prosecutor, casting a glance of annoyance at the hand that was still on his sleeve.

"About Christian being a mad-dog killer. Do you really believe that?"

Barshop pulled back from Brando's hand and stared at him. "What about Dag Drollet? Mr. Brando, you should really be ashamed." He turned abruptly and walked away, shaking his head.

Outside over 200 reporters were waiting for a statement, and Brando readily obliged.

Asked what advice he had given his son, he replied that he was close to his "nine children" and added, "I don't think I've said anything that would not be said by any father. I just kept telling him, 'Sometimes in life, you have to duke it out.'" Insisting that Christian's difficulties were exacerbated "because he's my son," he gave the accolade that his son had so yearned for: "He's tough. I'm proud of him." He then recalled his own difficult youth and talked openly about Christian's alcohol and drug problems, adding one of his own favorite tough-guy slogans, "Every time you get up off the canvas, you're stronger and better for it."

A reporter interrupted to ask if there was anything that could have been done to prevent the death of Dag Drollet. "Where is a feather dropped by a seagull on the heads of two thousand persons going to land?" he answered, resorting to one of his pseudo-Zen koans. "There are too many unknowns . . . ," he trailed off. "I don't know."

It took several more days to arrange for Christian's release, and finally, on August 15, Christian emerged from the county jail into the glare of flashing cameras and the din of seventy-five shouting reporters, some of whom had gathered before dawn. "I just want to go home and try to straighten this out," Christian managed to stammer, before his father interrupted to announce, "I am proud to have my son out of jail." Asked whether the murder case had changed his relationship with his father, Christian shrugged, still at a loss for words. Marlon quipped, "I got fatter and he got thinner."

It had been the same media circus that Brando's presence had created at the preliminary hearing, and over the next week his new cooperativeness was earning sympathy even from the tabloids.

Jacques Drollet was furious and tried to counter with an interview on "Inside Edition." But it was no contest. Later there came a strange new twist to Brando's moves when Albert and Lisette LeCaill received a letter on August 23, a communication that Jacques Drollet immediately reported to the DA's office:

> *Dear Lisette, Albert, and Tiairani,*
>
> *There is no way that we can bring back Dag. No way is money a substitute for a father's love. But, we understand that you have been mother and father to Tiairani since her birth, and so we address this letter to you.*
>
> *From Christian's heart and mine, we would like to give to Tiairani the sum of one million dollars U.S. ($1,000,000) as security for her lifetime. We give this to the baby with all our love and tears. Our hearts break for the whole family.*
>
> *I do not blame Jacques for the hard things he says about me and the family. If I were in his place, I might feel the same way. I hope the day will come when he and I can happily serve as grandfathers to Tuky.*
>
> *Please understand that there are no conditions attached to this offer. If Jacques wishes to continue his suit, so be it.*
>
> *We send you all our love to all the family.*
>
> *Marlon and Christian*

For anyone who had ever followed Brando's maneuvers, the divide-and-conquer strategy was obvious, since it was in the actor's interest to try to separate the LeCaills from the uncompromising and accusatory Drollet.

Brando would continue to try to exploit this angle for months to come, even though Dag's mother and stepfather refused to accept the offer. Soon the LeCaills and Drollet again demanded a DNA test to determine Tuki's paternity. "Marlon refuses to allow that," their L.A. attorney Marshall Morgan informed them. Morgan had received word from Shapiro that the actor considered it "an invasion of his family's privacy."

Despite Brando's extreme sensitivity about his family's privacy, on

August 27 it became public knowledge that the baby, Tuki, required treatment for drug addiction after being released from the hospital. The following day Cheyenne herself was admitted to the emergency room, allegedly because of another drug episode, and perhaps an overdose. Her psychiatrist, Dr. Yves Petit, requested that the court of Papeete put her under judicial safekeeping to protect her "against her own doings." Judge Gatti agreed, at the same time announcing his intention to place the baby with Cheyenne's mother, Tarita.

Two weeks later, on September 14, Cheyenne returned to Papeete's Palais de Justice, where she was required to give yet a third deposition under more extended questioning by Judge Gatti. Also present were Jacques Drollet, Drollet's attorney François Quinquis, and Maître Claude Girard, substituting for Marie Léou, Cheyenne's usual representative.

"In effect, as in the United States," Cheyenne explained, "I am legally a minor and thus dependent on my father, [and] I was afraid that he would keep me. Besides, I accused my father, in front of his lawyer, of complicity in the murder of Dag because I thought that he was fixated on *The Godfather* and that he was crazy on this subject. He was jealous of my life and of my happiness, and always wanted me to take care of him. Besides, when I was seventeen years old, he had asked me to the Beachcomber Hotel, and I had refused. However, I must tell you that I retracted my accusations of complicity that I made at the time of or just after Dag's death, because I was gravely traumatized, as I am again today . . ."

With the apparent allusion to incest left hanging, she was then asked to describe her movements before the shooting. Explaining that she and Christian had entered the house through the same door, she in front of him, she added that he was "arranging his knife and his revolver. . . . When I entered the television room," she continued, "I was obliged to advance because there was a little screen, and as the sofa was in front of the television. . . . As I have told you before, Dag was reclining and Christian was practically on top of him. I thought they were having fun. . . . In fact, I was thinking that Christian wanted to show his weapons to Dag and then tell him to stop hitting me."

Since there had been so many suppositions about her claims that Dag had abused her, she was specifically asked about her anger toward him. "I never said that I wanted Dag's death," she replied. "It is true that I told Dag that I dreamt of seeing him crucified. . . . When I was pregnant, Dag made me nervous. And he said that he did not want to see me. And when he came to see me, it was only to reproach me, and he also molested me. For my part I reproached him regarding his former girlfriend, Valérie Duguet, as well as other friends. And I recall having said sentences like, 'It's necessary to kill that guy,' or 'I'll break his face' and 'I'll kill his soul.' I remember perfectly having said that to several people . . . , but I said that under the influence of anger in an argument.

"As Dag didn't want to speak to me, I don't know if he had the intention of really leaving me. But for my part, I did not want to stay alone because I feared that my father would keep me."

Once again she repeated her feeling that there had been some sort of "complicity" between her father and Christian, that in the long conversation the two of them had had that afternoon, Marlon had told Christian to bring the gun to the house that night. She thought this was further confirmed by the fact that Christian had been *"énervé"* in an inexplicable fashion during dinner. "He told me that he was going to kill [Dag] like that, without reason. . . . I didn't pay any attention to that," she said. "Christian has always been a troubled boy, and I mean to say that he has a weak soul. . . . When I saw the weapons, I did make a connection with what Christian was talking about. I thought that he wanted to show them to Dag to make an impression on him." Pressed further on the subject of the gun and the threats, she showed considerable control. "I am sticking with the explanation that I have already given you," she insisted. "Know that I thought that the gun was not loaded because it seemed very light, but I knew that it was a gun."

On her previous statements to Dag's mother regarding Christian's feelings toward her, she became more explicit. "When I said [to Madame LeCaill] that Christian wanted more from me, that was true," she declared. "Several times I was made to feel that Christian loved me more than a sister—without, however, there having been any gesture between him and me. But, for example, when he came to see us at the house, he always made himself more handsome. By contrast, if I said that Christian was very jealous of Dag, I think that this must be attributed to my illness. . . . I [also] deny having said to Madame LeCaill that I was not able to say the whole truth to the judge . . . because it was 'necessary that I defend Christian.' "

Jacques Drollet, who had remained quiet throughout, now confronted Cheyenne with his suspicions about possible incestuous relations between her and Christian. She bristled. "I tell you again that the accusations which have been brought against me of having been or having had to submit to incestuous relationships are false, and I never spoke of that to anyone." Then she demanded, "Who told you about this subject?" Drollet replied to the judge, "It was Dag who approached me on the subject following some confidences from Cheyenne."

There was one final question: When asked why she had not allowed herself to be questioned by the American "judicial system," Cheyenne said, "I was not able to return to the United States because I was hospitalized, and I am still under treatment. If someone were to authorize it, I would be disposed to return to the United States."

Early in September 1990, Brando had made a surprise announcement of his own by calling his old standby, Army Archerd of *Variety*. For all his worry about a DNA test "invading his family's privacy," after all his years of zealously guarding his secrets, he now declared that he intended to pen his autobiography. "I'm looking for a publisher," he told Archerd. "I'll be my own agent." When Archerd suggested it might be hard to reach the actor, he laughed and said, "All voices bounce back in this canyon." He explained to the columnist that with Christian's case he had been "invaded so deeply by the press" that he had "been forced into this position. . . . No, it won't be painful," he added. "I have no inhibitions. There isn't anything I won't go into." Then he added a few dashes of his favorite cliché to explain his recipe for toughness: "Whatever doesn't kill you makes you stronger, even though it's a world of bruises."

Later that month Brando's London lawyer, Belinda Frixou, announced that she had been asked to represent the book and invited interested parties to stop by at her office on their way to the annual Frankfurt Book Fair. The news set off a multimillion-dollar bidding war with publishers worldwide eager to make Brando an offer he couldn't refuse. In response to reports that the actor had taken this extraordinary step to pay for Christian's legal defense, Frixou adamantly denied that money was the motive. "There've been so many different books about him, unauthorized biographies," she insisted, "that it is about time to set the record right and give everybody the correct version." She added that he would not be using a ghostwriter but "doing it totally himself. . . . He's a very good writer and has done scripts before," she said. "He's written passages and poems and is a writer I would say of—who would I compare him to? I simply can't—[he has a] descriptive, floral style. Very, very poetic."

Brando, she said, would be choosing a publisher not on the basis of money alone but only after meeting face-to-face with individual editors, and then Brando was "anxious to get going," since he planned to begin writing in earnest "in the next few weeks."

While Brando's legal representative was waxing lyrical about his prose style and his desire to write the book alone, Brando himself turned around and asked Philip Rhodes to ghost his autobiography. Seemingly forgetting that he had been furious with Rhodes only months before, he phoned his old friend and tried to entice him back into the inner circle. The makeup man listened as Brando tried to cajole him with the promise that he would be well paid. Rhodes refused to have anything to do with it. He also urged Marlon to drop the idea himself, reminding him that long ago the actor had made a vow never to reveal anything about his private life to the public. Brando, however, kept talking about the money, not only his own but what was in it for Rhodes. The fact was—and Brando knew it—Rhodes had kept detailed journals throughout his life, and everyone realized that Brando himself had a notoriously bad memory. If Brando could use these diaries, they might give him a chronology, which in fact he seemed incapable of putting together himself.

In early October 1990, at the same time Marlon was supposedly meeting potential publishers, Rhodes was approached again, not just by Brando but also by Caroline Barrett: If he didn't want to write the autobiography, would Rhodes be willing to turn over his journals? Recalling his resolution after Brando's tantrum on the set of *The Freshman* and his subsequent cold-shoulder routine, Rhodes turned her down flat. Given all that had happened, coupled with the added stress caused by Christian's arrest, Brando had reached the point of a "nervous breakdown," Rhodes thought. He even wondered aloud if his and Tom Papke's phones might be tapped. Or as he reminded Papke, "You can't let him into your mind to start bothering you. Like a priest, you must exorcise this demon."

On September 26, Marlon, Christian, and Miko arrived at Santa Monica Superior Court. As usual the press gathered, ready for any comments that might be tossed their way. In the courtroom the Brando men wore matching stoic expressions, as if they were presenting a unified front to Drollet, his son, Bjarn, and Albert LeCaill, all of whom had once again flown 5,000 miles to be present at the latest legal skirmish. In fact, though, the session was to be a short one; Steven Barshop asked the judge for a continuance so that he could pursue efforts to bring Cheyenne back to testify, and presiding Judge Robert Thomas agreed to the postponement.

Afterward Brando ventured out to the front of the courthouse to make his own announcements, again talking to the assembled reporters for nearly a half hour. Not surprisingly, he now adopted the strategy of blaming the victim by declaring that there was clear evidence that Dag had abused his daughter. "Cheyenne has suffered enormously," he said. "She's been beaten physically. We have clear proof of that. She's suffered a head injury, where her face was smashed and she had to have her face remade."

Whether Brando had conflated Cheyenne's injuries from her accident with his "clear proof" that Dag had beaten her was unclear, but facts didn't seem to stop him. "She's suffered a nervous breakdown," he continued. "She's had to be in a sanitarium under a doctor's care, and for that man [prosecutor Barshop] to keep chasing my daughter is unspeakable. As a father, I'm deeply offended." Brando was composed until he was asked about Cheyenne's baby boy. "Tuki is doing fine," he said. "He's healthy and strong. Cheyenne is doing her best." He then began to sob quietly.

In fact, though, Brando had never seen the baby, nor had he responded to Judge Gatti's repeated request that he present himself in Tahiti to give a deposition that might lessen the pressure on Cheyenne. Brando may have tried to convince Papke during the preliminary hearing that he was "just being a father" and "was not manipulating," but even his assistant had been skeptical. "In all those statements to the press—that was Marlon acting," said Papke. "I've never seen him genuinely affected by anything, even having his son in court for murder. The only time I saw real tears was when his German shepherd died."

In short, Brando may have had the instincts of a parent but the mind of a Mafia don.

On October 1, 1990, Shapiro presented an offer in which Christian would plead guilty to the lesser charge of "voluntary manslaughter with the use of a firearm." While Barshop was seriously considering this, publicly he adopted a wait-and-see attitude while the cops followed up several new leads on Christian's doings in Laurel Canyon. Meanwhile, coprosecutor Bill Clark continued to explore the possibilities of bringing Cheyenne back to testify.

On October 31, All Hallow's Eve in Tahiti, the day on which everyone gathers to light candles for the dead, Cheyenne visited Dag's grave with Alberto Vivian, her new companion. Under the full moon, she threw herself on Dag's grave and cried, "I've ruined many lives." After twenty-five minutes of uncontrollable sobbing, Vivian had to carry her screaming from the cemetery and drive her home.

According to later reports, Tarita had put Tuki to bed and was already asleep herself. Since Cheyenne was still agitated, Vivian decided to stay to try to calm her. He put on some records and they then went into Tuki's room, where Cheyenne softly sang a French lullaby to the baby boy asleep in his crib. After returning to the sitting room, Cheyenne supposedly told Vivian: "This is a terrible day for me. I am so depressed and so confused because so much is going on." She then told Vivian she was tired and kissed him good-night. Halfway home he had second thoughts and turned around. Back at Tarita's compound, he let himself into her room, but finding Cheyenne neither in bed nor with Tuki, he began to call for her and soon discovered that the bathroom door was locked. After he summoned Teihotu from his adjacent bungalow, the two men broke down the door and found Cheyenne on the floor, gagging and covered with vomit.

An ambulance rushed her eleven miles to the hospital. As emergency room medics began pumping her stomach, she went into cardiac arrest. The medics thumped her chest and gave her oxygen, but she lapsed into a coma. "Her heart was fibrillating," reported Daniel Pardon, the family's spokesperson. "We thought she would die. But her condition stabilized later that day, and the next morning she opened her eyes briefly and squeezed a nurse's finger on request, signaling that she was out of the coma."

Brando spoke to the doctors by phone, telling them that if Cheyenne was dying, he would come immediately, but if her condition improved his priority had to be Christian. In interviews, however, the actor denied that the overdose was an intentional suicide attempt. "Contrary to what people are saying, she simply took too much medication," he explained. "I hope her brain cells have not been irreversibly affected, but it is too early to say." Despite refuting the suicide story, he nevertheless went on to blame Steven Barshop and the entire district attorney's office. "I hold them directly, not indirectly, responsible for her present mental and physical state," Brando said. "She has given six contradictory versions of what happened on the night of the sixteenth to five different people, including Judge Gatti. To any jury she would hardly be a believable witness."

Although her condition improved and Cheyenne was released from the hospital, three days later she again tried to take her own life, this time by hanging herself from a tree with a dog chain. Brando now made no attempt to disguise what was happening. On the night of November 11, he agreed to speak to a *Los Angeles Times* reporter who had previously evidenced sympathy for Christian's cause. "Cheyenne hung herself," he said in an emotional voice. "She has been placed on life support systems. But we don't know if there's any brain damage or not." He reiterated that while he longed to be with her, he had been warned that he might be held by Tahitian authorities for questioning. "This case is tearing everyone apart," he added, again blaming the district attorney's office for trying to pressure his daughter to come back to testify.

In the battle being waged in the press, Brando went on the offensive, announcing that while his daughter was "the most precious thing in the world to me," he could not afford to jeopardize his son's trial by being detained in Tahiti. "The [expletive] judge is going to arrest me," he said angrily. "The [French authorities] would detain me by taking my passport, and I [would be] stuck in Tahiti."

Meanwhile, Cheyenne's Tahitian attorneys, Claude Girard and Marie Léou, had asked the court to declare her "mentally incompetent" and appoint Tarita as Tuki's legal guardian. At a competency hearing held on December 6, Dr. Bernard Ryckelynck, a court-appointed psychiatrist, testified to her medical history and present condition. After the birth of her baby, he explained, she was hospitalized in a locked ward, where it was noted that she "hit a nurse" on the maternity service, that she was talking to herself, and that "she had put her baby under a water faucet while laughing."

Dr. Ryckelynck had examined her on November 22, filing a report that read: "Her spontaneous expression was poor, her attention fluid or floating. When one asked her questions, she seemed not to hear; however, when one asked precise facts, she had some memory but spoke of them without any emotional investment. The only domain that released her emotional reactions and that she expressed with a moral sadness, which was evident, is the death of her lover. 'I no longer want to live,' she said. 'I want to die because it isn't possible that he is no longer here . . . never will I find another like him.' "

Jacques Drollet became furious when he saw Cheyenne on the streets of Papeete stalked by tabloid photographers and reporters, telling one of them that she would be happy to talk—for $75,000. (In fact, an interview was offered to *Paris Match,* reportedly by her friend Alberto Vivian, for $100,000.)

On December 21, Judge Joel Rudof of California Superior Court made his final decision and ruled against coprosecutor Clark's motion to compel Cheyenne to appear for testimony. It was the end of the road. Brando's daughter had been successfully put beyond the prosecutors' reach.

"In her absence, we knew were going to have to scramble," Clark conceded, noting that at trial the prosecution would need to establish (1) where the murder gun came from, (2) Christian's motive for confronting Dag, and (3) how many drinks Christian had had. Cheyenne would have been the key to tying all this up, he said, but he also thought that they could do it with other witnesses as well: Laurene Landon, Marlon, even possibly waiters from the restaurant. Landon had for the moment disappeared, however, and neither the cops nor the DA's office had been able to serve her with a summons to testify before a grand jury. Like Cheyenne, she too had been spirited away; whether she was simply behind the locked gates of the Mulholland compound or out of town, no one knew.

Meanwhile Barshop had been following up several leads that had come to him from an unlikely source. On November 6 the *National Enquirer* reported that it had uncovered evidence that three months before the shooting, Christian had "shot his best friend point-blank in the head—but the pal miraculously escaped death when the bullet only grazed his temple." The previous February, the story alleged, Christian was high on angel dust when he fired a pistol at the head of Ricardo Alvarez, one of the Down Boys. The prosecution realized that Alvarez's own narration of the incident to the tabloid offered enough information to start another investigation of Christian's propensity for violence—if not actually lay the basis for another felony charge.

Alvarez conceded that Christian, whom he called "Padrón," had a dark side. "He could turn downright nasty when he got too high." That night, he said, he, Billy Smith, and another friend drove to Christian's house, bringing along a case of beer and a bag of cocaine. "We pulled up to his house, and as soon as Christian saw us, he burst out of the door like a wild man. My heart nearly stopped when I realized he was waving a gun and firing into the air.

"One of the guys thought he could handle Christian's fury. He got out of the car carrying a twelve-pack of beer. Christian was on him in a flash. He held his gun on the guy with one hand while he beat him senseless with the other. The guy fell to the ground without once raising his hand in defense. Laurene was there sobbing," he added. "She begged us to leave, but it was already too late. Then Christian staggered over to the car. He reached through the window and pointed the gun right at driver Billy Smith's face.

" 'Padrón, this is crazy,' I spit out from the backseat. 'For God's sake, we're your friends.' . . . The next thing I knew a warm flow of blood streamed down the side of my face. I put my hand to my head and felt a two-inch burn above my left ear."

One of Alvarez's companions then confirmed what had happened. "The bullet was lodged in the back of the seat," he recalled. "The angle Christian had shot at somehow caused the bullet to graze Ricardo's temple, but didn't inflict a serious wound. . . . The guys took off in the car like a bat out of hell and ended up at [Smith's] mother's house. She cleaned Ricardo's wound and bandaged it up. Of course, none of us wanted to call the police or an ambulance. The driver didn't have a license and the guys were carrying drugs."

A few days later, the *Enquirer* reported, Christian ran into the friend whom he'd attacked before shooting Alvarez. "I said to Christian, 'Are you crazy? You could've killed someone.' Christian looked right through me, and said, 'It was nothing. What's the big deal? No one got hurt. Everything is fine.' "

Alerted to the story, the police immediately tried to track down those involved in the incident. Because the bullet that grazed Alvarez's face supposedly had lodged in the backseat of Smith's red Caprice, the police also traced the car, but Detective Monsue learned that it had been junked the previous September. He then interviewed Smith's mother, who confirmed that she had put salve on Alvarez's wound but remembered little else, denying that she had seen a bullet hole in her son's car or had dug the projectile out of the backseat. Alvarez remained "lost." Since it was common knowledge that the *Enquirer* had paid the ex–prop man at least $3,000 for his account, Barshop assumed that he had taken the money and run, fearing involvement with the police. The prosecutors and Detective Monsue, however, did locate and interview the other witness, Billy Smith.

Although investigators collected other stories of Christian's violence, by the end of December 1990 Barshop knew that he had exhausted all avenues for putting together a "murder one" case in the absence of Cheyenne's testimony. Judge Robert Thomas had set a trial date of January 14, 1991, and advised that he would grant no more continuances. Consulting with his superiors on Shapiro's earlier offer of a plea, Barshop got the okay from downtown to negotiate. He also discussed the plea offer with Drollet and the LeCaills, who weren't at all happy. "After talking to Jacques for over six months, I knew he wouldn't be receptive," the DA added, "which I could certainly understand. No matter what you say to him about the wisdom of pleading the case, the fact remains his son is dead. No matter what you predict as Christian's sentence, it's not sufficient. But I think he realized that my intentions were good." Drollet insisted, however, that he, Lisette, and Albert be allowed to make their voices heard at the sentencing hearing. Their greatest fear was that with all Brando's power, Christian might be shown leniency. In the final analysis, they felt, American justice was not only politics but an elaborate, often lopsided game won by whoever had the most cash.

On January 3, the prosecutor phoned Shapiro to accept his offer of a guilty plea to the charge of voluntary manslaughter. Shapiro then took the plea offer to Christian and his father, and in a discussion at Mulholland he convinced both that this was the best resolution to the case. How Shapiro prevailed, reportedly, was to assert his confidence that with the full battery of social workers, psychiatrists, and their medical examiner, he had a convincing case for leniency, so much so that the judge might even grant Christian a suspended sentence.

The next morning, Friday, January 4, Marlon did not make an appearance at his son's side when under gray and drizzling skies, Shapiro escorted Christian into the Santa Monica Courthouse. Barshop read the district attorney's official statement, declaring that because they had exhausted all available avenues for compelling Cheyenne to testify, "this was a case of voluntary manslaughter and should be treated as such," and within ten minutes Judge Thomas adjourned the session, having scheduled sentencing for February 26, 1991.

If Brando was hiding his anger and pain behind Mulholland's closed gates, Jacques Drollet was in equal, if not more agony. In his announcements to the press he expressed his fear that Christian would serve little prison time. "Marlon Brando is rich, and well known, and his lawyers are very clever," he said. "They will find a way to get Christian out." Outside the courtroom, Drollet handed the press photographs of Dag lying dead on the sofa, including the close-ups, which newspapers published worldwide. The pictures, along with Drollet's statements, seemed to shift the balance of public sympathy, and given the current concerns about "law and order," even the most liberal-minded had to wonder if Marlon Brando's son was going to "get away with murder." "How anger is replacing any pity that the star had," Kevin O'Sullivan and Richard Shears headlined their story in the London *Mail on Sunday* about the tragedy. They wrote, "The actor who was perhaps the greatest talent of his generation has chosen to live his life in the most gross kind of excess, with the self-destruct button never far away—and now it has happened. . . . Perhaps with a loving and attentive father to see them through this identity crisis, [his children] could have coped. Both Cheyenne and Christian disintegrated."

While Brando himself had often been perplexed by the problems he had seen in his offspring, he had never held himself responsible, choosing instead to blame his ex-wife Anna Kashfi for Christian's difficulties. With Cheyenne he blamed Dag and then the prosecutors, never for a moment acknowledging that his own Machiavellian ploys might have created the nightmare that so haunted her now.

Although Cheyenne remained under indictment in Tahiti, the Tahitian Court of Appeals had already ruled that she could go to France for treatment at the Clinique des Pages, an exclusive psychiatric facility on the outskirts of Paris. On January 8, only a few days after Christian's guilty plea, Brando's daughter flew to the French capital, accompanied by Tarita. Even in her emotionally unstable state, Cheyenne had begun to wonder aloud just what kind of a father Marlon had been. "I have come to despise my father," she claimed, "for the way he ignored me when I was a child. He came to the island maybe once a year, but really didn't seem to care whether he saw me or not. He wanted us, but he didn't want us."

For understandable reasons Jacques Drollet was equally unforgiving. Returning to Tahiti to await the sentencing hearing on February 26, Drollet agreed to another interview, knowing full well that Brando and Shapiro were continuing to marshal the media back in Los Angeles. Meeting for lunch with an American reporter at Le Belvédère, a restaurant near the peak of Mount Orohena, Drollet stared out the window at the rainbow that arched the sea below. He then opened the notebook he carried at all times to record everything that had happened since Dag's killing. Inside the front cover he had pasted a photograph of his murdered son. In solemn and grave tones he began by making allusions to his background, his Jewish ancestry, his service in the Free French navy, his recruitment by the Irgun, and no less, the vagaries of American justice. These were not idle references, the reporter realized, recalling that although Drollet was a schoolteacher by profession he had once fought for principles and was familiar with the use of firearms. With tears in his eyes but his jaw set, Drollet went on. He spoke of Brando as *"démoniaque."* Then he confessed to a flinty bent-on-revenge obsession with seeing the actor dead.

"Last week I went to Bjarn," he explained. "I said, 'You have a life to live. I am old. It is for me to do.' "

"Don't do this," the reporter cautioned. "You'll be killing yourself."

"I am an old man," he objected with a wan smile.

"No . . ."

Drollet shook his head, looking down at his notebook on the table in front of him. "Just call it Masada. . . . I don't discuss this anymore."

In Los Angeles Brando now arranged for his favorite *Los Angeles Times* reporter to do an exclusive—a heartwarming article about Christian as the true victim of the case. The results were predictable. Christian described how all his custody battles were held at the Santa Monica Courthouse, so it was a familiar place to him. "I've been coming through these doors since I was a kid."

"I grew up with an extremely violent mother," he was quoted. "She drank and we had a lot of problems. My whole family, except for my father, is alcoholic. . . . My family's so weird and spaced out. We'd have new additions all the time. Like I'd sit down at the table with all these strange people and say, 'Who are you?' "

On the morning of February 26, the Santa Monica Courthouse was again overrun by the media and spectators clamoring for a look at Marlon Brando, and, if anything, their numbers had swelled. Steven Barshop opened the hearing with a strong statement, outlining the witnesses and evidence he intended to present. Detectives Monsue and Kingsford would testify, and so, too, would several Down Boys, he said. While the Down

Boys' testimony might be inappropriate at a trial, it was wholly admissible under California law as "hearsay evidence" at a sentencing hearing. Barshop paused, quickly going on to make a point of the lack of cooperation from Mary McKenna Brando, who had agreed to be interviewed for the probation report but "will not talk to me." The same had been true of Laurene Landon, he said, but instead of asking for a "body attachment," he would rely on the report. The L.A. County coroner, Dr. Cogan, was to be called in order to refute the defense's forensic expert, and to further establish Christian's pattern of violence, Barshop announced that Stephen Hunio would confirm modifying his best friend's machine gun.

"And last," he declared, "it is my request under the law of the victim's impact . . . that the Drollet family have the right to be heard. Mr. Drollet has come from Tahiti to be here in this matter. The mother and child of Dag Drollet are here to be heard. The stepfather of Dag Drollet is here to be heard."

After showing the victim's crime-scene photos, presenting a report from Detective Monsue, and playing the tape of Christian's confession, Barshop put Billy Smith, one of the so-called Down Boys, on the stand. While Smith insisted that the name "was just a joke," not a real group, he testified that he had known Christian for nearly two years, lived near him in Laurel Canyon, and had partied with him, drinking and doing coke. Barshop asked Smith to recount the incident in which Christian had ordered him off his property, firing a gun over his head three times before shooting Ricardo Alvarez, who was sitting "obliviated" in the backseat of Smith's car. Smith confirmed it all and repeated what he had already told Barshop's investigators, including his claim that the group had smoked PCP and gotten drunk during the day. Barshop then elicited another story, this one an account of Christian using a hammer to knock out another Down Boy's headlights. As if to beat Shapiro to the punch, he then had Smith explain that Alvarez had received money from the *National Enquirer* to tell his story, but he himself hadn't.

Shapiro, however, thought he had found another motive for Smith's testimony—that the informant had been arrested for driving while intoxicated, a violation of his probation on another charge. Smith conceded that was so, and Shapiro now drove his point home: Hadn't Mr. Barshop offered to cut a deal, since the previous day his case had been continued pending Christian's sentencing? Smith agreed that he was hoping for leniency, but this did nothing to alter the "fact," as he put it, of his testimony.

David Butler, a firearms identification officer with the LAPD, was next up and repeated testimony that he had given at the preliminary hearing about the Sig-Sauer. The gun, he said, had a number of built-in safeguards to prevent an accidental discharge, and his analysis disputed Christian's claim that it had gone off because he "didn't know the hammer was back."

Now Barshop asked if Butler had been able to reconstruct the crime scene and determine the bullet's trajectory. Butler replied that once the bullet had finally been found and he had returned to Mulholland, the "carpet was out and damaged and moved." Barshop hadn't found it necessary to spell it out, but it took no great insight to conclude that between Cheyenne's quick flight from the country and the tampering with the crime scene, there had been plenty of behind-the-scenes maneuvering.

Barshop then called Steve Hunio, explaining that although the illegal weapons charge had been severed from the case, his testimony would go to the issue of Christian's propensity for violence. For the first time in the proceedings, Christian raised his head and looked up at the witness stand. Under Barshop's questioning, Hunio explained that Christian had been his closest friend for sixteen years. He said that his alcohol and drug problems had worsened from 1988, when he fell in with a bunch of bad people. "We grew apart because of that," he added with a note of sadness in his voice, then confirmed that he had modified Christian's MAC-10 to make it fully automatic. "I did it out of friendship," he said. "It wasn't a matter of money. He was very, very afraid of being kidnapped," he added, explaining Christian's rationale for wanting a machine gun. "He was absolutely paranoid, terrified of people coming into the house or hurting him or members of his family."

His testimony was forthright and clear, and after he left the stand, for one brief moment he turned and looked at the back of Christian's head. His expression was stony faced, but it was almost as if he were bidding his friend good-bye.

After a break Barshop brought Mary McKenna Brando, his hostile witness, to the stand. Nervous and trembling, she was forced to sit in the witness box as the DA read her three-page divorce declaration into the record. Having ascertained that this was a document prepared by her attorney and signed under penalty of perjury, he proceeded to list the complaints she had made about Christian's violence. It included her claim that he had threatened her life and physically assaulted her, once pointing a loaded rifle at her mother.

"Did you sign that document?" Barshop asked when he completed his recitation.

"Yes, but . . ."

"Thank you, ma'am," Barshop said, cutting her off. "I have no further questions."

On cross-examination, Shapiro asked her to explain. "I was angry at Christian at the time," she insisted. "I just listened to my lawyer. . . . There are, I guess, some exaggerations. I never said he pointed a loaded rifle at my mother. . . . Just ask my mother."

As if on cue, Mary's mother exclaimed from her seat, "No!" Marlon turned and gave her a warm smile.

"Christian was acting like a brat," Mary continued. "I wanted him to stop acting like a brat."

On the second day of the hearing, the defense presented its side of the case with a series of psychological and firearms experts. On the third morning, Shapiro called a character witness.

The courtroom, meanwhile, was buzzing with the question of whether Marlon himself would testify on Christian's behalf. Shapiro had informed neither the DA's office nor the public of the actor's intentions. Late in the morning, however, he asked to approach the bench, requesting a sidebar with Judge Thomas and Barshop. Ever the showman, the defense attorney took a beat and then announced to the judge, "The walrus wishes to speak."

Returning to his table, Shapiro had another joke ready.

"We have no more witnesses," he announced. There were audible groans of disappointment. "No," he added with a wide grin, "we will call Marlon Brando. We just wanted to see if the press was still awake."

As the audience laughed, Brando rose from his seat, his face expressionless. For the most important performance of his life, he had chosen to wear a rather old, somewhat frayed-looking black turtleneck and a rumpled cashmere blue blazer, its tailoring pulled out of shape by his enormous girth. Slowly he walked across the front of the courtroom to the witness stand. The clerk began to swear him in, and completed the recitation of the oath with the usual phrase, "so help you God?"

"No, I will not swear on God," he announced abruptly. "I will not swear on God, because I don't believe in the conceptional sense and in this nonsense. What I will swear on is my children and my grandchildren."

"We have a different oath we can give him," the judge said quickly, not to be rattled by Brando's outburst.

"Do you solemnly affirm that the testimony you may give . . . shall be the truth and the whole truth and nothing but the truth—"

"I do indeed," Brando interrupted.

"—And that this you do under the pain and penalty of perjury?"

"Yes, I do."

He then sat in the witness chair, but because of his weight—more than 300 pounds, it appeared—he had to shift sideways, his arm draped over the railing to support himself.

Announcing his name as "Marlon Brando Jr.," he responded in a muted, almost choked voice to Shapiro's request that he describe "the early childhood."

"You have to give me a minute or two to collect myself. I have never met this woman, and although I have talked to her on the phone, I haven't heard any of these stories . . . and would you ask these guys *to shut up . . .*"

Brando's emotion about Mrs. Hardy, an earlier defense witness whose testimony had limned Christian's duress as a child, had now given way to an angry snap at the two translators who sat several yards from him, rendering testimony in French for the benefit of the Drollet family. If the actor had set out to make a good impression on the court, he had already struck a false note, and he quickly realized it, apologizing to the judge and telling Shapiro that he had forgotten what the question was.

Reminded that the attorney wanted him to describe Christian's childhood, including "any traumatic experiences," Brando began a rambling narrative of his relationship with Anna Kashfi. He called her "as negative a person as I have met in this life," adding in his slightly off-the-mark vocabulary, "I think the tincture of what her character is can be encapsulated in the fact she is not in this courtroom today."

Brando told the court he had married Kashfi ("probably the most beautiful woman I have ever known") because she was pregnant and he didn't want his child to be illegitimate, but that the marriage soon ended. His voice grew angry as he described how she had lied to him about her Indian parentage. Shapiro simply let this undiminished antagonism spill out.

Once Kashfi moved out of his house—into an apartment he paid for, he was quick to point out—he admitted that he "led a rather wasted life, chased a lot of women." Then Brando detailed the continuing custody battles over Christian, mentioning that they had brought him to this courthouse many times. He had seen how Kashfi hired and fired nurses when the boy was young, how she was taking drugs, and he had to fight for his son—he couldn't simply back off and leave the child alone.

He recalled one ugly battle with Kashfi after she had gotten a court order requiring him to send a chauffeured limousine whenever Christian was to be delivered to Mulholland. One time Brando himself arrived to pick up his son, and Anna, he said, became irate with his explanation that he had done so because the limo was late. "She took a fencing foil, and beat me on the back with it, and it hurt a lot. I pretended that it didn't mean anything at all. . . . I have never said anything bad to Christian about his mother. I have always tried to tell him that his mother was ill."

He announced, "I think perhaps I failed as a father," and though "the tendency is always to blame the other parent," he admitted that "there were things that I could have done differently had I known better at the time, but I didn't."

When Shapiro tried to bring Marlon down to earth by asking specific questions, he initially responded by ranting about the judge who had first granted him custody—"Judge Rittenband, a known hater of women," which was, Brando said, "the only reason I got Christian."

Anyone who did not know the long history of Brando's custody battles wouldn't have had the faintest idea what he was going on about. If his reference to the unmarried Rittenband seemed inappropriate, though, there was more. Explaining that when he got Christian "he was just a basket case of emotional disorders," he began to rail against another judge, "Judge Scott . . . , who liked publicity," and who had returned Christian to Kashfi's custody. This, Brando charged, was a "barbarous decision" despite the "battery of psychiatrists" who all recommended that Christian stay with him.

Shapiro tried to establish that Brando had regained custody of Christian when he was thirteen, after years of court battles. Once again Marlon missed the point, asserting that these were not custody battles but hearings over visitation rights, and he continued to complain that Kashfi had told maids that he was "a nasty person, a vicious person, not to be trusted." As before, he suddenly stopped himself, his voice trailing off like that of an old, lost man: "It is all in the boxes somewhere stuck away."

Asked how far Christian went in school, Brando didn't answer directly, but recited what sounded like typical Marlon Zen-speak. "As far as I am concerned, Christian is still going to school." He then spoke warmly about his son's going to technical school, where "his tactics in welding were very good . . ." He was invited to be a teacher, "for which I was very proud, and he had to take his written tests, which scared him to death."

The recitation here was poignant, this grasping at Christian's small triumph. But when Shapiro got down to the facts again, trying to prompt Brando to give the answer he was looking for—how many years of formal education Christian had—Brando still didn't give an answer. Instead, he conceded that his son never paid any attention, ditched school, smoked grass, and often went out with his dogs, who "were very close to him."

"What about people who say Christian is the spoiled son of a rich and famous man?" Shapiro asked.

Now Marlon flared up again. "Then either they are a lying son-of-a-bitch or they don't know what they are talking about. Of all the children I have," he continued, "Christian from the beginning was the most independent. I offered him money. He didn't take it. He wanted his own identity. He struggles. He works hard and he struggles."

As Christian silently wept—now for the first time showing any real emotion in the courtroom—his father's anger returned to the fore, and he lashed out at the reporters with whom, he said, Christian "had to struggle." "This is the *Marlon* Brando case," he said heatedly. "If Christian were black, Mexican, or poor, he wouldn't be in this courtroom. Everyone wants a piece of the pie, including the—" He stopped himself abruptly.

"I want to direct your attention now to the events of May the sixteenth," Shapiro said, picking up the slack, "and I want you to relate to the judge when you first saw Christian that day, the day of this horrible event."

"What day is that?" Brando asked.

"The day of the death of Dag Drollet."

"Oh."

There were gasps in the courtroom. Jacques Drollet, who had been staring at Brando intently, now shook his head in angry despair. Shapiro continued, however, trying to lead Brando through the events of the evening, beginning with his brief conversation with Christian before the young man had left to take Cheyenne to dinner. Asked when his son and daughter returned, he was vague about the specific time. However, when Shapiro questioned him about seeing Christian upon his return, he deflected the question and digressed, pulling out of nowhere Barshop's earlier remark that he kept his guns under his bed.

Shapiro then segued into Christian's interest in guns. Insisting that Christian had only gone hunting with "Dag, the guy who was here yesterday," Marlon seemed to have become thoroughly addled. Presumably he meant Steve Hunio, who had testified the day before. That he could so blithely substitute Dag's name had Jacques Drollet livid with fury.

Brando was soon off on another long and confused digression: "I come from a long line of Irish drunks. My uncle . . . my mother's great uncle, I think. O'Gunn was his name. That is my family name. Miles O'-Gunn. He was a drunk."

The name, of course, was Myles Gahan, not O'Gunn, but he went on: "Both my sisters were drunks, and the only reason I use the word *drunk* is not to demean them. It just means that that is the way they identified themselves in Alcoholics Anonymous. I have been to Alcoholics Anonymous with my mother, my father . . . and why it didn't get to me, I don't know. I have never been a drunk, although I have drunk in my life. It just jumped over me, and [I] never abused any kind of substance. It may be food, I guess," he added, "but that will appear in the papers."

Shapiro again tried to rein him in, asking him to make the connection between his ordering Christian to bring the guns to Mulholland and his son's drinking. Christian, Brando answered, had brought the MAC-10, proudly telling him, "This is an Uzi." He stopped there, though, breaking the narrative. "Almost every crime that is committed—and if I am not correct, you can correct me, Judge—is committed with somebody having drunk alcohol and/or drugs, mostly *and* drugs." He had turned and addressed Judge Thomas directly, who refrained from comment.

"Did Christian bring up his weapons to your house?" Shapiro pressed.

"Damn right he did, because I told him I would—I would steal them, and I would. I wouldn't give a damn. I would go right in his house and take his property." Brando then explained how he had locked up Christian's motorcycle when he was eighteen. Now Shapiro interrupted and asked where the guns had been put, and if Christian knew their whereabouts. Brando's response presented a stranger picture yet—that Christian had brought the guns as ordered, then sneaked some of them out of the house. Later, on May 16, when Brando asked Christian directly, he'd confessed that he still had "the automatic."

Brando then explained that he had instructed Christian before dinner, "I want that, too, Christian. You got to bring that to me. Pick it up and bring it over here."

"Was Christian truthful with you?" Shapiro asked.

"Damn right he was truthful," Brando snapped. "That guy knows how to lie better than I do. And I am good at it, and it takes a bullshitter to catch one, and I know when he is lying. He knows when he is lying, and he is a bad liar. Christian could never tell a lie worth a damn, and he could never look at me in the face and tell me a lie. And he has tried, because he knew he couldn't get away with it. . . . With girls, I am sorry to say, he has lied as have I, your honor," he added, "and some of the rest of the gents around here. I state some of the ladies, too. I don't see a smile on her face . . ."

He had gestured toward someone in the audience, someone real or imagined—none of the reporters could tell—then apologized for "talking too much."

Shapiro brought Brando back to his memories of the night of May 16, asking him to recount his conversation with Christian after his son returned from dinner. It was a crucial point, but after briefly recalling that Christian had come into his bedroom and said, " 'Boy, did we have a great dinner, blah blah blah,' " Marlon claimed that he asked him if he had brought the gun. Christian had said yes, that it was "in the other room." Brando recalled asking his son what he and Cheyenne had talked about, and mentioning Cheyenne led Brando to another digression, this one about his daughter. "Mind you, Cheyenne has seven pieces of metal in her face," he said. "She came from Tahiti with a head like that, a green—a head as big as a watermelon, and she had been close to death on another occasion with what they call an ectopic pregnancy, which is a pregnancy on the wall of the outside of the woman's stomach someplace, womb or something, and she was off her nut. She was having a lot of emotional problems, behaving irrationally, which was totally unlike her or anything. She is a Tahitian. She thinks like a Tahitian, and I have always checked on the kids."

He then continued, explaining that Cheyenne had come to Los Angeles, and as he started to describe what he felt seeing his daughter in such terrible circumstances, he made a different connection. "I have to say something in retrospect to Jack," he began. "Speaking of daughters, which is not known to everybody . . ." He then told the story of the death of Jacques Drollet's daughter in the airplane crash. The comment was hurtful and betrayed as much about himself as about the Drollets. Whereas he had refused to meet with Albert LeCaill and Jacques's son Bjarn after Dag's death, he now presented himself as sympathetic, someone who understood another father's pain. "I remember putting my arms around him," he went on, "giving him my genuine affection and condolences . . . so he knows certainly what it feels like. He has had his share of anguish and misery."

"Whose son was killed here?" muttered a member of the press.

Saying that Jacques Drollet "had his share of anguish and misery," Brando seemed to be asking for Drollet's empathy while describing Cheyenne and Christian. But his inappropriate remarks seemed to originate in the incident the screenwriter Eoghan Harris had noted a few years ago, when Brando had watched his son trying to get in the driveway gate and admitted his problems with Christian. Harris had thought then how much Brando seemed to be watching himself in a movie, and indeed even here on the stand, he seemed to be playing the role of a stoic but grief-stricken father.

Brando stumbled on and chronicled other signs of his daughter's deterioration, recounting that during his last trip to Tahiti in March 1990, when he had taken the whole family to Tetiaroa, she had been "thin as a dime. . . . She wasn't eating," he said. "She would sit in her room, and she and Dag were fighting, and she didn't want Dag in there. One night she wouldn't talk to me. I would come in and sit down . . . , just start talking about the day or the wind or whatever it was, and so she would jump over the railing and just take off. Sometimes I would find her. Sometimes I wouldn't, but I wouldn't go looking for her."

Why Cheyenne was then so furious with her father wasn't clear, and Brando seemed to have no clue as he expressed his confusion about whether he went looking for her. "She used to sit under one particular tree," he continued, and then explained that his son, Teihotu, had told him that on one occasion Cheyenne had started to swim out toward Rimatuu, one of the atoll's other islands, and they had had to retrieve her in a boat.

Brando declared that he had felt frustrated but that one of Cheyenne's doctors in Tahiti had offered him some advice. While Cheyenne was "not nuts," the doctor said, he still suggested that Marlon bring her to the United States to have experts try to discover what was "wrong with her."

At that point Brando stopped himself, noticing the judge making signals to the attorneys.

"Want me to hurry up?" he asked.

"No," said Judge Thomas, instead informing him that he was adjourning for lunch.

The press and spectators spent lunch filled with speculation about Brando's performance. Was he really so out of it? Was it a performance? Was he simply manipulating, controlling even his own attorney with his digressions and asides? In the courthouse cafeteria, one pressman organized a $5 betting pool, the pot to go to whichever reporter came closest to guessing Christian's sentence.

When court reconvened at 1:45 P.M., Shapiro had evidently coached Brando, directing him to be more aware of the victim's family and to stop his sometimes self-revealing digressions.

"I just wanted to say," Brando began, almost in midsentence as he reseated himself on the witness stand, "I am sorry if I offended anybody in the courtroom. I give my apologies. I was kind of hysterical."

"Don't worry about it," replied Judge Thomas, eager to move on.

"Sorry, Judge," Brando repeated, then he turned back toward the courtroom and waited at last for guidance from Shapiro. The attorney now emphasized that he would be asking "some direct questions" and requested that the actor "just focus in on these areas for Judge Thomas, if you would."

"Okay," Brando said, brought to his mark. No director had been as forceful in years, and he seemed ready for another take.

Shapiro returned to the evening of the murder, reiterating Brando's conversation with his son after dinner, when Christian had told him that the gun was "in the kitchen someplace." Brando now resumed his account:

"And then I, as we were watching [TV], said, 'What did Cheyenne say?' And there was a pause, and he said, 'You don't want to know, Pop,' and I turned to him and I said, 'Listen, I want to know everything that Cheyenne says. Every single scintilla of information that you have got, I want to know what it is. I want to know what she said.'

"And he said, 'Believe me, Pop, you don't want to know,' and he got up and he left the room."

The next time he saw Christian, Brando claimed, was five minutes later. "He came into the room and looked weird," he told the court, "and he said, 'I killed Dag,' and I said, 'What are you talking about?' And he said, 'He is dead, Pop. I didn't mean to do it. He went for the gun, and it went off.'"

Brando recalled asking Christian if he had the gun because, as he said, he "wanted to smell the gun to see if it had been fired." It was only after smelling the gun and realizing it had been discharged that he "went right in the other room where Dag—where Dag was, and I am not lying. I swear to Christ on Tuki's life and soul. I saw Dag lying . . . and he still had a pulse, and I breathed into his mouth, and I called 911."

"Did you see the body being taken out?" asked Shapiro. He seemed to be feeding him, asking him to create the scene that he had insisted upon before, but again Brando was confused, substituting Dag's name for Jacques'.

"As much as it may not be believed by Dag, Lisette—that is, I loved Dag," he said. "He was going to be the father of my grandchild, and I talked to him a lot and about taking dope and giving dope to Cheyenne. . . . That was about a week before, because I had to find out from him what kind of drugs Cheyenne took." He recalled that she had mentioned ecstasy, though he didn't know what that was. Then he returned to the removal of Dag's body, the scene that Shapiro had prompted him to describe. "When they brought him out," he recalled, "I asked some officers to unzip the bag, and I wanted to say good-bye and admire him properly. I kissed him, told him I loved him and that is all—"

When Shapiro asked him, "Is there anything else that you would like to add to your testimony here today? Anything else you would like to say?" Brando looked across at the Drollet family. Having been annoyed by the translators, he now chose to address the Tahitians in French. With tears in his eyes, he began, "I cannot continue with the hate in your eyes," he said. "I'm sorry with my whole heart." He went on, starting to sob. He spoke of Dag's daughter, Tiairani, and her future, and how he had offered to take care of her needs. Tuki, he said, was their common grandson, their joint blood. Finally, he finished by reminding Jacques Drollet that he had loved Dag, that Dag was to be the father of his grandchild, and if the

Frenchman were only to look into his heart, he would have to acknowledge that that was true.

Throughout, Drollet stared back at him, and even though he, too, had tears in his eyes, there was not the slightest sign of forgiveness on his face.

Judge Thomas turned to Barshop, expecting his cross-examination. But for the past several hours the prosecutor had been watching Brando carefully, calculating his own moves. He was deeply distrustful of the testimony, suspecting that all the confusions, all the deflections, all the inability to answer a direct question was Brando at his best. "He may be acting," he had whispered to a colleague, and by the time Shapiro finished he had made up his mind. He was not going to ask for an encore or take the chance of allowing the greatest actor in the world to elicit more sympathy for himself and his son. "I have no questions," he told the judge, who then excused Brando from the stand.

"That will conclude our evidence in mitigation of punishment," Shapiro said, as Brando lumbered back to his seat, white and sweating, his breath coming in short gasps. As he sat down, Miko put his arm around him, but he stared vacantly ahead.

The Drollets, of course, had asked to be heard, and after a brief recess, DA Bill Clark introduced them. Such "victim impact statements" were a routine part of California sentencing hearings, but Lisette LeCaill transcended the usual. In her dignity and brevity she revealed a strength that far surpassed Brando's stream of consciousness. Standing tall and poised, dressed all in black, she spoke directly to the judge in short sentences, her French translated to the court. What she said, simply, was that she had loved her son and that she could not believe that his death had been an accident.

Lisette was followed by her husband, Albert LeCaill, who chose to speak in English. He disputed Marlon's claim that the actor had been "close" to Dag and his family. He said that during the time Cheyenne lived with them, he had never met either her father or her mother, that Lisette had met Tarita only twice, and that their phone calls to the house had never been to establish a friendship with him and Lisette. His voice then became indignant as he recalled how long it had taken Brando to notify them of Dag's death and that the actor had made himself unavailable when they so desperately needed news about what had happened.

"We try to meet Marlon . . . in Los Angeles," he recalled, "but I never have any chance neither to see him [nor] to speak directly to him.

"Mr. Brando knows our country," he continued, "knows our habits, and I was very shocked when I received by hand one letter from them offering us some amount of money. For sure it was a lot of money, but in my life I don't need to be bought. I have nothing to say, and I think that is the last thing I can say, just because Dag was like my son."

Jacques Drollet was the last to speak, rising from his seat and standing tall, speaking in almost perfect English. After a detailed, moving account of his son's childhood and relationship with Cheyenne, he arrived at the story of his son's death. Dag had told his father, "Marlon Brando likes me," Drollet recalled. But Drollet had been perceptive enough to advise his son that when Brando "is in Polynesia, he acts like a Polynesian, but Marlon Brando, when he is in Los Angeles, I don't know him." He made a brief reference to a visit to California years before with his half-brother, Leo Langomazino. Then, he had thought Brando was a rude boor and a slob, but today he only explained, "I really didn't like the way he was with us that day." As a result, he said, the many times he had visited Los Angeles, he had never called Brando nor gone to his house again.

Dag was "too confident," he continued, having thought that it was a simple matter, that by coming to Los Angeles to protect the woman who was carrying his baby, he would be accepted by Brando. But the question remained in his mind, he said. "Does Marlon Brando like Dag? We have evidence that . . . probably the last days he was on good terms with Dag." But, he insisted, at the beginning of the relationship, three or four years before, Brando "didn't like Dag. He didn't want Dag as his son-in-law. . . . I think [the Brando family] simply rejected him, and he didn't understand that. People from the islands are very naive. They are too good, to my knowledge. They welcome you. You are adopted as we adopted Marlon Brando."

Drollet went on to explain the difference between living in Tahiti and living in America to explain why Dag had been "too confident" of his safety. In Tahiti, he said, "we do not carry any guns. . . . The only gun we need is . . . to go spear fishing. That was the only gun Dag had." That was why he added that if someone pointed a gun in Dag's face, he would have laughed, just as Drollet would, too. "If anyone [would] come to me in Los Angeles," he explained, "and point a gun at me, I say, 'Hey, what is going on?' I will laugh at you, and I will be shot, just like Dag has been shot."

It was a poignant reminder of just how different Dag's upbringing and style of living had been from Christian's. He added that some people had wondered why Dag had not defended himself. "How could he?" he asked plaintively. "He did not believe it."

The judge had to be moved by Drollet's closing words: "Thank you, sir, for listening to me," he said simply. "Thank you for your patience. . . . Forgive my English. . . . We have suffered much, and we still suffer. We have lost a beloved son. Marlon [has] lost nothing. He has a son here. He has Tuki. He has Cheyenne . . ." And now Drollet made it clear just who he held responsible for everything, including the difficulties that Cheyenne and Christian were in. "If they are in such a shape, it is because of him, not of us. It is not our problem. We have suffered much. We still suffer. It is not easy for us to come here, and we came, and we thank you for giving us this opportunity to speak."

"Thank you, sir," Judge Thomas replied.

Neither Brando nor his son had stirred in their seats as they sat with downcast eyes. The audience, however, had been deeply affected by Drollet's statement, since after all the expert testimony, all of Brando's labyrinthine explanations and rationalizations, the father's speech had reminded everyone just who the victim was and whose son was now dead.

Barshop took the floor to insist on the maximum term prescribed by law—sixteen years.

"I clearly agree with Mr. Marlon Brando," he said, "that this is not the 'Marlon Brando Show,' nor should it be." Vehemently objecting to any implication that Christian Brando was being treated differently by either the DA's office or the court system because of who his father was, Barshop declared that he had heard many "blacks, browns, and poors in custody saying, 'Hey, Christian Brando's getting a better deal because he has got money. He has got a rich, famous, powerful family.'

"Christian Brando shot Dag Drollet in the face. Point-blank range," he continued emphatically. "We ask the punishment to fit the crime. There was, there is, and there has not been shown any struggle whatsoever."

Judge Thomas needed no recess during which to consider what would be a fit sentence. "The only thing everyone here can agree is that this was a tragic situation," he began. "I have heard very well presented information and evidence from both sides with respect to the aggravating and mitigating factors, and the court finds these factors to be of equal weight."

After three days of elaborate testimony, the scales of justice hung at an even balance, it seemed, and Solomon-like, Thomas now chose the middle course: six years for voluntary manslaughter and an additional four years on the gun charge, a total sentence imposed of ten years in state prison. With credit for the ninety days previously served, plus forty-five days for "conduct credit," Christian would be eligible for parole in about four and a half years.

Christian was hustled from the courtroom by the bailiff, with Marlon following after him through the rear exit. After the months of wooing the press, he had no more use for them. Shapiro had already had his chauffeur drive his Mercedes to the courthouse's rear exit, usually reserved for Corrections Department buses that take prisoners to jail. The area was caged off, with heavy bars and chain-link fences surrounding the driveway. Hundreds of photographers and reporters were now massed on the far side, shoving cameras and microphones through the bars. Brando walked out into the slight drizzle that had started to fall, his eyes hidden behind heavy wraparound sunglasses. Captured as if behind bars, he looked more like a Mafia don than anyone could have imagined—huge, unbowed, and if truth be told, genuinely frightening. He stepped into the Mercedes, the gate was lifted, and he was driven away.

In the days to come, Brando would suffer more sad and humiliating losses: Miko's wife, Jiselle, killed in a highway accident; his former daughter-in-law, Mary McKenna Brando, arrested for prostitution. Christian's former lover, Shirley Cumpanas, would pose nude for *Penthouse* and use a 900 number to tell sex secrets about her affair with Marlon Brando's son. Jocelyne Lew, another of Christian's lovers, sold her story to the tabloids. Taken all together, the Brando family was, as the French press called them, *"maudits"*—cursed. There did indeed seem to be a blight on the house of Brando, and like a Greek tragedy, it had been passed from one generation to the next.

For all the speculation and experts' disagreements during the sentencing hearing about what had actually happened the night of May 16, there was one piece of information that had never come to light: It was a glimpse into Brando's psyche that might have confirmed what Drollet and even

Cheyenne came to suspect—that Marlon Brando, wittingly, unwittingly, possibly as a result of his own limitations, had played a key role in the shooting, not by holding the gun, but by setting the stage and providing the emotional cues that led to the killing.

The subtext was simple. Years before, after Marlon had been seeing his therapist, G. L. Harrington, he had often told close friends that he had finally been able to come to terms with his past, with his volatile temper, his anger, his hatreds. While he had rarely ever talked about his mother, he spoke of his father and often recited anecdotes from his childhood to his own kids. Particularly, he had shared with Christian his boyhood escapades, his getting into trouble, his girlfriends, his having problems with his own "old man."

There was one event in Brando's life that one had to assume was an anecdote he would have told Christian, since it was an instance of his proving his manhood. During a conversation with one of his associates, when the two were discussing *Jericho* and the propensity for violence in human beings—guns and self-defense as well as heated anger—he spoke about his father as "a very, very tough hombre, a street fighter, a brawler." He explained that his father had often frightened him. He also made it clear that he had confronted him after his father had been "beating the shit out of my mother." He went on to relate how he had gone upstairs and retrieved his father's .45 and also a large trench knife, whereupon he threatened to kill his father if he continued to abuse his mother. In his high-adrenaline state, he then paused and stopped himself only at the last minute, realizing just how close he had come.

The episode was a partial source for his improv in *Tango*, yet as Brando described it, what he had done to protect his mother was a near blueprint for the confrontation between Christian and Dag. Had Christian heard the story often enough that, between his addled brain and borderline IQ, he thought he had received an implicit command from his father? If Brando, as Cheyenne suspected, had been the one to tell Christian that Dag was beating her, and in the same conversation instructed him to "bring his gun up to the house," had Christian taken this as a subtle challenge to do what Marlon had once done in similar circumstances? To protect his sister, just as his father had once protected his own mother? And so, had he gone to Laurene's house and picked up a .45 automatic and a *knife,* the same combination of weapons Brando had used to threaten his father? Then walked into Mulholland, pointed his weapon at Dag, and said, like his tough and honorable dad, "If you touch her again, I'm going to kill you"?

The likelihood of such a replay was chilling to contemplate, but not to be dismissed—certainly not in the context of the Brando household, where verbal communication had always been partial at best.

While Christian had been sentenced to only ten years in jail, with the likelihood that he would serve less than five years because of California's traditional "half-time" probation guidelines, it was his sister, Cheyenne, who would receive the harsher punishment: an indeterminate, possibly lifelong sentence of being shut away in psychiatric hospitals, with her father as the jailkeeper.

The prestigious Clinique des Pages specialized in the treatment of "acute cases," and once Cheyenne had been installed behind its thick, high walls, few people saw her for several months. She was reported to be "totally amorphous," her eyes *"dans le vague."* Later she would describe her accommodations there as very much like jail, "a little cell four meters by three, with a bad bed, a table, and an iron chair. I could not go out even for a walk," she claimed. "I did not even have a comb to do my hair. I spent my days sleeping, because of the medications that I was taking, or reading or listening to cassettes. Time went very slowly."

In early January, six weeks before Christian's sentence, Brando sent Tarita and Tuki to the French town of Le Vésinet, renting them an expensive apartment at the Hôtel Ibis. Here they would be close to Cheyenne.

The "cure" Cheyenne was reportedly taking seemed to be a throwback to the nineteenth century: "sleep therapy" and "forced rest." She made pottery, read, and played with Tuki when Tarita brought him to the clinic. She had requested a television in her $20,000-a-month room so that she could follow the trial, but her doctors refused, afraid that the sight of Christian in the dock would provoke a crisis. Nevertheless, a friend was able to reach Cheyenne after the verdict and told her of the ten-year sentence; the result was another suicide attempt, this time with an overdose of tranquilizers. "They had believed she was on the road to recovery," friends told the *Daily Express,* "but she became increasingly upset as the court case loomed." Medical sources said Cheyenne had managed to horde a large quantity of pills, probably from the clinic's pharmacy.

With Christian's sentencing, Brando was free to turn his attention to

Cheyenne. Her indictment in Tahiti had been useful in keeping her beyond Barshop's grasp, but she was still under the control of Judge Gatti. Her lawyers in Tahiti had appealed the magistrate's charge of complicity to murder. However, on April 9, 1991, the territorial court in Papeete upheld Gatti's ruling to keep Cheyenne under judicial control, arguing that there were still enough unanswered questions in the murder of Dag Drollet to warrant the charge of complicity.

Cheyenne's lawyers attempted to have Judge Max Gatti removed from the case; the request was rejected. Brando's response was to hire Cheyenne yet another lawyer, Jacques Vergès. Vergès had been an adviser to Pol Pot in Cambodia, but he later became internationally known as the spokesman and defender of Nazi war criminal Klaus Barbie, again conducting much of the case in the media.

For Jacques Drollet, watching Brando's machinations and learning about the notorious Vergès—a particularly vile choice to a Jew who had been a French freedom fighter—only strengthened his resolve. The fight now included three lawsuits—two civil and one criminal—and hearing Drollet's intention, Pat Quinn, like so many of Marlon's old friends, considered the irony of the situation. "Drollet's doing to Marlon what Marlon did to Clavell," she said. "I'm just sad that Christian has to be the sacrifice. I love Marlon, but he set this in motion a long time ago. The wheel has come full circle."

Brando himself continued to maneuver even before the sentencing hearing by resurrecting his idea of selling his autobiography. He started the ball rolling again with another phone call to columnist Army Archerd. He told Archerd that he had changed his mind about one thing; instead of handling the sale of the book himself, he had chosen his good friend George Englund to negotiate the deal. Englund, he said, was already in New York meeting with six publishers. Unmentioned was the fact that Englund was also agenting media rights to the story of Panamanian strongman and dope dealer Manuel Noriega.

During January 1991 Englund contacted major New York publishing houses, setting an asking price of $5 million. Discussions then ensued with six publishers, all of whom tendered offers. Random House's Harold Evans was summoned to Los Angeles for dinner on Valentine's Day. Evans spent a few days with Brando, and three weeks later, on March 11, 1991, the deal was closed for the officially reported purchase price of $3.5

million. But others said that the total price tag in fact exceeded $5 million, one of the most expensive single book deals in publishing history. Whatever Brando's contract stated in terms of hard, cold cash, the talk along Publishers Row was of the "signing on" price. Gossip had it that the actor had demanded, and Evans had agreed, that Brando receive a nonrefundable $750,000 bonus just for consenting to the contract.

Evans justified the extraordinary advance by reassuring everyone that Brando had promised to tell all. "Everything will be in the book," he announced cheerfully. "His career, his political involvement, his marriages, his children." "Recent events . . . have convinced me of the usefulness of retracing my steps," Brando himself declared in a press release, "if only to serve as a guide to my children to steer a course by, or more importantly to avoid one." Referring to the Brando family maid who had lived with them in Evanston, Marlon added, "I intend to disclose all of my life and the people in it, from my earliest memory of playing in my moonlit bed with the naked body of my sleeping, beloved Ermi to this present scribbling in my bed of another day." As anxious as Brando was said to be to get his version of the story before the public, he would continue to have problems writing. Some of his difficulties were due to an inability to curtail his ramblings as he lay in bed—not scribbling as he claimed in the press release, but taping. While Alice Marchak and other assistants might work from clips, doing what several people described as a "cut-and-paste job," Brando himself was suffering from his usual patchy memory. One time he allegedly tracked down Ursula Andress in Rome, his call rousing her in the middle of the night. Andress did not believe it was actually Brando, and she asked for a phone number so that she could call him back, which she did.

Almost immediately he explained the reason for his call: Had they ever gone to bed together?

In fact, they had, in the 1950s, and they supposedly spent the next two transatlantic hours reminiscing, with Marlon promising to pay for the expensive phone call. If Andress was miffed that Brando did not remember his fling with her, she didn't let on. But what was even more perturbing— and indicative—was how much about his life he had forgotten. It confirmed what friends had been thinking all along: How could he possibly write the book sitting alone up at Mulholland, making surprise long-distance calls, trying to wrestle with a past that had been so chaotic that he couldn't remember fucking Ursula Andress?

• • •

On September 25, 1991, *Variety*'s Army Archerd reported that Brando had finally flown to Paris to visit his daughter. Intending to mislead, Brando had actually planted the item and had arrived in Paris the week before. Cheyenne, known in the clinic as "Christine" and described as "psychotic, irascible, megalomaniac, and mythomaniac," had already been checked out of the facility on September 18. Presumably her release had been arranged by her father—unbeknownst to the media but, even more, behind the back of the authorities.

Part and parcel of the drama, Judge Max Gatti had flown from Tahiti, having scheduled another deposition with Cheyenne and her lawyer Jacques Vergès on October 23. But they awaited her arrival in vain. Gatti then checked with the clinic and was shocked to learn that Cheyenne had left more than a month before. Clinic officials explained that she had completed her "cure," and that they were not prison guards, nor were they compelled to implement the judge's judiciary orders. Gatti reported the disappearance to the French police, who immediately launched a nationwide search for Cheyenne and also for Brando, who was now suspected of having helped his daughter evade justice.

On October 22, Lisette LeCaill in Papeete received a phone call from Cheyenne. "I'm thinking about Dag," she said. "I need to talk to you. Tuki is doing very well—he looks like Dag. If I go back to Tahiti, I will give him to you, not to my mother."

When Lisette asked where she was calling from, Cheyenne lied and said she was at the Clinique des Pages.

On October 27 the police issued a warrant for Cheyenne's arrest. Gatti, meanwhile, was furious at the blatant violation of his court order. He had accepted the promises of Cheyenne's lawyers that once she had shown improvement at the French clinic, he could resume his questioning. Now Brando had succeeded in putting her beyond his reach.

Meanwhile attorney Vergès was playing games of his own with the press and had even granted an interview to "Current Affair." He confirmed that Cheyenne was in France with her father but refused to say exactly where. Asked about Brando's hiring him "to save his troubled daughter from a stalemate with the law," he spoke solemnly into the camera. "If she is sent back [to Tahiti], I think she may [try to] commit suicide again. Or her illness may become worse." When the "Current Affair" announcer referred to her and her father eluding the police, Vergès insisted, "She's not escaping justice. She is with her father and her father is not wanted. He is incognito. That's a difference." Vergès, however, may only have known the half of it.

Unaware that she was facing extradition or even that there was a warrant out for her, Cheyenne had obligingly set out with her father, who had arrived driving a new Volkswagen Golf, which he had presented to her as a gift. After leaving the clinic, they had made their way to Orléans, about two hours southwest of Paris, with Brando doing the driving, stony-faced, not saying a word. While he seemed angry and depressed, Cheyenne was happy not to have to talk. When they reached Orléans—installing themselves at the private estate of Brando's old friend Maria St. Just, the socialite, actress, and confidante of Tennessee Williams—he seemed more cheerful. Teihotu joined them there. What the next move was, though, was unclear. If there was a plan, Marlon didn't explain it, although he had been talking to his English lawyer, Belinda Frixou, and made a few references to taking a boat across the Channel and—as Clark and Barshop speculated—possibly returning from London to Los Angeles.

Kept in the dark about what was going to happen, and feeling isolated, Cheyenne became angry and accused her father of aloofness. Brando's response, as his daughter later recalled it, was to blurt out, "I am not God." She objected, accusing him of acting precisely "like God," not just with her but with all of his family, and she went on to call him "Svengali." Flailing but still receiving no response, Cheyenne flew into a rage and fled the villa, much as she had run out of the house in Tahiti when Brando refused to let her come see him on the set of *The Freshman* in 1989. The result was another auto accident. The VW rolled several times into a ditch and landed upside down. Fortunately, Cheyenne was not injured, and she walked back to the villa.

On the morning of November 15, the flight of Brando *père et fille* finally came to a halt in a small village outside Orléans where they had moved into a chateau owned by a friend of Maître Vergès. Cheyenne was having breakfast in the kitchen with her father when police officers knocked on the door. Brando admitted them and the police commanded Cheyenne to accompany them without resisting.

At 11:30 A.M. she was delivered to the Palais de Justice in Orléans, where she was served "face to face" with the arrest warrant ordering her return to Tahiti. Cheyenne remained patient, her face expressionless and impenetrable as she sat in the hallway. Arriving at one P.M. wearing his advocate's robes, Vergès assisted the police in completing the necessary paperwork while Cheyenne was put in a separate room, where she was carefully watched for any signs of instability.

Two days later two gendarmes accompanied her onto a French military jet that transported her back to Tahiti, and the following morning, November 18, 1991, she stepped off the plane into the bright Tahiti sunlight, with police officers at her side. She wore a bright red sweater, with thick red lipstick and dark glasses, and she looked brittle and hard. Thirty policemen were on the Tarmac to hold back the journalists who had awaited her arrival after a ten-month absence. But they had only a brief glimpse of her as she was immediately taken to Lutania prison for arrest formalities and then to a secured room at the nearby hospital.

For the next nine days Cheyenne was kept under guard, but on November 24 Jacques Vergès arrived, creating a flood of publicity for his client. In an airport interview, the attorney claimed that Judge Gatti's dossier against Cheyenne was "empty," and during the next several days he organized a media blitz designed simultaneously to disarm the judge, divide the civil from the criminal charges against Cheyenne, and most visibly, to put public opinion on her side.

On the third day after his arrival, Vergès convinced Judge Gatti to release his client on $1 million bail, or 100 million French Pacific francs, a historic amount in French Polynesia. "The million dollars will be paid in three weeks," the attorney assured the public. But the next day he announced that the bond would in fact never be paid. Cheyenne, he insisted, wasn't solvent. It seemed a lame argument, given the shares held by Cheyenne Brando in the capital and assets of Société Anonyme Tetiaroa, not to mention the financial worth of her father. Nevertheless, even without the required bail posted, Cheyenne was allowed to return to her mother and brother in their Punaauia compound not far from the LeCaills.

On November 30 Cheyenne stood on the Tarmac at Faaa Airport, wearing floppy coveralls and a white T-shirt. A UTA flight had just landed, and she waited as the two portable stairways were wheeled up to the first-class and coach doors, and the weary passengers stepped off. Beside her stood Vergès in a black silk suit, sporting Doctor No glasses and smoking a cigar, looking like an undertaker. He routinely patted Cheyenne on the back, as if to reassure her during the delay when more and more passengers came off the plane; there was still no sign of Tarita and Tuki, but after more luggage was off-loaded they finally appeared. Cheyenne's face broke into a wide smile as she saw her mother, carrying the baby in her arms, descend the stairs. Tuki was wide-eyed, an innocent-looking child who smiled as Cheyenne hugged him inside the terminal. Looking at him now, it was hard to imagine that the Drollets would have any doubts about his being Dag's child, the resemblance was so striking.

Meanwhile, as "the Tahitian Brandos" embraced at the airport, several miles away Jacques Drollet sat in the cemetery where he went every morning to "talk to Dag." For this sixty-eight-year-old man the battle of the last eighteen months was beyond any struggle he had ever fought before. And it was still far from over. The previous day Brando had appeared on American television accusing French justice, Judge Gatti, and the Drollets of "destroying my family." Vergès, too, was quoted in the morning's paper under a front-page headline, MISSION ACCOMPLISHED.

For two weeks prior to Cheyenne's return, island gossip had it that Drollet and Brando were about to meet to effect a reconciliation. It was said that Judge Gatti would arrange an official "confrontation" and the two men would explain themselves through their interposed attorneys. Vergès, however, had then entered the scene and Brando's strategy—if the report had any validity to begin with—seemed to have changed radically. "No chance that Marlon Brando comes to Tahiti," Vergès declared. "As usual," Drollet responded, "Marlon Brando would rather manipulate people from the shadows than come out to the sunlight and tell the truth."

Engaged in his own personal crusade for the past year and a half, Brando was apparently steadfast in his refusal to present himself for questioning. This represented perhaps the ultimate stalemate, which only exacerbated Drollet's fury in the face of what would happen next. Several days earlier, Vergès had proposed another meeting, what he called a *"réconciliation à la tahitienne"* between the two families. The months of grief and discouragement seemed to have broken the determination of Lisette, and it took no genius to see that the attorney was trying to use her to drive a wedge between Drollet and her husband, Albert LeCaill.

Earlier that morning, Cynthia Garbutt had telephoned Jacques Drollet's sister, Iris, to ask Albert and Lisette to come to the "prayer meeting" arranged for 9:30. "We want a gathering of the two families . . . to make peace for the sake of Tuki." Cynthia talked of "good prayers" and "sharing the pain, then both families will care for Tuki."

Iris instructed her to call the LeCaills herself, then she informed her brother. Drollet, naturally, refused to attend. But after leaving the airport, the Brando contingent had driven to the nearby home of Tarita's sister, Anna, where Albert and Lisette were waiting to meet them.

Cynthia had also asked a Protestant minister to be present. He opened with a prayer and then invited everyone to stand and express his or her feelings. The only one to do so was Albert. He thanked the minister for his choice of verses read from the Bible, verses dealing with a child's good life. Then addressing the group, Albert said, "God will judge even if you hide. At the moment, I tell you this [entire situation] will be judged by man, too, with regard to the good and the bad. The law of man and the law of God are the same. . . . I cannot hide this side of ourselves. I cannot talk only about the baby."

The ceremony was held entirely in Tahitian, and the gathering was "very cold," LeCaill later said. Neither Tarita nor Cheyenne showed any reaction to his statement, and nothing was said about Brando or the on-going investigation of Cheyenne.

The meeting had disbanded after twenty minutes, and alone, Lisette had then gone to Dag's grave. There she encountered her ex-husband, Jacques. "What will you do?" she asked him.

Drollet shook his head, still looking at his son's gravestone. "Continue my search for the truth," he replied. "I am also preparing my revenge. You remember how they have killed our son? It was horrible. I can never forgive that."

"But there is Tuki. . . . That baby is mine."

"You will have trouble with Cheyenne and Tarita," Drollet replied. "You will find out that you have been manipulated."

"I am more concerned about the living than the dead," she said. "I want to live in peace with Tarita's family. Tuki is our chance to revive Dag."

Drollet looked at her. "My God, our son is in that hole there. We cannot live in peace until we know."

In reality, Jacques-Denis Drollet was feeling a bit beaten, his health undermined by the stress and sleepless nights of the previous year, and a tooth infection and the antibiotics he was taking were making him feel even weaker. Yet he knew that the pursuit of the investigation would now most likely fall to him alone. Later that day, he wrote an open letter to the Tahitian dailies entitled "I've Had Enough." "I am fed up with people behaving like worms when my son has been killed," he said. "I'm fed up with people who pretend to be good neighbors and citizens but who make life miserable for their own children and kill other people's children." (The newspapers refused to publish his statement, citing the possibility of a lawsuit.)

Brando, meanwhile, was not sitting idle. While it appeared to legal authorities and the world at large that he was stonewalling, he was in effect manning a command post atop Mulholland Drive, planning his next moves. If he couldn't go to Cheyenne, then he would bring his daughter to Los Angeles. Like many of his previous maneuvers, this one would cost him a great deal of money.

The sums to date, in fact, were astronomical, even for a man of Brando's resources. In addition to huge legal fees (seven attorneys in Los Angeles, two in Paris, two in Tahiti, one in London, plus Harvard Law professor Alan Dershowitz, who'd been brought in to consult on Christian's appeal), there were doctor bills, countless airplane tickets (Vergès was said to travel only first-class), private detectives, expert witnesses, bodyguards, and the expenses of the jaunt in France, among other things. At one point during Christian's defense, it was rumored that Brando had even had to borrow $1 million from Michael Jackson. Now, despite his book advance, he had decided to go back to work.

Thus, when Alexander and Ilya Salkind came to him with a movie in November 1991, Brando was happy to sign on. Despite the prolonged lawsuit he had brought against them for *Superman,* they were willing to pay him $5 million for ten minutes of screen time. Never mind that the movie was *Christopher Columbus: The Discovery.* Never mind that his Indian friends were appalled that Brando would sanction the Columbus myth, the story of the "European oppressor" they found so denigrating to Native American history. Never mind, too, that Brando's costume promised to make him look like a float in the Columbus Day parade. Pure and simple, Brando needed the cash, and as old-time friends like Pat Quinn recognized, he was "putting his family first. . . . He needed the money to bring his daughter to Los Angeles and buy Cheyenne a house," Quinn said.

Once the production got under way, it was not long before the Salkinds ran into financial trouble, bouncing salary checks and not paying their bills. Reassuring creditors that the marquee value of Brando and Tom Selleck would guarantee "a sufficient flow of funds" at the box office brought cries of protest from Selleck, who objected that "they have no right to associate our names with their delinquencies." Brando, however, had made no comment before or during his twelve days in front of the cameras. Having made sure that he was paid in advance, he flew to Madrid in January 1992, did his stint, and, uneventfully, left for home.

Back in Los Angeles, however, he apparently had second thoughts about *Columbus,* much as he had had with *The Freshman.* He picked up the phone and once again called *Variety,* now airing his dissatisfactions. From the very start, he claimed, once he had been informed that the Salkinds were making a movie about Christopher Columbus, he had offered them his advice: "Having an appreciable knowledge of the historical facts that Christopher Columbus was directly responsible for the first wave of genocidal obliteration of the native peoples of North America," he said, "I wanted to make certain that the history of the interaction between Christopher Columbus and the indigenous inhabitants would be accurately portrayed." He insisted that he had persuaded Ilya Salkind to present Columbus not as the "idiotic person" featured in the original script but "as the true villain he was." Salkind had "agreed to my concept" after several hours of "taped and witnessed conversation," Brando said, adding that he had convinced the producer that if he used his ideas, the picture would make more rather than less money, "which was his primary, if not his only, consideration in making this film."

Conceding that he hadn't seen the final cut, Brando then launched another of his rectitudinous spiels. He was sure, he said, "that the Native Americans were presented with cruel inaccuracies, and as my contract specifically states that the producers are under the obligation to adhere to historical accuracy, I have no other recourse than to, at the very least, have my name removed from this picture." It sounded as if Brando was huffing and puffing his way toward another lawsuit.

Alexander Salkind seemed to be having a good laugh when asked to comment on Brando's charges. He gave an example of the kinds of changes Marlon had requested during their story conferences. "He wanted to have long fingernails and look horrible," he recalled, "and he wanted to have a Jewish girl in a cage burned in boiling oil because at that time the Spaniards were after the Jews." Letting Brando's bizarre ideas speak for themselves, Salkind added, "I didn't want to be cross with him, but . . . we didn't want to have a girl boiling in oil. We didn't want to make a horror picture. We wanted to make an adventure picture."

Despite threatening to bring his complaints to the Screen Actors Guild and also "to the courts" so that "the full light of world attention will eliminate these issues," Brando said nothing more as the movie opened to near unanimous pans—not because it was politically incorrect but because it was monumentally dull. Brando's cameo was singled out both for its lack of artistry and for what it said about his greed in taking the part in the first place. Calling his performance "little more than a series of reaction shots," *Entertainment Weekly* added that "his motivation—apart from the money, of course—seems to have been to do a movie so transparently unworthy of his gifts that it serves as further justification for his retirement."

During the early months of 1992, Cheyenne continued to live in the Punaauia compound with Tarita, Tuki, and Teihotu and his family. She was always watched, either by Tarita, by Cynthia, or by her brother, and her mother remained completely mute about what was happening. Although Cheyenne's bail had been lifted, she was still under indictment and Gatti vowed that he would not drop the case until he questioned Brando.

The case would soon change dramatically when, on April 13, Vergès announced that he would no longer be representing Cheyenne because of Brando's refusal to meet with questioners. Some sources claimed that Brando had in fact fired the attorney; Vergès insisted to the Parisian newspaper *Le Figaro* that he had resigned. Either way, Brando immediately hired yet another French lawyer, Jean-Yves Le Bourne, whom he quickly dispatched to Tahiti to be there in time to represent Cheyenne before Judge Jean-Bernard Taliercio, now replacing Gatti, on April 15, 1992.

In her fifth Tahitian statement, Cheyenne dropped a bombshell: "My father is constantly manipulating people," she said. "I am sure he asked Christian to kill Dag." What was just as headline-making was that she also reportedly alleged that her father had made sexual advances toward her. "I detest my father," Cheyenne was quoted as saying, "because he has always behaved in an unhealthy manner toward me." While she did not elaborate, she said she had turned down an invitation to live with Brando, adding "I refuse to be his maid or governess."

Meanwhile, directly and through his attorneys, Brando had renewed his campaign to bring her to Los Angeles. Still getting nowhere with the Tahitian courts, he tried to use his clout, "calling everyone he knew" of any influence. Having been in and out of France for four decades and still considered an even more important celebrity there than in America, he had many connections in Paris, among them the minister of culture, Jack Lang, who was allegedly approached to work out a deal with the U.S. State Department. In June, however, Jacques Drollet, through his own contacts, learned that Brando had been turned down.

As if that rejection had at last convinced Brando that his testimony was the key to Cheyenne's release, he finally agreed to submit to questioning by the French authorities. What Brando proposed—and what the authorities agreed to—was that he be deposed in the office of his attorney, Edward Medvene, by a U.S. attorney deputized by the Tahitians, and that Steven Barshop not be allowed to be present. The job fell to Assistant U. S. Attorney Gregory W. Jessner, and on June 19, 1992, the thirty-four-year-old government lawyer arrived at Medvene's Century City office with three pages of detailed questions submitted by the Tahitian judiciary.

For months Jacques-Denis Drollet had been hoping that Brando's testimony would at last put to rest the abiding mysteries surrounding his son's killing. Drollet had met with Gatti to formulate the interrogatory, and it was meant to probe the possible complicity of Cheyenne—and indeed Marlon himself—in the crime as well as in what Drollet suspected had been a cover-up after the shooting.

Unhappily, Drollet's hopes were dashed by the limited interrogation. Whether Jessner was intimidated or whether he simply hadn't done his homework, he failed to ask a significant number of the questions submitted by the French. More than that, he failed to follow up on many of Brando's frustratingly evasive answers. An even more major lapse was his allowing the transcript of the deposition to be sealed, as DA Bill Clark later discovered, and it took a complaint by *Paris Match* to unseal a federal court document that was supposedly open to the public.

As recorded by the court stenographer in fifty-four pages of transcript, Brando's responses took the form of fifty-six *I don't know*s, *I don't remember*s, or *I don't recall*s. When asked to describe the events of the evening of the killing, he replied, "It is all a smear now." Claiming not to remember the date of the shooting, he replied that all that remained from the incident were "little dots of recall. . . . I was stunned." After the shooting,

Christian, he said, was "withdrawn, silent, and distressed," while his daughter "had large emotional fluctuations, mood, behavior." About his own reaction to the violence, he explained, "I was very plainly deteriorating into a state of confusion."

Brando's testimony was also marked by his own mood swings. Sometimes exhibiting excessive, almost fawning politeness to the U.S. attorney, he would then inveigh against the Los Angeles police and the district attorneys as well as the press, all of whom were out to "nail somebody" and "create a big case," resulting in a "publicity trial." There had been a concerted "cover-up" for "political" reasons, he asserted—to help reelect the Los Angeles district attorney—and not satisfied with this, he drew an analogy to the lying of high U.S. public officials during Iran-contragate, including the president and the attorney general. He often fell into convoluted syntax, and while checking the later transcript for accuracy, he even changed every recorded "Yeah" to "Yes," presumably trying to strip his speech of any hint of slang or informality.

Most important, however, Brando was not just self-contradictory; at several points he was positively misleading. He was willing to explain that he had found the fatal bullet, but there was no mention of how he and Papke and one of his assistants had spent several days methodically reconstructing the shooting before turning it over to the police. He told how "the police tore the rug up" to find the "track of where the bullet was, where it had entered the rug, where it had gone underneath along the cement and stopped." This was an obfuscation, since it was he and his two assistants who had destroyed the carpeting and rearranged the furniture.

On the crucial issue of Cheyenne's abrupt departure three and a half weeks after the killing, Brando's distortions were even bolder. He insisted that he was ignorant of the date of her flight, as well as unaware at the time that she had been on the brink of receiving a subpoena. "I tried to persuade her not to. . . . I didn't want her traveling . . . [but] she wanted to go. So there wasn't much for me to do," he said. Jessner, ill-prepared, failed to stop him by pointing out that it was Brando himself who had purchased her ticket, covertly and within hours of her all-too-damning statement to detectives: "It's murder, in case you don't know it."

Although Judge Gatti had granted Cheyenne permission to leave Tahiti to go to France for treatment only on the condition that she surrender her passport and remain confined at the clinic in Le Vésinet, Brando also professed ignorance of this. Instead, he insisted that he was unaware that once Cheyenne had left the Clinique des Pages, the police would come after her with a warrant. This assertion was preposterous, since for months Brando had been in consultation with attorneys in French Polynesia, Los Angeles, London, and Paris; but again Jessner failed to confront his witness with what were obvious inconsistencies or the fact that the actor had accompanied his daughter, failed to inform authorities of her whereabouts, and moved her from one location to another several times as police closed in.

"[Cheyenne] never permanently got out of the hospital," Brando rationalized. "We had spent time at the behest and with the consent of the doctor in two locations other than the place in Vésinet . . . and one of the things that's difficult to appreciate is in the midst of all this chaos, pain, disorder, and pressure, there was the press trying to turn a dollar on this story. . . . Under normal circumstances, you become suicidal dealing with those people. But under these circumstances, it was just utterly impossible and only added to the extraordinary stress. So we found a place and always tried to keep it unknown so that we could have some semblance of order in our lives while we were waiting."

But the real question was, what were they *waiting* for? The answer to that would not become clear until steps were taken to bring Cheyenne to Los Angeles on August 1. And here again, it seemed, Brando knew no law other than his own when it came to what he called protecting his children.

On July 27, six weeks after her father's deposition, Cheyenne made an appearance at the office of Judge Jean-Bernard Taliercio to protest her continued confinement in French Polynesia. The judge began to ask his questions. With his first query, Cheyenne remained mute; with his second, she suddenly began shouting, insulting everyone—Taliercio, his secretary, her own lawyers. She began to throw things, becoming so out of control that police had to be called to escort her home. Stunned by the incident, Jacques Drollet attempted to get the transcript of the session. He was advised, however, that no report of the meeting was filed, unlike every other official session of the court.

The following day a formal appeal was filed, and two days later the Cour d'Accusation, the highest judicial body in French Polynesia, lifted Cheyenne's travel ban, citing her "nervous condition" and need for psychiatric care. Part of its decision, the court announced, was based on its sense that Brando had cooperated fully. Although the Tahitian court had awaited a transcript of Marlon's June 19 Los Angeles deposition, it had not been forthcoming. Suddenly, during the two days of the court's deliberation, a copy arrived—not through official channels, but reportedly hand-delivered by one of Brando's personal emissaries.

In Los Angeles, Assistant District Attorney Bill Clark was stunned by the Tahitian court's decision, and still frustrated that without Cheyenne's testimony, the real truth behind the murder of Dag Drollet would never be fully known. "I think she set Christian up, not knowing how far it would go," he said. "He killed the person that conceivably was the most important person in her life, even more than Marlon. And then from there she had to deal with the pregnancy and with her guilt, and she probably did get to the point where she really did not want to go on and twice tried to kill herself. And that might have been avoided by her coming forward and clearing the air, if only Marlon had let her."

If Brando failed to see the need for Cheyenne to purge herself, he still responded in the only way he knew how—with money and the help of lawyers. The key was gathering his offspring. After the death of Miko's wife on June 2, 1992, in a hit-and-run freeway accident, he brought Miko and his two-year-old son, Shane, up to Mulholland to live. But as early as mid-May he had also bought a new house in Sherman Oaks, less than fifteen minutes drive from Mulholland. With a guest villa, tennis courts, and a swimming pool, it was roomy, gated, and quiet. The former home of actress Kristy McNichol, the purchase price was close to $1 million, about $400,000 of which he put up in cash. After taking title his first step was to move in a loyal staff member and to assign Caroline Barrett to oversee the decoration and furnishing. The occupant-to-be had at first been a mystery to the press, with reporters first suspecting Cristina Ruiz and later twenty-three-year-old Avra Douglas; the latter name had begun to appear in the gossip columns as Brando's newest partner, although in reality she was a classmate and friend of his daughter Rebecca who had been hired to type the manuscript of Brando's autobiography.

Within weeks, however, it was not hard to identify the future occupant: Cheyenne. On August 1, 1992, Brando's Tahitian daughter quietly flew into LAX, accompanied by Teihotu and his wife and children.

In the days following her arrival, Cheyenne remained at her father's Mulholland aerie, lounging by the swimming pool. Soon Brando stalkers spotted her on Sunset Strip, accompanied by Teihotu, Rebecca, Avra Douglas, or Petra Barrett. Marlon had laid down the law that she was never to be given the keys to any of the family cars.

Cheyenne had still not moved into the Sherman Oaks house when one night in mid-December she knocked on her father's door and confronted him. He had been withdrawn, hanging his Do Not Disturb sign outside his bedroom, and not only did she feel isolated and alone, she missed Tahiti, her friends, and her baby.

The argument began in the usual way, with Cheyenne's halting questions, then it escalated. In no time at all she was yelling. She shouted at her father and once again accused him of having killed Dag. For the first time she was confronting him directly, and they fought physically. She punched him and, according to her account, he returned the blow, striking her in the mouth. Reeling, she went into the den where Dag was shot and sat on the floor in an almost catatonic state. A while later her father came into the room and told her, "There are some people here from CPC who are going to take you with them." His voice was gentle, and he added, "It's best for you to get some help because you need help."

When the attendants from the Community Psychiatric Center of Westwood entered, Cheyenne agreed to go with them, even though she was frightened. "I was afraid of these people," she later said, "because I knew that they had come to take me and that I could not defend myself in any way. But just before getting into the ambulance, my father did something that truly astonished me: He took one of my cigarettes and he smoked it, smoked it pretentiously."

Brando made arrangements to pay the hospital on a cash basis, and Cheyenne was registered under an assumed name.

There she fell into a routine, sitting in the same spot in the dayroom, hunched over and smoking. She neither watched television, which was on constantly, read, nor talked to anyone else seated nearby. "It was as if she was living entirely in her head," said Lorie Kligerman, one of the nurses assigned to Cheyenne. "If there was any affect at all, it was in connection with her vitamins, particularly the calcium she was taking."

How real, how rational her thinking was became open to speculation, but Cheyenne's antagonism was building. During a conversation with her father, she expressed her desire not only to be released but also to have her child with her. Again Brando told her that this was not a good idea. She exploded, erupting in another violent episode. Recalled Kligerman: "She kicked a four-foot hole in the wall and assaulted him." Later, still distraught, she told Kligerman that it had been "the biggest fight of her life," and in the course of explaining why they had the argument, the nurse said, she accused her father of telling Christian to kill Dag.

On December 20 Petra Barrett, came to see her, as she often had during the previous weeks. The two had always remained close. There was a regular routine for checking in visitors, but Cheyenne grew impatient, then angry when the nurse insisted that the usual procedure had to be followed, requiring Cheyenne to wait. Suddenly, as Kligerman was turning away, Cheyenne took a hard swing at her. Fifteen minutes later, the nurse said, she came to and found herself lying on the floor. "[Cheyenne's] fist came at me, and she knocked me out. I had a tooth broken and bruises all over my leg. I have no idea what she did to me when I was out."

Brando was in regular consultation with Dr. Robert Gerner, Cheyenne's therapist at CPC, about what kind of treatment should be pursued. Dr. Gerner seemed to realize that Brando himself was part of the problem, and he suggested moving Cheyenne to a treatment facility that would put some geographical distance between them—thus reducing the constant reminders of Dag's death.

Why the psychiatrist suggested Boyer House in Berkeley, California, Cheyenne had no idea. On February 2, 1993, she arrived at the boarding care home, a rundown, one-level unit situated behind a large ramshackle house on Woolsey Avenue, on the southern edge of the University of California campus. She knew no one in northern California, and she felt alone, afraid, and abandoned.

Cheyenne was known at Boyer House as "Susan Ferguson," the same name she had used at CPC, the clinic in Westwood. There was only one other live-in patient, and Cheyenne spent most of her time alone except for visits every two or three weeks from Rebecca, Avra Douglas, or Miko. Marlon himself stayed away, presumably at the suggestion of Dr. Gerner. Although the monthly tab was $12,750, Cheyenne cooked her own food. Her room was small, the floor covered in cheap linoleum, the furniture more like that of a Motel Six. She was again prescribed psychotropic drugs, which she sometimes refused to take, and after the first month she also failed to appear at her group therapy sessions. Since she hadn't been allowed to talk about Dag's death, she was still grieving, and her posttraumatic stress was all the greater with the feeling of being locked up and "controlled" by her father.

"He wants to control my perceptions," she said, insisting that he was having her therapist report to him after every session. "He wants to control everybody's life in a different way. He's the devil himself," she added. "We might all live in a dark zone, but his is worldwide." Marlon, who would not visit her in Berkeley for many months after her arrival, had been so dejected by her lack of improvement that when he phoned Philip Rhodes to make one of his routine overtures, he told him, "I don't know if she will get better. She'll probably be in an institution for the rest of her life."

"It had affected him so deeply," Rhodes later added, "that he said he could no longer talk about his daughter."

Day to day Cheyenne was allowed to go out during the afternoon, and often all she did was walk the streets alone, her eyes hidden behind sunglasses as she constantly smoked, listening to Depeche Mode or the soulful sounds of Chet Baker through the CD Walkman she always carried. One of her stopping-off points was the Buttercup Restaurant, a café on College Avenue, and six weeks or so after her arrival in Berkeley, she stopped in the café's entrance, lost in her own world of music and inner thoughts. A middle-aged woman came in behind her, but Cheyenne wasn't aware of her desire to pass through. The woman then spoke abruptly to her, trying to get her attention, and told her "not to block the doorway." Cheyenne wheeled around and hit her. Kathleen Grady, fifty-three, said she was shocked when "she just hauled off and slapped me across the face." The police were called, and Cheyenne was charged with battery in Berkeley Municipal Court. The result was a brief stay not in jail but at the psychiatric unit of Berkeley's Herrick Hospital. Grady would file a civil suit later the next year.

After a week in Herrick Cheyenne had calmed down sufficiently to be returned to Boyer House. Meanwhile, on May 27 in Tahiti, Judge Taliercio finally dropped all charges against her on the grounds that the case lacked merit. No one bothered to tell Cheyenne, though; it wasn't until many days later when she was talking to Cynthia Garbutt that she was given the news. Now she yearned more than ever to return to the island and her baby. But even though the Tahitian court had released her from the criminal indictment, she was still stuck in Berkeley with no idea of when, or how, she was going to get out.

During this period *Paris Match* reporters had continued to try to track her, canvassing all the major psychiatric facilities in San Francisco and its environs. Finally they got lucky when a staffer at Herrick Hospital confirmed that "Susan Ferguson" had been there for about a week in March but had since been returned to Boyer House. Staking out the residence, the reporters saw her take her daily walks, and when she seated herself on a bench near Sather Gate at the nearby University campus, they approached and asked if they could speak to her. She told them that she had been wanting to talk freely for quite a while, that she wanted the truth to come out. One of the journalists suggested that she might want to talk to her doctor before speaking to the press.

That night she phoned Dr. Gerner and told him that she felt it was time for her to speak, that she felt she had to do it. On June 8, 1993, two days later, Cheyenne met with the reporters for an interview that spread over three days. Sometimes she was moved to tears, sometimes she flared in anger, and sometimes her face lit up with a smile that was near incandescent as she described her life in Tahiti or talked about her son. She responded alternately in French and English, but no longer fearing criminal indictments or her father's presence, she could finally tell her story.

REPORTER: Five months after leaving L.A., how is your life today?

CHEYENNE: I'd say I've changed a lot. I completely stopped communicating with my father. We haven't spoken to each other for five months. February 20 was my birthday, but he didn't even send me a card. . . . He's probably fed up, so I guess I'm a lucky person. I think that here I have discovered his true nature. Sometimes it seems to me he doesn't have any conscience. He has this way of saying, "I would give my life for you," as he told me many times. But that's just not credible. He is a liar and he was lying when he said that.

REPORTER: You appeared in what is called "Brando's case," both as a capital witness—one of the keys to the inquiry—but you have also been described as an unstable witness—depressive, under sedation, with suicidal tendencies, and not very credible because you are suffering from deep psychological troubles. How did the doctors officially diagnose you?

CHEYENNE: They told me I was schizophrenic.

REPORTER: How did you react to this gloomy diagnosis?

CHEYENNE: I found it revolting that one would see me as insane.

There could not be a more absurd situation. After what I had been going through, I needed quiet and tranquility. I would have preferred to go to Tetiaroa to get some rest. Instead of that, they put me in a lunatic asylum. . . .

REPORTER: Your father has also said that you are brain-damaged because of your auto accident in Tahiti.

CHEYENNE: They have done two scans on me, and they didn't see any brain damage. As for my memory loss, it is just that I do not want to remember because of the shock and the pain.

REPORTER: If you had been allowed to testify in L.A. in June 1990, less than a month after Dag's death, what would you have told the court?

CHEYENNE: I would have said that my father was responsible for my fiancé's death.

REPORTER: And what evidence would you have given for such serious accusations?

CHEYENNE: The fact that my father asked Christian to bring his gun back home on that evening and also the fact that Christian unexpectedly got worked up against Dag during the dinner. He told me he was going to kill him, just like that, without any reason.

REPORTER: During the afternoon of May 16, your father and Christian had a long conversation that lasted maybe one hour. Did you hear about it?

CHEYENNE: I don't know what they told each other.

REPORTER: Your father explained in a very convincing way to the authorities that he had asked Christian to bring him back his gun because your brother would often drink and consequently your father wasn't comfortable knowing his son would walk around drunk with a gun in his pocket.

CHEYENNE: Why did he choose that particular evening?

REPORTER: Go back to the circumstances of your dinner with your brother the evening the murder took place. You said you didn't understand Christian's sudden anger at the table?

CHEYENNE: I was very pleased he had invited me for dinner. It was an opportunity to speak with a brother whom I had never really talked with before. He asked me how my life was. I told him: "No problem, with ups and downs, as for everybody." And suddenly he said: "I am going to kill him." I laughed. I told Christian: "You speak nonsense!"

REPORTER: Didn't you tell your brother during the meal that Dag would beat you?

CHEYENNE: No, not at all.

REPORTER: Did you have the feeling that Christian was setting you up during dinner?

CHEYENNE: No, I thought my father did that. I would think that my father probably talked about Dag and me to Christian on that day. And Christian is weak and crazy and his greatest joy in life, his nirvana, is to please Marlon Brando.

REPORTER: So Christian would have misinterpreted your father's words, and under the influence of alcohol lost control and the gun would have fired?

CHEYENNE: That's what I think about when I say that my dad is a very powerful man, much more powerful than one would believe.

REPORTER: Do you mean he did it through suggestion?

CHEYENNE: Autosuggestion.

REPORTER: It has been said that your father was angry at Dag for introducing his daughter to drugs. Was it Dag who made you a drug user?

CHEYENNE: No, not at all. I did drugs before knowing him. We used drugs with mutual consent, and we smoked marijuana a lot. We took acid just once, but it was a bad trip for both of us. But my father blamed Dag for the drugs because I used to explain everything to my father, and he never accepted the fact that I was using drugs. He was always blaming Dag for that.

REPORTER: How did your father make it clear that he didn't approve of your relationship with Dag?

CHEYENNE: One day, with very little notice, he arrived on the island and immediately called me to his hotel room in Punaauia. He said he wanted me to come back to L.A. to take care of him. He was sixty-three and I was seventeen. He was living with a woman, Yachiyo—she was still there and at his beck and call—and yet I was supposed to stay with him, cook his meals, be close to him. He actually used the phrase "take care of me." It was as if he was asking me to choose between him and my fiancé.

REPORTER: At the very beginning of the inquiry, you made this sensational revelation to the police officers. You said: "In case you didn't know, it's murder." What did you mean?

CHEYENNE: I thought about *The Godfather*. My father presented himself and his life in a different way, but *The Godfather* is one of his facets.

REPORTER: When you first saw the movie, you recognized your father under the godfather's features?

CHEYENNE: It was the image of the true Marlon Brando.

REPORTER: Watching *The Godfather,* it wasn't Don Corleone you were seeing?

CHEYENNE: No, it was my father in the flesh. Afterward, for a long time, I saw him as a myth. I saw that he had the mentality of the godfather, of the Mafia—the powerful man able to manipulate people as it pleases him. That's why I think my father has that power, and it reminded me of voodoo. That's why I said, "He is the demon." I believe that even today my father keeps a psychological influence over me, which I don't know how to get rid of.

REPORTER: You have made [the] allegation . . . that your father behaved in an unnatural way toward you. Will you now explain?

CHEYENNE: I have always been the "sacrifice" of Marlon Brando, his lamb for sacrifice, for his own personal happiness. I have said that I have been sexually abused by my father. My first memories go back to age seven.

REPORTER: Did you tell your mother about it?

CHEYENNE: No, I never told anybody about it, not even my mother.

REPORTER: How would you describe these "sexual abuses"?

CHEYENNE: My father acted in a strange way toward me, frequently touching my breast or giving me, on my bed, some massages, bouncing me on the bed as if he wanted me to mime for him the gestures of making love, like I'm having sex. He continued touching my breast even when I already was with Dag. To a certain degree, it was also a game on his part, and as a child I didn't always understand what was happening. He was also nice to me, taking walks, talking to me, but I was also very angry with him, because I remember now what he was doing to me.

REPORTER: What was it like living on Tetiaroa? Do you remember being with your father there?

CHEYENNE: I think my father was an alcoholic when he was there. I was told that he would drink whiskey and eat a mango at the same time. I lived on Tetiaroa for about two years. The longest he came was for about two or three months. . . .

REPORTER: When your father brought you to Los Angeles in August 1992, did you want to come?

CHEYENNE: Yes, but I thought it was for just a visit. . . . I didn't know I was supposed to stay a long time.

REPORTER: You didn't know he had bought a house for you?

CHEYENNE: No, he didn't talk about that. Maybe he thought he could isolate me.

REPORTER: Why did he want to do that?

CHEYENNE: I think he was worried I would say something wrong, or something I didn't mean.

REPORTER: What was it like living with him during those months?

CHEYENNE: He often went in his room and put on a Do Not Disturb sign. That was when he did his "exercise." He said he sat in the dark room and played tapes. He said they were "autosuggestion" tapes. I don't know what that is, but he was listening to voices—I think his own voice—for hours, at three in the morning. I didn't see him do this, but he always talked about it . . . his meditating.

REPORTER: Did you consider your father's hours of meditation a sign of spiritualism on his part? Did you think it was a good or bad thing?

CHEYENNE: Definitely a bad thing. From my knowledge of Buddhism, I would say that he's made a space for himself in that room so that nobody can touch him, that makes walls so he is no longer open.

REPORTER: Is he searching for his soul?

CHEYENNE: I don't think he has a soul, so he is not searching for it. He is a great *manitou*—that's Tahitian for guru. He likes to lead people . . .

REPORTER: Yes, people see him as a leader who has helped the Indians, black people, the underdog . . .

CHEYENNE: Well, they should see him walking around in his pajamas with a hole in his pants, a hole that is not supposed to be there. They would see that he just doesn't care when he comes and knocks on my door all the time. He is a hypocrite.

REPORTER: Did you ever wonder about your father's relations with women?

CHEYENNE: Yes, of course. He always broke the heart of all the women he went out with.

REPORTER: Whom are you thinking about?

CHEYENNE: About my mother first.

REPORTER: What about you. Do you think you are one of them?

CHEYENNE: No, I don't consider myself as one of his broken hearts. I realize now that I have always been his sacrifice and that Christian will always make him happy because he is his favorite child. So he has no hold over me anymore. My love for him is dead.

REPORTER: How do you think your father will react to this interview?

CHEYENNE: He will probably kill me. I'd rather not imagine it, even though I first spoke about it with my doctor.

REPORTER: Does an unforeseeable reaction coming from your father worry you?

CHEYENNE: A little bit, especially because I still live in the States. I know the risks I take by speaking because my mother will also be implicated in this. Maybe he will be so mad that he will stop supporting her in Tahiti. If I were in Tahiti, I would be less afraid. I have a house there and all my family lives nearby. So nothing bad could happen to me. He could not put me out on the street there.

When the *Paris Match* issue featuring Cheyenne's interview hit the newsstands in Paris in the early-morning hours of Thursday, June 17, 1993, it was approximately eleven P.M. California time. Brando had evidently been alerted: Cheyenne was suddenly incommunicado, and by Thursday noon the patients' phone at Boyer House was "no longer in service." Several weeks later she was moved to the psychiatric unit of Alta Bates Hospital in Berkeley, a more "structured" environment in which she was to continue her treatment. Boyer House then stood empty, the treatment group having decamped after Cheyenne's transfer, and Dr. Robert Gerner was apparently no longer involved with Cheyenne's therapy.

By the late fall of 1993, Marlon had phoned Alta Bates and scheduled a visit to see his daughter. Cheyenne herself had been trying to work out a better relationship with him, and while she still insisted that she wanted to return to Tahiti, she conceded she was willing to remain in Berkeley through the spring to "complete" her treatment. She also talked about the possibility of moving in with her new boyfriend. That prospect undoubtedly alarmed Brando and possibly moved him to make his call, since the boyfriend was by all appearances a fiftyish, bearded street person and fundamentalist Arab who sometimes criticized Cheyenne for profane and "ungodly" language. In adopting the role of Cheyenne's protector, he said that he, too, would be meeting with "Mr. Brando" to discuss her future.

What the two men thought of each other was a matter of speculation. In any case, by Christmas 1993 Cheyenne was allowed to return to Tahiti. Soon thereafter she was reported back in the hospital; by February 1994 she was released and returned to living in Punaauia with her mother and her brother. She remained stable as long as she took her medication, but when she didn't, she acted erratically. (Once she was sighted standing in the middle of Boulevard Pomare, Papeete's main thoroughfare stopping midday traffic.) Tarita still cared for her child, and Tuki reportedly found Cheyenne so difficult that he became upset when he was with her. Brando himself did not return to either Tahiti or Tetiaroa, and save for his fleeting contact with Cheyenne in Paris, still had never spent any time with his long desired grandson. His idyllic vision of Tahiti had been destroyed by the drawn-out legal proceedings, and the animosity of many Tahitians toward him for the death of one of their native sons must have been more than he could bear.

Throughout the months of Cheyenne's hospitalization, Brando remained in relative isolation, although columnist Liz Smith reported that he had resumed his dalliance with Cristina Ruiz, who was pregnant with a third child. But much as Cheyenne had described, he had indeed cut himself off from almost everyone except those who "obeyed" him, like Caroline Barrett and Alice Marchak, who both still assisted him with his book. Even he and George Englund had come to a parting of the ways, for in September 1993 the man whom Brando had always valued as a smooth operator had pulled a fast one and announced the unthinkable from a Brando loyalist: Rather than aid Brando with his writing, he would be penning his own memoirs. The past tense was probably telling, but his Warner Books publisher, Nansey Neiman, insisted that the two men had not "had a falling out" and that Englund's book would not be a "dirt-filled *Brando Dearest.*" Nevertheless, she hedged and added, "I think Mr. Brando has a very volatile personality. I know there have been periods in their lives when they haven't been talking."

If Marlon and Englund's friendship had bitten the dust by September 1993, so, too, had another old association in the actor's life: Just the month before, in August, Brando had filed suit in Los Angeles Superior Court against producer Elliott Kastner. In his court documents he claimed that a $1 million check he had received the previous April had bounced. The payment, he argued, was to ensure his appearance in Kastner's next movie, a musical version of *Treasure Island.* The prospect of Brando's taking on a singing role in this kind of nonsense no longer startled anyone, but in his filing, the actor insisted that he and Kastner had an oral agreement and that Kastner had put him under contract in order to use the Brando name to lure financing to his project. It was standard operating procedure for Kastner, and Brando had never objected before. The actor's complaint was only that the money hadn't been forthcoming. With several Hollywood plaintiffs winning substantial monetary awards plus punitive judgments for broken oral agreements, Brando was on solid legal ground, although his motivation was open to question: big bucks without having to work. But Brando's civil attorney, Edward Medvene, had no comment.

A musical *Treasure Island* wasn't ludicrous enough, it seemed, nor was the anticipated money from another court settlement. In February 1994 Brando decided to come out of retirement again, this time finding another big-money, little-work project. For a reported $3.25 million against 12¼ percent of the gross, he would appear with Johnny Depp in New Line's *Don Juan de Marco and the Center Fold.* Extraordinarily enough, Francis Ford Coppola was named as the executive producer. Had amnesia set in? Had Coppola forgotten the bitter lawsuit Brando had brought against him over *Apocalypse Now?* Or had the bearded director, now in his fifties, just decided to cash in?

If anything confirmed Marx's credo that "history repeats itself, first as tragedy, then as farce," it was the script for the movie in which Brando agreed to appear. After years in psychotherapy, after watching his daughter consigned to psychiatric clinics and mental hospitals, possibly for life, after enlisting psychiatrists to evaluate his son's 78 IQ, low self-esteem, and susceptibility to homicidal violence while drunk, he would now play the role of a psychiatrist himself. There was, unhappily, a bitter logic to it. In treating Depp's delusional, sex-addicted character, Brando, the aging psychiatrist, is supposed to learn the secrets of love.

With the project's announcement, industry pundits hailed Brando's return to the screen as a comic, while *Variety* reported that the actor had shed fifty pounds or more and soon followed up with the happy news that once in front of the camera he was cooperative, punctual, professional, *likable* in every way possible. But likable was not what Brando was about—never had been, never should be. The icon of our generation, the larger-than-life symbol of rebellion, antiestablishment values, and artistic commitment—in a sense, he owed us more. At least the question had to be asked: Isn't a genius who has pushed the boundaries and probed the depths of our psyche obligated to the culture to continue his quest? That may be both the responsibility and curse of a rare talent. In abrogating the first, it would seem that he found himself overwhelmed by the latter.

One afternoon about halfway through the production, during a freak afternoon thunderstorm, a friend of the actor was standing outside watching the lightning crack over the valley below Mulholland. He was surprised to see Brando emerge and stand barefoot, his arms across his chest, the wild wind blowing through his hair and whipping his kimono about his legs.

The actor then walked into the storm, like Lear on the heath, and shouted above the thunder, "I love the wind! When I die, I'm going to be part of it!" And as a bolt of lightning splintered the air, he turned and vanished into the house.

Sadly, Brando had already consigned himself to his supreme isolation. Over the past forty years, the theater had given way to Hollywood. Movies had been subsumed by his political and ecological activism. And now it had all been replaced by "family." But like King Lear he had discovered, too, that he was a "foolish fond old man." His dreams of a private, peaceful kingdom had been destroyed, and all that was left was a self-made prison where he could take upon himself "the mystery of things, as if we were God's spies," and ask of his own Cordelia her forgiveness.

N O T E S

Full references for all books cited in these notes can be found in the bibliography.

In the course of researching this book, more than 750 people were interviewed, many of whom I met or spoke with on multiple occasions. When the text clearly identifies the speaker—or when it is clear who provided information in the narrative—no citation is provided in this section.

INTERVIEWS

Ellen Adler [by Ati Citron]
Robert Aiken
Jay Presson Allen
William Allyn
Luana Anders
Edward Anhalt
Hy Anzell
Dr. Jacob Arlow
Sid Armus
Eliot Asinof
Alec Ata
Henrietta Aurell
Jim and Henny Backus
Dr. Seldon Bacon
Esther M. Johnson Baer
Parley Baer
George Baird
Peter Baird
Albee Baker
Dorothy Baldwin
Jay Baldwin
Vincent Baldwin
Marion Rouse Bales
Catherine Balfour

Lucinda Ballard
Martin Balsam
Robert Balzer
Temanava Bambridge-Babin
Dennis Banks
Bee Bee Barron
Steven Barshop
Sue Barton
Bobby Bass
Phil Batista
Barbara Baxley
Stephanie Beacham
Elizabeth Miller Beale
Bob Becker
Dorothy Behm de Rivera
Norton Bell
Dr. Leo Bellak
Vernon Bellecourt
Romona Bennet
Kay Phillips Bennett
Nancy Benolken
Eddie Benton-Banai
M. J. Bergfald
Andrew Bergman

Arthur Bergstrom
Bill Bernstein
Walter Bernstein
Bernardo Bertolucci
Charles A. Betcher
Roy Bishop
Jack Bittner
Mae Cooper Bittner
Roe Black
W. S. (Bill) Black
Julian Blaustein
Ben Blee
Debbie Bock
George Boosalis
Patricia Bosworth
Audrey Rouse Bower
Dorothy Bradford
Stewart Brand
Cheyenne Brando
Jocelyn Brando
Mary McKenna Brando
Johnny Brascia
Judith Braun
Margaret Brenman-Gibson
Roy M. Brewer
James Bridges
Richard P. Buehrer
Ruth Perejda Buehrer
Jean Bultman
Robert Burandt
William Burford
Niven Busch
Bill Cable
Reggie Cabral
Alice Calanca
Oscar Calanca
Frank Camellino
John Cameron
Donald Cammell
Murray Campbell
John Carbone
Gary Carey
James Carney
Morris Carnovsky
Mike Carroll
Michael J. Casey

Dave Cave
David Chasman
Janette Chevalier
Melvin ("Buddy") Chevalier
Robert ("Quill") Chevalier
Rosemarie Christensen
John Christiansen
Sharon Churcher
William Clark
Gerald Clarke
Elna Claussen
David W. Claypool
Chuck Clayton
Kathleen Cleaver
James Coburn
Cyrus ("Cy") Cochrane
Kay Cole
Peter Collier
Juleen ("J. C.") Compton
Norma Connolly
Margarite ("Betta") Cook
Phillip Cook
Wilber Cook
Tamar Cooper
Joan Copeland
Hubert Cornfield
Jack Costanzo
Rose Enevold Coy
Alice Cromie
Shirley Cumpanas
Irene Dailey
Stewart C. Dalrymple
Mallory Jones Danaher
Faith Dane
Bengt Danielsson
Charles Davis
Frances Taylor Davis
Dr. John Davis
Olga Davis
Dan Dayton
Samson DeBrier
Larry "D." DeCosta
Ada Deer
Richard Denman
Jean-Léon Destiné
David Diamond

Irene Diamond
Gordon Dickie
Edward Dmytryk
Shamus Donnell
Roger Donoghue
David Doyle
Ida Drecoll
Ruth Dresser
Jacques-Denis Drollet
Darren Dublin
Katherine Dunham
Robert Dunn
Dominick Dunne
Alex DuPrel
Chouteau Dyer-Chapin
Gary Ehman
Echo Ellick
Lucille Ellis
Bruce Ellison
Donald Ellsworth
Philip Ellwein
Ruth Emerson
Norman Enevold
Jack English
Richard Erdman
Richard Erdoes
Lee Falk
Stephen Farber
Sara Farwell
Ruth Small Felgar
Don Fera
Jesse Ferguson
Giselle Fermine
Robert G. Ferrero
Josephine H. Fescella
John Fesler
Jean Firman
Ken ("Bum Bum") Fish
James Mitchell Fite
Bob Flood
Sunshine Monroe Flood
Jack Forbes
"Wino Willie" Forkner
Robert Free
Judy Freed
Russell Friedman

Virgil Frye
Sidney J. Furie
Barbara Gale
Cynthia Garbutt
Robbie Garfield
Charles Garry
Sylvia Gasselle [by Ati Citron]
Daniel Gélin
William Gibson
Sir John Gielgud
Hal and Emmy Gifford
Dr. Sanford Gifford
Mary Elizabeth Gleason (Suydan)
Tommy Gomez
Gerald Goodrich
Mel Gordon
Morton Gottlieb
Dorothea Salinger Gould
Mab Gray
Everett Greenbaum
Dick Gregory
Alberto Grimaldi
Pat Grissom
Lawrence Grobel
Chaim Gross
Eddie Grove
Dan Gurler
Anna Marie Gustafson (Heini)
Dr. Frederick Hacker
David Hadley
Preston Haglon
William Haines
David Hajdu
Conrad Hall
Earl Hammond
Don Hanmer
Anna Kashfi Brando Hannaford
Don Hannula
Curtis Harrington
Eoghan Harris
Julie Harris
Neil Hawpetoss
Pierce Hayford
Roberta Haynes
Thomas Healy
Barbara Wright Heck

Frances Heflin
Jim Henderson
Standish Henning
Mike "Moon" Henrique
Bernard Herold
Denis Herrmann
Dolly Higgins
Heimata "Charlie" Hirshon
Jane Hoffman
Barbara Grimm Holland
George "Geordie" Hormel
John Hormel
Thomas Hormel
Geoffrey Horne
Ed Horst
Robert Hoskins
Ed Howard
Judy Howard
Robin Howard
Mrs. Billy Howell
John T. Hughes
Steve Hunio
Kim Hunter
Bella Itkin
Diana Ivarson
Anne Jackson
Eddie Jaffe
Dennis Jakob
Reverend Robert Jeambey
George Jenkins
Gregory Jessner
Marian Johnsen
Ben Johnson
Clarence Jones
Gloria Jones
Valerie Judd
Bernard Judge
George Justin
John Scott Kadderly
Jay Kanter
Elia Kazan
Janet Tiffany Keep
Gail Keith-Jones
Hugh Kelley
Kenneth Kendall
Herbert Kenwith

Frances Key
Michael Kidd
Detective Lee Kingsford
Don Kirby
Lorie Kligerman
Leo Knapp
Herman Knolte
Howard W. Koch
Reginald Kramer
Stanley Kramer
Isabel Kratville
Lillian Jankowski Kristan
William Kunstler
Dan Ladely
Chris Laffaille
Pat Lamberty
Laurene Landon
Mark Lane
Andrée Langomazino
Robert Lantz
Robert Lanum
Jack Larson
Sondra Lee
Jean-David Lefebvre
Jim Leigh
Leo Lerman
Jocelyne Lew
Eddie Lewis
Ira Lewis
Robert "Bobby" Lewis
Wilma Linneman
Sacheen Littlefeather
Marjorie Loggia
Cary Loftin
Joshua Logan
Richard Loving
Skip E. Lowe
Vermelle "Maggie" McCarter
Kevin McCarthy
Nan Prendergast McChesney
Joe Machlis
Janet McCloud
Luke McKissick
Larry McNichols
Richard McNutt
Mary Doyle McQuiggan

Charles H. Maguire
Karl Malden
Judith Malina [by Ati Citron]
Joseph L. Mankiewicz
Abby Mann
Daniel Mann
Janet Margolin
Stan Margulies
Henry Marasse
Ellen Marsden
Jack Martin
Henry Marx
Peter Matthiessen
Russell Means
Burgess Meredith
Daphne Merkin
Mike Metzger
Peter Metzger
Mary Ann and Jack Meyers
Ray and Lucille Meyers
Mildred Milar
Hervé Mille
Betty Wallace Miller
Doug Miller
Joan Claussen Molidor
Otto Molidor, Jr.
Louise Monaco
William Moneysmith
Detective Andrew R. Monsue
Lilliane Montevecchi
Robert "Sandy" Montour
William Marshall Morgan
Fernand Moskowitz
Roy Moseley
Thelma Schnee Moss
Robin Mundel
Mary Murphy
Natalia Danesi Murray
Vivian Nathan
Mildred Natwick
Dr. James T. Neal
Louise Neal
Dorothy Nebenzal
Harold Nebenzal
Dr. Peter Neubauer
Reverend Bob New

Harold Norse
Elliott Norton
Rudyard Norton
Michelle Noval
Maila Nurmi
Harvey Obenauf
Jim O'Brien
Kevin O'Brien
Dan O'Herlihy
Ann Lombard Osborne
Willis Overholser
Victor Pacellini
Tom Papke
Daniel Pardon
Elena Patera
Jack Peaco
Leonard Peltier
Arthur Penn
Leland Perry
Jurgen and Lynn Petersen
Carl H. Peterson
Lenka Peterson
Sheila Petry
André Philippe
Elsie Pickering
Maria Ley Piscator
David Pressman
Al Prince
Annie Prince
Augusta Prince
Taylor "Tap" Pryor
Doris Puffer
Gérard Pugin
Eleanor Purdy
Don Purrington
Moira Putnam
Mario Puzo
Anthony Quinn
Pat Quinn
François Quinquis
Henry Rakin
Phil Ramey
Robert Ramsey
Steve Randall
Paul J. Randolf
Toby Raphelson

Betsy Redfield
Joe Reed
Kenneth Relyea
Philip Rhodes
Don Richardson
Jan Lettieri Rinaldo
Henry Rittmeister
Margaret Roberts
Meade Roberts
Ralph Roberts
Bob Robideau
Nancy Robinson (Henderson)
Nan Morris Robinson
Yves Roche
Cleo Cooper Romaguerra
Norman Rose
Frank P. Rosenberg
Marion Rosenberg
John Rosenthal
William Roser
Alfred Roulet
Olivier Royant
Paul Rowsey
Paulette Rubinstein [by Ati Citron]
Al Ruddy
Mrs. William Russell
Nick and Nancy Rutgers
Raymond and Cécile Ruysseveldt
Marie Cui Ryan
Fred Sadoff
Terry Saeving
Eva Marie Saint
Dean St. Dennis
Sylvia Salinger
Maxine Sampson
Anita Sands
Edward W. Sawusch
Kenneth Sawusch
Kenneth Schar
Joyce Scheffey (Crosbie)
Bert Schneider
Irving Schneider
Ann and Clarence Scholl
Budd Schulberg
Larry Schulz
Vernon Scott

Bobby Seale
Charlotte Seiler
Walter Seltzer
Ralph T. Server
Robert Shapiro
Sam Shaw
Richard Shepherd
Bobby Sherman
Patricia Sherman
David Shumacher
Mary Lightbody Sides
Johnny Silver
Esther Steinberg Smith
Clayton Snow
Joan Snow
Anna Sokolow
Marilyn Sorel
John Souza
Joseph Spery
Bob Spitz
Betty Squier [by Jessica Portner]
Jacqueline Stallone
Maureen Stapleton
John Staver
David Stenn
Jack Sterley
Phil Stern
Stewart Stern
Helene Franklin Stewart
Phyllis Stewart
Sherry Stewart
Jeanelle Stovall
Ray Strand
Gil Stratton
Elaine Stritch
Dorothy Studer
Lester Stuft
James Sunderland
Charles and Esther Kimble Swan
Jack Swan
Charles B. Sweatt Jr.
Edwin "Bud" Sweeney
Billy Swift Hawk
Igor Tamarin
Jessica Tandy
Judge Jack Tanner

Daniel Taradash
Jimmy Taylor
Standish Thayer
Henrietta Duell Thibadeau
Joy Thomson
Isabel B. Threlkeld
Kenneth Tilsen
Kenneth Tobey
John and Nancy Todd
Unity Tomlinson
Peter Turgeon
Frank Underbrink
Judge Warren Urbom [by Bob Flood]
Frances Swift (Tiddy) Valade
William Valos
Napi Van Derek
Don Vanderspool
John Vari
Jacques Vergès
Byron Veris
Robert Vermuyten
Michelle Vignes
Michael "Mindy" Wager
Mike Walker
Eli Wallach
Frank Ward
Janet Ward

Dr. John Ward
Richard Waring
Frank Warner
Henry T. Warner
Oliver Washburn
Donny Waukechon
W. J. Weatherby
Turere Weaver
Dr. Arthur Weider
William Webster
Ray Martin Wells
Belle West
Bob White
Robert Whitehead
Jill Johnsen Will
Calder Willingham
Gordon Willis
Donald Windham
Shelley Winters
Bente Claussen Wolf
Carmelita Pope Wood
Yvonne Wood [by Eric Lindbom]
Bill Woodfield
Teresa Wright
Clarence Zermer
Mary Zion

1. *OMAHA:* **1893-1930**

PAGE

4   *"a man with a hole in the middle . . .":* Jocelyn Brando to PM.

8   *"find their voice":* Ann Braude, *Radical Spirits,* p. 201.

11   *"all my little friends went . . .":* Frances Brando Loving, interview for "Nebraskans in Film," Nebraska State Historical Society, 1981, p. 5.

12   *"The stage seldom sees a prettier . . .":* Omaha World-Herald, 4/14/25.

12   *"Julie, the young wife of Liliom . . .":* Omaha World-Herald, 1/13/26.

13   *"Mrs. Marlon Brando's acting . . .":* Omaha World-Herald, 10/26/26.

13   *"growing love of music . . .":* Omaha Bee-News, 10/21/26.

13   *"Amazingly true to life":* Omaha World-Herald, 5/11/27.

13   *"The stage set was very shadowy . . .":* Nancy Benolken to PM.

14   *". . . Just listen to her"*: Henry Fonda and Howard Teichmann, *Fonda: My Life*, pp. 29–31.

14   *"If it will make anybody . . ."*: *Omaha World-Herald* 1/27/34.

16   *"it smelled wonderful"*: Frances Brando Loving, interview for "Nebraskans in Film," Nebraska State Historical Society, 1981, p. 6.

18   *"You women stink!"*: Remark recalled by Geoffrey Horne to PM.

2. EVANSTON: 1930-38

PAGE

20   *"Dodie felt she got a little shortchanged . . ."*: Ann Lombard Osborne to PM.

21   *"It was like explosions . . ."*: Maxine Sampson to PM.

23   *"He was kicked out of class . . ."*: Jurgen Petersen to PM.

27   *"It was startling . . ."*: Nancy Benolken to PM.

27–28   *". . . a prominent brain surgeon . . ."*: Kay Phillips Bennett to PM.

28   *"I was struck drunk . . ."*: Letter from Dorothy Brando to David Salinger, 4/29/35; correspondence made available by Mrs. Sylvia Salinger.

29   *"were living beyond . . ."*: William Valos to PM.

29   *"It used to bother me . . ."*: MB quoted in *Silver Screen*, July 1950.

30–31   *"Bud has grown enormously . . ."*: Letter from Dorothy Brando to David Salinger, 2/12/37.

3. LIBERTYVILLE: 1938-41

PAGE

34   *"Dodie never complained . . ."*: Kay Phillips Bennett to PM.

35   *"something screwed up with the family"*: Marian Johnsen to PM.

36   *". . . a name for himself very quickly"*: Ray Meyers to PM.

39   *"Bud, you're a bum . . ."*: Remark recalled by Sherry Stewart to PM.

39   *"Bud, you're going to have to work . . ."*: Remark recalled by Jack Sterley to PM.

40   *". . . running away one day . . ."*: Sherry Stewart to PM.

40   *"There was one room that their mother . . ."*: Dorothy Behm de Rivera to PM.

43   *". . . I remember his antics . . ."*: Janet Tiffany Keep to PM.

44   *". . . beat out little tattoos . . ."*: Sunshine Monroe Flood to PM.

49   *"the peanut butter and jelly . . .":* Phyllis Stewart to PM.
52   *"Mama, Jamie's up on the hill . . .":* Jocelyn Brando to PM.

4. SHATTUCK: 1941-43

PAGE

63   *"How can you argue . . .":* Incident recounted by John Fesler to PM.

65–66 *"we were neither surprised . . .":* Letter from Marlon Brando Sr. to H. R. Drummond, 10/8/41; this and later correspondence of MB Sr. in this chapter provided by Shattuck–St. Mary's School, Faribault, Minnesota, which has copies on file.

68   *"You lay a finger on me . . .":* Incident recounted by Richard Denman to PM.

69   *"I didn't expect you to fail":* Letter from MB Sr. to MB Jr., 10/29/41; copy on file at Shattuck.

71   *"I have Marlon placed . . .":* Letter from Earle M. Wagner to MB Sr., 10/23/41; copy on file at Shattuck.

71   *"a new boy who shows great talent":* The Spectator, 10/29/41 (qtd. in Fred Leighton, "The Story of Brando's Shenanigans at Shattuck," *St. Paul Sunday Pioneer Press,* 2/5/56).

73   *"able to put that one-fourth . . .":* MB Jr.'s letter qtd. in letter from MB Sr. to Dr. Donald Henning, 11/27/41; copy of latter on file at Shattuck.

73   *"I feel that he must be . . .":* Letter from MB Sr. to H. R. Drummond, 11/29/41; copy on file at Shattuck.

76   *"Why don't we have a little . . .":* Incident recounted by Stewart Dalrymple to PM.

76   *"Don't ever put your hands . . .":* Incident recounted by Paul Rowsey to PM.

78   *"You son-of-a-bitch!":* Incident recounted by William Burford and others to PM.

79   *"Hey, Charlie . . .":* Incident recounted by Thomas Hormel to PM.

80   *"I wish I could be more optimistic . . .":* Letter from H. R. Drummond to MB Sr., 5/30/42; copy on file at Shattuck.

82   *"Why do you want . . .":* Remark recalled by Carmelita Pope to PM.

83   *"full-fledged member of our junior class":* Letter from H. R. Drummond to MB Sr., 8/13/42; copy on file at Shattuck.

84   *"I have just had a very interesting . . .":* Letter from H. R. Drummond to MB Sr., 10/28/42; copy on file at Shattuck.

85–87 The weekend in Mitchell, South Dakota, was recalled by Philip Ellwein to PM.

87   *"I thought I'd broken . . .":* Remark recalled by Joe Spery to PM.

94   *"The last eight guys up . . .":* Incident recounted by Stewart C. Dalrymple to PM.

95   *the drama teacher would himself be unceremoniously bounced:* Don Purrington, associated with Shattuck for close to fifty years and still active in alumni affairs, described Wagner's 1947 dismissal to PM: "He was put on the carpet one day. It had to do with his association with Mrs. Henning, and it was taken care of before her husband, the headmaster, returned from overseas. Wagner was put on the pan, and was sent out of there, just *bingo.*"

5. NEW YORK—SAYVILLE: 1943-44

PAGE

100   *"town idiot":* The experience was so unforgettably bad that Marlon would draw upon it almost thirty years later in his anguished monologue in *Last Tango in Paris.* Whether his coworker ever saw the film is unclear, but the man was still living in Libertyville in the mid-1980s.

101   *"A lot of sexual research . . .":* Qtd. in Tony Curtis and Barry Paris, *Tony Curtis,* p. 69.

101   *One of Germany's leading theater directors:* Background of Piscator and history of his Dramatic Workshop at the New School drawn from John Willett, *The Theatre of Erwin Piscator,* pp. 152–67, and C. D. Innes, *Erwin Piscator's Political Theatre,* pp. 97–130.

104   *"Easily the best acting . . .":* George Freedley, *New York Telegraph,* 5/24/44.

104   *"Piscator said, 'No, no, Marlon . . .":* Mae Cooper Bittner to PM.

105   *"No, I went to school with Stella":* Remark recalled by Elia Kazan to PM.

106   *"If it hadn't been for her . . .":* Remark recalled by Karl Malden to PM.

106   *she breathed theater from her first day:* Background of the Adler family and Stella Adler drawn from Lulla Rosenfeld, *Bright Star of Exile,* Wendy Smith, *Real Life Drama,* and Stella Adler, *The Technique of Acting.*

110   *"I taught Marlon nothing . . .":* Qtd. in Anna Kashfi Brando and E. P. Stein, *Brando for Breakfast,* p. 27.

111   *"was a very kind woman . . .":* Qtd. in Lawrence Grobel, *Conversations with Brando,* p. 149.

113   *"Very quickly you could tell . . .":* Stella Adler to Mel Gordon, April 1986.

116   *"sickly":* Remark recalled by Juleen Compton to PM.

119   *"To sum my activities up . . .":* MB to Dr. Donald Henning, 1/29/44; copy on file at Shattuck.

123   *"psychoneurotic grounds":* Darren Dublin to PM.

126   *"I gave her the mop . . .":* Remark recalled by Maureen Stapleton to PM.

131–32   Edith Van Cleve describes her lunch with Marlon's mother in Gary Carey, *Marlon Brando: The Only Contender*, p. 26.

135   *"I saw a marvelous view . . .":* Carlo Fiore, *Bud: The Brando I Knew*, p. 8.

136   *"fast-moving musical production . . .":* *Bay Shore* [N.Y.] *Sentinel*, 7/8/44.

137   *"screwing all over the place":* Fiore, *Bud*, p. 21.

137   *"was perfectly willing to share":* Ibid.

137   *"a man in a state of perpetual erection":* Ibid., p. 22.

138   *"Mr. Piscator, will you tell . . .":* Remark recalled by Elaine Stritch to PM.

139   *"There was a wonderful role . . .":* Joy Thomson to PM.

139   *" 'She* knows *I'd* never go into . . .": Fiore, *Bud*, p. 19.

139–40   *"To deny that I was sexually . . .":* Ibid., pp. 13–15.

140   *"thirteen or fourteen . . .":* Ibid., p. 15.

141   *"He's got no right . . .":* Remark recalled by Joy Thomson to PM.

142   *"screwing everything that moved":* Joy Thomson to PM.

142   *"Stella said that Piscator . . .":* David Diamond to PM.

6. *NEW YORK—PROVINCETOWN: 1944-47*

PAGE

144–45   *"I was so scared . . .":* Qtd. in Gary Carey, *Marlon Brando: The Only Contender*, p. 22.

146   *"Afterward everybody was saying . . .":* Qtd. in Richard Schickel, *Brando: A Life in Our Times*, p. 33.

153   *"a very spoiled girl . . .":* Juleen Compton to PM.

155   Background on Katherine Dunham and her dance school is from Lynne Fauley Emery, *Black Dance from 1619 to Today*, pp. 251–60.

155   Description of Papa Augustine's beliefs and background is based on interviews with Katherine Dunham and Jean-Léon Destiné.

157   *". . . Work will give you strength . . .":* Remark recalled by Lucille Ellis to PM.

163   *"I know how big . . .":* Incident recounted by Mike Henrique to PM.

164   *"Like a large number of men . . .":* Qtd. in Carey, *Marlon Brando*, p. 250.

166   *". . . Welch instructed Brando . . .":* Marguerite Cook to PM.

168–69   *"I thought Kazan would have . . .":* Qtd. in Carey, *Marlon Brando*, p. 29.

169   *"I'd heard Harold's first talk . . .":* Elia Kazan, *Elia Kazan: A Life*, p. 300.

169   *"I wouldn't have sat by . . .":* Ibid., p. 301.

170–71   Clurman's difficulty with MB's mumbling and projection is from Harold Clurman, *On Directing,* pp. 116–17, as is the account of the rope incident.

172   *"... a bucket of water ...":* Kazan's instruction recalled by Richard Waring to PM.

173   *"Maxwell Anderson must have written ...":* New York Times, 2/28/46.

173   *"more and more acquiring powers ...":* Qtd. in George Jean Nathan, *The Theatre Book of the Year 1945–1946,* p. 323.

173   *"The public is far better qualified ...":* Ibid.

174   *"Marlon ... if you want ...":* Remark recalled by Darren Dublin to PM.

175   *"It was like Stella ...":* Sondra Lee to PM.

176   *"... a Mixmaster up his ass":* Remark recalled by Kevin McCarthy to PM; see also Patricia Bosworth, *Montgomery Clift,* p. 137.

176   *"Whenever the two of them ...":* Qtd. in Bosworth, *Montgomery Clift,* p. 137.

176   *"... we went to somebody's apartment ...":* Qtd. in ibid.

178   *"Oh, I know what you expect ... what he would do":* Remark recalled by Robin Howard to PM. See also Cornell's remarks qtd. in Bob Thomas, *Brando: Portrait of the Artist as a Rebel,* p. 31.

179   *"way off the beat ... skin of the character":* Carlo Fiore, *Bud: The Brando I Knew,* pp. 63–64.

179   *"I sure was ...":* Qtd. in ibid., p. 67.

179–80   *"Marlon Brando gives a Marchbanks ...":* New York Times, 4/14/46.

180   *"managed to make something ...":* New York *Daily News,* 4/14/46.

180   *"Good try, Marlon!":* Harold Clurman, *All People Are Famous,* p. 259.

180   *"Don't you know ...":* Qtd. in Thomas, *Brando,* p. 31.

180   *"Hickory Dickory Dock":* Ibid. According to Thomas, Lunt later repudiated this often repeated anecdote.

180   *"... he'd bring the agency millions":* Qtd. in Carey, *Marlon Brando,* p. 42.

183   *"all these crazy Jews ...":* Igor Tamarin to PM.

184   *"... Brando was incredible ...":* Qtd. in Jerome Lawrence, *Actor: The Life and Times of Paul Muni,* p. 292.

184   *"you can learn from":* Qtd. in ibid.

184   *"How the hell can an actor ...":* Qtd. in ibid., p. 293.

184   *"moments of great warmth and charm ...":* Qtd. in ibid.

184   *"I was afraid I'd break up ...":* Qtd. in William Stott with Jane Stott, *On Broadway,* p. 96.

186   "THE JEWS HAVE BEEN PERSECUTED ...": Qtd. in Lawrence, *Actor,* p. 295.

187–88   *"We discussed the possible problems ...":* Robert Lewis, *Slings and Arrows,* p. 176; Brando's meetings with Bankhead recalled by Lewis to PM.

189   *"he squirmed. He picked his nose ...":* Qtd. in Brendan Gill, *Tallulah,* p. 73.

7. *NEW YORK—OFFSTAGE: 1945-48*

PAGE

196 *". . . the mentality of an ax murderer"*: Qtd. in Richard Schickel, *Brando: A Life in Our Times*, p. 22.

197 *"Wally climbed into the grocer's cart . . ."*: Qtd. in Tim Taylor, "Wally Cox and Mr. Peepers," *Coronet*, April 1955, pp. 93–94.

197 *". . . us ex-rugged fellows . . ."*: Wally Cox, *My Life as a Small Boy*, pp. 124–25.

205 *"If more people did that . . ."*: Qtd. in Joe Morella and Edward Z. Epstein, *Brando: The Unauthorized Biography*, p. 30.

205 *"Two hundred bucks for what?"*: Incident recalled by Igor Tamarin to PM.

205–6 *"Do you know how I make . . ."*: Qtd. in Truman Capote, "The Duke in His Domain," *The New Yorker*, 11/9/57.

208 *"Marlon had the run of my place . . ."*: Qtd. in Morella and Epstein, *Brando*, pp. 29–30.

8. STREETCAR *AND THE ACTORS STUDIO: 1947-49*

PAGE

219 *"I draw all my characters from myself"*: Qtd. in Donald Spoto, *The Kindness of Strangers*, p. 153.

221 *"an audition would prove . . ."*: Qtd. in Gary Carey, *Marlon Brando: The Only Contender*, p. 44.

222 *"I finally decided . . ."*: Qtd. in Bob Thomas, *Brando: Portrait of the Rebel as an Artist*, p. 42.

222 *"He didn't behave . . ."*: Irene Mayer Selznick, *A Private View*, p. 303.

224 *"They should have got John . . ."*: Remark recalled by Kim Hunter in Lillian Ross and Helen Ross, *The Player*, p. 321.

224 *"aggressive, unpremeditated . . ."*: Qtd. in Charles Higham, *Brando: The Unauthorized Biography*, pp. 78–79.

225 *"There are no 'good' . . ."*: Qtd. in Elia Kazan, *Elia Kazan: A Life*, p. 329.

225 *"keep things his way . . . does it leave us?"*: Qtd. in Michel Ciment, ed., *Elia Kazan*, pp. 180–81.

226 *"He slunk onto . . ."*: Selznick, *A Private View*, p. 304.

228 *"His squat gymnasium physique . . ."*: Truman Capote, "The Duke in His Domain," *New Yorker*, 11/9/57.

230 *"God and nature gave . . ."*: qtd. in Ciment, *Elia Kazan*, p. 184.

230   *"discovering a way . . .":* Steve Vineberg, *Method Actors,* p. 155.

230   *". . . miracle was in the making":* Kazan, *A Life,* p. 343.

231   *"What would I say . . .":* Ibid., pp. 345–46.

231   *"What we've got here . . .":* Qtd. in Thomas, *Brando,* p. 44.

231   *"In those days . . .":* Selznick, *A Private View,* p. 312.

232   "TRY NOT TO . . .": Telegram recalled by Peter Turgeon to PM; however, Carlo Fiore claimed that he had sent the telegram (*Bud: The Brando I Knew,* p. 95).

232   "RIDE OUT BOY . . .": Qtd. in Thomas, *Brando,* p. 45.

232   Reviews of *A Streetcar Named Desire* are quoted in Joe Morella and Edward Z. Epstein, *Brando: The Unauthorized Biography,* pp. 154–55.

233   *"uncomfortable and dangerous":* William Redfield, "Brando and Burton: One Might Have Played Hamlet, the Other Did," *New York Times,* 1/15/67.

233   Brando was the future: See Hal Hinson, "Some Notes on Method Actors," *Sight and Sound,* Summer 1984, pp. 200–205.

234   *"legitimate professional promotion . . . legitimate stage":* Qtd. in Thomas, *Brando,* p. 54.

234   *"The theater to me . . . to the distortion?":* Qtd. in Louis Levitas, "Portrait of the Actor as a Young Man," *New York Post,* 4/5/48.

234–35   *"It took me a long time . . .":* Qtd. in Capote, "The Duke in His Domain."

243   *"Brando's mother was . . .":* Harold Clurman, *All People Are Famous,* p. 260.

245   *in housekeeper Ermy's bed:* Brando himself suggested this when he announced that he would write his autobiography: "I intend to disclose all my life . . . from my earliest memory of playing in my moonlit bed with the naked body of my sleeping beloved Ermi [*sic*]" (qtd. in Gayle Feldman, "Random Buys Brando Memoir," *Publishers Weekly,* 3/29/91).

247   *Igor Tamarin walked in:* Incident recounted by Karl Malden to PM, and confirmed by Igor Tamarin to PM.

248–49   *"She wouldn't tell . . .":* Lawrence Grobel, *Conversations with Brando,* pp. 35–36.

250   *"For almost two-thirds . . .":* Marjorie Loggia and Glenn Young, eds., *The Collected Works of Harold Clurman,* p. 134.

251   *"Marlon was difficult . . .":* Qtd. in "Filmography: Jessica Tandy," *Premiere,* February 1992, p. 104.

251   *"I don't believe in that crap . . .":* Qtd. in Levitas, "Portrait of the Actor as a Young Man."

251   *"She learns a part . . .":* Qtd. in Theodore Strauss, "The Brilliant Brat," *Life,* 7/31/50.

251–52   *"If someone has . . .":* Jessica Tandy to PM.

252   *"It just looks terrible . . .":* Remark recalled by Carmelita Pope to PM.

253   *One night Malden sauntered:* Incident recounted by Karl Malden to PM.

254   *"Marlon, look, those are . . .":* Qtd. in Carey, *Marlon Brando,* p. 52.

254   *"One night I came . . .":* Qtd. in Helen Dudar, "The Real Marlon Brando," *New York Post,* 1/4/55.

254   *The same speechlessness:* Carey, *Marlon Brando,* p. 55.

255   *"All of a sudden . . .":* Qtd. in Fiore, *Bud,* p. 103.

256   *"My nose healed . . .":* qtd. in Morella and Epstein, *Brando,* p. 27.

258   *"I don't want . . .":* Remark recalled by Carmelita Pope to PM.

258   *"You know, you'll never . . .":* Remark recalled by Carmelita Pope to PM.

260   *"Brando said he wasn't . . .":* Gerald Clarke to PM; see also Clarke, *Capote,* p. 302.

262   *". . . a new crop of performers . . .":* David Garfield, *A Player's Place,* p. 46.

262   *"a common language . . .":* Lenka Peterson to PM; see also Garfield, *A Player's Place,* p. 54.

262   *"I wouldn't open . . .":* Remark recalled by Bobby Lewis to PM.

263   *"always next to . . . You stepped in what?":* Jane Hoffman to PM; see also Garfield, *A Player's Place,* p. 55.

265–66 *Eli Wallach played an FBI agent:* Incident recounted by Eli Wallach to PM; see also Garfield, *A Player's Place,* pp. 61–62.

267   *"these kids grow up fast":* Jerry Wald–Jack Warner memos, Jack Warner Collection, University of Southern California Library, Los Angeles.

9. HOLLYWOOD: 1949-54

PAGE

275   *"a paradisiacal dream . . . ever known":* Richard Schickel, *Brando: A Life in Our Times,* p. 57.

276   *"You know, Miss Bankhead . . .":* Remark recalled by Stanley Kramer to PM.

277   *"I was so drunk . . .":* Remark recalled by Pat Grissom to PM.

277   *"I didn't know . . .":* Qtd. in *New York Times,* 10/16/49.

278   *"Every once in a while . . .":* Ibid.

279   *"He was under enormous strain":* Fred Zinnemann, *Fred Zinnemann: An Autobiography,* p. 84.

279   *"I've got Marlon . . . let him be":* Conversation recalled by Karl Malden to PM.

279–80 *"When I first started . . .":* qtd. in Chris Hodenfield, "Mondo Brando," *Rolling Stone,* May 20, 1976.

280   *". . . breakthrough nature . . .":* Steve Vineberg, *Method Actors,* p. 157.

284–85 *"It was a fiasco . . .":* Incident recounted by Shelley Winters to PM; see also Winters, *Shelley: Also Known as Shirley,* pp. 280–84.

286–87   The first meetings between Brando and Hedda Hopper and Louella
         Parsons are recounted in George Eells, *Hedda and Louella*, p. 302 and p.
         278, respectively.

287   Life *magazine devoted six pages:* Life, 7/31/50.

288   *"When I first came . . .":* Qtd. in Sidney Skolsky, "Hollywood Is My
         Beat," *Hollywood Citizen News*, n.d.

289–90   *"He told me that he . . .":* Conversation with MB Sr. and incident with
         recording device recalled by Roe Black to PM.

292   *"Streetcar is an extremely . . .":* Qtd. in Rudy Behlmer, ed., *Inside Warner
         Bros. (1935–1951)*, p. 324.

293   *Warner and Feldman insisted:* Details on casting the film drawn from
         memos in the Jack Warner Collection, USC Library; see also Elia
         Kazan, *Elia Kazan: A Life*, pp. 384–86.

293–94   *"shaking like an autumn leaf . . .":* Alan Dent, *Vivien Leigh*, pp. 103–4.

294   *"Blanche is a woman . . .":* Leigh letter to Alan Dent, qtd. in *Sunday
         Telegraph* (London), 7/9/61.

294   *"Why do you always . . .":* Conversation qtd. in Alexander Walker,
         Vivien, p. 202.

294   *"I requested that Vivien . . .":* Kazan, *A Life*, pp. 386–88.

295   *". . . the way Stanley would live":* Incident recounted by Elia Kazan to
         PM.

295   *"Lucinda, I want to be . . .":* Remark recalled by Lucinda Ballard to PM.

296   *"How do you do?":* Conversation qtd. in *Los Angeles Times*, 9/12/50.

297   *"small talent, but the greatest . . .":* Kazan, *A Life*, p. 387.

299–300 *"I could not imagine . . .":* Dan Ben-Amotz, *Screwing Isn't Everything*, pp.
         481–82 (excerpt translated by Ati Citron).

301   *to sue the ranch owner:* Later MB Sr. took over the claims of his six
         co-complainants. After Black filed for bankruptcy, he and MB Jr.
         continued their suit. On July 3, 1954, the court awarded the Brandos
         $37,352, but Black Ranches and the National Bank of Denver
         countersued, arguing that MB Sr. had previously agreed to extend
         Black's note. The suit would be in appeals courts for the next twelve
         years.

302   *drafting an embattled defense:* Incident recounted by Joe Mankiewicz to
         PM; see also Kazan, *A Life*, pp. 388–93.

303   *"secretly, skillfully . . .":* Kazan, *A Life*, p. 435.

303   *"if someone spits . . .":* Kazan letter to Steve Trilling, Warner Bros.
         executive, qtd. in Behlmer, *Inside Warner Bros.*, p. 332.

305   *"After they shoot . . .":* Qtd. in Kazan, *A Life*, p. 396.

305   "Will he fuck her . . .": Qtd. in Leonard Mosley, *Zanuck*, p. 240.

307   *"was running a business . . .":* Kazan, *A Life*, p. 419.

307   *concessionary offer:* Meeting with Zanuck described in ibid. pp. 420–21.

309   *"I told him a peasant . . .":* Elia Kazan to PM; see also Kazan, *A Life*, p.
         428.

309   *"Don't be misled . . .":* Kazan, *A Life,* pp. 428–29.

310   *"fucking is not a big deal":* Ibid.

310   *"He was that way . . .":* Ibid.

312   *"No actor can play . . .":* Remark recalled by Sam Shaw to PM.

312   *"He was scaring . . .":* Sam Shaw to PM; see also Shaw, *Brando, in the Camera Eye,* pp. 88–89.

314   *"Russell is not only . . .":* Qtd. in Hedda Hopper, "Hollywood's New Sex-boat," *Photoplay,* July 1952.

316   *"the greatest actor of his time":* Qtd. in Shaw, *Brando,* p. 46.

316   *"You know, Tony . . .":* Remark recalled by both Anthony Quinn and Sam Shaw to PM.

317   *Marlon's response:* Incident recounted by Anthony Quinn to PM.

317   *"Marlon always gave me more . . .":* Qtd. in Gary Carey, *Marlon Brando: The Only Contender,* p. 73.

318   *"confessed Commie membership . . .":* Qtd. in Kazan, *A Life,* p. 453.

318   *"Not until I saw . . .":* Hedda Hopper, *Los Angeles Times,* 3/30/52.

318   *"too romantic . . .":* Remark recalled by Sam Shaw to PM.

319   *"All of us around here . . .":* Qtd. in *Los Angeles Examiner,* 12/22/51.

320   *second picture for Houseman:* Background of John Houseman drawn from his autobiography, *Front and Center.*

320   *an ideal director:* Background of Joseph L. Mankiewicz drawn from numerous film histories and PM interview with Mankiewicz.

320–21   *"Mankiewicz was in London . . .":* Houseman, *Front and Center,* p. 388.

322   *". . . I was captivated by him":* Dore Schary, *Heyday,* p. 259.

322   *"I'm sick to death . . .":* Qtd. in Charles Higham, "Brando's Back," *San Francisco Chronicle,* 1/22/89.

323   *"I accepted this role . . .":* Qtd. in Bob Thomas, "Marlon Brando Takes Diction Lessons for Role in *Caesar,*" *Hollywood Citizen News,* n.d.

324   *"Gielgud, who was justly celebrated . . .":* Houseman, *Front and Center,* p. 390.

325   *". . . to play overelaborately":* Remark recalled by Joe Mankiewicz to PM.

326   *"He thanked me very politely . . .":* John Gielgud with John Miller and John Powell, *An Actor and His Time,* p. 156.

326   *"impressed and flattered . . . act in the theater again":* Gielgud letter to PM, 8/1/88.

326   *"I did wrong to withhold . . .":* Qtd. in Victor S. Navasky, *Naming Names,* p. 202.

327   *"He told me he'd been to Washington . . .":* Qtd. in ibid. pp. 201–2.

327   *community was sickened:* For response of theater and film community to Kazan's testimony, see ibid., pp. 204–9, and Kazan, *A Life,* pp. 466–78.

332   *"Suddenly he had discovered . . .":* Houseman, *Front and Center,* p. 397.

332–33   *"I realize now . . .":* Qtd. in Bob Thomas, *Brando: Portrait of the Rebel as an Artist,* p. 54.

333   *"They would photograph . . .":* Gielgud et al., *An Actor and His Time,* pp. 155–56.

333   *"During that long week . . .":* Houseman, *Front and Center,* p. 398.

334   *"We did not want it shown . . .":* Ibid., p. 404.

334–35   The tabulation of the response cards is from ibid., p. 406.

335   *"Nothing but regal treatment . . .":* Variety, 5/11/53.

335   *"the best Shakespeare . . .":* Time, 6/1/53.

335   *"the delight and surprise of the film":* New York Times, 6/5/53.

335   *"After his amazing success . . .":* Dorothy Kilgallen, *American Weekly,* 7/19/53.

335   *"gained ground as an actor . . .":* Qtd. in Schickel, *Brando,* p. 80.

337   *"make big business . . .":* Qtd. in Gladys Hill, "It Isn't That I Don't Like Glamour," *Silver Screen,* July 1950.

338   Story of the bikers in Hollister drawn from *Biker* 4, no. 15 (8/10/77), pp. 4–5, 23.

338   *"It touched my sense . . .":* Qtd. in Donald Spoto, *Stanley Kramer,* p. 157.

339–40   *". . . Find another little town . . .":* Biker, 8/10/77, p. 23.

340   *"antisocial, if not downright communistic":* Qtd. in Thomas, *Brando,* p. 88.

340   *"Good sentiments must be rewarded . . .":* Goldwyn often repeated his slogan about good "thentimenths." See, for example, Jean Malaquais's description of a script meeting with Goldwyn in Peter Manso, *Mailer,* pp. 146–47. According to A. Scott Berg (*Goldwyn,* pp. 468–69), Goldwyn resisted the trend toward realism and criticized *The Wild One* for "making heroes of young men in black leather jackets."

340   *". . . ask questions later . . .":* Qtd. in Thomas, *Brando,* p. 88.

340   *Marlon made faces:* Charles Higham, *Brando: The Unauthorized Biography,* p. 136.

341   *"We can't do it . . .":* Qtd. in Thomas, *Brando,* p. 89.

345   *"started trading . . .":* Ibid., p. 90.

347   *"We started out . . .":* Qtd. in ibid., p. 91.

348   *"to take art, dramatic literature . . .":* Qtd. in *Los Angeles Times,* 9/12/50.

348   *"an actor whose sullen face . . .":* Time, 1/18/54.

10. WATERFRONT: 1953–54

PAGE

349   *"I have a thousand head . . .":* Qtd. in *Omaha World-Herald,* 1/20/53.

350   *"I knew that when word . . .":* Qtd. in Gary Carey, *Marlon Brando: The Only Contender,* p. 93.

351   *"Man, don't you get it? . . .":* Qtd. in William Redfield, "Brando and

Burton: One Might Have Played Hamlet, the Other Did," *New York Times,* 1/15/67.

351   *sort of gofering:* Valerie Judd to PM.

352   *"I don't want to work . . .":* Qtd. in Carlo Fiore, *Bud: The Brando I Knew,* p. 117.

352   *"Marlon Brando, who distinguished himself . . .":* Elliott Norton, *Boston Post,* 7/28/53.

354   *"When critics say . . .":* Elia Kazan, *Elia Kazan: A Life,* p. 500; in his interview with PM, however, Schulberg claimed that at the time of their first discussions, Kazan had not revealed this as a motive for either pursuing the project or scripting the final scene: "Kazan didn't say this at the time, so I think it's probably more hindsight."

355   *"Father John's effect . . .":* Budd Schulberg, *On the Waterfront: The Final Shooting Script,* p. 143.

355   *"I wrote down lines . . .":* Ibid., p. 145.

355   *"We became brothers":* Kazan, *A Life,* p. 487.

356–57   The account of Schulberg and Kazan's arrival in Hollywood and their meeting with Zanuck is drawn from Schulberg, *On the Waterfront,* pp. 146–48; Schulberg interview with PM; and Kazan, *A Life,* pp. 508–11.

357   *"The floor was littered . . .":* Schulberg, *On the Waterfront,* pp. 148–49.

357–58   The account of the meeting with Sam Spiegel is drawn from ibid., p. 150.

358   *"Frank had grown up . . .":* Kazan, *A Life,* p. 515.

359   *"Professional is one thing . . .":* Andrew Sinclair, *Spiegel,* p. 69.

359   *four sessions a week:* see Kazan, *A Life,* p. 816.

359   *"really screwed himself":* Schulberg to PM, confirming that both he and Kazan, with percentages, made more from the film than Brando did.

360   *"Do you want the world . . .":* Qtd. in Sinclair, *Spiegel,* p. 69.

360   *"Mumbles" and "the most overrated actor . . .":* Kitty Kelley, *His Way,* p. 228.

360   *"He fought like a tiger . . .":* Qtd. in Sinclair, *Spiegel,* p. 70.

360   *"To kill Sam Spiegel":* Qtd. in Kazan, *A Life,* p. 518.

360   *". . . saved our ass":* Qtd. in Schulberg, *On the Waterfront,* p. 151.

366   *"And take your girlfriend with you":* Budd Schulberg confirmed this ad-lib to PM.

367   *"if I was Mutt . . .":* Qtd. in Bob Thomas, *Brando: Portrait of the Rebel as an Artist,* p. 92.

367–68   Discussion of the taxi scene is drawn from Budd Schulberg and Charles Maguire to PM.

368   *"the finest thing . . .":* Qtd. in Carey, *Marlon Brando,* p. 99.

369   *"some serious trouble . . .":* Budd Schulberg to PM.

369   *Brando's conflicts:* Elia Kazan to PM.

370   *"He would never expose . . .":* Ibid.

370 Brando at Norman Mailer's party described in Peter Manso, *Mailer,* pp. 170–71.

371 *ran to Stella Adler's:* Eddie Jaffe recalled MB's description of anxiety attacks to PM.

372 *"Psychoanalysts, I've found . . .":* Elia Kazan to PM.

373 *"a sudden need . . .":* Qtd. in Charles Higham, *Brando: The Unauthorized Biography,* p. 145.

374 *"I'd like to drop you . . .":* Qtd. in Geoffrey T. Hellman, "Don't Take Notes on the Boyfriend," *New Yorker,* 4/20/55.

374 *". . . under a faucet . . .":* Qtd. in ibid.

374 *". . . You can't look . . .":* Qtd. in Higham, *Brando,* p. 146.

374 *"extremely practical":* Fiore, *Bud,* p. 130.

375 *"couldn't see anything wrong . . .":* Juleen Compton to PM.

375 *"the leader of the ass-kissers":* Igor Tamarin to PM.

377 *"not a heart attack":* Dodie's reassurance recalled by Kay Phillips Bennett to PM.

377 *"Sam, you've finally . . .":* Kazan, *A Life,* p. 527.

377 *without saying a word:* Brando conceded that he thought the film "was so terrible I walked out without even speaking to [Kazan]" (qtd. in Truman Capote, "The Duke in His Domain," *New Yorker,* 11/9/57).

380 *"Thank you very much":* MB acceptance speech qtd. in Maurice Zolotow, "Brando," *The American Weekly,* 1/14/57.

380 Posing for pictures and incidents backstage drawn from Mason Wiley and Damien Bona, *Inside Oscar,* pp. 250–53.

11. *FLAILING:* 1954-58

PAGE

381 *was besotted:* Leonard Mosely, *Zanuck,* pp. 258–65.

382 *"Marlon's left . . .":* Conversation qtd. in Gary Carey, *Marlon Brando: The Only Contender,* p. 101.

382 *"very sick and mentally confused":* Qtd. in numerous news reports, including *Los Angeles Times,* 2/4/54.

382 *"considerable sums" . . . "under a mental strain . . .":* New York *Daily News,* 4/2/54.

382 *"Marlon lazied himself . . .":* Helen Dudar, "Brando and Hollywood," *New York Post,* 1/6/55.

382 *"a high-priced harlot . . .":* Qtd. in Mosely, *Zanuck,* p. 264.

382–83 *"Brando was under treatment . . .":* New York *Daily News,* 4/2/54.

383 *"Not because of big-star temperament . . .":* Qtd. in John Mathews,

"Marlon and Marilyn," *Motion Picture Magazine,* May 1954, p. 13; see also New York *Sunday News,* 11/7/54.

384 *"like a United Nations diplomat":* New York *Daily News,* 4/2/54.

384 *Brando's "capture":* Louella Parsons, *Los Angeles Times,* 2/17/54.

387 *"it was just a year ago tonight . . .":* Qtd. in Mason Wiley and Damien Bona, *Inside Oscar,* p. 253.

389 *"Do you really want . . .":* Remarks recalled by Julian Blaustein to PM.

389 The chocolate soda incident is qtd. in Charles Higham, *Brando: The Unauthorized Biography,* pp. 151–52.

390 *"Mr. Dean appears . . .":* Qtd. in Carey, *Marlon Brando,* p. 119.

390 *"It was like Apollo . . .":* Kenneth Kendall to PM.

390 *"Jimmy was so adoring . . .":* Elia Kazan, *Elia Kazan: A Life,* p. 538.

391 *"Dean . . . had an* idée fixe *. . .":* Qtd. in Truman Capote, "The Duke in His Domain," *New Yorker,* 11/9/57.

391 *"throwing himself around, acting the madman":* Qtd. in ibid. In the Capote interview, Brando went on a bit grandly: "Towards the end I think he was beginning to find his own way as an actor. At least his *work* improved." He hadn't been untouched, however, after Dean's fatal auto crash in September 1955. The evening of the accident, he went to comfort Ursula Andress, Dean's most recent girlfriend (and once, briefly, his as well). "He was stilled," according to Maila Nurmi, who was also there, in her interview with PM. "He didn't say anything like 'One could have foreseen it.' Nor was he crying or overwhelmed." At the time of the Capote interview, Brando was considering narrating a documentary on Dean "to show he wasn't a hero; show what he really was—just a lost boy trying to find himself. . . . I'd like to do it—maybe as a kind of expiation for some of my own sins" (qtd. in Capote, "The Duke in His Domain"). Then he admitted that he remained excited about something for only "seven minutes" and, indeed, did not narrate this documentary.

392 Discussion with MB in his trailer recalled by Julian Blaustein to PM.

393 *". . . makeup play the part":* Qtd. in Gary Carey, *Brando,* p. 103.

394 *"from teenagers . . .":* Qtd. in Randall Riese and Neal Hitchens, *The Unabridged Marilyn,* p. 63.

394 *"A geek is the lowest form . . .":* Qtd. in *Los Angeles Times,* 4/11/54.

394 *picket lines: New York Times,* 10/2/54.

395 *"On his present European trip . . .":* Newsweek, 11/8/54.

395 *"I didn't think . . . unless he's sure":* Qtd in Aline Mosby, UP dispatch, *Beverly Hills Newslife,* n.d.

395–96 *"Spittoon rubbish . . . hardly begun":* Qtd. in *Los Angeles Times,* 11/1/54.

396 *"the only girl . . .":* Qtd. in ibid.

396 *"We are still . . .":* Qtd. in ibid.

396 *"He had better":* Qtd. in ibid.

396   *"perhaps by next June"*: Qtd. in *Los Angeles Examiner*, 11/10/54.

396   *"But I was very serious"*: Qtd. in *Los Angeles Times*, 11/9/54.

396   *"I do intend to marry the girl"*: Qtd. in Carey, *Marlon Brando*, p. 107.

397   *"I will not speak . . ."*: Qtd. in New York *Daily News*, 11/27/54.

397   *"The world will not wreck . . ."*: Qtd. in *Newsweek*, 11/15/54.

397   *"made a mistake . . ."*: Carlo Fiore, *Bud: The Brando I Knew*, p. 135.

399–400   "WANT VERY MUCH . . .": Qtd. in A. Scott Berg, *Goldwyn*, p. 471.

400   "BRANDO FEARFUL . . .": Collection of Joseph L. Mankiewicz.

400   "GOLDWYN TELLS ME . . .": Ibid.

400   *"I will not direct . . ."*: Joe Mankiewicz recalled his remark to PM.

401   *"Frank, I've never done . . ."*: Qtd. in Anna Kashfi Brando and E. P. Stein, *Brando for Breakfast*, p. 53.

402   *"He's supposed to . . ."*: Remark recalled by Joe Mankiewicz to PM. See also Fiore, *Bud*, pp. 146–47.

403   *"Please, I don't mind . . ."*: MB's conversation with Goldwyn recalled by Joe Mankiewicz to PM.

404   *"Where's Marlon?"*: Incident described by Bob Thomas, *Brando: Portrait of the Rebel as an Artist*, p. 108.

404   *"Frank is the kind of guy . . ."*: Carey, *Marlon Brando*, p. 115.

404–5   *"Marlon, my boy . . ."*: Qtd. in Thomas, *Brando*, p. 115.

405   *"It was the most terrifying . . ."*: Qtd. in ibid., p. 116.

406   *"Faithful in detail . . ."*: *Time*, 11/14/55.

406   *"Sam, You Made . . ."*: *New Yorker*, 11/16/55.

406   *"I've done enough . . ."*: Qtd. in Berg, *Goldwyn*, p. 474.

406   *"I wanted to effect . . ."*: Qtd. in Joe Morella and Edward Z. Epstein, *Brando: The Unauthorized Biography*, p. 81.

406   *"recently discovered impulse . . ."*: Qtd. in ibid., p. 79.

406   *script approval*: Dore Schary, *Heyday* p. 299.

407   *"If Marlon had wanted . . ."*: Qtd. in Thomas, *Brando*, p. 117.

407   *"laughed so hard . . ."*: Qtd. in ibid., p. 112.

409   *"Of all the countries . . ."*: Qtd in Kashfi and Stein, *Brando for Breakfast*, p. 62.

409   *"Americans don't even begin . . ."*: Ibid.

410–11   The conflict with Glenn Ford over cookies is reported by Thomas, *Brando*, p. 121.

411   *"I can't wait . . ."*: Qtd. in Carey, *Marlon Brando*, p. 122.

412   *". . . Beneath a dark stain . . ."*: Bosley Crowther, *New York Times*, 11/30/56 and 12/2/56.

414   *"Today the Indians . . ."*: Qtd. in Carey, *Marlon Brando*, pp. 123–24.

414   *"there is no more exciting . . ."*: Qtd. in Thomas, *Brando*, p. 132.

419   *"Herro, herro . . ."*: Qtd. in Kashfi and Stein, *Brando for Breakfast*, p. 66.

420   *"I'm just doing it . . ."*: Qtd. in Morella and Epstein, *Brando*, p. 64.

421   *"I don't like the ending . . ."*: Conversation recounted by Joshua Logan to PM; see also Logan, *Movie Stars, Real People, and Me*, pp. 97–98.

422	Trip to Japan via Hawaii drawn from Fiore, *Bud,* pp. 165–71.
423	*"stand at a distance . . .":* Qtd. in Thomas, *Brando,* p. 132.
424	*"What's the matter?":* MB's conversation with Garner is in ibid. pp. 124–25.
424	*"You must never . . .":* Logan, *Movie Stars,* pp. 103–5, which is also the source for the cigarette discussion.
425	*"I will not say . . .":* Fiore, *Bud,* pp. 178–80, which is also the source for MB's testing of Logan in the scene with Buttons.
425	*"Marlon wanted to be directed . . .":* Qtd. in Lawrence Grobel, "You Ought to Be in Pictures," *Movieline,* May 1994, p. 62.
426	*"He knows exactly . . .":* Logan, *Movie Stars,* pp. 110–11.
426	*"judging from the stills . . .":* Letter to Joshua Logan from Jack Warner, 2/5/57, Warner Bros. Archives, University of Southern California, Los Angeles.
426	*steal a few women:* see Fiore, *Bud,* pp. 188–89.
428	*"I knew from his conversation . . .":* Logan, *Movie Stars,* p. 101.
429	*"A comic novel . . .":* Gerald Clarke, *Capote,* p. 298.
429	*"Now, come on, Josh . . .":* Qtd. in Logan, *Movie Stars,* p. 105.
429	*"Don't let yourself . . .":* Qtd. in Clarke, *Capote,* p. 301.
429	*"He didn't know . . .":* Qtd. in ibid., p. 302.
429	*"Okay, but split . . .":* Qtd. in Fiore, *Bud,* p. 180.
429	*"Slim and trim as a boy":* Ibid., p. 181.
429–30	*"What an experience . . .":* Qtd. in Clarke, *Capote,* p. 302.
430	*"The secret to the art . . .":* Qtd. in ibid.
430	*"The little bastard . . .":* Qtd. in Thomas, *Brando,* p. 129.
430	*"I asked Marlon . . .":* Qtd. in Clarke, *Capote,* p. 302, where, however, Campbell is not mentioned by name. Clarke confirmed that Capote meant Campbell in interview with PM. Donald Windham disputed Capote's story in his interview with PM.
431	*"Oh, you were so wrong . . .":* Conversation qtd. in Logan, *Movie Stars,* pp. 106–7.
431	*"Here, of course, is the inevitable . . .":* Qtd. in Clarke, *Capote,* p. 303.
431–32	*"caused every bit . . .":* Ibid.
432–33	*"The last eight, nine years":* excerpts of MB's interview from Capote, "The Duke in His Domain."
433	*"You should have killed . . .":* Logan, *Movie Stars,* p. 120.
435	*"walk through":* Qtd. in Morella and Epstein, *Brando,* p. 64.
435–36	*"He was so tough . . .":* MB's conversation with Logan over this scene drawn from Logan, *Movie Stars,* p. 117.
436	*"He just played . . .":* Joshua Logan to PM.
436	*"were like fire horses . . .":* Logan, *Movie Stars,* p. 118.
437–38	*"Now, don't blame him . . .":* Injured arm anecdote is from ibid., pp. 118–19.
438	*"the first breakthrough . . . blithering idiot":* Ibid., p. 120.

438   *"a conventional role . . .":* Bosley Crowther, *New York Times,* 12/6/57.

438   *"Brando and his girl . . .":* Qtd. in Morella and Epstein, *Brando,* p. 186.

438   *"contribute in a telling . . .":* Qtd. in Thomas, *Brando,* p. 132.

439   *made her highly suspect:* See *New York Post,* 5/5/56.

440   *"separate the sheep from the goats":* Background and role of Roy M. Brewer in Hollywood blacklisting drawn from Victor S. Navasky, *Naming Names,* pp. 87ff and 265–66, and from Brewer's interview with PM.

443   *"It's me, Rita! . . .":* Kashfi and Stein, *Brando for Breakfast,* p. 103, and Anna Kashfi Brando Hannaford to PM.

443   *". . . it was my fault . . .":* Kashfi and Stein, *Brando for Breakfast,* pp. 87–88.

444–45   *"I guess it's my vanity . . .":* Qtd. in Fiore, *Bud,* pp. 205–7.

445   *". . . the absence of anxiety . . .":* Qtd. in Kashfi and Stein, *Brando for Breakfast,* p. 97.

445   *"Fox decided to make the film . . .":* Qtd. in *Cinema Texas,* program notes, University of Texas, Austin, 3/27/78, p. 102.

447   *"Well, I was watching . . .":* Qtd. in Robert LaGuardia, *Monty,* p. 172.

448   *Marlon himself retold:* Maureen Stapleton to PM; see also Patricia Bosworth, *Montgomery Clift,* p. 312.

448   *"Take Dean Martin":* Qtd. in Edward Dymtryk, *It's a Hell of a Life But Not a Bad Living,* pp. 101–2; Dmytryk also recalled this comment to PM.

448   *Dmytryk's politics:* Background of Dmytryk's HUAC testimony drawn from Dmytryk, *It's a Hell of a Life . . .* , and from Navasky, *Naming Names,* pp. 232–38.

449   *"threatening to expose . . .":* Anna Kashfi Brando Hannaford to PM; see also Kashfi and Stein, *Brando for Breakfast,* p. 76.

450   *"I'm changing the Nazi . . .":* Qtd. in Fiore, *Bud,* p. 203.

450   *"That's not true . . .":* Qtd. in *Cinema Texas,* program notes, p. 103, and Edward Dmytryk to PM.

450–51   *"We were going . . .":* Edward Anhalt to PM.

451   *Brando was mobbed: Los Angeles Times,* 6/17/57.

451   *"I was disturbed . . .":* Fiore, *Bud,* p. 213.

451–52   *"If you were writing . . .":* Qtd. in Philip K. Scheuer, "Threads of Power, Irony Bind 'Young Lions' Web," *Los Angeles Times,* 3/30/58.

452   *"An actor is an empty . . .":* Televised exchange qtd. in Richard Schickel, *Brando: A Life in Our Times,* p. 118.

455   *"This would have to happen . . .":* Qtd. in Higham, *Brando,* p. 184.

456   *"It doesn't work . . .":* Remark recalled by Edward Anhalt to PM.

457   *"Brando would appear . . .":* Edward Dmytryk to PM; see also Dmytryk, *It's a Hell of a Life,* p. 226.

457–58   *"There was a good deal . . .":* Qtd. in LaGuardia, *Monty,* p. 175.

458   *"Tell Marlon he doesn't . . .":* Qtd. in Bosworth, *Clift,* p. 319.

458   *"He's using about one-tenth"*: Qtd. in ibid.

458   *"momentarily berserk"* . . . *"He hadn't had . . ."*: Ibid., p. 320.

458   *"like pinholes . . ."*: LaGuardia, *Monty,* p. 172.

458   *". . . get finished with Monty . . ."*: Qtd. in ibid.

458–59   *"Irwin Shaw wrote . . ."*: Qtd. in Jess Stearn, "Riddles of Marlon Brando," New York *Daily News,* 3/18/58.

460   *"If Marlon's allowed . . ."*: Qtd. in Carey, *Marlon Brando,* p. 132.

460   *"Sit down and quietly reflect . . ."*: Remark recalled by Anna Kashfi Brando Hannaford to PM.

460   *"wasn't letting him . . ."*: Fiore, *Bud,* pp. 224–25.

460   *"If you do, she'll . . ."*: Ibid., p. 225.

461   *"Let her have anything . . ."*: Conversation in ibid., p. 228.

463   *"There is no Indian blood . . ."*: Qtd. in *Los Angeles Examiner,* 10/13/57.

463   *"She's as Indian as Paddy's pig"*: Glass's remark recalled by Walter Seltzer to PM. In her memoirs, Kashfi continued to insist that her deceased natural father had been Indian and that William Patrick O'Callaghan was her "stepfather" (*Brando for Breakfast,* p. 110).

463   *"I got into a big . . ."*: Anna Kashfi Brando Hannaford to PM; see also Kashfi and Stein, *Brando for Breakfast,* p. 114.

464   *"My heart aches for this little girl . . ."*: Hedda Hopper, *Los Angeles Times,* 11/14/57. Kashfi later denied speaking to Hopper (*Brando for Breakfast,* p. 115).

464   *"Reporters are all scum . . . passive coldness"*: Kashfi and Stein, *Brando for Breakfast,* pp. 101, 127.

465   *Sam Gilman was called:* James Bacon, "Brando Split with Bride Reported," *London Mirror News,* 12/12/57.

465   *"unregenerative Nazi . . ."*: Bosley Crowther, *New York Times,* 4/18/58.

466   *"is really just . . ."*: John McCarten, "Reluctant Dragon," *New Yorker,* 4/12/58.

466   *"Brando underplays . . ."*: Qtd. in Morella and Epstein, *Brando,* p. 188.

12. *TURNING A CORNER:* **1958-62**

PAGE

470   *he had encountered and become friends:* Background of script recounted by Frank P. Rosenberg to PM in interview; source for Peckinpah's recollection of being paid $3,000, which was then scale, is Garner Simmons, *Peckinpah,* p. 28.

470–71   Meeting with MB at Seltzer's home described by Rosenberg to PM.

472   *"a buddy . . . and who doesn't"*: Conversation qtd. in Carlo Fiore, *Bud: The Brando I Knew,* pp. 235–36.

472   Peckinpah's reaction to his firing confirmed in David Weddle, *"If They Move . . . Kill 'Em."*

473   *"Hollywood's newest Cinderella . . ."*: Los Angeles Mirror, 10/15/58.

474   *"Have you ever had a producer . . ."*: Conversation qtd. in Fiore, *Bud,* p. 246.

474   *"Malden usually plays losers"*: Kubrick-Brando exchange qtd. in ibid, pp. 237–38.

475   *"by the time he had finished . . ."*: Ibid, p. 237.

475   *"Just before we were to start . . ."*: Qtd. in G. Barry Golson, ed., *The Playboy Interviews,* pp. 627–28.

475   *"At a meeting, Brando had been urging . . ."*: Frank Rosenberg's version of Kubrick's remark about Nuyen and subsequent dismissal recounted in interview with PM.

476   *". . . I can direct the picture . . ."*: Remark recalled by Frank P. Rosenberg to PM.

476   *"with deep regret because of my respect . . ."*: Qtd. in Louella Parsons, *Los Angeles Examiner,* 11/20/58.

476   *"If he had hired . . ."*: Fiore, *Bud,* p. 243.

476–77   *"I usually direct myself . . . mark of maturity"*: Qtd. in Joe Hyams, "Standards Are High and So Is His Pay," *Los Angeles Times,* n.d.

477   Kashfi's attack on Brando recalled by Frank P. Rosenberg to PM.

477   *"grievous mental suffering . . ."*: New York *Herald Tribune,* 3/17/59.

477   *"I didn't want Christian . . ."*: From transcript of MB's testimony, Christian Brando's sentencing hearing, 2/28/91, pp. 241, 243.

478   *"something sexual"*: Anna Kashfi Brando Hannaford to PM.

478   *"the queerest . . ."*: Anna Kashfi Brando and E. P. Stein, *Brando for Breakfast,* p. 120.

478   *"Just the way Marlon was talking"*: Anna Kashfi Brando Hannaford to PM.

478   *"specialized in supplying . . . 'up your cloaca!' "*: Kashfi and Stein, *Brando for Breakfast,* p. 120.

479   *"I have the obligation . . ."*: Qtd. in "One-Eyed Jacks Information Guide," Paramount Pictures, 1961; see also Fiore, *Bud,* p. 252.

479   *"Our early-day heroes . . ."*: Qtd. in "One-Eyed Jacks Information Guide."

480   *"How would Ben Johnson play it?"*: Remark recalled by Ben Johnson to PM.

481   *Marlon had already spent:* Gary Carey, *Marlon Brando: The Only Contender,* p. 139.

481   *"Would you believe that . . ."*: Qtd. in Fiore, *Bud,* p. 249.

481   *"There is nothing so unusual . . ."*: Qtd. in Murray Schumach, *New York Times,* 5/24/59.

481   *"making a film, not a schedule"*: Qtd. in ibid.

481   *John Ford had often worked:* Johnson recalled telling MB about Ford in interview with PM.

481 *"Ah had my first heart attack . . .":* Remark recalled by Frank P. Rosenberg to PM.

482 *"I'm waiting for a wave":* Incident recounted by Frank P. Rosenberg to PM.

482 *"Good, we'll sit here and wait":* Remark recalled by Karl Malden to PM.

482 *". . . the wrong end . . .":* Conversation recalled by Sam Shaw to PM; see also Shaw, *Brando, in the Camera Eye,* p. 68.

482 *"Mr. Brando, don't you think . . .":* Remarks recalled by Ben Johnson to PM.

482 *11,000 feet: Time,* 3/24/61.

484 *To help himself visualize:* Schumach, *New York Times,* 5/11/59.

484 *"He just wouldn't settle . . .":* Qtd. in Lee Belser, "Brando's 'Reverence' for Other Craftsmen Lauded by Actress," *Los Angeles Mirror,* 7/20/61.

484 *". . . Directing by itself is hard enough . . .":* Qtd. in Joe Morella and Edward Z. Epstein, *Brando: The Unauthorized Biography,* p. 81.

485 *"I am still afraid . . .":* Qtd. in ibid.

489 *"Where is everybody?":* MB's becoming drunk and passing out on set drawn from Fiore, *Bud,* pp. 253–55. Sam Shaw and Philip Rhodes confirmed incident—as well as MB's insistence on doing "drunk scenes" actually drunk—in interviews with PM.

489 MB's firing of Carlo Fiore recounted in ibid., pp. 263–64, and confirmed by Karl Malden to PM.

490 *"They're going to complain . . .":* Frank P. Rosenberg recalled MB's remark and subsequent meeting to PM.

490 *"Freeman's full of crap":* Remark recalled by Walter Seltzer to PM.

490 *"Marlon, who dies today? . . .":* Remark recalled by Karl Malden to PM.

490 *"We've got the Brando name . . .":* Qtd. in Bob Thomas, "End Nearing on Actor's Own Film," *Hollywood Citizen News,* 5/23/59.

492 *"I wanted to notify you officially . . .":* Wrap party described and Mort Sahl quoted in Sidney Skolsky, "Hollywood Is My Beat," *New York Post,* 6/8/59.

492 *"I want this line . . .":* Archie Marchek described MB's method of cutting the film to Karl Malden, who related MB's remark and Marchek reply to PM.

493 *"I'm down at Paramount . . .":* Phone calls recounted in Fiore, *Bud,* pp. 265–66, 268.

494 *"Where we going . . .":* Incident recounted by Frank P. Rosenberg to PM. See also Charles Higham, *Brando: The Unauthorized Biography,* p. 201.

494 *"Now, it's a good picture . . .":* Qtd. in Bob Thomas, *Brando: Portrait of the Rebel as an Artist,* p. 155.

495 "One-Eyed Jacks *is a potboiler . . .":* Qtd. in *Newsweek,* 4/13/61.

496 *"I truthfully went . . .":* Jim Henagahn, *Hollywood Reporter,* 7/31/61.

497 *"probably the greatest living actor . . .":* Tennessee Williams, *Memoirs,* p. 83.

497   *"The Magnani part . . .":* Qtd. in Morella and Epstein, *Brando,* p. 76.

497   *"I had no intention . . .":* Qtd. in ibid.

500   *Arthur Krim quickly approved:* Richard Shepherd to PM, who also confirmed that Franciosa was paid his full salary, per Brando's dictates.

502–4   Description of *Fugitive Kind* rehearsals drawn from recollections of Meade Roberts to PM.

504   *"I only know my cue . . .":* Remark recalled by Maureen Stapleton to PM; she is also source for her conversation with Williams.

505   *"Why can't she . . .":* Remark recalled by Richard Shepherd to PM; similar remark made by MB directly to Anna Magnani ("Why don't you shave?") recalled by Sam Shaw to PM.

506   *"She'd tell the cameraman . . .":* Qtd. in Joe Morella and Edward Z. Epstein, *Paul and Joanne* p. 82.

506   *using a clamp:* Incident recounted to PM by associate producer George Justin, who added that while Magnani sometimes played "the grand prima donna, she was absolutely right to be furious" about this suggestion.

506   *"She's like a vacuum cleaner . . .":* MB's remark in phone call to Sam Gilman recalled by Meade Roberts to PM. In interview with PM, Maureen Stapleton recalled MB's making the same "vacuum cleaner" complaint to her.

506   *"a very suspicious man . . .":* Qtd. in Fred Baker, *Movie People,* p. 46.

507   *"maybe a little sophomoric . . .":* Richard Shepherd to PM.

507   *"a sadistic egocentric":* Qtd. in *Los Angeles Mirror,* 8/12/90.

508   *One resident, overhearing him:* Cynthia Fowler, "A Town Remembers," essay for NYU graduate school, May 1985, p. 1.

508   *". . . too good a job . . .":* Qtd. in ibid., p. 15.

511   *"she was very kind to me . . .":* Qtd. in Morella and Epstein, *Paul and Joanne,* p. 82.

511   *"I hated working . . .":* Qtd. in Judith Crist, *Take 22: Moviemakers on Moviemaking,* p. 66.

512   *continued to fly to California:* Thomas, *Brando* pp. 161–62.

513   *"I want to apologize . . .":* Remark recalled by Charles H. Maguire to PM.

514   *"Too much is too much . . .":* *Los Angeles Examiner,* 5/7/60.

514   *"Sordid" and "repelling":* *Los Angeles Times,* 5/7/60.

514   *"mumbling with marbles in his mouth":* *Variety,* 4/13/60.

514   *"This explosive woman . . . rock in my fist":* Qtd. in Morella and Epstein, *Brando,* pp. 76, 78.

514   *"But I haven't got enough time . . .":* Conversation qtd. in Dick Williams, *Los Angeles Mirror,* 8/12/60.

515–16   *"Tell MGM I'll do the picture . . .":* Qtd. in Thomas, *Brando,* p. 164.

516   *"I slapped her twice . . .":* Qtd. in *Los Angeles Times,* 11/19/59.

516   *". . . said child and his mother":* Qtd. in ibid.

517   *Judge Mervyn A. Aggeler:* Ibid.

517   *". . . None of them can stand . . .": Redbook,* December 1959.

517   *"an unidentified woman"* and *"heaped vilification":* Qtd. in *Los Angeles Examiner,* 1/8/60; in Kashfi and Epstein, *Brando for Breakfast,* pp. 156–57, Kashfi identifies the companion as "a twenty-one-year-old half-Hungarian, half-Filipino actress named Barbara Luna."

517   *"the necessity of good faith . . .":* Qtd. in *Los Angeles Examiner,* 1/8/60.

517   *"I'll be damned if I'll spend . . .":* Qtd. in Thomas, *Brando,* p. 164.

518   *"presents a microcosm of man's situation . . .":* Qtd. in ibid., p. 169.

519   *"the only films that interest me . . .":* Qtd. in Bengt Danielsson, "The Truth About the Film on *Bounty,"* Europa-Press AB, Stockholm, 1963, part I, p. 3.

519   *"The goddamn beach is black!":* Bengt Danielsson recalled remark to PM; also qtd. in Danielsson, "The Truth About the Film," part II, p. 1

519   *"was the first and last time . . .":* Danielsson, "The Truth About the Film," part II, p. 2; Danielsson confirmed in interview with PM.

520   *"I always felt an affinity . . .":* Qtd. in Golson, *Playboy Interviews,* p. 612 (originally published in *Playboy,* January 1979).

521   *"Would you like to adopt him?":* Conversation recounted in Kashfi and Stein, *Brando for Breakfast* pp. 157, 180; recalled by Anna Kashfi Brando Hannaford to PM.

521   *"acquired such phrases . . .":* Qtd. in *New York Post,* 10/14/60; see also *Los Angeles Times,* 10/14/60, and Kashfi and Stein, *Brando for Breakfast,* p. 179.

521   *"You are a great artist . . .":* Qtd. in *New York Post,* 10/14/60; see also *Los Angeles Times,* 10/14/60, and Kashfi and Stein, *Brando for Breakfast,* p. 179.

522   *"The picture's got to be spectacular . . .":* Qtd. in Danielsson, "The Truth About the Film," part II, p. 4.

522   *"What about putting in a scene . . .":* Qtd. in ibid., p. 2.

523   *"I love it down here . . .":* Comment recalled by Ridgeway ("Reggie") Callow in interview with author Rudy Behlmer; further remarks and recollections of Callow (now deceased) are also drawn from this transcribed interview, which is part of the oral history collection of the American Film Institute, Los Angeles.

524   *play drums into the night:* Danielsson, "The Truth About the Film," part IV, p. 2; Danielsson confirmed late-night drumming sessions to PM.

527   *"a social or philosophical . . . I want to put over":* MB's comments on script recalled by Bengt Danielsson to PM. See also his "Truth About the Film," part III, p. 2.

528   *". . . a thrilling adventure-story . . .":* Danielsson, "The Truth About the Film," part III, p. 2, and confirmed by Danielsson to PM.

528   *"was always completely sincere . . .":* Danielsson, "The Truth About the Film," part III, p. 3, and confirmed by Danielsson to PM.

529   *to play seaman John Adams:* Jimmy Taylor to PM. Taylor recalled that

the shoot was on hiatus while Rosenberg flew back to Los Angeles with Brando's latest request, which was eventually turned down; see also Thomas, *Brando,* p. 156; MB later insisted that he did not request a change in roles.

530   *"made no attempt . . .":* Danielsson, "The Truth About the Film," part IV, p. 2, and confirmed by Danielsson to PM.

531   *"Put that girl up . . .":* Remark recalled by Dave Cave to PM.

531   *"miles of film":* Jimmy Taylor to PM.

534   *"He's a great politician . . .":* Qtd in Thomas, *Brando,* p. 168.

534   *"Every time Trevor . . .":* Vivienne Knight, *Trevor Howard,* p. 142.

534   *The rivalry grew:* Jimmy Taylor recalled the one-upmanship to PM.

534   *"I can't honestly say . . .":* Qtd. in Thomas, *Brando,* p. 168.

535   *dictatorial but multifaceted:* Bengt Danielsson to PM.

536   *"No, Marlon don't want I see people":* Remark recalled by Gérard Pugin to PM.

536   *"The peppery Puerto Rican actress . . .":* *Los Angeles Mirror,* 4/20/61.

536   *"Don't send your son . . .":* Kashfi and Stein, *Brando for Breakfast,* pp. 181–82, and confirmed by Kashfi to PM.

536–37   *"He told me he had married . . .":* Kashfi and Stein, *Brando for Breakfast,* p. 180, and confirmed by Kashfi to PM.

537   *"Had he forgotten France Nuyen . . .":* Kashfi and Stein, *Brando for Breakfast,* p. 182, and confirmed by Kashfi to PM.

538   *"I don't give a damn . . .":* Qtd. in Gary Carey, *Marlon Brando: The Only Contender,* p. 157.

538   *"No, let's go back to the beginning . . .":* Standoff recalled by Jimmy Taylor to PM.

538   *". . . the whole bloody mess . . .":* Qtd. in Thomas, *Brando,* p. 172.

538   *"Sol, this Brando . . .":* Qtd. in ibid.

538   *"Did you ever hear . . . he came back":* Qtd. in Bill Davidson, "Six Million Dollars Down the Drain: The Mutiny of Marlon Brando," *Saturday Evening Post,* 6/16/62, pp. 21–22.

539   *"The arguments went on . . .":* Qtd. in ibid., p. 21.

540   *"Yes, she was jealous . . .":* Qtd. in *Los Angeles Times,* 6/30/61.

540   *"But I've had no sexual relations . . . lived with her since":* Qtd. in Kashfi and Stein, *Brando for Breakfast,* p. 180.

540   *"hidden away in a box":* Ibid.

540   *"a morally unfit father":* Ibid., p. 181.

540   *"it would have been gratuitously cruel . . .":* Ibid.

541   *"minimize this turmoil . . .":* Qtd. in ibid.

541   *"She couldn't have married . . .":* Qtd in *London Daily Telegraph,* 6/30/61.

542   *"You figure which salary bracket . . .":* Qtd. in Kurt Singer, "Marlon Brando Grows Up," n.d.

542   *"was a bore":* Qtd. in Thomas, *Brando,* p. 168.

543   *"Leo, I have to have money . . .":* Remark recalled by Nick Rutgers to
           PM.
543–44   *"I'll tell you why it cost . . .":* Qtd. in Vernon Scott, "At Last Brando
           Speaks About Costly *Bounty," Los Angeles Mirror,* 9/9/61.
544   *"Shall we dance?":* Carey, *Marlon Brando,* p. 160.
544   *"Dick, you shouldn't have done it":* Qtd. in ibid.
545   *"You're making the biggest mistake . . .":* Qtd. in Davidson, "Six Million
           Dollars."
545   *"For six weeks [Brando] sabotaged . . .":* Hedda Hopper, *Los Angeles
           Times,* 12/7/61.
545   *"That's a pretty damn good picture . . .":* Qtd. in Carey, *Marlon Brando,* p.
           161.
547   *"I am amazed that everything . . .":* Qtd. in Thomas, *Brando,* p. 177.
547   Description of shooting of final scene and comments made by MB and
           Ridgeway Callow drawn from Richard Loving's interview with PM and
           from Callow's interview with Rudy Behmer, oral history collection,
           American Film Institute.
550   *". . . in a professional manner . . .":* *Hollywood Reporter,* 6/25/62.
551   *"There is so much . . .":* Bosley Crowther, *New York Times,* 11/9/62.
552   *". . . a talented actor's revenge . . .":* Stanley Kauffmann, "Twenty Million
           Dollars Worth of Brando," *New Republic,* 12/8/62.
552   *"more eccentric than heroic . . .":* Pauline Kael, *Atlantic Monthly,* March
           1966, p. 74.
553   *"the* Post *settled and gave me some money":* Interview with Marlon
           Brando, *Playboy,* January 1979.
553   *"He was Sam Spiegel's . . .":* Qtd. in ibid.
554   *"Dear Brando, you pious fake . . .":* Letter qtd. with the kind permission
           of Mrs. George Glass.
555   *"MGM is making it difficult . . .":* *Variety,* 12/18/60.

13. *THE SIXTIES (I):* 1962-68

PAGE
560   *"churned out of a subway photo booth":* Gary Carey, *Marlon Brando: The
           Only Contender,* p. 172.
562   *"There are few countries left . . .":* Qtd. in Bob Thomas, *Brando: Portrait of
           the Rebel as an Artist,* pp. 194–95.
563   *"It is the job of the director . . .":* Qtd. in Michel Clerc, *Paris Match,* n.d.
563–64   *". . . one of the many performers . . .":* Qtd. in Kate Cameron, "Table Talk
           with Brando," New York *Sunday News,* 4/14/63.

564   *"children are the most satisfying thing":* Qtd. in Art Buchwald, "The New Brando," New York *Herald Tribune,* 4/27/63.

564   *"kiss your little brother . . .":* Qtd. in Anna Kashfi Brando and E. P. Stein, *Brando for Breakfast,* p. 185.

564–65   *"She could have no logical claim . . .":* Charles Higham, *Brando: The Unauthorized Biography,* p. 219.

565   *"tackled me on the front lawn . . .":* Kashfi and Stein, *Brando for Breakfast,* p. 186; Anna Kashfi Brando Hannaford to PM.

565–66   *one of the callers she frequently:* Anthony Summers, *Goddess,* p. 344.

566   *"When I got . . . out of the room":* Qtd. in Higham, *Brando,* p. 220.

566   *". . . in Rome recently":* Leslie Childe, *Daily Herald* (London), 10/20/62.

566   *suicide attempt seemed to follow the usual pattern:* In 1963, another woman actually did take her life after an affair with Brando, according to her daughter who volunteered to be interviewed after becoming aware that PM was writing this biography. Her mother, she said, was of Mexican descent and had worked as an extra on *Streetcar* and had a walk-on part in *The Ugly American.* The daughter, who was born in 1953, said she recalled Brando's visits to her divorced mother's home throughout the late fifties and early sixties. In September 1963, the mother killed herself with pills and alcohol because she was pregnant with Brando's child, the daughter asserted, and since the actor had "already married someone else" (presumably Movita), she felt she could neither support another child alone nor, as a Catholic, have an abortion. The daughter remembered Brando's coming to the funeral. After the publication of Brando's 1979 *Playboy* interview, the daughter sent Brando a telegram, and he telephoned her, remembering her as a little girl, and asked her to visit at Mulholland. After reassuring him that she was not claiming him as her *own* father, just trying to find out what he knew about her mother, she spent the day with him, and he confirmed his relationship with her mother.

567   *"The amazing odyssey . . .":* Herb Stein, "Brando's Opening Up Creates a Stir," *New York Morning Telegraph,* 5/12/63.

568   *"Directing interests me . . .":* Qtd. in Bob Thomas, "Brando's Farewell," *Newark Evening News,* 6/6/63.

568   *". . . an enemy of the people . . .":* Qtd. in "Brando Burnt Up by Gossip Writers," *New York World-Telegram,* 4/10/63.

568–69   *"Whatever professional dishonor . . .":* Bosley Crowther, *New York Times,* 4/12/63.

569   *"One of his best performances":* New York *Daily News,* 4/12/63.

569   *"stylized, mannered, and artificial acting":* Leo Mishkin, *New York Morning Telegraph,* 4/12/63.

569   *"to reduce injustice in this world":* Shana Alexander, "Rebel with a Cause," *Newsweek,* 3/3/75, p. 74.

569   *"designed to make Brando . . .":* Qtd. in Richard Schickel, *Brando: A Life in Our Times,* p. 147.

572   *"here is the screen's great masochist . . .":* Molly Haskell, "Bandit, Mutineer, and Pervert" (part 8 of "A Myth Steps Down to a Soapbox"), *Village Voice,* 9/6/73.

572   *"I've heard some wild stories . . .":* Conversation qtd. in Thomas, p. 197.

573   *"If an actor can be influential . . .":* James Bacon, "The New Brando: Marlon Turns Sociable to Sell Pictures," *Newark Evening News,* 7/14/63.

573   *She gave birth to a daughter:* Kashfi and Stein, *Brando for Breakfast,* p. 187; see also news reports about Cui's later paternity suit, e.g. *Los Angeles Times,* 7/20/63.

574   *"acute pyelonephritis . . .":* *New York Post,* 7/21/63.

575   *"the child is probably mine":* Cui's allegation that MB made this remark reported in *Los Angeles Times,* 8/7/63.

575   *"wasn't intimate . . .":* Qtd. in *New York Post,* 8/7/63.

575   *"Miss Cui still insists . . .":* Qtd. in *Los Angeles Times,* 8/7/63.

577   *"Who do you think you are . . .":* Incident recounted by Louise Monaco to PM.

580   *"I need the money . . .":* Qtd. in Thomas, *Brando,* p. 198.

581   *"Sixteenth-Century Fucks":* Qtd. in Rock Brynner, *Yul: The Man Who Would Be King,* p. 171.

581   *". . . close friends":* Ibid., p. 172.

581   *studio's inaugural press conference:* Incident described in ibid.

582   *One afternoon he ran amok . . . :* Ibid., p. 173.

584   *"Fox denied . . .":* *Hollywood Reporter,* 11/2/64.

584–85   *"It's like pushing a prune pit . . .":* Qtd. in Thomas, *Brando,* p. 198.

587   *"Looking back, I guess . . . I'd do it for nothing":* Qtd. in Joanne Stang, "Marlon Brando at Forty," *New York Times,* 11/29/64.

587   *"has his pick of directors . . .":* "Unseaworthy," *Newsweek,* 8/23/65.

587   *"Like many another great actor . . .":* Pauline Kael, "Marlon Brando: An American Hero," *Atlantic Monthly,* March 1966, p. 75.

588–89   MB's interview with the young reporter at press conference publicizing *Morituri* is qtd. in Thomas, *Brando,* pp. 199–200.

590   *". . . ran off with our son":* Qtd. in "Brando's Ex Seized in Fight over Son," *New York World-Telegram,* 12/8/64; the Bel Air Sands Hotel incident reported in numerous news reports; see also Higham, *Brando,* pp. 239–41. Kashfi had a somewhat different version of events in *Brando for Breakfast,* pp. 194–96, and in her interview with PM.

590   *"I've spent six years alone . . .":* Qtd. in "Anna's Story," *New York Journal American,* 12/9/64.

590   *". . . great physical harm . . .":* Qtd. in *New York World-Telegram,* 12/8/64.

591   *"a wide, swinging personality . . .":* "Judge Told Tarita's Son Is Brando's," *New York Post,* 2/17/65.

591   *"but I told him to spit it out":* Qtd. in "Witness Tells Anna Kashfi Suicide Hint," *Los Angeles Times,* 2/16/65.

591   *"with the primary purpose . . .":* "Brando Testifies He Married Both Wives in a Family Way," New York *Daily News,* 2/18/65.

591   *"being given away to a woman . . .":* Kashfi and Stein, *Brando for Breakfast,* pp. 1–98.

591–92   Excerpts from Frances Brando Loving's letters to Judge Rittenband quoted from file in Santa Monica District Court, case no. SMD: 8492, "Brando."

593   *Initially Marlon had ducked:* Kashfi and Stein, *Brando for Breakfast,* p. 199.

593   *"psychoneuroses, which at times . . .":* Qtd. in ibid.

593   *fined $200:* Ibid.

594   *"Your mother is wicked . . .":* Christian's alleged remark from Kashfi and Stein, *Brando for Breakfast,* p. 200.

594   *she regained full custody:* court files and many newspaper reports, e.g., "Brando Loses Custody of His Son," New York *Herald Tribune,* 10/1/65.

594   *"barbarous" . . . dependent on drugs:* Qtd. in ibid.

594   *"end up on the cutting-room floor":* Remark recalled by Jocelyn Brando to PM.

595   *"Schizoid . . . a potter's field of banalities":* *Newsweek,* 2/28/66.

595   *"a phony, tasteless movie":* Bosley Crowther, *New York Times,* 2/19/66.

595   *"a liberal sadomasochistic fantasy":* Pauline Kael, *The New Yorker,* 2/26/66.

597   *"Have you ever been in a fight? . . .":* MB's idea for scene recalled by Arthur Penn to PM.

597   *he insisted on more and more makeup:* Leonard Lyons, "The Lyons Den," *New York Post,* 6/30/65; other crew members confirmed this to PM; see also Higham, *Brando,* p. 244.

598   *". . . I'll just take the money . . .":* Qtd. in Thomas, *Brando,* p. 218.

598   *"casual it":* Pat Quinn to PM.

598   *"Five to go yet . . .":* Conversation between MB and Rhodes qtd. in Jeff Brown, "The Making of a Movie," *Holiday,* February 1966, p. 88.

599   *"Here I am . . .":* Qtd. in Elia Kazan, *Elia Kazan: A Life,* p. 750.

607   *"a successful businessman . . . famous actor son":* "Marlon Brando, Sr., 70, Is Dead in Hollywood," New York *Herald Tribune,* 7/19/65.

608   *"had climbed in bed . . .":* Thomas, *Brando,* p. 201.

610   *"Don't tell me about Marlon . . .":* Remark recalled by Walter Seltzer to PM.

612   *"Atta boy, Marlon! . . .":* Incident recounted by James Bridges to PM.

614   *"Jim has just done ..."*: Conversation between MB and Miller recalled by
       James Bridges to PM.

615   *"When I make a movie ..."*: Sidney Furie to PM. Furie's similar remarks
       about MB qtd. in Joe Morella and Edward Z. Epstein, *Brando: The
       Unauthorized Biography*, p. 116.

615   *"Be my guest"*: Conversation between MB and Saxon qtd. in Thomas,
       Brando, p. 203.

616   *"His heart, it bleeds ..."*: Jingle recited by Sidney Furie to PM; see also
       variation qtd. in Thomas, *Brando*, p. 204.

616   *"What the hell ..."*: MB/Furie argument qtd. in Morella and Epstein,
       Brando, p. 116. Sidney Furie also recounted this incident and MB's
       response to PM.

616   *"It takes me a long time ..."*: Qtd. in Morella and Epstein, *Brando*, p. 116,
       and confirmed by Furie to PM.

617   *"somnambulistic"*: Philip Scheuer, *Los Angeles Times*, 9/29/66.

617   *"... another dog ..."*: Pauline Kael, "Wrong Turns," *New Yorker*,
       9/24/66.

617   *"our most powerful young screen actor ..."*: Kael, "Marlon Brando," p. 72.

620   *"I hung out with Marlon ..."*: Qtd. in Robert Shelton, *No Direction
       Home*, pp. 345–46; see also Bob Spitz, *Dylan*, p. 279.

622   *Dr. Robert Kostichek*: UPI dispatch, 4/21/66.

622   *"There goes Soviet Loren!"*: Remark recalled by Jan Lettieri to PM.

622   *"Do you know, you have black hairs ..."*: Sophia Loren claimed MB
       whispered this to her, according to Jerry Epstein, *Remembering Charlie*,
       p. 184.

622   *"You must tell him off ..."*: Qtd. in ibid., p. 179.

622   *"Listen, you son-of-a-bitch ..."*: Qtd. in ibid.

622   *"little boy"*: Ibid.

623   *"I feel content ..."*: Qtd. in Weston Taylor, *News of the World*, 2/20/66.

623   *"My style of acting ... ninety miles an hour"*: Qtd. in Carey, *Marlon
       Brando*, pp. 188–89.

623–24 *"He was a mean man ... a monster of a man"*: Qtd. in interview with
       Marlon Brando, *Playboy*, January 1979, reprinted in G. Barry Golson,
       ed., *The Playboy Interviews*, p. 627.

624   *With other stars he provided*: *News of the World*, 3/12/66.

625   *"as proof of their friendship"*: Incident described in Kathleen Tynan, *The
       Life of Kenneth Tynan*, pp. 320–21.

628   *"It requires a statistician ..."*: Joe Hyams, "Brando," *News of the World*,
       1/1/67.

629   *she paid the insurance bond*: Patricia Bosworth, *Montgomery Clift*, p. 396;
       see also Kitty Kelley, *Elizabeth Taylor*, p. 253.

630   *"Marlon's not finished yet . . ."*: Qtd. in Bosworth, *Montgomery Clift,* p. 400.

630   *"He wasn't sure . . ."*: John Huston, *An Open Book,* pp. 372–73.

631   *"Marlon's immorality . . ."*: Richard Burton diary entry qtd. in Melvyn Bragg, *Richard Burton,* p. 223.

632   *"as little as possible"*: Lawrence Grobel to PM; see also Lawrence Grobel, *The Hustons,* pp. 576–77.

632   *"He gives you about twenty-five feet . . ."*: Qtd. in Chris Hodenfield, "Mondo Brando," *Rolling Stone,* 5/20/76.

632   *"it was* never *the same"*: Grobel, *The Hustons,* p. 581.

632   *"If you remember the scene . . ."*: Qtd. in ibid.

632   *"Later, during the filming . . ."*: Huston, *An Open Book,* p. 373.

633   *"trying to screw . . . propositioning everybody"*: Qtd. in Grobel, *The Hustons,* p. 582.

633   *"If I'd known . . ."*: Qtd. in ibid.

634   *"one of my best pictures . . ."*: Huston, *An Open Book,* p. 374.

634   *"anticlimactic and banal"*: Bosley Crowther, *New York Times,* 10/12/67.

634   *"People weren't willing . . ."*: Qtd. in Grobel, *The Hustons,* p. 583.

635   MB's 10/17/66, and 1/26/67 purchase of Tetiaroa for $270,000 confirmed in records on file in Conservation des Hypothèques, Bureau de Papeete, Tahiti.

638   *"ugly racialism"* and *"arrested development"*: Renata Adler, "*Candy,* Compromises Galore," *New York Times,* 12/18/68.

638   *"For sheer ignominious ineptitude . . ."*: *Newsweek,* 12/30/68.

639   *Kael cited Emerson's description*: Kael, "Marlon Brando," p. 75.

639   *"Marlon has yet to learn . . ."*: Qtd. in Bragg, *Richard Burton,* p. 306.

640   *"Brando was the American challenge . . ."*: William Redfield, "One Might Have Played Hamlet, the Other One Did," *New York Times,* 1/15/67.

640   *"he no longer cared . . ."*: Ibid.

640   *Molly Haskell*: Her essay, "A Myth Steps Down to a Soapbox," appeared in *The Village Voice* in nine parts in 1973: 6/14, 6/21, 6/28, 7/19, 7/26, 8/9, 8/30, 9/6, and 9/20.

643   *reviewers would point to this scene*: See, for example, Molly Haskell, "Taking the Rap for the Rest of Us" (part 9 of "A Myth Steps Down to a Soapbox"), *The Village Voice,* 9/20/73, p. 67.

644   Hubert Cornfield's recollections of directing *Night of the Following Day* and his allegations of what he termed MB's "betrayals" are drawn from his letter to PM, 6/19/94, which is quoted with his kind permission.

645   *"Hey, asshole . . ."*: Qtd. in Thomas, *Brando,* p. 213.

645   Description of MB's behavior in dining room based on notes on file in *Paris Match* reference library, "Brando au Touquet," p. 4.

647   *"The dialogue . . ."*: *Los Angeles Examiner,* 1/22/69.

647   *"never been worse . . ."*: Pauline Kael, *New Yorker,* 3/8/69.

14. **THE SIXTIES (II): 1963–71**

PAGE

648   *"join the romantic adventure . . ."*: Qtd. in Tony Thomas, *The Films of Marlon Brando,* p. 211.

648–49   *"I don't know, but . . ."*: Remark recalled by James Coburn to PM.

649   *at a reduced salary:* "He Shall Return," *New York Times,* 6/16/68.

649   *$750,000:* Salary confirmed by Alberto Grimaldi to PM.

649   *"Because he is not sure . . ."*: Harold Clurman, *All People Are Famous,* p. 261.

649–50   *"I guess everybody came late . . ."*: Qtd. in Vernon Scott, "Brando, Civil Rights Crusader," UPI dispatch, *St. Paul Sunday Pioneer Press,* 6/16/68.

650   *"mumbled a warning . . ."*: Taylor Branch, *Parting the Waters,* p. 805.

650   *"We are on a breakthrough . . ."*: Qtd. in ibid., p. 816.

651   *"I had never met any white man . . ."*: Qtd. in James Campbell, *Talking at the Gates,* p. 80.

651   *it was only Marlon who had replied:* Ibid.

651   *"They speak of prejudice . . ."*: Qtd. in "Brando Says Prejudice Exists in Film Industry," *New York Times,* 7/13/63.

652   *Cambridge, Maryland:* "Brando Says He'll Risk Jail in Cambridge," *New York Post,* 7/17/63.

652   *"She was tired . . ."*: Qtd. in Arthur Berman and Paul Weeks, *New York Post,* 7/21/63.

652   *"I'm sure some of the flowers . . ."*: The housing protest was well covered in the press—see, for example, Ralph Blumenfeld, "Brando Picketing—Despite His Doctor," *New York Post,* 7/28/63; "Brando Joins Pickets at House Trace," *Minneapolis Tribune,* 7/28/63; "Marlon Brando Is Jeered in Rights March on Coast," *New York Times,* 7/28/63.

653   *"We are here as devoted and peaceful representatives . . ."*: Qtd. in "Actors Rebuffed in Alabama Deny 'Rabble-Rousing' Charges," *New York Times,* 8/8/63.

654   *"This is another world . . . George Wallace"*: Qtd. in Stan Koven, "Brando Visits the World of the Alabama Negro," *New York Post,* 8/23/63.

655   *"the role of Mr. Citizen . . ."*: Qtd. in James A. Wechsler, *New York Post,* 2/24/64.

656   *"probably easier . . . racism in the industry"*: Ronald Brownstein, *The Power and the Glitter,* p. 172.

656   *segregated theaters:* New York *Herald Tribune,* 3/10/64; London *Daily Mirror,* 3/11/64.

656   *Christian Marquand: Paris Jour,* 3/11/64. This article referred to Marquand as one of MB's "best supporters" and commented on their "brief and mysterious sojourn" in Paris a few days before the London meeting.

657   *California Indian:* Sam Shaw, *Brando, in the Camera Eye,* pp. 78–79.

658   *"Most people in this country . . .":* Qtd. in "Brando Charges Blackmail of Indians," *New York World-Telegram and Sun,* 1/18/64.

658   *"a campaign of awareness": New York Times,* 1/21/64.

660   *"I tried to tell him . . .":* Qtd. in *Newsweek,* 3/16/64.

660   *"The hell he will . . .":* Qtd. in "Brando Arrested While Leading Indian 'Fish-In,' " AP dispatch, 3/3/64.

660   *Quillayute River:* "Marlon Gets Oopsy in an Indian Canoe," AP dispatch, 3/5/64.

661   *he joined singer Miriam Makeba:* New York *Daily News,* 3/11/64.

661   *". . . Baldwin was a fussy host . . .":* W. J. Weatherby, *James Baldwin,* pp. 270–71.

666   *"I was convinced that Marlon . . .":* Elia Kazan, *Elia Kazan: A Life,* p. 750.

666–67 *"I was meeting . . .":* Ibid., pp. 750–52.

667   *"He was so intense . . . worth and of himself":* Ibid., pp. 752–53; incident also recalled by Elia Kazan to PM.

668   *"J. Edgar Hoover hated black people . . .":* Interview with Marlon Brando, *Playboy,* January 1979, p. 126.

669   *"could be my own son":* Qtd. in *Los Angeles Times,* 4/13/68.

669   *"came out of the house with his hands up . . .": New York Post,* 4/28/71; see also "Brando and the Black Panthers," New York *Daily News,* 5/12/68; *New York Times,* 5/3/69; *Los Angeles Times,* 4/28/71; AP dispatch, 4/29/71.

670   *dye his skin: Newsweek,* 5/18/68.

672   *"There's a tendency for people . . .":* Interview with Marlon Brando, *Playboy,* January 1979, p. 136.

672   *"Understanding prejudice . . .":* Ibid.

673   *he reasserted his full commitment:* Vernon Scott, "Brando Tells Civil Right Role," UPI dispatch, 6/23/68.

673   *lobbying for gun control:* Robert Windeler, "Hollywood Writers and Actors Lead Fight on Movie Violence," *New York Times,* 6/17/68.

674   "I AM IMPATIENT . . .": Qtd. in *Variety,* 5/1/68.

674–75 "Hijacking" incident drawn from news accounts, e.g., *New York Post,*

12/6/68. Brando's own account is qtd. in Lawrence Grobel, *Conversations with Brando,* p. 139; see also Alice Marchak and Linda Hunter, *The Super Secs,* p. 170.

675   *Brando was to play William Walker:* Edward Said, "The Quest for Gillo Pontecorvo," *Interview,* November 1988, p. 1.

676   *"He was very demanding . . .":* Alberto Grimaldo to PM.

676   *"If he wanted a purple smile . . .":* Qtd. in Gary Carey, *Marlon Brando: The Only Contender,* pp. 202–3.

677   *". . . I shouldn't have been so stubborn . . .":* Qtd. in John Francis Lane, "Is Marlon Really Necessary?" *Show,* January 1970, p. 84.

678   *". . . What I would prefer . . .":* Qtd. in Roger Ebert, "Pontecorvo: 'We Trust the Face of Brando,' " *New York Times,* 4/13/69.

686   *"The conflict basically stems from fatigue . . .":* Hank Werba, "Brando Ultimatum Shifts Site . . . at 250G Cost," *Variety,* 6/17/69.

686   *"I did not want to blow . . .":* Interview with Marlon Brando, *Playboy,* January 1979, p. 138.

687   *Grimaldi would later sue:* Confirmed by Alberto Grimaldi to PM.

687–88   *"I've spent ten years . . .":* MB's statements and the description of evening in a nightclub are from Josh Greenfield, "Rapping and Zapping in Morocco with Marlon," *Life,* 3/9/70.

688   *"too intellectual"* and *"playing the classic . . .":* La Stampa and L'Unita reviews qtd. in "Italian Critics Hail Film but Rib Brando," AP dispatch, 12/23/69.

688   *"in some two years . . . antiracist theme":* Ibid.

688   *"one of Brando's finest performances":* Kevin Thomas, "Brando Hero of Burn!" *Los Angeles Times,* 12/16/70.

688   *"many unhappy . . .":* Playboy, January 1971.

688   *"a wonderful picture":* Interview with Marlon Brando, *Playboy,* January 1979, p. 138.

690   *"Oh, let me dream first":* Remark recalled by Alec Ata to PM.

690–91   Description of trip to Tetiaroa drawn from Jocelyn Brando to PM and from Marchak and Hunter, *The Super Secs,* pp. 239–53.

692   *"You didn't have my authorization . . .":* Remark recalled by Dave Cave to PM.

693   *"I was in Paris . . .":* Qtd. in Bob Thomas, *Brando: Portrait of the Rebel as an Artist,* p. 227.

694–95   *"a haven for artists . . .":* Introduction to the 1971 master plan, qtd. in 1983 update of master plan.

696   *World War II landing supply transport:* Description of bringing Caterpillar tractor to Tetiaroa from Bernard Judge interview with PM.

698   *"Wrap a pareu . . .":* Remark recalled by Conrad Hall to PM.

15. THE GODFATHER *AND* LAST TANGO IN PARIS: 1970-73

PAGE

702   *Paramount was euphoric:* See, for example, Rick Setlowe, "Paramount's Gamble Four Years Ago on Mario Puzo Has Really Paid Off," *Variety,* 9/30/70.

702   *"authentic" cast of "unknowns . . .":* Qtd. in Dan Knapp, *Los Angeles Times,* 9/13/69.

702   *"No way . . .":* Qtd. in "The Story Behind *The Godfather*," *Ladies' Home Journal,* June 1972, p. 67.

702   *The decision to go with Coppola:* Andrew Yule, *Life on the Wire,* p. 43.

703   *"He was the only Italian . . .":* Qtd. in Lawrence Grobel, "The Glory Days," *Movieline,* August 1993, p. 57.

703   *Once Coppola came aboard:* Meeting recalled by Mario Puzo to PM; see also "The Story Behind *The Godfather*," p. 67.

703   *Brando's response was low-key:* Bob Thomas, *Brando: Portrait of the Rebel as an Artist,* p. 234.

703   *At Ruddy's insistence:* "The Story Behind *The Godfather*," p. 67.

703   *"I assure you that Marlon . . .":* Qtd. in Michael Goodman and Naomi Wise, *On the Edge,* p. 122.

703–4   *he fell to the floor:* Incident recounted in ibid.

704   *take a screen test:* Joseph Gelmis, "Brando Got *Godfather* Job Only After High-Level Rows," *Newsday,* 6/25/72.

704   *". . . evidence that I was ruined":* Qtd. in Roger Duroule, "Marlon Brando," *Le Dimanche* (Paris), 8/28/72.

704   MB's makeup and *Godfather* "screen test" described by Philip Rhodes in interview with PM; see also Coppola's recollection qtd. in Goodman and Wise, *On the Edge,* p. 123.

705   *"the face of a bulldog . . .":* Qtd. in Thomas, *Brando,* p. 236.

705   *"He looks Italian . . .":* Qtd. in Gary Carey, *Marlon Brando: The Only Contender,* p. 213.

705   *"He's on the incentive plan . . .":* Qtd. in Joyce Haber, "Brando Earns Role on Own Film Test," *Los Angeles Times,* 2/2/71.

710   *"Thank God you were . . .":* Remark recalled by Stephanie Beacham to PM.

710   *the director's more flamboyant ideas:* Ira Zuckerman, *The Godfather Journal,* pp. 8–9.

710   *"Powerful people don't need to shout":* Qtd. in Thomas, *Brando,* p. 239.

711   *"I've always felt . . .":* Qtd. in Peter Biskind, *The Godfather Companion,* p. 22.

712   *"self-destructive bastard"* and Pacino's repeated screen tests are from Yule, *Life on the Wire,* pp. 44–45.

712 "... *I'm a brooder*": Qtd. in Grobel, "Glory Days," p. 57.

713 "*They had been talking*...": Qtd. in Arnold Hano, "When Brando Walked In, Everybody Turned to Stone," *TV Guide,* 11/16/74.

713–14 Description of rehearsal is drawn from Zuckerman, *Godfather Journal,* pp. 37–38, and from Yule, *Life on the Wire,* p. 48, in which Duvall is quoted.

715 "*If they fire you*...": Qtd. in "No 'Mafia' in Script: Godfather Problem," *San Francisco Examiner,* n.d., which is also source for Coppola's "Brando saved my neck ..."

715 *Paramount came close:* Grobel, "Glory Days."

715–16 "*I touched him! I touched him!*": The woman's remark and incidents while shooting scene drawn from Alice Marchak and Linda Hunter, *The Super Secs,* pp. 104–5.

716 "*Tallie's too pretty for the part*": Qtd. in Goodman and Wise, *On the Edge,* p. 129.

716 "*I don't like this scene at all*": Qtd. in Thomas, *Brando,* p. 243.

717 *Montana simply opened his mouth:* Incident recounted in ibid., p. 242.

717–18 "*You said you liked me*...": Qtd. in Bob Thomas, "Comeback of the Rebel," *Playgirl,* May 1974.

718 "*If you know your lines*...": Qtd. in Chris Hodenfield, "Mondo Brando," *Rolling Stone,* 5/20/76.

718 "*Actors like Coppola a lot*...": Qtd. in Biskind, *Godfather Companion,* p. 161.

718 "*I could understand how*...": Qtd. in "*The Godfather:* Triumph for Brando," *Newsweek,* 3/13/72.

718–19 *The major blowup between Willis and Coppola:* Incident recounted by Gordon Willis to PM.

720 "*Why didn't anyone tell me?*...": Remark recalled by Al Ruddy to PM.

720–21 Mooning incidents drawn from several accounts, including Zuckerman, *Godfather Journal,* pp. 79–80, and Marchak and Hunter, *The Super Secs,* pp. 106–8.

721–22 Stretcher incident recalled by Gordon Willis to PM.

723 Al Ruddy's conversation with MB about schedule delay recalled in his interview with PM.

724 "*incomprehensible attitudes*" and "*open hostility*": Alberto Grimaldi qtd. in "Italy Film Firm Sues Brando for $700,000," *Los Angeles Times,* 8/5/70, which also itemized Grimaldi's assertions of MB's behavior resulting in monetary damages; lawsuit further described by Grimaldi to PM.

726 *Brando was whispering obscenities:* Zuckerman, *Godfather Journal,* p. 117.

727 "*Have you any idea*...": Yule, *Life on the Wire,* p. 49.

727 "*From Brando I learned to come late*": "The Story Behind *The Godfather,*" p. 67.

727   "*Just once, I would like...*": Qtd. in Thomas, *Brando*, p. 246.

728–29   Luigi Luraschi phone call to Alice Marchak, frozen assets, and MB's "Figure something out" are drawn from Marchak and Hunter, *The Super Secs*, p. 131.

729   "*in great despair*"... "*In Bacon you see...*": Qtd. in Joseph Gelmis, "Talking *Tango* with Bertolucci," *Newsday*, 2/11/73.

730   "*He made me into the pig...*": Qtd. in Biskind, *Godfather Companion*, p. 25.

730   "*one of the most powerful statements...*": Qtd. in "*The Godfather:* Triumph for Brando."

730   "*He'd taken out...*": Qtd. in Grobel, "Glory Days," p. 57.

730   "*Marlon was desperately in need of $100,000...*": Qtd. in ibid., p. 58.

731   *Movita promptly filed suit:* Joyce Haber, "Brando, Ex-Wife Movita in Court Clash," *Los Angeles Times*, 7/3/72.

731–32   Kashfi's actions and Christian's problems as a child drawn from transcript of Virginia Harding's testimony in Christian Brando sentencing hearing, 2/28/91, pp. 234–35.

732   "*I found bottles of Jack Daniel's...*": Qtd. from ibid., pp. 245–46.

734   "*Disagreement?...*": Qtd. in "Swift Exit for Brando," *Los Angeles Times*, 10/28/71.

734   "*Let's talk about ourselves...*": Qtd. in "*Tango:* The Hottest Movie," *Newsweek*, 2/12/73.

734   "*I tried to develop... incredibly intelligent*": Qtd. in ibid.

734–35   "*Finished scripts are only necessary...*": Qtd. in New York *Sunday News*, 1/21/73.

735   "*An angel as a man...*": Qtd. in "Self-Portrait of an Angel and Monster," *Time*, 1/22/73.

736   "*It was a great synchronization...*": Qtd. in Mel Gussow, "Bertolucci Indicts *Last Tango* Indictment as Obscene," *New York Times*, 2/2/73.

736   "*He was so wonderful...*": Qtd. in Sally Quinn, "New York in 4/4 Time," *Washington Post*, 2/16/73.

736–37   Turndowns from Paramount and MGM from Peter Bart, *Fade Out*, p. 42.

737   "*That's four thousand dollars...*": Qtd. in Biskind, *Godfather Companion*, p. 24.

738   *Alice Marchak:* Marchak and Hunter, *The Super Secs*, p. 132.

738   "*...He started at such a violent pitch...*": Qtd. in Guy Flatley, "Bertolucci Is All Tangoed Out," *New York Times*, 2/11/73.

738–39   "*I'm a catastrophe...*": Remark recalled by Fernand Moskowitz to PM.

739   "*I make documentaries on actors...*": Qtd. in Joseph Gelmis, *The Film Director as Superstar*, pp. 119–20.

740   "*She was a Lolita... more natural...*": Qtd. in "Self-Portrait of an Angel and Monster."

740   First meeting of Maria Schneider and MB, including conversation, drawn from ibid. and from Judy Klemesrud, "Maria Says Her *Tango* Is Not Blue," *New York Times,* 2/4/73.

741   *"He knows what he wants to achieve . . .":* Qtd. in publicity release for *Last Tango in Paris,* United Artists, 1973 (Walter Alford, publicist).

741   *"Nearly every morning . . .":* Qtd. in Christina Kirk, "That Girl in *Tango,*" New York *Daily News,* 1/28/73.

742   *"I never felt any sexual attraction . . .":* Qtd. in ibid.

742   *"I decided that to suggest . . .":* Qtd. in "Self-Portrait of an Angel and Monster."

742   *". . . The picture is half-done . . .":* Qtd. in Marchak and Hunter, *The Super Secs,* p. 132.

743   *"I wanted to show it as . . .":* Qtd. in "*Tango:* The Hottest Movie."

743   *"I finally cut it out . . .":* Qtd. in "Last Tango in Paris," *Film Facts* 16, no. 1 (1973).

743   *"I want you to screw Maria . . .":* Conversation between Bertolucci and MB qtd. in Leo Janos, "The Private World of Marlon Brando," *Time,* 5/24/76.

743   *". . . I don't think Bertolucci . . .":* Qtd. in Hodenfield, "Mondo Brando."

743–44 *"Actresses and actors . . .":* Qtd. in Flatley, "Bertolucci Is All Tangoed Out."

744   *"we're both bisexual . . .":* Qtd. in Leonard Probst, "Maria Schneider of Last Tango," *Village Voice,* 2/8/73.

744   *"got worried about taboos . . .":* Qtd. in Tom Donnelly, "The Arts," *Los Angeles Times,* 3/3/74.

744   *"Well, he came as close . . .":* Qtd. in Hodenfield, "Mondo Brando."

744   *"How about I take . . .":* Limping incident recounted by Fernand Moskowitz to PM.

745   *Schneider's rear end:* "*Tango:* The Hottest Movie."

745   *"Instead of entering the character . . .":* Qtd. in "Self-Portrait of an Angel and Monster."

745   *"Forty years of Brando's life . . .":* Qtd. in ibid.

746   Giselle Fermine recalled her first meeting and subsequent friendship with Anna Kashfi to PM.

746   *". . . I was screaming . . .":* Fermine repeated Kashfi's story to PM.

747   *"Devi, it was evident . . .":* Anna Kashfi Brando and E. P. Stein, *Brando for Breakfast,* p. 242.

747–48 Kashfi's failure to return Christian to school and subsequent events during kidnapping incident drawn from ibid., and from Kashfi interview with PM, Fermine interview with PM, and court testimony in subsequent custody hearing.

748   *In later court testimony, Garey insisted:* Kashfi and Stein, *Brando for Breakfast,* p. 243.

748   *A screaming brawl:* Giselle Fermine to PM.

749   *he headed for Los Angeles:* New York *Daily News,* 3/10/72 and 3/11/72.

749   *drunk and disorderly charge:* New York *Daily News,* 3/10/72; see also Kashfi and Stein, *Brando for Breakfast,* p. 245.

749–50   Jay J. Armes's finding of Christian and James Wooster's admission that he and his cohorts had expected $10,000 are drawn from Armes's court testimony; Charles Higham, *Brando: The Unauthorized Biography,* pp. 280–81; and Kashfi and Stein, *Brando for Breakfast,* pp. 245–46.

750   *The judge postponed the hearing:* Time, 3/27/72.

750   *"very, very afraid of being kidnapped again":* Bill Cable to PM.

750   *"He never really liked to go . . .":* Steve Hunio to PM.

751   *"If the movie was about the military . . .":* Qtd. in "The Making of *The Godfather,"* Time, 3/13/72.

751   *"one of the most brutal . . .":* Vincent Canby, "Bravo, Brando's Godfather," *New York Times,* 3/12/72.

751   *"The role of Don Vito Corleone . . .":* Pauline Kael, "Alchemy," *New Yorker,* 3/18/72.

752   *". . . enhanced by our knowledge . . .":* Allen McKee, "Brando's Godfather," *New York Times,* 8/20/72.

752   *"Brando's heresy is that he refuses . . . his earlobe a little":* Shana Alexander, "The Grandfather of All Cool Actors Becomes the Godfather," *Life,* April 1971, pp. 40–42.

753   *"Success has made my life . . .":* Qtd. in "*The Godfather:* Triumph for Brando."

753   *"He could wind up . . .":* "Trade Sees Brando *Godfather* Share Maybe $1,500,000," *Variety,* 5/10/72.

754   *a certain "annuity":* New York *Times,* 4/9/72.

755   *"I don't know how . . .":* MB and Bertolucci conversation recounted by Bertolucci in "*Tango:* The Hottest Movie."

756   *"Give me some reminiscences . . .":* Qtd. in Flatley, "Bertolucci Is All Tangoed Out."

756   *"that made me think about milking . . .":* Qtd. in Hodenfield, "Mondo Brando."

758   *"I had the feeling . . .":* Qtd. in Flatley, "Bertolucci Is All Tangoed Out."

758–59   The account of the shooting of the dance hall scene is drawn from interviews by Fernand Moskowitz and Jean-David Lefebvre with PM. See also Sydney Edwards, "The Regenerated Brando," *San Francisco Chronicle and Examiner,* 4/30/72.

760   *"I will never make . . .":* Qtd. in "*Tango:* The Hottest Movie." Bertolucci added that MB told him, "I was completely and utterly violated by you" (ibid.). See also MB qtd. in Gussow, "Bertolucci Indicts *Last Tango* Indictment": "That's the last time I use up my energies."

760   *". . . Tahiti or the desert":* Qtd. in Hodenfield, "Mondo Brando."

760   *Brando returned to court with Christian: New York Times,* 5/9/72; Anna Kashfi Brando Hannaford to PM.

760   *Fernauld, a private school:* Christian Brando probation report and MB testimony in transcript of Christian Brando sentencing hearing, pp. 246–47.

760   *she claimed that it was his habit:* Steve Dunleavy, "Anna and the King of I Am," *News of the World,* 7/30/72.

761   *"We need him in Rome . . .":* Grimaldi's phone call and MB agreement to do looping drawn from Marchak and Hunter, *The Super Secs,* pp. 133–35.

761   *To circumvent the censors: Variety,* 9/27/72.

761–62   *"the most powerfully erotic film ever made . . .":* Pauline Kael, "Tango," *New Yorker,* 10/28/72.

762   *"sometimes brave . . .":* Vincent Canby, "Film Festival: *Last Tango in Paris," New York Times,* 10/16/72.

762   *the case goes to trial:* The case was ultimately dismissed by Italy's highest tribunal. See *"Last Tango* Cleared by Italy High Court," *New York Times,* 12/21/73.

762   *amounted to more than $100,000:* Mel Gussow, *New York Times,* 2/2/73.

762   *"the perfect macho soap opera . . .":* Grace Glueck, "I Won't Tango, Don't Ask Me," *New York Times,* 3/18/73.

763   *Admission to the film:* Quinn, "New York in 4/4 Time."

763   *the actress's "unnecessary revelations . . .":* "Movie Mailbag," *New York Times,* 2/25/73.

763   *"If you ask me about the fact . . .":* Qtd. in *"Tango:* The Hottest Movie."

763   *"I have no idea what . . .":* Qtd. in Hodenfield, "Mondo Brando."

764   *"traces of a drug . . .": New York Times,* 2/16/73.

765   *"if the family is able to reach . . .":* Ibid.

766   *"He was my brother . . .":* Qtd. in Janos, "The Private World of Marlon Brando."

16. **THE AMERICAN INDIAN MOVEMENT: 1972–76**

PAGE

769   *"Archerd yelled . . .":* Army Archerd's remark and backstage encounter with Sacheen Littlefeather both recalled by Howard Koch to PM.

769   *"I'm Apache . . .":* Qtd. in Mason Wiley and Damien Bona, *Inside Oscar,* pp. 477–78.

770   *"For two hundred years . . .":* Qtd. in Bob Thomas, *Brando: Portrait of the Rebel as an Artist,* pp. 263–65.

771   *"as sincere as anyone . . .":* Andrew Sarris, *Village Voice,* 4/5/73.

771   *"The simple answer is . . .":* Qtd. in Jerry Tallmer, "Faces Turned Pale," *New York Post,* 3/31/73.

771–72   Background of Sacheen Littlefeather from her interview with PM as well as Joan Smith, "Young Once, Indian Forever," *San Francisco Examiner (Image Magazine),* 7/3/88.

772–74   Littlefeather's meetings with MB and preparations for Oscar speech recalled by her to PM.

774   *"He's gonna win, Alice . . .":* Qtd. in Peter H. Brown and Jim Pinkston, *Oscar Dearest,* p. 141.

776–77   Background of Dennis Banks and Russell Means drawn from their interviews with PM and from Peter Matthiessen, *In the Spirit of Crazy Horse.*

777   Background of other AIM activists and description of their involvement in Wounded Knee from interviews with PM.

778   *"like Dien Bien Phu . . .":* Qtd. in *Voices from Wounded Knee,* p. 187.

779   *"The 1868 treaty . . .":* Matthiessen, *In the Spirit of Crazy Horse,* p. 83.

780   *they had driven to Trona:* Anna Kashfi Brando and E. P. Stein, *Brando for Breakfast,* p. 254.

780–81   *"I saw Marlon as a man . . .":* Sasheen Littlefeather to PM; see also Brown and Pinkston, *Oscar Dearest,* p. 148.

781   *in July 1973 Brando took a trip:* New York *Times,* 7/24/73.

782   *"a mystery woman":* Peter Citron, "Marlon Brando Hunts Boyhood Home in Omaha," *Omaha World-Herald,* 7/23/73; see also "Brando's Birthplace," *Omaha World-Herald,* 9/13/73.

782   *"He has been taken from me . . .":* Qtd. in Steve Dunleavy, "Anna and the King of I Am," *News of the World,* 7/30/72.

782   *"I agree 100 percent . . .":* Qtd. in "Indian Reservation," *London Daily Mail,* 4/3/73.

782   *"dropped his pants . . .":* Kashfi and Stein, *Brando for Breakfast,* p. 247.

783   *"Mom, I can't live up there . . .":* Remark recalled by Anna Kashfi Brando Hannaford to PM.

783   *"usually Alice who dealt . . .":* Steve Hunio to PM.

784   *"I came to give my support . . .":* Qtd. in "Brando Comes to St. Paul to Support AIM Defendants," *Minneapolis Tribune,* 1/26/74.

786   Script conferences and discussion about "Today" show recalled by Mark Lane and Abby Mann to PM.

787   *he had quietly donated:* "Gift to AIM Disclosed," *Minneapolis Star,* 1/26/74.

788   *Judge Frederick Nichol:* Matthiessen, *In the Spirit of Crazy Horse,* p. 89.

788–89   Background of Louis Moves Camp, story behind his testimony, and his mother's testimony are drawn from ibid., pp. 93–97, and Mark Lane interview with PM.

789   *he and Mann invited Judge Nichol:* "Brando Buys Lunch for Judge," *Minneapolis Star-Tribune,* 9/15/74; conversation at lunch recalled by Abby Mann to PM.

789   *"the FBI, which I have revered . . .":* Qtd. in Matthiessen, *In the Spirit of Crazy Horse,* p. 99.

791   *Christian was arrested:* Confirmed in LAPD records cited in "Christian Brando Probation Report," 1990; MB's "lecture" based on 1974 arresting officer's recollection to Detective Andrew R. Monsue in 1990, who recounted description to PM.

792   *"One time Jack caught . . .":* Bill Cable related Christian's description of the incident to PM.

792–93   *Brando took the extraordinary step:* "Wiring" of Christian's room and his response drawn from MB testimony, Christian Brando sentencing hearing, February 26–28, 1991.

795   *"I think giving up all my land . . .":* Qtd. in *Los Angeles Times,* 12/29/74.

796   *" 'Over my dead body' . . .":* "Sister Resists Brando Plan to Give His Land to Indians," *Los Angeles Times,* 12/30/74.

796   *"it's safe to assume . . .":* Qtd. in *Los Angeles Times,* 1/4/75.

796   *"I don't believe in honors . . .":* Qtd. in Jana Miller, "Hearings Make Brando 'Proud' of Native Nebraska," *Lincoln Star,* 2/18/74; see also Charles Higham, *Brando: The Unauthorized Biography,* p. 291.

797   *he tossed the . . . garment:* Dan Ladley recalled incident to PM.

797–98   Background of Menominee dispute and takeover of Alexian abbey drawn from interviews with those Warrior Society members qtd. in text, as well as from Dennis Banks and Russell Means; see also Matthiessen, *In the Spirit of Crazy Horse,* pp. 119–20, 139, 584–85.

799   *Marlon was as ill equipped:* Madison *Capital Times,* 1/31/75; interviews with Menominee Warrior Society also confirmed MB's attire to PM.

799   *to raise the $750,000:* Madison *Capital Times,* 1/31/75.

800   *Riding with them was Reverend James Groppi:* New York *Daily News,* 2/1/75.

802   *"I was up on the roof . . .":* Interview with Marlon Brando, *Playboy,* January 1979, p. 132.

803   *The governor ordered . . . white farmer was shot:* *Wisconsin State Journal,* 2/2/75.

803   *Two hours of shooting:* "Shooting Breaks Out near Novitiate, Indians Sign Agreement," *Shawano* (Wis.) *Evening Leader,* 2/3/75; "Indians Evacuate Alexian Novitiate," *Shawano Evening Leader,* 2/4/75; "Guard Evacuates Indians Peacefully After 34-Day Occupation of Abbey," *New York Times,* 2/4/75.

803   *"They were shooting bullets . . .":* Interview with Marlon Brando, *Playboy,* January 1979, p. 132.

803   *was voluntarily returned:* Madison *Capital Times,* 2/21/75.

804   Standing behind Means: "Brando Posts Bond for Means," Minneapolis Tribune, 4/17/75.

804   "You're going to have to kill us!...": Qtd. in Voices from Wounded Knee, p. 136.

806   MB's speech at Graham's fund-raiser and his reaction drawn from Bill Graham and Robert Greenfield, Bill Graham Presents, pp. 370–73.

806   "become very suspicious...": Elia Kazan, Elia Kazan: A Life, p. 753.

807   Mooning incident with Gillo Pontecorvo recalled by Dennis Banks to PM.

807   "They scared the shit...": Qtd. in Kashfi and Stein, Brando for Breakfast, p. 256.

808   "There were political problems...": Qtd. in Daily Mirror (London), 10/18/74.

808   Visit to John Foreman's apartment recalled by Dennis Banks to PM.

809–10   Background of shoot-out at Oglala drawn from Matthiessen, In the Spirit of Crazy Horse, pp. 136–92, and PM interviews with Dennis Banks and Leonard Peltier.

812   "I've sunk millions in this project...": Qtd. in Jim Watters, "I Just Want to Be Normally Insane," New York Times, 9/21/75.

812   "She's the daughter of...": Qtd. in Moira Hodgson, "I Saw Marlon Brando Shoot Jack Nicholson," Vogue, December 1975.

812   "Another day, another twenty-one grand": Qtd. in ibid.

812   "Has God's gift...": Qtd. in ibid.

813   "learned, human...a really neat man": Qtd. in Sheila Wheeler, "Hollywood on the Range," New Times, 5/14/76.

813   "was absolutely full of it": Qtd. in Joseph McBride, "Author McGuane Says Brando-Nicholson Breaks Behavior 'Willful and Capricious,' " Variety, 5/11/76.

813   "I always wondered why...": Qtd. in Leo Janos, "The Private World of Marlon Brando," Time, 5/24/76.

814   even McGuane conceded: Qtd. in McBride, "Author McGuane Says Brando-Nicholson."

814   "out of control...movie that surrounds him": Vincent Canby, "Missouri Breaks, Offbeat Western," New York Times, 5/20/76.

815   "thus far failed to find...": Qtd. in Paul Zimmerman, "Back in the Saddle," Newsweek, 8/11/75.

815   "They're probably monitoring...": Qtd. in Chris Hodenfield, "Mondo Brando," Rolling Stone, 5/20/76.

815   "Get my gun!...": Remarks recalled by Dennis Banks to PM.

817   Description of Oregon state troopers stopping Dennis Banks, Leonard Peltier, and others is drawn from PM interviews with Banks, Peltier, and Bruce Ellison, and from Matthiessen, In the Spirit of Crazy Horse, pp. 253–58.

817   Weapons found, MB ownership of motor home and station wagon, and inventoried list of MB credit cards and airline tickets confiscated confirmed in FBI memo, "To Bureau and All SAC; From Rapid City (70-10239) (P)," 11/14/75. The memo informed "all bureaus" that Banks and Peltier were "fugitives" and that they "and any companions should be considered extremely armed and dangerous."

818   *"The decision may come down . . .":* Dennis Banks recalled his conversation with MB and his decision to go to Tetiaroa to PM.

819   *Brando and Abby Mann visited:* Abby Mann recalled visits and his lobbying efforts to PM.

819   *". . . Even sympathetic liberals . . .":* Liz Smith, "Brando's Zeal Is Showing," New York *Daily News,* 4/9/76.

821   *already bent every rule:* Matthiessen, *In the Spirit of Crazy Horse,* pp. 277–83; and PM interviews with Leonard Peltier and Bruce Ellison. Description of trial drawn from Matthiessen, *In the Spirit of Crazy Horse,* pp. 290–319.

821   *"historic verdict":* Matthiessen, *In the Spirit of Crazy Horse,* p. 318.

821–22   MB's visit to trial and discussion of whether he should testify recalled by Bruce Ellison, Leonard Peltier, and Bob Robideau to PM.

822   *Internal FBI documents:* 6/27/75, File #MP70-10239, by SA Frederick Coward Jr., SA Vincent Louis Breci, SA J. Gary Adams [JGA:arw], dictated 6/29/75. Airtel/Confidential, 8/7/75, from SAC, Chicago, to Director, FBI. Daily Summary Teletype, 7:28 P.M., 8/13/75, from Rapid City, S.D., to Director, All Offices via Washington, Albuquerque, Butte, Denver, Detroit, Los Angeles, Milwaukee, Minneapolis, Oklahoma City, Omaha, Phoenix, Seattle. 11/14/75, to All Offices via Washington, from Rapid City. 2/20/76, Portland, Oregon; File #PD89-94, by SA Steven L. Hancock, SA Wayne C. Barlow [SLH:csa], dictated 2/17/76.

822   *the FBI's identification division:* 1/28/76, File #89-3229; to SAC Sacramento, re: RESMURS. 3/11/76, File #89-3229; to SAC Portland, re: RESMURS. 4/6/76, re: RESMURS.

823   *"such information not be sent . . .":* 11/14/75, File #DN70-4448, title RESMURS, interviewed 11/14/75, Salem, Oregon, dictated 11/21/75, SAC Theodore P. Rosack, Denver.

823   *"No, I am not the guilty one . . .":* Qtd. in Matthiessen, *In the Spirit of Crazy Horse,* p. 370.

17. *TAHITI: 1972-83*

PAGE

827   *"for some stupid reason":* Remark recalled by Taylor "Tap" Pryor to PM.

831   *". . . those who travel . . .":* National Tattler, 11/17/74.

831–32   Tape of MB conversation with Stewart Brand and Jay Baldwin transcribed and published in *The CoEvolution Quarterly,* Winter 1975, pp. 60–69.

836   *"I, too, have had . . .":* Qtd. in Gary Carey, *Marlon Brando: The Only Contender,* p. 250.

836   *"I am convinced the world . . .":* Qtd. in Leo Janos, "The Private World of Marlon Brando," *Time,* 5/24/76.

838   *"I've got to do this movie . . .":* Qtd. in Charles Higham, "Coppola's Vietnam Movie Is a Battle Royal," *New York Times,* 5/15/77.

838–39   Background of casting and financing *Apocalypse Now* drawn from Eleanor Coppola, *Notes on the Making of "Apocalypse Now";* Peter Cowie, *Coppola;* Michael Goodwin and Naomi Wise, *On the Edge.*

839   *Costs were rising:* Ibid. and in Higham, "Coppola's Vietnam Movie."

840   *Coppola returned to his home in Napa:* Goodman and Wise, *On the Edge,* p. 224, and Coppola, *Notes,* pp. 85–91.

841   *"I think he should be . . .":* Conversation between MB and Francis Coppola qtd. in Coppola, *Notes,* p. 128.

842   *". . . I may not know . . .":* Qtd. in Goodwin and Wise, *On the Edge,* p. 228.

844   *"delusions of grandeur" . . . "foolish pretensions":* Vincent Canby, "The Screen: *Apocalypse Now,*" *New York Times,* 9/15/79.

844   *"This man has become . . .":* David Denby, "Hollow Movie," *New York,* 8/27/79.

844   *"Gee, I don't know . . .":* Qtd. in *People,* 9/3/79.

844   *"I know . . . because we pay . . .":* Qtd. in Cowie, *Coppola,* p. 132.

845   *"I have a right . . .":* Qtd. in Carey, *Marlon Brando,* pp. 258–59.

845   *identified himself as "Mike":* See also "A Ham to the Very End," *Daily Express* (London), 11/14/79, in which it is reported that MB also used the name "Marcos" when making his calls.

848   *to play Jor-El as a "green suitcase":* "Dialogue on Film: Richard Donner," *American Film* 6, no. 7 (May 1981), p. 62.

848   *Coppola seconded this assessment:* Ibid.

848   *"Who knows? . . .":* Qtd. in "About the Production," Warner Bros., 1978.

848   *"When he finished . . .":* Qtd. in ibid.

848   *"In fact, Brando was . . .":* Qtd. in ibid.

848   *"I had even been figuring . . .":* Donner's awareness of MB's tight schedule and their conversation qtd. in Roderick Mann, "Superman Makes the Leap to the Screen," *Los Angeles Times,* 7/31/77.

849   *"solemn intonations" to "an old Vic ..."*: Andrew Sarris, *Village Voice*, 12/25/78.

849   *He also petitioned the Los Angeles Superior Court*: Los Angeles Times, 12/18/78.

849   *On December 26*: Los Angeles Times, 12/26/78; *Variety*, 12/27/78.

849   *new scheme of scooping algae*: MB explanation of project qtd. in Victor Davis, *Daily Express* (London), 5/2/77.

849–50 *"I didn't have any money ..."*: Qtd. in Lawrence Grobel, *Conversations with Brando*, p. 174.

851   *"Why don't you ever call me? ..."*: Conversation recalled by Everett Greenbaum to PM.

852   Background of *Playboy* interview described by Lawrence Grobel to PM; see also Grobel's introduction in his *Conversations with Brando*.

853   *Mann's scripts were "really bad"*: Qtd. in *Conversations with Brando*, p. 131.

853   *"I could open this up ..."*: Qtd. in ibid., p. 168.

853   *"vital in respect to ... It's the same old story"*: MB letter qtd. in ibid., pp. 171–72.

853   *"the success of 'Roots' ..."*: Qtd. in Victor Davis, *Daily Express* (London), 5/2/77.

853   *"he didn't want to play a nice guy"*: Qtd. in *Newsweek*, 12/11/78.

858   *"neurotic, a bisexual, a bigot ..."*: Qtd. in New York *Daily News*, 9/25/79.

858   *"quite perturbed about the book"*: Qtd. in New York *Daily News*, 8/31/79.

858   *he had retreated to his Oregon*: Jack Martin, *New York Post*, 10/19/79.

859   *"portraying the energy cartel ..."*: Qtd. in *New York Times*, 5/30/80.

859   *"But you've sold me"*: Qtd. in Roderick Mann, "Brando and Scott Mix in Formula," *Los Angeles Times*, 11/23/80, which also recounts the meeting as described by Steve Shagan (Avildsen later disputed this version).

859   *"It was Patton meets the godfather"*: Qtd. in ibid.

859   *"What are you going to ..."*: Conversation between Scott and MB qtd. in Tom Buckley, "At the Movies," *New York Times*, 5/30/80.

860   *"I think it's poison ..."*: Qtd. in *New York*, 12/8/80; *Variety*, 1/7/80.

860   *left on the cutting-room floor*: Playgirl, April 1981.

860   *"Appearing grotesquely fat ..."*: Variety, 12/3/80.

860   *he made arrangements to divide*: Reassignment documents filed in Conservation des Hypothèques, Bureau de Papeete, Tahiti, 9/20/79.

865   *Quincy Jones*: Wallace Terry, " 'Your Real Home Is Within,' " *Parade Magazine*, 11/18/90.

867   *"You know something? ..."*: Conversation between tourist and Tarita recalled by Al Prince to PM.

868   *"Everybody's looking for the one ..."*: Qtd. in Chris Hodenfield, "Mondo Brando," *Rolling Stone*, 5/20/76.

18. *THE EIGHTIES:* 1982-89

PAGE

869 *"... in search of true love":* Qtd. in Chris Rodley, "Marlon, Madness, and Me," *Time Out 20/20,* April 1989, p. 44.

869 *The film was to be called:* MB's description of plot in Lawrence Grobel, *Conversations with Brando,* pp. 178–81.

870 *an affair with a young woman:* Donald Cammell confirmed this in Rodley, "Marlon, Madness, and Me."

870 *threats on behalf of the family ... apologize:* Ibid., p. 44.

870 *"a very enticing premise" ... "He felt completely happy ...":* Ibid., pp. 44–45, and confirmed by Donald Cammell to PM.

870 *"He changed his mind ...":* Qtd. in Rodley, "Marlon, Madness, and Me," p. 45, and confirmed by Cammell to PM.

871 *"He maintained that he couldn't read it ...":* Qtd. in Rodley, "Marlon, Madness, and Me," p. 46, and confirmed by Cammell to PM.

872 *explanations for the ... lawyer's suicide:* Rian Malan, "The Final Deal: The Last Days and Shattering Death of a Hollywood Power Broker," *California,* December 1982.

872 *In the harsh afternoon sunlight:* Michael Leahy, "The Day the Pressure Cooker Blew," *Los Angeles,* January 1983.

872 *"made more money ...":* London *Daily Mirror,* 4/8/82.

872 *"I got fourteen million dollars ...":* Qtd. in Grobel, *Conversations with Brando,* p. 173.

872 *Strategically, Brando's timing:* Michael Goodman and Naomi Wise, *On the Edge,* pp. 345–47.

873 *would be more corporations:* As with MB's Black Elk Inc., a corporation established in 1976, he was nostalgic in choosing his corporations' titles: Peavine was named for sister Fran's rambunctious horse back in Libertyville, while Pipestone Inc. took its name from the material traditionally used by Plains Indians for sacred ceremonial pipes.

874 *"A former actress has filed ...":* London *Daily Mail,* 12/20/82 (from *Mail* correspondent in Los Angeles); see also *Washington Post,* 4/17/82.

875 *On December 3, 1983, he was arrested:* LAPD CLETS and DMV (91/10/91), Adult History: 12/3/83, LAPD—602 (K) (1) PC (Trespass; posted landmark; refused to leave—No dispo. shown).

876 *he was kicked out for "noncompliance":* According to "Christian Brando Probation Report," 1990, part of court record for sentencing hearing, February 26–28, 1991.

880 *assigning bookcase rows and shelf numbers:* The books were assigned to categories—for example, biography, civil rights, environment, law, politics, encyclopedias and other reference works; they were then organized and cataloged by shelf and row number. Prominent among

the specified sections were art, music, philosophy (both western and eastern), and psychology, the latter including volumes of writings by Freud, Karen Horney, Jung, R. D. Laing, Rollo May, and Wilhelm Reich. The poetry selection began with *1001 Yiddish Proverbs* and then ran to hundreds of volumes, including haiku and Chinese love poetry, collections of John Donne, Matthew Arnold, A. E. Houseman, Robert Frost, T. S. Eliot, Carl Sandburg, Dylan Thomas, *The Iliad,* and *The Odyssey,* and the complete Pelican Shakespeare. A major portion of shelves nearby was taken up with "intelligence"—a grouping that contained numerous works on the CIA as well as *The Pentagon Papers,* Frank Snepp's *Decent Interval,* a history of British intelligence, LeCarré's spy novels, and assorted books on spying and tradecraft. Close by was a shelf grouping labeled "mischief," which included *Getting Even II, Exotic Weapons, Methods of Disguise, Wiretapping and Electronic Surveillance,* and *How to Investigate Your Friends and Enemies.* There were scores of titles on Native Americans and Zen. In the fifth segment of shelves were all the "health" books, which ranged from well-known, best-selling diet books to studies of biofeedback, mediation, and "altered states of consciousness" and "tag-end" volumes, such as *The Power of Alpha Thinking, Life with Women and How to Survive It,* two copies of Norman Cousins's *Anatomy of an Illness, Medical Diseases in Tropical and Subtropical Areas,* two copies of Spock's *Baby and Child Care, A Child's Handbook on Divorce,* and Montessori's *Discovery of the Child.*

881   *$35.2 million:* See estimates in "Marlon's Millions: Acting for Dollars," *Entertainment Weekly,* 10/2/92, p. 28.

883   *"The black guy says . . .":* Bill Cable recalled Christian Brando's description of incident to PM; see also MB's own comment, "I've pointed loaded guns at people," qtd. in Grobel, *Conversations with Brando,* p. 129.

888–89   Description of MB eating at the Budapest Restaurant and ordering food delivered drawn from PM interview with Russell Friedman.

891   *"I've never quite understood what . . .":* Qtd. in Marshall Ledger, "The Ascent of Adrian Malone," *New York Times Magazine,* 3/15/81.

894   *"You look great . . .":* Conversation with MB about doing *Macbeth* recalled by Joseph Mankiewicz to PM.

901–2   *"I want to talk to you, Tony . . .":* MB conversation with Anthony Quinn recalled by Quinn to PM.

904   *"My dad's lawyers are pressuring . . .":* Remark qtd. in and conflict with Christian cited from "Declaration of Mary McKenna in support of request for an injunctive order" included in divorce petition filed by Marvin Mitchelson in Los Angeles County Superior Court, 6/2/86; settlement of $400 monthly support payment confirmed in the same court file, case #WED 47145.

906   *the rights to his story:* Fox Butterfield, *New York Times,* 1/29/87.

906   *"Nobody's done anything . . .":* Remark recalled by Pat Quinn to PM.

907   *announcing himself as producer: New York Post,* 7/21/87.

908   *grade B violent exploitation films:* Danny Peary, *Cult Movie Stars,* p. 310; the exception to her usual roles was *All the Marbles,* a comedy-drama about a female wrestling team managed by Peter Falk.

909   *"Christian later told me . . .":* Description of MB meeting with De Benedittis recalled by Bill Cable to PM.

910   *"It was one hundred forty pages . . .":* Rodley, "Marlon, Madness, and Me," p. 49, and confirmed by Donald Cammell to PM. Cammell told PM that this too was part of a "repetitive pattern in Marlon's life. It's called the giant jerk-off."

910   *"I'll do it for nothing":* Qtd. in Bob Thomas, *Cape Cod Times,* AP dispatch, 10/14/89.

910   *"a movie like this . . .":* Qtd. in *Premiere,* October 1989.

910   *"from a black perspective":* Qtd. in Robin Dougherty, "More than Marlon," *Boston Phoenix,* 9/12/89.

911   *"Nobody was talking . . .":* Qtd. in Thomas, *Cape Cod Times.*

911   *"As a fellow actor . . .":* Qtd. in ibid.

911   *through a tiny radio:* "Marlon's Main Line," *London Daily Mirror,* 10/12/89.

911   *"They brought her in . . .":* Conversation between Philip Rhodes and MB recalled by Rhodes to PM.

912   *"I don't need Brando . . .":* Donald Cammell to PM.

913   *"I can't believe I can feel . . .":* Qtd. in *News of the World,* 7/30/89.

914   *calling the director "out of the blue":* Fred Schruers, "Brando Giveth, and Brando Taketh Away," *Premiere,* September 1990.

914   *"I'm sorry it took so long . . .":* Qtd. in ibid.

914   *for a reported $3.3 million:* Ibid.

914   *Christian was telling friends:* Jeff Gottlieb, "Mutiny from the Bounty," *US,* 10/1/90.

915   *"He had deceived me . . .":* Cheyenne Brando to PM.

916   Cheyenne's accident, surgery in Los Angeles, and MB's vigil at her bedside drawn from Cheyenne Brando interview with PM and from news accounts (e.g., "Brando's Daughter Scarred in Crash," *Los Angeles Times,* 8/25/89).

916   *"He is the best . . .":* Qtd. in *Variety,* 8/15/89.

916   *"It's horrible . . .":* Qtd. in Murray Campbell, *Toronto Globe and Mail,* 8/31/89.

917   *"did not give much back":* "Brando Coulda' Been . . . ," *Omaha World-Herald,* 9/4/89.

917   *"A phone call was very nice . . .":* Qtd. in Janet Maslin, *New York Times,* 7/15/90.

917–18   *"have led to painful misunderstandings . . .":* "A Statement by Marlon Brando," letter issued by PMK Public Relations, New York, 9/11/89.

918 *"an unexpectedly deft comic actor . . ."*: Janet Maslin, *New York Times,* 7/20/90.

918 *"I swear on my children . . ."*: Qtd. in Army Archerd, *Variety,* 10/4/89; see also Jeannie Williams, *USA Today,* 10/5/89; alleged threat and MB denial confirmed by MB in interview, "Saturday Night with Connie Chung," 10/7/89.

918 *"brief exquisite characterization"*: Julie Salamon, *Wall Street Journal,* 9/21/89.

919–20 *"I was thinking about . . ."*: "Saturday Night with Connie Chung," 10/7/89.

920 *"Dear Bud, I was delighted to see you . . ."*: Letter to MB provided by Walter Seltzer to PM.

19. *THE SHOOTING: 1990–94*

PAGE

923 *"Man, I didn't mean to . . ."*: "Spontaneous remarks" made by Christian Brando after shooting at Mulholland on 5/16/90 to uniform officer Steve Cunningham; qtd. in LAPD "Follow-up Investigation" report, filed by Cunningham on 5/17/90, case #SA003367.

923–24 Investigation of crime scene by West Los Angeles homicide detectives Lee Kingsford and Andrew R. Monsue drawn from their LAPD "Follow-up Investigation" reports filed 5/17/90, and from PM interviews with both detectives.

924–25 MB's statements to police recalled by Detective Monsue to PM, as well as qtd. from "Follow-up Investigation," in which Monsue reported his questioning of MB on the night of the murder.

926 Cheyenne Brando's statements qtd. in Detective Lee Kingsford's "Follow-Up Investigation," in which he reported his questioning of Cheyenne the night of the murder.

926 Tarita's statements qtd. in Detective John Rockford's "Follow-up Investigation," in which he reported his questioning.

926 *"Get me Bill Kunstler now . . ."*: Remark recalled by Detective Monsue to PM. See also "Brando Case Is a Natural for Kunstler," *Los Angeles Times,* 5/29/90.

926–27 Prior ties between the Drollet and Brando families as well as Dag Drollet's background described by Jacques-Denis Drollet to PM.

927 Cheyenne's drug use and Dag's attempt to "get her away from drugs" described in Cynthia Garbutt's deposition, Cabinet du Juge d'Instruction, Papeete, Tahiti, 7/19/90; Jacques-Denis Drollet confirmed her drug problem to PM, as did Cheyenne herself in interview with PM.

927   *"I am the most beautiful girl . . ."*: Remark recalled by Jacques-Denis Drollet to PM.

928   *"aggression and instability . . ."*: Report of psychiatric evaluation, document #457-174, submitted to Appellate Court of Papeete, Tahiti, Dr. Bernard Ryckelynck, 11/22/90.

929   *hiding his passport:* Cynthia Garbutt's deposition, 7/19/90.

929   *not the father of her baby:* Dag Drollet repeated the remark to Cynthia Garbutt, who testified to it in her deposition, ibid.; also, Jacques-Denis Drollet to PM.

931   *None of Christian's friends:* Those friends who were aware of MB's long-term affair with Anita Kong (and also knew that Christian had considered Anita Kong and the wealthy Dr. Wiley "surrogate" parents) speculated that Bobby was Kong's son.

938–41   *The interrogation room where Christian:* Christian Brando's taped statement to police excerpted from transcription included as "Attachment G" in Los Angeles County Superior Court Filings, case #SA003367

941   *he phoned Cynthia Garbutt:* Garbutt recalled MB's request to PM, but later said he had been trying to reach Jacques Drollet "all night."

941–42   *"Don't you know your son . . ."*: Conversation with "Hard Copy" producer recalled by Jacques-Denis Drollet to PM; see also *Daily Mail* (London) interview with Drollet, 7/10/90.

942   *the loving patriarch:* See, for example, Fenton Bresler, *Daily Express* (London), 5/25/90.

947   *"This is going to come down . . ."*: Transcript, bail hearing, Division 91, West Los Angeles Municipal Court, Judge Rosemary Shumsky presiding, 5/22/90.

948   *"We primarily handle . . ."*: Ibid.

948   *"This case, for the purposes . . ."*: Ibid.

948   *"The court finds no basis . . ."*: Ibid.

949   *"There's no way to describe it . . . The messenger of misery . . ."*: Qtd. in *Los Angeles Times,* 5/23/90.

950   *Robert L. Shapiro: Los Angeles Times,* 6/12/90.

950   *"Christian just walked in . . ."*: Cheyenne's statement qtd. in LAPD "Follow-up Investigation," filed by Detective Andrew R. Monsue, case #90-08 15759, 6/12/90; confirmed by both Monsue and Cheyenne to PM.

950–51   The police attempts to return to Mulholland to question Cheyenne Brando described by Detective Monsue to PM; confirmed by Steven Barshop to PM.

951   *"he wanted a ticket . . ."*: Rosetta Valenti confirmed the request for a Qantas plane ticket for Cheyenne, departing Los Angeles on 6/15/90, to Detective Monsue in a police statement, case #90-08 15759, 8/9/90. Valenti declared that it was "well after noon" on 6/12/90 (the date of

Monsue's first interview with Cheyenne) that she had spoken to MB and Cheyenne about this flight to Tahiti.

951 *"When you take a look . . .":* Steven Barshop to PM. See also *Los Angeles Times,* 6/26/90; *New York Times,* 6/27/90.

951 *hospitalized for psychiatric observation:* Affidavit of Claude Girard and medical certificate from Dr. Yves Petit, psychiatrist, Vaiami Hospital, in which the doctor confirmed to Los Angeles prosecutors that on 7/6/90 Cheyenne was moved to "a locked [isolation] unit" because of her "disruptive behavior and incoherent talk" while in the maternity ward.

952 *Drollet filed a civil suit in Tahiti:* Confirmed by Jacques-Denis Drollet and his Tahitian attorneys, François Quinquis and Temanava Bambridge-Babin, to PM.

952 *"She cut off all her hair . . .":* Qtd. in *Star,* 8/7/90.

953 *"It's done. I killed him":* Recollection of Christian's remark from Cheyenne Brando's deposition, Cabinet du Juge d'Instruction, Papeete, Tahiti, 7/17/90; confirmed by Cheyenne Brando to PM.

953 *"A little later . . .":* Tarita's description of shooting from Tarita Teriipaia's deposition, Cabinet du Juge d'Instruction, Papeete, Tahiti, 7/13/90.

953 *Brando's office manager confirmed:* Cynthia Garbutt's deposition, 7/19/90.

953 *charging her with complicity:* USA Today, 7/19/90.

954 *"The reality is that . . .":* Qtd. in *Daily Mail* (London), 7/10/90; similar remarks made by Jacques-Denis Drollet in interview with PM.

955–58 *the preliminary hearing began:* Testimony and descriptions of proceedings at Christian Brando's preliminary hearing, July 23–24, 1990, Los Angeles Municipal Court, Judge Larry Fidler presiding, drawn from court transcript and press clippings as well as author's personal observations, notes, interviews, and interpretations.

958–61 *decided to air their dissatisfactions:* Jacques-Denis Drollet and Albert LeCaill to PM.

961 *a $100 million wrongful-death suit:* Confirmed by William Marshall Morgan and Jacques-Denis Drollet to PM.

961 *"How can you shoot someone . . .":* Qtd. in *Star,* 8/7/90; similar remarks made by Jacques-Denis Drollet in interview with PM.

961 *presumably because his passport:* Although Christian Brando's release on bail was expected to be immediate (given MB's assumed wealth), Robert Shapiro's legal assistant announced that Christian's passport "has not been found" (UPI dispatch, 7/26/90). It was then reported that the delay was in fact due to Brando's "scrambling" to try to raise the $10 million bond, even though Shapiro had told the judge that the amount of bail "was not an issue." Shapiro, however, continued to insist that the real

problem was the alleged missing passport—see *Los Angeles Times* (8/8/90): "As days, and then weeks passed [after the preliminary hearing], Brando remained in jail, [Shapiro] said, because the family was unable to find his passport." It should be noted that, according to Papke, six days before Shapiro made this statement on 8/7/90, MB himself had taken possession of Christian's passport; Papke had picked it up from the offices of attorney Daniel Stormer, the initial co-defense counsel with whom Kunstler had deposited all papers and documents in the Christian Brando case when he had been replaced by Shapiro. (That the passport was with these materials was logical since Kunstler had actually brought the passport to the first bail hearing, 5/22/90, and volunteered to turn it over to the judge on the spot; see transcript and Kunstler's twice repeated statement: "We have his passport here for surrender to the court.")

964   *"Dag was killed by Christian . . .":* Qtd. from testimony, interrogation of Cheyenne Brando, Cabinet du Juge d'Instruction, Papeete, Tahiti, 7/30/90.

964   *"Marlon Brando will always remember . . .":* Jacques-Denis Drollet to PM; similar remarks qtd. in *Sunday Mirror* (London), 8/5/90.

964   *"She said that she hoped to see us . . .":* Cheyenne's phone call to Albert LeCaill, just after midnight, 8/7/90, and to Lisette LeCaill the following morning, were testified to by the LeCaills in declarations filed with both Judge Gatti in the Tahitian court and the Los Angeles District Attorney's office.

964   *"But why didn't he do anything . . .":* Qtd. from Maeva Bonno's description of her conversation with Cheyenne in her declaration to the Tahitian court subsequently filed with the Los Angeles District Attorney's office.

965   *slashed his bail to $2 million:* Upset by the judge's reduction of bail, the prosecutors filed an affidavit of prejudice against him; each side was entitled to one peremptory challenge, and immediately Judge Robert Thomas was assigned to preside in Christian's trial (*Los Angeles Times,* 9/5/90).

965   *". . . I want to know . . .":* William Clark recalled incident to PM (although Steven Barshop did not remember MB grabbing his arm). MB also recounted this exchange to Lawrence Grobel but omitted Barshop's reply (*Conversations with Brando,* p. 191).

965   *"I don't think I've said anything . . .":* Qtd. in *Los Angeles Times,* 8/10/90; in the statement that most upset the Drollet family, MB apologized for "blathering," then said that he could take the press attacks on himself: "I've got a hide that thick," he explained, holding two fingers wide apart and seemingly unaware that this might not be an appropriate metaphor in a shooting case.

965–66   *"I just want to go home . . .":* Qtd. in *Los Angeles Times,* 8/16/90, which is also source for MB's remarks.

966   *". . . There is no way that we can bring . . .":* Communication from MB filed with L.A. District Attorney's office as exhibit attached to declaration from Albert and Lisette LeCaill.

967–69   *". . . I am legally a minor . . .":* Testimony qtd. from interrogation of Cheyenne Brando, Cabinet du Juge d'Instruction, Papeete, Tahiti, 9/14/90.

969   *"I'm looking for a publisher . . .":* Qtd. in *Variety,* 9/7/90.

969–70   *"There've been so many different books . . .":* Qtd. in *Los Angeles Times,* 9/26/90.

971   *"Cheyenne has suffered enormously . . . doing her best":* Qtd. in *Los Angeles Times,* 9/27/90.

972   *All Hallow's Eve:* Incident described by Alberto Vivian to *Star,* 11/20/90.

972   *lapsed into a coma: Los Angeles Times,* 11/2/90.

972   *"Her heart was fibrillating . . .":* Qtd. in *People,* 11/19/90.

972   *his priority had to be Christian:* In fact, MB had been advised by his attorneys not to travel to Tahiti because the French authorities might hold him there for questioning in their own investigation of the case. Although Steven Barshop had reassured Robert Shapiro that he had no objection to MB's flying to his daughter's bedside, MB continued to blame the L.A. District Attorney's office for preventing him from being with Cheyenne (see *Los Angeles Times,* 11/9/90).

972   *"Contrary to what people are saying . . .":* Qtd. in *People,* 11/9/90.

972   *"I hope her brain cells . . .": Star,* 11/20/90.

972–73   *"I hold them directly . . .":* Qtd. in *Los Angeles Times,* 11/9/90.

973   *"Cheyenne hung herself . . .":* Qtd. in *Los Angeles Times,* 11/13/90.

973–74   *"hit a nurse" . . . "Her spontaneous expression was poor . . .":* Qtd. from medical report read into record at hearing on petition to appoint a guardian "for the incapable adult Cheyenne Brando . . . and her son Tuki," Family Court, Tribunal of the First Instance of Papeete, Tahiti, 12/6/90. At the conclusion of the hearing, the judge appointed three guardians for Cheyenne and Tuki: MB's Tahitian attorney, Claude Girard; her brother Teihotu; and MB's "commercial representative," Cynthia Garbutt. See also *Los Angeles Times,* 12/8/90.

974   *Judge Joel Rudof: Los Angeles Times,* 12/22/90.

974–75   *"shot his best friend point-blank . . .":* Ricardo Alvarez's story qtd. in *National Enquirer,* 11/6/90.

976   *did locate and interview:* Transcription of tape-recorded interview of William Emmette Smith III, 11/5/90; entered into evidence as Exhibit H for prosecutors' "Statement in Aggravation," in Christian Brando's sentencing hearing, Los Angeles County Superior Court, Santa Monica, February 26–28, 1991.

976   *Friday, January 4:* MB's not being at his son's side for guilty plea was explained by Robert Shapiro: "He was in no emotional position to come out today" (qtd. in *Los Angeles Times,* 1/5/91).

977   *"Marlon Brando is rich . . .":* Qtd. in ibid; similar remarks made by Jacques-Denis Drollet in interview with PM.

977   *"How anger is replacing any pity . . .":* Kevin O'Sullivan and Richard Shears, *Mail on Sunday* (London), 1/6/91.

977   *"I have come to despise my father . . .":* Cheyenne Brando to PM; see also Peter Manso and Olivier Royant, "J'Accuse Brando," *Paris Match,* 6/24/93.

978   *"Last week I went to Bjarn . . .":* Jacques-Denis Drollet to PM.

978   *"I've been coming through these doors . . .":* Qtd. in *Los Angeles Times,* 2/26/91.

978–93   *On the morning of February 26:* Sentencing hearing, *The People of the State of California vs. Christian Brando,* Los Angeles County Superior Court, Santa Monica, Judge Robert W. Thomas presiding, February 26–28, 1991. All testimony qtd. from court transcript of proceedings; description and summaries of proceedings drawn from author's personal observations, notes, and interviews.

993   *eligible for parole:* Steven Barshop confirmed to PM; see also *USA Today,* 3/1/90. Robert Shapiro later filed an appeal of the sentence, arguing "mitigating circumstances," but Judge Thomas denied it without comment (*USA Today,* 6/26/91).

995   *"They had believed she was . . .":* *Daily Express* (London), 3/4/91.

996   *upheld Gatti's ruling . . . the request was rejected:* La Dépêche de Tahiti, 4/10/91.

996   *yet another lawyer, Jacques Vergès:* La Dépêche de Tahiti, 8/28/91, and *USA Today,* 9/12/91.

996–97   *the deal was closed:* Gayle Feldman, "Trade News," *Publishers Weekly,* 3/29/91.

997   *"Everything will be in the book . . .":* Qtd. in ibid.

998   *"psychotic, irascible . . .":* *Libération* (Paris), 11/16/91.

998   *Gatti then checked with the clinic:* France Soir (Paris), 10/28/91.

998   *"I'm thinking about Dag . . .":* Cheyenne Brando's phone call described by Lisette LeCaill to PM.

998   *police issued a warrant: People,* 10/27/91.

999   Description of Cheyenne's trip with MB drawn from her interview with PM; see also Manso and Royant, "J'Accuse Brando."

999   *police commanded Cheyenne:* La Dépêche (Paris), 11/16/91; *Les Nouvelles* (Paris), 11/16/91; *Le Parisien,* 11/16/91.

1000   *a French military jet:* Al Prince, "The Brando Saga Returns to Tahiti," *Tahiti,* January 1992.

1000   *on $1 million bail:* Ibid.

1000– Description of Cheyenne's reunion with Tarita and Tuki at airport
1001   drawn from author's personal observations, notes, and interviews; see
        also Olivier Royant and Peter Manso, "L'Exploit de Maître Vergès,"
        Paris Match, 12/12/91.

1001   *"No chance that Marlon Brando . . .":* Qtd. in Prince, "The Brando Saga."

1001   *"Marlon Brando would rather . . .":* Jacques-Denis Drollet to PM and qtd.
        in Prince, "The Brando Saga."

1001–2 Description of gathering of the two families drawn from PM interview
        with Albert LeCaill; see also Royant and Manso, "L'Exploit de Maître
        Vergès."

1002   *"What will you do? . . .":* Conversation recalled by Jacques-Denis Drollet
        to PM.

1004   *"they have no right to associate . . .":* Qtd. in Judy Brennan and Linda
        Moor, "Salkinds' Crew in Columbus Daze," *Variety,* 4/21/92.

1004   *"Having an appreciable knowledge . . .":* Qtd. in Judy Brennan, "Brando
        Wants No Credit for *Columbus* Pic," *Variety,* 4/21/92.

1004–5 *"He wanted to have . . .":* Qtd. in *Entertainment Weekly,* 5/22/92; Bernard
        Weinraub, "It's Columbus Against Columbus . . . ," *New York Times,*
        5/21/92.

1005   *"the full light of world attention . . .":* Qtd. in Brennan, "Brando Wants
        No Credit."

1005   *"little more than a series . . .":* *Entertainment Weekly,* 9/4/92.

1005   *"My father is constantly manipulating . . . maid or governess":* Qtd. from
        testimony, interrogation of Cheyenne Brando, Cabinet du Juge
        d'Instruction, Papeete, Tahiti, 4/15/92; also qtd. in *Daily Express*
        (London), 4/16/92; *New York Newsday,* 4/16/92.

1006–8 *"It is all a smear now . . .":* MB's responses qtd. from transcript, United
        States District Court, Central District of California, In Re: Letter
        Rogatory from the Court of First Instance of Papeete, French Polynesia,
        Misc. No. 28697: Deposition of Marlon Brando, 6/19/92. See also
        "Brando Cover-up?" *Entertainment Weekly,* 10/2/92.

1008   *she suddenly began shouting:* Jacques-Denis Drollet to PM: he also stated
        that no transcript of the hearing was filed because of the outburst and
        suspension of the proceedings.

1010   *"There are some people here from CPC . . .":* Remark recalled by
        Cheyenne Brando to PM when she described her stay with MB in Los
        Angeles and her subsequent hospitalization; see also Manso and Royant,
        "J'Accuse Brando."

1011   *"She kicked a four-foot hole . . .":* Lorie Kligerman to PM; see also *USA
        Today,* 2/17/93.

1012   *". . . she just hauled off . . .":* Qtd. in *San Francisco Chronicle,* 3/2/94, which
        reported the filing of the civil suit.

1013–18 *Cheyenne met with the reporters:* Cheyenne Brando qtd. from transcribed interview; excerpts published in Manso and Royant, "J'Accuse Brando."

1019   *Cristina Ruiz, who was pregnant:* Liz Smith, *Los Angeles Times,* n.d. (c. April 1993).

1019   *"I think Mr. Brando has . . .":* Qtd. in *New York Times,* 9/22/93.

1019   *Brando had filed suit: Los Angeles Times,* 8/19/93.

1020   *For a reported $3.25 million: Variety,* 2/17/94.

BIBLIOGRAPHY

Adams, Cindy. *Lee Strasberg: The Imperfect Genius of the Actors Studio.* Garden City, N.Y.: Doubleday, 1980.

Adler, Stella. *The Technique of Acting.* New York: Bantam, 1988.

Alleman, Richard. *The Movie Lover's Guide to New York.* New York: Harper & Row, 1985.

Anger, Kenneth. *Hollywood Babylon.* San Francisco: Bell Publishing/Straight Arrow, 1981.

Bach, Steven. *Final Cut: Dreams and Disaster in the Making of "Heaven's Gate."* New York: Morrow, 1985.

Baker, Fred. *Movie People.* London: Abelard-Schuman, 1972.

Barck, Oscar T., Jr. *A History of the United States Since 1945.* New York: Dell, 1965.

Bart, Peter. *Fade Out: The Calamitous Final Days of MGM.* New York: Morrow, 1990.

Bates, Brian. *The Way of the Actor: A Path to Knowledge and Power.* Boston: Shambhala, 1988.

Battcock, Gregory, ed. *The New American Cinema: A Critical Anthology.* New York: Dutton, 1967.

Beath, Warren Newton. *The Death of James Dean.* New York: Grove Press, 1986.

Behlmer, Rudy, ed. *Inside Warner Bros. (1935–1951).* New York: Simon & Schuster, 1985.

Ben-Amotz, Dan. *Screwing Isn't Everything.* Tel Aviv: Metziuth Publishers, 1979.

Bentley, Eric. *The Theatre of Commitment and Other Essays on Drama in Our Society.* New York: Atheneum, 1967.

Berg, A. Scott. *Goldwyn: A Biography.* New York: Knopf, 1989.

Bigsby, C. W. E. *A Critical Introduction to Twentieth-Century American Drama.* Vol. 2. Cambridge: Cambridge University Press, 1984.

Biskind, Peter. *The Godfather Companion.* New York: Harper Perennial, 1990.

Blum, Daniel. *A New Pictorial History of the Talkies.* New York: Putnam, 1968.

Blumenthal, John. *The Official Hollywood Handbook.* New York: Simon & Schuster, 1984.

Boller, Paul F., Jr., and Ronald L. Davis. *Hollywood Anecdotes.* New York: Morrow, 1987.

Bordman, Gerald. *The Oxford Companion to American Theatre.* New York: Oxford University Press, 1984.

Bosworth, Patricia. *Montgomery Clift: A Biography.* New York: Bantam, 1979.

Bragg, Melvyn. *Richard Burton: A Life.* Boston: Little Brown, 1988.

Branch, Taylor. *Parting the Waters: America in the King Years 1954–63.* New York: Simon & Schuster, 1988.

Brando, Anna Kashfi, and E. P. Stein. *Brando for Breakfast*. New York: Crown, 1979.

Braude, Ann. *Radical Spirits: Spiritualism and Women's Rights in Nineteenth-Century America*. Boston: Beacon Press, 1989.

Brenman-Gibson, Margaret. *Clifford Odets: American Playwright: The Years from 1906 to 1940*. New York: Atheneum, 1982.

Brown, Dee. *Bury My Heart at Wounded Knee*. New York: Pocket, 1970.

Brown, Peter H., and Jim Pinkston. *Oscar Dearest: Six Decades of Scandal, Politics and Greed Behind Hollywood's Academy Awards, 1927–1986*. New York: Harper & Row, 1987.

Brown, Peter Harry, and Patte B. Barham. *Marilyn: The Last Take*. New York: Dutton, 1992.

Brownstein, Ronald. *The Power and the Glitter: The Hollywood-Washington Connection*. New York: Pantheon, 1990.

Brynner, Rock. *Yul: The Man Who Would be King*. New York: Simon & Schuster, 1989.

Burne, Jerome, ed. *Chronicle of the World*. Mt. Kisco, N.Y.: ECAM Publications, 1989.

Campbell, James. *Talking at the Gates: A Life of James Baldwin*. New York: Penguin, 1991.

Campbell, Sandy. *B: 29 Letters from Coconut Grove*. Verona, Italy: privately printed, 1974.

Carey, Gary. *Marlon Brando: The Only Contender*. New York: St. Martin's, 1985.

Chaillet, Jean-Paul, and Elizabeth Vincent. *Francis Ford Coppola*. Translated by Denise Raab Jacobs. New York: St. Martin's, 1985.

Chapman, John, ed. *The Burns Mantle Best Plays of 1947–48*. New York: Dodd Mead, 1948.

Ciment, Michel, ed. *Elia Kazan, An American Odyssey*. London: Bloomsbury, 1988.

Clarke, Gerald. *Capote: A Biography*. New York: Simon & Schuster, 1988.

Clurman, Harold. *All People Are Famous (Instead of an Autobiography)*. New York: Harcourt Brace Jovanovich, 1974.

———. *On Directing*. New York: Macmillan, 1972.

Cole, Toby, and Helen Krich Chinoy, eds. *Actors on Acting*. New York: Crown, 1989.

Coppola, Eleanor. *Notes on the Making of "Apocalypse Now."* New York: Limelight Editions, 1979.

Cowie, Peter. *Coppola*. New York: Scribners, 1989.

Cowie, Peter, and Derek Elley, eds. *International Film Guide—1988*. New York: Zoetrope, 1987.

Cox, Wally. *My Life as a Small Boy*. New York: Avon, 1961.

Crim, Keith, et al., eds. *The Perennial Dictionary of World Religions*. San Francisco: Harper & Row, 1981.

Crist, Judith. *Take 22: Moviemakers on Moviemaking*. New York: Viking, 1984.

Crow Dog, Mary, and Richard Erdoes. *Lakota Woman*. New York: HarperCollins, 1990.

Curtis, Tony, and Barry Paris. *Tony Curtis: The Autobiography*. New York: Morrow, 1993.

Dalton, David. *James Dean: The Mutant King*. New York: St. Martin's, 1974.

Daniel, Clifton, ed. *Chronicles of the Twentieth Century*. Mt. Kisco, N.Y.: ECAM Publications, 1988.

Danielsson, Bengt. *Tahiti: Circle Island Tour Guide*. Singapore: Koon Wah Press, 1981.

Dardis, Tom. *Some Time in the Sun*. New York: Limelight Editions, 1976.

Davis, Miles, with Quincy Troupe. *Miles: The Autobiography*. New York: Simon & Schuster, 1989.

Day, A. Grove, ed. *The Lure of Tahiti: An Armchair Companion*. Honolulu: Mutual Publishing, 1986.

Deloria, Vine, Jr.. *Custer Died for Your Sins: An Indian Manifesto*. Norman, Okla.: University of Oklahoma Press, 1988.

Dent, Alan. *Vivien Leigh: A Bouquet*. London: Hamish Hamilton, 1969.

Didion, Joan. *The White Album*. New York: Pocket, 1979.

Dmytryk, Edward. *It's a Hell of a Life but Not a Bad Living*. New York: Times Books, 1978.

Douglas, Kirk. *The Ragman's Son: An Autobiography*. New York: Pocket, 1988.

Dunne, John Gregory. *The Studio*. New York: Limelight Editions, 1968.

DuPrel, Alex W. *Tahiti Blue: Modern Tales of the South Pacific*. Tahiti: Les Editions de Tahiti, 1990.

Easty, Edward Dwight. *On Method Acting*. Florence, Ala.: House of Collectibles, 1966.

Eells, George. *Hedda and Louella*. New York: Putnam, 1972.

Ellwood, Robert S., ed. *Eastern Spirituality in America*. Mahwah, N.J.: Paulist Press, 1987.

Emery, Lynne Fauley. *Black Dance from 1619 to Today*. Pennington, N.J.: Princeton Book Company, 1972.

Epstein, Jerry. *Remembering Charlie: A Pictorial Biography*. New York: Doubleday, 1989.

Eyraud, Arlette. *Tahiti Today and All Its Islands*. Paris: Les Editions du Jaguar/Les Editions J.A., 1990.

Farber, Stephen, and Marc Green. *Hollywood Dynasties*. New York: Fawcett Crest, 1984.

———. *Hollywood on the Couch*. New York: Morrow, 1993.

Fergusson, Francis. *The Human Image in Dramatic Literature*. New York: Doubleday/Anchor, 1957.

Fiore, Carlo. *Bud: The Brando I Knew*. New York: Delacorte, 1974.

Fitzgerald, F. Scott. *The Last Tycoon*. New York: Penguin, 1941.

Fonda, Henry, and Howard Teichmann. *Fonda: My Life*. New York: New American Library, 1981.

Fowler, Gene. *Good Night, Sweet Prince: The Life and Times of John Barrymore*. San Francisco: Mercury House, 1989.

Freeman, Lucy. *Why Norma Jean Killed Marilyn Monroe*. Chicago: Global Rights, 1992.

Friedrich, Otto. *City of Nets: A Portrait of Hollywood in the 1940s*. New York: Harper & Row, 1986.

Froug, William. *The Screenwriter Looks at the Screenwriter.* New York: Dell, 1972.

Garfield, David. *A Player's Place: The Story of the Actors Studio.* New York: Macmillan, 1980.

Gavin, Jane. *Intimate Nights: The Golden Age of New York Cabaret.* New York: Grove Weidenfeld, 1991.

Geist, Kenneth L. *Pictures Will Talk: The Life and Films of Joseph L. Mankiewicz.* New York: Scribners, 1978.

Gelmis, Joseph. *The Film Director as Superstar.* Garden City, N.Y.: Doubleday, 1970.

Gielgud, John, with John Miller and John Powell. *An Actor and His Time.* New York: Penguin, 1979.

Gill, Brendan. *Tallulah.* New York: Holt, Rinehart & Winston, 1972.

Gitlin, Todd. *The Sixties: Years of Hope, Days of Rage.* New York: Bantam, 1987.

Goldman, Eric F. *The Crucial Decade—And After: America 1945–1960.* New York: Vintage, 1960.

Goldman, William. *Adventures in the Screen Trade: A Personal View of Hollywood and Screenwriting.* New York: Warner Books, 1983.

————. *The Season: A Candid Look at Broadway.* New York: Long Light Editions, 1969.

Golson, G. Barry, ed. *The Playboy Interviews.* Chicago: Wideview Books, 1981.

Gomery, Douglas. *The Hollywood Studio System.* New York: St. Martin's, 1986.

Goodwin, Michael, and Naomi Wise. *On the Edge: The Life and Times of Francis Coppola.* New York: Morrow, 1989.

Graham, Bill, and Robert Greenfield. *Bill Graham Presents: My Life Inside Rock and Out.* New York: Doubleday, 1992.

Graham, Sheilah. *Confessions of a Hollywood Columnist.* New York: Morrow, 1969.

Graziano, Rocky. *Somebody Up There Likes Me.* New York: Simon & Schuster, 1955.

Green, Abel, and Joe Laurie, Jr. *Show Biz: From Vaude to Video.* New York: Henry Holt, 1951.

Greenbaum, Everett. *The Goldenberg Who Couldn't Dance.* New York: Harcourt Brace Jovanovich, 1973.

Gregg, Rodman, ed. *Who's Who in the Motion Picture Industry, 1991,* Beverly Hills, Calif.: Packard House, 1991.

Grobel, Lawrence. *Conversations with Brando.* New York: Hyperion, 1991.

————. *The Hustons.* New York: Scribners, 1989.

Grun, Bernard. *The Timetables of History: A Horizontal Linkage of People and Events.* New York: Touchstone/Simon & Schuster, 1982.

Halliwell, Leslie. *Halliwell's Film Guide.* 6th ed. London: Paladin Grafton, 1988.

————. *Halliwell's Filmgoer's Companion.* 9th ed. London: Grafton, 1988.

Hart, Moss. *Act One: An Autobiography.* New York: Random House, 1959.

Hartnoll, Phyllis, ed. *The Oxford Companion to the Theatre.* 3rd ed. London: Oxford University Press, 1967.

Haskell, Molly. *From Reverence to Rape: The Treatment of Women in the Movies.* New York: Penguin, 1974.

Hay, Peter. *Broadway Anecdotes.* New York: Oxford University Press, 1989.

————. *Movie Anecdotes.* New York: Oxford University Press, 1990.

————. *Theatrical Anecdotes.* New York: Oxford University Press, 1987.

Hecht, Ben. *A Child of the Century.* New York: Simon & Schuster, 1954.

Hethmon, Robert T., ed. *Strasberg at the Actors Studio.* New York: Viking, 1965.

Hickenlooper, George. *Reel Conversations: Candid Interviews with Film's Foremost Directors and Critics.* New York: Citadel Press, 1991.

Higham, Charles. *Brando: The Unauthorized Biography.* New York: New American Library, 1987.

Hirsch, Foster. *A Method to Their Madness: The History of the Actors Studio.* New York: Da Capo Press, 1984.

Holden, Anthony. *Laurence Olivier.* New York: Atheneum, 1988.

Holley, Val, with David Loehr. *James Dean: Tribute to a Rebel.* Lincolnwood, Ill.: Publications International, 1991.

Houseman, John. *Front and Center.* New York: Simon & Schuster, 1979.

Howe, Irving. *World of Our Fathers.* New York: Harcourt Brace Jovanovich, 1976.

Huston, John. *An Open Book.* New York: Ballantine, 1981.

Hymowitz, Carol, and Michaele Weissman. *A History of Women in America.* New York: Bantam, 1978.

Innes, C. D. *Erwin Piscator's Political Theatre.* London: Cambridge University Press, 1972.

Izod, John. *Hollywood and the Box Office: 1895–1986.* New York: Columbia University Press, 1988.

Johnson, Paul. *A History of the Jews.* New York: Harper & Row, 1987.

Jones, David Richard. *Great Directors at Work: Stanislavsky, Brecht, Kazan, Brook.* Berkeley, Calif.: University of California Press, 1986.

Kael, Pauline. *5001 Nights at the Movies.* 2nd ed. New York: Henry Holt, 1991.

Kaplan, Mike, ed. *Variety: Who's Who in Show Business.* Rev. ed. New York: Garland Publishing, 1985.

Katz, Ephraim. *The Film Encyclopedia.* New York: Crowell, 1979.

Kauffmann, Stanley. *Before My Eyes: Film Criticism and Comment.* New York: Da Capo Press, 1974.

————. *A World on Film: Criticism and Comment.* New York: Dell, 1958.

Kay, Robert S. *Tahiti and French Polynesia: A Travel Survival Kit.* Berkeley, Calif.: Lonely Planet Publications, 1985.

Kazan, Elia. *Elia Kazan: A Life.* New York: Knopf, 1988.

Kelley, Kitty. *Elizabeth Taylor: The Last Star.* New York: Simon & Schuster, 1981.

————. *His Way: The Unauthorized Biography of Frank Sinatra.* New York: Bantam, 1986.

Knight, Vivienne. *Trevor Howard: A Gentleman and a Player.* New York: Beaufort, 1986.

Kolker, Robert Phillip. *Bernardo Bertolucci.* New York: Oxford University Press, 1985.

Kritsberg, Wayne. *The Adult Children of Alcoholics Syndrome: From Discovery to Recovery.* Pompano Beach, Fla.: Health Communications, 1985.

LaGuardia, Robert. *Monty: A Biography of Montgomery Clift.* New York: Avon, 1977.

Lawrence, Jerome. *Actor: The Life and Times of Paul Muni.* New York: Samuel French, 1974.

Lawrenson, Helen. *Whistling Girl.* Garden City, N.Y.: Doubleday, 1978.

Leon, Ruth. *Applause: New York's Guide to the Performing Arts.* New York: Applause Books, 1991.

Lewis, Robert. *Slings and Arrows: Theater in My Life.* New York: Stein & Day, 1984.

Litwak, Mark. *Reel Power: The Struggle for Influence and Success in the New Hollywood.* New York: New American Library, 1986.

Logan, Joshua. *Movie Stars, Real People and Me.* New York: Delacorte, 1978.

Loggia, Marjorie, and Glenn Young, eds. *The Collected Works of Harold Clurman.* New York: Applause Theatre Books, 1994.

Loos, Anita. *Kiss Hollywood Good-by.* New York: Ballantine, 1974.

Lutyens, Mary. *Krishnamurti: The Years of Awakening.* New York: Avon, 1975.

MacCann, Richard Dyer. *Film: A Montage of Theories.* New York: Dutton, 1966.

McClintick, David. *Indecent Exposure: A True Story of Hollywood and Wall Street.* New York: Dell, 1982.

McGaa, Ed Eagle Man. *Mother Earth Spirituality: Native American Paths to Healing Ourselves and Our World.* San Francisco: HarperCollins, 1990.

Macgowan, Kenneth. *Behind the Screen: The History and Technique of the Motion Picture.* New York: Dell, 1965.

McGuane, Thomas. *The Missouri Breaks: An Original Screenplay.* New York: Ballantine, 1976.

McLelland, Doug. *Star Speak: Hollywood on Everything.* Boston: Faber & Faber, 1987.

McMurtry, Larry. *Film Flam: Essays on Hollywood.* New York: Simon & Schuster, 1987.

McWilliams, Carey. *Southern California: An Island on the Land.* Salt Lake City: Peregrine Smith, 1973.

Manchester, William. *The Glory and the Dream: A Narrative History of America 1932–1972.* New York: Bantam, 1973.

Manso, Peter. *Mailer: His Life and Times.* New York: Simon & Schuster, 1985.

Mantle, Burns, ed. *The Best Plays of 1943–44.* New York: Dodd Mead, 1944.

———. *The Best Plays of 1944–45.* New York: Dodd Mead, 1945.

———. *The Best Plays of 1945–46.* New York: Dodd Mead, 1946.

———. *The Best Plays of 1946–47.* New York: Dodd Mead, 1947.

Marchak, Alice, and Linda Hunter. *The Super Secs.* Los Angeles: Charles Publishing, 1975.

Marx, Arthur. *Goldwyn: A Biography of the Man Behind the Myth.* New York: Norton, 1976.

Matthiessen, Peter. *In the Spirit of Crazy Horse.* New York: Viking, 1980.

Miller, Arthur. *Time Bends: A Life.* New York: Grove Press, 1987.

Moldea, Dan E. *Dark Victory: Ronald Reagan, MCA, and the Mob.* New York: Penguin, 1986.

Mordden, Ethan. *The American Theatre.* New York: Oxford University Press, 1981.

Morella, Joe, and Edward Z. Epstein. *Brando: The Unauthorized Biography.* New York: Crown, 1973.

———. *Paul and Joanne: A Biography of Paul Newman and Joanne Woodward.* New York: Delacorte, 1988.

Mosley, Leonard. *Zanuck: The Rise and Fall of Hollywood's Last Tycoon.* Boston: Little Brown, 1984.

Mourousi, Yves. *Le Destin Brando.* Paris: Editions Michel Lafon, 1991.

Nathan, George Jean. *The Theatre Book of the Year 1945–1946: A Record and an Interpretation.* New York: Knopf, 1946.

Navasky, Victor S. *Naming Names.* New York: Viking, 1980.

Nickens, Christopher. *Brando: A Biography in Photographs.* New York: Doubleday, 1987.

Norse, Harold. *Memoirs of a Bastard Angel.* New York: Morrow, 1989.

Oppenheimer, Jerry, and Jack Vitek. *Idol: Rock Hudson.* New York: Bantam, 1986.

Oumano, Elena. *Paul Newman.* New York: St. Martin's, 1989.

Ouspensky, P. D. *A New Model of the Universe: Principles of the Psychological Method in Application to Problems of Science, Religion and Art.* New York: Vintage, 1971.

Packard, William, David Pickering, and Charlotte Savidge, eds. *The Facts on File Dictionary of the Theatre.* New York: Facts on File, 1988.

Parker, John. *Five for Hollywood.* London: Macmillan, 1989.

Peary, Danny. *Cult Movie Stars.* New York: Fireside/Simon & Schuster, 1991.

Peyser, Joan. *Bernstein: A Biography.* New York: Ballantine, 1987.

Phillips, Cabell. *The 1940's: Decade of Triumph and Trouble.* New York: Macmillan, 1975.

Pincus, Edward. *Guide to Film Making.* New York: New American Library, 1969.

Putigny, Bob. *Tahiti and Its Islands.* Singapore: Les Editions du Pacifique/Times Editions, 1989.

Redfield, William. *Letters from an Actor.* New York: Viking, 1967.

Rhode, Eric. *A History of the Cinema from Its Origins to 1970.* New York: Da Capo Press, 1976.

Riese, Randall. *The Unabridged James Dean: His Life and Legacy from A to Z.* Chicago: Contemporary, 1991.

Riese, Randall, and Neal Hitchens. *The Unabridged Marilyn: Her Life from A to Z.* New York and Chicago: Congdon & Weed, 1987.

Robe, Lucy Barry. *Co-Starring Famous Women and Alcohol.* Minneapolis: CompCare Publications, 1986.

Robertson, Nan. *Getting Better: Inside Alcoholics Anonymous.* New York: Morrow, 1988.

Robertson, Patrick. *The Guinness Book of Movie Facts and Feats.* New York: Abbeville Press, 1991.

Rosenfeld, Lulla. *Bright Star of Exile: Jacob Adler and the Yiddish Theatre.* New York: Crowell, 1977.

Ross, Lillian. *Picture.* New York: Penguin, 1952.

Ross, Lillian, and Helen Ross. *The Player: A Profile of an Art.* New York: Limelight Editions, 1984.

Saquet, Jean-Louis. *The Tahiti Handbook.* Translated by Nancy and Dominique Benard. Singapore: Te Fenua/Editions Avant et Après, 1989.

Satterfield, Archie. *The Home Front: An Oral History of the War Years in America: 1941–45.* New York: Playboy Press, 1981.

Schary, Dore. *Heyday: An Autobiography.* Boston: Little Brown, 1979.

Schessler, Ken. *This Is Hollywood: An Unusual Guide.* La Verne, Calif.: Ken Schessler Publishing, 1978.

Schickel, Richard. *Brando: A Life in Our Times.* New York: Atheneum, 1991.

———. *Schickel on Film: Encounters—Critical and Personal—with Movie Immortals.* New York: Morrow, 1989.

Schnayerson, Michael. *Irwin Shaw: A Biography.* New York: Putnam, 1989.

Schulberg, Budd. *On the Waterfront: The Final Shooting Script.* New York: Samuel French, 1980.

Seckler, Dorothy Gees. *Provincetown Painters 1890s–1970.* Syracuse: Visual Artist Publications, 1977.

Selznick, Irene Mayer. *A Private View.* New York: Knopf, 1983.

Shaw, Sam. *Brando, in the Camera Eye.* New York: Exeter Books, 1979.

Shelton, Robert. *No Direction Home: The Life and Music of Bob Dylan.* New York: Ballantine, 1986.

Shipman, David. *The Story of Cinema: A Complete Narrative History from the Beginning to the Present.* New York: St. Martin's, 1982.

Simmons, Garner. *Peckinpah.* Austin: University of Texas Press, 1982.

Simon, John. *Movies into Film: Film Criticism 1967–1970.* New York: Dial, 1971.

Sinclair, Andrew. *Spiegel: The Man Behind the Pictures.* London: Weidenfeld and Nicolson, 1987.

Smith, Wendy. *Real Life Drama: The Group Theatre and America, 1931–1940.* New York: Knopf, 1990.

Spiritual Community Guide #6: The New Consciousness Sourcebook. Pomona, Calif.: Arcline Publications, 1985.

Spitz, Bob. *Dylan: A Biography.* New York: Norton, 1989.

Spoto, Donald. *Camerado: Hollywood and the American Man.* New York: New American Library, 1978.

———. *The Kindness of Strangers: The Life of Tennessee Williams.* New York: Ballantine, 1986.

———. *Stanley Kramer: Film Maker.* New York: Samuel French, 1978.

Squire, Jason E., ed. *The Movie Business Book.* New York: Simon & Schuster, 1983.

Stine, Whitney. *Stars & Star Handlers: The Business of Show.* Santa Monica, Calif.: Round Table Publishing, 1985.

Stott, William, with Jane Stott. *On Broadway.* Austin: University of Texas Press, 1978.

Strasberg, Susan, *Bittersweet.* New York: Putnam, 1980.

Summers, Anthony. *Goddess: The Secret Lives of Marilyn Monroe.* New York: New American Library, 1985.

Swan, John H. *The Libertyville Fire Department: Past, Present and Future.* Libertyville, Ill.: Libertyville Firemen's Association, 1985.

Taraborrelli, J. Randy. *Michael Jackson: The Magic and the Madness.* New York: Ballantine, 1991.

Taylor, Theodore. *People Who Make Movies.* New York: Avon, 1967.

Thomas, Bob. *Brando: Portrait of the Rebel as an Artist.* London and New York: W. H. Allen, 1973.

Thomas, Tony. *The Films of Marlon Brando.* Secaucus, N.J.: Citadel Press, 1973.

Tynan, Kathleen. *The Life of Kenneth Tynan.* New York: Morrow, 1987.

Urdang, Laurence, ed. *The Timetables of American History.* New York: Simon & Schuster, 1981.

Utley, Robert M. *Billy the Kid: A Short and Violent Life.* Lincoln, Neb.: University of Nebraska Press, 1989.

———. *The Lance and the Shield: The Life and Times of Sitting Bull.* New York: Henry Holt, 1993.

Vanden Heuvel, Katrina, ed. *The Nation 1865–1990: Collections from the Independent Magazine of Politics and Culture.* New York: Thunder's Mouth Press, 1990.

Vickers, Hugo. *Cecil Beaton: A Biography.* New York: Donald I. Fine, 1985.

Vineberg, Steve. *Method Actors: Three Generations of an American Acting Style.* New York: Schirmer Books, 1991.

Voices from Wounded Knee, 1973: In the Words of the Participants. Akwesasne Notes, Mohawk Nation at Akwesasne via Rooseveltown, New York, 1974.

Walker, Alexander. *Vivien: The Life of Vivien Leigh.* New York: Weidenfeld & Nicolson, 1987.

Wall, Steve, and Harvey Arden. *Wisdomkeepers: Meetings with Native American Spiritual Elders.* Hillsboro, Ore.: Beyond Words Publishing, 1990.

Wayne, Jane Ellen. *Marilyn's Men: The Private Life of Marilyn Monroe.* New York: St. Martin's, 1992.

Weatherby, W. J. *James Baldwin: Artist on Fire.* New York: Donald I. Fine, 1989.

Weddle, David. *"If They Move . . . Kill 'Em": The Life and Times of Sam Peckinpah.* New York: Grove, 1994.

White, Stewart Edward. *The Betty Book.* Columbus, Ohio: Ariel Press, 1937.

Wiley, Mason, and Damien Bona. *Inside Oscar: The Unofficial History of the Academy Awards.* New York: Ballantine, 1986.

Willett, John. *The Theatre of Erwin Piscator.* New York: Holmes & Meier, 1979.

Williams, Dakin, and Shepherd Mead. *Tennessee Williams: An Intimate Biography.* New York: Arbor House, 1983.

Williams, Tennessee. *Memoirs.* Garden City, N.Y.: Anchor Press/Doubleday, 1983.

Winters, Shelley. *Shelley: Also Known as Shirley.* New York: Ballantine, 1980.

————. *Shelley II: The Middle of My Century.* New York: Simon & Schuster, 1989.

Woititz, Janet Geringer. *Adult Children of Alcoholics.* Pompano Beach, Fla.: Health Communications, 1983.

Wood, Robin. *Arthur Penn.* New York: Praeger, 1970.

Yule, Andrew. *Fast Fade: David Puttnam, Columbia Pictures, and the Battle for Hollywood.* New York: Delacorte, 1989.

————. *Life on the Wire: The Life and Art of Al Pacino.* New York: S.P.I. Books, 1992.

Zierold, Norman. *The Moguls: Hollywood's Merchants of Myth.* Los Angeles: Silman-James Press, 1969.

Zinnemann, Fred. *Fred Zinnemann: An Autobiography: A Life in the Movies.* New York: Scribners, 1992.

Zuckerman, Ira. *The Godfather Journal.* New York: Manor Books, 1972.

A C K N O W L E D G M E N T S

This book does its best to depict with accuracy the often complex and contradictory events of its subject's life. More than 750 people were interviewed over a period of eight years, some interviews filling more than twenty hours of tape. Follow-up sessions were routine, especially when earlier testimony was unclear or ambiguous. The transcript totaled over sixty thousand pages. Secondary materials such as news stories, magazine profiles, studio memos, court transcripts, and previously published biographies were used in preparing for interviews as well as for corroborative purposes. The locales of the research included Tahiti, France, England, Israel, as well as more than half the states in the continental U.S.

My premise has always been that memory is fragile. Recollection is everyone's second chance. A book like this must continually "triangulate"—compare multiple versions of a single event, taking as the truest the approximation woven by all. To the extent that the writing of a history is a reconstruction, in those instances where disagreements among sources could not be resolved through further interviewing or by referring to secondary materials, I have sought to acknowledge divergent points of view, as well as the bias of individual speakers. To do so, I believe, is the only responsible way to write biography.

In certain instances, sources requested the right of review of transcript; where this was the case, the opportunity to revise was granted only in the interest of accuracy, which is to say to clarify and sharpen, not to sanitize. I have taken care to ensure that the substance and attitude of individual speakers have not been lost.

Plainly, a book of this kind cannot happen without the participation of many, and I owe a debt of gratitude to all those who gave of their time and energy. For some, the culling up of personal memories was difficult, and I wish to express my thanks and my hope that the book itself justifies their participation. Several sources, as well as individuals who supported this project in other ways, cannot be acknowledged by name; they know who they are, and I regret that I cannot thank them publicly.

This project could not have been completed without the assistance of city, county, and state libraries and historical societies, among them: Evanston (Ill.) Historical Society; Douglas County Historical Society (Omaha); Nebraska State Historical Society (Lincoln); Hall County Historical Society (Grand Island, Neb.); Libertyville-Mundelein (Ill.) Historical Society (Libertyville); Boston Public Library; and Omaha Public Library. Similarly, for invaluable assistance with documents and materials pertaining to Brando's stage work and films, as well as background on the motion picture industry and New York theater world, I am grateful to: the Museum of Broadcast Communications (Chicago); Museum of Television and Radio (New York); Doheny Library,

University of Southern California, (Los Angeles); UCLA Arts Library, Special Collections (Los Angeles); the Margaret Herrick Library, the Academy of Motion Picture Arts and Sciences (Los Angeles); Louis B. Mayer Library, American Film Institute (Los Angeles); Morris Library, Special Collections, Southern Illinois University (Carbondale, Ill.); New York Public Library for the Performing Arts; Pacifica Film Archive (Berkeley, Calif.); Goodman Theatre Archives (Chicago); and the Katherine Dunham Center of the Performing Arts (East St. Louis, Ill.). For materials on other aspects of the actor's life, I wish to thank the Omaha Community Playhouse; Shattuck–St. Mary's School (in particular, the indefatigable Millie Marple, school archivist); New York Psychoanalytic Institute Library; Yivo Institute for Jewish Research (New York); the Theosophical Society (Wheaton, Ill.); National Council on Alcoholism (New York); Center of Alcohol Studies, Rutgers University (New Brunswick, N.J.); Raymond Fogelman Library, New School for Social Research (New York); Yale Medical Library (New Haven); and the Syracuse University Library, Special Collections.

I benefited enormously from the research and logistical help of a number of assistants in different parts of this country, as well as abroad. Chief among those to whom I owe a huge debt of gratitude are: Rebecca "Becky" Burcham and Ati Citron in New York; Bob Flood in Omaha; Paul Smith in Faribault, Minnesota; Jessica Portner, Peggy Biscow, and, most of all, Eric Lindbom in Los Angeles; Dana Bartholomew, Sophie Marnette, Ethan Michaels, Kevin Cook, and Mitch Ikuta in Berkeley; Alexander Kara in Paris; Al Prince and Denis Herrmann in Tahiti; Helen Fielding in London; Sandy Thomas in Hawaii; and also Bet MacArthur, Wayne Worcester, and Ivor Irwin. Thanks, too, to my brother, Victor, for invaluable help with translations from the French. To Alice Ruckert, my assistant of more than ten years now, I cannot adequately express my gratitude for seeing this project through from the beginning.

For editorial assistance, my thanks to Trent Duffy and Craig Nelson at Hyperion, who more than worked overtime, and also to the late Jeanne Bernkopf, who helped during the early phases of the book. To the eagle-eyed Peggy Garry at Hyperion, my gratitude, too. For assistance with photographs, my thanks to those who dug into their personal albums to supply pictures, as well as to Deborah Bull at PhotoSearch in New York for photography research and also for pulling the pictures together. To Lois Wallace, my agent, once again kudos and my gratitude.

For logistical support in various forms, my thanks to Karen Nobile of Saab USA and Thomas McGurn of BMW of North America; IBM for its state-of-the-art 750C ThinkPad; Klaus Messner of the ever accommodating Sunset Marquis Hotel in Hollywood; the staff of the Park Hyatt in San Francisco; Kenmark Office Supply and Shank Painter Printers on Cape Cod; and, also, Alice Waters and Bill Staggs of Berkeley's Chez Panisse, as well as Joseph Le Brun and Paul Harrington at the Town House in Emeryville for providing sustenance par excellence, often at the last minute when one appeared out of the blue, without a reservation. Likewise, Kristel Pratt Kent and her husband, Dale, welcomed me to Omaha, and their hospitality is something I shall remember for a good long time to come.

To editors Wayne Lawson at *Vanity Fair;* Peter Bloch at *Penthouse;* John Rezek and Steve Randall at *Playboy;* Peter Biskind at *Premiere;* and to my colleagues at *Paris Match,* Christopher Laffaille, Olivier Royant, Françoise Joyes, and Jacques Lange, my appreciation for their continued encouragement.

Most of all, though, more personal thanks are due to friends who saw to my well-being throughout the eight years it took to complete this project; their understanding, energy, reassurance, and support sometimes seemed to make all the difference in the world. In particular, I thank: Jim Landis, Ray and Lee Elman, Peter Kuhn, David Fechheimer and Corinne Cadon, Mel Gordon, Tom and Leslie Goldstein, Robert Lesser, Marlon and Kathi Langner, Jack Martin, Ralph Singer, Steven Simmons, Dr. David Case, Nick Von Hoffman, Diana Trilling, Jerome Traum, Dan and Patricia Ellsberg, and also Bill and Jane Scott.

Finally, my greatest debt is to Ellen Hawkes. She assisted in the completion of this work in too many ways to enumerate, and, without her help burning the midnight oil there is little question that the manuscript could not have been finished to deadline. As always, she serves as my severest critic and my surest prop; indeed, my source of balance.

I N D E X